BUSINESS INFORMATION

HOW TO FIND IT, HOW TO USE IT

SECOND EDITION

BY MICHAEL R. LAVIN

ORYX PRESS
1992

The rare Arabian Oryx is believed to have inspired the myth of the unicorn. This desert antelope became virtually extinct in the early 1960s. At that time several groups of international conservationists arranged to have 9 animals sent to the Phoenix Zoo to be the nucleus of a captive breeding herd. Today the Oryx population is nearly 800, and over 400 have been returned to reserves in the Middle East.

Library of Congress Cataloging-in-Publication Data
Lavin, Michael R.
    Business information : how to find it, how to use it / by Michael
R. Lavin. — 2nd ed., new and expanded ed.
        p. cm.
    Includes bibliographical references and index.
        ISBN 0-89774-556-6 (cloth) — ISBN 0-89774-643-0 (paper)
    1. Business—Research—Handbooks, manuals, etc.   2. Reference
books—Business—Bibliography.   3. Business—Bibliography.
4. Business—Data bases—Directories.   I. Title.
HF5356.L36   1991
650'.072—dc20   91-28129
                                                               CIP

Contents

List of Exhibits   v

List of Figures   vi

Preface   vii

Acknowledgments   xii

PART I: Introduction   1
Chapter   1: Sources and Forms of Business
   Information   3

PART II: Getting Started   23
Chapter   2: Locating Experts   25
Chapter   3: Finding Reference Materials   42
Chapter   4: Finding Books, Documents, and Statistical
   Reports   61
Chapter   5: Searching Journals, Newspapers, and
   News Services   82

PART III: Information about Companies   111
Chapter   6: National Business Directories   113
Chapter   7: Specialized Business Directories   136
Chapter   8: Corporate Finances: Private
   Companies   158
Chapter   9: Corporate Finances: Public
   Companies   182
Chapter 10: Basic Investment Information   200
Chapter 11: Special Investment Situations   227
Chapter 12: Investment Advice and Analysis   249

PART IV: Statistical Information   273
Chapter 13: Introduction to Statistical
   Reasoning   275
Chapter 14: The Census of Population and
   Housing   293
Chapter 15: General Economic Statistics   326
Chapter 16: Industry Statistics   347

Part V: Special Topics   373
Chapter 17: Information on States and Local
   Areas   375
Chapter 18: Marketing Information   398
Chapter 19: Business Law Sources   425
Chapter 20: Taxation and Accounting   452

Appendix: Keeping Up to Date   473

Title Index   477

Subject Index   493

List of Exhibits

Exhibit 2-1 *State Administrative Officials Classified by Function* 31

Exhibit 2-2 *Encyclopedia of Associations* 35

Exhibit 3-1 *Encyclopedia of Business Information Sources* 44

Exhibit 3-2 *Directory of Periodicals Online* 55

Exhibit 4-1 *Standard Industrial Classification Manual* 63

Exhibit 4-2 *Statistics Sources* 74

Exhibit 4-3 *Statistical Reference Index* 77

Exhibit 4-4 *Predicasts Forecasts* 79

Exhibit 5-1 *ABI/INFORM* 88

Exhibit 5-2 *Predicasts F&S Index United States* 91

Exhibit 5-3 *PTS PROMT* 93

Exhibit 6-1 *Standard & Poor's Register of Corporations, Executives and Industries* 118

Exhibit 6-2 *Standard Directory of Advertisers* 121

Exhibit 7-1 *Directory of Corporate Affiliations* 147

Exhibit 7-2 *Official Gazette of the Patent and Trademark Office* 152

Exhibit 8-1 *Quarterly Bank and Savings & Loan Rating Service* 167

Exhibit 8-2 *RMA Annual Statement Studies* 173

Exhibit 8-3 *Statistics of Income: Corporation Income Tax Returns* 175

Exhibit 9-1 *Moody's Industrial Manual* 191

Exhibit 10-1 *The Wall Street Journal*—Listed Stock Quotes 207

Exhibit 10-2 *The Wall Street Journal*—OTC Stock Quotes 210

Exhibit 10-3 *The Wall Street Journal*—Mutual Fund Quotes 211

Exhibit 10-4 *The Wall Street Journal*—Bond Quotes 213

Exhibit 10-5 *Daily Stock Price Record* 218

Exhibit 10-6 *Standard & Poor's Security Owner's Stock Guide* 221

Exhibit 11-1 *Moody's Dividend Record* 244

Exhibit 12-1 *Zacks Earnings Forecaster* 259

Exhibit 12-2 *Value Line Investment Survey* 261

Exhibit 12-3 *Moody's Industry Review* 266

Exhibit 13-1 *Economic Indicators*—Semilog Graph 286

Exhibit 13-2 *Survey of Buying Power Data Service*—Buying Power Index 289

Exhibit 14-1 *Census of Population*—Table of Contents 305

Exhibit 14-2 *Census of Population*—Table Finding Guide 306

Exhibit 14-3 *Census of Population and Housing, Summary Tape File 3-A* 310

Exhibit 14-4 *Census of Population, Chapter B: General Population Characteristics* 318

Exhibit 15-1 *Survey of Current Business* 339

Exhibit 16-1 *Census of Manufactures: Geographic Series* 351

Exhibit 16-2 *Census of Manufactures*—Product Tables 352

Exhibit 16-3 *Census of Retail Trade: Merchandise Line Sales,* Table 1 354

Exhibit 16-4 *Census of Retail Trade: Merchandise Line Sales,* Table 2 355

Exhibit 16-5 *Dun's Census of American Business* 365

Exhibit 17-1 *Sourcebook of Zip Code Demographics* 385

Exhibit 17-2 *ACCRA Cost of Living Index* 392

Exhibit 18-1 *LNA/Arbitron Multi-Media Service* 401

Exhibit 18-2 *Simmons Study of Media and Markets* 420

Exhibit 19-1 *United States Reports* 432

Exhibit 19-2 *Shepard's Federal Labor Law Citations* 436

Exhibit 19-3 *Labor Relations Reference Manual* 442

Exhibit 19-4 *Labor Relations Cumulative Digest and Index* 443

Exhibit 20-1 *Federal Taxes 2nd Citator, 2nd Series* 462

List of Figures

Figure 1-A   Ways of Looking at Information   5
Figure 5-A   Additional Periodical Indexes for Business Research   100
Figure 7-A   International Trademark Classification   151
Figure 8-A   Corporate Balance Sheet   160
Figure 8-B   Corporate Income Statement   161
Figure 11-A   Primary Financial Disclosure Forms and Reports   228
Figure 11-B   Guide to Secondary Sources of Disclosure Filings   246
Figure 13-A   Consumer Price Index Data, All Cities (1967=100)   283

Figure 13-B   Histogram and Cumulative Frequency Ogive   287
Figure 14-A   1990 Census Questionnaire: Complete Count versus Sample Questions   296
Figure 14-B   Geographic Units in the Census   301
Figure 14-C   Important Census Relationships   302
Figure 14-D   Translating Demographic Questions into Census Format   323
Figure 19-A   Sources of Federal Judicial Decisions   433
Figure 20-A   Sources of Federal Tax Decisions   456

Preface

Information, rather than oil or steel, is likely to become the most precious commercial resource, and the company that can gather, evaluate, and synthesize information ahead of its rivals will have a competitive advantage.

The New York Times,
May 13, 1990

Timely, accurate business information—its value is clear, but knowing how to find it is another matter. When confronted with a research project, or even a request for a few simple facts, businesspeople seldom know how to launch their campaign. Once started, they proceed in a lurching, haphazard manner, trusting to luck and a small network of familiar contacts. And the ability to locate needed information is only the first step; business researchers also need to act upon what is found. To be useful, information must be understood, evaluated, integrated with what is already known, and applied to specific situations. This book can be the catalyst for accomplishing these goals.

SCOPE AND PURPOSE

Business Information: How to Find It, How to Use It combines in-depth descriptions of major business publications and databases with explanations of concepts essential for using them effectively. For beginning researchers, the book is designed to develop critical skills, including how to begin a research project, where to look for needed information, and how to understand what is found. For more experienced readers, the book will serve to hone those skills, to introduce advanced techniques, and to suggest alternatives to familiar methods. Readers in both categories should also gain a greater appreciation of the enormous diversity of published information and the wide range of specific questions which can be answered.

Business Information requires no prior knowledge of economics or business. Every discussion begins with an explanation of the basic concepts necessary to understand the resources described. As much as possible, publications and databases are not merely described, but put in perspective. When similar materials are available from competing publishers, the sources are compared. When different approaches are possible, this too is discussed. Two overriding themes are found throughout the book: the importance of planning a search strategy, and the need to develop a critical eye when using business information. Readers are encouraged to categorize their information needs, explore a variety of methods, and evaluate what they uncover. Topics have been chosen because they represent regularly encountered information requests.

Equally important is what the book is not intended to do. First, *Business Information* should not be viewed as a comprehensive guide to the literature of business. Although hundreds of resources are introduced, they represent a small portion of the publishing universe. More extensive guides, including Lorna Daniells' classic *Business Information Sources*, are listed in Chapter 3. However, no guide to the literature, no matter how extensive or well done, can come close to listing all the materials at the researcher's disposal. There is simply too much published information to be captured in the pages of a single book, and new resources appear every day. Second, the book is not a guide to the "core" resources in business. The titles have been chosen for several reasons: they are authoritative, respected works; they are among the most frequently used by researchers; they best illustrate the concepts under discussion; they display unique features; and/or they reflect the rich diversity of published information. Still, the selections represent the author's personal preferences and biases. In many cases, the items are widely available in medium or large librar-

ies, but others are more specialized and not as readily found. Some are surprisingly affordable; others are quite expensive. And just as it would be impossible to create a comprehensive guide to business literature, it is equally impossible to devise a universal core collection. Each researcher's personal list would vary considerably, depending on needs and circumstances.

INTENDED AUDIENCE

The first edition of *Business Information* grew out of a course taught to graduate library school students and practicing librarians. It was written to be both a classroom text and a hands-on manual. This dual objective remains unchanged in the revised and enlarged second edition. The book was also written for businesspeople, and for students and researchers outside the library world. The need to develop business information skills is evident in many occupations besides librarianship. Journalists, market researchers, community planners, economic development officers, legislative aides, public officials, entrepreneurs, personnel managers, secretaries and administrative assistants, management consultants, union representatives, private investigators, information brokers, attorneys and paralegals, consumer advocates, and a host of others will find this book helpful in their daily work. *Business Information* is also appropriate as a textbook in disciplines outside library science—for courses in marketing, finance, strategic management, business research methods, business journalism, and legal research, to name a few.

The original intent behind a second edition was to incorporate the many changes which have taken place since publication of the first edition in 1987. However, the scope of the project quickly expanded. The first edition was aimed primarily at readers with little background in business research. I was surprised (and pleased) to discover that more experienced readers were turning to it as well. Why have so many found it useful? One reason is that most business librarians and researchers are self-taught or learn on the job. The book was welcomed because it summarized and organized knowledge that readers had gained piecemeal, through years of discovery. A more important set of reasons follows from the vast expanse of business information—no researcher, regardless of how experienced, dedicated, or talented, can know everything. Because the range of topics in *Business Information* is fairly broad, readers will undoubtedly encounter unfamiliar publications and subjects. Finally, many business publications are complex.

The uses and limitations of a major tool may not be clear to the casual observer. A title may be packed with appendices and other special features unrelated to the book's main purpose. Even for familiar titles, it is easy to overlook their less obvious uses. As a consequence, the second edition goes "beyond the basics," exploring many topics in greater detail and suggesting more sophisticated search strategies.

The warm reception accorded the first edition of *Business Information* has been gratifying. In many libraries, a well-worn copy can be seen within arm's reach of the reference desk. Librarians consult it when helping a patron with an unfamiliar topic, or to jog the memory during a hectic moment. It is also useful for describing materials which are unavailable in the researcher's own library. Patrons welcome the book when they need a basic concept explained, when they are about to embark on a complex project, or when they need to relate what they know to the broader world of published information. In many libraries it is also used in staff training programs.

These patterns of use, combined with the favorable comments and suggestions received, were the impetus for an expanded version. Those who benefited from the coverage of basic topics will be relieved to see this material remains—the second edition will continue to serve as an introduction to business research. At the same time, the book now contains far more to interest the experienced researcher. It is doubtful that any reader will encounter a single chapter containing no new information. This more ambitious approach presented several challenges. One was balancing the introductory material with the more advanced. Another was knowing when to stop. On the whole, I believe the result is a highly versatile tool. For classroom and staff training purposes, instructors can omit individual publications, chapter sections, or entire chapters with no loss of continuity.

CHANGES TO THE SECOND EDITION

The most significant changes to the second edition are the expanded discussion of previously treated topics and the inclusion of many new topics. Other modifications are the more extensive coverage of electronic products, and the greater emphasis on research strategies.

The preface to the first edition talked about the rapidly changing nature of business publications, but as I began this revision, the phenomenal pace of such changes took me by surprise. So much of the first edition is now obsolete or no longer correct that the older book should be retired from service. Describing business re-

sources is like trying to measure a melting snowflake. In the three years it took to create this edition, numerous sections had to be completely rewritten two, or even three times because fundamental changes occurred to the sources under discussion. Standard resources cease publication and new ones rise to take their place. Even enduring publications don't remain constant. Titles change, as do formats, frequencies, contents, and publication objectives. Changes have been incorporated up until press time, but once again, much will become outdated quickly. The cutoff date for major revisions was June 1991.

Other changes have resulted from fundamental developments in business and information—new legislation, upheavals in the economy, financial innovations, and advancements in technology. For example, sweeping changes in income tax policy took place in 1986, too late to be incorporated in the first edition. In 1989, important changes in trademark law were instituted. Major legislation on foreign trade was also enacted in the late 1980s, including adoption by the United States of the Harmonized Commodity Classification System. Another adjustment with profound ramifications for business researchers was a major revision of the government's Standard Industrial Classification system, the first since 1972.

In some cases, changes occur on a scheduled basis. For example, the U.S. Bureau of the Census produces massive new economic reports every five years and demographic reports every ten years. As of this writing, publications from the 1987 Economic Census are nearly complete, but few products from the 1990 Census of Population and Housing have appeared.

Perhaps the most notable change in business information has been the increasing importance of electronic databases, especially CD-ROMs. When the first edition was written, only two CD-ROM products were in widespread use by business researchers, and few others even existed. The promise of CD-ROM technology was discussed briefly in the first edition, but few people could have predicted the explosive growth and tremendous popularity of this medium.

Much of the new and expanded coverage that marks the second edition was prompted by feedback from readers across the country. The most frequent suggestions involved stock dividends, mergers, accounting pronouncements, private companies, market share, and news services. Six chapters are completely new and all others have been enlarged. Readers may quibble over the inclusion or omission of particular subjects, or the amount of

attention devoted to them. The lengthier discussions generally deal either with topics frequently encountered by researchers or those which are especially complex.

Another change is the greater emphasis on research strategy. The first edition stressed the importance of evaluating search results, and this remains a key feature of the second edition. Business researchers must always question the value of what they find, asking such questions as "Where does the information come from?" "Does it have any weaknesses?" and "Is it accurate and reliable?" Once again, these issues are addressed in every chapter. However, the second edition makes a greater attempt to place specific resources in a research framework. Every chapter concludes with a discussion of how to apply information to the research process. Finally, the reading lists following every chapter have been enlarged and completely updated, and a separate list of periodical titles has been added as an appendix.

The result of these enhancements is a book considerably larger than the first edition. On the other hand, the chapter on job hunting and consumer information has been deleted entirely. This was done to reduce the book's growing unwieldiness. Although these topics are important and popular, the chapter was sufficiently different from the rest of the book to make it the logical choice for deletion.

One of the most frequent comments about the first edition, both in published reviews and in remarks made to the author, was the limited information about online databases. The scant treatment was intentional, in part because the enormity of the topic could easily swamp the discussion of printed media, but mostly for another reason. Because many business databases were expensive, and because many beginning researchers and smaller libraries had limited access to them, I then felt it was unfair to grant extensive coverage to databases in a beginning guide. Any reservations regarding this matter have long since disappeared. Online databases have become such an integral and widespread part of business research that the subject cannot be ignored. Even researchers with no online access should be aware of the wealth of available resources, how they differ from printed products, and the important advantages they offer. However, as with the printed sources, only a small number of representative titles are described. The addition of even these selected databases has contributed greatly to the increased size of the new edition, but their inclusion has enhanced the total presentation enormously.

ORGANIZATION

The book is organized into five sections. Part I introduces ideas and methods important to all business research. These include how business information is used, its characteristics, the sources of published and unpublished data, and the forms in which publications and databases appear. Part II is devoted to the tools which determine where to look for information—the directories, indexes, bibliographies, and catalogs which describe other business sources. (This section is the most extensively enlarged, reflecting the preeminence of this stage in the research process.) Part III surveys the challenging task of investigating companies, both private and publicly held. Research needs in this area cover directory data, financial profiles, investment information, and specialized news. Part IV deals with statistical data of various types: demographic, economic, and industrial. A separate chapter introduces general statistical concepts and research problems. Part V explores four special topics—information about local areas, business and labor law, marketing, and taxation and accounting.

In every chapter, key concepts and terminology are introduced before the related information products are described. The number of major resources varies per chapter, from about a dozen to 25 or more. Many additional publications are described briefly or mentioned as examples. Chapters conclude with discussions of strategic issues—the research problems encountered, how to initiate a project, choosing the best tools, and how to cope with information overload.

For those wishing to pursue various topics further, lists of additional readings are provided. These lists are selective, and the emphasis is on popular, rather than scholarly, materials. Items on the lists are diverse, containing books, reports, journal articles, and brief stories from popular magazines. The following guidelines were used to select the readings: to include materials which explore important topics the book could not cover in greater detail; to list readings which illustrate important points or present a perspective different from my own; to identify unusual or seemingly unrelated stories the reader would be unlikely to uncover except by chance; and, finally, to highlight well-written pieces which might be fun to read. Product reviews were not emphasized because the resources they describe change so quickly. However, reviews have been included where they emphasize important points about the nature of business information sources. The best way for researchers to keep abreast of new and changing publications is to read newsletters and professional journals. The appendix offers a selective list of such current awareness tools.

The book is structured so that beginning topics appear first, followed by more detailed or sophisticated discussions. One problem was deciding where to insert individual publications. It is surprisingly difficult to categorize many business sources, especially those which address several needs. Throughout the book, frequent references are made to related discussions in other chapters. In several cases, summary tables are included to show relationships among various resources.

Most authors of guides to the business literature also wrestle with the question of format versus subject. This work is arranged by topic, with multiple formats (government documents, CD-ROMs, microfiche, etc.) discussed in all chapters. Such an approach is especially important for contrasting the features of electronic and printed sources. Despite the powerful features of online databases and CD-ROMS, printed sources will serve the researcher equally well or better in many situations. To offset any problems this integrated technique presents, Chapter 1 provides a brief introduction to each format.

A few words should be said regarding other standard features. The lists of "Major Sources Discussed" found at the beginning of most chapters indicate neither all the titles covered in the chapters nor the most important. The lists are intended only to give a general sense of the chapter's content.

For major research tools, the publisher's name and frequency of publication are given. The primary frequency is identified, together with any subsequent updates or cumulations. Standard bibliographic nomenclature is used—bimonthly, semiannual, annual, biennial, quinquennial, and so forth. Many publications are produced in several formats; a single product may be available in print, on CD-ROM from several publishers, and offered online through many vendors, with each variation differing in some respects. Product descriptions have attempted to capture salient features, but space considerations prevented lengthy format comparisons for every publication.

FINAL THOUGHTS

Many additional topics could have been included in this work. However, because the book came perilously close to becoming a two-volume set, additional material was discarded in the planning stages, and much was

deleted in the final editing. I would have preferred to reproduce many more sample pages and describe many more publications, but in order to keep the book's size manageable, useful, and affordable, some limits had to be set. As in the first edition, specialized topics such as real estate, insurance, import and export management, and operations research were excluded. And once again, the most significant omission involves sources of foreign business information. Conducting international research is increasingly vital for all businesses, but the topic requires a book of its own. It is my fervent wish that some day such a guide will be written for American researchers.

Several chapters mention new reference sources or databases which were still under development at the time this manuscript was submitted. I understand the high fatality rate among publishing projects, especially in the burgeoning field of CD-ROMs. Those which are mentioned have been included because they promise to be truly important additions to the researcher's tool box, or because they will offer a distinct alternative to other resources discussed. Such inclusions have been kept to a minimum.

In closing, I would like to return to a comment made earlier—no business researcher knows everything. Of course, this includes myself. Like most of my peers, much of what I know is self-taught, gained through working as a reference librarian, consultant, trainer, and instructor. I have learned a great deal over the years not only from reading and exploration, but also from colleagues, library patrons, students, and publishers' representatives. Creating this book (and its predecessor) provided an enormous, accelerated education. In many instances, it forced me to confront topics with which I was unfamiliar or even uncomfortable. It also provided the motivation to seek answers from many knowledgeable individuals: specialists in a particular field, as well as the publishers and database producers themselves. In many cases, it took dogged determination to verify answers to seemingly simple questions. I hope readers will benefit from this process. What makes the topic so continually fresh after years of practice is the tremendous learning which takes place every day. I have striven to improve this edition in all respects. Comments, suggestions, and corrections are welcomed.

Michael R. Lavin
Buffalo, NY
June 1991

Acknowledgments

Many individuals have lent assistance and support during the writing of this book. My thanks go first to my coworkers at Lockwood Memorial Library, State University of New York at Buffalo. The enthusiasm and team spirit shown by the staff provide an ideal environment in which to work and grow. Special thanks are extended to Don Hartman and Ed Herman for sharing their considerable expertise, to Gayle Hardy for her unflagging support and practical suggestions, and to Judith Adams for granting release time to complete the project. Colleagues at the Buffalo & Erie County Public Library have once again provided help. In particular, Joyce Davoli of the Business and Labor Department has extended innumerable favors large and small.

Business publishers of every type have been extraordinarily helpful. Many have provided review copies of reference materials and many more have offered valuable insights into their products. Special thanks are due to Beth Dempsey at Gale Research, who was especially generous in sending materials for review. Several online vendors also extended help, with free access to a variety of their products. Two firms that warrant special mention are CompuServe, Inc. and Mead Data Central, both of which provided complimentary passwords for lengthy periods.

As always, John Wagner and Art Stickney at Oryx Press have been extremely supportive. So too have many librarians and researchers across the country, who have taken the time to acknowledge their appreciation for the first edition and offer suggestions for the second.

And to my wife and son, I offer heartfelt thanks once again. They have put up with a great deal during the writing of this book, and have exhibited steadfast patience and understanding throughout the ordeal. This book is dedicated to Irene and Andrew, with love.

PART I
Introduction

CHAPTER 1
Sources and Forms of Business Information

TOPICS COVERED

1. The Value and Cost of Information
2. Secondary Information from External Sources
3. Characteristics of Business Information
4. Where to Look for Information
   a. Government Agencies
   b. Libraries
   c. Trade Associations and Other Nonprofit
      Organizations
   d. Private Companies
5. Types of Business Publications
   a. Trade Journals and Newspapers
   b. Other Periodical Sources
   c. Business Information Services
   d. Microforms
6. Online Databases
   a. Benefits of Online Systems
   b. Types of Databases
   c. Menu-Driven Systems
   d. Nonprofit Databases
7. Other Electronic Information Sources
   a. CD-ROM Products
   b. Computer Tapes
8. Some Parting Comments
9. For Further Reading

Faced with the results of a wrong decision or a missed opportunity, most of us have said, "If only I had known about that beforehand!" Knowledge makes the difference between success and failure in such circumstances, and knowledge comes from information. Most people accept the truism that knowledge is power, but obtaining needed information is not always a simple task. Major corporations have discovered that information is a resource to be managed and they have constructed sophisticated computerized systems to organize the flow of information within the firm. Despite these efforts, gathering useful intelligence from outside the organization remains a haphazard effort for many companies. Most people who need to conduct business research are simply not skilled in doing so.

This chapter acquaints the reader with the nature of business information: its basic characteristics, who produces it, and what packages it comes in. The discussion offers a glimpse at the kinds of publications available and where they can be found, setting the stage for the more detailed chapters to follow. Topics to be covered include the economics of information, ways of looking at information, problems associated with researching business topics, and the sources and forms of business information. While the emphasis of this book is on published materials, this chapter also introduces some sources of unpublished data.

THE VALUE AND COST OF INFORMATION

Information is a valuable commodity—knowing something is usually preferable to not knowing it. But beyond contributing to the individual's fund of knowledge, why does information have intrinsic worth? Stated simply, information reduces uncertainty. The more we know about a situation, the more certain we are about possible outcomes. The more certainty we possess, the less risk we face in making decisions and planning for the future.

Information has two valuable applications: problem solving and strategic planning. Problem solving is the more obvious use—applying information to specific decision-making situations. Research can unearth potential problems, reveal possible solutions, suggest variations to more obvious alternatives, determine what is physically possible, and uncover what others have done in similar situations. Furthermore, information helps the decision-maker assess the probable outcomes of alternative decisions, the advantages and disadvantages to each, and even whether the proposed solution has worked in the past. In summary, information can provide new ideas, verify what the researcher believes to be true, prevent costly mistakes, and, in the very best case, actually solve the problem at hand.

Long-range planning is possibly the most important application of information in the business world. When used in this strategic sense, information is often called intelligence. Intelligence is gathered by collecting individual bits of data, piecing them together, and analyzing the results to discern important patterns or trends. Intelligence relies on information sources outside the organization; by scanning the environment, the researcher can recognize potential threats and opportunities before it is too late to do something about them. Change, whether political, social, economic, or technological, poses the greatest challenge to management's ability to plan. The use of information for strategic purposes largely determines whether the firm anticipates change, or is controlled by it.

Intelligence gathering supports strategic planning activities in many ways. Information can be used to evaluate the marketplace by surveying changing tastes and needs, monitoring buyers' intentions and attitudes, and assessing the characteristics of the market. Information is critical in keeping tabs on the competition by watching new product developments, shifts in market share, individual company performance, and overall industry trends. Intelligence helps managers anticipate legal and political changes, and monitor economic conditions in the United States and abroad. In short, intelligence can provide answers to two key business questions: How am I doing? and Where am I headed?

For all its value, information carries numerous problems and costs. All researchers must confront an inescapable fact: information is a boundless resource, and no one can acquire all possible information on a given topic. The sheer mass of available data makes research difficult, and most material unearthed in a search will be irrelevant to the user's immediate needs. Furthermore, information is usually published piecemeal in a variety of sources and seldom found in precisely the required form. These difficulties make research time-consuming, and few researchers have unlimited time. The scope of a search is almost always determined by the project deadline.

These concerns are important, because information always has a cost. Whether users hire a consultant, purchase existing publications, or track down their own answers, each method has a direct cost. Information also has such indirect costs as delayed and wrong decisions and foregone opportunities. Estimated costs can often be misleading; people frequently believe that insignificant questions will be simple to research, when the exact opposite is often true. A "big question" may be easier to answer because someone else has already done the research.

The hardest problem in business research is determining the point at which the benefits of information justify the costs. Benefits may be hard to assess, or may accrue long after the information is first obtained. More information is preferable to less; yet, in practical terms, perfect information is unattainable. Researchers must assess the reliability and accuracy of what they uncover and decide whether or not to continue searching. As already suggested, time constraints can make this an academic question. A second factor is the magnitude of the consequences. The potential profit or loss to the individual or organization is an excellent gauge of the information's importance. Another consideration is whether the information addresses a recurring problem or can be applied to similar situations in the future.

Each person constantly weighs the costs and benefits of information, but two other matters affect the balance. First, the problem at hand is usually not the only task vying for the researcher's attention; and second, the knowledge, skills, and interests of the researcher help determine the path an investigation will take. In the final analysis, all these factors have an impact on the amount of searching to be done.

SECONDARY INFORMATION FROM EXTERNAL SOURCES

Information comes in many forms and from many sources. There are several ways of looking at information, but this discussion will focus on how information is generated. Figure 1-A distinguishes between internal and external information, and between primary and secondary sources. Internal information is created within the organization, while external information is acquired from the outside. Primary information is produced specifically

for the problem at hand. Secondary information is a by-product of some other task, which is then applied to the matter under consideration.

FIGURE 1-A. Ways of Looking at Information

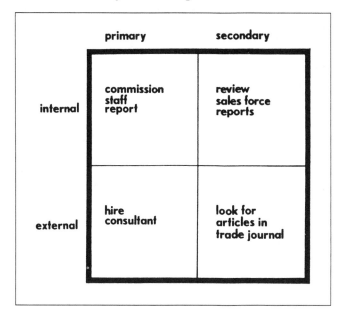

Figure 1-A provides examples of each of the four categories in this typology. A toy manufacturer interested in feedback on its new line of action figures has numerous ways to obtain the information. Using the direct approach, the firm's marketing department could observe children playing with the toys in a controlled environment. Alternatively, the manufacturer could hire a market research firm to conduct an opinion survey of parents. Both methods utilize primary sources, since information is gathered to answer the firm's specific question. The first method is generated internally, the second externally.

Secondary information is generally less costly than primary information, but may not fit the company's exact needs. The monthly reports filed by the firm's sales staff are an internal source of secondary information that could indicate the reaction of toy store owners to the new product. An external source might be an article in a trade magazine that discusses consumer attitudes toward military and action toys. Secondary information is easier to acquire than primary and should always be investigated before conducting original studies. Many texts explain how to conduct primary research, but little has been written on secondary research methods. The purpose of this book is to introduce techniques for obtaining external secondary business information—the most difficult to manage, least utilized, but most cost-effective information category.

CHARACTERISTICS OF BUSINESS INFORMATION

Another important concept is the distinction between public and proprietary information. Public information is available to anyone who wishes to use it. Though some public information is free, one must usually pay to obtain it. Realistically, public information is limited to those who can afford it or can find such free alternative sources as public libraries. The keys to locating public information are knowing where to look and being willing to pay the price.

"Public" is not always synonymous with published. Many types of information are not widely disseminated, but producers are willing to share them with those who ask. Conversely, just because something is a matter of public record does not guarantee it will be easily accessible. For example, local municipalities may keep detailed records of the licenses and permits they grant, but may not keep statistics which summarize licensing activities.

In contrast, proprietary information is owned by, and for the sole use of, the organization which created it or contracted to have it produced. In the classification scheme shown in Figure 1-A, proprietary information can be internal or external, primary or secondary. Many types of business information are strictly proprietary, collected for the use of the organization and not available to outside researchers. Examples could include sales records, personnel files, market research, trade secrets, and minutes of board meetings. Although certain limited categories of business information must be made public by law, most company records are exempt from such provisions.

A third category of business information is neither fully public nor private, but falls into a gray area known as controlled publications. Use of these materials is restricted to "qualified subscribers" and is usually unavailable to the general researcher. An example of this category is information collected by trade associations for the sole use of their members. A well-known case is the Multiple Listing information collected by firms belonging to a local board of Realtors. The information is shared only among board members and their customers.

The existence of controlled information is often widely known. Summary conclusions from such reports may even appear in the news media, while the actual document remains frustratingly unavailable to the public. The familiar Arbitron radio and television ratings, for example, are available only to broadcasters and advertis-

ing agencies. The inaccessibility of proprietary information is a major stumbling block to business research, and a problem seldom encountered in other fields.

Business sources also differ from other publications in being produced by firms that specialize in a narrow field. For this reason, few business reference sources are seen in bookstores and other common outlets, but must be obtained directly from the publisher. On the other hand, the publishing industry in recent years has witnessed incredible consolidation. Major business publishers such as McGraw-Hill and Dun & Bradstreet have acquired numerous independent publishers in a bid to become highly diversified information providers. These new-formed giants own dozens of subsidiaries which produce business books, reference materials, newsletters, journals, online databases, and syndicated intelligence services.

A conspicuous example is the International Thomson Organization, Ltd. Originally a British publisher of local newspapers, Thomson has grown to become one of the largest diversified information companies in the world, and is now headquartered in Toronto. During the past two decades, the firm has acquired some of the most respected names in reference book and business publishing, including Gale Research. Most of Thomson's affiliates are quite specialized, such as prominent business law publishers Warren Gorham & Lamont, Inc., the Clark Boardman Company, and Callagan & Company. Many Thomson publishers focus on individual industries. Among them are Ward's Communications (automotive), Jane's Information Group (aviation and defense), American Banker, and the Medical Economics Company. Despite this diversity, Thomson has made a special effort to acquire producers of financial and investment information. Each of the following titles is produced by a different Thomson subsidiary, and each is a renowned publication or database in its field: the *Bond Buyer, Investext, Spectrum Ownership Profiles, Trademarkscan, Wiesenberger Investment Company Service, Sheshunoff Bank Quarterly Ratings*, and the *Merger Yearbook*.

Two final points should be made about highly diversified publishers like Thomson International. First, a major corporation such as Thomson acquires firms as much for the recognition factor as for product quality. Although a publication, database, or syndicated service may not be unique, frequently a single name stands above the rest in the public mind; companies like Sheshunoff and Jane's become synonymous with the information they provide. In other words, business publishers may be quite specialized, but their names are often widely

known. Second, despite the solid reputations of leading publishers, researchers should realize that business publishing is highly competitive. Because of the lucrative market for business intelligence, several companies may publish virtually identical materials. In the investment arena, for example, Standard & Poor's Corporation and Moody's Investors Service produce many similar publications. This competition is beneficial to users of business information because it offers freedom of choice. Similar products may differ in price, arrangement, level of coverage, and other key features. However, seldom is one publication clearly superior; each one provides a variety of important benefits its competitor does not.

Another interesting characteristic of business publications relates to the ways they are used. Researchers frequently need very specific, brief facts rather than in-depth studies of a subject. Such data are often found as a minor part of a larger publication, and important information can show up in the most unlikely places. This has significant ramifications for the business researcher. It is not enough to know what types of publications are available; researchers must also be familiar with the contents of major works. How does one source differ from another? What information is unique? How are the data presented? What time period is covered? Does the work contain graphs, indexes, appendices, or other special features? These are questions to consider when examining a reference source for the first time. Many published guides can lead the business researcher to appropriate reference sources, but no guide is a substitute for first-hand knowledge of important publications.

Users also need timely information. To capture rapidly changing events, many business publications are sold on a subscription basis, and take the form of newspapers, magazines, loose-leaf services, electronic databases, and other formats which can be updated quickly and easily.

Literally any type of business information can be published, no matter how unlikely. Since information can be the key to business success, managers are usually willing to pay for it when the need arises. Entrepreneurs have capitalized on this willingness by publishing the most specialized resources imaginable. For example, numerous companies compile and repackage local real estate data based on tax filings and other public records kept by local governments. Researchers can quickly obtain ownership and valuation data on a specific property without stepping foot in the state. The leading publisher is Real Estate Data, Inc. (better known as the REDI Real Estate Information Service). This Florida-

based firm provides current parcel identification maps and tax rolls for several hundred counties throughout the nation.

Never assume information is unavailable just because its existence seems unreasonable. The experienced researcher will discover valuable information even when common sense indicates it would be too limited in purpose or too costly to publish. Researchers can also outsmart themselves by relying on rules of thumb that are not always true. For example, only publicly held corporations must divulge financial information to the public, yet Dun & Bradstreet compiles extensive financial reports on private companies. The safest way to view business publishing is to believe that virtually anything is available for a price.

The use of computers is another reason for the abundance of business information. Because large amounts of data can be electronically stored and reorganized by publishers, a multitude of products which were formerly too expensive or difficult to create are now available. Printed publications such as directories, statistical compendia, and financial services are more timely, powerful, and comprehensive than ever before. However, the widespread use of computers has done little to reduce the cost of business information to the researcher. More often than not, published information is expensive. This is especially true of specialized publications with limited markets, but even standard reference works can be costly. The costs of building a broad-based reference collection are further increased by the need for constant updating. This doesn't mean that all business publications are expensive; many can be obtained quite cheaply and some are even free. And for infrequently consulted publications, online databases are an economical alternative to purchasing printed materials.

A discussion of the characteristics of business information must conclude with a warning to serious researchers. There is a genuine need to understand where business information comes from. Before using any publication, it is wise to determine how and for what purpose the material was compiled. An ever-present danger is to misuse or misunderstand information because of unwarranted assumptions made by the researcher. Do statistical publications provide complete count data, or simply estimates? If estimates are used, how are they obtained? Is financial information about a company provided solely by the firm, or is corroborative material used? This book tries to point out the limitations of important publications and the potential pitfalls in using them. Comments are also provided on how to evaluate

business publications. However, it is the responsibility of the researcher to be certain he or she understands the nature of the information being used.

WHERE TO LOOK FOR INFORMATION

A major frustration facing business researchers is deciding how to get started. The less one knows about a topic, the harder it is to proceed. This is more than a case of simple inertia. A central paradox of information gathering is how to determine what is needed when the researcher has no clear understanding of what is available. A familiarity with basic categories of information and the forms in which they appear can greatly reduce such "information paralysis."

The first question every researcher should ask is: "Who knows what I need to know?" In answering, consider whether it is reasonable to expect the information to exist, and who is likely to have it. One of the most engaging aspects of business research is the continual surprise of finding obscure, but necessary information. For example, a study on "International Trade in Rhinoceros Products" by the International Union for Conservation might seem bizarre to anyone except the person who needs it.

When investigating the likelihood that specific sources exist, always ask: "To whom would this information be important?" In the case of rhinoceros products, a conservation group would be a good guess. Skilled researchers must be imaginative and persistent because the best source of information is not always the obvious one. One might find local statistics on the number of mobile homes at the county health department rather than the assessor's office or the department of inspections and licenses. To give an idea of the variety of organizations that provide business information, some of the major sources are introduced in this section. Publications describing these organizations in greater detail will be introduced in Chapter 2.

Government Agencies

Governments can be the most prolific and useful sources of business information. Local, state, and federal agencies are bountiful repositories for all kinds of information. For example, local school boards administer student censuses; state transportation departments conduct traffic count studies on major highways; and the

U.S. Commerce Department compiles lists of foreign companies seeking to purchase American-made products.

Researchers who utilize the vast resources of the United States government quickly appreciate the highly organized federal information system. The U.S. Government Printing Office (GPO) is the largest publisher in the free world; its products can be purchased by mail, telephone, or through GPO bookstores in major cities. What's more, centralized collections of government publications are widely available to the public. Nearly 1,500 public and academic libraries across the country are official depositories for federal documents. The U.S. government is also a major compiler of computer databases, from online files to magnetic tapes. The Superintendent of Documents already supplies CD-ROMs to local depository libraries, and a pilot program is under way to explore the feasibility of distributing other electronic files. A full range of computerized information might soon be disseminated freely to the public through the depository system. How does the researcher find needed information from the thousands of printed reports, microforms, and databases published each year? The task is made simpler by the many indexes, directories, and catalogs produced by the government and by commercial publishers. Some of the most important finding tools are introduced in Chapter 4.

Federal agencies also have resident experts on every subject imaginable, and many are not only willing, but happy to share their knowledge with interested outsiders. Guides to government experts are covered in Chapter 2. When seeking unpublished documents, citizens turn to the provisions of the Freedom of Information Act (FOIA), which stipulates that certain categories of documents must be made available to requesting individuals. Experienced researchers know there is more than one way to obtain answers from the government, and determination usually pays off.

Information from state governments may not be as easy to obtain as federal data, and the form of organization varies from state to state, but this source of information should not be overlooked. The state commerce department, attorney general's office, department of state, and banking and insurance commissions are all rich sources of business data. Staff members of legislative committees and local offices of state legislators can be excellent starting points when tracking down elusive government information. All 50 states have a state library agency, and most have a central research library where published documents are housed. Most state governments also publish organizational manuals, directories, and statistical abstracts.

Local agencies can be the most frustrating to deal with because government services are dispersed among counties, cities, and other jurisdictions. Local governments may produce and store useful material, but they do not necessarily assume the task of disseminating information or assisting researchers. Some of the more helpful agencies for research purposes are the county or city planning department, the county clerk's office, and the various tax departments. Independent agencies, such as regional planning boards and economic development agencies can also be quite helpful. Researchers seeking local government information are best advised to follow all leads and to visit agencies in person. Local information may also be obtained from such nongovernment sources as public libraries, newspaper offices, public utility companies, and chambers of commerce.

Libraries

Libraries of all types should be among the first sources of business information to investigate. While libraries create little in the way of primary information, they excel at collecting, organizing, and retrieving secondary materials. The first public library to provide distinct service to the business community was the Newark Public Library, which established a separate business branch at the turn of the century. By the 1950s, most central libraries in major cities had a business department or branch, and today even medium-sized libraries have respectable business collections. Librarians are familiar with the needs of their community and are happy to assist in any research problem.

Many colleges and universities have established specialized business libraries. Leading universities such as Harvard, Stanford, Columbia, and the University of Pennsylvania have outstanding business libraries, but even medium-sized colleges house well-rounded business collections in a general library. Finally, several thousand special libraries in the United States are associated with corporations or nonprofit organizations. New York City alone has hundreds of specialized business libraries located in organizations as diverse as the Federal Reserve Bank and the Advertising Research Foundation. Some special libraries are closed to the public, but many allow outside researchers to use materials in the library by appointment.

Although libraries of every kind are a wonderful source of free business information, remember that the library staff can only provide limited assistance to each patron. Librarians can answer specific questions and guide the user to appropriate information sources, but

they should not be expected to perform in-depth investigations. To minimize frustration, researchers must be willing to learn about basic reference tools and to orient themselves to library organization and procedures.

For those uninterested in conducting their own research, some large public and university libraries have autonomous research departments that will answer more involved business inquiries for a fee. Another alternative is to hire a free-lance researcher or information broker. Private research firms are available in most major cities, and several firms are national in scope. Two well-known information brokers are the FIND/SVP Information Clearinghouse in New York City and Washington Researchers, Ltd. in the District of Columbia.

Trade Associations and Other Nonprofit Organizations

A third source of high-quality business information is trade associations. These are voluntary organizations whose members are companies involved in the same type of business or industry. Associations deal with matters of mutual concern to their members, and common activities include promoting the industry, establishing standards and codes of ethics, and engaging in political lobbying. A primary function of the trade association is to provide information services to its members. Most groups maintain research departments, and many have extensive libraries. An association exists for just about every conceivable business activity, from the International Goat Association to Pickle Packers International. Not every group shares information with nonmembers, but the researcher will generally find it worthwhile to contact such organizations.

Numerous other nonprofit organizations can provide business information. Many research centers are prolific publishers of economic and business reports. Research foundations or "think tanks" may be highly partisan in outlook, or they may strive to remain politically neutral. Examples of highly respected research organizations are the Brookings Institution, the National Bureau of Economic Research, the RAND Corporation, the American Enterprise Institute, the Tax Foundation, the Conference Board, and the Urban Institute.

Another type of nonprofit organization is the university research center. Independently funded centers at major universities study all kinds of issues, including business and economic topics. Though many focus on regional concerns, especially at state universities, others are well known for the quality of their work at the national level. The Salomon Brothers Center for the Study of Financial Institutions, located at New York University, and Columbia University's Center for International Business Cycle Research are examples. Other nonprofit groups such as labor unions and public interest groups should also be considered when undertaking research.

Private Companies

The profitable nature of business intelligence makes the private sector another important source of information. Large corporations such as McGraw-Hill, Inc. and the Metropolitan Life Insurance Company have sophisticated research departments that produce high-quality business reports. Nationally known consulting firms such as Arthur D. Little, Inc. are also excellent sources of original business research. Many consultants have developed strong reputations for expertise in specialized areas. Forecast International/DMS is well known for research on aerospace and defense, for example. The range of companies existing solely to provide business information is truly incredible. Companies that publish business materials or package information for a fee will be discussed in the next section, which deals with published forms of business information.

When pursuing information, the researcher should be open to using any and all possible resources, published or otherwise. Imaginative research means looking beyond standard sources. On the other hand, it is sometimes easy to overlook the obvious. For example, one of the best places to obtain information about a company is from the company itself. Every researcher is faced with a limitless number of options, so it can be helpful to begin an investigation by thinking of broad categories rather than specific solutions. Although all options could not be covered in such a brief treatment, this section has endeavored to introduce some of the most important sources of business intelligence.

TYPES OF BUSINESS PUBLICATIONS

Just as there are many suppliers of business information, the material itself comes in many packages. Some publications appear in common forms, like books and newspapers, while others are more specific to the business world. Each has special characteristics, so it is worth discussing the principal categories in some detail. This section is intended as an introduction only. Specific examples of each category will be provided throughout the book.

Trade Journals and Newspapers

The trade journal is one of the most widely used, versatile, and affordable forms of business publication. A trade journal is a magazine devoted exclusively to the needs of a particular industry. Several thousand trade journals are published in the United States, covering most types of business activity. The diversity of titles is remarkable, ranging from *American Funeral Director* to *Professional Carwashing*. Trade journals are typically published monthly or bimonthly, though some appear fortnightly or even weekly. The largest publishers, such as McGraw-Hill, Penton, Chilton, and Cahners, produce more than 20 journals each, covering a variety of industries. Other large publishers specialize in a particular field; Lebhar-Friedman, for example, issues more than ten journals on various retailing industries. However, most trade publishers restrict their output to one or two titles.

Trade journals commonly provide a broad range of news and current information about the industries they cover. They may list personnel changes in leading companies, announce new products or major contracts, and warn of impending changes in government regulations or other important events. They also publish detailed articles on industry trends and discuss management techniques of interest to their readers. The advertisements are an especially useful source of intelligence because they are geared to the industry in question. Many journals also provide ongoing industry statistics, some of which are difficult to find elsewhere. Examples of titles with important current statistics are *Automotive News*, which provides a weekly report on U.S. car sales by manufacturer, and *Oil & Gas Journal*, which publishes weekly data on refinery output by product and region.

Special issues of trade journals are another vital source of information. Many periodicals publish special features on the same topic every year. Most are included with the basic subscription, but some must be purchased separately. Common topics include directories of companies within the industry, ranked lists of leading firms, buyer's guides listing major suppliers to the industry, salary surveys, "year in review" issues, and annual industry forecasts. Annual statistical publications that appear as special issues of such journals as *Progressive Grocer* and *Dealerscope Merchandising* have become classic sources of industry information.

A close cousin to the trade journal is the industry newspaper. Trade papers and tabloids generally appear more frequently than trade journals, typically on a daily or weekly basis. They resemble general newspapers in that they concentrate on current news rather than in-depth articles. Some are well known to the general public, such as *Women's Wear Daily*, *Billboard*, and *Daily Variety*; others, like *Advertising Age*, are read by businesspeople outside the industry; but most are intended for the industry alone. An interesting subgroup is the trade paper which provides detailed commodity price information. Examples are *American Metal Market* and *Chemical Marketing Reporter*.

Other Periodical Sources

Many other journals and newspapers are of interest to the business researcher. General magazines such as *Business Week* contain well-written articles on all aspects of business. Magazines like *Forbes, Fortune,* and *Inc.* carry detailed stories profiling individual companies and executives. Others, such as *Business Month, Across the Board,* and *Nation's Business,* concentrate on broad management, economic, and political trends. Professional journals, such as *Business Marketing, Personnel Journal,* and *Management Accounting,* are aimed at practitioners of particular management activities. Academic journals report the cutting edge of scholarly research, but the more popular business-school reviews are written as much for the business executive as the academic community. These journals summarize research findings for the general reader, and frequently present stimulating and controversial ideas. Articles in the better journals, from the famous *Harvard Business Review* to the lesser-known *Business Horizons,* are widely read and quoted. Finally, some business periodicals are comprised solely of statistical tables, and are often the most effective means of rapidly releasing such information. These journals may be published by government agencies (the U.S. Bureau of Labor Statistics' *Employment and Earnings*), or by nongovernment sources (Dun & Bradstreet's *Current Economic Indicators*).

No discussion of business periodicals would be complete without special mention of *The Wall Street Journal.* This renowned business newspaper has been published every business day since 1889 and has become an American institution. Though best known for its detailed coverage of the stock market, it is not simply a financial paper. The *Journal's* hallmark is investigative and analytical stories on all areas of business.

The format of the *Journal* underwent significant reorganization in October 1988, expanding coverage in such areas as technology, small business, law, and personal finance. The paper now appears in three standard-

ized sections, enabling the busy reader to quickly find topics of interest. An especially useful feature, familiar to long-time *Journal* readers, is the daily "What's News" section, which offers a quick, two-column summary of the day's events. The paper also carries more than ten rotating columns on various subjects, at least two of which appear each day. The topics range from "Tracking Travel" to "The Labor Letter." The daily investment columns are another popular feature, especially "Abreast of the Market," and the influential "Heard on the Street." The *Journal* can also surprise and delight first-time readers with its humorous pieces, excellent political coverage, country profiles, and book, movie, art, and theater reviews. Of course, it is packed with such daily financial and economic data as dividend announcements, corporate earnings reports, daily stock prices, and current economic indicators. Because of its long tradition of reporting reliable, unbiased news on a timely basis, *The Wall Street Journal* is without question the nation's premier business publication.

Business Information Services

Information "services" are another means of disseminating news to the business community. A service is a current awareness publication with several distinguishing characteristics: ongoing updates, narrow focus, a limited audience, and no advertising. Three major types of publication meet these criteria—newsletters, looseleafs, and syndicated intelligence services.

Newsletters differ from other periodicals in several additional respects. They are slender publications, often containing only 10 or 12 pages per issue. Many are published by a self-employed individual working out of a home or small office, and most also have very small circulations. Several thousand business newsletters are published in the United States. The most common type is the investment advisory letter (discussed in Chapter 12), but there are many others. For sheer diversity, few categories of publication can match the newsletter. *Keep Watching,* for example, carries stories on the causes and prevention of shoplifting; *Sludge* provides in-depth coverage of the treatment and disposal of municipal and industrial waste. Because of their narrow focus, newsletters often carry information not found anywhere else. And despite their limited distribution, many exert considerable influence; *Platt's Oilgram News* and *Scrip World Pharmaceutical News* are just two newsletters considered indispensable in their respective industries.

Loose-leaf services are publications designed to be stored in ring binders, so that revised material can be added easily by replacing an existing page with a new one. This format is familiar to the legal community, but is also a convenient method of transmitting business information. Such services can be updated monthly, weekly, or even daily to ensure the most current, accurate information possible. Loose-leafs are especially valuable for constantly changing subjects such as business law and corporate finance. The loose-leaf format is especially well suited to bring together voluminous information from a variety of sources and organize it in a coherent system. One of the best illustrations of this technique is the complex field of income taxes. Loose-leaf tax services gather the entire body of tax law and practice into a unified set of books and present the information in a manageable way. Tax laws, regulations, IRS rulings, and court decisions are grouped together by topic and updated continuously.

A handful of publishers specialize in producing loose-leaf services, and each of them issues dozens of products. Some of the biggest names in the loose-leaf field are Commerce Clearing House, the Bureau of National Affairs, and Prentice Hall. The publications of these and other companies will be discussed in in Chapters 19 and 20.

Syndicated intelligence services are less prevalent than newsletters and loose-leaf services and can be quite expensive. These services are the product of massive, ongoing surveys to obtain information unavailable through other methods. Instead of conducting research for a single customer, compilers of intelligence services concentrate on subjects with wider appeal, and sell the results to anyone who wishes to buy them. The most common areas for this type of publication are financial information and market research. The classic example of the financial intelligence service, Dun & Bradstreet's credit reporting, is introduced in Chapter 8.

Few areas of business publishing are as fascinating as market intelligence reports. Syndicated marketing services can provide the subscriber with an unbelievably detailed picture of how, where, and to whom individual products are advertised and sold. These subscription services are offered by market research firms employing a variety of survey techniques. Syndicated reports can provide demographic profiles of the people who buy a particular product, identify the best-selling brands in different parts of the country, list companies with the largest market share, determine who reads which magazines or watches what television shows, and innumerable

other useful facts. Some research firms specialize in a particular field. The Beverage Marketing Corporation, for example, focuses on the alcoholic beverage, soft drink, and bottled water industries, while Dataquest, Inc. follows computer-related industries. Other companies produce a broader range of major reports. The A.C. Nielsen Company and Audits & Surveys, Inc. are large, well-known providers of diversified services. Further discussion of syndicated marketing reports can be found in Chapter 18.

Many firms also provide onetime studies of market trends, either as multi-client studies or "off-the-shelf" reports. A multi-client study is proposed by a research firm and sponsored in advance by clients solicited by the researcher. Each sponsor then receives a copy of the resulting study. An off-the-shelf report results from a study with no advance sponsors; the producer of the report is betting that there is sufficient interest in the results to make the effort worthwhile. As an example, a research firm might conduct a thorough investigation of the market for laptop computers in Europe, then offer to sell the report to any companies interested in entering that market. These studies become outdated quickly, and they are expensive to obtain, usually starting at $800 or more for each report. Dozens of research firms in the United States, Europe, and the Far East engage in this type of publishing. Among the biggest U.S. firms are Frost & Sullivan, Inc., FIND/SVP, Inc., and Predicasts, Inc.

Microforms

Microfilm and microfiche publications enable the user to store large amounts of information in a small space. Enterprising publishers have discovered the additional benefit of collecting documents from a diversity of individual sources and reproducing them for sale on a single reel of film or packet of fiche. In the past, users wishing to maintain a comprehensive file of corporate annual reports, for example, had to contact hundreds of companies, keep track of what was received, process the incoming mail, and file the reports. A large collection took an enormous amount of space, and keeping more than the most current reports was impractical. To counter these difficulties, micropublishers collect paper reports and reproduce them on microfiche; users then choose from a number of subscription plans to create a customized, manageable collection of documents.

Any body of publications that is voluminous and time consuming to acquire is a perfect candidate for microform publishing. Suppliers of business information now offer an amazing variety of microfilm subscrip-

tions, including nondepository U.S. government documents, telephone books from across the country, manufacturers' catalogs, and state industrial directories.

Many microform collections are self-contained research systems, including detailed indexes to the publications themselves. Greenwood Press's *Urban Documents Microfiche Collection,* which reprints local government reports from the largest cities and counties in the United States and Canada, is supported by its quarterly *Index to Current Urban Documents.* University Microfilm International's (UMI's) *Transdex Index* is a monthly guide to the astonishing collection of foreign documents translated by the U.S. Joint Publications Research Service (JPRS). The JPRS translations include economic, political, medical, and technical articles and reports from all over the world. The publications are available on microfiche from the U.S. government or from UMI. By acquiring large microform collections, subscribers can instantly build extensive library collections.

This discussion has only scratched the surface of business publishing. Many additional formats can be of use to the researcher. Patents, court cases, company catalogs, brokerage reports, and house organs are a few of the other publications that deal with business topics. But the type of publication is not necessarily important to the user; the information itself is the researcher's ultimate goal, not the package in which it comes. However, certain types of information may be more likely to appear in a specific form, or may be used more conveniently in one format than another. Changes in business law may be found most readily in loose-leaf services, for example, while the results of an ongoing consumer survey may be available only through a syndicated intelligence service. The diligent researcher should utilize a diversity of formats when seeking elusive information. Background on a small local company might be found in printed directories, industry newsletters, a microform collection of regional publications, and an assortment of other resources. In most cases, no single source will provide sufficient information, but gleaning essential facts from a variety of publications will provide the needed answers.

ONLINE DATABASES

The power of the computer to store, organize, and disseminate vast amounts of information has truly revolutionized business publishing. Computerized indexing and typesetting enable publishers to produce up-to-the-minute reference books unknown in the past. But the real revolution in business information is the emergence of

electronic communication that bypasses the printed document and allows the user to interact with the publication in a variety of new ways. There is great diversity among computerized products, but the remainder of the chapter will explore the electronic media of greatest interest to business researchers, beginning with online databases.

The first commercially available online systems were introduced nearly 20 years ago, and have become an integral part of business research An online database is a file of information stored in a centralized computer and accessible to subscribers in remote locations via telecommunications systems. In the past, searchers used dumb terminals or teleprinters to communicate with the host system, but today most people use microcomputers to conduct an online search. The user establishes an account with the database supplier (hereafter called the vendor), searches the database whenever needed, and in most cases pays only for the actual searching that is done. The database vendor serves as an intermediary between dozens of information producers and the researchers wishing to access their files. Many producers also publish the contents of their database as printed reference works and CD-ROM disks.

Benefits of Online Systems

Computer databases have many advantages over printed materials. First, having access to databases saves the researcher the cost of purchasing thousands of dollars of reference works. Why spend $400 on a business directory which is consulted only a few times each year, when most database vendors charge only for the actual usage? Second, many types of information are simply not available in any other form. The researcher who ignores computer databases closes the door on a panorama of unique information sources. More rapid updating of information is an obvious advantage of databases. Many online systems also offer the option of printing the results of a search in a variety of customized formats, so that the user obtains information in exactly the form required. A subtler advantage is that large online systems can help overcome the incredible fragmentation of published information. Many online vendors offer global search capabilities, allowing access to the contents of dozens of databases simultaneously, the equivalent of instantly reading dozens of different reference books at the same time. The researcher need not worry that less obvious sources of information are being overlooked, or that time constraints are limiting the number of sources consulted. The most important benefit the computer offers researchers is the incredible speed and power of electronic re-

trieval. Users can utilize an assortment of sophisticated commands to bring pinpoint accuracy to a search. Taken together, these capabilities make online searching one of the most powerful tools at the researcher's disposal. However, online databases *do not* completely replace other research methods. Databases have drawbacks, including the amount of time required to become proficient in their use and to keep skills polished. Specialized reference books are still the most efficient way to locate certain types of business information.

But traditional research tools such as library card catalogs and printed periodical indexes can be cumbersome and time-consuming to use. The researcher can find material easily only if the cataloger or indexer has placed it under some variation of the concept being sought. A further constraint is the need to know the vocabulary and filing rules of the printed source. With computer databases, the user can search for a specific word wherever it appears, whether it is an official index term or not. Many online vendors offer versatile command languages which enable the user to perform very sophisticated searches. One common type of command is called the logical (or Boolean) operator. By using the commands AND, OR, and NOT, the searcher can identify records exhibiting a combination of characteristics. The OR operator, for example, allows the user to combine a string of synonymous terms to broaden a search. AND is used to link two or more disparate concepts by locating items containing all of the terms in the same record. (A record is an individual item in the database. If the databases lists journal articles, then the description of each article comprises a single record.) The proximity operator allows the user to look for words as they appear in relation to one another (word A within five words of B, word A in the same paragraph as word B, etc.) Field searching permits the user to specify the portion (or field) of a record where the information must appear. Searchers can then limit the search to words appearing in the title of the article, the lead paragraph, the company name field, or elsewhere. Other limiting commands can narrow the search results by date, language, country, or similar characteristics.

To illustrate, assume a researcher wants to know more about the concept of "critical success factors" (CSF) in management. He or she could tap into a database called *ABI/INFORM* to quickly find several hundred articles on this topic. By using proximity operators, the system will identify every occurrence of that phrase in the database, whether it is the subject of the article or not. The results could be narrowed using the AND operator to find those articles discussing both CSF and the subject term "Strategic Planning." Using the NOT operator, articles which talk about project management are ex-

cluded. Finally, the results could be restricted to articles providing practical guidelines for implementing the CSF technique, written in English during the past five years. As an alternate approach, the searcher could focus on the use of CSF in a particular setting—within an industry, such as banking, or a specific functional application, such as human resource management. Thus online searching not only enables the user to locate "needle-in-the-haystack" information, but to limit a large body of relevant literature to a more manageable size. Exhibit 5-1 (in Chapter 5) shows a typical record from *ABI/INFORM*, as retrieved through a variation of the above-mentioned searches.

Types of Databases

There are three broad database categories: bibliographic, full-text, and factual. Bibliographic databases refer the user to information in other publications. They may cover journal and magazine articles, newsletters and newspapers, books, dissertations, conference proceedings, research reports, or any other type of publication. The database can be searched by specific topic, author, type of document, time period, or dozens of other access points, taken singly or in combination. Some bibliographic databases provide only indexing to the publications they cover, but many provide abstracts (brief summaries) of the articles as well. *ABI/INFORM* is a bibliographic database; many others are introduced in Chapters 4 and 5.

Full-text databases provide complete documents that have been stored in a computer file. The user can request the text of magazine articles, newspaper stories, special reports, and even entire encyclopedias. Full-text services offer the advantage of instantaneous access to the article or publication needed. In the past, if the material was unavailable locally, the researcher had to resort to interlibrary loan or to a commercial document delivery service. The cost of printing an article from an online database is often inexpensive, and usually compares favorably to other delivery modes. An important question to ask, however, is what constitutes "full-text." Online access to full-text files presently excludes photographs and other graphics accompanying an article. In some cases, the online version may also exclude tables and other supporting information, and many full-text files omit news briefs, events calendars, reviews, and other short features.

Another advantage of full-text is the ability to search for words or names that appear anywhere in the text, regardless of whether they are the focus of the

article. For example, someone trying to verify that Cracker Jack popcorn snacks were introduced in 1892 at the World's Columbian Exposition in Chicago could locate the answer in minutes via a simple search of the full-text newspaper files available on the NEXIS group of databases. A trivia column in the *Boston Globe* had answered the exact question by contacting the public relations staff of Borden, Inc. It is highly unlikely that this article would have been located if the text of the newspaper was not available online.

A final advantage of full-text systems is their incredible timeliness; many files are updated continuously throughout the day. For up-to-the-minute information, full-text news wire services can be an unparalleled source of business intelligence. Wire stories can be searched by subscribers of DIALOG, NEXIS, and other leading vendors, can with little real-time delay. Whether they provide general, financial, or corporate news, wire services can give a more detailed version of the story than appears in a newspaper or magazine. Major electronic news wires are described in Chapter 5.

Factual databases provide the user with answers to specific nonbibliographic questions, and are among the most interesting databases to use. They may list directory information, statistics, or financial data. Specialized databases can provide airline schedules, credit ratings, patent and trademark filings, stock and bond quotations, and even movie reviews. For the innovative business researcher, factual databases are extremely versatile tools. Electronic directories can be used to generate customized mailing lists, identify links between companies, rank firms by size within an industry, and find elusive information about executives. Online financial services can be used to select companies which meet stated criteria, monitor portfolios, identify emerging trends, or compare the performance and position of several companies quickly and easily. Statistical databases enable the researcher to locate hard-to-find data, obtain newly released figures before they appear in print, and create tables with many years of historical data. Information from factual databases of all types can also be downloaded to a microcomputer file for further manipulation by the user's word processing, database management, spreadsheet, or mapping software.

The differences among the three types of databases are not always clear; in fact, a significant trend in the online industry is the emergence of databases which merge the characteristics or functions of several files. In particular, a number of business databases now combine bibliographic records with directory information. For example, the *Company Intelligence* database from Infor-

mation Access Company contains information on over 100,000 firms. Each record provides a brief company description together with citations to approximately ten recent journal and newspaper stories on the firm.

Several thousand online services are presently marketed by dozens of database vendors. Because of the businessperson's need for current information and the corporation's willingness to pay for it, one can choose from an extraordinary number of business-related databases. One of the largest, most diversified vendors of online services is DIALOG (DIALOG Information Services Inc., now a subsidiary of Knight-Ridder, Inc.). DIALOG offers more than 350 databases, approximately two-thirds of which have direct business applications. Business information on DIALOG runs the gamut from company directories, financial services, and statistical files, to news wires, periodical indexes, and full-text files of newspapers, journals, and newsletters. The BRS Search Service (BRS Information Technologies, now part of Maxwell Online, a subsidiary of Maxwell Communication Corporation, PLC) has fewer offerings than DIALOG, but it too has numerous files of interest to business researchers, including several factual and full-text databases. Most of the business databases on BRS are also available through DIALOG, but a few, such as the index to *Investor's Daily*, are found on BRS alone.

Several major vendors have concentrated on supplying full-text services for searchers who do not have large libraries at their disposal. The pioneer in the creation of such files was Mead Data Central, Inc. (a subsidiary of the Mead Corporation), whose LEXIS/NEXIS databases offer electronic editions of a growing number of publications, including exclusive rights to the online version of the *New York Times*. LEXIS/NEXIS business offerings include corporate annual reports, state corporation filings, Wall Street brokerage reports, and the complete text of newsletters, trade journals, and local business newspapers. Two other full-text vendors are VU/TEXT (VU/TEXT Information Services, Inc., another subsidiary of Knight-Ridder) and DataTimes (DataTimes Corporation, a subsidiary of the Oklahoma Publishing Company); each supplies the complete text of daily newspapers from cities around the country. NewsNet (NewsNet, Inc.) is a full-text provider of business newsletters online. Dow Jones News/Retrieval offers sole access to the online version of *The Wall Street Journal* and the Dow Jones news wire, among the several hundred full-text titles it makes available. Even DIALOG has added many full-text files to its system.

Many other vendors offer major business databases. Reuters Ltd. provides extensive online statistics for economic and industry analysis, plus numerous U.S. and foreign financial and full-text databases. The H.W. Wilson Company produces an array of bibliographic files under the WILSONLINE logo, including *Business Periodicals Index* and *Biography Index*. Such European systems as Pergamon Financial Data Services (Pergamon Orbit Infoline, Ltd., another Maxwell subsidiary) and Data-Star (a subsidiary of Radio-Suisse AG, owned in part by the Swiss government) contain both American and foreign databases, and are being marketed aggressively to researchers in the United States. Each boasts a diversity of bibliographic and nonbibliographic business files, searchable using powerful command systems similar to their American competitors. Data-Star is especially noteworthy because it offers U.S. subscribers significant connect-hour discounts during certain times of the day.

The researcher should also be aware that many specialized vendors provide expensive subscription services exclusively to business customers. Most of the vendors mentioned up to this point charge a nominal annual service fee in addition to the billings for actual usage. Others, such as LEXIS/NEXIS and NewsNet, assess a modest monthly subscription fee in addition to usage charges. Except for these costs, the most popular systems can be characterized as "pay-per-use" services. In contrast, some database vendors sell their services to corporate clients for hefty annual subscriptions plus usage fees. Services of this type are not as widely known, and have a smaller base of subscribers. They are used most heavily by corporate libraries and other research units in large organizations. To distinguish them from their better-known counterparts, they will be referred to throughout this book as "corporate-oriented services." Examples are ADP Network Services, Inc. and DRI/McGraw-Hill.

Menu-Driven Systems

For many years, database searching was the exclusive domain of librarians and other trained information professionals. Vendors like DIALOG, Data-Star, BRS, and Mead utilize complex command structures that require training and practice to master. This does not mean that novices are unable to search them, only that considerable experience is required to use them efficiently and well. In the past, most people had to rely on a librarian or information broker to perform searches for them. Individuals conducting their own searches had to use the

databases heavily to maintain searching skills and to justify the investment in online training. That situation has changed dramatically in recent years with the growing popularity of more user-friendly databases. These "end-user systems" utilize a series of menus to guide the searcher through each step. They are being marketed to anyone with a personal computer, a modem, and a need for information, whether at home or work. CompuServe (CompuServe, Inc., a subsidiary of H&R Block), and Dow Jones News/Retrieval (Dow Jones & Company, Inc.) have far outstripped DIALOG and BRS in the number of individual subscribers reached. Traditional vendors have responded by introducing menu-driven systems of their own. DIALOG now offers The Knowledge Index and The Business Connection, user-friendly subsystems of the parent service. DIALOG has also begun offering individual databases in menu-driven format as well. BRS entered the end-user market with BRS/After Dark and BRS/Colleague.

A new wrinkle in end-user searching is based on the videotext systems which have become popular in Europe. Videotext is distinguished by more sophisticated graphics and the presence of advertising to off-set subscription costs. The major player in this country is PRODIGY (Prodigy Services Company, a joint venture of IBM and Sears). It offers home shopping, financial services, consumer product evaluations, entertainment, news, and business information, all for a flat monthly fee.

Most menu-driven systems are designed for home use, but several have important business applications. CompuServe is best known for its recreational databases, bulletin boards for hobbyists, and electronic shopping networks, but many of its offerings are relevant to business research. CompuServe is one of the few major vendors providing access to such popular databases as the *Institutional Broker's Estimate System*, *SUPERSITE*, and the *Value Line DataFile*. Some business-related services are not available to basic CompuServe subscribers, only to those paying a higher monthly fee.

A more obvious choice for end-user business searching is the Dow Jones News/Retrieval system. Although an increasing number of Dow Jones offerings can be searched using a powerful command language, the system's major appeal continues to be its menu-driven databases. As one might expect, the emphasis is on financial information, but the selection is quite extensive. Users can find Dun & Bradstreet reports, stock quotes, foreign news services, corporate financial reports, and a diversity of stock market advice and analysis.

Most CompuServe subscribers are home users, but the vast majority of Dow Jones searchers are corporate customers.

How do menu systems differ from their command-driven alternatives? To move through the databases, users must select from a continuing series of menu choices until they arrive at the desired information. Choices are strictly limited to what appears on the various menus. Moving from one step to the next is simple, but cumbersome, and many researchers who know exactly what they want find this approach frustrating. The tradeoff is apparent: menu systems are simple to use, but limited in their capabilities; command systems are extremely versatile, but complex and more difficult to master. Most experienced searchers eschew the menu systems, but such avoidance is really a form of computer-search snobbery. Menu systems can be valuable research tools because many useful business databases are available nowhere else, and many are tailor-made for answering specific reference questions. Particularly when the request itself is simple, menu-driven databases can be the most cost-effective option for providing quick information.

Nonprofit Databases

With few exceptions, business databases are expensive to access, regardless of the type of system upon which they reside. Government-produced databases offer more reasonably priced alternatives, even when found on commercial systems. Products from government agencies include bibliographic files, numeric databases, and electronic directories. For example, the complete text of the U.S. Commerce Department's *Commerce Business Daily* can be searched on DIALOG and several other vendors. It lists major federal contract awards and requests for proposals issued by civilian and military agencies. Databases compiled by state agencies also appear on commercial systems. A discussion of state databases for corporate research is found in Chapter 8.

Numerous state and federal agencies have created electronic bulletin boards from which business researchers can obtain the latest news and statistical information. Participants on the U.S. Bureau of the Census bulletin board system, for example, can view and download summary data from many of the most recent Census surveys the same day data are released. Governments also maintain hundreds of in-house databases containing public information. Although access is restricted to agency personnel (which in some cases includes govern-

ment contractors), researchers with specific questions may be able to obtain needed information by contacting the appropriate office.

The catalogs of academic and public libraries are another source of online information which should not be overlooked by business researchers. Libraries of all sizes have converted their traditional card catalogs into electronic databases with sophisticated searching capabilities. As more libraries begin to offer remote access to these catalogs, researchers will be able to dial up vast amounts of information from their home or office, virtually free of charge. Many libraries are even appending other databases to their online catalog systems, with files ranging from internally produced directories of community agencies to commercial products such as *Business Periodicals Index* and electronic encyclopedias. Libraries are also linking their online catalogs into regional and statewide networks, allowing users to search enormous databases of shared resources. In addition, several nationwide catalog networks, formerly available only to library employees, are becoming increasingly accessible to end-users. These formidable research tools will be discussed in Chapter 4.

OTHER ELECTRONIC INFORMATION SOURCES

Online systems remain the most heavily used electronic sources for business searching, but they are by no means the only medium at the researcher's disposal. Important business databases can be found with increasing frequency on CD-ROMs, magnetic tape files, and diskettes for microcomputers.

CD-ROM Products

An extremely popular alternative to online information retrieval has emerged in recent years—database searching on Compact Disk-Read Only Memory (CD-ROM). Using laser technology, information producers are able to store an incredible amount of data on a single compact disk (or disc). Because a single CD can hold up to 1,500 times the data on a floppy diskette, large databases can be installed on a microcomputer for local use. The CD-ROM disk is read by computers using a special CD player. As a result, researchers now can acquire the current contents of a heavily used database on compact disk and search the file as often as they want.

The contents of the CD cannot be altered or added to in any way; data on old disks are superseded by completely revised editions.

The first commercially available CD-ROM database was unveiled in 1985, though larger 12-inch optical disk products had previously been available. Since that time, several hundred CD-ROM databases have been released by a myriad of publishers, and many more appear each month. Publications on CD-ROM range from the complete text of the multi-volume *Oxford English Dictionary* to automotive parts catalogs. As with online databases, CD-ROM search software may utilize a system of menus, a sophisticated command structure, or both. CD-ROM products are designed as end-user products. In general, they are easy to use, offering a variety of search prompts, status messages, and instructional displays at every step. Most are updated on a continuing basis—quarterly, monthly, or even weekly. In some cases, subscribers purchase the disks outright; in others, they lease the most recent edition and return superseded disks.

Business-related CD-ROMs are among the fastest growing products. Like their online counterparts, they include bibliographic, full-text, and factual databases. The most prolific category of business CDs is the factual database. Products range from corporate directories, such as Dun & Bradstreet's *Million Dollar Disc,* to demographic statistics, such as Slater Hall Information Products' *Population Statistics*, and even to geographic information systems, such as Chadwyck-Healey's *Supermap.*

Full-text products for business cover everything from financial reports to periodical articles. Two types of full-text disks are currently on the market. The first reproduces the text portion of the document only, with the characters entered into the database in ASCII format. The user can search any word or phrase appearing in a record, but photographs, drawings, and graphs are not available. An example is University Microfilm International's *Business Dateline.* The second type of full-text disk employs optical scanning technology to reproduce an exact replica of the original article, including all graphics. With this system the text cannot be searched; in fact, nothing in the database is searchable unless the producer adds its own indexing. In some cases, optically scanned products are intended simply as a document storage medium, much like microfilm or microfiche. Instead of issuing thousands of sheets of fiche per year, the new medium allows the publisher to store the same amount on several dozen CDs. A few ingenious information companies have combined the searching

power of their existing databases with the convenience of full-text optical scanning. The user consults the traditional bibliographic index to locate articles, which are then automatically linked to the location of the complete article or report on a separate disk. Two spectacular examples are University Microfilm International's *Business Periodicals Ondisc* (which can be searched using the powerful *ABI/INFORM* database) and Disclosure, Incorporated's *Laser D/SEC* (which likewise is linked to the sophisticated searching power of *Compact D/SEC*).

An especially interesting development among business CD-ROMs is the trend toward products which combine an assortment of databases on a single disk. *CD/Corporate*, part of Lotus Development Corporation's Lotus One Source family of databases, brings together investment data from Media General Financial Services, Inc., abstracts of periodical articles from Predicasts and UMI/Data Courier, and much more. *Computer Select*, from Ziff Communications Company, combines full-text articles from popular computing magazines, abstracts to articles from over 100 additional trade journals and newspapers, specifications for thousands of computer hardware and software products, profiles of 11,000 companies in computer-related industries, and a dictionary of computing terminology.

Similarly, many producers of CD-ROMs are combining disk subscriptions with software allowing access to an online database for additional information. Users of the Lotus One Source disks may select a menu item called *CD/Newsline* to tap into a segment of the Dow Jones News/Retrieval database. Both DIALOG and H.W. Wilson offer disk subscribers dial-up access to a variety of databases to update their CD-ROM searches. Subscribers to Dun & Bradstreet's *Dun's Reference Plus*, a directory of several million U.S. companies, can dial into the full D&B database to order complete company reports.

The U.S. government has also embraced CD-ROM technology. Following the lead of the Bureau of the Census, several agencies are now issuing CD-ROM databases. Most existing products are numeric or factual. Many are available through the depository library system, and more will follow. The software for searching these files is not always sophisticated or user-friendly, but government distribution of these important files is a welcome development indeed.

CD-ROM technology has its drawbacks, including less timely updating than online files, the cost of setting up multiple workstations, and the need to purchase numerous products to obtain broad subject coverage. Unless the subscriber invests considerable time, effort,

and money into networking, each disk can be used by only one user at a time. One of the biggest frustrations is the lack of standard search software. Dozens of search systems are in use, and subscribers to multiple products will need to master a diversity of them. For this reason, it may make sense to focus on families of similar products. For business research, product families using a common search language include InfoTrac (Information Access Company), DIALOG OnDisc (DIALOG Information Service), ProQuest (University Microfilms International), SilverPlatter (SilverPlatter Information, Inc.), WILSONDISC (H.W. Wilson Company), and Lotus One Source (Lotus Development Corporation).

Computer Tapes

Less common than CD-ROMs or online databases is the sale or lease of data tapes. Many producers of electronic databases make copies of tapes available to customers for use on their own computers. Among the types of data files available for purchase are bank regulatory reports, demographic data, and stock price information. This option might seem a bit exotic, but many large corporations, planning agencies, and universities routinely use tapes produced by commercial firms, nonprofit research organizations, and government agencies. The federal government alone compiles hundreds of statistical files, from the National Oceanic and Atmospheric Administration's *Earthquake Database* to country surveys from the *CIA World Data Bank*. Many current data sets are available directly from the issuing agencies, while hundreds more are distributed by the Federal Computer Products Center, an arm of the government's National Technical Information Service. Historical files can be ordered through the National Archives, which also operates a referral service to lead researchers to appropriate sources of government data files.

Major universities have established centralized data tape archives to collect such materials and help researchers use them. Individuals interested in tape files should also be aware of the Inter-university Consortium for Political and Social Research (ICPSR), a network which provides publicly available data files to member universities. Located at the University of Michigan, ICPSR presently boasts more than 300 member institutions around the world. Its tape depository contains over 1,400 machine-readable data sets in all areas of the social sciences. Political data and public opinion surveys are strongly represented in the collection, but a wealth of statistical information for business and economic re-

search can also be found. Relevant files cover such topics as demographics, employment, income, housing, consumer behavior, health care, and government finance. Some of the more popular ongoing files are the *Consumer Expenditure Survey* from the U.S. Bureau of Labor Statistics, the *Current Population Surveys* from the U.S. Bureau of the Census, *International Monetary Statistics* from the International Monetary Fund, and the *Survey of Consumer Attitudes and Behavior* conducted by the University of Michigan's Survey Research Center. ICPSR also produces a number of online databases for research purposes. These are accessible through ICPSR's Consortium Data Network (CDNet). *ICPSR Variables* is a detailed online index to the actual survey questions appearing in several hundred popular tape files. It is a powerful tool for identifying data series on a specific topic, or for comparing how questions are asked in different surveys. The *Survey Methodology Information System* is a bibliographic index to articles, books, conference papers, and unpublished reports relating to survey design and methods.

Although most computer tape files contain statistical records, some bibliographic and full-text tapes are also being introduced. As mentioned earlier, larger university and public libraries are acquiring tapes of periodical indexes such as *Business Periodicals Index*, the *Academic Index*, and *ABI/INFORM*. Several companies have produced user-friendly software which enables searchers to access these tapes directly from the library's online catalog. What was once a rarity is gradually becoming commonplace in large libraries despite the considerable costs of mounting such a system.

For the moment, most business researchers don't have access to locally mounted (on-site) bibliographic or numeric tape files. However, there is a wide selection of business data available on diskette. Smaller files of all types are being sold for use with microcomputers. Some contain data only, and must be used in conjunction with commercially available software. Other products have their own customized software and are sold as standalone systems. Either way, microcomputer data files can be used in combination with other software such as spreadsheets, statistical packages, or mapping programs. Users can reorganize data, perform additional computations, and produce sophisticated maps and graphs.

Diskettes containing economic, financial, and demographic data are the most popular, but nonstatistical files such as company directories are also common. Examples of commercial products sold on diskette include DRI/McGraw-Hill's *Metro Insights City Analyzer*, which contains economic profiles of major U.S. metropolitan areas, and *Value/Screen II*, a collection of stock market information from Value Line, Inc. The federal government also markets a selection of diskette products, ranging from the Bureau of the Census's *County Business Patterns* to the U.S. Department of Labor's *Dictionary of Occupational Titles*.

As with printed products, the form in which electronic information is available is not as important as knowing where to find it. Indeed, as more and more products become available in electronic form, the differences in formats will become less obvious. The researcher sitting at a microcomputer in the library or office may have no idea whether the database being used is part of a CD-ROM network, a locally mounted computer tape, or a remote online system. Much of the preceding section was presented to illustrate the incredible diversity of products available and to underscore the substantial impact of technology on business information. Despite the dazzling promise of electronic information, printed products remain the best source to consult in many cases. Though online databases and CD-ROMs offer exciting capabilities for retrieving and reorganizing information, many printed resources are perfectly suited to a specific information request.

The bewildering array of information formats—paper, microform, and electronic—may seem to present more confusion than help, but the diversity of choices provides the researcher with enormous flexibility. The individual who wants to subscribe to a compendium of economic statistics may have the option of selecting a journal, a yearbook, a floppy diskette, an online database, or an electronic bulletin board. For library users, the variety of formats increases the likelihood that an individual library will have the information in question.

SOME PARTING COMMENTS

Information is valuable to the business community and an extraordinary range of material is available to those who know where to look. But, do managers take advantage of secondary information sources? Numerous studies indicate that they do not. When making business decisions, executives depend upon people, rather than publications, to obtain the information they need. Decisions are often based on subjective factors, not data. Managers typically skim through a handful of publications on a routine basis—a business magazine, a daily newspaper, a few trade journals, and perhaps an intelligence service. Personal contacts are often the principal

way in which executives keep up on things. In other words, most businesspeople rely on passive methods of gathering intelligence.

If information is such a critical resource, why is it so often ignored or underutilized? One reason is human nature, which leads all of us to resolve our personal information needs in the same haphazard ways. The sheer volume of information is a formidable barrier to its use. Also, decision-makers prefer to see information summarized, with clearly stated conclusions. To the degree that lower-level managers seek information from secondary sources, senior executives do receive the benefit of business research. But the greatest reason secondary information remains unused is that too many businesspeople are unaware of what is available, while those who understand its value frequently have no idea how to find what they need.

Researching secondary business sources is not a skill taught in business schools (or most other places, for that matter), but it is a skill worth learning. Whether you are a librarian, manager, journalist, market researcher, or free-lance investigator, and whether you seek information for yourself or someone else, this book should prove helpful in achieving that goal. The remaining chapters introduce specific types of business information, examples of where it can be found, and how to interpret what is discovered.

Becoming an "information specialist" is a lifelong process, but it begins with accepting the point of view that information is a powerful tool when used to its potential. The purpose of this book is to present a systematic approach to a complex subject. For those who are new to the field of business research, it should provide a solid grounding for further study. To those already engaged in research, the material is intended to hone skills previously developed. Regardless of your interests, it is hoped you will find the world of business information both helpful and fascinating.

FOR FURTHER READING

A few of the topics touched upon in this chapter are explored more fully in the following articles and publications. Researchers in a variety of disciplines have begun to examine ways to measure the economic value of information technology in the business organization. Two notable works are *The Information Edge* by N. Dean Meyer and Mary E. Boone (2nd ed., Dow Jones-Irwin, 1989) and *Information Economics* by Marilyn M. Parker

and Robert J. Benson (Prentice Hall, 1988). Rather than focusing on information technology, the works below look at the role of business information. One of its major uses is to obtain competitor intelligence; selected works on this topic are described in the reading list following Chapter 8. The materials describing electronic databases are meant to highlight the differences among different types. Books and articles on database searching techniques are found at the end of Chapter 3.

Use and Value of Business Information

Garvin, Andrew. *How to Win with Information or Lose without It* (Washington, DC: Bermont, 1980).

Garvin is president of FIND/SVP, one of the most successful information brokerage firms in the U.S. Here he discusses the importance of information for decision-makers and how to obtain needed facts. The value of this book is in its outlook toward the information-seeking process, with an emphasis on how to deal with "information paralysis."

Meyer, Herbert E. *Real World Intelligence: Organized Information for Executives* (New York: Weideneld & Nicolson, 1987).

Presents an overview of the intelligence function, using examples from the government, the military, and business. As former vice chairman of the U.S. National Intelligence Council, the author provides an interesting perspective for business researchers. This unusual book is lively, perceptive, well written, and concise. Though somewhat general in its coverage, the examples ring true and the arguments are convincing.

Newsome, James, and Claire McInerney. "Environmental Scanning and the Information Manager." *Special Libraries* 81 (Fall 1990): 285–93.

Introduces the concept of environmental scanning in business organizations, its uses and value. Describes basic components of a scanning program and suggests ways the corporate library can become active in the process.

Ullmann, John E. "Coping with Bad News." In *Global Corporate Intelligence*, edited by George S. Roukis, Hugh Conway, and Bruce H. Charnov. (New York: Quorum, 1990): 109–22.

Most discussions of strategic intelligence focus on its value in identifying emerging opportunities. This piece explores major threats which may come to light from the information-gathering process, and how companies should react to bad news.

Characteristics of Business Information Users

Aguilar, Francis. *Scanning the Business Environment* (New York: Macmillan, 1967).

This landmark work, based on the author's doctoral dissertation, studies the ways in which senior executives acquire and use information. The book discusses both active and passive scanning methods and their impact on executive decisions. Though published more than 20 years ago, this study offers many insights which remain valid today.

Daft, Richard L., Juhani Sormunen, and Don Parks. "Chief Executive Scanning, Environmental Characteristics, and Company Performance: An Empirical Study." *Strategic Management Journal* 9 (March/April 1988): 123–39.

Chief executives were interviewed in 50 manufacturing companies to determine the methods and frequency of environmental scanning. The findings indicate that scanning is most often employed in situations of greatest uncertainty. The study also shows that CEOs in profitable companies engage in scanning more often than their counterparts in less profitable firms.

Littlejohn, Alice C., and Lois Benson-Talley. "Business Students and the Academic Library: A Second Look." *Journal of Business & Finance Librarianship* 1, No. 1 (1990): 65–88.

This study of library behavior among business students at California State University Long Beach discovered that use of the library has increased dramatically in recent years, but students still possess limited library research skills.

Reid, David M. "Data Access and Issue Analysis in Strategic Planning." *Marketing Intelligence & Planning* 7, No. 1/2 (1989): 14–18.

Summarizes a study of corporate data-gathering practices, based on interviews with CEOs from more than 100 firms in diverse industries. Reid concluded most companies have a surprisingly poor understanding of their customers, their competitors, and the marketing environment because they have no formal structure for collecting strategic intelligence.

Wurman, Richard Saul. *Information Anxiety* (New York: Doubleday, 1989).

"Information anxiety," which the author defines as "the ever-widening gap between what we understand and what we think we should understand," is the price we pay for living in an information-rich society. In a shamelessly gimmicky book, packed with eye-catching graphics, epigrams, quotes, and anecdotes, the author suggests techniques for coping with this modern ailment. Wurman has a breezy style and a wonderful knack for coining phrases like the "uh-huh syndrome" and "overload amnesia." Many readers will balk at the book's disjointed presentation and Wurman's endless capacity for self-promotion, but everyone will find nuggets of wisdom in this entertaining jaunt.

Online Databases

Pfaffenberger, Bryan. *Democratizing Information: Online Databases and the Rise of End-User Searching* (Boston: G.K. Hall, 1990).

Explores two key questions: whether database technology has the potential to create an "information democracy," where the most unsophisticated users have access to electronic data; and whether end-user searching will become as common as using the telephone. In a carefully developed analysis, the book reviews the history of database technology, the "unanticipated need" for search intermediaries, and the promise of such new technologies as front-end search software, CD-ROMs, and artificial intelligence. At the outset, the author states his sympathy for the goal of successful end-user searching, but most of this monograph examines the barriers to achieving it.

Suozzi, Patricia. "By the Numbers: An Introduction to Numeric Databases." *Database* 10 (February 1987): 15–22.

Introduces basic concepts related to numeric files available through online systems.

Tenopir, Carol, and Jung Soon Ro. *Full Text Databases*. New Directions in Information Management, no. 21. (New York: Greenwood, 1990).

Summarizes recent research in the field of full-text databases, much of it conducted by Tenopir herself. Topics include how well full-text systems perform, and how effectively people search them. Several introductory chapters describe the characteristics of full-text databases, how they differ from bibliographic files, the vendors, the different types, and descriptions of representative databases. Covers both online and CD-ROM media. Concluding chapters summarize the ramifications of research findings for searchers and database producers.

Other Electronic Information Systems

Chen, Ching-chih, and Peter Hernon, eds. *Numeric Databases* (Norwood, NJ: Ablex, 1984).

A wide-ranging collection of essays on numeric databases, with an emphasis on machine-readable files produced on computer tape.

Eaton, Nancy L., Linda Brew MacDonald, and Mara R. Saule. *CD-ROM and Other Optical Information Systems: Implementation Issues for Libraries* (Phoenix, AZ: Oryx Press, 1989).

A sound and thorough introduction to library implementation of CD-ROM products, including a clear, concise explanation of what they are, how they work, and the hardware involved. Other topics covered are library applications of CD-ROM, retrieval methods and software-related concerns, the impact of CDs on library service, and future policy considerations. Several case studies of successful library implementation are presented.

Gerken, Ann. "What Is a Data Archive and What Should the Information Specialist Know About Managing Locally Maintained Numeric Data Files?" *Database* 11 (August 1988): 60–65.

An excellent primer on the basic characteristics of numeric tape files and the key considerations in establishing a collection of computerized data tapes.

Lewis, Peter H. "Where Libraries Are Leading the Way." *New York Times* (May 13, 1990): F–8.

A brief overview of how libraries are at the forefront of innovations in computerized information storage and retrieval.

O'Leary, Mick. "Local Online: The Genie Is Out of the Bottle—Part I." *Online* 14 (January 1990): 15–18.

Discusses the growing popularity of locally mounted bibliographic tape files, and lists some of the database providers offering on-site licensing. Part II of the article, which appears in the March 1990 issue, compares the costs and benefits of on-site licensing to CD-ROM workstations.

Quint, Barbara. "How Is CD-ROM Disappointing? Let Me Count the Ways." *Wilson Library Bulletin* (December 1987): 32–34.

To temper the almost universal enthusiasm for CD-ROM technology exhibited by librarians, gadfly Quint suggests some limitations when compared to online systems. An important commentary from an incisive and humorous observer.

Wenzel, Patrick. "Microcomputer-based Access to Machine-readable Databases." *Reference Services Review* No. 1/2 (1988): 51–55.

Explores the seldom-discussed world of commercial data files available on floppy diskette.

PART II
Getting Started

CHAPTER 2
Locating Experts

TOPICS COVERED

1. People: The Untapped Information Source
2. Directories of Government Agencies
   a. Federal Executive Agencies
   b. The United States Congress
   c. State and Local Agencies
3. Directories of Libraries and Librarians
4. Directories of Associations
5. Universities and Nonprofit Research
   Organizations
6. Fee-Based Research Services
7. How and When to Ask for Help
8. For Further Reading

MAJOR SOURCES DISCUSSED

- *United States Government Manual*
- *Federal Executive Directory*
- *Congressional Staff Directory*
- *State Administrative Officials Classified by Function*
- *State Data and Database Finder*
- *World Chamber of Commerce Directory*
- *Directory of Special Libraries and Information Centers*
- *Encyclopedia of Associations*
- *Research Centers Directory*
- *Burwell Directory of Information Brokers*
- *International Directory of Marketing Research Companies and Services: The GreenBook*
- *Consultants and Consulting Organizations Directory*

The best researchers know that information seeking is not simply a matter of looking at books or tapping into databases. In many situations, the quickest and most effective way to find what you need is to contact people who are willing to share their own expertise, whether for free or otherwise. Of course, many businesses employ professionals who sell their knowledge and information skills for a fee, including law firms, management consultants, market research firms, private detective agencies, document delivery services, and information brokers. Obtaining professional advice doesn't always require hiring a specialist, however. A phenomenal amount of expert information is available at no cost, and for less effort than one might think. The trick is knowing where to look and how to ask. Unlike fee-based services,

the potential providers of free business information usually don't advertise in the Yellow Pages. Still, the telephone can be one of the most powerful tools at the researcher's disposal.

PEOPLE: THE UNTAPPED INFORMATION SOURCE

Experts are everywhere. In most cases, the simplest way to find them is to identify the settings in which they work: government agencies, trade associations, universities, libraries, think tanks, and other information organizations. Some groups are more oriented toward sharing information than others. Libraries, for example, are in

the business of providing free information, and a good librarian won't hesitate to offer professional advice. While most government information specialists are employed primarily to gather, organize, and/or analyze data for other purposes, many are quite willing to answer questions from the public. Another outstanding source of free and inexpensive information is the trade association, though some restrict their services to members only. When seeking expert assistance, look beyond the obvious sources. Journalists can be surprisingly helpful, especially if they can obtain information from you in return. Editors of trade journals and newsletters closely follow narrow areas of interest and are aware of the latest developments in their field. They can also be an excellent source of leads, and may be happy to refer you to other experts. Business reporters for daily newspapers can be extremely helpful when background is needed on local companies, executives, or economic conditions. Finally, you can contact the author of an exceptionally relevant book or article.

Published directories can guide researchers to the experts they seek. Most directories are compiled annually, though some are updated on a less frequent basis. They usually provide current names, addresses, phone numbers, and reasonably detailed descriptions of the appropriate organizations. The purpose and activities of the organization, the information it specializes in, and the names of key people are also common elements of directory listings. Most have indexes by subject, geographic location, and personal name. Others have indexes to the type of service offered, type of client served, or special research capabilities provided.

For an overview of major information sources, an excellent place to start is the *Business Organizations, Agencies, and Publications Directory,* compiled by Gale Research, Inc., a leading publisher of indexes and directories. This biennial handbook describes more than 23,000 companies, nonprofit organizations, and publications of interest to business researchers. The topics in its 44 chapters run the gamut from university business schools to major trade fairs. The most noteworthy sections are those on trade associations, business libraries, document delivery services, research centers, and government agencies. The chapters on business publications highlight periodical indexes, databases, directories, newsletters, and more. Much of the information is taken from the more specialized Gale publications described below, but this directory is highly recommended as a single-volume guide to a wide array of major sources. Two other features make it a valuable resource even for libraries with extensive directory collections. First, because it covers such a diversity of organizations, the Master Index can be a time saver when the exact nature of the organization is unknown. Second, the descriptions are fairly lengthy—in some cases more informative than those in more specialized Gale directories.

The remainder of this chapter is devoted to descriptions of published guides which can lead the researcher to the most appropriate sources of expert advice. For guidance in tracking down other important directories, consult *Directories in Print*, described in Chapter 3.

DIRECTORIES OF GOVERNMENT AGENCIES

Government employees can be an unparalleled source of information on any topic imaginable. The structure and activities of federal, state, and local governments are far-flung and complex. A major problem for researchers is identifying the most appropriate agencies to help with a particular situation. Knowing the responsibilities, organization, and services of government agencies can save hours of fruitless phone calls. Once a likely resource is identified, the researcher can even find the names and numbers of individuals within the organization by job function. Looking for a detailed manual of government structure? Biographical information on government experts? Up-to-date lists of telephone contacts? An extensive collection of guides and directories is at your disposal. Many are produced by the various governments themselves; others are compiled by commercial publishers.

The federal government is a logical place to start when looking for research assistance, if only because its information-gathering apparatus is so extensive. Federal agencies employ specialists on every conceivable subject, from apples to zircons, and many are pleased to share their expertise with legitimate callers. This is not to suggest that government information specialists are waiting for people to ask them what they know, but they can be highly approachable and helpful nonetheless.

Because the U.S. capital is also the world information capital, guides to Washington-based information sources are abundant. Directories are available on subjects ranging from lobbying groups to political action committees. An excellent all-purpose guide to the capital scene is the *Washington Information Directory,* published annually by Congressional Quarterly, Inc. It covers both government and nongovernment organizations in a topical arrangement, with a brief description of

each. Included are listings of executive agencies, consumer groups, major trade associations, labor unions, foreign embassies, and addresses for the Washington press corps. Comparative tables list contacts for various functions within major governmental departments, such as agency librarians, legal counsels, and equal employment officers. A variety of "Handy Reference Lists" provide information on related areas such as the names of state governors and mayors of major cities.

A newer research tool, produced annually by Columbia Books, Inc., is *Washington [Year]: A Comprehensive Directory of the Key Institutions and Leaders of the National Capital Area.* Like the previous publication, it covers government agencies, trade associations, labor unions, and the media. It also identifies a diversity of additional organizations and individuals: major companies, universities, hospitals, research centers, museums, social and professional clubs, community affairs groups, and more. By covering both national institutions located in Washington and prominent local organizations, it serves as a guide to the power structure of this vitally important city.

Federal Executive Agencies

The executive branch of the federal government is a likely starting point for information on regulatory issues, current statistics, industry background, world economic developments, and a host of other business concerns. One way to identify federal agencies is to contact a local office of the Federal Information Center (FIC), a telephone assistance service established to help citizens locate government information. An FIC operator will generally refer you to an appropriate agency for further information. To find the phone number of the Federal Information Center nearest you, consult the government listings in your local telephone directory. A second approach is to delve into one of the dozens of published guides to federal information services. The publications below are among the most useful introductions to the organization and personnel of executive agencies.

United States Government Manual (U.S. Office of the Federal Register—Annual).

This inexpensive guide to the federal government profiles all agencies of the executive, legislative, and judicial branches, but cabinet departments, independent agencies, and quasi-governmental organizations are presented in the most detail. *The Manual* presents encyclopedic articles that explain the history, purpose, and powers of each governmental unit. Organizational charts, the title of the legislation which authorized the agency, and the pertinent section of the *Code of Federal Regulations* dealing with the agency are provided. Addresses and phone numbers of regional offices, together with the names and titles of key personnel, can also be found. Subagencies are treated in similar fashion, showing the relationship to the parent organization. Freedom of Information Act information is cited for all executive agencies. Other useful features include listings of agency libraries, sources of additional information, and contacts for such major functions as procurement and employment opportunities. *The Manual* contains a subject/agency name index, an index to personnel, and appendices listing defunct organizations and common acronyms. For users who need more specific information, some agencies publish their own directories or telephone contact lists.

Federal Staff Directory (Staff Directories, Ltd.—Semiannual).

This invaluable guide to 30,000 of the top-ranking employees of the executive branch covers staff members in the Office of the President, cabinet departments, independent agencies, and quasi-official organizations. Included are top decision-makers in the diplomatic corps and chief military officers. Information is arranged by agency, with a subject/keyword index and a personal name index. For each agency, phone numbers are provided for directory assistance, Freedom of Information Act requests, recorded messages, and other important contacts and services. A unique supplement contains biographical information on approximately 2,600 key officials. Taken together, the two sections enable the researcher to identify the most appropriate expert on a given topic. The *Directory* is published in hardcover each December, with a paperback revision issued in July. Staff Directories, Ltd. also publishes the *Judicial Staff Directory*, and the *Congressional Staff Directory*. The latter title is described later in the chapter.

Federal Regulatory Directory (Congressional Quarterly, Inc.—Irregular).

Published every three to four years, this basic handbook begins with an excellent overview of the regulatory process, then describes the major administrative agencies and their regulatory powers. Thirteen of the most prominent agencies are profiled in depth, giving a history of the organization, its legislative authorization, powers, method of operation, recent events, outlook for the future, and biographical information on key officials. The second part of the guide offers briefer descriptions of

the other regulatory bodies. For every agency, the *Directory* lists regional offices, sources of additional information, and major publications. The chapters in the *Code of Federal Regulations* pertaining to each agency are also cited. Personal name and subject indexes are included. The 6th edition appeared in 1990.

Federal Executive Directory (Carroll Publishing Company—Bimonthly).

Researchers in need of the most current phone listings for government officials, or wishing to update information found in more detailed publications, can consult this extensive directory of more than 80,000 federal employees. Revised every two months, the *Federal Executive Directory* lists personnel alphabetically by name, as well as by agency and job title. Executive agencies, members of Congress, and congressional staff members are covered in great detail. For example, Department of State listings specify names and numbers for individual "country desks." After major elections, separate "Transition" sections highlight recent changes in personnel. Designations are given for unconfirmed political nominees and individuals in acting positions. Special features include a directory of federal libraries, toll-free government hot lines, agency public affairs offices, and a detailed keyword index to agencies and functions. Carroll also publishes the *Federal Regional Executive Directory,* which lists 30,000 key federal employees in local and regional offices.

Another producer of current telephone listings is Monitor Publishing Company. Its *Federal Yellow Book* lists 35,000 key officials in the executive branch, including independent agencies and commissions. Congressional offices are covered in a separate publication. Entries in the *Federal Yellow Book* are arranged by agency, with a separate section for selected regional offices. Like the Carroll directory, it provides a personal name index, and a keyword agency index, but subject access is not as good. The *Yellow Book* is organized extremely well; each agency section begins with a table of contents, a guide to buildings and abbreviations, and a list of important numbers. Though updated only quarterly, its level of detail is exceptional.

How to Find Business Intelligence in Washington (Washington Researchers Publishing—Irregular).

From the title, this work might seem to be a step-by-step guide to navigating the corridors of Washington, but it is predominantly a directory of federal agencies which collect business-related data. Most listings do include a variety of descriptive information, however. For each major agency, a general overview is given, followed by listings of subagencies within the organization. Entries include the address, phone number, and, in most cases, the name of a general contact person. For some agencies, separate names and phone numbers are given for specific functions, and toll-free hotlines are listed where available. A brief description of the information-gathering activities is provided for each subagency. At the end of every agency chapter is a supplemental section listing the following information: departmental libraries, documents rooms, regional offices, Freedom of Information Act offices, and significant agency publications. These useful supplemental sections describe "what you can get" from each agency. The directory is updated infrequently, but once the appropriate agency is identified, researchers can turn to the more current federal directories listed above. A more significant drawback is the lack of a detailed subject index. Although a brief chart lists the agencies primarily responsible for major topics, it is insufficient. Researchers will need to browse this guide extensively to use it effectively. Still, it is a unique and important reference tool. The 10th edition was issued in 1991.

Washington Researchers, a well-known consultant for locating government information, also publishes *Who Knows: A Guide to Government Experts*. This guide provides subject access to government employees who specialize in particular industries, markets, countries, or other business topics. The subject index is quite specific, covering such products as benzoic acid and billiard cloth. For major topics, several experts from different agencies may be found, providing the user with alternative perspectives. This directory is updated more frequently than its sibling publication, but is still irregular. The 11th edition appeared in 1991. A third publication from Washington Researchers, *How to Find Information about Companies*, is introduced in the reading list following Chapter 8.

Federal Statistical Directory, *William R. Evinger* (Oryx Press—Irregular).

Now published commercially, this former U.S. Office of Management and Budget guide lists executive agencies which gather and disseminate statistical information. Entries are arranged by agency, following the pattern set by the *Government Manual.* Some 4,000 agency personnel are identified, together with phone numbers, job titles, and/or areas of concentration. The directory lists executives as well as the individuals directly dealing with statistical programs. Emphasis is placed on the data series or publications upon which each person works. Agency libraries and publications offices

are also cited. Appendices list state contacts for cooperative statistical programs sponsored by such agencies as the Bureau of Justice Statistics. Other appendices provide a bibliography of government publication catalogs, a list of frequently called numbers, and directories of Federal Information Centers and Government Printing Office Book Stores. A personal name index is also included. The principal weaknesses of this useful guide are its infrequent revisions (it is updated every four to five years) and the absence of a subject index. However, it does provide important insights into the structure of the federal statistical system, with a detailed picture of how each statistical agency is organized. When used together with the more current executive directories described earlier, the *Federal Statistical Directory* can be an effective point of entry to government data sources. The 28th edition was published in 1987; a new version, including a subject index, is due in late 1991. A more current, though less detailed guide to federal statistical experts can be found in the annual *Statistics Sources*, described in Chapter 4.

The United States Congress

Congressional offices can be especially helpful for tracking the status of legislation, locating timely research results, and cutting through the maze of federal bureaucracy. Staff members working for congressional offices or standing committees can lead researchers to government publications and unpublished committee reports, and provide expert information of their own. Often they are among the most experienced and knowledgeable people in Washington. The following guides offer detailed information on the people and structure of Congress as well as current directory information.

Congressional Directory (U.S. Joint Committee on Printing—Biennial).

Also known as the *Official Congressional Directory,* this is the government's guide to members of Congress, their aides, and employees of the Capitol. It provides brief biographies of every U.S. senator and representative and lists their committee assignments and their Washington and district offices. A separate section profiles every committee, its chair, members, and key staff. Chronological tables show when each member's term will expire, and a ranked list indicates who has served the longest continuous terms. The *Congressional Directory* also provides brief information on key people in the executive and judiciary, and lists U.S. diplomats and foreign service officers.

Additional features of the *Directory* include floor plans of the Capitol Building, maps of every congressional district, statistical tables, and listings of journalists assigned to cover the Congress. Because it is published biennially, in conjunction with each new Congress, the *Directory* is usually somewhat dated and should be supplemented by the *Federal Executive Directory* or the commercial publications described below.

Congressional Staff Directory (Staff Directories, Ltd.—Semiannual).

Like its executive staff counterpart, the *Congressional Staff Directory* is remarkably detailed. Names, job titles, and phone numbers are provided for 20,000 legislative personnel. Biographical profiles of more than 3,000 key staffers give their educational and career backgrounds and areas of interest. Business researchers will find certain listed organizations especially useful, including the Office of Technology Assessment, the Congressional Research Service, the General Accounting Office, and the Congressional Budget Office.

The *Directory* contains much that is also found in the *Official Congressional Directory*, but two unique features are brief descriptions of the powers and duties of major committees, and an alphabetic index to towns and cities in the United States, listing the representative for each. The *Congressional Staff Directory* is published semiannually, in April and September. Researchers who wish more rapid updating and who need less detailed information can subscribe to an "Advance Print" issued in February. Data from the *Congressional Staff Directory* are also available on a set of floppy diskettes with its own software.

Another especially interesting guide to Congress is the *Almanac of American Politics*. Compiled biennially by the publishers of the widely respected *National Journal*, the *Almanac* offers a nonpartisan analysis of congressional performance. In addition to biographical information on senators and representatives, it provides editorial comment on their views, reputations, and status. Pertinent facts include their voting record on key bills, data on campaign contributions and expenditures, and recent election results. A unique feature is the comparative rating of each member's performance, gathered from such political groups as the ACLU, the American Conservative Union, and the Chamber of Commerce of the United States. The full text of the latest *Almanac* is searchable online through LEXIS/NEXIS.

Congressional Yellow Book (Monitor Publishing Company—Quarterly).

The most current guide to congressional personnel is the *Federal Executive Directory* mentioned above, but the *Congressional Yellow Book* is a timely directory covering Congress only. It lists U.S. senators, representatives, their staffs, officials of congressional support agencies, and members of caucuses and other unofficial organizations. This directory provides more detailed information than its competition from Carroll Publishing, including full-page profiles and photographs of each member of Congress. Other useful features are a brief but fairly extensive analysis of the jurisdiction of every congressional committee, a listing of zip codes by congressional district, and boundary maps. However, the *Yellow Book* has no subject or personal name indexing, and is updated four times per year rather than six.

State and Local Agencies

A variety of directories are published for each of the 50 states. Most state governments produce organizational manuals (sometimes called "blue books"), telephone directories, publication catalogs, and statistical yearbooks. Commercial publishers within each state also produce valuable reference guides to complement official publications. Directories of local agencies and organizations are published at both the state and local levels. Aside from collecting directories for the states and communities dealt with most frequently, librarians and researchers can consult several national publications which compare state and local organizations across the country. The following publications list state agencies, state information services, local government executives, and chambers of commerce. While chambers are generally not government agencies, many serve in a quasi-official capacity.

State Yellow Book (Monitor Publishing Company—Semiannual).

The most current addresses and phone numbers for state government personnel can be found in the following two directories. Monitor's *State Yellow Book* provides access to approximately 30,000 officials in state government, including the executive, legislative, and judicial branches. Entries give the officials' names, titles, and phone numbers. The directory is arranged by state; executive agencies within each state are grouped according to level, beginning with the governor's office and continuing to cabinet departments, commissions, and so on. Brief state profiles are given, as are lists of military installations within the state. An appendix lists intergovernmental organizations to which state officials belong. A personal name index is divided by state, and the functional index to agencies is fairly general and not complete.

Carroll Publishing Company produces a similar directory, but it appears three times per year. Like its competitor, Carroll's *State Executive Directory* is arranged by state and lists approximately 35,000 officials. Both publications include listings for Guam, American Samoa, Puerto Rico, and the Virgin Islands. The *Yellow Book* is broader in scope, including legislators, legislative committees, and judges at the supreme and appellate levels. The only officials outside the executive branch appearing in the Carroll directory are found in an appendix listing legislators' names and phone numbers. However, the *State Executive Directory* does have better indexing. The keyword index to agencies is quite detailed, and the personal name index appears in a single alphabet.

State Administrative Officials Classified by Function (Council of State Governments—Biennial).

This basic directory covers principal administrative agencies in all states, the District of Columbia, and United States territories and possessions. Listings are brief, citing agency name, address, phone, and the highest ranking official. Arrangement is by function, then subdivided by state. Approximately 150 categories are designated, including such specific activities as ombudsman, unclaimed property records, and state fair managers. This functional arrangement is invaluable because different agencies may perform the same task from one state to another, and because departmental names can vary among the states. As shown in Exhibit 2-1, consumer affairs activities are primarily administered by attorney generals' offices (or their equivalents), but consumer agencies may also operate as independent boards, agencies at the departmental level, and divisions of other departments, ranging from agriculture to community affairs. The directory provides no indexes by personal name or state, and is only updated biennially, but it is convenient and affordable.

The Council of State Governments also publishes two companion directories. *State Elective Officials and the Legislatures* lists legislators, elected executive officers, and judges of each state's highest court. For every state and territory, executive and judicial listings appear first, followed by legislators in alphabetical order. Additional details are found in *State Legislative Leadership, Committees & Staff*, including names of legislative officers, and the chairpersons and key staff members of standing committees.

EXHIBIT 2-1. *State Administrative Officials Classified by Function*

CONSUMER AFFAIRS

(Investigates and mediates consumer complaints of deceptive and fraudulent business practices.)

ALABAMA
Dennis Wright
Consumer Protection Div.
Off. of Attorney General
11 S. Union St.
Montgomery, AL 36130
(205) 242-7335

ALASKA
Robert E. Mintz
Chief
Consumer Protection
Section
Dept. of Law
1031 W. Fourth Ave.,
Suite 110
Anchorage, AK 99501
(907) 279-0428

ARIZONA
Patrick Murphy
Financial Fraud Div.
Off. of Attorney General
1275 W. Washington,
#259
Phoenix, AZ 85007
(602) 542-3702

ARKANSAS
Steve Clark
Attorney General
Off. of Attorney General
323 Center, #200
Little Rock, AR
72201-2610
(501) 682-2007

CALIFORNIA
Michael A. Kelley
Director
Dept. of Consumer
Affairs
1020 N St., Rm. 516
Sacramento, CA 95814
(916) 445-4465

COLORADO
Thomas McManus
Director
Antitrust/Consumer
Protection
Dept. of Law
1525 Sherman St., 2nd Fl.
Denver, CO 80203
(303) 866-3611

CONNECTICUT
Mary M. Heslin
Commissioner
Consumer Protection
Dept.
165 Capitol Ave.
Hartford, CT 06106
(203) 566-4999

DELAWARE
Donald Williams
Director
Div. of Consumer Affairs
Dept. of Community
Affairs
820 N. French St., 4th Fl.
Wilmington, DE 19801
(302) 571-3250

FLORIDA
Helen Webb
Acting Director
Div. of Consumer
Services
Agriculture & Consumer
Services Dept.
Mayo Bldg.
Tallahassee, FL
32399-0800
(904) 488-2221

GEORGIA
Barry Reid
Administrator
Off. of Consumer Affairs
Off. of Planning &
Budget
205 Butler St., SE, Plz.-E
Atlanta, GA 30334
(404) 656-1760

HAWAII
Philip Doi
Director
Off. of Consumer
Protection
Rm. 520, 250 S. King St.
Honolulu, HI 96813
(808) 548-2560

IDAHO
Jim Jones
Attorney General
Off. of Attorney General
State Capitol
Boise, ID 83720
(208) 334-2400

ILLINOIS
Neil F. Hartigan
Attorney General
500 S. Second St.
Springfield, IL 62706
(217) 782-1090

INDIANA
James C. Spencer
Assistant Director
Div. of Consumer
Protection
Off. of Attorney General
125 W. Market
Indianapolis, IN 46204
(317) 232-6331

IOWA
Richard Cleland
Director
Consumer Protection Div.
Off. of Attorney General
Hoover State Off. Bldg.
Des Moines, IA 50319
(515) 281-5926

KANSAS
Art Weiss
Deputy Attorney General
Consumer Protection Div.
Off. of Attorney General
Judicial Ctr.
Topeka, KS 66612
(913) 296-3751

KENTUCKY
Frederic J. Cowan
Attorney General
State Capitol, Rm. 116
Frankfort, KY 40601
(502) 564-7600

MAINE
Harry Gaddinge
Acting Superintendent
Bur. of Consumer Credit
Protection
State House Station #35
Augusta, ME 04333
(207) 289-3731

MARYLAND
William Leibovici
Chief
Consumer & Investor
Affairs Div.
Off. of Attorney General
7 N. Calvert St.
Baltimore, MD 21202
(301) 576-6550

MASSACHUSETTS
Paula Gold
Secretary
Executive Off. of
Consumer Affairs
1 Ashburton Pl.
Boston, MA 02108
(617) 727-7755

MICHIGAN
Fredrick H. Hoffecker
Assistant in Charge
Consumer Protection Div.
Attorney General
Law Bldg., 6th Fl.
Lansing, MI 48913
(517) 335-0855

MINNESOTA
Doug Blanke
Assistant Attorney
General
Consumer Div.
Off. of Attorney General
117 University Ave.
St. Paul, MN 55155
(612) 296-7575

MISSISSIPPI
Tray Bobinger
Director
Consumer Protection Div.
Off. of Attorney General
Gartin Bldg., 5th Fl.
Jackson, MS 39201
(601) 359-3680

MONTANA
Brinton B. Markle
Attorney-Unit Manager
Consumer Affairs Unit
Dept. of Commerce
1424 Ninth Ave.
Helena, MT 59620
(406) 444-4313

NEBRASKA
Denise Frost
Attorney
Consumer Fraud Section
Off. of Attorney General
P.O. Box 94906
Lincoln, NE 68509-4906
(402) 471-3833

NEVADA
Shari Compton
Commissioner
Div. of Consumer Affairs
Dept. of Commerce
2501 E. Sahara Ave.,
#202
Las Vegas, NV 89518
(702) 486-4150

NEW HAMPSHIRE
John Arnold
Attorney General
208 State House Annex
235 Capitol St.
Concord, NH 03301-6397
(603) 271-3658

NEW JERSEY
James J. Barry Jr.
Director
Div. of Consumer Affairs
Dept. of Law & Public
Safety
1100 Raymond Blvd.,
Rm. 504
Newark, NJ 07102
(201) 648-4010

56 State Administrative Officials Classified by Function 1989-90

State Legislative Sourcebook, Lynn Hellebust (Government Research Service—Annual).

The *State Legislative Sourcebook* is an outstanding reference tool describing the legislative process and structure for the 50 states, the District of Columbia, and Puerto Rico. Each state chapter begins with an explanation of how a bill becomes a law, an outline of how the legislative bodies are organized and when they meet, and listings of key officials. Another useful feature is the extensive guide to information sources in each state. Addresses and phone numbers for bill status advice, bill delivery requests, and commercial bill tracking and document delivery services are provided. Publishers of state blue books, telephone directories, regulatory registers, statutes, databases, political newspapers, and general reference books are identified.

State Data and Database Finder (Information USA, Inc.—Irregular).

This exceptionally useful compendium provides detailed explanations of the types of data collected by state governments, tips on how to obtain the data, and state-by-state agency directories. The guide is arranged by subject, with 38 topics ranging from crime statistics to unclaimed property. It also covers specific state programs such as Census data centers and industrial development incubators. The book is a gold mine of advice on state government procedures, including freedom of information requests, procurement policies, and licensing and permit requests. It covers an incredible variety of information collected or compiled by state governments: bank financial statements, company directories, motor vehicle records, labor statistics, and more. Of special interest to business researchers are the descriptions of databases maintained by state agencies, with information on the availability by format (printouts, mailing labels, computer tapes, online access), size of the file, and cost. Agency listings specify phone numbers for each type of information request, the types of reports or filings available, price, and ordering procedures. Added features include a combined subject/name/geographic index, a chart indicating the types of data available for each subject category, and an introductory chapter on how to do research at the state level. The latest edition appeared in 1989.

A more specialized guide to state resources is produced by Washington Researchers Publishing. *How to Find Company Intelligence in State Documents* provides a brief introduction to the types of company information collected by state agencies and how researchers can acquire them, together with a directory of the appropriate agencies for each state.

Municipal/County Executive Directory (Carroll Publishing Company—Annual).

Many guides to local government are published, but this service is easily the most comprehensive. Nearly 50,000 elected, appointed, and career officials of counties, cities, villages, townships, and other municipalities are listed. To be included, localities must meet minimum population requirements (counties greater than 25,000 and municipalities greater than 15,000). The *Directory* is arranged geographically, then subdivided by agency name. The municipal section is arranged alphabetically by place name, with a geographic index by state; the county section is arranged by state, then subdivided by county. In both sections, officials' names, titles, addresses, and phone numbers are given, together with a general switchboard number for every government unit. For smaller jurisdictions, separate appendices list the names of the chief executives only. Personal name indexes are provided for both municipal and county officials. The service is also available as two separate directories, one for counties and one for municipalities. Aside from the narrower focus, the advantage of these editions is that both are updated twice per year.

World Chamber of Commerce Directory (World Chamber of Commerce Directory—Annual).

One of the best bargains in local information resources is this inexpensive directory of chambers of commerce and similar organizations. Though it has undergone several name changes, many long-time subscribers use its original title, *Johnson's Directory*. It lists more than 10,000 chambers, boards of trade, tourist bureaus, and local economic development agencies in the United States and Canada, arranged by state or province, then by local place name. Address, phone number, and chief executive name are identified for each. Other organizations related to community development are also found here. For every state, addresses are given for regional offices of the U.S. Small Business Administration, the state economic development department, and the major utilities serving the state. A supplementary directory lists states and communities which have produced videos on their area. Also included are appendices with extensive international information. Names, addresses, and phone numbers are provided for foreign chambers of commerce in the United States and abroad, and U.S. and foreign embassies worldwide. Each appendix is arranged by country.

DIRECTORIES OF LIBRARIES AND LIBRARIANS

There are literally thousands of libraries in the United States, from the small-town public library to the most sophisticated research facility. Many reference librarians specialize in particular research areas, and many are subject experts in their own right. The best librarians are not only familiar with library resources, but nonlibrary alternatives as well, and can be outstanding sources of research leads. Innumerable library directories are published, from regional guides to specialized sources such as *Directory of Government Document Collections and Librarians.* Membership rosters for library associations are also abundant. Of particular interest to business researchers is the annual *Who's Who in Special Libraries*, the official membership guide to the Special Libraries Association. Few biographical works focus on librarians; the most comprehensive is the *Directory of Library & Information Professionals*, a biennial guide from Research Publications, Inc. Of all the library-related directories, the following two are especially useful.

American Library Directory (R.R. Bowker—Annual).

This massive publication lists some 30,000 libraries of all types in the United States and Canada. The bulk of the entries are for public libraries, but the *Directory* includes 4,600 academic libraries, 8,900 special libraries, and 1,700 government libraries. Among the special libraries are those located in hospitals, corporations, law firms, and research organizations. All libraries are listed geographically regardless of type. Each entry provides information on founding date, staff size, number of volumes owned, subject matter collected, and major departments. Many listings also include data on budget size, special collections, and names of department heads. The complete contents of this important directory are also available online through DIALOG; like the printed version, the information is revised annually. A multitude of searchable variables makes the online version a powerful research tool. Users can quickly locate individual librarians, identify libraries with specialized collections and services, and generate customized lists of institutions by utilizing a combination of characteristics, from staff size to number of periodical subscriptions.

Directory of Special Libraries and Information Centers (Gale Research, Inc.—Annual).

Although the *American Library Directory* includes special libraries, this excellent source from Gale Research offers more comprehensive coverage, with over 19,000 collections in the United States and Canada. It lists libraries in corporations, nonprofit organizations, and government agencies, as well as specialized departments in public and academic libraries. Entries are similar to those in the Bowker directory, but may also include descriptions of the services offered, computer facilities, online capabilities, in-house publications, such as catalogs or indexes, and, most important, whether the library may be used by outside clientele. Arrangement is alphabetical by name of organization, with subject, geographic, and personal name indexes. The international section profiles the most important research libraries in 120 countries. Gale also publishes the information by subject in three smaller volumes covering "Business, Government, and Law," "Computers, Engineering, and Science," and "Health Sciences." This version is known collectively as the *Subject Directory of Special Libraries and Information Centers*, and each of the three volumes may be purchased separately.

DIRECTORIES OF ASSOCIATIONS

Two comprehensive guides to trade associations and other membership organizations in the United States are essential tools for answering a variety of research needs. For researchers consistently involved in investigating a particular topic or industry, a personal or institutional membership in a relevant association can be an extremely worthwhile investment. For more occasional needs, many associations are willing and able to provide limited assistance and referral to nonmembers. Many also publish research reports and other helpful materials.

Encyclopedia of Associations (Gale Research, Inc.—Annual).

The *Encyclopedia of Associations* has grown steadily since its first publication and now contains listings of over 22,000 membership organizations. In addition to trade and professional associations, the directory includes labor unions, foreign boards of trade in the U.S., public interest groups, and other organizations important to business researchers. The *Encyclopedia* also covers athletic groups, religious societies, fraternal organizations, social clubs, hobby organizations, Greek-letter societies, and such offbeat and humorous groups as the National Society for the Prevention of Cruelty to Mushrooms.

An alphabetical index is arranged by keyword, so the user need not know the exact name of the organization being sought. The keyword index also lists defunct

organizations and former names of existing groups. Another feature of the index is the inclusion of several thousand organizations that are *not* associations; these groups are described in 13 other directories, most of which are published by Gale. The index then refers the user to one of these publications for further information. This unusual addition is included because a surprising number of businesses, government agencies, foundations, and research centers have names that sound like associations.

Exhibit 2-2 illustrates the detailed coverage of this indispensable tool. Descriptions of associations include founding date, size of membership and staff, number of state and local affiliates, and budget size. Listings also discuss the nature and purpose of each group, if and when it holds annual meetings, and the titles of any ongoing publications. Volume 2 contains a geographical index to the national associations and a personal name index to association executives. For an additional fee, subscribers may receive two updating services published between editions: one lists major changes to existing listings, the other lists newly founded associations.

Gale also produces two companion publications: *International Organizations* describes over 10,000 multinational and foreign national associations; and *Regional, State, and Local Organizations*, published in five volumes, covers nearly 50,000 groups below the national level.

Online and CD-ROM versions of the *Encyclopedia of Associations* are produced. Each contains the listings from all three editions of the printed books, bringing information on 80,000 organizations together in a single computerized file. The online version is updated twice yearly on the DIALOG system and can be searched using a variety of key variables. Such characteristics as founding date, budget, or staff size can be combined with broad subjects or geographic areas to create very specific lists for research or marketing purposes. Another advantage of the online service is its ability to quickly identify newsletters, journals, statistical reports, and other serial publications produced by trade and professional associations. The semiannual CD-ROM version, called *Gale GlobalAccess: Associations*, also utilizes DIALOG software.

NTPA: National Trade & Professional Associations in the United States (Columbia Books, Inc.—Annual).

For researchers interested strictly in business-related associations, this is a much more focused directory. *NTPA* lists 6,300 organizations, with coverage limited to trade associations, professional organizations, and labor unions with national memberships. In fact, most of the

organizations herein are quite substantial; fully two-thirds have budgets greater than $50,000 per year, and several hundred have annual revenues in excess of $5 million.

Listings are similar to those in the Gale directory, though *NTPA's* descriptions are briefer. Unique features are an index to associations by budget size, an acronym index, and a separate directory of association management companies together with the names of the groups they manage. An interesting introductory chapter discusses the history and nature of trade associations. A notable drawback is the lack of a keyword index; unless the user knows the exact name of the organization, identifying it can be difficult. To counter this deficiency, the publisher provides fairly detailed subject, geographic, and executive name indexes. Columbia also publishes a companion directory called *State and Regional Associations*. Similar in purpose and content to the national edition and also appearing annually, it covers 5,000 prominent associations at the state level, with organizations arranged by state, then alphabetically by name. Like its national counterpart, *State and Regional Associations* includes indexes by subject, acronym, budget size, and executive names.

UNIVERSITIES AND NONPROFIT RESEARCH ORGANIZATIONS

A number of directories list nonprofit organizations, universities, and government agencies engaged in research activities. Directories of this type can lead the user to sources of published and unpublished information, computerized data files, and experts willing to share their knowledge. Depending on the type of organization, they may have secondary information available for sale, or they may conduct customized studies on a contractual basis.

Locating faculty members with specific backgrounds and research interests can be an especially frustrating task. The directories listed below can help identify institutions, but they are not necessarily the best resources for pinpointing individuals. On the other hand, if the person's name is known, but not the institution, the *National Faculty Directory* is an outstanding reference tool. Published annually by Gale Research, it lists the names, titles, addresses, and phone numbers of nearly 600,000 teaching faculty in over 3,400 institutions of higher learning. Biographical profiles of college faculty can be found in many general sources, ranging from traditional "Who's Who" type directories to more in-

EXHIBIT 2-2. *Encyclopedia of Associations*

★3960★   AMERICAN MULE ASSOCIATION (Animal Breeding) (AMA)
6725 Union Rd.   Phone: (805) 238-4867
Paso Robles, CA 93446   Roxy McIntosh, Exec.Sec.
Founded: 1977. **Members:** 700. **Staff:** 1. Individuals interested in breeding, racing, showing, and raising mules. Encourages the development of public interest in mules through the promotion and sponsorship of public mule contests; seeks to educate the public regarding the history, breeding, and raising of mules. Plans to: establish an association for the prevention of cruelty to mules and other animals; encourage the scientific development and scientific breeding of finer mules; provide for community recreation through the sponsorship of contests, races, and exhibitions of mules. Establishes rules for mule contests, races, and exhibitions, and standardizes election and equipment of judges, directors, and spokespersons for such functions. Compiles racing statistics. **Committees:** Packing and Driving; Performance; Racing. **Divisions:** Packing; Racing.

Publications: *Newsletter,* monthly.

Convention/Meeting: semiannual.

★3961★   AMERICAN OSTRICH ASSOCIATION (Animal Breeding) (AOA)
601 Bailey   Phone: (817) 877-1300
Ft. Worth, TX 76107   Susan Cook, Exec.Dir.
Founded: 1987. **Members:** 536. People who promote ostrich raising as a potential food, leather, and feather industry. Provides information about raising ostriches; maintains exhibits at state fairs and stock shows. **Telecommunications Services:** Fax, (817)877-1218.

Publications: *Newsletter,* monthly. **Advertising:** accepted. ● *Ostrich Report,* quarterly. Magazine. **Advertising:** accepted.

Convention/Meeting: annual - always August; also holds periodic meeting.

★3962★   ANGORA GOAT RECORD AND REGISTRY (Animal Breeding) (AGRR)
1451 Sisson   Phone: (616) 765-3056
Freeport, MI 49325   Susan and Donald Drummond, Co-Presidents
Founded: 1985. **Members:** 25. Individuals who own and breed angora goats. Seeks to preserve and purify the breed. Operates North America Genetic Recovery Program, through which the registry breeds purebred angora females with registered angora males in an effort to upgrade the purity of the breed. Compiles statistics pertaining to angora goats; maintains angora goat registry. **Computerized Services:** Lineage information on genetic recovery angora goats.

★3963★   EMPRESS CHINCHILLA BREEDERS COOPERATIVE (Animal Breeding) (ECBC)
P.O. Box 402   Phone: (303) 697-4421
Morrison, CO 80465   Gail V. Sanden, Gen.Mgr.
Founded: 1965. **Members:** 600. **Staff:** 2. **Local Groups:** 41. Breeders of chinchillas for fur. Conducts research; supervises live animal and pelt shows. **Formed By Merger Of:** Farmers Chinchilla Cooperative of America (founded 1950), National Chinchilla Cooperative of America (founded 1950), and National Chinchilla Breeders of America (founded 1938).

Publications: *Empress Chinchilla Breeder Magazine,* monthly.

Convention/Meeting: annual.

★3964★   INTERNATIONAL LLAMA ASSOCIATION (Animal Breeding) (ILA)
P.O. Box 37505   Phone: (303) 756-9004
Denver, CO 80237   Sandy Chapman, Gen.Mgr.
Founded: 1982. **Members:** 1400. **Staff:** 2. **Budget:** $350,000. **Regional Groups:** 11. Breeders and owners of llamas. Provides education on the care and use of llamas. (Llamas are animals native to the Chilean and Peruvian Andes.) **Committees:** Alpaca Owner; Importation; Legislative; Packing; Public Relations; Research; Wool; Workshops.

Publications: *ILA Membership Directory,* annual. ● *ILA Newsletter,* 6/year. ● Also publishes brochures.

Convention/Meeting: annual jamboree, with performance events and exhibits.

★3965★   INTERNATIONAL NUBIAN BREEDERS ASSOCIATION (Animal Breeding) (INBA)
P.O. Box 130   Phone: (503) 895-2742
Creswell, OR 97426   Shirley Gardner, Sec.
Members: 500. Objective is to promote the Nubian dairy goat breed. Holds specialty shows throughout the country. Bestows all-American awards for excellence in shows and merit awards for the greatest amount of milk produced in a year. **Formerly:** National Nubian Club.

Publications: *Newsletter,* 8/year.

Convention/Meeting: annual. 1990 Santa Rosa, CA; 1991 Little Rock, AR; 1992 West Springfield, MA.

★3966★   LLAMA ASSOCIATION OF NORTH AMERICA (Animal Breeding) (LANA)
P.O. Box 1882   Phone: (702) 265-3177
Minden, NV 89423   Virginia Christensen, Adm. Office
Founded: 1980. **Members:** 1200. **Staff:** 1. Llama and alpaca owners and breeders; interested others. Sponsors research and youth programs related to the care of llamas.

Publications: *Breeder's List,* 3/year. ● *LANA Binder,* quarterly. ● *LANA Membership Directory,* annual. ● *LANA News,* quarterly. Newsletter. ● Also publishes youth program material.

Convention/Meeting: annual conference, with llama show and exhibits.

★3967★   MINIATURE DONKEY REGISTRY OF THE UNITED STATES (Animal Breeding) (MDR)
2901 N. Elm St.   Phone: (817) 382-6845
Denton, TX 76201   Betsy Hutchins, Exec. Officer
Founded: 1958. **Staff:** 2. Maintained by the American Donkey and Mule Society (see separate entry). Owners of registered miniature donkeys. (Miniature donkeys measure no more than 36 inches high at the withers, range in color from mouse gray to reddish brown to black, and have a dark stripe that runs down the back and across the shoulders to form a cross.) Assists purchasers in locating breeders in their vicinity; provides information about the breed to the public. Compiles statistics. Maintains miniature donkey registry (stud book) and mailing list of users services; issues registration certificates. **Convention/Meeting:** none.

★3968★   MOHAIR COUNCIL OF AMERICA (Animal Breeding) (MCA)
516 Central Natl. Bank Bldg.   Phone: (915) 655-3161
San Angelo, TX 76901   Brian J. May, Exec.Dir.
Founded: 1966. **Members:** 10,500. **Staff:** 4. Mohair growers throughout the U.S. Promotes the use of mohair. Maintains fabric library; conducts cooperative advertising and promotion with mills, manufacturers, and retailers. Sponsors competitions; compiles statistics; bestows awards.

Convention/Meeting: semiannual board meeting.

★3969★   NATIONAL BOARD OF FUR FARM ORGANIZATIONS (Animal Breeding) (NBFFO)
c/o Robert Buckler
405 Sibley St., Suite 120   Phone: (612) 293-0054
St. Paul, MN 55101   Robert Buckler, Exec.Dir.
Founded: 1944. **Members:** 45. **Staff:** 2. **Budget:** $100,000. **Regional Groups:** 3. **State Groups:** 25. **Local Groups:** 17. Federation of state and regional associations of ranch raised mink and fox producers, with a combined membership of 2000. Fosters breed improvement of ranch raised mink and fox. Works with U.S. Department of Agriculture in collecting mink production statistics; sponsors annual short course; conducts research; bestows awards. **Committees:** Forward Planning; National Policy; Research; Short Course Program.

Publications: *Research References on Mink and Foxes,* annual. ● *Seminar Proceedings,* annual. ● Also publishes research bibliography.

Convention/Meeting: annual conference, with seminar.

★3970★   NATIONAL BUFFALO ASSOCIATION (Animal Breeding) (NBA)
10 Main St.
P.O. Box 580   Phone: (605) 223-2829
Ft. Pierre, SD 57532   Nancy Stirling, Exec.Dir.
Founded: 1966. **Members:** 900. **Staff:** 3. **Budget:** $120,000. Active members (500) are owners of buffalo; associate members (372) and honorary members (28) are people interested in but who do not own buffalo. Purposes are to: promote buffalo and buffalo products, namely meat and hides; seek fair and equitable regulations in the control of disease and in the movement of buffalo or buffalo products, both intrastate and interstate; promote and develop recreation connected with buffalo. Presents awards; offers specialized education program. Maintains hall of fame; compiles statistics. **Committees:** Heritage; Legislature; Marketing; Public Relations; Research.

Publications: *Buffalo Chip,* periodic. Newsletter. ● *Buffalo Magazine,* bimonthly. ● *Directory,* annual. ● Also publishes *Buffalo Management and Marketing* and *Buffalo Ranchers' Handbook.*

Convention/Meeting: semiannual, with exhibits and seminar.

★3971★   NATIONAL PEDIGREE LIVESTOCK COUNCIL (Animal Breeding) (NPLC)
One Holstein Pl.   Phone: (802) 254-4551
Brattleboro, VT 05301   Zane Akins, Sec.-Treas.
Founded: 1911. **Members:** 53. **Staff:** 1. **Budget:** Less than $25,000. Federation of breeders of beef and dairy cattle, horses, swine, sheep, goats, and ponies. Member organizations register pedigrees of animals, maintain records of ownership, foster breed improvement, and promote respective breeds. Conducts national advertising campaigns and programs of herd improvement; emphasizes youth involvement. Bestows awards. **Telecommunications Services:** Fax, (802)254-8251. **Formerly:** (1985) National Society of Live Stock

From *Encyclopedia of Associations,* 25th edition, Volume 1, edited by Deborah M. Burek. Copyright © 1990 by Gale Research Inc. Reproduced by permission of the publisher.

depth publications such as *Contemporary Authors* and *Who's Who in Economics*. The *Biography and Genealogy Master Index* from Gale Research is a name index to the individuals covered in dozens of major biographical sources. This excellent research tool is published annually, with five-year historical cumulations. It indexes over 250 directories and reference services, including *Who's Who in America* and the *Current Biography Yearbook*. Many specialized guides to authors, researchers, and professionals are covered. The index is also available online through DIALOG.

One way to identify faculty specializing in particular fields is to perform a literature search, using bibliographic guides to books, periodical articles, and other publications to locate individuals who have written extensively on a topic. Perhaps the best method is to plug into the so-called "invisible college." By contacting a faculty member at a local school, or even a nationally known university, the researcher can obtain leads on experts elsewhere in the country. The directories listed below are designed to assist in two areas: obtaining addresses of individual schools, and locating specialized research organizations.

Research Centers Directory (Gale Research, Inc.—Annual).

This unique directory describes over 12,000 nonprofit research organizations in universities, foundations, and other settings. It covers the full spectrum of disciplines, from the sciences to social and cultural studies. Extensive coverage is given to business, economics, and public policy. Several indexes enhance the value of the *Directory*: the names of the centers and host organizations are listed, together with name changes and defunct groups; acronyms, major project names, titles of databases, and annual conferences are indexed; and an index of special capabilities lists the centers by type of computer, scientific equipment, or other facility. Each entry mentions the center's founding date, method of governance and funding, purpose, type of research activities, annual research budget, staff size, publications, and special capabilities. Information is updated between editions by a supplement service.

Gale also publishes three related directories, each updated on an irregular basis. The *Government Research Centers Directory* covers U.S. government facilities, from the Department of Agriculture's Meat Animal Research Center to the Bureau of the Census's Population Estimate Research Unit. The *International Research Centers Directory* covers both nonprofit and commercial centers outside the United States; approxi-

mately 6,000 centers in 145 countries are identified. The *Research Services Directory* lists more than 4,000 commercial firms that offer some type of research service. Most of the companies in this third source are consulting or marketing research firms, though a variety of other services are represented.

All four directories can be searched online in a single database called *Research Centers and Services Directory*. It is available exclusively on DIALOG, with semiannual updates. Another Gale publication useful for identifying both nonprofit and commercial research organizations is the *Information Industry Directory*, described in Chapter 3.

HEP: Higher Education Directory (Higher Education Publications, Inc.—Annual).

HEP is the most convenient guide to college addresses, phone numbers, key administrative officials, and quick background information. This service lists approximately 4,000 accredited degree-granting institutions, with coverage of the United States, Puerto Rico, and other U.S. possessions. Included are junior colleges, four-year schools, and universities. Entries are arranged by state, then by institution name. *HEP* provides the following additional facts on each school: date established, enrollment, affiliation, accreditation, degrees offered, and calendar system. A supplemental section describes national and regional accrediting organizations, state educational agencies, and consortia and associations in higher education. Indexing is by administrators' names and by name of institution.

Researchers may also want to consult more detailed guides to schools and their programs. *American Universities and Colleges,* sponsored by the American Council on Education, is published every four years by Walter de Gruyter, Inc. Other extensive works include *Peterson's Graduate Programs* (Peterson's Guides, Inc., annual in five volumes); the *College Blue Book* (Macmillan Publishing, Inc., biennial in five volumes); and *Barron's Guide to Graduate Business Schools* (Barron's Educational Series, Inc., biennial in one volume).

FEE-BASED RESEARCH SERVICES

Innumerable companies offer information-related services. The publishers and database producers listed throughout this book are one type of information provider, and guides to these organizations are described in Chapters 3 and 4. But three types of fee-based information specialists are appropriate to discuss at this point:

market research firms, consultants, and information brokers. Companies generally turn to specialized research services when they have insufficient in-house expertise, when a project is extremely complex, when they seek objective outside advice, or when they know other organizations have ready access to the information needed. The decision to pay someone else to conduct research on your behalf should never be made without verifying the reputation, qualifications, and track record of any prospective researcher. It is also imperative that both parties completely understand the extent of the research to be done, how it will be undertaken, the form which the final report will take, and all fees involved. For large projects, it is wise to specify these points in writing. Establishing long-term relationships with professionals you can trust can be a satisfying part of the research process. Sometimes it's nice to know there are others to turn to when faced with a knotty research problem.

The task does not have to be a major project to warrant outside help. Many firms can provide fast, expert assistance on small jobs. This is especially important when information is needed immediately. Document delivery services, for example, can provide publications and/or public documents on demand for a fee. Many such companies can rapidly deliver virtually any public document filed with the federal government, as well as state, local, and foreign government filings. Examples of this type of organization are Federal Document Retrieval, Research Information Services, Inc., and the Washington Service Bureau, all with headquarters in Washington, D.C. Other delivery firms specialize in retrieving government publications, back issues of journals, or foreign publications, and some can search for virtually any type of book, article, or report. The directories listed below represent the leading guides to various types of fee-based research organizations, including document delivery companies.

Burwell Directory of Information Brokers (Burwell Enterprises, Inc.—Annual).

This guide to more than 1,000 organizations which specialize in locating sources of secondary information is compiled by Helen Burwell, publisher of the *Information Broker* newsletter. Regarded as the premier directory of its kind, it profiles services ranging from library research and database searching to document delivery and customized report writing. Included are library consulting firms and fee-based services in public and academic libraries. Organizations are represented from around the country and in more than 30 other nations.

Each entry provides organization name, address, phone number, and contact person. Descriptions include the subjects handled by each firm, the services offered, founding date, and background on the history and qualifications of principal researchers. Firms are listed alphabetically within each state or country, with indexes by organization name, city, personnel, subject, and service capabilities.

FISCAL Directory of Fee-Based Information Services in Libraries (FYI/County of Los Angeles Public Library—Biennial).

FISCAL, a "Discussion Group" of the Association of College and Research Libraries, is comprised of academic libraries which sponsor fee-based research centers. The *FISCAL Directory* is a joint venture of FISCAL and FYI, the fee-based service at the County of Los Angeles Public Library. It describes more than 200 libraries which perform on-demand research and document delivery for a fee, including those in academic, public, and corporate libraries. Each organization is afforded a two-page listing, with detailed descriptions of services offered, fee schedules, billing options, delivery methods, research specialties, online capabilities, and staff. Indexes provide access by subject specialty, geographic area, and online vendor.

Individuals seeking to hire local database searchers will also find Gale's *Online Database Search Services Directory* useful. Published on an irregular basis, this guide offers in-depth descriptions of the capabilities and services of organizations which perform online searching for a fee. Of the 1,700 sources covered, most are public and academic libraries, though information brokers and other private firms are included. Descriptions explain the search request procedure of each organization, fee structure, the subject areas and databases in which they specialize, vendor access, and related services offered. Listings are arranged geographically. Indexes provide additional access by subject, database specialization, vendors used, organization name, and personnel.

International Directory of Marketing Research Companies and Services: The GreenBook (New York Chapter of the American Marketing Association—Annual).

The *GreenBook* is the best known and most complete guide to marketing research companies. This annual publication describes over 1,300 firms that conduct surveys, audits, product testing, and other marketing studies. The narrative portion of each entry is provided by the firm itself, and the *GreenBook* has plenty of paid

advertisements for further information. It is indexed by geography, personnel, services provided, industries served, and computer software capabilities.

Two other helpful sources are *Bradford's Directory of Marketing Research Agencies*, and the *Research Service Directory*. *Bradford's,* published by a company of the same name, covers approximately 1,500 research firms and marketing consultants. Standard listings are very brief, but firms may pay a fee if they wish to describe their services in greater detail. Geographic, personnel, and service indexes are provided. It appears somewhat irregularly, usually every one to two years. The second publication, also known by the names *Directory of Research Services* and *MRA Blue Book,* profiles the 750 firms belonging to the Marketing Research Association, Inc. Unlike *Bradford's,* the listings are reasonably lengthy. An especially useful feature is the index to specialized research capabilities, such as permanent access to shopping malls and sophisticated telephone banks. It is revised annually.

Consultants and Consulting Organizations Directory (Gale Research, Inc.—Annual).

Over 16,000 consulting firms are listed in this Gale directory, with indexing by city, subject (including "industries served"), company name, and key personnel. The length of each listing varies, depending on the amount of information supplied by the respondent. A typical entry includes name, address, principal officers, date founded, staff size, facsimile and other telecommunications capabilities, and a concise statement of the firm's activities and services. Longer listings may provide a more detailed description of the firm, branch office locations, and titles of recent publications or sponsored conferences. Approximately 10% of the companies also disclose annual revenue figures. Data from the *Directory* are available online through the Human Resources Information Network (HRIN).

Another excellent guide is Dun & Bradstreet's annual *Dun's Consultants Directory.* It covers 25,000 consulting firms by name, geographic location, and consulting specialty, with a geographic index to branch locations. Although the description of each company's services is not as detailed and the indexing is not as complete, the basic information is similar to Gale's. For most firms, *Dun's* cites the year started, officers' names, a brief description, and branch locations. *Dun's* has many more listings than its competitor, and is more likely to include consultants' sales figures and total employment size for any given firm.

Directory of Management Consultants (Kennedy and Kennedy, Inc.—Irregular).

The *Directory of Management Consultants* focuses on firms which offer management advice. Revised every two to three years by the editors of *Consultants News,* it provides lengthy descriptions of 800 of the most reputable firms in the United States. The *Directory* contains an index of industries served and an extremely detailed index to consulting specialties.

Membership directories of consultants' associations can also provide leads for management advice. Several national and international groups publish detailed directories, including the Association of Management Consulting Firms and the Institute of Management Consultants. Companies in many other service industries can provide important advice and information for research purposes. Numerous trade directories can help identify more specialized service firms. Among the most useful are the *Standard Directory of Advertising Agencies, O'Dwyer's Directory of Public Relations Firms, Emerson's Directory of Leading U.S. Accounting Firms,* the *Martindale-Hubbell Law Directory*, and *Pro File: The Official Directory of the American Institute of Architects.*

HOW AND WHEN TO ASK FOR HELP

For many people, the biggest barrier to asking for expert advice is simply a lack of confidence, but even the most intrepid researcher can improve interview results by following a few basic rules.   You should never ask professionals for free advice if giving information is what they or their firm does for a living. Even when the request seems like fair game, if the expert indicates he or she would be happy to help you for a fee, you should respect that wish. Fortunately, lots of people are willing to freely share what they know if they are approached correctly.

Before making any personal contacts, it is essential to prepare for the interview. First, make sure you have a clear idea of what you want to know. Next, spend some time identifying the most likely sources of information. It is a waste of your time and the respondent's to contact organizations which are clearly inappropriate. Understanding the nature of the organization you are calling is a good way to start. Third, make a list of specific questions to ask. Finally, it usually helps to do some preliminary research on the topic before making any

personal contacts. This will provide general background, help you to phrase questions, and allow you to put the responses in some frame of reference.

The first rule of successful interviewing is to make a good initial impression. Interviewing is definitely a people skill, and it takes practice to become good at it. Your attitude will have a lot to do with how you come across to a respondent. You should strive to be friendly, open, confident, and even optimistic. A dose of humility never hurts; show respect for the other person's abilities, but don't be obsequious. These attitudes will increase the chances that the expert will give you some time, and will make it far easier to develop a conversational rapport as the interview continues. Expect that the person is willing to talk to you; if not, you can always go on to the next prospect. The most important point to get across in the opening conversation is who you are and what you are doing. Don't be evasive—explain why you need the information. Not only will this clarify your purpose to the other individual, it will lend legitimacy to your request, help to dispel any suspicions, and set the stage for the interview. Above all, don't pose as someone you are not. If you are working on a confidential project, say so, but still try to give the respondent a sense of who you are. During the interview, don't ask vague, convoluted, or trivial questions. Though planning is important, don't adhere rigidly to your list of questions—allow respondents to say what they want in their own way. Develop good listening skills, and show interest in what is said. Though it is usually fine to let a respondent talk at length, there are times you will need to redirect the conversation. Follow any promising new avenues suggested by the previous answers. Don't hesitate to probe, as long as this is not done in an aggressive manner. When a particular response doesn't answer the question, rephrase it. Also, be sensitive to the other person's concerns. If the respondent seems to be getting nervous about the time, close the interview, but ask if you can call back if you think of additional questions. Finally, never be afraid to show ignorance; feigning knowledge is never a wise policy.

Not everyone will agree to help you with your research. One way to encourage cooperation is to share a little bit of what you know. Experts are always anxious to learn additional facts, and most people are more cooperative in a two-way exchange. Better yet, be willing to share the results of your final research, when appropriate. If it is clear that the person cannot or will not help, it never hurts to ask them for further leads. Remember, there are always alternative sources of information. For example, data on business conditions in a particular locality may be kept by planning departments at the municipal, county, regional, and state levels, as well as by industrial development agencies, chambers of commerce, privately financed development councils, and university research centers. This variety of data sources leads to another important point: because organizations have different missions, each one may provide a different slant on the same topic. Turning to multiple sources can give you a more balanced picture and corroborate previously gathered information.

The key to success is in not giving up after the first rejection. Even when the correct organization has been identified, you may not start with the right person.

Everyone has experienced being shunted from one phone number to another when seeking information. Often one branch or office is blissfully unaware of what another is doing, even if the two are neighbors. This is frustrating, but the rewards for persistence make the effort worthwhile. Sometimes meandering is unavoidable, especially if the topic is unfamiliar. The best way to minimize false starts is to do some research before hand, using the types of tools described in this chapter.

When is it appropriate to seek expert advice? The most direct answer is: "Always, if the information need is important." Even brief advice from an expert can save time, effort, and needless mistakes, so researchers should get in the habit of utilizing human resources. Mapping a plan of attack is always recommended before embarking on a new research effort. Situations where expert advice is especially valuable include when you don't know quite how to get started; when it's a subject you know little about; when the published resources are less helpful than expected; when it's difficult to evaluate the quality of information turned up so far; when published information is not timely enough; and, of course, when you're in a hurry. Is it worth making 30 phone calls to find a reliable answer? Use the same guidelines you would in consulting reference books and other published sources. Only you can decide how much effort is warranted. Of course there are also times you may feel the need to bring in paid consultants or researchers to help with a problem, but it's truly amazing how much can be uncovered with a little initiative.

This chapter has tried to provide readers with new and useful ideas to encourage imagination and open-mindedness in their pursuits. Unfortunately, most individuals have a fairly narrow view of information resources. Some researchers are book oriented, others are people oriented. Generally speaking, librarians turn most readily to published information. Businesspeople, on the other hand, are usually more comfortable with

informal networks of personal contacts. Some types of research lend themselves naturally to one avenue rather than the other; most journalists, for example, obtain almost all of their information from interviews and observation. The important point is that almost every research problem can benefit from both published and people resources.

FOR FURTHER READING

This reading list covers several loosely related areas. Interviewing is a vital but often overlooked research skill. Some of the guides described in the list following Chapter 3 offer brief discussions of interviewing techniques, but the titles below are more extensive. Most were written for journalists and writers, but many of the points are extremely pertinent to business researchers. A second category deals with obtaining expert information, including working with consultants and information brokers. The third topic focuses on the government as an information provider. Much was said in Chapters 1 and 2 about the value of government experts and publications. To put the discussion in perspective, a darker view is presented here. A variety of restrictions and problems related to government information are outlined in these articles and reports. Viewpoints from both sides are presented.

Interviewing Techniques

Brady, John. *The Craft of Interviewing* (Cincinnati, OH: Writer's Digest Books, 1976).
    Seasoned interviewer Brady passes on tips of the trade in a lively and instructive presentation. Of special interest is the chapter on conducting phone and mail interviews.
Donaghy, William C. *The Interview: Skills and Applications* (Dallas, TX: Scott, Foresman, 1984).
    A textbook approach to interviewing techniques. Most important concerns are addressed, including interview preparation, structuring the interview, the opening and close, asking questions, probing, handling resistance, listening, and taking notes. Part II describes the different types of interviews, from employment selection to counseling to market research. The most relevant chapter deals with the "information interview."

Metzler, Ken. *Creative Interviewing: The Writer's Guide to Gathering Information and Asking Questions.* 2nd ed. (Englewood Cliffs, NJ: Prentice Hall, 1989).
    Despite its subtitle, this useful book is not just for writers. Among the topics covered are the stages of the interview, conversational dynamics, planning the interview, developing listening skills, how to ask questions, and note taking.
Tyson, Kirk W. "Gathering Non-Published Information from External Sources." In his *Business Intelligence: Putting It All Together.* (Oak Bridge, IL: Leading Edge Publications, 1986): 59–73.
    Gives tips on how to use interviewing techniques to gather business intelligence. Tyson, president of the Competitor Intelligence Group, discusses both who and how to ask. The advice on telephone interviewing is especially good. An appendix provides a table of questions researchers most frequently need to ask, together with the types of organizations most likely to provide the answers.

Government Agencies

"Federal Information Policies: Why Should the Academic Community Be So Concerned?" *Library Issues: Briefings for Faculty and Administrators* 10 (November 1989): 1–4.
    This briefing provides an overview of current government policies which threaten the dissemination of information in the United States. The briefing focuses on OMB Circular A130 which contains numerous recommendations for curtailing the federal government's role as an information provider.
Fricker, Richard L. "Information, Please: Is the FOIA a Myth?" *American Bar Association Journal* 75 (June 1990): 57–61.
    Examines the reasons why the Freedom of Information Act doesn't always work the way it was intended, including the wide variations in response among different agencies. Several examples of poor government response are discussed.
Gutman, Richard. "Getting Uncle Sam to Open Up." *The Compleat Lawyer* 6 (Spring 1989): 18–21.
    A nuts-and-bolts explanation of how to request information under the FOIA, including a sample request letter.
Kent, Calvin A. "The Privatization of Government Information: Economic Considerations." *Government Publications Review* 16 (March/April 1989): 113–32.
    An economist outlines the arguments for and against privatization of the government's information dissemination activities. Evaluation of major studies on both sides of the issue are presented, concluding with a critique of OMB Circular A-130. Although the author, director of Baylor University's Center for Private Enterprise, recommends a middle course of action, he clearly sees benefits to privatizing some aspects of government information, and increasing fees for others.

Mackenzie, Angus. "Who Wants to Know?" *California Lawyer* 5 (April 1985): 39–43.

Describes the use of the Freedom of Information Act by businesses to obtain competitor intelligence and information for litigation purposes. Discusses methods that companies can use to prevent the government from disclosing confidential information about themselves, including "reverse FOIA" lawsuits.

McClure, Charles R., Ann Bishop, and Philip Doty. "Federal Information Policy Development: The Role of the Office of Management and Budget." In *United States Government Information Policies,* edited by Charles R. McClure, Peter Hernon, and Harold C. Relyea. (Norwood, NJ: Ablex, 1989): 51–76.

Describes the central role played by the OMB in determining information policy. The authors suggest OMB focuses too much on the cost of providing information and too little on how their decisions affect users. Recommendations are made for reassessing OMB's responsibilities.

Perritt, Henry H. "Government Information Goes On-Line." *Technology Review* 92 (November/December 1989): 60–67.

Summarizes major policy concerns related to government provision of electronic databases for public access, including the major issues of price and competition with the private sector.

Consultants and Other Fee-Based Research Services

Golightly, Henry O. *Consultants: Selecting, Using, and Evaluating Business Consultants* (New York: Franklin Watts, 1985).

Golightly, an elder statesman of the consulting industry, offers sage, forthright, and pithy advice on the use of business consultants. Topics include what consultants do, why businesses should use them, whether their services are worth the cost, how to tell when they are needed, how to identify and select good ones, how to oversee their work and evaluate their performance, and how to secure employee cooperation. A concluding chapter presents some interesting thoughts on the common mistakes managers make when dealing with consultants.

Lunden, Elizabeth. "Quality Control in Fee-Based Library Services: Who Cares?" In *Fee-Based Services: Issues and Answers,* The Second Conference on Fee-Based Research in College and University Libraries, University of Michigan, 1987. (Ann Arbor, MI: University of Michigan Libraries, 1987): 31–40

Discusses issues of quality in delivering fee-based information, the characteristics of a quality product, and how to improve it.

Rugge, Sue. "What to Expect from an Information Consultant." *Online* 12 (March 1988): 48-50.

Unlike other fields of consulting, where the client's expectations may be better defined, those who hire "information consultants" often have little idea of what constitutes good service. Rugge, an experienced consultant with a national reputation, describes the attributes and abilities of a good information broker, the nature of the consultant/client relationship, and the types of services fee-based researchers can provide.

Shenson, Howard L. *How to Select and Manage Consultants: A Guide to Getting What You Pay For* (Lexington, MA: Lexington Books, 1990).

A newer title, similar in many respects to Golightly, but providing more detail on a variety of issues, including setting fees, determining overhead, judging the consultant's qualifications, evaluating the proposal, and negotiating the contract. A short, but interesting chapter offers tips on getting "free" advice during the consulting process. Shenson is an experienced management consultant and editor of a popular newsletter for the consulting industry.

Stern, Bruce and Scott Dawson. "How to Select a Market Research Firm." *American Demographics* 11 (March 1989): 44-46.

Tips on identifying and evaluating potential research firms, including the importance of obtaining written proposals and the benefits of building long-term relationships with good service providers.

CHAPTER 3
Finding Reference Materials

TOPICS COVERED

1. General Guides to the Literature
2. Guides to Directories
3. Guides to Periodicals and Other Serials
   a. General Serials Directories
   b. Trade Journal Directories
   c. Newsletter Directories
   d. Newspaper Directories
   e. Guides to Special Issues
4. Guides to Specialized Business Publications
5. Guides to Computerized Information Sources
   a. Directories of Online Databases
   b. Specialized Online Directories
   c. CD-ROM Directories
   d. Directories of Magnetic Tape Files and Diskettes
6. Honing Research Skills
7. For Further Reading

MAJOR SOURCES DISCUSSED

- *Encyclopedia of Business Information Sources*
- *Directories in Print*
- *Ulrich's International Periodicals Directory*
- *Business Publications Rates & Data*
- *Oxbridge Directory of Newsletters*
- *Editor & Publisher International Year Book*
- *Business Rankings Annual*
- *Findex: The Directory of Market Research Reports, Studies and Surveys*
- *Information Industry Directory*
- *Directory of Online Databases*
- *Fulltext Sources Online*
- *CD-ROMs in Print: An International Guide*
- *Directory of Computerized Data Files: A Guide to U.S.Government Information in Machine Readable Format*

Samuel Johnson wrote: "Knowledge is of two kinds. We know a subject ourselves, or we know where we can find information upon it." To know the answers ourselves certainly seems preferable; at the very least, it saves us the trouble of looking it up. Realistically, there will probably be more instances in our lives when we don't know the answer than when we do. The accelerating rate at which knowledge is created makes it impossible to learn and retain everything that is relevant to us. And even if we could, it is unlikely we would be able to anticipate all our future information needs. That is where research skills come into play. Knowing where to look is the researcher's stock-in-trade, but numerous finding tools are published to assist novice and expert alike. The focus of this chapter is on these guides—the directories, handbooks, and bibliographies that can lead the user to the proper source of information.

Learning what reference materials are available is a vital part of the research process, but a bewildering array of published materials exists for every business topic imaginable. Finding exactly the right source to address a specific question often seems like an overwhelming task. Common sense might suggest that a particular type of publication must exist, but identifying it when needed can be challenging. Library catalogs are frequently too general for specific inquiries, and popular guides such as *Books in Print* typically do not cover specialized reference works. One of the best ways to learn about potentially useful information sources is to consult guides to

the reference literature. The tools introduced in this chapter are designed to help the user locate the harder-to-find publications so important to business research. They are presented according to the format of the publications they cover. All types of reference works are explored: printed materials such as directories, journals, and newsletters; specialized business services such as loose-leaf services and market research reports; and electronic media, including online databases, CD-ROMs, and magnetic tape files.

GENERAL GUIDES TO THE LITERATURE

Given the enormous scope of business publishing, it is no small accomplishment to compile a broad-based guide to major business information sources. A fair number of attempts have been made, but only two books serve as reasonably current guides to the full spectrum of published information: *Business Information Sources*, and the *Encyclopedia of Business Information Sources*. Neither is comprehensive—there are far too many reference sources for a single book to cover—but each presents thousands of titles on a multitude of topics. Both guides cover specialized reference tools and serial publications, as well as more traditional publications such as business encyclopedias, dictionaries, handbooks, and even textbooks. Although totally different in format and style, both works are minor masterpieces which belong in every business library.

Business Information Sources, Lorna Daniells (University of California—Revised Edition, 1985).

The undisputed classic in the field of business information is this wide-ranging work compiled by the former business bibliographer of Harvard University's prestigious Baker Library. Daniells shows a rare talent for selecting and describing the most representative and useful publications for business research. The book is divided into 21 chapters, each covering a specific type of information. It begins with a chapter on "Locating Facts" and ends with a basic book list for the beginning researcher or small library. About half of *Business Information Sources* is devoted to basic reference materials, and half to the literature of specific disciplines such as marketing and banking. These latter chapters include not only reference sources, but standard textbooks and books written for the practicing manager. This feature makes it especially useful for identifying sources of introductory information on management topics. Each entry is ac-

companied by a brief but well-written summary of the work. A thorough author and title index to the publications is also provided. The value of this excellent finding guide cannot be overstated; no researcher should be without it. A new edition is scheduled to appear in late 1991.

Encyclopedia of Business Information Sources (Gale Research, Inc.—Irregular).

Instead of presenting topics in broad categories, the *Encyclopedia of Business Information Sources* takes a dictionary approach, listing specific subjects in an alphabetical arrangement. A typical page can be seen in Exhibit 3-1. The works mentioned are not annotated, as they are in Daniells, although one-third of the listings include a brief note describing the scope or purpose of the work. The real value of the *Encyclopedia* is its breadth of coverage. It provides mini-bibliographies on more than 1,000 subjects, from corporate culture to urban development, and thousands of major business publications are cited. Four types of headings are used: products (e.g., typewriters or water beds), businesses (e.g., telephone answering services or home improvement companies), management functions (e.g., personnel management or public relations), and general subjects (e.g., agriculture or retirement). The *Encyclopedia* also provides information on topics of current interest, such as insider trading or desktop publishing. The amazing diversity of subjects includes such surprising topics as hypertension, vocabulary, humor, and other nonbusiness subjects of potential interest to the businessperson. The generous use of cross-references leads the user to the appropriate subject heading.

Under each subject, topics are divided by type of material. Sixteen categories are used as standard subdivisions, including Handbooks & Manuals, Indexes & Abstracts, Periodicals, and Directories. Most subjects also cite sources of unpublished information such as trade associations and research centers. This exceptional guide is completely updated every two to three years; the 8th edition was released in 1991.

Gale also publishes similar guides for several other subjects, including the *Encyclopedia of Public Affairs Information Sources*, the *Encyclopedia of Legal Information Sources*, and the *Encyclopedia of Health Information Sources*. The *Encyclopedia of Geographic Information Sources* emphasizes business and economic information about the 50 states and more than 300 major U.S. cities. The 4th edition was released in 1987 and the companion volume covering foreign countries followed in 1988.

EXHIBIT 3-1. *Encyclopedia of Business Information Sources*

INTEREST
See also: MONEY

GENERAL WORKS

How to Forecast Interest Rates: A Guide to Profits for Consumers, Managers and Investors. Martin J. Pring. McGraw-Hill, Publishing Co., 1221 Ave of the Americas, New York, NY 10020. (800) 262-4769 or (212) 512-2000. 1986. $11.95.

The Money Market. Marcia Stigum. Dow Jones-Irwin, 1818 Ridge Rd., Homewood, IL 60430. (800) 634-3961 or (312) 790-6000. 1989. $62.50. Third edition. Covers interest rates, commercial paper, the credit markets, financial futures, options, etc.

HANDBOOKS AND MANUALS

Controlling Interest Rate Risk: New Techniques and Applications for Money Management. R.B. Platt. John Wiley and Sons, Inc., 605 Third Ave., New York, NY 10158. (800) 526-5368 or (212) 850-6465. 1986. $34.95.

Financial Compound Interest and Annuity Tables. Financial Publishing Co., 82 Brookline Ave., Boston, MA 02215. (617) 262-4040. 1980. $65.00. Sixth edition. 1986. Supplement. $22.50.

Lake's Monthly Installment Interest and Discount Book. A. V. Lake and others. A. V. Lake and Co., P.O. Box 1595, Beverly Hills, CA 90213. $28.00. Sixth edition.

PERIODICALS AND NEWSLETTERS

Banking Safety Digest. Warren G. Heller, editor. Veribanc, Inc., Post Office Box 461, Wakefield, MA 01880. (800) 442-2657 or (617) 245-8370. Quarterly. $69.00 per year. Newsletter. Covers deposit insurance, bank failures, federal regulations, etc. Prints lists of the nation's largest safe banks and safe banks offering the highest certificate of deposit yields for various maturities.

Banxquote: High Yield Federally Insured Banking. Masterfund, Inc., 575 Madison Ave., New York, NY 10022. (212) 888-8430. Monthly. $125.00 per year. Newsletter. Provides information concerning the highest interest yields available at federally insured banks and savings institutions.

Barron's: National Business and Financial Weekly. Dow Jones and Co., Inc., 200 Liberty St., New York, NY 10281. (212) 808-7200. Weekly. $99.00 per year.

Grant's Interest Rate Observer. Grant's Interest Rate Publishers, 233 Broadway, Suite 4005, New York, NY 10279. (212) 608-7994. Biweekly. $375.00 per year. Newsletter on interest rate trends, money markets, and fixed-income investments.

Interest Rate Forecast; Analysis of Bond and Money Market Trends. J. Anthony Boeckh, editor. BCA Publications, 3463 Peel St., Montreal, PQ, Canada H3A 1W7. (514) 398-0653. Monthly. $525.00 per year.

Interest Rate Service. World Reports Ltd., 280 Madison Ave., Suite 1209, New York, NY 10016. (212) 689-7442. Monthly. $900.00 per year.

Investors High Yield Safety Report. Veribanc, Inc., Post Office Box 461, Wakefield, MA 01880. (800) 442-2657 or (617) 245-8370. Monthly. $315.00 per year. Newsletter. Provides ratings by color codes and stars of banks and savings institutions offering high interest rates to depositors.

Money Reporter: The Insider's Letter for Investors Whose Interest is More Interest. Marpep Publishing, Ltd., 133 Richmond St., W., Toronto, ON, Canada M5H 3M8. (416) 869-1177. Weekly. $185.00 per year. Newsletter. Canadian interest-bearing deposits and investments.

One Hundred Highest Yields Among Federally-Insured Banks and Savings Institutions. Advertising News Service, Incorporated, P.O. Box 088888, North Palm Beach, FL 33408. (800) 327-7717 or (305) 627-7330. Weekly. $84.00 per year. Newsletter.

RESEARCH CENTERS AND INSTITUTES

Veribanc, Inc. Post Office Box 461, Wakefield, MA 01880. (800) 442-2657 or (617) 245-8370. Conducts research relating to the financial condition of individual banks, savings and loan associations, credit unions, and bank holding companies. For a fee, will provide a detailed rating of a particular institution or lists of institutions in various safety categories.

STATISTICS SOURCES

Interest Rates on Selected Consumer Installment Loans at Reporting Commercial Banks. Board of Governors of the Federal Reserve System, Washington, DC 20551. (202) 452-3000. Quarterly.

Selected Interest and Exchange Rates. Board of Governors of the Federal Reserve System, Washington, DC 20551. (202) 452-3000. Weekly. $15.00 per year.

Statistical Annual: Interest Rates, Metals, Stock Indices, Options on Financial Futures, Options on Metals Futures. Chicago Board of Trade, Education and Marketing Services Dept., 141 W. Jackson Blvd., Chicago, IL 60604. (800) 621-4641 or (312) 435-3500. Annual. $15.00. Includes data on GNMA CDR Futures, Cash-Settled GNMA Futures, U. S. Treasury Bond Futures, U. S. Treasury Note Futures, Options on Treasury Note Futures, NASDAQ-100 Futures, Major Market Index Futures, Major Market Index MAXI Futures, Municipal Bond Index Futures, 1,000-Ounce Silver Futures, Options on Silver Futures, Kilo Gold Futures.

INTERIOR DECORATION

ABSTRACTING AND INDEXING SERVICES

Art Index. H. W. Wilson Co., 950 University Ave., Bronx, NY 10452. (800) 367-6770 or (212) 558-8400. Quarterly. Annual cumulations. Service basis. Subject and author index to periodicals in art, architecture, industrial design, city planning, photography, and various related topics.

DIRECTORIES

American Society of Interior Designers - Membership List. American Society of Interior Designers, 1430 Broadway, New York, NY 10018. (212) 944-9220. Annual. Membership.

Directory of Home Furnishings Retailers, Including Full-Line Home Furnishing Stores, Furniture Stores, Bedding Stores & Wholesale Distributors. Chain Store Guide Information Services, 425 Park Ave., New York, NY 10022. (212) 371-9400. Annual. $259.00. Firms with a minimum of $1 million in annual sales. Generally includes product lines, sales volume, year founded, key personnel, and related information.

GUIDES TO DIRECTORIES

Published directories list all manner of organizations, people, and business firms. Major directories of research organizations were introduced in Chapter 2, and some of the most important company directories will be discussed in Chapters 6 and 7, but thousands of other sources are available for business research. The following three titles cover the complete spectrum of directory publishing, and are the best resources for identifying directories on virtually any topic.

Directories in Print (Gale Research, Inc.—Annual).

This indispensable guide lists over 10,000 directories published in the United States. It is divided into 16 broad categories, from Science to Arts & Entertainment. However, the majority of listings are for directories of companies and other business-related publications. Hundreds of business activities are represented by such titles as the *Tent Rental Directory*, the *Sandblasting Companies Directory*, and the *Genetic Technology Sourcebook*. The emphasis is on national and international directories, though some regional publications are described. Extensive coverage is afforded to directories published as special issues of periodicals, and to microforms, online databases, and other nonprint directories. Information on each source includes the scope and size of the directory, the content of a typical entry, the arrangement, indexing, and price. Listings are especially useful for ordering purposes because they cite the frequency of each publication and the time of year it is published. Subject and keyword/title indexes are provided.

Directories in Print formerly included local publications, until its growing size made such inclusions impractical. Gale now compiles *City & State Directories in Print*, which lists publications covering individual states, cities, or local areas. The 5,000 entries include city directories, cross-reference directories, chamber of commerce rosters, and state industrial directories. Listings are arranged geographically by state, with title/keyword and subject indexes. The first edition appeared in 1990; future editions will be published biennially.

Another tool for identifying directories is the *Guide to American Directories* from B. Klein Publications. It covers approximately 7,500 publications, but many are such nondirectory sources as bibliographies, periodicals, and statistical compendia. However, the *Guide to American Directories* concentrates on business topics and includes many directories not found in the Gale publication. Entries are arranged alphabetically by subject, and

accessed by a title index. Directories dealing with a particular geographic area are listed under that state or city. Each entry cites the publisher's address, price, and type of coverage. Although the directory has appeared at irregular intervals, the publisher plans to revise the book biennially beginning with the 12th (1989) edition.

Trade Directories of the World (Croner Publications, Inc.—Monthly Updates).

Unlike Gale and Klein, Croner issues information in loose-leaf binders with monthly updates. Also, the contents are limited almost completely to trade and business directories, with a strong emphasis on publications of interest to importers and exporters. The title is somewhat misleading, since nearly one-third of the book is devoted to directories of American firms. More than 3,000 publications are described, covering every major country in the world. Arrangement is by region and country, then subdivided alphabetically by title. Indexes provide access by subject, publisher, and, for U.S. directories, by state and city. A special index highlights import/export guides by country. Addresses for U.S. and foreign publishers are given, with foreign companies arranged by country. Each entry lists the title (in three languages), publisher, frequency, price, and a brief description of contents.

Although *Trade Directories of the World* has been published for more than 30 years, it is not without weaknesses. Lack of a master index by title makes it difficult to locate information on a specific publication. Furthermore, the use of entry numbers rather than titles in the existing indexes makes them cumbersome to use. Although the loose-leaf pages are revised through monthly mailings, the listings are not as current as one might suspect. However, all entries are updated at least once every two years. For these reasons, this guide is not as widely used as it should be. Still, *Trade Directories of the World* is an important finding tool because it includes many publications not seen in other reference works.

GUIDES TO PERIODICALS AND OTHER SERIALS

A small armada of serial directories guides users through the endless sea of periodical sources. Distinctions among them tend to blur, and the titles themselves can be misleading, but most emphasize a particular type of serial. For the purposes of this discussion, a serial is defined as any publication appearing on a recurring basis,

at a regularly stated interval—daily, weekly, monthly, biennially, and so forth. By their nature, business reference sources tend to be serial publications, and many of the guides introduced elsewhere in this chapter also give extensive coverage to serials. Because serials are so vital to business research, the following guides are indispensable. Most focus on periodical publications—those serials which appear more frequently than once per year. These include journals and magazines, newspapers, and newsletters.

General Serials Directories

One way to find out about serials titles is to utilize the services of a subscription agent such as EBSCO Industries, Inc., Readmore Publications, Inc., or the Faxon Company. Firms such as these serve as intermediaries between publishers and libraries, and they maintain extensive serials databases. Many provide their customers with printed directories containing basic information on serials titles, including current prices. EBSCO's annual *Librarians' Handbook*, for example, lists more than 100,000 serials currently in print. Several vendors also provide their customers with online access to information; an example is Faxon's *INFOSERV* database, which is updated daily.

For detailed information about serials, most researchers turn to published directories. The following guides identify both periodicals and other types of serials. Coverage includes annual publications, loose-leaf services, newspapers, journals, and even irregular serials—those publications appearing on a recurring basis, but with inconsistent frequency. These tools are comprehensive and diversified, and each covers thousands of serials of every type and on any subject.

Ulrich's International Periodicals Directory (R.R. Bowker—Annual, with Quarterly Updates).

Ulrich's, a leading name in serials directories for over 50 years, is a massive three-volume work that provides bibliographic and ordering information for more than 110,000 publications from 197 countries. In fact, less than half of the publications are from the United States. Since merging with *Ulrich's Annual and Irregular Serials*, it covers all types of recurring publications, and the contents are almost evenly divided between periodicals and other types of serials. Information is grouped into broad subject classifications, with additional access through a title index. Each entry lists the publisher, address, frequency, language, and price. Most

listings also cite the year the serial was first published, the editor's name, former titles, circulation data, availability online or in microform, where it is indexed, and a brief description of scope or contents. Appendices include a list of serials that have recently ceased to exist, separate directories of titles available online and of major online vendors, an index to publications of prominent international organizations, and a list of periodical indexes and abstracts.

Information from the Bowker database is also available as a microfiche publication, as an online service through DIALOG and BRS, and as a CD-ROM product known as *Ulrich's Plus*. Electronic data bring added research capabilities. Because the printed directory lists titles under fairly broad headings, it can be tedious trying to locate publications on a specific topic. Searching the online or CD-ROM versions, users can combine characteristics such as country of origin and keywords to quickly locate the most relevant possibilities. Serials frequently have variant titles, so users of the print version must often guess under which title a particular publication will be listed; searching by keyword in the online or CD-ROM database usually eliminates this problem. A fairly high number of data entry errors are present, especially in the assignment of field codes, but this should not deter use of this essential resource. The online version is updated monthly; the CD-ROM appears quarterly.

The Serials Directory: An International Reference Book (EBSCO Publishing—Annual, with Quarterly Updates).

When it debuted in 1986, *The Serials Directory* had many features that *Ulrich's* did not, but with each succeeding year, the differences between them become less noticeable. The only difference in scope is *The Serials Directory* lists general daily newspapers, while *Ulrich's* excludes local papers and covers subject-oriented ones only. With approximately 120,000 entries, EBSCO's directory is also slightly larger than *Ulrich's*. However, because the two publishers obtain their information in completely different ways, a surprising number of serial titles are unique to each directory. Comparing the "Accounting" sections of both books showed more than 50% of the titles in each one were not duplicated in the other.

The entries in both directories are also quite similar, though the EBSCO source tends to provide a greater number of narrative descriptions and lists Library of Congress classification numbers for most titles. EBSCO and Bowker both indicate the names of the relevant indexing services for every periodical title, which is

extremely valuable for research purposes. Both use similar subject headings, but they are equally prone to list some publications under less relevant headings. EBSCO has been criticized by librarians for relying too heavily on automated indexing and providing too little human editing. For example, a management journal called *Operations Research* continues to appear under the heading "Medicine—Surgery." Fortunately, the quality is improving with each new edition. And, like Bowker, EBSCO now offers a CD-ROM edition. Called *The Serials Directory/EBSCO CD-ROM*, it contains up to 23 searchable variables for each listing. The disks are updated quarterly. An online service called EBSCONET is also produced, but is only available to customers of EBSCO's subscription agency.

Standard Periodical Directory (Oxbridge Communications—Annual).

The *Standard Periodical Directory* (*SPD*) lists 70,000 titles, with coverage restricted to material published in the United States and Canada. Although the total number of entries is far fewer than in *Ulrich's* or *The Serials Directory*, the *SPD's* great strength is extensive coverage of newsletters, association publications, house organs, and other hard-to-locate materials. Another advantage *is* the geographic limitation; more than half of the titles in the EBSCO and Bowker directories are foreign. For researchers interested only in North American publications, the *Standard Periodical Directory* makes wading through foreign listings unnecessary.

The *SPD* does not emphasize nonperiodical sources; only 15% of the listings are annual, biennial, or irregular serials. However, it does describe a large number of loose-leaf services and a respectable sampling of directory publications. A complete entry contains the title, former titles, address, publisher, sponsoring organization, editors, key personnel, year founded, availability in other formats, subscription price, circulation data, and the cost of placing a typical ad. Lacking is information on where each publication is indexed, but this feature is promised for future editions.

Trade Journal Directories

Because trade journals play such an important role in business research, it is essential to locate them by specific subject. The *Encyclopedia of Business Information Sources* is a convenient subject guide to major trade journals, but its coverage is generally limited to the most prominent titles in each field. The broad-based serials directories from EBSCO, Bowker, and Oxbridge describe several thousand trade journals each, but the subject headings are usually too broad to allow easy access by industry. The two sources described below address these deficiencies by providing detailed subject listings and more comprehensive coverage.

Business Publication Rates and Data (Standard Rate & Data Service—Monthly).

Standard Rate & Data Service (SRDS) publications (described in Chapter 19) are not considered directories as such, but they can be extremely helpful in identifying sources of information. SRDS provides current, detailed data on advertising rates for various types of media, and *Business Publication Rates and Data* does so for several thousand trade journals and general business magazines. The *Business Publication* edition also has several advantages as a periodical finding guide. First, it is revised monthly, ensuring that the user will be viewing the most current information possible. Second, it eschews periodicals of little or no interest to the business researcher. Third, it uses particularly useful subject and industry classifications. Finally, each entry includes an excellent statement of editorial policy, providing an especially clear description of the journal's purpose and contents. SRDS also appends a directory of the leading publishers of trade journals, together with the titles produced by each.

The Source Directory of Predicasts (Predicasts—Annual, with Supplements).

The Source Directory lists the major publications indexed in Predicasts databases and printed products. Predicasts is a leading compiler of periodical indexes for business research, with a reputation for in-depth coverage of industry news, analysis, and statistics. More than 1,300 industry-specific publications are identified in *The Source Directory*, including trade journals, annual statistical reports, business newspapers, and government-produced serial publications. The main section is an alphabetical listing of titles with address and ordering information. Part 2 is a geographical subject index by region and country. Part 3 is an industry index arranged by four-digit SIC code. (The SIC system will be introduced in Chapter 4.) Because the SIC structure is such a convenient and popular method of organizing business information, *The Source Directory* serves as a quick and simple guide to publications that cover particular industries.

Newsletter Directories

Business newsletters are another font of specialized industry information. Many of the serial directories mentioned in this chapter provide some coverage of newsletter publications. But because newsletters have a limited audience, they can be difficult to track down. Trade associations are major producers of specialized newletters, and the electronic editions of the *Encyclopedia of Associations* are good resources for identifying titles published by this type of organization. (In 1988, Gale released an extremely useful set of directories entitled *Association Periodicals*, but as of this writing a second edition is not planned.) The three directories listed below are excellent guides to newsletters from all types of publishers. Each provides access to resources which might otherwise be lost to the researcher.

Newsletters in Print (Gale Research, Inc.—Biennial).

Over 10,000 newletters from the U.S. and Canada are identified and described in this valuable guide. Publications are grouped into 32 broad categories, with detailed indexes by subject, title, and publisher name. Each lengthy entry cites title, publisher, address, sponsoring organization (if other than publisher), founding date, frequency, size, former titles, price and circulation data, and an excellent summary of the newsletter's contents. Listings also indicate whether the newsletter is available online, and its intended readership. Two interesting appendices list newletters offered to subscribers free of charge and newsletters available online. The directory is also available online through the Human Resource Information Network (HRIN).

Oxbridge Directory of Newsletters (Oxbridge Communications—Annual).

The more than 21,000 listings for U.S. and Canadian newsletters found in this publication are taken from Oxbridge's flagship *Standard Periodical Directory*, but the descriptions are more detailed. Information includes publisher, address, founding date, frequency, size, price, and audience type. Editorial descriptions are fewer and briefer than in *Newsletters in Print*, but Oxbridge does provide some notable information which Gale does not. Because the *Directory* is also intended for suppliers to the newsletter industry, Oxbridge lists names for such key positions as circulation manager, art director, and production manager. The method of printing and the name of the printing company are also given. Although there is no subject index, the topical groupings are more detailed than those provided by Gale. A complete title index, an index to major publishers, and a subject guide to newsletters which sell mailing lists of their subscribers are also included.

Legal Newsletters in Print (Infosources Publishing—Annual).

Approximately 1,700 titles, representing every area of the law, are listed in this specialized guide. The directory provides extensive coverage of business-related topics, including taxation, accounting, and even industry-specific newsletters with strong legal content. It also covers such traditional business law topics as securities regulation, bankruptcy, and antitrust. Newsletters are defined to include membership bulletins, reporting services, and even binder-type newsletters. The main section is organized by title, with a publisher index, a list of publications no longer available, and an extensive subject index. Two special subject headings are used for broad-based newsletters which track important court decisions and pending litigation. *Legal Newsletters in Print* also offers detailed descriptions of the newsletters. Each entry provides information on publisher, editor, ISSN, founding date, frequency, price, circulation, number of pages, physical description, and former titles. Many entries also indicate the presence of an index, whether the title is indexed elsewhere, if the title is also available online or in microform, whether back issues are available, and if it contains book reviews. A brief annotation describing the newletter's editorial content can also be found.

Newspaper Directories

Local newspapers are an invaluable source for uncovering trends in regional economic development, biographies of business executives, background on small companies, and news about the local operations of national corporations. Standard Rate & Data Service publishes several useful guides to newspapers in the United States. They are intended primarily as manuals of advertising rates, but they provide extensive information on the operations of each paper. *Newspaper Rates and Data* lists daily newspapers from across the country, while *Community Publication Rates and Data* covers specialty and weekly newspapers. The sources listed below are more traditional directories of newspapers in the U.S. and abroad.

Editor & Publisher International Year Book (Editor & Publisher Company, Inc.—Annual).

This bible of the newspaper industry describes 1,600 daily newspapers from around the world. It also covers major weeklies, foreign language papers in the U.S., and specialty publications such as black, religious, and college newspapers. A separate section lists suppliers of equipment and services to the industry. Newspaper entries provide data on circulation, subscription rates, wire services used, supplements and special issues, detailed information on editorial and administrative personnel, and production specifications. Listings are arranged geographically, by country, state, and city.

A companion directory, the *Editor & Publisher Syndicate Directory*, gives information on companies providing syndicated cartoons, comic strips, editorials, contests, puzzles, and specialty columns. Information is accessible by syndicate name, feature title, author or artist, and subject.

Another popular guide to newspapers is the five-volume *Working Press of the Nation*, issued annually by the National Research Bureau. Though intended primarily as a guide to publicity outlets, researchers will find it helpful for a variety of purposes. Volume 1 covers daily, weekly, and specialty newspapers in the United States, providing information similar to the *Editor & Publisher International Year Book*. Separate sections list news and photo wire services, syndication services, and national magazine supplements. Volume 2 lists approximately 5,000 magazines of all types. Volume 3 describes the news services and personnel of television and radio stations around the country, while Volume 4 is a guide to feature writers and news photographers. The final volume, "Internal Publications," is a directory of 2,800 house organs published by corporations and nonprofit organizations. These are newsletters and glossy magazines written primarily for the employees and customers of the respective organizations.

Gale Directory of Publications and Broadcast Media (Gale Research, Inc.—Annual).

The *Gale Directory*, formerly known as the *Ayer Directory of Publications*, is one of the oldest periodical directories in the country. Coverage is evenly divided between newspapers and other periodicals; in addition to newspapers, some 1,300 newsletters and 11,000 popular magazines and trade journals can be found here. Beginning with the 1990 edition, it also covers about 10,000 television, cable, and radio stations and networks in the United States, Puerto Rico, and Canada. Volume 1 contains the descriptive listings of publications and broadcast stations, arranged geographically by state and city.

Volume 2 provides indexes by title/keyword, type of publication, and broad subject. A unique geographic index to editors' names and addresses is useful for marketing purposes.

The descriptions in Volume 1 are limited to basic information, but do include important facts. For publications, entries cite the founding date, key staff members, physical size, circulation data, subscription price, and general information on advertising rates. For broadcast media, call letters, channel, network affiliation, staff members, name of owner, the top three local programs, and summary ad rates are listed. Although the newspaper descriptions are brief, Gale lists nearly 2,000 dailies and 8,500 weeklies.

Because newspapers, periodicals, and broadcast stations are interfiled geographically, the *Gale Directory* is an excellent guide to sources of local information as well as local publicity outlets. It is especially useful for profiling the publishing activity in a given city. The indexing by category allows users to identify publications by target audience, including Hispanic, black, female, Jewish, and foreign-language readers. In 1989, the *Gale International Directory of Publications* was introduced. This biennial provides geographic access to about 5,000 foreign newspapers and periodicals.

Guides to Special Issues

Special issues of magazines and trade journals are really reference books within a periodical. They are inexpensive and readily available; in most cases, single copies can be purchased by nonsubscribers. One way to identify major special issues is through conventional periodical indexes. Unfortunately, general indexes seldom indicate the recurring nature of the articles they index. A few indexes to business periodicals do make an effort to highlight special issues; one of the most useful is *PAIS International*, introduced in Chapter 5. Certain guides to specialized reference sources also cover recurring features of periodicals, including *Industry Data Sources* and the *Statistical Reference Index*, both described in Chapter 4. A number of directories devoted exclusively to special issues have been published, but very few are revised on an ongoing basis. The following two are among the best.

Guide to Special Issues and Indexes of Periodicals, *Miriam Uhlan* (Special Libraries Association—Third Edition, 1985).

This handy resource lists regularly appearing special issues of periodicals in 1,300 American and Canadian magazines, with an emphasis on trade journals.

Periodicals are arranged alphabetically, and each entry lists the dates when special issues typically appear. Examples of such issues include annual convention previews, year-in-review features, and quarterly financial surveys. The *Guide to Special Issues* also indicates whether each magazine compiles an annual index to its articles, and whether issues contain indexes to advertisers.

A major drawback to this publication, and others like it, is the lack of frequent revisions. The 3rd edition appeared in 1985; as of this writing, plans for a new edition are doubtful. This is especially limiting because magazine editors constantly change the dates and frequency of these "regular" issues, and new features appear every year. Unfortunately, the Uhlan directory is the only publication of its type which has ever been updated.

Business Rankings Annual (Gale Research, Inc.—Annual).

Though revised annually, this publication has a much narrower focus than other special issue directories, restricting its coverage to articles which contain ranked lists. One of the most popular features of business periodicals is the annual ranking. Famous surveys such as *Business Week*'s review of the highest paid executives, or *Forbes*'s listing of the 400 wealthiest individuals receive wide media coverage when they are released. Most business rankings are more obscure, but they are no less interesting to researchers and to those being ranked. For many years, the staff of the Business Library of the Brooklyn Public Library has maintained an in-house index to publications containing such rankings. By examining every issue of more than 1,000 journals, newspapers, financial services, and other serials received by the Library, they identify several thousand relevant articles each year. Many are regular features of the publications in question, while others are onetime reports. They represent an enormous body of useful, otherwise hard-to-find data. The index covers a variety of company rankings: the major firms in a specific industry, the leading companies exhibiting a particular characteristic, and the largest firms by city or other level of geography. In addition, rankings of occupations by salary, cities by percentage of black population, business magazines by circulation, and other non-company lists can be found. Of special interest are the rankings of brand names, which can provide background on market share. (A more specialized ranking guide from Gale Research, the *Market Share Reporter*, is introduced in Chapter 18.)

Beyond identifying the publications where rankings can be found, the *Business Rankings Annual* actually specifies the names of the top five or ten firms in each ranked list. A complete alphabetical index to all the named companies is also compiled, enabling the researcher to quickly determine that Equitable Life Assurance was a top-ranked company on six different surveys, for example. The biggest drawback is the somewhat convoluted subject indexing. To illustrate, all of the lists which rank states by specific characteristics are indexed first under "States," then subdivided by topic. Most users would approach an index of this type by the attribute itself ("Business Failures—States"), not the other way around. In many cases, considerable effort is required to identify the appropriate subject heading. Even so, the *Business Rankings Annual* is a unique and important finding tool.

GUIDES TO SPECIALIZED BUSINESS PUBLICATIONS

Identifying specialized reference materials such as syndicated intelligence services can be difficult. Few are listed in general-purpose finding tools such as *Ulrich's* or *Books in Print*. One way to keep track of the more elusive reference products is to maintain your own collection of publishers' catalogs. The leading compilers of loose-leaf services, microforms, and market research reports issue extensive catalogs of their own products. But to establish such a collection, the researcher must have a sense of who the producers are. Another way to identify these specialized services is to request catalogs from firms which operate as distributors for other publishers. Two leading distributors of market reports are Off-the-Shelf Publications, Inc. (Commack, NY) and the FIND/SVP Information Clearinghouse (New York City). Their catalogs, updated several times each year, are excellent guides to market reports. Both companies also produce their own reports, though the Commack company operates in this capacity under the name Business Trend Analysts. Two leading producers of market studies, Frost & Sullivan, Inc. and Arthur D. Little, Inc., have created online indexes to their own reports, but these are exceptions to the rule.

How else to learn about specialized business information services? Guides to the literature devoted exclusively to business topics can be helpful, but finding the specific title you seek can be a hit-or-miss proposition. One of the best guides to a diversity of nontraditional business information services is an online database called *Industry Data Sources*, which is introduced in Chapter 4. Unfortunately, even this outstanding finding tool is rather spotty in its coverage of specialized resources. Another solution lies in format-specific guides. For example,

several guides to microform publications are available, though few are well-suited to the business researcher's needs. The Meckler Corporation's annual *Guide to Microforms in Print* offers detailed author/title access, but the subject index is much too broad to be useful. The best way to learn about business microforms is to peruse the catalogs of publishers specializing in this field. To identify them, consult Meckler's *Microform Market Place: An International Directory of Micropublishing*, which describes the major activities of more than 350 leading firms. A more specialized resource is Chadwyck-Healey's *Micropublishers' Trade List Annual*, a yearly microfiche reproduction of catalogs and brochures from nearly 300 microform issuers worldwide. No indexing is provided for the set, but if the user knows the publisher of the item in question, this is a handy way to obtain detailed information.

The directories described below offer more extensive coverage of two categories of elusive business publications: market research reports and loose-leaf services.

Findex: The Directory of Market Research Reports, Studies and Surveys (Cambridge Information Group—Annual, with Update).

Findex is a guide to commercially available business reports from over 500 major research firms. Formerly published by FIND/SVP, this truly unique directory covers syndicated intelligence services, Wall Street analysts' reports, off-the-shelf market research, and multi-client studies, with an emphasis on industries, products, and markets. The publications themselves are expensive; even the onetime studies range in price from $500 to $2,500 each. Because of these high costs, the usefulness of *Findex* might seem limited, but it can be a gold mine of hard-to-locate research results. Some 10,000 reports are covered, though this number includes older studies that are still in print. *Findex* is arranged by broad industry category, with a separate section of company-specific reports. Detailed indexes are compiled for publisher, title, geographic area, and subject access. Each entry provides a short summary of the report, together with price, publisher, availability, and publication date or frequency. A complete directory of publisher addresses is also included. The annual issue is updated by a mid-year supplement. Subscribers who need more current information may call a toll-free Update Service. *Findex* is also accessible as an online database of the same name, available exclusively through DIALOG.

Legal Looseleafs in Print (Infosources Publishing—Annual).

The only finding tool geared specifically toward loose-leaf services unfortunately restricts its coverage to publications with a legal orientation. This means that loose-leaf sources of financial and investment information cannot be found here, but *Legal Looseleafs in Print* is still a worthwhile guide for business researchers. "Legal" is defined broadly, so business law sources and legal services aimed at the nonlawyer are both covered extensively, including guides to business practices, policies, and how-to manuals. The range of legal topics is comprehensive, covering such areas as products liability, patents and trademarks, pension plans, and the environment. Numerous industry-specific legal reporters can also be found. Policy-oriented publications cover business start-up, corporate planning, foreign trade, collective bargaining and employee benefits. A total of 3,400 loose-leaf titles are listed. Entries give authors, publishers, founding dates, price, frequency, number of volumes, and updating costs. The arrangement is alphabetical by title, with fairly specific subject indexing. Separate sections list titles by publisher, titles which are no longer available, and publisher addresses.

GUIDES TO COMPUTERIZED INFORMATION SOURCES

The number and diversity of electronic business resources is staggering, with many new products appearing each month. Happily, quite a few current directories can guide users through this maze. The first two directories described below cover the gamut of electronic sources, including online databases, CD-ROMs, diskettes, and computer tapes. The publications in the remaining sections focus on specific electronic formats.

Information Industry Directory (Gale Research, Inc.—Annual).

This unusual guide provides background information on more than 4,500 organizations, products, and services related to electronic information. Both commercial firms and nonprofit groups are covered. The first volume describes information sources in the United States and abroad, and the second provides multiple access points. In addition to a useful Master Index, Volume 2 contains separate title indexes for databases, printed publications, and software, and indexes by personal name, geographic location, and subject. An Index to Function/Service Type categorizes organiza-

tions by the type of product or service they provide—CD-ROMs, magnetic tapes and floppy disks, abstracting services, consulting, data collection, etc.

Entries are arranged alphabetically by name of organization, with separate descriptions for individual products and services where appropriate. The detailed descriptions include a breakdown of staff size, year founded, clientele served, publications, computer-based products and services, and sources of information. Many of the listings describe organizations and products not found in any other major reference tool. The arrangement by organization name can be frustrating, but it offers a useful alternative to more traditional directories, and the excellent Master Index makes it quite easy to use.

Federal Data Base Finder (Information USA, Inc.—Irregular).

Matthew Lesko, a well-known expert on information sources from government agencies, produces this commercial guide to more than 4,000 federal data products. (Lesko is also the publisher of the *State Data and Database Finder,* described in Chapter 2.) The *Federal Data Base Finder* lists online databases, publicly available computer tape files, and data diskettes produced by the federal government. Coverage of online services is limited to those available directly from federal agencies; government-produced data distributed through commercial vendors are excluded. Some databases are interactive systems available to the public on a subscription basis, while others are electronic bulletin board systems with news, summary statistics, and other current information for public dissemination. However, files directly searchable by the public are few; most databases are accessible only to government employees. In these instances, the directory identifies who to contact and what to ask for. Armed with specific knowledge, the researcher can frequently obtain printouts by mail or brief information by phone. The service may be free, or available at a modest cost.

The directory is arranged by issuing agency, with descriptions of data products available directly from the agency. Titles are listed alphabetically regardless of format. At the end of every agency section is a list of additional tape products offered by the government's two principal tape distributors—NTIS and the National Archives. Database descriptions contain brief summaries of file contents, costs, methods of inquiry, and contact persons or offices. Types of variables and time periods are specified, and, in many cases, order numbers and prices are given. A fairly detailed subject index is provided, and the table of contents lists all database titles by agency. The directory is updated every two to three years. The 3rd edition appeared in 1990.

Although the 3rd edition of the *Federal Data Base Finder* incorporates several improvements, it still has weaknesses. Many descriptions are rife with jargon or lack sufficient detail. Because the entries appear in narrative form, it can be difficult to pick out key facts about products, and descriptions don't always contain the same elements. A standardized directory format, highlighting such key characteristics as file size, price, and time period would enhance usability. And because all formats are intermingled, it would be helpful to use codes or symbols to differentiate tapes, diskettes, and online files. Additional indexes are also needed, including a master title index, a list of subagencies, and a guide to data categories (directory information, micro-data, time series, etc.). Despite these shortcomings, the *Federal Data Base Finder* is valuable for its comprehensive coverage. Few researchers will peruse this extensive guide without discovering potentially useful government files.

A more current, though briefer guide to federal online databases can be found in a supplement to the annual *Statistics Sources*, described in Chapter 4.

Directories of Online Databases

There is a wide selection of guides to online databases, some of which are available online themselves. The publications below are leading sources of current information about online services.

Computer-Readable Databases: A Directory and Data Sourcebook (Gale Research, Inc.—Annual).

The first major directory to online information was compiled by Martha E. Williams in 1976. Updated on an irregular basis, it enjoyed four editions under Williams's direction, but with varying titles and publishers. Acquired by Gale Research in 1989, *Computer-Readable Databases* now appears annually. The directory describes individual databases, database producers, and vendors in three separate sections. The first section also covers several hundred CD-ROMs, magnetic tape files, diskettes, and electronic bulletin boards. A detailed subject index, a master index (including former names, variant titles, and publication names), and an index to CD-ROM products enhance the value of this important guide. Two additional indexes list the databases available on each online system, and the titles issued by every database producer.

The lengthy database descriptions in *Computer-Readable Databases* include a number of points not covered by competing directories. Among them are the method of indexing employed, typical data elements, the titles of available user aids, and toll-free numbers for user

assistance. Listings also provide more detailed information on print, microform, or CD-ROM counterparts than typically can be found in other online directories. With over 6,000 detailed database profiles, it is one of the most comprehensive and best resources available. The *Directory* can also be searched online via DIALOG, on a file of the same name. Users of the online version can employ a combination of search categories to easily identify databases which exhibit specific characteristics. For example, the researcher can quickly locate full-text databases which are also available as CD-ROMs, or financial databases with numeric data available on floppy diskette.

Directory of Online Databases (Cuadra/Gale—Semiannual, with Updates).

Cuadra Associates, a leading name in the database industry, has produced the *Directory of Online Databases* since 1979. When Gale Research announced in early 1991 its acquisition of rights to Cuadra's publications, many subscribers assumed the *Directory* would be merged with Gale's own *Computer-Readable Databases*. However, because the two subscription lists overlap so slightly, Gale plans to maintain both directories in their present form. The decision is surprising, given the similarity of the publications, but it offers users a choice between two excellent research tools.

The *Directory of Online Databases* describes online sources in all subject areas, with representation from around the world. One of the most comprehensive directories published, it lists 600 vendors and more than 4,000 databases. Included are so-called "invisible databases," files which exist as part of a larger database. Complete revisions are published in January and July, with supplements appearing in April and October. It is also available as an online product called the *Directory of Online and Portable Databases*. This version is updated quarterly and is offered through Data-Star, ORBIT, and Questel.

Entries in the print *Directory* are arranged alphabetically by title, with indexing by subject, producer, vendor, and country of origin. Also included is a guide to the telecommunications systems used by each service, and a directory of addresses and phone numbers for all producers and vendors. Information on each database includes a description of the contents, the type (bibliographic, directory, etc.), language, time span, frequency, cost, subscription conditions, and whether the file is also available in CD-ROM format.

The *Directory of Online Databases* is similar in most respects to *Computer-Readable Databases*. The format, scope, size, and indexing are virtually identical, and both offer separate directories for database producers and vendors. The most noticeable differences are Cuadra's more frequent updates and Gale's lengthier database descriptions. However, each directory lists many databases the other does not.

A similar, though less popular guide to online resources is the *DataBase Directory Service* from Knowledge Industry Publications. It appears annually, with a midyear supplement and a monthly updating service. Online, it is available through BRS as the *Knowledge Industry Publications Database*. Both versions cover 3,200 databases, mostly from the U.S. and Canada. The information provided for each database resembles that of the Cuadra directory. A typical description includes a summary of the contents, subjects covered, source of information, size of the database, time covered, updating frequency, print equivalents, publisher, vendors, price, and availability restrictions.

Datapro Directory of On-Line Services (Datapro Research Division of McGraw-Hill—Monthly Updates).

This alternative to more traditional database directories is issued in loose-leaf format, and provides descriptions of 2,400 databases from 900 producers, extensive profiles of 43 major vendors, and numerous special features. Indexing is by company name, title, and subject. Each vendor profile is four to five pages in length, and covers the history of the service, its competitive position, subject strengths, support services, and facilities. Also included is a "hands on" evaluation of the service: its structure, command language, documentation, and more. Producer profiles are much briefer, but each contains information on the company's principal business, its parent company, revenues (when available), products, type of customers, and even future plans. The descriptions of the databases themselves are similar to those found in other directories, but also include information on documentation and training services.

Included is an impressive array of background articles: "Tutorials" provide instruction on important skills such as assessing the cost of an online search; "Feature Reports" survey the impact of such emerging areas as E-Mail, CD-ROM, and international search capabilities. Subscribers also receive a monthly newsletter with news and commentary on current industry trends. Despite Datapro's loose-leaf approach, the main profiles of vendors and databases are infrequently updated. The *Directory* is also less comprehensive than its competitors. However, newcomers to database searching will find the *Datapro Directory* useful for its producer-oriented format, lengthy profiles, and extensive supplementary materials.

Specialized Online Directories

The following publications are more specialized guides to online databases, covering full-text databases and indexes to periodicals included in leading data files.

Books and Periodicals Online: A Guide to Publication Contents of Business and Legal Databases (Books and Periodicals Online, Inc.—Annual, with Supplements).

This important index provides title access to the periodical coverage of numerous online databases. Although directories like *Ulrich's* and *The Serials Directory* usually indicate where a periodical is indexed, this service examines online access in detail. For example, the researcher trying to track down a story which appeared in *Business Month* magazine could determine that the journal was indexed in *Trade & Industry Index* and *Accountants*, abstracted in *ABI/INFORM, Management Contents*, and *PTS PROMT*, and available in full-text on *Magazine ASAP*. Based on this information, the article could be located using the most appropriate database to which he or she had a subscription. *Books and Periodicals Online* includes newspapers, magazines, journals, newsletters, loose-leaf services, wire services, and reference books. Most of the periodicals relate to business, but there is strong coverage of legal publications as well. Listings are arranged by periodical title, with a detailed description of the database contents, format, and time period. The directory is easy to use and clearly indicates the different ways the same periodical is covered by several databases, or even by the same database offered through different vendors. A separate list of periodicals by database is marred by numerous omissions, and a subject index would be helpful, but neither flaw seriously impairs the usefulness of the guide. A directory of database vendors and producers is also provided.

Directory of Periodicals Online; Indexed, Abstracted, and Full-Text: News, Law, & Business (Info Globe—Annual).

Another guide to the coverage of periodicals in online databases is the *Directory of Periodicals Online* (*DPO*). Introduced in 1985 by Federal Document Retrieval, Inc., it was the first publication of its kind. Because of its strong Canadian content, (*DPO*) was purchased in 1989 by Info Globe, the electronic publishing division of the Toronto *Globe and Mail*.

DPO is by no means limited to Canadian sources; also indexed are databases appearing on major online systems in the United States, plus a few European vendors. It indexes the journal coverage of several hundred databases, representing more than 8,000 periodicals in business, law, and general news. Information on each periodical includes previous titles, frequency, subjects covered, and the databases on which it can be found. A separate section describes each database, including its format, coverage, frequency, and vendors. Exhibit 3-2 shows a typical page from *DPO*. In the case of *New England Business*, seven online databases are listed as covering this monthly journal in some manner. The user can then consult the second section to determine which online vendors offer the databases mentioned.

The major drawback to the *Directory of Periodicals Online* is its two-part arrangement, requiring a two-step process to determine how a particular journal is treated by each database. As an example, four different types of online coverage are available for *New England Business*: *Business Dateline* includes the full text of articles; *ABI/INFORM, Management Contents*, and *PTS PROMT* provide abstracts; *PAIS* creates brief annotations; and *Trade & Industry Index* and *Newsearch* merely cite the bibliographic information. Unless the researcher is familiar with the databases, the descriptions in the second section must be consulted to determine this. And with only annual revisions, *DPO* is not as current as *Books and Periodicals Online*. However *DPO* offers several advantages over its competitor, notably the coverage of more periodical titles and the inclusion of a broad subject index.

Fulltext Sources Online (BiblioData—Semiannual).

Unlike the preceding two services, this index deals exclusively with the periodical coverage of full-text databases. Before *Fulltext Sources Online*, trying to determine whether a periodical had an online counterpart was a haphazard process. General sources such as Cuadra's *Directory of Online Databases* identify single-title databases such as the *Electronic Washington Post* and the *Harvard Business Review Online*, but not the contents of multiple-title files such as *Trade & Industry ASAP* or *Business Dateline. Ulrich's* provides a separate index to online periodicals, but again, only for single-title files.

Fulltext Sources Online is a detailed index to the hundreds of periodicals available in full-text through nearly two dozen major vendors. Included in the directory are journals, magazines, newsletters, and wire services in all subject areas. Arranged alphabetically by periodical title, each listing indicates the vendors, the database names, and the dates of coverage online. For newspapers and wire services, entries also include the update frequency and lag time. Subject and geographic indexes are provided, as are a guide to databases by vendor and a directory of vendor addresses.

EXHIBIT 3-2. *Directory of Periodicals Online*

New Civil Engineer
DATABASE(S): Infomat International Business

New Directions
DATABASE(S): Canadian Business & Current Affairs

New Directions for Women
ISSN: 0160-1075
FREQUENCY: Bimonthly
DATABASE(S): Book Review Index

New Electronics
DATABASE(S): Index New Zealand; Infomat International Business

New England Business
PUBLISHER: New England Business Corporation
ISSN: 0164-3533
FREQUENCY: Monthly
SUBJECTS: Business - New England
DATABASE(S): ABI/INFORM; Business Dateline; Management Contents; Newsearch; PAIS International; PTS PROMT; Trade & Industry Index

New England Economic Indicators
PUBLISHER: Federal Reserve Bank of Boston
ISSN: 0548-4448
FREQUENCY: Monthly
SUBJECTS: Economic Conditions - New England
DATABASE(S): PAIS International

New England Economic Review
PUBLISHER: Federal Reserve Bank of Boston
ISSN: 0028-4726
FREQUENCY: Bimonthly
SUBJECTS: Economic Conditions - New England
DATABASE(S): ABI/INFORM; Business Periodicals Index; PAIS International

New England Journal of Business and Economics
NOTES: See Northeast Journal of Business and Economics

New England Journal of Human Services
PUBLISHER: Osiris Press, Inc.
ISSN: 0227-996X
FREQUENCY: Quarterly
DATABASE(S): PAIS International; Social Work Abstracts (SWAB)

New England Journal of Medicine
PUBLISHER: Massachusetts Medical Society
ISSN: 0028-4793
FREQUENCY: Weekly
SUBJECTS: Medicine
DATABASE(S): AgeLine; Courier Plus; Magazine Index; Newsearch; Social Work Abstracts (SWAB); Trade &

Industry Index

New England Journal of Prison Law
NOTES: See New England Journal on Criminal and Civil Confinement

New England Journal on Criminal and Civil Confinement
FORMER TITLE: New England Journal of Prison Law
ISSN: 0740-8994
FREQUENCY: Semiannual
DATABASE(S): Index To Legal Periodicals; Legal Resource Index; Newsearch

New England Law Review
PUBLISHER: New England School of Law
ISSN: 0028-4823
FREQUENCY: Quarterly
SUBJECTS: Law - New England
DATABASE(S): Index To Legal Periodicals; Legal Resource Index; Newsearch

New England Quarterly
PUBLISHER: Northeastern University
ISSN: 0028-4866
FREQUENCY: Quarterly
DATABASE(S): Book Review Index

New England Review / Bread Loaf Quarterly
PUBLISHER: Middlebury College
ISSN: 0736-2579
FREQUENCY: Quarterly
DATABASE(S): Book Review Index

New Era: Japan
PUBLISHER: The Telecommunications Association
FREQUENCY: Biweekly
SUBJECTS: Telecommunications - Japan
DATABASE(S): New Era: Japan; PTS Newsletter Database

New Federation
DATABASE(S): Canadian Business & Current Affairs

New Hampshire Bar Journal
PUBLISHER: New Hampshire Bar Association
ISSN: 0548-4928
FREQUENCY: Quarterly
SUBJECTS: Bar Associations - New Hampshire
DATABASE(S): Index To Legal Periodicals; Legal Resource Index; Newsearch

New Hampshire Business Review
PUBLISHER: Business Publications, Inc.
ISSN: 0164-8152
FREQUENCY: Semimonth
SUBJECTS: Business - New Hampshire
DATABASE(S): Business Dateline; PTS PROMT

New Internationalist
PUBLISHER: PAC Ltd
ISSN: 0305-9529
FREQUENCY: Monthly
DATABASE(S): Canadian Business & Current Affairs; Canadian Periodical Index

New Jersey Business: the magazine of the New Jersey Business & Industry Association
PUBLISHER: New Jersey Business & Industry Association
ISSN: 0028-5560
FREQUENCY: Monthly
SUBJECTS: Business - New Jersey
DATABASE(S): PAIS International

New Jersey Law Journal
PUBLISHER: American Lawyer Newspapers Group, Inc.
ISSN: 0028-5803
FREQUENCY: Weekly
SUBJECTS: Courts - New Jersey; Law - New Jersey
DATABASE(S): Legal Resource Index; Newsearch

New Jersey Lawyer
PUBLISHER: New Jersey State Bar Association
ISSN: 0195-0983
FREQUENCY: Bimonthly
SUBJECTS: Bar Associations - New Jersey; Lawyers - New Jersey
DATABASE(S): Index To Legal Periodicals; New Jersey Lawyer; WESTLAW Texts and Periodicals

New Jersey Success
PUBLISHER: Success Publishing Co.
ISSN: 0886-9995
FREQUENCY: Monthly
SUBJECTS: Business - New Jersey
DATABASE(S): Business Dateline; PTS PROMT

New Law Journal
PUBLISHER: Butterworth & Co.
ISSN: 0306-6479
FREQUENCY: Weekly
DATABASE(S): Index To Legal Periodicals; Legal Resource Index; Newsearch

New Leader: a biweekly of news and opinion
PUBLISHER: American Labor Conference on International Affairs
ISSN: 0028-6044
FREQUENCY: Biweekly
SUBJECTS: International Relations; Labor
DATABASE(S): Book Review Index; Courier Plus; Magazine Index; Newsearch; PAIS International; Readers' Guide To Periodical Literature

New Left Review
PUBLISHER: B De Boer
ISSN: 0028-6060

Books and Periodicals Online and the *Directory of Periodicals Online* also provide coverage of full-text databases, but neither does so as completely as *Fulltext Sources Online*. For *New England Business*, it identifies several files which its competitors do not, and this is by no means an isolated case. Researchers and librarians who rely extensively on full-text databases for searching or document delivery will find this an indispensable publication.

CD-ROM Directories

At the end of 1988 there were fewer than 300 commercially available CD-ROM titles; by year-end 1990, the number had quadrupled. The best way to keep up with this rapidly changing field is to read the new product announcements in such periodicals as *Information Today*. General reference tools, though less timely, are also useful. For example, both *Ulrich's* and the *Directory of Online Databases* indicate whether a source is also available in CD-ROM format. The *Information Industry Directory* and *Computer-Readable Databases* even provide separate indexes to CD-ROMs. The directories described below offer more extensive coverage of compact disk products.

CD-ROMs in Print: An International Guide (Meckler Corporation—Annual).

The full range of CD-ROM products, from geographic information systems to digitized sound effects packages, is covered by *CD-ROMs in Print*. Most entries, however, represent more traditional materials— bibliographic, numeric, and directory databases. The 1991 edition describes approximately 1,400 CD-ROM. Listings provide basic information on the content, frequency, technical specifications, price, and subscription terms for each disk. Because several firms can participate in the creation of a compact disk product, *CD-ROMs in Print* distinguishes among them. Each entry lists the provider of the data, the designer of the software, and the publisher of the disk. Where appropriate, a distributor's name is also provided. A note indicates whether potential subscribers can preview the product, through either a free trial offer or demonstration diskette. Addresses and phone numbers for the four categories of company are listed in separate directories found at the back of the book. Other supplemental sections include a fairly detailed subject index and an index to product type (full text, abstract, statistical, etc.) *CD-ROMs in Print* also lists new products yet to be published, many of which may never appear in print. Though useful, these descriptions would be less

confusing in a separate section of the directory. *CD-ROMs in Print* is updated monthly through a supplement appearing in Meckler's *CD-ROM Librarian* magazine.

A similar guide to CD-ROMs is published by Learned Information, Inc., but the current edition is unavailable for review as of this writing. Though intended as an annual publication, the *Optical Publishing Directory* encountered production difficulties following release of the third edition in 1988. However, the 1988 edition was similar to the Meckler directory of the same year in every respect: arrangement, scope, content, size, and indexing. The *Optical Publishing Directory* stressed such characteristics as subscription terms and content, where *CD-ROMs in Print* emphasized software and ROM drive specifications; otherwise, the product descriptions were also similar. A revised edition is scheduled for mid-1991; thereafter, publication should resume on a yearly basis.

Directory of Portable Databases (Cuadra/Gale— Semiannual).

Most listings in Cuadra's *Directory of Portable Databases* describe CD-ROMs, but fairly ample coverage is given to databases on floppy diskette and magnetic tape—hence the rather obscure title. The April 1991 edition lists more than 950 CD-ROM products, some of which are unique to this publication. Entries are similar to those in Cuadra's *Directory of Online Databases*, citing the publisher, database type, language, geographic scope, time span, frequency, and a fairly lengthy description of content. Also identified are the data provider, system requirements, software used, and subscription details. The *Directory* is divided into three sections, one for each type of medium. Some duplication occurs because many databases are available in more than one format. Indexes are provided by subject, publisher, and distributor, with a master index to titles and names. An appendix lists online databases which have corresponding portable products listed in the *Directory*. This is particularly useful because the same database may go by several names depending on the format.

The *Directory of Portable Databases* is the only publication to compare CD-ROM databases to their equivalents in other "portable" formats. It also is one of the few sources to give explicit coverage to databases on floppy diskette, and is one of the most current sources of information tracking this rapidly growing field. The *Directory* is also available online through Data-Star, ORBIT, and Questel. Called the *Directory of Online and Portable Databases*, it combines the contents of both Cuadra/Gale publications.

Directories of Magnetic Tape Files and Diskettes

Data on computer tape and diskette have been among the most difficult information sources to identify. Directories of microcomputer-based products are particularly scarce. Produced by government agencies, nonprofit organizations, and even commercial publishers, the business products in this format include demographic and economic statistics, local area profiles, mailing lists, and financial and investment services. Aside from brochures and catalogs distributed by the producers themselves, there are few reliable guides to such products. Notable exceptions are the *Directory of Portable Databases* and the *NTIS Listing of Data Files on Floppy Diskette*, which is limited to products compiled by federal agencies.

Guides to microcomputer software are abundant, including directories, buyers' guides, indexes, and product reviewing services. Unfortunately, these publications emphasize so-called applications software; actual data products are seldom found among their listings. One of the few periodicals which follows developments in data diskettes, the quarterly *Social Science Computer Review*, emphasizes products used for instructional purposes rather than continuously updated data files. One of the better ways to locate smaller data files is simply to identify organizations which publish the needed information in other formats (print, online, etc.), then contact them to see whether subfiles are available on diskette. *Directories in Print, Computer-Readable Databases*, and a few other reference tools include such information in their listings.

Locating data tapes for use on larger computer systems is also difficult. However, a variety of guides to data files are beginning to appear. The Research Libraries Information Network (RLIN), an online system produced by the Research Libraries Group, Inc., contains extensive information on data tapes. An RLIN database called *Machine-Readable Data Files* contains complete cataloging records for several hundred tape products owned by participating university libraries and data archives. Unfortunately, the future of this database is uncertain as of this writing. Descriptions of machine-readable files can also be found in various print directories. Government agencies such as the U.S. Bureau of the Census issue publication catalogs which describe their computer products. Another useful guide to government files is the *Federal Database Finder*. Tapes created and sold by commercial firms and nonprofit organizations can be found in the *Information Industry Directory*. The

Research Centers Directory is another useful source of descriptive information on tapes from nonprofit groups. A few tape products can also be found in some online directories, most notably *Computer-Readable Databases*. Descriptions of new tapes containing demographic, economic, or social data can be found in specialized periodicals. Two examples are the *IASSIST Quarterly*, a newsletter from the International Association for Social Sciences Information Service and Technology, and the *Population Index*, a quarterly publication of the Population Association of America. The directories below are among the most comprehensive guides to locating published tape files.

Directory of Computerized Data Files: A Guide to U.S. Government Information in Machine Readable Format (U.S. National Technical Information Service—Annual).

The closest thing to an official, one-stop shopping guide to publicly available government tape files comes from the National Technical Information Service (NTIS). Because the data-gathering activities of the government are highly decentralized, even this massive directory is not a comprehensive source. Compiled by the Federal Computer Products Center, it profiles 2,000 files, all of which can be ordered directly through NTIS. Though the Federal Computer Products Center has in stock tape files from more than 100 U.S. agencies, the *Directory of Computerized Data Files* only lists tapes from about 50 of the major data producers. The listings are arranged according to 27 broad topics, with indexes by agency and tape number. A detailed subject index is also given. Besides a description of the file contents, each entry gives technical characteristics, price, ordering information, and the NTIS technical report number for the accompanying documentation manual. Information is also updated several times per year by a brochure entitled *Recent Releases from the Federal Computer Products Center*, and by a quarterly newsletter called *Center Line*. Related NTIS publications are the *Listing of Datafiles on Floppy Diskette* and the *Directory of Computer Software*.

The best commercial guide to government data files is *Federal Statistical Data Bases: A Comprehensive Catalog of Current Machine-Readable and Online Files*, by William R. Evinger. Published in 1988 by Oryx Press, there are no plans for a revised edition. Though similar to the government's directory, it is not simply a reprint or reworking of NTIS data. Evinger has assembled information on 2,500 products from over 100 federal agencies. It includes less popular files available through NTIS, and those tapes available only through the producing agency. The directory is arranged by agency, with title and subject indexes. The descriptions of each file are

easier to read than those in the NTIS directory, with information on geographic coverage, time period, and related files clearly identified. For non-NTIS products, Evinger also provides the addresses and phone numbers of agency contacts.

ICPSR Guide to Resources and Services (Inter-university Consortium for Political and Social Research—Annual).

ICPSR, the largest nongovernment tape archive in the world, was briefly introduced in Chapter 1. Its *Guide to Resources and Services* includes a complete catalog of the Consortium's holdings, with lengthy descriptions of each data set and its accompanying documentation manuals. The directory is arranged in broad subject categories, with a title index and a personal name index to principal investigators. A separate volume provides detailed subject access. A quarterly newsletter, the *ICPSR Bulletin*, serves as an updating service between editions. Information can also be retrieved online, with the full text of the catalog offered through ICPSR's CDNet service, and descriptive listings for most ICPSR files found on RLIN's *Machine-Readable Data Files*.

HONING RESEARCH SKILLS

The directories, bibliographies, indexes, and handbooks presented in this chapter provide many starting points for locating needed information. But how can one use these aids to best advantage? As suggested in Chapter 1, it is often helpful to think of categories of information. Is the most likely source a newsletter? A loose-leaf service? A database? Would it be better to contact a government official? The editor of a trade journal? A consultant? Even when multiple sources of information are appropriate, experienced researchers address problems systematically, investigating one category at a time until the search is completed. These are the reasons finding tools tend to be organized by type of resource.

No researcher can ever hope to know all sources of business information. The number of resources is virtually limitless, and the array of guides to those sources is also formidable. Basic finding tools can overlap confusingly in scope and purpose. To deal with the problem, become familiar with the characteristics of as many major guides as possible. In this way, the researcher can identify the best tool for the job at hand. Some titles are known for their detailed descriptions or evaluations, others for their thorough indexing or special features. A publication can be the obvious choice in a particular

situation because it is updated more frequently or contains more listings than its competitors. Although the diversity of guides may seem overwhelming, researchers are fortunate to have so many specialized tools at their disposal.

Basic finding tools help the user move beyond comfortable research habits. Most people tend to consult those resources they are most familiar with. But routine responses can lead to incomplete answers; there is simply too much information available, and too many new resources appearing all the time. It pays to consult finding tools even when a reasonable answer can be found in a publication close at hand, or from a familiar contact. The use of finding guides is an important way to expand one's fund of knowledge. Experience is important, but the researcher must be willing to stretch to improve his or her abilities. There is no substitute for personal familiarity with information sources, and the regular use of finding guides will add to that working knowledge on a daily basis.

FOR FURTHER READING

The topics covered in this list relate to general research skills, including the basics of online searching and how to evaluate reference products. The final section describes leading bibliographies of major business reference tools. Two of the better textbooks on library research are the *Guide to the Use of Libraries and Information Sources*, 6th ed., by Jean Key Gates (McGraw-Hill, 1989), and *A Guide to Library Research Methods*, by Thomas Mann (Oxford University Press, 1987). The titles cited in the first section are intended for the general reader with minimal research skills.

General Research Methods

Berkman, Robert. *Find It Fast: How to Uncover Expert Information on Any Subject* (New York: Harper & Row, 1987).
Presents a step-by-step approach to research, with an emphasis on identifying sources of expert information. Basic information on libraries, government documents, reference books, and more. Includes a separate section of sample searches.

Horowitz, Lois. *Knowing Where to Look: The Ultimate Guide to Research.* Revised ed. (Cincinnati, OH: Writer's Digest Books, 1988).

This excellent manual provides a combination of research tips and basic sources of published information. The author covers a wide range of topics, with a fairly extensive chapter on computer databases.

Roel, Ronald E. *Research Any Business Question, Fast and Professionally* (Brentwood, NY: Caddylak Publishing, 1985).

This work deals specifically with business research. It covers both the research process and basic sources of information. An unusual feature is the emphasis on forms and checklists, examples of which are provided throughout.

Tyson, Kirk W. *Business Intelligence: Putting It All Together* (Oak Brook, IL: Leading Edge Publications, 1986).

A guide to obtaining business information from published and unpublished sources. The coverage of published sources tends to be skimpy and outdated, but the book has plenty of useful advice.   Its greatest strength is in discussing how to make use of information once it's acquired. Also covered is the importance of developing a research strategy, how to conduct telephone interviews, and how to turn intelligence into information. Numerous tables and worksheets help readers focus their research projects.

Washington Researchers. *Business Researcher's Handbook: The Comprehensive Guide for Research Professionals* (Washington, DC: Washington Researchers Press, 1983).

This unique manual was written for practicing consultants and free-lance researchers. It provides a thorough examination of how to conduct research as a business venture. The work emphasizes the client-researcher relationship and how to produce a research report.

Online Research Techniques

Fenichel, Carol H., and Thomas Hogan. *Online Searching: A Primer.* 3rd ed. (Medford, NJ: Learned Information, 1989).

This brief treatment covers the basics of online searching: what it is, who provides it, and how it is done. Highly recommended for a first look at the technical aspects of computer searching.

Harter, Stephen P. *Online Information Retrieval* (San Diego, CA: Academic Press, 1986).

This more advanced guide is valuable for its coverage of search strategies and techniques. Does the best job of any text on how to formulate a search and evaluate the results.

Shaw, Debora. "Nine Sources of Problems for Novice Online Searchers." *Online Review* 10 (October 1986): 295–303.

A wonderful overview of common mistakes made by beginning searchers, including search tactics, the mechanics of searching, and database selection.

Evaluating Reference Materials

Gray, Richard A. "Reviewing Reference Publications—The Importance of Relevant Subject Knowledge: Selected Case Studies." *Reference Services Review* 18 (Spring 1990): 7–16.

Tackling the question of why so many reviews of reference books are mediocre, Gray suggests reviewers lack the necessary subject expertise to do an accurate, insightful job. To support this conjecture, he critiques a number of good and bad reviews.

Herther, Nancy K. "How to Evaluate Reference Materials on CD-ROM." *Online* 12 (March 1988): 106–108.

Given the high cost, popularity, and uneven quality of the CD-ROM products which have come to market, it is not surprising that numerous articles counsel readers on how to select and evaluate these materials. Herther's brief piece is one of the best, focusing on practical concerns of database value and quality.

O'Dell, Judith E. "Factors Used in Selecting Online Databases." In *Proceeedings of the Ninth National Online Meeting, 1988.* (Medford, NJ: Learned Information, 1988): 287–91.

This short paper introduces basic considerations in choosing database vendors and search services.

Raitt, David. "Evaluating CD-ROMs: An Observational Perspective." In *Proceedings of the Tenth National Online Meeting, 1989.* (Medford NJ: Learned Information, 1989): 343–53.

Focuses on the large number of substandard databases, and suggests that many publishers rushed to get a product on the market without adequate research or planning. Most interesting is the author's list of common CD-ROM shortcomings, with examples of poorly designed or unneeded products.

Stevens, Norman. "Evaluating Reference Books in Theory and Practice." *Reference Librarian* No. 15 (Fall 1986): 9–19.

Outlines the basic characteristics of a good reference book and suggests methods for evaluating new reference publications.

Guides to Information Sources

Scanlan, Jean M., Ulla de Stricker, and Anne Conway Fernald. *Business Online: The Professional's Guide to Electronic Information Sources* (New York: Wiley, 1989).

A beginning guide to major business databases in a variety of categories, including financial reports, business news, accounting and taxation, and company directories. A discussion of whether to perform your own online searching or hire a fee-based searcher is especially well done.

Strauss, Diane Wheeler. *Handbook of Business Information: A Guide for Librarians, Students, and Researchers* (Littleton, CO: Libraries Unlimited, 1988).

Like the book you are reading, Wheeler's work combines explanations of basic business concepts with descriptions of major information sources. It covers a greater number of topics, though usually in briefer fashion. Chapters 1 through 8 introduce important reference sources by format, ranging from online databases to directories. The remaining 10 chapters discuss publications by subject category, including banking, insurance, and real estate. There is a useful chapter on general reference sources, such as business dictionaries and encyclopedias, and an excellent section on the importance of pamphlet and clipping files. Among the appendices is a list of free publications of value to researchers.

Vocelli, Virginia S. "Core List of Printed Business Reference Sources." In *The Basic Business Library: Core Resources*, 2nd ed., edited by Bernard S. Schlessinger. (Phoenix, AZ: Oryx Press, 1989): 5–53.

A list of 177 "core" reference publications recommended for smaller libraries. Each entry includes a description of the work's authority and scope, plus commentary on why it is recommended and for what types of libraries. Although the list is necessarily subjective and somewhat unbalanced in its coverage, it has proven popular with librarians and other researchers seeking advice on selecting business reference books.

CHAPTER 4
Finding Books, Documents, and Statistical Reports

TOPICS COVERED

1. The Standard Industrial Classification System
2. Types of Bibliographic Resources
3. Finding Books on Business Topics
   a. Online Library Networks and Library Catalogs
   b. General Trade Bibliographies
   c. Specialized Business Catalogs
   d. Subject Bibliographies
   e. Book Reviews
4. Identifying Book Publishers
5. Guides to Government Publications
6. Locating Statistical Information
7. Incorporating Books and Documents into Business Research
8. For Further Reading

MAJOR SOURCES DISCUSSED

- *Standard Industrial Classification Manual*
- *Books in Print*
- *Harvard Business School Core Collection: An Author, Title, and Subject Guide*
- *Literary Market Place: The Directory of American Book Publishing*
- *Monthly Catalog of United States Government Publications*
- *Government Reports: Announcements & Index*
- *Statistics Sources*
- *DataMap: Index of Published Tables of Statistical Data*
- *American Statistics Index*
- *Statistical Reference Index*
- *Industry Data Sources*
- *Predicasts Forecasts*

The publications introduced in Chapters 2 and 3 consisted of basic guides for locating people, organizations, and reference materials which can aid in the research process. They are tools to consult in the initial stages of a project, when mapping a strategy and identifying the likeliest approaches to follow. The resources outlined in Chapters 4 and 5 are used in succeeding steps—publications which will lead to the actual information needed. Indexes, abstracts, bibliographies, and catalogs refer the user to information on a specific topic. How do I locate a recent book on sexual harassment in the workplace? Are there any government studies on privatization in Eastern Europe? Can I get a statistical report analyzing the buying habits of social security beneficiaries? There are hundreds of reference works to choose from, and selecting the most appropriate materials requires effort and forethought. The resources described in this chapter represent the most widely used bibliographic tools for identifying business information published in books, government documents, and statistical reports. Chapter 5 will introduce major indexes for locating periodical articles and news stories.

THE STANDARD INDUSTRIAL CLASSIFICATION SYSTEM

Many business publications organize their contents according to various classification systems. Classification is the arrangement of information into categories so that similar concepts are grouped together. Familiar library systems like the Dewey Decimal Classification and the Library of Congress Classification are adequate for organizing business books, but are not detailed enough for more specialized business needs.

Many systems classify business information by product or industry. The most widely used method in this country is the Standard Industrial Classification (SIC), which was devised by the U.S. Office of Management and Budget (OMB) as a guideline for reporting business statistics. The Bureau of the Census and other federal agencies use it to collect and publish data on business activity, but the system also enjoys nonstatistical uses.

The OMB intended to update the SIC codes every five years in conjunction with the Economic Census, but actual revisions have been less frequent. The official source of definitions for SIC numbers is the *Standard Industrial Classification Manual*. The latest edition was published in 1987, and is available in book form, magnetic tape, and floppy diskette. The completion of the 1987 edition was significant because the previous full revision occurred in 1972.

The goal of the classification structure is to encompass the full spectrum of economic activities in the United States. Each four-digit SIC number represents a particular kind of business. The codes range from 0100 to 9999, as seen below.

MAJOR GROUP	DESCRIPTION
01–09	Agriculture, Forestry, and Fisheries
10–19	Mining and Construction
20–39	Transport, Communications, and Utilities
50–59	Wholesale and Retail Trade
60–69	Finance, Insurance, and Real Estate
70–89	Other Service Industries
91–94	Government Services
99	Nonclassifiable Industries

Thus, all wholesale and retail businesses have an SIC code beginning with 5, all codes for manufacturing industries begin with 2 or 3, and so on. The system is hierarchical, and industries may be classified in broad two- or three-digit groupings, as well as the more specific four-digit codes. As an example, nonelectrical machinery is given the designation 35, while internal combustion engines are classified under 3519.

Why is the SIC system important to business researchers? Briefly stated, whenever business activities or organizations are counted, sorted, listed, or compared, the Standard Industrial Classification is likely to be used. SIC numbers appear extensively in business directories, financial services, statistical publications, periodical indexes, and industry reports. Many of the reference sources described throughout this book use the SIC system as a convenient way of organizing their contents. It is particularly useful for retrieving information from online databases. For example, *Predicasts Forecasts* utilizes a modified SIC structure to summarize statistical information on hundreds of industries.

The Standard Industrial Classification serves as a uniform way of describing the structure of American industry. It is vague to say a company is in the motion picture business. Is the speaker describing a film studio? A production company? A distributor? A casting service? Defining the business as part of SIC 7832 ("Motion picture theaters, except drive-ins") is both more precise and universally accepted. The researcher investigating that industry could consult business directories, periodical indexes, and statistical sources under SIC 7832 to quickly find pertinent material. The SIC system is used by virtually all types of business publications, so it is essential that researchers become familiar with its arrangement.

The SIC system is not without drawbacks. The principal weakness is the infrequent revision of the *Manual*. Newly emerging industries may not be assigned a code number for years, a serious difficulty in the vigorous and rapidly changing American economy. Also, four digits are often insufficient to classify specific products or services. Many descriptions at the four-digit level are too broad, and many industries are lumped together in "not elsewhere classified" categories. Exhibit 4-1, taken from the SIC *Manual*, illustrates a typical "catchall" category—in this case, miscellaneous repair shops. Notice the diversity of establishments which do not warrant SIC numbers of their own, from septic tank cleaning to taxidermy shops. Also notice how little these activities have in common. A third shortcoming is that the basic structure was established nearly 50 years ago, when the focus of our economy was quite different. As a result, manufacturing industries are usually covered quite well, retail and wholesale trades less well, and service industries worst of all.

A final difficulty follows naturally from the emphasis on manufactured goods; the SIC concept is best suited to product-oriented activities because the classification structure focuses on the material from which products are

EXHIBIT 4-1. *Standard Industrial Classification Manual*

SERVICES   377

Industry
Group
No.   Industry
           No.
769   **MISCELLANEOUS REPAIR SHOPS AND RELATED SERVICES—Con.**

        7699   **Repair Shops and Related Services, Not Elsewhere Classified—Con.**

           musical instrument repair; septic tank cleaning; farm machinery repair; fur-
           nace cleaning; motorcycle repair; tank truck cleaning; taxidermists; tractor
           repair; and typewriter repair.

Agricultural equipment repair
Antique repair and restoration, except
  furniture and automotive
Awning repair shops
Beer pump coil cleaning and repair
  service
Bicycle repair shops
Binoculars and other optical goods
  repair
Blacksmith shops
Boiler cleaning
Boiler repair shops, except manufactur-
  ing
Bowling pins, refinishing or repair
Camera repair shops
Catch basin cleaning
Cesspool cleaning
China firing and decorating to individ-
  ual order
Cleaning and reglazing of baking pans
Cleaning bricks
Coppersmithing repair, except construc-
  tion
Covering textile rolls
Dental instrument repair
Drafting instrument repair
Engine repair, except automotive
Farm machinery repair
Farriers (blacksmith shops)
Fire control (military) equipment repair
Furnace and chimney cleaning
Furnace cleaning service
Gas appliance repair service
Glazing and cleaning baking pans
Gun parts made to individual order
Gunsmith shops
Harness repair shops
Horseshoeing
Industrial truck repair
Key duplicating shops
Laboratory instrument repair, except
  electric
Lawnmower repair shops
Leather goods repair shops
Lock parts made to individual order
Locksmith shops
Luggage repair shops
Machinery cleaning
Mattress renovating and repair shops
Measuring and controlling instrument
  repair, mechanical

Medical equipment repair, except elec-
  tric
Meteorological instrument repair
Microscope repair
Mirror repair shops
Motorcycle repair service
Musical instrument repair shops
Nautical and navigational instrument
  repair, except electric
Organ tuning and repair
Piano tuning and repair
Picture framing to individual order, not
  connected with retail art stores
Picture framing, custom
Pocketbook repair shops
Precision instrument repair
Rebabbitting
Reneedling work
Repair of optical instruments
Repair of photographic equipment
Repair of service station equipment
Repair of speedometers
Rug repair shops, not combined with
  cleaning
Saddlery repair shops
Scale repair service
Scientific instrument repair, except
  electric
Septic tank cleaning service
Sewer cleaning and rodding
Sewing machine repair shops
Sharpening and repairing knives, saws,
  and tools
Ship boiler and tank cleaning and
  repair—contractors
Ship scaling—contractors
Stove repair shops
Surgical instrument repair
Surveying instrument repair
Tank and boiler cleaning service
Tank truck cleaning service
Taxidermists
Tent repair shops
Thermostat repair
Tinsmithing repair, except construction
Tractor repair
Tuning of pianos and organs
Typewriter repair, including electric
Venetian blind repair shops
Window shade repair shops

Reprinted from the *Standard Industrial Classification Manual*, published by the U.S. Office of Management and Budget.

made. A good example is the SIC treatment of recycling operations. Though waste recycling is an activity of growing economic importance, the 1987 revisions make no specific provisions for it. Part of the problem is that many types of materials are recycled—paper, glass, aluminum, plastics, and so on. The SIC system groups processors of recycled materials together with original manufacturers. Makers of recycled paper are grouped under SIC 2621 (Paper Mills), for example. Similarly, the codes ignore the many firms involved in the materials

recovery industry; companies which collect, sort, and process trash for later recycling are grouped under the broad umbrella of SIC 4953 (Refuse Systems).

Some of the shortcomings noted are due to the government's self-imposed limitations. In order to obtain a unique SIC number, an industry must have "economic significance" as determined by an OMB-established algorithm. Certainly, many of the services listed in Exhibit 4-1 represent fairly esoteric businesses. But other activities subsumed under SIC 7699 are quite

common, including chimney cleaning establishments, picture framing shops, and piano tuning services. Nonetheless, they do not constitute a large enough percentage of the total U.S. economy as defined by the OMB formula. A subtler restriction results from the principle that there be a single, "primary" SIC number assigned to any business establishment. An establishment which engages in several types of activities will be described by the SIC code which represents the largest portion of its output. This presents a special problem in industries where complementary activities are undertaken by the same establishment. A good example of this occurs in retail operations which also service the type of product they sell. Notice in Exhibit 4-1 that many of these services commonly take place in a retail establishment. If establishments that *only* repair bicycles are few in number or small in aggregate sales, the industry will never receive its own SIC code. Other problems associated with the classification structure will be raised in Chapters 13 and 16.

Because of the limitations of the SIC system, many producers of business information (including the Bureau of the Census) have created their own classification numbers based on the OMB's framework. In fact, the system was designed with this possibility in mind. Five, six-, or seven-digit extensions are quite common in business publications, as are completely new four-digit codes. An expanded SIC number is shown below.

CLASS	DESCRIPTION
36	Electrical equipment
363	Household appliances
3631	Household cooking equipment
36311	Electric ranges
363117	Microwave ovens

This example was taken from Predicasts, Inc., a publisher of numerous printed reference tools which are organized under a SIC-based classification system. Because Predicasts has made so many revisions to the original system, they now refer to their numbers as "Predicasts Product Codes."

Departures from the official SIC codes are useful not only for added specificity, but for side-stepping inherent weaknesses in the system. As an example, return to the case of the recycled products discussed above. Predicasts has handled the problem by departing from the government's product orientation. They have extended the 4953 code to 49532 for "Solid Waste Recovery." This category is further broken down to distinguish between municipal operations and private enterprises. What's more, individual subdivisions have been created for glass, metal, and other materials. In this

way, all recycling operations are not only identified explicitly, they are grouped together. The codes are used to identify transportation, sorting, and manufacturing operations. No matter that the 4953 codes remove recycling factories from the manufacturing classifications entirely; Predicasts frequently takes liberties of this nature in the interests of improved accessibility. The exception to their happy solution involves paper recycling. As one of the oldest and largest recycling activities, it received its own Product Code (262102) long ago.

The SIC system is not a mandatory standard followed by all publishers, which presents potential problems to business researchers. In some cases, users of business reference tools need to recognize when a SIC number has been modified or invented. Numbers created by the Office of Management and Budget have four digits at the most; any SIC code longer than that has been created by some other organization for its own use. In the case of four-digit numbers, recognizing whether a particular code is "official" becomes less obvious. When conducting SIC-based research across several publications, start with the codes given in the *Standard Industrial Classification Manual*. This will help identify numbers coined by someone else.

A related problem comes with the inevitable transition from an older, obsolete edition of the *Manual* to the latest version. This is especially important in the period following a major revision. When the 1987 *Manual* was released, it took more than two years for major commercial publications to incorporate the changes. Several major publishers, including Predicasts, decided not to adopt the revised codes because their own modifications had become so extensive in the intervening years. Potential confusion in comparing old numbers to new is lessened by using "bridge" tables which appear at the back of the *Manual*. These appendices show the relationships between new numbers and their predecessors, and vice versa.

Despite its weaknesses, the basic structure of the SIC system is sound and logical. It is a widely used and fundamental tool for business research.

TYPES OF BIBLIOGRAPHIC RESOURCES

Bibliographic tools come in a variety of formats, address a multitude of needs, and span the universe of publication types. Library catalogs, whether displayed in card files or on computer screens, are probably the most familiar example of a bibliographic guide. They direct the user to specific publications in a particular

library or library system, and can be consulted by author, title, subject, and other access points. Indexes, subject bibliographies, and similar tools serve much the same purpose, though their coverage is not usually restricted to an individual library's collection. They may appear as books, as microforms, or in a variety of electronic formats. For this discussion, all types of bibliographic guides will be referred to generically as indexes. An index leads the user to specific information, by subject, title, or any other characteristic being sought. Specialized indexes exist for every type of material imaginable. They may cover scholarly communications (doctoral dissertations, working papers, or conference proceedings), official documents (patents, court cases, or environmental impact statements), news services, editorials, speeches, essays in books, or even public opinion polls. Whatever the coverage, indexing tools can describe materials in a number of ways. The most basic index merely lists author, title, and publisher. More sophisticated services provide abstracts or other narrative summaries of the items being indexed.

An important characteristic of any indexing service is the vocabulary it adopts to describe subject terms. If you are searching for books on employee benefits, what word or phrase do you look under: "Fringe benefits?" "Benefits, employee?" "Compensation?" "Nonwage benefits?" A good index will provide cross-references leading to the appropriate term, but it helps to know if some standard vocabulary has been adopted. When using any index, the first step is to identify the best terms to consult. Verifying the appropriate terminology before beginning a search saves time and improves the quality of the search results. One standard vocabulary, the Library of Congress Subject Headings (LCSH), is used in the catalogs of almost every major library in the United States. Many of the tools covered in this chapter also rely on LCSH for subject indexing. Its wide usage allows researchers to move from one index to another without learning a new language. LCSH employs very specific headings and covers every imaginable discipline, from philosophy to astrophysics. To assist users with the system, the Library of Congress compiles an extensive guide to LCSH terminology, titled simply *Library of Congress Subject Headings*. Its pages not only identify the proper terms to consult under LCSH, but are also filled with cross-references and lists of related terms. It is available through the U.S. Government Printing Office in book form, on microfiche, and on CD-ROM. (The latter format is known as *CDMARC Subjects*.) The book version, issued as a massive three-volume set, is now updated annually. The microfiche and CD-ROM versions are revised quarterly, with each new issue superseding its predecessor. Every researcher should become comfortable with using *Library of Congress Subject Headings*.

FINDING BOOKS ON BUSINESS TOPICS

Books, special reports, collections of essays, book chapters, and other onetime publications frequently represent the best, most convenient source of needed information. There are few ongoing, comprehensive bibliographies specific to business topics, so the catalog of a major public or academic library is a good place to begin a search for business monographs. Other options include remote online databases, general trade bibliographies, specialized business catalogs, and subject bibliographies. A few of the most basic reference tools in each category are introduced below.

Online Library Networks and Library Catalogs

Conducting an online search of a shared cataloging network is probably the closest a researcher can come to generating a comprehensive list of books on a given subject with a minimum of effort. Bibliographic utilities, as they are sometimes called, contain millions of catalog records contributed by many different libraries. A half-dozen major catalog networks are used in North America; the largest and best known is OCLC. An alternative is to consult the catalog files of the nation's largest library—the U.S. Library of Congress.

OCLC Online Union Catalog (Online Computer Library Center—Continuous Updating).

The Online Computer Library Center is a nonprofit consortium of 9,000 libraries, including the Library of Congress and the New York Public Library. The *OCLC Online Union Catalog*, with records on more than 19 million unique titles, is the result of the largest cooperative library venture in the world. The database contains descriptions of books, government documents, serials, audio-visual items, maps, microforms, and other library materials. Information is updated continuously through the day, and records also indicate which member-libraries own a particular title.

Despite its extensive holdings, for many years the OCLC system was not the boon to researchers that it might have been. In the past, the search capabilities of

OCLC were spectacularly unimpressive (with no subject access, for example), and the search protocol was quite rigid. It was used almost exclusively by library employees, and direct access by the public was rare. To counter these limitations, researchers could turn to a more flexible, commercial version of the database available through BRS. Called *OCLC EASI Reference*, the file is actually only a subset of the parent database. It contains bibliographic records for materials published within the most recent four years. New records are added quarterly and older material is deleted once each year. In addition to subject access, *EASI Reference* is searchable on all relevant fields, including author, publisher, language, publication date, and document type or format.

In early 1990, OCLC unveiled a more versatile alternative to its traditional service. The new system is called EPIC, and it provides access to a variety of bibliographic databases, including the *OCLC Online Union Catalog*. Searching can be done either through a series of menus or by using a familiar command language. More than 20 indexed fields are searchable, including language, place of publication, and frequency. Subscriptions to EPIC are available directly through OCLC, or, with prior arrangements, as a gateway service via CompuServe or EasyNet.

The newest OCLC enhancement is a menu-driven system called *The FirstSearch Catalog*, which provides basic Boolean searching of the full OCLC database. *FirstSearch* is designed for end-user searching, and the price structure will allow many libraries to provide direct access to their patrons. OCLC also plans to offer additional databases through this service, including the GPO *Monthly Catalog*. The system is scheduled for release in the late summer of 1991.

National Union Catalog: Books (U.S. Library of Congress—Monthly, with Cumulations).

The extensive catalog records of the Library of Congress (LC) can be searched through OCLC, but LC offers bibliographic tools of its own. The venerable *National Union Catalog: Books* (*NUC*) has been produced for decades. It contains records of monographs cataloged by the Library of Congress during that period, plus unique records supplied by over 1,000 contributing libraries. In print form, *NUC* is issued monthly, with quarterly and annual cumulations. Access is primarily by title. A more flexible version of *NUC* appears on microfiche. The main section is arranged by accession number (in order of processing), with separate indexes by author, title, series title, and subject. The indexes are updated monthly, and cumulated on a year-to-date basis.

The Library of Congress portion of *NUC* is fully searchable on a database called *LC MARC-Books*, which is updated weekly. It contains information on nearly three million books cataloged since 1968, and is available online through DIALOG and WILSONLINE.

General Trade Bibliographies

Many standard reference tools also provide subject access to published books. Trade bibliographies, compiled with the cooperation of the book publishers themselves, serve as ongoing catalogs of current publishing. The two most comprehensive trade bibliographies in the United States are the *Cumulative Book Index (CBI)* from the H.W. Wilson Company, and the *American Book Publishing Record (ABPR)* from R.R. Bowker. Either, or both, can usually be found in most larger libraries. Both are issued monthly, with annual cumulations. Both list recently published books in all disciplines, including business. Otherwise, they are different in their approach. The *Cumulative Book Index* collects information on all English-language books, regardless of country of publication. Access is by author, title, and subject in a single alphabet. Library of Congress subject headings are used. Entries typically list the author, title, publisher, and pagination of the book. When available, the price, ISBN, series title, and other data are provided. The bibliography is also available online through WILSONLINE (updated twice each week) and as a WILSONDISC CD-ROM (updated quarterly).

The *American Book Publishing Record* limits its coverage to books published in the United States. *ABPR* affords no direct author, title, or subject access, but the entries are arranged by Dewey Decimal Classification, so similar topics are grouped together. A detailed subject index to the Dewey groupings is appended to help identify the most appropriate sections to consult. One advantage of *ABPR* over *CBI* is the amount of detail shown. *ABPR* entries provide fairly complete library cataloging records for every title. Library of Congress Subject Headings are used as descriptors within each entry, so the user can get a general idea of the book's contents. *ABPR* has no online or CD-ROM equivalent at this time.

Books in Print (R.R. Bowker—Annual).

Few bibliographic tools are more widely used or better known than *Books in Print (BIP)*. This enormous work lists nearly every book currently available for sale in the United States. At any one time, well over 800,000 titles are included. The listings are arranged in separate volumes by author, title, and subject. A supplemental volume provides directory information for all publishers

represented in the set. *BIP* is issued annually in the fall, with a mid-year supplement during the spring. Information is updated through Bowker's *Forthcoming Books*, a bimonthly guide to new and soon-to-be-released titles. All the information from the Bowker database is also available online via DIALOG and BRS (both updated monthly), and as a bimonthly CD-ROM called *Books in Print Plus*. Computer searching in either format allows the user to identify books by keyword, or to combine subjects with such other characteristics as price range, publication date, and audience level.

Specialized Business Catalogs

A typical example of the many indexes to specific forms of business monographs is *University Research in Business and Economics*, an annual compilation from the Association for University Business and Economic Research. It lists monographs, research series, working papers, and other materials published by business schools which are members of the Association. Information is organized by broad subject classification, with indexes by author and by issuing school. Some research organizations produce indexing services which cover their own books, reports, and journals. Examples include the Conference Board's annual *Conference Board Cumulative Index*, Business International, Ltd.'s quarterly *Business International Publications Index*, and the RAND Corporation's quarterly *Selected RAND Abstracts*.

Another specialized bibliographic service is the library acquisitions list, through which a library informs its users of recently received books. Acquisitions lists of well-known business collections are frequently available on a subscription basis. An example is *Recent Additions to Baker Library*, a monthly list from the library at Harvard's Graduate School of Business Administration. A few business libraries also publish extensive catalogs.

The following two publications are narrower in scope than such massive resources as *NUC*, *CBI*, and *ABPR*.

Bibliographic Guide to Business and Economics (G.K. Hall—Annual).

One of the few comprehensive bibliographies specific to business materials, this guide lists business-related books cataloged by the Research Libraries of the New York Public Library, supplemented by the MARC tapes of the Library of Congress. The catalog provides access by author, title, and subject, interfiled in a single alphabet. Complete bibliographic descriptions are pro-

vided for books, reports, conference proceedings, and a variety of other publications. Other titles in the G.K. Hall series include the *Bibliographic Guide to Law* and the *Bibliographic Guide to Government Publications*. The latter is available in two editions, one for publications of state, regional, and federal agencies in the U.S., and one for the publications of foreign governments.

Harvard Business School Core Collection: An Author, Title, and Subject Guide (Baker Library—Annual).

Another annual bibliography, though much more selective, is this catalog from the Harvard Business School's incomparable Baker Library. It is not a complete record of the Library's holdings, but a catalog of Baker's "Core Collection": a small browsing library of approximately 3,500 volumes. The collection provides users with a brief selection of recent, representative titles on a diversity of business topics, reflecting the current research and teaching interests of the Business School. It is heavily slanted toward textbooks, but handbooks and popular works are included, as are some scholarly publications and classics in management literature. The collection is weeded each year to make room for new additions and to maintain its manageable size. Although not intended as a list of the "best business books," nor as a guide to purchasing for other libraries, the *Harvard Business School Core Collection* is an exceptionally useful introduction to important books on most business topics. The catalog is divided into four parts, arranged by principal author, title, Library of Congress Subject Heading, and geographic area. A descriptive catalog record is provided for every entry.

Subject Bibliographies

A third approach to locating book material is through subject-specific bibliographies compiled by scholars, librarians, or other experts in the particular field of study. Book-length bibliographies are usually the result of extensive research and will list many more titles than would be discovered through a simple check of a library catalog or bibliographic utility. In addition, most subject bibliographies organize the entries in a more usable form than a simple alphabetical arrangement, and almost all are annotated. Many publishers produce ongoing bibliographic series on business topics, including Gale Research, Oryx, Garland, and Greenwood. A particularly extensive series is published by the Council of Planning Librarians. Topics covered by recent titles in the "CPL Bibliography" series range from desktop publishing to privatization.

Identifying subject bibliographies is not difficult. One method is to consult guides to the business literature such as *Business Information Sources*. Another is to check library catalogs or trade bibliographies. Most provide subject access, and subdivide topics by type of publication or treatment. Those which utilize Library of Congress Subject Headings are especially helpful because LC provides a standard subdivision for "Bibliography." In some cases the headings are fairly evident, as with "Homeless People—Bibliography." Usually it is best to consult the guide to LC subject headings, however. For example, a bibliography on the American farm crisis is just as likely to be found under "Agriculture—Economic Aspects—United States—Bibliography" as it is under "Farms—United States—Bibliography." The *OCLC Online Union Catalog*, the *Cumulative Book Index, Books in Print*, and Hall's *Bibliographic Guide to Business and Economics* all list subject bibliographies by LCSH.

The *Bibliographic Index*, published by H.W. Wilson, covers not only book-length bibliographies, but bibliographies appearing as parts of books or in journal articles. To be included, a bibliography must contain 50 or more citations. All subjects are covered, including fairly good representation of business topics. The service appears three times per year, including an annual cumulation. Listings are arranged by LC subject headings. The index is also available online through the WILSONLINE system, with semiweekly updates. Data in the online file go back to late 1984.

Book Reviews

A final method for researching books is to identify reviews. Several periodicals are devoted exclusively to reviewing recent works in business. One of the most extensive is the quarterly *Business Library Review* from Gordon and Breach Publishers. Many general reviewing sources also have reasonable coverage of important new business books, including *Booklist, Kirkus Reviews,* and *Choice*. Popular business magazines and scholarly journals also carry book reviews.

How can the researcher quickly locate evaluations of a specific book? Many major periodical indexes provide access to book reviews by book title, author, or both. One of the most thorough is the *Business Periodicals Index*. Online periodical indexes can offer additional access to book reviews by subject. The *Trade & Industry Index* is particularly useful in this regard. The electronic versions of *Books in Print*, both online and CD-ROM, now include the complete text of all book reviews appearing in Bowker periodicals, including *Publishers Weekly* and *Library Journal*.

Beyond these resources, two specialized tools provide direct access to thousands of book reviews from all types of magazines, newspapers, and journals. H.W. Wilson's *Book Review Digest* covers reviews appearing in approximately 100 well-known journals. Arrangement is by author, with title and subject indexing. In addition, it reproduces brief extracts from the actual reviews. To be included, a book must be reviewed in two or more of the periodicals covered by the service. *Book Review Digest* is published ten times per year, including quarterly and annual cumulations. It is also available online through WILSONLINE (updated twice weekly), and as a WILSONDISC CD-ROM (updated quarterly).

The fastest and simplest method of locating specific book reviews is to consult the *Book Review Index* from Gale Research. It lists all book reviews appearing in nearly 500 periodicals, from general interest magazines to scholarly journals. A special effort has been made to include the book supplements to major newspapers, from the *Washington Post Book World* to the *Times Literary Supplement* of London. Entries are arranged by author, with a title index. Under each entry is a list of journals in which a review appeared, together with the date and page of the issue. The *Book Review Index* is updated bimonthly, with quarterly and annual cumulations. The full index is also searchable online via DIALOG. Unfortunately, the online file is only updated three times per year. No subject indexing is provided in either the print or online versions, but searching online for key words appearing in book titles can bring fruitful results.

IDENTIFYING BOOK PUBLISHERS

Countless guides list publishers of every variety. They range from directories of names and addresses only, such as K.G. Saur's annual *Publishers' International ISBN Directory*, to more specialized sources, such as R.R. Bowker's *Publishers' Trade List Annual*, which reproduces publishers' catalogs in their entirety. A quick source of directory information is the "Publishers" volume of *Books in Print*, which lists names, addresses, and phone numbers for more than 25,000 U.S. publishers and their imprints. Another convenient Bowker directory, *Publishers, Distributors & Wholesalers of the United States*, is available in book form and as an online database through DIALOG. For lengthier profiles of individual companies, the following two directories are recommended.

Literary Market Place: The Directory of American Book Publishing (R.R. Bowker—Annual).

The *LMP* offers brief but informative descriptions of 2,500 major book publishers in the United States. For each firm, a detailed list of the management and editorial staff is given, together with a summary of publishing activities. The latter category includes the type of material published, the names of imprints used, the number of titles in print, and the number of new titles per year. This directory has traditionally focused on the activities of the largest publishers in the country, but, for the first time, the 1990 edition also includes a separate section describing 400 smaller presses. Also listed are book clubs, book review syndicates, micropublishers, and companies that provide services to the publishing industry, such as stock photo agencies, clipping services, and computerized typesetting firms. Addresses and phone numbers for all of the above publishers and organizations are reproduced in a separate "Industry Yellow Pages." Another section of *LMP* describes major reference books and periodicals for the publishing industry. Bowker's annual *International Literary Market Place* contains similar information for foreign publishers on a country-by-country basis.

Publishers Directory (Gale Research, Inc.—Annual).

With almost 20,000 firms represented, Gale's *Publishers Directory* is one of the most comprehensive guides to the U.S. publishing industry, and Canadian publishers are also represented. Many entries profile "little publishers"—those firms existing outside the mainstream of commercial publishing. Examples are small presses that produce regional, foreign language, and other special interest materials, and museums and other nonprofit organizations that publish books. An important feature for business research is the inclusion of hundreds of firms which specialize in business reference material. Entries in the *Publishers Directory* are similar to those in *LMP*, though with less emphasis on company personnel. Subject, geographic, and keyword indexes are provided.

GUIDES TO GOVERNMENT PUBLICATIONS

For many areas of business research, information from the federal government can be a vital component. Chapter 2 introduced sources for identifying appropriate agencies and personnel. The ability to quickly locate government publications is an equally important skill, and many catalogs and indexes have been created to assist in this process. This chapter can only provide the briefest introduction to the topic. Entire books have been written on how to locate government documents, several of which are listed in the guide to further reading at the end of the chapter. Additional tips on locating statistical reports from the government are given in Chapters 14, 15, and 16. Laws, regulations, and congressional publications are discussed in Chapters 19 and 20.

Most federal publications are distributed by the Government Printing Office (GPO) and the National Technical Information Service (NTIS). Neither is a publisher in the traditional sense, since they have no editorial control over the documents they distribute. However, both agencies produce a huge number of publications. The GPO issues more than 50,000 titles per year, while NTIS releases an additional 60,000. The combined output represents a huge, diverse body of information no researcher can afford to ignore.

The GPO is the official printer for documents produced by government agencies. Many of the resulting publications are distributed to Depository Libraries, sold to the public by the GPO, or both. The Superintendent of Documents, a division of the GPO, administers the Depository Library Program described in Chapter 1. This group also assigns classification numbers (called SuDoc numbers) to the publications. The basic arrangement of the SuDoc numbering system is by agency, subagency, and type of publication. For example, anything beginning with the SuDoc designation "L" refers to publications from the Department of Labor. Some of the subagencies are designated as follows:

L2   Bureau of Labor Statistics
L35   Occupational Safety and Health Administration
L37   Employment and Training Administration

This notation is important to researchers because most Depository Libraries keep their government documents in a segregated collection organized by SuDoc number.

Depository Libraries do not receive all government publications. Most participating libraries are Selective Depositories, choosing to acquire documents in certain categories only. And not all GPO publications are made available through this program. Some must be purchased, while others can be obtained only through the issuing agencies. What's more, not all federal publications pass through the GPO. A considerable number of government reports are published by NTIS and fall outside the SuDoc system. Of greater concern, a huge percentage of reports are printed and distributed by the agencies themselves. Although federal law requires agencies to make publications available to the Superintendent

of Documents, this mandate is not strictly followed or enforced. Materials which fall through the cracks, called fugitive documents, can be difficult for researchers to identify and acquire. No one knows how many publications the government actually produces, but various studies have estimated the percentage of nondepository documents to be anywhere from 50% to 90% of the federal publishing output. Although this number is dismally high, it includes NTIS documents which are really not fugitive items. Among the best ways to track down fugitive documents are to contact the libraries of individual agencies, to consult the printed catalogs and bibliographies which some agencies publish, to search large bibliographic utilities such as OCLC, and, for documents with strong statistical content, to check the incomparable *American Statistics Index*, introduced later in the chapter.

The National Technical Information Service serves as a clearinghouse for technical reports describing research conducted by or for the government. Most of these reports summarize research done on an agency's behalf by nongovernment organizations such as universities, consulting firms, and nonprofit groups. The reports are submitted by government contractors to the agencies which funded the research. NTIS is also charged with distributing foreign technical reports covering topics of importance to American research efforts. Dozens of organizations around the world cooperate with NTIS in this manner; foreign reports comprise 30% of the total NTIS collection. Of those documents received directly from U.S. sources, approximately 75% are submitted by NASA, the Department of Energy, and the Environmental Protection Agency.

While the majority of NTIS reports deal with the applied or natural sciences, many relate to the social and behavioral sciences, including economics and management. But NTIS is not heavily utilized by business researchers because NTIS documents aren't as readily available as those from the GPO. Fewer researchers are aware of the agency, and those who are may not have easy access to the reports. Also, less than 10% of NTIS titles are grouped in business, management, or economics categories.

Despite the small percentage of business documents, the quality of business information in NTIS is quite good. Reports frequently deal with the latest business trends or cover subjects which can be difficult to find in other ways. Recent examples include an analysis of the independent video industry in Great Britain, a study of employee turnover among women blue-collar workers, and a look at business uses for "smart card" technol-

ogy. Other routinely found NTIS documents are World Bank country studies and economic reports from the CIA. Documents grouped outside traditional management categories can also be relevant to business research. Technological concerns are inextricably tied with business research, and NTIS is an outstanding source of information on computer technology, pollution control techniques, manufacturing processes, new uses for raw materials, and energy conservation. NTIS is also the primary distributor of government data tapes in machine-readable format.

How do researchers obtain NTIS documents? Few technical reports from NTIS are available through the Depository Program; instead, they are sold directly by the agency. Anyone can order a report from NTIS, in paper copy or microfiche. Another option is to purchase a blanket order to broad categories of reports through the "Selected Research in Microfiche" (SRIM) program. NTIS organizes its documents into more than 400 subject categories. SRIM subscribers can designate any combination of categories for purchase; they will automatically receive all titles published in that category during the year. Subscribers can opt to purchase a customized index to their SRIM collection, updated quarterly, or they can subscribe to one of the standardized indexes described below. Many research libraries have extensive SRIM collections that make a vast storehouse of information accessible quickly and conveniently, especially when used in conjunction with NTIS indexes on CD-ROM or online.

Many guides to government publications are compiled by commercial publishers. One of the most useful is the annual *Bibliographic Guide to Government Publications*, mentioned earlier. Most commercial bibliographies are fairly specialized, however, including the *Guide to U.S. Government Directories* from Oryx Press, and John Andriot's popular *Guide to U.S. Government Publications*, an annual from Documents Index. The latter is a guide to government serials and titles in series, noteworthy for the way it traces changes in SuDoc numbers over time. The finding tools listed below constitute the major catalogs, indexes, and databases produced directly by NTIS and the GPO.

Monthly Catalog of United States Government Publications (U.S. Government Printing Office—Monthly, with Cumulative Indexes).

The major tool for finding information on federal government publications is the *Monthly Catalog*, known affectionately as *MoCat*. Although published continu-

ously since 1895, it did not assume its present form until July 1976. At that time the Government Printing Office began utilizing the OCLC cataloging system to create an electronic database of *Monthly Catalog* entries. This important decision caused several notable changes for researchers: 1. Because the catalog is easier to produce, it now contains many new features making it simpler to use; 2. GPO was forced to conform to national library standards, including the use of Library of Congress Subject Headings; 3. As an electronic database, it is searchable online through several vendors, and on numerous CD-ROM products.

Although the *Monthly Catalog* is the most comprehensive guide to the publications of the United States government, it is not all-encompassing. It covers documents sent by agencies to the Superintendent of Documents, whether the items are for sale by the Government Printing Office or not. This includes all items made available to Depository Libraries. (Users can identify those included in the Depository Program by the presence of a bullet, followed by an "Item number" in the *Monthly Catalog* entry.) The vast majority of publications in *MoCat* are depository items, though a surprising number are not sold by the GPO. This is because the government has cut back on the number of titles it sells, concentrating instead on publications with the broadest appeal. Also included are descriptions of government periodicals and loose-leaf services; these can be found in a special issue called the *Periodicals Supplement*, released each year in January or February. Excluded from *MoCat* are most technical reports distributed by NTIS, most audio-visual materials, some publications intended for internal agency use only, and fugitive publications which escape the attention of the Superintendent of Documents. Another limitation is that it may take many months after release before a publication appears in the *Monthly Catalog*.

MoCat provides bibliographic descriptions for 20,000 new publications yearly. Each entry provides agency name, individual author (where appropriate), title, series name, size, number of pages, and subject headings. Also found are SuDoc numbers, Depository Item numbers, and, for ordering purposes, the GPO stock numbers and prices. Entries are arranged by SuDoc number, effectively bringing together all the titles by each agency. Additional access is provided through indexes by LC subject headings, keywords, titles, authors, series titles and numbers, and GPO stock numbers. Monthly indexes are cumulated semiannually, annually, quinquennially, and decennially. The cumulations also provide indexes by SuDoc number.

Despite cumulative indexes, one of the biggest drawbacks to using the *Monthly Catalog* is that users must have an approximate idea of when a publication appeared in order to find it. To counter this problem, a number of commercial firms have reproduced the complete catalog on microfilm or rolling microfiche. These services are updated monthly or bimonthly, with each new edition superseding the old. This enables the user to quickly search more than 20 years of publications in a single, updated file. Several companies produce such catalogs, including the *Government Publications Index* from the Information Access Company, and the *Government Documents Catalog Service* from Auto-Graphics, Inc.

These microform products are produced from GPO data on computer tape. Many libraries with online catalogs purchase the GPO tapes and load them directly on their catalog systems; library patrons can then search for government documents in the same way they look for books. GPO tapes can also be accessed through commercial online vendors, including BRS, DIALOG, and WILSONLINE.

Finally, the *Monthly Catalog* can be found on CD-ROM from no fewer than seven publishers. Included are CD-ROM versions of the Auto-Graphics and IAC products described above. Other producers are Marcive, Inc., the Brodart Company, SilverPlatter Information, Inc., the H.W. Wilson Company, and OCLC, Inc. Most are updated monthly or bimonthly, and many support sophisticated searching capabilities. The IAC version, available as part of its InfoTrac system, is by far the simplest to use, though not as comprehensive as some of its competitors. Although it affords access by agency, author, title, series, subject, and keyword, users cannot search by SuDoc number or date. For ease of use combined with sophisticated searching capabilities, Auto-Graphics's *Government Documents Catalog Service* (sometimes called *IMPACT*, after the software used) is a good choice. *IMPACT* offers easy-to-follow menus enabling searching by keyword, various document numbers, and basic agency, title, and subject retrieval. Searches can be limited by date, and Boolean logic is supported. Menus for the latter operations are cumbersome, however. The *MARCIVE GPO CAT/PAC* also combines menu searching with Boolean capabilities and is fairly simple to use. The most flexible search capabilities are offered by *GPO on SilverPlatter*.

GPO Sales Publications Reference File (U.S. Government Printing Office—Bimonthly).

The *PRF* is a microfiche listing of all government documents currently in print and available for sale. Listings give the agency, title, publishing date, SuDoc number, and usually a brief description of the contents. Information for ordering includes the GPO stock number, price, stock status, weight, and type of binding. The listings are arranged in a single alphabet by title, author, series, subject, and title keyword. Separate indexes by GPO stock number and by SuDoc number can also be found. The fiche is updated six times per year and each new edition supersedes the earlier versions.

PRF lists what is currently available for sale, regardless of when it was published. However, the *Monthly Catalog* includes publications not sold through GPO, but available either from Depository Libraries or directly from issuing agencies. For this reason, researchers attempting a comprehensive document search should use the *Monthly Catalog*. The *PRF* is attractive because it is cumulative and extremely easy to use. This should be the first source consulted when you want to purchase a document. The file is also available online through DIALOG, with biweekly updates.

Another GPO sales catalog is actually a series of publications called *Subject Bibliographies*. More than 200 are available, and each one is free from the GPO. The *Subject Bibliographies* provide short lists of popular titles sold by the government. Each list is devoted to a specific topic such as housing, foreign trade, or the Census. Individuals interested in receiving updated bibliographies can request a free index to all of the titles in the series by contacting the Government Printing Office. A second free resource is called *Government Periodicals and Subscription Services*, also known as "Price List 36." This annual catalog of the periodicals and loose-leaf publications sold through GPO also appears as an online database available through CompuServe.

Government Reports: Announcements & Index (U.S. National Technical Information Service—Semimonthly, with Annual Cumulations).

Only about 10% of the reports distributed by NTIS can be found in the *Monthly Catalog*, and those are mainly depository items. *Government Reports: Announcements & Index (GRA&I)* is a complete listing of reports sold by NTIS, together with technical reports distributed by other government clearinghouses. The service provides especially strong coverage of defense contracting, aerospace engineering, and energy research. NTIS distributes a potpourri of documents, and *GRA&I* offers an unpredictable diversity of coverage. Anything from sta-

tistical compendia to conference proceedings to translations from the government's Joint Publications Research Service are likely to show up. *GRA&I* also lists bibliographies done in support of government research efforts, patents owned by the government, data tapes available from NTIS, and documentation manuals for tape users.

The printed edition of *GRA&I* is really a current awareness service. Each semimonthly issue is divided into 38 broad categories, from Civil Engineering to Administration & Management. The broad groupings are then further divided into approximately ten subtopics. The user interested in research on inventory management, for example, can simply turn to the appropriate section in each issue to scan the titles of the most recent reports. Of greater importance, *GRA&I* gives lengthy abstracts for every report. Indexes are provided by subject (which NTIS calls keyword), personal and corporate author, and a variety of numbering systems, including NTIS order number, contract number, and series number. *GRA&I* offers no title indexing with each issue, though an annual title index is produced separately on microfiche. The other indexes are cumulated once per year in a six-volume bound set.

GRA&I is an admittedly cumbersome source for retrospective research, and the lack of monthly or quarterly cumulations doesn't help. A welcome alternative to the printed index is the computerized version, available online and as a CD-ROM subscription. The *NTIS Bibliographic Data-Base* is offered online by at least eight vendors around the world, including BRS, DIALOG, and Data-Star. The file contains more than 1.2 million records from 1964 to the present; new records are added twice per month. The database is searchable using a wide selection of variables, including corporate source, sponsoring agency, document type, and country of publication. At present, three companies produce a CD-ROM version of the database—OCLC, DIALOG, and SilverPlatter. Each is updated quarterly. One cautionary note: unlike the *Monthly Catalog*, which utilizes standard LC subject headings, NTIS supports several different controlled vocabularies designed by the Department of Defense, the Energy Department, NASA, and other agencies. Users undertaking a comprehensive search will need to work harder to identify all relevant subject terms.

NTIS also publishes subsets of the full *GRA&I* service as *NTIS Abstract Newsletters*. There are about 27 titles in the series, conforming to the broad categories in *GRA&I*. In this way, subscribers can receive bulletins on specific topics such as health care or library science. Every newsletter is updated weekly, so they are a bit

more current than the complete service. All have annual subject indexes. One of the most popular titles in the series is *Business & Economics: An Abstract Newsletter.* Other business-oriented *NTIS Abstract Newsletters* cover manufacturing, computers, management, public administration, and behavior theory.

LOCATING STATISTICAL INFORMATION

Statistics are without question one of the most frustrating categories of business information to confront. This is because statistical data are so abundant. Thousands of sources are published, covering everything from microchips to potato chips. Such data are usually needed quickly, yet finding precisely the right figures, in the form needed, and covering the geographic area and time period specified can be like searching for the proverbial needle in a haystack. Tips on conducting statistical searches will be offered throughout the book, but several exceptional finding tools have been developed to save hours of fruitless hunting.

Statistics Sources (Gale Research, Inc.—Annual).

Statistics Sources is a remarkably detailed guide to thousands of statistical publications, databases, and sources of unpublished information. Over 20,000 subject terms are employed, including every major country in the world. The sample page shown in Exhibit 4-2 offers a hint of the variety of subjects and sources, and the amount of detail provided. The emphasis is on business statistics, but figures on health, social conditions, political trends, and other areas are covered too. Three types of headings are used: products or industries, geographic areas, and general subjects. Headings are subdivided further by specific characteristics like wages, employment, production, and foreign trade. Listings for foreign countries cite the nation's central statistical office, its statistical abstract, and the primary source of financial information.

Among the supplemental sections is a bibliography of key statistical publications. It covers major compendia from the United States and abroad, as well as statistical dictionaries, directories, and other finding tools. Commercially available online databases are also listed. Another important section is the directory of government telephone contacts, arranged by subject, with government experts listed by name. A third supplement, listing statistical databases compiled by the federal government, includes online services, data tapes, and diskette products. No other finding tool covers such a diversity of data resources. *Statistics Sources* is highly recommended as

the first place to look when mapping a strategy for statistical research. Gale also publishes the *Statistical Services Directory*, which lists several thousand organizations that regularly produce statistical reports.

DataMap: Index of Published Tables of Statistical Data (Oryx Press—Annual).*

DataMap is an index to the tables appearing in individual reports. Fewer than 30 publications are covered in the last edition, but the indexing is amazingly thorough, covering nearly 14,000 statistical tables. The chosen publications are among the most popular statistical compendia found in libraries; the intent was to create a research tool to assist users in locating the data most readily available in common sources. Most of the titles are reports from the U.S. government and the United Nations, but popular commercial publications can also be found. Among the reports indexed are the *Statistical Abstract of the United States*, the *CRB Commodity Year Book*, the *County and City Data Book*, the *International Financial Statistics Yearbook*, and the *World Almanac and Book of Facts*. Two surprising titles are the United States summary volumes for the *Characteristics of the Population* segment of the decennial Census, and the annual *Index to International Public Opinion*.

To first-time users, *DataMap* appears confusing, but it is quite simple to use. More than 10,000 specific subject headings are listed in Part III of the index. Once the appropriate heading is found, the user is led to the descriptions of individual tables found in Part II. For example, someone interested in the frozen food industry would look under "Frozen Foods" in the index and find about 30 references, ranging from "Capital Expenditures (by Year)," to "Vegetables (Amount/by Commodity/by Region)." The terms in parentheses indicate the "secondary characteristics" of the data tables, meaning the form of the variable, the time period, and the geographic area covered. Continuing with the example of frozen vegetable production, the researcher immediately knows the table is broken down by individual commodity and by region. The designation following this entry is "AS 0247," referring to that heading in Part II. A quick check of Part II identifies the title of the table, indicates the data covers the period from 1976-1985, and tells the user it can be found on page 180 of the 1986 edition of *Agricultural Statistics*.

The biggest drawback to *DataMap* is the time lag in indexing. Because the book is published annually, because the production cycle for such a massive undertaking is lengthy, and because many of the sources it indexes are themselves delayed, *DataMap* refers to a significant

---

*NOTE: *DataMap* ceased publication as of 1991.

EXHIBIT 4-2. *Statistics Sources*

STATISTICS SOURCES, Thirteenth Edition - 1990

GAMBIA - TAX REVENUES

International Monetary Fund, Nineteenth and H Streets, NW, Washington, D.C. 20431; "Government Finance Statistics Yearbook."

GAMBIA - TELEPHONE CALLS - INTERNATIONAL

American Telephone and Telegraph Communications, Customer Information Center, Post Office Box 19901, Indianapolis, Indiana 46219; "The World's Telephones."

GAMBIA - TELEPHONE TRAFFIC

American Telephone and Telegraph Communications, Customer Information Center, Post Office Box 19901, Indianapolis, Indiana 46219; "The World's Telephones."

GAMBIA - TELEPHONES - BUSINESS AND RESIDENCE

American Telephone and Telegraph Communications, Customer Information Center, Post Office Box 19901, Indianapolis, Indiana 46219; "The World's Telephones."

GAMBIA - TELEPHONES IN USE

American Telephone and Telegraph Communications, Customer Information Center, Post Office Box 19901, Indianapolis, Indiana 46219; "The World's Telephones."

Statistical Office of the United Nations, Publishing Service, New York, New York 10017; "Statistical Yearbook," section on Communications - Telephones in use.

GAMBIA - TOURISM

Statistical Office of the United Nations, Publishing Service, New York, New York 10017; "Statistical Yearbook," section on Transport - International tourist travel.

GAMBIA - TRACTORS IN USE

Statistical Office of the United Nations, Publishing Service, New York, New York 10017; "Statistical Yearbook," section on Agriculture - Tractors in use.

GAMBIA - TRADE BY COMMODITY

Food and Agricultural Organization of the United Nations (FAO) Via Delle Terme di Caracalla, 00100 Rome, Italy; "The State of Food and Agriculture."

Statistical Office of the United Nations, Publishing Service, New York, New York 10017; "Foreign Trade Statistics for Africa."

GAMBIA - TRADE STRUCTURE

Food and Agricultural Organization of the United Nations (FAO) Via Delle Terme di Caracalla, 00100 Rome, Italy; "The State of Food and Agriculture."

Statistical Office of the United Nations, Publishing Service, New York, New York 10017; "Foreign Trade Statistics for Africa."

Statistical Office of the United Nations, Publishing Service, New York, New York 10017; "Statistical Yearbook," section on External Trade - Trade structure of developing countries.

GAMBIA - TRADE WITH DEVELOPING COUNTRIES

Food and Agricultural Organization of the United Nations (FAO) Via Delle Terme di Caracalla, 00100 Rome, Italy; "The State of Food and Agriculture."

Statistical Office of the United Nations, Publishing Service, New York, New York 10017; "Statistical Yearbook," section on External Trade - Trade structure of developing countries.

GAMBIA - UNEMPLOYMENT

International Labour Office, I.L.O. Publications, CH-1211, Geneva 22, Switzerland; "Yearbook of Labour Statistics."

GAMBIA - VITAL STATISTICS RATES

Statistical Office of the United Nations, Publishing Service, New York, New York 10017; "Statistical Yearbook," section on Population - Vital statistics rates.

World Health Organization, Office of Publications, Geneva, Switzerland; "World Health Statistics: Vital Statistics and Causes of Death."

GAMBIA - WAGES

International Labour Office, I.L.O. Publications, CH-1211, Geneva 22, Switzerland; "Yearbook of Labour Statistics."

GAMBIA - WELFARE EXPENDITURES

International Monetary Fund, Nineteenth and H Streets, NW, Washington, D.C. 20431; "Government Finance Statistics Yearbook."

GAMBLING AND GAMBLERS - ARRESTS

U.S. Department of Justice, Federal Bureau of Investigation, Ninth Street and Pennsylvania Avenue, NW, Washington, D.C. 20535; "Crime in the United States."

GAMES, TOYS, ETC. - ADVERTISING EXPENDITURES

Television Bureau of Advertising, Incorporated, 477 Madison Avenue, New York, New York 10022; from data compiled by Broadcast Advertisers Reports, Incorporated, 800 Second Avenue, New York, New York 10017.

GAMES, TOYS, ETC. - EXPENDITURES

U.S. Department of Commerce, Bureau of Economic Analysis, 14th Street between Constitution Avenue and E Street, NW, Washington, D.C. 20230; "The National Income and Product Accounts of the United States, 1929-1982," and "Survey of Current Business," July issues.

GAMES, TOYS, ETC. - FOREIGN TRADE

U.S. Department of Commerce, Bureau of the Census, Suitland, Maryland 20233; monthly report, "U.S. General Imports and Imports for Consumption, Schedule A - Commodity by Country."

GAMES, TOYS, ETC. - MANUFACTURE

U.S. Department of Commerce, Bureau of the Census, Suitland, Maryland 20233; "United States Census of Manufactures: 1982," and "Annual Survey of Manufactures."

GAMES, TOYS, ETC. - PRODUCER PRICE INDEXES

U.S. Department of Labor, Bureau of Labor Statistics, Washington, D.C. 20212; "Producer Price Indexes."

GARAGES - See GASOLINE SERVICE STATIONS AND GARAGES

GARDENS - HOME - CHARACTERISTICS - GARDENING

National Gardening Association, 180 Flynn Avenue, Burlington, Vermont 05401; annual report, "National Gardening Survey," and unpublished data based on data from the Gallup Organization, Princeton, New Jersey.

1175

---

amount of older information. As an illustration, subscribers received the 1990 edition in mid-1990; the most current titles indexed were 1989 publications, but the majority of data in those publications cover the previous year. The two-year lag should not discourage users by any means. If data on frozen vegetable output were found in the 1989 edition of *Agricultural Statistics*, the same data probably will appear in subsequent editions. It is also likely that a footnote in the table will refer to a monthly or quarterly report which updates the annual data.

Experienced librarians and researchers tend to ignore *DataMap* because the publications it indexes are so familiar. This is a mistake. In fact, *DataMap* is a useful tool precisely because it covers well-known, pedestrian sources. A common mistake many researchers make when faced with an unfamiliar statistical question is to plunge instantly into highly specialized data sources. How embarrassed the searcher then becomes when, after a lengthy period of fruitless digging, the answer is found quietly waiting in the *World Almanac*! A quick check of *DataMap* will circumvent this problem immediately. If the data are found in the index, the source document will most likely be an arm's reach away. If not, the researcher can dive into more esoteric publications without wondering if the obvious has been overlooked.

American Statistics Index (Congressional Information Service—Monthly).

The Congressional Information Service has resolved an enormous, long-standing research problem with imagination and flawless execution. Their *American Statistics Index* (*ASI*) successfully provides a comprehensive, ongoing guide to the statistical publications of the federal government. CIS is a private company specializing in guides to government documents. To produce the *American Statistics Index*, CIS employees visit government offices daily to obtain current statistical reports as they are published. The documents are then thoroughly indexed by CIS, and abstracts are written to describe each one. Coverage of federal agencies is so thorough that many of the documents never show up in the *Monthly Catalog*.

ASI indexes the actual tables and graphs appearing in government publications. It differs from *DataMap* in its monthly updating, its coverage of several thousand documents (including 700 government periodicals), and its lengthy abstracts of the statistical tables. Users simply consult the subject or title index to locate a specific document, then turn to the abstract section for further information.

Although the subject headings are fairly broad, the index lists the titles of the individual tables rather than the title of the whole document. Another index provides access by series title and/or report number for those items issued by the government in numbered series. And the unique and ingenious "Index by Categories" identifies statistics on major subjects according to the form ("category") in which they are presented. Categories include various geographic, demographic, and commodity breakdowns. For example, the federal government produces a number of reports on school enrollment in the United States, but the researcher might need that information in a specific format. If a comparison of enrollments in various cities were needed, the user could consult the Index by Categories under "Cities," which would then be subdivided by the broad topic of "Education." On the other hand, if the researcher needed national statistics on school enrollment by age, the Index by Categories could be consulted under "Age." It is often helpful to combine the two approaches, looking under the specific topic in the Subject Index, as well as a broad heading in the Category Index.

Abstracts are grouped according to the agency that produced the document, then subdivided by type of report, such as monthly, annual, or special study. The abstracts are unusual, however, because each one describes individual tables within a report. If there are 40 tables in a document, every one will be listed. Thus, researchers can focus on the exact information needed, and not wonder whether the report contains the required data. Each abstract also provides complete bibliographic information to assist the user in purchasing the document from the Government Printing Office or locating it in a Depository Library. CIS also sells the documents on microfiche, either through customized blanket orders, or as individual "on demand" orders. This is especially important because so many of the documents are neither sold by GPO nor available as depository items. In fact, more than 40% of the publications appearing in *ASI* are nondepository items, making it an essential resource for identifying fugitive documents.

These features constitute a remarkable achievement in business information; the *American Statistics Index* is an indispensable reference tool. Researchers can identify statistical reports on every imaginable topic, from elevator accidents to Mikhail Gorbachev's political appearances. The service is also valuable for locating nonstatistical information; any publication containing a substantial number of tables is fair game for *ASI*, including narrative studies, congressional testimony, and annual reports of government agencies. *ASI* is also helpful

for comparing similar data from different agencies. For example, a researcher interested in statistics on terrorist bombings can find both the State Department and the FBI perspectives. This is especially important for economic data, where several agencies may measure the same events using different definitions and methodologies.

CIS also publishes two related guides. The *Index to International Statistics (IIS)* covers publications of intergovernmental organizations. Included are major annual, monthly, and special reports from nearly 100 multinational groups. Among the major organizations covered are the Organization of Economic Cooperation and Development, the General Agreement on Tariffs and Trade, NATO, the Organization of American States, the World Bank, the European Community, and various United Nations agencies. Specialized organizations range from OPEC to the International Sugar Commission. Another CIS guide, the *Statistical Reference Index (SRI)*, is described below in greater detail. Both *IIS* and *SRI* follow the same format as *ASI* and both have complete microfiche sets available for purchase. The *American Statistics Index* can be searched online via DIALOG, but the other two services have no online equivalents. However, all three indexes are available on a quarterly CD-ROM product called the *Statistical Masterfile*. The system supports Boolean logic, as well as proximity, truncation, and field searching. Users may search all three indexes simultaneously, or in any combination. The early versions were disappointing due to cumbersome search routines and slow response time. Although many problems have been resolved by subsequent upgrades, more improvements are needed to make this a truly useful CD-ROM.

Statistical Reference Index (Congressional Information Service—Monthly, with Quarterly and Annual Cumulations).

The *Statistical Reference Index*, a guide to several thousand statistical publications from nonprofit organizations, commercial publishers, and selected state agencies, is a powerful all-purpose business research tool. *SRI* can never be as comprehensive as *ASI*; instead, it provides selective coverage of the most authoritative nongovernmental sources of data, with an emphasis on recurring statistics unavailable from federal agencies.

SRI's volumes are divided into two parts, one for indexing, the other for detailed abstracts of the tables themselves. The major index is by subject and name, with additional indexes by titles, categories, and issuing sources. Because the organizations which conduct the research are not always the same as those which issue the reports, *SRI* also provides access by compiler in its

"Index by Subjects and Names." The abstracts are organized by type of publisher in the following manner: associations, business organizations, commercial publishers, independent research organizations, state governments, and universities. Well-known organizations of all kinds are represented, including the A.C. Nielsen Company, the American Bar Association, the Brookings Institution, and the Gallup Poll. Not only are annual studies covered, but quarterly and monthly surveys as well. And like *ASI*, the *Statistical Reference Index* can be used as a guide to narrative reports that contain substantial statistical tables.

An outstanding feature of *SRI* is the extensive coverage given to recurring statistical articles from periodicals, including business magazines and trade journals. Exhibit 4-3 illustrates how periodicals are covered by the service. A typical entry describes *Chilton's Jewelers' Circular/Keystone*, a monthly journal from the Chilton Company offering detailed coverage of the jewelry industry. The initial paragraph describes the editorial focus of the journal and indicates some of its major sources of data. The next section describes the statistical columns found in every month's issue, plus any quarterly and annual recurring features. Note that the statistical tables are described in detail. Finally, under the heading "Statistical Features," month-by-month coverage is given to every article containing significant tabular information. Among the articles listed are an annual salary survey appearing in the November issue, and an annual article on the industry outlook for the coming year, published in the January issue.

SRI focuses on business, economic, and industry statistics, but users can also find reasonable coverage of political and social concerns. Among the indexed business reports are market studies, company rankings, industry surveys, forecasts, and opinion polls. Researchers can quickly locate data on industry-wide financial ratios, corporate finances, consumer behavior, market share, industry production, and state economic conditions from every imaginable type of source. Many of the publications are widely quoted popular reports, while others are extremely specialized. Consider this sampling of titles covered by *SRI*: the American Medical Association's *Socioeconomic Characteristics of Medical Practice*; "Tastes of America," an annual survey of dining habits conducted by *Restaurants and Institutions* magazine; *World Military and Social Expenditures*, a well-known study from a nonprofit research group called World Priorities; and the *Impact of Travel on State Economies*, an annual study from the U.S. Travel Data Center, the leading nonprofit source of travel research.

EXHIBIT 4-3. *Statistical Reference Index*

C2150–6.912   Chilton Co.

Includes 10 tables showing survey response on the following:

a. Types of equipment purchased in past 12 months, by food industry segment; outlook for most important packaging developments in next 2 years; and main concerns regarding CAP/MAP (controlled/modified atmosphere packaging).

b. Package inspection equipment in use, and capabilities; types of containers produced at plant facilities; and current and planned use of selected new packaging technologies.

C2150–7   CHILTON'S JEWELERS' CIRCULAR/KEYSTONE
Monthly.
ISSN 0194-2905.
SRI/MF/not filmed

Monthly trade journal (with an additional issue midyear) reporting on trends in jewelry and watch manufacturing and marketing. Covers retail and wholesale operations, product development, prices, and trade. Data are from Jewelers Board of Trade (JBT), American Watch Assn, *Jewelers Circular Keystone* (JC-K) original research, and other sources.

Issues contain numerous feature articles and editorial depts. Statistical features include the following:

a. Monthly "Management" section, with monthly JBT feature, including 1 text table showing new jewelry businesses and failures, by business type and region; firms receiving increase and decrease in JBT credit ratings; number and average value of credit claims placed with JBT for collection; and number of jewelry retailers, wholesalers, and manufacturers; for month 3-4 months prior to cover month, and same month of previous year.

b. Monthly "Indicators" section, including data on jewelry industry stock market activity, and sales and earnings of selected jewelry companies; and 5 monthly tables, listed below.

c. Quarterly feature presenting current wholesale prices for colored stones, pearls, and diamonds, based on data from *Gemworld Pricing Guide*. Feature appears in the "Gemstones" section of the Feb., May, Aug., and Nov. issues.

d. Annual jewelers' directory and almanac issue (published in June), including detailed jewelry industry statistics.

e. Other statistical features, including annual articles on retail jewelry industry salaries, jewelry sales outlook, and gemstone supply-demand and price outlook.

An annual editorial index appears in the Feb. issue.

Monthly JBT and "Indicators" features appear in most issues; occasionally some tables are omitted when space is limited or data are unavailable. Quarterly feature on wholesale prices appears as explained above. All additional features with substantial statistical content are described, as they appear, under "Statistical Features." Nonstatistical features are not covered.

Subscription price includes several additional issues published throughout the year. These issues, providing nonstatistical information for specific trade shows, are mailed on a regional basis. SRI does not cover these regional issues.

Availability: Jewelers' Circular/Keystone, Circulation Department, Chilton Way, Radnor PA 19089, industry subscribers $28.00 per yr., single copy $4.00, others $75.00 per yr., single copy $4.00.; SRI/MF/not filmed.

Issues reviewed during 1988: Nov. 1987-Oct. 1988 (P) (Vol. CLVIII, Nos. 11-12; Vol. CLIV, Nos. 1-10); and 1988 Directory [Sept. 1988 issue is in 2 parts].

MONTHLY INDICATOR TABLES:

[Data generally are shown for latest available month (ranging from 1 to 6 months prior to cover date), with comparisons to same month of previous year. Tables [1-4] also show data for year to date, with change from same period of previous year. Tables [3-5] occasionally are shown as text statistics.]

[1-2] Imports and exports dollar value [for watches/clocks, gemstones by type, pearls, finished jewelry, and, (imports only) synthetic and imitation stones].

[3] Vital statistics [births, deaths, marriages, and divorces].

[4] Jewelry-store sales [includes sales value for current and several previous months, based on Commerce Dept data; and/or sales change for current month, based on JC-K Retail Jewelers Panel reports].

[5] Precious metals prices [New York market prices for gold, silver, and platinum; also shows price ranges for previous month; table title may vary].

STATISTICAL FEATURES:

C2150–7.901: Nov. 1987 (Vol. CLVIII, No. 11)
CASH REWARDS PAY OFF FOR MORE JEWELERS, ANNUAL FEATURE

(p. 42-45) Annual survey article, by George Holmes, on jewelry store employee earnings, 1986. Data are from a JC-K retail panel survey of member jewelers, representing over 500 employees. Includes 6 tables showing the following:

a. Salary medians and ranges; distribution of employees by salary range; and percent of employees receiving extra income from commissions/bonuses/profit sharing; all by position, with salary detail for male and female managers, 1986.

b. Percent of respondents offering various types of incentives to sales personnel, and using formal plans for determining salary increases and measuring sales performance; and distribution of respondents by payroll as percent of sales.

For description of previous article, see SRI 1987 Annual under C2150-7.801.

HOW TO CREATE A COMPENSATION PLAN

(p. 46-58) By Hedda S. Walowitz. Article, with 3 undated tables on employee benefit programs of small businesses, showing the following: types of health insurance offered, percent of full-time employees with employer-provided health insurance, and business owners' reasons for instituting employee retirement plans, all by business size (annual gross receipts). Data are from National Federation of Independent Business Foundation.

JEWELERS FOR THE 21st CENTURY: PART 2

(p. 60-70) By William G. Shuster. Part 2 of a 2-part series of articles on jeweler characteristics, and opinions on jewelry store management, ethics, and national issues, by sex and region. Data are from a JC-K survey of retail jewelry store owners, officers, and managers. No survey date is given.

Includes 30 tables showing survey response on the following, by sex and/or region: selected management policies and personnel issues; importance of customer rapport; business ethics; discount pricing; most important product lines in next 10 years; business outlook; gemological training; and selected social and political issues.

For description of Part 1, see SRI 1987 Annual under C2150-7.810.

C2150–7.902: Jan. 1988 (Vol. CLIV, No. 1)
JEWELERS RAISE THEIR FASHION IQ

(p. 40-42) By Cindy Edelstein. Article on jewelers' fashion consciousness. Data are from a recent JC-K retail jeweler panel survey.

Includes 5 tables showing survey response on sources of fashion information, including specific magazines read; extent to which fashion trends influence retailers' merchandise choices; and fashion factors with greatest impact on jewelers' business.

JEWELERS' '88 OUTLOOK: BLUE SKIES, BUT SOME STORMY CLOUDS, ANNUAL FEATURE

(p. 58-61) Annual article, by William G. Shuster, on jewelry sales outlook for 1988. Data are from a JC-K retail jeweler and supplier panel survey.

Includes 5 tables showing the following for retailers and suppliers: outlook for business activity, profits, and sales, with selected regional detail for suppliers; and expected impact of Oct. 1987 stock market drop.

COLORED STONES IN 1988: FEEDING A VORACIOUS APPETITE, ANNUAL FEATURE

(p. 66-67) Annual article, by Hedda S. Walowitz, with 1 table showing colored gemstone price, supply, and demand outlook, by type of stone, 1988. Data are from a JC-K survey of gem dealers.

For description of previous article, see SRI 1987 Annual under C2150-7.803.

C2150–7.903: Feb. 1988 (Vol. CLIV, No. 2)
JEWELERS ON TV

(p. 232) Brief article, with 1 listing of top 15 jewelry stores ranked by expenditures for local TV advertising, 1986, with percent change from 1985. Data are from Television Bureau of Advertising, based on Broadcast Advertisers' Reports.

JEWELRY RATES LOW IN BUYING SPREE SURVEY

(p. 240) Article summarizing selected findings from the "Lifetime Women's Pulse Poll," a 1987 opinion survey of 991 women conducted by Lifetime Cable TV.

Includes 2 tables showing survey response concerning how respondents would spend a gift of $5,000 that had to be spent on themselves, and factors influencing decisions to try new styles.

A full-text microfiche collection of the reports appearing in *SRI* can be purchased. But because most of the indexed publications are copyrighted, CIS cannot obtain permission to reproduce every report. For example, the journal seen in Exhibit 4-3 is not available, as indicated by the designation "SRI/MF/not filmed." Still, approximately 70% of the reports can be obtained from CIS on fiche. A blanket subscription to the microfiche provides an extensive, self-contained business research system.

Industry Data Sources (Information Access Company— Monthly).

This sizable online database provides abstracts for more than 100,000 published reports containing financial and marketing data, with an emphasis on products and industries. The indexed publications include journal articles, dissertations, conference proceedings, and government documents, but *Industry Data Sources* concentrates on such recurring sources of industry information as newsletters, directories, statistical yearbooks, special issues of periodicals, syndicated intelligence services, online databases, and similar serial publications. Aside from *Findex* (introduced in Chapter 3), it is one of the few indexes with extensive coverage of in-depth market surveys.

Industry Data Sources focuses on publications containing statistics, but a great deal of narrative material is also covered. It offers fairly powerful search capabilities, which is important given the size of the database. For example, the reports are indexed by SIC number as well as by subject headings. The database also utilizes a searchable field called "Data Descriptors," which categorizes the nature of the statistics found in each report. These categories are of two types: the attributes being measured (e.g., growth rates, market shares, etc.); and the form of measurement (e.g., annual, composite, average, percent). *Industry Data Sources* is a valuable resource because of the excellent indexing and the sheer diversity of publications it covers. By using this extensive database, the researcher will uncover many specialized reports that might otherwise be overlooked. *Industry Data Sources* is available through DIALOG and Data-Star.

Predicasts Forecasts (Predicasts, Inc.—Quarterly).

Predicasts Forecasts limits itself to publications that offer projections of future business and economic activity. In addition to leading the user to specific statistical publications, it summarizes the actual data from each source. Forecasts are gathered from hundreds of periodicals, market studies, and government reports. Since information is geared toward products and indus-

tries, *Predicasts Forecasts* is organized by product code, using the same modified SIC system seen in other Predicasts publications. Forecasts are also included for general economic and demographic characteristics, such as the national birth rate and Gross National Product. These are given alphanumeric codes beginning with the letter E.

Exhibit 4-4 shows a typical page from *Predicasts Forecasts*; the data appeared in the July 1989 issue. Product A is the principal commodity being presented, and Product B (where applicable) shows a relationship to the primary product. For example, forecasts can be found which show expenditures for computer equipment by the toiletries industry, consumption of packaging by the industry, and similar interrelationships. The data are given for a base year, a short-term forecast, and a long-term projection. The unit of measurement and source document are also cited. In the case of shaving preparations, the base year figure is from 1987, and sales were measured at $727 million. A long-term forecast for 1992 predicts that sales (in constant dollars, adjusted for inflation) will rise to $935 million. The information was obtained from the December 1988 issue of *Soap/Cosmetics/Chemical Specialties*. Researchers wishing to see more detailed information may consult the journal to read the full article, or they may order a reprint from the Predicasts document delivery service. Notice in Exhibit 4-4 the diversity of sources, even for the fairly narrow industry of toiletries. Forecasts were found in government documents (the *U.S. Industrial Outlook*), mainstream business journals (*Chemical Week*), newspapers (*Chemical Marketing Reporter*), specialty trade journals (*Drug & Cosmetics Industry*), and newsletters (*Technology Forecasts*).

Predicasts *Worldcasts* indexes industry and economic forecasts for foreign countries, regions, and the world. *Worldcasts* is available in two editions: one organized geographically by region and country, the other by product code. Data from all of the Predicasts forecasting services are also available online through DIALOG and Data-Star. On DIALOG, they appear on two separate files, each updated monthly; the database with domestic forecasts is known as *PTS U.S. Forecasts*. On Data-Star, the U.S. and international files are combined, with quarterly updates. The *Predicasts Basebook*, another of the company's statistical services, is discussed in Chapter 16.

EXHIBIT 4-4. *Predicasts Forecasts*

PREDICASTS

SIC	PRODUCT A	EVENT	QUALIFIER	YEARS B	S	L	QUANTITIES B	S	L	UNIT OF MEASURE	SOURCE JOURNAL	DATE	PAGE	Annual Growth
	Detergent Alkylates (Continued)													
28432 30	Detergent Alkylates	consump by	laundry powders	86	to	92	–	-1.3%	–	growth/yr	Chem Mkt R	08/15/88	25	– %
28432 30	Detergent Alkylates	consump by	liquid laundry detergents	86	to	89	100.	+7.5%	–	growth/yr	Chem Mkt R	08/15/88	25	– %
28432 32	Alkylbenzene Sulfonates NEC	consumption	(linear)	88	–	–	100.	105.	–	index	C&E News	01/23/89	38	5.0%
2844 TOILETRIES														
28440 00	Toiletries	expend for	computer equipment,software & svcs	88	–	92	490.	–	638.	mil $	Chem Week	03/29/89	45	6.9%
28440 00	Toiletries	expend for	computer industrial equipment	88	–	92	12.	–	17.	mil $	Chem Week	03/29/89	45	9.1%
28440 00	Toiletries	expend for	computer industrial equipment	88	–	92	2.5	–	2.6	% of EDP	Chem Week	03/29/89	45	1.0%
28440 00	Toiletries	expend for	computer software	88	–	92	54.	–	113.	mil $	Chem Week	03/29/89	45	20.3%
28440 00	Toiletries	expend for	computer software	88	–	92	11.1	–	17.7	% of EDP	Chem Week	03/29/89	45	12.4%
28440 00	Toiletries	expend for	computers & auxiliary equipment	88	–	92	199.	–	256.	mil $	Chem Week	03/29/89	45	6.5%
28440 00	Toiletries	expend for	computers & auxiliary equipment	88	–	92	40.6	–	40.1	% of EDP	Chem Week	03/29/89	45	-4%
28440 00	Toiletries	consump of	aerosol & spray containers	88	–	93	178.8±	–	275.	growth/yr	Chem Mkt R	02/27/89	27	9.1%
28440 00	Toiletries	consump of	alcohols	87	–	92	164.	–	211.	mil 87$	S&C Spec	12/00/88	24	5.2%
28440 00	Toiletries	consump of	cosmetic ingredients	–	–	–	–	–	2.7	bil $	D&C Ind	05/00/89	6	– %
28440 00	Toiletries	consump of	cosmetic ingredients	87	to	92	1815.	–	4450.	growth/yr	D&C Ind	05/00/89	6	– %
28440 00	Toiletries	consump of	cosmetics additives	87	92	00z	330.	2650.	390.	mil $	S&C Spec	05/00/89	83	7.2%
28440 00	Toiletries	consump of	essential oils	87	to	92	–	–	–	mil 87$	S&C Spec	12/00/88	24	3.4%
28440 00	Toiletries	consump of	ethanol	–	89	–	–	20.	–	% of prodB	CPI Purch	04/00/89	41	– %
28440 00	Toiletries	consump of	fats	87	–	92	73.	–	85.	mil 87$	S&C Spec	12/00/88	24	3.1%
28440 00	Toiletries	consump of	flavor & perfume materials	87	–	92	1200.	–	1500.	mil lbs	Tech Fore	08/00/88	13	4.6%
28440 00	Toiletries	consump of	fragrances	87	90	95	39.	42.	48.	mil lbs	Chem Mkt R	11/23/88	34	2.7%
28440 00	Toiletries	consump of	fragrances	87	to	–	–	+3.%	–	growth/yr	Chem Mkt R	08/01/88	9	– %
28440 00	Toiletries	consump of	inorganic pigments	87	–	92	29.	–	34.	mil 87$	S&C Spec	12/00/88	24	3.3%
28440 00	Toiletries	consump of	packaging ics	88	–	93	1.7±	–	2.1	bil $	Chem Mkt R	02/27/89	27	4.4%
28440 00	Toiletries	consump of	petroleum products	87	–	92	218.	–	273.	mil 87$	S&C Spec	12/00/88	24	4.7%
28440 00	Toiletries	consump of	pigments	87	–	92	30.	–	35.	mil 87$	S&C Spec	12/00/88	24	3.2%
28440 00	Toiletries	consump of	polymers	87	–	92	179.	–	238.	mil $	Chem Mkt R	10/10/88	31	5.9%
28440 00	Toiletries	consump of	polymers	87	–	92	179.	–	238.	mil $	Chem Mkt R	12/00/88	24	5.9%
28440 00	Toiletries	consump of	raw materials	–	89	–	–	1.4	–	bil $	Chem Mkt R	01/02/89	21	– %
28440 00	Toiletries	consump of	raw materials	87	–	92	1221.	–	1501.	mil 87$	S&C Spec	12/00/88	24	4.3%
28440 00	Toiletries	consump of	surfactants	87	–	92	169.	–	196.	mil 87$	S&C Spec	12/00/88	24	3.1%
28440 00	Toiletries	consump of	surfactants	87	to	–	–	+3.%	–	growth/yr	Chem Mkt R	10/10/88	31	– %
28440 00	Toiletries	expend for	computer consulting & services	88	–	92	46.	–	65.	mil $	Chem Week	03/29/89	45	9.1%
28440 00	Toiletries	expend for	computer consulting & services	88	–	92	9.4	–	10.2	% of EDP	Chem Week	03/29/89	45	2.1%
28440 00	Toiletries	expend for	computer personnel	88	–	92	178.	–	187.	mil $	Chem Week	03/29/89	45	1.3%
28440 00	Toiletries	expend for	computer personnel	88	–	92	36.4	–	29.3	% of EDP	Chem Week	03/29/89	45	-5.3%
28440 00	Toiletries	employ c⁴	production workers	87	88	89	63.4	70.5	71.2	000 worker	US Outlook	01/00/89	15-4	6.0%
28440 00	Toiletries	employ	(industry)	87	88	89	36.7	41.7	42.2	000 worker	US Outlook	01/00/89	15-4	7.3%
28440 00	Toiletries	shipments		88	88	89	10.9	11.3	11.7	bil 82$	US Outlook	01/00/89	15-4	3.7%
28440 00	Toiletries	shipments	(product)	87	88	89	11.1	11.4	11.7	bil 82$	US Outlook	01/00/89	15-4	2.7%
28440 00	Toiletries	imports		87	88	89	437.	461.	490.	mil $	US Outlook	01/00/89	15-4	5.9%
28440 00	Toiletries	exports		87	88	89	384.	487.	580.	mil $	US Outlook	01/00/89	15-4	22.9%
28440 00	Toiletries	sales		87	–	92	10.3	–	12.5	bil 87$	S&C Spec	12/00/88	24	4.0%
28440 00	Toiletries	sales	(ethnic)	88	–	92	732.	–	987.	mil $	S&C Spec	02/00/89	24	7.8%
28440 00	Toiletries	consumption	(cosmetic additives)	–	89	–	1.7	10.	2.1	bil $	Chem Mkt R	01/02/89	21	– %
28440 00	Toiletries	consumption		88	–	93	750.	–	912.5±	bil $	Packaging	04/00/89	38	4.4%
28440 00	Toiletries	consumption		88	–	89	100.	120.	136.8	mil 87$	Chem Week	04/12/89	33	4.1%
28440 00	Toiletries	after-tax profit		87	–	89				index	Chem Mkt R	06/20/88	29	17.0%
Shaving Preparations														
28441 00	Shaving Preparations	expend for	ingredients	87	–	92	252.	–	340.	mil $	D&C Ind	05/00/89	6	6.2%
28441 00	Shaving Preparations	consump of	cosmetics additives	87	92	00z	252.	340.	510.	mil $	S&C Spec	05/00/89	83	5.6%
28441 00	Shaving Preparations	sales	(incl bath soaps)	87	–	92	727.	–	935.	mil 87$	S&C Spec	12/00/88	24	5.2%
Perfumes & Colognes														
28442 00	Perfumes & Colognes	expend for	ingredients	87	–	92	380.	–	580.	mil $	D&C Ind	05/00/89	6	8.9%
28442 00	Perfumes & Colognes	consump of	cosmetics additives	87	92	00z	380.	580.	1055.	mil $	S&C Spec	05/00/89	83	8.2%
28442 00	Perfumes & Colognes	consump of	fragrance materials	87	to	92	–	+8.8%	–	growth/yr	D&C Ind	05/00/89	6	– %

B-259

INCORPORATING BOOKS AND DOCUMENTS INTO BUSINESS RESEARCH

The topics introduced in this chapter may seem unrelated, but each represents a relatively underutilized portion of the business literature. When faced with a major project, most researchers turn naturally to reference books, databases, and periodicals. The types of finding guides introduced in Chapters 3 and 5 seem more than adequate to lead the user to the most appropriate information sources. Books are frequently thought too general, or too outdated, to be useful. Government documents are seen to be esoteric and too difficult to find. The fact that most libraries banish their government publications to separate collections in basements or annexes only reinforces their unfamiliarity to the public. Statistical publications may seem like the keystone to business research, but they too are commonly overlooked. Researchers turn to them when explicitly asked to retrieve numeric data, but seldom to buttress nonstatistical work or to locate narrative reports accompanying statistical tables.

Government publications can make an important contribution to most research projects, being widely available and easy to locate (once you learn how). Unfortunately, it is rare for even the most accomplished business researchers to think of a source such as *Government Reports: Announcements and Index* when embarking on a search. Monographic material is usually treated in a similar manner. Books offer a level of thoroughness and detail which other resources can never match, and provide useful background for the work to follow.

The quality of business research can suffer from lack of imagination, and from an overly strong attachment to the familiar. All of us tend to respond reflexively to information requests. When faced with a statistical question, for example, we turn to a statistical source. No matter that "better" numbers might be found more readily in a book or journal article. There are several ways to combat this intellectual inflexibility; all of them have been stated earlier, but all are worth repeating. First, work on strengthening good research habits by remaining open to creative approaches. Second, utilize guides to the literature to extend the boundaries of the familiar. And third, always take the time to outline a research strategy. The more ambitious the project, the more critical the plan, but even the most straightforward information requests can benefit from a little forethought.

FOR FURTHER READING

Little has been written about the SIC system. In addition to the materials described below, a few more articles can be found in the reading lists for Chapters 6 and 16. For readers wishing to keep abreast of trends in business book publishing, two resources are recommended. Each year in the first March issue of *Library Journal*, Susan DiMattia selects and reviews the best business books of the previous year, and observes the current fads and patterns in publishing. In a different vein, *Publishers Weekly* conducts an annual survey of the market for business books. The *PW* survey, which typically appears in an August issue, identifies the best-selling titles, summarizes industry performance, and solicits comments from leading publishers.

The listings relating to government documents focus on the publications, finding tools, and computerized databases of the federal government. Background reading on the government's role as an information provider can be found in the lists following Chapters 2 and 15.

Standard Industrial Classification System

Kern, Richard. "At Long Last! Changes in the SIC System." *Sales & Marketing Management* 136 (April 28, 1986): 8+. The author describes the process which ultimately led to the 1987 SIC revisions. In fact, this article appeared about midpoint in the arduous journey: the OMB first announced plans for revision in a February 1984 issue of the *Federal Register*, and the final revisions did not appear until an October 1987 issue. Kern does a good job summarizing the proposed changes, most of which were eventually adopted.

PTS User's Manual (Cleveland OH: Predicasts, 1989).
For a look at modified SIC codes, browse through the complete "Predicasts Product Codes" found in this manual. Remember, Predicasts decided not to incorporate the government's 1987 revisions because the publisher's own modifications have departed substantially from the official SIC framework over the years. This system remains one of the best designed and most detailed industry classifications in the U.S. The *PTS Manual* displays the codes in both numeric and alphabetical listings.

U.S. Office of Management and Budget, Federal Committee on Statistical Methodology. *A Review of Industry Coding Systems.* Statistical Policy Working Paper, no. 11. (Washington, DC: U.S. Government Printing Office, 1984). Although federal statistical agencies use the SIC system as the basis of collecting and reporting industry data, surprising differences are found in the coding procedures used by various agencies. This report explores the basic principles which underlie the SIC system, the sources used by government agencies to collect data, and the interagency

sharing of industry-coded data. The report is intended for statistical policy-makers within the government, but anyone with a serious interest in industry classification will find it enlightening.

Guides to Book Reviews and Other Selection Tools

Bellanti, Robert, and Tracey Miller. "Business and Management." In *Selection of Library Materials in Applied and Interdisciplinary Fields*, edited by Beth Shapiro, and John Whaley. (Chicago: American Library Association, 1987): 10–31.

This essay describes numerous sources for identifying and evaluating business books and reference works. Also discusses how business publishing differs from other fields.

Murphy, Marcy, and Sajjad ur Rehman. "Reviewing Management Literature." *Library Quarterly* 57 (January 1987): 32–61.

An important bibliometric study of the journals which provide the best coverage of book reviews for newly published business materials. Among the most productive sources identified are a handful of well-known trade journals of the publishing industry, several professional library journals, and a few leading management periodicals.

Ternberg, Milton G. "Selecting and Acquiring Business Materials." *Collection Building* 9, No. 1, (1988): 22–31.

Discusses the different types of business publications typically found in business libraries and the selection tools used to identify them. Includes a list of major scholarly and practitioner journals which regularly contain book reviews.

Government Documents

Bower, Cynthia. "Federal Fugitives, DNDs and Other Aberrants: A Cosmology." *Documents to the People* 17 (September 1989): 120–26.

A fascinating look at the shadowy world of fugitive federal documents. Bower introduces three types of fugitives: nondepository items for sale by the GPO; "depository" items which somehow are never distributed to Depository Libraries (which the author terms DNDs); and government materials not published by the GPO. Based on an in-depth study conducted by the author over several years.

Geahigan, Priscilla C., and Robert F. Rose. *Business Serials of the U.S. Government.* 2nd ed. (Chicago: American Library Association, 1988).

An annotated guide to 176 of the most important business-related serials published by the federal government. Arranged by broad topic, with title and subject indexes.

Kelly, Melody S., and Frank Lee. "Access to Government Information: Recommended Bibliographies, Indexes, and Catalogs." In *The Basic Business Library: Core Resources*, 2nd ed., edited by Bernard S. Schlessinger. (Phoenix, AZ: Oryx Press, 1989): 142–50.

A short list of guides to the literature of government publications, including textbooks, commercial indexes and bibliographies, and major government catalogs.

Robinson, Judith Schiek. *Tapping the Government Grapevine: The User-Friendly Guide to U.S. Government Information Sources* (Phoenix, AZ: Oryx Press, 1988).

An enjoyable and understandable introduction to the sometimes intimidating world of government information. Topics range from the organization of the federal information system to sources of nonprint data. Appealing graphics, clear prose, and real-world examples make this a definite first choice.

Sears, Jean L., and Marilyn K. Moody. *Using Government Publications* (Phoenix, AZ: Oryx, 1985–1986).

For a more detailed look at government documents, this two-volume work is highly recommended. The authors take the reader step-by-step through the research process, beginning with the basics of searching, and moving on to specific research tasks. The wide range of topics includes legislative history, patents and trademarks, military specifications, and much more. Many chapters are devoted to sources of statistical data, from personal income to foreign trade.

Shill, Harold B. "NTIS and the Privatization of Government Information" In *United States Government Information Policies: Views and Perspectives*, edited by Charles R. McClure, Peter Hernon, and Harold C. Relyea. (Norwood, NJ: Ablex, 1989): 205–33.

Describes attempts during the Reagan administration to privatize NTIS, and suggests potential consequences of such action. A good introduction to the history and role of NTIS.

Zink, Steven D. *United States Government Publications Catalogs.* 2nd ed. (New York: Special Libraries Association, 1988).

An annotated bibliography of over 300 publications catalogs issued by federal agencies. Unfortunately, many agency catalogs and bibliographies tend to have a short life span, and as time passes, some of the items here will doubtless cease to exist. On the other hand, this is the most comprehensive, up-to-date guide available. The importance of this tool cannot be overstated; researchers who rely exclusively on the catalogs of the GPO and NTIS will miss a surprisingly large world of fugitive documents.

CHAPTER 5
Searching Journals, Newspapers, and News Services

TOPICS COVERED

1. Indexes: The Key to Periodical Literature
    a. Types of Indexes
    b. Beyond Indexes
2. General Business Indexes
3. Subject-Oriented Indexes
    a. Accounting and Finance
    b. Marketing and Advertising
    c. Personnel and Labor Relations
    d. Other Journal Indexes
4. Indexes to News Sources
    a. National Newspapers
    b. Regional News
    c. Newsletter Databases
    d. Wire Services
5. Which Index Is Best?
6. For Further Reading

MAJOR SOURCES DISCUSSED

- *Business Periodicals Index*
- *Business Index*
- *ABI/INFORM*
- *Predicasts F&S Index United States*
- *PTS PROMT*
- *PAIS International in Print*
- *Accountants' Index*
- *FINIS: Financial Industry Information Service*
- *PTS Marketing and Advertising Reference Service (MARS)*
- *Personnel Management Abstracts*
- *Wall Street Journal Index*
- *Business Dateline*
- *PTS Newsletter Database*
- *PR Newswire*

Almost any substantial research project will benefit from the use of periodical literature. Periodicals cover every possible industry, topic, and discipline, and they are specialized in a way few other resources can be. A trade journal or newsletter which follows a narrow field month after month develops a familiarity with that topic few experts can match. And, periodicals are current, easy to obtain, and generally inexpensive. The main problem in using them is their overwhelming numbers. Sifting through thousands of business periodicals, representing millions of potentially valuable articles, is a daunting task.

How does the researcher locate specific information in journals? One approach is to use the periodical directories mentioned in Chapter 3. Guides like *Business Publication Rates and Data* and the *Encyclopedia of Business Information Sources* will quickly identify significant periodicals in a particular field. The researcher can then scan recent issues to locate relevant articles. This type of focused browsing narrows the hunt to the most likely or useful journals, locates the most current articles in those journals, and reveals pertinent articles which would go undiscovered using other methods. But

such "directed serendipity" can be time consuming, and the researcher will miss highly relevant articles that appear in other types of magazines.

A second approach is to use the year-end indexes many journals compile for the articles in their own publications. These annual indexes can generally be found in the December or January issue of the magazine, or as a separate year-end supplement, but not all publications will have them. The most efficient method is to utilize broad-based periodical indexes and abstracts. Most offer highly specific subject headings, and a single indexing service can provide coverage of hundreds of periodical titles. Such indexing leads the researcher to relevant articles regardless of the type of journals in which they are located.

INDEXES: THE KEY TO PERIODICAL LITERATURE

There is at least one index or abstracting service for every discipline imaginable, and business-related indexes account for a substantial percentage of this output. Including online bibliographic databases, more than 200 periodical indexes are devoted entirely to business topics or have a strong business focus. Because management is such an interdisciplinary activity, nonbusiness indexes, from economics and computer science to psychology, law, and political science, must also be considered.

Types of Indexes

Most people are familiar with the *Readers' Guide to Periodical Literature*. Typical indexes to business periodical articles resemble the classic *Readers' Guide* format quite closely. Under each subject heading, article titles are listed, together with the author's name, the journal title, volume number, date, and pagination. Some indexes offer additional descriptive information, such as whether the article contains illustrations, tables, bibliographies, or other supplemental materials. Many online and CD-ROM indexes also include the names of the people, institutions, and companies mentioned in the article, the country or geographic location involved, and the type of article (editorial, interview, company profile, etc.). Not only does this serve to describe the material in greater detail, but it provides the researcher with more access points when conducting a search. Many indexes summarize articles with brief annotations to give a sense

of what the article is about. In a variation of this approach, the business indexes of Predicasts supply an annotation in lieu of the article's title. A common technique in newspaper indexes is to include both the headline and the lead sentence of each article.

A more sophisticated version of the annotation is the abstract, a carefully written summary of the publication being indexed. The best abstract writers strive to highlight the main points, state the conclusions reached, and even summarize the supporting statistical evidence. Good abstracts also include as many keywords from the article as possible. Abstracts may be a single sentence or they may run to several hundred words. However, the goal is to be concise, and typical abstracting publications limit their summaries to about three brief sentences. Abstracting services are useful bibliographic tools for several reasons. First, a well-written abstract will enable the researcher to determine whether the article is worth obtaining and reading. Second, if sufficiently detailed, it can provide the reader with specific answers, avoiding the need to consult the actual article. For example, abstracts in *PROMT* summarize statistical tables found in the periodicals it covers. And third, abstracts in electronic form (online databases, CD-ROMs, or locally mounted tapes) provide additional keywords to search.

A related service, the digest, is characterized by summaries lengthier than an abstract. Digests may utilize extracts or abridgments of the original text, or paraphrase key ideas. But the main difference between digests and abstracts is that abstracts are designed to give the researcher a sense of the publication's content before reading it, while the digest usually serves as a substitute for the complete document. For example, several publishing companies have tried to market "book briefs," offering executives and other busy readers 8-to-12-page summaries of popular new business books. An interesting example for business periodicals is *Operations Research/Management Science: International Literature Digest*. This monthly publication from the Executive Sciences Institute covers the scholarly literature of operations research. The one-to-two-page digests summarize the authors' research methodology and findings, including all essential mathematical formulas. Subscribers also receive an annual author and subject index.

Most indexing tools enable retrospective searching of publications by topic or author. Citation indexes meet a different need, allowing the researcher to work forward in time instead of backward. This is done by identifying subsequent articles which cite an earlier work, either in a footnote or bibliography. In this way, when a researcher

locates an important publication, he or she can find later articles which build upon, review, or refute the original work. Citation searching can be especially useful when the traditional subject approach produces meager results; by concentrating on citations to known works, the researcher can identify other writers working on the same topic. The major citation service which covers business-related topics is the *Social Sciences Citation Index*, compiled by the Institute for Scientific Information, Inc. Published three times per year with annual and quinquennial cumulations, this massive index covers more than 1,500 journals in the social and behavioral sciences, including management and economics. Though somewhat confusing to first-time users, it is the most effective tool for conducting a citation search of the scholarly literature. The index is also available online through BRS, DIALOG, and Data-Star, and as a CD-ROM product.

No matter what type of indexing service is being consulted, the researcher should become familiar with its organization and language. Does it use any unusual alphabetizing rules? Does it routinely omit certain categories of publication or types of articles? Are place names handled differently than other subject headings? Are certain topics covered in a separate section of the index? Failing to check such basic facts may result in an incomplete or unsuccessful search. Some indexes have a very simple structure, presenting information according to some brief classification scheme and providing very broad subject access. Others are quite detailed, utilizing thousands of subject headings and dozens of standardized subdivisions. Many online databases use brief descriptors rather than lengthy subject headings. Multiple descriptors are then assigned to each article. In this way, the researcher can combine the terms in a variety of ways to obtain greater flexibility in searching. Because every indexing service has a unique point of view, most use a controlled list of terms created by their own editorial staff. If the controlled vocabulary is especially large or complex, the company may publish a separate guide to subject headings or a thesaurus of descriptor terms. A thesaurus can be especially useful for identifying broader and narrower terms used in the index and for suggesting related topics to investigate. A number of business indexes provide extensive thesauri or lists of subject headings, including *ABI/INFORM*, *PAIS*, and *Work Related Abstracts*.

Some indexing services rely on an indexing structure not of their own devising. In most cases, the system used is the Library of Congress Subject Headings (LCSH), introduced in Chapter 4. Although the LCSH terms used to describe business topics are not always the best, a surprising number of business databases have adopted the system, from *Business Periodicals Index* to *PAIS International*.

Beyond Indexes

Current awareness services seek to keep the subscriber abreast of the latest articles in a given area. One way to track current articles on a specific topic is to hire a clipping service or other fee-based research company. The firm will scan each new issue of designated newspapers and journals looking for information on your subject and send you copies on a routine basis. Such companies can be identified through the *Editor & Publisher International Year Book*, the *Literary Market Place*, and the *Burwell Directory of Information Brokers*.

Another option is electronic clipping services. Generally known as Selective Dissemination of Information (SDI) systems, they provide the subscriber with a customized printout of recent publications, updated automatically on a recurring basis. The client establishes an SDI account with the vendor, then specifies the databases to be searched, the subjects to be included, and, in some cases, even the journal titles to be scanned. The service can be canceled or amended any time the customer wishes. Most major online vendors offer SDI services. Users of the "DIALOG Alert" service, for example, can receive daily, weekly, or monthly reports via regular mail, or sent to their electronic mail account. When the topic to be searched is reasonably specific, SDI is a surprisingly affordable and efficient way to keep up with the latest news or research in a given area.

Many published resources can also help readers track recent articles by subject. Newsletter and digest systems are primarily current awareness publications. For example, *The International Executive*, a journal of the American Graduate School of International Management, looks like a typical abstracting service, but contains no cumulative index. Every issue includes digests of significant articles in international management, each one two to four pages in length. A popular new trend in current awareness is the melding of periodical indexes with directory or financial data on a single database. In this way, researchers can obtain a quick profile of a company together with recent news and analytical articles. The first of these electronic products was Lotus Development Corporation's *CD/Corporate* on CD-ROM. A newer example is *Company Intelligence*, an online database from Information Access Company, which is

also available on CD-ROM as *Company ProFile.* It combines directory information from *Ward's Business Directory* with selected article citations from the *Business Index* and news stories from *PR Newswire. Company ProFile* itself can be combined with *Investext* and the complete *Business Index* to form an integrated system called *General BusinessFile.*

GENERAL BUSINESS INDEXES

The business indexes most likely to be found in libraries of all types are those which cover the widest range of topics. For indexing of general topics in popular magazines, students and researchers turn to tools like *Readers' Guide Abstracts* (H.W. Wilson Co.), the *Magazine Index* (Information Access Company), and *Periodical Abstracts Ondisc* (University Microfilms International). For broad coverage of business subjects, a variety of similar products are available.

Business Periodicals Index (H.W. Wilson Company— Monthly, with Quarterly and Annual Cumulations).

This outstanding index covers nearly 350 journals in business and economics. The choice of magazines to be indexed is made by a nationwide panel of librarians after extensive customer polling. The intent is to include the most popular and representative titles in a wide range of fields. The list is completely reevaluated every five years. Types of journals include general business magazines, financial publications, practitioner journals for disciplines like accounting and personnel management, and a selection of major trade journals. Many widely read academic journals are covered, but highly theoretical material is not emphasized. Indexing focuses on industries, companies, current business news, major economic events, public policy concerns, and management practice.

All articles are indexed by subject, and major topics are further divided by subheadings. Indexing terms include company names, geographic locations, personal names, and general subjects in a single alphabet. No author indexing is available, but stories about a person are indexed under the individual's name. The indexing is superb, with each article placed under very specific subject terms. *Business Periodicals Index* uses Library of Congress Subject Headings, but adds its own terminology when LCSH is insufficient. Issues are compiled monthly (except August), with quarterly and annual cumulations.

BPI's most noticeable flaw is that bibliographic information for each article can be difficult for first-time users to decipher. Journal titles are abbreviated (with a guide to abbreviations in the front of each index), and volume, date, and page designations are confusing. Regular users will not consider this a problem. More serious is the lack of timeliness in content. Although each month's index arrives promptly, the magazines covered are often several months old. However, the high caliber of the indexing makes this an acceptable tradeoff between speed and quality. Finally, *Business Periodicals Index* covers fewer journals than many of the major indexes, but the coverage reflects those journals most widely available in libraries.

BPI is also offered online through WILSONLINE and as a WILSONDISC CD-ROM; both services contain data beginning with June 1982. The CD-ROM version is searchable in a menu-driven "Browse Mode" or a command-driven "Expert Mode." Disks are revised quarterly, but WILSONDISC subscribers may update any disk search by using a free WILSONLINE password, an excellent bonus because the online files are updated twice weekly. An enhanced product, *Wilson Business Abstracts* will become available in the late summer of 1991. It will provide the same coverage and indexing as *BPI,* plus 50- to 150-word abstracts for nearly every article, dating back to June 1990. This new product will be available on CD-ROM and online, with no print equivalent.

Business Index (Information Access Company— Monthly).

The *Business Index* is similar in purpose to *BPI,* but it indexes many more publications. Included in the service is full coverage of more than 300 business periodicals, fairly extensive indexing of *The Wall Street Journal* and the business section of the *New York Times,* in-depth coverage of more than 50 local business magazines and newspapers such as *Crain's Chicago Business,* and selective indexing for hundreds of nonbusiness periodicals.

The three formats of the *Business Index*—microfilm, CD-ROM, and online—are sufficiently different to require separate explanations. The microfilm version is issued on a single reel of film containing approximately three years of indexing in one alphabet. Subscribers receive a new reel of film each month, completely superseding the previous one. With every new reel, the earliest data are deleted and the latest month is added. Articles indexed under each subject heading are arranged chronologically, with the most recent information appearing

first. Approximately every two years, subscribers receive an archival set of microfiche covering the period from 1986 to the present. A second set of fiche covering 1979 through 1985 is also available.

While the cumulative coverage is convenient, the microfilm format is frustrating to use. Winding through the alphabet takes time, and there are no photocopying capabilities. One of the most persistent complaints from users involves the poor quality of the accompanying microfilm readers; the film frequently unwinds from the reel, the machines break easily, and the plastic screens can be difficult to read.

IAC resolved these technical problems in 1985 with the popular InfoTrac family of CD-ROMs. Unfortunately, an InfoTrac version of the *Business Index* wasn't created until recently. Other InfoTrac products, including the *General Periodicals Index*, provided extensive business coverage, but they were no substitute for the more specialized index. In a typical business search, twice as many articles were retrieved using the *Business Index*.

The CD-ROM version of the *Business Index* made its long-awaited debut in January 1991 and is remarkably simple to use. InfoTrac workstations include specially designed keyboards with uniquely labeled function keys. A user with no prior knowledge of CD-ROMs can begin searching InfoTrac with no instruction whatsoever. The disks are updated monthly, and each contains the most recent three years of indexing. Subscribers can lease an annual archival disk covering the prior four years.

The online version is called the *Trade & Industry Index*. It is updated monthly, but daily additions are supplied on a separate file called *Newsearch*. Online coverage goes back to 1981. A third database, *Trade & Industry ASAP*, provides the full text of approximately 250 journals. *Trade & Industry Index* is available on the DIALOG system; *Newsearch* is available on BRS and DIALOG; and the *ASAP* file can be found on BRS, DIALOG, and NEXIS, though the contents vary slightly on each system.

The key differences among the three formats involve search capabilities and the types of materials covered. The microfilm version is the least sophisticated product. Access is primarily by subject, though limited author indexing is provided. Subjects include companies, industries, products, brand names, and general topics in a single alphabet. Modified LCSH terminology is employed, with numerous subheadings. The InfoTrac version employs the same subject approach, but author indexing is much more extensive. Keyword searching and limited Boolean capabilities are also available, but

only after the user tries a standard subject search. Another difference is the presence of abstracts for selected articles. The abstracts are derived from other IAC databases, notably the *Health Index* and the *Computer Database*.

By far the most sophisticated version is the *Trade & Industry Index*. All major fields are indexed, with complete Boolean and proximity search capabilities. The *Trade & Industry Index* also contains the full text of articles from more than 85 of the journals it indexes, plus the full text of corporate press releases from *PR Newswire*, both going back to 1983. While the complete text of these stories may be printed or viewed online, the user cannot search for words in the text on this file. Complete search capabilities for the entire articles are provided on *Trade & Industry ASAP*.

With nearly two million records in the file, obtained from sources as varied as trade journals, newspapers, local business publications, and corporate press releases, *Trade & Industry Index* is one of the most comprehensive business databases on the market.

All three formats offer advantages not found in Wilson's *Business Periodicals Index*. Many more journals are covered, and the indexing is more timely. The journal titles, dates, and pages are completely spelled out for each listing. More flexible subject headings reflect newly developing business topics; coined phrases, jargon, and new terminology are used more extensively than in *BPI*, and indexing by brand name is common. The index also employs more subject subdivisions than the Wilson publication. Topics are subdivided by standard phrases such as "investment activities," "market share," and "product evaluations." Finally, *Business Index* covers more articles by company name than *BPI*.

At one time the *Business Index* was justly criticized for overall poor quality, but more care is now given to data entry, and many indexing problems have been corrected. However, the quality of indexing in the Wilson service is still consistently superior. A potentially frustrating characteristic of the *Business Index* results from its indexing style. Because IAC makes such heavy use of subject subdivisions, one must scan many screens of information to avoid missing pertinent information. The problem is compounded by the size of the index, with its multiple years of data. There is nothing intrinsically wrong with using extensive subdivisions in an index; when researching a very narrow topic, such detailed indexing can be a real time saver. However, it presents a definite disadvantage for users seeking an overview of a topic. The placement of closely related articles under several subtly different subheadings is

especially annoying. This should not deter users from consulting the *Business Index* when needed. Because of the size of the database, the number of journals covered, and the speed with which they are indexed, it remains an important resource. Those who wish to use it on a regular basis should take the time to study its idiosyncrasies.

IAC has also created two microfilm services, the *Business Collection* and the *Magazine Collection,* which can be used in conjunction with the InfoTrac products. Available on a subscription basis and updated biweekly, they offer the complete text of articles from hundreds of periodicals, reproduced on numbered microfilm cartridges. The *Business Collection* covers approximately 400 business periodicals dating back to 1982. Users of the *Business Index* or the *General Periodicals Index* on CD-ROM can immediately turn from the index to the *Business Collection* to obtain many of the articles found in their search. To browse individual journal titles, users can consult the printed *Issue Guide* which lists the cartridge numbers where each issue can be found.

ABI/INFORM (Data Courier, Inc.—Weekly Updates).

ABI/INFORM, one of the first online abstracting services to cover management and business topics, is accessible through DIALOG, BRS, NEXIS, and ten other systems. It has no print equivalent, but a CD-ROM version called *ABI/INFORM Ondisc* is updated monthly and has most of the search capabilities which make the online service such a powerful tool.

In both formats, *ABI/INFORM* provides citations and abstracts to 800 business and economics journals. Approximately half are "core" journals indexed in their entirety; the other half are given selective coverage. Even for the core titles, *ABI/INFORM* excludes book reviews, ephemeral columns, and brief news items. Titles are predominantly from the U.S., though some 25% are published abroad; Great Britain, Canada, Australia, Germany, and Japan are the foreign countries most heavily represented. Over 99% of the articles are written in English.

ABI/INFORM is the most comprehensive multidisciplinary index to the scholarly literature of management. However, journals are not limited to academic titles; coverage also includes general business magazines, practitioner journals, and some trade periodicals. All management disciplines are represented, and related fields such as health care management, telecommunications, and computing are covered extensively. The abstracts are consistently well-written and fairly long, usually about 250 words. Exhibit 5-1 presents two typical *ABI* abstracts, displayed in the CD-ROM format.

In either format, the database is accessible by author, keyword in title, journal title, publication date, publication year, subject, and words in the abstract. Subject access includes company name (since June 1986), industry, and geographic area, as well as general subjects. *ABI* users can search by specific descriptors such as "Strategic Planning," broader classification codes (2310 for Planning), or a combination of both. Additional codes allow limiting by article treatment: "how-to" articles, theoretical presentations, case studies, biographical profiles, articles with strong statistical content, and so on. Searchers can further limit results by the type of organization (nonprofit, small business, multinational company) and by management function (personnel, marketing, planning, etc.) Another useful indexing device is the inclusion of the article's focus or perspective. For example, searchers can combine a subject with terms like "Advantages," "Problems," "Applications," or "Implementations." Other commonly used descriptors include "Market Share," "Trends," "Predictions," and "Economic Impact." More creative indexing terms—"Manycompanies," "Manycountries," and "Manyindustries"—have been coined to assist in locating articles of a comparative nature.

Chapter 1 gave an example of how *ABI* could be used to quickly identify practical articles on the use of "Critical Success Factors" in the strategic planning process. The two records shown in Exhibit 5-1 were among those retrieved by this search. Notice that "Critical Success Factors" is not a subject descriptor (designated in the CD-ROM version as "Terms"), but "Success," "Critical," and "Factors" are. This is typical of the style of post-coordinated indexing adopted by *ABI*; the compilers avoid phrases as indexing terms unless the expression itself is quite popular. Instead, they focus on the words within the phrase, so the searcher must use the Boolean operator AND to identify articles where all three words appear as descriptors. This idiosyncrasy takes getting used to, but is employed to keep the controlled vocabulary at a comfortable size. The approach affords greater flexibility to indexers and searchers alike. For example, innumerable single-word modifiers have been established as formal descriptors; among them are "Direct," "Equal," "Partial," "Real," and "Small." As a result, new descriptors for every fleeting buzz-word in the management literature are unnecessary; instead, most phrases can be constructed through a combination of adjectives and nouns. A researcher seeking articles on skilled workers or a skilled labor force could construct a search in the following manner on the DIALOG system:

skilled/df and (workers or employees or labor)/de

EXHIBIT 5-1. *ABI/INFORM*

```
87-30217
Title:     Using Critical Success Factors in Planning
Authors:   Jenster, Per V.
Journal:   Long Range Planning (UK) Vol: 20 Iss: 4 Date: Aug 1987
           pp: 102-109  Jrnl Code: LRP  ISSN: 0024-6301
Company:   Iowa Farmatics Inc
Terms:     Strategic planning; Factors; Success; Factors; Design; Processes;
           Information systems; Systems design; Models
Codes:     2310 (Planning)
Abstract: A strategy planning and strategic control process, which is tightly
   integrated with the firm's information system, is introduced. This approach
   is designed to assist directors and senior managers in executing and
   monitoring their strategies. This design method incorporates 9 steps: 1.
   Provide structure for design process. 2. Determine general forces affecting
   strategy. 3. Develop a strategic plan or modify the current plan. 4. Identify
   a chosen number of critical success factors. 5. Determine who is responsible
   for which crucial areas. 6. Select the strategic performance indicators. 7.
   Develop and integrate appropriate reporting procedures. 8. Implement and
   initiate system use by the senior personnel. 9. Establish evaluating
   processes and methods. Through suitable introduction, this approach can
   create an integrated strategic context within which top management and key
   personnel can execute the strategy and maintain a competitive edge for their
   firm.


88-36854
Title:     Planner's Guide: Critical Success Factors
Authors:   Freund, York P.
Journal:   Planning Review Vol: 16  Iss: 4  Date: Jul/Aug 1988  pp: 20-23
           Jrnl Code: PLR  ISSN: 0094-064X
Terms:     Corporate planning; Corporate objectives; Strategic business units;
           Problems; Strategy; Success
Codes:     2310 (Planning)
Abstract: Identification of critical success factors (CSF) can be an effective
   technique for focusing strategic direction and investment within an
   organization.  CSFs must be important to the attainment of overall corporate
   goals as well as being measurable and controllable.  In addition, they should
   be relatively few in number, expressed as tasks, applicable to all similar
   companies in the industry, and hierarchical in nature.  A CSF methodology
   found to be more successful in medium-sized and large companies calls for: 1.
   a determination of success factors of the overall business, followed by
   identification of specific contributions by individual business units, 2.
   the determination of CSFs for each business unit's component functional
   areas, 3.  the development of strategies in each area to leverage competitive
   strength and overcome weaknesses, 4.  the development of measurement tools,
   and 5.  establishment of reporting processes and producers.  The effective
   use of CSFs by an insurance company is detailed.
```

This would retrieve any records where "skilled" appeared as a single-word descriptor ("df") together with any of the other three words, appearing in the descriptor field. In the latter case, "de" is used because any of the three words could be part of a lengthier phrase, as in "blue collar workers" or "government employees." Remember, single words aren't used exclusively; many popular phrases have also been designated as descriptors.

A complete thesaurus of *ABI*'s controlled vocabulary terms (both words and phrases) is published. And for those users unaware of the single-word approach, a free-text or keyword search usually provides adequate results. The articles in Exhibit 5-1 would be retrieved using the phrase "Critical Success Factors" or the acronym "CSF" because they appear in the article titles or abstracts, which are rich in identifying words and phrases.

The CD-ROM product is similar to the online version in all major respects. Almost every field accessible online can be searched via the disk, and the record contents are identical. The online version dates back to 1971, while the current disk covers the most recent five years in a rolling cumulation, with the earliest month dropped from each monthly update. Two retrospective disks cover 1971-1980 and 1981-1986. Purchasers of the second retrospective disk have been promised a free cumulative update each year to prevent a gap between the current and retrospective files. Differences between the two versions are minor, but online searching is definitely more flexible. For example, search results on the CD can only be printed in two formats, the citation or the full record. The CD software automatically looks for plural and singular forms of every word, a feature which cannot be turned off. A single-word search of the descriptor field on CD-ROM will also retrieve phrases where the word is part of a descriptor phrase; a search for "responsibility" will also retrieve "corporate responsibility" and "social responsibility," for example. This can present problems, given the nature of the indexing structure. On many online systems, searchers can indicate a range of years to be searched or sort the search results, capabilities lacking in the CD-ROM. A more significant difference is that the online product is updated weekly, as opposed to the monthly updates on disk.

Despite its minor limitations, *ABI/INFORM Ondisc* is one of the best CD-ROMs available today. It is powerful, flexible, and easy to use. Most people can begin rudimentary searching with little or no prior instruction. For these reasons, *ABI/INFORM Ondisc* has quickly become one of the most popular CD-ROMs in business libraries. Selected company and industry records from *ABI* can also be found on another CD-ROM service called *CD/Corporate*, part of the Lotus One Source family of databases.

A companion product, *Business Periodicals Ondisc* (*BPO*), combines the complete text of approximately 350 business journals with the powerful *ABI/INFORM* indexing system. The articles are stored on optical disks which the subscriber receives at the rate of about 50 per year. This represents about half of the journals indexed on the *ABI* database. Because the disks are produced by optical scanning, the text of the actual articles cannot be searched, but keywords in the *ABI* abstracts can. When searching for topics on the *ABI/INFORM* portion of the system, the *BPO* user is notified whenever an appropriate article is available on the full-text system. He or she is then instructed to insert the appropriate optical disk and the software immediately locates the article. The full text, complete with photographs and other graphics, can then be viewed on an oversize screen or printed on a laser printer. If the user simply wants to view recent issues of a particular journal, a table of contents file can be browsed on screen. While the cost of the system is prohibitive for most would-be subscribers, its availability opens a new avenue of document delivery. For many organizations, the convenience of one-step retrieval and compact storage will make *BPO* a welcome product.

Predicasts F&S Index United States (Predicasts, Inc.—Weekly, with Cumulations).

Formerly known as the *Funk & Scott Index of Corporations and Industries*, *Predicasts F&S* provides detailed coverage of more than 750 trade journals, newspapers (including *The Wall Street Journal*), government documents, and special studies—some 2,000 titles in all. The focus is on material dealing with individual companies and the industries to which they belong. It is published weekly, with monthly, quarterly, and annual cumulations. Each issue appears in two parts: a company name index and an index to industries and products. In both sections, subject subdivisions are used to identify the specific aspect of the company or industry being discussed. Examples of these subdivisions are "Products and Processes," "Facilities and Equipment," "Capital Expenditures," "Resources and Resource Use," and "Market Information." The industry section utilizes a classification structure based on the SIC system. There are two important points to remember when using this structure: the numbering system is extended beyond four digits to achieve remarkable specificity, and Predicasts does not strictly adhere to the U.S. Office of Management and Budget industry definitions. Where the government lists smaller activities under miscellaneous categories, Predicasts assigns unique code numbers. In fact, the Predicasts numbering system has departed so often from the SIC standard that they call their classification numbers "product codes." An extensive alphabetical index to the codes is included in every issue. The industry section also indexes articles which include economic or demographic statistics; these are classified under codes beginning with the letter E. For example, articles on various interest rates begin with the code E56 and articles on life expectancy are found under E136. Articles about local, national, and international government activities are assigned codes beginning with 9, then further divided by the level of government, the function, and even the agency name. Finally, articles on small businesses, multinational corporations, and conglomerates are grouped under codes beginning with 99.

Exhibit 5-2 shows a sample page from the company section of *Predicasts F&S*. Notice that indexed stories include both news reports and in-depth articles. Cross-references to affiliated company names are provided. Also notice *Predicasts F&S* does not list the article title, but writes a descriptive phrase to give the user a clearer idea of the article's contents. Because all Predicasts indexes emphasize articles containing statistical information, summary data are included in the article description wherever possible. Because of this focus on data, and because it covers such a diversity of trade journals, *Predicasts F&S* is an indispensable guide to company and industry information not easily found through other means.

International coverage of business topics is augmented by two companions to the U.S. edition: *Predicasts F&S Index Europe* and *Predicasts F&S Index International*. The two foreign indexes are organized in three sections—company name, industry, and country or region. All three publications cover articles discussing events taking place within that geographic area, regardless of where the article originated; the foreign editions contain articles from U.S. publications and vice versa. This perspective also applies to company locations, focusing on where the event takes place, not where the firm has its headquarters. For example, an article about a European branch of an American company would be found in *Predicasts F&S Index Europe*, not the U.S. edition. The three *Predicasts F&S* indexes are also available as a combined online file called *PTS F&S Index*. The initials refer to the "Predicasts Terminal System," the name given to Predicasts's family of online products. The database is updated weekly, with records back to 1972. It can be searched on DIALOG, BRS, and Data-Star.

A CD-ROM version of *Predicasts F&S* was unveiled in early 1991, with records dating back to January 1990. Called *F&S Index Plus Text*, the disk contains more than its online counterpart. Approximately 80% of the records on disk are augmented by information from the *PTS PROMT* database, which is described below. *PROMT* records on disk provide abstracts, verbatim extracts, or, in the case of selected shorter articles, the complete text. *F&S Index Plus Text* combines the powerful SilverPlatter search software with Predicasts's detailed indexing. Searchable fields include Predicasts product codes, event codes, country, company name, publication date, and source; words in the text can also be searched. Searches can be limited to those records containing text, and the distinction between extracts and full text is always identified in the record. *F&S Index*

Plus Text is available in both U.S. and International editions, with monthly updates. A variety of subscription plans are offered, and subscribers automatically receive annual archival disks. This exciting new product will undoubtedly become extremely popular among librarians and researchers alike.

PROMT (Predicasts, Inc.—Monthly).

Predicasts also produces several abstracting services; most are available in print and online. The company's flagship service is *PROMT*, which stands for "Predicasts Overview of Markets and Technology." The printed and online versions are quite different, and will be described separately.

Many citations found in the three *Predicasts F&S* indexes are reproduced with abstracts in the printed version of *PROMT*. But where the *F&S* products index 2,000 publications, *PROMT* covers only half that number, and concentrates on the most substantial articles in each. However, it is difficult to make direct comparisons of the two because they are quite different in many respects. While *Predicasts F&S* provides broad coverage of all types of company and industry news, *PROMT* focuses on stories involving products, markets, and technology. Users can locate company-specific and industry-wide information on market share, product trends, sales and consumption data, emerging technologies, new products, research and development expenditures, marketing strategies, and similar subjects. *PROMT* also includes mergers, company finances, and other topics not directly related to products and markets. *Predicasts F&S* offers more extensive coverage in the areas of government regulation, labor, economic conditions, and other general business trends. And *Predicasts F&S* provides more thorough coverage of the journals it indexes.

The most obvious difference between the two is that *PROMT* contains abstracts, which range from three sentences to paragraphs of 200 words or more. Each abstract presents as much factual information as possible, including names, dates, and places. Statistical data are cited whenever possible. In fact, many of the abstracts contain no narrative, simply summarized statistical tables.

The abstracts are organized by industry, but instead of using Predicasts's detailed product codes, arrangement is according to broad industry groups such as chemicals or electronics. Major groupings are subdivided, with about 500 categories in all. Every issue contains a fairly detailed index, listing company names, trade names, products, and countries in a single alphabet. Although the abstracts are not reprinted in an annual cumulation, the index section is cumulated in the quar-

EXHIBIT 5-2. *Predicasts F&S Index United States*

COMPANIES 409 **Goldome Realty Credit**

Earnings were $11.6 mil in FY ended 7/1/89, vs $1.3 mil in FY88 Feedstuffs 08/14/89 p6
Financial performance, 1988 OTC Review 09/00/89 p34
Golden Princess Mining 1041000
Signs pact for Alban Explorations to buy 100% stake in gold project, NV Mining Jrl 05/26/89 p408
Golden Recycle 5093121
Affiliate of Coors (Adolph)
Mounts ASKO computer-assisted slitting sys for secondary aluminum, CO Light Mtl 12/00/88 p24
Golden Reward Mining 1041000
Is 33.33% sold by VenturesTrident Limited Partnership to MinVen Gold SkilMining 01/21/89 p13
To install a gold ore stacking, reclaiming and handling system SkilMining 02/18/89 p22
To produce 65,000 oz/yr of gold at Golden Reward property, SD Mining Jrl 01/13/89 p26
To produce 50,000 oz/yr of silver at Golden Reward property, SD Mining Jrl 01/13/89 p26
Golden State Foods 5140000
Food processor, McDonald's supplier, considers possible merger NY Times N 10/14/89 p19
Revenues data, 1988 Forbes 12/11/89 p226
Golden State Newsprint 2621020
May add recycled newsprint mill to triple cpcty at Pomona, CA, mill PaperAge 10/00/89 p3
May build major recycled newsprint mill at Pomona, CA PIMA 11/00/89 p16
May add 2nd, 230,000 m tpy 100%-recycled newsprint machine at mill, CA Pulp,Paper 11/00/89 p31
Studies feasibility for world-class recycled newsprint mill; Pomona, CA AmePaGrl 10/00/89 p1
Golden Temple Bakery 2043019
Has introduced its Golden Temple Bran Mornin' Muesli cereal LooFoEd 12/12/88 p226F
Golden Valley 2030020
Strategizes to raise earnings from microwave popcorn and french fries Barrons 10/23/89 p20
Golden Valley Microwave 2030000
Intros microwaveable flavored-popcorn line under 'Act II' brand name Vend 02/00/89 p15
Introduced frozen/refrigerated Act I Extra Butter Microwave Popcorn LooFoEd 02/28/89 p5
Reports FY88 net income of $16.817mil vs $12.346mil in FY87 WSJ (NJ) 02/14/89 pB12
Return on equity analysis Forbes 11/13/89 p220
Financial forecast, 1990 Fin World 10/17/89 p60
SEC probes for allegedly inflating co earnings & misusing funds Bus Week 07/10/89 p30
Issued patent by US Patent & Trademark Office for laminated packaging Snack Food 12/00/89 p6
Golden West Financial 6120000
See also World Savings & Loan, affiliate
Has final talks about acquiring two failed thrifts with govt aid, FL WSJ (NJ) 12/20/88 pA4
Acquires Ohio Valley S&L and First Border Savings under FSLIC auspices Am Bank 12/20/88 p3
Chief executive compensation data, 1988 Forbes 05/29/89 p214
Chief executive officer performance award Fin World 04/04/89 p87
Management profile Wall St T 06/12/89 p93903
Return on equity analysis Forbes 01/09/89 p241
Sales and earnings growth rates analysis Forbes 01/09/89 p96
Reports 1988 net income of $138.35 mil or $4.41/shr WSJ (NJ) 01/24/89 pB6
Sales & profits listed w/those of leading savings & loans, 1988 (table) Bus Week 03/20/89 p97
Earnings estimate, 1989 Fin World 05/02/89 p66
Shareholder equity data, 1988 Euromoney 06/00/89 p96
EPS annual growth rate data, 1978-88 Fortune 06/05/89 p372
Earnings growth rate estimate, 1990 Fin World 12/12/89 p61
Financial performance projtn, 1989 Forbes 01/09/89 p96
Financial analysis Value Line 02/10/89 p1164
Financial forecast, 1989 Forbes 05/01/89 p312
Financial analysis Value Line 05/12/89 p1163
Financial analysis Value Line 08/11/89 p1163
Financial analysis Value Line 11/10/89 p1163
Originations of single-family home loans rose 92% to $3.8bil in 1988 Am Bank 01/25/89 p2
Among largest savings institutions ranked by 1988 assets (table) Fortune 06/05/89 p372
Golden West Publishing 2711000
Affiliate of Media General
Offered for sale for undisclosed terms by Media General WSJ (NJ) 10/18/89 pB6
Media General to sell this unit for undisclosed sum NY Times N 10/19/89 p49
To be sold by Media General Edit Publ 10/28/89 p35
Golden Zone Resources 1041000
Determines open-pit mineable gold reserves totaling 370,000 tons, AK Mining Jrl 05/05/89 p344
Goldenberg Candy 2621000
To rebuild existing manufacturing plant in Philadelphia, PA Vend 01/00/89 p8
To resume full production at Philadelphia candy plant in 5/89, PA Vend 04/00/89 p7
To resume full production of Peanut Chews, Chew-ets candy at PA plant USDiJo 05/00/89 p5
Golder Thoma & Cressey 6720000
To form Golder Thoma Cressey Fund II to buy Careercom for $121 mil NY Times N 08/12/89 p19
Forms GTC Restaurant Group with foodservice veteran V Lambiase NatnsRestr 06/26/89 p18
Affiliates to jtly acquire Charter-Crellin for $27/shr NY Times N 03/02/89 p28
Affiliate will acquire Charter-Crellin with Nicholas Feder & Jaffe WSJ (NJ) 03/02/89 pB11
Leads group that seeks to acquire Careercom for $121 mil or $11/shr WSJ (NJ) 08/14/89 pC14
To assign $2.1mil in Postal Instant Equity to Kane-Miller for buyout WSJ (NJ) 01/31/89 pC27
Golder Thoma Cressey Fund II 6720000
To be formed to buy Careercom for $121 mil in cash, or $11/shr NY Times N 08/12/89 p19
Goldfield 1000000
Will produce 381k oz of non-placer gold in 1989 Metal Bul 09/04/89 p19
Reports net income of $2.772mil in year ending 12/31/88 WSJ (NJ) 03/03/89 pC6
Reports net income of $2.772mil in year ending 12/31/88 WSJ (NJ) 03/06/89 pB5
Reported net income of $2.771 mil in 1988, vs $229,000 in 1987 Am Mtl Mkt 04/19/89 p5
Goldfoil Manufacturing 3497000
New hot stamping foil plant has 1 of world's widest vacuum metallizers, CA Mod Plast 11/00/89 p143
Goldhirsh Group 2794000
To launch qtrly lifestyle mag tentatively titled 'Inc Plus' Ad Age 10/30/89 p71
Golding Industries 2260006
Sold by Publicker Ind for $43.8mil to Joseph Littlejohn & Levy new co WSJ (NJ) 03/29/89 pA2
Publicker Industries sells to new firm for $43.7mil NY Times N 03/30/89 p26
Goldman Financial 6720000
May acquire mfr of gear equipment Gleason Works NY Times N 06/15/89 p28
Offered $20/shr for Gleason in friendly bid WSJ (NJ) 06/15/89 pC16
Seeks Gleason for $120 mil or $20/shr MetalwNews 06/19/89 p5
Takeover bid of $120 mil or $20/shr is rejected by Gleason directors WSJ (NJ) 06/30/89 pA6
Gleason rejects $120 mil bid as insufficient MetalwNews 07/10/89 p8
Goldman Sachs 6211000
See also Amerace, affiliate
See also Wheeling-Pittsburgh Steel, affiliate
Organizations & Institutions
Has established an asset management div, as has Salomon Brothers Pensions 05/15/89 p4
Forms BroadPark Partnership w/ Citibank to provide loans for takeovers WSJ (NJ) 04/04/89 pA5
To jtly set up US real estate venture in 1/90 Jpn Econ J 11/25/89 p34
Buys 34% in Wheeling-Pittsburgh for $13.9 mil from resigning chrmn NY Times N 01/28/89 p21
Acquires 34%, or 1.75 mil shares, of Wheeling-Pittsburgh Steel Am Mtl Mkt 01/30/89 p16
Acquires 34% hldg in Wheeling-Pittsburgh Steel for $13.98 mil or $8/shr WSJ (NJ) 01/30/89 pB8
Acquires 34% of Wheeling-Pittsburgh Steel for about $13.9 mil Am Mtl Mkt 02/06/89 p2
To buy 49% stake in new partnership for auto parts spun off by SPX NY Times N 03/07/89 p37
Buys 9.7% stake in Anchor Glass Container for investment purposes NY Times N 08/22/89 p27
Buys 9.7% stake in Anchor Glass Container WSJ (NJ) 08/22/89 pB2
Has had $225mil invested in it by 7 big undisclosed insurance cos NY Times N 03/30/89 p26
Daiichi Mutual Life to buy part of a nonvoting preferred stock issue Jpn Econ J 04/08/89 p15
Management Dynamics
Changes corp culture, internal policies to cope with changing mkt Forbes 09/18/89 p150
Products & Processes
New stock portfolio mgmt unit is offered $200 mil from wealthy people WSJ (NJ) 07/27/89 pC1
To assist Shearson Lehman Hutton in plan to offer unbundled stock units WSJ (NJ) 01/30/89 pC1
Will form an asset management division NY Times N 05/09/89 p37
Will manage financial futures trading in US for Yasuda Trust & Banking Jpn Econ J 08/12/89 p18
Expenditures & Obligations
One of 5 US securities firms teaming up for shared global net CommWeek 10/30/89 p2
People
To eliminate 65 jobs or less than 5% of staff in fixed-income dept NY Times N 01/31/89 p33
Plans to selective staff cuts due to cyclical industry pressures NY Times N 05/18/89 p32
To likely lay off more than 200 employees in strategic review WSJ (NJ) 05/18/89 pC12
Market Information
Foreign exchange market share forecast, 1989 Euromoney 05/00/89 p79
With Salomon Bros has contracted with AMR to stop unwanted takeover WSJ (NJ) 08/30/89 pA3
US debt & equities underwritten by yr & mkt shr for 1987-88, table WSJ (NJ) 01/03/89 pC1
Global debt & equity underwriting and mkt shr by yr for 1987-88, table WSJ (NJ) 01/03/89 pC19
Junk bond underwriting and market share by year for 1987-88, table WSJ (NJ) 01/03/89 pC19
Financial Data
Merger and acquisitions advice activity by deal value in UK data, 1988 Euromoney 02/00/89 p100
Mergers and acquisitions advice by deal value in US data, 1988 Euromoney 02/00/89 p100
Mergers and acquisitions advice by number of deals in US data, 1988 Euromoney 02/00/89 p100
Merger and acquisition financial activity for US clients data, 1988 Euromoney 02/00/89 p100
Merger & acquisition financial deals for European clients data, 1988 Euromoney 02/00/89 p102
Merger and acquisition financial advice activity for UK clients data, 1988 Euromoney 02/00/89 p102
Merger and acquisitions advice ranked by number of deals worldwide data, 1988 Euromoney 02/00/89 p96
Merger and acquisitions advice ranked by deal value worldwide data, 1988 Euromoney 02/00/89 p98
Merger and acquisitions advice ranked by crossborder deal value data, 1988 Euromoney 02/00/89 p98
Merger & acquisition deals with Europe buying into US data, 1988 Euromoney 02/00/89 p98
Lead management of new Eurobond issues arranged in 1988 Euromoney 09/00/89 p162
Eurobonds lead and co-lead managed in 1988 Euromoney 09/00/89 p162
Eurobond issues co-managed in 1988 Euromoney 09/00/89 p166
Fixed-rate Eurobond issues arranged in 1988 Euromoney 09/00/89 p168
Fixed-rate Eurobond issues lead managed in 1988 Euromoney 09/00/89 p168
US dollar-issued Eurobonds arranged in 1988 Euromoney 09/00/89 p170
Canadian dollar-issued Eurobonds arranged in 1988 Euromoney 09/00/89 p172
Private sector-issued Eurobonds arranged in 1988 Euromoney 09/00/89 p180
Lead manager of US issuers brought to Eurobond market in 1988 Euromoney 09/00/89 p184
International equity issues offered in 1988 Euromoney 09/00/89 p188
International equity offerings lead and co-lead managed in 1988 Euromoney 09/00/89 p188
Euro medium-term notes arranged in 1988 Euromoney 09/00/89 p200
All domestic issues sold in US during 1988 Euromoney 09/00/89 p201
Domestic debt issues offered in 1988 Euromoney 09/00/89 p201
Domestic equity issues arranged in 1988 Euromoney 09/00/89 p202
Preferred stock issues arranged in 1988 Euromoney 09/00/89 p202
Common US equity issues arranged in 1988 Euromoney 09/00/89 p202
Mortgage-backed debt arranged in 1988 Euromoney 09/00/89 p203
Off-the-shelf debt issues arranged in 1988 Euromoney 09/00/89 p203
Holds 2.87% share of US dollar-denominated Eurobonds issued in 1988 Asian Bus 10/00/89 p67
Revenues data, 1988 Forbes 12/11/89 p220
Goldome 6020000
Manufacturers Hanover gets Fed permission to acquire 11 branches Am Bank 09/28/89 p3
Goldome Bank 6030000
Will sell Goldome Strategic Investments, investment advisory svcs unit WSJ (NJ) 07/26/89 pC5
Is selling 11 offices to Manufacturers Hanover Trust, NY Am Bank 10/02/89 p3
Plan to sell 11 branches to Manufacturers Hanover is being opposed, NY WSJ (NJ) 05/05/89 pC13
To have over $50 mil added to its 1989 net income through asset sales Am Bank 10/02/89 p3
Sold the Instabank ATM network to the New York Cash Exchange (Nyce) Am Bank 11/17/89 p12
Has completed the sale of 11 branches to Manufacturers Hanover Trust Am Bank 11/14/89 p16
Has sold 11 branches in the New York area to Manufacturers Hanover, NY WSJ (NJ) 11/14/89 pA8
Seen as strengthening retail banking business, while tightening costs WSJ (NJ) 03/28/89 pB11
Restructuring plan includes 5-6% job reductions in 1990 Am Bank 10/24/89 p1
Targeting mass consumer market & using CEO TA Cooper as TV spokesperson BankAdNews 05/22/89 p1
Asked by Gannett to apologize to shareholders for USA Today type report BankAdNews 04/17/89 p1
Introduced Co-Op Equity Line loan service for co-op owners in mid-1/89 BankAdNews 02/20/89 p5
Reports 1988 deficit of $119.1mil, after fifth straight quarterly loss Am Bank 02/21/89 p3
Financial performance projtn, 1989 Forbes 01/09/89 p96
Among largest thrifts ranked by deposits for 1988 (table) Am Bank 05/26/89 p8
Goldome Bank for Savings 6020000
Bank hldg co lost $63.1 mil in 4th-qtr 1988, $119.1 mil loss for year NY Times N 02/18/89 p19
Goldome Realty Credit 6162000
Will close 21 offices in 11 states in the next 3 mo NY Times N 04/08/89 p19

terly and year-end issues. This arrangement offers users an alternative to the more traditional *F&S* products. As a current awareness service, *PROMT* allows subscribers to browse the abstracts for recent news. For retrospective research, the cumulative indexes can be consulted.

The online version is called *PTS PROMT*. Available on DIALOG, BRS, Data-Star, and CORIS, it is both larger and more powerful than the print version. The most significant difference involves content—the online version provides access to a huge assortment of additional resources, including financial reports. *PTS PROMT* contains selective abstracts for *The Wall Street Journal*, corporate press releases, nearly 200 local newspapers and magazines from the U.S. and Canada, corporate annual reports, Wall Street analysts' reports (from the *Investext* database), registration statements for new stock offerings, market research reports, and stories from *COMLINE*, a Japanese news service. Predicasts also adds selected abstracts from two of its own industry-specific databases, the *Marketing and Advertising Reference Service (MARS)*, and *Aerospace/Defense Markets and Technology*. The most recent enhancement to *PTS PROMT* is the addition of the complete text of articles from selected journals. At present, about 150 titles are represented, but the number is growing. Keywords in the text are not searchable, but users can display or print the complete article. To provide keyword access, Predicasts compiles abstracts or verbatim extracts for those articles reproduced in full.

Because *PTS PROMT* is so large and contains information from so many sources, it is frequently referred to as a "megafile." The database now holds approximately two million records, with some 200,000 more added per year. The size of the file can also be a hindrance, slowing response time and retrieving unwanted information. To counteract these obstacles, searchers can specify publication type, effectively omitting abstracts from annual reports, press releases, or other irrelevant categories. Predicasts also distinguishes between major and minor descriptors in its indexing, so results can be limited to articles with more extensive coverage of the topic. Traditional limiting devices such as language, publication date or year, and country can also be employed.

PTS PROMT has powerful searching capabilities. Users can identify articles by company name; by company codes such as DUNS numbers, ticker symbols, or CUSIP numbers; by product names; and by Predicasts's extensive product codes. Two other important search

devices are by event code and special feature. Event codes identify the type of activity being discussed in the article, from use of resources to marketing procedures. The codes are reasonably detailed and bring enormous versatility to a search. The special features code identifies articles with a particular focus, such as those presenting detailed statistical tables or providing information on a single company. For example, a searcher on the DIALOG system looking for worldwide statistics on sales of medical lasers could build any of the following components into the search strategy:

PC=3832848 (the product code for medical lasers)
EC=65 (the event code for sales and consumption)
CC=0 W (the geographic code for the world)
SF=Table(identifies articles with statistical tables as a special
    feature)

Exhibit 5-3 represents two of the records retrieved employing several of the search statements cited above. The first is a summary of a statistical table appearing in an industry newsletter; the second is a summary of a market research report sold for $1,895. Notice how detailed the second abstract is, including the generous use of numerical information. The article from *Laser Focus World* actually contained four additional tables and each one received a separate abstract in *PTS PROMT*. Searchers will encounter some duplication, with five abstracts describing the same article; however, the five taken together can serve as a reasonable substitute for the original article. A related problem is that both *Predicasts F&S* and *PROMT* index brief news items appearing in journals. Because article length is not indicated in the citation, users can be misled by a particularly promising citation or abstract. The problem is ameliorated now that many articles are reproduced online in full.

PTS PROMT is updated daily, making it an incredibly current source of information. It is an enormous file covering virtually every industry, and representing a variety of information sources. Detailed abstracts are coupled with extensive search codes to enable very precise retrieval. For most online searches, it is best to begin with *PTS PROMT* before moving to smaller, more specialized Predicasts files, including *Predicasts F&S*.

The *PTS PROMT* database is not available on CD-ROM in its entirety, but two disk products offer selected *PTS PROMT* records. *CD/Corporate*, a member of the Lotus One Source family, offers selected current *PTS PROMT* records for the companies and industries it covers. The second optical product is *F&S Index Plus Text*, described above.

EXHIBIT 5-3. *PTS PROMT*

```
                                                        02180084
World markets for medical lasers by application 1980-1992
     Laser Focus World    April, 1989    p. 61
     ISSN: 0740-2511

     World: Medical lasers sales ($ mil)
                              1988        1990        1992
Surgical
  Nonophthalmic              163         200         230
  Ophthalmic                  84         105         120
Diagnostic                    56          67          80
Therapeutic                   34          30          30
Accessories                   53          63          70
Total                        390         465         530
Source: Arthur D Little


PRODUCT: *Lasers for Medicine (3832848); Laser Accessories (3832820)
EVENT:   *Sales & Consumption (65)
COUNTRY: *World (0 W)


               ***************************


02560474
Medical  Lasers  in  a  New  Era:  ARGON/KRYPTON  LASER MARKET: Revenue and
  Revenue Growth Rates
     Research Studies-MIRC    July 28, 1989    p. IV-34+

     The  argon-krypton  laser market was a significant one in 1985. At that
time,  physicians  were satisfied with purchasing a laser that offered both
the  blue-green  light  or argon and the red light of krypton. Revenues for
the laser were at a peak of $11.8 mil in 1985. Since that time, the sale of
the  system  has  begun to slow. Other technologies, including diode lasers
and tuneable dye lasers, have begun to displace the instrument. Revenues in
1989  were  $6.3  mil.  By  the end of the forecast period the need for the
argon/krypton  laser  will  begin  to  disappear.  Revenues are expected to
decline to $3.7 mil by 1995.
     Revenue growth for argon/krypton lasers will be negative throughout the
forecast  period.  In 1986 laser revenues took their most dramatic downturn,
declining  by  20%.  In 1988 it diminished to about 16.9%. In 1991, revenues
are  projected  to  take  a  dramatic dip because dye and diode lasers will
begin  to  take over both replacement and new argon/krypton sales. In 1995,
revenuσágrowtϕáwil∞ probabl• declinσ b• abouʃ 5%/yϩáunti∞áthσ laseϩ becomes
one  that  is  rarely sold. Due to the maturity of the market, growth rates
will  fluctuate  between  (4.3%) and (5.4%) between 1993-95. Occasional
replacement  sales  to ophthalmologists will cause the variance noted among
these  years.  The  compound  annual revenue growth rate for this period is
estimated at (7.4%).      The price of the  221-page study is $1,895.

Copyright 1989 Market Intelligence Research Company, Inc. For further
information,  call  MIRC  and  ask  for  an  office  automation  account
executive.415-961-9000.

PRODUCT: *Gas Lasers (3832811); Lasers for Medicine (3832848)
EVENT:   *Sales & Consumption (65)
COUNTRY: *United States (1USA)
```

PAIS International in Print (Public Affairs Information Service—Monthly, with Quarterly and Annual Cumulations).

PAIS International in Print resulted from the merger in 1991 of the *PAIS Bulletin* and the *PAIS Foreign Language Index*. The Public Affairs Information Service, a nonprofit association of libraries, has published the index since 1915. Although not strictly a business tool, *PAIS* includes an enormous amount of business information. It covers periodical articles, books, government documents, conference proceedings, reference sources, and other publications that touch on topics of interest to public policy. Over 1,600 journals are indexed on a selective basis, including several hundred written in French, German, Spanish, Italian, or Portuguese.

Business subjects found in *PAIS* include the role of business in society, business law, regulatory concerns, multinational corporations, general economic conditions, and management practices. *PAIS* affords constant surprises. For example, every issue contains a heading for "Directories," under which can be found the titles of numerous business directories that have been published either as books or special issues of periodicals. Other useful subject subdivisions include "Statistics" (e.g., "Banking—Statistics"), "Public Opinion" (e.g., "Stockbrokers—Public Opinion"), and "Size" (e.g., "Corporations—Size"). Although not an abstracting service, *PAIS* includes single-sentence annotations describing the contents of most articles and publications.

The index is also available in electronic formats. *PAIS International Online* is offered through DIALOG, BRS, and Data-Star, and is updated monthly. Compact disk versions are available from two publishers. *PAIS on CD-ROM* is published by PAIS itself. Searching can be done in a browsing mode, or two different command-driven modes with full Boolean capabilities. Unfortunately, searching is both cumbersome and restrictive, requiring needless extra steps and permitting no proximity searching. A more elegant search system is offered by SilverPlatter's *PAIS International*. Both CD-ROM products are updated quarterly. The contents of all CD-ROM and online versions are identical to the printed index, including the brief annotations. All computerized versions also provide a built-in thesaurus and journal list.

Many other indexes look at business information from an economic, social, or political perspective. Some, like the *Alternative Press Index* and the *Left Index* (both published quarterly), provide viewpoints outside the mainstream. Three additional public policy indexes are noteworthy for business research. The *Index to U.S. Government Periodicals*, from Infordata International, is compiled quarterly with annual cumulations. It covers nearly 200 periodicals published by the federal government, from glossy magazines to obscure newsletters. Whether they offer insights into the operations of specific agencies, hint at changes in government policy, or add to the debate on controversial topics, government periodicals often provide news and viewpoints not found in other publications. The main shortcoming of the *Index to U.S. Government Periodicals* is the lengthy lag time in publishing. A more current guide to government periodicals is the *American Statistics Index*, described in Chapter 4. Although *ASI* only indexes articles containing significant statistical content, more than 700 government periodicals are covered.

The *Index to Periodical Articles Related to Law*, compiled by Glanville Publications, first appeared in 1958. It covers law-related articles found in nonlegal journals. In fact, beginning with the 1989 issues, it specifically excludes any articles which are oriented toward the law itself. Also excluded are any journals covered by Wilson's *Index to Legal Periodicals* or IAC's *Current Law Index* (both described in Chapter 19). Instead, the Glanville service covers economic, social, political, medical, and behavioral topics which have an impact on the law. Approximately 250 journals are indexed. Titles range from business journals such as *Accounting Review* to general-interest magazines, including *Playboy* and *Penthouse*. It is cumulated annually and quinquennially. In 1989, a 30-year cumulation was issued.

Another unique indexing tool is the *Future Survey*, produced by the World Future Society. This fascinating service provides abstracts and reviews for journal articles, books, and other documents that provide insights on future world events. The potential impact of current decisions and trends are emphasized, as are all manner of speculation, forecasts, and projections. Both descriptive and prescriptive articles are included. The abstracts are grouped into 18 categories, ranging from food and agriculture to defense and disarmament. Strong coverage is given to the world of work, corporate structure, government regulation of business, and the domestic and international economies. The *Future Survey* is published monthly, with annual cumulations.

SUBJECT-ORIENTED INDEXES

The periodical indexes described so far represent major services providing the broadest possible coverage of business topics. Most indexes, however, offer in-depth treatment of narrower topics. Some cover only those materials produced by a single organization, such as the

Business International Publications Index and similar products mentioned in Chapter 4. Others concentrate on a particular form of publication, like newsletters. However, most periodical indexes focus on a specific subject or discipline, ranging from the *Insurance Periodicals Index* to *Urban Transportation Abstracts*.

Accounting and Finance

Accounting is far more than simple bookkeeping. The discipline possesses a substantial body of literature, much of which overlaps with finance. Accountants are concerned with cost control, budgeting, management information systems, auditing of management practices, analysis of investment opportunities, and the impact of financial policies on the organization. General sources like *ABI/INFORM* and *Business Periodicals Index* devote ample space to accounting and finance topics, but researchers will find more specialized tools extremely helpful. Likewise, the banking industry enjoys several indexing sources which provide more detailed coverage than general business indexes. The profiles below highlight some of the best tools for research in accounting and finance. Sources devoted exclusively to taxation are described in Chapter 20.

Accountants' Index (American Institute of Certified Public Accountants—Quarterly, with Annual Cumulation).

The library staff of the AICPA compiles the *Accountants' Index*, a nearly comprehensive guide to periodicals, books, book chapters, special reports, conference proceedings, government documents, and official pronouncements of regulatory bodies. Over 300 periodicals are indexed, covering everything from academic journals to popular magazines. Even newsletters from the major accounting firms are indexed. The scope is international, with representative English-language publications from all over the world. Topics related to accounting are included, ranging from systems analysis to organizational structure.

The *Accountants' Index* provides subject, author, and title indexing in a single alphabet. Subject headings are quite specific, and geographic subdivisions are used. Researchers can look up the name of an organization or accounting firm, a regulation, an accounting principle, or even an item on a financial statement to quickly locate the desired topic. Accounting rules are indexed under the name of the promulgating body and the rule number. Users interested in FASB Statement 87, which establishes guidelines for reporting pension fund finances, can consult "Financial Accounting Standards Board Statements—Statement 87." Under this heading are references to the actual pronouncement, as well as to technical bulletins, commentaries, news stories, editorials, scholarly research, and other publications dealing with the rule. The major flaw in this important tool is the significant lag in publishing. The quarterly issues are usually about ten months behind, and the fourth quarter, which is also the annual cumulation, is even tardier. Those seeking more timely access can turn to the online version of the index, called *Accountants*. The database is available exclusively on the ORBIT Search Service. Despite its lateness, the *Accountants' Index* is the premier resource in accounting because of its comprehensive coverage and outstanding subject access.

Accounting Articles is a monthly loose-leaf service from Commerce Clearing House, Inc. It is similar in purpose to its AICPA competitor, though it covers fewer than half the journals. Although updated monthly, its delay in coverage is not much better than that of the *Accountants' Index*. However, *Accounting Articles* provides short but detailed abstracts for all of its articles. It is arranged in a classified format, with a subject index appearing as an appendix. Users following the latest developments in a narrow field may prefer this arrangement for current awareness purposes, but most researchers will find it tedious and confusing. For one thing, the classification structure is not presented in a single cumulation; instead it is repeated in every monthly report. After six months, the monthly reports are cumulated. Every five years the loose-leaf reports are removed from the binder and replaced with a hardbound quinquennial cumulation. In the meantime, researchers conducting a comprehensive study need to consult several years of semiannual reports plus the latest monthly reports. Subject indexing is incomplete and convoluted. Despite the advantages offered by abstracts and monthly updating, *Accounting Articles* should be a secondary choice for most researchers.

FINIS: Financial Industry Information Service (Bank Marketing Association–Semimonthly Updates).

The leading online database for research on banking and other financial institutions is *FINIS* (pronounced "fee-NEE"). Though produced by the Bank Marketing Association (BMA), it covers more than marketing. Specifically, *FINIS* deals with all areas of the financial services industry, including credit unions, savings and loan associations, insurance companies, and securities brokers. Marketing topics are emphasized, but users can also find articles on personnel issues, government regu-

lation, new technologies, and other concerns. It is especially good for researching news about specific companies, products, and services. Excluded are most articles dealing with economic conditions, monetary policy, and similar macroeconomic issues. *FINIS* provides detailed indexing and well-written abstracts for all stories.

The database is compiled by the staff of the BMA Information Center, and reflects that library's holdings. More than 200 periodicals are indexed, including banking magazines, scholarly journals, industry newsletters, the publications of the Federal Reserve banks, house organs from leading commercial banks, and popular business magazines and newspapers. Selected monographs are also indexed, as are case studies and marketing plans submitted to the BMA from banking students. In addition to searching for authors, journal titles, subject descriptors, and keywords in titles or abstracts, *FINIS* allows searchers to identify articles by named persons, by geographic location, by company or product name, and, for articles which discuss individual banks, by the asset size of the institution. BMA produces a guide to the subject terms utilized in the database, called the *Thesaurus of Financial Services Marketing Terms*. *FINIS* is available on DIALOG, BRS, NEXIS, and Pergamon Financial Data Services.

American Bankers Association Banking Literature Index (American Bankers Association—Monthly, with Annual Cumulations).

The *Banking Literature Index* is also compiled by the professional staff of a trade association library. Although the Bank Marketing Association is affiliated with the American Bankers Association, the two indexes are completely independent. However, they are extremely similar in many respects. The *Banking Literature Index* covers slightly fewer journals than *FINIS*, but considerable overlapping occurs. The major difference in indexing is one of emphasis. *FINIS* offers broader coverage of nonbank institutions, but the focus is on marketing concerns. The ABA index restricts its coverage to banks and bank-type institutions, but gives greater emphasis to general management, regulatory, legal, and tax issues. It does include monetary policy and other economic issues within its purview. The *Banking Literature Index* contains no abstracts, nor is it available online. It is easy to use, however, and the index terms are usually quite specific. Twice each year, the index reproduces a complete guide to the subject headings used, including extensive references to broader, narrower, and related terms.

Another option for banking articles is *The Fed in Print*, a semiannual guide to the publications of the research departments at all Federal Reserve banks. In-

cluded are newsletters, journals, annual reports, conference proceedings, research papers, and other special studies. Topics covered are surprisingly varied, including forecasts of business conditions, studies of the behavior of financial markets and instruments, profiles of regional economies, and official news from the Federal Reserve Board. Many articles are well-written stories of popular interest. Indexing is quite specific. For example, articles about Federal Reserve regulations can be found easily by name (e.g., "Regulation Q"). *The Fed in Print* is compiled by the staff of the Federal Reserve Bank of Philadelphia, and is free to interested libraries and researchers. A final resource is the online version of the *American Banker*, the daily newspaper considered to be the industry bible. It is available on DIALOG, Data-Star, NewsNet, NEXIS, and several other systems. On most, it is updated daily.

Marketing and Advertising

Surprisingly few marketing-specific indexes and databases have been created. The two major resources in the United States are available online only. The third source profiled below covers articles on marketing theory, with an emphasis on U.S. and British publications.

PTS Marketing and Advertising Reference Service (MARS) (Predicasts, Inc.—Daily Updates).

Predicasts conducted an extensive survey of information professionals before designing the *MARS* database. Unveiled in 1985, the resulting online service was custom-made to meet the needs of anyone researching topics in advertising, media, or consumer marketing. *MARS* indexes over 140 marketing periodicals, focusing on professional advertising journals, trade publications in the consumer products industries, scholarly journals in marketing, the advertising columns of major newspapers, and off-the-shelf market research studies. The real power of *MARS* lies in its versatile indexing system, which provides an assortment of unique access points. For example, users can search for articles by advertising agency, trade name, advertising spokesperson, or slogan. Predicasts has designed a special classification system to identify major marketing concepts, from media use to target markets. The system is so detailed that researchers interested in ad campaigns can specify whether they want to find articles on copy and layout, ad testing, new campaign launchings, or award-winning ads. When researching the advertising industry, *MARS* can quickly identify agency profiles, executive and account changes, financial data, and trends in agency service. *MARS* also covers the media business, from company mergers to

advertising costs. The search results in any of these areas can be limited by article type, from editorials to company profiles, or by special features in the article, such as pictures, charts, or tables. The more familiar indexing fields seen in *PTS PROMT* and *Predicasts F&S* can also be utilized, including product, event, and country codes; and company names.

This extensive use of specialized subject classifications and advertising concepts allows searchers to locate specific articles in ways the more general databases do not. For example, someone interested in advertisers' use of older celebrities to convey a "grandparent" image could use a variety of codes, including campaign themes, spokespersons, and consumer attitudes, to locate articles discussing this trend. Then using the named people cited in these records, the search could be redirected to identify specific campaigns using spokespersons such as Wilford Brimley or Art Carney. *MARS* is clearly designed to meet the specialized needs of a particular audience. The file is available on DIALOG and Data-Star, with daily updates on both.

Advertising and Marketing Intelligence Abstracts (The New York Times Company—Daily Updates).

Advertising and Marketing Intelligence Abstracts (*AMI*) is available exclusively on the NEXIS system and covers fewer than half the journals in *MARS*. Despite its smaller size and the absence of many special features, *AMI* will frequently locate articles not found on the competing service. The reason lies partly in the subtle differences of editorial policy between the two databases and partly in differing indexing methods. *MARS* utilizes a highly structured approach, with classification codes for products, events, and advertising concepts. *AMI* relies on more traditional subject headings. The different outcomes can be seen by using the example of elderly spokespersons described above. Despite the detailed codes available in *MARS*, there is no way to search directly for the topics of age, grandparents, or senior citizens without resorting to keywords in the title or abstract. *AMI* provides fairly specific subject headings, in this case using the term "Aged." Other subject headings to incorporate into this search include "Ad Campaigns," "Celebrities," "Actors and Actresses," and "Endorsements." While *AMI* has no special code for spokespersons, the user can search by named persons in the article. Some of the same records were found on both databases, but each file identified several articles not located through the competing service.

AMI abstracts are briefer (generally one to three phrases in length), but they make extensive use of searchable keywords. Most articles have at least four subject headings assigned, and additional fields are employed for company names, named persons, and geographic terms. Users can also search by author, journal title or code, date, document type, and presence of illustrations. Both databases will yield good results for most searches, but due to its size and flexibility, *MARS* is usually the best place to start.

Market Research Abstracts (Market Research Society—Semiannual).

Market Research Abstracts is a guide to scholarly articles, covering topics as varied as consumer behavior and industrial distribution. Strong emphasis is given to research techniques and methodology. Thirty-five publications are covered, including most of the leading academic marketing journals. Selective indexing is done for such nonmarketing titles as the *Journal of Applied Psychology* and the *Harvard Business Review.* The journal list is evenly divided between British and U.S. titles. Because so few journals are covered, only about 400 articles are indexed each year. The abstracts are arranged in seven broad categories, with keyword and author indexing. For those interested in academic research, this is a focused guide to the standard literature in the field.

Personnel and Labor Relations

Whatever the research need in personnel or labor relations, several indexing sources offer a truly multidisciplinary perspective.

Personnel Management Abstracts (Personnel Management Abstracts—Quarterly, with Annual Cumulation).

This excellent guide is a wide ranging index to the literature of personnel management, industrial psychology, and labor relations, with strong coverage of organizational behavior, labor economics, and other related disciplines. Nearly 100 journals are indexed. The editors clearly understand their subject: abstracts are concise, but informative, and the arrangement is logical. Topics are grouped into several dozen broad categories, reflecting commonly researched topics. Examples include "Arbitration," "Employee Benefits," "Job Design," "Motivation," and "Organization Development." An author index is included, as is a supplementary section with abstracts of recent books in personnel management. Detailed subject or keyword indexes are not provided, so unless the topic clearly falls into one of the broad categories, searching can be difficult and frustrating.

An alternative, entitled *Personnel Literature*, is published by the federal government. It is a monthly index to the publications received by the library of the U.S. Office of Personnel Management. Coverage is not restricted to public employment issues, and the range of topics mirrors that of *Personnel Management Abstracts*. A number of differences can be seen between the two. The government publication provides no abstracts, but it does index books and government reports as well as journal articles. Fewer subject categories are used in *Personnel Literature*; many are quite similar to those of *Personnel Management Abstracts*, but others are unique. More important, the government provides an annual subject/keyword index under the title *Personnel Literature Index*. Perhaps the best feature of the government publication is that it is affordable to even the smallest libraries.

For an even broader view of personnel issues, *Human Resources Abstracts* is an interesting choice. It is a multidisciplinary index, with a definite orientation toward social concerns. The index defines its province as "human, social, and manpower problems," but the focus is otherwise difficult to characterize. The traditional subjects of personnel management and labor economics are covered, but sociological topics are equally represented. Articles range from delivery of social services, to immigration, to sex roles in the work place, to cross-cultural studies of organizational behavior. Over 250 journals are selectively indexed, and some books are also covered. Arrangement is by broad classification, with subject and author indexing. *Human Resources Abstracts* is issued quarterly by Sage Publications, with cumulated indexes in the fourth quarter.

Work Related Abstracts (Harmonie Park Press—Monthly, with Cumulative Index).

Work Related Abstracts is unquestionably the most complete guide to the literature of labor relations, but it also covers a variety of other human resource topics. Published in loose-leaf format, it is organized into 20 sections, from "Compensation and Fringe Benefits" to "Human Behavior at Work." Each section is updated monthly, and a complete subject index also appears monthly, with quarterly and annual cumulations. Articles span the continuum from scholarly to eminently practical. News events are also covered. A unique feature is the extensive indexing of trade union magazines and newspapers, sources seldom seen in other guides. As a result, in-depth reporting on individual unions and industries can be found, including a lengthy section on current contract settlements. *Work Related Abstracts* is also an excellent vehicle for locating labor's viewpoint on topics of interest. The abstracts are quite brief, sometimes little more than annotations. Another weakness is the substantial delay in publishing; monthly issues are typically received about ten months late. Still, the indexing is very thorough, and the publication is simple to use. Subscribers also receive a biennial guide to subject headings. Because of its focus on labor issues, *Work Related Abstracts* is an essential resource for anyone doing research in collective bargaining or industrial relations.

Other Journal Indexes

Management is an orphan discipline, falling outside the realm of more traditional fields of study. However, most management topics touch upon other areas of study in some way. This is especially true of the social sciences, such as urban planning and sociology, and of the applied sciences like industrial engineering and cybernetics. For many types of business research, consulting a nonbusiness index may be the most sensible approach. *Psychological Abstracts,* for example, provides comprehensive indexing for all areas of industrial psychology, including conflict resolution, job satisfaction, and human factors engineering. *Communication Abstracts* deals with all facets of communication, from mass media to interpersonal communications. Slightly more than 200 scholarly and trade journals are indexed in fields as diverse as psychology, communication theory, management, journalism, and law. Strong coverage is given to the newspaper and broadcasting industries, advertising, public relations, government regulation, public opinion, cognitive processes, and consumer behavior. *Sociological Abstracts* examines industrial sociology and organizational behavior. Among the topics are corporate culture, occupations, community development, and public opinion. *Women Studies Abstracts* covers current research and opinion found in feminist and women's studies journals, including the areas of employment, finance, and marketing.

An excellent example of a multidisciplinary index for business research is *Geographical Abstracts: Human Geography*. Human geography explores a diversity of topics, including demography, transportation, resource use, urban studies, community planning, economic development, and tourism. Although most of these subjects are also studied by other social scientists, geographers present a unique viewpoint not found in the traditional business literature. *Geographical Abstracts* provides vir-

tually comprehensive coverage of journals, books, conference proceedings, reports, theses, and dissertations. Topics are arranged by major category, with several subdivisions. Detailed subject and author indexing is lacking in each issue, but an annual subject index is available as a separate subscription. The index is also available online exclusively through DIALOG as part of the *GeoBase* file. *GeoBase* can be searched by author, title, subject, geographic location, language, publisher, corporate source, and journal name.

Technical topics such as engineering and computer science can have particularly strong interest to the business researcher. Many indexes are oriented toward technology, yet provide extensive coverage of management issues, company news, and so on. An excellent example of the overlap between business and engineering can be found in *Computer and Control Abstracts*, which also resides on a popular online database called *INSPEC*. Most articles indexed by this service focus on the engineering and design of computer systems, but many deal with business applications of computer technology, from assembly line automation to financial information systems. Conversely, titles can often be deceiving, and promising indexes may have little coverage of business topics. Identifying nonbusiness indexes which might have relevance to business research can be difficult. It is easy to overlook unfamiliar sources when planning a research strategy, but the effort becomes critical when multidisciplinary assignments are undertaken. Less obvious indexing tools can often provide exactly what is needed, but the number of possible choices is daunting. What's more, the extensive use of online searching in the business world has spurred an incredible proliferation of databases. Many online indexes have no print counterpart and many are unbelievably specialized. For example, dozens of online services are devoted exclusively to the in-depth coverage of a single industry. The DIALOG system alone boasts more than 20 industry-specific indexes, from *Coffeeline* to the *Materials Business File*. In the interests of widening research horizons, it is important to move beyond general business sources. Figure 5-A is a list of some of the more prominent specialized indexes.

INDEXES TO NEWS SOURCES

A salient characteristic of business research is the importance of up-to-date information; the ability to keep up with the latest developments is essential. Most of the periodical indexes mentioned in this chapter provide coverage of recent news events, as reported in newspapers, popular magazines, or trade publications. Some, such as *Trade & Industry Index* and *PTS PROMT* even include corporate press releases. Many specialized services also provide timely access to news events. Some offer the broadest possible coverage, others give exclusive attention to business and economic topics. Researchers today can choose from traditional print indexes and news digests or interactive wire services and full-text databases to monitor ongoing events, or to search for specific news items. Generally speaking, the resources described below are easy to use and widely available.

National Newspapers

Major newspapers with a national readership can be an outstanding source of business information. Their in-depth analysis and investigative reporting frequently yield answers not found in other publications. And because they appear daily, newspapers are usually the first to publish fast-breaking stories. National papers also cover their local metropolitan scene. Information on government contractors and high-tech companies inside the Washington beltway, for example, can be found in the *Washington Post*. Prominent newspapers such as the *New York Times*, the *Washington Post*, the *Los Angeles Times*, and the *Christian Science Monitor* provide extensive coverage of national economic and business events. These publications are well indexed in a variety of reference tools. All four papers have their own printed indexes; the *New York Times Index*, for example, is issued semimonthly with annual cumulations. Online indexing of newspapers is also widely available, and several services cover a variety of important papers in a single database. *Trade & Industry Index* covers *The Wall Street Journal* and business articles from the *New York Times*, while *PTS PROMT* offers selective indexing for a variety of papers.

For more extensive treatment of national papers, researchers can turn to three other extremely convenient resources. The New York Times Company produces *Information Bank Abstracts* (or *ABS* for short), found exclusively on NEXIS. It provides comprehensive indexing for the *Times* itself, but unlike the printed index, contains brief, well-written abstracts. *ABS* also covers about 60 other major publications. These are indexed selectively, with an emphasis on business articles. Leading titles include *The Wall Street Journal*, the *Christian Science Monitor*, the *Los Angeles Times*, the *Financial Times* of London, the *Economist*, *Forbes*, and the *Far*

FIGURE 5-A. Additional Periodical Indexes for Business Research

International Business and Management

Asia-Pacific Database. (I) on.
(Aristarchus Knowledge Industries—Biweekly)

Canadian Business Index. (I) pr, on, cd.
(Micromedia, Ltd.—Weekly)

Infomat International Business. (AB) on.
(Predicasts—Weekly)

International Executive. (AB) pr.
(American Graduate School of International
Management—3x/year)

SCAD Bulletin. (AN) pr, on.
(Service Central Automatise de Documentation, European
Economic Community—Weekly)

SCIMP: European Index of Management Periodicals.
[Selective Cooperative Index of Management Periodicals]
(I) pr, on, cd.
(European Business Schools Librarians Group—10x/year)

Social Sciences

Current Contents: Social and Behavioral Sciences. (I) pr,
on.
(Institute for Scientific Information—Weekly)

Population Index. (AB) pr.
(Population Association of America—Quarterly)

Social Sciences Index. (I) pr, on, cd.
(H.W. Wilson Company—Quarterly)

Sociological Abstracts. (AB) pr, on, cde.
(Sociological Abstracts, Inc.—5x/year)

Economics

Index of Economic Articles. (AB) pr, on, cd.
(American Economics Association—Annual)

International Bibliography of Economics. (I.) pr, on.
(Tavistock Publications—Annual)

International Development Abstracts. (AB) pr, on.
(Elsevier/Geo Abstracts—Quarterly)

Journal of Economic Literature. (AB) pr.
(American Economics Associations—Quarterly)

Rural Development Abstracts. (AB) pr, on, cd.
(C.A.B. International—Quarterly)

Public Administration and Health Care Management

Health Planning and Administration. (AB) on, cd.
(U.S. National Library of Medicine—Monthly)

Hospital Literature Index. (I) pr, on, cd.
(American Hospital Association—Quarterly)

Sage Public Administration Abstracts. (AB) pr.
(Sage Publications, Inc.—Quarterly)

Environment

Environment Abstracts. (AB) pr, on, cd.
(Bowker A&I Publishing—Monthly)

Pollution Abstracts. (AB) pr, on, cd.
(Cambridge Scientific Abstracts—Bimonthly)

Urban Studies

Sage Urban Studies Abstracts. (AB) pr.
(Sage Publications, Inc.—Quarterly)

Urban Affairs Abstracts. (AB) pr.
(National League of Cities—Monthly)

Urban Transportation Abstracts. (AB) pr.
(U.S. Transportation Research Board—Semiannual)

Management Science, Operations Research, and Statistics

Current Index to Statistics: Applications, Methods, and
Theory. (AB) pr, on, cd.
(American Statistical Associations—Annual)

International Abstracts in Operations Research. (AB) pr.
(International Federation of Operational Research
Societies—Bimonthly)

Operations Research/Management Science: International
Literature Digest. (AB) pr.
(Executive Sciences Institute—Monthly)

Statistical Theory and Methods Abstracts. (AB) pr.
(International Statistical Institute—Quarterly)

Computer Science and Computing Industry

Artificial Intelligence Abstracts. (AB) pr, on, cd.
(Bowker A&I Publishing—Monthly)

Computer Database. (I) on., cd.
(Information Access Company—Biweekly)

Computer Literature Index. (AN) pr.
(Applied Computer Research Inc.—Quarterly)

Computer Select. (AB) cd.
(Ziff Communications—Monthly)

Computing Reviews. (AB) pr, on.
(Association for Computing Machinery—Monthly)

Microcomputer Index. (AB) pr, on.
(Learned Information, (Inc.—Bimonthly)

Engineering and Technology

Applied Science and Technology Index. (I) pr, on, cd.
(H.W. Wilson Company—Monthly)

CAD/CAM Abstracts. (AB) pr, on, cd.
(Bowker A&I Publishing—Monthly)

Energy Information Abstracts. (AB) pr, on, cd.
(Bowker A&I Publishing—Monthly)

Engineering Index. (AB) pr, on, cd.
(Engineering Information, Inc.—Monthly)

Ergonomics Abstracts. (AB) pr.

FIGURE 5-A. Additional Periodical Indexes for Business Research (continued)

(Ergonomics Information Analysis Centre—Quarterly)

Robotics Abstracts. (AB) pr, on, cd.
(Bowker A&I Publishing—Monthly)

Agribusiness, Biotechnology, and Food Industries

Agribusiness U.S.A. (AB) on.
(Pioneer Hi-Bred International—Biweekly)

BioBusiness. (AB) on.
(BIOSIS—Weekly)

BioCommerce Abstracts and Directory. (AB) on.
(BioCommerce Data, Ltd.—Semimonthly)

Reference Point: Food Industry Abstracts (AN) pr.
(Food Marketing Institute—Monthly)

Chemical and Pharmaceutical Industries

Chemical Business Newsbase. (AB) on.
(Royal Society of Chemistry—Weekly)

Chemical Industry Notes. (AB) on.
(American Chemical Society—Weekly)

Pharmaceutical News Index. (I) on.
(UMI/Data Courier—Weekly)

Miscellaneous Industries

Aerospace/Defense Markets & Technology. (AB) pr, on.
(Predicasts—Monthly)

Insurance Periodicals Index. (AB) pr, on.
(NILS Publishing Company—Monthly)

(AB)—Abstracts available	pr—Printed product
(AN)—Brief annotations	on—Online database
(I)—Indexing only	cd—CD-ROM

(NOTE: Where products are available in different formats, titles are for printed products. Online and CD-ROM equivalents may have variant names.)

Eastern Economic Review. The file can be searched by author, subject descriptor, named person, geographic term, company names, or words in the title or abstract. Searches can be limited by date, journal or newspaper title, article type (editorial, etc.), or type of illustration. *ABS* is updated daily, with records from the *Times* and the *Journal* appearing within 24 hours of publication.

UMI/Data Courier, a division of University Microfilms International, produces *Newspaper Abstracts.* It covers the *New York Times,* the *Washington Post, The Wall Street Journal,* the *Christian Science Monitor,* the *Los Angeles Times,* the *Chicago Tribune,* the *Boston Globe,* and the *Atlanta Constitution.* It is available as a monthly CD-ROM called *Newspaper Abstracts Ondisc,* and as an online database. The online product has undergone a variety of changes in recent years. It can now be found as part of UMI's *Newspaper and Periodical Abstracts,* available exclusively on DIALOG. In addition to the eight newspapers indexed on CD-ROM, online coverage includes approximately 20 other newspapers and more than 400 magazines and journals. By the end of 1991, periodical coverage will double to nearly 1,000 titles. The file is presently updated weekly, but will soon change to daily updates.

The *National Newspaper Index (NNI)*, a product of the Information Access Company, comes in three forms: a microfilm workstation similar to the *Business Index,* an InfoTrac CD-ROM, and an online database. The film

version can be searched by subject only, but the CD-ROM provides basic keyword and Boolean capabilities. The online version, available on BRS and DIALOG, can be searched using various indexed fields and special features. The *National Newspaper Index* is updated monthly in all its formats, though daily updates can be found online through a separate database called *Newsearch.* The online files also carry several news wire services, including the *Reuters Financial Report. NNI* provides no abstracts and it covers fewer publications than its competitors. To counter this deficiency, it offers far more extensive subject indexing than either *ABS* or *Newspaper Abstracts.*

Every conceivable newspaper of national renown is also available electronically in full text. NEXIS, for example, offers exclusive access to the electronic edition of the *New York Times.* A significant advantage of full-text searching over other options is that the user can look for any occurrence of a word or name instead of being limited to subject indexing. And what was once a rarity is now commonplace; the full text of *USA Today* can be searched on four different systems, and the *Washington Post* on at least six.

The latest innovation in newspaper access is full-text CD-ROM databases. Three publishers, University Microfilms International (UMI), NewsBank, Inc., and DIALOG Information Services are presently offering

such products. Article coverage from all three is virtually complete, with the exception of obituaries, paid advertising, certain syndicated features, and similar restrictions. These are not optically scanned disks, so no graphics are available. Instead, the text of articles is keyed in by hand and read in ASCII format. NewsBank and UMI disks are updated monthly, and lag time is typically four to eight weeks; DIALOG disks are issued quarterly. All three systems provide extensive search capabilities, including field limiting, Boolean, and free-text retrieval.

The first title in UMI's *ProQuest Newspapers Ondisc* series, the *Washington Post*, was released in early 1991. Three additional newspapers are due in the summer of 1991, with five more to follow. As of this writing, the debut of the *ProQuest* version of *The Wall Street Journal* is imminent, though it will be sold only to public and academic libraries. The *New York Times* will be available in 1992. Subscriptions for each *ProQuest* newspaper cover articles from the current year plus the two previous years. Archival disks with older articles will be available for each title. For those newspapers covered by UMI's *Newspaper Abstracts*, *ProQuest* disks will also provide complete indexing and brief abstracts.

NewsBank's full-text products, issued in a series called *NewsBank CD News*, are also beginning to appear as of this writing. The *Boston Globe*, the *Chicago Tribune*, and the *Christian Science Monitor* are presently available. An additional 10 papers are in development, and NewsBank ultimately plans 40 more. While UMI is focusing on major national and regional newspapers, NewsBank is also targeting smaller-circulation papers. Initial versions of *NewsBank CD News* provide simple, but powerful menu-driven searching. Later versions will offer two additional modes for more sophisticated searching. DIALOG presently has seven titles on disk, including the *Boston Globe* and the *Los Angeles Times*.

Newspapers devoted entirely to business topics are especially well indexed online. *Investor's Daily* does not have an electronic equivalent in full text, but it can be searched online via BRS. The file is called the *Investor's Daily Database* and it contains indexing and abstracts dating back to 1986. The service is produced by Bowker Business Research and is updated monthly. The *Journal of Commerce and Commercial* is indexed selectively in a number of online databases, including *Information Bank Abstracts*, *ABI/INFORM*, *Trade & Industry Index*, and *PTS PROMT*. The full text of the paper is also searchable on VU/TEXT and DIALOG. The *Financial Times* of London, an outstanding source of international business news, is available as a full-text online database

through DIALOG and NEXIS, and is updated daily. A separate file called *Financial Times Company Abstracts* is offered through DIALOG and Data-Star. The latter service provides abstracts only for those stories containing corporate news or company profiles. *The Wall Street Journal* is covered by many general indexes, from *Newspaper Abstracts* to *PTS PROMT*. More detailed guides to this indispensable newspaper are described below.

Wall Street Journal Index (University Microfilms International—Monthly, with Quarterly and Annual Cumulations).

The Wall Street Journal is widely acclaimed as the official chronicle of American business activity, so the index to the *Journal* is an indispensable tool for business research. From 1958 through 1989, the index was compiled and published by the staff of Dow Jones and Company. Beginning with the January 1990 issue, production has been taken over by UMI/Data Courier, the publisher of *Newspaper Abstracts*. UMI has kept most of the structure and special features of the Dow Jones version intact, adding enhancements of its own.

The new and old versions are similar in appearance to other printed newspaper indexes, with one significant difference: the *Wall Street Journal Index* is divided into two sections, one citing company-specific articles, the other dealing with general news stories. The company section is arranged by corporate name, while the general section combines subject terms, geographic names, organizations, and people in a single alphabet. The general section also uses the titles of some of the most popular columns as indexing terms. Examples include "Heard on the Street," and "Your Money Matters." Corporate name indexing is quite detailed, but researchers accustomed to more specific subject indexing may find the broad subject headings frustrating. However, the *Wall Street Journal Index* uses many specific terms where appropriate. Examples include "Boycotts," "Generic Products," "Insider Information," and "Military Weapons." The problem lies more with broader topics such as "Economic Policy" or "Employment," which may cover several pages of closely printed listings in the annual index. Of course this problem is common to most printed newspaper indexes; the format is designed to allow users to follow events over a period of time. But for those seeking a specific story, unless the approximate date of the event is known, the researcher will need to do a bit of scanning to locate it. UMI has ameliorated the problem somewhat by subdividing the most general terms geographically. Thus, under "Budgets and Budgeting," there will be subheadings for "United States," "New York State," and so on.

Articles in both sections of the index are listed in chronological order. Exceptions include book, movie, and theater reviews (arranged alphabetically by the name of the work being reviewed), and death notices (alphabetized by the name of the deceased). Stories are not indexed under the reporter's byline except for material from the editorial pages.

Differences between the old and new versions of the index are minimal. Instead of adopting the Dow Jones subject headings, UMI uses the terminology created for *Newspaper Abstracts*. For example, Dow Jones listed articles about federal agencies directly under the agency name (State Department, Treasury Department, etc.), while UMI groups them together using "United States" as a preface (U.S. State Department, U.S. Treasury Department). In the old version, letters to the editor were arranged by the letter writer's name; the UMI version lists them chronologically, but provides separate indexing by the writers' names. UMI has also enhanced access to book reviews by listing them by title, then repeating the listings in a second grouping arranged by book author. Another enhancement is the inclusion of a code to indicate whether the length of the article is short, medium, or long. Finally, UMI provides quarterly cumulations to the index, a service not available in the old version. Otherwise, the structure of the index remains the same, including all of the features mentioned above. UMI has also agreed to continue indexing *Barron's*, another important newspaper from Dow Jones. The *Barron's* index appears as an appendix to the annual cumulation of the *Wall Street Journal Index*.

The UMI version does not cite article titles in the index. Instead, listings provide a brief annotation describing the article's content. The annotations are written by UMI staff and usually consist of a single sentence, two or three lines long. The annotations are precise, well written, and incorporate important facts, such as names, dates, and financial data. The old version used a combination of article titles and annotations to impart the article's content. For example, *The Wall Street Journal* has long been noted for its lengthy, three-part headlines for major stories. In these instances, the old index would cite the headline verbatim. In cases of shorter, less informative headlines, the old index would give the article title followed by the lead sentence. In some cases the headline was sufficiently vague, so the staff of the *Index* would create their own annotation, relying heavily on the wording of the original article. However, in both the Dow Jones and UMI versions, the annotations are concise and descriptive.

Annotations in the *Wall Street Journal Index* are sufficiently detailed to provide a chronology of a particular event, in some cases eliminating the need to look up the actual articles on microfilm. Annotations are particularly useful in providing a quick overview of a company's recent history. They can even serve as a convenient source of financial data; all corporate earnings and dividend reports from the *Journal* are indexed, including the amounts and the dates involved. Day-by-day closing values of the Dow Jones Industrial Average are listed on the inside cover of each issue.

UMI also provides online and CD-ROM access to the *Index*, through the *Newspaper Abstracts* database described above. Both versions offer more information than can be found in the printed index, but the annotations and indexing terms are identical. The disk and online services include the actual headline, the reporter's byline, and a list of all subject headings assigned to the article (in most cases, one to three headings are assigned). The databases are searchable by subject, company name, named person, article length, byline, and keywords in the headline and/or annotation. UMI refers to the latter as the abstract. UMI will soon offer full-text access to *The Wall Street Journal* on CD-ROM as part of its *ProQuest Newspapers Ondisc* series.

Another way to locate articles from *The Wall Street Journal* is through Dow Jones's own online database. The Dow Jones News/Retrieval system provides exclusive access to the complete text of all editions of the *Journal* and the Dow Jones wire service (described later in this chapter). Complete coverage of the *Journal* goes back to January 1984, with more selective coverage to June 1979. The database is called *Dow Jones Text-Search Services*, but is commonly known as *TEXT*. It is available as a menu-driven system or as a command system with full Boolean- and proximity-search capabilities. The search language closely resembles the system used on BRS. Additional full-text files on *TEXT* are listed as separate menu items on the database, and include the *Washington Post*, *Business Week*, *Fortune*, and many more. Although Dow Jones News/Retrieval is the only online system providing direct online access to *The Wall Street Journal*, the database can be reached through "gateway" arrangements with such vendors as DataTimes.

A subfile of *TEXT* is also available through Dow Jones News/Retrieval. Called *Dow Jones News* (*DJNEWS*), it holds the most recent 90 days of full-text articles, but cannot be searched by words in the text. Users can select articles from a menu of recent headlines,

or can search by stock ticker symbol or Dow Jones subject codes. Articles from the *Journal* on *TEXT* and *DJNEWS* are both updated daily.

The Wall Street Journal is indexed by an impressive array of reference services. The following list summarizes the variety of options available to researchers:

1. *Wall Street Journal Index* (print) UMI/Data Courier.
2. *National Newspaper Index* (microfilm, CD ROM, and online) Information Access Company.
3. *Business Index* (microfilm and CD-ROM) Information Access Company.
4. *Trade & Industry Index* (online) Information Access Company.
5. *General Periodicals Index* (CD-ROM) Information Access Company.
6. *Information Bank Abstracts* (online) New York Times Company.
7. *Predicasts F&S Index* (print, CD-ROM, and online) Predicasts, Inc.
8. *PTS PROMT* (online) Predicasts, Inc.
9. *Newspaper and Periodical Abstracts* (online) UMI/Data Courier.
10. *Newspaper Abstracts Ondisc* (CD-ROM) UMI/ Data Courier.
11. *Dow Jones News* (online) Dow Jones & Company.
12. *ProQuest Newspapers Ondisc* UMI/Data Courier.

Numbers 1-5 provide indexing only, numbers 6-10 include annotations or abstracts, and numbers 11-12 provide the complete text. Many of these choices are variations on a basic product, but researchers can still select from indexing done by five different organizations. Some of these services only index major articles, but many are quite thorough in their coverage (notably numbers 1-2 and 8-12). Also, many subject-oriented indexes cover the *Journal* selectively, including *FINIS*, *PAIS*, *Personnel Literature Index*, and the *Future Survey*.

Regional News

University Microfilms International publishes indexes to more than two dozen daily papers around the country, including the *Atlanta Constitution*, the *Boston Globe*, and the *Denver Post*. Where published indexes don't exist, many cities offer some type of unpublished access. Although newspaper morgues (clipping files) may not be open to the public, historical societies, public libraries, and even universities have traditionally compiled indexes to their local papers, and many now reside on in-house computer systems. A few libraries even sell subscriptions to printed editions of their indexes. But these alternatives make long distance research difficult. Short of visiting the cities themselves, one has to contact the organizations which compile the indexes and ask them to consult their files and supply the articles. And in cases where such organizations cannot comply, the researcher then must hire a locally based document delivery service.

The best method of remote access to out-of-town news stories is to search full-text newspaper databases. The researcher can instantly obtain a complete copy of the article regardless of what city the newspaper is from. The NEXIS system includes about 20 daily papers in its large full-text line-up. Another service, DataTimes, offers over 25 newspapers, including several from Canada. One of the most complete full-text services is VU/TEXT, which boasts over 45 daily papers. Though VU/TEXT is owned by Knight-Ridder, Inc., many of its offerings are not Knight-Ridder papers. All of the papers are updated within 72 hours of publication, many within 24 hours. The user can search all papers simultaneously, a group of files within a geographic region, or a single newspaper. Since DIALOG was acquired by Knight-Ridder, the company has begun adding full-text newspapers to that system as well. There are 28 titles available on DIALOG as of this writing, with plans to add one or two per month until all VU/TEXT titles are available. They can be searched individually or in the combined *Papers* file. The advantage of using DIALOG is its more sophisticated capabilities.

An enormous amount of business news never makes the daily papers. Local business events are also covered by regional business periodicals, most of which are published weekly or monthly. Magazines like *New England Business* and newspapers like *Crain's Chicago Business* closely follow the local scene. In addition to news briefs, these publications typically include biographies of prominent executives, company profiles, surveys of the local economy, and even ranked lists of major businesses. Several indexing services provide coverage of these sources, including the *Business Index, Trade & Industry Index*, and *PTS PROMT*. Full-text services are found in a variety of formats. Both NEXIS and VU/ TEXT provide business papers among their selections. The two most wide-ranging sources of regional news are described below; both act as selective "clipping services."

Business Dateline (UMI/Data Courier—Weekly Updates).

With more than 150 publications, the most extensive full-text coverage of regional business publications online can be found on *Business Dateline*. In addition to regional business periodicals, several wire services and daily newspapers are covered, including the *Christian Science Monitor* and the *Washington Post*. The database does not reproduce stories from every periodical cover-to-cover, but concentrates on substantive articles with information on local companies, industries, executives, or business conditions.

Business Dateline utilizes the same search features found on *ABI/INFORM*, including Data Courier's descriptor terms, industry codes, and management function codes. Numerous other access points have been created for this file, including SIC number, dateline, company location, and region of the country. And because the complete articles are reproduced online, the user can search for words in the text. The database can be found on seven major systems, including DIALOG, BRS, Dow Jones, NEXIS, and VU/TEXT. A CD-ROM version of the database, *Business Dateline Ondisc*, contains stories dating back to 1985, and monthly updates are provided. Unlike UMI's *Business Periodicals Ondisc*, this is not a complete reproduction of all the journals, replete with graphics. *Business Dateline Ondisc* provides the text only, in ASCII format, just like the online version.

Business NewsBank Index (NewsBank, Inc.—Monthly, with Quarterly and Annual Cumulations).

Selected business stories from local papers are also available on a microfiche collection called *Business NewsBank*. Access to the fiche is provided through the *Business NewsBank Index*, in print and on CD-ROM. The service reproduces significant stories from 450 daily newspapers and 150 weeklies. The focus is on company and industry news. In print form, the index appears in two sections. A geographic section is arranged by state, then city or town. Within each location, the stories are subdivided by industry. The second index is by name and subject, including industries, company names, and personal names in a single alphabet. The subject index is further subdivided by type of news, such as mergers, lawsuits, and earnings reports. Subscribers receive a new set of microfiche each month along with the index. Articles on the fiche are batched by industry in 13 broad categories, so users can browse current issues by topic. The indexing is quite good, the system is easy to use, and the microfiche is clearly reproduced. With many more newspapers covered, it is a useful alternative to *Business Dateline*.

A companion product predates *Business NewsBank* by many years. Called the *NewsBank Index*, it provides the same type of access to daily newspapers, but concentrates on a broad range of public affairs issues, the arts, and biographical articles. Reviews and editorials are reproduced as well as news stories. The collection is divided into 15 categories, including health, law, transportation, and environment. Though most of the categories include stories of interest to business researchers, there is a separate category for "Business and Economic Development," where the bulk of the business-specific articles appear. The index itself is divided into parts, with a separate publication indexing all the business-related stories regardless of category. While *Business NewsBank* focuses on companies, executives, and industries, its older cousin covers everything else. There is surprisingly little overlap between the two. For example, *Business NewsBank* will cover stories on specific banks, and profiles of the banking industry at the local level; *NewsBank* will identify stories on national and international banking issues (bank failures, fraud, deregulation, interest rates, etc.) as seen in local papers, together with local case studies. The latter approach allows researchers to compare regional disparities in the way national stories are presented and provides an array of opinions via editorials from hundreds of newspapers. Stories of national importance are also covered in greater detail by the hometown paper where the event occurs. Of course all of these advantages can be pursued using online services such as NEXIS and VU/TEXT, but no online system covers as many cities as *NewsBank*. The tradeoff is between selective subject coverage and wider geographic scope.

Electronic indexing of the *NewsBank* services is available through a CD-ROM product called the *NewsBank Electronic Index*. Separate disks are available for *NewsBank* and *Business NewsBank*, or they may be purchased together.

Newsletter Databases

Business news can also be followed through an industry-specific approach, which usually means industry newsletters. Newsletters often provide more detailed and sophisticated coverage of a topic than trade journals in the same industry. Although some print indexes and general business databases include a handful of newsletters within their scope, the best way to gain access to this important category of information is to conduct an online search of full-text files. Newsletters are important be-

cause they are timely, extremely focused, very detailed, and often contain information not found anywhere else. They can also provide a specialized slant on the news. Many newsletters can be found on large systems such as NEXIS and CompuServe, but two more specialized services are usually the best places to begin a full-text search: the *PTS Newsletter Database* and NewsNet. A special category of industry newsletter, the Wall Street analyst's letter, is introduced in Chapter 12.

PTS Newsletter Database (Predicasts—Daily Updates).

Since its introduction in 1988, the *PTS Newsletter Database* has been steadily adding new publications to its file. As of this writing, over 400 newletters are available in full text. The offerings span a variety of industries, but there is particularly strong coverage of telecommunications, defense, aerospace, and other high-tech fields. Nonindustry newsletters can also be found, including those which track governmental and regulatory developments, foreign economic concerns, and international trade issues. The emphasis is on North America and Europe, but letters from Japan, Latin America, the Middle East, and other areas are represented. The database is not heavily indexed; users can search for words in the text, titles, journal names, article length, and publication date. The only additional indexing is by industry category; every article within a publication is assigned the industry code of that publication. These are not the familiar Predicasts product codes, but a list of 28 broad groupings such as "Financial Services" or "Packaged Goods." The *PTS Newsletter Database* can be found on DIALOG and Data-Star; on DIALOG it can be searched as a menu-driven system or in the standard command mode.

NewsNet (NewsNet, Inc.—Continuous Updating throughout the day).

NewsNet is not an individual database, but an entire online system devoted to newsletter coverage. Established in 1982, it now carries nearly 500 newsletters in their entirety, and like the *PTS Newsletter Database*, continues to expand. Both Predicasts and NewsNet provide strong coverage of telecommunications, electronics, and international business. Some overlap occurs in the titles carried, but each service boasts many unique offerings. Both divide their files into broad subject categories, though NewsNet's are a bit more diverse. And both support Selective Dissemination of Information (SDI) and global search services. NewsNet searching is not as flexible, but online updating is extremely fast, and some publications appear online before the print subscribers receive their newsletters through the mail. Be-

cause NewsNet is an online vendor like DIALOG or BRS, it carries other databases besides newsletters, including wire services, business directories, and financial services.

Wire Services

Teletype reporting from news bureaus has been a long-time staple of the news business, but such services are fairly limited for research purposes. The advent of online search systems has wedded the news-gathering expertise of the wire services to the interactive query capabilities of online databases. Now, instead of being limited to what comes across the teletype, subscribers can retrieve specific information whenever it's needed. The effectiveness of these interactive news wires is demonstrated by how quickly they have become mainstays of the online industry. Virtually every major online vendor offers a selection of wires, and the most popular are truly ubiquitous. News from the Associated Press can be searched on more than nine online services, for example. Worldwide coverage is also available from numerous specialized wires. Major news bureaus like Reuters have always had strong international coverage, but now databases from individual countries can be easily searched. NEXIS offerings are especially diverse, including wire services from Great Britain, China, Japan, Taiwan, and the Soviet Union. Another multinational wire service is International Access Company's *Newswire ASAP*, exclusively on DIALOG. This database presently carries 12 general, corporate, and financial wires from the U.S., Japan, Germany, and other countries.

Several dozen specialized business wires are readily available. Those covering financial news are introduced in Chapter 11. Other business wires present a wider view of the news. The most famous is the *Dow Jones News Service*, popularly known as the Broadtape. Though many of its stories ultimately appear in *The Wall Street Journal*, the wire service offers continuous updating; reporters add breaking stories to the file within minutes of gathering the information. The Broadtape is found on two separate files, both offered exclusively through the Dow Jones News/Retrieval Service. *Dow Jones News* contains the continuously updated stories, which remain in the file for 90 days. This database is menu driven, but users have several search options. They can scan the headlines of the latest major stories, search for stories on publicly traded companies by specifying a stock symbol, or retrieve stories by industry or topic by using broad subject codes. The second file with stories from the

Broadtape can be found as part of the *Dow Jones Text-Search Services* (*TEXT*) family of databases. This file carries the stories older than 90 days, together with the most important stories from the current database. There are two major advantages to searching the database on *TEXT*: full-text coverage dates back to June 1979, and all indexed fields and text can be searched using a powerful command language. Another general business service is *Knight-Ridder Financial News*, available on DIALOG, VU/TEXT, and several other systems. *Knight-Ridder* emphasizes data on U.S. and foreign financial markets, with detailed tables for commodity prices, stock index, and other timely figures.

Electronic publicity services are databases which reproduce the complete text of press releases from thousands of corporations, government agencies, and other organizations. Such services might seem like an unwelcome vehicle for corporate hype, but they are truly invaluable sources of information on companies, products, and markets. They are especially important for providing detailed information which otherwise would never be seen; most print publications only have room for the most significant stories. *PTS New Product Announcements*, another Predicasts database, focuses on press releases which introduce new products or services. Users can search according to company or brand name, product name, or even by Predicasts's detailed product codes. Other searchable fields include special features (whether the release provides price information, specifications, etc.), the product use, geographic area, and publication date. The file is found on DIALOG and Data-Star. Two other well-known publicity files are described below.

PR Newswire (PR Newswire Association, Inc.—Updated Continuously).

The PR Newswire Association is the nation's oldest and largest organization of its kind. For a fee it reproduces press releases from client organizations and makes them available to online searchers. Contributors include companies, labor unions, stock exchanges, trade associations, philanthropic groups, universities, and public relations firms. The majority are U.S. organizations, and approximately 80% of the database deals with business news. Every type of business announcement is carried, including earnings announcements, new securities offerings, personnel changes, litigation, major contracts, and new products. The file can be searched by company name or ticker symbol, product, state, or broad section heading. Any words in the title or text can also be retrieved. The *PR Newswire* is offered by Dow Jones,

DIALOG, NEXIS, NewsNet, and VU/TEXT. Portions of the file also reside on other databases: three from the Information Access Company (*Trade & Industry Index*, the *National Newspaper Index*, and *Newswire ASAP*) and the above-mentioned *PTS New Product Announcements*. The Information Access Company now includes the complete text of news releases from *PR Newswire* on its new CD-ROM product, *Company ProFile*. The disks contain the most recent six months of *PR Newswire* articles in a rolling cumulation, and will only include stories about those companies covered by *ProFile*—approximately 100,000 firms. This marks the first time a full-text wire service is available on disk.

A similar, but smaller online database is called the *Business Wire*, produced by a company of the same name. It is identical in most respects to its competitor; the same types of information and the same fields are searchable on both, though the *Business Wire* provides a dateline instead of a state of origin. On some online systems it is even combined with the *PR Newswire* to form a single file. The *Business Wire* can be found on all the services listed above, plus CompuServe and several lesser-known systems.

WHICH INDEX IS BEST?

No library can afford to subscribe to all the printed indexes which are published, and no researcher can keep track of all the available online files. But do we really need so many indexes? If all the searcher needs are a few randomly chosen, fairly relevant, reasonably current articles, just about any index might do. But if the chosen index doesn't cover the type of information needed, then even minimal results will be hard to obtain. And in most cases, business research requires more than a cursory investigation. For important projects, there are no easy shortcuts, unless the researcher is prepared to accept superficial results. The use of a single index is guaranteed to result in an incomplete answer. Even with access to "megafiles" like *PTS PROMT* or *Trade & Industry Index*, there is no such thing as one stop shopping. No single database can track every important business periodical, and each index approaches its subjects differently. By consulting several indexing tools, the user will almost always improve the results of the search. Some duplication is bound to occur, but many indexes can be used before the effect of diminishing returns becomes pronounced. The researcher alone must determine how much effort is worthwhile and how much information can be digested.

The type of research usually dictates which indexes are most appropriate. For example, when conducting a lengthy retrospective search, an index without cumulations would not be a wise choice. Conversely, when looking for the latest news, printed indexes with long time lags are virtually useless. Become familiar with as many major tools as possible. When exploring an index or database for the first time, think about ways it could be helpful in the future, and in what ways it is unique. Subject matter is an important consideration, of course. For research in labor relations, it usually makes sense to begin with a specialized service like *Work Related Abstracts* before approaching general purpose indexes. Consult such guides to the literature as the *Encyclopedia of Business Information Sources* and the *Directory of Online Databases* to identify specialized indexes. On the other hand, if you want to focus on coverage in popular magazines, then a source like *Business Periodicals Index* or the *Magazine Index* is an appropriate place to start.

If you know that a specific journal affords strong coverage of your topic, a useful technique is to identify the sources which index that journal. Not only will the identified index provide you with detailed access to your journal of choice, it will most likely cover similar periodicals as well. For print indexes, *Ulrich's* is a handy tool for determining which indexes cover a particular journal. For online databases, *Books and Periodicals Online* and the *Directory of Periodicals Online* perform a similar function. EBSCO's *Index and Abstract Directory*, an annual spin-off of *The Serials Directory*, focuses on approximately 30,000 periodicals covered by at least one indexing service. As with *Ulrich's*, the user of the EBSCO directory can look up a journal title and identify the indexes in which it appears. But the *Index and Abstract Directory* also provides a second section which reproduces the complete journal lists from 700 indexing publications. Since one of the best ways to gain understanding of an index is to see what periodicals it covers, scanning the lists in the EBSCO directory is much faster than examining the indexes themselves.

When searching online, the availability of multi-file searching can be an enormous boon. Full-text services such as Dow Jones News-Retrieval, NewsNet, and NEXIS offer global search capabilities, allowing the user to execute the same search in a number of databases simultaneously. One of the most inexpensive ways to browse many databases at the same time is offered on the DIALOG system. Using their DIALINDEX service, the searcher can enter a single query to quickly determine how many "hits" occur in each specified database. In this way, the searcher obtains clues to identify the most likely files without entering the databases themselves.

Every index presents a particular point of view. The effect of indexing perspective may not be obvious at first, but it can have a significant impact on research results. Take the case of the person seeking journal articles on home equity loans. *The Fed in Print* might emphasize the economic impact of this type of loan—how it affects consumer spending, savings rates, the money supply, or the construction industry. *FINIS* might stress the demand for such loans, the variety of loan packages available, and how banks are promoting these instruments. *Readers' Guide* might focus on personal finance concerns—articles explaining what a home equity line of credit is, how to obtain one, and whether it's a sensible way to borrow money.

Even when two periodical indexes (whether they be online databases or printed products) appear virtually identical in major respects, experienced researchers quickly learn that one is never better than another for all purposes. Throughout this chapter, many similar pairs of indexes have been introduced; in most comparisons, an obvious superiority is not apparent. Depending on the topic at hand, one may be better in a certain situation, while a competing index will be preferred in another. It is far more likely, however, that both sources will contribute unique elements to a search. Where comprehensive results are important, a thorough checking of all of the most relevant publications is worth the additional effort.

To demonstrate the point, compare the performance of the *Business Index* to that of the *Business Periodicals Index* in a specific search. As we have seen, the two are similar in many ways. To find articles on corruption in federal defense contracting, either index would be a reasonable selection. Consulting *Business Periodicals Index*, the user finds a subject heading for "U.S. Department of Defense—Contracts and Procurement," but no subdivisions for fraud or corruption. Taking another approach, the searcher locates a heading for "Government Contracts—Fraud." Neither heading is exactly what is wanted, but scanning both will result in a suitable number of relevant articles.

The *Business Index* uses the more popular phrase "Defense Contracts." Numerous subdivisions are found under this heading, and several are pertinent, including "—Crime," "—Corruption," "—Ethical Aspects," and "—Investigations." The greatest number of relevant articles turn up under the latter subdivision, but the others are also worthwhile. In this instance, the *Business Index*

lists many more articles within a given time span than does *BPI*. But because of the proliferation of subdivisions, the researcher needs to scan the entire topic to identify the most likely categories. The question is whether this specificity serves a purpose. Although one might argue that the four subdivisions connote slight differences in meaning, the same types of articles were found under each. To summarize the results, *BPI* located fewer articles but took far less effort; the *Business Index* identified many more stories, but required persistence to do so. And a casual use of either one would have yielded minimal results; as is so often the case, neither index provided an ideal solution. For an in-depth investigation of this topic, any number of additional sources would prove fruitful. All periodical indexes make some contribution to the business literature, and most have a place in the research process. There are some badly flawed products on the market, but these are rare. The surest way to obtain good research results is to select the best combination of tools for the job. Each indexing source has unique editorial guidelines, prompting the would-be user to ask myriad questions. What types of journals are included in the index? Is the information current? What is the geographic scope? How specific are the subject terms? Are there additional access points important to the search? Does the index offer any special features? Does it focus on particular types of articles? Are abstracts provided? If so, how detailed are they and what facts do they emphasize? As you examine the publications described in this chapter, these are the questions to ask.

The quality of any index is dependent on the intellectual decisions made by its compilers. The selection of indexing terms, the writing of abstracts, and even the choice of which publications to include will largely determine how well the researcher can use a particular tool. Computerized databases may result in more successful results because they offer greater flexibility (searching for keywords in a title or abstract, for example), but even electronic indexes have their weaknesses. However, as more full-text databases become available online and on CD-ROM, the problems of dealing with bibliographic structures of human design can be by-passed. Full-text products offer options which were unimagined in years past. In a sense, the complete document now becomes its own index, and the researcher can retrieve articles based on the actual language used by the author. For this reason, full-text databases should be included in any discussion of indexing services. Whether the database consists of a single journal or an extensive collection of periodicals, it should be viewed as an alternative to the more traditional bibliographic tools.

That is not to say that full-text searching presents no problems of its own, or that subject searching in an index can often result in faster, better outcomes. But business researchers now have many more resources at their disposal. As information technology continues to advance at an accelerating rate, the choices available in a typical research project will increase proportionately. In the future, the present arsenal of research tools may become obsolete, replaced by all-encompassing data banks driven by artificial intelligence programs. Until that day arrives, the researcher's best resources are experience, ingenuity, and diligence.

FOR FURTHER READING

Periodical indexes, especially those available online or in CD-ROM format, are among the most frequently reviewed reference products. The sampling of reviews included here has been selected to emphasize important points regarding the various types of indexes and abstracts, to give the reader a sense of how such products should be evaluated, and to provide a taste of the incredible diversity of periodical indexes on the market today.

Periodical Indexes

Bursuk, Barbara. "A Comparison of Online Marketing and Advertising Sources: AMI and MARS." *Database* 12 (April 1989): 72-74.

A short, but observant comparison of the two leading periodical indexes in marketing, stressing the difference in index structures and how it effects online retrieval.

Ensor, Pat. "ABI/INFORM Ondisc: Patron Evaluations in an Academic Library." *CD-ROM Librarian* 4 (October 1989): 25-30.

A cogent review of this outstanding CD-ROM index, followed by a summary of a user survey conducted at Indiana State University.

Karp, Nancy. "ABI/INFORM on CD-ROM: How Does the Disk Stack Up?" In *Proceedings of the Ninth National Online Meeting, 1988.* (Medford, NJ: Learned Information, 1988): 141-48.

An expert and thorough comparison of *ABI's* CD-ROM and online formats. Although this review treats an earlier version of the CD software than the Ensor article, the pertinent changes in the later version are fairly minor.

Kroeger, Marie. "Using UnCover (Article Access) in a University Library." *Reference Services Review* 18 (Winter 1990): 69-76.

Describes *UnCover*, a massive electronic file based on the tables of contents from nearly 10,000 periodicals of all types. The database is available online through CARL (the

Colorado Alliance of Research Libraries) and is updated with remarkable speed. Users can search by keywords in the journal title, article title, or article annotation. They may also view the complete tables of contents from a particular issue of a periodical. Although the search capabilities are somewhat limited, the enormous scope and rapid updating make this an attractive alternative to more traditional periodical indexes.

Ojala, Marydee. "Business Periodicals Index and ABI/INFORM." *Database* 10 (December 1987): 70-72.

Another article which illustrates the importance of indexing structure in seemingly similar periodical indexes. Of course there are also significant differences in content between these two well-known resources, and Ojala captures the salient features of each with her characteristic brevity and verve.

———. "Predicasts Casts a Wide Net." *Online* 14 (July 1990): 73-77.

Keeping up with the latest changes to the ever-growing *PTS PROMT* database is a full-time job. Even describing the wide range of unrelated sources covered by *PTS PROMT* is a challenging task. One of the most recent efforts is this update by an astute observer of the online scene.

Reid, Richard C. "Reflections on an Electronic Ball of String: Changes in PROMT." *Database* 10 (October 1987): 48-62.

This lengthy piece was the first to analyze *PTS PROMT* after it became a so-called "megafile." The database has undergone many subsequent changes, but here is an overview of many of the most important components of this indispensable file. Also compares search results of *PTS PROMT* with those of another megafile—*Trade & Industry Index*.

Shorthill, Rachel R. "Unexpected Online Sources for Business Information." *Online* 9 (January 1985): 68-78.

Many nonbusiness files contain excellent business references. The author examines *PsychINFO*, *ERIC*, *Health Planning & Administration*, and *PAIS* for coverage of business topics. A large body of business-related articles was found in each, and many items were not duplicated in other databases. A complete list of the business journals indexed in the four databases is given.

News Services

Jaffurs, Alexa. "Newspapers on CD-ROM: Timely Access to Current Events." *Laserdisk Professional* 2 (May 1989): 19-26.

A point-by-point comparison of the *National Newspaper Index*, *Newspaper Abstracts Ondisc*, and the *Newsbank Electronic Index*.

Kubli, Mary K. "Choices in Online Newsletter Retrieval: NewsNet Versus the PTS Newsletter Database." *Database* 12 (February 1989): 39-46.

A comparative review of the two major full-text databases for business-related newsletters.

Ojala, Marydee. "Business Information on Newswires—Why Wire Watchers Watch All Wires." *Online* 12 (July 1988): 75-79.

This article identifies the problems inherent in using online wire services. Discusses the various search strategies necessary when using different wires, the propensity for many wire services to reside within larger databases, and other concerns.

———. "Newspaper Databases—The Abstract and Index Approach." *Online* 13 (January 1989): 90-97.

Despite the increasing popularity of full-text newspaper databases, the more traditional online indexes and abstracts offer certain advantages to searchers. Ojala compares the online versions of the *National Newspaper Index* and *Newspaper Abstracts* with the *Information Bank Abstracts*.

Full-Text Retrieval and Delivery Services

Browning, Marilyn M., and Leslie M. Haas. "Is 'Business Periodicals Ondisc' the Greatest Thing Since Sliced Bread? A Cost Analysis and User Survey." *CD-ROM Professional* 4 (January 1991): 37-41.

A well executed analysis and review of UMI's revolutionary *Business Periodicals Ondisc*. The central question is whether this expensive system is a cost-effective way to provide journal access or simply a more convenient alternative to other delivery modes. The authors examined the per-copy costs of operating the system, explored options for underwriting the cost, and studied the use of the system in their library. In addition to reporting the results of the study, the article provides an extremely balanced summary of the system's strengths and weaknesses.

Halperin, Michael, and Barbara Ann Holley. "Business Collection and Business Periodicals Ondisc: Streamlining Periodical Retrieval." *Database* 12 (December 1989): 28-43.

An earlier look at *BPO* compares it to IAC's full-text microfilm system. The article highlights an important point for librarians and researchers—a variety of alternatives are now available for full-text article retrieval and delivery.

Pagell, Ruth. "Searching Full-Text Periodicals: How Full Is Full?" *Database* 10 (October 1987): 33-36.

The author points out the difficulty in determining the extent to which articles are excluded from full-text files. Surprisingly, the contents of the same database may vary from one vendor's system to another. Although the article is now a few years old, the general points made are still valid today.

PART III
Information about Companies

CHAPTER 6
National Business Directories

TOPICS COVERED

1. Content of Business Directories
2. How Businesses Are Organized
   a. Companies Versus Corporations
   b. Corporate Affiliations
   c. Company Management
3. Directories of Leading Firms
4. Comprehensive National Directories
5. Guides to Manufacturing Firms
6. Research Strategies
   a. Problems Encountered Using Directories
   b. Ready-Reference Searches
   c. Detailed Company Research
7. For Further Reading

MAJOR SOURCES DISCUSSED

- *Standard & Poor's Register of Corporations, Executives and Industries*
- *Million Dollar Directory*
- *Standard Directory of Advertisers*
- *Ward's Business Directory of U.S. Private and Public Companies*
- *Macmillan Directory of Leading Private Companies*
- *Online Information Network*
- *Dun's Electronic Business Directory*
- *Dun's Market Identifiers*
- *Dun's Business Identification Service*
- *Trinet U.S. Businesses*
- *U.S. Manufacturers Directory*
- *Reference Book of Manufacturers*
- *Thomas Register of American Manufacturers*

One of the largest categories of business research is the investigation of companies. Whether the information sought is for in-depth analysis or a simple address query, the first recourse is usually a business directory. Familiarity with directory sources is the key to using them well. The sources described in this chapter are among the most commonly used guides to general company information in the United States. Chapter 7 will introduce more specialized directories.

CONTENT OF BUSINESS DIRECTORIES

Company directories may vary considerably in scope, degree of coverage, and form of organization, but they possess certain similarities. Most directories provide access in at least two of the following three ways: company name, geographic location, and product or industry. Directories can be published by commercial firms, associations, or government agencies, and can range in price from nominal to prohibitively expensive.

Business directories are intended primarily as location guides, directing the user to a name, address, or phone number. Most publications also provide additional information: names of key executives, descriptions of products or services, ballpark measures of the company's size, and similar characteristics. Some directories indicate whether a company is owned by another firm, whether it is publicly traded, when it was founded, or even what other companies provide its principal services (e.g., the name of its bank, advertising agency, or the type of computer it uses).

Directories can do more than answer location questions. They can be used to verify the spelling of company and executive names, identify officers in specific positions, determine what a company does, find a list of product names, or track down corporate name changes. Directories are used by the nonbusiness community to make consumer complaints, prepare for a job search, order replacement parts for household products, or raise funds for nonprofit organizations. In the business world, directories are essential for compiling lists of companies that meet desired qualifications—the largest companies in a geographic area, the manufacturers of a given product, the leaders in a specific industry. Lists like these can be used to solicit customers, seek out potential suppliers, identify the competition, assess merger candidates, attract new companies to the area, or conduct market research on a city.

How are business directories compiled? Publishers usually send questionnaires to the companies to be listed. In most instances, it is beneficial for a company to appear in a widely used directory. Inclusion is usually free to the listed company, although there may be a fee for such additional coverage as a boldface heading, a company logo, or advertising. Alert marketing managers make sure their firms are listed, and some advertising consultants specialize in helping clients obtain directory coverage. Some directory publishers limit inclusion to companies that meet specified criteria such as a certain sales volume or number of employees. Others attempt to be comprehensive, scanning telephone books and mailing lists to locate as many entries as possible. The most sophisticated directory publishers utilize every resource at their disposal to verify and update information, including press releases, news wires, government reports, and direct contact with listed firms.

Directories appear in many forms, from printed books to microfiche. Electronic access to directory listings provides more versatile, powerful data retrieval. Searchers no longer need to know the exact form of a company name, or even the first word in the name. Online databases and CD-ROM directories enable users to search for any word in the company name, or to combine characteristics to pinpoint vaguely known firms. Databases can be searched by multiple variables, so users can generate a list of firms which meet a specified combination of criteria. Many systems allow the user to sort search results to create company rankings by various characteristics, from company size to zip code. Searchers can usually select the form of the output, from brief mailing labels to detailed profiles. Some systems even create customized reports comparing data on several companies in a single table.

HOW BUSINESSES ARE ORGANIZED

To use business directories skillfully, the researcher must understand why information appears the way it does, and how it's likely to be found. An introduction to some basic concepts of business organization will help achieve this objective.

Companies Versus Corporations

Most people use words like "establishment," "firm," "corporation," and "industry" interchangeably. Commonly used business terms often have specialized economic or legal meanings. Properly speaking, an establishment is any single location of a business, while an enterprise is the company as a whole. An industry is the total group of companies engaged in a similar business activity. Banking and chemical manufacturing are examples of industries. An understanding of such definitional differences is essential to business research, and can explain why certain types of information are more readily available than others.

The word "company" is an inclusive term for any type of business organization. A company can be a proprietorship, a partnership, or a corporation. The sole proprietorship is the simplest and most common form of business organization. Any individual may form a proprietorship with little cost or effort. The major legal requirement is that the founder register the business name with the local government where the company will reside. Such an "assumed name" is frequently referred to as a "dba," which stands for "doing business as." A partnership is an association of two or more people for the purpose of jointly owning a business. Registering a partnership is similar to filing a proprietary name, although the partners may also wish to draft "Articles of Copartnership" to specify their mutual rights and obligations.

A corporation is a special type of company—an "artificial legal being" created by state charter, endowed with specific powers, and capable of surviving the deaths of its owners. Unlike a proprietorship or partnership, the corporation exists in the eyes of the law as an entity separate from the owners. In the United States, a business may incorporate in any one of the 50 states, regardless of where it resides. The state grants the corporate charter and approves the corporation name, because no two corporations in the same state may have deceptively similar names. The Articles of Incorporation also authorize the number of shares of stock that can be issued; the

owners receive these shares in proportion to their degree of ownership. The shares may usually be sold or transferred at any future time.

Why incorporate? A major reason is the concept of limited liability. In theory, the owner of a corporation only risks the money put into the corporation; the owner's personal assets are protected from creditors, lawsuits, and other potential claims against the corporation. Incorporation also affords the business with additional means for financing growth. If a company wishes to sell stock as a method of raising capital, it must first incorporate. Not all corporations sell stock to the public; most U.S. corporations are privately held (also called closely held). Ownership of stock in a closely held corporation is limited to a small group of people; the stock of a publicly held corporation can be purchased by anyone who wants to invest in the firm.

Federal and state laws require that certain information on publicly held corporations must be divulged to the public. Other forms of business, including the private corporation, are under no such restrictions; in fact, most businesses guard information about themselves very carefully. Thus, publicly held corporations are generally simpler to investigate than other types of businesses.

Depending how the concept is defined, there are as many as 16 million companies in the United States; even the narrowest view results in some 10 million businesses. Many of these have no employees other than the owner, and many are home-based businesses. Out of this enormous universe, approximately 2 million firms are incorporated. Once again depending on the definition, somewhere between 15,000 and 30,000 of these corporations are publicly traded, so only a very small percentage of companies are required to disclose important information to the public. This means that business directories may be one of the only sources of easily acquired information for the majority of firms in the United States.

Companies are listed in business directories according to their official nomenclature, not their popular designations. Businesses spend a great deal of effort designing, promoting, and protecting brand names and trademarks in order to achieve market recognition. Although brands are usually recognized by consumers more readily than the official name of the company, the two are quite often different. In fact, a company may use numerous brands to identify individual products or services in its marketing mix. Strategies for investigating brand names will be explored in Chapter 7.

Corporate Affiliations

The concept of affiliated companies is another key to corporate organization. A large firm may have plants, branch offices, or sales outlets located throughout the world, and to organize such a far-flung network, it may be organized into divisions and subsidiaries. A subsidiary is a distinctly separate firm controlled by a "parent" company through the ownership of a majority of the subsidiary's stock or assets. When 100% of the firm's stock has been acquired by the parent, it is called a wholly owned subsidiary. Within a single large company there may be a complex hierarchy of relationships because a subsidiary itself can own other companies. Such occurrences usually result from successive corporate takeovers.

While a subsidiary is a separate legal entity, often with its own president and board of directors, a division is typically an organizational device for clarifying the structure of the firm. A division is a section of a company which performs a distinct function or operation. Divisions may be organized by product, territory, type of customer (such as consumer and industrial divisions), or function (such as a data processing division). In practice, distinctions between subsidiaries and divisions are often unclear. Companies acquired by a parent firm may maintain their identities as subsidiaries, or be integrated more fully as divisions; the choice is made by the parent company. In fact, a parent can choose to call an affiliate whatever it wishes. After a whirlwind decade of buyouts, mergers, and spin-offs, relationships among affiliated companies have become extremely complex. Just remember that subsidiaries and divisions have parent entities.

Although "affiliate" can be used as a generic word to indicate either a subsidiary or division, it is more precisely defined as a company controlled by another firm that does not own a majority of the controlled firm's stock. Some degree of control can be exercised through ownership of less than a majority of stock, or through shared boards of directors, substantial loans made by the controlling company, or dominant supplier relationships. To be an affiliate in a practical sense, however, the degree of control must be significant.

Determining whether a firm is owned or controlled by another is not always simple because there are other relationships which do not involve ownership rights. Most are simply marketing arrangements which have arisen due to the specialized nature of an industry. A franchise, for instance, is a series of outlets owned by independent managers, as opposed to a chain, where the outlets are owned by the same firm. In a franchise

agreement, the franchise owner licenses the company name to independent businesses. For a continuing fee, the franchise owner offers the franchisee various types of assistance, such as financing, training, standardized products or techniques, and large-scale advertising. Another corporate relationship, the joint venture, has two or more companies contractually agree to work together to achieve a goal. The firms may simply work together on a specific project, or they may establish a new company jointly owned by all companies participating in the venture.

In certain industries, other intercompany relationships are common business practice. Grocery chains, for example, are often owned by large food wholesalers; the wholesaler owns some of the stores, while others are owned independently and supplied by the wholesaler. These so-called "voluntary chains" are also characteristic of the retail drug business, auto parts stores, and other retail industries. Automobile dealers, soft drink bottlers, and hotel chains are other examples of industries that utilize unique marketing relationships.

The world of company organization is labyrinthine. Questions like "Is this company locally owned?" or "How are these companies related?" can be difficult to answer. Two firms can have no formal relationship with one another, yet have close ties because the same person owns both. Business directories can be extremely helpful in sorting out complex company affiliations, but using them may be only the first step in obtaining a true picture of the company's structure.

Company Management

Another important question is who runs the company. For small firms, this is usually a simple matter, but large organizations have complex power structures. Titles such as president, chief executive officer, chief operating officer, and chairman of the board do not have the same meaning from one company to the next, because the individuals in these positions do not exercise the same degree of authority. Some firms are notorious for handing out inflated titles; a single company may have dozens of executive vice presidents. Corporations also have boards of directors, whose members are elected by the owners or shareholders. The relationship between a corporation's managers and the elected directors can be confusing. In theory, the directors are legally responsible for the stewardship of the corporation. In practice, there are strong boards and weak boards; each corporation is left to develop its own governing structure.

In many companies, even the employees are unclear about the formal and informal authority in the firm. The amount of such information that can be gleaned from business directories is usually limited. A good way to understand corporate structure is to look at a firm's organizational chart. Although this information might seem quite basic, such charts are rarely published and may be difficult to obtain. One of the few organizations which reproduces the organizational charts of major companies is the nonprofit Conference Board. Diagrams of organizational structure for 500 leading corporations are found in the *Conference Board Chart Collection*. Seventeen major industry categories are represented. The publication appears in loose-leaf format and is updated continuously; each chart is revised at least once every three years. The complete service is expensive, but charts can be ordered individually or by industry group. Although the *Chart Collection* covers only a small fraction of the major companies in the United States, it can be extremely helpful in identifying industry-specific patterns of organization. Finally, business directories typically provide information only on the key officers in the company. Important middle management positions such as personnel director or sales manager are simply not identified in many national directories.

DIRECTORIES OF LEADING FIRMS

Inclusion in a business directory is usually based upon the size of the company, a geographic area, a type of product, or a special function. Geographic scope can be international, national, statewide, or local. Industry or "trade" coverage focuses on companies engaged in a specified type of activity or group of related activities. Special purpose directories provide access to information otherwise difficult to obtain, such as by brand name or parent company.

National business directories make no attempt to limit themselves to specific industries or types of business. Their purpose is to cover either the most significant companies in the country, or to supply as comprehensive a list of all companies as possible. National business directories are published for virtually every industrialized nation in the world, and the largest countries may have several. In the United States, a wide selection is available. The directories described below present listings for leading U.S. firms. When information is being sought on a large or well-known company, it makes sense to look here first.

Standard & Poor's Register of Corporations, Executives and Industries (Standard & Poor's Corporation—Annual, with Updates).

The *Standard & Poor's Register* comes closest to being a "Who's Who" of American companies. Published continuously since 1928, it is probably the best-known business directory in the nation. It contains listings on over 55,000 companies, including some 1,000 Canadian firms and several hundred companies from other countries. All publicly traded companies are eligible for inclusion, plus any private companies with either annual sales in excess of $1 million or more than 50 employees. Although these criteria seem straightforward, only a fraction of the eligible firms are listed in the *Register*. S&P's editorial staff exercises considerable judgment, listing firms of interest to the widest possible business audience. For example, international coverage is limited to the largest foreign companies with a presence in the United States.

The directory is issued in three volumes each year: Volume 1 is an alphabetical listing by company name; Volume 2 is a directory of executives and board members; and Volume 3 is a set of indexes to the first volume. In addition to name, address, and telephone number, the company information appearing in the *Register* is fairly extensive, as Exhibit 6-1 illustrates. Each listing includes the names and titles of key officers; annual sales or revenues; number of employees; the SIC numbers that best describe the company; and the principal bank, accounting firm, and law office with which the company does business. Whenever relevant, the directory includes the name of a parent company or the stock exchange where its securities are traded. As seen in Exhibit 6-1, Family Circle is a subsidiary of the New York Times Company, and Familian Pipe & Supply is a division of the Familian Corporation. Contrast these firms with Family Dollar Stores, a publicly traded corporation listed on the New York Stock Exchange as well as several regional exchanges. Although personal names are generally limited to the senior executives, S&P provides the names of the principal engineering, research, and purchasing officers for many companies. The *Register* also lists board members, even for firms which are not publicly traded. For Family Circle, the asterisks indicate officers who sit on the board, while the names near the bottom of the listing indicate outside directors. Finally, companies may pay an advertising fee to the publisher to have their corporate logo reproduced in the listing.

Volume 2 gives biographical information on more than 70,000 leading executives and directors, though this represents fewer than 20% of the names mentioned in Volume 1. Each biography summarizes the individual's principal business affiliation, and the names of other companies on whose boards he or she serves. Whenever available, biographies include personal data such as home address, place of birth, alma mater, year of graduation, degrees held, and professional memberships.

Volume 3 contains a series of indexes, primarily by industry arrangement (grouped by SIC number) and by geographic location. The geographic index is arranged by state; within each state a few major cities are specified (about 80 in all), followed by "rest of the state" groupings. The entries within both the SIC and geographic indexes are arranged alphabetically by company name to facilitate referral to Volume 1.

Volume 3 also carries an obituary section of executives who have died in the preceding year, and a listing of companies and individuals appearing in the *Register* for the first time. A "Corporate Family Index" rounds out the specialized access. This section consists of an alphabetic index of affiliate companies, and a directory of parent companies and their subsidiaries. Both parts act only as cross-references to the firms appearing in the *Register*. The annual directory is updated three times per year in a cumulative paperback supplement, which indicates corporate address changes, personnel shifts, and other corrections.

The *Register* is also produced in online and CD-ROM formats. The CD-ROM, *Standard & Poor's Corporations*, is published by DIALOG Information Services and updated six times per year. The disk also includes information from *Standard & Poor's Corporation Records* and summary data from *Compustat* (both introduced in Chapter 9). The *Register* portion is divided into two files, one for company listings, the other for executives. The system utilizes powerful search commands familiar to DIALOG customers, but is also accessible through an easy menu mode. Both modes allow searching by field, sorting by variable, designing customized output, and creating comparative tabular reports. The online version, similar in most respects to the compact disk, is available through DIALOG and LEXIS/NEXIS. On both systems it is mounted as two separate files. The biographical portion is updated semiannually, and the corporation file is updated quarterly. Both the online and disk products contain information not found in the print version of the *Register*. For example, the company's founding date is listed whenever possible. A field for market territory is included, indicating whether the firm does business on a regional, national, or international basis. The electronic versions also distinguish between primary and secondary SIC codes. This is help-

EXHIBIT 6-1. *Standard & Poor's Register of Corporations, Executives and Industries*

CORPORATIONS   983

Sales: $10Mil   Employees: 60
*Also DIRECTORS —Other Directors Are:
Mary T. Cohn
PRODUCTS: Linen goods
S.I.C. 2269

FALLS CITY INDUSTRIES, INC.
565 Starks Bldg., Louisville, Ky. 40202
Tel. 502-589-1151
*Pres & Treas—James F. Tate
*V.-P—Marvin Cherry
Secy—Rucker Todd
Accts— KPMG Peat Marwick, Louisville, Ky.
Primary Bank— Liberty National Bank & Trust Co. of Louisville
Primary Law Firm—Brown, Todd & Heyburn
Revenue: $42Mil   Employees: 400
Stock Exchange(s): OTC
*Also DIRECTORS —Other Directors Are:
S. Gordon Dabney   Martin J. Duffy, Jr.
George M. Goetz   Shelton R. Weber
Frank B. Hower, Jr.   Edward W. Rhawn
Joe M. Rodes   Joseph B. Woodlief
PRODUCTS: Motor carrier
S.I.C. 4212; 4213

FALLS CITY TOBACCO CO., INC.
1806 W. Main St., Louisville, Ky. 40203
Tel. 502-584-6234
*Pres—Edward L. Friedberg
*V-P & Treas—Norman Friedberg
*V-P (Sales)—Jean S. Friedberg
Accts— Deloitte & Touche
Primary Bank— First National Bank of Louisville
Sales Range: $2—3Mil   Employees: 5
*Also DIRECTORS —Other Directors Are:
E. L. Friedberg (Mrs.)
BUSINESS: Dealers, stemmers, redryers of leaf tobaccos
S.I.C. 2141

FALLS DAIRY DIVISION
(Associated Milk Producers, Inc.)
Jim Falls, Wis. 54748
Tel. 715-382-4113
Div Mgr—Ervin Purdeu
Sales: Over $120Mil   Employees: 175
PRODUCTS: Powdered whey, cheese
S.I.C. 2022

FALLS MACHINE SCREW CO., INC.
680 Meadow St., Chicopee, Mass. 01013
Tel. 413-592-7791
*Pres—Raymond J. Perreault
V-P—Larry N. Ottoson
*Secy & Treas—M. Dorothy O'Malley
Accts— Leo E. DeJordy, Chicopee, Mass.
Primary Bank— Bank of New England, N.A.
Sales Range: $2—5Mil   Employees: 48
*Also DIRECTORS —Other Directors Are:
Leo E. DeJordy   Louis E. Dupuis
W. Harvey Perreault
PRODUCTS: Screw machine products
S.I.C. 3451

FALLS METAL WORKS, INC.
409 Main St., Little Falls, N. J. 07424
Tel. 201-256-1300
*Pres—Robert Vander May
Sales: $2Mil   Employees: 57
*Also DIRECTORS
PRODUCTS: Sheet metal work, deburring machines
S.I.C. 3444; 3541

FALLS PROVISION CO., INC.
521 East St., Chicopee, Mass. 01020
Tel. 413-594-4373
Pres—S. Partyka
V-P—M. Partyka
Accts— Stanley Kuta, East Longmeadow, Mass.
Primary Bank— Chicopee Savings Bank
Primary Law Firm—Cooley, Shrair, Alpert, Labovitz & Dambrov
Sales Range: $2—5Mil   Employees: 34
PRODUCTS: Sausages
S.I.C. 2013

FALLS STAMPING & WELDING CO.
(Subs. Target Stamped Products Corp.)
2900 Vincent Street, Cuyahoga Falls, Ohio 44222
Tel. 216-928-1191
*Pres & Chief Exec Officer—Roy Van Kangan
Compt—Arthur C. Liddy
Oper Mgr—James Spahn
Accts— Meaden & Moore Inc., Cleveland, Ohio
Primary Law Firm—Buckingham, Doolittle & Burroughs
Sales: $5Mil   Employees: 35
*Also DIRECTORS
PRODUCTS: Metal stampings & assemblies; auto parts, pneumatic wheels, appliance parts
S.I.C. 3469; 3429; 3465; 3714

FALLS STEEL TUBE & MANUFACTURING CO.
418 N. Center St., Newton Falls, Ohio 44444
Tel. 216-872-0981
*Chrm—Charles W. Kenworthy
*Pres—Ray L. Hicks
*V-P (Engr)—Theodore R. Ugrin
*V-P (Sales)—William B. Sewell, P.O. Box 397, Brighton, Mich. 48116
*Secy & Treas—Mary R. Force
*Asst Secy-Treas—Clyde G. Hicks
Accts— Ernst & Young, Youngstown, Ohio
Primary Bank— Bank One, Eastern Ohio, N.A.
Primary Law Firm—Squire, Sanders & Dempsey
Sales Range: $8—10Mil   Employees: 65

*Also DIRECTORS —Other Directors Are:
Victor R. Beltram
PRODUCTS: Automotive exhaust systems; steel tubing
S.I.C. 3714; 3317

FALSTAFF BREWING CORPORATION
312 W. 8th St., Vancouver, Wash. 98660
Tel. 206-695-3381
*Chrm, Pres & Chief Exec Officer—Lutz Issleib
V-P—William M. Bitting
V-P (Sales)—Gary Damveld
Secy—John Schiess
Sales: $39.35Mil   Employees: 259
Stock Exchange(s): NAS
*Also DIRECTORS —Other Directors Are:
Bernard Orsi
PRODUCTS: Beer
S.I.C. 2082

FALSTROM CO.
Falstrom Court, Passaic, N. J. 07055
Tel. 201-777-0013
*Chrm & Pres—Clifford F. Lindholm, II
*V-P & Treas—Francis Vucci
*Secy—A. W. Lindholm, Jr.
Purch Agt—F. Tichacek
Per Dir—Y. Alessandrini
Plt Mgr—Leon Juchniewicz
Accts— Demetrius & Co., Florham Park, N. J.
Primary Bank— Trust Company of New Jersey
Employees: 200
*Also DIRECTORS —Other Directors Are:
James Hollyer   Clifford F. Lindholm, III
PRODUCTS: Metal fabrication in steel, aluminum & magnesium; consoles, metal housings & chassis, custom light & heavy weldments, special alloy metal parts, stampings
S.I.C. 3499; 3449; 3469

HERMAN FALTER PACKING COMPANY
384 Greenlawn Ave., Columbus, Ohio 43216
Tel. 614-444-1141
*Pres & Treas—Carl Falter
*V-P & Secy—James Falter
Primary Bank— BancOhio
Sales: $18Mil   Employees: 100
*Also DIRECTORS
PRODUCTS: Meat packing
S.I.C. 2011

FAMCO, INC.
216 Junia Ave., Winston-Salem, N. C. 27108
Tel. 919-721-1500
*Pres—James R. Flynt, Jr.
*Exec V-P (Ind Maint Serv) & Secy—Fred E. Marshall
*Treas—James R. Flynt, Sr.
Per Dir—Ed West
Purch Agt—Wayne Reed
Chief Engr—Keith Light
Traffic Mgr—John Southern
Acctg Mgr—Jerry Wiles
Accts— Bruce E. Hall & Co., Winston-Salem, N. C.
Primary Bank— Central Carolina Bank & Trust Co., N.A.
Primary Law Firm—Womble Carlyle Sandridge & Rice
Sales: $6Mil   Employees: 68
*Also DIRECTORS
PRODUCTS: Job shop metal fabrication (custom); aircraft ground support equip.; ind. maint.
S.I.C. 3499; 3537; 7692

FAMCO MACHINE DIVISION
(Belco Industries Inc.)
1001-31st St., Kenosha, Wis. 53140
Tel. 414-654-3516
*Pres, Plt & Purch Mgr—William Blasi
*Exec V-P—Paul Ehrlich
*V-P (Sales & Engr)—D. K. Loukidis
Accts— Altschuler, Melvoin & Glasser, Chicago, Ill.
Primary Bank— First National Bank of Kenosha
Primary Law Firm—Rosenfeld, Rotenberg, Schwartzman, Hafron & Shapiro
Sales: $4Mil   Employees: 40
*Also DIRECTORS
PRODUCTS: Arbor & foot presses, squaring shears, air presses
S.I.C. 3542

FAME TOOL & DIE CO., INC.
Woodford Ave. Ext, Plainville, Conn. 06062
Tel. 203-225-0800
*Pres—Maryann E. Cichowski
Accts— Eugene Scibek, Plainville, Conn.
Primary Bank— Burritt Interfinancial Bancorp
Primary Law Firm—Weber & Marshall
Sales Range: $1—2Mil   Employees: 12
*Also DIRECTORS —Other Directors Are:
F. Cichowski, Jr.   R. Cichowski, Sr.
F. A. Cichowski
PRODUCTS: Metal stampings, tools, dies, jigs & fixtures
S.I.C. 3544

FAMIGLIA BRANDS INC.
75 Amity St., Jersey City, N. J. 07304
Tel. 201-451-2222
*Chrm & Chief Exec Officer—R. T. Alberti
*Pres, Secy & Treas—S. J. Kronstadt
Accts— Herman J. Dobkin & Co., New York, N. Y.
Primary Bank— Ramsey Savings & Loan
Primary Law Firm—Spengler, Carlson, Gubar, Brodsky & Frischling
Sales: $2.30Mil   Employees: 50
Stock Exchange(s): OTC
*Also DIRECTORS —Other Directors Are:
J. Goldfinger   R. Kanter
J. Mondlak

PRODUCTS: Frozen & fresh pasta products
S.I.C. 2098

FAMILIAN CORP.
7651 Woodman Ave., Van Nuys, Cal. 91402
Tel. 818-786-9720
*Chrm—Leonard Shapiro
*Pres—Bernard J. Shapiro
*Chief Fin Officer & Treas—Leonard D. Gross
Accts— Deloitte & Touche, Los Angeles, Cal.
Primary Bank— Wells Fargo Bank, N.A.
Revenue: $317Mil   Employees: 1,100
*Also DIRECTORS —Other Directors Are:
Allan Shapiro   D. Shapiro
S. Schoen
PRODUCTS: Plumbing, heating supplies & equip. & related products
S.I.C. 5074; 3431; 3634

FAMILIAN PIPE & SUPPLY CO.
(Div. Familian Corp.)
7651 Woodman Ave., Van Nuys, Cal. 91402
Tel. 213-873-5050
*Pres—Bernard J. Shapiro
*Exec V-P—Leonard D. Gross
*Sr V-P (Sales)—Jerry Grosslight
V-P (Sales & Mktg)—Gary Grosslight
*V-P (Purch)—David Shapiro
V-P—Ron Solloway
Treas—Brigitte Ware
Secy—Barbara J. Cohen
Accts— Price Waterhouse, Los Angeles, Cal.
Primary Bank— Wells Fargo Bank, N.A.
Primary Law Firm—Hunton & Williams
Sales: $450Mil   Employees: 1,400
*Also DIRECTORS —Other Directors Are:
John Chislett   Jeremy Lancaster
Jeffrey Unickel
PRODUCTS: Plumbing, heating & industrial supplies (distr.)
S.I.C. 5074; 5085

THE FAMILY CIRCLE, INC.
(Subs. The New York Times Company)
488 Madison Ave., New York, N. Y. 10022
Tel. 212-593-8000
*Chrm—William H. Davis
*Vice-Chrm—William T. Kerr
*Pres—Arthur Hettich
Sr V-P—David L. Gorham
*Sr V-P—Benjamin Handelman
*Sr V-P—Michael E. Ryan
Sr V-P & Publ—Thomas C. Redd
V-P (Fin)—Richard H. Steinman
V-P (Mfg)—Vito Colaprico
V-P (Adv & Sales)—James Fraguela
V-P (Plan & Devel)—Robert L. Neary
V-P (Trade Rel)—John Pfreinder
*V-P (Cir)—Jesse W. Iverson
V-P—David P. F. Hess
V-P—James W. Wall
Secy—Truman W. Eustis, III
*Asst Secy—Solomon B. Watson, IV
Accts— Deloitte & Touche, New York, N. Y.
Primary Bank— Chemical Bank
Sales: $114.54Mil   Employees: 500
*Also DIRECTORS —Other Directors Are:
George Edwards   Sydney Gruson
Arthur Ochs Sulzberger
BUSINESS: Magazine publishing
S.I.C. 2721

FAMILY DOLLAR STORES, INC.
P. O. Box 25800, Charlotte, N. C. 28212
Tel. 704-847-6961
*Chrm & Treas—Leon Levine
*Pres & Chief Oper Officer—Ralph D. Dillon
*Sr V-P, Secy & Gen Coun—George R. Mahoney, Jr.
Sr V-P (Store Oper)—Richard H. Griner
Sr V-P (Fin)—C. Scott Litten
Sr V-P (Adv)—John D. Pleir
Sr V-P (Data Proc)—Albert S. Rorie
Sr V-P (Real Estate)—Stephen G. Simms
V-P (Human Resources)—Terry A. Cozort
V-P (Distr & Transp)—Owen R. Humphrey
V-P (Fin)—David J. Krause
V-P (Loss Prevention)—Robert S. Parker
V-P & Cont—C. Martin Sowers
V-P (Store Oper)—Phillip W. Thompson
Dir Distr & Fleet Transp—Frank Beglin
Mdse Transp Mgr—Curtis Beatty
Fleet Mgr—Calvin Harvel
Accts— Laventhol & Horwath, Charlotte, N. C.
Primary Bank— NCNB National Bank of North Carolina
Primary Law Firm—Parker, Poe, Thompson, Bernstein, Gage & Preston
Sales: $669.50Mil   Employees: 6,400
Stock Exchange(s): NYS, BST, PAC, MID, PSE
*Also DIRECTORS —Other Directors Are:
Mark R. Bernstein   Thomas R. Payne
BUSINESS: Retail discount stores
S.I.C. 5331

FAMILY ENTERTAINMENT AMERICA INC.
22842 Via Cordova, South Laguna, Cal. 92677
Tel. 714-499-5661
*Pres—A. D. Hengstler
*Exec V-P—Ron Stevens
*Treas—J. R. Rodriguez
*Secy—Tommi Thornbury
Accts— James L. Zaccagni, San Antonio, Texas
Stock Exchange(s): OTC
(Continued on next page)

ful for omitting companies which may only be marginally involved in an industry. The computerized products also designate whether the firm is public, private, or a subsidiary.

Electronic access affords all kinds of search capabilities not found in the printed product. Users can identify companies within a specified range of sales; list all the major clients of an accounting firm, bank, or law firm; find out if executives serve on the boards of other companies; list key businesspeople who have graduated from a particular university; or locate firms exhibiting a specified combination of attributes. Records can also be retrieved by keyword in the company name or business description. The results of any search can be sorted by a number of variables, including zip code, founding date, and size.

Million Dollar Directory (Dun's Marketing Services—Annual).

The *Million Dollar Directory* consists of five annual volumes: the first three provide company information in alphabetical sequence, and the fourth and fifth volumes contain industry and geographical indexes to the set. The directory is published as a by-product of Dun & Bradstreet's credit reporting services, but does not contain the famed D&B credit ratings. However, with coverage of approximately 160,000 companies, it is one of the largest business directories in printed form. To be included, a company must meet one of the following criteria: net worth (i.e., net assets) greater than $500,000; annual sales greater than $25 million; or 250 or more employees. Although net worth is a yardstick for inclusion, that figure is not reported in the company listings.

Detailed company descriptions are found in the alphabetic section. Most information is similar to that in the *Register*, including address, phone number, key executives and directors, SIC numbers (as many as six are listed in order of importance), sales volume, and number of employees. Parent company is given where applicable. Features of the *Million Dollar Directory* not found in S&P include: founding date; ticker symbols for publicly held firms; the company's state of incorporation; and special symbols to designate publicly held companies, importers, exporters, and corporations which do not have "Corp." or "Inc." in their names. Dun & Bradstreet also assigns a unique nine-digit "DUNS number" to every company; this identification system has become significant beyond Dun & Bradstreet products because many other business databases now include the numbers in their listings as a method of identifying individual firms. (DUNS is a coined acronym for Data Universal Numbering System.) Once the DUNS number is known,

researchers can simplify online searching in many databases (including directory, financial, and bibliographic files) by merely entering this numeric code.

Several other differences between the *S&P Register* and the *Million Dollar Directory* are worth noting. First, Dun & Bradstreet tends to include more executive names in its listings. Second, for companies which have major divisions, the *Million Dollar Directory* provides information about them within the parent listing. This is because Dun & Bradstreet has always considered divisions to be "branch" locations. In contrast, Standard & Poor's will give divisions their own listings, providing they meet the publisher's criteria for inclusion. Both directories afford separate coverage of subsidiaries, but again only if the subsidiary meets the publishers' size criteria.

The indexes in the final volumes of the set are similar to the *Register's*, with two main exceptions. First, Dun & Bradstreet repeats the full address of each company in the index section to facilitate the compilation of mailing lists. Also, D&B provides a useful cross-tabulation of companies in its SIC index. While Standard & Poor's subdivides its SIC listings alphabetically by name of company, Dun & Bradstreet arranges the listings first by industry code, then by geography within each SIC grouping. The variation gives users a definite choice between the two publications. The *Million Dollar Directory* is physically cumbersome; each volume is a heavy, unwieldy book with bindings that do not hold up to heavy usage. The directory is also more expensive than its Standard & Poor's counterpart, but it is three times larger.

Which of the two should a library or company purchase? Users looking for a selective list of the very largest firms might turn to the *S&P Register*, while those in need of a more inclusive guide might consider the *Million Dollar Directory*. However, the decision may not be that simple. Even though the Standard & Poor's publication is much smaller, it contains many companies not found in its larger competitor, and of course it offers unique features. Organizations that do a great deal of company research, or consult directory information frequently, should consider more than one major directory, and most large libraries have both on hand. For users who prefer the D&B approach but don't need such a massive resource, there is an abridged publication called the *Million Dollar Directory Top 50,000 Companies*.

The *Million Dollar Directory* is also available in electronic formats. The online version is available exclusively through DIALOG, and provides information not seen in the printed directory. Added features include a

differentiation between total company employees and employees at the headquarters location, and a special designation for firms with a single location (i.e., those with no branches, divisions, or subsidiaries). The electronic editions also list the DUNS numbers for parent companies, and, where applicable, the ultimate parent. This allows compilation of a corporate "family tree," showing all affiliated companies and how they relate to one another. Search results can be sorted according to many variables, and tabular reports which compare the characteristics of numerous companies can be designed.

The *Million Dollar Disc* on CD-ROM does not use DIALOG software. It further differs from the online product by including biographical profiles of executives from more than 10,000 companies. The latter data are derived from a D&B publication called the *Reference Book of Corporate Managements*, discussed in Chapter 7. Users may search using a Basic menu-driven mode, or a Detailed mode with full Boolean capabilities. In the Basic mode, information can be retrieved by company name, SIC code, sales volume, employee size, name of executive, or DUNS number. Sales and employment size values can be searched by pre-set ranges, or the user can create customized ranges. The Basic mode can also identify publicly traded firms, importers, and exporters. The Detailed version affords more flexibility and power, and the results of a Basic search can be carried over to this mode by pressing a single function key. A major drawback is that no keyword searching is possible on the company name field; users must know the beginning words in the name in order to retrieve the record. As of this writing, major enhancements are being added, and should be available shortly. The *Million Dollar Disc* is updated quarterly.

Standard Directory of Advertisers (National Register Publishing Company—Annual, with Updates).

The *Standard Directory of Advertisers (SDA)* fills a need not met by other national directories. Also called the "Advertiser Red Book," it describes some 25,000 companies with large national advertising budgets. According to the publisher, these firms account for 95% of all consumer goods and services sold in the United States. Although it covers fewer companies than other national directories, *SDA* lists the most asked-about firms and offers information not readily found in other sources.

Subscribers may choose a classified edition or a geographic edition. The information is identical in both, but the listings are arranged differently. For the sake of simplicity, the structure of the classified edition will be described. Entries are organized according to 51 product

groupings, from cleaning agents to farm equipment. An alphabetical index to company names appears at the front, and two companion publications provide additional indexing. The first contains indexes by brand names, executives, and SIC numbers; the second provides geographic access by city and state. The brand index includes 62,000 heavily advertised product names, and refers the user to the company which owns the brand.

SDA's uniqueness lies in its focus on marketing information. Exhibit 6-2 shows a typical page from the directory. Included are the advertising agency (or agencies) that handles each company's account, and the names of account executives. The company's total advertising budget is frequently cited, together with the amount spent on each ad medium. For example, the Dr. Pepper Company spent $114 million advertising its products in a recent year, more than half of which went to network and cable television. Even where dollar amounts are omitted, listings usually describe the type of advertising utilized, from billboards to trade catalogs; as indicated by the codes on the bottom of the page, 24 media categories are specified. Entries also indicate whether firms distribute nationally or regionally. For companies using exclusive dealerships, the number of outlets is given. The "Red Book" makes a special effort to identify key middle managers not covered in other directories. The emphasis is on marketing positions, but service managers, public relations officers, and personnel officers may also be listed. Brand names are listed in most company entries, providing a more recognizable picture of what the company does. To illustrate, compare the listing for Falstaff Brewing in Exhibit 6-2 with the Standard & Poor's entry in Exhibit 6-1. Though S&P shows that Falstaff is a fairly large, publicly traded company, the name might not mean much to readers outside the company's home region. *SDA* lists Narragansett, Ballantine, and other Falstaff brands.

The *Standard Directory of Advertisers* also contains some surprises. Because it covers organizations with large advertising budgets, some government and nonprofit agencies, such as the Pennsylvania State Lottery, the Salvation Army, and the California Raisin Advisory Board, are listed.

Information is updated through a bi-weekly "Ad Change" bulletin and five cumulative paperback supplements. *SDA* is an excellent source of information on brand names, new products, advertising budgets, and other marketing issues. It is also a sensible choice for smaller libraries which cannot afford the more expensive national directories, and for public libraries which receive consumer requests.

EXHIBIT 6-2. *Standard Directory of Advertisers*

BEER, ALE & SOFT DRINKS

Class. 14B

40319-002

DAD'S ROOT BEER
(Sub. of The Monarch Co.)
651 W. Washington St., Ste. 401
Chicago, IL 60606
Tel.: 312-559-9200
Telex: 206641UD
Telefax: 312-559-1816

Approx. Number Employees: 15
Fiscal Year-end: 12/31/88

S.I.C.: 2086
Dad's Root Beer & Sugar Free Dad's
Root Beer

Michael Flynn (Pres.)
Marie Centenail (Controller)
John Evanson (Mktg. Mgr.)

Advertising Agency:
19868-000
Scott Ross, Ltd.
550 Frontage Rd., Suite 2033
Northfield, IL 60093
Tel.: 708-446-1948

(Advertising Appropriations: $204,000;
Daily Newsp. $2,000; Business Publ.
$5,000; Premiums, Novelties $5,000;
Spot Radio $10,000; Spot T.V.
$50,000; Exhibits (Show, Indus. Films)
$12,000; Point of Purchase $10,000;
Co-op Adv. $100,000; Audio/Visual
$10,000)
(Media: 1-4-9-13-15-16-17-19-21)
Distr.: Natl.; Intl.

14818-001

DELAWARE PUNCH CO.
(Sub. of Barq's, Inc.)
601 Poydras St., Ste. 1925
New Orleans, LA 70130
Tel.: 504-524-5142
Telefax: 504-524-3861

Approx. Sales: $10,000,000
Approx. Number Employees: 10
Fiscal Year-end: 9/30/89

S.I.C.: 2087
Beverage Concentrate

John Oudt (Chm. Bd.)
John Koerner (Pres.)
Joseph Corizzo (V.P.-Sls.)
Richard Hill (V.P.-Mktg.)
Don Woods (Dir.-Sls.)
Fred C. Walters (Mktg. Services Mgr.)

Advertising Agency:
2162-000
Peter A. Mayer Advertising, Inc.
324 Camp St.
New Orleans, LA 70130
Tel.: 504-581-7191
Telefax: 504-581-3009
—Frank Montagnino (Acct. Exec.)

July
(Advertising Appropriations:
$1,000,000)
(Media: 1-2-4-9-13-16-17-19-21-22)
Distr.: Natl.; Intl.

14825-000

DIXIE BREWING CO., INC.
2537 Tulane Ave.
New Orleans, LA 70119
Tel.: 504-822-8711

Approx. Sales: $11,000,000
Approx. Number Employees: 85

S.I.C.: 2082
Dixie Beer, Coy International Private
Reserve, Coy Light Beer, Dixie Amber
Light, New Orleans Best, New Orleans
Best Light, Coy, Coy Marathon

Kendra Elliott Bruno (Pres.)
Joseph Bruno (Exec. V.P.)
J. Michael Bruno (Natl. Sls. Mgr.)

Advertising Agency:
Direct

Dec.
(Advertising Appropriations: $68,900;
Spot Radio $3,000; Product Samples
$10,000; Point of Purchase $5,000;
Cable T.V. $50,000)
(Media: 13-17-19-23)
Distr.: Reg.

46704-001

DR PEPPER COMPANY
(Sub. of Dr Pepper/Seven-Up
Companies, Inc.)
8144 Walnut Hill Lane
Dallas, TX 75231
Tel.: 214-360-7000
Telefax: 214-360-7980

Fiscal Year-end: 12/31/89

S.I.C.: 2086; 2087
Soft Drinks; Dr Pepper, Seven-Up, Diet
Seven-Up, Cherry Seven-Up, Welch's
Carbonated Soft Drinks & I.B.C.
Rootbeer & Creme Soda

John R. Albers (Pres. & Chief Exec.
Officer)
True H. Knowles (Exec. V.P. & Chief
Oper. Officer-Dr Pepper)
John M. Kilduff (Sr. V.P.-Sls.)
John Clarke (Sr. V.P.-Mktg.)
Bill Tolany (V.P.-Mktg. Services)

Division:
46704-002
Fountain Food Service
8144 Walnut Hill Lane
Dallas, TX 75231
Tel.: 214-360-7000
S.I.C.: 2086; 2087

Subsidiary:
46704-006
Premier Beverages
(See Separate Listing)
8144 Walnut Hill Ln.
Dallas, TX 75231

Advertising Agencies:
2695-000
Rives Smith Baldwin Carlberg
5444 Westheimer Rd.
Houston, TX 77056
Tel.: 713-965-0764
Telefax: 713-965-0135
(Fountain Food Service Div.)

3435-001
Young & Rubicam New York
285 Madison Ave.
New York, NY 10017
Tel.: 212-210-3000

Jan.
(Advertising Appropriations:
$114,118,000; Daily Newsp.
$1,962,000; Consumer Mags.
$263,000; Business Publ. $68,000;
Outdoor (Posters, Transit) $559,000;
Network Radio $103,000; Spot Radio
$4,729,000; Network T.V. $32,677,000;
Spot T.V. $30,959,000; Cable T.V.
$2,798,000; Misc. $40,000,000)
(Media: 1-3-4-5-13-14-15-16-23-24)
Distr.: Natl.; Intl.

14826-000

THE DOUBLE-COLA COMPANY
3350 Broad St.
Chattanooga, TN 37408
Tel.: 615-267-5691
Telex: 558-436 DBL COLA CTA
Telefax: 615-267-0793

Approx. Sales: $17,200,000
Approx. Number Employees: 24
Fiscal Year-end: 12/31/88
Year Founded: 1927

S.I.C.: 2086

Flavor Mfr., Double Cola, Ski, Jumbo,
Diet Double Cola, Chaser

Noorally K. J. Dhanani (Chm. Bd.)
Alnoor K.J. Dhanani (Vice Chm. Bd.)
L.E. Shanks (Pres.)
John H. Kirby (V.P.-Sls.)
Karl Sooder (V.P.-Mktg.)
M. H. Sanborn, Jr. (V.P. & Dir.-Intl. Sls.)
Leland Myers (Controller)

Advertising Agencies:
39620-000
S & S Public Relations
40 Skokie Blvd.
Northbrook, IL 60062
Tel.: 312-291-1616
—Diane Shrago (Sr. V.P.)

209-000
ARS Advertising Inc.
1001 Reads Lake Rd.
Chattanooga, TN 37415
Tel.: 615-875-3743
Telefax: 615-875-5346
(Corp.)
—Robert Thatcher (Acct. Supvr.)

Oct.
(Advertising Appropriations:
$3,000,000)
(Media: 1-4-5-6-7-8-9-10-13-15-16-17-
18-19-21-22)
Distr.: Natl.; Intl.

14827-000

DRIBECK IMPORTERS, INC.
57 Old Post Road No. 2
Greenwich, CT 06830
Mailing Address: P. O. Box 4000
Greenwich, CT 06836
Tel.: 203-622-1124
Telefax: 203-622-0533

Approx. Sales: $60,000,000
Approx. Number Employees: 57
Year Founded: 1964

S.I.C.: 5181
Importers of Beck's Beer & Dribeck
Light Beer

Walter Driskill (Pres. & Chief Exec.
Officer)
Thomas H. Schwalm (Exec. V.P.-Sls. &
Mktg.)
E. A. Kennedy (Exec. V.P.-Fin.)
Virgil Abbatiello (V.P.-Sls.)

Advertising Agency:
39021-008
Della Femina, McNamee WCRS, Inc.
(A Eurocom WCRS Della Femina Ball
Co.)
350 Hudson St.
New York, NY 10014
Tel.: 212-886-4100
—Jerry Della Femina (Acct. Exec.)

Oct.-Nov.-Dec.
(Advertising Appropriations:
$6,000,000)
(Media: 3-13-15-19-21-23)
Distr.: Natl.; Intl.

14828-000

EASTERN BREWING CORP.
334 Washington St.
Hammonton, NJ 08037
Tel.: 609-561-2700
Telefax: 609-561-9441

Approx. Sales: $20,000,000
Approx. Number Employees: 80

S.I.C.: 2082; 2086
Brewery; Malta El Sol & Malta Dukesa
Non-Alcoholic Beverage, Milwaukee
Premium, Canadian Ace & Fox Head
Beer

James Penza (Pres.)
Thomas Fatato (Treas. & Sec.)

Advertising Agency:
1397-200
Font & Vaamonde Associates, Inc.
183 Madison Ave., Suite 1402
New York, NY 10016
Tel.: 212-686-2230
Telefax: 212-545-4883

Sept.
(Advertising Appropriations: $300,000)
(Media: 1-2-5-13-14-23)
Distr.: Reg.

14829-000

EFCO IMPORTERS
P.O. Box 741
Jenkintown, PA 19046
Tel.: 215-885-8597
Telex: 240-812 EFCO UR
Telefax: 215-885-4584

Approx. Sales: $2,500,000
Approx. Number Employees: 10

S.I.C.: 5181; 5149
Importers of Beer, Mineral Water &
Soft Drinks, Specialty Foods, Health
Foods

Martin N. Friedland (Pres.)

Advertising Agency:
2251-000
Stan Merritt Inc./Advertising
369 Lexington Ave.
New York, NY 10017
Tel.: 212-867-4650
Telefax: 212-983-5832
(Brahma Beer, Hughi Soups, Zwicky
Cereals, Belle-vue Beer)
—Dick Goebel (AE)

Jan.
(Advertising Appropriations: $100,000)
(Media: 1-3-16-17-21)
Distr.: Natl.

40128-010

**FALSTAFF BREWING
CORPORATION**
(Affil. of General Brewing Co.)
312 W. 8th St.
Vancouver, WA 98660
Tel.: 206-695-3381

Approx. Number Employees: 1,750

S.I.C.: 5181; 4225
Falstaff, Narragansett Lager, Krueger
Beer, Krueger Pilsner, Krueger Ale,
Haffenreffer Lager, Croft Ale,
Narragansett Ale, Hanley Pilsner, Boh
Beer, Pickwick Ale, Ballantine Beer &
Ale

Paul Kalmanovitz (Chm. Bd.)
Lutz Isseleib (Pres.)

Advertising Agency:
Direct

(Media: 1-2-3-4-5-13-15-16-19)
Distr.: Natl.

27509-002

FAYGO BEVERAGES, INC.
(Sub. of National Beverage Co.)
3579 Gratiot Ave.
Detroit, MI 48207
Tel.: 313-925-1600
Telefax: 313-571-7611

Approx. Sales: $100,000,000
Approx. Number Employees: 350

S.I.C.: 2086
Mfr. Soft Drinks; Faygo

Stan Sheridan (Pres.)
Harvey Lipsky (V.P.-Research & Devel.)
Al Chittaro (V.P.-Sls.)
Rick Zaksas (Dir.-Mktg.)
Robert Schmeltzer (V.P.-Opers.)
(continued—next page)

12. Network Radio 13. Spot Radio 14. Network T.V. 15. Spot T.V. 16. Exhibits (Show, Indus. Films) 17. Product Samples 18. Yellow Page
Adv. 19. Point of Purchase 20. Newsp. Distr. Mags. 21. Co-op Adv. 22. Audio/Visual 23. Cable T.V. 24. Misc.

329

Ward's Business Directory of U.S. Private and Public Companies (Gale Research, Inc.—Annual).

This publication has changed title, publisher, format, and scope several times since its first appearance in 1965. Though now published by Gale Research, the editorial work on *Ward's* is conducted by the Information Access Company (IAC). Size restrictions are no longer imposed as criteria for inclusion. IAC identifies potential listings by scanning several thousand publications for significant news stories. *Ward's* now covers more than 100,000 of the largest public and private companies in the United States. Despite the lack of size criteria, it basically remains a directory of leading firms; only about 5% of the listings are for companies with less than $2 million in sales.

In 1990, *Ward's* underwent significant changes which addressed its most serious deficiencies, most of which involved format. Prior editions inhibited access by dividing company listings into two volumes by size of firm. Company listings now appear in a single alphabet. The old format also displayed listings in a tabular presentation, which made it difficult to read and imposed limitations on the amount of data which could be shown. The entries for each company now present more information, using a standard directory format. Finally, *Ward's* is now published as a more durable, easier to handle hardcover set.

Every entry is verified annually through contact with the listed company. Data on publicly traded firms are obtained from the *Disclosure Online* database. All listings include such expected items as address, phone, type of business, and chief executive's name. SIC numbers are arranged in order of importance, beginning with the firm's primary classification. Additional facts are employee size; sales volume; key executives; immediate parent; type of establishment (division, subsidiary, private, public, etc.); whether the company is an importer, exporter, or both; and founding date, where available. A serious problem in earlier editions was the rounding of sales figures to the nearest million and number of employees to the nearest hundred. This sounds reasonable, but for smaller companies, "less than 100," is not particularly meaningful. Sales and employee size data are no longer rounded.

One limitation continues to hamper the quality of *Ward's* listings. Whenever IAC cannot obtain sales figures from the companies themselves, estimates are calculated. These are generated primarily by comparing the firm to companies with similar employment size within its industry. Approximately 30% of the listings have sales estimates, indicated by an asterisk after the number.

Ward's is now issued as a four-volume set. Volumes 1 and 2 contain the full company descriptions, arranged alphabetically by firm. Volume 3 lists companies geographically by state and zip code, and includes several summary tables analyzing various characteristics of the listed companies. Volume 4 offers company rankings by sales within four-digit SIC grouping. The "Rankings" volume will be discussed in greater detail in Chapter 8. The print edition of *Ward's* has become quite popular for its special features, including the zip code index, the company rankings, and the coverage of many smaller firms not found in comparable sources.

Online and CD-ROM versions of *Ward's Business Directory* are also available. The online database, *Company Intelligence*, is produced by the Information Access Company and offered exclusively through DIALOG. It combines citations to recent news stories (taken from IAC indexes) with the basic company descriptions seen in *Ward's*. The service is updated daily. On CD-ROM, *Ward's* data are published as part of IAC's *Company ProFile* disk.

A new competitor to *Ward's* is the *Directory of Blue Chip Companies*, from American Business Directories. It covers approximately 120,000 establishments with 100 or more employees. The publication is a by-product of the *Online Information Network*, described later in the chapter. Listings are less detailed than *Ward's*, providing address and phone; name and title of chief executive or manager; up to three SIC numbers (expanded to six digits); and codes for employee size and sales volume. Access is also less extensive. The main listings are alphabetical, with a second section arranged by state and city.

Macmillan Directory of Leading Private Companies (National Register Publishing Company—Annual).

The *Macmillan Directory* describes approximately 6,500 major privately held companies plus their subsidiaries, for a total of 12,500 firms. In addition to listing standard data such as employees, sales, officers, year founded, and SIC numbers, *Macmillan* is one of the only directories to divulge financial and operating statistics for private firms. Important figures include total assets, liabilities, net worth, fiscal year-end, number of manufacturing plants, and number of U.S. and foreign offices. *Macmillan* also does a more thorough job than Standard & Poor's and D&B in identifying each company's major service providers; users can frequently find the firm's pension manager and insurance company, for example. Basic data on subsidiary companies are given within each parent-company entry. The main section is arranged

by parent company, with a master index to all firms. Additional indexes provide access geographically by state and city, and by SIC number.

To be listed in the *Macmillan Directory*, companies must have sales of $10 million or more. Sources used to identify these firms include the other specialized directories compiled by the publisher, and articles from journals and newspapers. Users should note that *Macmillan* covers fewer than 20% of the private companies which meet its stated sales criterion. Still, the publication has grown substantially with each new edition. Despite its limited coverage, this invaluable source of hard-to-find data should be a welcome addition to any researcher's tool kit.

COMPREHENSIVE NATIONAL DIRECTORIES

The directories introduced above provide data on the largest companies in the United States. But what about the millions of smaller firms? Given the huge number of companies in the United States, and the many new ones appearing each year, no single directory could ever list every firm in existence. However, company databases of extraordinary size are now readily accessible. The directories described in this section, whether in microfiche or electronic formats, strive to be as complete as possible within their defined scope. The smallest one lists 5 million establishments, the largest boasts more than 8 million. Still, even the largest databases fall short of universal coverage.

There is a clear tradeoff in business publications between the number of companies covered and the amount of information provided on each firm. With few exceptions, the directories described below will offer nowhere near the detail found in the guides to large companies. In many cases, comprehensive directories list little more than names, addresses, and phone numbers. But these directories are important because of their enormous size. They are also establishment-based, meaning they list information on individual locations of a company, not just its headquarters. For these reasons, the directories are especially useful for verifying the existence of a firm, tracking down an address or phone number when a company's general location is unknown, and, in the case of online databases, identifying a company when only a portion of its name is certain. They are also an ideal way of determining whether a proposed business name is already being used by another firm. For more extensive research projects, comprehensive directories are well-suited for compiling mailing lists, investigating the size and scope of an industry, identifying the competition in your market area, or developing a neighborhood business profile. National in scope, they are one of the best ways to identify the extent of a company's domestic locations, whether manufacturing plants, service outlets, branch offices, chain stores, or even independent franchises. And of course they can be the perfect source for checking on quick facts about smaller companies. Given their extensive coverage, any one of them is a logical starting point when conducting company research.

Online Information Network (American Business Information, Inc.—Monthly).

The *Online Information Network,* one of the largest business directories in the United States, is compiled by a mailing list producer in Omaha, Nebraska. Formerly titled the *Instant Yellow Page Service,* it is a nationwide company directory based on the complete contents of the Yellow Pages from 4,800 phone books. The publisher's promotional literature boasts information on 14 million U.S. businesses, but data are actually available for approximately 9 million establishments. (Many businesses place ads under more than one Yellow Page heading, so the publisher counts every listing.) Even so, with 9 million records, the *Online Information Network* is an amazing compilation. The source of the data makes this service unique, with information on many establishments not found in typical business directories. For example, professional practices are heavily represented, from dentists to marriage counselors. Listings for many nonprofit organizations may also be found, including schools, art galleries, museums, libraries, hospitals, and associations.

The database is menu driven, and users can search by company name, SIC code, subject heading, telephone exchange, or a variety of geographic variables, including three- and five-digit zip codes. Successive menu choices allow the user to broaden the previous step by adding additional industries or geographic areas, or to narrow the search by combining industry, geographic, and size variables. Information is updated on a monthly schedule as new phone books are received. Two additional databases are available on the system: a separate directory of more than 500,000 manufacturing establishments in the United States, with supplemental information obtained from the companies themselves; and a database of the 4.3 million householders with the highest income in the country. The latter provides name, address, telephone number, and an age indicator (telling whether the person is above or below 50 years of age).

The "Instant Yellow Pages" portion of the database is the mainstay of the service. Searchers can request either a profile of a specific company, or can generate lists of firms meeting specified characteristics. Company profiles cite the name of the firm, the address (including zip code), the phone number, the classified subject headings under which ads appeared in the phone book, a designation for the type of ad, and the year a listing first appeared. Because phone book publishers use different subject terms, American Business Information has created standardized headings for use in the database. In addition, the publisher assigns relevant SIC numbers to every establishment. These are modified SIC codes, extended to six digits for increased detail. The first four digits are always the official codes from the *Standard Industrial Classification Manual*. The publisher also adds supplemental information obtained annually from the companies themselves. Most listings now contain an executive's name, sales volume, and employee size. Every record is also indexed according to sales and employee size categories (e.g., "Code D: Sales from $2.5- to $5 million"), enabling users to search for companies falling within a specified range. When exact figures on sales are not provided by the listed company, the publisher uses an estimation technique to assign an appropriate code. The method is similar to that used by *Ward's Business Directory*, based upon the government's industry-specific ratios of sales per employee.

Like most menu-driven systems, the output options are limited—users can select from three formats for company listings. For a single company search, the full profile is provided. For multiple name searches and for industry or geographic searches, the detailed list of subject headings and SIC codes for each company is omitted; users can then select either a brief format of basic address information, or an enhanced format including sales volume, employee size, and contact person. Search results can also be sorted by company name, zip code, or SIC number.

Subscriptions to the service are available directly through the publisher. No minimum usage is required, but a modest annual subscription fee is charged. The publisher does not participate in telecommunication networks such as Telenet or Tymnet, so subscribers must make a long distance call to Omaha when using the database.

Information from the database is available in a variety of other media. American Business Information's primary business is supplying customized mailing labels and prospect lists for marketing purposes. They also publish some 1,200 annual directories with nationwide listings based on such specific Yellow Page categories as "Health Clubs," "Pet Kennels," "Shoe Stores," and "Chain Saw Dealers." An alternative to this subject approach is a series of state business directories, described in Chapter 7. Customers can also order data from the publisher on magnetic tape or floppy diskette.

A CD-ROM product, called the *American Business Disk*, contains most of the data found online for all 9 million establishments. It is menu-driven and updated semiannually. Records can be searched by company name, SIC code, or subject heading, and results can be limited by state, city, or zip code. Values cannot be searched by range, but users can truncate both zip codes and SIC codes to obtain broader groupings. Once a search is executed, the initial screen provides an alphabetical list of company names, the city where each is located, and a phone number. Users can then request the complete record for any individual listing one at a time. The system also includes an alphabetical index of Yellow Page subject headings so the most appropriate search terms can be identified. Only one record can be printed at a time, an intentional limitation designed to protect the publisher's mailing list operations. Still, the *American Business Disk* is an exciting and affordable product for subscribers who need to perform frequent address and phone number checks.

A separate disk product has been designed exclusively for direct marketing purposes. Called *Business Lists-On-Disc*, it generates both printed lists and mailing labels, and provides the same background information found on the *American Business Disk*. The software to *Business Lists-On-Disc* contains a counter which records the number of listings printed or downloaded. Subscribers pay an annual licensing fee based on the number of listings used, with a minimum of 1,000 names. Screen displays can be viewed at no charge; they are excluded from the pricing count.

Dun's Electronic Business Directory (Dun's Marketing Services—Quarterly).

This comprehensive directory, formerly called *Dun's Electronic Yellow Pages*, no longer obtains its information from telephone listings, but from the extensive records of Dun & Bradstreet itself. New names are acquired through an agreement with the Bell operating companies, but that is the extent of the database's relationship to telephone books. Nearly 8.5 million establishments are listed, and all data are verified at least once per year by telephone or mail survey. In addition to the expected types of businesses, the database contains information on professional practices (including law firms

and doctors' offices), trade associations and other membership organizations, hospitals, and government organizations.

In addition to basic directory information, *Dun's Electronic Business Directory* provides SIC numbers, county of residence, and a designation indicating the employee-size category. Like its competitor, Dun & Bradstreet has added to the value of its database by assigning more detailed SIC numbers to each establishment. Numbers are expanded to eight digits, in a system which D&B calls "SIC 2 + 2." The level of specific access afforded by the "2 + 2" system cannot be overemphasized. Additional features include DUNS numbers, type of company (headquarters, branch, single location, etc.), and a code for the size of the city in which the establishment is located. For medical and legal practices, the firms' specialties are also cited. Although sales data are never given, each record indicates whether additional information can be found on a companion database called *Dun's Market Identifiers.*

In the United States the database is available exclusively through DIALOG, and the records are updated quarterly. Because of DIALOG's powerful search capabilities, and the fact that virtually every data field in a record is indexed, researchers can utilize the file in a myriad of sophisticated ways. For example, one could generate a list of independently owned convenience stores with a single location, fewer than ten employees, and located in a southern city with a population greater than 50,000. The database designates self-employed professionals as "firms." For group practices of all types, duplicate records are generated for the group itself and for the individual practitioners, so searchers will need to restrict search results to firms in order to eliminate the duplication. Search results can be sorted according to a variety of variables, output can be customized, and search results can be summarized in tabular reports.

Dun's Market Identifiers (Dun's Marketing Services—Quarterly).

For many years the extensive company data compiled by Dun & Bradstreet was available only to customers of their Credit Services division. Libraries and nonsubscribers had to be content with the much smaller files found in the *Million Dollar Directory* and other print sources. The most significant breakthrough in making D&B's directory data available to a wider audience took place in the early 1980s, when the company unveiled *Dun's Market Identifiers* (*DMI*), offered exclusively through DIALOG. Inclusion was originally limited to firms with total employees of five or more, or sales of $1 million or more, plus their subsidiaries and branches. In

1990, all size restrictions were abandoned, and coverage was expanded to over 7 million establishments. All listings are updated at least once every 18 months.

Although more companies are found on *Dun's Electronic Business Directory*, *DMI* contains records for all firms for which D&B can verify additional background information. Enhancements include business descriptions; officers' names and titles; date of incorporation; sales volume for the most recent available year; number of employees (both total and at that location); historical data on sales and employment; sales growth; net worth; the company's bank and accounting firm; parent companies and their DUNS numbers; the physical size of the company's facility and whether it is owned or rented; and, where appropriate, the number of customers. Once again, the "SIC 2 + 2" system is utilized. Data for headquarters are more extensive than for branch locations.

Researchers are frequently disappointed by the large number of *DMI* records which have no sales data available. D&B treats divisional headquarters as branches, and it never lists sales figures for branches. According to Dun & Bradstreet, once these listings are removed from the discussion, fully 80% of the remaining records identify sales, and approximately 25% also include historical figures. If information on company sales is critical, you can determine its availability for a given firm without printing the complete record. Furthermore, when searching for companies with particular characteristics, the results can be limited to those records with recent sales data; *DMI* now indicates the exact date when a company's figures were last revised. The distinction between records with or without sales data is somewhat blurred because *DMI* also contains some estimated data (designated by an E). In some cases where actual sales figures are not available from the company itself, D&B feels confident in formulating an estimate. Like many business publishers, they utilize an industry-specific sales/employee ratio, but do not rely on government statistics to do so. Because Dun & Bradstreet possesses such an enormous file of financial information, they are frequently able to generate their own ratios. But ratio-based estimates are only created for industries where D&B has sufficient actual data upon which to draw. This is more likely to be the case for manufacturing concerns than for retail or service establishments.

Virtually every data field in *DMI* is fully indexed, so searchers can identify companies by size, industry, type, location, executive's name, or any other variable contained in the record. Additional characteristics can be identified through a "Special Features" field; these in-

clude whether the firm is minority owned, its legal status (corporation, partnership or proprietorship), if it's a home-based business, and whether it imports or exports. Also, every record links an establishment to the other firms in its corporate family, making it a simple matter to generate extensive lists of subsidiaries, divisions, or branches, or to identify immediate and ultimate parents.

Dun's Business Identification Service (Dun & Bradstreet Credit Services—Semiannual).

This invaluable but limited directory is a microfiche listing of approximately 5 million companies, with an additional one million cross-references from alternate names and dba's. The listings come from Dun & Bradstreet's enormous database of company credit reports, but no credit ratings are given in this service. Subscribers may receive the fiche in alphabetical order, or geographically by state. Each entry gives the company name; address (minus the zip code); and a symbol indicating if it is a branch, headquarters, single location, or cross-reference. The lack of zip codes and phone numbers is frustrating, but once a location is known, researchers can call Directory Assistance, consult the U.S. Postal Service's annual *National Five-Digit ZIP Code and Post Office Directory*, or turn to other print directories. The extensive use of abbreviations also presents problems. First, it is unwise to rely on the *Business Identification Service* to verify a company's legal name. Second, the way a company will be listed is quite unpredictable. Although standard abbreviations are employed, there is little consistency in determining where they are used. Even the first word is shortened where necessary, so it doesn't take much to throw a word well outside its normal alphabetizing sequence. Of course the reason for these weaknesses is the sheer size of the publication. In order to weigh-in at a reasonable size, the length of each listing had to be limited to a single line.

The *Business Identification Service* was not intended as a traditional business directory, though it can function in that capacity. D&B had two main reasons for producing the service. Used with the *Dun & Bradstreet Reference Book of American Business* (described in Chapter 8), it serves as a guide to the credit reports available from Dun & Bradstreet. It also provides a structure for subscriber companies to use in organizing their own records, based on the unique ten-digit DUNS numbers. Because D&B credit ratings are frequently consulted by the business community, because the D&B database is so large, and because the numbering system is convenient, many companies utilize DUNS numbers in setting up their customer accounts. The microfiche

thus serves as a current guide to DUNS numbers for millions of companies. The publisher encourages this usage and counsels subscribers on how to assign their own unique numbers for accounts not carried by D&B.

There are a number of important ways the researcher may use the *Business Identification Service*. It is a convenient source of addresses for millions of companies and thousands of nonprofit organizations and government agencies. Next, it can serve as a starting point for researching elusive companies, especially since dba's and trade names are extensively cross-referenced. While the service tells little about each firm, once its location and true name are known, other resources can be consulted for additional information. Third, since it includes branch locations, it can be a quick source of information on how far-flung a company's operations actually are. Because trade names are linked to corporate names, the fiche is especially useful for identifying local owners of national franchises. Finally, it is a convenient starting place for determining who else is using a prospective name for a new business.

The *Business Identification Service* is expensive. But unlike other publications from Dun & Bradstreet Credit Services, it is available to libraries and to those who don't subscribe to D&B credit reports. And aside from the more limited *Reference Book of American Business*, it is the only nonelectronic directory which lists millions of establishments in a single source.

A smaller, but more affordable alternative is the *National Business Telephone Directory*, published by Gale Research. It covers 425,000 establishments with 20 or more employees. Multiple locations of a single firm are listed, provided each location meets the publisher's guidelines for inclusion. Entries cite address and phone number, including zip code and area code. As with *Dun's Business Identification Service*, headquarters and single-location establishments are designated. A separate section highlights Fortune 500 companies and their larger branches and subsidiaries. This is basically a directory for users in need of a convenient, single-volume source of company listings. Unfortunately, revisions are infrequent and irregular. As of this writing, the latest edition was issued in 1989.

Trinet U.S. Businesses (Trinet America, Inc.—Quarterly).

The *Trinet* database has been constructed using a diversity of sources: state and local government records, news clippings, listings from Trinet's parent (American Business Information), and from a Trinet subsidiary which publishes local business directories. For many

years, the published database was limited to establishments with 20 or more employees, but in late 1989, Trinet added many new records from its unpublished files. Now, any company with sales volume in excess of $1 million is included, plus its affiliates and branch locations. This expansion more than tripled the size of *Trinet U.S. Businesses* to approximately 7.5 million establishments. Every company record is now verified by phone or mail at least once per year, and all listings are compared to the U.S. Postal Service's "National Change of Address" file semiannually.

Trinet provides information on individual establishments, which it calls "locations." For each location *Trinet* lists address, phone number, county and metropolitan area, primary and secondary SIC numbers, a unique Trinet identification number (TN), sales, number of employees, type of location (branch, headquarters, public, private, ultimate parent, etc.), and an estimate of market share. The latter figure is obtained by comparing the sales at that location to the total industry sales of all establishments in the *Trinet* database. In addition to searching these indexed fields using Boolean operators, numeric fields can be searched using relational operators such as "greater than" or "less than," or by specifying a range of values. Basic information on the headquarters location is also given in every branch listing.

Trinet obtains sales data for publicly traded companies through an agreement with Disclosure, Incorporated, but sales figures for all private companies and all individual locations of public companies are estimated. According to Trinet officials, fully 90% of contacted locations refuse to provide sales data, and the 10% which do report figures tend to exaggerate. For publicly held companies and large private companies which disclose total sales figures, the estimated data for each location is adjusted proportionately so the sum of all establishment data agrees with the company total. Here again, estimates are calculated based on industry-specific ratios of sales per employee devised by the U.S. Department of Commerce. This is a fairly crude estimation technique, and the figures are further degraded when respondents provide only approximations of their work force or when an SIC number is assigned incorrectly. Also remember that locations with less than $1 million in sales volume are not represented in the database unless they are related to a parent company found in *Trinet*. This means that industry sales estimates and company market shares are incomplete, especially for industries heavily represented by smaller firms.

A companion file, the *Trinet Company Database*, summarizes information on all multi-location companies found in the *Trinet U.S. Businesses* database. If Company A (a firm with over $1 million in sales) had 30 locations, each would be described in the larger file, while a single, summary listing would appear in the *Company Database*. Company listings cite the total number of employees, the number of establishments, and total company sales. Sales data are further divided into manufacturing versus nonmanufacturing, and by the major SIC categories of the firm. No specific figures are reported for individual locations and subsidiaries; this information must be retrieved through the larger database. *Trinet* is available on DIALOG, LEXIS/NEXIS, and several corporate online services.

Two pre-formatted special reports can be ordered using the *Trinet* establishment database. A "Line of Business Report" (LOB) is available for any parent company in the file. This format creates a tabular summary of sales, number of establishments, percent of total company sales, and market share for every industry in which the company is engaged, arranged by SIC number. On DIALOG, reports are generated by specifying the unique company number (TN) assigned by Trinet, and requesting an LOB using DIALOG's "Report" format. The second specialized report provides a tabular summary of market share by company for any designated four-digit SIC code. *Trinet* generates the report by summing all sales figures for relevant locations of the company and ranking each company's totals. Up to 50 companies are listed per industry.

Listings in the *Trinet* database often contain errors, and as one might expect, the sales estimates can be way off base. For these reasons, it is advisable to compare *Trinet* data to listings from other directories. However, *Trinet* frequently offers information on business locations not seen in other national directories, including D&B sources.

GUIDES TO MANUFACTURING FIRMS

Manufacturing industries no longer occupy a preeminent position in our economy, but the 1987 Census counted over 350,000 U.S. manufacturing establishments with at least one employee. Manufacturers differ from other firms because they create tangible products. Manufacturing is not limited to heavy industry and the processing of raw materials; consumer goods of all types also come under this umbrella. Sometimes trying to

determine just what is considered a manufacturing firm can be confusing. Logging firms and fish hatcheries are not manufacturers, but sawmills and seafood canneries are. The best way to determine whether an industry engages in manufacturing is to consult the *Standard Industrial Classification Manual.*

For research purposes, the major difference between investigating a manufacturer and another type of firm is the need to find out about the products as well as the company. Manufacturing directories tend to be either buyer's guides, which focus on the actual products, or more traditional directories describing the firms. Leading examples of both types are discussed below.

U.S. Manufacturers Directory (American Business Information, Inc.—Annual).

The *U.S. Manufacturers Directory*, a by-product of the *Online Information Network*, lists more than 120,000 companies, but coverage is limited to manufacturers with 25 or more employees. Both headquarters and branch locations are included. Many manufacturers do not advertise in local Yellow Pages because their products are distributed nationally, so additional *Directory* listings are obtained from a variety of publicly available sources. Every entry is then verified on an annual basis through direct contact with the listed companies.

Company information is fairly limited, but the *U.S. Manufacturers Directory* is a useful and versatile tool, especially for researchers without access to the more extensive online resources. The *Directory* is more than a simple phone book. Supplemental data include the name and title of the principal executive at that location, up to three SIC numbers, and coded designations of the company's employee size and sales volume. Seven employee-size categories are used, from under 25 employees to more than 1,000. Similarly, nine groupings of sales figures are used, ranging from less than $500,000 to over $100 million.

The *Directory* is organized in three sections. The main listings are arranged alphabetically. The other sections provide addresses and phone numbers only, arranged by four-digit SIC number and by city. With its multiple access points and affordable price, the *U.S. Manufacturers Directory* is a likely resource for a variety of research needs, from identifying a manufacturer's branch locations, to determining the major companies in a given industry or geographic area.

Electronic access, through the previously mentioned *Online Information Network*, is more detailed. In addition to sales categories, exact figures can be found

for most online listings. The database is also much larger, covering approximately 500,000 manufacturing establishments.

Another company-oriented manufacturing guide is *Marketing Economics Key Plants: Guide to Industrial Purchasing Power*. The two-volume set is published approximately every two years by the Marketing Economics Institute, Ltd. Coverage is limited to factories with more than 100 employees; approximately 40,000 establishments are listed. Volume 1 is arranged geographically by region, state, and county, then by four-digit SIC number; Volume 2 lists establishments by SIC category first, then by state and county. The same company data appears in both volumes, presented in tabular form. Each entry cites the company address, phone, SIC number, and number of employees rounded to the nearest hundred. The quality of the physical book has declined in recent years, with a flimsy paperback binding, faded type, and small print. However, the directory remains popular, particularly among sales managers and marketers. Listings limited to the largest manufacturing facilities help users target their marketing efforts. Subscribers who don't need national coverage can purchase any of eight regional editions.

Reference Book of Manufacturers (Dun & Bradstreet Credit Services—Semiannual).

This two-volume directory from the credit reporting division of the Dun & Bradstreet Corporation is unquestionably the most comprehensive printed guide to manufacturing companies. D&B likes to use the phrase "Reference Book" in its publication titles, so don't confuse this source with two similarly named books. Derived from the same massive database as the other Dun & Bradstreet products described in this chapter, the *Reference Book of Manufacturers* covers approximately 400,000 establishments, including multiple listings for firms with more than one location. However, access is by company name only. The headquarters address is always listed first, followed by branch operations. Entries provide DUNS number, street address, mailing address where applicable, brief product description, employee-size code, year established (if founded within the previous ten years), and, when available, the Dun & Bradstreet credit rating.

Although the *Reference Book of Manufacturers* doesn't afford users the flexibility found in the *U.S. Manufacturers Directory*, its sheer size and the presence of D&B ratings make it an important ready-reference tool. Extensive use of cross-references for dba's and other variations of company names is also valuable.

Unfortunately, the book is only available to subscribers of D&B credit reports, so few public or academic libraries have it.

Thomas Register of American Manufacturers (Thomas Publishing Company—Annual).

An alternative approach to information on manufacturers is to focus on their products. The best example of this type of directory is the massive *Thomas Register*. One of the most recognizable reference works in any business library, it is also one of the most remarkable business directories ever devised. The *Thomas Register* is a comprehensive, detailed guide to the full range of products manufactured in the United States. It makes no distinctions based on company size. Covering only manufacturing companies, it strives for complete representation within that scope.

The first edition in 1906 was a single volume easily held in one hand. The 1991 edition was published in 25 oversize volumes, and the set has been growing steadily each year. It now contains information on 148,000 manufacturers, with cross-references to over 110,000 brand names. Literally hundreds of thousands of products are listed under 50,000 classifications. This enormous reference tool may seem intimidating and confusing, but it is simple and convenient to use once one becomes familiar with its arrangement.

The *Thomas Register* is primarily a classified listing of products, much like a telephone book's Yellow Pages. The emphasis is on products, not companies. For example, companies in the auto parts industry are listed in the *Thomas Register* under the parts they manufacture—headlights, windshield wiper blades, car door handles, etc. It is this amazing degree of specificity that makes the publication so remarkable. Headings as specialized as "hog machine knives" and "bolt head trimming machines" may be found. Also remarkable is the range of products covered, from ball bearings to locomotives. Products are not limited to heavy industry; the set covers the full scope of American manufacturing. The only exclusions are food and food-related products, which are covered in the separate *Thomas Food Industry Register*, and chemical products, which are given superficial coverage at best. Otherwise, products are as varied as weather vanes, Christmas trees, auditorium seats, garbage trucks, calendars, feathers, and burial vaults.

The directory is divided into three parts. The bulk of the information is located in the "Products and Services" section, which comprises volumes 1-16 of the 1991 edition. An idiosyncrasy of the set is that products are listed under inverted headings, such as "Handles: Screwdriver" and "Handles: Mattress." Major headings

and their subdivisions can be quite lengthy; machinery subdivisions cover 600 pages of small print, valves 300 pages, and wire 200 pages. This system is useful on the whole, but it does not ensure that similar products will be grouped together. For example, "Coatings" and "Shelves" are used as broad headings, but "Hand Tools" and "Fasteners" are not.

This unique arrangement also results in incongruities because of the vagaries of the English language. An example is the heading for "Cases," under which are found subdivisions for packing cases and museum cases, as well as suitcases, sample cases, instrument cases, and violin cases. An advantage to this type of arrangement, however, is that products can be further subdivided by their properties, such as the material they are made from. Separate listings under metal, wood, leather, plastic, and glass can be a significant time saver when seeking a specific type of product. To determine the correct inverted heading (which is not always obvious), the user can consult an index of terms at the end of the "Products and Services" volumes.

Companies listed under each product heading are arranged geographically, to help users identify local suppliers. The value of the set is enhanced by display ads placed in each product category. The information found in these paid advertisements can often lead to exactly the firm being sought.

The second part of the *Thomas Register* is a two-volume "Company Profiles" section, an alphabetical directory of all companies whose products are listed in the main volumes. Each entry cites company name, address, phone numbers, and a brief description of the products manufactured. Entries may also include parent/subsidiary relationships, the name of the chief executive officer, and a list of cities where the company has major manufacturing facilities. Finally, most companies are assigned an "asset rating" that can give researchers a general idea of company size based on total tangible assets. Advertising can also be found in the "Company Profile" section. Ads here frequently list names of officers and addresses of sales offices and distributors around the country. Rounding out this section is an extensive brand name index to the company names.

The third section is the "Catalog File," sometimes referred to as the "ThomCat." These seven volumes reprint company catalogs for over 1,200 firms. The catalogs are useful not only to obtain a more complete picture of the company being researched, but also to locate specific product information, photographs, and engineering specifications. To indicate which companies have provided a catalog, a boldface reference appears

next to the firm's name each time it is mentioned in the other volumes. Because of its longevity, scope, and reasonable price, the *Thomas Register* is one of the most widely available business directories.

Information from the set is also reproduced as an online database, and more recently, as a CD-ROM disk. The online service can be searched exclusively through DIALOG, and the disk is also produced by DIALOG. Both are updated semiannually. Search capabilities on either electronic version are virtually identical, though CD-ROM users will find the menu mode to be simpler. The electronic editions provide information not found in the printed volumes. For every company, a more detailed list of product offerings is available. When applicable, descriptions also include important product specifications, such as hardware compatibility. Listings of company executives and their job titles are more prevalent in the electronic editions. Each record also includes a complete list of the company's brand names. Finally, companies are assigned SIC numbers as well as the traditional Thomas product headings. Users can search the database by keywords in the subject headings and the product descriptions. In this way researchers are less dependent upon the convoluted terms assigned by the publisher, and will generally locate additional firms not uncovered through a manual search. Similarly, users approaching the printed directory may be unable to find the correct heading simply because they don't know what the item is called. A purchasing agent looking for manufacturers of screws used to hold together notebook binders might be stymied without electronic access to *Thomas*. The keyword approach will quickly reveal that they are called binding posts, and can be found in the directory under "Posts: Binding." Another important benefit is the ability to combine terms and concepts through Boolean logic. Someone looking for manufacturers of embroidered shoulder patches will have limited success using the printed directory. Headings can be found for "Emblems" and for "Embroiderers," but nothing more specific. Some likely candidates can be deduced from words in the company names or information in the advertisements, but the electronic formats will produce better, faster results by simply combining the two subject terms. If keyword searching produces too many irrelevant listings, the user can combine keywords with SIC codes for greater precision.

A related database on DIALOG is called *Thomas New Industrial Products*. This is a full-text electronic version of a monthly journal from Thomas Publishing called *Industrial Equipment News*. The online edition is updated weekly and contains articles going back to 1985. It provides summarized manufacturers' press releases describing their new products.

Two competing publications are less extensive than the *Thomas Register*. *MacRae's Blue Book*, an annual three-volume set, has been issued by MacRae's Blue Book, Inc. since 1893. It contains product listings, a company directory, and an extensive brand name index. *MacRae's* is especially useful for identifying local outlets for national manufacturers, since many listings include addresses of regional sales offices. Coverage is restricted to original equipment manufacturers, excluding firms which provide goods for further processing by other manufacturers, and company catalogs are no longer reproduced.

A third choice after *Thomas* and *MacRae's* is the four-volume *U.S. Industrial Directory* by Cahners Publishing. This annual set is limited strictly to industrial products. Company catalogs are not reproduced, but the *Directory* includes a "Literature Index" to 6,000 manufacturers' catalogs available free of charge. The Cahners and MacRae's directories are considerably smaller than *Thomas*, providing data on approximately 45,000 companies each.

Sweet's Catalog File (The Sweet's Group—Annual).

Another massive guide to manufacturers' products is the famous *Sweet's Catalog*, published by a division of McGraw-Hill Information Services. It reproduces full-color catalogs from hundreds of companies, but coverage is restricted to firms which manufacture products related to building and construction. The range of products is extensive, from bicycle racks to skylights. Because of this diversity, *Sweet's* is indispensable for contractors, engineers, and building supply outlets, as well as for architects, designers, and interior decorators. Its 18 volumes cover 16 broad categories, including exterior site work, masonry, thermal & moisture protection, electrical systems, paints & finishes, and furnishings. Such specialized areas as hospital fixtures and conveying systems are also covered. Volume 1 provides indexes by company name, trade name, and type of product. Also found in this volume is a six-part reference guide to building materials. Called "Selection Data," it discusses the properties and uses of each product type, then gives comparative tables citing the specifications of different brands. Sweet's also publishes seven specialized catalog services, covering areas such as industrial construction and foreign manufacturers. Subscribers to the *Sweet's Catalog File* receive a CD-ROM index to manufacturers and product specifications called *SweetSearch*.

Another extensive guide to manufacturers' catalogs is produced by Information Handling Services (IHS). Its *Vendor Catalog Service* is available on microfilm cartridges which are updated six times per year. The complete "Master Catalog Service" contains 95,000 catalogs from 25,000 manufacturers and distributors of industrial products. As of this writing, a full subscription costs approximately $20,000 per year. Subsets of the collection focusing on specific product categories are available in two formats: "Full Service Catalogs" present the complete catalogs for each company, and "Vendor Side-by-Side Services" compare all manufacturers' offerings for each product line, with extracts from each catalog. IHS also produces a set of indexes to the complete collection, and these can serve as useful detailed and up-to-date manufacturers directories. Volume A, "Vendor Name Listing," cites company names, addresses, phone and fax numbers, and product categories, together with references to the microform collection. Volume B, "Brand/Trade Name," is one of the most extensive guides to industrial brand names extant. Volume C, "Product Locator," is an alphabetical index of products, giving the companies which manufacture them and their locations in the microform collection. The directories are also updated six times per year, and can be purchased without a subscription to the microfilm.

RESEARCH STRATEGIES

Where does the researcher begin to look for directory information? With millions of companies and hundreds of publications, the choices are endless. The strategy adopted will depend upon the resources available, the searcher's knowledge of individual directories, and the type of information required. The following sections discuss the problems inherent in using directories, how to approach ready-reference questions, and how to conduct more detailed directory research.

Problems Encountered Using Directories

There are numerous pitfalls associated with using business directories. Some are inherent in using any directory, while others are peculiar to business publications. The largest problem is locating the most current information, since every directory is outdated before it is published. The greatest turnover is in corporate personnel; officers are promoted from within or leave the company entirely. Even directories that provide supple-

ments or appear semiannually cannot guarantee the most current information possible, and few online directories are updated more frequently than four times per year.

A particularly troublesome problem is judging the accuracy of the data. In addition to the inevitable transpositions and typographical errors, publishers may unintentionally receive misinformation from the companies appearing in the directory. Telephone queries from directory publishers are frequently answered by employees with an incomplete understanding of the firm. Respondents to direct mail surveys can easily misinterpret a question, providing total company sales instead of sales for the local plant, or listing only production workers instead of all employees.

When interpreting directory information, it is best to consult any explanatory material found in the front of the publication. Making unfounded assumptions is a serious mistake. Abbreviations and symbols used to designate executive positions, monetary amounts, and other data can lead to confusion. Awareness of the units of measure adopted by the publisher is also important, especially where rounded numbers are employed. A subtler, more serious problem occurs when researchers misinterpret what is being measured. What are the criteria for inclusion in the directory? What is the universe from which companies are chosen? Where does the information come from? Many directories use estimation techniques to arrive at sales figures, which may not be apparent to the user.

Another hazardous assumption is to select a company based on too little information. A simple mistake is to choose the wrong company because it has a similar name to the firm being sought. The number of companies in the United States with similar names is extraordinary, and thousands of new names are filed each year. Terms like American, National, Data, and Technology are commonplace in company nomenclature. A large directory may list dozens of names which begin with the same word or sound.

Directory idiosyncrasies are another problem. Each publication has its own quirks of organization, presentation, and filing. Alphabetizing is a particularly knotty problem. Company names frequently begin with an initial, a person's first name, a number, or an acronym. The best directories will provide cross-references from a popular name like "3-M" to the company's actual name (Minnesota Mining and Manufacturing Company), but most will not. Eponymous company designations may be listed under the person's first or last name, and two hyphenated surnames may be misinterpreted as a first and last name. Situations like these present a number of

choices for alphabetizing. Better directories offer a guide to their filing methods, but many do not, and the worst do not even maintain a consistent system throughout. Directories which heavily abbreviate names present serious barriers to searching, whether online or in print. An ironclad rule of using any online or printed business directory is to search for a particular name in a variety of ways if it is not found under what appears to be the obvious form. In this respect, electronic databases can be better resources than their printed equivalents because searchers can combine characteristics, truncate, or use keywords as additional access points. Online databases and CD-ROMs which allow scanning of a company name index are invaluable. An example is the EXPAND feature available on most DIALOG databases.

Ready-Reference Searches

Locating a company address and phone number can be surprisingly difficult. When nothing about the company is known beforehand, the task is definitely more challenging. Brand names posing as company names, misspelled words, and transposed personal names can lead to fruitless searching. Occasionally, the name itself may suggest a clue to location or industry, but even the best assumptions can lead the searcher astray. Plenty of "Dayton Companies" are located outside Ohio. Begin a blind search with comprehensive directories, because they have the largest number of listings. Electronic databases are particularly well-suited because of their enormous size and their ability to identify firms by keyword. Paying $5 for a single address from quick computer search is less expensive than an hour of wasted time. For those without access to computerized resources or extensive print directories like *Dun's Business Identification Service*, a number of more readily available sources are worth consulting. The *Thomas Register*, *Ward's Business Directory*, the *Directory of Blue Chip Companies*, the *Million Dollar Directory*, and the *U.S. Manufacturers Directory* each list over 100,000 companies, making any one of them a likely first choice.

To reduce the frustration of blind searching, determine as much as possible about the company before you start looking. If the general location of the firm, or its type of business (or both) is known, the choice of directories is simpler. Knowing that a manufacturer is located in Michigan, the researcher might first check regional directories. Realizing the company is a food processor might suggest guides specific to the grocery industry. Knowing the company is listed on the New York Stock Exchange makes *Standard & Poor's Register* a good bet,

and a well-known consumer products company is likely to be found in the *Standard Directory of Advertisers*. Unfortunately, in these situations researchers may run the risk of outsmarting themselves. Making hasty assumptions about the nature of a company or the contents of a directory may cause the searcher to eliminate the very source with the needed answer. For example, many seemingly small firms are listed in the *Million Dollar Directory*, and many manufacturing directories also list wholesalers.

When a lengthy search fails to uncover a company address, it is time to question the facts. The name may be garbled, it may be a brand name, the location or type of business may be incorrect, or the entity may not be a business enterprise at all. Many corporations are nonprofit or religious organizations, though this may not be apparent from the name. Sources such as *Dun's Business Identification Service* and the *Online Information Network* can help identify nonprofit corporations, as can more specialized guides like the *Encyclopedia of Associations* and the *Research Centers Directory*. A more specialized publication comes from the government itself. Nonprofit and religious corporations must apply for tax-exempt status, and the U.S. Internal Revenue Service issues an annual directory of organizations currently enjoying that designation. Its *Cumulative List of Organizations* lists the name of every relevant group in alphabetical order. The only additional information given is the city of residence, and no geographic or subject indexes are provided. Still, with approximately 300,000 names listed, it can cut short many fruitless company searches.

Another set of possibilities is that the company may have gone out of business, been acquired by another firm, or simply changed its name. These are situations where online searching can help immeasurably, but printed alternatives also abound. Newspaper and journal indexes may shed light on recent events. When available, a quick check of directories from earlier years may determine the approximate time a previously known name "disappeared." Many large libraries maintain historical collections of printed directories, and the complete file of the *Thomas Register* from 1906 to the present can be purchased on microfilm. Once a state of residence is identified, researchers can contact the government agency which maintains corporation records for that state. Several commercial publishers even compile historical and current guides to defunct companies. The process of researching obsolete names through published sources will be described more fully in Chapter 11.

A seemingly straightforward directory question can develop into a major research problem. There is a limit to the time anyone can spend locating an individual address, but if the request is important, a diligent search may pay off. Persistence and creativity make a difference. Sometimes an answer comes through dogged determination: consulting state directories one by one, or even phone books for major cities in a region may be acceptable if the need warrants it. Experienced researchers generally develop an uncanny sense of where to look, based on the accumulation of many hard-learned lessons. Every researcher or librarian develops his or her own favorite sources and strategies for a given situation. This is generally fine, but remember there is a danger in failing to try new or seldom-used methods.

Detailed Company Research

A search for background information in company directories is usually a two-step process. A first step is to determine anything useful about the company in a general directory, followed by a check of more detailed publications. As an example, *Thomas Register* may indicate the target company is a manufacturer of aircraft parts. This knowledge can lead the pursuer to an assortment of aerospace directories for additional information. When fairly specialized information is required, the search strategy may be different. Knowing something about the company helps, but understanding the content of directories becomes crucial. Some facts can be found in only a few sources, while others appear everywhere. The name of the chief executive, a sales estimate, or the number of employees are common elements of almost any directory listing. The year a company was founded, its state of incorporation, or the name of the firm's ad agency are much rarer. A specialized question will automatically narrow the search, and a thorough knowledge of major directories will save time. Online databases are valuable because they often include data not found in other sources. In fact, many computerized directories offer information unavailable in their printed counterparts. More importantly, electronic databases allow the researcher to use directory information in more efficient, precise, and versatile ways. For example, few printed directories provide access to companies by zip code, but virtually any online directory allows the user to compile customized zip code sorts.

A common problem in company research is finding conflicting information in different sources. Large companies may be listed in numerous directories, but the information doesn't always coincide. When discrepancies are found, which publication should be believed? The user must rely on what is known about each publication. For example, Trinet bases sales data on a mathematical estimating technique, while Standard & Poor's reports figures supplied by the companies themselves. It may turn out, however, that neither presents the real picture. Estimates are not the only cause of discrepancies in directory listings. How a responding company interprets a publisher's questionnaire can make a significant difference in the resulting information, and some companies may intentionally provide disinformation or exaggerate their size. The date information was collected is equally important. Are sales figures based upon last year's performance, or newer data? Even employment figures can vary significantly during the year, especially in highly seasonal industries. Outright mistakes are also common, even in highly regarded publications. Any element of a company's listing can be reported incorrectly in reputable directories, not just the statistical information. An important rule is to verify information in more than one source whenever possible. Determining which of two differing entries is closer to the truth may not be possible, but researchers can make an attempt. A third source can sometimes shed light on the problem, but can also further complicate the picture. In most cases users must be willing to accept the answer which seems most reasonable based on what else is known, or be prepared to conduct additional research.

In many situations, the researcher doesn't have time to consult multiple sources. When speed is imperative, which source should be consulted first? There is no easy answer to this question either. Every user of business directories forms opinions based upon personal experience. Some people refuse to use sources such as *Ward's* or *Trinet* because of the estimated figures. Others are highly suspicious of Dun & Bradstreet data because they've encountered erroneous information. It is probably unwise to reject any publication out of hand; all major business publishers strive to be as accurate and reliable as possible. The choice of directory depends not only on the reputation of the publisher, but the objective of the publication, the source of its information (if known), the recency of publication, and its convenience of use. Again, if the answer is important, it is unwise to rely on a single source.

FOR FURTHER READING

The following titles provide a closer look at some of the concepts introduced in this chapter. The materials on corporate names are included as a reminder not to take names for granted in the research process (and because they're fun). Related reading lists can be found in Chapter 7 (brand names and trademarks) and Chapter 11 (name changes and corporate ownership).

About Directories and Their Compilers

Bartko, Maxim C. "Business Compilers: Who's Who and Why." *Catalog Age* 7 (April 1990): 95-100.
Describes the major compilers of comprehensive business-to-business directory databases used for mailing list purposes: Dun & Bradstreet, TRW, Trinet, American Business Lists, Ed Burnette, and others.

Ojala, Marydee. "SIC Codes Revisited: Dun's Goes Marching Two by Two." *Online* 13 (November 1989): 84-89.
A critical look at D&B's extended six- and eight-digit SIC codes from a database searcher's perspective. The "SIC 2 + 2" system is now used in *Dun's Market Identifiers* and other directory databases.

———. "Targeting Prospects with Online Databases: Telemarketing and Business List Building." *Online* 13 (March 1989): 96-99.
Discusses one of the most important uses of online directory databases, the types of searches for which they are best suited, and examples of some of the most pertinent databases.

Tafel, Linda L. "Dun's Electronic Yellow Pages." *Database* 12 (June 1989): 63-66.
A brief review of this popular online file, including a discussion of how it has changed over the years.

Corporations and Organizational Structure

Chandler, Alfred. *Strategy and Structure* (Cambridge, MA: MIT Press, 1962).
This classic history of the development of modern corporate structure tells the story of the innovative organizations which created the forms of corporate organization common today.

Dent, Harry S. "Corporation of the Future." *Small Business Reports* 15 (May 1990): 55-63.
Noted futurist Dent speculates on the increased blurring of lines among corporate affiliations. Due to the pressures of global competition and product/service specialization, Dent sees the need for corporations to have characteristics of both large and small companies. One way to accomplish this is through greater use of "strategic alliances and networks": more joint ventures, stronger ties between suppliers and customers, and increased use of subcontractors.

Duncan, Robert. "What Is the Right Organizational Structure?" *Organizational Dynamics* 7 (Winter 1979): 59-79.
A short, well-written introduction to basic concepts in organizational design. Discusses the strengths and weaknesses of functional, decentralized, and mixed organizations and the types of environments best suited to each. A decision-tree model is presented to assist the manager in selecting the most appropriate structure.

Kaestle, Paul. "A New Rationale for Organizational Structure." *Planning Review* (July/August 1990): 20-27.
Examines the forces driving the current changes in organizational structure, including greater competitiveness and new information technology. A notable trend in the 1980s was "deconglomeration," where highly decentralized parent companies began to shed unrelated subsidiaries. The author discusses the tradeoff in benefits between centralization and decentralization, and provides three case studies to illustrate the innovative ways large corporations are restructuring.

Managers, Directors, and Power in the Corporation

Byrne, John A. "The Limits of Power." *Business Week* (October 23, 1987): 33-35.
This short piece states that the trappings of power with which today's CEOs surround themselves often belie the true extent of their authority. Such factors as decentralization, the growing power of directors, investment bankers, and others outside the executive suite, and the gargantuan size of far-flung corporate empires, all contribute to the erosion of control. Also noteworthy is the increasing preoccupation of CEOs with external factors such as defending against corporate takeovers.

Lamb, Robert Boyden. *Running American Business: Top CEOs Rethink Their Major Decisions* (New York: Basic Books, 1987).
A fascinating look at how decisions are made in major corporations. Lamb, an editor with *Fortune* magazine, bases his conclusions on numerous interviews conducted with top CEOs over a span of years. The book begins with a discussion of the realities of decision making, and the executive network to which most CEOs belong (what Lamb terms the "phantom club"). Succeeding chapters are devoted to different categories of executive decisions, including takeovers, marketing strategies, and choosing successors. Case studies in which CEOs describe the events in their own words are provided.

Mace, Myles L. *Directors: Myth and Reality*. Revised ed. (Cambridge, MA: Harvard University, 1986).

A pioneering study on the responsibilities and duties of directors in U.S. corporations. This work was originally published in 1971. A follow-up study conducted by Mace in the 1980s indicated that very little had changed since the original research was reported.

Mintzberg, Henry. "The Manager's Job: Folklore and Fact." *Harvard Business Review* 68 (March/April 1990): 163-76. This classic article, reprinted from the July/August 1975 issue, was one of the first to investigate common myths about executive behavior. Among Mintzberg's principal findings: most of an executive's typical day is taken up by activities which are fast-paced, brief, and diverse; managers have surprisingly little control over their time; information processing is a key part of the manager's job; and executives strongly prefer oral communication (phone calls, meetings) to written reports.

———. *Power In and Around Organizations* (Englewood Cliffs, NJ: Prentice Hall, 1983).

A thought-provoking examination of formal and informal power, and the ambiguities of management roles.

Company Names

Charmasson, Henri. *The Name Is the Game: How to Name a Company or a Product* (Homewood, IL: Dow Jones-Irwin, 1988).

A thorough discussion of the functions served by company and brand names, the importance of choosing the best name possible, and the legal and marketing concerns to consider in the naming process. Plenty of advice is provided, plus lots of examples of good and bad names.

Napoles, Veronica. *Corporate Identity Design* (New York: Van Nostrand Reinhold, 1988).

Examines how names and symbols can help define a corporation's public identity. The focus is on important concepts for designing a corporate logo, but the reasons for changing the company's name are also discussed.

Townsend, Bickley. "Cashing In on Corporate Identity: An Interview with Clive Chajet." *American Demographics* 12 (July 1990): 42-43.

Revealing comments on the relationship among corporate image, company name, and brand strategy. The process of developing a new company name is also discussed. Chajet is the CEO of Lippincott & Margulies, the PR firm that created the names Duracell and Infiniti, among others.

CHAPTER 7
Specialized Business Directories

TOPICS COVERED

1. Geographic Directories
   a. State Industrial Directories
   b. Other Directories for States and Regions
   c. Telephone Books
   d. City Directories
   e. Local Business Directories
2. Trade Directories
3. Special Purpose Directories
   a. Biographical Directories
   b. Corporate Affiliations
4. Searching for Brand Names and Trademarks
   a. Registered Versus Unregistered Trademarks
   b. Classification of Registered Trademarks
   c. Specialized Trademark Publications
5. Putting It All Together
6. For Further Reading

MAJOR SOURCES DISCUSSED

- *Colt Microfiche Library of State Directories*
- *State Business Directory Series*
- *Microcosm*
- *Thomson Bank Directory*
- *Reference Book of Corporate Managements*
- *Who's Who in Finance and Industry*
- *Directory of Corporate Affiliations*
- *Brands and Their Companies*
- *Official Gazette of the United States Patent and Trademark Office*
- *Trademark Register*
- *Compu-Mark Directory of U.S. Trademarks*
- *Trademarkscan-Federal*

What makes business directories so important, anyway? With thousands on the market, can any research need justify such proliferation? Aside from identifying company addresses and phone numbers, directories can identify suppliers, create mailing lists, and answer quick facts about a company. But far too many researchers fail to exploit another use—directories can be powerful resources for conducting in-depth company analyses. In fact, almost every detailed search should begin with directories. There are four principal reasons for this. First, it is difficult to begin a major research project if little is known about a firm. The basic nature of the company will largely determine the subsequent direction a search will take. Even a cursory check of directory sources will begin to fill in the blanks and prevent false starts. A related point is that librarians and researchers are frequently given misinformation, resulting in lengthy wild goose chases. Verifying facts before embarking on a thorough search will save endless frustration.

Second, the information uncovered in directories can provide clues which will suggest areas worth investigating. Does the firm have strong ties to other companies? Does it limit its market to a particular geographic area? Is it engaged in heavily regulated activities? Without the preliminary data found through directories, these are questions which might not surface until the final stages of the project, if at all. Third, a thorough comparison of different directory listings can corroborate information found elsewhere, and help resolve discrepancies found in conflicting reports. Finally, directories can actually provide answers not discovered through other means, especially for small private companies. Directories should be viewed as valuable sources of company intelligence.

Most company directories are compiled with a very specific purpose or audience in mind. While the publications in Chapter 6 offer general coverage of domestic companies, the sources described below take a narrower approach. Some focus on a specific geographic area, some on individual industries or products. Other specialized directories provides access to biographies of key executives and directors, relationships among different firms, rankings of companies, and guides to brand names. Because researching trademarks is itself quite specialized, a separate discussion of this type of information will be provided.

GEOGRAPHIC DIRECTORIES

State, regional, and local directories come in many forms and are published by a variety of organizations. No one could afford the money and effort required to subscribe to all local directories published in the United States, but large libraries attempt to collect publications from a variety of major cities and states. Some of the most frequently encountered geographic directories are telephone books, city directories, local business rosters, and state industrial directories.

State Industrial Directories

State directories offer a diversity of research options. Some cover a cluster of counties within a state or across the boundaries of neighboring states; others include companies from two or more entire states. Most, however, are limited to firms within a single state. Two categories of state and regional publications will be discussed: those which list manufacturing firms only, and those which include nonmanufacturers.

The most detailed state business directories are the so-called industrial directories. Some include large wholesalers, construction companies, or mining concerns among their listings, but most limit coverage strictly to manufacturing operations. In the past decade, the number of commercial publishers in this field has grown, and the leading producers have expanded their output. As a result, almost every state is now represented by at least two different industrial directories, and many states offer three or more. Industrial directories vary in scope, size, frequency, and price. Many are annuals, but a significant number are biennial, and the smallest may appear on an irregular basis only. Size depends on manufacturing activity in the state; agricultural states may list only a few

hundred companies in their directories. Almost all state directories are accessible by company name, product or industry, and geographic location.

Industrial directories are produced by both nonprofit organizations and commercial publishers. Nonprofit groups publish directories in at least 40 states. Most of these are compiled by state agencies such as commerce departments or departments of economic development. Others are generated by statewide chambers of commerce or university research centers. A host of commercial publishers also compile industrial directories. Major commercial firms make their data available as printed directories, customized mailing lists, and floppy diskettes. Some produce publications for more than one state, but even the largest publishers specialize in particular parts of the country. The following companies each publish directories for six or more states: Manufacturers News, Inc. (Midwest and East Coast); MacRae's Bluebook, Inc. (Northeast and Mid-Atlantic); Commerce Register, Inc. (Northeast); the George D. Hall Company (East Coast); and the Harris Publishing Company (Midwest and Mid-Atlantic). Manufacturers News now produces directories outside its traditional areas, including Kentucky and Texas. MacRae's Bluebook has substantially reduced its output. In the early 1980s, the company tried to produce a publication for every state, but has now scaled back its efforts to a mere 8 directories covering 15 states.

Two questions face the library or company wishing to build a collection of state industrial directories: "Which publisher do I choose for my state?" and "How do I achieve national coverage at minimal cost?" A simple answer to the first question is to buy as many as you can afford. For researchers and organizations who continually investigate local firms, purchasing several directories for the same state is a wise investment. For those who can't, the key variables in comparing directories for a single state are frequency of publication, number of listings, amount of detail, and price. Directories published by nonprofit organizations are usually cheaper than their commercial counterparts, and coverage is often identical (or even greater). In some cases, the nonprofit publication is the clear choice. Where more than one commercial publication is available, each will have its strengths and weaknesses. Hall's directories usually contain more company listings than their competitors, but they offer less information on each firm. Commerce Register includes more information than most publishers, including the company's founding date, its principal bank, accountant and law firm, and company directors as well as officers. Each publisher provides

unique data in its listings. Manufacturers News cites the type of computer used by each manufacturer. MacRae's listings indicate the size of each plant and provide separate figures for the number of plant and administrative employees.

Can any library truly justify building a representative collection from all 50 states? Absolutely. State directories offer a number of advantages over national business directories. First, they cite information on individual plant locations rather than the whole company. Listings usually include the names of local managers, the number of employees, and the products manufactured at each plant. Second, concise descriptions of smaller companies may not show up in any other directories. Third, state publications can provide information not easily found in other sources. Finally, a set of 50 state directories will provide more comprehensive coverage than the major national directories—some two to three times as many establishments as found in the *Thomas Register* or *Million Dollar Directory*. Even researchers with access to extensive sources such as *Dun's Market Identifiers* will find state industrial directories invaluable. No matter how similar information may be from one source to another, each directory provides worthwhile data, and the amount of duplication between similar sources is much less than one might expect.

There is no inexpensive way to obtain national coverage. Large libraries wishing to purchase directories for every state have three alternatives. The first is a subscription to the *Colt Microfiche Library*, described below. A second is to establish a standing order with a directory distributor, covering as many states as possible. Several of the directory compilers themselves serve as distributors for other publishers, including Manufacturers News and Harris Publishing. Both options are convenient, but limit the freedom to select specific publishers. There is no guarantee that the choices made by Colt or a distributor will result in the best products for your library's needs. To maintain such freedom requires contacting different publishers on a state-by-state basis to place individual orders. The quickest way to compare the content, size, and format of the competing products is to consult *Directories in Print* and *City & State Directories in Print*.

Unfortunately few libraries, corporations, or individuals can afford to build a national collection. Developing a more modest library of state directories can begin in a number of ways. A good start is to purchase directories for one's own and neighboring states. Another suggestion is to purchase sources for the largest industrial states, as the budget allows. Begin with New York, Ohio, Illinois, New Jersey, and Pennsylvania, and add Michigan, Massachusetts, Texas, and California when possible. Acquiring different states in alternate years is another way to stretch purchasing power. A final suggestion is to acquire multi-state directories such as the *Directory of Central Atlantic States Manufacturers* or the *Directory of New England Manufacturers*, both by George D. Hall. When conducting company research, however, there is no such thing as too many directories.

Colt Microfiche Library of State Directories (Colt Microfiche Corporation—Semiannual).

The *Colt Microfiche Library* provides the complete text of industrial directories for all 50 states. One publication is reproduced for each state, with the selections made by the Colt staff. All types of publishers are represented, including nonprofit agencies, small commercial publishers, and bigger firms like MacRae's and Harris. Taken together, the directories provide information on more than 300,000 plant locations. Because many state directories are updated biennially or irregularly, *Colt* subscribers will not receive a new edition for every state each year. However, approximately 90% of the current titles have been updated within the past two years. (Directories for states with fewer firms, such as Montana and Alaska, are published infrequently.) To minimize delays, subscribers receive two fiche shipments per year.

While expensive, an annual subscription to the *Colt Microfiche Library* is cheaper than purchasing 50 directories in paper copy. Of course *Colt* also has disadvantages. For frequent users, the microfiche format is a hindrance. There can also be a considerable delay between the time a directory appears in print and the *Colt* subscriber receives it on fiche, even with semiannual mailings. Finally, the directories chosen will not always be the ones you would have preferred. The *Colt* service is clearly not for everyone, but it offers convenient access for researchers and libraries alike.

Other Directories for States and Regions

Guides to nonmanufacturers also present various options. "Service directories" cover companies engaged in retail or wholesale trade, transportation and construction, and business or personal services. Most are produced by industrial directory publishers, so they are virtually identical in format and content to their manufacturing counterparts. The best examples are compiled for heavily populated states such as California, Massachusetts, Illinois, and Ohio. Unfortunately, far too few states are represented by publications of this type. For those wishing to purchase directories for broad geographic areas, other options are available, including a new series

of regional products from Dun & Bradstreet. Less expensive directories are produced for many areas of the country, but most are little more than regional telephone books.

State Business Directory Series (American Directory Publishing Company—Annual).

State Business Directories is a series of 48 individual state directories. Volumes for the remaining states—New York and California—will be available in late 1991. The series is published by a division of American Business Information, Inc., the producer of the *Online Information Network* and the *U.S. Manufacturers Directory*, both described in Chapter 6. Like their sibling directories, the books in this series reproduce information found in the Yellow Pages of telephone directories across the country. For example, the *Virginia Business Directory* contains listings for 178,000 companies, obtained from 71 phone books across the state. Users will find these directories limited for researching companies. Listings basically cite the address (including zip code), phone number, and an indication of the type of ad placed in the phone book. A separate section on manufacturing companies reproduces the basic information found in the *U.S. Manufacturers Directory*, including the codes for employee size and sales volume category. This section lists information by SIC number and by city. Manufacturers represent a small proportion of each directory's content, however.

The bulk of the information in the *State Business Directories* is contained in the classified section. Businesses are listed according to the headings used in the Yellow Pages themselves. Because the various phone book producers use different subject headings, American Directory Publishing has created standard headings based on those most commonly used. The series includes every business category found in phone books, from barber shops to apartment buildings. A second section in each directory repeats the company listings alphabetically by city. Finally, the publisher provides a useful statistical section giving business counts by city, county, zip code, SIC code, and subject heading. The great value in these state publications is their sheer comprehensiveness. For research on a limited geographic area, the *State Business Directories* are a sensible and affordable way to obtain company listings for a variety of purposes. The only serious limitation is lack of an alphabetical index to company names.

Thomas Regional Industrial Buying Guides (Thomas Publishing Company—Annual).

A less extensive group of geographic directories is compiled by the publishers of the *Thomas Register*. This series covers manufacturing and nonmanufacturing firms, but again provides no background information on the listed companies. Entries are presented in two sections, one alphabetical by company name, the other classified by type of business, then subdivided by city. Though the directories appear identical to the *Thomas Register*, they are more than regional versions of their bigger cousin. In addition to manufacturing firms, the directories include wholesalers, manufacturer's representatives, and some service firms. The type of company is indicated in parentheses after every listing. Unlike the *Thomas Register*, coverage of consumer products is minimal. Each directory focuses on a region within a state or group of states. Fifteen titles are available, representing the Midwest, Northeast, and Mid-Atlantic regions only. All books are issued annually, and any title is available free to customers located within the area being covered.

Since the breakup of AT&T, most of the Bell operating companies have ventured into business directory publishing. Many now produce regional industrial Yellow Pages similar to those from Thomas Publishing. An excellent example is the *Ameritech Industrial Yellow Pages* series. Twelve different editions are published for various areas in the eastern half of the country. Each one offers a classified guide to industrial products and services and an alphabetical directory of companies. Company listings cite street address, zip code, area code, phone number, and a designation of company type. Ameritech directories are also offered free to qualified subscribers located within each service area.

Dun's Regional Business Directories (Dun's Marketing Services—Annual).

In response to customer demand for local business directories, D&B unveiled its *Microcosm* series several years ago. But *Microcosm* (described later in this chapter) failed to meet the needs of many subscribers. Rather than repackaging data from *Microcosm*, *Dun's Regional Business Directories* offer a genuine alternative to the older product. They provide background information on the largest companies within a specified economic region. Most regions transcend an individual metropolitan area, and many cross state boundaries. For example, the Hartford regional directory covers seven counties in Connecticut plus another four in Massachusetts. Thirty directories are presently available, with more to follow.

D & B intends to make each directory in the series approximately the same size and price. To do so, coverage is limited to the 20,000 largest establishments ranked by employment size, with certain adjustments made to portray local business conditions as accurately as possible. The focus is on individual company locations, not just headquarters. The main section of each directory is arranged geographically by zip code, with indexes by company name and SIC code. Two additional features are ranked lists of the top 1,000 companies in the region (by sales and by employment size), and a statistical analysis of firms by SIC category. Company listings cite the number of employees at that location; the SIC number; key executives; whether the firm is a branch or headquarters; and, where applicable, the name of the parent company. Publicly traded firms are identified, together with their stock exchanges and ticker symbols. Headquarters listings also cite company sales volume, total company employment, and founding date.

Telephone Books

An "inexpensive" but labor intensive way to build a collection of local directories is by maintaining a phone book library. In the United States, about 4,800 phone books are issued by the so-called Regional Bell Operating Companies (RBOCs), plus nearly as many "non-Bell" directories from independent phone companies. Many communities have separate books for households and businesses, and even Yellow Pages can be divided into books for consumer services and for "Business-to-Business Listings." In addition to the "official" phone book, most major cities also have at least one directory published by a commercial firm other than the local phone company. Phone books are sometimes the only source of a current address or phone number, and are also inexpensive sources for compiling mailing lists or community business profiles.

Most public and academic libraries maintain collections of phone directories. Individuals and companies may purchase out-of-town books at reasonable prices through the business office of the local phone company. Businesspeople may find it useful to own books for major cities like New York, Chicago, and Washington, as well as for cities where they do business. An alternative to ordering a large phone book collection each year is to purchase the following microform service.

Phonefiche (University Microfilms International—Updated Continuously).

This microfiche collection reproduces the complete contents of telephone books for communities with populations greater than 25,000. Both White and Yellow Pages are included. Although UMI is unable to obtain permission to reproduce every phone book it would like, more than 90% of the targeted communities are included on the fiche. There is some duplication because UMI reproduces each book in its entirety, and many communities appear in more than one directory. To assist users in identifying the correct directory to consult, subscribers receive a copy of UMI's *Community Cross-Reference Guide*, a detailed index to the cities, towns, and villages found in the collection. Although a minimum order is required, purchasers can choose from a variety of plans to create a customized phone book collection. Each directory is updated annually and subscribers receive fiche shipments throughout the year, as the books are filmed.

City Directories

City directories are compiled by private companies through door-to-door surveys of city residents, including businesses. Because such a project entails great effort, directories are not available for some large U.S. cities.

The largest producer of city directories is the R.L. Polk Company in Detroit. Polk publishes approximately 1,400 local directories and maintains offices in 800 cities. The company has a directory library at its headquarters and several smaller libraries in regional offices; these offices will answer telephone requests for directory information at no charge to Polk subscribers. Most other companies engaged in this type of publishing limit their activities to individual metropolitan areas or regions. Public and academic libraries generally collect city directories for their localities only, though larger libraries may subscribe to directories for other major cities. These libraries also provide free directory assistance by telephone. In many cases, city directory questions account for a large percentage of telephone requests received by the library.

The format of Polk titles is typical of most city directory publishers. Polk directories are divided into four sections—an alphabetical listing of people and companies (white pages), a street index (green), a telephone number index (blue), and a classified business directory (yellow). The street index lists occupants by their addresses, and the numeric listing of phone numbers

shows who owns them. These indexes can be used to identify "blind" phone numbers or addresses, compile local mailing lists, plan door-to-door or telephone canvasses, trace overdue accounts for credit collection, and conduct neighborhood profiles on a block-by-block basis for market research.

Because the directories are compiled through personal interviews, they include information on individuals with no phone and those with unlisted numbers (providing they respond to the survey). Inclusion in the classified section is free, so businesses that don't advertise in phone books may be found here. The classified section also lists colleges, apartment buildings, clubs, associations, and trade unions. Information on individuals includes occupation, where employed, whether the respondent owns or rents the residence, and the number of adults in the household. Business listings provide the owner's or manager's name and a description of the business.

There are drawbacks to city directories. Some cities are not surveyed every year, and even in cities that are, the information becomes outdated quickly. Householders are free to refuse participation in the survey, and even the classified section may have numerous omissions. A final concern is accuracy; misinformation can easily creep into such a large undertaking. Because of these problems, the city directory is best used in conjunction with phone books and other sources to ensure accurate and comprehensive coverage.

A second type of directory available in many cities (including those with no true city directory) is called a cross-reference directory. These publications achieve similar results to city directories by simply feeding information from local phone books into a computer, which cross lists entries by address and by phone number. As a consequence, the more detailed information on householders and businesses which can be found in a city directory is absent from the cross-reference publications. The Ohio firm of Haines and Company produces "Criss+Cross Directories" for more than 60 communities throughout the country, and its products are fairly typical of this type of publication. Access in Haines directories is strictly by street address and phone number, with no personal name index. Haines adds the year each listing first appeared in the phone book; this serves as an indicator of the length of residence for each household and business. Other leading publishers of cross-reference services are Dickman Criss-Cross Directories, Inc., with approximately 50 books covering New York, Pennsylvania, and Ohio, and the Bresser Company, with some 20 guides to communities in Michigan.

Local Business Directories

Another important source of company information is local directories which specifically cover the business community. Most are published by chambers of commerce, but they may also be compiled by newspapers, public utility companies, neighborhood business associations, or commercial publishers. Chamber of commerce directories vary widely from city to city. Some are merely membership rosters; others are more comprehensive directories including nonmember firms. Some only list company name, address, and a brief description; others cite additional information on each firm. Most are arranged both alphabetically and by type of business. More sophisticated chambers may also produce specialized directories of firms that import or export products, of industrial park tenants, of shopping malls and office buildings, or other categories of local interest. Others offer customized mailing lists or computer printouts. Researchers can identify the addresses and phone numbers of chamber offices across the country through the *World Chamber of Commerce Directory*, introduced in Chapter 2.

A more limited source of local directories is the local business association. Organizations for purchasing agents, personnel officers, real estate brokers, and other professionals abound at the local level. Groups such as these may be difficult to locate because many have no fixed address. Some organizations, however, are quite large and have permanent locations and full-time staffs. If all else fails, researchers can identify national associations through sources such as Gale's *Encyclopedia of Associations*. National organizations can generally provide callers with the current address of a local chapter. A similar resource can be found in such community organizations as neighborhood business associations, support groups for minority- and women-owned businesses, and downtown merchants associations.

Commercial publishers also compile business directories for metropolitan areas. Most restrict their activities to a single region, but two publishers are more diversified.

Microcosm (Dun's Marketing Services—Semiannual).

The most extensive national collection of local business directories is this microfiche series from Dun & Bradstreet. A separate set of fiche is compiled for every major metropolitan area in the country—approximately 300 in all. For less populous states like Alaska, Wyoming, and North Dakota, the fiche cover the entire state. In most cases, however, the geographic boundaries follow those used by the U.S. Bureau of the Census in

defining its Metropolitan Statistical Areas—basically one or more counties surrounding a large city. Unlike *Dun's Regional Business Series*, no establishment-size restrictions are imposed. *Microcosm* represents the most all-encompassing guide to local business communities available in nonelectronic form. Each *Microcosm* product provides listings for every location of every company for which D&B has data, so directories vary in size and price.

Every *Microcosm* directory is arranged by SIC number, by company name, and geographically by city or town. The complete company listing is reproduced in all three sections. As with other products from Dun's Marketing Services, company names are limited to 30 characters in length, so abbreviations are frequently used. Where applicable, dba's and other trade styles are included in addition to the firm's corporate name. The balance of the information found in *Microcosm* listings is limited: DUNS number, complete address, phone, the name of the principal executive, SIC numbers, number of employees at that location, and an indication of company status (headquarters, branch, or single location). The focus on individual establishments is important, often providing more listings than can be seen in a telephone book. It is also a great source for names of branch managers and for comparative size of local offices. And the SIC and geographic listings are excellent for conducting local market profiles.

Contacts Influential (Contacts Influential Marketing Information Services—Annual).

Contacts Influential is an exceptionally useful series of local directories. The publisher recently became a division of Trinet, Inc., and fewer cities are covered now than in years past. The company currently has operations in seven states, including Florida, Texas, and California. A total of 25 directories are currently issued. They are more expensive than most locally produced resources, but *Contacts Influential* guides provide extensive information in a variety of presentations. The main section of each directory is arranged by company name and lists key officers, type of business, employee size category, type of location, and how long the company has been in business. Other sections include a numeric index to phone numbers (similar to those seen in city directories), an index by street name (grouped by zip codes for marketing purposes), and an index to company personnel. The "Market Planning Section" provides a statistical overview of industries by SIC number within each zip code. For cities where *Contacts Influential* is published, the directory is an excellent source of local business intelligence.

TRADE DIRECTORIES

Trade directories focus on a specific type of industry rather than a geographic area. The variety in this category is enormous, and it is difficult to generalize about them. Some trade directories provide detailed information on each company, but more often they serve as buyer's guides, emphasizing product information. Titles can be misleading; what may seem like a directory *of* an industry can turn out to be a directory *for* an industry. An example is the *Candy Industry Buying Guide*, which lists companies that supply equipment and raw materials to candy manufacturers rather than naming the candy companies themselves. Trade directories can be published by professional and industry associations, trade journals, or other commercial publishers. An association often restricts coverage to members of its group, as with the American Institute of Real Estate Appraisers' *Directory of Members*. Major trade journals produce company directories as an annual feature of the magazine, such as the *Hardware Age Who Makes It Buyer's Guide*. These special issues are received automatically by journal subscribers, but can be purchased separately for a minimal cost. Journal publishers may also produce trade directories which are not part of the journal subscription, though they are generally more expensive than membership directories or buyer's guides. Such directories are often quite detailed, providing specialized company information and industry statistics. The *Keystone Coal Industry Manual* and the *Progressive Grocer's Marketing Guidebook*, both annual publications of MacLean Hunter Media, Inc., are examples of this type of directory. Many nonjournal publishers also produce trade directories.

There are several thousand trade directories published in the United States. Titles range from the *American Book Trade Directory* to the *Directory of the Pickle Industry*. Every conceivable industry has at least one directory of its own. Manufacturing is by far the largest industry category for which trade directories appear. Major industries such as aerospace, electronics, and chemicals are well covered, and directories of consumer products are also widely available. Manufacturing directories also exist for firms that supply specialized products to other industries. Coverage of retail stores is scant, but some retail directories do exist. There are directories of department stores, drug stores, convenience stores, health food stores, and more, but none is comprehensive in scope. One of the best series of retail directories, the *Chain Store Guides*, is produced by Lebhar-Friedman, Inc., a leading publisher of trade journals. Each of the 12

directories provides detailed background on chain store operators, though the information varies according to the type of industry. Typical listings include such data as the number of units operated, their locations, merchandise lines carried, sales volume, sales per square foot, breakdown of sales by customer type, and form of ownership. Guides to mail order companies are popular, and several excellent directories are available. Directories of wholesalers are especially difficult to locate, although many manufacturing directories include major wholesalers for that industry.

Directories of service companies can be indispensable for researchers because service firms are seldom covered in national business directories unless the company is quite large. Service directories may be aimed at the consumer market, with listings of real estate brokers, airlines, or employment agencies. Others concentrate on services to other businesses, such as manufacturers' representatives, public relations firms, customhouse brokers, or public warehouses.

Because of the enormous number of trade directories published, it is impossible to provide a lengthy list in this chapter. Specific information on trade directories can be found by consulting Gale's *Directories in Print* and other guides covered in Chapter 3. A single title is described below to illustrate the amount of detail such publications can provide.

Thomson Bank Directory (Thomson Financial Publishing—Semiannual).

The best guide to banks in the United States is this comprehensive "Bankers Blue Book" formerly called the *Rand McNally Bankers Directory*. Published continuously since 1876, it describes nearly 15,000 U.S. banks, their 45,000 branches, and 60,000 foreign banks around the world. The first two volumes cover the United States, including national and state commercial banks, bank holding companies, trust companies, mutual savings banks, and Edge Act corporations. Also covered are American offices of foreign banks. Savings and loan associations, mortgage banks, credit unions, and other financial service firms are not covered. Volume 3 profiles non-U.S. banks engaged in foreign exchange or foreign trade operations.

Entries are arranged geographically by state and city, regardless of whether the establishment is a headquarters or a branch. However, a separate section is devoted to bank holding companies. An alphabetical index is found in Volume 1. For every headquarters location, an extensive array of data is provided in addition to name, parent company, address, phone, and names

of key executives. Users can quickly identify the type of bank and form of charter, the founding date, summary financial information, whether accounts are insured by the FDIC or other federal agencies, whether the bank is a member of the Federal Reserve Board, its correspondent banks, its automated clearinghouse, whether it participates in any wire networks, and any trade organizations to which it belongs. Most listings also reproduce the bank's logo, a list of branch locations, and subsidiary names. Some listings even reproduce the bank's current slogan. An especially useful feature is the inclusion of every bank's state and national ranking by asset size. The researcher can easily determine that a particular bank is the tenth largest in its state and ranks 320th nationwide. Less detail is provided for branches, but users can typically identify the branch manager and the location of the headquarters.

A separate "Financial Services Directory" presents tabular comparisons of every bank, charting 21 major banking services and indicating whether each bank provides them. Services range from trust and estate planning to accounts receivable financing. A buyer's guide section shows classified listings for companies which provide bank supplies, equipment, and services. Another set of directories lists all automated and paper clearinghouses. A statistical section in Volume 1 offers summary data on the banking industry and a ranking of the 500 largest firms. Finally, a reference section provides background information on the banking system, including addresses and names for the Federal Reserve Banks, state banking agencies, and national trade associations. Similar statistical and regulatory information is given for every state. The publisher also compiles two related directories: the *Thomson Savings Directory*, and the *Thomson Credit Union Directory*.

A competitor to Thomson is *Polk's World Bank Directory* by the R.L. Polk Company. Volume 1 covers banks in North America and appears semiannually; Volume 2 covers the rest of the world and is issued annually. *Polk's* is arranged in the same fashion as the Thomson directory, covers virtually the same banks, and provides much the same information. It too offers a separate section on bank holding companies. Much of the supplementary material seen in the *Thomson Bank Directory* is absent from *Polk's*, and users may be frustrated by the lack of an alphabetical index. On the other hand, the bank descriptions are quite similar, and Polk includes a few minor items not given by its competitor, including the number of branches owned by each bank, and the name of the bank attorney.

SPECIAL PURPOSE DIRECTORIES

A final category of business directories is a more eclectic grouping, which will be referred to here as the special purpose directory. These sources are generally of two types: they may describe firms with common characteristics; or they provide researchers with unique access to company data, recasting traditional directory information in more usable forms. Such directories may list companies that meet a stated criterion, they may compare companies in ranked lists, or they may identify firms by designations other than their actual names. The difference between trade and special purpose directories is often blurred, since their objectives often overlap. The *Direct Marketing Market Place* for example, not only lists mail order companies, but firms that provide services to the direct mail industry, and companies which utilize direct mail as a major portion of their marketing strategy. The *Directory of American Research and Technology* covers corporations that have extensive laboratory facilities as well as firms which offer commercial research services. Some directories identify and describe companies engaged in similar businesses, but which transcend a single industry. A good example is the guide to high-technology companies, which can include a diversity of industries from defense electronics to biotechnology. Examples are *BioScan* and the *Corporate Technology Directory*. The latter source, also known as *CorpTech*, offers fairly detailed descriptions of more than 30,000 firms that develop or manufacture high-tech products and services. It is available in print form, on disk, and online through the ORBIT system.

A common category of special directory identifies particular functions or personnel within a company. Examples include the *Law & Business Directory of Corporate Counsel*, which lists in-house lawyers employed by major corporations, and the *National Directory of Corporate Public Affairs*, a guide to companies which have executives in charge of community relations or public affairs. Many directories highlight companies that exhibit special concern for social issues, or a lack thereof. The *Taft Corporate Giving Directory* is an annual survey of major corporations with company-sponsored foundations or philanthropic programs; *U.S. and Canadian Business in South Africa* is an irregular publication of the Investor Responsibility Research Center, and its focus is quite evident. Another common type of directory shows relationships between companies and their service providers, such as *Who Audits America*, a guide to the leading publicly traded companies in the United States and their public accounting firms, and the

Corporate Finance Blue Book, which identifies companies' financial service providers, from outside pension fund managers to insurance underwriters.

The most prevalent category of specialized directory identifies companies with common characteristics other than their industry or geographic location. Characteristics include the way in which the companies do business, how they are organized, or specific activities in which they are engaged. Marketing arrangements are a popular topic of specialized directories, from franchise organizations to mail order companies. There is even a guide to companies which utilize manufacturer's agents. Other directories cover firms by their type of ownership, especially minority- and women-owned businesses. Special purpose directories deal with both mundane and unusual issues. Examples range from directories of firms that own large computer systems, to descriptions of companies which sponsor formal training and internship programs.

Several guides cover companies that import and export products. The very best is an annual set from Journal of Commerce, Inc. The *Directory of United States Importers* and the corresponding *Directory of United States Exporters* provide information on over 30,000 companies in the United States, Puerto Rico, and Canada which export their own products, import goods for further processing or resale, or import/export items for other companies. Included are manufacturers, wholesalers, retailers, manufacturer's representatives, export buyers, brokers, and agents. Data are collected from the actual customs documents filed at major U.S. and Canadian ports.

The remainder of the chapter will discuss some of the most frequently consulted special purpose directories, including biographical publications and guides to corporate affiliations. Because researching registered trademarks involves specialized tools and techniques, a separate section of this chapter is devoted to trademark and brand name sources. Other specialized directories are introduced elsewhere in the book. Directories which list companies in ranked order are described in Chapter 8; guides to defunct companies and corporate name changes are covered in Chapter 11.

Biographical Directories

One method of finding biographical information on business leaders is to search newspaper and periodical indexes, especially those covering local and regional publications. An alternative approach is to request business reports from Dun & Bradstreet Credit Services.

Although these invaluable reports are best known for their corporate credit ratings and payment histories, they also contain brief background information on the principal executives of each firm. A further description of D&B reports is given in Chapter 8.

Surprisingly few biographical directories offer extensive business coverage. General publications such as *Who's Who in America*, published by Marquis Who's Who, list only the most nationally prominent business executives. Marquis also publishes four regional directories which contain many more listings than the national edition. These guides, such as *Who's Who in the East*, include many business executives. Because Marquis produces so many biographical sources, they also compile an annual *Index to Who's Who Books*, which serves as an alphabetical guide to all the names appearing in its various directories. A second index to biographical directories, the massive *Biography and Genealogy Master Index*, was briefly described in Chapter 2.

Only three national directories specialize in executive profiles. Volume 2 of the S&P *Register* has already been introduced. The following sources are also extensive guides devoted exclusively to business coverage.

Reference Book of Corporate Managements (Dun's Marketing Services—Annual).

This four-volume set from Dun & Bradstreet provides an alternative approach to executive information. Instead of listing corporate officers alphabetically, their biographies are arranged by company name. Coverage is limited to 12,000 major firms in the United States. Although all types of companies are listed, surprisingly strong coverage is given to banks, financial service firms, and retail firms. Like the listings found in *Standard & Poor's*, the information on each person is brief. However, while S&P covers more companies, Dun & Bradstreet describes many more people—more than 170,000 in all. (Standard & Poor's limits biographical listings to the most senior executives and directors in every firm.) For the companies covered by the *Reference Book of Corporate Managements*, the publisher attempts to include as many executives as possible, down to the vice president level. While some companies only cite one or two executives, as many as 65 biographies can be found for a single company.

The personal information in the *Reference Book* includes year of birth, marital status, colleges attended (with dates and degrees), military service (with dates and rank), employment history, and principal outside affiliations. The first three volumes are arranged alphabetically by company, with a brief description of each firm and the biographical profiles. Volume 4 contains indexes to the

set, including personal names, companies arranged geographically by state and city, and a SIC index to all companies. Data from the *Reference Book of Corporate Managements* are also available in CD-ROM format, as part of the *Million Dollar Disc*.

Another interesting guide is the annual *Directory of Directors in the City of New York and Tri-State Area*. It has been published continuously since 1898 by a firm now called the Directory of Directors Co., Inc. The focus is on the officers, directors, partners, and trustees of the leading business and legal establishments in New York City. Selected companies in New Jersey, Connecticut, and downstate New York are also included. This directory does not offer biographical information, but home addresses are frequently cited, and each person's outside business and civic affiliations are listed. The directory is arranged by personal name, with a company index. The publisher also produces a similar guide for the Boston area.

Who's Who in Finance and Industry (Marquis Who's Who, Inc.—Biennial).

This well-known directory from Marquis is not limited to corporate executives and directors. Educators, association managers, government officials, and other business-related individuals are included. Approximately 23,500 people are described, far fewer than those covered in the competing directories. However, inclusion is highly selective, determined by each person's achievements or position.

The listings in *Who's Who in Finance* are the most detailed of the three major directories. In addition to birth date, marital status, education, career history, and outside business affiliations, most listings provide the names of parents, children, and spouse; marriage date; professional certifications; publications; religious and political affiliation; and memberships in clubs, lodges, professional and trade associations, and civic organizations. In most cases, both business and home addresses are given. Listings are arranged alphabetically by personal name, with no additional indexes. Data from this directory can also be searched on CD-ROM, as part of Lotus One Source's *CD/Corporate*.

Corporate Affiliations

A rich variety of directories provide information on parent and affiliate companies. Several general-purpose directories show affiliate relations, including the *Standard & Poor's Register*, the *Macmillan Directory of Leading Private Companies*, and *Dun's Market Identifiers*. Many directories focus on multinational relation-

ships. Examples are the *Directory of American Firms Operating in Foreign Countries*, the *Directory of Japanese Affiliates and Offices Operating in the U.S. and Canada*, the *Probe Directory of Foreign Direct Investment in the United States*, and the *Directory of Foreign Manufacturers in the United States*. The three publications described below are the most extensive guides to corporate affiliations in this country.

Directory of Corporate Affiliations (National Register Publishing Company—Annual, with Updates).

This "Who Owns Whom Red Book" describes 4,000 parent companies that own other firms or have large independent divisions. Approximately 40,000 of these "corporate children" are included. The *Directory of Corporate Affiliations (DCA)* is now published in two volumes. Volume 1 contains an alphabetic master index and the main descriptions, arranged by parent companies. Volume 2 carries a geographic index by city and state, a SIC index, and a personal name index to executives. In the main section, parent firms are presented alphabetically, with pertinent information such as address, business description, officers, state of incorporation, and sales volume. Additional information, such as stock exchange, total assets and liabilities, net worth, and year founded may also be seen. Under each parent is a list of affiliates in hierarchical order. Data on subsidiaries are limited, but typically include address, chief executive, and line of business, together with sales volume and number of employees, when available. The degree of ownership (100% or less) is also indicated for each subsidiary. Exhibit 7-1 shows how the directory presents information, which can be somewhat confusing at first glance. In the case of Champion International, the company has three operating units: the Paper Division, the Dairypak Division, and the Forest Products Division. All three names are followed by the number 1 in parentheses, which indicates they represent the first rung in the affiliate hierarchy. Those entries with a (2) designation report directly to one of the divisions. For example, the Sartell Mill reports to the Paper Division and the Bonner Mill reports to the Forest Products Division. Also notice the diversity of affiliations shown in the Exhibit. Champion International lists divisions and individual plant locations, while the Chancellor Corporation owns a variety of subsidiaries.

An especially useful feature of the *Directory of Corporate Affiliations* is the annual list of "Mergers, Acquisitions, and Name Changes." The annual summary appears at the front of Volume 1, and is supplemented by a ten-year historical guide to changes in the status of parent companies. *DCA* is updated five times per year in a brief *Corporate Action* newsletter.

A companion publication called the *International Directory of Corporate Affiliations* is sold separately. While there is some overlap between the two directories, the international edition focuses on foreign companies with U.S. operations and American firms with a presence abroad. Approximately 1,200 foreign parents and 1,500 domestic parents are described, together with 30,000 affiliated firms. The first section is arranged by foreign parent, with information on U.S. and foreign subsidiaries and divisions. A second section lists American parents with foreign affiliations. Two geographic indexes are arranged by states and cities in the U.S., and by country and city for the rest of the world. A trade name index is also provided.

Listings from both editions can be searched online or on CD-ROM, as the *Corporate Affiliations* database. It is available exclusively through DIALOG in both formats, and is updated quarterly. Virtually every field is fully searchable, including employee size, all financial data, all geographic variables, SIC numbers, and state of incorporation. The number of affiliates for every parent and the degree of ownership for every subsidiary are also indexed. This means that users can quickly identify all parent companies in Illinois with net worth greater than $50 million and more than five subsidiaries, or all subsidiaries in food processing industries which are less than 100% controlled by their parent.

America's Corporate Families: The Billion Dollar Directory (Dun's Marketing Services—Annual).

This two-volume directory from Dun & Bradstreet is similar to its competitor in most respects, but covers more parent companies. Over 9,000 ultimate parents are listed, together with 45,000 subsidiaries and divisions. To be included, parent companies must have net assets over $500,000 and more than one subsidiary. All 9,000 parent firms are also found in the *Million Dollar Directory*, and the corporate descriptions are virtually identical. Besides the information on corporate relationships, *America's Corporate Families* offers many affiliate listings not seen in the *Million Dollar Directory*, and most descriptions of subsidiaries and divisions provide information on sales, employment size, and chief executive. Relationships are shown in hierarchical fashion, with numeric designations indicating the order in which companies report to their parents. All firms are indexed geographically and by SIC number, and a master index to company names is also provided. Volume 2 of *America's Corporate Families* covers multinational relationships,

EXHIBIT 7-1. *Directory of Corporate Affiliations*

Section 2 — Parent Companies

Larry Barron *(Mgr.-Pur.)*
Mitchell Frederick *(Quality Control)*

Subsidiary:
6803-109
Gateway Homes, Inc. **(2)**
P.O. Box 728, Hwy. 78 East
Guin, AL 35563
Tel.: 205-468-3191   (100%)
Mfrs. Single-Section Homes
S.I.C.: 2452; 3448
Tex Johnson *(Gen. Mgr.)*

† 6804-000

🏁 **Champion**
Champion International Corporation

One Champion Plaza
Stamford, CT 06921
Tel.: 203-358-7000   **NY**
Telex: 91522
Telefax: 203-358-7495
CHA—(NYSE PS Bo Ci MW Ph)
Assets: $6,699,885,000
Earnings: $456,445,000
Liabilities: $3,354,928,000
Net Worth: $3,344,957,000
Approx. Sls.: $5,128,513,000
Emp: 30,400
Fiscal Year-end: 12/31/88
Major Mfr. of Printing & Publication
Papers
S.I.C.: 2621; 2631; 2656; 2672; 2677;
2678; 2679; 2435
Andrew C. Sigler *(Chm. Bd. & Chief
Exec. Officer)*
Aubrey L. Cole *(Vice Chm.)*
William R. Haselton *(Vice Chm.)*
Kenwood C. Nichols *(Vice Chm.)*
L. C. Heist *(Pres. & Chief Oper. Officer)*
William H. Burchfield *(Exec. V.P.)*
B. Taggart Edwards *(Exec. V.P.)*
Mark A. Fuller, Jr. *(Exec. V.P.)*
Richard E. Olsen *(Exec. V.P.)*
John A. Ball *(Sr. V.P.)*
Gerald J. Beiser *(Sr. V.P.-Fin.)*
Marvin H. Ginsky *(Sr. V.P. & Gen.
Counsel)*
C. William Gray *(Sr. V.P.)*
Judson Hannigan *(Sr. V.P.)*
Philip R. O'Connell *(Sr. V.P. & Sec.)*
Frank Kneisel *(V.P. & Treas.)*
Austin A. Moore, Jr. *(V.P. & Controller)*
Gerald J. O'Connor *(V.P. & G.M.)*
Michael P. Corey *(V.P.-Corp. Plng.)*
Thomas F. Volpe *(V.P.-Tax Affairs)*
John H. Hildenbiddle *(V.P.-Creative
Services)*
Nick Van Nelson *(V.P.-Govt. Affairs)*
John Johnson *(V.P.-Corp. Engrng.)*
Richard J. DiForio *(V.P.-Environment)*
Bartley L. Reitz *(V.P.-Mngmt.
Information Services)*
Robert W. Turner *(V.P.- Public Affairs)*
Board of Directors:
Robert A. Charpie
Aubrey L. Cole
William R. Haselton
Frederick G. Jaicks
Howard W. Johnson
Elizabeth J. McCormack
Sybil C. Mobley
H. Barclay Morley
Walter V. Shipley
Andrew C. Sigler
Edward O. Vetter
Richard E. Walton
5000-000
Manufacturers Hanover Trust
Co.*(Transfer Agent)*
P.O. Box 24975, Church Street
Station
New York, NY 10249
21870-006
Arthur Andersen & Co.*(Auditors)*
1345 Avenue of The Americas

New York, NY 10105
Tel.: 212-708-4000

Divisions:
6804-014
Champion International Corp., Paper
Div. **(1)**
One Champion Plaza
Stamford, CT 06921
Tel.: 203-358-7000
Coated & Uncoated Fine Printing Papers, Cut-
Size Business Papers, Envelope Papers,
Form Papers, Converting & Specialty Papers
S.I.C.: 2621
Mark A. Fuller, Jr. *(Exec. V.P.)*
Robert E. Tiemeyer *(V.P.-Sls. & Marketing-
Newsprint & Pulp)*
Robert W. Sexton *(V.P.- Sales & Marketing-
Kraft Paper & Board)*
L. S. Barnard *(V.P.-Sls., Printing & Writing
Papers)*
Earle Bensing *(V.P.-Sls., Conv. & Dairypak)*
Ted Robinson *(V.P.-Sls., Publ. Papers)*
Thomas V. Zeuthen *(V.P. & G.M., Nationwide
Papers)*

Plants & Mills:
6804-049
Bucksport Mill, Champion International
Corp. **(2)**
P.O. Box 1200, River Rd.
Bucksport, ME 04416
Tel.: 207-469-3131
Mfr. Coated Paper
S.I.C.: 2671
6804-051
Courtland Mill, Champion International
Corporation **(2)**
P.O. Box 189
Courtland, AL 35618
Tel.: 205-637-2741
Mfr. Printing & Writing Papers
S.I.C.: 2621
6804-052
Lufkin Mill, Champion International
Corporation **(2)**
P.O. Box 149
Lufkin, TX 75901
Tel.: 409-634-8811
Mfr. Newsprint
S.I.C.: 2621
6804-053
Roanoke Rapids Mill, Champion
International Corporation **(2)**
P.O. Box 580
Roanoke Rapids, NC 27870
Tel.: 919-537-6011
Kraft Paperliner Producer
S.I.C.: 2621
6804-050
Sartell Mill, Champion International
Corp. **(2)**
P.O. Box 338
Sartell, MN 56377
Tel.: 612-251-6511
6804-054
Sheldon Mill, Champion International
Corporation **(2)**
P.O. Box 23011
Houston, TX 77228-3011
Tel.: 713-456-8780
Newsprint Mill
S.I.C.: 2621
6804-044
Champion Dairypak Div. **(1)**
801 5th Ave.
Belvidere, IL 61008
Tel.: 815-544-2186
Mfrs. Microwave Trays
S.I.C.: 3589
David Hunter *(Gen. Mgr.)*

Plant:
6804-055
Canton Plant, Champion Dairypak Div.
(2)
P.O. Box 175
Canton, NC 28716
Tel.: 704-646-2000
Mfr. Bleached Paperboard
S.I.C.: 2631
6804-045
Champion International Corp., Forest
Products Div. **(1)**
One Champion Plaza
Stamford, CT 06921
Tel.: 203-358-7000
Plywood & Lumber Mfg.
S.I.C.: 2435; 2621
Byron T. Edwards *(Exec. V.P.)*

Mills:
6804-056
Bonner Mill, Forest Products Div. **(2)**
Drawer 7
Bonner, MT 59823
Tel.: 406-258-5511

Stud Mill
S.I.C.: 2421
6804-057
Camden Mill, Forest Products Div. **(2)**
P.O. Box 200
Camden, TX 75934
Tel.: 409-398-2511
Plywood Veneer
S.I.C.: 2435
6804-058
Citronelle Plant, Forest Products Div.
(2)
P.O. Box 365
Citronelle, AL 36522
Tel.: 205-866-2415

†★ 6805-000
CHAMPION PARTS, INC.
2525 W. 22nd St.
Oak Brook, IL 60521
Tel.: 708-573-6600   **IL**
Telefax: 312-573-0348
Year Founded: 1947
CREB—(OTC)
Assets: $96,049,000
Earnings: $1,621,000
Liabilities: $66,737,000
Net Worth: $29,312,000
Approx. Sls.: $129,480,000
Emp: 2,400
Fiscal Year-end: 12/31/88
Remanufacturer of Automotive Truck &
Tractor Parts
S.I.C.: 3714
Charles P. Schwartz, Jr. *(Chm. & Chief
Exec. Officer)*
Donato A. Savini *(Pres. & Chief Oper.
Officer)*
Robert C. Mikolashek *(V.P.-Mfg.
Opers.)*
Leonard D. O'Brien *(V.P.-Fin., Sec. &
Treas.)*
Kevin J. O'Connor *(V.P.-Sls. & Mktg.)*
Frederick Pochowicz *(Personnel Dir.)*
Gary Esterling *(Dir.-Mktg.)*
Robert Smith *(Data Processing Dir.)*
Board of Directors:
Charles P. Schwartz, Jr.
Robert Feitler
Donald H. Freeman
J. R. Gross
Raymond F. Gross
Gary Hopmayer
Edward Kipling
Fredrick C. Meyers
Raymond Perelman
Donald G. Santucci
Donato A. Savini
4291-000
Adams, Fox, Adelstein & Rosen*(Legal
Firm)*
208 So. LaSalle St.
Chicago, IL 60604
Tel.: 312-368-1900
4292-000
Exchange National Bank*(Transfer
Agent)*
120 So. LaSalle St.
Chicago, IL 60603
Tel.: 312-443-6745
22354-051
Touche Ross & Co.*(Auditors)*
One Illinois Center, 111 E. Wacker
Dr.
Chicago, IL 60601

Divisions:
6805-001
Hope Div. **(1)**
1501 W. Ave. B
Hope, AR 71801
Tel.: 501-777-8821
S.I.C.: 3714
6805-003
Northeast Div. **(1)**
Lock Haven, PA 17745
Tel.: 717-962-2151
S.I.C.: 3714
6805-005
Texas Div. **(1)**
200 W. Vickery Rd.
Ft. Worth, TX 76101
Tel.: 817-336-9741
S.I.C.: 3714
6805-049
Western Division **(1)**
2696 So. Maple
Fresno, CA 93725

Tel.: 209-233-2577
S.I.C.: 3714

●
10889-000
CHANCELLOR CORPORATION
745 Atlantic Ave.
Boston, MA 02111
Tel.: 617-728-8500   **MA**
CHCR—(OTC)
Assets: $247,494,000
Earnings: $3,521,000
Liabilities: $205,589,000
Net Worth: $41,905,000
Approx. Rev.: $48,664,000
Emp: 75
Fiscal Year-end: 3/31/88
Leveraged Lease Financing of
Transportation, Medical &
Communication Equip.
S.I.C.: 7359
Vincent W. Garrett *(Chm. & Chief Exec.
Officer)*
Walter E. Huskins, Jr. *(Vice Chm.)*
W. Barry Tanner *(Pres. & Chief Oper.
Officer)*
John J. Flynn *(Exec. V.P.)*
John Bresnahan *(Exec. V.P.)*
William C. Sprong *(Sr. V.P. & Treas.)*
Frederick R. H. Witherby, Jr. *(V.P.)*
Kathleen R. Maloney *(V.P. & Gen.
Counsel)*
Board of Directors:
Vincent W. Garrett
A. David Case, O.C.
Kenneth V. Cox
Bruce M. Dayton
G. Edwin Graham
Walter E. Huskins, Jr.
Marks H. Lockhart
Michael Scott Morton
W. Barry Tanner
23509-001
Csaplar & Bok*(Legal Firm)*
One Winthrop Square
Boston, MA 02110
3918-002
State Street Bank & Trust Co.*(Transfer
Agent)*
225 Franklin St.
Boston, MA 02110
Tel.: 617-786-3000

Subsidiaries:
10889-001
Chancellor Asset Corporation **(1)**
745 Atlantic Avenue
Boston, MA 02111
Tel.: 617-728-8500
S.I.C.: 7359
10889-002
Chancellor DataComm, Inc. **(1)**
745 Atlantic Avenue
Boston, MA 02111
Tel.: 617-728-8500
S.I.C.: 7359
10889-003
Chancellor Financial Sales & Services,
Inc. **(1)**
745 Atlantic Avenue
Boston, MA 02111
Tel.: 617-728-8500
S.I.C.: 7359
John T. Kraska *(V.P.)*
Thomas W. Martin *(V.P.)*
Robert M. Ross *(V.P.)*
Brian Stucker *(V.P.-Lease Origination)*
10889-004
Chancellor Fleet Corporation **(1)**
745 Atlantic Avenue
Boston, MA 02111
Tel.: 617-728-8500
S.I.C.: 7359
James P. Campbell *(V.P. & Reg. Mgr.)*
Alexis F. Donghi *(V.P. & Reg. Mgr.)*
John M. Jaje *(V.P. & Reg.Mgr.)*
Mark A. Paul *(V.P.-Remarketing)*
Joseph M. Tollus *(V.P.-Materials Handling)*
10889-005
Chancellor Management Corporation
(1)
745 Atlantic Avenue
Boston, MA 02111
Tel.: 617-728-8500
S.I.C.: 7359
10889-006
Valmont Financial Corporation **(1)**
11213 Davenport, Ste. 303
Omaha, NE 68154
Tel.: 402-691-6240   (100%)
Emp: 15

(continued next page)

---

† Refer to the International Directory of Corporate Affiliations for information about foreign holdings.

and lists parent companies in three separate sections: companies based in the United States, Canadian parents, and other foreign companies. The format is otherwise identical to Volume 1.

A more extensive guide to company affiliations is published by Dun & Bradstreet's British subsidiary. *Who Owns Whom* is an annual six-volume set issued in four editions: the United Kingdom and Ireland, Continental Europe, Asia and Australia, and North America. Compared to the sources described above, *Who Owns Whom* offers little information on each firm. The parent company address is given, along with the names of affiliate firms, their countries of incorporation and type of affiliation, and the SIC codes for every company. The alphabetical index also indicates the percentage of ownership exercised over each subsidiary. The subsidiaries are listed in hierarchical order. No addresses are given for affiliates, nor any background data on parent companies. *Who Owns Whom* doesn't limit coverage to companies with ties to the United States; its 25,000 parent companies and 275,000 subsidiaries make it the most comprehensive guide to the worldwide operations of major businesses. Each edition is divided into three sections. The first is arranged by country and lists all parent companies with headquarters in that country, followed by each firm's worldwide affiliates. The second section lists all foreign parents with subsidiaries in the region, arranged in a single alphabet. The third section is an alphabetical master index to all parents and affiliates. The complete set is expensive, but information from the directories is available online through Pergamon Financial Data Services.

SEARCHING FOR BRAND NAMES AND TRADEMARKS

Brands are not always identical to the names of the companies that own them, but people are more likely to recognize brand names. Many business directories contain brand name indexes to help locate the proper company. Some of the most extensive guides are the *Standard Directory of Advertisers*, the *Thomas Register*, and *MacRae's Blue Book*. A variety of more specialized resources are also available to assist in a brand name or trademark search. Before introducing them, some basic concepts will be covered, including the difference between registered and unregistered trademarks, the registration process, and common types of trademark research.

Registered Versus Unregistered Trademarks

A trademark is a distinctive word, phrase, symbol, or design placed on a product or service to distinguish it from those of other companies. A trademark identifies an individual product or service and a trade name identifies the entire company, but for the purposes of this discussion the terms will be used interchangeably. There are also special types of trademarks called service marks, certification marks, and housemarks, but all of these terms impart the notion of a brand name.

From a marketing perspective, the purpose of a brand is to generate customer recognition, reassure buyers of consistency and quality, and provide the focus for advertising and promotional campaigns. From a legal point of view, a trademark is intended to designate the source of a product or service, to protect both consumer and producer from deceptive practices, and to protect the trademark owner against the use of that mark, or a deceptively similar one, by anyone else in the same type of business. Not all trademarks are registered; the registration of a name or design is completely at the owner's discretion. Under United States law, legal rights to trademarks are actually acquired through commercial use of the mark, not through the act of registration. Registration basically provides the owner with an official record of that use, making it simpler to defend against infringement. Trademarks are registered nationally with the U.S. Patent and Trademark Office (PTO) and may be renewed indefinitely as long as they remain in use. Registered trademarks are identified by the symbol® or the phrase "Reg. U.S. Pat & T.M. Office." Unregistered marks may be identified by the symbol™.

A related category of marketing designation is the burgeoning field of merchandise licensing. A famous individual such as Bill Blass, or the owner of such copyrighted creations as "Batman" or "Garfield" may enter into contractual relationships with companies to allow the use of their names and creations. A licensed name or design may be used simultaneously by as many companies as obtain the rights to their use. The owner of a trademark may also license that mark to other companies, but in order to do so it must be registered. This is generally done to capitalize on popular products and symbols by marketing unrelated products using the same imagery. A good example would be licensing Teenage Mutant Ninja Turtles trademarks for use on clothing, school supplies, and other nontoy items. In most cases, however, a trademark is generally identified with one company only.

Prior to 1989, a domestic company wishing to register a trademark in the United States had to prove that it was already using the name in commerce. This put American companies at a disadvantage because the U.S. was one of the only industrialized nations with such a stringent requirement. Sweeping revisions in federal law changed that limitation as of November 1989. Now companies need only demonstrate a bona fide intent to use a proposed trademark within three years. However, to be eligible for registration with the Patent and Trademark Office, the product or service must be sold in interstate trade. Any brand intended for sale within a single state may have a trademark registered with the state government.

Certain additional requirements must be met before a trademark application is accepted by the PTO. For example, the mark cannot use or suggest an obscene or slanderous meaning, the name of living persons cannot be used without their permission, and no flag or symbol of the federal or state governments or their agencies may be used. The trademark cannot be confusingly similar to a previously registered mark unless the word is considered a "weak trademark." Words suggesting the general attributes of a product—universal, mighty, acme—are considered weak trademarks and can be used simultaneously by more than one company as long as the products themselves are not similar.

Federal trademarks are registered for a period of ten years. New marks must pass an additional test. Before the sixth year of the initial registration period expires, a statement must be filed with the PTO avowing that the product or service is still in commercial use. A trademark may be renewed indefinitely for ten-year periods, assuming it continues to be used.

The process of registering a trademark follows several steps. If an application is accepted by the PTO it is assigned a Serial Number (SN), and the name and design are then published for opposition in the government's weekly *Official Gazette: Trademarks*. The general public then has 30 days to challenge the mark, charging that the new name or design will cause confusion in the marketplace. If no challenge is received, the trademark is duly registered in the normal course of business at the Patent and Trademark Office. Registrations are batched on a weekly basis, assigned a Registration Number in chronological order, and republished in the *Gazette* as fully registered. The government actually maintains two trademark registries, called Principal and Supplemental. The Principal Register is for trademarks that meet all requirements of the PTO, are published for opposition, and are subsequently registered. The Supplemental Register is for weaker marks not meeting Patent

and Trademark Office standards. They are considered Supplemental because the name is deemed less distinctive in the public mind than a Principal mark would be. A Supplemental trademark is not published for opposition.

The act of registering a trademark does not end the owner's obligations; the mark must be protected throughout its life from becoming identified with the generic product it represents. Numerous firms have lost exceedingly valuable marks because, in the public mind, the brand name became interchangeable with the category of product it represented. Successful trademarks can lose their status if the owner allows the name to be used in a generic sense. Bayer lost the use of "aspirin" as a trademark because they failed to combat the careless use of the name. Widely recognized terms such as thermos, cellophane, linoleum, and harmonica have become part of our language as a result of this process. Dozens of current trade names are in constant danger of losing their trademark status to "genericide"; Xerox, Kleenex, Styrofoam, Q-tips, Teflon, Scotch Tape, Formica, and Vaseline are all examples.

Trademark status is exhibited primarily by advertising, labeling, and packaging. Not only must the trademark's use be demonstrated, it must also be carefully protected. The name should be highlighted or capitalized when seen in print, it should never be made into a plural or adjectival form, and its appearance should never vary. The company must make an active effort to promote its unique identity in the public mind. For example, the generic name of the product should be mentioned in company literature, as in "Sanka brand decaffeinated coffee" and "Band-Aid brand adhesive bandages." Because such universally known products have become household words, it is often difficult for the researcher to determine whether the name is generic or not. A quick way to find out is to consult a standard dictionary, whether unabridged or a desk edition. The current editions of better-quality works such as the *Random House Dictionary of the English Language*, *Webster's New Collegiate Dictionary*, or the *American Heritage Dictionary* indicate whether many common names are trademarks or not. However, the best way to determine if a name is registered is to consult the specialized publications described later in this section.

Classification of Registered Trademarks

Many reference tools have been created to help researchers investigate registered trademarks. Essential to the proper use of these publications is an understand-

ing of the classification systems used by the government. Prior to 1974, a U.S. Trademark Classification was utilized; after this time, the PTO switched to the International Classification System. Both are very broad groupings of products and services; each uses about 50 general categories, including several catchall classes.

The Patent and Trademark Office continues to assign U.S. Classification numbers to new trademarks, even though it has switched to the International system. Registrations are listed in the *Official Gazette* under the International number with the U.S. number in parentheses. Ultimately, as pre-1974 trademarks expire or are renewed, the older classification system will be phased out.

The basic structure of the International Classification is shown in Figure 7-A. To the uninitiated searcher, the method of selecting the appropriate class for a type of product can seem baffling. For example, Class 11 for "Environmental Control Apparatus" embraces air conditioners, furnaces, sun lamps, and sewage disposal units. It also covers stoves, refrigerators, and barbecue grills, which might seem like stretching the definition. Stranger still, bathtubs, toilets, electric fixtures, and light bulbs also find their way into Class 11. The average searcher looking at the general classification outline would probably have no idea where to find trademarks for light bulbs. Exhibit 7-2 is a page from the *Official Gazette* that lists trademark applications for International Class 9, "Electrical and Scientific Apparatus." Grouped together on that single page are marks for telecommunications equipment, a fax machine, computer programs, a camera, and the "Doctor Who" television show! The system abounds with additional, equally strange decisions, such as placing coat hangers under Class 26 for "Fancy Goods," and flea collars under "Pharmaceuticals" in Class 5. These classifications may be defensible to one degree or another, but they are certainly not conducive to easy searching.

In order to understand the logic imposed on these groupings, each class must be examined in its entirety rather than relying on a general outline of classifications. The PTO's *Index to Trademark and Service Classes* provides an alphabetical guide to the classification systems used for trademarks. It is not available for sale or public distribution from the PTO or the Government Printing Office, nor is it received by federal Depository Libraries. However, it may be consulted at the Patent and Trademark Office, or at many Patent Depository Libraries (PDLs), which contain special resources for use in patent and trademark research. Approximately 60 PDLs have been established in the United States; most are located in large public and university libraries. Subject indexes to trademark classes can also be seen in the *Trademark Register* and *Trademarkscan-Federal*, commercial publications described in the following section.

Specialized Trademark Publications

Two situations require trademark research: a comprehensive investigation of registered marks to determine whether the proposed name or design for a new company, product, or service is already being used; and a search to identify the owner of a known trademark. The first type is vastly complex and, like patent searching, is best left to experts. Investigating the record for previously registered trademarks is an integral part of new product research. Errors or omissions in such a search can be costly mistakes; failure to uncover an existing trademark or having a new name contested can result in millions of dollars in wasted market research, advertising, and production costs. Attempting to identify the owner of a specific trademark is a simpler task, though it may take several steps. For the persistent investigator who has already consulted general brand name directories with no success, several of the publications introduced below may yield better results. The first title described below covers both registered and unregistered names, and is not intended as a comprehensive resource. All others are devoted exclusively to federally registered trademarks.

Brands and Their Companies (Gale Research, Inc.— Annual, with Supplements).

An excellent single source for identifying brand names and their owners is this extensive guide from Gale Research, formerly called the *Trade Names Dictionary*. The 1990 edition lists about 230,000 brand names from approximately 40,000 companies. Coverage is limited to producers of consumer goods and services only. Much of the information is gathered from approximately 100 different trade directories containing their own brand name indexes, but fully half of the listings are obtained from the companies themselves.

The two-volume directory is arranged in two sections: the bulk of the set is an alphabetical listing of brand names; Volume 2 also provides a separate directory of company names and addresses. For brand names, each entry provides a brief product description, the company name, and the source where the information was obtained. Defunct popular names (mostly automobile brands) and former brand names now in the public

FIGURE 7-A. International Trademark Classification

Products

Class 1	Chemicals
Class 2	Paints
Class 3	Cosmetics and Cleaning Preparations
Class 4	Lubricants and Fuels
Class 5	Pharmaceuticals
Class 6	Metal Goods
Class 7	Machinery
Class 8	Hand Tools
Class 9	Electrical and Scientific Apparatus
Class 10	Medical Apparatus
Class 11	Environmental Control Apparatus
Class 12	Vehicles
Class 13	Firearms
Class 14	Jewelry
Class 15	Musical Instruments
Class 16	Paper Goods and Printed Matter
Class 17	Rubber Goods
Class 18	Leather Goods
Class 19	Non-Metallic Building Materials
Class 20	Furniture and Articles Not Elsewhere Classified
Class 21	Housewares and Glass
Class 22	Cordage and Fibers
Class 23	Yarns and Threads
Class 24	Fabrics
Class 25	Clothing
Class 26	Fancy Goods
Class 27	Floor Coverings
Class 28	Toys and Sporting Goods
Class 29	Meats and Processed Foods
Class 30	Staple Foods
Class 31	Natural Agricultural Products
Class 32	Light Beverages
Class 33	Wines and Spirits
Class 34	Smokers' Articles

Services

Class 35	Advertising and Business
Class 36	Insurance and Financial
Class 37	Construction and Repair
Class 38	Communication
Class 39	Transportation and Storage
Class 40	Material Treatment
Class 41	Education and Entertainment
Class 42	Miscellaneous

domain are also listed. These features are useful because the current status of brand names is not always known. However, the directory makes no distinction between registered and unregistered trademarks. Another excellent feature is a thorough explanation of the alphabetizing conventions utilized. Because brand names often employ numerals, initialisms, punctuation marks, and personal names, this is a necessary finding aid. Users should examine this section, since several peculiar alphabetizing standards are used, including filing under "the," and listing personal names under the individual's first name (e.g., Gloria Vanderbilt is filed under G).

Three companion guides are published in Gale's *Trade Names Directory* series. *Companies and Their Brands* provides reverse access to the information found in the main directory. Here the user looks up the company name to see a complete list of its current brands. The other two directories are the foreign equivalents to the U.S. set. *International Brands and Their Companies* and *International Companies and Their Brands* provide the same treatment for more than 15,000 companies outside the United States, and their 50,000 brands. All four directories are now available online through DIALOG's *Trade Names Database*.

Official Gazette of the United States Patent and Trademark Office: Trademarks (U.S. Patent and Trademark Office—Weekly).

The weekly *Gazette* is divided into two publications, one for patents and one for trademarks. *Trademarks* contains news about trademark law, listings of contested names, and other current information. The heart of each issue is devoted to trademarks published for opposition, new registrations, and canceled, amended, and renewed registrations. New registrations are divided into Principal and Supplemental registers. Each issue provides an index to the registrants appearing in that issue, arranged by company name.

The section entitled "Marks Published for Opposition" is where all trademarks in the Principal Register are first seen. Listings are arranged according to the International Classification system; those marks assigned multiple classifications are listed first. Each mark is assigned a consecutive Serial Number. Exhibit 7-2 illustrates a typical page from this section. If a mark utilizes a design or a stylized logotype, it is reproduced in black and white. If the name is registered with no design, it is listed in plain block letters. Each listing also indicates the filing date, the date the mark was first used, the company name and city of the applicant, a description of the product or service the mark represents, the former U.S. Classifica-

EXHIBIT 7-2. *Official Gazette of the Patent and Trademark Office*

MARCH 27, 1990   U.S. PATENT AND TRADEMARK OFFICE   TM 63

CLASS 9—ELECTRICAL AND SCIENTIFIC APPARATUS

SN 73-565,718. GTE PRODUCTS CORPORATION, STAMFORD, CT. FILED 10-28-1985.

SYLVANIA BLUE DOT

OWNER OF U.S. REG. NOS. 536,749 AND 1,325,543.
FOR DISK CAMERAS (U.S. CL. 26).
FIRST USE 4-16-1985; IN COMMERCE 4-16-1985.

———————

SN 73-586,368. BRITISH TELECOMMUNICATIONS PUBLIC LIMITED COMPANY, LONDON, ENGLAND, FILED 3-6-1986.

PRIORITY CLAIMED UNDER SEC. 44(D) ON UNITED KINGDOM APPLICATION NO. 1251071, FILED 9-26-1985, REG. NO. B1251071, DATED 11-14-1988, EXPIRES 9-26-1992.
OWNER OF U.S. REG. NO. 1,489,931.
THE MARK CONSISTS, IN PART, OF THE LETTERS "BTI".
SEC. 2(F) AS TO THE WORDS "BRITISH TELECOM".
FOR TELEPHONES, RADIO PAGING RECEIVERS, TELEX TRANSMITTERS AND RECEIVERS, FACSIMILE TRANSMITTERS AND RECEIVERS, ELECTRONIC MAIL UNITS, MESSAGE SWITCHING UNITS, TELECONFERENCING UNITS, MODEMS, ANTENNAS, AND SATELLITE DISHES, ALL FOR USE IN PROVIDING DATA VOICE AND IMAGE COMMUNICATIONS BY ELECTRONIC, OPTICAL AND DIGITAL MEANS THROUGH THE MEDIUM OF RADIO TRANSMISSION (U.S. CLS. 21 AND 26).

———————

SN 73-588,159. PYRAMID TECHNOLOGY CORPORATION, MOUNTAIN VIEW, CA. ASSIGNEE OF OFFICE AUTOMATION SYSTEMS, INC., SAN DIEGO, CA. FILED 3-17-1986.

PYRAMID

OWNER OF U.S. REG. NO. 1,434,515.
FOR COMPUTER PROGRAMS, NAMELY, FONT GENERATING PROGRAMS FOR LASER PRINTER CONTROLLERS (U.S. CL. 38).
FIRST USE 9-19-1984; IN COMMERCE 9-19-1984.

CLASS 9—(Continued).

SN 73-604,675. KABUSHIKI KAISHA KENWOOD, TA KENWOOD CORPORATION, TOKYO, JAPAN, FILED 6-13-1986.

ILLUSTPHONE

PRIORITY CLAIMED UNDER SEC. 44(D) ON JAPAN APPLICATION NO. 43066/1986, FILED 4-25-1986, REG. NO. 2136303, DATED 5-30-1989, EXPIRES 5-30-1990.
FOR FACSIMILE TRANSMITTER USED TO TRANSMIT LETTERS AND/OR DRAWINGS BY MEANS OF WIRE, WIRELESS, PHONE, WIRELESS SETS AND TELECOPIER MACHINES (U.S. CL. 21).

———————

SN 73-623,858. BRITISH BROADCASTING CORPORATION, THE, AKA BBC, LONDON, ENGLAND, FILED 10-3-1986.

PRIORITY CLAIMED UNDER SEC. 44(D) ON UNITED KINGDOM APPLICATION NO. 1274096, FILED 8-8-1986, REG. NO. 1274096, DATED 8-8-1986, EXPIRES 8-8-1993.
FOR PRE-RECORDED AUDIO AND VIDEO TAPES, CASSETTES AND DISCS, PHONOGRAPH RECORDS, CINEMATOGRAPHIC FILMS, AND COMPUTER PROGRAMS (U.S. CLS. 21, 36 AND 38).
FIRST USE 0-0-1980; IN COMMERCE 0-0-1980.

———————

SN 73-624,540. NORISTAN LIMITED, WALTLOO, PRETORIA, SOUTH AFRICA, ASSIGNEE OF NORIDATA SYSTEMS (PROPRIETARY) LIMITED, WALTLOO, PRETORIA, SOUTH AFRICA, FILED 10-7-1986.

NORIMED

PRIORITY CLAIMED UNDER SEC. 44(D) ON SOUTH AFRICA APPLICATION NO. 86/5260, FILED 8-12-1986, REG. NO. 86/5260, DATED 8-12-1986, EXPIRES 8-12-1996.
FOR COMPUTER SOFTWARE PROGRAMS USED FOR THE MANAGEMENT OF MEDICAL DOCTOR'S PRACTICE (U.S. CL. 38).

Reprinted from the *Official Gazette of the Patent and Trademark Office*, published by the U.S. Patent and Trademark Office.

tion number (in parentheses), and any explanatory information or disclaimers accompanying the application. When the trademark becomes registered, the basic information is republished in the *Gazette*. The "Registrations Issued" section lists the registration number, the name of the trademark, the registrant, and the former U.S. Classification. For the user who needs to refer to the design, each listing also cites the Serial Number and the date the application was first published in the *Official Gazette*.

The *Gazette* provides no cumulative indexing; the weekly issues are intended chiefly as a current notification service. However, the publication also serves as the official record of applications and trademark registrations. Separate indexes, directories, and databases are available from the PTO and from commercial publishers. These serve as cumulative listings of registered trademarks, but each refers users to the appropriate issues of the *Official Gazette* for further information. As long as the Registration Numbers are known, anyone can also order individual trademark filings from the PTO. These single sheet descriptions contain additional information not found in the *Gazette*, including the registrant's latest known address and the most recent renewal date.

The *Official Gazette* can be ordered in paper directly through the PTO, or on microfiche via the U.S. Government Printing Office. Individuals wishing to purchase older volumes can do so through a commercial firm called Compu-Mark, which has produced a historical microfiche set called *U.S. Federal Trademarks Official Gazette*.

Index to Trademarks Registered with the United States Patent and Trademark Office (U.S. Patent and Trademark Office—Annual).

This is an annual cumulation of the company names cited in the weekly "List of Trademark Registrants" section of the *Gazette*. Under each company name is a list of trademarks registered, renewed, or canceled during the previous year, together with its registration number and date of publication in the *Gazette*. For renewed marks, the original registration date is given, which is extremely helpful for historical research. For each company, the firm's city of residence and dba (if any) is also cited. There are two drawbacks to using this publication. First, it takes nearly 12 months after the publication of the year-end issue of the *Gazette* before the cumulative index appears. Second, unless the user knows the year a trademark was registered or renewed, searching can be time-consuming. On the other hand, by examining the current year's issues of the *Gazette* plus 20 years of the *Index*, researchers can compile a reasonably comprehensive list of a company's currently registered marks.

Trademark Register (Trademark Register, Inc.—Annual).

The *Trademark Register* is a cumulative listing of every registered mark issued since 1881 and currently in force at the time of publication. Information on trademarks can be located in two sections, each using a different classification scheme. Trademarks issued or renewed after September 1973 are organized under the International Classification System. Marks registered or renewed prior to that time are found under their U.S. Classification number. In both sections, the trademarks are listed alphabetically within each class. This arrangement means both sections must be consulted in order to perform a thorough search. On the bright side, the number of marks classified under the old system grows smaller every year, and should completely disappear by 1994.

Because the *Trademark Register* provides no single alphabetical listing by trademark, the researcher must be careful to identify appropriate classification numbers before beginning the search. The broad outline of classification titles is entirely insufficient to lead users to the proper category, but an excellent subject index to class numbers is found at the rear of the volume. For frequent trademark searchers, this unique feature alone presents a compelling reason to purchase the book.

Like most trademark guides, the *Register* cannot be used alone in any practical sense because it is designed as an index to the *Official Gazette*. Each entry gives only the name of the trademark, its International and U.S. class numbers, the Registration Number, and the date of publication. The *Register* cites the date each mark's registration is announced in the *Gazette* rather than the date it was first published. To see what a mark looks like requires looking first in the issue of the *Gazette* when the mark was registered, and then to the earlier issue when it was published for opposition.

The publisher produces several companion volumes to the *Trademark Register*. The *Trademark Owners Register* is a company name index complete with company address. The *Trademark Design Register* reproduces the designs for some 15,000 recently issued trademarks and is indexed by trade name, company name, and class.

Compu-Mark Directory of U.S. Trademarks (Compu-Mark U.S.—Annual, with Quarterly Updates).

A simpler to use, but more expensive alternative to the *Trademark Register* is Compu-Mark's annual ten-volume index. The set is divided into two parts: one arranged by classification number, the other alphabetically by trademark name. The classified section lists

trademarks alphabetically within each International Classification group. Entries for each trademark in the Principal Register include trade name, Registration Number, and the date and page of the *Official Gazette* where the mark was first published, something the *Trademark Register* doesn't do. *Compu-Mark* also lists trademark applications which are still pending. The information on pending trademarks is identical to that for registered marks except that the Serial Number is listed rather than the Registration Number. Other features found in the classified volumes are the names of each applicant or registrant, whether the mark is an original registration or a renewal, whether the mark appears in the Principal or Supplemental Register, and whether it includes a design element. None of these features are found in the *Trademark Register*.

The second part of the service, called the "All Classes Directory," provides an alphabetical listing of all trademarks, regardless of classification. This arrangement is not available in the *Trademark Register*. *Compu-Mark* indexes multi-word trade names under each keyword in the name, not just the first word. The keyword indexing appears in both the classified volumes and the "All Classes" edition. Even registered slogans are fully indexed in this manner. These features make the set a much easier, and much more powerful resource, for both single-name look-ups and in-depth classified searches.

Though ease of use is one of *Compu-Mark*'s main virtues, name searching still requires two steps. To locate the owner of a specific mark, the researcher checks the name index, which indicates the appropriate section to consult in the classified volumes. The classified listings contain the complete information, including the registrant's name and the date of publication in the *Official Gazette*. *Compu-Mark* offers one other advantage: cumulative quarterly supplements make it a more current resource than the *Trademark Register*. On the other hand, *Compu-Mark* assumes the user is intimately acquainted with the International Classification system. Not even a rudimentary subject index to classifications is provided, and lack of indexing presents serious problems for individuals who need to search by category.

Researchers may also access the service through *Compu-Mark U.S. On-Line*. This system includes both federal and state registrations, as well as canceled, expired, and abandoned trademarks since 1960. It is updated biweekly. The online version also provides information on transfer of trademark ownership and other supplementary data found on the trademark filings themselves. Users must subscribe to the system directly through the publisher.

Trademarkscan-Federal (Thomson & Thomson—Weekly).

The *Trademarkscan* database is available exclusively on DIALOG, and is quite affordable, especially for quick, single-name look-ups. *Trademarkscan* covers all trademarks currently registered or pending with the U.S. Patent and Trademark Office. A separate database, *Trademarkscan-State*, has information on filings at the state level. *Trademarkscan* cites both publication dates from the *Official Gazette*: the date it appeared for opposition, and the registration date. Records also contain ownership history—the renewal owner (if different from the original registrant), and the assignee, where ownership has been sold or transferred to a different company.

Users can search *Trademarkscan* by trade name, company name, assignee, product or service class, description, keyword, and a variety of date variables. Searchers can also limit results to active marks, to foreign registrants, or to marks with design elements only. In fact, more than 40 fields are fully indexed, giving the researcher unprecedented access to trademark information. *Trademarkscan* indexers also create cross-references which enable phonetic searching, regardless of how names are spelled. Given the enormous variations in trade names, this is an invaluable capability. Another command allows the user to locate a specified string of characters no matter where they appear in a name, even if they represent a string of letters in the middle of a word. A final capability, available to subscribers with enhanced DIALOG software, is the power to view and print the actual graphics of marks containing design elements. Users can also search by design code, retrieving all images representing a particular object, animal, or concept.

The complete federal and state *Trademarkscan* databases, including design images, are now available on CD-ROM. Both titles are updated monthly, with current disks superseding previous ones. Because of file size and graphic capabilities, *Trademarkscan-Federal* is divided into two disks, with each containing a portion of the classification schedule. The system uses the powerful DIALOG OnDisc software, with search capabilities virtually identical to the online system.

Trademarks/CD-ROM (U.S. Patent and Trademark Office—Irregular).

Three pilot versions of this government-produced CD-ROM were issued between January 1990 and July 1991. Regular production will begin in October 1991, with biweekly updates. The disk will be distributed to Patent Depository Libraries, and may be used by the

public at these locations. There are presently no plans to sell subscriptions or to make the disk available to GPO Depository Libraries. Like the commercially produced trademark databases, *Trademarks/CD-ROM* contains information not published in the *Gazette*, including a verbal description of the mark's appearance, the renewal history, and the full address of the registrant.

Twenty-four fields are indexed and searchable, including the design description, class, and type of mark. Boolean capabilities are fully supported, and the system is quite simple to use. Like *Trademarkscan*, this product allows keyword searching, phonetic searching (though the user must specify the feature as a separate command), and left-, right-, and internal truncation. The PTO is currently discussing plans to add image capabilities to the disk. A significant drawback is that records are displayed in chronological order, with the earliest registered marks showing first. This in itself is not a problem, but the initial display only shows the trademark name and the date. Users must then scroll through each full record to learn more. Also, the publication date cited is the registration date, not the date published for opposition. Compared to *Trademarkscan* on disk, the system is slow and cumbersome, but it is a welcome alternative for those without access to commercial products.

PUTTING IT ALL TOGETHER

Directories can be extremely valuable for in-depth company research. To learn "everything" about a firm, as many directories as possible should be used, with each one contributing additional data to the total fund of knowledge. A meaningful profile may emerge only after many bits of information are collected, and thoughtful analysis is brought to bear. Comparing data from directory listings may be the only way to obtain information on a small private company, but it can be useful in researching large firms as well. Usually the larger the company, the greater the chances that something will be found.

Consider the case of the Trexalong Company, a fictitious manufacturer of exercise equipment for physical therapy and related medical applications. Before beginning, our researcher realizes she should verify the information she was given. The *Million Dollar Directory* confirms the spelling, the legal name, and that the company is a Delaware-registered corporation located in Scranton, Pennsylvania. Sales are listed at $200 million and there are approximately 170 employees. It does not appear to be publicly traded, nor is it a subsidiary of

another firm. Executive names are listed, and their surnames allow a preliminary assumption that it is not a family-owned business. Other national directories confirm this basic information with only minor discrepancies. The *Macmillan Directory of Leading Private Companies* indicates assets, liabilities, and net worth figures for the firm. *Dun's Market Identifiers* also confirms much of the information uncovered so far, and further indicates the company owns its headquarters, employs 80 people at that location, and has 1,100 customers. *Dun's Business Identification Service* shows that six additional locations for the company are scattered across the country. Further, the company does business at two of these locations under the name "Flextrack Products." The *Online Information Network* identifies an additional location under the dba. The *Directory of Corporate Affiliations* calls this location a division, and shows the company also owns the Health Speed Corporation, a manufacturer of stationary bicycles.

Background on individual locations comes from the *U.S. Manufacturers Directory*, *Dun's Electronic Business Directory*, *Trinet*, and state industrial directories for each of the states where the firm has a presence. The resulting data show that only two of the locations are manufacturing facilities, that both are small, and both make parts for the final product. Another location turns out to be a warehouse facility, and three others look like regional sales offices, all of which is confirmed later in *MacRae's Blue Book*. Sales and employment-size data for the three manufacturing plants more or less conform to the company totals found earlier. Additional information on the subsidiary is also uncovered.

To identify the company's major competitors, the researcher scans the rankings in *Ward's*, but encounters a snag; the industry groupings are too broad, and even the four-digit SICs aren't specific enough for this industry. But the *Thomas Register* has been overlooked. It doesn't give rankings, but at least the names of competitors can be obtained. Besides, maybe Trexalong has a product catalog included in the set. As it happens none is found, but a half-page ad is almost as good. It looks as though Trexalong specializes in cardiovascular exercise and measurement devices for hospitals. Returning to the question of competitors, a variety of headings are checked in the classified section. Unfortunately, none are specific enough. Moving to the online version of *Thomas*, the researcher combines medical and exercise terms in a search and identifies three likely competitors. Trade directories of medical equipment verify that two of these do indeed make cardiovascular devices. Better yet, a more specific ad for Trexalong indicates that the com-

pany prides itself on its sophisticated equipment and state-of-the-art technology. On a hunch, she consults the *Corporate Technology Directory*, which bears further fruit. The brief narrative in *CorpTech* explains that the company sells exclusively to hospitals and that they developed many of the advances used in their equipment, then goes on to describe the equipment's unique features more thoroughly. The *Directory of American Research and Technology* adds to the picture: a small research facility is located at the company headquarters.

Continuing her pursuit, the researcher turns to the *Standard Directory of Advertisers*, and uncovers an approximate figure for advertising expenditures, and the media used in advertising. Most of this effort is aimed at business publications, direct mail to businesses, and trade shows, which reinforces information that the product is not sold to retail customers. Several brand names are also listed. *Trademarkscan* reveals that all of them are registered, and identifies the registration dates. Previously consulted directories indicated the company was founded a scant six years ago, and biographical directories show that three of the company's principals graduated from the same university shortly before the founding date: one with a degree in physiology, one in mechanical engineering, and one in finance. Another officer, an older man, is listed as the president of a company called Armstrong Exercise Equipment. A second look at the *Million Dollar Directory* indicates that Armstrong is also located in Scranton, and was founded in 1963.

Finally, our searcher returns to another lead suggested by the national directories. Several sources note that Trexalong is an exporter. The *Directory of United States Exporters* indicates the company exports exclusively to Canada, and a substantial proportion of total sales are accounted for by these exports. Canadian business directories uncover locations in Toronto and Montreal not shown in American sources. Any number of other directories could be consulted to further add to the portrait. Some will simply verify what was previously found; some will uncover new information; and some will fail to contribute anything of value.

Is this type of research simple? Not really. Is it always necessary to do such a thorough job? Of course not. Aren't there easier ways to find some of this information? Sometimes. Are such spectacular results common? It's doubtful. Putting all reservations aside, the message contained in the Trexalong example is quite simple: never underestimate the power of business directories to assist with exhaustive research projects. The Trexalong example is realistic in the sense that not all leads proved rewarding, and not all data could be verified in a variety

of sources. It also shows that there is more than one way to find information, even if the route is somewhat circuitous. For the resourceful investigator willing to think about the meaning behind the data, directories can be richly rewarding tools. But directory information cannot stand alone; it is easy to jump to erroneous conclusions based on directory information alone. Periodical articles, government records, press releases, and other sources of company information should also be used whenever possible. In the Trexalong example, a good feature article from a local Scranton newspaper or business magazine might have answered many questions explicitly, obviating the need for such painstaking research. On the other hand, directories are essential for verifying what is found elsewhere.

How can you determine the most efficient route to take? As the Trexalong case points out, one step often leads logically to the next, but there is seldom a single best approach. A second tack is to utilize the global search capabilities of large online systems. This is one of the fastest ways to plumb the diversity of published resources, including directories and full-text databases.

FOR FURTHER READING

Although a great deal has been written about specific electronic business directories (those available online or via CD-ROM), few articles explore the characteristics of printed directories, and fewer still examine specialized business sources. Some of the more notable articles are listed below. The balance of the reading list covers a diversity of issues related to trademarks and brand strategy.

Specialized Directories

Cheney, Debora, and Sharon Malecki. "Industrial Directories: A Closer Look." *RQ* 26 (Winter 1986): 221–30.
   An introduction to the content, standard features, and uses of state and regional industrial directories.
Farin, Philip. "Directory Listings Ad Up to Sales." *Sales and Marketing Management* 124 (May 19, 1980): 64–71.
   An interesting view of trade directories from the perspective of the listed companies. The advantages and disadvantages of advertising in trade directories are discussed.
O'Keefe, Philip. "Get Discovered with Directories." *Business Marketing* 72 (June 1987): 130–37.
   Where Farin explores free listings in trade directories, O'Keefe discusses the importance of placing paid ads in business directories. The article describes various types of directories, including national, regional, business-to-business yellow pages, and industry-specific.

Ransom, Kevin. "Stodgy R.L. Polk Begins Taking Risks." *Crain's Detroit Business* (August 3, 1987): 1+.
A rare portrait of R.L. Polk, the nation's largest producer of city directories.

Trademarks

Alexander, Jack. "What's in a Name? Too Much, Said the FCC." *Sales & Marketing Management* 141 (January 1989): 75–78.
A revealing look at the government's power to invalidate trademarks which have entered the popular vocabulary. In this case, the offending name was Formica. The author outlines the successful campaign undertaken by the Formica Corporation to protect this valuable trademark from "genericide."

Baird, Stephen R. "Putting the Cart Before the Horse in Assessing Trademark Validity: Toward Redefining the Inherently Generic Term." *Journal of Corporation Law* 14 (Summer 1989): 925–72.
Articles in law reviews are seldom recommended for casual reading, but researchers can learn much by even skimming this thoroughly researched analysis. Describes the legal foundation and purpose of trademark protection from both a public and corporate perspective, then describes the various types of trademarks, arranged from strongest to weakest.

Oathout, John D. *Trademarks: A Guide to the Selection, Administration and Protection in Modern Business Practice* (New York: Scribner's, 1981).
A straightforward manual on trademark basics. Although some information has been superseded by the Trademark Reform Act, most of the discussion remains valid.

Porsch, Robert J. "The New Trademark Law." *Direct Marketing* (August 1989): 80–82.
An overview of the most significant changes in this important legislation.

Springhut, Milton. "Trademark Double-bind Eased." *High Technology Business* (November/December 1989): 4.
A brief discussion of why the ability to reserve trade names before actual use is so important to the competitive standing of the United States.

U.S. Patent and Trademark Office. *Basic Facts About Trademarks* (Washington, DC: U.S. Government Printing Office, 1988).
The government updates this informative pamphlet approximately every three years. Includes a complete list of the International Trademark Classification and sample application forms.

United States Trademark Association. *Trademark Management: A Guide for Executives* (New York: Clark Boardman, 1982).
Another guide to managing and protecting trademarks, by the leading association of trade name owners.

Van Slyke, Paul C. "Sweeping Trademark Revisions Now in Effect." *Marketing News* (December 18, 1989): 2.
A short, but exceptionally well-written summary of the Trademark Revision Act.

CHAPTER 8
Corporate Finances: Private Companies

TOPICS COVERED

1. Financial Statements
   a. The Balance Sheet
   b. The Income Statement
   c. Other Financial Statements
2. Credit Reports
3. Researching Regulated Companies
4. Federal, State, and Local Government Records
5. Making Financial Comparisons
   a. Financial Ratios
   b. Company Rankings
6. Strategies for Researching Private Companies
7. For Further Reading

MAJOR SOURCES DISCUSSED

- *Dun & Bradstreet Reference Book of American Business*
- *Duns Financial Records Plus*
- *Branch Directory and Summary of Deposits*
- *Quarterly Bank and Savings & Loan Rating Service*
- *Best's Insurance Reports*
- *RMA Annual Statement Studies*
- *Industry Norms and Key Business Ratios*
- *Almanac of Business and Industrial Financial Ratios*
- *Statistics of Income*
- *Dun's Business Rankings*

Business directories are definitely limited in their capabilities. When researchers need information on how well a company is doing, they must turn to financial sources. Business publications offer an avalanche of financial information on publicly traded firms, but locating data on private (or closely held) companies is much more challenging. Because closely held companies are not required by law to disclose financial information to the public, they do not publish annual reports, nor do they share information about themselves with major business publishers. The same research restrictions hold true for subsidiaries of publicly held firms; the parent corporation reports consolidated information on the company as a whole, making subsidiary data much harder to find. Obtaining background information on private companies, subsidiaries, and divisions is possible, but comes at a greater cost of time, effort, and money.

This chapter will survey an assortment of techniques for investigating these more elusive firms. Among the sources covered are credit reports, records filed with government agencies, company rankings, and financial ratios. A brief discussion of publications which profile banks, insurance companies, and similarly regulated organizations is included here because many of these firms are not publicly traded. Almost all of the strategies examined in this chapter are also appropriate for researching public companies, but more effective methods will be described in Chapters 9 through 12.

FINANCIAL STATEMENTS

No meaningful discussion of financial research is possible without some knowledge of how financial transactions are recorded. Understanding financial statements and reports requires a grasp of rudimentary accounting concepts. Only the most basic terms will be introduced in this chapter. Some excellent books written for the novice are listed at the end of this chapter.

Accounting is the systematic recording of financial events. The methodology of accounting is determined by generally accepted accounting principles (GAAP), the

rules accountants follow. The framework of GAAP has been developed over the years through a combination of widely adopted, traditional practices and the pronouncements of professional accounting groups such as the Financial Accounting Standards Board (FASB).

Accountants must follow the basic principles of objectivity, full disclosure, conservatism, and consistency. The first three deal with notions of fairness, honesty, and prudence, but the fourth principle is worth discussing. GAAP often allows the accountant to choose from several equally acceptable approaches to record a transaction. For example, a company may use one of several methods of valuing its inventory. The principle of consistency states that the accountant cannot capriciously switch from one method to another from year to year. Otherwise the company would use the method which presented its finances in the most favorable light at that moment. Changes in accounting methods must be fully explained in the statement itself.

Financial statements are generated from the day-to-day transactions of the firm. Daily data are then categorized and totaled on a monthly and annual basis. The resulting statements capture the important financial history of the company, serving as a report on the firm's performance.

The Balance Sheet

The Statement of Financial Position, also called the Statement of Financial Condition or Balance Sheet, presents a quick picture of the company's value.

If you were to tally the dollar value of all the items you own, and subtract all the money you owe, the result would be an estimate of your net worth. The idea is essentially the same for a company, except it is an ongoing process. The resulting statement is a portrait of the firm's worth at a specific point in time, usually the last day of its fiscal year. It's called a Balance Sheet because the statement is divided into two sides, which by definition must be equal. The basic formula for this equality is:

Assets = Liabilities+ Equity

Assets are the tangible and intangible items owned by the firm; liabilities are the amounts owed by the company; and equity is the amount contributed by the firm's owners. The justification for the equation is straightforward. A company can acquire assets by borrowing (creating a liability), or by using the owners' own funds (creating equity). Equity comes from money contributed by the owners, and from the portion of company profits reinvested in the firm.

The two figures on the right-hand side of the equation represent claims against the assets; their sum must equal the left-hand side. The basic equation can be reconfigured to state this relationship from another point of view:

Assets - Liabilities = Equity

Seen in this light, equity is another way to say net worth.

Figure 8-A is an abbreviated example of a Balance Sheet for the fictitious Wealthy Corporation. Assets are divided into items that are current and fixed. Current assets are cash and items easily convertible to cash, as well as assets having a life of less than one year. Accumulated depreciation represents the amount of fixed assets "used up" since they were first acquired. The concept of depreciation is often misunderstood or viewed as an accounting gimmick. People intuitively understand that most tangible assets decrease in value with age. Depreciation is a way of accounting for the finite life of physical items, and the eventual need to replace them.

Liabilities are also divided into current and long-term categories, depending on their life span. Current obligations are paid within a year from the date they are incurred, while such long-term debts as mortgages can remain on the books for many years. Equity is the amount of capital contributed by the stockholders plus accumulated retained earnings. Retained earnings are the portion of each year's profits kept in the firm instead of being distributed to the stockholders as dividends.

The Income Statement

The Income Statement, also called the Profit and Loss Statement or Earnings Statement, records the flow of money in and out of the company through the year. It is perhaps more understandable to nonaccountants than the Balance Sheet because it is akin to what each of us does when constructing a budget or reconciling a bank statement. In one sense the Income Statement is the more important document because it measures the earning power of the company. Assets really have value only in their ability to generate income for the firm. If a company continually operates at a loss, its net assets will drain away, and sooner or later it will cease to exist. Profit, which accountants call net income, is the point of the whole exercise, "the bottom line." The final step on the Income Statement is to divide net income by the number of shares of stock to determine a value for "Earnings Per Share."

FIGURE 8-A. Corporate Balance Sheet

Wealthy Corporation of America
Statement of Financial Position
Period Ending December 31, 1990

Assets

Current Assets:

Cash	$19,526
Marketable Securities	35,680
Accounts Receivable	281,940
Inventories	468,148
Total Current Assets	805,294

Fixed Assets:

Property & Plant	2,744,390
Equipment	809,215
Less: Accum. Depreciation	(1,116,773)
Total Fixed Assets	2,436,832
TOTAL ASSETS	$3,242,126

Liabilities

Current Liabilities:

Accounts Payable	480,952
Notes Payable	42,750
Total Current Liabilities	523,702

Long-Term Debt:

Mortgage	1,087,334
Bank Loan	399,083
Total Long-Term Debt	1,486,417
TOTAL LIABILITIES	2,010,119

Equity

Common Stock	855,780
Accumulated Retained Earnings	376,227
TOTAL EQUITY	1,232,007
TOTAL LIABILITY AND EQUITY	$3,242,126

Figure 8-B is the Income Statement for Wealthy Corporation. It begins with an amount for total revenues during the year and progressively subtracts expenses until net income is determined. Figure 8-B illustrates a multiple-step approach, which separates both income and revenue by category. This format presents a truer picture of the firm's operations. Notice that "other revenue" is segregated from "total sales." In this case, additional revenue might have been generated from the interest earned by the "marketable securities" listed on the Balance Sheet. The firm could also have rented space in its facility to another company, sold some of its equipment, or conducted other transactions which would earn income outside its normal line of business. By separating "other revenue," the reader of the statement can determine the firm's gross profit. The key figure in the Income Statement for this calculation is "Cost of Sales" (sometimes called Cost of Goods Sold or CGS), which measures costs directly attributable to the creation or acquisition of the product the company manufactures or sells. Such costs include raw materials and the portion of labor devoted to manufacturing the product. For most manufacturing and retail businesses, Cost of Sales is the largest category of expense. The difference between sales revenue and Cost of Sales is the gross profit, sometimes referred to as gross margin.

The Balance Sheet indicates the firm's financial status; the Income Statement portrays financial activity. Put another way, the Balance Sheet is static, representing the firm at a specific point in time; the Income Statement is dynamic, showing what has occurred over a period of time. The Balance Sheet shows what the firm is worth; the Income Statement shows what it has earned. The Balance Sheet tells whether the firm is solvent, while the Income Statement indicates whether it is profitable.

Other Financial Statements

Two other statements further explain the data from the Balance Sheet and Income Statement. The Statement of Stockholders' Equity is a report which shows how the firm's capital structure changes from one year to the next, including new issues of stock and stock buy-backs. It may go by numerous other designations, including Changes in Shareholders' Equity and Statement of Capitalization. Dividend disbursements and the accumulation of retained earnings appear either as part of the Income Statement itself, or on the Statement of Stockholders' Equity. An abbreviated version of the retained earnings data for Wealthy Corporation might look like this:

Retained Earnings, Dec. 31, 1989	$320,935
Add: Net Income, 1990	134,860
Less: Dividends Paid, 1990	(79,568)
Retained Earnings, Dec. 31, 1990	$376,227

FIGURE 8-B. Corporate Income Statement

Wealthy Corporation of America
Statement of Income
For the Year Ending December 31, 1990

Sales	$3,853,278
Less: Cost of Sales	3,108,566
Gross Profit	744,712
Less: General & Admin. Expenses	553,730
Operating Profit	190,982
Add: Other Revenue	49,160
Earnings Before Interest and Taxes	240,142
Less: Interest Expense	74,092
Net Income Before Taxes	166,050
Less: Provision for Income Tax	31,190
Net Income	134,860
Common shares of stock outstanding	75,000 shares
Earnings Per Share	$1.80

The fourth financial report found in annual disclosure documents is the Statement of Cash Flows, which shows where the company's year-end cash balance came from. It links one year's Balance Sheet to the next by showing how cash was generated and used. The statement is divided into three sections, showing cash flows from operations, investing, and financing. For example, cash can be received as the result of net income (operations), interest earned (investing), borrowed money (financing), or additional stock (financing). Note that the first two examples are reflected in the Income Statement and the latter two on the Balance Sheet, so the Statement of Cash Flows also links the other statements together.

Despite the existence of GAAP, little uniformity exists in accounting terminology. For example, common stock is also referred to as capital stock, paid-in capital, stockholder's equity, ownership interest, and shareholder's investment. Even the recognizable "bottom line" can be called net income, net earnings, net profit, income after taxes, and profit.

CREDIT REPORTS

Many novice business researchers believe that financial statements for closely held companies are completely unavailable. In truth, modern commerce would not function smoothly if companies couldn't evaluate the credit worthiness of their business customers. Businesses, like individuals, establish credit ratings based on their bill-paying history, earning power, and net worth. Credit reports on companies not only provide a payment record and analysis of the firm's financial status, they are also an excellent source of background information. Credit agencies gather data from a hodgepodge of sources, but the actual financial statements are generally supplied by the rated companies themselves. Because it is in their best interest to maintain a good credit rating, organizations volunteer financial data to reporting services. However, submissions are not required to be audited by an independent accounting firm. In fact, the majority of credit reports contain unaudited financial data, and researchers should always be careful when using such information.

The leading supplier of business credit information, the Dun & Bradstreet Corporation, was founded in 1841. D&B offers a wide variety of financial intelligence products, but credit reports form the backbone of the company's services. Dun & Bradstreet maintains offices in major cities throughout the country, from which reporters and analysts collect information on millions of American companies. Data are supplied by banks, creditors, government records, published news reports, and interviews with executives from the respondent companies. A report is considered current if the key information has been updated within the past 18 months, but most records are revised at least once a year. A customer request to D&B for information on a company with no current information will automatically initiate a special update search. The publisher has compiled information on more than 4 million firms, representing 9 million business establishments, the most extensive source of background information on private companies in the United States.

The basic D&B credit document is called a *Business Information Report*, and varies in length; a typical report is about four pages. The focus of each report is the company's credit history, highlighting payments made, debts outstanding, and bills past due. Most reports include abbreviated financial statements submitted by the companies themselves, though some firms decline to provide this information. A major source of intelligence utilized by D&B reporters is public information found in county clerks' offices and various local courts. In the life of a company, significant events of all types become a matter of public record: liens and judgments against the firm, mortgages and other secured loans, bankruptcy proceedings, and changes in the legal status of the corpo-

ration. A Dun & Bradstreet report also includes a discussion of the company's operations, its history, biographical information on its principals, a description of its products or services, comments on its facilities and customer base, and the famous Dun & Bradstreet credit rating. The ratings actually represent a combination of the rated company's credit history and its financial strength as measured by net worth. For many companies, several additional reports can be ordered, including a *Payment Analysis Report* and a *Credit Advisory*. Subscribers can order reports by telephone or online. They can be received in a variety of ways, including U.S. mail, fax, and online delivery. The online system is called *DunsPrint*. For non-D&B subscribers, the NewsNet system now offers a "gateway" to Dun & Bradstreet's online files. NewsNet users can obtain most of the basic D&B reports.

The price schedule for D&B products is based on "Units," with a basic *Business Information Report* (delivered through the mail) priced at one Unit. Specialized reports, services, and delivery systems are generally priced above one Unit. To become a D&B subscriber, customers must purchase a minimum of 100 Units in advance every year. If those are used before year-end, additional Units can be purchased in blocks of 50. Any unused Units beyond the first 100 can be carried forward to the following year. Not everyone can become a D&B subscriber, however; the publisher reserves the right to restrict access to its credit products.

Dun & Bradstreet controls some 90% of the market for commercial credit reports. Most of its competitors focus on narrowly defined industries such as apparel firms. Only one company can boast a broad-based database large enough to challenge D&B. TRW Business Credit, a division of TRW, Inc., maintains records on 9 million establishments in the United States, approximately the same number as D&B. TRW reports, called *Business Profiles*, differ from D&B's *Business Information Reports* in that they consist almost entirely of payment history data and public filings. TRW provides no financial statements, and none of the useful D&B information on company history, executive biographies, or operations. On the other hand, the payment information is often more extensive, with a great deal of statistical analysis given. Financial information on approximately 6,000 publicly traded corporations is contributed by Standard & Poor's; sales figures and other descriptive information on large private companies is obtained from the *Trinet* databases described in Chapter 6. The two systems also differ in pricing; TRW reports generally cost less. Furthermore, no minimum subscription is required; TRW actively solicits the smaller customer.

Subscribers can order TRW reports by telephone, through the publisher's own online system, or via the *TRW Business Profiles* database available on the NewsNet system. The reports found on NewsNet are identical to those delivered directly through TRW.

In the past, both credit systems lacked information on sole proprietorships, particularly those with no employees. TRW was the first to provide personal credit information on the owners of small companies. Its *Small Business Advisory Reports* draw upon TRW's enormous database of consumer credit ratings. Dun & Bradstreet recently offered a similar service called "Interact." Since D&B doesn't have a corresponding consumer credit division, it obtains data from Equifax, Inc., a major TRW competitor in the consumer market.

The accuracy of D&B's database should be discussed. Every experienced researcher knows that no information source can be taken at face value. Errors of all types creep into any database, and a file as enormous as Dun & Bradstreet's will have its share of mistakes. For decades, D&B enjoyed an unassailable reputation in the business community, and the firm was widely perceived as the provider of reliable, accurate information. In October 1989 *The Wall Street Journal* published a front-page story which made damaging allegations about D&B's credit operations. Unrealistically high quotas were allegedly encouraging D&B employees to cut corners, and in some cases to even fabricate information. Dun & Bradstreet responded quickly; data-gathering methods were improved, a customer hot line was installed, and additional quality control procedures were instituted. Errors will continue to appear in Dun & Bradstreet records, ranging in seriousness from wrong phone numbers to inaccurate credit ratings. But Dun & Bradstreet remains a responsible and respected information producer. Like most reputable business publishers, D&B is eager to correct mistakes which come to its attention. More importantly, the publisher possesses one of the most remarkable fonts of information on privately held companies. However, business researchers should always look at information critically. Evaluation of data involves a healthy dose of common sense and the ability to compare new intelligence to what is already known. Relying on a single source of information usually leads to trouble.

Dun & Bradstreet Reference Book of American Business (Dun & Bradstreet Business Credit Services—Bimonthly).

Subscribers to D&B reports also receive this six-volume directory as part of the service. The basic subscription includes semiannual updates to the set, but customers can pay extra to receive bimonthly revisions.

The *Reference Book* serves as a printed index to the 4 million U.S. companies for which current *Business Information Reports* are available. Companies are arranged geographically by state, and further divided by city, town, or village. Each listing cites the company name, its primary SIC number, telephone number, credit rating, types of reports available, and, for firms less than ten years old, the founding date. DUNS numbers are not given. Numerous cross-references are provided for divisional names and trade names. This is limited information, but the directory is intended primarily as an index to the full database, and as a quick guide to credit ratings. Until recently, the *Reference Book* was only sold to subscribers of D&B's credit reporting service. Beginning in 1991, nonsubscribers can now purchase the complete set or individual regional volumes.

The *Reference Book of Manufacturers*, described in Chapter 6, is available only to subscribers of the D&B credit reports, though it is not included in the basic subscription. The *Reference Book of Manufacturers* differs from the *Reference Book of American Business* in several respects: it covers manufacturers only; it includes more basic directory information (e.g., address); and arrangement is by company name.

The best features of both publications are combined in a CD-ROM product called *Duns Reference Plus*. Again, it is available only to subscribers of the credit reports. Like the *Reference Book of American Business*, company name, credit rating, and types of available D&B reports are cited for every entry. In addition, the user will find a list of primary and secondary SIC numbers, the year founded, the complete address and phone number, the DUNS number of the firm, its parent (where applicable), and a list of trade names and divisions. For subsidiary firms, the searcher can retrieve the record for the parent company at the touch of a function key. Once a company has been identified, a communications package allows the user to automatically order a full report from D&B and download it onto the PC. *Duns Reference Plus* also has several weaknesses. First, a company can be retrieved only by telephone number, DUNS number, or name and location. For the latter search, both characteristics must be entered; the searcher must know the city and state in which the company is located in order to retrieve the record by company name. Finally, no screening capabilities are available, even for the limited data fields listed in the file. Users cannot generate a list of firms by SIC number, county, or D&B rating, and Boolean searching is not possible. The system was clearly designed as an electronic version of the printed books, enabling the user to quickly order a specific company report.

D&B's primary customers are corporate credit managers, who usually know the address, phone number, and/or DUNS number of the firms about which they are inquiring. For this reason, most D&B products require the user to know one or the other of these characteristics in order to retrieve information. The *Reference Book of American Business* is arranged by city. *Duns Reference Plus*, the telephone inquiry service, and the NewsNet gateway are generally accessible only by DUNS number, name/city, or phone number. *DunsPrint* allows certain types of company screening, but its search capabilities are limited as well. For direct access by company name, researchers can turn to two other D&B products introduced in Chapter 6: *Dun's Business Identification Service* on microfiche and *Dun's Market Identifiers* online. More flexible access to D&B financial data is offered by the following database.

Duns Financial Records Plus (Dun & Bradstreet Business Credit Services—Quarterly).

Researchers who need fewer than 100 D&B reports per year can pursue one of three alternatives. First, the new "D&B Express" service allows nonsubscribers to order a single report by telephone, though they will pay substantially more than a traditional customer. Only the *Business Information Report* is available under this plan. Second, NewsNet subscribers can obtain online reports via the gateway system mentioned earlier. The third option is to utilize an online database offered on both DIALOG and Dow Jones News/Retrieval. Called *Duns Financial Records Plus* (*DFR*), it provides partial information from the D&B files. Slightly less than 2 million firms are represented here. Records provide the same company history, biographical data, and operations summary found in the *Business Information Report*, and the directory information from the *Dun's Market Identifiers* database. Approximately one-third of the records cite financial information, including one to three years of summary data from the company's Balance Sheet and Income Statement, 14 financial ratios, and industry norms for those same ratios. No credit ratings or payment histories are available.

On DIALOG, many of the key financial variables are fully searchable, as are all words in the text. A list of companies can be ranked by user-defined characteristics, and comparative tabular information can be displayed. Users can also restrict a search to those records containing financial data. Search results can be printed or downloaded in a variety of standard or customized formats. *DFR* is definitely an expensive database, but the greatest cost is in printing the company records. Subscribers to D&B reports may find it makes sense to use *DFR* for screening only. Substantial savings can be realized by

printing selected portions of the report only, or by printing the resulting DUNS numbers from *DFR*, then ordering the full reports directly from Dun & Bradstreet.

The *DFR* database on the Dow Jones system is more limited in its capabilities. Companies can be retrieved only by company name, DUNS number, or telephone number. Likewise, the only output formats are the complete record, the financial record, or the textual profile.

As of this writing, users of the *Duns Financial Records* database on DIALOG can expect to spend about $95 for a full report with no credit data. Considering that a typical report is only two pages, and that many contain limited financial data, readers might consider this price excessive. In contrast, a basic *Business Information Report* costs D&B subscribers about $18. Nonsubscribers can obtain the same report through the "D&B Express" service for $60, or through the NewsNet gateway for $45. This comparison illustrates why many businesspeople consider a D&B subscription a worthwhile investment. More than 80,000 organizations are presently D&B subscribers, and the publisher answers approximately 90,000 information requests each day.

RESEARCHING REGULATED COMPANIES

Certain categories of business are required to submit financial and operating information to government agencies even though they are not publicly traded. These regulated industries are generally involved in activities which have a profound impact on the public welfare. Banks, public utilities, and airlines are prominent examples of this type of company. The deregulation movement which began in the late 1970s has reduced the number of industries which are subject to detailed reporting requirements, but thousands of companies must still submit financial statements to regulatory agencies. Many of the companies which fall within regulated industries are also publicly held. On the other hand, many are private, and others are subsidiaries of larger firms. In fact, if it weren't for reporting regulations, many public companies could conceal information at the operating level simply by forming a holding company.

Researchers should consider three additional points. First, publicly held companies in some industries are exempt from disclosing data to the U.S. Securities and Exchange Commission. Instead, they file financial statements with their principal regulatory agency. This mechanism is most commonly demonstrated by firms in bank-related industries. Second, though an industry may not be required to submit reports at the federal level, individual states compel certain types of financial disclosure. The best example is the insurance industry. A final point involves the dissemination of government reports. Though disclosure filings may be public record, they are not necessarily widely distributed. Obtaining copies of regulatory reports usually requires some effort. The companies themselves may send them on request, which is generally true of banks and utilities. In other cases, documents can be examined in the company's offices, a situation common in the broadcasting industry. Of course, the regulatory agencies themselves will usually provide disclosure documents on demand for a fee, but identifying the appropriate contact can be tricky.

A case in point is the disclosure mechanism for the banking and thrift industries. Although many banks and savings and loan associations are publicly traded, many others are "mutuals," legally owned by their depositors. Regardless of ownership, all institutions are required to file reports with various federal and state banking agencies. The principal financial documents which banks submit are the Consolidated Statement of Condition and the Consolidated Report of Income. These statements are also known as "Call Reports." They constitute the legally mandated financial statements which banks must file, in contrast to the voluntary, condensed statements distributed to depositors and the general public. Both types of Call Reports are submitted quarterly, with a final report at year-end. The Statement of Condition is a detailed Balance Sheet reporting on more than 600 items. The Report of Income chronicles over 150 income and expense categories. Most banks now submit a "Consolidated Report of Condition and Income" as a single document, under guidelines established by the Federal Financial Institutions Examination Council. A combined report typically consists of some 30 pages of standardized financial tables; narrative commentary is optional and appears at the end of the report. Despite the uniformity of these documents, it is important for researchers to remember that they are filed with the appropriate regulatory agency for each bank, not with a centralized depository.

Because of the diversity of regulatory bodies, Call Reports can be difficult to track down. Those filed with the U.S. Federal Deposit Insurance Corporation (FDIC) are available directly through the agency's Disclosure Group, but requests must be made in writing. Call Reports submitted to the Federal Reserve Board (the Fed) are sold through the National Technical Information Service (NTIS). Reports filed with the Fed, the FDIC,

and the Federal Home Loan Bank Board (FHLBB) are also available in electronic formats, as quarterly magnetic tapes. Several commercial firms have tried offering these reports in comprehensive microfiche collections, but such ventures have generally met with little success. Disclosure, Incorporated currently provides microfiche copies on demand, but also includes the complete text of selected bank reports on its *Laser D* system. More will be said about this remarkable CD-ROM product in Chapter 9. Call Reports are also distributed through corporate-oriented online vendors, including ADP Data Services, the WEFA Group, and CompuServe's Business Information Service.

The public utilities industry also has extensive financial reporting requirements. Terminology for this industry runs contrary to traditional financial nomenclature in that "privately owned" refers to investor-owned firms. Publicly owned utilities are those operated by government entities or communities.

The U.S. Energy Information Administration publishes an annual guide called *Financial Statistics of Selected Electric Utilities*. It covers approximately 1,500 of the largest electric utilities, representing all types of firms. Detailed financial and operating data are displayed in tabular form, with five companies compared on a single page. Less detailed, but more convenient data are produced by a commercial firm called Public Utilities Reports, Inc. Its annual *P.U.R. Analysis of Investor-Owned Electric and Gas Utilities* offers two-page profiles for more than 200 utility companies which sell stock. Electric utilities which belong to the Edison Electric Institute (a leading trade association) submit detailed operating data on an annual Uniform Statistical Report. Results are used to compile the Institute's *Statistical Yearbook*, but company-specific reports can be obtained from the firms themselves. Another source for utility companies, *Moody's Public Utility Manual*, will be discussed in Chapter 9.

Background information on companies in many regulated industries are frequently summarized in commercial publications. Some secondary publications are little more than directories, but they do include selected financial data and business summaries. An example is the annual *International Directory of Nuclear Utilities*, compiled by a research firm called NUEXCO. Others choose to display data in tabular form, presenting brief comparisons of numerous companies on a single chart. Some even calculate various performance ratings, and rank firms by noteworthy characteristics.

Perhaps the most useful commercial sources are those which combine narrative and tabular information in convenient, well-organized company profiles. The following publications are based upon regulatory data.

Branch Directory and Summary of Deposits (Decision Research Sciences, Inc.—Annual).

The crazy-quilt of regulatory jurisdictions for banks makes identifying the appropriate reporting agency for a particular bank difficult. An array of commercial publications obviate the need to contact government agencies directly, however. The *Thomson Bank Directory* and *Polk's Bank Directory* (both introduced in Chapter 7) provide summary financial statements for many banks. More detailed information can be found in *Moody's Bank & Finance Manual*, described in Chapter 9. Another useful service is the *Branch Directory and Summary of Deposits*, a 16-volume set arranged geographically, with each volume covering a particular state or region of the country. Data are gathered from all federal bank regulators, state agencies, and from private sources such as Thomson Financial Publishing. It is one of the few titles which surveys banks, thrifts, and credit unions in a single publication. The focus is on industry statistics by geographic area, and financial profiles of banks and branches. Statistical tables summarize total bank deposits and number of offices by type of institution at the county and zip code levels. Financial data for individual banks is also presented by county and town. This section cites total deposits and deposits by type for every banking institution in the country. A complete list of branch offices for every bank and thrift includes the year each office was opened, three years of comparative deposit figures, and the percentage of the bank's total deposits held by that branch. The set is expensive to acquire in its entirety, but researchers interested in a particular region will find a single-volume purchase to be a worthwhile investment. Data are also sold on magnetic tape and floppy diskette.

An alternative is to acquire publications produced by government banking agencies. Much of the data on branch bank deposits, for example, can be found in a multi-volume annual series from the FDIC called the *Data Book: Operating Banks and Branches*. However, this publication only covers FDIC-insured institutions. Much of the information in the *Branch Directory* is not easily found in government publications, and some is available only on computer tape.

Quarterly Bank and Savings & Loan Rating Service (LACE Financial Corporation—Quarterly).

The financial statements of banks are quite different from those of other companies, and analyzing bank reports requires a certain expertise. Four key attributes

are used by bank regulators to evaluate a financial institution's performance and strength: Capital adequacy, Asset quality, Earnings, and Liquidity. A fifth characteristic, Management, is a nonfinancial variable which regulators and analysts also consider when evaluating a bank. The five attributes comprise the so-called CAMEL factors. A variety of commercial publications utilize some variation of CAMEL to compare bank finances. In addition to providing tabular data on thousands of banks, these publications attempt to evaluate each bank by assigning a composite letter rating.

One of the best banking guides for a general audience is the *Quarterly Bank and Savings & Loan Rating Service*, from LACE Financial Corporation. LACE is an acronym for "Liquidity, Asset-quality, Capital, and Earnings," a proprietary version of the CAMEL method. Dr. Barron Putnam, president of LACE Financial, conducted much of the empirical research which led to the CAMEL model. The LACE service lists comparative data for every federally insured bank and S&L in the United States and Puerto Rico. The publication is divided into three sections: the first ranks the 100 largest bank holding companies by LACE rating, the second compares financial characteristics for banks, and the third does the same for savings and loans. Institutions in the latter two sections are both arranged by state and city. For every listing, the bank's total assets and net income are cited, together with approximately ten financial ratios. Ratios measure such characteristics as primary capital, loan loss reserves, and noninterest income. The book's preface explains each ratio, and suggests acceptable levels in every category. For four of the most important ratios, each institution is then compared to all other banks in the same asset-size category, showing its percentile rank. Ten size categories, called "Peer Groups," are used for comparative purposes in assigning both percentiles and letter ratings. Weights are assigned to each ratio to determine the composite rating within each Peer Group. Ratings range from A+ to E. Most banks in good financial condition will receive a B rating, while those with serious problems will be rated D or E.

Exhibit 8-1 demonstrates the standard presentation of LACE data. The Vectra Bank of Federal Heights, Colorado, had total assets of $15 million as of December 1990. The second column indicates the bank had a loss of $32,000 for the year. The fifth column of numbers, labeled "nonperf. loans/capt," calculates the ratio of nonperforming loans to bank capital—the lower the number, the better. In the case of Vectra, the ratio is 22.2%, placing the bank in the 17th percentile of its Peer

Group. In general, the bank is not performing well. Its overall rating is D, where it has remained for more than a year (except for a C rating earned in the third quarter of 1990).

Sheshunoff Bank Quarterly Ratings and Analysis, produced by Sheshunoff Information Services, Inc., also calculates ratios and composite ratings for every federally insured bank in the country, arranged by state and city. Basic data are supplemented by a variety of special tables providing rankings by key variables. Like its competitor, a separate section compares the largest bank holding companies. Both LACE and Sheshunoff include summary data on trends in the banking industry, complete with graphs and/or maps. There are numerous differences between the two resources. Each uses a different methodology in determining bank ratings, focuses on particular characteristics and ratios, and assigns different weights in calculating the composite values. Sheshunoff assigns ratings strictly by Peer Group, while LACE makes adjustments to reflect the fact that some types of banks are performing badly as a group. Another limitation is that Sheshunoff only assigns ratings from A+ to C; banks which fall below a C rating are given an NR (not rated) designation. Furthermore, Sheshunoff utilizes a curve to assign ratings within each group, a practice which LACE eschews. A major advantage to Sheshunoff is that it reports more than twice as many ratios for each bank, including figures on loans by type. Sheshunoff also provides more special features, including state-by-state averages, and a series of rankings by key characteristics, from net income to the amount of foreign loans. But Sheshunoff only gives ratings for the current period, while LACE cites ratings from each of the four preceding quarters, plus the latest two year-end ratings. This is important because one of the best ways to measure a bank's performance is to examine changes over time. LACE is also a more affordable service, and includes banks and S&Ls in a single volume. To gain the same coverage, Sheshunoff subscribers must purchase a companion publication called *Sheshunoff Savings and Loans Quarterly Ratings and Analysis*.

Sheshunoff data are also available in several electronic formats, including diskette and CD-ROM. Diskettes are issued by type of institution and geographic area. The name of the disk product, which appears as part of the Lotus One Source series, is *CD/Banking*. The complete set provides key financial ratios, Sheshunoff ratings, and data on branch deposits for banks, S&Ls, and credit unions. Customers can select from a variety of subscription plans. The service is updated quarterly.

EXHIBIT 8-1. *Quarterly Bank and Savings & Loan Rating Service*

PAGE 24

U.S. BANK RATINGS FOR INSURED COMMERCIAL AND SAVINGS BANKS—DATA FOR MARCH 1991

COLORADO

BANK NAME	CITY	TOTAL ASSETS (MIL)	NET INCOME (000)	LIQUIDITY TI-VL A/AST	/PCT	ASSET QUALITY NONPERF ASTS CAPT PCT	ASTS	CAPITAL TIER 1 CAPITAL AST	PCT	LOSS RESV. ASTS	NET INT INC	NON INT INC	OVER HEAD EXP	PROV TO RESV	NET INC M91	PCT	NET INC D90	D/M 89	D/M 90	J/S 90	S/M 90	D/M 90	M/91
OMNIBANK UNIVERSITY HIL	DENVER	20	51	-2.8	25	23.6	16	11.96	86	0.88	4.7	1.5	4.8	0.00	1.00	57	0.26	B	B	B	B	B	B
RESOURCES IND BK	DENVER	14	211	15.7	90	28.2	11	13.94	92	2.73	10.4	1.0	4.8	-.16	5.73	99	-0.44	E	B	B	B	C+	B
SOUTHWEST ST BK	DENVER	91	62	-1.6	56	22.7	16	10.04	74	0.51	4.3	1.3	3.8	0.29	0.27	16	0.53	C+	C	E	E	C	A-
TRI ST BK	DENVER	43	35	-0.0	54	18.9	21	7.24	30	1.05	4.3	1.0	3.8	1.04	0.35	11	0.27	C+	B-	C	C	C+	B+
UNION B&TC	DENVER	92	143	-15.3	7	11.4	17	6.86	23	0.61	4.7	0.8	4.4	0.30	0.64	24	0.96	C+	C	C	B	B	C+
UNION NB OF COLORADO	DENVER	15	-240	3.6	55	8.1	45	5.91	9	1.58	2.8	0.7	6.4	4.37	-6.40	0	-4.55	D	D	D	E	D	D
UNITED BK OF BEAR VALLE	DENVER	125	505	20.8	98	6.8	62	7.06	26	1.36	4.8	0.7	3.3	0.00	1.63	92	-0.09	B	B	B	D	C+	A
UNITED BK OF CHERRY CRK	DENVER	65	135	23.5	98	42.9	35	3.65	5	2.48	4.3	1.3	4.3	0.80	-3.18	34	-3.18	C+	C+	C+	D	C+	B
UNITED BK OF DENVER NA	DENVER	2,332	7,714	-14.9	39	25.5	18	5.19	5	2.18	3.0	3.1	3.5	0.02	1.24	77	-1.24	B	C+	B	B	B	B
UNITED BK OF MONACO NA	DENVER	85	268	14.9	97	20.4	17	5.88	9	1.43	3.2	3.7	3.5	0.38	1.24	71	0.13	C+	C	C	D	C	C+
UNITED BK OF SKYLINE NA	DENVER	53	-105	-10.8	16	92.7	12	4.78	9	4.76	4.2	2.0	7.6	0.00	-0.72	8	-4.41	D	D	D	D	D	D
VECTRA BK	DENVER	47	-10	-12.4	67	27.8	12	6.67	19	0.99	4.5	0.8	4.9	0.36	-0.09	8	-0.31	C+	C+	C+	B	C+	C+
WOMENS BK NA	DENVER	19	-9	6.4	67	16.2	16	6.69	20	0.49	5.3	0.6	5.2	0.11	-0.20	9	-1.30	B	B	B	D	B	B
YOUNG AMERICANS BK	DENVER	84	-228	-9.6	19	18.3	21	7.85	43	1.35	4.6	0.4	4.4	0.13	-1.21	69	1.20	C+	C+	C+	C	C+	C
(cont.)	DENVER	8	-25	-6.7	9	0.2	75	13.35	90	0.09	4.4	0.4	4.4	0.05	-1.18	6	-3.15	B	B	C	D	C	C+
SNOW BK NA	DILLON	22	38	7.6	72	13.6	29	5.33	64	0.95	4.6	1.7	5.2	0.09	0.69	35	1.18	B+	B+	B	B+	B	C+
DOLORES ST BK	DOLORES	40	118	-13.7	7	5.3	59	6.09	50	0.25	3.4	0.5	1.8	0.20	1.17	66	1.06	B+	A	A	A	A	B
DOVE CREEK ST BK	DOVE CREEK	12	135	-12.3	7	64.5	73	6.31	68	1.00	3.4	0.7	4.3	0.15	0.50	25	0.55	C+	C+	E	B	C+	B
BURNS NB OF DURANGO	DURANGO	66	184	-1.8	74	20.7	17	9.40	9	0.49	4.4	3.4	3.6	0.00	1.14	63	0.64	C+	C+	C	C	C+	C+
DURANGO NB	DURANGO	6	7	6.8	51	20.7	17	6.71	20	1.00	5.7	3.4	5.0	0.00	0.46	33	0.42	C+	C	B	C	C+	C+
FIRST NB OF DURANGO	DURANGO	88	243	-5.3	36	3.1	76	8.71	58	0.51	4.5	1.1	3.8	0.37	1.10	59	1.11	B	B	B+	B+	B	B+
UNITED BK DURANGO NA	DURANGO	47	-98	16.2	95	6.0	56	5.17	11	1.85	4.3	1.9	5.6	1.90	-0.78	4	-0.03	C+	B	B	B	B	B+
ALPINE BK	EAGLE	14	-23	-9.2	7	15.0	28	6.08	55	0.97	4.3	2.3	4.3	0.14	-0.66	33	-0.79	B	B	B	C+	B	B
FIRST BK OF EAGLE COUNT	EAGLE	28	95	-9.6	69	9.6	35	8.52	55	0.91	4.4	1.1	3.5	0.21	1.35	79	0.74	B	B	B	B	B	B
COLORADO IND BK	EATON	4	-15	-10.2	5	9.6	35	7.99	46	1.52	5.4	1.5	5.0	3.38	-1.45	6	3.37	C	C	C+	B	B	B
EATON BK	EATON	21	46	-7.3	12	13.6	39	7.85	39	1.03	5.0	0.9	3.8	0.00	0.83	45	0.86	C+	C+	C+	B	C+	C+
FIRSTBANK EDGEWATER NA	EDGEWATER	3	-12	70.6	95	10.6	39	5.85	52	0.04	3.2	4.4	11.1	0.14	-2.29	27	-2.66	C	C	B-	D	C	NB
CENTENNIAL NB	ENGLEWOOD	5	-85	-29.8	0	41.8	79	8.31	50	0.56	5.2	1.1	7.1	0.23	-0.90	4	-0.47	D	C	B	C+	C	C+
CENTRAL BK SE NA	ENGLEWOOD	43	24	49.3	99	14.8	27	5.73	9	0.60	5.1	1.7	4.5	0.48	-0.81	4	-0.31	B	B	B-	B	C+	C+
FIRST BK ARAPAHOE YOSEM	ENGLEWOOD	22	24	2.5	50	14.8	27	5.89	9	0.62	5.1	1.7	5.8	0.37	0.46	23	-0.79	B	C+	C+	C+	C+	C+
FIRST INTERSTATE BK	ENGLEWOOD	21	18	-2.9	25	1.9	80	7.10	27	0.99	5.0	1.5	5.1	0.06	0.34	19	-0.39	B	C	C	B-	C	B
FIRST INTERSTATE BK NA	ENGLEWOOD	141	465	11.8	96	1.7	90	9.54	69	0.97	5.0	1.3	6.3	0.57	1.33	80	1.11	D	A	A	B-	A	B+
LINCOLN NB OF ENGLEWOOD	ENGLEWOOD	179	380	17.0	97	0.0	98	6.85	23	1.58	4.3	1.0	6.3	0.81	0.11	88	0.13	C	C	B	B	B	C
MEGABANK OF ARAPAHOE NA	ENGLEWOOD	69	75	-4.6	31	27.0	13	6.65	7	0.00	3.0	0.7	4.4	0.00	2.22	98	0.13	B	C+	B+	C	C+	C
OMNIBANK ARAPAHOE	ENGLEWOOD	36	32	-23.7	0	5.8	53	10.49	78	0.57	3.0	0.6	4.4	0.84	2.95	50	0.89	C	B	C+	C	C	C
PROFESSIONAL BK COLORAD	ENGLEWOOD	13	-61	-12.9	24	53.8	15	4.09	9	1.57	3.7	1.2	7.6	0.00	-0.98	55	-0.36	C	C	B	C	D	D
REPUBLIC NB	ENGLEWOOD	17	-41	-17.4	3	24.0	16	4.36	15	1.73	4.8	1.4	7.6	0.23	-1.50	3	-2.19	C	C	B	B	E	D
TECNATIONAL BK	ENGLEWOOD	41	-35	-12.7	85	59.7	2	4.78	4	1.87	5.0	1.7	7.7	1.13	-0.40	18	-0.58	E	E	C+	E	D	D
UNITED BK OF ARAPAHOE N	ENGLEWOOD	10	-626	-3.6	45	59.7	2	4.39	4	3.44	4.0	1.3	3.9	6.91	-3.45	4	-1.68	C+	D	C	C	D	D
VECTRA BK ENGLEWOOD	ENGLEWOOD	67	-44	-11.0	6	44.2	11	7.64	39	0.95	4.0	1.6	6.3	0.00	-0.83	5	-0.62	B	C+	C	C	D	D
FIRSTBANK OF ERIE	ERIE	21	7	15.2	75	25.9	74	7.12	28	1.14	3.8	1.8	4.4	0.58	-0.51	35	-0.85	B-	B	B	B	C+	B
PARK NB	ESTES	14	6	18.4	93	2.0	0	7.60	38	0.28	3.6	0.8	4.9	0.06	0.06	14	0.55	B+	A	A	A	B	C+
ESTES PARK BK	ESTES PARK	35	86	-0.5	66	0.0	74	8.77	59	0.86	4.3	1.8	4.6	0.14	0.98	52	1.06	B	B	B	B	A	B
FIRST NB OF ESTES PARK	ESTES PARK	27	71	-0.5	51	9.7	42	8.64	57	0.69	4.7	0.5	3.8	0.12	1.04	57	1.20	C+	C+	C+	C+	C+	C+
BANK OF EVERGREEN	EVERGREEN	35	107	-4.2	33	15.0	28	7.61	38	0.67	6.6	1.7	5.9	0.45	1.24	71	1.56	C+	B	B	B	C+	B
COLORADO NB - EVERGREEN	EVERGREEN	67	147	9.6	93	26.4	17	5.37	7	1.47	4.6	1.8	7.4	0.82	0.86	39	0.57	C+	B	B	B	C+	C+
EVERGREEN NB	EVERGREEN	19	-332	10.3	80	74.8	17	5.80	45	2.95	4.3	1.0	5.8	4.43	-6.98	10	-4.49	B	B	C+	C	E	D
BANK OF FAIRPLAY	FAIRPLAY	9	-14	-15.5	0	22.2	17	7.93	17	0.96	4.3	1.0	6.8	0.14	-0.64	10	-0.22	C+	C	C	C	C	C
VECTRA BK FED HGHTS	FEDERAL HEIGHTS	15	-32	-34.8	0	22.2	17	5.55	7	1.07	3.5	2.2	6.8	0.18	-0.83	15	-1.23	C+	C+	C+	D	C+	B
FIRST NB OF FLAGLER	FLAGLER	36	153	-6.7	23	2.8	72	14.56	93	0.48	4.0	0.3	1.9	0.00	1.71	91	1.97	A	A+	A+	A	A	A
FIRST NB OF FLEMING	FLEMING	19	19	-7.8	48	49.0	6	7.34	34	1.96	4.6	1.1	4.3	0.42	1.47	78	1.57	E	E	E	E	E	E
FIRST NB OF FLORENCE	FLORENCE	20	40	-4.6	19	39.9	10	7.39	34	1.18	4.3	0.9	4.5	1.01	0.81	43	0.26	D	D	C+	D	C	C
CENTURY BK FT COLLINS	FORT COLLINS	25	24	-6.6	13	29.5	21	6.38	15	1.33	4.7	1.4	4.3	1.01	0.39	21	-0.74	C+	C+	C+	C+	C+	C+
FIRST CMNTY IND BK	FORT COLLINS	18	60	2.4	49	14.3	28	10.89	81	2.14	5.8	0.0	3.2	0.38	1.36	79	0.96	C+	C+	B	B	B	B

Several other companies provide bank ratings of one type or another. All publications are complex and require study before they can be used comfortably. They also crowd a great deal of data on a single line, making the tables somewhat difficult to read. LACE is the simplest to use, in part because it reports fewer variables. (LACE was designed for the library market, and the format was simplified based on comments from librarians.) For researchers in need of quick, easy-to-use comparisons, LACE is an appropriate service. And for those who prefer a single rating, LACE is clearly the best resource. In contrast, Sheshunoff is frequently the publication of choice for sophisticated users because of its larger selection of standard ratios. Sheshunoff is also the best known of the services. Not only has it been around the longest, it is often quoted in major financial newspapers and magazines.

Relying on a single letter-rating to evaluate a bank's standing can be misleading, but such services can help in making comparisons. Users should take the time to study the methods used in deriving the reported information. In the case of bank ratings, this means also becoming familiar with the specialized terminology and concepts of the banking industry.

Best's Insurance Reports (A.M. Best Company— Annual, with Updates).

The financial operations of the insurance industry are monitored by state agencies. Insurance companies may be publicly traded or mutually owned by their policy holders, but in either case financial disclosure is required. The most respected source of company profiles for this industry is the A.M. Best Company. Its annual *Best's Insurance Reports* has been published for nearly 100 years and is still the most frequently cited reference book in this field. *Best's Reports* covers virtually every insurance company doing business in the United States. Each listing typically offers summary financial statements, a breakdown of how the company's funds are invested, a history of the firm, a summary of management activities, ownership information, officers and directors, types of insurance written, the states in which it is licensed to operate, financial ratios, a brief analysis of operations, and the well-known Best's Rating. Two editions cover life and health insurance companies and property and casualty insurers. A companion set is published for foreign insurance companies. Those wishing to obtain more current information on insurance company activities, ratings changes, and other news have a variety of options. *Best's Insurance Reports* customers automati-

cally receive subscriptions to both editions of the monthly magazine *Best's Review*. They may also subscribe to *Best's Insurance Management Reports*, a weekly newsletter which includes *Best's Rating Monitor*. *Advance Company Reports* is a loose-leaf service that supplies revised company profiles before they appear in the annual bound volumes. Finally, researchers who follow the insurance industry on a daily basis may wish to use *BestLink*, A.M. Best's online database.

An alternative to Best's publications is *Standard & Poor's Insurance Rating Service*. This quarterly loose-leaf covers 200 of the leading insurance companies worldwide. Though it follows fewer firms than *Best's Insurance Reports*, it presents the information in more succinct fashion, with more narrative commentary. Each "Rating Analysis" is a four-page report which discusses the company's strategy, and provides a review of recent events, an analysis of operating and financial performance, and an explanation of how the rating was determined. The service also includes reports on trends in the insurance industry at home and abroad.

FEDERAL, STATE, AND LOCAL GOVERNMENT RECORDS

Companies in heavily regulated industries are not the only ones faced with government reporting requirements. Both public and private companies must file a diversity of reports and forms with agencies at all levels of government. Much of this reporting supports the government's administrative, enforcement, or statistical efforts, and is sealed from public viewing to protect the privacy of the filing companies. However, numerous company files are accessible to the public. Depending on the agency and the document, public records can be obtained in several ways. Many federal and state agencies maintain heavily used document rooms, where staff members are available to assist the public. Some honor requests by phone, but most do so only by mail or in person. Many have adopted standard request forms, and most require a fee for document delivery. Certain records may not be readily available, in which case the researcher may need to submit a Freedom of Information Act letter.

Most local government records are available for personal inspection and copying only, with little or no phone or mail service. Furthermore, such records may not be well-indexed, or may be filed or recorded in broad chronological groupings. Certain types of reports must also be submitted to public libraries or other designated

locations for community inspection. This is typical of transcripts of public hearings directly affecting the community, such as requests for utility rate increases, new broadcast licenses, and permits for waste disposal sites and energy transmission pipelines. An interesting example of a local depository network involves mortgage disclosure reports. All financial institutions which grant mortgages must submit an annual statement to their principal regulatory agency. The report details the institution's lending patterns within the community, broken down by Census Tract. The reports are forwarded to the Federal Financial Institutions Examination Council, which designates a Central Depository for every metropolitan area in the United States. Depositories are usually public libraries or local planning agencies, and they are required to make the disclosure reports available for public inspection.

"Public" does not mean published, nor does it necessarily mean that documents are easy to obtain. The researcher generally needs to know where to look, what to ask for, and how to request it. Because the information is often quite narrow in focus, the results may not be worth the effort required to obtain them. Clearly, this type of research is not for everyone, nor is it appropriate for every situation. At the very least, however, all business researchers should be aware of the broad potential offered by public filings. Several of the directories introduced in Chapter 2 are good starting points for identifying relevant government agencies and their services, but the following discussion will highlight some of the most useful possibilities.

State agencies which regulate securities transactions can be an excellent source of financial information. Public or semi-public companies not required to file reports with the U.S. Securities and Exchange Commission may have to file disclosure statements under state "Blue Sky Laws" (so named because they were enacted to protect consumers against investment opportunities with no more value than a piece of sky). Even privately held companies may be forced to file reports when they acquire a smaller public company. The agency handling inquiries about these filings varies from state to state. Many states have established an independent securities commission. If not, disclosure statements are filed with a securities division located within another agency. In many states it is the department of state, the commerce department, or the banking department, though the appropriate agency can be as different as the attorney general's office, the state auditor, or the insurance commission.

Business franchises may also be required to file financial documents at the state level. Because potential investors need to evaluate the soundness of a franchise opportunity, some states require the offering company to submit a packet of information before doing business in that state. Most utilize a format known as the Uniform Franchise Offering Circular (UFOC). Such franchise kits usually provide a history of the organization, a list of pending litigation against the firm, biographical information on the principals (including criminal convictions and bankruptcy judgments), franchise requirements, financial statements, and even a financial profile of an "average" franchise owner. They may also provide a picture of the company's future plans, market studies, and other useful data. The data are required even if the franchise is privately owned or is a subsidiary of another firm. At present, only 15 states mandate such disclosure documents. Other states are covered by the Federal Trade Commission's Franchise Rule, which merely requires the franchise sponsor to make an unreviewed prospectus available for inspection. But if a company has franchises located across the country (or even throughout a region), the chances are good that you'll be able to find a state which has UFOC data on file. Information from franchise kits can also be found in other forms. Several annual publications summarize key facts from major franchise filings. One of the best is the *Source Book of Franchise Opportunities* from Business One Irwin. Listings include the company's founding date, the year it first offered franchises, whether it belongs to any trade associations for the franchise industry, the number of total units in operation, the number which are company-owned, the states in which it is registered, the distribution of franchises by state, basic financial data, the fees charged to franchisees, and the types of support offered. And Buckmaster Publishing, a producer of corporate reports on microform, has announced the imminent debut of a new microfiche collection consisting of the Offering Circulars for the nation's 500 largest franchises.

What about other types of closely held companies? As a rule, all corporations must file an annual report in their state of incorporation to indicate they are still in operation. In most states, the report is actually a brief form, indicating little more than name, address, and perhaps the names of officers and directors. However, more than ten states require such additional information as the value of total assets or annual sales. The same state agencies also maintain the original incorporation papers on file, together with any subsequent amendments. Again, these reports are not as revealing as one might hope. In

most states, the principal officers of the corporation are not required to sign the documents; as long as the name and address of a registered agent (usually the corporation's attorney) appears, the law is satisfied. However, incorporation papers and annual reports can answer such questions as the date the firm was first incorporated, when mergers or acquisitions took place, previous names, and whether the company still exists. In most states the appropriate depository of corporate registration data is a corporations department or the corporations division of the department of state.

Numerous other documents are required at the federal, state, and local levels. Most are quite specific, and may provide only a few relevant pieces of information, so government filings are most helpful when used in conjunction with other information sources. At the federal level, researchers can obtain detailed information about a company's pension finances from the U.S. Department of Labor's Pension and Welfare Benefits Administration, and background on certain products and processes from the U.S. Environmental Protection Agency's Office of Toxic Substances. At the state level, companies which have received government loans or other financial help will have filed reports with the state development agency which granted the assistance. Companies embarking on major construction or expansion projects may be required to produce detailed environmental impact statements which can reveal an extraordinary amount of information on the firm's operations. Depending on the size of the project, such reports are filed with either the state or the federal government.

Local filings can be especially enlightening for smaller companies. Deeds, mortgages, and property tax records can be a useful source of information, and many localities index these records by name as well as property location. Such files can tell researchers what real property a corporation or individual owns, when it was acquired, and the assessed valuation for tax purposes. Civil judgments imposed on a local corporation by most courts in the county are generally filed at the county level. Information on liens, unpaid taxes, and other financial obligations are also on file. A particularly interesting local record tracks information on secured transactions. Under the Uniform Commercial Code, whenever a person or company pledges security against a loan, the lender can file a report with the county clerk's office in the county where the collateral resides, as well as with the department of state. Data on secured loans from so-called UCC filings can be a valuable source of information on

company operations and finances. They do not specify the dollar value of specific transactions, but they can shed light on activities the researcher may not be aware of.

Recent advances in technology are making state and local records more accessible. Some state agencies now sell computer tapes; others sell printouts or mailing lists on a onetime or subscription basis. For example, many states sell a daily, weekly, or monthly list of new business incorporations. Several states have even created online databases to provide subscribers with motor vehicle data or corporation registrations. Unless the researcher has a recurring need to investigate companies in a particular state, subscribing to such services is not practical. However, several private companies have begun constructing nationwide databases which will ultimately include numerous agencies from every state. Dun & Bradstreet already makes extensive use of state and local filings in its credit reports, but the two most comprehensive databases of state filings are *Information America* (produced by an Atlanta company of the same name) and *Prentice Hall OnLine* (from Prentice Hall Legal & Financial Services). Each utilizes a variety of methods to acquire data, including purchasing tapes and serving as gateways to states' own online systems. Their data vary from state to state, but the most commonly encountered files are corporation records, UCC filings, bankruptcy records, and local liens and judgments. Both publishers offer extremely easy, but flexible menu-driven search systems, coupled with electronic ordering of full-text documents. Users can search by company name within state, or can specify the type of filing required. Both systems allow global searching by name of company. The user can specify all filings within one state, a single type of filing in all states, or all filings in all states. Prentice Hall has the more extensive service, with 60 million filings of various types from 27 states. Information USA currently offers access to filings from 20 states, and is somewhat easier to use. Other state filing services usually offer narrower geographic coverage. The *INCORP* library on LEXIS/NEXIS, for example, has databases for approximately 15 states, including limited partnership and trademark filings.

MAKING FINANCIAL COMPARISONS

An alternative method of analyzing privately held firms is to compare the company in question to similar corporations within the same industry. Even if detailed financial data on the private firm are unknown, reasonable assumptions may be based on what *is* known. One

way to do this is to look at the financial statements of publicly traded firms with similar characteristics. Another is to examine industry-wide financial averages or norms. Two types of publications can aid in this process—company rankings and financial ratios.

Financial Ratios

The problem facing all users of financial information is how to interpret the data. For any given company, do the numbers represent good news or bad? Does the company have an acceptable gross profit? Is the net income reasonable for that volume of sales? Is the level of inventories too high? Does the company have too much debt? These and other pertinent questions can be answered best through the use of financial ratios. Ratios provide a standard of comparison for company performance. By recasting items from the Balance Sheet and Income Statement into ratios or percentages, a better picture of the firm's financial health emerges. In other words, the items in a financial statement rarely impart meaning in and of themselves; they must be compared to other statements or to industry averages.

There are two ways to perform a numerical study of financial statements: common-size analysis and ratio analysis. The common-size method converts every line on a financial statement into a percentage of the total amount. Each item shown on the Income Statement will be converted to a percentage of total revenues, and each item on the Balance Sheet will appear as a percentage of total assets. The numbers for Wealthy Corporation in Figures 8-A and 8-B show that general and administrative expenses comprise 14% of total sales, and fixed assets represent 75% of total assets. Common-size analysis enables comparison of two companies regardless of their respective sizes.

Ratio analysis compares one item on the financial statement to another, instead of to the whole. Obviously any two numbers can be compared to one another, but it makes sense to focus on the most meaningful relationships. For example, it is useful to compare total debt to total equity on the Balance Sheet in order to determine how much of the firm's assets is funded through borrowing. Another key measure is to compare interest expenses to Earnings Before Interest and Taxes (EBIT). This ratio, called "Times Interest Earned" measures the company's ability to meet debt obligations. Over the years, accountants and financial analysts have developed dozens of other standardized ratios for statement analysis. Ratios may be employed to compare the performance of the

company over time, by looking at how its ratios change from year to year. The company's ratios may also be compared to those of its competitors, to similar firms, or to the industry as a whole. It is fairly simple to obtain industry-wide norms for common financial ratios.

Because ratios comprise an essential source of information for analyzing company performance, many publications provide data on industry averages in ratio form. Industry norms are derived by combining data from hundreds (or even thousands) of individual financial statements and calculating average values. Data are obtained on both private and public companies. The financial statements themselves come from several sources. Dun & Bradstreet collects statements on several million privately held companies, and therefore has an ideal database for calculating ratios.

Income tax returns filed by corporations, partnerships, and proprietorships are another excellent source. While individual returns are not released to the public, the IRS does compile composite financial statements for major industries. Industry ratios also come from trade and professional associations, which collect financial statements from their members for just such calculations. Again, data on individual companies remain confidential, but aggregate numbers are published.

Industry averages are best measured through use of median values. The median is the middle value in an array of numbers ranked in descending order from strongest to weakest. Using a mean value or other type of average could be misleading since exceptionally high or low numbers could distort the average. The most detailed ratio publications also cite values for upper and lower quartiles. The upper quartile represents the number midway between the median and the topmost value; the lower quartile is the number appearing mid-way between the median and the bottom value. Dividing the list into fourths in this way gives a better sense of how the numbers are distributed. Numbers above the upper quartile or below the lower quartile are farthest from the norm. It also helps determine where a particular company would appear in the ranked list. Companies in the upper quartile have a better performance than those in the lower.

Comparability is another convention frequently seen in ratio publications. It is unwise to make generalizations about corporate finances based upon the behavior of all companies within an industry. Larger firms generally exhibit different financial characteristics than smaller ones, so it is important to compare companies of similar size. For almost all industries, the most meaningful way

to determine size is by total assets. The best ratio publications not only present data by industry, but break the results of each industry into asset-size categories.

Medians, quartiles, and asset-size groupings make it possible to estimate the financial characteristics of private companies without access to their complete financial statements. Multiplying a firm's sales or total assets by common-size percentages for its industry allows construction of hypothetical statements, for example. This technique only works to the extent that the company's performance approximates the industry norm, which may not be the case at all. The more actual numbers known, the greater the degree of confidence with which unknown values can be estimated. Ratios can also be used to evaluate the validity of financial estimates arrived at by other means, or to analyze unaudited figures obtained from other sources; if the given numbers lie well outside industry norms, their accuracy may be questioned. However, techniques such as these should be used with extreme caution, and compared to what else is known about the company.

RMA Annual Statement Studies (Robert Morris Associates—Annual).

Robert Morris Associates is a highly respected national organization of bank loan officers. RMA surveys its membership annually to obtain sample financial statements of businesses seeking bank financing. The Association feeds the data into a computer to determine financial norms for over 375 industry groups. The resulting publication, *Annual Statement Studies*, has appeared regularly for over 60 years, and is used widely by bankers, accountants, financial analysts, and researchers of all kinds.

Exhibit 8-2 shows a sample page from the 1990 publication. Each two-page table provides summary data for a four-digit SIC grouping, in this case SIC 5511, New and Used Car Dealers. (Note, Exhibit 8-2 shows only the second page.) As shown in the upper left corner of the table, data from 2,342 companies were used to generate the averages for this industry, of which 185 were based on unqualified statements. This section provides the reader with some sense of the nature of the data used to compile the ratios. An unqualified report is one which has been fully examined by an independent auditor and meets generally accepted accounting principles. A "Compiled" report was submitted by the company management, with no audit, verification, or review. The left side of the page cites data for all companies in the industry sample for the most recent three years. The right side shows the current data, divided into six categories, grouping similar sized companies by annual sales. The page not

shown presents the same information, but sorted by six asset size categories. If fewer than 10 firms appear in any category, the information is suppressed for that group.

The top three sets of rows represent common-size analysis for the industry—assets, liabilities, and income data. As the Exhibit shows, 66.4% of auto dealers' assets were held in the form of inventory during the 1989/90 period, which is not surprising given the nature of the business.

The next group of rows provides data for 16 popular financial and operating ratios. The Quick Ratio, for example, is obtained by dividing the most liquid current assets by the current liabilities; it measures the company's ability to meet current obligations. RMA includes operating ratios that compare more specific information, such as the line comparing Officers' Compensation to Total Sales. For each ratio, the three figures represent the upper-quartile value, the median, and the lower quartile. In the case of the Debt/Worth Ratio, the median value for all companies is 4.4 (i.e., the amount of debt is 4.4 times the amount of net worth). In some cases, not all companies were used to compute a certain ratio, because some of the financial statements are incomplete. In these instances, the number appearing to the left of the ratio in parentheses indicates the actual number of statements used to calculate that ratio. Also notice the boldface numbers appearing to the left of the three ratios dealing with inventories, receivables, and payables. These represent alternative methods of presenting the ratios in question. Each is obtained by dividing the number 365 by the ratio, resulting in a "turnover" figure. For example, the "days' inventory turnover" reflects the average number of days any item remains in inventory. Using the numbers shown in Exhibit 8-2, the median inventory turnover for all companies is 68 days.

The last two rows on each page represent the total dollar amount of sales and assets for all companies in the survey, so that industry-wide Balance Sheets and Income Statements may be calculated using the percentages from the common-size analysis. In other words, the percentages in the common-size analysis can be recast as dollar values represented the aggregate finances for all companies in the sample.

To first-time users, *Annual Statement Studies* may appear baffling, but an enormous amount of data is presented in a meaningful way. Definitions and explanations for ratios are provided in the preface of the publication. The book also provides a subject index to industries, an index by SIC number, and a bibliography of more specialized sources of financial ratios published by other organizations, complete with its own subject index.

EXHIBIT 8-2. *RMA Annual Statement Studies*

RETAILERS - AUTOS- NEW & USED SIC# 5511   467

Comparative Historical Data			Type of Statement	Current Data Sorted By Sales					
267	208	185	Unqualified	1	5	7	20	70	82
24	16	12	Qualified				1	3	8
329	293	333	Reviewed	4	13	29	85	128	74
335	304	297	Compiled	14	28	30	77	104	44
1577	1472	1515	Other	12	75	120	332	624	352
6/30/87-3/31/88	6/30/88-3/31/89	6/30/89-3/31/90		242(6/30-9/30/89)			2100(10/1/89-3/31/90)		
ALL 2532	ALL 2293	ALL 2342	NUMBER OF STATEMENTS	0-1MM 31	1-3MM 121	3-5MM 186	5-10MM 515	10-25MM 929	25MM & OVER 560
%	%	%	**ASSETS**	%	%	%	%	%	%
5.7	5.4	5.2	Cash & Equivalents	6.5	6.4	5.0	5.2	4.7	5.9
8.6	8.8	8.5	Trade Receivables - (net)	6.0	6.1	7.1	7.0	8.5	11.0
66.0	65.7	66.4	Inventory	67.2	70.1	72.4	71.4	67.1	57.8
2.8	2.9	2.9	All Other Current	3.2	2.6	2.1	2.2	3.1	3.6
83.1	82.7	83.0	Total Current	82.8	85.1	86.7	85.7	83.4	78.3
9.8	10.1	9.8	Fixed Assets (net)	13.7	9.5	8.8	8.1	9.5	12.0
.5	.6	.7	Intangibles (net)	.0	1.1	.7	.7	.7	.6
6.5	6.6	6.5	All Other Non-Current	3.4	4.2	3.8	5.5	6.4	9.1
100.0	100.0	100.0	Total	100.0	100.0	100.0	100.0	100.0	100.0
			LIABILITIES						
52.0	52.1	54.5	Notes Payable-Short Term	49.8	51.7	56.2	57.0	55.7	50.7
1.3	1.4	1.4	Cur. Mat.-L/T/D	2.0	1.2	1.2	1.3	1.6	1.4
5.5	5.9	5.8	Trade Payables	6.0	5.2	4.9	5.5	6.0	6.0
.5	.5	.3	Income Taxes Payable	.4	.3	.5	.2	.4	.3
7.1	6.4	6.4	All Other Current	4.0	6.5	4.5	5.7	6.6	7.3
66.4	66.3	68.4	Total Current	62.2	64.9	67.3	69.7	70.2	65.8
8.3	8.4	9.1	Long Term Debt	10.9	9.0	8.3	8.3	9.5	9.4
.1	.1	.1	Deferred Taxes	.1	.0	.1	.0	.1	.2
1.3	1.5	1.5	All Other Non-Current	2.4	1.1	.5	1.5	1.5	2.1
23.9	23.7	20.8	Net Worth	24.4	25.0	23.8	20.5	18.7	22.5
100.0	100.0	100.0	Total Liabilities & Net Worth	100.0	100.0	100.0	100.0	100.0	100.0
			INCOME DATA						
100.0	100.0	100.0	Net Sales	100.0	100.0	100.0	100.0	100.0	100.0
14.5	14.1	14.0	Gross Profit	24.9	16.2	14.5	14.0	13.6	13.3
13.6	13.3	13.5	Operating Expenses	25.8	16.2	14.0	13.6	13.1	12.5
.9	.8	.5	Operating Profit	-.9	.0	.5	.3	.5	.8
-.3	-.3	.2	All Other Expenses (net)	.5	.9	.3	.2	.2	.0
1.2	1.1	.3	Profit Before Taxes	-1.3	-.9	.2	.1	.4	.8
			RATIOS						
1.4	1.4	1.4		1.8	1.6	1.5	1.4	1.3	1.4
1.2	1.2	1.2	Current	1.3	1.2	1.3	1.2	1.2	1.2
1.1	1.1	1.1		1.1	1.1	1.1	1.1	1.1	1.0
.3	.3	.3		.3	.3	.3	.2	.3	.3
(2516) .2	(2282) .2	(2328) .2	Quick	.1 (119)	.2 (184)	.1 (512)	.1 (924)	.2 (558)	.2
.1	.1	.1		.1	.1	.1	.1	.1	.2
4 103.5	4 100.1	3 104.5		1 481.0	3 114.6	3 129.6	3 114.7	3 110.9	5 80.4
6 61.2	6 59.1	6 60.0	Sales/Receivables	3 124.3	6 61.1	6 62.0	6 64.8	6 63.5	7 50.6
10 37.9	10 36.9	10 37.2		13 27.6	11 32.4	11 33.8	9 42.9	9 39.5	11 32.3
51 7.1	50 7.3	51 7.1		83 4.4	72 5.1	73 5.0	63 5.8	51 7.1	42 8.7
66 5.5	65 5.6	68 5.4	Cost of Sales/Inventory	104 3.5	111 3.3	94 3.9	79 4.6	64 5.7	52 7.0
85 4.3	83 4.4	87 4.2		183 2.0	152 2.4	111 3.3	99 3.7	79 4.6	68 5.4
2 174.3	2 169.5	2 166.1		0 UND	1 284.1	2 235.1	2 166.8	2 161.3	2 154.9
3 107.5	4 103.6	4 101.8	Cost of Sales/Payables	5 74.8	4 85.4	3 113.5	3 106.8	4 101.0	4 101.8
5 66.8	6 64.8	6 62.8		14 26.2	9 39.7	6 57.5	6 60.4	5 67.1	6 63.7
17.1	17.1	17.8		5.0	8.3	10.2	16.1	21.3	22.6
27.8	29.1	31.4	Sales/Working Capital	14.4	15.1	19.0	24.6	36.4	43.1
60.5	67.8	93.9		43.7	38.3	35.0	61.0	127.9	236.4
4.2	3.9	2.2		2.2	2.1	2.2	1.9	2.2	2.9
(2276) 2.1	(2051) 2.0	(2182) 1.3	EBIT/Interest	(25) 1.1	(113) 1.0	(173) 1.3	(486) 1.2	(869) 1.3	(516) 1.5
1.2	1.2	.7		.1	.1	.8	.7	.6	.9
6.7	7.8	4.7			3.5	4.9	3.7	4.3	7.0
(649) 2.3	(568) 2.4	(560) 1.3	Net Profit + Depr., Dep., Amort./Cur. Mat. L/T/D		(16) .6	(33) .6	(111) 1.0	(224) 1.3	(174) 1.8
.6	.7	-.2			-1.3	-1.9	-.2	-.5	.3
.1	.2	.2		.1	.1	.1	.1	.2	.2
.3	.4	.4	Fixed/Worth	.4	.3	.3	.3	.4	.4
.8	.8	1.1		2.1	.9	.7	.8	1.1	1.2
2.1	2.1	2.4		1.7	1.6	1.7	2.5	2.8	2.3
3.8	3.8	4.4	Debt/Worth	3.6	4.0	3.9	4.2	5.0	4.1
7.0	7.1	9.5		11.1	9.1	6.4	9.4	11.1	8.5
38.1	36.8	26.8	% Profit Before Taxes/Tangible Net Worth	30.6	14.9	20.2	19.7	28.9	33.4
(2405) 18.7	(2155) 19.0	(2134) 9.7		(26) 1.5	(108) 1.4	(174) 6.3	(473) 6.5	(835) 10.2	(518) 15.4
5.3	5.9	-5.5		-18.4	-27.5	-4.4	-6.1	-7.2	.3
8.4	9.0	5.7		8.8	4.3	5.4	4.5	5.5	7.0
4.0	3.8	1.6	% Profit Before Taxes/Total Assets	.4	.1	1.5	.9	1.5	2.8
.7	.7	-1.7		-4.4	-4.5	-1.9	-1.9	-2.1	-.5
135.4	128.7	137.5		172.5	119.7	145.9	143.9	144.0	115.8
68.0	64.7	68.1	Sales/Net Fixed Assets	34.9	51.9	66.8	75.0	74.2	61.2
33.1	32.2	32.3		16.1	16.6	27.5	38.2	36.3	29.3
5.2	5.2	5.1		4.0	4.1	4.0	4.7	5.3	5.6
4.2	4.3	4.1	Sales/Total Assets	2.8	2.9	3.4	3.9	4.4	4.5
3.4	3.5	3.4		1.5	1.8	2.6	3.2	3.7	3.7
.2	.2	.2		.4	.2	.1	.2	.2	.2
(2212) .3	(1995) .3	(2044) .3	% Depr., Dep., Amort./Sales	(22) .7	(93) .4	(150) .3	(439) .3	(825) .3	(515) .3
.5	.5	.5		1.5	.7	.6	.5	.5	.5
.4	.4	.4		2.2	.9	.6	.5	.2	.2
(1584) .7	(1438) .7	(1550) .7	% Officers' Comp/Sales	(15) 3.8	(69) 1.3	(115) 1.0	(338) .9	(659) .6	(354) .5
1.3	1.2	1.3		5.1	2.2	1.6	1.5	1.0	.8
44926029M	43860500M	45679259M	Net Sales ($)	16292M	243829M	759197M	3855655M	15093893M	25710393M
11024093M	10485463M	11182257M	Total Assets ($)	9425M	108175M	268646M	1057627M	3595961M	6142423M

©Robert Morris Associates 1990   M = $thousand   MM = $million
See Pages 1 through 15 for Explanation of Ratios and Data

Reprinted with permission from Robert Morris Associates. RMA cautions that the Studies be regarded only as a general guideline and not as an absolute industry norm. This is due to limited samples within categories, the categorization of companies by their primary Standard Industrial Classification (SIC) number only, and different methods of operations by companies within the same industry. For these reasons, RMA recommends that the figures be used only as general guidelines in addition to other methods of financial analysis.

Sources range from *Operating Ratios for the Typographic Industry* to *Aerospace Facts and Figures*. Complete address and price information is provided for each.

Industry Norms and Key Business Ratios (Dun & Bradstreet Business Credit Services—Annual).

Similar to the RMA publication, though more expensive, *Industry Norms and Key Business Ratios* is generated from D&B's unique database of business credit reports, and draws upon the financial statements of more than a million companies. It covers 800 industry groups, more than twice the number available in RMA, but less information is given for each industry. Although median and quartile figures are presented, data are not grouped by size of company, and no historical information is provided. D&B calculates 14 ratios, while RMA provides 16. In addition to common-size analysis, Dun & Bradstreet calculates a "typical" Balance Sheet and summary Income Statement for each industry; this is done by multiplying the common-size percentages by the median total assets and sales for that industry group. The common-size presentation of Income Statement data is much briefer than for Balance Sheet items.

In addition to the "Desk-Top Edition" described above, D&B also sells more detailed ratio data to commercial customers in 15 different editions covering specific industry segments. Various formats offer breakdowns by asset size, geographic region, and time period. Each can be purchased in printed format or on floppy diskette. Industry norms from D&B also appear in several other products. Selected company and industry ratios are presented in several of Dun & Bradstreet's more specialized credit reports. Company and industry comparisons are also found in the *Duns Financial Records Plus* database. The online reports typically cite eight industry norms and four key ratios for every company.

Almanac of Business and Industrial Financial Ratios (Prentice Hall, Inc.—Annual).

Another frequently used source of ratios has been compiled for many years by Leo Troy, a professor of economics at Rutgers University. The numbers are based on summary statistics generated by the U.S. Internal Revenue Service. Computer tapes from the IRS tabulate the total dollar value of business tax returns line by line. Troy uses this aggregate data to calculate figures in common-size and ratio form. Although the publication appears annually, there is a considerable time lag before IRS data are made available—generally about three years.

Other weaknesses are also a direct consequence of using IRS data. Industry breakdowns are less detailed than those seen in RMA and D&B; only 180 SIC codes are listed. And because tax returns for proprietorships and partnerships don't contain Balance Sheet data, common-size Balance Sheets are not calculated here. On the other hand, detailed Balance Sheets are found on corporate tax returns, and Troy uses these to calculate some of his ratios. Also, data appearing on the IRS tapes are estimates based on a sampling of all returns. Still, more than 100,000 establishments are used in the sample.

Troy's publication does offer some significant advantages. Data from Income Statements are more detailed than those found in most other sources. For example, common-size analysis for rent, advertising, interest, and other specific expenses is given. Figures are divided into 12 asset-size categories, plus totals for all companies. In addition to the common-size analysis for income and expense items, ten ratios are calculated. For every industry, separate tables are provided for companies which reported a profit, and for all firms (including those with no taxable income during that year).

Several other publishers produce ratio sources based on IRS tapes. An annual from Schonfeld & Associates, Inc., *IRS Corporate Financial Ratios*, covers the same 180 industries found in Troy, but only for corporate returns. Because corporations must file more detailed data with the IRS, this publication is able to calculate more than 70 ratios in all. Data for companies reporting net income and those without net income are listed on the same table, but only four size categories are provided. Unlike the tables from Troy, only ratios can be found; no common-size percentages are given.

Statistics of Income (U.S. Internal Revenue Service—Annual).

The IRS itself publishes a series called *Statistics of Income*, which summarizes industry assets, liabilities, and income and expenses from its computer tapes. The series has been produced annually since the 1950s and is presented in four volumes: Corporations, Partnerships, Sole Proprietorships, and Individuals. The Corporation volume, for example, is based on a stratified sample of approximately 85,000 corporate tax returns. It presents aggregate data for major Balance Sheet and Income Statement items for broad industry groupings. Separate tables are given for all firms and for those reporting taxable income.

Exhibit 8-3 shows a sample page from *Statistics of Income: Corporation Income Tax Returns*. It illustrates the three main differences between IRS data and the information found in commercial sources like Troy's. First, only major industry groups are presented. In this case, combined data can be found for all auto dealers and automotive service stations; separate figures are not

EXHIBIT 8-3. *Statistics of Income: Corporation Income Tax Returns*

Corporation Returns/1986

RETURNS WITH NET INCOME

Table 3—Balance Sheets, Income Statements, Tax, and Selected Other Items, by Major Industry—Continued

[All figures are estimates based on samples—money amounts are in thousands of dollars]

					Major industry—Continued					
				Wholesale and retail trade—Continued						
				Retail trade						
Item	Total	Building materials, garden supplies, and mobile home dealers	General merchandise stores	Food stores	Automotive dealers and service stations	Apparel and accessory stores	Furniture and home furnishings stores	Eating and drinking places	Miscellaneous retail stores	Wholesale and retail trade not allocable
	(43)	(44)	(45)	(46)	(47)	(48)	(49)	(50)	(51)	(52)
Number of returns, with net income	332,985	25,900	5,863	25,486	55,944	24,792	22,069	58,579	114,352	1,767
Total assets	**434,023,511**	**21,937,235**	**156,316,034**	**47,632,578**	**62,596,594**	**23,929,483**	**16,213,078**	**46,127,494**	**59,271,015**	**1,325,414**
Cash	27,605,573	1,813,808	4,592,707	3,289,088	5,067,449	1,953,461	1,457,103	3,854,295	5,577,661	123,063
Notes and accounts receivable	81,488,247	4,352,862	44,337,122	4,094,947	8,458,799	3,968,287	4,051,413	3,200,590	9,024,227	249,401
Less: Allowance for bad debts	1,677,175	136,228	633,361	31,875	190,661	124,485	136,266	66,426	357,874	4,661
Inventories	118,855,041	8,101,889	30,248,517	11,882,124	31,022,301	8,633,014	6,411,705	1,468,484	21,087,008	355,216
Investments in Government obligations	10,236,695	192,076	9,166,908	368,356	75,391	*3,945	*34,396	55,314	340,310	—
Other current assets	20,141,677	719,950	9,902,279	1,818,724	1,914,115	985,533	557,703	2,259,752	1,983,621	118,823
Loans to stockholders	5,439,941	149,801	668,166	521,007	740,707	437,018	184,820	2,058,570	679,851	*38,786
Mortgage and real estate loans	6,271,536	125,374	4,997,873	95,437	191,386	38,913	42,354	305,304	474,895	*2,835
Other investments	37,465,867	899,374	17,385,006	2,823,389	1,621,276	2,289,544	728,221	4,962,735	6,756,321	133,788
Depreciable loans	159,773,415	8,224,215	40,766,621	30,047,966	19,430,421	8,285,547	4,105,039	28,187,091	20,726,515	453,800
Less: Accumulated depreciation	68,282,820	4,023,212	14,850,290	12,400,062	9,163,285	3,492,058	1,933,764	11,705,935	10,714,215	234,103
Depletable assets	462,209	*24,386	—	*270,308	41,178	*3,860	*69	*18,254	104,154	*47
Less: Accumulated depletion	88,382	*2,176	—	*14,210	*12,703	*2,772	—	*8,698	47,823	*30
Land	12,190,884	993,355	2,342,679	2,095,279	1,875,730	173,859	245,621	3,363,808	1,100,554	64,831
Intangible assets (amortizable)	7,015,306	114,926	891,004	1,280,087	356,004	297,725	96,260	2,638,580	1,340,720	*9,785
Less: Accumulated amortization	1,529,543	26,513	151,629	308,623	116,795	80,447	26,093	452,942	366,501	*1,839
Other assets	18,655,041	413,348	6,652,430	1,800,636	1,285,280	558,540	394,497	5,988,718	1,561,592	15,673
Total liabilities	**434,023,511**	**21,937,235**	**156,316,034**	**47,632,578**	**62,596,594**	**23,929,483**	**16,213,078**	**46,127,494**	**59,271,015**	**1,325,414**
Accounts payable	56,422,522	3,228,839	16,847,611	9,587,431	5,713,545	3,589,399	2,497,135	4,387,946	10,570,615	196,594
Mortgages, notes, and bonds payable in less than one year	56,488,735	2,311,556	17,637,131	2,015,873	24,929,214	908,914	1,393,845	2,328,871	4,963,331	196,379
Other current liabilities	57,998,372	1,649,909	34,205,558	4,501,624	4,464,819	2,444,698	1,843,006	3,736,661	5,152,097	89,064
Loans from stockholders	11,200,050	707,263	1,087,980	848,928	2,020,104	900,667	531,211	2,638,461	2,465,435	57,938
Mortgages, notes, and bonds payable in one year or more	77,635,056	3,357,434	27,514,442	10,337,033	7,581,896	3,045,586	1,875,303	14,980,481	8,942,881	216,311
Other liabilities	20,184,586	510,912	9,623,906	2,581,531	1,201,106	642,422	893,235	2,592,996	2,138,478	23,759
Capital stock	18,181,943	1,230,059	4,033,172	2,304,335	3,000,937	1,739,127	740,882	1,750,782	3,382,649	68,734
Paid-in or capital surplus	28,964,224	1,157,823	11,620,580	3,866,589	1,388,371	1,838,007	761,343	4,028,259	4,303,252	109,955
Retained earnings, appropriated	808,236	*23,985	267,032	*25,021	54,754	*20,914	244,023	107,872	64,636	—
Retained earnings, unappropriated	106,266,760	7,406,784	33,513,788	12,011,983	11,854,311	8,748,284	5,329,924	10,305,327	17,096,359	322,830
Retained earnings, 1120S	6,110,357	877,709	378,847	451,633	1,532,409	312,598	602,757	567,573	1,386,832	*83,727
Less: Cost of treasury stock	6,237,328	525,039	414,012	899,403	1,144,871	261,132	499,586	1,297,736	1,195,550	*39,876
Total receipts	**1,032,357,027**	**54,792,536**	**184,670,209**	**206,754,270**	**273,526,780**	**49,881,828**	**36,679,361**	**75,663,550**	**150,388,491**	**2,986,305**
Business receipts	998,500,003	53,554,665	173,510,150	202,840,886	267,845,352	48,550,441	35,472,277	69,799,329	146,926,904	2,900,933
Interest	6,705,623	240,116	3,229,499	419,792	989,707	371,091	236,349	634,576	584,493	10,053
Interest on Government obligations:										
State and local	895,631	14,156	735,628	20,194	16,578	8,959	40,292	26,880	32,945	*292
Nonqualifying interest and dividends	338,776	27,352	4,957	9,825	162,812	9,963	26,325	38,838	58,704	*501
Rents	5,587,177	238,125	1,609,078	552,397	931,928	105,845	127,614	1,340,447	681,743	23,449
Royalties	611,126	13,829	6,786	9,623	4,379	151,444	*801	301,747	122,516	*270
Net short-term capital gain reduced by net long-term capital loss	164,615	1,419	19,651	18,898	23,510	2,758	8,590	15,998	73,791	*1,969
Net long-term capital gain reduced by net short-term capital loss	3,515,374	90,690	1,238,566	848,373	272,285	58,493	35,889	734,424	236,655	*10,917
Net gain, noncapital assets	1,352,456	76,776	137,825	179,711	376,903	19,589	43,475	350,782	167,395	*836
Dividends received from domestic corporations	374,234	17,233	154,050	41,829	33,124	63,226	5,592	25,786	33,394	*1,031
Dividends received from foreign corporations	361,146	12,873	106,109	83,806	*584	*1,512	—	*151,242	*5,019	*2,133
Other receipts	13,950,865	505,304	3,917,911	1,728,936	2,869,619	538,507	682,157	2,243,501	1,464,932	33,922
Total deductions	**1,002,250,610**	**52,713,742**	**177,547,388**	**202,935,042**	**269,447,122**	**47,508,007**	**35,032,654**	**72,073,600**	**144,993,055**	**2,889,613**
Cost of sales and operations	712,732,597	38,689,453	110,108,352	155,436,174	228,038,484	28,583,132	22,581,079	29,702,705	99,593,223	2,051,690
Compensation of officers	15,260,907	1,366,038	664,113	1,086,130	3,768,241	983,651	1,126,881	1,897,903	4,367,950	117,818
Repairs	4,774,895	244,076	1,003,876	1,057,224	649,931	170,792	141,342	919,523	588,129	13,928
Bad debts	2,479,245	240,509	1,022,170	134,918	279,876	215,002	153,310	72,267	361,192	7,662
Rent paid on business property	23,294,993	726,401	5,408,569	3,175,528	2,428,928	2,760,202	1,144,069	3,739,741	3,911,556	40,721
Taxes paid	18,350,246	1,008,354	4,358,647	2,683,949	2,871,013	1,111,271	733,161	2,905,655	2,678,195	50,000
Interest paid	13,587,518	644,523	5,635,269	1,178,811	2,238,743	494,082	362,090	1,542,593	1,491,406	36,861
Contributions or gifts	451,691	21,184	142,488	80,381	48,035	47,904	17,239	30,966	63,494	995
Amortization	586,403	18,446	123,356	65,070	53,891	55,411	15,295	128,748	135,165	955
Depreciation	17,218,154	782,050	3,742,107	3,292,567	2,759,221	933,018	426,026	2,945,371	2,337,794	55,269
Depletion	34,374	*3,251	*5,576	8,719	8,248	*1,989	*749	1,717	4,125	—
Advertising	17,407,326	695,705	4,816,917	2,092,280	2,745,074	1,234,279	1,497,216	1,827,465	2,498,391	37,235
Pension, profit-sharing, stock bonus, and annuity plans	3,242,948	195,736	990,832	533,945	349,555	146,222	149,981	275,091	601,585	22,019
Employee benefit programs	5,520,934	205,079	1,000,251	1,879,236	903,536	240,859	122,563	466,236	703,174	12,650
Net loss, noncapital assets	175,520	4,738	13,218	17,018	18,144	14,844	33,832	40,012	33,714	*1,186
Other deductions	167,132,859	7,877,178	38,511,647	30,213,090	22,286,207	10,515,346	6,527,821	25,577,608	25,623,963	440,625
Total receipts less total deductions	30,106,417	2,078,795	7,122,822	3,819,228	4,079,658	2,373,822	1,646,707	3,589,950	5,395,436	96,692
Constructive taxable income from related foreign corporations	401,329	8,259	*141,110	52,006	1,565	1,148	—	188,404	8,838	—
Net income	29,592,013	2,072,897	6,528,304	3,851,040	4,064,645	2,366,011	1,606,415	3,731,388	5,371,314	96,400
Income subject to tax	24,251,758	1,614,029	6,238,456	3,437,037	2,890,601	2,039,317	1,284,720	2,772,403	3,975,195	60,992
Income tax, total	9,276,919	587,796	2,643,447	1,356,682	997,240	812,922	459,166	1,036,785	1,382,880	19,408
Regular and alternative tax	9,148,167	582,018	2,622,060	1,330,408	973,873	810,254	456,828	1,002,012	1,370,714	19,317
Tax from recomputing prior-year investment credit	88,512	5,453	11,018	18,599	21,830	2,633	1,589	16,569	10,821	*91
Additional tax for tax preferences	39,802	*325	*10,368	7,676	1,538	*35	749	17,766	*1,345	—
Foreign tax credit	350,840	9,212	97,171	61,364	37	4,122	—	176,890	2,037	—
U.S. possessions tax credit	*64,030	—	—	2,998	—	—	—	—	483	60,549	—
Orphan drug credit	—	—	—	—	—	—	—	—	—	—
Nonconventional source fuel credit	*120	*113	—	—	—	—	—	—	7	—
General business credit	857,600	21,986	308,256	151,621	84,939	26,812	9,140	172,371	82,475	1,005

Footnotes at end of table. See text for "Explanation of Terms" and "Description of the Sample and Limitations of the Data."

Reprinted from *Statistics of Income: Corporation Income Tax Returns*, published by the U.S. Internal Revenue Service.

given for new car dealers. Second, asset-size categories for each industry are not listed. A separate table gives some size breakdowns, but only for broad sectors of the economy (e.g., manufacturing). Finally, no ratios are calculated. *Statistics of Income* presents raw tax return data from which users can calculate their own ratios. Column 47 gives data for auto dealers and service stations which reported taxable income for 1986. Notice that 55,944 tax returns were filed in this category. But the data in this publication are based on a total sample of 85,000 corporations nationwide, so IRS economists use estimation techniques to derive the industry totals seen in these tables. For example, the IRS estimates total industry revenues (i.e., "Total Receipts") for corporations which realized a profit in this category were $273.5 billion. By adding the values from several tables for a given business grouping, researchers can estimate total industry sales and expenditures. This provides an alternative to data in publications from the Bureau of the Census or from commercial sources. Note, however, that figures from six separate tables must be added to obtain industry totals. This is because numbers are published in three volumes (for corporations, proprietorships, and partnerships) and each volume presents tables for companies with net income and those without.

The *Statistics of Income* series lacks industry detail, but the government also publishes a more extensive service called the *Statistics of Income Source Book*. It provides similar data, broken down by four-digit SIC codes. Figures at the four-digit level are also divided into the same 12 asset categories seen in Troy. The *Source Book* appears in three editions covering corporations, partnerships, and proprietorships. The other drawback is the time lag; *Statistics of Income* generally appears about three years after the tax year ends. Researchers in need of more current trends in business income can turn to a quarterly journal from the IRS called the *SOI Bulletin*. Summary tables from the IRS tapes are always published in the *Bulletin* first.

Other Sources of Financial Ratios

Numerous other ratio publications are available. *Financial Studies of the Small Business*, an annual service from Financial Research Associates, is based on contributions from more than 1,000 participating accounting firms; approximately 25,000 financial statements are used. The emphasis is on smaller companies. Data are tabulated for three asset sizes, plus all-company totals. Common-size Balance Sheets and Income Statements are given, together with 16 median and quartile

ratios. The service includes measures of operating costs, including expenses for labor, advertising, rent, insurance, and executive salaries. A total of 70 industry groups are analyzed, with an emphasis on retail and service firms.

The government produces several additional guides, including the Federal Deposit Insurance Corporation's annual *Statistics on Banking*, and the *Quarterly Financial Report for Mining, Manufacturing and Trade Corporations* published by the Bureau of the Census. Other ratio publications are compiled by trade associations or trade journals, most of which focus on very narrow industries. Some are widely used, such as Cornell University's *Operating Results of Mass Retail Stores* or the National Restaurant Association's *Restaurant Industry Operations Report*. Most are much more obscure, such as the National Paperbox and Packaging Association's *Key Ratio Survey of the Folding Carton and Rigid Box Industry*.

To identify the more specialized guides, two publications are particularly helpful. In addition to the bibliography in RMA's *Annual Statement Studies*, an excellent guide is the *Statistical Reference Index*, introduced in Chapter 4. Dozens of industries are represented, including convenience stores, business form manufacturers, and supermarkets. The complete text of most reports indexed in *SRI* can be purchased on microfiche from the Congressional Information Service at a reasonable price.

Which ratio publication to use? That depends upon the industry group being investigated and the type of ratio needed. Each publication has strengths and weaknesses. The products from Dun & Bradstreet and Schonfeld are expensive, while RMA and Troy are quite reasonable. Troy provides data not found in the other two, but is not a timely source. D&B offers the most detailed coverage of industry groups, but lacks breakdowns by asset size. The guide from Financial Research Associates is excellent for analyzing small businesses, but follows too few industries. The best overall product is probably *Annual Statement Studies*. In terms of number of industries covered, variety of ratios calculated, amount of detail, and price, the RMA publication is an excellent choice. RMA is also the only major source which presents ratios by sales category as well as asset size.

Company Rankings

A second way to compare company performance is to determine where a firm appears on a ranked list of competitors. Americans are fascinated by lists, rankings,

and superlatives, but rankings have numerous weaknesses. They may be based on educated guesses, they may obscure important information in their attempt to simplify, they may rank firms that should not be compared, or they may use meaningless standards of comparison. Whether a company appears first or second frequently results more from definitional hair-splitting than any meaningful evaluation. Despite such concerns, rankings can impart useful information for research purposes. They can indicate each firm's relative position, and present an overall picture of the market and its key players. Rankings can also indicate whether a firm is losing ground from one year to the next, and who its principal competitors are. Such interpretations should always be made with care, and should be based on more than a single variable.

The most famous ranking in American business is the annual "Fortune 500." *Fortune* magazine has compiled this directory every year since 1955. The issue appears in April or May and ranks the 500 largest publicly owned industrial firms by sales volume. The 500 companies are also ranked according to eight other measures. *Fortune* also produces a list of the 500 largest nonindustrial firms (actually six separate lists representing a total of 500 firms) which appears in June. The two lists can be purchased as a separate publication called the *Fortune Directory*.

The "Forbes 500 Annual Directory," compiled annually since 1917, also appears in an April or May issue. As with its competitor, companies are included based on sales, but only three additional categories—profits, assets, and market value—are ranked. Industrial and non-industrial firms are ranked in a single list. *Business Week's* "Top 1000: America's Most Valuable Companies" selects companies according to the current market value of their outstanding stock. The companies are listed in a single ranking, and in separate industry comparisons. An extensive array of additional variables is given for each company.

The three lists described above focus exclusively on publicly traded companies. One of the best rankings of closely held companies is *Forbes* annual list of the 400 largest private companies ranked by sales. It usually appears in a December issue of the journal. The "Inc. 500" is *Inc.* magazine's annual guide to the fastest growing privately held companies. (*Inc.* also produces a corresponding guide to the 100 fastest growing small public firms.) Local and regional business newspapers and magazines are also noted for their coverage of the largest private firms in their areas. Most rankings, however, include both public and private firms in a single list. They are now common annual features of many general business magazines and trade journals. Most rankings compare obvious virtues: the largest, the most profitable, the fastest growing. Others are based upon more subjective characteristics such as the best-run firms, the most admired executives, the best companies to work for, or the most socially responsible. Some journal articles are incredibly detailed in their comparisons. *Financial World*, for example, ranks stock brokerage firms by a variety of measures, from responsiveness to customers' needs to overall service.

Some periodical publishers produce separate guides to rankings, such as *American Banker's* annual book of *Top Numbers*. Ranked lists can also be found as supplements to standard business directories or statistical yearbooks, ranging from the *Thomson Bank Directory* to the *New York Stock Exchange Fact Book*. Even government agencies publish company rankings; the U.S. Department of Defense compiles an annual directory of the largest military contractors, for example. For researchers who want to generate their own rankings, a wide selection of online databases and CD-ROMs can assist in the process. Virtually any electronic database which enables the user to sort records by one or more numeric variables is ideal for generating customized lists.

Most published rankings focus on the top 100 or 500 companies in their fields, but a handful of sources are more inclusive. The two directories described below represent the most extensive printed guides to U.S. company rankings.

Dun's Business Rankings (Dun's Marketing Services, Inc.—Annual).

Dun's Business Rankings covers some 9,200 companies, of which 45% are privately held. Rankings are presented by state, by SIC number, by private companies only, by public companies only, and in a single, nationwide list. For each of these arrangements, rankings are arrayed by number of employees and by sales volume, making a total of ten ranked categories. With so many rankings to choose from, this publication is more versatile than most. Rather than simply churning out the 10,000 biggest companies, the compilers took an industry-by-industry approach. Because every type of business has its own peculiarities, D&B constructed unique size criteria for each SIC grouping, making the industry listings more meaningful. For example, food stores needed total sales of $500 million to be considered, while furniture stores only required sales of $25 million. A complete table of listing criteria is included in the preface.

Each listing contains the firm's address and phone number, its primary SIC code, the number of employees, sales volume, relevant rankings for the particular section, and, for publicly traded companies, the ticker symbol. The publication also includes a separate directory of key executives arranged by company and function, an index of divisional names used by the parent companies, and an alphabetical guide to the ranked firms, including their national rankings and the number of employees at the headquarters location.

Dun's Business Rankings does have several serious weaknesses. Few SIC numbers are broken down to four digits; most are presented at the three-digit level, and some groupings either combine several three-digit SIC categories, or broaden the category to the two-digit level. This forces comparisons which shouldn't be made. For example, Category 85 combines pens, costume jewelry, buttons, novelties, miscellaneous notions, and manufacturing industries not elsewhere classified. Because the four-digit SIC numbers are listed for each company, users can scan the list for appropriate comparisons, but the results may not be worth the effort. Of the 44 companies listed in Category 85, only four are pen manufacturers. The other 40 listings represent an unbelievable amalgamation of firms, including three casket companies. This is admittedly an extreme example (as any would be that included the infamous "not elsewhere classified" codes), but it is not atypical of the problems encountered using *Dun's Business Rankings*.

Other limitations of this source are less obvious, but potentially more serious. The most significant is that total company sales are used, which distorts the company comparisons. A company engaged in a single industry will be overshadowed by a larger, diversified company even if the smaller firm is the leader in that industry. Conversely, because only primary SIC numbers are considered, secondary SICs will not be reflected in their appropriate categories. Finally, because D&B does not provide sales data by division, many leading companies are automatically excluded from their business rankings. Papermate is a division of the Gillette Company, so it doesn't show among the leading pen companies.

Ward's Business Directory: Ranked by Sales within 4-Digit SIC (Gale Research, Inc.—Annual).

Ward's Business Directory was introduced in Chapter 6, but the fourth volume of the set is such a comprehensive guide to company rankings that it deserves its own description. For each SIC category, companies are ranked by sales. Listings are tabular and include such additional company information as the address and phone,

the number of employees, and the type of firm. For divisions and subsidiaries, the name of the parent company is given on the line below. To improve the readability of the tables, every third listing appears in bold print.

Because reporting firms tend to provide approximate sales figures, many companies within an industry will appear to have the same sales volume, a phenomenon that becomes more pronounced the further down one moves in the rankings. When viewing a list of dozens of companies with the same figures, one might question the value of a ranked list; on the other hand, it may be sufficient to learn that an industry is comprised of several tiers of companies, including large clusters of similarly sized firms. At least a company's relative position in the industry becomes known.

As discussed in Chapter 6, many of *Ward's* sales figures are simply crude estimates. Another problem is almost the opposite of one exhibited by *Dun's*. *Ward's does* include divisional breakdowns; in some cases the directory goes so far as to list major plant locations of a firm. Unfortunately, each one is ranked separately within the industry. The headquarters location may show up as the second largest in the industry, its largest plant as number 5, and its remaining factories as numbers 33 and 62. This distorts an already confusing array. For divisions and plant locations which fall within the same industry, the publisher needs to group them together. Indenting affiliate listings under the headquarters location would show the true order of the list and still identify component parts of a larger firm. *Ward's* fixed another problem in 1990 by grouping companies at the four-digit SIC level. The directory has also added coined SIC numbers for diversified financial companies and for general conglomerates.

Trinet U.S. Businesses, introduced in Chapter 6, employs a more sensible methodology for rankings. In its "Share of the Market" reports, industry sales data are obtained by summing revenues of all relevant locations owned by the company. Because modern corporations are so diversified, this is the only reasonable way to approximate sales by line of business. Unfortunately, it is virtually impossible to obtain sales data at the establishment level, making the use of estimates unavoidable. The resulting composites are no better than the estimates upon which they are built.

Does this mean that the major guides to company rankings are useless? No, only that they should be used with great caution. At worst, they can help identify those companies worthy of further research. By comparing the lists from several ranking sources, the user may be able to gain enough insight to make additional assumptions.

Whenever possible, it is well worth the effort to find more focused rankings compiled by trade associations or specialty journals. These too can be added to the total fund of knowledge. The more a researcher learns about an industry, the more confidently he or she can assess the accuracy of a ranked list.

STRATEGIES FOR RESEARCHING PRIVATE COMPANIES

There may be an abundance of information on any given private company, but ferreting it out can take time, effort, and skill. Instead of being conveniently arranged in comprehensive annual reports or well-written profiles, information on private firms is scattered across a myriad of published and unpublished sources. Even when information is unearthed, individual bits must be fitted together like pieces of a puzzle. Constructing a larger picture requires analytical skill, ingenuity, and even guesswork. It is almost always necessary to draw conclusions based in part on assumptions.

Because this type of research can be so complex, now is a good time to quickly review some of the strategies suggested in this, and previous chapters. One of the simplest ways to begin research on a closely held company is to obtain a Dun & Bradstreet credit report. Another is to search newspaper and journal indexes, especially those covering the company's home-town publications. Indexes to trade journals and industry newsletters can be equally helpful. In the past, searching through indexes was a daunting task due to the enormous number of printed products. The process was all the more frustrating because most indexes would produce little of value. And it seemed that many of the most promising publications weren't covered by any of the printed indexes. Much of this frustration has been swept away by the advent of online systems with global search capabilities, and by the appearance of numerous full-text databases. Another excellent source is wire services focusing on corporate press releases, such as *PR Newswire*. Even if little is found through an online search, at least the process is conducted with speed and confidence. When indexes and full-text databases fail, scanning unindexed periodicals can be an effective, though time-consuming technique. Even advertisements can provide meaningful clues to a company's plans and activities.

Information on private companies can be found in many other ways. The preceding discussion of public filings offers ample proof of that assertion. Chapter 7

illustrated the benefits of comparing data from different directories. Many directories are notable for their inclusion of other financial data beyond the traditional sales estimate. The *Macmillan Directory of Leading Private Companies* cites total assets, liabilities, and net worth as reported by the responding companies. Other directories offer mini-profiles of listed companies, and may include brief indicators of the firms' financial, operating, and market characteristics. Examples include *Progressive Grocer's Marketing Guidebook* (Progressive Grocer) and the *Securities Industry Yearbook* (Securities Industry Association). Both are annual directories.

The creative researcher can also turn to a variety of indirect publications and methods. Wall Street research reports, introduced in Chapter 12, may discuss private companies if they are major competitors to publicly held firms. Similarly, disclosure documents of publicly held firms sometimes mention private companies with which they do business. Electronic databases such as *Disclosure Online*, *PTS Annual Reports Abstracts*, *Standard & Poor's News*, and *Investext* are ideally suited for locating small facts buried in larger reports. One way to investigate subsidiaries is to go back to the time the company was acquired by its parent. When a publicly traded firm purchases another company (either public or private), a great deal of information is usually revealed. Even if the transaction occurred several years earlier, such detailed information can provide a useful base upon which to develop further leads. The same is true of formerly public companies which have "gone private" through a leveraged buyout.

Another indirect approach is to make assumptions about a private company's finances based on industry norms or the characteristics of similar companies. These methods can be extremely risky, but when combined with other intelligence can yield useful results. A more general approach is to derive information from studies of the entire industry. This is especially helpful when it becomes necessary to make educated assumptions about a company. Background on the structure, behavior, and trends of the industry or market of which the company is a part can contribute to this process enormously, as can industry-wide statistics from governments and trade associations. Researchers should also investigate unpublished sources such as consultants, government officials, editors of trade journals and newsletters, and other industry experts.

All of the above options require skill, time, or money to pursue. As with any information request, the researcher must weigh the need against the effort and expense required to obtain the desired results. It seldom

makes sense to pursue every research option, so the individual needs to determine which options sound reasonable for a given company or situation. Undertaking in-depth research on private companies often requires the instincts and patience of a private detective or investigative journalist, but the results definitely can be rewarding.

FOR FURTHER READING

This list begins with guides to financial statements. Most titles are intended for the nonaccountant. The next section identifies guides to researching private companies, though some cover both public and private firms. The third explores commercial credit reports and government filings as sources of private company data. The final section examines the importance of competitor intelligence and how to obtain it. Many of the techniques for acquiring competitive intelligence are especially relevant for researching private companies.

Financial Statements

Bernstein, Leopold A. *Analysis of Financial Statements*. 3rd ed. (Homewood, IL: Dow Jones-Irwin, 1990).
This is the classic textbook on statement analysis. Another excellent choice is George Foster's *Financial Statement Analysis*, 2nd ed. (Prentice Hall, 1986).

Haller, Leon. *Making Sense of Accounting Information: A Practical Guide for Understanding Financial Reports and Their Use* (New York: Van Nostrand Reinhold, 1985).
Truly a guide for the nonaccountant. Haller assumes no prior knowledge of financial information, and provides plenty of real world illustrations.

Tracy, John A. *How to Read a Financial Report: Wringing Cash Flow and Other Vital Signs Out of the Numbers*. 3rd ed. (New York: Wiley, 1989).
A short, readable guide to analyzing financial statements, written for nonaccountants. Each chapter distills important principles into a brief presentation, incorporating changes in federal income tax law and accounting standards.

Woelfel, Charles J. *Financial Statement Analysis* (Chicago: Probus, 1988).
This excellent guide presents a different slant. The first 70 pages introduce key accounting concepts. A discussion of statement analysis explains the differences among the types of analysis: horizontal, vertical, common size, and ratio. Another chapter deals with interim statements and segment analysis.

Researching Private Companies

DIALOG Information Services. *Field Guide to Company Intelligence* (Palo Alto, CA: DIALOG, 1988).
Search techniques for locating company information on both private and public firms using DIALOG databases. Includes online news reports, directory listings, biographical information, product announcements, and background on corporate structure and subsidiary relationships. Numerous search examples are given.

Karp, Nancy S. "Private Company Information in Selected CD-ROM Databases." *CD-ROM Professional* 13 (July 1990): 36-40.
Compares the search features, content, and performance of four popular CD-ROM products for retrieving information on large private companies: *ABI/INFORM*, *CIRR*, *General Periodicals Index*, and *CD/Private*.

Washington Researchers. *How to Find Information About Companies*. 8th ed. (Washington, DC: Washington Researchers, 1991).
Washington Researchers issues numerous guides to business research, but this title offers the best overview of information sources—state and federal governments, trade associations, libraries, publications and databases, and private information services. The work is primarily an annotated directory/bibliography, but tips are provided on how to approach government agencies, using the Freedom of Information Act, and beginning a research project.

Credit Reports and Public Filings

Kaufmann, David J. "The UFOC Crush: How to Read the UFOC Without Feeling Overwhelmed." *Entrepreneur* (January 1990): 75-82.
Explains the importance of the Uniform Franchise Offering Circular for researching companies that sell franchises.

Ojala, Marydee. "Business Credit Reports Online." *Online* 15 (July 1991): 83-86.
A thorough discussion of TRW and D&B reports, as available through the NewsNet gateways.

Pritchard, Teresa and Susan Hutchens. "Remote Access to Corporate Public Records: Scanning the Field." *Database* 14 (April 1991): 24-27.
A comparison of state public records available online through Information America, Prentice Hall, and Mead Data Central.

Roberts, Johnnie L. "Credibility Gap: Dun's Credit Reports, Vital Tool of Business, Can Be Off the Mark." *The Wall Street Journal* (October 5, 1989): A-1, A-10.
An eye-opening investigation of the Dun & Bradstreet practices which resulted in outdated or erroneous credit reports. This front-page story caused a great deal of negative publicity for an already beleaguered D&B. The firm has since moved to correct many of the weaknesses chronicled here.

Competitor Intelligence

Fuld, Leonard M. *Competitor Intelligence: How to Get It—How to Use It* (New York: Wiley, 1985).

Of the many books on competitor intelligence published within the past five years, Fuld's is the most practical. The discussion of business publications is weak, but the exploration of unpublished information sources is without equal. Numerous unusual and imaginative ways to investigate companies are described, stressing the importance of a systematic campaign to pursue all avenues of intelligence. Fuld also wrote a follow-up book called *Monitoring the Competition: Find Out What's Really Going On Out There* (Wiley, 1988). The second work focuses on how to set up a monitoring system within an organization.

McGonagle, John J., and Carolyn Vella. *Outsmarting the Competition: Practical Approaches to Finding and Using Competitive Information* (Napierville, IL: Sourcebooks, 1990).

Another good introduction to the concept of competitor intelligence, including discussions of research strategies, legal and ethical issues, and special research situations such as subsidiaries and privately held companies.

Porter, Michael E. *Competitive Strategy: Techniques for Analyzing Industries and Competitors* (New York: Free Press, 1980).

Porter, a leading expert in competitive strategy, has written the definitive book on the uses of competitor intelligence. While much of the book stresses market positioning, it is essentially a how-to manual for researchers interested in industry analysis.

Vella, Carolyn M., and John J. McGonagle. *Competitive Intelligence in the Computer Age* (New York: Quorum, 1987).

An earlier book by Vella and McGonagle that focuses on creative database searching for competitive intelligence. Unlike many books on competitive intelligence, considerable attention is devoted to disinformation—where it comes from and how to recognize it.

CHAPTER 9
Corporate Finances: Public Companies

TOPICS COVERED

1. Privacy and Public Disclosure
2. Disclosure Statements
   a. Annual Reports to Stockholders
   b. Form 10-K Reports
   c. Proxy Statements
3. Secondary Sources of Disclosure Data
   a. Summary Financial Services
   b. Full-Text Systems
   c. Other Sources of Company Profiles
4. Navigating the Publishing Maze
5. For Further Reading

MAJOR SOURCES DISCUSSED

- *Compact D/SEC*
- *Moody's Manuals*
- *Standard & Poor's Corporation Records*
- *PTS Annual Reports Abstracts*
- *Laser D/SEC*
- *SEC Online*
- *NAARS*
- *Worldscope Company Profiles*
- *Compustat PC Plus*

Many of the techniques introduced in the previous chapter are equally appropriate for investigating public firms: credit reports, public filings, company rankings, and industry ratios can all be used in researching any kind of company. Unlike private firms, however, detailed financial data on public companies are abundant and often found in convenient packages. In fact, so much information exists that the problem really is deciding what to look at first.

Anyone investigating public companies can utilize primary source documents provided by the companies themselves, or commercial publications which draw from original sources. They can delve into lengthy reports or skim brief summaries, focus on financial statements alone or turn to news items, commentary, and analysis. Statistical tables, rankings, and other specialized reports make company comparisons simple. Numeric data contained in electronic publications can be searched, sorted, and rearranged in any combination. Information is disseminated in every conceivable medium: newsletters, loose-leaf services, microfiche, CD-ROMs, online systems, and more.

This chapter will introduce examples of all these categories. Major topics include primary disclosure documents, commercially produced company profiles, full-text databases, and guides to comparative data. We'll begin with an introduction to basic disclosure concepts, then explore exactly what a public company is, and what kind of information it must divulge.

PRIVACY AND PUBLIC DISCLOSURE

Public companies constitute a tiny fraction of all firms in the United States, but they are responsible for most of the nation's business activity. But what does "public" really mean? All such corporations sell stock to the general public, but this is a fairly vague statement. To say that a public company must have more than a certain number of stockholders doesn't truly capture the principle behind public ownership either. A better way to think about public companies is to consider how people become shareholders. Anyone who wishes to acquire stock in a public company may do so by purchasing shares on the open market. In private firms, the stock-

holders are typically the principals in the company—the founders, members of their families, key employees, and perhaps others who have a direct relationship with it. If a stockholder in a private company wishes to reduce his or her investment in the firm, the stock could be sold or transferred to anyone the owner chooses, but normally it would be offered to the existing stockholders. There is no ready marketplace for buying and selling shares of private companies.

A gray area separates the publicly owned company and the truly private entity. The government has created many exceptions to the broad definition of "public," making the distinction between the two categories less than clear. For example, some firms may need to raise more capital than can be obtained from the immediate group of principals, yet don't wish to "go public." An alternative is to consult a business broker or investment banker who specializes in arranging company financing. Such a specialist may sell stock to a venture capital firm, a financial institution, or a small group of sophisticated investors. Depending on the details of the transaction, such deals are called either private placements or limited offerings. Another gray area is the so-called intrastate offering, where small local corporations sell stock only to investors within their own state. In these cases, outsiders own stock in the firm, but the firm falls outside federal disclosure laws.

We can better understand what financial disclosure entails by examining the purpose behind it. During the speculative frenzy of the late 1920s, unprecedented numbers of small investors were duped into buying stock of little or no value. The devastating stock market crash of 1929 was the catalyst behind two key pieces of legislation: the Securities Act of 1933 and the Securities & Exchange Act of 1934. Their provisions were based on the principle that the public has the right to know any and all "material information" about publicly traded companies. Material information was defined as any knowledge that would affect the financial decisions of a prudent investor. For example, it would be important to know about an impending lawsuit which could seriously decrease a company's profits, or even bankrupt the firm. A less dramatic example would be a company that sold some of its assets for $100 million, then reported the income together with its regular operating profits. Any onetime or unusual event (known to accountants as an extraordinary item) which distorts the true picture of a company's performance would thus be considered material.

But even public companies have a right to privacy. Disclosure laws do not give investigators access to all information about a firm. The type of information that must be disclosed is generally restricted to broad financial data and news of material events. The firm must report revenues, expenses, and profit, together with a summary of its assets and liabilities. Information on a company's marketing strategies, production costs, and other day-to-day operations is not subject to disclosure requirements. Stockholders have a right to know the salaries and fringe benefits received by key executives, but the hourly wages paid to rank-and-file employees is proprietary information. Trade secrets are also closely guarded by each firm.

Some companies do not issue stock at all, yet must report financial information to various governments under other laws. The patchwork of federal and state regulations makes it difficult to know just what types of information might be available on any given firm, or where to find it. However, except for those corporations traded in the public marketplace, information from disclosure documents is not widely published. Still, unpublished government filings can be an invaluable source of corporate information. A good example of non-SEC filings can be seen in the gray area of quasi-public companies mentioned earlier. Firms which utilize private placements, limited offerings, or intrastate offerings may be required to submit information to the federal government, or to state governments under other laws. As mentioned in Chapter 8, all states have enacted "Blue Sky" laws to protect consumers against disreputable companies and brokers who promise the sky when making investment offerings. Even corporations bound by federal securities laws must also submit information to state authorities. The North American Securities Administrator's Association, an organization of state financial regulators, has made great strides toward uniformity of Blue Sky laws. The Uniform Securities Act has been adopted by more than 40 states as of this writing. Another variation of company financing which can affect disclosure rules is the limited partnership. Although these entities are not corporations and do not issue stock per se, investor participation in such ventures can be widespread. Therefore, certain partnerships must meet stringent reporting requirements: "public limited partnerships" file special disclosure documents, and "master limited partnerships" file the same reports as public stock companies.

Subsidiaries of publicly held companies are not required to file separate disclosure documents; relevant information on affiliate organizations is attributed to the parent company. Financial reports are termed "consolidated statements" because they summarize the activities of the total company, including affiliates. The government requires some reporting by "business segment," which will be discussed later, but segment data are limited. The bigger the parent, the more difficult it is to research a single component of its operations. For this reason it is frequently as challenging to uncover information on a subsidiary or division as it is on a strictly private company.

DISCLOSURE STATEMENTS

For publicly held corporations, the best source of financial information is the company itself. Recurring reports generated through the disclosure process are an excellent starting point for financial research. Some reports are filed with the Securities and Exchange Commission, some with a stock exchange, and others are sent directly to stockholders. All three types are available to the general public at little or no cost. Public companies are required to file three major reports annually. The Annual Report to Stockholders (ARS) and the Proxy Statement are sent to the company's shareholders, and the 10-K Report is filed with the Securities and Exchange Commission. Additional reports are files under particular circumstances, such as the occurrence of unexpected material events or the issuance of new securities. These event-oriented filings will be discussed in Chapter 11.

Annual Reports to Stockholders

The best known disclosure document is probably the Annual Report to Stockholders (ARS), a glossy, upbeat brochure mailed each year to every stockholder of record. Annual Reports generally contain lots of photos, graphics, and considerable narrative in addition to the financial statements themselves. Many surveys have been conducted to evaluate the use of corporate reports by the public. Some indicate the ARS is the most heavily used source of information by general investors, while others say it lags far behind newspapers, published advisory services, and recommendations from stockbrokers. Whichever assessment is true, Annual Reports are distrusted by most people, and are seldom used to their fullest potential. Annual Reports are commonly viewed as little more than public relations pieces.

Certainly there is some truth in this belief. Annual Reports are, without question, designed to present the best possible picture of the company. However, the actual financial statements must be audited by an independent CPA, and the narrative information must be consistent with the financial facts. Bad news can certainly be played down, explained away, or minimized by euphemistic prose, but it cannot be ignored. What's more, both Generally Accepted Accounting Principles and SEC regulations dictate that certain categories of information *must* appear in an Annual Report.

When used properly, an Annual Report can be an excellent source of worthwhile information. The Annual Report tells what the company is doing, what it plans to do, how it is organized, and what foreign activities it is engaged in. It can shed light on management's philosophy as well as its justification for the company's behavior. The photographs can provide a vivid glimpse of products and properties of the firm. At the very least, the Annual Report suggests how the company views itself, and how it presents itself to the public.

Professional analysts approach an Annual Report from front to back, beginning with the numbers. While the financial statements are the heart of the report, the narrative sections are often extremely helpful. Every Annual Report contains the "Letter to Shareholders," (sometimes called the "President's Letter") in which the president or chairman of the board reviews the past year and presents the outlook for the coming year. This section reflects the personality of the chief executive, and varies in tone and content. Some are brief; others are remarkably lengthy. Some say little of merit; others are informative or even blunt. The President's Letter also imparts a sense of mood—whether the company is aggressive or defensive, proud or pessimistic, growing or retrenching. Much of the remaining narrative is simply a discussion of the past year's activities, and it varies considerably from one report to another. Most, however, organize the discussion according to the different operations within the company.

Two mandatory narrative sections appear in the financial portion of the Annual Report. The "Auditor's Report" is the signed statement of an independent CPA attesting that the financial contents meet Generally Accepted Accounting Principles. It affirms the auditor's opinion that the numbers represent the facts and are consistent with previous years' data. Most Annual Reports receive unqualified approval from the auditor, but readers should be alert to any auditor reservations or qualifying remarks. The "Management Discussion and

Analysis of the Results of Operations and Financial Condition" ("Management Discussion" for short) is one of the most important and informative sections of the report. Here the firm comments specifically on the data in the financial statements. This is not only a summary of the numbers, but an analysis of how the company's actions affected its performance and financial position, what the numbers mean, and how they were arrived at. The SEC requires the firm to discuss the past three years of company performance in this section.

The financial information in an Annual Report consists of the four financial statements described in Chapter 8. The Balance Sheet typically provides two years of data, while the Income Statement, Stockholders' Equity Statement, and Cash Flow Statement generally report three years of activity. A separate table summarizing key figures for additional years is also required; this table cites data from the previous five, ten, or eleven years. A final component of the tabular section presents financial data in ratio form. Financial data in the Annual Report are updated by a brief, unaudited "Interim Report" which is sent to stockholders quarterly.

The last part of the Annual Report's financial section contains the footnotes to each statement. These notes can be fairly lengthy, and the section may go on for several pages. The footnotes are frequently overlooked by unsophisticated readers, but they are among the most significant parts of the Annual Report. Together with the "Management Discussion," they clarify important facts not evident from the numbers. When GAAP allows the company a choice of accounting methods, as in the cases of inventory valuation or asset depreciation, footnotes describe the method used. Footnotes spell out contingent liabilities, such as pending law suits, which could have a detrimental effect on the company's profits. They also describe the characteristics of the firm's long-term debt, extraordinary income and expenses, and other matters not obvious from the financial statement alone. Finally, they point out any changes in accounting methods adopted during the period covered.

Annual Reports also contain supplementary financial data made mandatory in recent years. "Segment Data" specify key figures by line of business. For example, if a chemical firm engaged in three separate activities, segment data might show total sales for each line of business in the following manner:

Total Sales (In Millions of Dollars)

Year	Solvents	Adhesives	Plastics	Total
1990	$16.7	$15.8	$6.9	$39.4
1989	16.1	14.2	3.5	33.8
1988	15.8	13.4	0	29.3

Segments do not translate into breakdowns by subsidiary. The company in the example above might not have any subsidiaries; the three activities could be carried out at different plant locations or divisions. More likely, the segment data represent an amalgamation of parent and affiliate operations—the parent company might produce solvents and adhesives, Subsidiary A might produce adhesives and plastics, and Subsidiary B might produce plastics alone. Segment data reflect consolidated figures, but if the reader knew the company only had one subsidiary that dealt with plastics, and that unit was acquired in 1989, it could be inferred that the figures described the chemical subsidiary specifically. With small, well-defined companies, segment data can provide useful information about subsidiaries. For large companies, the line of business groupings tend to be too broad to offer such specific insights.

In order for segment data to appear in the ARS, each line of business must comprise 10% of total revenues, net income, or assets of the firm. However, companies have considerable latitude in how they define segments. A firm engaged in the manufacture of envelopes, business forms, and gummed labels could easily choose to present no segment data at all, claiming the firm was engaged in the single activity of producing business supplies. Of course, much of the narrative information in many reports can be considered coverage of business segments. Most large firms find it convenient to review the past year's accomplishments by product category. However, this type of discussion is not mandatory, as the segment statistics are. Other supplemental information seen in Annual Reports includes selected quarterly data for the previous year, financial highlights, and, occasionally, a discussion of the firm's efforts to be a good corporate citizen (called a social responsibility report).

The ARS is automatically sent to every owner of the firm's stock within 60 days of the end of its fiscal year (FY). Not all firms have fiscal years ending in December. Many companies are engaged in businesses which exhibit a definite seasonal pattern, and their FY mirrors this cycle. In addition to mailing reports to stockholders, the news media, and various "stakeholders" in the firm, most companies maintain mailing lists of others who wish to receive the document each year. Almost every moderately sized public and academic library maintains a file of Annual Reports for selected companies. Firms generally print enough copies of the report to ensure its availability to anyone who requests one.

Larger business libraries also subscribe to hundreds (or even thousands) of Annual Reports on microfiche. Several microform publishers provide package plans for

corporate reports. A private company called the Godfrey Memorial Library has been producing micrographic corporate reports since the early 1950s. Other microfiche publishers are Disclosure, Inc., the Q-Data Corporation, and Buckmaster Publishing. The latter publisher limits its coverage to the "Fortune 1000" companies. Bechtel Information Services, a fifth provider of fiche reports, was recently acquired by Disclosure, Inc.

Microfiche subscriptions are convenient, but they are less timely than printed reports, and the color graphics do not reproduce clearly. The electronic products introduced later in the chapter also have their weaknesses. To obtain current reports rapidly and in their complete form, there is still no substitute for the original document.

Form 10-K Reports

The principal document public companies must file with the SEC is the Form 10-K, also called the 10-K Report. The "form" is an itemized list of questions which must be addressed, but the resulting document is a detailed and lengthy financial publication. The 10-K Report is unadorned, with no artistic photos, striking graphs, or flowery narrative, but it is an essential document for serious corporate research.

The 10-K avoids most of the company hype which readers of the Annual Report find suspect. It also follows a standard format mandated by the SEC, which makes finding information somewhat simpler. For example, Item 1 always describes the activities of the business, and Item 8 always presents the financial statements. Most important, the 10-K Report has much more specific information about the company than will be found in its glossier counterpart. Of course, the Annual Report also contains information not found in the 10-K, so the two documents should be used together. In 1980 the government issued sweeping new regulations resulting in the "Integrated Disclosure System." An important change was the increased comparability of financial data appearing in the two reports. Another change was a substantial increase in the amount of information that must be disclosed in the reports. To offset this burden, companies are now permitted to reprint entire sections of one report in the other, instead of listing the same information twice. In fact, one report may simply refer to a section of another published document when meeting the new disclosure requirements. This freedom presents problems to the user—what is found in the 10-K for one firm may be incorporated in the ARS for another, and vice versa.

Some companies combine the two under one cover to save money, but most firms continue to release separate reports.

What, then, does the 10-K contain that the Annual Report does not? When reporting to the SEC, the corporation must describe how the firm does business, albeit in broad terms. This includes brief sections on its products, markets, and distribution channels. Many reports provide estimates of market share and the degree of competition in the industry, if such factors are significant. A discussion of the company's research and development activities and patent ownership can usually be found here. Next, the 10-K lists all subsidiaries of the company and the major properties it owns. The firm must also discuss the extent of foreign operations, what raw materials it uses and where they come from, seasonal variations in sales, and other matters affecting the company's operations. It must divulge environmental safety problems, legal proceedings, its dependence on a few large customers, and other areas of vulnerability.

The 10-K must also present information on the ownership and management of the company, but it may do this by referring to other disclosure documents. Some firms present this information directly in the 10-K, but most refer to data appearing in the Proxy Statement. Finally, the 10-K may contain a large section of exhibits pertinent to the company. Such exhibits might include the text of a new bond indenture, a major government contract, the details of a joint venture with another firm, or amendments to corporate bylaws. The 10-K is updated by a quarterly 10-Q Report.

The 10-K Report is not as readily available as the ARS. In most cases, it is not sent to stockholders unless they ask for it; however, the inside cover of the Annual Report gives instructions for ordering one. Libraries do not collect paper copies of 10-K Reports to the extent that they acquire Annual Reports, though many of the largest business libraries have 10-K collections. The SEC itself operates Public Reference Rooms in its regional offices, and disclosure documents may be examined there. Many commercial document retrieval services provide rapid delivery of SEC filings for a fee. Among the best known are Disclosure, Inc., the Washington Service Bureau, Inc., and Research Information Services, Inc.

Data from SEC filings are accessible electronically through a diversity of CD-ROM and online products. A number of these will be described later in the chapter. A more frequently encountered medium for 10-K Reports is microfiche. The Securities and Exchange Commission has long recognized the importance of disseminating these documents as efficiently as possible; at the same

time, the agency has faced the problem of storing such a massive accumulation of files. For these reasons, the SEC has contracted with private publishers to reproduce disclosure documents on microfilm. Beginning in the early 1970s, Disclosure, Inc. obtained an exclusive contract to provide this service. In 1985, Bechtel won the contract, but Disclosure regained it in early 1991 by acquiring the Bechtel company from its parent. Disclosure (via the Bechtel contract) automatically receives all SEC documents to be filmed, including Annual Reports and Proxies. But because SEC filings are public documents, and anyone has the right to reproduce them, the Q-Data Corporation also provides micrographic services.

Both companies offer customers a variety of subscription plans, but building a comprehensive collection is expensive. Because Disclosure is the SEC's exclusive distribution agent, it provides fiche copies more quickly than its competitor. And because the publisher receives original copies of the documents it films, the fiche are often more legible. Both companies also obtain financial reports from other regulatory agencies. Disclosure is noted for its documents relating to publicly traded banks and savings & loan companies. Q-Data obtains reports from state regulatory agencies and other sources of disclosure documents for smaller public companies. Also, Q-Data's production methods allow it to provide microfiche at a much lower cost. First, Q-Data reproduces only the most significant exhibits to each document, which reduces the total size of the collection. (The basic report is reproduced in full, however.) Second, Disclosure films each document on one sheet (or packet) of fiche, while Q-Data includes several documents on a single sheet. This enables libraries which cannot afford the more expensive service to maintain a 10-K collection, though it is arranged in a less convenient manner. Q-Data subscribers must consult the publisher's company-name index in order to locate a specific report in the collection.

Beginning sometime in 1992, researchers will have virtually instantaneous online access to all SEC filings as they are released. The system, known as Electronic Data Gathering, Analysis and Retrieval (EDGAR), will completely automate the disclosure filing process. A contract to implement the system was awarded to the BDM Corp. in January 1989. EDGAR will generate more than 14 million pages of documents annually, and subscribers can receive updated computer tapes daily. The SEC's Public Reference Rooms will have dedicated EDGAR terminals to provide online access to documents, but commercial vendors will be free to mount the tapes on their own systems. Mead Data Central, an EDGAR subcontractor, will provide full-text online access through its LEXIS/NEXIS service, complete with full Boolean capabilities. Disclosure, Inc., another EDGAR subcontractor, will continue to be the official disseminator of microfiche and paper copies of SEC documents for the eight-year life of the current contract. Although EDGAR will not abolish printed disclosure documents, it will enable users to retrieve information more quickly than ever before.

Proxy Statements

The Proxy Statement is the official notice sent to all stockholders before the firm's annual meeting. By law, all shareholders must receive the report before management may solicit proxy votes. The Proxy Statement contains background material on all matters to be voted on at the meeting. If, for example, a vote is to be taken on changing the employee stock option plan, the Proxy will cover the details of the proposal, including the text of the existing plan. Information is prepared by the company, and thus represents management's views on each topic. Shareholders' proposals must also be included in the report. This phenomenon has become increasingly important in recent years, especially concerning matters of executive compensation, voting rights, financial policies directly affecting shareholder wealth, and social issues like animal testing and environmental protection. Since management generally opposes outside proposals, the Proxy provides a brief "supporting statement" from the proposal's sponsor, followed by the "company response" and management's recommendation.

The Proxy Statement is usually the official information source on ownership and management of the company. Biographical information for all directors is provided, together with their photos and data on their ages, salaries, benefits, and stock ownership. Briefer data are given for key executives, including salaries and stock holdings. A total figure for salaries paid to all executives, and a summary of the stock ownership of major stockholders can also be found. Proxy Statements are also primary documents for background on proposed mergers. Such reports are extremely detailed, covering background on the transaction, management's justification for it, a profile of the merger partner or acquisition target, details on how the deal will be financed, and the company's post-merger plans. Such reports usually include the complete text of the merger agreement as an appendix.

SECONDARY SOURCES OF DISCLOSURE DATA

Commercial publishers have been providing summarized financial data on public companies since the late nineteenth century. Two firms, Moody's Investors Service and Standard & Poor's Corporation, dominated the market for many decades, but now face stiff competition from an array of newcomers. Electronic publishing has completely revolutionized the availability of financial information.

Secondary sources offer many advantages over the original documents. The single most important benefit is convenience; secondary sources bring together information on thousands of companies in a single resource and organize it in an easy-to-use fashion. They will often cull the most pertinent data from mounds of original material, enabling users to locate important facts much more quickly. The approaches taken by financial publishers are varied; some present bare-bones snapshots, some provide fairly comprehensive company profiles, and others reproduce primary documents in their entirety.

Summary Financial Services

Business researchers can choose from a mind-boggling assortment of commercially produced financial resources. Some publications quote from source documents verbatim, while others summarize data and present the results in well-indexed, standardized formats. Certain summary services restrict coverage to Annual Reports or 10-Ks, while others rely on a diversity of disclosure documents. Many services combine summaries of SEC filings with information from corporate press releases or secondary news sources. A noteworthy trend in electronic publishing is the combination of disclosure data with information from other financial databases. *Compact D/SEC* includes figures from the *Spectrum Ownership* and *Zacks* databases. *CD/Corporate* combines financial statements with a diversity of related data contributed by a half-dozen commercial publishers, including abstracts of journal articles, full-text analysts' reports, and market performance measures.

The publications below are noted for their extensive reporting of corporate financial statements.

Compact D/SEC (Disclosure, Incorporated—Monthly).

Compact D/SEC, better known by its former name (*Compact Disclosure*), contains lengthy extracts from major SEC documents for over 12,000 corporations. Its powerful capabilities and user-friendly approach have made it one of the best-selling CD-ROMs for business libraries. Like other CDs using DIALOG software, *Compact D/SEC* allows the user to search via an "Easy Menu Mode" or a more sophisticated "DIALOG Emulation Mode." The latter does almost everything that can be done on DIALOG's online system, and the menu version is itself surprisingly powerful. Subscribers can receive disks monthly, quarterly, or annually, depending on their needs and budgets.

Every record contains summary information from the 10-K Report, Proxy, 8-Ks, the most recent 10-Qs, and, for newly public companies, the Registration Statement. For many companies, the Management Discussion and President's Letter are reproduced in full from the Annual Report to Stockholders. Although exhibits are not reproduced, a complete list of them is given for every company. Supplemental information is provided from two outside databases, *Zacks Earnings Estimates* and *Spectrum Ownership*. (*Spectrum* is described in Chapter 11, and *Zacks* in Chapter 12.) However, complete data from *Spectrum* is only available on *Compact D/SEC* for an additional fee; basic subscribers receive summary data only.

Although it doesn't contain the full text of any disclosure documents, *Compact D/SEC* provides extensive reports—a typical record is about 12 pages. Each begins with a company profile, including a narrative description of the firm, its address, state of incorporation, stock exchange and ticker symbol, primary and secondary SIC codes, DUNS number, and, where relevant, the company's most recent ranking on the Forbes and Fortune 500s. *Compact D/SEC* is also a convenient source for determining a company's CUSIP number, a frequently encountered identification number assigned to companies and their securities. (CUSIP stands for the American Bankers Association Committee on Uniform Securities Identification Procedures.) The profile section cites the number of shareholders, number of shares outstanding, number of employees, the auditor, legal counsel, and stock transfer agent. This section concludes with a five-year summary of sales, net income, Earnings Per Share, and a business segment report.

The bulk of each company report is comprised of the quarterly and annual financial statements. Data are reasonably comprehensive, listing most major lines from the Balance Sheet, Income Statement, and Cash Flow statement. Additional tabular information includes the most recent quarterly financials, key ratios, and summary stock price, ownership, and dividend figures. For annual data, users can choose between a three-year or a five-year comparative display. The complete text of footnotes to

the financial statements is fully searchable, creating an invaluable resource for accountants and financial analysts. Nonfinancial information is also fairly extensive. For every company, a complete list of all documents filed with the SEC in the previous 12 months is given, together with the date of each filing. A list of subsidiaries can be found, as can lists of directors and officers, their ages, and salaries.

Compact D/SEC offers phenomenal retrieval capabilities. Over 200 variables can be searched, as well as words and phrases in the text portions of the record. Literally every line of every financial statement is indexed and fully searchable. For any numeric field, the user can specify a range of values to search. The searcher can also distinguish between annual and quarterly data when constructing a query. Results can be limited by stock exchange, fiscal year, type of filing, or numerous other options. The ability to perform company screening is extraordinary; companies with virtually any combination of financial characteristics can be identified and ranked in numerous ways. The portion of the record providing financial ratios is especially useful for this type of activity.

Not all of these capabilities are available in the Easy Menu Mode, but dozens of the most significant measures can be searched in this scaled-down version. The menu system allows the user to call up a succession of windows to identify the required variables and combine them with other characteristics. Sixteen basic menus are further divided by sub-menus. For example, the geographic menu allows the user to search by state of residence, state of incorporation, city, zip code, or telephone area code. The financial menu provides search options for 76 variables, approximately half the number searchable on the full "DIALOG Emulation Mode." Fairly sophisticated text searching is also available on the menu version. In both modes, users can sort search results and display or print them in a variety of formats. Both modes allow users to select from standard formats or to define their own formats by designating the portions of the record they wish to print. Users can also create customized tables which compare key variables for all companies retrieved in the search. Finally, search results can be downloaded in several formats for further manipulation by word processing, spreadsheet, or database management software.

Other CD-ROMs available from Disclosure are *Compact D/Canada, Compact D/Worldscope,* and *Compact D/'33.* The latter service covers Registration Statements and Prospectuses.

The *Disclosure* database is also available online from at least eight major vendors. The most powerful version is found on DIALOG (as *Disclosure Online*), and conforms almost completely to the expert version of *Compact D/SEC.* Other command-driven systems offering *Disclosure Online* include BRS, Data-Star, and NEXIS/LEXIS. More limited, menu-driven versions can be found on Dow Jones News/Retrieval and CompuServe. On most systems, *Disclosure Online* is updated weekly, but only the most recent year of reports is provided. Individuals needing to conduct historical research will need to consult older editions of the compact disk, which date back to 1986.

Moody's Manuals (Moody's Investors Service—Annual, with Updates).

Moody's, a subsidiary of Dun & Bradstreet, has published the famous *Moody's Manuals* since 1909. The title actually represents a set of books with information grouped together by type of company. The set currently consists of the following eight parts:

Bank & Finance Manual (4 vols. plus updates)
Covers banks, insurance companies, real estate investment trusts, and other financial firms.

Industrial Manual (2 vols. plus updates)
Covers industrial firms listed on stock exchanges.

International Manual (2 vols. plus updates).
Covers major publicly traded foreign companies.

Municipal & Government Manual (2 vols. plus updates)
Covers federal, state, and local governments, and government agencies which issue bonds.

OTC Industrial Manual (1 vol. plus updates)
Covers industrial firms which trade Over-the-Counter.

OTC Unlisted Manual (1 vol. plus updates)
Covers smaller, less active OTC firms which are not part of the NASDAQ system.

Public Utility Manual (2 vols. plus updates)
Covers gas, electric, and telephone utilities.

Transportation Manual (1 vol. plus updates)
Covers railroads, airlines, trucking, and shipping companies.

Each annual book is accompanied by a loose-leaf volume with weekly or semiweekly *News Reports.* To alleviate the potential confusion seven separate titles could cause, three times each year Moody's also produces a *Complete Corporate Index* to the set.

Moody's Manuals provide detailed profiles of more than 15,000 companies and thousands of municipalities. The data are gathered from 10-K Reports, Annual Reports to Stockholders, and other disclosure documents, as well as news sources. The manuals offer four different levels of coverage, ranging from less than a single page to 12 pages of closely printed material. Companies must pay a fee to Moody's in order to receive the three detailed levels of coverage, but any firm can receive minimal coverage at no cost. The most complete level provides seven years of comparable financial data, financial ratios, and extensive narrative, including the full text of the President's Letter to Shareholders. The other levels of coverage give successively fewer years of data, and less narrative.

The company descriptions in each volume are not arranged alphabetically, but by level of coverage, and in some cases also by type of company or geographic location. For this reason, users must employ the alphabetical index that appears in the blue-paged section at the front of each volume. This section also contains a list of company names no longer covered by Moody's due to mergers, bankruptcies, name changes, or other reasons. Each title in the set has a "Special Features" section on blue pages in the middle of the volume. The contents of the special features vary according to the subject of the manual, but they are mainly statistical tables or special lists. For example, the *Transportation Manual* cites statistics on rail and air traffic. The "Special Features" sections in several volumes also contain geographic and SIC indexes to company listings.

The amount of information is impressive, especially for the more detailed levels of coverage. Every report begins with a summary of the capital structure of the company (the outstanding shares of stock, total value of long-term debt, etc.), its founding date, a history of mergers and name changes, and a list of subsidiaries. A summary of the business, a list of major properties, and a directory of officers and executives rounds out the first part of the report. Exhibit 9-1 shows the beginning of a medium-length Moody's report—the first page of a three-page summary of the Loctite Corporation. Most information is taken from the company's 10-K Report. The description of products is quite detailed, though the Annual Report to Shareholders undoubtedly presents the same information in a more colorful and interesting manner. When available, Moody's also cites sales by business segment. In this case, Loctite reports by geographic segment rather than line of business.

The next section is comprised of summary financial statements, with comparable data from previous years. The more detailed reports also provide key financial and operating ratios for the company. Due to lack of space, only the most important figures from the financial statements are given, as determined by Moody's editorial policy. Also, footnotes to statements are given in the briefest manner. These factors make it worthwhile for the researcher to consult the actual source documents to obtain a more complete financial picture.

The final section of each report is a summary of the firm's securities. Each outstanding class of stock and bond issued by the company is described in reasonable detail. For stocks, the number of shares authorized and outstanding, the par value (if any), the voting rights, and dividend history are outlined. Also indicated are the names of the transfer agents, the registrar, and the stock exchange where the security is traded. For bonds, the date of issue and date of maturity, the dollar denomination and number of bonds issued, and the contractual characteristics of the bond are spelled out. The Moody's bond rating is also given for each bond. (The meaning of all this will become clearer after reading Chapter 10.)

Other information in Moody's depends upon the type of company being described. The *Public Utility Manual*, for example, includes maps that identify the geographic area the utility services and its principal transmission lines or gas pipelines, as well as detailed data on its rate structure.

For researchers without access to primary documents, or who wish to compare many companies quickly, Moody's is an excellent source of reliable information. Although many companies pay a fee for added coverage, accuracy does not suffer; Moody's has a great stake in maintaining its reputation. *Moody's Manuals* also provide convenient ready-reference information. They can be used to find a company's state of incorporation, its founding date, its stock transfer agent, the number of shareholders, and many other quick facts. The *Manuals* enjoy enormous popularity in the business community and are likely to be found in any library with even a modest business collection.

Much of the data from the *Moody's Manuals* is also accessible in electronic form. Information can be retrieved online via a set of databases offered exclusively through DIALOG. The records are divided into three separate databases: *Moody's Corporate Profiles* contains information seen in the annual *Moody's Manuals*; *Moody's Corporate News—U.S.* reproduces the stories found in the *News Reports*; and *Moody's Corporate News—International* offers news reports from *Moody's*

EXHIBIT 9-1. *Moody's Industrial Manual*

LOCTITE CORPORATION

CAPITAL STRUCTURE

LONG TERM DEBT Issue	Rating	Amount Outstanding
1. Notes payable	. . . . . .	$39,330,000

CAPITAL STOCK Issue	Par Value	Shares Outstanding
1. Common	$0.01	17,988,104

HISTORY

Incorporated in Delaware on May 13, 1988 to succeed a company of the same name originally incorporated in Connecticut in 1953.

In 1970 acquired International Sealants, S.A., Corp., and its' subsidiaries for 850,000 com. shs. and cash.

On Oct. 2, 1972, acquired through merger Permatex Co., Inc. in exchange for 324,000 com. shs. Also in 1972 acquired remaining 62.5% of common stock of Permatex Co.'s affiliate in Mexico.

In 1973, Co. acquired, Douglas Kane Group Ltd., Welwyn Garden City, Hertfordshire, England, for about 126,000 Co. com. shs.

On June 28, 1974, acquired Woodhill Chemical Co., and Woodhill Chemical Sales Corp. for $8,500,000 cash and notes.

In 1985, Co. formed Loctite El Systems Inc. in Rocky Hill Connecticut.

In Nov. 1986, acquired remaining interest in Luminescent Systems, Inc.

In Oct. 1986, acquired 51% interest in Societe Francaise d'Assembage Mecanique et d'Etancheite for $15,500,000 in cash.

In July 1987, acquired Repco-Loctite Pty. Ltd, an Australian joint venture company.

In Jan. 1988, Co. acquired total ownership of Krelinger-Loctite N.V., its joint venture company in Belgium.

In July 1989, Co. acquired Fabbrica Adesivi Sigillanti Italiana S.p.A. of Cerano, Italy.

In 1990, Co. acquired Banite Inc., of Buffalo, N.Y.

BUSINESS & PRODUCTS

Company has as its principal line of business the manufacture and sale of adhesives, sealants and related specialty chemical products.

Company manufactures and sells a broad range of chemical sealants and adhesives having different chemical properties designed to suit a wide variety of applications. Special and standard equipment for the application of adhesives and sealants is also marketed by the Company, along with a variety of specialty chemical items which are ancillary to the sealants and adhesives line. The principal products are anaerobic sealants and adhesives and cyanoacrylate adhesives.

Anaerobics: Anaerobic sealants and adhesives remain liquid in the presence of air but cure in the absence of air. These liquids are used to replace or augment mechanical means for locking, sealing, retaining and structurally bonding machine elements, providing extra strength and reliability to these assemblies, and increasing resistance to loosening or damage caused by shock or vibration. Anaerobic sealants and adhesives can be used without solvent removal processes, and in many cases permit the relaxation of machining tolerances. The net result is less complexity in manufacture and assembly operations for the user, frequently providing substantial overall cost savings.

Anaerobic sealants and adhesives have an indefinite shelf life and are produced with a wide variety of chemical and physical properties to meet the demands of their numerous industrial applications. They are used primarily on metal surfaces in equipment such as vehicles, household appliances, electronic equipment, and numerous other mechanical subassemblies.

Cyanoacrylates: Cyanoacrylate adhesives differ from anaerobic sealants and adhesives in that they cure upon exposure to moisture, which is present in trace amounts on the surfaces to be bonded. They cure in times ranging from a few seconds to several minutes to form thin, transparent bonds. Because of the speed and strength of cyanoacrylate bonds, these materials require care in handling and use.

In general, cyanoacrylates have a shelf life in excess of one year and do not require extensive surface preparation prior to use. Cyanoacrylate adhesives may be used to bond metal, plastics, rubber, glass, ceramic, or wood, either together or in combination. Typical uses include the assembly of certain rubber and vinyl products, glass containers, auto accessories, electronic components, and office equipment, especially where speed of cure is an important consideration.

Other Sealants, Adhesives and Related Products: The Company manufactures and sells other engineering adhesives, principally silicone adhesives and sealants, as well as epoxies and modified acrylic adhesives; ultraviolet light and primer cured sealants and coatings used in a wide variety of industrial applications; a line of home and auto-care products for consumer use, including high viscosity, noncuring sealants which are used principally to coat conventional gaskets, and rust converters; and other related specialty chemicals, principally lubricating, and cleaning compounds.

Other Products: The Company manufactures and sells a small amount of other products, primarily for household use, including metal-care products and cleaners for tile, porcelain, wood, metal, and fiberglass surfaces.

Company began, in 1986, to manufacture and sell electroluminescent lamps, a new and versatile type of lighting device.

Sales By Geographic Area, years ended June 30:

(in millions)	1989	1988	1987
United States	$211.0	$191.7	$165.6
Europe	180.5	171.4	126.7
Other foreign	83.9	72.1	56.7
Eliminations	(18.8)	(18.3)	(11.2)
Total	$456.5	$416.9	$337.8

PRINCIPAL PLANT & PROPERTIES

Listed below are principal plants and physical properties of Co. and its subsidiaries.

Domestic & Foreign

Costa Rica	Brazil
Connecticut (5)	United Kingdom (3)
Illinois	Ireland (2)
New Hampshire (3)	West Germany (2)
Kansas	Italy (2)
Ohio (2)	Spain
Puerto Rico	Austria
Canada	South Africa
Mexico (4)	Japan
Hong Kong	Australia (2)

Chile (2)	Colombia
France (2)	Korea
Belgium (2)	

SUBSIDIARIES

Owns entire capital stock of following companies:
Loctite Argentina S.A.
Loctite Automotive & Consumer Products Pty. Ltd. (Australia)
Loctite Puerto Rico, Inc.
Loctite Canada, Inc.
Loctite Brasil, Ltda.
Loctite Belgium S.A.
Loctite Quimica. Chile, Ltda.
Loctite de Colombia, S.A.
Societe Francaise d'Assemblage Mecanique et d'Etancheite (France)
Loctite (U.K.) Limited
Loctite (Ireland) Limited
Loctite Deutschland G.m.b.H.
Loctite (Italia) S.p.A.
Loctite Europa Ges.m.b.H. (Austria)
Loctite (Japan) Corp.
Loctite Australia Pty. Limited
Loctite Co. de Mexico, S.A. de C.V.
Compania Loctite de Centro America, S.A. (Costa Rica)
Loctite (South Africa) Pty. Ltd.
Loctite Espana, S.A.
Permatex Industiral Corp.
Loctite Luminescent Systems Inc.
Loctite (Services) Ltd. (Korea)
Loctite Switzerland A.G.
Loctite (Asia) Ltd. (Hong Kong)
  Joint Ventures:
K.F. Teknikk A/S (Norway)
Permatex de Venezuela, C.A.
Loctite (China) Co. Ltd.
La Compagnie de Materiel et d'Equipments Techniques (France)

MANAGEMENT

Officers
K.W. Butterworth, Chmn. & Chief Exec. Off.
T.F. Patlovich, Vice-Chmn.
David Freeman, Exec. Vice-Pres. & Chief Oper. Off.
R.L. Aller, Vice-Pres., Chief Fin. Off. & Treas.
E.F. Miller, Vice-Pres. & Sec.
J.R. Reck, Vice-Pres.
G.B.E.M. Briels, Vice-Pres.
Dante Pippolo, Vice-Pres.
E.L. Daisey, Vice-Pres.
R. Parker, Vice-Pres. & Contr.

Directors
Jurgen Manchot
Jack H. Schofield
Robert E. Ix
Frederick B. Krieble
K.W. Butterworth
Roman Dohr
John K. Armstrong
Stephen T. Trachtenberg
Robert H. Krieble
David Freeman
Theodore Patlovich
Wallace Barnes

Auditors: Price Waterhouse.

Annual Meeting: In Nov.

General Counsel: Day, Berry & Howard.

No. of Stockholders: Sept. 8, 1989, 2,299.

No. of Employees: June 30, 1989, 3,512.

Executive Office: 10 Columbus Blvd., Hartford, CT 06106. **Tel.:** (203) 520-5000.

General Office: 705 N. Mountain Rd., Newington, CT 06111. **Tel.:** (203) 278-1280.

INCOME ACCOUNTS

COMPARATIVE CONSOLIDATED INCOME ACCOUNT

YEARS ENDED JUNE 30

(in thousands of dollars)

	1989	1988	1987	1986	1985
Net sales	456,498	416,880	337,802	266,788	231,479
[1]Cost of sales	174,220	162,441	138,787	111,163	91,868
Research & devel. exps.	17,258	14,576	11,995	10,051	8,761
[1]Selling, gen. & admin. exps. . . .	185,356	174,047	139,835	108,747	95,980
Operating income	79,664	65,816	47,185	36,827	34,870
Investment income	10,150	6,549	5,344	5,742	6,429
Interest expense	5,812	11,014	7,732	7,738	10,082
Other income	dr2,060	dr438	84	294	dr20
Foreign exchange gain	dr4,120	409	482	dr1,090	288
Earnings bef. inc. taxes	77,822	61,322	45,363	34,035	31,485
Income taxes	23,346	19,472	14,698	10,862	11,042
Net earnings	54,476	41,850	30,665	23,173	20,443
Retained earnings beg. of year . .	189,738	167,748	147,610	131,854	137,319
Cash dividends	16,193	10,890	8,540	7,417	7,297
Stock repurchase	5,648	8,970	1,987	. . . . . .	18,611
Retained earn. end of year	222,373	189,738	167,748	147,610	131,854
SUPPLEMENTARY P. & L. DATA					
Maint. & repairs	5,548	4,801	4,147	3,267	2,674
Depreciation	9,373	9,263	8,317	6,979	6,012
Taxes other than income	. . . .	. . . .	. . . .	. . . .	6,082
Rents	8,328	7,572	6,268	4,644	3,781
Advertising	25,292	26,274	18,876	16,047	14,979

[1]Includes related portions of items shown under "Supplementary P. & L. Data" below statement.

International Manual. Each database is updated weekly. The differences in content between the printed and online publications are considerable. First, *Corporate Profiles* covers only those firms which are listed on the New York or American Stock Exchanges or the National Market System—approximately 5,000 companies. Excluded are smaller over-the-counter companies, government entities, and those banks, utilities, and transportation firms which are not publicly traded. On the other hand, *Corporate News—U.S.* provides updates on all domestic companies covered by the *Manuals*, not just the 5,000 or so found in *Corporate Profiles*. Another difference is the supplemental information available for selected companies. The database contains additional financial analysis and outlook for about 900 companies with high investor interest; this corresponds to the information presented in a publication called *Moody's Handbook of Common Stocks*. Finally, the full report from the *Moody's Manuals* is not reproduced online. Missing are such sections as the stock and bond profiles, the corporate history, and the list of officers and directors.

Moody's Corporate Profiles provide extensive financial data, including five years of numbers from Income Statements and Balance Sheets, capitalization summaries, ten key ratios, quarterly dividend and earnings figures, and five years of annual stock price summaries. Though the file is not as detailed or powerful as *Disclosure Online*, more than 40 financial variables can be searched, and most can also be sorted. Additional ready-reference data include the company's address, ticker symbol, stock exchange, DUNS number, primary and secondary SIC codes, and business description.

The *Corporate News* file employs an extensive list of standard event codes, which makes searching for specific types of news quite simple. Over 100 codes are used, ranging from EC=373 (joint ventures) to EC=260 (new plants or plant expansions). The file is especially useful for identifying stories on new stock and bond issues, changes in bond ratings, and similar financial events. A second advantage is the ability to quickly retrieve quarterly earnings and dividend announcements. It also contains stories dating back to January 1983, which is important because few libraries keep superseded volumes of the printed news reports, and because the *Corporate Profiles* database contains only the current year's report for each company. A related benefit is that the news file retains summary information from previous annual reports. Finally, the narrative is quite concise, typically ranging from a single sentence to several paragraphs. However, some information from the annual reports, including tabular data and the President's Letter,

may go on for several pages. The major weakness of the *Corporate News* files is that financial data cannot be searched numerically.

A recently improved CD-ROM disk, *Moody's Company Data*, actually contains more information than is found online. Financial data are given for approximately 10,000 firms (all publicly traded companies in the printed *Manuals*), plus year-to-date information from the loose-leaf *News Reports*. Summary information from *Moody's Handbook* is provided as an added feature. The disk does not utilize DIALOG software, but the system is menu-driven and on-screen directions are fairly clear. Experienced users can by-pass menus by using various key combinations. Some 140 financial variables are fully searchable, as are nearly 30 text variables. Results can be sorted, and customized comparative reports can be built. Keyword searching is supported, including Boolean capability. The disk is updated monthly, but quarterly subscriptions are available. A second disk containing data and news on foreign companies, called *Moody's International Plus*, is offered separately.

Standard & Poor's Corporation Records (Standard & Poor's Corporation—Annual, with Updates).

This publication from S&P is similar to the *Moody's Manuals* in most important respects, but there are noteworthy differences. The most obvious are size and format. The *Corporation Records* are published entirely in loose-leaf format and arranged alphabetically. Moody's is also more comprehensive than its competitor, both in the number of companies and the amount of information. What Moody's takes 20 volumes to cover, Standard & Poor's does in 7. The *Corporation Records* contain detailed reports on 9,000 companies plus news reports on these and 4,000 additional firms. The difference in size is largely due to minimal coverage of banks and financial companies, and no coverage of municipalities.

An advantage of the Standard & Poor's service is its faster updating. The main volumes of the *Corporation Records* are revised quarterly instead of annually, and the corresponding news service provides subscribers with late-breaking corporate information every business day. The updates appear in the seventh volume, called *Standard & Poor's Daily News*. In fact, the editorial offices where the *Corporation Records* are produced resemble the city desk of a newspaper. The investor awaiting the latest corporate earnings information will generally see it in Standard & Poor's before it appears in Moody's. The *Daily News* service also contains useful special features. For example, weekly lists of new stock offerings and registration statements filed with the SEC can be found

in every Monday's issue. And unlike other popular news services, it provides a continuously cumulating index, making it a simple matter to locate all the recent stories on a given company. The other aspect of Standard & Poor's timeliness is more subtle. Because the base volumes are updated quarterly, the complete annual report on a company appears in print much sooner.

Like the Moody's set, *Corporation Records* contains several levels of coverage depending on the fee paid by the companies appearing in the volume. Narrative information is generally kept to a minimum, though a firm may pay to print the "President's Letter." Maps and other special features seen in Moody's *Public Utility* and *Transportation* manuals are absent in S&P. What's more, the most complete level of coverage only provides two years of comparative data, as opposed to seven years in Moody's. Standard & Poor's does list a ten-year summary of earnings, however. Finally, the financial tables in S&P are compressed and utilize extensive abbreviations, making them more difficult to read than those in Moody's.

Aside from these differences, the information in both publications is similar. Capitalization, description of securities, and lists of subsidiaries, properties, and officers can all be found in the *Corporation Records*. Like Moody's, the S&P volumes also contain special tables with industry statistics and company lists. Where Moody's has a geographic index to company names, S&P has a more complete index by SIC number. The *Corporation Records* also compiles an extensive "Cross-Reference" index to subsidiaries and name changes which is more comprehensive than Moody's list of "Additional Companies No Longer Included." The cross-references and *Daily News* features are the strongest selling points of the Standard & Poor's service, but Moody's remains the better choice for corporate profiles. Moody's also seems to be the clear favorite among users of financial information. However, because both Moody's and S&P offer many of their publications to libraries as extremely reasonable package deals, both services can be found side-by-side in many business collections.

Data from the set are also available online through DIALOG and LEXIS/NEXIS, and on CD-ROM. On DIALOG, the online version is divided into three files, *Standard & Poor's Corporate Descriptions* and two *Standard & Poor's News* databases, one with retrospective stories going back to 1979 and one with the most recent few years. On LEXIS/NEXIS, the database is divided into two files, *Corporate Descriptions* and *Daily News*. On both systems, the news file is updated daily and the *Corporate Descriptions* file is revised every two

weeks. In many respects, the online files from Moody's and Standard & Poor's are quite similar. Both focus on financial data and both present fairly detailed Balance Sheets and Income Statements. A significant difference is in the number of variables which can be searched. Although neither Moody's nor S&P index every financial characteristic in their respective databases, Moody's provides access to more than twice the number its competitor does. There is also a slight difference in emphasis between the two products. Moody's presents five years of financials, while S&P gives two or three years. Conversely, Standard & Poor's lists ten years of annual stock prices and dividend payments, where Moody's lists only five. Another difference is that S&P reproduces its entire printed report online, which Moody's does not. This means that *Standard & Poor's Corporate Descriptions* includes lists of subsidiaries, company histories, and detailed descriptions of stock and bond offerings. Finally, where the online versions of *Moody's Manuals* restrict coverage to approximately 5,000 companies, all 9,000 companies with full profiles are found in S&P's online products. The news files from Standard & Poor's are very similar to their Moody's counterparts. Both contain retrospective information (S&P's going back to 1979), both utilize standardized event codes (though S&P uses fewer of them), and both offer news stories as well as financial tables. Users should also note that data from Annual Reports appear on the *News* files before they end up on the *Corporate Descriptions* database.

The CD-ROM version of the *Corporation Records*, called *Standard & Poor's Corporations*, was introduced in Chapter 6. It differs from the online version in that it also contains directory information on private companies and executive biographies (both taken from the *Standard & Poor's Register*), and selected financial statistics from S&P's *Compustat* database. Otherwise, the disk is similar to its online cousin. It utilizes DIALOG software, and is searchable in the familiar "Easy Menu Mode" and the "DIALOG Emulation Mode."

PTS Annual Reports Abstracts (Predicasts, Inc.— Monthly).

This Predicasts database contains partial records from the Annual Reports of approximately 4,000 companies, including foreign firms traded on U.S. exchanges. Information on each company is divided into three separate reports. The "Corporate Establishment" records offer a brief profile of the company, citing address, sales volume, number of employees, and Predicasts product codes. The "Tabular" records provide three to five years of abbreviated financial data, including sales and net income by segment, research and development costs, and

capital expenditures. The "Textual" records contain excerpts from the narrative portions of the Annual Report, and focus on management goals, marketing strategies, research activities, new products, and plans for new facilities and future acquisitions.

The records are brief, but *PTS Annual Reports Abstracts* can be a useful alternative to more detailed financial databases. Researchers comfortable with Predicasts product and event codes will find the indexing especially helpful. The database is also searchable by employee and sales size, fiscal year, city, state, zip code, telephone area code, stock exchange, and words and phrases in the text. Except for sales volume, no financial variables can be searched. The database is available on DIALOG and Data-Star. Many of the Textual records are also found in the *PTS PROMT* file.

Full-Text Systems

Until recently, users had no choice but to consult paper documents and microfiche collections to obtain full-text information. Today several electronic options exist, and when the EDGAR system becomes fully operational, there will be more.

Laser D/SEC (Disclosure, Inc.—Updated Continuously).

Originally dubbed *LaserDisclosure*, this CD-ROM is not designed for traditional financial searching. Instead, it is an electronic document delivery system, a high-tech replacement for microfiche or paper collections. *Laser D* stores the complete text of disclosure reports on optical disks. At present, subscribers receive approximately 100 disks per year, each containing up to 28,000 pages of information. Virtually all significant SEC documents are included: 10-Ks, 8-Ks, 10-Qs, Proxies, Annual Reports to Stockholders, Registration Statements, Prospectuses, and so-called Williams Act filings, complete with graphics, photos, and exhibits. Subscribers can select the complete collection or certain types of documents only. The service covers all companies in the Disclosure database, with reports dating back to January 1989. Other products in the series are *Laser D/International*, which delivers annual reports for 7,000 foreign companies, and *Laser D/Banking*, which covers 700 banks and savings institutions.

To retrieve a report, the searcher types the name, ticker symbol, or disclosure number of the company being sought, and the system responds with a list of documents available for that company, citing the type of report and the filing date. From that menu, the searcher selects the desired document, and is prompted to insert the disk containing the text of that report. The user can

then read the full report on screen, use tabs to jump to designated areas of the report, or specify pages to be reproduced on a high-resolution laser printer. The disks themselves are produced using optical scanning technology, and except for the tab feature, no indexing enhancements are provided. This means that no subject or keyword searching is possible on the text itself, nor can the user download documents to another computer file.

The publisher moved quickly to remedy the lack of sophisticated search capabilities on the full-text system. Now subscribers can choose an integrated package which combines *Compact D/SEC* with *Laser D*. Users can search for specific data in *Compact D/SEC*'s financial summaries and narrative extracts; the system will then refer to the appropriate disk containing the full report. The actual searching is done on the abstracting service, not the full-text files. Of course searchers can still view a complete menu of a company's filings if they wish.

Even without the link to *Compact D/SEC*, *Laser D* offers compact, convenient document storage and retrieval capabilities. For those who have suffered through the effort of filing and refiling thousands of fiche, searching for missing fiche, losing documents due to carelessness, or making due with poor photocopies, *Laser D* answers a multitude of needs. Required reports are found in seconds, with no fumbling or false starts. One of the most important benefits is the variety of documents included. No longer will users of 10-K Reports be frustrated to learn that needed data are listed in the ARS; both documents are readily accessible on the laser system. Well-labeled function keys make the system simple to use, and reports are updated rapidly. The publisher promises that documents appear within ten working days of their release by the SEC, and subscribers generally receive one or two new disks per week. Perhaps best of all, *Laser D* compares favorably in cost to an equally comprehensive microfiche collection. Potential subscribers will need to assess the expense of making copies from the laser printer, however. Another factor to consider is that only one person can retrieve reports at a time, unless the subscriber invests in additional workstations or Disclosure's impressive "Jukebox" system.

SEC Online (SEC Online, Inc.—Semiweekly).

One database allows direct full-text searching of all records simultaneously. *SEC Online* provides the complete text of 10-Ks, 10-Qs, Annual Reports, and Proxies exactly as they are reported by the filing companies. Approximately 6,000 companies are covered: those listed on the New York and American Stock Exchanges plus 2,000 major firms on the NASDAQ system. Filings for listed stocks are available from 1987 to the present;

coverage of NASDAQ companies begins with January 1990. *Laser D/SEC* covers far more firms, though it is likely that smaller public companies will be added to *SEC Online* in the future. Another gap in coverage is the absence of most exhibits from the 10-Ks and Proxies, though lists of exhibits are included.

The database is available in both online and CD-ROM formats. LEXIS/NEXIS, DIALOG, and INVESTEXT/PLUS offer online access. The LEXIS and DIALOG versions are similar in most respects. The file did not become available on DIALOG until December 1990, but the same time period is covered on both systems. In both, tables of contents are added to each report, enabling rapid access to relevant sections of the document. Each document is divided into standard fields (called segments on LEXIS), so users can limit searching to a specific part of the record. The information is divided into four separate subfiles, one for each type of document. In this way, users can limit a search to Proxy Statements only, or they can search all documents at once in a combined file. Unfortunately, only the text portions of the reports are searchable. The financial statements can be retrieved, but numeric screening is not possible, making *SEC Online* less powerful than *Disclosure Online*.

SEC Online is now available on CD-ROM from Standard & Poor's Compustat Services as *Compustat Corporate Text*. Competing versions are due by late summer 1991: SilverPlatter Information's *SEC Online on SilverPlatter* and Lotus Development's *CD/Corporate: SEC Filings* (available as a Lotus One Source database). The three products are similar in most respects. Like the online counterparts, only the text portion of records are searchable on disk; financial tables are present in the records, but numeric data cannot be searched. The S&P and Lotus versions contain all filings seen online, with monthly updates. For the moment, the SilverPlatter version will provide only 10-Ks and 20-Fs, with quarterly updates, but the company plans to enhance the scope and frequency soon. Aside from the search software employed by each, the most noticeable difference is how data are divided on the disks. For example, SilverPlatter separates the database by type of company; manufacturing firms are one one disk and all other companies are on a second.

How does CD-ROM access to *SEC Online* compare with *Laser D*? All four publishers offer substantial discounts to academic and library customers, but *Laser D* is by far the most expensive. On the other hand, it is also the most comprehensive system, with cover-to-cover reproduction, including graphics and exhibits. Furthermore,

SEC Online provides fewer types of documents, and doesn't support the powerful financial searching capabilities of *Compact D/SEC*. While *Laser D* does not allow simultaneous full-text searching of all documents, extensive portions of text can be searched through the *Compact D/SEC* portion of the system. The tradeoff between cost and features is clear; for the many potential subscribers who can't afford the more sophisticated *Laser D* system, *SEC Online* offers convenient, full-text access to basic documents.

NAARS (American Institute of Certified Public Accountants—Weekly).

NAARS stands for the *National Automated Accounting Research System*, an online file of financial data gathered from Annual Reports to Shareholders. Approximately 4,200 firms are included, representing companies listed on the New York and American Stock Exchanges, as well as larger over-the-counter firms. Each record contains only the audited portions of the Annual Report: financial statements, footnotes, and the auditor's reports. Excluded are the President's Letter and other narrative sections of the report, photos, and graphics. Five years of Annual Reports are presented, but data from an archival file can be retrieved through a special request to the AICPA.

NAARS indexing was designed by the technical staff of the AICPA and reflects areas of greatest interest to accountants. Descriptor codes are assigned to identify major events experienced by each company. Approximately 60 codes are used, ranging from "FOREFF" (the economic effect of foreign exchange) to "CHGAUD" (change in auditor). Users can thus search for companies showing particular accounting attributes—all firms which have received a qualified auditor's report or instituted changes in accounting methods, for example. Like all LEXIS/NEXIS databases, records are divided into "segments," but in this case segments are identified for every key line and section in the financial statements. All words in the text of the auditor's statement and the footnotes are also searchable. Combining descriptor codes with segment searching allows users to focus on specific characteristics, such as firms which have merged ("ACQUIS") and whose annual reports mention pensions in the footnote segment. Other searchable segments include company name, ticker symbol, stock exchange, SIC code, date, and auditing firm. Unfortunately, the only financial segments which can be searched arithmetically are sales, net income, total assets, and net income. Accountants find *NAARS* especially helpful for identifying how other companies have chosen to describe a particular transac-

tion, but all researchers will find it well-suited for event-related screening. *NAARS* is available exclusively on the LEXIS/NEXIS system.

Other Sources of Company Profiles

Recognizing that some researchers and librarians might not require comprehensive financial data, many publishers compile abbreviated reference tools. The quarterly *Corporate 1000 Yellow Book* from Monitor Publishing Company provides single-page descriptions of the thousand largest publicly traded companies in the United States. The *Corporate Directory of U.S. Public Companies* offers briefer profiles for the more than 12,000 publicly traded companies which submit 10-K Reports. Listings cite the number of shares outstanding, the number of shareholders, the annual dividend, total and current assets, total and current liabilities, the Price/Earnings Ratio, and five years of sales, net income, and Earnings Per Share data. Also cited are the company's auditor, legal counsel, stock transfer agent, executives and directors, major stockholders and their percentage of ownership, major subsidiaries of the firm, and a brief business description. The format is a model of concise but valuable information. Eight indexes provide access from a variety of perspectives, including major stockholders, officers and directors, and Fortune and Forbes rankings. The *Corporate Directory* is published annually in two volumes by Walker's Western Research, a subsidiary of the Cambridge Information Group. Another popular service from the same publisher is *Walker's Manual of Western Corporations*. This venerable publication profiles approximately 1,500 publicly traded companies located in the western states, including Alaska and Hawaii. Five years of financial statements are given, together with business summaries, stock ownership information, capitalization data, and selected narrative from the Annual Reports. Geographic and SIC indexes are provided. *Walker's Manual* is published annually, with quarterly updates.

A broad selection of more specialized company profiles are available, but most concentrate on single industries. Such services often include information on subsidiaries and divisions in addition to publicly held firms. Examples are the following three annual titles from Fairchild Publications: the *Electronic News Financial Fact Book & Directory*, *Fairchild's Financial Manual of Retail Stores*, and *Fairchild's Textile & Apparel Financial Directory*.

A final category of financial services standardizes data in easily comparable tabular formats. Many of the investment publications covered in Chapters 10 and 12 are renowned for this approach, from *Media General* to the *Value Line Investment Survey*. Where enhanced information is concerned, there is considerable overlap between popular investment services and the more sedate financial publications, but several publications are based heavily upon primary disclosure documents.

Worldscope Company Profiles (WD Partners—Annual).

Worldscope, created by the research firm of Wright Investor's Service, is now a joint venture of Wright and Disclosure, Inc. It provides comparative information on nearly 6,400 of the largest companies from the United States and 23 other countries. Coverage will be expanded to approximately 9,000 firms in the near future. Every company receives a single-page profile, with six years of standard financial data reported in the currency of its native country. Key performance measures are reported as ratios, growth rates, or in U.S. dollars to enable company comparisons by country or industry. For these measures, country and industry norms are also calculated. Extensive tables of company rankings provide additional comparisons. *Worldscope* is issued annually as an eight-volume set of hardbound volumes. It is also available as a quarterly CD-ROM called *Compact D/Worldscope* and as an online database.

The CD-ROM utilizes the same search system as *Compact D/SEC*. Five years of data display on screen, but users can download ten years of comparable figures. The online version is offered through several systems, including CompuServe and Dow Jones News/Retrieval. It can be searched only by company name or ticker symbol, with no financial screening possible. Output is available in ten standardized formats, ranging from a brief company profile to a full report averaging 12 pages. The major advantage of the online version is more extensive company information. Instead of the 100 or so key variables listed in the print and CD-ROM products, the online system presents more than 400 detailed measures from the financial statements. Only four years of historical coverage are offered, however. Online updates occur monthly.

Compustat PC Plus (Standard & Poor's Compustat Services, Inc.—Weekly).

Compustat differs from the other resources discussed in this chapter by being almost entirely numeric in content, and by providing extensive historical data. It is one of the most important databases for scholarly research in corporate financial structure and investment

performance. A more extensive magnetic tape file of *Compustat* data has been available since 1962, but the CD-ROM did not appear until 1987. The following discussion is limited to the compact disk version.

Compustat contains a wealth of current and retrospective data on some 7,000 active firms, plus historical data for 5,000 companies which are no longer traded. Data fields include major items from the financial statements, selected footnotes, plus measures of stock performance. In all, several hundred variables are presented for every company. *Compustat* adjusts all variables for differences in accounting methods, and presents them in a standardized format. Another advantage is the length of time for which figures are presented. Annual financials are reported for 15 years, quarterly financials for 5 years, segment data for 7 years, and monthly market data for 7 years. Industry composites are also provided. The software is quite sophisticated, enabling the user to screen on most variables, display results in a variety of formats, and perform as many as 50 mathematical operations on the data. This complexity is a strength, but can also be a source of frustration. Researchers wishing to manipulate the data to its fullest capability will need to spend hours learning the system. The publisher maintains an excellent toll-free support line to assist users.

Compustat is not just a tool for sophisticated financial analysts. Users who wish to generate basic information can utilize more than 60 pre-formatted reports. Generating a report is done by entering a few simple commands, and subscribers receive a 200-page manual called the "Report Library," which gives examples of every standard report. The reports are diverse and should accommodate most basic users' needs. Examples range from straightforward financial statements to segment data by line of business. Reports can provide historical trends for one company or compare several firms in a single table. Electronic assistance is provided through detailed help screens, a directory of ticker symbols, and an online thesaurus of financial codes.

Another drawback to *Compustat* is its high price. Weekly updates are available, but this service is understandably expensive. Subscribers may opt for monthly, quarterly, or even annual updates instead. For the annual version, a substantial price reduction is offered to educational institutions. A separate database called *I/B/E/S* (introduced in Chapter 12) is available on the system for an additional fee.

Compustat can also be searched online. The same data fields and companies are represented, but time series go back further—up to 20 years for annual financials. The online product is updated weekly and is offered

through a number of the more sophisticated corporate vendors, including ADP Data Services. Abbreviated information from *Compustat* can be found on the *Standard & Poor's Corporations* disk.

NAVIGATING THE PUBLISHING MAZE

When investigating the basic financial condition and structure of public companies, the need seldom arises to map a detailed research strategy. Because data are easily found in an assortment of convenient packages, research is fairly straightforward. The nature of the inquiry and the amount of detail required will largely determine which sources are used. In most cases the only preliminary step is the need to verify that the firm is traded publicly. For companies listed on leading stock exchanges or national markets, this is an easy task. The SEC produces an inexpensive annual called the *Directory of Companies Required to File Annual Reports with the Securities and Exchange Commission*. The alphabetical indexes to *Standard & Poor's Corporation Records*, or the paperback supplement to the *Moody's Manuals* are both handy resources. Another excellent source is *Compact D/SEC*, which includes even smaller companies which report to the SEC. Customers of Disclosure, Inc. also receive a free annual directory of all companies in the database, entitled *SEC Filing Companies*. Even such familiar directories as *Standard & Poor's Register* and the *Directory of Corporate Affiliations* indicate whether major companies are publicly traded.

There are two problems in identifying a company's public status, however. The first is that nothing remains constant in the business world. Private firms go public, public firms are acquired by other companies, and, in some cases, public companies are taken private. Because changes occur so rapidly, researchers should never assume that they know a company's present status. Many publications provide valuable assistance in tracking corporate changes on a current basis, including the *Wall Street Journal Index* and *Standard & Poor's Daily News*. Online databases are especially helpful for keeping up with recent changes, including full-text news sources and periodical indexes. Specialized guides for researching corporate changes will be covered in Chapter 11.

The second problem is that not all public companies must file 10-K Reports with the SEC. Verifying the status of smaller public firms or quasi-public corporations can be extremely difficult, and there are no comprehensive directories for such companies. A worthwhile guide to some of the more obscure public companies is a semian-

nual directory called the *National Stock Summary*. This publication is described in Chapter 10. The techniques used for researching private companies can also lead to information on elusive public and quasi-public companies, but no single strategy will guarantee results.

Once a corporation has been identified as public, nearly any one of the sources described in this chapter can provide needed information. The key question to address before selecting a publication involves format. For in-depth background on a company, primary documents are perfectly adequate to the task. For quick summaries, comparative reports, current news, and ready-reference data, commercial publications are best. In either case, the choice of formats is formidable. For public documents, users can turn to paper or microfiche collections in libraries, utilize full-text online or optical systems, or call a document delivery specialist. An even greater diversity exists for commercial products. Specific information requests can present a challenge only because similar publications treat data differently. Various electronic databases may highlight certain variables and ignore others, or may cover only particular types of SEC documents or categories of companies. Every researcher will develop favorite publications and search techniques. Information of some type is readily available, even for individuals and organizations with limited resources.

Of course there is more to researching a public company than locating basic financial data. A public company's actions are affected strongly by events in the financial marketplace. It is highly likely that individuals gathering information on public companies will require at least some data on the firm's investment performance. The following three chapters will continue the discussion of publicly traded companies, but from an investor's perspective.

FOR FURTHER READING

A great deal has been written on financial disclosure, corporate annual reports, and the role of the SEC. Much of the material is quite technical, intended for accountants and securities lawyers. On the other hand, a surprising number of guides have been written for the beginning investor. For example, each April many popular newspapers and magazines run articles on how to read financial reports. Others summarize trends in the current year's batch of reports. The following titles represent a variety of books and articles that should be understandable to beginners.

The SEC and Corporate Disclosure Policy

Phillips, Susan M., and J. Richard Zecher. *The SEC and the Public Interest* (Cambridge, MA: MIT Press, 1981).
  The economic impact of the SEC as a regulatory agency is examined here. Although this insightful book is fairly short, the authors touch on a diversity of issues: the equality of access to investment information, the relationship between stockholder and manager, the cost of SEC reporting, and the Commission's effectiveness in creating a national marketplace. Several case studies are analyzed, including the deregulation of brokers' fixed commissions on the NYSE, a slow process which culminated in 1975. An introductory chapter provides a quick history of stock exchanges and the SEC.

Skousen, K. Fred. *An Introduction to the SEC*. 4th ed. (Cincinnati, OH: South-Western, 1987).
  A brief overview of the SEC. This handy guide discusses the historical events which preceded the founding of the SEC, the organization of the Commission, the laws which it administers, and its impact on the accounting profession. The two meatiest chapters deal with the registration process and the corporate reporting requirements under the 1933 and 1934 Securities Acts. Although the book is fairly short, Skousen places the SEC in its proper perspective better than most longer works, and does so without getting bogged down in detail.

U.S. Securities and Exchange Commission. *The Work of the SEC* (Washington, DC: The Commission, 1986).
  This booklet, revised every few years, describes the six major laws which the SEC enforces. Also included is a guide to the various organizations within the SEC, plus tips on how to obtain information from them. The explanations are fairly clear, making this a good choice for those looking for a brief guide to securities laws.

Wechsler, Dana and Katarzyna Wandycz. "An Innate Fear of Disclosure." *Forbes* (February 1990): 126-28.
  Since 1976, publicly held companies have been required to disclose key financial data by business segment or line of business. Many companies define segments broadly to avoid more detailed reporting, which presents problems for financial analysts, researchers, and investors.

Annual Reports to Shareholders

Bernstein, Judith R. "Corporate Annual Reports in Academic Business Libraries." *College & Research Libraries* 47 (May 1986): 263-73.
  Describes how college and university business libraries manage their collections of corporate financial reports in fiche and paper.

Hector, Gary. "Cute Tricks on the Bottom Line." *Fortune* (April 24, 1989): 193-200.

Provides examples of common techniques used by companies to downplay negative information in the annual report.

Herring, Jerry. *Annual Report Design: A Guide to the Annual Report Process for Graphic Designers and Corporate Communicators* (New York: Watson-Guptil, 1990).

Although clearly focusing on the PR function of annual reports, this slick handbook also describes the legal requirements, including what must be included and how it must be presented. It provides interesting insights for the user of annual reports, by disclosing the techniques employed by corporate image specialists.

Linden, Dana Wechsler. "Lies of the Bottom Line." *Forbes* (November 12, 1990): 106-12.

The author decries some of the accepted accounting principles which can be used to inflate a company's reported net income. Examples are given of particularly egregious abuses contained in recent company reports.

Lipay, Raymond J. *Understand Those Financial Reports* (New York: Wiley, 1984).

The author utilizes a question-and-answer approach to explain the basics of financial statements. The section on auditors' statements and footnotes is especially good. Lipay also takes pains to distinguish the usefulness of the annual report to shareholders as compared to the 10-K.

SRI International. *Investor Information Needs and the Annual Report* (Morristown, NJ: Financial Executives Research Foundation, 1987).

This fascinating study examines the information needs of investors—both professional and individual—and how they are met by corporate annual reports. It covers their perceptions of annual reports, their usage of other sources of financial information, the benefits and weaknesses of the ARS, and what corporations should be doing to produce more objective, meaningful reports.

Thomsett, Michael C. "The Annual Report." In his *Investor Factline: Finding and Using the Best Investment Information*. (New York: Wiley, 1989): 63-84.

An easy-to-read introduction to the annual report from the investor's viewpoint.

SEC Disclosure Filings

Disclosure, Inc. *A Guide to SEC Corporate Filings* (Bethesda, MD: Disclosure, 1990).

This handy pamphlet summarizes the content of all major reports filed with the SEC, including the various registration statements, acquisition reports, and insider filings. A "Quick Reference Chart" compares the contents of each report. The guide is available free to Disclosure customers, and is revised frequently.

Herdman, Robert K., Robert D. Neary, and Robert E. Rossell. *SEC Financial Reporting: Annual Reports to Shareholders, Form 10-K, Quarterly Financial Reporting.* 2nd ed. (New York: Matthew Bender, 1990 with annual updates).

This single-volume loose-leaf service presents basic guidelines for financial reporting in SEC disclosure reports. Subtitle to the contrary, the focus is on 10-Ks and 10-Qs. Additional chapters discuss the special requirements of banks and insurance companies. Annual updates highlight recent changes and proposed rules for financial reporting.

Levine, Sumner N. "10-K and Other SEC Reports." In his *Financial Analyst's Handbook*, 2nd ed. (Homewood, IL: Dow Jones-Irwin, 1988): 438-51.

Another short primer on principal SEC filings, including itemized lists of what is reported in each.

Sherwood, Diane. "SEC's 'Equal Access' EDGAR." *Information Today* (February 1989): 3-4.

Reports the SEC's long-awaited awarding of the contract for the EDGAR system to a consortium headed by BDM Internal, Inc. The article also provides a brief description of the proposed system and how it will be available to researchers.

Commercial Sources of Disclosure Data

Begue, Linda S., and Melissa B. Mickey. "Researching SEC Filings Online." *Business Information Alert* 1 (March 1989): 1-3+.

A short guide to leading online systems from Bechtel, Disclosure, SEC Online, and the States News Service.

Hutton, Debra J. "LaserDisclosure: A Product Profile." *Laserdisk Professional* 3 (March 1990): 56-59.

Brief description of Disclosure's amazing full-text optical system. The article was written before several important enhancements were unveiled, including the addition of *Compact D/SEC*'s sophisticated search capabilities.

Nicol, Margaret W., and Christina M. Darnowski. "Online Access to SEC Filings." *Database* 12 (August 1989): 28-33.

Fairly detailed comparison of 13 online databases containing a diversity of information from various SEC filings, including brief explanations of major SEC documents. A separate chart relates each type of filing to the databases on which they can be found.

CHAPTER 10
Basic Investment Information

TOPICS COVERED

1. The Investment Process
   a. Financial Intermediation
   b. Equity and Debt Financing
2. Types of Securities
   a. Stocks
   b. Bonds
   c. Investment Companies
   d. The Money Market
3. How to Read Financial Listings
   a. Listed Stock Quotations
   b. Over-the-Counter Stock Quotes
   c. Mutual Fund Listings
   d. Bond Quotations
4. Basic Sources of Financial Quotations
   a. Published Quotations
   b. Electronic Quote Systems
   c. Telephone Inquiry Services
5. Summary Investment Data
6. Choosing the Right Source
7. For Further Reading

MAJOR SOURCES DISCUSSED

- *The Wall Street Journal*
- *Investor's Daily*
- *Barron's National Business and Financial Weekly*
- *National Monthly Stock Summary*
- *National OTC Stock Journal*
- *Daily Stock Price Record*
- *Standard & Poor's Security Owner's Stock Guide*
- *Media General Plus*
- *Standard & Poor's Bond Guide*
- *Moody's Bond Record*
- *Stocks, Bonds, Bills, and Inflation Yearbook*

The world of investments is complex and has a language all its own. What's more, the nature of investing undergoes continual transition; as the economic and regulatory environments change, new types of financial instruments emerge and become popular. Many of the investment vehicles available today were nonexistent in the 1970s. Complex and changing though they are, these instruments fuel our economy, and are partly responsible for the American standard of living. This chapter will introduce basic concepts of investing in a simple manner, so that users wishing to work with investment publications will understand their scope and purpose.

THE INVESTMENT PROCESS

"Investments" is used in this book to mean the concept of securities. A security is a financial instrument which represents a claim on an asset, and is negotiable on the open market. Possession of a security provides the holder with a claim to ownership of something of value, or to the right to receive income from an asset, or both. For example, if you own the mortgage to a piece of real estate, you are entitled to receive a stream of mortgage payments of both interest and principal. If the mortgagor defaults on those payments, you then have a claim against that piece of real estate. What makes a security different from a deed, an IOU, or some other legal or financial

document is that a ready marketplace exists at all times for the buying and selling of the security. Most people would recognize stocks and bonds as different forms of securities, but many other securities exist, with a corresponding marketplace for each. A security is itself an asset because it represents the right to something else of value. If these ideas are not completely understandable at this stage, they should become clearer as the chapter progresses.

Financial Intermediation

The legal concept of property has long been a part of Western culture, but the idea of a security is comparatively new. Securities as we know them came into being in the sixteenth century along with the growth of corporations, but did not become a force of consequence until the Industrial Revolution. Opening a coal mine or building a toll road took more resources than one individual could amass. Furthermore, the larger the capital outlay, the greater the risk that an investment would not return a profit. These two motivations—capital formation and risk sharing—led investors to pool their resources through the creation of securities. An excellent example of this process is the method used to finance voyages of discovery to the New World. Explorations not funded by royal treasuries were usually financed through the formation of a corporation. Individual investors pooled their resources to enable such a venture, and with luck reaped a percentage of the profits in return.

When economists look at the world, they see two financial sectors: net lenders, who have a surplus of capital; and net borrowers, who have a deficit. The borrowing sector is made up of business firms and governments, while the lending sector is composed of individual households. Each household is a "surplus money unit," providing the capital to fuel the economy. That certainly is true if household members invest directly in stocks, in other securities, or have savings in some form of bank account. But it is equally true for household members who own insurance policies, belong to a pension plan, contribute to social security, or even own a checking account. The way in which your money is used by financial institutions, with or without your knowledge (and whether you think of it as your money or not), is called financial intermediation.

Intermediation is the process of bringing the economy's net borrowers and net lenders together. Intermediaries include all types of financial institutions. In the most straightforward example, a bank accepts deposits of various kinds from individuals and lends these deposits to borrowers, who then pay the bank interest for the use of the funds. The bank then pays some portion of the interest to the depositors.

The money to power this economic engine results from a circular flow: businesses and governments, acting as employers, pay workers for services provided, then borrow it back again through intermediaries. The savings and investment cycle draws new life from productivity increases and technological innovation, generating new capital through economic growth.

Equity and Debt Financing

Let's say you've just invented an amazing device or conceived of a wonderful new business idea. If you wanted to start your own company to take advantage of this innovation, where would you obtain the funding? You could borrow money from a rich relative, sell all your worldly possessions, or take out a second mortgage on your house. You might try a guaranteed loan from the U.S. Small Business Administration or a local industrial development agency. You could turn to a group of investors called venture capitalists, who provide funds in return for a percentage of your profits. You might even sell stocks or bonds in your company. Consider the following table and try to determine the difference between columns I and II.

SOURCES OF FUNDS

Column I	Column II
Liquidate your assets	Borrow from friends
Seek partners	Apply for a bank loan
Solicit venture capital	Seek government assistance
Sell stock	Sell corporate bonds

The funding choices in column I require you to use your own money or share ownership in the firm with someone else, while the options in column II merely obligate you to pay back a debt. Equity and debt financing are the only two ways money can be raised. This is another way of looking at the basic accounting equation introduced in Chapter 8: Assets = Liabilities + Equity.

This equation clarifies the difference between stocks and bonds. A stock is a certificate which represents a proportional share of ownership in a corporation. A bond is a security which represents a loan to be repaid. If you own 1,000 shares of stock in a company with a total of 10,000 shares outstanding, you own one-tenth of that business. This means you are entitled to one-tenth of the

profits that are distributed, or one-tenth of the firm's net worth should it be liquidated. On the other hand, if you own a $1,000 corporate bond, you will receive the $1,000 principal at the end of the bond's life, plus regular interest payments until it matures. Bondholders have no other claims against the company, and no ownership relationship. Stocks are equity instruments and bonds are debt instruments. Stocks and bonds are seldom used to finance a new company because investors are reluctant to take risk in an unknown firm. They are typically more comfortable financing the growth of existing companies with established track records.

TYPES OF SECURITIES

One can invest in many kinds of securities, and each type has many variations. This section will introduce basic concepts involving the most common forms of investments—stocks, bonds, investment companies, and money market instruments.

Stocks

The most widely held type of security is common stock. Stocks are normally purchased in round lots of 100 shares each. Because stock ownership can and does change hands frequently, transfer agents are hired by each firm to keep track of its stockholders. This enables "shareholders of record" to exercise their voting rights and to receive dividend payments (their percentage of corporate profits).

Many companies also issue shares of preferred stock, so named because it has a pre-established dividend rate which must be paid before common shareholders receive a dividend. Preferred stock is a hybrid between stocks and bonds because it has characteristics of both. Holders of preferred stock enjoy ownership rights as common stockholders do, and they receive a fixed rate of return as bondholders do. To summarize, owners of both common and preferred stock have three fundamental rights: the right to vote on important matters affecting the company, the right to receive a proportion of corporate profits in the form of dividends, and the right to sell the stock at any time.

An important distinction to make regarding any security involves primary and secondary markets. The initial offering of a company's stock to the public takes place in the primary market. Any subsequent trading of stock among the public occurs in the secondary market. Many people view the secondary market as little more than legalized gambling, but it plays a vital role in the economy. If stockholders had no guarantee that they could sell their shares whenever they needed or wanted to, few people would ever buy stock. This thriving secondary marketplace makes securities a liquid asset. The primary market could not exist without the secondary market.

The primary market is comprised of dozens of firms called investment banks or stock underwriters. An investment bank handles all the details and underwrites all the risk to the firm when a company "goes public." If the underwriter believed $5 per share was a realistic market price for a new stock, and the firm needed to raise $5 million, the underwriter would try to sell a million shares of stock. The underwriter would pay the firm $5 million (less a fee) and assume the risk of selling the shares to the public to recover the money. The firm now has its $5 million and doesn't much care who buys the stock or who trades it thereafter. Obviously the world is a little more complicated than this. For example, underwriters usually form syndicates to share the risk of a new stock issue, and syndicates rarely issue stock without some assurance that the sale will be 100% subscribed. The underwriting process also occurs any time an established publicly traded firm issues additional new stock for expansion purposes. Though oversimplified, this discussion presents a basic picture of how the primary market functions.

The secondary market is the medium through which existing stock is traded from one owner to another. It is comprised of stock exchanges and the Over-the-Counter market (OTC). A stock exchange is a physical place where people meet to buy and sell stock in a two-way auction. Most exchanges have informal roots; they began in coffee houses and taverns and gradually became institutionalized. All industrialized nations have at least one stock exchange, and the United States has several. The two nationwide stock exchanges in this country are the New York Stock Exchange (NYSE) and the American Stock Exchange (AMEX). There are also small regional stock exchanges in Chicago, San Francisco, Philadelphia, Boston, and several other cities. The New York Stock Exchange is the largest exchange in terms of dollar amounts traded. It is known as the "Big Board" because stocks of the largest public companies are traded there.

All stock exchanges in the United States operate in much the same way. Large brokerage firms pay a fee to obtain one or more "seats" on the exchange, because only member firms are allowed to trade there. Similarly, for a

company's stock to be listed on the exchange, it must meet the requirements set by the exchange. Since the NYSE is the largest, it has the most stringent listing requirements, involving the number of shareholders, total shares outstanding, sales volume, and other factors. When an individual wishes to buy or sell shares in a listed company, he or she must place the order with a local stockbroker. If the broker's firm is a member of the exchange, the order is transmitted to the floor of the exchange. If the broker is not a member, the transaction is conducted by a member firm which charges the nonmember broker a fee.

The price of a share of stock at any moment is determined by the give-and-take of the auction process—the price other buyers are willing to pay, and the amount of money sellers are willing to accept. What if no one wants to buy or sell when you want to trade? To accommodate such situations, the exchange appoints member firms to act as "specialists" for specific stocks. The specialist stands ready at all times to buy or sell shares in that stock to assure an orderly market.

The Over-the-Counter market is not a physical place, but a network of dealers who belong to the National Association of Stock Dealers (NASD), and participate in a computerized trading system called NASDAQ (NASD Automated Quotation). Stock dealers buy and sell stock for their own inventory, as opposed to stockbrokers who conduct trades on someone else's behalf. Like other merchants, stock dealers buy merchandise at wholesale and sell at retail. Dealers in the OTC market act like a specialist on the New York Stock Exchange. Each dealer agrees to "make a market" in a select group of OTC stocks. An actively traded OTC stock may have more than a dozen market makers around the country, while a small, inactive stock may only have one or two. All market makers stand ready to buy or sell stock in the companies they specialize in at any time. The difference between what they are willing to sell the stock for and the price they will pay to buy it is their markup—the source of the dealer's profit. To summarize, a stock exchange is a physical place where representatives for buyers and sellers meet to trade on an auction basis; the Over-the-Counter market is a network of dealers who transact business on a retail basis.

The Over-the-Counter system is the marketplace for companies that have recently gone public or are too small to meet the listing requirements of an exchange. Many large firms are eligible for listing on a national exchange, but choose to remain unlisted. Banks, insurance companies, and firms in high-tech industries are frequently seen among the OTC ranks. Other prominent OTC companies include well-known manufacturers of consumer goods such as Nike and Adolph Coors. In recent years the NASDAQ system has given the national stock exchanges keen competition for eligible companies. There are about 1,200 firms listed on the NYSE and another 800 on AMEX, but the NASDAQ system has about 4,000 companies. That in itself is not a challenge to the exchanges, but the volume of NASDAQ trading has been steadily increasing. In addition, the NASD won the right in May 1983 to form a "National Market System" for its most heavily traded stocks. Information on stocks in the National Market System is now reported in the same way as data on NYSE and AMEX stocks.

A few parting remarks should be made about the structure of the stock market. First, in addition to NASDAQ, several other computer trading networks exist. The Intermarket Trading System (ITS) provides a computer link among the NYSE, the AMEX, and five regional exchanges. This is helpful because of "dual listings" for stock. Although companies listed on the New York Stock Exchange cannot be listed on the American Stock Exchange (or vice versa), nationally listed stocks may be listed simultaneously on any regional exchanges. The regional exchanges do list a small number of local companies not traded elsewhere, but the bulk of the trading on regional exchanges is for NYSE and AMEX stocks that are dually listed. The Intermarket Trading System provides consolidated information on stock trades anywhere in the network so that traders may be sure of obtaining the best price. More than 80% of the volume of trading activity in NYSE companies is done on the floor of the exchange, but tracking prices on dually listed companies improves the quality of available information. Another computer network for stock information is the Instinet System, which reports trading activity among large institutions. Institutional investors such as pension funds and insurance companies play a significant role in today's market. Because they usually trade large blocks of stock, it is often simpler for them to deal directly with one another through Instinet, by-passing the exchanges altogether.

Many OTC stocks are not part of the NASDAQ system because they trade very infrequently, or because they fail to meet NASD requirements. Some are even too small to meet SEC filing requirements. The exact number of non-NASDAQ companies is unknown, but is somewhere between 6,000 and 9,000 firms. These lesser-known stocks are often referred to as unlisted stocks, or penny stocks, though neither is an accurate label. Actually, penny stocks are any which sell for less than a dollar per share (though some definitions include stocks which

sell below two dollars). Penny stocks can be listed on regional exchanges, the NASDAQ system, or can be traded by OTC dealers which specialize in such securities. Penny stocks have always been regarded as risky investments, but in recent years they have acquired an infamous reputation. This is largely due to the alarming number of indictments against penny stock brokers who allegedly perpetrated massive stock frauds. One of the reasons that such crimes are possible is that information on non-NASDAQ stocks is difficult to obtain. To combat the problem, the NASD has recently unveiled a second computer network to report data on these more elusive securities. The OTC Bulletin Board reports timely price quotes supplied by more than 100 market makers. As of this writing, nearly 3,000 non-NASDAQ companies are represented in the system.

Bonds

Corporate bonds are typically issued in denominations of $1,000 and have a life of ten years or more. As with stocks, if buyers did not have the confidence of knowing bonds could be sold at any time, few people would be willing to purchase them. In the primary market, the original bond buyer is indirectly loaning the company $1,000 for each bond purchased. If the original buyer sells the bond, it then enters the secondary market where it is traded back and forth among investors through the rest of its life. The secondary market exists because companies cannot be expected to redeem a bond every time someone wishes to turn one in. Corporate bonds may be listed on the NYSE, the AMEX, or traded over-the-counter.

It can be difficult to grasp the idea that the price of a bond in the secondary market can vary from day to day. After all, if the bond is worth $1,000 when it matures, why wouldn't it be worth that amount throughout its life? The simplest answer is that its market price depends on the forces of supply and demand. However, the primary reason for daily price fluctuation relates to the behavior of interest rates. When a standard bond is issued, it has an assigned "coupon rate" of interest which does not change over the life of the bond. The coupon rate is determined by the underlying strength of the company (the risk of the investment) and the prevailing rates of interest in the marketplace. If a bond had a coupon rate of 8%, it would pay interest in the amount of $80 per year (8% x $1,000 = $80). Interest on corporate bonds is typically paid in equal semiannual installments, so in this case the bond holder would receive two $40 payments each year.

If the prevailing rate of interest for new bonds changed to 10% five years later, the holder of the 8% bond could receive a higher rate of interest by selling the existing bond and buying a new one. Real world investment decisions are more complicated than the example of two different bonds. The bond holder actually has a choice between keeping the original bond or investing in a wide variety of alternative securities which may pay a higher yield. What would be worth $1,000 at maturity may be worth much less today because of these alternative investment opportunities. Also consider that a one-year-old bond is worth intrinsically more than an 18-year-old bond. The holder of the year-old bond might expect 19 years of future interest payments, while the holder of a similar bond of eighteen years could expect only two more years of payments. Bond valuation is tied to the concept of "time value of money." Because money can earn interest, a dollar held today is worth more than a dollar received in the future. This phenomenon creates an interesting relationship between bond prices and their interest rates. As bond prices increase, interest rates decrease.

This inverse relationship can be demonstrated by the notion of current yield. A bond's current yield is calculated by dividing its annual interest payment by the current price of the bond. If an investor paid $1,000 for a bond (which is called buying at par), the current yield would be equal to the coupon rate. If more than $1,000 was paid (buying at premium), the current yield would be less than the coupon rate. If less than $1,000 was paid (buying at discount), the current yield would be more than the coupon rate. Using the example of an 8% bond, consider the difference in yield if it were purchased for $1,000, $800, and $1,200 respectively:

$80/$1,000 = 8%

$80/$800 = 10%

$80/$1,200 = 6.7%

The coupon rate of interest does not vary; the current yield fluctuates with daily price changes.

A third way to describe a bond's interest rate is to calculate its "yield to maturity" (YTM). The current yield is a simple measure of what a bond is worth on a particular day; YTM is a more complex measure of the bond's yield if it were purchased that day, held to maturity, and the interest payments were reinvested at current rates. These three measures are standard ways of comparing one bond to another, but none of them represents the actual yield to the investor. The true rate of return for any investor can only be calculated based on the purchase price, the time it was held, and the selling

price. There are many other types of bonds besides the standard corporate bond. The United States government issues Treasury Bonds, and shorter-term debt instruments called Treasury Notes. Corporations established by the federal government in order to finance public policy goals can issue Agency Bonds. The Federal National Mortgage Corporation (Fannie Mae) is one example of this type of organization. Bonds issued by state and local governments are called municipal bonds. Municipals can be issued by governmental units, such as the State of California or New York City; by state-created corporations, such as the New York State Urban Development Corporation; by state and local authorities, such as bridge, water, and sewer authorities; and by local school districts. Another debt instrument is the zero coupon bond; this is a corporate or government bond that doesn't pay a coupon interest rate, but is sold far below its face value. The absence of interest payments is countered by the difference between the price paid for the bond and its redemption value.

Even though they have significant differences, stocks and bonds possess similarities as well: both are introduced in the primary market and traded on the secondary market, both can be sold at any time by their owners, and both have two sources of income associated with them. A stock can earn a stream of dividend payments while it is owned, plus earn a capital gain if it is sold for more than it was purchased. A bond earns a stream of interest income and can also be sold for a capital gain.

Investment Companies

An investment company provides a medium for small investors to pool their funds so they might participate in the same markets as larger investors. For example, the minimum denomination of a U.S. Treasury bill is $10,000. An individual with $5,000 could not purchase a T-bill, but two investors with the same amount could do so together. Thus the creation of an investment company allows investors to participate in markets from which they would otherwise be excluded. An investment company also reduces financial risk. Putting all investment eggs in one basket is risky, but in a diversified portfolio, the poor performance of one security could be partially offset by the success of another.

The most common type of investment company is the mutual fund, which allows individuals to purchase a percentage of a large portfolio of securities managed by the Fund. Each contributor receives shares in the Fund to signify the proportion of ownership. In addition to reduced risk, each shareholder presumably benefits from the professional full-time management of the portfolio. If 1,000 investors each contributed $5,000 to create a mutual fund, the Fund would have $5 million to invest in securities. If the Fund gave each investor 100 shares, the initial value of each would be $50. The share value would fluctuate from day to day as the prices of the underlying securities in the portfolio changed. Because the costs of operating the Fund are deducted from the value of the portfolio, the price per share is called the Net Asset Value (NAV). In the meantime, shareholders in the Fund would also receive dividends based on interest or dividends paid by the underlying securities. The Fund managers could change the composition of the portfolio as market conditions dictated. New investors could also buy shares in the Fund at its current NAV, and the additional capital would be used to enlarge the portfolio. Theoretically, there is no limit to the number of shares a mutual fund can issue.

The portfolio of a mutual fund can be comprised of any type of security—stocks, bonds, municipal bonds, money market instruments, or even precious metals— but most funds specialize in a particular form of investment. Mutual funds specify their investment goals, whether to earn high dividends, to appreciate in value in the long term, or to buy speculative securities and hope to make large capital gains. Funds can specialize by investing in foreign securities, "high tech" opportunities, or even stocks of companies that exhibit social responsibility. An important distinction among mutual funds is whether they are "load" or "no-load" funds. No-load funds do not charge a commission for purchasing shares, while load funds do.

Two other types of investment companies, closed-end funds and fixed-unit investment trusts, issue a fixed number of shares and no more. Shares in a closed-end fund must be acquired from an existing shareholder. Closed-end funds are listed on stock exchanges and sold like stock; otherwise they are identical to mutual funds in all respects. A unit investment trust issues shares with a fixed life and a portfolio that does not change over that life. Portfolios of unit trusts are typically made up of tax exempt securities, such as municipal bonds. The John Nuveen Company and several other firms are well known for creating and selling unit trusts, and each company may have dozens of trusts on the market at one time. One of the few publications to provide lengthy descriptions of individual unit trusts is *Moody's Bank & Finance Record.*

The Money Market

The money market involves any type of debt security having a maturity of less than one year. Stocks, bonds, and mutual funds are considered long-term investments that are part of the capital market. Money market instruments usually have terms of about 90 days, and some have maturities of only one day. They are often issued by corporations or financial institutions to raise large sums of money quickly for a brief period of use. The secondary market for money market instruments has become quite active, and numerous money market mutual funds have been created to allow small investors to participate.

The U.S. Treasury bill (T-bill) is a good example of a money market security. T-bills are used by the federal government to finance about one-fourth of the national debt. Because they are the most actively traded security in the world, many investors consider them the closest equivalent to currency. T-bills are issued in minimum denominations of $10,000 and in units of $5,000 thereafter. They are sold at weekly auctions by the 12 Federal Reserve Banks and their branches. Purchase of new issues remains active for about a week, and after the first day they may be bought at commercial banks for a fee. The auction by the Federal Reserve Banks and the remaining sales by banks constitute the primary market for the bills. Once T-bills are sold, they may be resold and purchased in the secondary market, which consists of dozens of government securities dealers who specialize in this activity.

New bills are auctioned by the Federal Reserve every Monday, and are issued to buyers the following Thursday. Investors may also enter a noncompetitive bid, and will pay the average price for that week's issue. T-bills have maturities of three months, six months, or a year, meaning they will be redeemable on a Thursday, 13, 26, or 52 weeks after their purchase.

Treasury bills do not pay a coupon rate of interest, but are sold at discount and redeemed at full face value. The difference between the price paid and the amount redeemed is the interest on the investment. If a 90-day bill is auctioned for $9,785.60 and redeemed for the full $10,000, this represents an annual interest rate of 8.58%. Because T-bills are short-term instruments, the price of bills traded on the secondary market is closely related to the price of newly issued bills. *The Wall Street Journal* reports both the weekly auction price for new bills and the daily price of trading on the secondary market every day.

HOW TO READ FINANCIAL LISTINGS

Stock quotations and other financial listings appear in most daily newspapers and even on cable television, yet most people pass them over with little thought. To the mildly curious, they appear incomprehensible—page after page of tiny print with strange abbreviations and arcane symbols. For business researchers, financial listings can offer important information and are worth learning to use.

Listed Stock Quotations

Financial quotations are generated by sophisticated computer systems that monitor trading activity in securities markets and summarize the results. The quotes that appear in daily newspapers are transmitted to the local papers by national news wire services such as the Associated Press and United Press International. The formats and abbreviations used by each wire service differ only slightly. Quotes in most newspapers are for the previous day's trading. Exhibit 10-1, from *The Wall Street Journal*, shows typical quotations for companies listed on the New York Stock Exchange. For dually listed stocks, prices are based on consolidated activity as reported on the Intermarket Trading System. This is why stock tables for the New York and American exchanges are usually labeled "Composite Trading." *The Wall Street Journal* relies on data supplied by the Associated Press, as does the *New York Times* and most other major newspapers. This 12-column format is nearly identical to that seen in daily papers across the country, though some papers use an abbreviated eight-column format.

Begin with the third column, which indicates the name of each stock. Company names are abbreviated, which is where confusion starts. To see what each abbreviation represents, understand that they are not stock ticker symbols. A ticker symbol is a code of one to three letters assigned to each company by the stock exchange (or a code of four to five letters for NASDAQ securities). The codes are used to report each stock transaction as it occurs on the floor of the exchange. The symbols do not always provide likely clues to the name of the company they represent, and one must be a seasoned stock-watcher to follow the ticker with any accuracy. Ticker symbols are increasingly important because investment information in popular online databases such as Dow Jones News/Retrieval are indexed by these codes. For this reason, the *Journal* does include the ticker symbol in the

EXHIBIT 10-1. *The Wall Street Journal*—Listed Stock Quotes

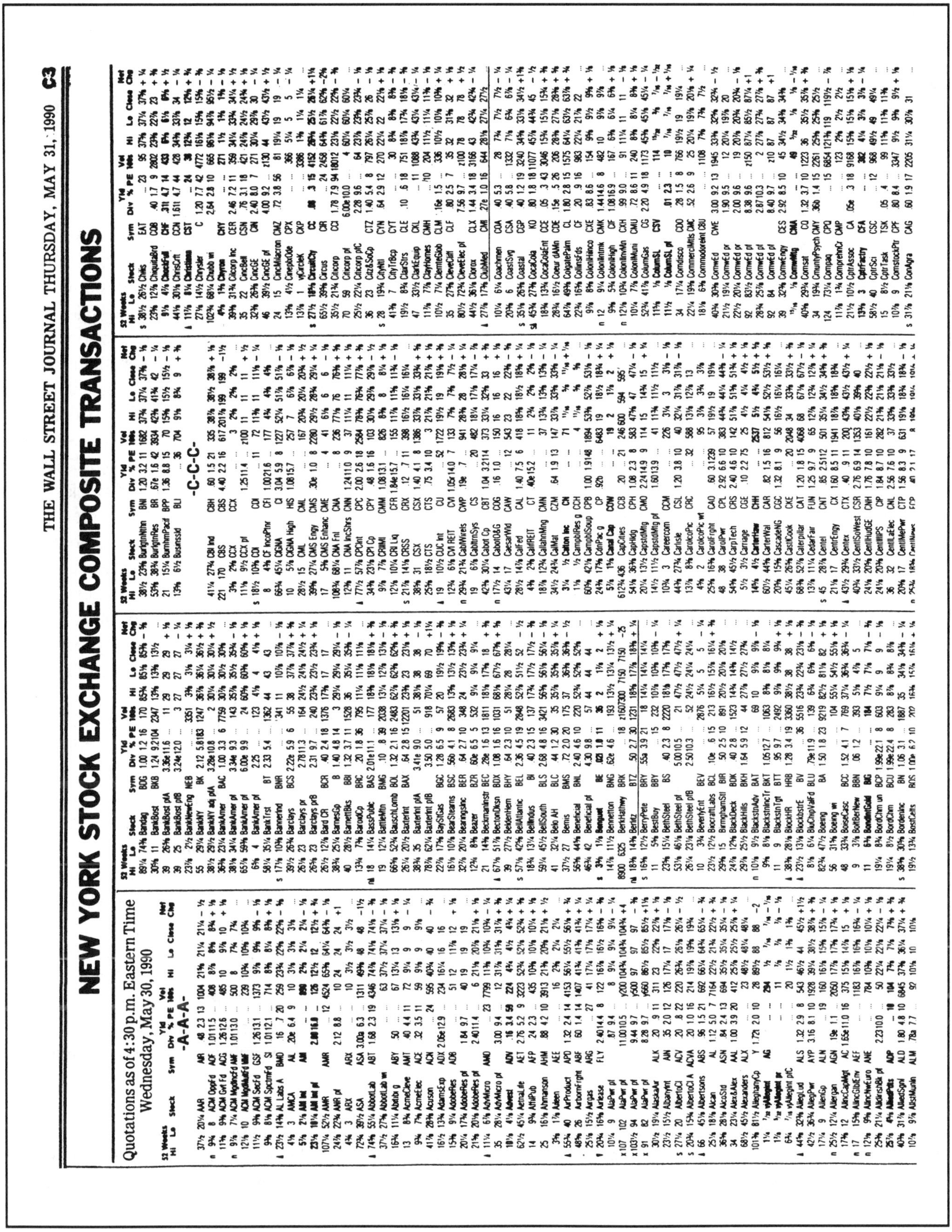

THE WALL STREET JOURNAL THURSDAY, MAY 31, 1990   C3

NEW YORK STOCK EXCHANGE COMPOSITE TRANSACTIONS

Quotations as of 4:30 p.m. Eastern Time
Wednesday, May 30, 1990

fourth column of data. This is also helpful as an additional reference to assist readers in locating the correct company, but the tables are not arranged by these codes. Ticker symbols are not intended for use in an alphabetized list.

The designations in column three are simple abbreviations of each company's name, created by the wire services. For well-known names, an abbreviation is usually sufficient to identify the company. Exhibit 10-1 lists easily recognized names like Clorox, Coca Cola, and Citicorp, as well as reasonably evident ones like Colgate Palmolive or Clark Equipment. Many abbreviations are less apparent, especially for companies which are not household names. The key to using financial tables is knowing that the abbreviations are alphabetized as though the company's name were fully spelled out. Thus CptrTask (Computer Task Group) comes before ComstockPtr (Comstock Partners). When in doubt, locate a nearby abbreviation you do recognize and proceed from there. For additional help, general reference sources such as the *Standard & Poor's Stock Guide* spell company names in full. Users can thus compare information in the *Stock Guide* to stock tables in the newspaper to help decipher listings. Another method is to consult specialized guides to newspaper abbreviations, although these are not updated very frequently. Such guides list companies in three alphabets—by name, newspaper abbreviation, and ticker symbol. Two recent books are Howard R. Jarrell's *Common Stock Newspaper Abbreviations and Trading Symbols* (Scarecrow Press, 1989) and Gerald Warfield's *Investor's Guide to Stock Quotations and Other Financial Listings* (3rd ed., Harper & Row, 1990).

When using newspaper stock tables, it makes sense to verify which exchange a company is listed on before proceeding to the tables. Also, some companies are popularly known by names other than their legal designation. Alcoa is actually the Aluminum Corporation of America, for example. This is why Conrail (the Consolidated Rail Corp.) is listed before ConEdison (Consolidated Edison) in Exhibit 10-1.

Now let's examine what the data in each listing mean. Look at the entry for Club Med (ClubMed) in the Exhibit. Five of the columns deal with the price of the stock. Columns 1 and 2 show the price range over the previous 52 weeks. Club Med stock sold for as high as $27^7/8$ and as low as $17^3/8$. The "High," "Low," and "Close" columns indicate the price activity for this particular day. In trading through the day, the highest price Club Med sold for was $28^1/8$, and the lowest was $27^1/4$. The close of $27^1/2$ describes the last sale of Club Med

common stock that day, regardless of when in the day it occurred. What do the numbers mean? Stocks listed on the New York and American exchanges are quoted in minimum amounts of one-eighth of a point, which is equivalent to $12^1/2$ cents. Club Med's high price of the day translates to $28.125 per share, or $2812.50 for a round lot of 100 shares. When referring to stock prices, it is not necessary to make this conversion; the accepted practice is to cite the figures as they appear in the stock tables.

The column labeled "Div" indicates the annual dividend paid by the company. The numbers reflect an estimate for current year dividends based on the latest quarterly payment. It is reported on a per-share basis. Therefore, Club Med is expected to pay common shareholders an annual dividend of $.27 per share for the current year. The column marked "yld" calculates the annual yield this dividend represents if the stock were purchased at this day's closing price, expressed as a percentage ($.27/$27.5 = 10%). The "P-E Ratio" listed in the next column is a standard measure of stock performance that will be discussed in the next chapter.

The column labeled "Vol 100s" shows how many shares of Club Med stock sold on this day. Because stock is sold in 100-share lots, the amount is reported in hundreds; the 644 amount translates to 64,400 shares traded. The last column indicates the change in price over the previous day's trading. It is calculated by subtracting the previous day's closing price from the current day's close, and it can reflect an advance or decline in price. For Club Med, the three dots in this column indicate no change over the previous day's close. The negative number for the stock above it (Clorox) denotes a decline of $1/4$ of a point over the day before. Notice that most stocks fluctuate very slightly from day to day, but may have a wide fluctuation over a year's time. Two other designations are present in the Club Med listing. The underlining seen in Exhibit 10-1 actually appears in *The Wall Street Journal* listing. This indicates that Club Med stock traded more actively on this day than it usually does. The top 40 stocks exhibiting this behavior to the greatest degree are so indicated every day. The pyramid symbol preceding the number in the first column indicates the highest price reached on this day represents a new high for the preceding 52 weeks. Stock tables employ a number of symbols and footnotes to highlight or further describe listings. Guides to the symbols used by the different tables can be found in each day's listings.

Over-the-Counter Stock Quotes

The presentation of OTC quotes seen in daily newspapers is less standardized than those for listed stocks. Large, actively traded OTC companies eligible for inclusion in NASDAQ's National Market System (NMS) are quoted in the same fashion as stocks listed on an exchange (prices are reported on a "high," "low," and "close" basis). Some 2,600 securities are represented on the National Market System, and many newspapers across the country present the full list. Smaller papers may opt to print an abridged version of the National Market System, representing the 1,000 or even 600 most active stocks on the list. Daily newspapers may also provide some information on NASDAQ stocks which are not part of the NMS. Many present the so-called "NASDAQ National List," which covers several hundred of the most actively traded stocks not eligible for listing on the NMS. Newspapers with more extensive financial coverage also publish "Supplemental" or "Additional" tables for NASDAQ stocks that are traded less actively. Local papers often feature a special list of OTC quotes for companies which are headquartered in the region or have a large facility there. These lists are usually provided by local offices of major OTC dealers. Most dailies do not provide coverage of all NASDAQ stocks, and no daily paper offers listings for non-NASDAQ companies.

OTC listings that are not part of the National Market System are quoted differently, reflecting the fundamental distinction between OTC stocks and those listed on an exchange. Exhibit 10-2, also taken from *The Wall Street Journal*, shows typical NASDAQ stock quotations. Notice the price quotes do not resemble Exhibit 10-1. Because OTC stocks are not sold at auction, and because many do not trade actively, high, low, and close quotations are not applicable. Remember that individual dealers make a market in OTC stocks by buying and selling for their own inventory. The bid price is the amount a dealer will pay to buy a stock from you, and the asked price is the amount the dealer will sell the stock for. The difference, or "spread," is the dealer's markup, the source of his or her profit. Generally, the less active the stock, the wider the spread. Bid and asked prices of inactive stocks may not fluctuate for weeks at a time. The OTC listings in newspapers show the highest asking price and lowest bid price quoted by all market makers for that stock in the NASDAQ system. The prices in the tables represent the range within which the individual investor may negotiate with a dealer.

OTC quotations may be traded in fractions less than eighths. Because profits can be made with narrow spreads, OTC securities are often traded in sixteenths or thirty-seconds of a dollar. For example, the bid price of General Nutrition Center's preferred stock (GnNtr pf) shown in Exhibit 10-2 is 3/32, which translates to $.09375, or slightly more than nine cents per share. This is an example of a penny stock.

Mutual Fund Listings

Quotations for mutual funds are quite simple to read as long as the user remembers the idea behind a fund. There are only four columns of information in a typical mutual fund listing. Individual funds are grouped by the company that sponsors them, as shown in Exhibit 10-3. Mutual fund companies may be stock dealers like Prudential Bache, subsidiaries of insurance companies like Mutual of Omaha, investment advisory firms such as Value Line, or companies which do nothing but manage mutual funds. The tables seen in most financial papers do not report prices on all mutual funds, only the 800 or so quoted on the NASDAQ system. To be accepted on NASDAQ, a fund must have a minimum of $25 million in assets and 1,000 shareholders. Newspapers which provide more extensive coverage of funds include *Investor's Daily* and *Barron's*. Specialized sources of mutual fund information will be introduced in Chapter 12.

The key to a fund's price is the daily value of its portfolio. The column labeled "NAV" represents the Net Asset Value of each fund as it was calculated that day. Figures are reported in dollar amounts, not fractions. Mutual funds aren't sold back and forth between individuals directly; if an individual wishes to sell some of his or her shares, they must be redeemed by the fund company itself, which will then resell them to another investor. Few firms charge a redemption fee, so the NAV may be thought of as the amount an investor would receive when selling the shares. The offer price listed in the next column is the price an investor pays to purchase shares in the fund. An "N.L." in this column stands for "no load," which means the fund does not charge a commission for the purchase of shares. The offer price for a no load fund is identical to the NAV. Some mutual fund tables list the NAV and Offer Price as the bid and asked price, which is in fact what they really are. The last column in a standard quotation is the change in the Net Asset Value over the previous day's trading. By law, mutual funds are required to calculate the NAV at least once each day.

EXHIBIT 10-2. ***The Wall Street Journal*—OTC Stock Quotes**

THE WALL STREET JOURNAL THURSDAY, MAY 31, 1990 **C5**

NASDAQ BID & ASKED QUOTATIONS

Stock	Div	Sales 100s	Bid	Asked	Net Chg.
-A-A-A-					
ACSEn		244	2 5/16	2 1/2	+1/16
AG Aut		153	3 7/16	3 1/2	...
ALPNT		201	1 11/16	1 7/8	−1/16
APA		21	6 3/4	7 1/4	+1/4
ATC		165	4 3/4	5	...
ATC wt		22	2	2 7/32	...
ATNN		396	1 3/4	1 13/16	...
ATS Mny		40	1	1 1/8	...
Abatix		8	3	3 1/4	...
ActnSt pf		13	2 7/8	3	...
Adelph h		45	13 1/2	14 1/4	...
AdvEn un		10	5 11/16	6 3/16	...
AdCpt		50	1 7/8	2 1/8	−1/16
AdGrav		37	1	1 1/8	...
AdvLog		148	17 1/4	17 3/4	+1/4
AdNMR		60	1	1 1/8	...
AdvLfe		310	3	3 1/8	+1/8
Advatex		160	3 1/4	3 3/8	...
AerSyE		5	4 3/8	4 5/8	...
Aeroson		23	1 1/8	1 1/4	...
Agrpost		33	3 5/8	3 7/8	...
Agristr		70	3/4	13/16	...
AirSen		250	15/16	1	...
AirInt		348	2 3/8	2 7/16	+1/8
Ajay		69	1	1 1/8	+1/32
Ajay un		10	6 1/4	7 3/8	...
Alcide		27	1	1 1/8	...
Alden	.12e	9	3 5/8	4	...
AlexEn		25	1	1 1/16	...
AllATV		50	3 3/4	4	...
Alphal h		711	6 1/16	6 1/4	+1/16
AlsFrm		13	5/8	1	...
Amribc	.20	2	16 1/4	16 3/4	...
AAcft		5201	29/32	15/16	+1/32
AmBdy		55	3 1/4	3 1/2	...
ABsCpt		528	6 1/8	6 5/16	...
ACty pf	1.50	70	16	16 3/4	...
AClaim		74	10 1/2	11 7/8	+1/2
AMConf		50	2 1/2	2 3/4	−1/8
AmDrg		593	1 5/16	1 3/8	+1/16
AShd rt		10	1 1/4	1 3/8	+1/8
AIM 84	3.00e	12	14	14 3/4	...
AIM 85	1.44e	8	13 1/2	14 1/4	...
AMobl		160	2 1/8	2 3/8	−1/8
ARecr	.16	34	7 5/8	7 7/8	...
ASafty s		93	1	1 1/16	...
ASCls un		110	6 1/8	6 3/8	...
Amrhst s		51	3 1/4	3 3/8	...
Ampal pf	.32	10	5 7/8	6 3/8	−1/8
Amtech		6	3	3 1/4	−1/16
AnlySur		7	1 5/8	1 3/4	...
AndGp h		113	2 3/8	2 3/4	−1/4
Angecn		114	4 1/4	4 3/8	...
Apco	.68e	2	4 7/8	5 1/4	+1/8
ApogRb		126	2 1/4	2 3/8	...
ApogeTc		40	4 7/8	6	+5/8
ApdMicr		5	2	2 1/4	...
Aquant		2558	2 7/8	2 15/16	+1/4
ArchPt		152	2 7/16	2 9/16	...
ArchCm		427	18	18 1/8	+1/4
Arcus		52	5 3/4	6 1/8	...
Ardenln		2	1 3/8	1 3/4	...
Artagph		150	2 13/16	2 15/16	−1/8
AtristG	.10e	150	5 1/8	5 3/8	...
ASEA	1.13e	41	128	129 1/4	−3/4
Astec wt		2	1	3	...
AtlExp		115	1 5/8	1 3/4	+3/16
Ault		164	2 1/4	2 1/2	−1/8
AuraSy		210	3 5/8	3 3/4	−1/16
Aurora		83	1 13/16	1 15/16	...
AuthDis		106	1 3/4	2	...
Avery		415	1	1 1/16	−5/32
AvonRnt		50	2 1/4	2 7/16	−1/4
-B-B-B-					
BI Inc		464	12	12 1/4	−1/4
BallJwl		97	2 1/8	2 1/2	−1/8
BkMd		19	9	11	−2
Barrie		180	2	2 5/16	−1/4
BargRs		340	2 3/4	3	+1/8
BrgRs un		91	10 5/8	11 1/4	+1/4
Bayly		9	1 5/8	2 1/4	...
Belcor s		5	1 7/8	2 1/8	...
Belmac		211	5 1/4	5 3/8	+3/8
BenhnA		61	1 7/8	2	−1/8
BntnOG		89	14 3/4	15	+1/4
BrnLel		65	1 1/8	1 3/8	−1/16
vjBcst pf		108	14	14 1/2	+3/4
BimdDy		1	3 1/2	3 3/4	...
Bioject		159	2 5/8	2 7/8	−1/8
Biomch		100	1 7/8	2 1/32	...
Biomc un		20	6 3/4	7 1/2	−1/8
Bioplst		137	3 3/8	3 1/2	+1/4
Biopore		21	1 1/4	1 9/16	...
BioTcG		592	2 7/16	2 1/2	+1/16
BiVasc		z50	1 3/8	1 1/2	...
BirdC pf	1.85	10	16	17	...
BobBrk		164	11/16	13/16	...
Bomed		15	7/8	1	...
Bwater	.33e	13	8 1/2	8 3/4	...
BrentB s	.40	1	13	13 1/2	...
Brilund		72	3 7/8	4 1/4	...
BristHd		10	1 7/8	2	...
BrstR un		7	1 5/8	2 1/8	...
Bdcstln s		14	7 1/4	8	...
BldrDsg		1430	3/8	13/32	...
BldDg wt		20	1/32	1/8	...
-C-C-C-					
CBL Med		9	3 1/2	3 5/8	...
CM Com		278	7 5/8	8	+3/8
CP Ovrse		4	3/8	1/2	...
CTEC B		z30	21 5/8	22 1/4	...
C3 pf		110	1/4	1/2	...
CblApic		113	3/4	13/16	−1/16
CblAp un		30	2 3/4	2 7/8	−1/4
CblC un		105	2 1/4	2 1/2	...
CalJam		190	5 1/4	5 3/8	−1/8
Fisons	.82e	231	25	25 1/8	...
Flexwat		145	1	1 3/8	−1/8
Foliage		105	1 15/16	2 1/16	...
Foreind		71	3 5/16	3 1/2	...
-G-G-G-					
GTS		29	3 5/8	3 7/8	...
GnCom		244	2 13/16	3	+1/16
GnKinet		14	7 3/4	8 1/4	...
GnNtr pf		218	3/32	5/32	...
GnPrcl		6	6 1/2	6 3/4	...
Gentnr		36	1 5/8	1 3/4	...
GeoTek		50	1 1/2	1 3/4	...
Gexa		5	1	1 1/8	−1/16
GlobVn		143	1 1/2	1 11/16	−1/4
GloV un		25	2 1/4	2 3/4	−3/8
GoVide		1071	7 1/8	7 1/4	...
GoVid wt		550	3 9/16	3 11/16	...
GoldCo		2	2 3/8	2 3/4	...
GldStd		225	1 5/16	1 7/16	...
GldKngt		1	12 1/8	12 1/2	...
GldNth		45	7/8	1 1/8	−1/4
GldQual		254	1 1/8	1 7/32	−1/32
GrdVly		110	2 7/16	2 9/16	...
GrayEl		220	5 3/8	5 7/8	+1/8
GrtOak		239	1 1/2	1 5/8	...
GOak un		2	4 1/2	5 1/8	...
GrnstR		211	1 1/8	1 5/16	...
Group	.01e	68	1/8	5/32	...
Grudge		2139	2 1/32	2 1/16	...
-H-H-H-					
HOH un		30	4 1/4	5	+1/4
HQ OfcS		409	5 1/8	5 1/4	...
HQ Ofln		344	1 5/8	1 7/8	+1/16
HQOI un		37	6 3/8	6 15/16	+1/8
Halador		80	7/16	15/32	+1/32
Hrrier s		z50	3 1/4	3 7/16	...
HaywdS	.40e	8	14	16 3/4	...
HlthCr		55	11/16	7/8	−1/16
Hlthtek		36	4 1/4	4 3/4	...
Hecks		153	3 1/8	3 3/8	−1/8
Helnet		15	3 3/4	4 1/4	...
HemaC		20	2 3/4	2 7/8	+1/4
Herblfe		871	1 31/32	2 1/32	+1/32
Highldr		21	3 1/4	3 7/16	−1/8
Himed		105	1 1/16	1 1/8	...
Himed un		10	3 3/4	4 1/8	...
HUSB		z58	1	1 1/2	...
Hmcall un		5	3	3 1/2	...
-I-I-I-					
I-Flw un		59	3 1/16	3 1/4	−1/8
Incomnt		126	1 7/16	1 9/16	...
Illo un s		76	29	29 1/2	−1 5/8
ImagEn		558	27/32	7/8	+1/32
ImgFl un		2	16	17	...
Imreg		93	1 1/4	1 3/8	−1/8
InHome		364	1 1/2	1 9/16	+1/8
IHme un		30	1 13/16	1 7/8	+3/32
Inamed		175	1 3/8	1 9/16	+1/16
IndBkgp	.72	5	14 1/4	15 1/4	...
IndEnt		39	2 3/8	2 1/2	−1/8
IndSqS	1.50	35	14	14 3/4	...
IndlBn	.48b	1	22	23 1/4	...
InfMgt		190	2 3/16	2 5/16	...
InfMg wt		50	1	1 3/32	...
InfMg un		10	9 9/16	10 1/4	...
Infrsnc		233	3 1/4	3 5/16	+1/16
InldGld		60	1 1/8	1 3/16	...
InstCp	.26e	10	11 7/8	12 1/2	+1/8
Integral		10	9	9 3/4	...
Intek		41	7/8	1	...
Intrclm		20	2	2 1/2	...
IntEnt		128	1/8	3/16	...
IntLfe s		4	7 1/4	7 3/4	+1/8
Intfrn		81	7 3/4	8	+1/8
IBS		60	2 1/4	2 3/8	...
IntlBus		112	1 3/8	1 5/8	...
IntCon		158	5/8	11/16	...
IntMove		157	2	2 1/16	...
IntPlat		30	3/8	1/2	...
IntlSup		105	1 1/8	1 3/8	...
IntYog		2	4 3/4	5 1/4	...
Intrnu		111	2 5/8	2 21/32	+3/32
Intrnu un		46	10 7/8	11 1/2	+1/4
Intphrm		128	6	7	−1/2
Isomet		19	5 1/4	6	...
Isramc		427	4 19/32	4 11/16	−3/32
-J-J-J-					
J2 Com		30	2 3/4	3	...
JPhil un		10	3 1/4	3 1/2	−3/8
JeffBcp	.50r	101	10 1/2	12	...
JenfCv		35	2 1/4	2 3/8	...
JrnEd un		23	3	3 1/4	...
-K-K-K-					
KCR		78	1 1/8	1 5/16	...
KnCtyL	1.12	12	36 1/4	36 3/4	...
KelyOil		118	11 5/8	11 7/8	+3/8
KyInvst	.35e	z10	12 1/2	13 1/2	...
Kleinrt		z50	14 1/2	16	...
Knwldg		180	1	1 1/16	−1/32
Krisch		200	13/16	15/16	...
KushLk		416	2 1/16	2 3/16	...
-L-L-L-					
LSB SC	.60b	17	13 7/8	15 7/8	...
LasVDsc		111	2 1/8	2 3/8	+1/8
LaserP		94	2 1/16	2 3/16	+1/8
LsrRc un		2	6 3/8	6 3/4	...
Lasrtch		122	1 1/4	1 5/16	+1/16
LaurlSv	.24	z50	12 1/4	13 1/2	...
Leak X		320	2 1/2	3	...
Leak X wt		150	1 1/4	1 3/4	...
Leeco		31	2 1/8	2 1/4	...
Leroy		462	6 1/2	7 1/4	+1 1/2
Lery un		35	8	9 1/4	+2 1/4
Levon		54	7/32	5/16	...
LibNBk	†	20	3 1/4	3 3/8	...
Play un		63	1 3/16	1 5/16	−1/16
PlexusR		12	1 3/4	2 1/8	...
PlrMol		73	1 5/32	1 7/32	...
PolutRs		60	1	1 3/8	−3/16
PolRs un		92	1 3/8	1 5/8	−1/8
Polymrx		65	2 3/8	2 5/8	−1/8
PoolEn		1349	13 1/8	13 3/8	+1/4
PwSpec		26	3 3/16	3 1/4	+1/16
PrabRbt		5	1 1/8	1 1/4	...
PfdHme		349	1 1/16	1 3/16	...
Prestek		82	13	13 3/4	+5/8
PrmEgy		25	1 15/16	2 1/16	...
PrfBcp s		30	7 1/2	8 1/4	...
PrftTc		213	3 1/2	3 3/4	...
Protch		168	2 7/8	3 1/4	...
PsycCp		279	4 7/8	5	−1/16
PubcoC		300	3/8	13/32	...
Purflw		511	7 1/2	7 3/4	...
Q Med		136	2 1/8	2 3/8	−1/4
QSR		83	3 3/8	3 3/4	+1/8
Qdrax		65	4 1/4	4 3/8	...
Quartzl		45	2 1/4	2 3/4	−1/4
-R-R-R-					
RCM		1605	4 3/8	4 1/2	+5/16
RF&P	1.00	1	31	31 3/4	−1/4
R Med h		279	9/16	5/8	...
RSI Hld		9	7/16	17/32	...
RadaEl		1034	2 15/16	3	...
RamHO		285	10 3/4	11 1/4	+1/2
Ramtrn		188	5 7/16	5 1/2	...
RndAcc		54	1 7/16	1 9/16	...
Raster		81	20	21 1/4	−1
Raycom		140	1 1/4	1 13/32	...
ReaGld		1	2 1/16	2 1/4	...
RegFdl	.40	2	12 1/2	13 1/2	...
Rntrak		155	1 1/2	1 3/4	+1/8
RepHlt		815	7 3/4	8 1/2	...
RepWste		203	7	7 1/4	...
RschFt		12	3 7/8	4 1/2	...
Ripley		z60	3	4	...
Roadmst		325	1 1/32	1 1/16	+1/32
Robesn		20	23/32	7/8	...
RckyMt		44	1 1/16	1 5/16	...
RkMt un		9	1 3/16	1 5/16	...
Rodime	.02e	50	7/32	1/4	...
RoosInv		50	1 5/8	1 3/4	−1/16
RossInd		10	2 1/8	2 1/2	...
Ryka		263	1 13/16	1 7/8	+1/16
-S-S-S-					
SI Hand		20	4 5/8	5	−1/4
SK Tch		223	4	4 1/8	−1/16
SOI Ind		62	1 7/8	2 1/8	...
SSMC pf		481	31 1/4	32 1/2	...
STOR		10	7	7 1/4	...
S2 Golf		281	3 1/16	3 1/4	...
SageAnl		238	4 1/4	4 1/2	−1/8
SIM wt s		1638	13	13 1/4	−1/4
Sandata		5	1 7/16	1 19/32	−1/32
Santos	.58e	6	13 1/4	13 1/2	+1/8
Saztec		4	3	3 3/8	...
ScanG s		402	1 1/8	1 1/4	−1/8
Scllm un		54	6 1/2	7	...
ScreBd s		29	9 1/8	9 1/2	...
Scorpn		51	1 1/8	1 1/4	...
SelTrn		117	13/16	15/16	...
Selvac		113	1 1/8	1 5/32	...
Senetek		666	2 13/16	2 7/8	−1/16
SenrSv		25	3 1/4	3 1/2	...
ShrdTc		325	3 7/8	4 1/8	...
Shredta		558	2	2 1/8	+1/16
ShrtShd		1545	4 3/8	4 15/32	+7/16
ShrtTke		50	1 13/16	2	...
SkyChill		126	4 1/4	4 3/8	...
Smtl wtA		297	6 7/8	7 1/4	+1/8
Smtl wtB		995	2 5/8	2 7/8	+1/8
SftwrDv		226	8 1/8	8 3/8	−5/8
Solltec		648	1 3/4	2 1/4	...
SolvEx		1021	2	2 1/8	−3/16
SonexR		93	15/16	1 1/16	−1/16
SonoTk		50	2 7/8	3	−1/8
SouEdc		30	4	5	...
SoPcPt		1810	23/32	25/32	+1/16
Sthld pf h	†	520	9/32	3/8	−1/32
SpecRet		116	1 1/2	1 5/8	...
Spctrln		463	1 13/16	1 7/8	+1/16
SprtTch		40	4 1/4	4 1/2	...
StdOil s		214	5 1/4	5 7/8	−1 3/8
StateBc	.33r	z34	11	12 3/4	...
StrlMed		230	2	2 1/32	+1/8
StevelC		35	2	2 1/8	...
Steve wt		25	3/8	1/2	...
StrtAm s	.02e	5	1 9/16	1 3/4	...
SuburB		11	5 1/4	5 1/2	...
Sulcus		91	2 1/8	2 1/4	+1/8
Sulcus un		235	4 7/8	5 3/8	+1/4
SumtFn		23	9 3/4	10 3/4	...
SumitNt	†	16	6 3/4	8 1/4	...
SumitTc		1329	14 1/2	14 5/8	+1/8
SunrsPr		6	2 3/4	3	...
SunrTc		344	5 3/16	5 3/8	+1/16
Sunrst		50	5 7/8	6 1/2	+1/8
SupRt pf	†	23	7 3/4	8 1/2	...
SuprSol		64	3	3 1/8	...
Swank		4	1 1/4	1 1/2	...
Syntc pf		10	6	6 3/4	...
Synthe		152	1 1/32	1 1/8	...
-T-T-T-					
TEL Off	1.15e	44	4 3/8	4 5/8	...
TSS un		43	4 3/8	4 1/2	+3/8
Tauntn		117	10 1/2	11 1/2	...
Techne		150	2 3/8	2 1/2	...
Tecngn		86	1 3/16	1 5/16	...
TcRsh un		z20	480	520	...
TelArt s		72	2 3/16	2 5/16	...
Telenet		64	1 1/2	1 7/8	...
Telt un		10	3	3 3/8	...
Tenet		20	1 1/8	1 3/8	...
TeraM g		5	1/8	3/16	...

EXHIBIT 10-3. ***The Wall Street Journal*****—Mutual Fund Quotes**

C18 THE WALL STREET JOURNAL THURSDAY, MAY 31, 1990

MUTUAL FUND QUOTATIONS

Wednesday, May 30, 1990

Price ranges for investment companies, as quoted by the National Association of Securities Dealers. NAV stands for net asset value per share; the offering includes net asset value plus maximum sales charge, if any.

	NAV	Offer Price	NAV Chg.
AAL Mutual:			
CaGr p	11.66	12.24	+ .01
Inco p	9.43	9.90	+ .01
MuBd p	9.85	10.34	.....
AARP Invst:			
CaGr	29.91	NL	+ .04
GiniM	14.94	NL	+ .03
GthInc	24.68	NL	+ .06
HQ Bd	14.77	NL	+ .04
TxFBd	16.44	NL	.....
TxFSh	15.13	NL	.....
ABT Funds:			
Emrg p	9.47	9.94	.....
GthIn p	9.76	10.25	− .01
SecIn p	9.80	10.29	− .02
UtilIn p	12.84	13.48	− .03
AHA Bal	10.84	NL	+ .01
AdsnCa p	18.30	18.87	+ .04
ADTEK	9.70	9.70	.....
AFA NAv	12.06	12.66	.....
AFA Tele	18.06	18.96	− .11
AIM Funds:			
Chart p	6.89	7.29	+ .01
Const p	9.28	9.82	.....
CvYld p	10.83	11.37	+ .05
HiYld p	6.39	6.71	+ .02
LimM p	9.75	9.92	.....
Sumit	8.25	.....	+ .02
Weing p	12.90	13.65	+ .03
A M A Family:			
ClaGt p	8.96	NL	+ .01
GlbGt p	22.87	NL	+ .13
GlbIn p	19.39	NL	+ .03
GIST p	9.88	NL	.....
USGv p	8.49	NL	+ .01
AMEV Funds:			
AstAl p	11.96	12.52	+ .02
Capitl p	15.85	16.64	+ .01
CaAp p	17.63	18.46	+ .03
Fidcr p	26.37	27.61	+ .03
Grwth p	21.63	22.71	+ .05
HiYld p	7.10	7.43	.....
TF MN	9.60	10.05	+ .01
TF Nat	9.82	10.28	+ .01
US Gvt	9.49	9.94	+ .01
AcornF	43.45	43.45	− .02
Afuture	10.24	NL	+ .10
Advance America:			
EqInc	10.37	10.89	+ .07
TF Inc	9.68	10.16	.....
US Gov	9.16	9.62	+ .01
Advest Advant:			
Govt p	8.26	8.26	+ .01
Gwth p	14.18	14.18	+ .04
HY Bd p	7.66	7.66	+ .02
Inco p	10.50	10.50	+ .02
Spcl p	12.68	12.68	− .01
AlgrSCp t	16.86	16.86	+ .05
AlgerG t	15.22	15.22	− .02
Alliance Cap:			
Allan p	6.21	6.57	+ .01
Balan p	11.51	12.18	+ .01
Canad p	6.48	6.86	+ .08
Conv p	9.16	9.69	+ .03
Count p	17.23	18.23	.....
Govt p	8.09	8.56	+ .01
GrInc p	2.68	2.84	− .01
HiYld p	5.27	5.58	+ .01
Intl p	17.55	18.57	+ .06
ICalT p	12.18	12.75	+ .01
InsMu	9.40	9.84	+ .01
MonIn p	11.27	11.93	+ .03
Mortg p	8.52	9.02	+ .02
MuCA	9.58	10.03	.....
MuNY	8.92	9.34	.....
NtlMu	9.52	9.97	.....
Quasr p	21.21	22.44	+ .02
ST MIa p	9.79	10.09	+ .02
ST MIb t	9.79	9.79	+ .02
Survy p	11.37	12.03	+ .03
Tech p	24.17	25.58	− .11
AlpnCA	9.90	10.29	.....
Altura Funds:			
Grwth	12.66	NL	+ .02
Inco f	9.94	NL	+ .01
Amer AAdvant:			
Balan	10.65	NL	+ .02
Equity	11.24	NL	+ .01
FixIn	9.74	NL	+ .01
Amer Capital:			
Cmstk	15.89	17.37	+ .03
CpBd p	6.43	6.75	+ .02
Entrp p	12.24	12.99	+ .01
Exch	84.31	.....	+ .50
FdMg p	12.53	13.15	+ .03
FdAm p	11.48	12.18	+ .03
GvSc p	9.91	10.40	+ .02
Harbr p	14.06	14.92	+ .06
HiYld p	6.17	6.48	+ .01
MunB p	18.75	19.69	+ .01
Pace p	25.52	27.08	+ .04
Provid	4.53	4.88	.....
TEHY p	10.75	11.29	.....
TxE I p	10.77	11.31	.....
Ventr p	16.43	17.43	+ .02
AExpEV	12.99	13.26	+ .03
American Funds:			
A Bal p	11.18	11.86	+ .01
PBHG	12.15	12.76	+ .06
Trend	13.79	14.48	+ .01
CarilCa	11.38	11.98	+ .02
Carneg Cappielo:			
EmGr p	9.97	10.44	+ .03
Grow p	17.94	18.78	+ .06
TRetn p	11.90	12.46	.....
Carnegie Funds:			
Govt p	9.15	9.58	+ .02
TEOhG	9.00	9.42	.....
TENHI	9.51	9.96	.....
Cardnl	11.15	12.19	.....
CrdnlGv	8.67	9.10	.....
Cnt Shs	19.24	NL	+ .05
ChpHY p	10.94	11.99	.....
Chestnut	101.32	NL	+ .03
CIGNA Funds:			
Agrsv p	14.37	15.13	+ .02
GvSc p	9.75	10.26	+ .02
Grth p	15.04	15.83	− .02
HiYld p	8.29	8.73	− .01
Inco p	7.43	7.82	+ .02
MunB p	7.65	8.05	.....
Util p	12.90	13.58	− .05
Value p	16.40	17.26	− .05
Citibank IRA-CIT:			
Balan f	2.23	NL	+ .02
Equit f	2.51	NL	+ .02
Incom f	1.94	NL	.....
ShtTr f	1.67	NL	.....
Clipper	42.27	42.27	− .05
Colonial Funds:			
AGold p	19.03	20.41	− .02
CalTE	6.95	7.30	+ .01
CpCsh p	43.40	44.29	− .02
CCsII p	41.49	42.34	.....
DvsdIn	7.13	7.65	+ .15
Fund p	20.21	21.67	+ .03
GvSec p	10.62	11.39	+ .02
Gwth p	12.77	13.69	+ .02
HiYld p	5.82	6.11	− .01
Incom p	6.17	6.48	+ .01
IncPls	8.55	9.17	+ .02
IntEq p	18.83	19.77	+ .23
MATx	7.06	7.41	.....
MI TE	6.48	6.80	.....
MN TE	6.86	7.20	.....
NY TE	6.58	6.91	.....
OhTE	6.78	7.12	.....
SmlIn p	13.44	14.11	+ .04
TXIns p	7.59	7.97	.....
TxEx p	12.87	13.51	.....
US Gv p	6.98	7.33	+ .01
US Id p	17.71	18.59	+ .01
Colonial VIP:			
DvRet t	11.05	11.05	+ .03
FdSec t	9.80	9.80	+ .01
Gwth t	11.96	11.96	+ .05
HiInc t	8.55	8.55	.....
HYMu t	9.82	9.82	− .01
InfHd t	11.14	11.14	.....
Co DTE	9.92	10.32	.....
Columbia Funds:			
Fixed	12.42	NL	+ .02
Grth	24.60	NL	+ .02
Muni	11.52	NL	.....
Specl	44.92	NL	+ .16
Common Sense:			
Govt	10.75	11.53	+ .02
Grwth	13.59	14.85	+ .02
GrInc	13.60	14.86	+ .04
MunB	12.30	12.91	+ .01
CwlthBI	2.08	2.25	.....
Compass Capital:			
EqInc x	10.34	10.83	− .04
FxdIn x	9.80	10.26	− .04
Grwth x	11.24	11.77	− .02
ShInt x	9.93	10.40	− .05
Composite Group:			
BdStk p	10.46	10.90	+ .02
Gwth p	11.04	11.50	+ .03
InFd p	8.17	8.51	+ .01
NW50 p	22.94	24.02	+ .05
TxEx p	7.07	7.36	.....
USGv p	9.84	10.25	+ .01
Conn Mutual:			
Govt	10.36	10.85	+ .03
Grwth	13.60	14.51	+ .02
TotRet	13.00	13.87	+ .02
Copley	13.85	NL	− .02
Counsellors Fd:			
CapAp	11.56	NL	+ .05
EGth	13.77	NL	+ .07
FixInc	9.39	NL	+ .01
IntEqu	12.81	NL	+ .05
IntGvt	10.10	NL	+ .01
NYMu	9.53	NL	+ .01
CtryCa	17.46	18.00	− .01
Cowen t	11.01	11.57	+ .03
CownOp p	12.71	13.36	+ .02
CmbldG	10.52	10.52	+ .02
DR Funds:			
Bal	10.24	NL	+ .02
Equity	11.71	NL	+ .02
EurEq	10.21	NL	+ .09
Dean Witter:			
AmVI t	15.15	15.15	+ .03
CalTF t	11.89	11.89	+ .01
EqStrat	26.29	NL	− .47
EurEm p	13.50	14.14	+ .02
Evergreen Funds:			
Evgrn	12.20	NL	+ .03
TotRtn	18.10	NL	+ .03
ValTm	12.18	NL	+ .01
LtdMk	17.65	NL	.....
ExcelMid	2.89	3.03	− .02
ExcHY p	7.26	7.62	+ .01
FBL Gth t	11.00	11.00	+ .01
FPA Funds:			
Capit	14.16	15.14	+ .02
NwInc	9.56	10.01	+ .01
Parmt	12.81	13.70	+ .06
Peren	20.73	22.17	+ .05
Fairmt	15.11	NL	+ .07
Federated Funds:			
FCCT	7.75	NL	.....
Exch	57.13	NL	+ .07
FBF	8.98	NL	+ .02
FIGT	9.53	NL	+ .01
FFRT	9.18	NL	− .01
GNMA	10.90	NL	+ .02
FGRO	20.81	NL	+ .07
FHYT	7.92	NL	.....
FIT	10.15	NL	+ .01
FIMT	9.84	NL	.....
FSIMT	10.12	NL	.....
FSIGT	9.93	NL	+ .01
FSBF	15.29	NL	+ .03
FST	23.51	NL	+ .02
FGVT	9.18	NL	+ .03
Fenimre	14.38	15.14	.....
Fidelity Invest:			
AgTF r	11.36	11.36	+ .01
A Mgr	11.16	NL	+ .02
Balanc	11.18	NL	+ .04
BluCh	15.34	15.65	+ .02
CA TF	11.14	NL	.....
CA In	9.56	NL	+ .01
Canad r	14.49	14.79	+ .12
CapAp r	16.50	16.84	+ .04
CngS	122.37	.....	+ .16
ConnT	10.55	NL	.....
Contra	17.92	NL	+ .05
CnvSc	11.76	NL	+ .03
DisEq	14.21	14.65	+ .03
Eq Inc	25.58	26.10	+ .11
EqIdx	13.85	NL	+ .01
Europ r	17.86	18.22	+ .05
Exch	84.24	.....	+ .36
Fidel	18.37	NL	+ .05
FlexB	6.69	NL	+ .01
Fredm	15.55	NL	+ .08
GloBd	11.23	NL	+ .02
GNMA	10.20	NL	+ .02
GovtSc	9.36	NL	+ .02
GroInc	17.42	17.78	+ .05
GroCo	20.95	21.60	+ .04
HiInc	6.78	NL	.....
HiYld	12.24	NL	+ .01
InsMu	10.92	NL	.....
IntBd	9.84	NL	+ .02
IntGr r	14.03	14.17	+ .02
LtdMn	9.19	NL	.....
LowP r	10.53	10.53	+ .02
Magln	59.80	61.65	+ .13
MI TF	10.87	NL	+ .01
MA TF	11.03	NL	+ .01
MN TF	10.36	NL	+ .01
MtgSc	10.05	NL	+ .01
MunBd	8.05	NL	.....
Oh TF	10.63	NL	+ .01
NJ HY	10.43	NL	+ .01
NY HY	11.56	NL	.....
NY Ins	10.76	NL	.....
OTC	20.71	21.35	+ .10
Ovrse	29.85	30.77	+ .03
PcBas r	14.60	14.90	+ .09
Puritn	13.45	13.72	+ .03
RealEs	9.12	NL	+ .05
ShtBd	9.25	NL	.....
ShtTGv	9.85	NL	+ .01
Sht TF	9.45	NL	.....
SpcSit	18.47	19.39	+ .04
TX TF	10.30	NL	+ .01
Trend	43.72	NL	+ .08
UtilInc	11.73	NL	+ .01
Value	28.59	NL	− .04
Fidl Inv Instit:			
CTAR r	8.20	NL	.....
EqP G	17.45	NL	+ .08
EqP I	11.31	NL	+ .05
IP LTD	10.05	NL	+ .01
IP SG	9.37	NL	.....
TE Ltd	10.52	NL	+ .01
QualD	10.77	NL	.....
Fidelity Selects:			
SIAir r	11.76	12.00	+ .01
SIAGI r	16.43	16.77	− .07
SIBio r	17.35	17.70	+ .10
SIBrd r	12.85	13.11	+ .04
SIBrk r	8.70	8.88	+ .05
SIChe r	24.69	25.19	+ .04
SICmp r	14.39	14.68	+ .01
SIDef r	12.76	13.02	+ .04
SIElec r	10.45	10.66	+ .03
SIEUt r	10.74	10.96	− .02
SIEng r	17.59	17.95	+ .09
SIEnS r	14.00	14.29	+ .27
SIEnv r	12.46	12.71	+ .07
SIFnS r	30.67	31.30	+ .10
SIFd r	24.78	25.29	+ .11
SIHlth r	52.28	53.35	+ .22
SIInd r	13.09	13.36	.....
Franklin Mgd Tr:			
CpCsh p	20.05	20.36	− .03
InvGd p	8.38	8.73	+ .01
RisDv p	11.38	11.85	.....
Freedom Funds:			
Envrn p	10.12	10.60	+ .07
EqVal t	11.21	11.21	+ .01
Globl t	11.68	11.68	.....
GlbIn t	9.76	9.76	+ .01
Gold t	14.86	14.86	+ .02
GvtIn t	9.80	9.80	+ .03
MgTE t	10.72	10.72	+ .01
RgBk t	11.28	11.28	+ .03
FmntMA	11.08	NL	+ .01
FundTrust:			
Aggr fp	14.06	14.27	+ .13
Grth fp	13.44	13.64	+ .14
GroI fp	14.36	14.58	+ .15
Inco f	9.29	9.43	+ .01
GIT Invst:			
EqSpc	18.17	NL	+ .05
HiYd	10.55	NL	.....
InMax	7.15	NL	.....
TFVA	10.95	NL	.....
GNA p	9.53	9.53	+ .02
GS CapG	11.65	12.33	.....
GT Global:			
Amer p	14.69	15.42	.....
Bond p	10.63	11.16	.....
Euro p	11.40	11.97	.....
GvInc p	10.04	10.54	.....
HltCr p	13.48	14.15	.....
Intl p	9.19	9.65	.....
Japan p	15.63	16.41	.....
Pacif p	12.51	13.13	.....
Wldw p	13.85	14.54	.....
GW Sierra Tr:			
CalBd	9.93	9.93	.....
GvSec	9.87	9.87	+ .01
GrInc	10.31	10.31	+ .01
Galaxy Funds:			
Bond	9.86	10.32	+ .02
Equity	11.21	11.74	+ .02
Gabelli Funds:			
Asset t	16.95	16.95	+ .01
CnvSc	10.71	NL	+ .01
Gwth p	17.72	NL	+ .10
Value p	9.63	10.19	+ .02
GatwyGr			unavail
GatwyIn			unavail
Geico fp	17.00	NL	− .02
Gen Elec Inv:			
ElfDiv	12.05	NL	.....
ElfGI	12.67	NL	+ .08
ElfnIn	10.75	NL	+ .01
ElfnTr	32.28	NL	− .01
ElfnTx	10.96	NL	+ .02
S&S	36.40	NL	+ .03
S&S Lg	10.94	NL	+ .02
GenSec	11.98	12.62	− .01
Gintel Group:			
CaAp p	14.04	14.04	− .10
Erisa p	33.68	33.68	− .10
Gintel	78.13	78.13	− .30
Gradison Funds:			
EstGr p	17.95	NL	+ .02
GvIn p	12.65	12.91	+ .03
OpGr p	14.24	NL	+ .04
Grnspg	13.03	NL	− .03
GwWsh p	13.02	13.71	.....
Grth Ind	8.36	8.36	+ .04
Guardian Funds:			
Bond	11.79	NL	+ .01
ParkA	21.78	22.81	+ .04
Stock	21.50	NL	+ .03
HTInsE p	11.21	11.74	+ .05
HanColo	9.35	9.82	+ .01
Harbor Funds:			
CapAp	13.42	NL	+ .06
Grwth	13.24	NL	+ .06
Intl	17.72	NL	+ .05
Value	13.39	NL	− .01
Hartwell Fds:			
EGth	17.92	18.81	+ .26
Gwth	20.61	21.64	+ .01
HrvstG p	9.40	9.97	+ .04
HeartG p	9.05	9.48	+ .01
HeartId p	14.18	14.85	+ .08
Helmsman Fds:			
DscEq	10.74	NL	− .03
GrEq	11.97	NL	+ .05
Inco	9.48	NL	+ .01
IncEq	11.23	NL	.....
Heritge p	12.10	12.60	+ .02
HrtgCv p	9.24	9.63	.....
HiMark	10.97	NL	+ .01
Home Group:			
GvSec	9.29	9.75	+ .02
GroInc	12.44	13.06	− .04
HY Bd	7.75	8.14	.....
NatTF p			unavail
Hor Man	19.43	NL	.....
Hummer	16.88	NL	− .01
Huntingtn Fds:			
Globl	13.77	14.09	− .04
Hard	13.36	13.67	− .08
HiInc	12.97	13.27	+ .02
IAI Funds:			
Apollo	13.05	13.05	− .01
Bond	9.83	9.83	+ .03
IntFd	11.24	11.24	+ .03
Region	20.12	20.12	− .02
Resve	10.21	10.21	.....
Stock	16.04	16.04	.....
IDS Group:			

Returning to Exhibit 10-3, the first listing is for AAL Mutual's Capital Growth Fund. The Net Asset Value is $11.66 per share. Since this is a load fund, the offering price of $12.24 per share is higher than the NAV.

Bond Quotations

Bonds listed on the New York and American exchanges are quoted in most daily newspapers, but prices on Over-the-Counter bonds are not as readily accessible. Exhibit 10-4 illustrates the most common format for bond quotations. Bond abbreviations are similar to those of their corresponding stocks, but not necessarily identical. Bond prices are quoted as percentages of par. Since most bonds have a par value of $1,000, the figure can be converted to a dollar amount by multiplying the number by 10. For example, the closing price for Boise Cascade (BoisC) is reported in the Exhibit as 105 1/2, which translates into $1,055 per bond. Advest (Advst) bonds are selling at a discount on this day, with a price of $750.

Many companies have more than one bond issue outstanding at one time and, as can be seen in Exhibit 10-4, some companies have quite a few. The numbers immediately following each company abbreviation distinguish the individual bonds of each firm. Two key characteristics are identified: its coupon rate of interest, and its year of maturity. The example of American Telephone & Telegraph (ATT) illustrates how bonds are differentiated. The first ATT bond carries a coupon rate of 5 5/8% annually, which means each bond pays the holder $56.25 per year (.05625 x $1,000). The "95" following the coupon rate indicates the bond can be redeemed at some point in 1995. The "s" seen after the coupon rate in some quotations is merely a device used to separate the interest rate from the maturity. This is a convenience to make reading the table easier and is shown where the interest rate does not contain a fraction. Other columns in the exhibit give the closing price and the net change over the previous day's close. The volume of trading is listed as the actual number of bonds sold. For example, the "10" appearing in the quotation for Boise Cascade reports ten bonds were sold that day. The current yield represents the relationship between the bond's coupon rate and its current price.

Many other securities quotations can be consulted on a daily basis. Most daily newspapers only carry stock, bond, and mutual fund listings, but papers with extensive financial coverage will include quotes for options, futures, foreign securities, federal and municipal bonds, and more. Space does not permit an analysis of all quotations available, but the previously mentioned *Investor's Guide to Stock Quotations* provides a detailed and interesting discussion of all major financial listings and how to decipher them.

BASIC SOURCES OF FINANCIAL QUOTATIONS

The raw data used for investment analysis are available in a variety of forms. Daily, weekly, and monthly publications provide information on securities prices, volume of trading, and other key measures of investment performance. Many nonprint sources are also available. The remainder of the chapter will introduce representative sources of basic financial data.

Published Quotations

Investment data available in the local newspaper are usually limited, but several daily or weekly newspapers specialize in reporting financial information, including extensive market quotes. Users of all kinds rely on securities quotations for a variety of reasons. Tracking the price fluctuations in certain bellwether securities can provide information on the performance of the economy as a whole. Investors follow the current day's prices, of course, but retrospective data are also important. Technical analysts rely on historical data to graph a security's performance and predict trends. Attorneys use historical price data when valuing estates, and tax preparers need historical quotes to determine their clients' capital gains. Because of this wide interest in security prices, users can subscribe to all sorts of quotation sources. The choice of printed publications has dwindled in recent years, due in part to the widespread use of computerized quotation services. The *Media General Financial Weekly*, for example, has ceased publication as a newspaper, though it remains available in electronic format. One of the most useful print sources for detailed stock quotes, the weekly *Commercial & Financial Chronicle*, dropped its security listings after it was sold to another publisher.

The Wall Street Journal (Dow Jones—Five Times per Week).

The *Journal* is the most frequently consulted financial daily in the United States. It provides much more than just securities quotations, but the detailed financial tables are one reason for its popularity. The data are

EXHIBIT 10-4. *The Wall Street Journal*—Bond Quotes

provided by a variety sources, including information compiled by Dow Jones itself. Stock quotes for the New York and American exchanges come from the Associated Press, while NASDAQ quotes are provided by UPI. Daily listings for NYSE and AMEX stocks and bonds exclude data for securities that did not trade that day, but the Monday issue of the paper contains a separate list of bid and asked prices for stocks not traded in the previous week. Where most newspapers offer listings for the National Market System only, the *Journal* also publishes daily tables for additional heavily traded NASDAQ stocks. NASDAQ quotes for less heavily traded stocks appear in a special table in Monday's *Journal*.

Other quotations include mutual funds, bonds, stock options, commodity futures, a diversity of options and futures contracts for indexes and interest rates, cash prices for selected commodities, and a separate table for daily oil prices. The *Journal* also carries brief listings for most regional exchanges, two major Canadian exchanges, American Deposit Receipts (certificates representing foreign stocks and bonds traded in this country, denominated in U.S. dollars), and a select list of quotes from foreign stock exchanges. A complete roster of U.S. Treasury securities appears daily, as does a list of federal agency bonds. As with most daily papers, it provides only the briefest coverage of municipal bonds on a daily basis, but a special list of "inactive, but widely-held" municipals can be seen on Mondays. Detailed foreign exchange data are reported daily. For 50 countries, exchange rates are given both in U.S. dollars and the national currency. Most currency tables only allow the user to measure exchange rates with the United States, but the *Journal* also provides a separate grid which, for ten leading countries, shows each country's exchange rate in relation to the other nine. This cross-rates table is supplied daily by Bank America. Every Monday, a more extensive list of exchange rates for nearly every country in the world is published, again compiled by Bank America.

Financial statistics in *The Wall Street Journal* are not limited to price quotations. A daily "Digest of Earnings Reports" summarizes quarterly corporate income statements as they are released by the companies. Upcoming dividends on stocks are also listed daily, as they are announced by the firms. Other daily tables show new stock offerings, changes in bond ratings, and interest rates on recently issued corporate bonds. Data from well-known proprietary sources appear on a daily or weekly basis. These include average yields on bank certificates of deposit (from Banxquote Money Market, on Fridays), the best and worst performing mutual funds (from Lipper

Analytical Services, daily, with Lipper indexes reported on Mondays), and insider trading data (from Invest/Net, Inc., on Wednesdays). The *Journal* also provides a detailed monthly list of short selling activity on the NYSE, and a popular quarterly table that compares the profits of 500 major corporations.

A broad array of general market barometers also appears daily in the *Journal*. For example, a series of tables and graphs shows the hour-by-hour fluctuation of the four Dow Jones Stock Averages (to be discussed in the next chapter). The "Stock Market Data Bank" cites daily summaries for seven other stock market averages which are carefully watched by investors, and three "Diaries" describe the behavior of the New York and American Exchanges and the Over-the-Counter market. The Diaries summarize trading activity on each of the three markets: the total shares traded, the number of stocks that went up in price ("advances"), the number that declined, and the number of stocks which reached a new high or low that day. The individual stocks that had the highest volume of trading and those which had the largest fluctuation in price (up and down) are listed separately. Additional tables give an index of stock prices by industry group (compiled by Shearson Lehman), and the P/E ratios and yields for each of the Dow Jones indexes. A detailed "Bond Data Bank" also appears daily. A rotating daily feature is found on the front page of the "Money and Investing" section. Called "Investment Insight," it presents popular market indicators in tabular and graphic form. Examples include stock price averages from foreign stock exchanges, rankings by yield of the 30 stocks comprising the Dow, and various bond indexes calculated by Merrill Lynch. All of the tables mentioned above, from the "Data Bank" to "Investment Insight," save the reader the chore of gleaning summary information and highlights from the thousands of quotations appearing in each day's paper.

Covering investment quotations is not the *Journal*'s sole purpose, but the paper does an excellent job in the scant pages it allots to the task. Despite the emergence of newcomers in financial publishing, and the enduring presence of respectable dailies like the *New York Times*, the *Journal* remains the leading business newspaper in the country.

Investor's Daily (Investor's Daily, Inc.—Five Times per Week).

In April 1984, William J. O'Neil, the publisher of several investment advisory services, launched an alternative to *The Wall Street Journal* called *Investor's Daily*. This paper eschews the lengthy, wide-ranging articles

that are the hallmark of the *Journal* and concentrates on investment information. Stories are brief, emphasizing news of public companies, economic conditions, and market behavior. The majority of pages are devoted to financial tables. For these reasons, *Investor's Daily* should not be viewed as a replacement for *The Wall Street Journal* as the main source of general business news. It is an excellent source of additional information, and many serious investors subscribe to both publications. *Investor's Daily* does present numerous articles analyzing companies and industries in the news. To assist readers in locating articles of interest, a weekly "Index of Investor's Daily Features" appears on Fridays. This column provides an alphabetical index to the companies and industries covered in special articles during the prior three months.

The great strength of *Investor's Daily* is the quality of its financial tables. These include many statistical measures not seen in standard listings, and often unique to the O'Neil database. The stock quotes are billed as "The World's Most Intelligent Stock Tables." They include standard information such as 52-week highs and lows; daily high, low, and closing prices; daily change; and P/E ratios; but also contain four other useful calculations. Among them are rankings for every stock based on earnings performance and relative price strength. Both measures are reported on a scale of 1-99. Bond tables cite Standard & Poor's bond ratings and Yield To Maturity calculations. Other significant differences are daily tables measuring industry performance for 196 industries and detailed graphs of stock performance for companies in the news. Up to 100 such graphs are printed daily. Most of the quotation tables and statistical summaries in the *Journal* can be found in *Investor's Daily* as well, from foreign exchange rates to earnings announcements. Many are virtually identical, but others are not. In some instances the *Journal* offers more detail; in others, *Investor's Daily* has the advantage. For example, the *Journal* prints more proprietary data from other sources, and a broader array of market indicators. *Investor's Daily* provides more extensive quotes for securities outside the mainstream markets, such as foreign issues, thinly traded NASDAQ stocks, and convertible bonds. Another advantage to *Investor's Daily* is that few statistical features appear on a rotating basis; virtually every table is published daily.

For several years, *Investor's Daily* was not covered by any periodical indexes. Retrospective access is now available online through the *Investor's Daily Database*, offered exclusively on BRS. It contains both bibliographic citations and abstracts to articles, updated monthly. The database is compiled by Bowker Business Research. The complete text of *Investor's Daily* is also available electronically through LEXIS/NEXIS.

Barron's National Business and Financial Weekly (Dow Jones & Company—Weekly).

This tabloid-sized weekly, published since 1921, ranks with *Fortune, Forbes*, and *Business Week* as one of the best-known business periodicals in the United States. *Barron's* is written exclusively for investors, and is frequently consulted for its detailed financial tables. The "Market Week" section takes up about one-third of each issue, and is made up of two parts. The "Week's Market Transactions" presents over 50 pages of securities quotations, while the "Market Laboratory" offers five pages of financial statistics.

Barron's is received by subscribers on Monday, and contains investment data for the previous week. The format of financial tables is similar to its daily cousin, *The Wall Street Journal*, although *Barron's* lists the high, low, and closing prices for the week as a whole. For many investors, this is a welcome alternative to following a security's price from day to day. The tables in *Barron's* also list prices for every security, whether traded the previous week or not. Tables are easier to read than those in the *Journal*; larger print and more spacing create listings that are much less cramped. Finally, the stock tables give slightly more data than standard listings, showing more complete information on dividends and corporate earnings.

The "Week's Transactions" also provides more comprehensive coverage of NASDAQ stocks, fairly good coverage of regional and Canadian exchanges, and stock option tables laid out in a very convenient format. This section includes other helpful features such as a listing of dividend payments made the previous week (as opposed to dividends declared), and a list of research reports recently published by Wall Street analysts.

The "Market Laboratory" section provides summary measures of security performance similar to the *Journal*'s "Data Bank," but in more complete fashion. It is considered the most convenient form of comprehensive market information available on a weekly basis. In fact, many of the rotating features shown in a Monday or Wednesday issue of the *Journal* can be found more readily in *Barron's*. Some of the special features in this section are a list of new stock issues due the following week, a list of companies currently being analyzed by major Wall Street brokerage houses, a summary of "large block" stock transactions (trades of more than 10,000 shares), and "Barron's Group Stock Averages." *Barron's*

also prints data from other proprietary sources, such as the "Lipper Mutual Fund Performance Averages," yields on various bank deposits from the *Bank Rate Monitor* and *Rate%Gram*, and credit card interest rates from *Bankcard Barometer*. The sources of these outside statistics tend to vary over time, but they offer diverse coverage of financial markets. Unquestionably, *Barron's* offers the most diverse compilation of market indicators of any investment publication.

National Monthly Stock Summary (National Quotation Bureau—Monthly, with Cumulations).

The best source of prices for non-NASDAQ stocks is not sold to libraries or members of the general public. The *National Daily Quotation Service*, known to the investment community as the "Pink Sheets," is a daily service, available only to brokers, dealers, and other investment professionals. It provides bid and asked prices for about 11,000 OTC stocks. Data are submitted by OTC market makers across the country. For those without access to the "Pink Sheets," the Bureau sells two non-controlled publications: the *NQB Monthly Price Report*, and the *National Monthly Stock Summary*.

The *NQB Monthly Price Report* covers all stocks found in the "Pink Sheets," but gives monthly and annual prices only. The format is a bit cumbersome to deal with, which is one reason why the service is found in so few libraries. It is issued as a stapled packet of 8 1/2" x 14" sheets of newsprint, printed on both sides. Every listing cites the previous month's high and low bid price, the closing bid and ask price for the month, the net change from the previous month, the price range for the year, and whether the current price represents a new high or low for the year. Additional facts include the NASD symbol for the stock, whether the stock is traded through NASDAQ, an indication of whether the stock is marginable under Federal Reserve regulations (i.e., investors can buy shares on credit), and whether the company underwent any recent changes in capital structure. Newly issued stocks are also designated. The *Monthly Price Report* is not recommended for everyone, but for researchers, investors, and libraries in need of frequent OTC quotes, the service is invaluable.

An alternative publication from the National Quotation Bureau is a paperback service entitled the *National Monthly Stock Summary*. Unlike the *Monthly Price Report*, it is located in many large public libraries. The information found here is more detailed in some respects and less so in others. One noticeable difference between the two services is that the *National Monthly Stock Summary* reports on both OTC and listed stocks. For stocks traded on an exchange or through NASDAQ, it cites the closing price for the previous month. For non-NASDAQ stocks, it lists the closing bid and ask prices for every reporting market maker. This information identifies who the market makers are and shows comparative market prices. For those stocks where no recent prices have been reported, the service quotes the latest available figures and the date. A history of major capital changes and historical price ranges can be found for many stocks. The *National Monthly Stock Summary* is also an excellent source for locating prices and terms for stock warrants.

A hardcover cumulation of the *National Monthly Stock Summary* is issued twice per year, in January and July. In addition to the information found in the other monthly issues, the semiannual editions list the company address, its transfer agent, the number of shares outstanding, and any former names. It also serves as a guide to defunct firms and an index to name changes. These features make it one of the best resources for verifying the existence of obscure stocks. Corresponding monthly and semiannual publications are also published for the bond market, under the name *National Monthly Bond Summary*. The two semiannual editions can be purchased directly from the National Quotation Bureau, or from another commercial publisher, Facts On File. The Facts On File editions are reprinted under the titles *Directory of Publicly Traded Stocks* and *Directory of Publicly Traded Bonds*.

Investors and researchers accustomed to seeing daily quotes for listed and NASDAQ stocks might question the usefulness of price information that is reported only once a month, but the importance of these publications from the National Quotation Bureau cannot be overemphasized. First, readers should remember that the price of a thinly traded stock may vary little over the course of a month. Even when prices fluctuate, these services provide a general idea of the range in which a stock is trading. For many purposes, including income tax reporting, this is usually sufficient. And for those who need a more precise current quote, brokers are typically happy to oblige.

National OTC Stock Journal (OTC Stock Journal, Inc.—Biweekly).

The *National OTC Stock Journal* publishes stock tables for the complete NASDAQ list, but its real value is the price data on non-NASDAQ companies. End-of-week bid prices are cited for approximately 1,400 unlisted stocks. Information is gathered directly from the market makers by telephone. The *National OTC Stock Journal* also prints an extensive list of new stock registrations and a brief guide to insider trading activity. The bulk of each issue is taken up by news articles and other

narrative features. Though it tracks far fewer stocks than the previously mentioned publications, this service is noteworthy for its more current quotes.

Several other newspapers and magazines publish stock quotes for regional listings and OTC firms. A number of these popular periodicals are aimed at small investors, and most are issued monthly. A good example is *Individual Investor*, which offers articles, syndicated columns, listings of new securities offerings, earnings reports, insider trading data, and several stock tables. The latter include an extensive NASDAQ list and a guide to more than 400 "Pink Sheet" stocks. The NASDAQ list cites monthly high and low, a mid-month closing price, a 52-week high and low, and monthly percent change. Data in this table are provided by Media General Financial Services. The non-NASDAQ list reports bid and ask prices for a single day (with about 1 1/2 months time lag), plus a 52-week price range. This information comes directly from the National Quotation Bureau. *Individual Investor* is published by Financial Data Systems, Inc. Another popular newspaper is a biweekly tabloid from PSN Communications, Inc. called *Today's Investor*. It offers general articles for the small investor, plus stock tables for NASDAQ and for several regional exchanges.

Daily Stock Price Record (Standard & Poor's Corporation—Quarterly).

Since the early 1960s, the *Daily Stock Price Record* (*DSPR*) has been the most convenient printed guide to retrospective prices. It is published in three editions, one each for the NYSE, the AMEX, and the Over-the-Counter market. All NYSE and AMEX stocks are cited, and about 6,000 OTC firms. The OTC volumes are divided into three parts, covering mutual funds, banks and insurance companies, and all other firms. Otherwise, the listings are alphabetical by company name. Every volume provides daily quotes for the entire quarter, with all the prices for a company displayed on a single page.

Exhibit 10-5 is a sample page from the NYSE edition for the fourth quarter of 1984. Using the example of Chesebrough Ponds, we can see that 27,700 shares were traded on Friday, November 23, and the closing price was $36 per share. The high was 36 4/8 and the low was 35 6/8; the symbol preceding 35 6/8 indicates this was also the low price for the week. Following each week of data are three figures: the total volume traded that week (123,600 shares), a ratio of relative strength compared to the Dow Jones Industrial Average (2.99%), and the average closing price over the past 30 days (35 7/8). At the bottom of each page is the current Earnings Per Share based on the previous four quarterly earnings ($3.18 per share), the latest quarterly dividend paid ($.48

per share), and the annualized divident ($1.92 per share). Below these figures is the monthly volume of shares that investors "sold short" in the past year.

Every issue of the *DSPR* also contains a brief section called "Major Technical Indicators," which provides day-by-day statistics for popular stock market measures. Statistics appearing here include the Dow Jones Industrial Average, the Standard & Poor's 500, the volume of odd-lot trading, NYSE Advances and Declines, and the Dow Jones Average Bond Yields.

Electronic Quote Systems

Electronic quotation sources have completely opened the world of securities price research. What was once a time-consuming task has become quite simple for those with access to specialized databases. Quotations of all types are readily available electronically, from stocks to commodities futures. Whether the request is for up-to-the minute quotations or a price from ten years ago, there are a number of alternatives to printed sources. Quotes can be retrieved via dedicated terminals, online systems, floppy diskettes, and other media. The following section presents a brief overview of the possibilities, limited for brevity to stock quotes.

Price data can be obtained through dedicated systems called ticker services and quotation terminals. A stock ticker provides continuous trade-by-trade quotations throughout the day, as transactions occur. Quotations can be reported via teletype machines, electronic display boards, or video terminal. Even people not interested in the stock market recognize ticker quotations because they are a common component of cable television programming. The summary data from ITS appears in the daily newspapers, but the consolidated ticker system records each transaction as it happens. Ticker displays seen on the floor of a stock exchange or in the office of a large brokerage firm report the transactions on a virtually instantaneous basis. This is known as "real time" data. Most ticker displays available to the general public report data with a 15- or 20-minute time lag.

Ticker services are not interactive; the viewer can only watch price information as it scrolls by. Other systems have been designed to enable the user to request and retrieve specific information for stock prices on demand. The most sophisticated interactive systems are called quote terminals, dedicated computer terminals which allow the user to type requests on a keyboard and review the information on a video screen. Leading producers of quote terminal systems are Quotron Systems, Inc.; Automatic Data Processing, Inc. (ADP) and its

EXHIBIT 10-5. *Daily Stock Price Record*

	CHESEBROUGH PONDS INC COM				CHEVRON CORPORATION COM				CHICAGO&N WESTN TRANSN CL A				CHICAGO MILWAUKEE CORP COM				CHICAGO MILWAUKEE CORP PR PFD $5				
	TICKER SYMBOL		THOUS SH OUTSTANDING		TICKER SYMBOL		THOUS SH OUTSTANDING		TICKER SYMBOL		THOUS SH OUTSTANDING		TICKER SYMBOL		THOUS SH OUTSTANDING		TICKER SYMBOL		THOUS SH OUTSTANDING		
	CBM			34065	CHV			342109	CNW			15974	CHG			2452	CHG *			478	
	VOL	HIGH	LOW	CLOSE	VOL	HIGH	LOW	CLOSE	VOL	HIGH	LOW	CLOSE	VOL	HIGH	LOW	CLOSE	VOL	HIGH	LOW	CLOSE	
10/1	603	36-03	35-06	35-07	1851	36-03¤	35-07	36	425	27-06	27-03	27-03	154	172-04	168	168	7¤	71	70-06	71	10/1
2	701	35-07	35-02	35-04	3958	36-04	36	36-02	133	27-02¤	27-01	27-01	58	167-04¤	162-04	166	11	70-04¤	68	68	2
3	559	35-04¤	35	35-02	2398¤	36-06	36-01	36-06	30	27-03	27-01	27-01	37	170-06	166-02	170-02	20	69	68-04	69	3
4	415	35-06	35-02	35-04	1359	36-06	36-02	36-05	153	27-07	27-01	27-07	105¤	177	172	174	16	70	69-04	70	4
5	2278¤	36-05	36	36-02	1844	36-05	35-07	36-01	617¤	28-03	27-04	28-01	91	176	174-06	175			69-04	70-04	5
	4556		2.98	35-03	11410		3.08	35-07	1358		2.34	27-04	445		14.65	140-02	54		5.89	67-06	
8	99	36-04	36-01	36-03	798¤	36	35-05	35-06	2802	28¤	26	26-01	77	175-04¤	172-04	175-04	1	69-06	69-06	69-06	8
9	263	36-04	36-01	36-03	1432	35-06	35-01	35-02	423	26-03	26	26-02	49	177-02	174	175-02	11	69-04	69	69	9
10	225	36-03	36	36-03	4655	35-02	34-03	34-06	1167	27-05	26-04	27-02	150¤	180	175-02	177-04	43¤	70-04	69-04	69-06	10
11	423	36-03¤	35-07	36-01	1620	34-07¤	34-02	34-04	1232¤	28-06	27-03	28	34	178-06	177-04	178-02	2	69-02	69-02	69-02	11
12	421¤	36-05	36	36-03	2070	35-01	34-04	34-07	456	28-06	28-01	28-04	22	177-06	176	176	35	69¤	67	67-04	12
	1431		3.05	35-03	10575		2.91	35-07	6080		2.36	27-02	332		15.06	142-03	92		5.85	67-07	
15	506	36-07	36-03	36-05	1809¤	35-06	34-07	35-04	313¤	28-06	28	28-02	74	178¤	176-02	177	6¤	68-02	67-04	68-02	15
16	324	36-05¤	36-01	36-04	1561	35-02	34-04	34-07	412	28-04	28	28	13	178	177	178			68	68-04	16
17	269	36-05	36-01	36-04	6718	34-04	33-03	33-04	274	28-05	28-01	28-02	132	180-04	177-06	180	18	67-06	67	67	17
18	1284	37-01	36-03	37-01	7366	33-04¤	32	33	1166	28-03	27-06	27-06	18	180-02	179-06	180	3	67-04	67	67-04	18
19	582¤	37-05	36-03	36-03	7249	33-01	32	32-07	1633	28¤	26-04	26-04	109¤	183-04	179-02	182-06	18	67-02¤	66	66	19
	2965		3.02	35-03	24703		2.69	35-07	3798		2.26	27-01	346		14.68	144-04	45		5.50	68-01	
22	303	36-07	36-03	36-04	4487	33-01¤	32-03	32-03	2811	27-06¤	26-04	27-03	33	183-04¤	182-06	183-04	67	65-02¤	62-04	63-06	22
23	596	36-07	36-01	36-04	4228	33-01	32-04	32-05	446	28-04	27-05	27-07	114	191	184	190	29¤	68	64-02	67-04	23
24	3086	37¤	36	36-05	5142	33-01	32-05	33	330	28-04	27-03	28-04	47	192	190-06	191-06	8	67-04	67-04	67-04	24
25	931¤	37-01	36-05	36-07	5005¤	33-04	32-07	33-02	240¤	28-05	28	28-03	38¤	192-02	189	189	2	67-02	66-06	66-06	25
26	816	36-07	36-01	36-01	1945	33-04	32-07	33-04	131	28-01	27-04	27-04	31	190-04	189-06	190-02	10	66	66	66	26
	5732		3.04	35-04	20607		2.74	35-07	3958		2.34	26-07	263		15.60	147	116		5.51	68-03	
29	685¤	36-06	36-02	36-04	9093	33-02¤	32-03	32-03	128¤	27-04	26-06	26-06	61	195	191	195	8¤	65-04	65	65	29
30	1317	36-06	36-02	36-05	10882¤	33-04	32-04	33-01	201	26-06	25-06	26-02	42¤	195-06	193-04	194	24	65-02	64-02	65-02	30
31	760	36-05¤	36	36	4367	33-01	32-05	32-06	908	26-05¤	25-05	26-04	77	193-02¤	189	189	3	64-04	64-02	64-02	31
11/1	1191	36-06	36	36-03	4657	33-02	32-07	33-02	176	26-05	26-02	26-03	36	191-06	189	191-02	18	65-02¤	63-06	64-04	11/1
2	1840	36-05	36	36-04	3863	33-03	33-01	33-02	194	26-01	25-05	25-05	5	191-04	191	191	1	65	65	65	2
	5793		2.98	35-04	32862		2.73	35-06	1607		2.16	26-05	221		15.71	149-04	54		5.29	68-03	
5	499	36-07¤	36-02	36-07	X 5245	33-01¤	32-06	33-01	1586	25-04	24-07	25-03	20¤	190	188-04	188-04	10¤	65-02	64-04	64-06	5
6	616	37-02	36-07	37	2942	33-05	33	33-04	142¤	26-01	25-03	25-06	31	187-06	185-06	186			64-04	65	6
7	509¤	37-03	36-07	37	4055	33-04	33-01	33-03	187	25-06	25-05	25-05	11	185-02	184-06	184-06	18	64	64	64	7
8	272	37-02	36-03	36-07	2875	33-05	33-02	33-04	472	25-06¤	24-04	24-07	12	185	184-04	184-06	13	63-02	62-06	63-02	8
9	604	37-03	37	37-02	2460¤	33-07	33-02	33-02	103	25	24-06	24-07	61	184¤	180-02	180-02	33	62-06¤	62	62	9
	2500		3.00	35-05	17577		2.72	35-05	2490		2.02	26-02	135		15.03	151-04	74		5.14	68-02	
12	127	37-03	37	37-03	2701	33-02	32-05	33	186¤	24-06	24-02	24-04	36	180-04	179-02	179-04	34	61-04¤	59	59-06	12
13	447	37-03	36-07	37-01	2043	33-01¤	32-04	32-07	803	24-05	24-02	24-04	9	179¤	178-04	178-05	6	60	59	59	13
14	730	37-03	36-06	36-06	1860	33-02	32-06	32-07	175	24-06	24-02	24-02	132¤	184-06	179-02	183-04	17	61-04	59-04	61-02	14
15	529¤	37-04¤	36-03	37	3794¤	34	32-07	33-06	64	24-03¤	24-01	24-01	21	184	183	183	6¤	61-06	61-06	61-06	15
16	309	37-04	36-03	36-03	2915	33-07	33-02	33-02	192	24-04	24-01	24-01	72	181-04	179-04	180	2	61-06	61-06	61-06	16
	2142		3.06	35-06	13313		2.79	35-04	1420		2.00	26	270		15.17	153-03	65		5.11	68	
19	145¤	36-07	36-02	36-03	2784	33-05	32-06	32-07	158	24-01	23-03	23-06	17¤	180	180	180			61	61-06	19
20	560	36-05	36-02	36-04	2652	33-02	32-06	33-02	85	24	23-06	23-07	1	180	180	180	4¤	61	61	61	20
21	254	36-06	36-02	36-02	1860	33-05¤	32-05	33-03	60	23-05¤	23-02	23-04	30	180¤	179-04	179-04	13	60-04¤	60	60	21
22	HOLIDAY				HOLIDAY				HOLIDAY				HOLIDAY				HOLIDAY				22
23	277	36-04¤	35-06	36	3294¤	33-07	33-03	33-05	398¤	24-06	23-04	24-05	3	180	179-06	179-06	1	60	60	60	23
	1236		2.99	35-07	10590		2.79	35-02	701		2.04	25-07	51		14.96	155	18		4.99	67-06	
26	570¤	36-02	35-07	35-07	2805¤	33-04¤	32-05	32-06	192¤	25-07¤	24-07	25-02	19¤	179-04	177-04	177-04	13¤	59-04	58	58	26
27	X 2561	35-01	34-01	34-05	3018	33-03	32-05	33-01	75	25-04	25	25-03	10	177-06	176-04	176-04	31	57	56	56-06	27
28	2511	34-05	33-06	33-07	2815	33-04	32-07	33-02	82	25-06	25-01	25-02	50	176-02	173-04	173-06	2	56	56	56	28
29	419	34-01	33-05	33-07	2599	33-03	33	33	116	25-04	25-01	25-02	28	173-02¤	172-04	173	21	55-04¤	53-04	54-04	29
30	1314	33-07¤	33-03	33-05	2712	33-01	32-05	33-01	373	25-02	25	25-02	4	173	172-04	173	13	54-06	54-02	54-06	30
	7375		2.83	35-07	13949		2.76	35-01	838		2.11	25-06	111		14.49	156-03	80		4.56	67-02	
12/3	2573¤	33-07	33-04	33-05	4516	33¤	32	32-02	69¤	25-03	24-03	24-04	7	173¤	172	172	4	54-04¤	54	54-04	12/3
4	1661	33-04	32-06	33	2864	33-03	32-03	32-07	73	24-05	24-01	24-02	96	175-02	172-03	173-06	20	56-02	54-06	56-02	4
5	1441	33-01	32-06	32-06	2463	33-02	32-04	33	88	24-04	23-07	23-07	17	174-04	173-04	173-04	8	56-06	55-06	56	5
6	1620	32-07	32-05	32-05	5614¤	33-04	32-07	32-07	253	24-04¤	23-06	24-03	23	174-04	173	174-04	7	56-02	55-04	56-02	6
7	1732	32-05¤	32-01	32-04	2414	33	32-03	32-04	104	24-05	24-01	24-03	71¤	182-04	174-04	182-04	32¤	60-04	56-04	60	7
	9047		2.78	35-06	17871		2.80	34-07	587		2.08	25-05	214		14.90	157-07	71		4.80	66-07	
10	1187	32-07¤	32-01	32-06	2896¤	33-01	32-03	33-01	103	24-06	24	24-06	154¤	190-02	184	187	79¤	66-02¤	61	63-04	10
11	541	32-07	32-04	32-07	1759	33	32-06	32-07	204¤	25	24-05	25	22	187-06	186-04	187	15	64	63-06	64	11
12	1694	33-01	32-05	33	3077	33-01	32-02	32-03	136	25	24-04	24-05	26	188	186-04	186-04	11	64-02	63	63	12
13	529¤	33-04	32-06	33-01	4237	32-02	31-05	31-06	129	24-06	24	24	172	186-06	180	181-04	4	63	62-04	62-04	13
14	1173	33	32-05	32-06	3368	32¤	31-01	31-01	120	24-02¤	23-07	24-01	43	181¤	179-04	180	2	62	61-04	61-04	14
	5124		2.83	35-06	15337		2.71	34-05	692		2.05	25-04	417		15.52	159-04	111		5.34	66-06	
17	587	33¤	32-04	33	2804	31-05	31	31-03	98	24-01	23-07	23-07	54	180-02¤	179	180	6	62-04¤	62	62-04	17
18	767	33-07	33-03	33-05	8036¤	31-07	31-01	31-06	467	24-01	23-02	23-04	59	185	180-04	184	21	64-04	63	64-04	18
19	1094¤	35	33-06	34-03	4910	31-06	30-03	30-05	824	24-01	23-02	23-07	31	185	183	183	18	65-04	64-04	64-04	19
20	817	34-05	33-07	33-07	5086	31-01¤	30	30-03	373	23-07¤	23	23-04	204¤	188-04	180	187-06	21	65-04	64-02	65-04	20
21	525	34-01	32-05	32-07	5703	30-04	30-01	30-01	584¤	24-02	23-05	24-02	217	188	182-04	186-07	46¤	68-04	66-04	66-04	21
	3790		2.81	35-05	26539		2.52	34-03	2346		1.95	25-03	565		15.60	160-07	112		5.44	66-04	
24	306¤	33-03¤	32-07	33-02	2847	31¤	30-02	31	54	24-02¤	24	24	22¤	187-06	186-04	186-07	10¤	68-04	67	68	24
25	HOLIDAY				HOLIDAY				HOLIDAY				HOLIDAY				HOLIDAY				25
26	327	33-03	33-01	33-01	2111	31	30-04	30-04	158	24-01	24	24	16	186-04	185	185	7	68-02	67-04	67-04	26
27	154	33-03	33-01	33-01	2615	30-07	30-05	30-06	368	24-04	24	24-03	110	186-04	184	185	2	67-04	67-04	67-04	27
28	578	33-03	33	33-02	3006¤	31-06	30-05	31	498¤	25-06	24-01	25-06	207	186¤	183-02	186	4	67-04¤	66-04	66-04	28
	1365		2.75	35-04	10579		2.55	34-01	1078		2.02	25-03	355		15.38	162-02	23		5.61	66-03	
31	848¤	33-05¤	33-01	33-05	3337¤	31-04¤	31	31-02	792¤	26-04¤	25-05	26-04	74¤	187-06¤	186-02	186-02	4¤	67¤	66-04	66-04	31
EARN	1.920			$ 3.18	2.400			$ 4.40				$ 2.56				$ 1.37					EARN
DIV	.480				.600																DIV

SHORT INT																				
	FEB	12823	AUG	28401	FEB	178996	AUG	398930	FEB	55158	AUG	30463	FEB	7847	AUG	-	FEB	-	AUG	-
	MAR	37841	SEP	25999	MAR	208268	SEP	359544	MAR	46700	SEP	32725	MAR	3000	SEP	-	MAR	-	SEP	-
	APR	49854	OCT	15100	APR	724889	OCT	486755	APR	72100	OCT	60225	APR	-	OCT	-	APR	-	OCT	-
	MAY	42501	NOV	34069	MAY	703037	NOV	552855	MAY	37600	NOV	48797	MAY	-	NOV	-	MAY	-	NOV	-
	JUN	24700	DEC	23399	JUN	454437	DEC	401336	JUN	17600	DEC	43925	JUN	-	DEC	-	JUN	-	DEC	-
	JUL	33700	JAN	-	JUL	298543	JAN	-	JUL	18575	JAN	-	JUL	-	JAN	-	JUL	-	JAN	-

4TH QTR 1984

Reprinted by permission of Standard & Poor's Corporation.

Bunker Ramo subsidiary; Telerate, Inc.; and Reuters Holdings. These quotation terminals can produce the latest trading information and retrospective price summaries on a particular stock, and also display ongoing ticker information. They are normally seen only in the offices of brokers, analysts, and professional money managers. Many systems are quite sophisticated, allowing the user to interact with other software packages, to view a several markets simultaneously, and to execute trades.

A third way to retrieve stock quotes electronically is through one of several dozen online services. These databases can be accessed through popular vendors such as Compuserve, VU/TEXT, NewsNet, and Dow Jones News/Retrieval; through more specialized corporate-oriented vendors; or directly through the producers. Many provide current quotes only, such as DIALOG's menu-driven *DIALOG Quotes and Trading*. Quotron offers a system to personal investors called *Quotdial*, which disseminates current quotes during and after business hours. The subscriber can choose between a real time service and a 15-minute delay. Dow Jones News/Retrieval offers both current and retrospective quote databases. *Dow Jones Enhanced Current Quotes* reports prices for stocks on the New York, American, Midwest, and Pacific exchanges, and NASDAQ issues. Prices are updated through the day with a 15-minute lag. A real-time version is also available. *Dow Jones Historical Quotes* covers the same securities, but prices only date back one year. The user can specify a single date, or daily values for a pre-set 12-day period. Monthly price summaries are available back to 1979 and quarterly summaries to 1978.

One of the most extensive, and best-known online services is the *Tradeline* database, now produced by IDD Information Services. It offers up to 15 years of daily high, low, and closing prices for thousands of stocks and other securities. Current prices are updated only once per day, but the database can be searched in a variety of ways, and financial screening is possible. *Tradeline* is offered through a number of distributors, including Dow Jones and CompuServe, though the capabilities vary by vendor. On several systems, *Tradeline* goes under other brand names; the best-known of these is probably *Fastock II*, the version available through ADP Data Services. *Media General*, another popular guide to stock prices, is introduced later in the chapter.

Still other formats can be used to obtain stock price data. One alternative is to subscribe to quotes on floppy diskettes. Companies such as Standard & Poor's and Value Line offer investors ongoing subscriptions to regularly mailed diskettes, usually updated monthly. Systems of this type usually include software for analyzing investment portfolios. Large institutions and academic researchers can turn to magnetic tape products for retrospective securities quotes. The organization which pioneered the collection of securities prices by computer is the University of Chicago's Center for Research in Security Prices (CRSP, pronounced "Crisp"). The Center has been producing the *CRSP Common Stock Master File* and its subfiles for many years. Adjusted daily values are compiled for stocks on the New York and American exchanges beginning with 1962; monthly values for NYSE companies date back to 1926, but monthly AMEX values are provided only to 1962. For researchers conducting sophisticated financial or accounting research in a mainframe environment, CRSP tapes are an outstanding resource. Regardless of the media, electronic delivery of stock data offers great flexibility in retrieval and display. And many electronic databases enable users to tabulate, analyze, and graph data using other software packages.

Telephone Inquiry Services

A simple phone call can put the person seeking financial quotes in touch with firms which provide answers for a fee. Fees vary, but an average price is about $8 to $10 per quote, with a minimum charge for small orders. This is an expensive alternative if a large number of quotes is requested, but when a few prices are needed quickly, it is a sensible solution. Some quote suppliers require payment in advance, some allow users to maintain a deposit account, and others only handle requests submitted in writing (which belies their status as a "phone service"). For example, the company library at the Standard & Poor's Corporation provides quotations for a fee, but users of the service must agree to pay a minimum monthly fee. Another long-standing service is the National Quotation Bureau (NQB), publisher of the daily "Pink Sheets." Because they have been in business since 1913, NQB has an enormous database of quotations to draw upon. Finally, large public libraries can provide a few quotations over the telephone for free, or will invite callers to use their back files of financial publications in person. The public library should always be consulted before paying a commercial quotation service.

SUMMARY INVESTMENT DATA

Often a researcher or investor needs quick information that goes beyond a simple quotation. Others require easy-to-read tables with an assortment of data on many companies. Numerous publications summarize standard measures of a security's performance. They can be used to answer specific questions or to help the investor choose securities that meet stated specifications.

Once again, there are numerous formats. Popular investment newspapers and magazines may offer such tables. For example, *Financial World*, a highly regarded semimonthly journal, provides a monthly supplement called "Independent Appraisals." It presents an assortment of key measures for the 3,000 stocks with the largest market capitalization. Data include Earnings Per Share and six other widely followed investment ratios, the percentage of stock owned by institutions, the 52-week price range, and the percent change in price over the previous three months. Information is supplied by Investor's Daily, Inc.

A second medium for summary data is the specialized financial publication. *Worldscope* and some of the other products introduced in Chapter 9 could be included in this group. Many advisory newsletters could also be classified here, especially publications rich in data, such as the *Value Line Investment Survey*. Examples of advisory services can be found in Chapter 12. Online databases and CD-ROM products are particularly appropriate for searching and presenting comparative investment data. The quintessential product of this type is *Compustat PC Plus*, which contains both financial and market data. Publishers of major financial magazines and reference guides frequently contract with Compustat to create specialized tables. The most visible example is the quarterly "Corporate Scoreboard" in *Business Week*.

A different approach to investment data is to examine the performance of the stock market as a whole. Hundreds of statistics measure trends in market behavior, from the famous Dow Jones Industrial Average to more obscure indicators. Almost all of the publications described in this chapter offer current figures on market barometers to one degree or another, including *Barron's*, *Investor's Daily*, and *The Wall Street Journal*. Many investment advisory newsletters contain a variety of market indicators, and some of the most popular will be discussed in Chapter 12. Investors also need to compare current trends to past market performance, and a variety of statistical services provide extensive tables of historical data. Several will be introduced in the following section.

The products presented here are representative examples of the many specialized investment services appearing in print or electronically. Some focus on comparative information for individual stocks, others study general investment trends.

Standard & Poor's Security Owner's Stock Guide (Standard & Poor's—Monthly).

One of the best bargains in financial publications is the monthly S&P *Stock Guide*, which lists detailed background data on several thousand stocks in convenient summary form. Exhibit 10-6 shows a typical listing from the *Stock Guide*. Data on each stock appear on a single line covering two pages. Figures include the previous month's price range, historical price range, current dividend information, corporate earnings, and a summary from the annual balance sheet. Because so much information is provided in so crammed a space, S&P provides a detailed guide to the table format in every issue.

The *Stock Guide* is a convenient and easy ready-reference tool. It can be used to determine a stock's ticker symbol, whether listed options are traded in the stock, what stock exchanges it is listed on, and how the firm's fiscal year runs. The *Stock Guide* culls key information and presents it in a standard format, so it is useful for investment screening. For example, the second page in Exhibit 10-6 shows that Allegheny Power (Number 22) has paid dividends continuously since 1935, but Alexander Energy (Number 12) has not paid a dividend since its inception.

The fifth column on the first page of each entry indicates Standard & Poor's rating for preferred stocks (similar in nature to a bond rating), or a "ranking" for common stocks based upon the strength of each company's earnings. The footnotes at the bottom of the second page indicate where stock splits or stock dividends have occurred. For many companies, S&P analysts have estimated future earnings. Separate sections at the rear of each month's issue provide summaries for preferred stocks, mutual funds, and variable annuities. Other features include lists of companies whose rankings have changed, new stocks, name changes, and brief tables of market statistics.

Media General Financial Services Database (Media General Financial Services—Weekly).

This well-known database provides a variety of financial and investment measures for companies on the New York and American exchanges, the National Market System, and selected NASDAQ firms—approximately 5,000 companies in all. *Media General* can be searched on DIALOG, Dow Jones, and CompuServe.

EXHIBIT 10-6. ***Standard & Poor's Security Owner's Stock Guide***

10 ALB-ALL — Standard & Poor's Corporation

¶S&P 500 •Options Index	Ticker Symbol	Name of Issue (Call Price of Pfd. Stocks)	Market	Com. Rank. & Pfd. Rating	Par Val.	Inst. Hold Cos	Inst. Hold Shs. (000)	Principal Business	Price Range 1971-88 High	1971-88 Low	1989 High	1989 Low	1990 High	1990 Low	Apr. Sales in 100s	April, 1990 Last Sale Or Bid High	Low	Last	%Div Yield	P-E Ratio
		Alberto-Culver Cl'B' (Cont.)																		
1	ACV.A	Class'A'(1/10 vtg)	NY,Ph	A−	22¢	56	5018		14⅛	6⅜	20¾	12¾	19¾	15¾	1587	19¼	16½	17¼	1.2	14
¶2•[1]	ABS	**Albertson's, Inc**	NY,B,M,P	A+	1	295	28827	Food supermkts: food-drug	38¾	1 3/16	60¼	36⅝	60⅜	48¾	13394	60⅜	55	57¼	1.7	20
3	ALCCC	**ALC Communications**	OTC	NR	1¢	22	3121	Long distance telephone svc	10¼	⅞	5	1⅜	2⅝	¾	3729	1	13/16	⅞B	...	d
¶4•[2]	AL	**Alcan Aluminium Ltd**	[3]NY,B,C,M,Mo,P	B	No	411	124547	Aluminum mfr/finished prod	25¼	3⅜	25⅛	20⅛	24½	18⅞	71739	21⅞	19⅜	20	5.6	6
5	ALCD	**Alcide Corp**	OTC	NR	1¢	18	3734	R&D microbiocidal chemistry	8¼	1 3/16	4¼	7/16	1 5/16	7/16	11608	1 5/16	⅞	1 5/16B	...	d
¶6•[4]	ASN	**Alco Standard**	NY,B,M,Ph	A	No	198	19330	Dstr office supplies & equip	30	1 5/16	36⅝	25⅜	35⅜	28⅛	8986	32	30⅜	31⅛	2.7	12
7	ADNEA	**Alden Electronics'A'**	OTC,B	B+	1	9	505	Mfr facsimile commun'ns eq	11	¼	4⅞	3⅞	4⅜	3⅜	85	3⅝	3⅜	3⅜B	3.6	15
8•[5]	ALDC	**Aldus Corp**	OTC	NR	No	68	4047	Desktop publishing software	37¼	13½	24½	12¼	22¼	15	35713	21¾	16¾	21½B	...	19
9	ABSB	**Alex Brown Inc**	OTC	NR	10¢	44	4204	Invest't bank'g,brokerage	28	8¼	14½	9½	11¾	9½	9575	11½	10⅞	11B	2.0	9
¶10•[6]	AAL	**Alexander & Alex Sv**	NY,B,P	↓B	1	159	25678	Insurance brokerage & agency	42⅜	7⅛	34	22⅝	31½	24½	10310	28⅞	24⅞	25½	3.9	18
11•[7]	ALEX	**Alexander & Baldwin**	OTC	A	No	166	18875	Shipping,sugar, R.E.,truck'g	36¾	1 11/16	39½	31¼	38	27¾	21930	31¾	28½	30¼B	2.9	12
12	AEOK	**Alexander Energy**	OTC	C	1¢	5	676	Oil & gas expl,dev,prod'n	5⅛	⅜	⅞	½	1	11/16	1335	1	⅞	⅞B	...	d
13	ALX	**Alexander's, Inc**	NY,B,M	B−	1	29	1468	Dept stores, N.Y.,N.J.,Conn	77	2	71¾	50¼	57⅜	45½	1115	51⅜	46	47⅞	...	d
14	ALFA	**Alfa Corp**	OTC	A	1	12	1370	Insurance holding company	·18¼	⅞	12¼	9¾	12	9⅜	953	11¾	10	10½B	3.8	11
15	AFN	**Alfin Inc**	AS,M	B−	1¢	10	519	Mkts imported fragrances	40	2⅛	4⅝	1½	2⅛	1½	1030	2⅛	1½	1⅝	...	d
16	ALCO	**Alico, Inc**	OTC	B+	1	38	1379	Citrus fruit: cattle-Florida	26½	1½	39	22½	32¼	27½	747	31½	27½	27½B	0.7	24
17	BMD	**A.L. Labs Cl'A'**	NY,M,Ph	NR	20¢	48	4156	Pharmac'ls:animal health prod	17¼	3⅝	18½	13	22⅝	17	3566	22⅝	21	21	0.8	20
18	Y	**Alleghany Corp**	NY,B,M,Ph	B	1	70	3765	Insur:title,prop:fin'l svcs	107⅝	5½	101½	67¾	89¾	81⅞	302	85¾	83	84⅜	s.	9
19	AG	**Allegheny Int'l**	NY,B,M,P	D	66⅔¢	17	952	Mfr consumer products	55⅜	1¼	2⅜	⅛	¾	¼	3376	9/16	7/16	½	...	d
20	Pr C	**$11.25 cmCv Pfd(100:SF100)vtg**	NY,M	D	No	9	291	small appliances, barbecue	98	7½	15⅛	7/16	1¼	7/16	382	1	¾	⅞B	...	..
21	ALS	**Allegheny Ludlum**	NY,Ph	NR	10¢	94	9808	Major stainless steel mfr	36⅛	15⅛	41⅝	29¼	43⅝	36⅝	5888	43	39½	40	3.0	7
22	AYP	**Allegheny Power Sys**	NY,B,C,M,P,Ph	A	2½	261	21076	Electric utility hldg co	53½	11¾	42½	35⅜	42⅛	36¾	10910	39¼	36¾	37	8.5	10
23	ALGH	**Allegheny&West'n Energy**	OTC	B	1¢	35	2549	Oil & gas explor,devel,prod'n	31	3¼	9¼	6½	10⅛	7½	7035	9⅞	8¼	8½B	...	20
24	ALN	**Allen Group**	NY,B,M,P,Ph	↓B−	1	47	4644	Auto accessories: testing eq	27¼	2	16⅞	9	15⅜	10⅛	8280	15⅜	11⅝	14⅛	...	17
25	Pr A	**$1.75cm Cv•Exch Pfd([52]26.225)**	NY,M	B+	No	22	1324	truck prod:mobile commun'ns	28⅞	9¼	19⅞	11½	18¼	15⅛	355	18¼	17	18¼	9.6	..
26	AORGB	**Allen Organ Cl'B'**	OTC	A−	1	28	769	Mfr electronic organs	40⅜	1 1/16	39	27	38⅛	34½	147	37	35½	35½B	†1.3	11
27•[8]	AGN	**Allergan, Inc**	NY	NR	1¢	196	40914	Opthalmic/dermatologic prod	...	...	25½	15⅝	18⅝	12¼	24624	16⅛	14½	15¾	1.9	20
28	AC	**Alliance Cap Mgmt L.P.**	NY,Ph	NR	No	20	16636	Investment management svcs	11⅜	9⅝	16	10½	17⅜	14¾	5874	17¼	14¾	15⅝	10.2	17
29	ANE	**Alliance New Europe Fd**	NY	NR	1¢	..	...	Closed-end invest-cap apprec	...	...	...	...	12⅛	9⅝	39349	12⅛	9⅝	10⅜	...	..
30	ALLP	**Alliance Pharmaceutical**	OTC	NR	1¢	28	2653	Dvlp,mfr med'l/pharmac'l prod	11⅛	2	14½	7⅞	12½	8¼	4109	10¾	8¼	8¾B	...	d
31	ALNT	**Alliant Computer Sys**	OTC	NR	1¢	29	3216	Mfr/mkts computer systems	37	3⅜	7	3	8⅛	5⅝	16718	7¼	5⅞	6½B	...	28
32	ALIC	**Allico Corp**	OTC	NR	1¢	10	798	Mfr mobile homes	17½	⅜	13/16	1/16	½	¼	628	⅜	⅜	⅜B	...	d
33	ALLC	**Allied Capital**	OTC	NR	1	21	1947	Closed end invest co,SBIC	19	1⅜	20¼	15¾	19¼	17½	2541	19¼	17¾	18B	†6.8	11
34	ALGR	**Allied Group**	OTC	B−	No	17	775	Ins hldg:prop,casualty,life	15¼	8½	13½	9⅝	13½	12¼	365	13½	13	13⅛B	3.7	7
35	ADP	**Allied Products**	NY,B,M,P	↓C	5	36	1992	Metal fab:farm,auto,fasten'r	45½	5⅝	27⅝	7⅛	9⅜	5⅜	3059	7⅜	5⅜	5⅜	...	d
36	ARAI	**Allied Research Corp**	OTC	NR	10¢	9	531	Subsid mfrs defense prod	9⅜	⅛	3⅜	1½	2¾	2	1139	2¾	2¼	2 7/16B	...	d
¶37•[1]	ALD	**Allied-Signal Inc**	NY,B,C,M,P,Ph,To	B	1	421	74367	Aerospace,automotive,fibers	54½	15⅜	40⅜	31¾	37½	32½	46107	36¾	34¼	35⅛	5.1	10
38	ALU	**Allou Health&Beauty'A'**	AS	NR	.001	1	.5	Dstr hlth & beauty aid prod	...	...	3	1⅞	2¾	1¾	770	2½	2⅛	2⅜	...	5
·39	WS	**Wrrt(Pur1com/1 Cl'B'wrrt at $5)**	AS	NR	No	..	...		...	...	11/16	¼	⅜	3/16	529	⅜	¼	⅜	...	..
40	SAI	**Allstar Inns L.P.**	AS	NR	No	7	824	Economy motel chain	12⅜	3¼	7⅞	1⅜	2⅛	¾	2021	1½	¾	⅞	...	d.
41	ALM	**Allstate Muni Income Tr**	NY,M,Ph	NR	1¢	4	26	Closed-end investment co	10¾	8⅞	10⅞	10	10⅝	9⅞	6611	10⅜	9⅞	9⅞	⊙7.9	..
42	ALT	**Allstate Muni Income II**	NY,M,Ph	NR	1¢	5	17	Closed-end investment co	10¼	9¼	10⅛	9¼	10⅛	9¼	6018	9⅞	9¾	9⅝	7.6	..
43	ALL	**Allstate Muni Income III**	NY,Ph	NR	1¢	..	...	Closed-end diversified inv co	...	...	10	8⅞	9½	8⅜	2547	8⅞	8⅜	8⅝	7.3	..
44	AMO	**Allstate Muni Inc Opport**	NY,Ph	NR	1¢	4	14	Closed-end investment co	10⅜	9⅞	11⅛	9¾	11⅛	10	4226	10½	10	10	8.4	..

Uniform Footnote Explanations-See Page 1. Other: [1]Ph:Cycle 3. [2]ASE:Cycle 3,To:Cycle 2 [3]Ph,To,Vc [4]NY:Cycle 3. [5]P:Cycle 1. [6]CBOE:Cycle 2. [7]ASE:Cycle 1. [8]Ph:Cycle 1. [51]Fiscal Sep'85. [52]®$3.91,'89. [53]Fiscal Mar'88 & prior. [54]12 Mo Dec'88. [55]®$1.04,'89. [56]Accum on Pfd. [57]Incl petition liabs. [58]Fiscal Dec '86 & prior. [59]12 Mo Sep '87. [60]Subsid Pfd M$. [61]Co opt to exch for $25 amt 7% Cv 2011. [62]Thru 5-14-90 scale to $25 in'96. [63]8 Mo Dec,'88. [64]©$0.20,'89. [65]Excl subsid pfd [66]Fiscal Mar'86 & prior. [67]9 Mo Dec. [68]9 Mo Dec,'87. [69]Incl cap gains:short $0.04,long $0.0166,'89. [70]©$0.0018,'90. [71]Incl cap gains:short $0.056,long $0.015,'89. [72]©$0.0003,'89.

Common and Convertible Preferred Stocks — ALB-ALL 11

Splits • Index	Cash Divs. Ea.Yr. Since	Dividends Latest Payment Period $	Date	Ex. Div.	Total $ So Far 1990	Ind. Rate	Paid 1989	Financial Position Mil-$ Cash& Equiv.	Curr. Assets	Curr. Liab.	Balance Sheet Date	Capitalization Lg Trm Debt Mil-$	Shs. 000 Pfd.	Com.	Earnings $ Per Shr. Years End	1985	1986	1987	1988	1989	Last 12 Mos.	Interim Earnings Period	$ per Shr. 1989	1990	Index
1•	1986	Q0.05	5-20-90	4-30	0.10	0.20	0.18	...	...	...		...	...	9905	Sp	0.09	0.34	0.64	0.99	1.12	1.20	6 Mo Mar	0.45	0.53	1
2•	1960	Q0.24	5-25-90	5-7	0.44	0.96	0.74	63.9	659	565	11-02-89	199	...	67270	Ja	1.29	1.50	1.88	2.44	P2.93	2.93				2
3	...	None Paid			...	Nil	...	0.24	43.8	161	12-31-89	21.4	4500	13735	Dc	p[51]d2.15	d4.63	d0.50	d2.64	Δd2.09	d2.32	3 Mo Mar	Δd0.02	d0.25	3
4•	1939	†Q0.28	6-18-90	5-14	†0.56	1.12	†1.12	247	3471	2095	12-31-89	★1179	10800	±228259	Dc	*d0.97	*0.97	1.68	3.85	3.58	3.16	3 Mo Mar	1.16	0.74	4
5	...	None Since Public			...	Nil	...	0.02	3.71	0.39	11-30-89	...	1	23410	My	d0.12	d0.13	d0.10	d0.10	d0.10	d0.10	6 Mo NovΔ	d0.06	d0.06	5
6•	1965	Q0.21	3-10-90	2-13	0.21	0.84	0.78	37.8	866	536	9-30-89	166	123	40280	Sp	1.16	1.33	1.81	2.33	[52]3.94	2.70	6 Mo Mar	2.38	1.14	6
7	1976	0.12	4-25-90	4-6	0.12	0.12	0.10	1.78	8.69	2.04	12-30-89	0.86	...	±2015	Mr	0.64	0.40	0.42	0.20	...	0.22	40 Wk DecΔ	0.23	0.25	7
8	...	None Since Public			...	Nil	...	58.6	80.4	12.8	12-31-89	...	...	p13589	Dc	*0.04	0.21	0.66	1.15	1.21	1.15	3 Mo Mar	0.33	0.27	8
9•	1986	Q0.05½	5-11-90	4-25	0.11	0.22	0.17½	Equity per shr $10.23			3-31-89	24.4	...	16139	Dc	1.14	1.59	1.29	0.46	P0.65	1.20	3 Mo Mar	d0.39	0.16	9
10	1922	Q0.25	3-30-90	2-26	0.25	1.00	1.00	756	1825	1656	9-30-89	216	...	±40297	Dc	d0.19	*1.04	*1.53	*1.57	P1.45	1.45				10
11•	1902	Q0.22	6-7-90	5-4	0.42	0.88	0.80	23.6	127	92.9	12-31-89	206	...	46096	Dc	1.50	1.65	2.29	Δ2.70	4.38	2.53	3 Mo Mar	2.87	1.02	11
12	...	None Since Public			...	Nil	...	2.31	4.16	4.52	12-31-89	12.0	...	7227	Dc	0.01	d0.50	[53]d0.17	[54]d0.16	d0.07	d0.07				12
13	...	0.10	9-9-80	8-20	...	Nil	...	23.9	97.1	43.8	7-29-89	50.8	...	4976	Jl	1.11	Δ0.59	0.27	Δd0.86	□4.20	d0.75	28 Wk Feb	□5.15	0.20	13
14•	1974	Q0.10	6-1-90	5-9	0.19	0.40	0.34½	Equity per shr $7.68			12-31-89	37.7	...	20928	Dc	0.61	0.70	0.87	1.20	1.09	0.94	3 Mo Mar	0.31	0.16	14
15•	...	None Since Public			...	Nil	...	2.89	12.1	1.93	1-31-90	0.81	...	6688	Jl	0.63	0.85	d1.92	0.22	0.03	d0.12	6 Mo Jan	0.20	0.05	15
16•	1973	A0.20	11-17-89	10-23	...	0.20	0.20	8.44	16.0	8.40	11-30-89	...	...	7092	Au	1.04	0.71	0.50	Δ1.11	1.24	1.13	6 Mo Feb	0.55	0.44	16
17•	1984	Q0.04	4-26-90	4-6	0.08	0.16	0.12	3.22	121	77.1	9-30-89	101	...	±11171	Dc	0.60	0.61	0.73	0.87	P[56]1.06	1.06				17
18•	...	2%Stk	4-27-90	3-27	2%Stk	Stk	2%Stk	Equity per shr $80.06			12-31-88	p188	...	p6569	Dc	12.29	11.42	9.01	6.99	P8.42	9.02	3 Mo Mar	1.11	1.71	18
19	...	0.35	1-1-86	12-9	...	[56]Nil	...	File Bankruptcy Chapt 11				[57]759	4730	10859	Sp	d13.08	[58]d17.97	[59]d44.39	d5.10	d7.80	d8.50	6 Mo Mar	d1.65	d2.35	19
20	...	2.81¼	7-1-86	6-17	...	Nil	...	Cv into 1.724 shrs com, $58				...	1916	...	SF 4% fr 12-1-91 $100							Accum $42.187 to 4-1-90			20
21	1987	Q0.30	4-2-90	2-22	0.30	1.20	1.05	79.1	458	220	12-31-89	67.8	...	22337	Dc	...	...	2.27	4.81	5.94	5.46	3 Mo Mar	1.52	1.04	21
22	1935	Q0.79	3-30-90	3-6	0.79	3.16	3.10	54.8	441	391	12-31-89	1578	[60]266	52789	Dc	3.59	4.03	4.05	3.96	3.72	3.73	12 Mo Mar	3.87	3.73	22
23	...	0.075	9-6-88	8-9	...	Nil	...	15.0	62.3	28.4	9-30-89	55.6	...	8109	Je	1.81	2.13	2.17	0.55	0.41	0.42	6 Mo DecΔ	0.14	0.15	23
24•	...	0.14	10-9-87	9-22	...	Nil	...	22.7	186	72.9	12-31-89	101	2300	8386	Dc	1.82	d1.23	d2.40	0.20	1.83	0.85	3 Mo Mar	1.26	0.28	24
25	1986	Q0.43¾	5-15-90	4-24	0.87½	1.75	1.75	Cv into 0.909,$27.50				...	2300	...	Dc	...	b0.08	n/a	n/a	n/a	...				25
26•	1954	†0.16	3-9-90	2-16	†0.16	0.46	†0.42	28.9	38.6	1.60	9-30-89	...	...	±1504	Dc	2.77	2.43	2.96	3.07	P3.21	3.22	3 Mo Mar	0.72	0.73	26
27	1989	0.07	6-15-90	5-21	0.14	0.30	0.05	85.6	432	348	9-30-89	94.3	...	67128	Dc	...	...	...	p0.88	P0.86	0.80	3 Mo Mar	0.26	0.20	27
28	1988	0.48	2-16-90	2-5	0.48	1.60	1.49	Equity per shr $1.99			12-31-89	0.42	...	28000	Dc	...	...	...	[63]0.43	0.90	0.90				28
29	...	Plan annual div			...	...	...	Net Asset Val $11.04			4-27-90	...	...	★21009	Dc	...	...	...	...	...	...				29
30	...	None Paid			...	Nil	...	34.7	36.0	1.87	12-31-89	8.57	...	13335	Je	d0.52	d0.80	d1.09	d0.92	d4.12	d3.98	6 Mo DecΔ	d0.48	d0.34	30
31	...	None Since Public			...	Nil	...	38.4	82.3	25.6	9-30-89	40.4	...	12625	Dc	d0.58	*0.28	*0.34	Δ*d3.27	P0.17	0.23	3 Mo Mar	0.01	0.07	31
32	...	None Since Public			...	Nil	...	0.40	1.68	6.02	8-26-89	0.41	...	p5042	Fb	0.75	d1.71	d2.92	d1.84	...	d0.32	9 Mo NovΔ	d1.69	d0.17	32
33•	1963	Q0.18	3-30-90	3-12	0.18	1.23	†[64]1.79	Equity per shr $8.21			12-31-88	29.4	[65]...	5867	Dc	▲[66]1.15	▲[67]1.10	1.36	1.48	P1.61	1.61				33
34	1985	Q0.12	3-30-90	3-13	0.12	0.48	0.44	Equity per shr $14.85			9-30-89	48.5	...	6818	Dc	0.79	1.29	1.76	Δ1.51	P1.87	1.77	3 Mo Mar	0.55	0.45	34
35	...	2%Stk	11-15-82	10-4	...	Nil	...	3.31	360	188	9-30-89	133	456	5013	Dc	*Δ1.14	3.36	d0.77	0.74	□Pd4.70	d4.89	3 Mo Mar	0.80	0.61	35
36	...	None Paid			...	Nil	...	4.75	19.3	20.4	9-30-89	5.91	...	4056	Dc	0.64	0.63	0.32	d2.12	Pd1.84	d1.84				36
37	1887	Q0.45	6-8-90	5-14	0.90	1.80	1.80	525	4141	3227	12-31-89	1903	...	p144000	Dc	d3.28	3.26	*3.55	3.10	3.55	3.60	3 Mo Mar	0.85	0.90	37
38	...	None Since Public			...	Nil	...	0.12	26.9	20.0	12-31-89	0.07	...	2580	Mr	d0.64	*0.09	*0.34	0.67	...	0.50	9 Mo DecΔ	0.52	0.35	38
39	...	Terms&trad. basis should			be checked in detail			Wrrts expire 7-10-94				...	...	1200	Mr	...	...	...	...	...	...	Callable fr 7-11-90 at 50¢			39
40	1987	0.25	11-15-89	9-25	...	Nil	1.00	1.20	1.65	4.98	12-31-89	166	...	13155	Dc	...	...	‡[68]0.10	□d0.18	d0.42	d0.52	3 Mo Mar	□d0.10	□d0.20	40
41	1987	M0.06½	6-22-90	6-4	0.39	⊙0.78	[69]0.837	Net Asset Val $10.09			4-20-90	...	...	31714	Au	...	...	...	§10.20	§10.36	...				41
42	1988	0.061	6-22-90	6-4	[70]0.368	⊙0.73	[71]0.803	Net Asset Val $9.78			4-20-90	...	...	★30000	Dc	...	...	...	§9.72	...	...				42
43	1989	0.05¼	5-25-90	5-7	0.252	0.63	0.08¼	Net Asset Val $9.33			4-20-90	...	...	★6011	Dc	...	...	...	...	...	...				43
44	1988	0.07	5-25-90	5-7	0.35	0.84	[72]0.78	Net Asset Val $9.34			4-20-90	...	...	20368	My	...	...	...	...	§9.56	...				44

•Stock Splits & Divs By Line Reference Index [1]2-for-1,'90. [2]2-for-1,'87. [4]3-for-2,'87,'89. [6]2-for-1,'87. [9]Adj for 5%,'86:3-for-2,'87. [11]3-for-2,'86:2-for-1,'88. [14]2-for-1,'87. [15]2-for-1,'86. [16]4-for-1,'87. [17]3-for-2,'86. [18]No adj for approx$41.81dstr,'86:Adj to 2%,'90. [24]5-for-4,'86. [26]Adj to 5%,'88. [33]3-for-2,'86:5-for-4,'87,'88.

Reprinted by permission of Standard & Poor's Corporation.

The type and amount of information varies depending on which vendor is selected, but the most extensive version is found on DIALOG.

The DIALOG database, called *Media General Plus*, offers five years of summary data from annual financial statements, an impressive list of financial ratios (also reported for five years), and 16 periods of quarterly sales, net income, and dividends. Detailed stock price histories give one year of daily prices and 60 periods of monthly data. Also available is background on the industry of which the firm is a part, and a table of comparative ratios for the industry. *Media General* is an excellent source of several measures difficult to locate through other means. One example is Beta Coefficients for companies and industries (Betas will be introduced in Chapter 12). Other variables include stock price momentum, several moving averages of stock price, and measures of insider trading and short-selling activity.

With the exception of stock price data, literally every item in the DIALOG record is searchable. The potential for screening is enormous, and users can search not only by financial variables, but by industry, exchange, location, fiscal year, and recency of information. The database is also useful for obtaining financial profiles of entire industries. Searchers can print results in a variety of standardized formats, self-defined formats, or customized tables of comparative data.

Media General on Dow Jones and CompuServe is much less versatile. For purposes of comparison, the Dow Jones version will be described. Each record on Dow Jones is much shorter; the emphasis is on market data, with no annual or quarterly financials. Because Dow Jones produces its own quotation database, no stock prices are seen in this version either. Also, none of the DIALOG search features are available. Users can search by industry, company name, or ticker symbol only. A final weakness is the limited options for displaying results. Company reports are available in two standard formats: the first compares two companies side by side, the second compares a company to its industry. Similarly, two different industries can be compared. Selected information from *Media General* can be found on CD-ROM via Lotus's *CD/Corporate*.

Standard & Poor's Bond Guide (Standard & Poor's—Monthly).

The *Bond Guide* is similar in purpose and format to the *Stock Guide*, but provides summary data on corporate bonds listed on the New York and American exchanges. It is somewhat confusing to use because each listing contains two types of data: one row provides information on the company as a whole, and the following row (or rows) gives data on individual bond issues. Company statistics emphasize information of special interest to bond holders, such as the "fixed charges times earnings" ratio, which measures the firm's ability to meet interest payments. Data on each bond include the exchange it is listed on, whether it is a registered or bearer bond, the months when interest payments are made, the S&P bond rating, price and yield information, and redemption provisions. The *Bond Guide* also contains sections on major foreign and convertible bonds, and provides an abbreviating listing (with ratings only) for several thousand municipal bonds. Lists are provided showing bonds which have been reviewed or whose ratings have been changed in the previous month. Like the *Stock Guide*, it can be used for ready-reference, or for investment decisions.

Moody's Bond Record (Moody's Investors Service—Monthly).

This source is similar to the S&P *Bond Guide*, but easier to use and more comprehensive. It includes data on the same types of bonds, plus other types of debt offerings, such as major issues of commercial paper and corporate notes. No company data appear, only information on individual securities. *Moody's Bond Record* lists standard information such as the current bond price, the date issued and price paid at issue, the presence of a sinking fund to pay off the bond, and the dates when interest is paid. Like Standard & Poor's, analysts at Moody's assign bond ratings to each bond. Moody's and S&P ratings are usually, but not always similar for a particular bond. *Moody's Bond Record* has a separate section on municipal bonds which resembles the list in *Standard & Poor's Bond Guide*. Moody's rates far more municipalities then S&P, so this section is much more extensive. Separate sections also list ratings for industrial revenue bonds and short-term loans to municipalities. *Moody's Bond Record* also provides a guide to firms whose ratings have been changed or reviewed recently.

Stocks, Bonds, Bills, and Inflation Yearbook (Ibbotson Associates, Inc.—Annual).

Historical information on stock market performance is useful for numerous purposes: to detect financial cycles and predict future changes, to place current markets in perspective, and to compare long-term yields of various investment opportunities. By studying past market behavior, analysts can reach important conclusions about different securities and how they perform. For all of these applications, few resources are as widely followed as the *SBBI Yearbook*. It provides historical rates

of return for common stocks, corporate and government bonds, and U.S. Treasury Bills. Seven basic time series are tracked. Two series measure the performance of different types of stocks: the index of larger stocks is based on the popular Standard & Poor's 500; smaller stocks are studied using a unique portfolio of more than 2,000 firms, including listed stocks whose capitalizations fall into the lowest quintile on the NYSE. Corporate bonds are measured by the highly regarded Salomon Brothers High-Grade Corporate Bond Index. Both long- and intermediate-term government bonds are followed, using data from the CRSP database. Short-term rates are tracked via Treasury Bill data, again taken from the CRSP files. Rates of return for the stock and government bond series are further divided into two components, measuring income and capital appreciation. For comparative purposes, the rate of inflation (as measured by the Consumer Price Index) is also cited. Tables cite monthly figures dating back to 1926 for all basic series.

The variables in the *SBBI Yearbook* have been carefully chosen as the best measures of investment performance. In addition to the basic series, ten derived series are calculated. These measure inflation-adjusted returns, four different risk premia, and the real interest rate. The model used to create these average investment yields was created in the mid-1970s by Roger Ibbotson (then director of CRSP, the University of Chicago's Center for Research on Securities Prices) and colleague Rex Sinquefield. A complete book of tables first appeared in 1977. From the beginning, the research has attracted considerable interest from both the academic and financial communities; today, *SBBI* data are quoted in numerous articles, utilized in scholarly studies, and avidly followed by portfolio managers. The authors subsequently founded a financial consulting firm which publishes the updated tables each year.

For those who don't require such detailed data, an abbreviated version of the *Yearbook* appears in monographic form. Published by the Research Foundation of the Institute of Chartered Financial Analysts, the book is called *Stocks, Bonds, Bills, and Inflation: Historical Returns*. The fourth edition appeared in 1989. Fewer tables are provided in the monograph, mostly because no monthly data are cited, and the book is updated less frequently. However, the two versions are identical in all other respects. For example, both contain extensive narrative sections describing the methodology of the study and analyzing the results. Additional chapters evaluate alternative measures of investment return, explain how to use historical data for financial analysis, and discuss how to determine the appropriate cost of capital. Data

tables are also available as a diskette product called *SBBI/PC*. Regardless of the version used, *SBBI* is the most authoritative source of historical investment yields.

Security Price Index Record (Standard & Poor's Corporation—Annual).

This annual S&P guide provides alternative data for historical analysis. Most tables track the performance of the 500 stocks which constitute the Standard & Poor's Composite Stock Index, a widely followed investment measure. Averages are given for Earnings Per Share, Price/Earnings ratio, dividends per share, Book Value, and stock yields. The stock price indexes themselves are also cited, for both the composite and for individual industry groups. Additional measures include average bond prices, bond yields by type and grade, and preferred stock prices and yields. For most series, monthly and annual averages are given for 50 years, and weekly averages for 10 years.

Another source of limited historical data is the *Business One Irwin Investor's Handbook*, an annual paperback from Business One Irwin. The various Dow price indexes are cited daily for the previous two years, together with monthly values for 20 years, quarterly figures for 35 years, and annual averages for 75 years. Averages for earnings, dividends, and P/E ratios are given, in this case for the components of the Dow and for the New York Stock Exchange. Other variables include the Barron's Confidence Index, trading volume on the New York Stock Exchange, and price indexes for selected foreign stock exchanges. Most stock and commodity exchanges produce their own statistical yearbooks, as does the National Association of Security Dealers. An excellent example is the *New York Stock Exchange Fact Book*, which provides extraordinary detail on all aspects of NYSE activity. Both past-year and historical figures are cited. An especially useful feature compares the results of periodic surveys of investor behavior conducted by the NYSE.

CHOOSING THE RIGHT SOURCE

The resources discussed in this chapter, both print and electronic, are only a representative sampling of basic investment products available. The link between information and success is widely perceived by the investment community. As a consequence, a blizzard of data is available from hundreds of sources. For the library trying to select publications for its collection, the reputation of the publisher, the longevity and popularity of the item, and the quantity and uniqueness of information are

factors to consider. To the researcher or investor making a private purchase, the choice is often based on the format of the material and the user's familiarity with it. But to both librarian and end-user, no single publication can ever serve as the sole source of investment statistics.

Almost every source has characteristics to recommend its use. Even publications similar to one another in most ways will have unique features to distinguish them. Choosing the best publication for a particular purpose can be difficult. The most helpful advice is to become familiar with as many sources as can serve your basic needs.

If the researcher has access to numerous sources of investment information, which should be tried first? For something as uncomplicated as a stock quote, the choices are staggering. Users can look to a daily newspaper, an online system, a telephone inquiry service, or a variety of other sources. Often, the form in which the data are needed becomes the deciding factor. If a day-by-day listing of prices over a month's time is required, then the *Daily Stock Price Record, Media General*, or *Dow Jones Historical Quotes* are all appropriate selections. If a weekly or monthly summary of price trends is wanted, *Barron's* or Standard & Poor's *Stock Guide* would suffice. Publications with background data on stocks are even more diverse. The researcher must remember the types of variables included by each product, and the form in which they are presented.

Keeping all of this straight can be a gargantuan task, especially for those who don't work with investment data on a regular basis. One way to ease the burden is to consult indexes to the investment literature. An outstanding resource is the *Investment Statistics Locator* by Karen Chapman, which was published by Oryx Press in 1988. This invaluable tool indexes data found in more than 20 major reference publications, from Standard & Poor's *Stock Guide* to the *New York Times*. The user can look under one of several hundred investment variables to see where data can be found, how they are presented, and how often they appear.

Another approach is to take a broader view of reference sources. Rather than trying to memorize everything found in a particular publication or database, focus on its general nature and purpose. It is more important (and easier) to remember how sources differ than how they are alike. Keep track of which publications contain hard-to-find information or present data in unique ways. To obtain quotes for non-NASDAQ stocks for example, turn to specialized sources such as the *National Stock Summary* or the *National OTC Stock Journal*.

The sources covered in this chapter have emphasized very basic information about investment instruments. The following chapter will introduce more specialized investment tools.

FOR FURTHER READING

Many excellent books have been written on all aspects of investing for the beginner and for the advanced practitioner. Materials range from the most basic introductions to in-depth scholarly treatments. Dozens of books are published each year to promote a particular investment strategy or point of view. The following list is not meant to be comprehensive, but is intended as a starting point for readers interested in understanding investments in greater detail.

General Investment Guides

Amling, Frederick. *Investments: An Introduction to Analysis and Management*. 6th ed. (Englewood Cliffs, NJ: Prentice Hall, 1989).
  Amling's widely used textbook is recommended to the beginning investor as an introductory guide.
Apostolou, Nick, and D. Lawrence Crumbley. *Keys to Understanding the Financial News* (New York: Barron's Educational Series, 1989).
  A pocket guide to fundamental economic and investment concepts. Over 40 topics are covered in rudimentary two-to three-page summaries. The purpose is to assist readers in understanding the terms heard on the evening news and read in the daily newspapers, as well as to assist investors in using financial data. Coverage is eclectic, and includes such topics as stock exchanges, technical analysis, leveraged buyouts, and the GNP.
Downes, John, and Jordan Elliot Goodman. *Finance & Investment Handbook*. 3rd ed. (New York: Barron's Educational Series, 1990).
  A massive work providing encyclopedic coverage of investment topics. Part I consists of 30 short articles describing major investment opportunities. Parts II and III provide lengthy articles explaining how to read financial statements, ticker tapes, and financial quotations in newspapers. Part IV is an extensive dictionary of investment terms. Part V, taking up the second half of the book, contains numerous directories and statistical tables for ready-reference. Now in its third edition, this useful compendium is revised frequently.

Hardy, C. Colburn. *Dun and Bradstreet's Guide to Your Investments* (New York: Harper and Row, Annual).

A general guide to a wide variety of investments, this popular resource is updated yearly to reflect changes in regulations and investment trends.

Reddy, Michael T. *Securities Operations: A Guide to Operations and Information Systems in the Securities Industry* (New York: New York Institute of Finance, 1990). This wonderful handbook offers a unique look at the "back room" operations of securities firms. The description of the little-understood world of clearing services (organizations such as the Depository Trust Corporation and the National Securities Clearing Corporation) is especially enlightening.

Thomsett, Michael C. *The Mathematics of Investing: A Complete Reference* (New York: Wiley, 1989).

A much-needed layperson's guide to the arithmetic of investment. The guide begins with detailed explanations of basic concepts—the time value of money, interest rate relationships, and the effects of taxation and inflation. Additional chapters explore the math necessary to understand such specific securities as mutual funds, bonds, options, and real estate. A final chapter summarizes the importance of utilizing simple mathematical analysis when making investment decisions and monitoring your portfolio.

Warfield, Gerald. *The Investor's Guide to Stock Quotations and Other Financial Listings*. 3rd ed. (New York: Harper and Row, 1990).

This indispensable manual provides practical explanations of how to read financial tables of all types. It offers the most thorough explanation of this topic to be found anywhere. A comprehensive directory of ticker symbols and stock abbreviations rounds out the coverage.

Weiss, David M. *Traders: The Jobs, the Products, the Markets* (New York: New York Institute of Finance, 1990).

A basic explanation of the work done by securities traders and market specialists. Individual chapters are devoted to major participants in the process, including OTC market makers, exchange specialists, and bond traders. Each chapter gives an introduction to the nature of the securities being traded, the institutional framework, how trading works, and what traders do. For those seeking an easy-to-follow look at the behind-the-scenes operations of securities markets, this is the best.

Wurman, Richard Saul, Alan Siegel, and Kenneth M. Morris. *The Wall Street Journal Guide to Understanding Money & Markets* (New York: ACCESS Press, 1989).

A profusely illustrated explanation of fundamental investment concepts. Much of the information is arranged in brief question/answer format, interspersed with a jumble of multi-colored charts, maps, and sample documents. This unusual style is the signature of works by Wurman and his ACCESS Press. While some may find the jumpy, highly visual presentation unsettling, others will be quite comfortable with its "video" look. The discussions are clear and concise, making this an ideal guide for ready reference, browsing, or a quick introduction to the topic.

Stocks

Engel, Louis, and Brendan Boyd. *How to Buy Stocks.* 7th revised ed. (New York: Bantam, 1984).

Probably the most widely read introduction to the stock market, this paperback has enjoyed many editions.

Little, Jeffrey B., and Lucien Rhodes. *Understanding Wall Street.* 2nd ed. (Blue Ridge Summit, PA: Liberty House, 1987).

This small paperback is one of the simplest and most understandable introductions to the stock market still available.

Rosenberg, Claude N. *Stock Market Primer.* Revised ed. (New York: Warner Books, 1981).

Rosenberg's book is a common-sense introduction that concentrates on do's and don'ts for the beginner.

Teweles, Richard J., and Edward S. Bradley. *The Stock Market.* 5th ed. (New York: Wiley, 1987).

A revised edition of the classic text by George Leffler, this is probably the most comprehensive introductory work available.

Weil, Henry. "Uncovering the Pearls in the Pink Sheets." *Money* (November 1988): 123-28.

One of the better descriptions of the "Pink Sheets," it includes a discussion of investment strategies focusing on unlisted stocks, and information about other reporting services covering these elusive securities.

Other Topics

Haslem, John A. *Investor's Guide to Mutual Funds* (Englewood Cliffs, NJ: Prentice Hall, 1988).

A wonderful introduction to the complexities of mutual funds. Haslem discusses the differences between mutual funds and other investment companies, types of funds, the advantages and disadvantages of investing in mutual funds, the responsibilities and functions of fund managers, how to choose a fund, how to understand the prospectus, how to purchase or redeem shares, and how to judge the fund's performance. Throughout the book, Haslem stresses the importance of information, reminding investors to do their homework and to ask questions.

Holt, Robert L. *The Complete Book of Bonds.* Revised ed. (New York: Harper & Row, 1985).

Provides a fine introduction to the subject, with an emphasis on corporate bonds.

Stigum, Marcia. *The Money Market.* 3rd ed. (New York: Dow Jones-Irwin, 1989).

Marcia Stigum is the leading authority on this topic and her book is sophisticated but well written. With its encyclopedic coverage, it is the "bible" for short-term debt securities.

Teweles, Richard J., and Frank J. Jones. *The Futures Game: Who Wins, Who Loses.* 2nd ed. (New York: McGraw Hill, 1987).

A massive, though readable and fairly nontechnical introduction to commodities futures. As the subtitle implies, the authors present a realistic assessment of this turbulent arena. Every conceivable issue is dealt with, including the purpose of futures markets, how they behave, how the trading system works, the reasons for price fluctuations, and the role of the broker. Specific instructions are offered for would-be investors. A list of sources of additional information is provided.

Thomsett, Michael C. *Getting Started in Options* (New York: Wiley, 1989).

An excellent beginning guide to stock options. The prolific Thomsett has a talent for explaining complex topics concisely and understandably.

CHAPTER 11
Special Investment Situations

TOPICS COVERED

1. Following Investment News
2. New Securities Offerings
3. Corporate Ownership
   a. Cumulative Ownership Sources
   b. Insider Trading Reports
4. Merger-Related Activities
5. Tracking Corporate Changes
6. Dividend Announcements
7. Keeping Things Straight
8. For Further Reading

MAJOR SOURCES DISCUSSED

- *SEC Abstracts*
- *Federal Filings*
- *Investment Dealers' Digest*
- *Spectrum Ownership Profiles*
- *Vickers Stock Traders Guide*
- *Insider Trading Monitor*
- *Mergers & Acquisitions*
- *IDD M&A Transactions*
- *M&A Filings*
- *Capital Changes Reports*
- *Predicasts F&S Index of Corporate Change*
- *Directory of Obsolete Securities*
- *Moody's Dividend Record*

Every day a torrent of business news floods the air waves, daily newspapers, and weekly magazines. Yet the typical citizen remembers little about recent business events. When it does capture public attention, business news is equated with Wall Street. Financial news tends to be the most dramatic, and often the most important business information relayed through the media. Much of it revolves around specific events in the life of public corporations—new issues of stock, joint ventures, debt offerings, changes in ownership, mergers, and other transactions affecting the firm's capital structure. The financial press cover such events in extraordinary detail, supplying investors, managers, and researchers with vital business intelligence. Popular business magazines and newspapers cover investment stories well, and some of these are listed in the Appendix. Newspaper indexes and news wires are discussed in Chapter 5. Researchers can also turn to an impressive battery of online databases, newsletters, and specialized information services to investigate corporate developments. Many news publications are actually advisory letters, a topic taken up in Chapter

12. The present chapter examines specialized investment guides which present detailed financial news in a well-organized, retrievable manner.

FOLLOWING INVESTMENT NEWS

Investors rely on financial information services to keep abreast of market news, identify recent transactions which meet specified characteristics, and research the financial history of individual corporations. Because material information about public securities must be registered with the SEC, the federal government is a nearly boundless repository of up-to-date company data. A wide range of significant events are covered by disclosure regulations. Summary descriptions of major SEC filings can be seen in Figure 11-A. Most of these documents cover specific occurrences, such as mergers or new security offerings, but general events of an unscheduled nature are reported on SEC Form 8-K. Depending on the event, an 8-K report may be brief or

FIGURE 11-A. Primary Financial Disclosure Forms and Reports

Periodic Reports

Annual Report	STK	Annual financial report to shareholders.
10-K	SEC	Annual financial report to SEC.
10-Q	SEC	Quarterly financial report to SEC.
20-F	SEC	Annual report filed by foreign firms.
Proxy Statement	STK	Notification of matters to be voted upon at annual shareholders meeting.

Mergers/Acquisitions/Tender Offers

14D-1	SEC	Notification of tender offer made by outside firm or individual.
14D-9	SEC	Management response to tender offer.
13E-4	SEC	"Self tender" (offer made by the firm itself).
13E-3	SEC	Notification of leveraged buyout or similar act to take firm private.

Institutional Ownership

13-F	SEC	Quarterly report submitted by all institutions with equity assets greater than $100 million.
13-G	SEC	Annual report submitted by institutions or individuals owning 5% or more of a company's stock.

Insider Holdings

13D	SEC	Signals purchase of 5% or more of a firm's stock, including the purpose of the acquisition. (5% owners are not technically insiders.) Schedule 13D is frequently the first warning of an intended takeover.
Form 3	SEC	Initial report of securities transaction filed by corporate officers, directors, and 10% owners.
Form 4	SEC	Amended report of all subsequent transactions by officers, directors, and "ten percenters."
Form 144	SEC	Preliminary notice by insider that they intend to sell "unregistered" stock (originally acquired through employee stock option plan or other means outside the normal market).

Registration of Securities

Registration Statement	SEC	Used to register securities before they are offered to the public. Nearly two dozen forms used, depending on type of transaction. Common filings include Forms S-1 and S-2.
Prospectus	STK	Public offering of a security in the primary market, including offer price.

Miscellaneous

8-K	SEC	Report of an unscheduled event of a material nature.

NOTE: Rules for filing insider trading forms have recently undergone major revision.
SEC = Reports filed with the U.S. Securities and Exchange Commission.
STK = Reports sent to stockholders or prospective investors.

fairly lengthy. Reported news ranges from the unexpected death of a CEO to the announcement of a government investigation against the company. To assist both filers and researchers, the SEC established eight event categories. When filing a Form 8-K, companies must report events by Item number, as follows:

Item 1.   Changes in corporate control.
Item 2.   Acquisition or sale of assets.
Item 3.   Bankruptcy or receivership.
Item 4.   Change of auditor.
Item 5.   Other material events.
Item 6.   Resignations of directors.
Item 7.   Financial statements and exhibits.
Item 8.   Change in fiscal year.

Because 8-Ks and other filings are an important source of business news, wire services and news bureaus maintain desks at the SEC's Media Room to monitor new filings. Document delivery services also maintain a constant watch for new filings, as do dozens of commercial publishers who repackage the information in a myriad of forms. The sources included in this chapter were chosen to illustrate the diversity of quality products available. The first group introduces publications and databases which offer broad coverage of all types of SEC filings. The remainder describe information services with a narrower focus.

SEC News Digest (U.S. Securities and Exchange Commission—Five times per Week.).

For many years the government has published this daily news service for the investment community. Although the *News Digest* still exists, it is no longer sold through the Government Printing Office, nor distributed to Depository Libraries. Its availability is one of the SEC's best-kept secrets. It is intended primarily as a press release to the news media, but government agencies, universities, and the regulated companies themselves may also obtain it at no charge. Users in the private sector must order the *News Digest* through Disclosure, Inc. (the official contractor for distribution of SEC documents) at a hefty subscription price. The contents of the *News Digest* are reprinted by several commercial publishers. It can even be searched online in its entirety on the LEXIS Financial Information Service. The SEC has tentative plans to distribute the *News Digest* on a wider basis via its own electronic bulletin board or other electronic delivery system.

Each day's issue provides a diversity of news, including a list of closed and open meetings to be held by the Commission, official announcements, and a summary of administrative, civil, and criminal proceedings

initiated against companies, brokers, and investors by the Commission. The heart of the *News Digest* is the section listing the previous day's disclosure filings. Included are merger-related documents covered under the Williams Act, new securities registrations, previously filed registrations which have become effective, and 8-K reports. Among the omitted documents are reports on insider transactions, and routine filings such as 10-Ks, 10-Qs, and Proxies.

Document descriptions vary in length, depending on the type. For example, the roster of 8-K filings is little more than a simple notification that the documents were filed. These entries cite the name of the filing company, the state, relevant SEC Item Numbers, the date of the event, and whether it is an amendment to a previously filed 8-K. For Williams Act filings, data are more detailed, listing the name of the company, the filing party, the form used, the class of security, its CUSIP number, the date of the acquisition, the number and percentage of shares involved, the percentage owned prior to this transaction, and whether the document is a new filing or an amendment. Descriptions of new securities registrations are also reasonably informative. These entries indicate the name of the firm, its address and phone number, the type of form, the class of security, the number of shares and dollar amount, the SEC file number, filing date, the name of the underwriter, and a designation for initial offerings. The complete text of all documents cited in the *News Digest* can be ordered for a small fee from the SEC's Public Reference Room.

SEC Today (Washington Service Bureau, Inc.—Five times per Week).

The publisher of this commercial newsletter is a major document delivery provider specializing in SEC reports. In one form or another, everything found in the *News Digest* appears in *SEC Today*, but it also offers additional information and disseminates news more quickly. *SEC Today* focuses on recent disclosure filings. Information is brief, since the newsletter is intended primarily as a notification service. Readers can order the full text of any document directly from the publisher. The listings of 8-Ks, securities registrations, and Williams Act filings are virtually identical to the government publication, though the publisher alters the format somewhat. The roster of 8-K filings is basically a rearrangement of the government's presentation, for example. The guide to new registrations is also similar, though it adds a brief description of the business and a designation for initial public offerings. The biggest difference can be seen in the Williams Act filings. Though it doesn't

provide a CUSIP number or the prior holdings, *SEC Today* does cite the direction of change which the transaction represents (i.e., purchase or sale), the nationality of the filer, and, for amended documents, the amendment number.

The appendix to each issue is a reproduction of the news briefs dealing with administrative announcements and proceedings from the previous day's *SEC News Digest. SEC Today* also contains related news stories and listings of securities cases filed with the U.S. Supreme Court. A unique weekly feature is the list of "No-Action Letters" issued by the SEC. These are opinions issued by the legal staff of the Commission in response to specific inquiries made by investors, brokers, securities issuers, and stock exchanges. No-Action Letters can provide invaluable assistance in interpreting areas of securities law. The Washington Service Bureau also publishes a weekly loose-leaf service called *SEC No-Action Letters Index and Summaries*, which provides subject and name access to these interpretations, together with abstracts of each letter. A separate microfiche subscription reproduces the complete text of each letter.

Many other newsletters and loose-leaf services covering the SEC are devoted to legal and administrative concerns rather than providing lists of disclosure filings. Examples include the *Federal Securities Law Reporter* from Commerce Clearing House and *Securities Week* from McGraw-Hill. Most are published weekly or monthly, and many are also available online as full-text databases. When researching legal and regulatory issues, these services are preferred, but for up-to-date coverage of news and disclosure filings, the *SEC Today* or the *SEC News Digest* are appropriate choices.

SEC Abstracts (States News Service—Daily).

For research purposes, *SEC Today* suffers from a lack of retrospective indexing, and the brevity of its listings. Both problems are addressed by major online databases which provide more detailed abstracts of disclosure documents. Databases such as *Compact D/SEC* and *SEC Online* focus on quarterly and annual filings, but *SEC Abstracts*, available exclusively on the LEXIS Financial Information Service, emphasizes event-oriented documents. The database is compiled by the States News Service, a wire service which specializes in tracking federal government activities. The firm's staff members in the media room at the SEC supply subscribers in the news media with stories on locally based companies. *SEC Abstracts*, sometimes called *SEC Abstracted Filings*, is derived from this activity. The database contains descriptive summaries of filings for mergers, insider trading, new securities offerings, and other material

events of an unscheduled nature. The file is updated daily, and new records generally appear in the database within 48 hours of being filed with the SEC. The earliest records date back to 1983.

The database has four subfiles: *ACQUIS* deals with merger-related filings, *EVENTS* tracks unscheduled events as reported on Form 8-Ks, *INSIDE* covers the stock transactions of corporate insiders, and *REGIS* reports on new securities registrations. The subfiles can be searched singly, all together, or in various combinations. Information found in the records depends on the type of document filed. *ACQUIS* and *INSIDE* descriptions are quite brief, with no narrative summary. For example, records covering insider trades cite the company name, the filing person, that person's relationship to the firm, the date of the transaction, filing date, the type of transaction, the amount of stock which changed hands, and the insider's total holdings. Records in the *EVENTS* and *REGIS* subfiles are usually more detailed. Abstracts for 8-K reports provide basic data on the company, plus a narrative description of the event, usually between 30 and 60 words in length. Users will find them concise but informative. If the 8-K lists more than one event, each is described, and the SEC's standard Item Number is given.

SEC Abstracts utilizes the same powerful search system found in other LEXIS/NEXIS files, including Boolean and proximity operators. Users can search for any keyword contained in the record, or can restrict results to specific characteristics—type of form, transaction, filing person, underwriter, and so on. The only numbers which can be searched are dates, and, for new security offerings, the amount registered.

Federal Filings (Federal Filings, Inc.—Continuous Updating).

A similar database is produced by Federal Filings, a subsidiary of Dow Jones & Company. Commonly referred to as *FEDFILES*, it covers the same types of records as its competitor, but has some significant differences. Reports are updated continuously throughout the day, making this an excellent way of monitoring the latest news possible. The user enters a simple command to view a list of all current day's filings displayed chronologically. Since the system is designed for tracking recent events, records remain in the system for approximately 90 days only. Because the system is menu-driven, none of the search capabilities seen in *SEC Abstracts* are available. To offset this limitation, the database is well indexed, and users can access records in unique ways. Once a menu category is selected, report titles can be quickly scanned to identify only those abstracts of interest. Users can scan filings by type of

company, choosing from any one of approximately 100 industry codes. Every record is also assigned a code for document type and at least one subject code. Searching can be done by such useful categories as announcements of special stockholders' meetings, bankruptcies, and antitrust news. Company name searching is possible, but Dow Jones also provides access by ticker symbol. Most records are about the same length as those in *SEC Abstracts*.

FEDFILES contains abstracts to documents and publications not found in *SEC Abstracts*, including summaries of antitrust reports issued by the U.S. Federal Trade Commission and abstracts of 10-K and 10-Q reports for approximately 500 leading corporations. *FEDFILES* also contains abstracts to selected stories from daily newspapers across the country, accessible by industry, company, or topic. *FEDFILES* is now available as a subfile on a combined Dow Jones database called *Wires*, which features seven wire services in one file. Though *FEDFILES* offers certain advantages, *SEC Abstracts* is more appropriate for pinpoint searching or for retrospective access.

NEW SECURITIES OFFERINGS

Whether a privately held firm is first "going public" (called an initial offering, or IPO), or a public company is issuing additional securities, the SEC demands detailed disclosure filings called Registration Statements. There are many varieties of Registration Statement, depending on the type of company and nature of the transaction.

For an initial registration (an IPO), the required document is typically an "S" form. The general report filed by most new companies is called Form S-1. Forms S-2 and S-3 are used by existing public companies issuing a new class of security, such as preferred stock or a new bond offering. Because the public is presumed to be informed about widely traded public companies, less information is required for these additional offerings. Form S-4 is required for new offerings made in conjunction with a corporate merger, and Form S-8 is needed when securities are issued for purposes of employee stock options or other benefit plans. Other categories of Registration Statements are "F" forms, covering foreign companies which offer securities in the United States, and "N" forms, used by mutual funds and other investment companies.

Public companies issuing additional shares of an existing class of security (more shares of common stock, for example) must also file disclosure documents. This process is called a trading registration. The requisite document in most cases is Form 8-A, but Form 8-B is used when a public company changes its name, and therefore must change the name of its registered securities.

Most Registration Statements created for an initial offering have common characteristics. Part I of the document specifies pertinent information on the offering, including how much is to be raised, the name of the underwriting firm, the underwriter's commission, and how the funds will be used by the company. It also provides information on the company itself—its debt and equity structure, history, nature of the business, ownership, management compensation, product lines, and audited financial statements. For an initial stock offering, this is the first time the public has access to detailed financial information about a previously private company. Part II of the Registration Statement consists of supporting documentation required by the SEC. The exhibits in Part II typically include corporation bylaws, insurance policies, and major contracts.

Once approved by the SEC, Part I ultimately becomes the sales brochure for the new issue, a document known as the Prospectus. Before attaining such approval, Part I can be used as a preliminary public announcement. Because portions of the document's cover are printed in red ink, the investment community refers to the preliminary announcement as a "Red Herring." Despite its promotional nature, the final Prospectus is typically a plodding document drafted by attorneys. But the SEC requires issuing firms to divulge certain types of unflattering information in the Prospectus. For example, if a company is brand new, with no record of sales or operations, the speculative nature of the investment must be spelled out in detail. In fact, the Registration Statement and Prospectus must specify any major risks inherent in the nature of the business. Registration Statements can be ordered on demand from commercial document delivery firms such as Disclosure, Inc.

A similar document is the Listing Application, which is required by the stock exchange where the security will be traded. Whenever a company seeks to be listed on a stock exchange, or a listed company issues new stocks or bonds, a listing application must be submitted. Since new securities are frequently issued when a corporate merger is enacted, Listing Applications are an excellent source of information on merger details, including background on both parties in a transaction.

Numerous secondary sources provide information on new securities issues. Many newspapers and journals list new stock and bond offerings, including such popular publications as *Barron's, The Wall Street Journal*, and the *Commercial & Financial Chronicle. Investor's Daily* prints an especially detailed list in every issue, with each day's report summarizing several months of the most recent offerings. Listings can also be seen in periodicals specializing in the OTC market, including the *National OTC Stock Journal. Moody's Manuals* and *Standard & Poor's Daily News* are convenient sources of new issue data because they are well-indexed, both in print and electronically. The print versions of both services also provide year-end summaries of major new issues.

Many advisory services focus on Initial Public Offerings as an investment strategy. Standard & Poor's monthly *Emerging and Special Situations* provides brief company profiles of selected IPOs, but no cumulative list of offerings. Over half of each newsletter is devoted to recently issued stocks that are now traded in the secondary market (also called the aftermarket). Some of the information is reprinted from S&P's *OTC Stock Reports*, introduced in Chapter 12. A more official source of new issue information is the daily *SEC News Digest*. Another comes from the New York Stock Exchange, whose *NYSE Weekly Bulletin* contains a complete roster of recent Listing Applications. Commercial reporting services such as the *SEC Today* offer yet another research option.

The most rapid and efficient retrieval of registration information is usually afforded by electronic databases. Two of the better systems—*FEDFILES* and *SEC Abstracts*—have been introduced already. Another important, though unlikely source is *PTS PROMT*, described in Chapter 5. It includes lengthy abstracts of S-1 Registration Statements, and employs detailed indexing, including Predicasts product and event codes.

Detailed summaries of all new issue filings are now available on CD-ROM through Disclosure's *Compact D/ '33*. (The title refers to the Securities Act of 1933, the law governing securities registration.) Every record includes a description of the security, the transaction type, background on the company, the names of underwriters and legal and financial advisors, fees incurred by the company, related companies in the transaction (the parent of a spin-off firm, the target of a takeover, etc.), the complete text of the narrative portion of the record, and a history of documents filed in the case. All important portions of the form are represented. Like other products in the *Compact D* series, it affords sophisticated, yet user-friendly searching. Virtually all portions of the record may be searched. Disks are updated monthly, with information dating back to January 1990.

Secondary publications also exist for other types of securities registrations. Electronic services like *SEC Abstracts* and *Compact D/'33* include bonds, for example, but the most comprehensive source for debt issues is the daily *Blue List of Current Municipal and Corporate Offerings*. This authoritative guide is produced by the Blue List Publishing Company, a division of Standard & Poor's. For each new security, the *Blue List* cites the issuer, amount, rate and maturity date, purpose, yield or price, and underwriter. The *Bond Buyer*, a daily tabloid from American Banker/Bond Buyer devotes extensive coverage to stories on new municipal and corporate offerings. The complete text of this paper is also searchable online through DIALOG, NEXIS, and NewsNet. S&P's *CreditWeek* and *Moody's Bond Survey* provide weekly coverage of major corporate and municipal bond issues. Both are described in Chapter 12.

Investment Dealers' Digest (Dealers' Digest, Inc.—Weekly).

Dealers' Digest, Inc. looks beyond SEC filings to obtain information. The company is in constant contact with the investment banks which do the actual underwriting. Their best-known publication is a weekly magazine entitled *Investment Dealers' Digest*, which provides well-written stories on securities news, underwriting trends, and other topics of interest to investment bankers. Every issue also features numerous rosters of recent underwriting activity. The section begins with a list of securities registered with the SEC during the previous week, differentiating between initial offerings and shelf registrations. Entries specify the company, filing date, type of document, SEC file number, underwriter, expected offering date, and the details of the transaction. The list is arranged by company name. A second section is a chronological listing of new issues by expected offering date. This chart is broken down by stocks, corporate debt, and municipals. The next table is arranged by underwriting firm, and reviews the status of each underwriter's recent offerings. The final list surveys the performance of new stock issues in the secondary market, listing the initial offering price, current market price, and price change since first issued. Statistical summaries of new issue activity by industry and type of security can also be found. Dealers' Digest also produces two weekly newsletters: *Going Public: The IPO Reporter* focuses on trends in the IPO market and provides details on forthcoming offerings; the *Private Placement Letter* covers new securities offerings in the private placement market.

Directory of Corporate Financing (Dealers' Digest, Inc.—Semiannual).

Because *Investment Dealers' Digest* is not a convenient source for retrospective searching, Dealers' Digest publishes a semiannual reference guide known as the *Directory of Corporate Financing*. The format is similar to the weekly journal, with access by company, type of offering, and underwriter. Information can also be found on joint ventures, mergers, and major private placements. Excellent statistical summaries are included. An especially popular feature is the ranked lists of underwriters by dollar volume of new issues. Composite rankings are given as well as separate lists by type of security. For researchers investigating historical trends, comparing the underwriting activity of various investment banks, tracking developments within a single company, or looking for a comprehensive review of the previous year's events, this directory is an invaluable resource. IDD Information Services, Inc., a subsidiary of Dealers' Digest, produces two comprehensive online databases with reports dating back to 1972. The main service is *IDD Domestic and International New Issues*, which is updated daily and available through direct subscription with the publisher.

Another source of retrospective data is the *Initial Public Offerings Annual*, from Omnigraphics, Inc. Coverage is limited to IPOs listed on the New York or American exchanges or the NASDAQ system. Each entry gives a standard five-page summary of the company's Prospectus. Included are a description of the business, summary financial statements, the terms of the offering, capitalization, and the use of proceeds statement.

The major competitor to Dealers' Digest, Inc. is the Securities Data Company. Their SDC Financial Database System consists of approximately ten major files, including several comprehensive services for new securities issues. The *Domestic Public New Issues Database* provides detailed information on all new issues offered since 1970. Subfiles are created for different categories of securities, including common stock, corporate bonds, convertible bonds, and mortgage-backed instruments. Separate files cover foreign offerings, private placements, and municipal securities. Descriptions are extensive, including provisions of the offering, listings of underwriters, and background on issuing firms. Information is obtained through prospectuses, news stories, and contacts with underwriters. Customers must subscribe to the SDC system directly through the publisher. The menu-driven files are easy to use and offer sophisticated capabilities for searching and reporting. Databases are updated daily. SDC also compiles statistics and rankings on underwriting activity, retrieved online as special reports. Summary findings are reported quarterly as a feature of *The Wall Street Journal*.

CORPORATE OWNERSHIP

The question of who really owns a company becomes blurred when speaking of public corporations. As far back as the 1930s, astute observers of corporate America began analyzing the difference between ownership and control. Under the law, a corporation is owned jointly by its stockholders. If two million stockholders have voting rights, then there are two million owners of the firm. But how this ownership relates to responsibility and authority is open to interpretation. Most shareholders purchase stock as an investment, not to influence the direction of "their" company. In fact, many investors don't exercise the voting rights they possess.

According to theory, the board of directors—which is elected by the stockholders—keeps an eye on management for the collective owners. The board is legally entrusted with the stewardship of the corporation. But theory often diverges from real-world behavior, and the role of the board varies considerably from company to company. For many firms, both day-to-day operations and long-term strategies are determined by corporate management. Management's success is measured quantitatively by market share, net income, the price of the stock in the marketplace, and dividends paid to stockholders.

By law, the major decisions affecting the company's future must be approved by a majority of owners attending the annual meeting of the firm. Most stockholders trust management's decisions. Management is allowed to solicit proxy votes from the stockholders by mail, and proxies in management's favor are usually sufficient to carry the day. For one thing, the largest stockholders in most corporations are other institutions. Pension funds, insurance companies, banks, and other institutional investors own huge blocks of stock in almost every major public corporation. Pension funds alone own more than 25% of the outstanding common stock in the United States. Institutions may or may not keep a particular stock in their portfolio for long periods of time, but many are unconcerned with their ownership rights. Traditionally, institutional investors have ignored their tremendous voting power and turned proxies over to management. This has changed somewhat in recent years, particularly

in areas of "social responsibility" and in matters affecting the vested interests of the institutional investor, but lack of voting remains a fact of corporate life.

Two ownership issues concern investment researchers: the composition of ownership, and insider trading activities. The first topic centers on how much control is exercised by leading shareholders. A group of like-minded individuals with large holdings can exert substantial influence on company management, and can play a key role in takeover battles. Of special interest is the percentage of stock owned by institutional investors, not only for their ability to exercise voting rights, but because of their market power. If a pension fund or insurance company decides to sell an enormous block of stock at once, it can have a jarring effect on the company's stock price.

A company's ability to identify shareholders is essential for soliciting proxy votes and for mailing dividend checks. Millions of shares of stock change hands each day, so most corporations hire transfer agents to keep track of current owners. A transfer agent is an organization, usually a large bank, which maintains a list of its client's stockholders. Whenever a share of stock changes hands, the information is relayed to the transfer agent, who updates the list.

Understandably, this can be a complicated task. The agent often does not know the true owner of the stock. For example, many investors simply do not take possession of their stock certificates. They are content to receive monthly statements from their broker citing the activity in their trading account, while allowing the broker to hold the certificate on their behalf. This is called holding a stock in "street name" only; the transfer agent's records show the broker as the stock owner. The broker passes proxy statements on to the actual owner, just as dividend checks are forwarded. Sometimes even the broker's name is not listed with the transfer agent. Brokers don't want to shuffle stock certificates back and forth with each trade, so stock clearinghouses hold certificates for stockbrokers and institutional investors, then keep track of the transfers. The records of the issuing company's transfer agent show the clearinghouse as the owner of the stock.

Disclosure regulations prevent clearinghouses from being a haven of anonymity. The SEC requires insiders, institutional investors, and others with extensive holdings in the company to divulge information about their trades soon after they are executed, or to register their holdings on a regular basis. An insider is defined as a senior executive or director of the firm, together with anyone owning 10% or more of the outstanding stock. An institutional investor is generally any organization with more than $100 million in invested assets. The SEC also imposes reporting requirements on individuals or institutions which own between 5% and 10% of a firm's stock, although such investors are not technically considered insiders. In many cases they own the stock for investment purposes only, but in others the purchase of large blocks can be the opening bid in a takeover attempt. Additional disclosure regulations relating to takeovers will be discussed later in the chapter.

Although the illegal excesses of the 1980s have made "insider trading" a pejorative term, such activities usually involve legitimate investment transactions. What *is* against the law is utilizing inside information to make a profit in the stock market. If an executive or director knew potentially damaging news before it was announced to the public, that person could sell whatever stock they owned before the negative news caused the stock's price to decline. Potential insider abuse is one reason companies must divulge material information to the public immediately. But insiders have a right to buy and sell stock in their company just as anyone else. Stock options, bonuses, and other employee benefit programs can make executives owners of sizable blocks of stock. Insiders, institutional investors, and other large shareholders have a legal obligation to report their trading activities to the SEC.

Corporate insiders must file SEC Form 3 when they acquire their first stock in the firm, and Form 4 for every subsequent transaction involving their company's stock. Institutional owners must file Forms 13-F or 13G on a periodic basis. Individual investors who purchase or own more than 5% of a company's stock must file Forms 13D or 13G, depending on the situation. Another disclosure document covers "restricted stock." A common example involves insiders who acquire shares through employee stock option plans. Under SEC rules, such stock must be held by the purchaser for a minimum period. Before reselling it, the insider must file Form 144, a "Notice of Proposed Sale." This prohibits options holders from exercising the option and immediately reselling the stock for a profit.

In January 1991, the SEC revised the rules on insider disclosure for the first time since 1934. This was done because the broad definition of "insider" created a huge volume of paperwork, and because a large percentage of insiders were delinquent in submitting filings. The new rules exempt lower-level executives from disclosure requirements, but impose stricter penalties on the remaining insiders who fail to file.

An investor or researcher might need corporate ownership information to obtain a profile of a company's ownership characteristics, or to monitor stock transactions as they take place. The latter situation usually involves tracking insider activities or merger transactions, both of which will be discussed later.

Cumulative Ownership Sources

Disclosure documents provide information on major stockholders, but are not always the most convenient source for constructing a company ownership profile. Because ownership filings are submitted by the stockholders themselves, and because they are updated as transactions occur, the individual documents do not offer a composite picture of a company's owners. Such a profile can inform investment decisions. Some investors feel that companies with a large percentage of institutional owners are especially vulnerable, or that their stock price is more volatile. Others like to buy stock in such firms on the assumption that institutional money mangers are savvy investors. Ownership profiles can also identify companies which have a controlling interest in another firm, though one is not a subsidiary of the other. Lawyers, labor unions, public interest groups, and community leaders have an interest in knowing who owns a company, for social, political, or legal reasons.

How can an interested party obtain cumulative ownership information? Annual Proxy Statements describe stock holdings for certain insiders and institutional investors, but the lists are incomplete. Financial services like *Standard & Poor's Stock Guide*, *Media General*, and *Compact D/SEC* provide data on the percentage of stock held by institutions and/or the number of institutional owners, but no names are given. The best way to obtain a breakdown of ownership by company is to utilize a commercial publication or database which cumulates information from disclosure documents. These services may track individual owners, institutional investors, or both, and they present data in convenient tables arranged by company name.

Spectrum Ownership Profiles (CDA Investment Technologies, Inc.—Various Frequencies).

Presently, only one service publishes complete, cumulative lists of corporate ownership by company name. CDA Investment Technologies compiles data from SEC ownership filings, summarizes them by company name, and publishes the results on a monthly, quarterly, or semiannual basis. Coverage is limited to companies on the New York and American exchanges,

and on the NASDAQ system. Six separate "Spectrum" services are published. The main title, *Spectrum 6—Insider Ownership*, is issued twice each year. This is a complete list by company name of all officers, directors, and 10% stockholders together with the number of shares owned, and the amount of any recent trades. A companion service, *Spectrum 5—Five Percent Ownership*, covers the details for current trading activities of 5% owners, and is updated monthly. The other publications in the "Spectrum" series, all published quarterly, are as follows:

> *Spectrum 1—Investment Company Stock Holdings Survey.* A listing of stocks owned by mutual funds, arranged by name of stock.
>
> *Spectrum 2—Investment Company Portfolios.* This companion to *Spectrum 1* provides the same information arranged by name of mutual fund.
>
> *Spectrum 3—Institutional Stock Holdings Survey.* Similar to *Spectrum 1*, except it lists the stock holdings of banks, insurance companies, pension funds, and endowment funds. Data are arranged by name of stock.
>
> *Spectrum 4—Institutional Portfolios.* This companion volume to *Spectrum 3* lists the same information by name of institutional owner.

Data from the Spectrum files can also be searched in electronic formats. Under an agreement with Disclosure, Inc., CDA makes its information available through an online database called *Disclosure/Spectrum Ownership*. Each company record cites general data on the firm (SIC code, stock exchange, ticker symbol, former name, and number of outstanding shares), together with listings of all institutional, insider, and 5% owners. Ownership information includes the total number of shares owned by each person or institution and the date of the latest filing for each. For every ownership category, summary statistics on the number of owners, the total shares, and their market value are given. The database is updated quarterly and is available through DIALOG, BRS, Dow Jones, and CompuServe. On Dow Jones and CompuServe it can be searched by company only. The system is much more flexible on DIALOG and BRS, where most numeric and text variables can be searched, including shareholders' names. Another online option is a direct subscription through CDA itself. The information on this version is updated daily, but an annual subscription fee is required. Finally, the files can be found on the SDC Financial Database System, produced by the Securities Data Company. (CDA and SDC are both owned by International Thomson.)

Researchers who refer to ownership data frequently may prefer the CD-ROM alternative. Subscribers to *Compact D/SEC* can receive *Disclosure/Spectrum Ownership* on disk for an additional charge. The information is presented as part of the Disclosure record. Readers should note that the standard subscription to *Compact D/ SEC* provides summary data from "Spectrum," including the number of owners by type and the percentage of ownership by type. Subscribers to the enhanced version of the disk will find more complete Spectrum reports.

Vickers Stock Traders Guide (Vickers Stock Research Corporation—Quarterly).

Vickers tracks institutional stock ownership only. The main publication is *Vickers Stock Traders Guide*, a two-volume manual combining information similar to that found in *Spectrum 1* and *Spectrum 3*. It provides complete information on stock ownership by 4,600 mutual funds, trust companies, college endowments, and insurance companies. Ownership of both U.S. and Canadian stocks are followed. Data are arranged by the name of the stock, with a list of each owning institution's total holdings and any transactions conducted in the previous quarter. The set also includes three ranked lists in every issue: the top 100 stocks held by institutions (ranked by volume of shares held), the top 100 stocks purchased during that period (ranked by dollar volume), and a similar list of the top 100 stocks sold. A second two-volume manual, the *Vickers Portfolio Guide*, gives the same information, arranged by institutional owner. In addition to a complete list of each institution's holdings and recent transactions, it cites the total dollar value of its stock portfolio. The service is similar to *Spectrum 2* and *Spectrum 4*.

Vickers data can also be found online via the LEXIS Financial Information Service. The database is similar to the printed product, being divided into two subfiles. The first, *Vickers Securities Report*, corresponds to the printed *Traders Guide*. For each stock, it profiles the holdings of all institutions with a significant position in that firm. It cites the transactions from the previous quarter, the total holdings, and the percentage of the institution's entire portfolio invested in this stock. Summary data are also compiled for each stock, including a list of the top ten institutions owning the stock, and a statistical analysis of total institutional ownership and trading. The second file, *Vickers Institutional Holdings*, contains detailed data by institution, and corresponds to the *Portfolio Guide*. For each institutional investor, a current list of the organization's stock holdings is given. Every report also provides summary analysis which includes a ranking of the institution's top ten stock holdings and a breakdown of holdings by industry group. For both files, numeric data in the holdings and transactions segments can be searched arithmetically.

Insider Trading Reports

Vickers and *Spectrum Ownership* offer cumulative profiles of stock ownership. A second approach is to use newsletters or online services that report transactions as they are filed. Aside from the news services described earlier, most publications of this type focus on insider trading. The following services provide ongoing coverage of new transactions, with varying degrees of currency.

Insider Trading Monitor (Invest/Net Group, Inc.— Daily).

Invest/Net is the SEC's official contractor for providing information on insider transactions. Its *Insider Trading Monitor* is available on DIALOG, ADP Data Services, and directly through the publisher. The latter two services offer continuous updating throughout the day, while DIALOG's file is revised once per day.

On DIALOG, the *Insider Trading Monitor* creates a separate record for every transaction. Each record lists data on the company as well as the trade. For companies, the name, address, phone, ticker symbol, CUSIP number, SIC code, and total number of shares outstanding are provided. The description of the trade includes the insider's name and position, whether the ownership is direct or indirect, the type of security, the nature of the transaction, the number of shares involved, the average price, and the insider's total holdings. The database can be searched by most variables, including company and insider's name, insider's position, transaction type, industry, and many numeric attributes. For example, searchers can retrieve all the stock sales within the chemical industry, made by CEOs, involving more than 5,000 shares, and occurring within the past nine months. DIALOG's Report feature can compile comparative tables for different companies, or generate customized lists by company or person. Unlike the *Spectrum* database, *Insider Trading Monitor* can also generate a comprehensive history of transactions by person or company. The records begin with 1984.

The version available directly from Invest/Net is a menu-driven system. Options allow searching by company name, ticker symbol, or insider's name. Other menu selections provide daily and weekly summaries of the most recent transactions. Ranked lists can be generated of the stocks traded most actively by insiders over the past 90, 180, or 360 days. A unique feature to this version

is a subfile with detailed descriptions of all Form 144 filings. These "Notices of Proposed Sale" must be filed by all insiders who intend to sell shares of restricted stock—notably stock acquired through employee benefit plans.

Invest/Net also provides a variation of their database on Dow Jones News/Retrieval. Called *Corporate Ownership Watch*, it offers less sophisticated search capabilities. However, it does include data from filings other than Forms 3 and 4. All 13D and 14D filings, which report transactions of 5% owners and tender offers, are covered. Only transactions from the previous 18 months remain on the database, but this version allows the user to display a comprehensive list of all insider holdings for a given company, an option unavailable through DIALOG. Another useful feature is the inclusion of the insider's percentage of ownership. *Corporate Ownership Watch* can be searched by name of filer, company name, or ticker symbol. Users can also view a list of the current day's filings by type, or a summary of the week's 25 largest transactions. Invest/Net also offers the latter feature as a weekly syndicated column seen in numerous business periodicals and general newspapers.

Insiders' Chronicle (Chronicle Publishing Company— Weekly).

This weekly newsletter is an extremely current printed source for tracking the latest insider transactions. Listings are arranged by company name, with separate tables for each stock exchange. For every stock with insider trading, the names of the individuals, the amounts purchased or sold, the dates of the transactions, the price, the amount of stock now owned, and the person's relationship to the company are shown. Because this is essentially an investment advisory service, additional features are provided. The cover article is an analysis of a company in the news, from an insider trading perspective. A list of the 15 companies with the largest volume of sales and the 15 firms with the largest volume of purchases is compiled. Company profiles are given for the four or five companies with the largest volume of insider trading as reported in the previous issue of the *Chronicle*. A statistical summary of the week's trading activity is also compiled. A quarterly summary of transactions is included with the subscription. Numerous other newsletters cover insider trading activity, but the *Insiders' Chronicle* is the most popular and simplest to use.

Official Summary of Securities Transactions and Holdings (U.S. Securities and Exchange Commission— Monthly).

The government's guide to insider transactions is more of a retrospective summary than a current news service. Every issue provides an alphabetical list of stocks, with a breakdown of acquisitions and sales by insiders' names. For each transaction, the following data are given: the insider's relationship to the firm, whether the transaction was direct or indirect, the date of the trade, its nature (open market trade, exercise of stock option, etc.), the amount bought or sold (and when reported, the average price per share), and the filer's total holdings. The publication is compiled for the SEC by Invest/Net. The major drawback to the *Official Summary* is the considerable delay in publishing. Though issued monthly, new editions don't appear until several months after the cover date, and the time period designated on each issue refers to the filing period, not the dates of the transactions. However, it is a more affordable alternative to the expensive commercial services.

MERGER-RELATED ACTIVITIES

Business in the 1980s seemed to be dominated by corporate mergers and acquisitions, also known as M&A activity. The decade saw over 2,000 major announcements per year, and the frantic pace of corporate takeovers is only now abating. Other decades have seen extensive merger activity, but the 1980s were unique for many reasons. The most spectacular characteristic was the breathtaking magnitude of the largest takeovers; record-breaking deals were surpassed repeatedly, until multi-billion dollar transactions seemed commonplace. The decade also saw an endless stream of legal and financial innovations including junk bond financing and novel anti-takeover defenses. The merger arena has become increasingly complex and fluid. Because the potential exists in any major transaction for all parties to make a great deal of money, the value of current, accurate information becomes obvious. Thus, an amazing growth in merger databases, newsletters, and reference materials also marked the decade. Although an entire book could be spent on this topic, the following section will provide a brief guide to some of the best-known sources of information.

Players on the M&A scene employ an arcane, colorful language, so a few essential concepts must be explained. A merger takes place when one company

acquires all of the stock or all of the assets of another firm, but there are many kinds of merger transactions. Only a few hundred of the deals which occur each year result in the merger of two publicly traded companies. Other types of mergers involve a public corporation acquiring a privately held company, the combination of two private firms, or the acquisition of a company by a group of private investors. Sometimes a publicly held company will sell one of its subsidiaries, a transaction referred to as a divestiture or sell-off. A less-frequent occurrence is a spinoff, when a subsidiary issues stock of its own and becomes a public company, independent of its former parent. In a leveraged buyout (LBO), the purchasers borrow heavily in order to finance their acquisition. Companies purchased through an LBO are thus saddled with a substantial burden of debt. The debt is most often paid off by subsequently selling a portion of the acquired company's assets, subsidiaries, or divisions. Many LBOs are initiated either by a group of company managers who wish to become sole owners of the firm, or by investment companies which see an opportunity to profit from the transaction. In either case, when a publicly held corporation is sold through an LBO, it generally becomes a private company. With all the LBOs and mergers of the past decade, many formerly public companies have either lost their independent identity or have "gone private."

Information about mergers is obtained from disclosure filings and the news media. When publicly held companies are involved, the participants must submit disclosure documents known collectively as Williams Act reports. The two major filings are Forms 14D-1 and 13D. The first is submitted by companies attempting to purchase another company in the open market (called a tender offer). The second is filed by individuals purchasing 5% or more of a company's stock with the intent to obtain substantial voting control or otherwise influence the management of the firm. News stories, including press releases from the participants themselves, are the primary source of information on private transactions. The business media can also provide additional details on mergers involving public companies.

When researching merger information based on SEC filings, two final points should be remembered, especially where online databases are concerned. First, acquiring companies frequently create "shell corporations" for the express purpose of transacting the merger. Shells usually have the word "Acquisitions" or "Holdings" in the name, and frequently refer to the target company in the title as well. For example, when Kohlberg Kravis Roberts & Company, the leading LBO deal maker

in the country, initiated its takeover of RJR Nabisco in 1988, it formed the RJR Acquisition Corporation. SEC documents will generally list the shell company as the "Reporting Person," so researchers should expand an online query beyond the field for acquiring company and look for the company name in the text or abstract fields also. Each Williams Act filing covers a particular type of transaction. Form 14D-1 deals with tender offers, Form 13E-3 with LBOs, and so on. When searching online systems, it is helpful to limit a search to specific document types. In general, researchers investigating merger-related activities should become familiar with the various filings and with merger terms and concepts.

An extraordinary variety of databases, newsletters, and reporting services utilize information from disclosure filings, company announcements, and the media to provide extensive, organized analysis of merger transactions as they unfold. General business indexes and news databases can be useful in conducting merger research, but the following sources provide specific coverage of M&A activities.

Mergers & Acquisitions: The Journal of Corporate Venture (MLR Publishing Company—Bimonthly).

Mergers & Acquisitions magazine is respected for its excellent articles on trends in merger techniques and strategy, but its value for business researchers is the "M&A Rosters" found in most issues. The Rosters list every corporate acquisition over $1 million which the publisher can identify, including private transactions. Entries cite the names of the buying and selling companies, the type of transaction, the basic terms of the deal, a brief description of both parties, and, when available, the sales and net income of one or both companies. Although some listings say only "undisclosed amount," many do include the purchase price. Entries are grouped by broad SIC category. Because of the industry arrangement, and because both public and private transactions are covered, *Mergers & Acquisitions* is a wonderful source for researching the market value of companies by type of business.

The journal is published bimonthly, but the Rosters appear quarterly, in July, September, January, and March. Deals transacted in the first quarter of the year are reported in the July/August issue, and so on. The November/December issue reports on an annual conference sponsored by the publisher, and the May/June issue is the annual "Almanac and Index." The latter volume includes articles which review the previous year's activities, plus numerous summary tables. Here can be found statistics by type of deal, industry, and size of transaction, together with rankings of the largest mergers and divestitures of

the year. A company index provides an alphabetical list of every buyer and seller mentioned in the previous year's issues. A more complete version of the Rosters can be found online as the *M&A Data Base*, offered through ADP Data Services. The online version will be described later in the chapter.

IDD M&A Transactions (IDD Information Services—Daily).

IDD Information Services is a subsidiary of Dealers' Digest, Inc., a leading source of information on world securities markets. The *IDD M&A Transactions* database offers extremely powerful searching capabilities, with records updated daily. Facts are gathered from SEC disclosure filings, corporate news releases, major financial publications and wire services, and the publisher's ongoing contacts with major investment banks. The database emphasizes companies in the United States and Great Britain, but major deals in other parts of the world are included. For U.S. companies, both public and private transactions are followed, with a cutoff of $1 million or more. For British companies, all publicly announced transactions are covered. Records date back to 1984.

Up to 178 data fields can be found in each report. Major areas of information are descriptions of both parties, key characteristics of the transaction, the techniques used, a narrative summary of the terms, the status of the deal, information on the financial and legal advisors employed by both sides, fees paid, and summary financial statements of the target company. For publicly held companies, background on the tender offer is given, as are recent stock prices, per share data, financial ratios, and premiums paid over current market value. Virtually every numeric and textual field in the record can be searched, and controlled vocabulary terms facilitate searching. Standardized fields include transaction type, deal status, attitude (friendly versus hostile), and the techniques or defense tactics used. Approximately 20 subject terms describe acquisition techniques, from tender offers to "dutch auctions." Another seven terms describe defensive tactics such as "poison pills" and "scorched earth" policies. In both instances, as many headings are assigned as appropriate.

The incredible detail of each record (especially for publicly held companies), coupled with the extensive indexing, make *IDD M&A Transactions* a remarkably versatile research tool. When searching by company name, users can easily differentiate between target and acquiring companies. Another distinction is between public and private deals. Companies actively contemplating a future merger can be identified by searching the

status field for the terms "Seeks Buyer" or "Seeks Target." Likewise, searchers can distinguish between completed and pending deals; even stories in the rumor stage can be identified. Any combination of characteristics can be combined for pinpoint results—deal value, SIC code of either party, country, state of incorporation, type of deal, source of funds, or financial attributes of the target company. The database is offered on the DIALOG system or directly through the publisher. It is also available on CD-ROM from DIALOG, utilizing the same search system found on other DIALOG On Disc financial databases, and from Lotus Development Corporation, as part of the Lotus One Source series. The Lotus disk, *CD/M&A*, is a menu-driven system with more limited screening capabilities. For current Lotus subscribers, *CD/M&A* costs about the same as the DIALOG version, but is more expensive for non-Lotus customers. Both are updated monthly.

Some of the information in the database can also be found in a weekly publication from Dealers' Digest. *Mergers & Acquisitions Report* follows a traditional newsletter format, with brief stories on deal announcements, regulatory changes, financing trends, and other news events. Every issue contains a summary of recent transactions presented in tabular form, but coverage is limited to deals of $100 million or more. Listings are abbreviated versions of the complete online entries, but include background on both parties, a description of the deal, and quick data on the price, type, status, and attitude.

A similar online service, called the *M&A Data Base*, is produced by MLR Publishing. This is the electronic version of the "M&A Rosters" seen in *Merger & Acquisitions* magazine. Like the IDD database, the MLR service focuses on public and private deals of more than $1 million, and is updated daily. It also includes stock price and per share information for publicly held companies. The MLR version is limited to transactions taking place in the United States or involving U.S. companies, and records date back to 1979. The database utilizes fewer indexed fields, though with approximately 100 searchable variables it is still a powerful system. The *M&A Data Base* also allows the user to perform certain arithmetic operations on numeric variables (e.g., identifying all records where variable A is 10% greater than variable B), a feature not found on the IDD system. The *M&A Data Base* is found exclusively on ADP Data Services, marketed primarily to the corporate community.

Another corporate-oriented online system is available from the Securities Data Company, as part of their SDC Financial Database System. The *Merger and Cor-*

porate Transactions Database covers 400,000 transactions dating back to 1981. The service is menu-driven, powerful, and updated daily. Users can view a Daily Activity Report, examine rankings of merger advisors based on different deal characteristics, create summary reports of merger volume, and obtain descriptions and histories of specific mergers. Background on publicly traded target companies includes five years of key financial figures. Screening can be done on any of 400 characteristics, including detailed codes by type of transaction or defense tactic. The SDC service also offers the ability to perform basic statistical analyses online.

M&A Filings (Charles E. Simon & Company—Daily).

Two other M&A online products are distinctly different in purpose and scope from the products described above. *M&A Filings* is produced by Charles Simon & Company, a major document delivery and research service for SEC documents. Information is based exclusively on Williams Act filings, and is therefore limited to transactions involving public companies. Approximately 35 data fields are indexed, so it is a less versatile system than the products described above. On the other hand, it boasts a number of useful features not offered by its competitors. Because it provides fairly lengthy abstracts of the SEC filings, surprisingly detailed information can be found. For the same reason, users can design very specific searches using keywords in the text. *M&A Filings* employs a controlled vocabulary to identify specific types of transactions. Simon utilizes nearly four times as many subject terms as the IDD database. This makes it extremely easy to identify very specific transaction characteristics, from deals requiring a covenant not to compete to those offering a "golden parachute" to management. *M&A Filings* can be searched by industry, geographic variables, and key financial characteristics. Because the information reported varies according to the type of disclosure document filed, users are advised to study the database documentation before constructing a search.

Records consist of abstracts of primary source documents, so researchers will often need to use news oriented databases to track subsequent developments in a merger-related transaction. Williams Act filings report the initiation of a merger action, not necessarily the outcome. *M&A Filings* enables the user to differentiate between original filings and amendments, but it is frequently impossible to determine if a deal was completed based on primary documents alone. The IDD and MLR products will update each record as new information is announced. *M&A Filings* is available exclusively on DIALOG, and is updated daily, with a one-day time lag

for most records. Reports date back to early 1985. The complete text of any SEC document in the database can be ordered through Charles Simon.

Another online service based on SEC filings can be found on the *ACQUIS* subset of *SEC Abstracts*, described earlier. The abstracts are briefer than those from Charles Simon, and no numeric searching is possible. Records can be searched by filing company, type of document, date, subject, or keywords in the text of the abstract.

Mergerstat Review (W.T. Grimm & Company—Annual).

A different approach to merger information is provided by sources which summarize the previous year's activities. Annual reviews can put the merger phenomenon in a broader perspective, comparing similar deals, analyzing industries, obtaining market prices for valuing a private business, locating ready reference data, and following general merger trends. Most annual publications combine narrative articles with statistical analyses and ranked lists of major deals. In addition to the "Almanac" issue of *Mergers & Acquisitions* magazine, there are three widely followed annual reviews.

Mergerstat Review, produced by the W.T. Grimm division of Merrill Lynch, emphasizes statistical tables, but offers a diversity of additional information. Detailed statistical summaries are provided for acquisitions, divestitures, management buyouts, tender offers, LBOs, and even canceled deals. Data are based on an analysis of all deals valued at $1 million or more and involving at least one party from the United States. Canceled deals are subtracted to calculate data on net merger transactions. The publication is one of the best sources for historical analysis; annual figures are reported back to 1963, and, in many cases, quarterly statistics are given for the previous 15 years. A variety of tabulations are presented by type of transaction, form of payment, industry breakdown, country of buyer, and state in which the deal took place. Most tables cite the number of transactions, median price, Price/Earnings ratio, and premium paid over current market value. *Mergerstat Review* offers a variety of company rankings, including a list of the largest deals of the year, the largest in U.S. history, the largest deals by type, and record-breaking transactions by industry. The final section is devoted to "Transaction Rosters" which cite details of merger-related activities which took place in the previous year. The first is a list of deals completed or pending; the second is a list of cancellations. The first roster is not comprehensive. The publisher lists only those deals for which a price was announced and for which the acquired company's annual sales are known. Of the 2,366 net transactions followed by Grimm in 1989, for example, only 369 are reported in the "Roster."

The two other major yearbooks are the *Merger & Acquisition Sourcebook* and the *Merger Yearbook*. The first is produced by the Quality Services Company, which also publishes several periodicals on the subject. The *Merger & Acquisition Sourcebook* provides a much more complete roster of major transactions than *Mergerstat*, including separate lists of foreign transactions, cancellations, and other breakdowns by type. In each section, deals are listed by SIC number, with fairly detailed information on each transaction. For example, the listings on public companies cite three years of sales, net income, and net worth for the acquired company, the price of the target company's stock at the time of the announcement, the price and terms of the deal, the Price/Earnings ratio and other analytical measures, brief background on the purchaser, and a narrative description of the transaction. Other sections highlight the largest mergers of the preceding year and present summary statistics by industry. Unlike the *Mergerstat Review*, a company name index is provided. Data from the *Sourcebook* are updated by a current newsletter called the *Acquisition/Divestiture Weekly Report*. The company also publishes the *Corporate Growth Report*, a monthly journal on trends and techniques in the acquisitions and buyout field.

The *Merger Yearbook* is now compiled by the Securities Data Company. The publication has undergone several title changes, and is frequently referred to as the *Yearbook on Corporate Acquisitions, Leveraged Buyouts, Joint Ventures, and Corporate Policy*. It is similar to the *Sourcebook*, with a variety of rosters, ranked lists, and an index to company names. Entries cite the basic terms of each transaction, background on the parties involved (with financial data where available), and the type of deal. It differs from *Mergerstat* and the *Merger & Acquisition Sourcebook* in describing joint venture activities, and in providing brief survey articles on trends in the field. Beginning with 1990, a companion international edition is available. SDC also publishes two periodicals. The *Yearbook's* updating service is a weekly newsletter called *Mergers and Corporate Policy*; their monthly guide to trends in merger activity is the *Merger Management Report*. They also publish the *Merger and Corporate Transactions Database* described above.

TRACKING CORPORATE CHANGES

Merger-related activity is only one way in which corporations undergo changes in structure or name. Corporations change names for numerous nonfinancial rea-

sons: to reflect a significant shift in mission, to change image or personality, or to jettison an old name in favor of a more modern sound. Companies may cease to exist, through bankruptcies or other forms of dissolution. Investors are also interested in capital changes within the firm, such as stock splits and new stock issues. Keeping track of these changes can be difficult. Fortunately, several excellent publications report data on a broad range of changes—reorganizations, mergers, name changes, capital adjustments—in a consolidated, organized fashion.

Periodical indexes in printed or electronic form can be an excellent way of identifying or verifying organizational changes. Disclosure tracking services like *FEDFILES* are particularly appropriate, but are limited to certain types of transactions. Directories which list subsidiary relationships are also useful. The *Directory of Corporate Affiliations*, described in Chapter 7, provides the added benefit of a bimonthly *Corporate Action* newsletter. Even summary financial services are helpful in following name changes. Records in *Compact D/SEC* can be searched by a standard field called "Company Cross-References," which includes former names. The printed versions of both *Moody's Manuals* and *Standard & Poor's Corporation Records* contain indexes to former and alternate names. The semiannual editions of the *National Monthly Stock Summary*, introduced in Chapter 10, offer excellent access to name changes, mergers, and defunct companies, alphabetically by name.

The following section will introduce three specialized services exclusively designed to track changes in corporate structure or identity.

Capital Changes Reports (Commerce Clearing House—Weekly).

Capital Changes Reports (also known as *Capital Changes Reporter*) is a loose-leaf service designed for income tax purposes. The seven-volume set chronicles the changes in capital structure of publicly traded corporations. Data are arranged alphabetically by company name, with a separate "New Matters" section covering the most recent changes. The basic alphabetical entries are updated periodically to incorporate all changes reported in "New Matters." Thorough indexing makes it easy to find all relevant transactions in both sections. Each company listing provides a chronological record of major financial events. Like the histories in *Moody's Manuals* and S&P's *Corporation Records*, the service cites the date of incorporation, plus the exact dates of major acquisitions, mergers, and name changes. It also

lists any transaction which alters the number of outstanding shares of a company's stock, such as stock splits, stock dividends, and new stock offerings.

Because the service is designed to help investors assess the taxable income and capital gains of stock transactions, the tax implications of each event are listed. For this reason, the amount of detail is more than most non-tax users require. Still, the service is fairly straight-forward. Researchers investigating name changes, bankruptcies, and other aspects of corporate history will find *Capital Changes Reports* a convenient resource. Other features of the service include a listing of securities pronounced "worthless" by the U.S. Treasury Department (i.e., companies which have gone bankrupt, had their charters revoked, etc.), and historical coverage of corporate dividends.

Prentice Hall, a major competitor of Commerce Clearing House, offers a set of volumes called *Capital Adjustments*. It is similar in most respects to the CCH publication except historical data appear in hardcover volumes which are updated by two loose-leaf volumes.

Predicasts F&S Index of Corporate Change (Predicasts—Quarterly, with Annual Cumulations).

This service from Predicasts is the only periodical index devoted to tracking changes in corporate structure. It covers the same wide selection of journals, newsletters, newspapers, and reports found in other Predicasts services, but focuses only on articles involving corporate change. Listings provide a single phrase summary of each article. Stories can be located by company name, Predicasts product code, or type of transaction. The latter access is afforded through a "Special Tabulations" section which indexes events under one of eight categories, including joint ventures, bankruptcies, and name changes.

Directory of Obsolete Securities (Financial Information Service—Annual).

Obsolete securities guides help investors identify the value of old stocks. Individuals who find or inherit old stock certificates may be surprised to discover the company still exists under another name. One of the most convenient ways to research obsolete stocks is to consult the *Directory of Obsolete Securities*. This cumulative directory covers thousands of corporate identities which have ceased to exist since 1927. *Obsolete Securities* lists publicly held companies which are now defunct due to bankruptcy, liquidation, or charter cancellation; firms which have been absorbed by another company or changed name; and publicly traded corporations which have "gone private." Each listing indicates what happened to the company and when, as well as the current name if the

company was absorbed. The directory cumulates each year, so researchers only need to consult the latest edition.

Another source of defunct securities is the multi-volume *Robert D. Fisher Manual of Valuable and Worthless Securities*, which continues the *Marvyn Scudder Manual of Extinct or Obsolete Securities*. The Scudder service was first published in 1926, and the combined set currently totals 15 volumes. Two predecessor volumes date back to 1910. The Fisher/Scudder manuals are much more comprehensive than the *Directory of Obsolete Securities*, but more time-consuming to consult since there is no cumulative index.

DIVIDEND ANNOUNCEMENTS

One reason to invest in stocks and mutual funds is the stream of income from dividends. Dividends are the percentage of a company's profit distributed to its stock-holders. As owners of the company, stockholders are entitled to participate in the firm's profits. The size of the dividend payment is determined by the corporation's board of directors, but for common stock, the board is under no obligation to declare such a dividend. The directors meet quarterly to set the amount of the next payment and the "date of record." This is the date on which the official list of stockholders' names will be checked to determine who receives the dividend payments. Because millions of shares of stock are traded each day, transfer agents must keep track of stockholders' names and addresses on computer lists. Because it takes several days after every stock transaction before the new owner's name is recorded, the stock exchanges and the NASD have established rules for determining the "ex-dividend date" for their stocks. The ex-date is generally four business days prior to the date of record. Owners of mutual funds also receive dividends, based on the total dividend payments of the underlying stocks in the fund's portfolio. Mutual funds generally send dividend checks on a monthly basis.

Several other concepts are linked with the notion of dividends. A stock dividend is a dividend paid in shares of the company's stock; shareholders receive some specified amount of new stock for every share they already own. A stock split usually occurs when the company feels the price of its stock has reached such a high level that individual investors cannot easily afford to purchase a round lot of stock. A 2-for-1 split means every existing share of stock is now divided into two; each stockholder now owns twice as many shares. If the stock was trading

at $100 per share before the split, it will trade for approximately half that amount immediately following the split. A right is a certificate created by the company and sent to every stockholder of record. It entitles the holder to purchase additional shares for a specified amount of money within a certain period of time, as described in the terms of the rights subscription. Rights differ from stock options in several respects, notably in being issued directly to existing shareholders. Warrants are a special category of rights, and are issued simultaneously with a new issue of stock or bond. They are generally included in a securities underwriting to make the new issue more attractive to investors. All of these transactions can be complicated, and have important tax and investment ramifications for the issuer and stockholder alike. Because they have certain characteristics related to dividends, information on stock splits, stock dividends, rights, and warrants are usually described in dividend reporting services.

Dividend announcements are a regular feature of financial newspapers such as *Barron's* and *Investor's Daily*. However, information appears in the news media as it is received by the companies. Investors and researchers need information that is both current and cumulative, so specific data can be quickly retrieved by company name. Referring to monthly and annual issues of the *Wall Street Journal Index* is one way to identify announcement dates and amounts, but the information is buried among the rest of the news on each company. *Capital Changes Reports* from Commerce Clearing House and *Capital Adjustments* from Prentice Hall both contain extensive sections summarizing historical payment information, but this is intended for retrospective research. Most summary financial and investment sources provide brief information on dividends, but data are not particularly detailed. The best way to quickly find both current and historical payment information is to consult specialized dividend services.

Moody's Dividend Record (Moody's Investors Service—Semiweekly, with Cumulations).

Both Moody's and Standard & Poor's publish dividend reporting services. Aside from minor variations, the two publications are virtually identical. Both services provide timely, detailed information on the dividends of stocks and mutual funds, indicating the amount of the dividend and relevant dates affecting payment. *Moody's Dividend Record* and *Standard & Poor's Dividend Record* are available through a variety of subscription plans.

Both services are extremely comprehensive, covering virtually all public companies and mutual funds in the United States and Canada, plus major foreign stocks traded in this country. Because the dividends of some investment companies and public utilities are subject to certain tax benefits, both publications include a year-end guide to the tax status of dividends. For both services, the tax supplement is issued in three installments.

To understand dividend listings, look at the example of Anheuser-Busch in Exhibit 11-1, which is taken from *Moody's Dividend Record*. The company paid a dividend of 18 cents per share for the first two quarters in 1989 and 22 cents for the last two quarters. The top line shows the annual dividend was 80 cents. For purposes of comparison, the previous year's dividend is also given, in this case 66 cents. The listing also indicates this is common stock with a par value of $1.00 per share, and that the company is listed on the New York Stock Exchange. Four columns of dates are also given for each company. The date declared is the date the board of directors met to determine the amount of the dividend to be paid. The date payable is the date the dividend checks will actually be mailed to stockholders. The date of record and ex-date were described earlier, but let's use the example of Anheuser-Busch to clarify the matter. If you owned stock in this company on February 3, you would be entitled to receive a dividend check for the first quarter. If you had sold your shares on February 4, you would not be entitled to a dividend even though the date of record is February 9. Exhibit 11-1 also illustrates several other points about dividend reporting services. Angeles Mortgage Investment Trust is an investment company which pays monthly dividends. Anglo American Telephone is a company with several classes of stock, namely four different issues of preferred stock. The payment history for each class is outlined. Analysts International is a company which declared quarterly dividends, experienced a 5-for-4 stock split, and issued stock rights all in the same year. Note the details of the transactions are spelled out in some detail.

The dividend guides from both S&P and Moody's provide the same descriptions, include complete year-end cumulations, offer tax-effect supplements, and have virtually identical special features in their year-end issue. These include an annual calendar of ex-dividend dates, a 15-year statistical summary of dividend activity, a list of firms which underwent stock splits or issued stock dividends, a directory of companies with dividend reinvestment plans, and a guide to all rights offerings which took place in the previous year. The rights list in S&P is

EXHIBIT 11-1. *Moody's Dividend Record*

January 1, 1990 — MOODY'S DIVIDEND RECORD — Page 15

Amt.	Date Declared	Ex-Div Date	Date of Record	Date Payable
AMWEST INSURANCE GROUP, INC.				
Com. (p0.01)		Pd '89 0.20	'88 0.20	ASE
0.05Q	Nov 23 '88	Dec 23 '88	Dec 31 '88	Jan 15
0.05Q	Mar 31	Apr 3	Apr 7	Apr 15
0.05Q	Jun 8	Jun 26	Jun 30	Jul 15
0.05Q	Sep 5	Sep 25	Sep 30	Oct 16
0.05Q	Nov 20	Dec 22	Dec 31	Jan 15 '90
ANAC HOLDING CORP.				
15.25% Exch. Pfd. (p0.01) **OTC** Last dist. stock, 3-15-88.				
ANACOMP, INC.				
Com. (p1) **NYS** Last div. 3cQ, 8-10-83.				
ANADARKO PETROLEUM CORP.				
Com. (p1)		Pd '89 0.30	'88 [1]0.35	NYS
0.075Q	Jan 27	Feb 22	Feb 28	Mar 8
0.075Q	Apr 27	May 24	May 31	Jun 14
0.075Q	Aug 1	Aug 24	Aug 30	Sep 13
0.075Q	Oct 27	Nov 22	Nov 29	Dec 13
[1] Plus rights dist.				
ANALOG DEVICES, INC.				
Com. (p0.166) **NYS** Last dist. rights, record 2-12-88. Last dist. 4-for-3 split, 4-14-86.				
ANALYSIS & TECHNOLOGY, INC.				
Com. (np)		Pd '89 0.145	'88 0.125	NAS
0.145A	Mar 10	Mar 27	Mar 31	Apr 25
ANALYSTS INTERNATIONAL CORP.				
Com. (p0.10)		Pd '89 [1]0.48	'88 0.42	NAS
0.12Q	Jan 16	Jan 25	Jan 31	Feb 15
0.12Q	Apr 20	Apr 25	May 1	May 15
[2][3][4][5]rights	—	—	Jun 30	—
0.12Q	Jun 15	Jun 28	Jul 5	Jul 19
5-for-4split	Jun 15	Aug 15	Jul 20	Aug 14
[6]0.12Q	Oct 18	Oct 25	Oct 31	Nov 15
[1] Plus rights dist. Incl. 36c paid prior to 5-for-4 split. [2] 1 Com. stock Purchase Right for each sh. held. Expiration date: 6-30-99. [3] Each right entitles holder to purchase 1 sh. of Com. stock at $100. [4] 20% or more of Com. stock must be purchased or an offer for 20% or more of Com. stock must be made before rights can be exercised. [5] Co. will redeem rights at 1c each before announcement of 20% being acq. [6] Initial div. after 5-for-4 split.				
ANALYTIC OPTIONED EQUITY FUND				
Com. (np)		Pd '89 0.36	'88 1.072854	
0.0759Q	Dec 30 '88	Dec 30 '88	Dec 30 '88	Dec 30 '88
0.001954CG	Dec 30 '88	Dec 30 '88	Dec 30 '88	Dec 30 '88
[1]0.655CG	Dec 30 '88	Dec 30 '88	Dec 30 '88	Dec 30 '88
0.14Q	Mar 31	Mar 31	Mar 31	Mar 31
0.10Q	Jun 30	Jun 30	Jun 30	Jun 30
0.12Q	Sep 29	Sep 29	Sep 29	Sep 29
[1] Short-term.				
ANANGEL-AMERICAN SHIPHOLDINGS LTD.				
ADR (SPONSORED)		Pd '89 0.75	'88 —	NAS
0.50	—	Mar 27	Mar 31	Jun 7
0.25	—	Aug 25	Aug 31	Oct 10
0.85 apx	—	Dec 5	Dec 11	Jan 24 '90
ANCHOR FINANCIAL CORP.				
Com. (p6)		Pd '89 0.35	'88 0.25	NAS
0.35A	Jan 10	Jan 25	Jan 31	Feb 28
ANCHOR GLASS CONTAINER CORP.				
Acqd. by Vitro, Sociedad Anonima				
Com. (p0.01)		Pd '89 [1]0.02	'88 0.08	NYS
0.02Q	Feb 24	Mar 2	Mar 8	Mar 28
	No action taken on 6-28-89 div.			
[2][3][4][5]rights	—	—	Sep 1	—
[1] Plus rights dist. [2] 1 Pfd. stock Purchase Right for each sh. held. Expiration date: 8-31-90 [3] Each right entitles holder to buy 0.01 sh. of Jr. Ptc. Pfd. A stk. at $55. [4] 20% or more of Com. stock must be purchased of an offer for 20% or more of Com. stock must be made before rights can be exercised. [5] 1c paid within 10 days after announcement of acq. of 20% or more of Com. stk.				
ANCHOR MACHINE & MANUFACTURING LTD.				
Com. (np)		Pd '89 0.015	'88 —	TSE
nb0.015Q	Nov 13	Nov 17	Nov 23	Dec 1
ANDERSON INDUSTRIES, INC.				
Com. (p1) **OTC** Last div. 11cQ, 4-24-84.				
ANDOVER BANCORP INC.				
Com. (p0.10)		Pd '89 0.80	'88 0.74	NAS
0.20Q	Jan 20	Feb 6	Feb 10	Mar 10
0.20Q	Apr 21	May 8	May 12	Jun 9
0.20Q	Jul 21	Aug 7	Aug 11	Sep 8
0.20Q	Oct 20	Nov 6	Nov 10	Dec 8
ANDREA RADIO CORP.				
Com. (p0.50)		Pd '89 0.54	'88 0.72	ASE
0.18Q	Feb 23	Feb 28	Mar 6	Mar 31
0.18Q	May 22	May 31	Jun 6	Jun 20
0.18Q	Sep 14	Sep 20	Sep 26	Oct 10
ANDRES WINES LTD.				
Cl. A Cv. Com. (np)		Pd '89 0.598	'88 0.598	TSE
b0.1495Q	Oct 26 '88	Dec 22 '88	Dec 30 '88	Jan 13
b0.1495Q	Feb 8	Mar 27	Mar 31	Apr 14
b0.1495Q	May 25	Jun 26	Jun 30	Jul 17
b0.1495Q	Sep 13	Sep 25	Sep 30	Oct 13
b0.1495Q	Oct 26	Dec 21	Dec 29	Jan 12 '90
Cl. B Cv. Com. (np)		Pd '89 0.52	'88 0.52	TSE
b0.13Q	Oct 26 '88	Dec 22 '88	Dec 30 '88	Jan 13
b0.13Q	Feb 8	Mar 27	Mar 31	Apr 14
b0.13Q	May 25	Jun 26	Jun 30	Jul 17
b0.13Q	Sep 13	Sep 25	Sep 30	Oct 13
b0.13Q	Oct 26	Dec 21	Dec 29	Jan 12 '90
ANGELES CORP.				
Com. (New) (np) **ASE** Last div. k50%, 12-2-83.				
ANGELES FINANCE PARTNERS				
Dep. Units		Pd '89 0.5621	'88 2.0491	ASE
0.1823M	Dec 16 '88	Dec 23 '88	Dec 30 '88	Jan 13
0.1868M	Jan 17	Jan 25	Jan 31	Feb 14
[1]0.193M	Feb 21	Feb 22	Feb 28	Mar 14
[1] Assets & liabilities transferred to Angeles Finance Trust in exch. for shares of Cl.A Com. & Cl.B Com. stock.				
ANGELES FINANCE TRUST				
Cl. A Shs. Ben. Int. (np)		Pd '89 1.66	'88 —	ASE
n0.20M	Mar 17	Mar 27	Mar 31	Apr 14
0.20M	Apr 14	Apr 24	Apr 28	May 12
0.20M	May 16	May 24	May 31	Jun 14
0.193M	Jun 15	Jun 26	Jun 30	Jul 14
0.193M,	Jul 14	Jul 25	Jul 31	Aug 14
0.185M	Aug 16	Aug 25	Aug 31	Sep 14
0.163M	Sep 18	Sep 25	Sep 29	Oct 13
0.163M	Oct 17	Oct 25	Oct 31	Nov 14
0.163M	Nov 16	Nov 24	Nov 30	Dec 14
ANGELES MORTGAGE INVESTMENT TRUST				
Cl. A Shs. Ben. Int. (np)		Pd '89 1.65	'88 —	ASE
n0.165M	Feb 21	Feb 22	Feb 28	Mar 14
0.165M	Mar 16	Mar 27	Mar 31	Apr 14
0.165M	Apr 14	Apr 24	Apr 28	May 12
0.165M	May 16	May 24	May 31	Jun 14
0.165M	Jun 15	Jun 26	Jun 30	Jul 14
0.165M	Jul 14	Jul 25	Jul 31	Aug 14
0.165M	Aug 16	Aug 25	Aug 31	Sep 14
0.165M	Sep 18	Sep 25	Sep 29	Oct 13
0.165M	Oct 17	Oct 25	Oct 31	Nov 14
0.165M	Nov 16	Nov 24	Nov 30	Dec 14
ANGELES MORTGAGE PARTNERS LTD.				
Units		Pd '89 0.3392	'88 1.8306	ASE
0.1694M	Dec 16 '88	Dec 23 '88	Dec 30 '88	Jan 13
0.1698M	Jan 17	Jan 25	Jan 31	Feb 14
Converted into 1 Cl. A sh. of Angeles Mortgage Investment Trust.				
ANGELICA CORP.				
Com. (p1)		Pd '89 0.76	'88 [1]0.72	NYS
0.19Q	Nov 30 '88	Dec 9 '88	Dec 15 '88	Jan 3
0.19Q	Mar 1	Mar 9	Mar 15	Apr 3
0.19Q	May 24	Jun 9	Jun 15	Jul 3
0.19Q	Aug 30	Sep 11	Sep 15	Oct 2
0.20Q	Nov 29	Dec 11	Dec 15	Jan 2 '90
[1] Plus rights dist.				
ANGELL REAL ESTATE CO., INC.				
Com. (p0.01)		Pd '89 1.52	'88 1.14	NYS
0.38Q	Dec 1 '88	Dec 23 '88	Dec 31 '88	Jan 31
0.38Q	Mar 2	Mar 27	Mar 31	Apr 28
0.38Q	Jun 9	Jun 26	Jun 30	Jul 31
0.38Q	Sep 21	Sep 26	Oct 2	Nov 1
ANGLO AMERICAN COAL CORP. LTD.				
Ord. (pR0.50)		Pd '89 R3.30	'88 R3.35	LON
[1]R2.05	—	Jun 5	Jun 2	Jun 23
[1]R1.25	—	Nov 27	Nov 24	Dec 29
[1] Before 15% So. Afr. tax to U.S. res.				
ADR		Pd '89 0.927	'88 0.905	OTC
[1]0.318	—	Nov 18 '88	Nov 25 '88	Jan 18
[1]0.609	—	May 26	Jun 2	Jul 11
[1]0.362 apx	—	Nov 17	Nov 24	Jan 17 '90
[1] After 15% So. Afr. tax to U.S. res.				
ANGLO AMERICAN CORP. OF SOUTH AFRICA LTD.				
Ord. (pR0.10)		Pd '89 R2.70	'88 R2.25	LON
[1]R0.70	—	Dec 27 '88	Dec 23 '88	Jan 20
[1]R2.00	—	Jun 19	Jun 16	Aug 2
[1]R0.85	—	—	Dec 22	Jan 19 '90
[1] Before 14.59755% So. Afr. tax to U.S. res.				
ADR		Pd '89 0.869	'88 0.798	NAS
[1]0.238	—	Dec 19 '88	Dec 23 '88	Feb 6
[1]0.631	—	Jun 12	Jun 16	Aug 17
[1]0.248 apx	—	Dec 18	Dec 22	Feb 5 '90
[1] After 14.59755% So. Afr. tax to U.S. res.				
ANGLO AMERICAN GOLD INVESTMENT CO. LTD.				
Ord. (New) (pR1)		Pd '89 R13.50	'88 R13.65	LON
[1]R7.00	—	Apr 3	Mar 31	May 3
[1]R6.50	—	Oct 2	Sep 29	Nov 3
[1] Before 14.9461% So. Afr. tax to U.S. res.				
ADR (NEW)		Pd '89 0.419	'88 0.479	NAS
[1]0.22	—	Mar 27	~~Mar 31~~	May 18
[1]0.199	—	Sep 25	Sep 29	Nov 20
[1] After 14.9461% So. Afr. tax to U.S. res.				
ANGLO AMERICAN INVESTMENT TRUST LTD.				
Ord. (pR0.50)		Pd '89 R30.90	'88 R18.10	LON
[1]R23.70	—	May 8	May 5	Jun 9
[2]R7.20	—	Oct 30	Oct 27	Dec 5
[1] Before 14.9989% So. Afr. tax to U.S. res. [2] Before 14.9993% So. Afr. tax to U.S. res.				
ADR		Pd '89 7.246	'88 1.888	OTC
[1]7.246	—	May 1	May 5	Jun 26
[2]2.183 apx	—	Oct 23	Oct 27	Dec 20
[1] After 14.9989% So. Afr. tax to U.S. res. [2] After 14.9993% So. Afr. tax to U.S. res.				
ANGLO CANADIAN TELEPHONE CO.				
4.50% Pfd. (p50)		Pd '89 2.25	'88 2.25	TSE
b0.5625Q	Jan 9	Jan 10	Jan 16	Feb 1
b0.5625Q	Apr 5	Apr 10	Apr 14	May 1
b0.5625Q	Jun 30	Jul 10	Jul 14	Aug 1
b0.5625Q	Oct 4	Oct 6	Oct 13	Nov 1
$3.15 Pfd. (p50)		Pd '89 3.15	'88 3.15	TSE
b0.7875Q	Jan 9	Jan 10	Jan 16	Feb 1
b0.7875Q	Apr 5	Apr 10	Apr 14	May 1
b0.7875Q	Jun 30	Jul 10	Jul 14	Aug 1
b0.7875Q	Oct 4	Oct 6	Oct 13	Nov 1
ANGLO CANADIAN TELEPHONE CO. (cont.)				
$2.90 Pfd. (p50)		Pd '89 2.90	'88 2.90	TSE
b0.725Q	Jan 9	Jan 10	Jan 16	Feb 1
b0.725Q	Apr 5	Apr 10	Apr 14	May 1
b0.725Q	Jun 30	Jul 10	Jul 14	Aug 1
b0.725Q	Oct 4	Oct 6	Oct 13	Nov 1
$2.65 Pfd. (p50)		Pd '89 2.65	'88 2.65	TSE
b0.6625Q	Jan 9	Jan 10	Jan 16	Feb 1
b0.6625Q	Apr 5	Apr 10	Apr 14	May 1
b0.6625Q	Jun 30	Jul 10	Jul 14	Aug 1
b0.6625Q	Oct 4	Oct 6	Oct 13	Nov 1
ANGLOVAAL LTD.				
Ord. (pR0.50)		Pd '89 R7.60	'88 R6.50	LON
[1]R2.50	—	Dec 12 '88	Dec 15 '88	Jan 20
[1]R5.10	—	Jul 3	Jun 30	Aug 4
[1]R3.00	—	—	Dec 15	Jan 19 '90
[1] Before 15% So. Afr. tax to U.S. res.				
ANHEUSER-BUSCH COMPANIES, INC.				
∘ Com. (p1)		Pd '89 0.80	'88 0.66	NYS
0.18Q	Dec 20 '88	Feb 3	Feb 9	Mar 9
0.18Q	Apr 26	May 3	May 9	Jun 9
0.22Q	Jul 26	Aug 3	Aug 9	Sep 8
0.22Q	Oct 25	Nov 3	Nov 9	Dec 8
ANIMED, INC.				
Com. (p0.01) **NAS** Last div. nk100%, 7-26-84.				
ANR PIPELINE CO.				
$2.675 Pfd. (p1)		Pd '89 2.675	'88 2.675	NYS
0.66875Q	Jan 27	Feb 9	Feb 15	Mar 1
0.66875Q	May 1	May 9	May 15	Jun 1
0.66875Q	Aug 1	Aug 9	Aug 15	Sep 1
0.66875Q	Sep 1	Nov 9	Nov 15	Dec 1
$2.12 Pfd. (p1)		Pd '89 2.12	'88 2.12	NYS
0.53Q	Jan 27	Feb 9	Feb 15	Mar 1
0.53Q	May 1	May 9	May 15	Jun 1
0.53Q	Aug 1	Aug 9	Aug 15	Sep 1
0.53Q	Sep 1	Nov 9	Nov 15	Dec 1
ANSONIA DERBY WATER CO.				
Com. (np)		Pd '89 0.60	'88 0.74	OTC
0.20Q	—	Dec 19 '88	Dec 26 '88	Dec 30 '88
0.20Q	Mar 15	Mar 20	Mar 27	Mar 31
0.20Q	Jun 14	Jun 20	Jun 26	Jun 30
0.20Q	Sep 13	Sep 19	Sep 25	Sep 29
ANTE CORP.				
Com. (p0.01)		Pd '89 nil	'88 nil	OTC
1-for-2rv.sp	Eff. 8-15-89			
1-for-3rv.sp	Eff. 11-1-89			
ANTHONY INDUSTRIES, INC.				
Com. (p1)		Pd '89 [1]0.4654	'88 [2]0.44	NYS
0.11Q	Dec 5 '88	Dec 20 '88	Dec 27 '88	Jan 3
0.11Q	Feb 28	Mar 2	Mar 8	Apr 4
0.11Q	May 5	May 30	Jun 5	Jul 6
0.11Q	Aug 10	Aug 30	Sep 6	Oct 3
[3]0.0254	Aug 14	Aug 30	Sep 6	Oct 3
[4]k5%	Nov 22	Nov 28	Dec 4	Dec 29
0.11Q	Nov 22	Dec 22	Dec 29	Jan 5 '90
[1] Also 5% in stock. [2] Incl. 33c paid prior to 3-for-2 split. [3] Due to redemption of Com. stock Purchase Right, eff. 3-10-86. [4] Cash paid for fractions at $15 a sh.				
ANZ BANKING GROUP				
ADR **OTC** Last div. $0.098 (proceeds from sale of rights), 8-31-88. Last reg. div. $0.088, 7-25-88. After 15% Australian tax to U.S. res.				
AOI COAL CO.				
Com. (p0.30)		Pd '89 0.05	'88 0.05	ASE
0.05A	Nov 1	Nov 27	Dec 1	Dec 15
AON CORP.				
∘ Com. (p1)		Pd '89 1.37	'88 1.26	NYS
0.32Q	Jan 20	Feb 2	Feb 8	Feb 21
0.35Q	Mar 17	May 3	May 9	May 22
0.35Q	Jul 28	Aug 2	Aug 8	Aug 21
0.35Q	Sep 15	Nov 1	Nov 7	Nov 20
APA OPTICS, INC.				
Com. (p0.01)		Pd '89 k100%	'88 —	NAS
nk100%	Mar 13	Apr 3	Mar 24	Mar 31
APACHE CORP.				
∘ Com. (p1.25)		Pd '89 0.28	'88 0.28	NYS
0.07Q	Dec 16 '88	Dec 23 '88	Dec 30 '88	Jan 31
0.07Q	Feb 8	Mar 27	Mar 31	Apr 28
0.07Q	May 4	Jun 26	Jun 30	Jul 31
0.07Q	Sep 13	Sep 25	Sep 29	Oct 31
0.07Q	Dec 8	Dec 22	Dec 29	Jan 31 '90
APCO ARGENTINA INC.				
Ord. (p0.01)		Pd '89 0.59	'88 0.24	NAS
0.15	Dec 12 '88	Dec 19 '88	Dec 23 '88	Jan 6
0.14	Mar 13	Mar 20	Mar 27	Apr 7
0.16	Jun 14	Jun 19	Jun 23	Jul 10
0.14	Aug 11	Sep 18	Sep 22	Oct 6
APEX MUNICIPAL FUND, INC.				
Com. (p0.10)		Pd '89 0.298745	'88 —	NYS
n0.082104M	Sep 6	Sep 11	Sep 15	Sep 28
0.071532M	Oct 6	Oct 13	Oct 19	Oct 30
0.073275M	Nov 6	Nov 13	Nov 17	Nov 29
0.071834M	Dec 4	Dec 11	Dec 15	Dec 28
APOGEE ENTERPRISES, INC.				
Com. (p0.333)		Pd '89 0.19	'88 0.155	NAS
0.04Q	Jan 20	Jan 30	Feb 3	Feb 16
0.05Q	Apr 25	May 1	May 5	May 23
0.05Q	Jul 31	Aug 7	Aug 11	Aug 29
0.05Q	Oct 20	Nov 1	Nov 3	Nov 16

Reprinted with permission from Moody's Investors Service.

obtained from Prentice Hall's *Capital Adjustments* service; Moody's list comes from CCH's *Capital Changes Reports*.

Differences between the services are minor. Moody's includes a separate section of dividends paid by bond funds, and also has wider coverage of foreign securities. The other noticeable differencě is the frequency of publication. The Moody's service appears twice weekly, and data continuously cumulate. The second issue of the week supersedes the first, the month-end issue supersedes the weeklies, and the year-end issue covers the entire year. In other words, at any one time, the user need only refer to the latest few weekly issues plus the most current month to see the complete year-to-date activity. In contrast, the S&P service is available under several subscription plans, with daily, weekly, or quarterly updates. Similar cumulations make it easy to retrieve data, but S&P relies a bit more on company-name indexes than on completely reprinting all the information with each update.

KEEPING THINGS STRAIGHT

Chapters 9, 10, and 11 introduced a dizzying range of investment publications and databases. While every product is intended for a particular purpose or market, distinguishing one from another requires a level of familiarity which occasional users can't possibly develop. To assist readers in sorting through this tangle of related sources, Figure 11-B presents a brief comparison of leading sources. The table indicates the type of data presented, their formats, and the categories of documents upon which they are based. Most of these resources are based upon SEC filings, which are themselves numerous and potentially confusing. Figure 11-A presents a list of the most important SEC filings organized by type.

Some of the information services available to investors are expensive, even by the standards of business publishing. Though many of the products introduced in the preceding chapters can be found in libraries of all types, a typical information center can afford only a fraction of the total. And these sources, diverse though they may be, are not the only ones on the market. Many more sophisticated services are aimed exclusively at professional money managers. A final observation is that research needs in the investment arena can change completely from one request to the next. One moment the need is for the most recent information possible, the next it's for a comprehensive overview.

One of the best methods of dealing with both the diversity and ever-changing nature of investment information is through online databases. Access to one or two diversified online vendors such as DIALOG, LEXIS/NEXIS, or Dow Jones can solve innumerable research problems. Online products not only offer access to more products, they are usually much more flexible than their printed counterparts. In some cases, the same database can be used for tracking current events, conducting financial screening, and obtaining detailed company profiles or histories.

The next question is how to select from among the incredible diversity of online products. In some situations, the type of database required is fairly obvious. This is generally true when information is sought about a specific event, such as a merger. But far too often, the purposes and capabilities of databases overlap. So-called "event studies" can present an especially challenging task. This type of research attempts to identify all cases in which a specific type of transaction took place over a given period of time. For example, the searcher wants to generate a list of all public companies which spun-off a subsidiary through the use of stock dividends. The first task is to identify databases which might cover this type of event. Dividend reporting services seem like an obvious choice, but other possibilities may come to mind. Because a new class of stock is created in the transaction, databases which summarize Registration Statements could be appropriate. Many merger-related files include divestitures in their coverage, so here is another option. The searcher should now ask several additional questions: Does the database cover the required time period? Do individual records provide the necessary information? Is event coverage comprehensive, or are certain transactions excluded by definition? And perhaps most important, is the file indexed in a way which facilitates accurate searching?

In this case, the searcher might consult the online *TEXT* version of *The Wall Street Journal*, combining variations of the terms "spin-off" and "dividend." Unfortunately, "spin-off" has several meanings in the business literature, and many irrelevant stories are retrieved. A way to combat this problem is to use databases which assign unique codes to different events. The *Wires* file on Dow Jones makes generous use of such codes, but none is given for this event. Happily, the corporate news files from both Moody's and Standard & Poor's employ specific codes for spin-offs, and a number of relevant stories are retrieved in each. Other databases might also yield satisfactory results, but this example illustrates an

FIGURE 11-B. Guide to Secondary Sources of Disclosure Filings

GUIDE TO SECONDARY SOURCES OF DISCLOSURE FILINGS

SOURCE	DATA	ARS	10-K	Proxy	10-Q	8-K	Regist	Mergers	Insider	Institut
Compact Disclosure	F,N,T	Part	Part	Part	Part	Notif	Notif	Notif	(1)	(1)
Compustat	F,N		Abst		Abst					
Corporate Text (SEC Online)	F,N,T	Full	Full	Full	Full					
FEDFILES	C		(2)	(2)	(2)	Abst	Abst	Abst		Annot
IDD M&A	C,F			Abst				Abst		
Insider Trading Monitor	C								Abst	
Insiders' Chronicle	C								Annot	
Investment Dealers' Digest	C							Annot		
Laser Disclosure	F,N,T	Full	Full	Full	Full	Full	Full	Full		
M&A Database	C,F							Abst		
M&A Filings	C							Abst		
Media General	F		Abst		Abst					
Moody's Manuals	F,N,T	Abst	Abst		Abst		Annot			
NAARS	F,N	Full(3)								
Official Summary	C								Annot	
PTS Annual Reports	F,T	Abst								
SEC Abstracts	C					Abst	Abst	Abst	Abst	
SEC News Digest	C					Notif	Annot	Annot		
SEC Online	F,N,T	Full	Full	Full	Full					
SEC Today	C					Notif	Annot	Annot		
Spectrum Ownership	C								Annot	Annot
Standard & Poor's Corp.	F,N,T	Abst	Abst		Abst		Annot			
Vickers	C									Annot

Data Codes: F = Financials; T = Text; N = Footnotes; C = Current News
Format Codes: Full = Full Text; Part = Partial Text; Abst = Abstracts or Extracted Data;
            Annot = Brief Annotations; Notif = Notification Only

(1) Abstracts available in enhanced version
(2) Major companies only
(3) Audited patrons only

important characteristic of financial news searches—indexing structure is frequently the primary factor in database selection.

A final point is relevant to both electronic and manual searches. A combination of resources may be required to solve a particular research problem, especially where comprehensive information is sought. Regardless of the need, numerous resources are available, in a multiplicity of formats. So while this abundance of choices might cause some confusion, in the long run it enables the researcher to work more effectively. The trick is to select the best tools for the job at hand.

FOR FURTHER READING

Stories of corporate ownership, insider trading, mergers and acquisitions, and initial public offerings seem to dominate the business press. Background materials to help you understand these important concepts are listed below. Guides to the various SEC reports mentioned in this chapter can be found in the reading list at the end of Chapter 9.

Going Public

O'Flaherty, Joseph S. *Going Public: The Entrepreneur's Guide* (New York: Wiley, 1984).
A more personal view of initial stock offerings, from an entrepreneur who successfully took several firms public. Especially useful is the extensive section on the aftermath of going public, including the reporting responsibilities, and the difficulties of adjusting to the new environment.
Slutsker, Gary. "When It Sounds Too Good to Be True." *Forbes* (June 26, 1989): 256–57.
Warns investors to be cautious when reading the exaggerated claims found in some prospectuses. Several examples are given to drive the point home.
Sutton, David P., and M. William Benedetto. *Initial Public Offerings: A Strategic Planner for Raising Equity Capital* (Chicago: Probus, 1988).
A step-by-step introduction to the process of going public. Covers the reasons for going public, the planning process, the role of underwriters, the stock offering, trading in the aftermarket, and the ongoing responsibilities of a publicly traded company. Several chapters discuss the content and preparation of registration statements and prospectuses.
Thomsett, Michael C. "The Prospectus." In his *Investor Factline: Finding and Using the Best Investment Information*. (New York: Wiley, 1989): 85–100.
Describes the content of a typical prospectus and offers tips on what investors should look (and look out) for.

Corporate Ownership and Insider Trading

Berle, Adolf A., and Gardiner C. Means. *The Modern Corporation and Private Property*. Revised ed. (New York: Harcourt Brace and World, 1968).
This seminal work, first published in 1933, explored the nature of modern corporate ownership. The authors concluded that the sheer size of public corporations inevitably placed the reigns of power in the hands of managers, not stockholders. Moreover, the goals of managers are generally different from those of the owners.
Buck, Edwin A. *Investing In and Profiting From Legal Insider Transactions* (New York: New York Institute of Finance, 1990).
This is a "how-to" guide for investors, but researchers will find it useful for the discussions of the insider reporting process. The basic SEC filings are described, together with an introduction to the stock trading behavior of insiders. Buck is the editor of the Vickers *Weekly Insider Report*.
Epstein, Edward Jay. *Who Owns the Corporation: Management vs. Shareholders*. A Twentieth Century Fund Paper. (New York: Priority Press, 1986).
More than 50 years after Berle and Means presented their thesis, the debate continues to rage regarding corporate ownership. In this work, Epstein chronicles excesses in management's exercise of authority during the early 1980s, especially those related to mergers and takeovers. He examines the issue of ownership from both a legal and financial perspective. The appendices list the results of major proxy contests, "greenmail" payments, and "golden parachute" settlements occurring between 1980 and 1986.
Gillis, John G. "Insider Trading." In *Financial Analyst's Handbook*, 2nd ed., edited by Sumner N. Levine. (Homewood, IL: Dow Jones-Irwin, 1988): 1765–1808.
Introduces the key legal principles governing insider trading, with reference to landmark cases. Covers the reasons behind the legislation and rulings, their history, and the importance of disclosure compliance.

Mergers and Acquisitions

Adams, Walter, and James W. Brock. *Dangerous Pursuits: Mergers & Acquisitions in the Age of Wall Street* (New York: Pantheon, 1990).
This critique of megamergers makes the argument that such deals take capital away from more productive pursuits such as investments in new plants and equipment, research, and new product development. The authors, long-time proponents of a strong antitrust policy, lay much of the blame for the excesses of the 1980s on lax enforcement. Although the book covers familiar ground, it provides a highly readable overview.

Davidson, Kenneth M. *Megamergers: Corporate America's Billion-Dollar Takeovers* (Cambridge, MA: Ballinger, 1985).

For a balanced, in-depth look at the merger phenomenon, this is an excellent place to start. Davidson covers a wide range of issues in a well-organized manner: the steps involved in the merger process, the players, the laws, a brief history of twentieth-century merger waves, the reasons why companies decide to acquire other firms, and the consequences of such extensive merger activity. Issues are discussed from a variety of perspectives, including economic, legal, financial, and social.

Halperin, Michael, and Steven J. Bell. "Business Students Find Leverage Online: Searching the M&A Files." *Online* 12 (July 1988): 58–62.

Comparative review of two leading M&A databases: *M&A Filings* and the lesser-known *M&A Database*.

Ojala, Marydee. "Dealing with a Full Deck: Mergers and Acquisitions Databases." *Database* 12 (June 1989): 85–95.

A comparison of two M&A databases available on DIALOG: *IDD M&A Transactions* and *M&A Filings*. Sample searches and database records are reproduced. The article also provides a summary of the major SEC filings related to merger activity.

Other Corporate Changes

Gargiulo, Albert F. *The "Questioned Stock" Manual: A Guide to Determining the True Worth of Old Securities* (New York: McGraw-Hill, 1979).

A fairly detailed discussion of how to trace the value of old stocks, including the use of published guides, hiring fee-based researchers, and checking state corporation files.

Kanner, Bernice. "The New Name Game." *New York* 20 (March 16, 1987): 16–17.

A flurry of corporate name changes took place in the late 1980s as major companies sought to redefine their identity. The result was a menagerie of meaningless names such as Navistar, Primerica, and USX, many of which elicited public confusion and even ridicule. The author describes the process which led to two of the more memorable "namelifts": Allegis and Unisys.

CHAPTER 12
Investment Advice and Analysis

TOPICS COVERED

1. The Role of Advisory Services
2. Predicting Investment Performance
3. Key Market Indicators
   a. Stock Indexes
   b. Earnings Per Share
   c. Price/Earnings Ratio
   d. Book Value
   e. Price Volatility
   f. Bond Ratings
4. Brokerage Reports
5. Commercial Advisory Sources
   a. Stock Market Letters
   b. Industry Analysis
   c. Mutual Fund Services
   d. Bond Advisory Services
6. Selecting Investment Publications
7. For Further Reading

MAJOR SOURCES DISCUSSED

- *The Wall Street Transcript*
- *Investext*
- *Zacks Earnings Forecaster*
- *Value Line Investment Survey*
- *Standard & Poor's Stock Reports*
- *The Market Guide*
- *The Outlook*
- *Standard & Poor's Industry Surveys*
- *Moody's Industry Review*
- *Wiesenberger Investment Companies Service*
- *Mutual Fund Values*
- *Moody's Bond Survey*

The final component of investment research is locating advisory information. Advisory sources constitute the most prolific area of financial publishing. Hundreds of magazines, newsletters, and loose-leaf services offer analysis and recommendations to the serious investor. Sources vary from simple to sophisticated, from broad in scope to narrowly focused. Many are well-known, respected publications which have been sold for many years; others are aimed at a limited market segment. Many are reasonably affordable, while some are prohibitively expensive. This chapter will examine the role of advisory publications in the investment community, the categories of sources available, and criteria for judging their value.

THE ROLE OF ADVISORY SERVICES

Investment advisory services are publications offering commentary, analysis, forecasts, or recommendations on investment topics. They appear in many forms, but the most common is the brief newsletter format. For purposes of this discussion, the terms newsletter and advisory service are used interchangeably. Some newsletters are purely factual, providing raw data for investment decisions. Others are strictly "action letters," giving specific advice on what securities to buy and sell at what time. Most newsletters fall somewhere between these two extremes, providing a mixture of data and recommendations. Typical services cover only one type of investment vehicle: stocks, bonds, mutual funds, precious metals, real estate, etc. Most specialize even further, utilizing a certain analytical technique or investment theory.

Does all this information and advice affect the price of securities? Can newsletters actually determine marketplace behavior? If enough people follow it, a particular recommendation will become a self-fulfilling prophecy. However, securities markets are too large and complex to be swayed greatly by specific advice. There are simply too many players in the game, with too many diverse motivations and beliefs to be subject to direct influence. On the other hand, the price of a stock with only 10,000 shares outstanding will react much more dramatically to the actions of a few investors than will a stock with millions of shares. The possibility of information directly affecting the market does exist.

Several additional factors operate to minimize the effect of investment advice. First, far too much advice is available from too many sources for any single suggestion to be widely followed. Investors must sift through mountains of information to make decisions, and most are too sophisticated to blindly follow the advice of any one guru. Also, there is much conflicting advice. The investor acting on positive advice will offset the actions of another following negative advice. A related point is that few investment advisors have large followings. Most newsletters have fewer than 5,000 subscribers, and many can operate profitably with only a few hundred. An action-oriented newsletter may enjoy enormous popularity for a brief time, but popularity waxes and wanes with the current success of a newsletter's predictions. Another mitigating factor is the remarkable speed in which investment information is acted upon. By the time a piece of news begins to circulate, the market price has already adjusted to it, and the opportunity for quick profit has passed. Of course, rumor also influences the marketplace, sometimes more heavily than verified facts. But acting on a rumor can be extremely risky.

Despite these disclaimers, there are instances where the market has demonstrated unusual behavior following a popular investment recommendation. A spectacular example took place in January 1981, when Joseph Granville, the flamboyant publisher of the *Granville Market Letter*, warned readers to "sell everything" immediately. The following day saw a $40 billion selling panic attributed by many analysts to Granville's actions. Whether he caused the sellout, or predicted it with uncanny accuracy, is impossible to determine, but such a phenomenon is rare indeed. Granville's subsequent following declined drastically due to similar radical predictions that failed to materialize. For the balance of the 1980s, his newsletter performed poorly compared to other advisory services.

The Granville experience illustrates several key points about the newsletter industry. First, it is virtually impossible for a newsletter to provide outstanding advice year in and year out. Second, it is difficult to predict earthshaking financial events; they occur unexpectedly. Analysts and newsletter publishers who do so once can seldom duplicate their stunning feat. And third, even if advisory services can have an influence on securities prices, there is no telling when or why.

Another example of the fickle nature of securities markets is demonstrated by the inconsistent results of recommendations made on the PBS television show "Wall Street Week with Louis Rukeyser." The audience has been estimated as high as ten million viewers, making it the most widely followed advisory medium in America. With such a large audience and outstanding reputation, "Wall Street Week" has enormous potential to influence stock market behavior. Research has shown that many of the recommendations made on the show are not acted upon by large numbers of investors, and there is no discernible pattern to explain why particular advice is accepted or ignored. Many analysts on Wall Street and in the academic community believe that even when a recommendation noticeably affects the behavior of a security, the results will be short-term in duration. The price of a stock recommended on Friday's "Wall Street Week" might rise on Monday morning, but will decline to former levels shortly thereafter. It takes more than someone's advice to influence security prices in the long run. Investors who try to benefit from such "blips" in price must remember that taxes on capital gains, brokers' fees, and other transaction costs have a way of eroding short-term profits.

Since no investment advisor is omniscient, and no one has an unblemished record of success, what is the value of investment advice? Some say it is impossible to "outperform the market" in the long run. Although an investor might do very well for a short time, it is the nature of an average to reduce everyone's performance to that level over the long haul. Whether one believes this theory or not, the key to success in investing is to be right more often than wrong. Investment newsletters are valuable because they aid in making informed decisions.

If newsletters have the potential to influence the market, does the possibility to influence newsletters also exist? Just how susceptible is investment news to manipulation and fraud? For one thing, it benefits the holder of investment information to disseminate what he or she knows. In pari-mutuel betting, telling others about a "hot tip" drives down the odds and reduces potential profit. But in securities markets, convincing others of a tip can

help make the prediction come true. The potential for abuse is enormous, and the rewards are equally so. The era of the "robber barons" is infamous for its unscrupulous manipulation of investment information. And at the height of the 1920s speculative frenzy, Wall Street plungers bribed newspaper reporters to print profitable fabrications. The securities laws of the 1930s reduced such manipulation by instituting standardized reporting systems and by outlawing spurious practices. Today, all publicly traded companies are required to report material information to the public, and corporate insiders are forbidden from profiting from withheld information. The SEC, the stock exchanges, and the NASD all monitor sudden, unexplained changes in securities prices. Financial newspapers and magazines have also adopted strict ethical codes to govern employees' behavior. Reporters tend not to be gullible; they are trained to consider the source of their stories, look for unseen motivations, and verify facts. With so much information available from the companies themselves, from the government, and from thousands of investment advisors, it is unlikely that small investors can obtain tips which no one else has.

But real world events prove that these safeguards are not always sufficient to prevent fraud. Insider trading and stock manipulation do occur, and can be difficult to detect. For example, some investors profit from a decline in a stock's price by engaging in "short selling," a perfectly acceptable investment practice. However, powerful short sellers have been known to form syndicates to drive down a stock's price through organized campaigns. Using rumor and exaggerated fact, syndicates can affect the price of a weakened stock by disseminating negative information to other investors and the media.

Collusion between reporters or newsletter publishers and market manipulators also occurs, as does trading on financial news before it is reported, but such activities are believed to be rare. Several celebrated cases in the 1980s showed that even the most reputable publications aren't immune to scandal. Both *The Wall Street Journal* and *Business Week* were embroiled in incidents where employees or printing contractors traded on information before it was published. In all instances, the abuse was uncovered and safeguards were quickly initiated. Both publishers readily admit there is no foolproof protection against corruption. Investment professionals agree that it is impossible to prevent even inadvertent news leaks, let alone blatant abuses. Considering the volume of investment news published each year, such happenings are remarkably infrequent.

PREDICTING INVESTMENT PERFORMANCE

What makes the price of a security fluctuate? The honest response is that no one really knows, but there are plenty of contributing factors. To say price is determined by supply and demand is to oversimplify. It also begs the question, since it fails to explain what causes supply and demand. Many things do, of course, including the price and availability of alternative investments, the amount of credit available, the state of the economy, investor confidence, the financial health of the underlying company, and a host of psychological factors.

A common explanation for the day-to-day behavior of securities markets is the news of the day. Fluctuations in the total market are frequently attributed to election results, pronouncements from the Federal Reserve Board, and other political and economic news. But any explanation is merely conjecture, and any single reason, no matter how logical, is oversimplification. The stock market crash of October 1987 has been studied more thoroughly than any financial event in recent history, yet no one can identify one isolated event which triggered the panic. There is no question that news events affect the decisions of individual investors, and thus the market. What is not known is the degree to which news has an effect. Some analysts feel it is a major consideration only when the news is completely unexpected. Others say news will only affect security prices briefly, after which the market returns to its "normal" course.

It is harder still to predict how the market will react to a particular piece of news. For example, conventional Wall Street wisdom states that wars send stock prices plummeting, yet when the United States invaded Grenada, and when the Persian Gulf war began, stock prices took dramatic upward turns. In many cases it would be just as accurate to base investment decisions on astrological conditions, which some investors do.

So what causes price changes for individual stocks? All theories of price fluctuation place importance on expectations. Because investors purchase securities in the hope of future gains, they base their decisions on what they believe will happen in the future. The most commonly followed school of investment is called fundamental analysis. Fundamentalists examine what they believe to be the underlying causes of price behavior in the economy at large and within individual companies. Fundamental analysts are concerned with such issues as corporate earnings, the characteristics of industries as a whole, new product announcements, pending lawsuits,

the success of competing companies, and the impact of governmental regulations. Technical analysts are not concerned with these issues at all. A pure technician believes that investment performance can be predicted solely on past price behavior, because securities exhibit identifiable cyclical patterns. Technical analysts graph daily price behavior for securities and examine peaks and troughs to determine the precise time to buy or sell. For this reason, they are frequently called market timers or chartists. To many technicians, information about the company itself is completely irrelevant; only the ups and downs of market price are important. To help them gauge these transitions, innumerable advisory services are published which chart investment performance in graphic form.

Other theories abound. Contrarians, for example, believe that the "herd" is always wrong, and invest accordingly. The thinking behind this strategy is that financial trends are cyclical, and by the time prevailing Wall Street wisdom becomes common knowledge, new trends are about to emerge. Another interesting school of thought, followed mostly by the academic community, is the "random walk" theory. It states that individuals can no more predict the price of securities than one can predict where a drunk will walk. A more extreme version, the "perfect market theory," believes all investment information is assimilated by the market immediately, and prices adjust before anyone can take advantage of new information. The image of the marketplace lurching about in drunken confusion is vivid and believable, but the theory is clearly unacceptable to most investors, because random success refutes the efforts of all investors following a more systematic approach.

KEY MARKET INDICATORS

Many statistical measures of investment performance have been devised, especially for the stock market. Some, like dividend yields and 30-day moving averages measure the performance of individual stocks. Others, like stock indexes and advance-decline ratios evaluate the market as a whole. Investment indicators for individual firms can be used to track changes over time, or to compare the company to industry and market norms. Some measures require the compilation of large amounts of data, while others are fairly simple to calculate. No single measure is ever adequate to describe or predict a security's performance, so wise investors will examine a variety of measures. A few of the most basic statistical concepts will be introduced below.

Stock Indexes

A stock index, sometimes called a stock average, is a way of tracking the performance of the entire stock market. One could add together the closing prices of every stock sold and calculate an average price, but an easier alternative would be to select a representative sample and calculate an average for that group from day to day. This is the basic idea behind a stock index. There are many indexes to choose from, but the most familiar is the Dow Jones Industrial Average (abbreviated as DJIA, or the Dow). The Dow is an index of the price of 30 "blue chip" industrial stocks. It does not measure the average price of the individual stocks, because the sum is no longer divided by 30. In the years the Dow has been calculated, the value of the divisor has steadily decreased to reflect stock splits declared by each of the component companies.

The Dow is measured in points rather than dollars. If the DJIA drops from 2689 to 2682, for example, it has declined by seven points, and the average price of a share of stock is certainly not $2682. The only clear meaning the Dow imparts is in relation to itself; it is a relative measure of changes over time. The Dow has been criticized for many reasons. Despite its weaknesses, it remains the universally accepted measure of market behavior by virtue of tradition—it has been calculated every day for more than 100 years. There is also a Dow Jones Transportation Average composed of 20 stocks, a Utilities Average of 15 stocks, and a composite figure that measures all 65.

A broader measure of market performance is the Standard & Poor's 500, which was devised in the 1950s. The stocks comprising the S&P 500 account for about 80% of the value of stocks traded on the New York Stock Exchange. Unlike the Dow, the S&P figure is a true index, using a base period of 1941/43 = 10. The Standard & Poor's Index is comprised of 400 industrials, 20 transportation stocks, 40 utilities, and 40 financial stocks. Other well-known measures include the NYSE Index, the AMEX Index, and the NASDAQ Index, each of which measures all stocks traded in its respective domain. Widely followed indexes are also computed by Barron's, Value Line, and other financial publishers.

Current and historical data on stock indexes are published in many of the sources listed in Chapter 10. Detailed data for numerous indexes can be found in *The Wall Street Journal*, *Investor's Daily*, and *Barron's*. The *Journal* even reports hour-by-hour values for the Dow, as well as a table of historic highs and lows and the current value of the divisor used to calculate the index. The daily

issues of the *Journal* lists the names of the individual companies which comprise the DJIA. Day-by-day listings for the Dow also appear with varying frequency in the following publications: monthly, quarterly, and annually in the *Wall Street Journal Index*; quarterly, in the *Daily Stock Price Record*; and annually, in *Standard & Poor's Statistical Service* and the *Business One Irwin Investor's Handbook*. A compilation of DJIA values from their inception can be found in *The Dow Jones Averages, 1885-1990* published by Business One Irwin. This is by no means a comprehensive list; the Dow is easily the most ubiquitous investment statistic in the United States.

Earnings Per Share

Corporate earnings are watched closely by the investment community. Earnings means the net income (or profit) reported on the firm's annual and quarterly income statements, not the dividend payout established by the board of directors. Net income is important to investors because it is the *source* of dividends paid to stockholders, and the source of retained earnings invested back into the company. Because earnings are the primary engine of growth in the firm, corporate earnings are a key factor in assessing the future price of a stock. The standard measure of corporate income used by investors is Earnings Per Share (EPS). It is calculated by dividing the annual net income of the firm by the total number of shares of common stock outstanding. The EPS figure is thus a useful method of comparing performance of companies of unequal size. For example, two companies may each have net income of $10 million, but one firm may have 10 million shares of stock outstanding, while the other only has 2 million. The EPS would be $1 per share for the first firm, but $5 for the second.

Earnings Per Share is affected by both the company's earnings and the number of shares outstanding. All things being equal, if a firm's earnings increase, so does its EPS. A company's earnings can be "diluted" when additional stock is issued. Dilution can occur when a stock split is declared, when convertible bonds are exchanged for common stock, or when a firm underwrites a new issue of common stock.

Price/Earnings Ratio

The most frequently used measure for comparing stocks is the Price/Earnings Ratio, which incorporates Earnings Per Share data. The P/E Ratio is calculated by dividing the most current closing price of the stock by the latest annual EPS. While the denominator thus remains stable for long periods, the value of the numerator fluctuates daily as the stock's price changes. For a company with Earnings Per Share of $5 and a current stock price of $50 per share, the P/E Ratio would be 10 times earnings. If the stock were selling at $30, the P/E would decline to 6 times earnings. Because corporate earnings fuel stock growth, it is no surprise that a statistic which relates stock price to company earnings is an important measure.

Investors are often puzzled by how to interpret this ratio. Generally, a low P/E indicates a strong investment because corporate earning power is high relative to the price of the stock. On the other hand, stock prices are based upon investor expectations, so a high P/E ratio can indicate investor confidence in the company. High growth companies traditionally have higher P/E values to reflect their greater potential. A rule of thumb is the higher the ratio, the more speculative the stock.

A company's P/E Ratio is a measure of the stock's relative value, best compared to the P/E of other stocks, or groups of stock. The key to interpreting the ratio is finding an appropriate standard of comparison. Over the past 40 years, the average P/E for the companies comprising the Dow Jones Industrial Average has been about 15, but the average fluctuates widely from one decade to the next. Clearly, it is important to consider a stock's P/E in relation to the whole market; it makes a difference whether the general price trend is rising or falling. Price/Earnings Ratios also vary by type of company, so the average ratio for the entire industry must be examined. Finally, the P/E can be measured against the company's own past performance. A falling ratio is usually seen as a good sign, especially where earnings have increased.

The fact that P/E Ratios are calculated daily for all stocks in the standard quotation tables demonstrates the importance of this key measure. Also, an average P/E Ratio is commonly calculated for the stocks which make up the Dow. Comparative ratios for firms within an industry can be found in such sources as *Media General*, *Standard & Poor's Industry Surveys*, and *Moody's Industry Review*. The latter two are introduced later in the chapter.

Book Value

What is a stock *really* worth? The easiest answer is that a stock is worth its current market price—what someone is willing to pay for it. Another measure of

worth is the underlying value of the company. A simple measure of the company's worth is its Book Value, calculated by dividing the net assets of the company by the number of shares of common stock outstanding. Net assets equal net worth, and net worth is stockholders' equity plus retained earnings, so Book Value is a measurement of how much has been "put into" the firm. Book Value becomes meaningful when compared to the current price of the stock. In general, if a stock is selling for considerably less than the Book Value, it is undervalued—a potential bargain. If the stock is selling for considerably more than the Book Value, it is overvalued. As with P/E ratios, it is difficult to make blanket statements about this figure. When prices in the stock market decline for an extended period, for example, stocks tend to sell below Book Value. But in a bull market, a stock selling below Book Value could be either an undervalued sleeper, unnoticed by investors, or a company with serious problems.

Price Volatility

Another way to measure a stock's performance is to examine its price movement over time. A stock that fluctuates widely is viewed as a risky investment because of the uncertainty of its price in the future. Volatility can be measured by calculating a moving average for the price over a period of time, then measuring the variance or standard deviation around that average. Stocks with larger standard deviations are riskier investments. This calculation measures unsystematic risk, meaning the risk that can be reduced by diversifying the stock portfolio.

A more important measure of risk is the Beta Coefficient. Beta values measure systematic risk—risk not reducible through diversification. The Beta Coefficient compares the fluctuation in an individual stock's price to the fluctuation of the entire market. A Beta value of 1 indicates the stock moves in concert with the market. A Beta greater than 1 means the stock is more volatile than the market; a Beta less than 1 shows less volatility.

Some of the more widely available sources of Beta values include *Media General, Value Line Investment Survey,* and *Standard & Poor's Stock Reports. Media General* computes two Beta Coefficients for each stock: one tracks volatility in a declining stock market, the other measures volatility in an advancing market. Beta Coefficients calculated in one publication will be different from those seen in every other source. The computations depend on how the market is defined; the variation of a single stock's price from the market average depends upon how many stocks are used to determine that average. *Value Line* calculates Beta based on the 1,700 stocks it follows each week, while *Media General* considers its total market to be the 4,000 stocks it regularly follows. A stock's price volatility can be compared to any group of stocks the analyst chooses to use.

Bond Ratings

One of the most important designations of a bond's quality is its bond rating. Ratings reflect a bond's investment risk, measuring the ability of the bond issuer to meet its debt obligation. The higher the rating, the less likely the company will default on paying interest or principal on the bond.

Three major agencies rate corporate and municipal bonds: Moody's Investor Service, Standard & Poor's Corporation, and the Fitch Investor Service. Moody's is the oldest and largest, followed closely by S&P in terms of the number of bonds rated. Fitch plays a limited role in this field but offers an alternative to the two industry giants. For many years, the ratings provided by the two leaders were similar in most instances, but in recent years divergent opinions have become more common. Large brokerage houses also issue bond ratings, but these ratings do not have the influence of the independent agencies. Conflict of interest is an issue, since many investment firms which publish ratings also underwrite new bonds.

It is difficult for a corporation or government to issue new bonds without receiving a rating from one of the independent agencies. Since the bond rating is an important measure of investment risk, it has a profound effect on the interest rate the bond issuer must pay to investors. Rating agencies receive hefty fees from the bond issuer to perform the analysis, as well as an annual fee for monitoring each bond's status.

The rating for each bond is determined by a thorough examination of the issuing company's position and the characteristics of the bond itself, as described in a legal contract called the bond indenture. In looking at the covenants of an indenture, especially for corporate bonds, the agency bases ratings on whether a sinking fund has been established to cover repayment on the bond's principal, whether the bond is secured by a mortgage or other collateral, whether claims of the bondholders are subordinate to other debtors, and whether there is a dedicated revenue source to cover interest payments. For corporate bonds, the company's financial position is critical, but the raters also look at pending events, market share, and

other pertinent factors. Ratings for municipal bonds are determined by the presence of a budget surplus or deficit, the size of the tax base, how successful the municipality is at collecting taxes, the economic climate of the area, and similar concerns. For municipal bonds, another factor enters into the rating process. Governments and agencies can purchase insurance from one of several organizations which will indemnify bondholders against default by the issuer. For bonds insured by MBIA, Inc. and AMBAC, Inc., the highest rating is always given.

BROKERAGE REPORTS

Most investors are familiar with research reports from major brokerage firms. The largest stockbrokers and dealers maintain extensive research departments to support their sales, counseling, and trading activities. Securities analysts employed by these firms usually specialize in a particular industry group and follow the performance of securities in that industry. Thus they become adept at spotting trends, recognizing trouble spots, and picking up market news and rumor. Investment advice from large brokerage firms is widely followed, so companies that issue securities cooperate with Wall Street analysts to a surprising degree. Analysts will visit or contact the firms fairly frequently. They typically have access to corporate information unavailable to most others, including direct contact with senior executives in the firm.

A common belief is that analyst reports do little more than tout stocks which brokers are trying to move. At the very least, there is a suspicion of conflict of interest. Would a broker make critical comments regarding one of its biggest customers? Undoubtedly, analysts' reports are not always completely objective, but such instances are thought to be rare. The primary audience of these documents is large institutions and sophisticated money managers. Because stockbrokers' reputations depend upon the quality of advice they give, their analysts' opinions tend to be expert and reliable. Analysts are extremely well-paid, experienced, and independent. Of course no one is correct all the time, but reports generated by analysts in major brokerage firms are an important source of quality investment information.

Thousands of reports are produced each year. Publications typically appear as special reports on an industry or firm, or as summary newsletters released weekly or monthly. Special reports provide in-depth analysis, and range in length from several pages to several hundred. Periodicals may print excerpts from more detailed re-

ports, summarize the current investment climate, and recommend specific securities. Some periodicals are wide-ranging in coverage, others are devoted to specific industries or investment categories. Many brokerage houses also produce general newsletters on current economic conditions. Reports are sent to the branch offices to be used as sales tools and to solicit new customers. Preferred customers may receive free reports on a regular basis, but individuals can usually receive a particular report for the asking. A few broker's newsletters are available on a paid-subscription basis, but most are not. Such publications are intended for use by the brokerage house and its customers, so they are usually not found in their original form at public and academic libraries.

Researchers investigating a company or industry should include brokerage publications among their list of major sources. Industry reports are an excellent way to obtain a quick overview of a particular line of business as well as analysis of current trends and comparisons of leading firms. Company reports can provide important insights into marketing strategy, distribution channels, management outlook, new products, industry cost structure, market share, and even company history. Analysts' reports may also offer background on privately held companies which compete with public firms. These reports also contain interesting commentary on political and regulatory events, new technology, environmental concerns, and virtually any other topic relating to company performance.

A related information source is the executive speech. CEOs are commonly invited to make presentations before meetings of leading investment analysts. The most prestigious group, the New York Society of Securities Analysts (NYSSA), holds such meetings weekly. Executives are asked to discuss their company's plans and operations in detail, and to field questions from the audience. Transcripts of these meetings are available in print and online from a variety of sources.

Because of their sheer numbers and their importance to the investment community, brokerage reports and executive speeches can be obtained in indirect ways also. Especially dramatic advice is picked up by syndicated financial columnists and by mainstream sources such as *The Wall Street Journal*. Information on analysts' activities are also available. *Barron's* weekly column, "At the Financial Analysts," lists companies being reviewed by Wall Street firms, as do several other publications. The *Directory of Investment Research* by Nelson Publications provides an annual list of the research staffs of major investment firms together with the companies and industries they cover. Investors can use these services to identify sources of specific reports.

For many years, Wall Street reports were largely inaccessible. Brokers did not sell reports to the general public; investors had to obtain individual publications from the brokers themselves, or rely on snippets of information appearing in the financial press. A more significant problem was that no catalogs or indexes kept track of available reports or their contents. Now other options are available in both print and electronic media. Several services reproduce thousands of reports from dozens of brokerage firms.

The Wall Street Transcript (Wall Street Transcript Corporation—Weekly).

The longest-lived secondary source of brokerage reports is *The Wall Street Transcript*, called *TWST* by its publisher. This tabloid-size newspaper was founded in 1963 by corporate attorney Richard A. Holman, who saw the need for a medium to communicate Wall Street research to the general investing public. *TWST* is quite expensive, but it contains an enormous amount of unique or hard-to-find information. Each issue consists of some 70 pages of small print covering information on more than 300 different companies every week. *TWST* contains little advice from its own staff; rather, it reproduces recommendations, news, and comment from a variety of Wall Street sources.

Much of the information appears in two weekly sections: "Broker Reports" reprints lengthy extracts of current brokerage publications, while "Wall Street Roundup" provides highlights of additional brokerage reports. Another section, "Corporate Reports on File," prints paid news releases from the companies themselves, including interim earnings statements, joint-venture announcements, news of corporate expansions, and other developments. Other sections include reprints of recent speeches made by corporate executives before the NYSSA; interviews with leading executives, analysts, and money managers; guest columnists who comment on special topics; and rumors of corporate takeovers and "softer" news.

TWST also sponsors a forum for analysts to comment on investments outside their own brokerage reports. Every issue contains transcripts of several meetings convened by the publisher to discuss investment topics. For example, "Corporate Critics Confidential" is a weekly feature which allows unnamed analysts to comment on the performance of chief executives in a given industry. The paper also sponsors between one and three "Roundtable Discussions" each week. The roundtables are conducted by Holman, who interviews five analysts specializing in the same industry. Each roundtable provides detailed analysis—often ten pages or more—including industry overview and outlook, and

analysis of leading firms in the field. These informative columns often cover small segments of larger industries seldom covered in other sources. Roundtable discussions are frequently supplemented with a report on insider trading within the industry and other special features.

TWST can be confusing to first-time users, but is worth becoming familiar with. Whether the searcher requires investment advice or background on companies and industries, *TWST* is a convenient source. Its usefulness is enhanced by excellent indexing; every issue contains a detailed table of contents and a cumulative index for the month to date. A year-to-date index appears every three months and an annual index is published in January. The complete text of the paper is available online through VU/TEXT. The database is called *Warndex*, and is updated weekly. The publisher has also announced plans to produce a CD-ROM version of the paper.

Investext (Thomson Financial Networks—Weekly).

One of the most comprehensive and powerful guides to analysts' reports is an online database called *Investext*. This service provides the complete text (minus pictures and graphs) for more than 150,000 investment reports dating back to 1982. Virtually every major Wall Street broker and investment bank is represented, as are regional houses from around the country. Canadian, European, and Asian brokers are also covered. In all, the output from 125 investment houses can be found. The complete text of speeches made before the New York Society of Securities Analysts are also provided, as are reports from an independent investment service called *The Market Guide*, which focuses on smaller OTC companies. (This resource will be described in greater detail later in the chapter.)

Investext is available online from DIALOG, BRS, Data-Star, the LEXIS Financial Information Service, and NewsNet. Versions with limited searching capabilities can be found on Dow Jones and CompuServe. The producer also operates its own online system called INVESTEXT/PLUS. The database is updated weekly on most systems, although there is a two to four week lag before current reports can be seen. Another way to search the database online is through *PTS PROMT*, which only provides brief abstracts of the reports, but offers Predicasts's more detailed indexing.

On the more sophisticated online services, such as DIALOG and Data-Star, the user can retrieve records based on keywords in the text of the reports, or by utilizing a variety of indexing terms. Each record is indexed by type of report (industry or company), company name, SIC codes, ticker symbols, analyst (i.e., author), corporate source (i.e., brokerage house), and

publication date. Thomson has also created a unique list of 53 broad industry categories, 1,500 product terms, and about 50 general business topics, such as litigation, divestitures, and corporate structure. A particularly useful feature is the ability to limit keyword searching to terms as they appear in titles, section headings, or table headings. These capabilities enable the researcher to retrieve information from analysts' reports that cannot be found in any other way. In addition to company and industry reports, *Investext* covers newsletters produced by brokerage houses, and general reports on economic and financial conditions. The latter category can be retrieved using the industry term "Economic Forum."

The most confusing aspect of *Investext* is the way each document is presented. Every report is divided into a Table of Contents record and a Text record. The Contents record provides the bibliographic and indexing information, together with a list of the section headings and tables contained in the report. The Text records are broken into "pages" on DIALOG, "paragraphs" on Data-Star. These are actually screens of approximately 3,000 characters of words and numbers. Every report consists of one Table of Contents record and a varying number of Text records, depending on the length of the report. On DIALOG, this can be deceptive, since 140 retrieved records may only represent 20 actual reports. To determine the actual number of reports retrieved, limit the results to the Table of Contents records (on DIALOG, the command is DT=Contents). A browsing format can be used to quickly scan the bibliographic information for each report (Format 3 on DIALOG). To display the full text of a single report, request the document by its unique Report Number, listed on the contents page. This mechanism was created to distinguish between indexing information and words in the text of the document, but is not the most elegant way to achieve this goal. Data-Star avoids this by allowing the use of standard output formats to select either the full report or just the "paragraphs" containing the desired information. The record structure definitely requires getting used to, especially on DIALOG, but it is a minor idiosyncrasy.

The other drawback to *Investext* is the high cost of printing a complete report. The average *Investext* report is seven "pages," but many reports are more than 100 pages in length. The cost of printing a single lengthy report or multiple shorter reports can be prohibitive. For this reason, many researchers use the database most often in one or more of the following situations: to retrieve quick facts about a company or industry; to display only the key portions of a lengthy report, especially numeric tables; to identify reports covering a specific combina-

tion of terms or subjects, then use other means to acquire the actual text; or, when a full report must be obtained immediately, and no other means are available. Its most important advantage is clearly the ability to search the full text of so many diverse documents quickly and effectively. *Investext* customers can also receive a useful monthly newsletter from the publisher at no cost. *New Research Reports* provides a complete roster of all reports recently added to the database, arranged by company name and industry.

Two CD-ROM products provide selected full-text records from the online service. *CD/Corporate* on Lotus One Source contains company reports only, typically limited to one or two pages. Keywords in the text are not searchable; users basically retrieve reports by company name. *Investext* is also available from the Information Access Company as an InfoTrac CD. The complete text of all reports appear on a two-disk set, though only the most recent 12 months are covered. The product is updated monthly; the earliest month drops off as each new month is added. The InfoTrac product is searchable by company name, industry, product, SIC code, author, or brokerage house. Unfortunately, no Boolean search capabilities are offered, nor can words in the text be retrieved. However, the product is simple to use and offers quick, convenient access to brokerage reports.

Zacks Earnings Forecaster (Zacks Investment Research, Inc.—Biweekly).

Because net earnings are such a key measure of company performance, investment analysts typically forecast Earnings Per Share data one or more years in advance. Several publishers compile records of Wall Street analysts' projections, but the guide from Zacks Investment Research is the most frequently seen in libraries. *Zacks Earnings Forecaster* performs a similar function to *The Wall Street Transcript*, but instead of reproducing highlights of brokerage reports, it focuses on estimates of EPS made by 150 different U.S. and Canadian investment firms. The earnings of approximately 4,000 companies are covered. Each biweekly issue cumulates all new and revised estimates submitted to Zacks during the current quarter. The listing for each company shows a forecast from at least one analyst, and usually from several, plus Zack's latest consensus forecast.

Exhibit 12-1, from a May 1991 issue, shows four separate projections for Citicorp's 1991 Earnings Per Share, ranging from a low of $.75 to a high of $1.50. The first column of data indicates Citicorp's actual earnings for 1990, which were $1.53 per share. Below the indi-

vidual estimates is a Zacks consensus forecast for 1991 ($1.27). Exhibit 12-1 also shows the date each forecast was made, the names of the brokerage firms and individual analysts, the fiscal-year end to which the estimate refers, and, in the "From" column, the analyst's previous estimate. Prudential Securities' forecast went from $1.50 per share to $1.00 per share, which is shown in the next column as a decrease of $.50. The space following this column indicates (with an asterisk) those estimates which have been revised in the current issue of the publication. For convenience, the direction of change is also indicated to the left of the company name. Many analysts also provide forecasts for the following fiscal year. In the case of Citicorp, three analysts have done so, including the newly reported figure from Interstate/Johnson Lane.

The database is available online through Dow Jones News/Retrieval, the LEXIS Financial Information Service, several of the more specialized corporate vendors, and directly from Zacks. On most systems it is known as *Zacks Earnings Estimates*. The online version emphasizes consensus forecasts rather than individual estimates. The file is updated weekly on Dow Jones, monthly on LEXIS, and daily on the publisher's own system. Estimates from Zacks can also be found on CD-ROM through *Compact D/SEC*. Data appear as part of the basic company report. Every *Compact D/SEC* record cites composite estimates for the next two fiscal years, together with the high and low estimates for both periods. Only the composite (mean) values are given; individual brokers' estimates are not provided.

A competing forecast service, produced by Lynch, Jones & Ryan, is the *Institutional Broker's Estimate System*, also known as *I/B/E/S*. Though similar in most respects to *Zacks*, the service is marketed primarily to professional money mangers. *I/B/E/S* offers more coverage than *Zacks*, with over twice as many brokerage houses represented worldwide. Where *Zacks* focuses on U.S. companies and some Canadian firms, its competitor also provides extensive reporting from Canada, Australia, Europe, and the Far East. Lynch, Jones publishes several printed reports, including monthly consensus forecasts, and weekly changes in individual estimates. The *I/B/E/S* database can be searched online through many vendors, though most are corporate-oriented systems. The only general-purpose vendor to offer *I/B/E/S* is CompuServe, where composite estimates are given for approximately 3,500 U.S. firms, with weekly updates. The file can be searched by ticker symbol or company name only. A basic record lists composite forecasts for the current fiscal year, the following year, a projected annual growth rate in earnings for the next five years, and a one-year projection for the stock's P/E Ratio. CompuServe also offers an expanded report for each company, which includes statistics on the number of analysts making estimates, the number of estimates revised upward and downward in each of the previous three weeks, and the high and low estimates. Finally, data from *I/B/E/S* are available on CD-ROM, via the enhanced edition of *Compustat PC Plus*.

Standard & Poor's Earnings Guide (Standard & Poor's Corporation—Monthly).

The newest competitor to the Zacks service is this concise monthly handbook from Standard & Poor's. The *Earnings Guide* provides consensus earnings forecasts on 3,000 companies, contributed by 130 analyst firms. Each monthly issue provides revised forecasts for the current and following year, plus a five-year projected growth rate. Individual projections from each analyst are not reported, only the mean, high, and low values. The number of analysts contributing to the consensus report is also indicated. Data are presented in comparative tables similar to those seen in S&P's *Stock Guide*. Additional company data include the latest actual EPS, the Book Value, and the Standard & Poor's stock rating. A handful of useful screening lists are also compiled, including a summary of companies whose forecasted earnings have undergone the most significant changes in the past month. Although the *Earnings Guide* covers fewer companies and offers less detail, it is a more affordable alternative to *Zacks Earnings Forecaster* and is extremely convenient to use.

COMMERCIAL ADVISORY SOURCES

Investors have definite personalities and financial objectives. Some are risk-averse and others are risk-takers. Many adhere to a particular theory or follow a single strategy to the exclusion of other methods. But all of them try to second-guess what the market will do. Most newsletters adopt a particular way of looking at the market, and hope to find subscribers with similar views. It would be impossible to comment on even a fraction of the newsletters available today, so this section will discuss services which concentrate on analytical information rather than recommendations alone.

EXHIBIT 12-1. *Zacks Earnings Forecaster*

```
           ZACKS EARNINGS FORECASTER ESTIMATE CHANGES DURING LAST THREE MONTHS      May 24, 1991

            LAST REP                                    C U R R E N T  F I S C A L  Y E A R    N E X T  F I S C A L  Y E A R
            EPS($)    DATE      BROKER      ANALYST     FYE    TO    FROM   CHANGE    FYE    TO    FROM   CHANGE
            dilution                                          ($)   ($)    ($)              ($)   ($)    ($)
+CINCINNATI GAS  4.11  4/22/91  PRUDENTIAL  B ABRAMSON  12/91  3.80   3.75   0.05
 Zacks Consensus:      QTR  6/91:  0.65               ANNL:   3.56                  ANNL:  3.65

-CINEPLEX ODEON  -3.34  3/28/91  SEIDLER AM  J LOGSDON  12/91  0.00   0.05  -0.05
-CINEPLEX ODEON         3/28/91  SUTRO & CO  S HILL                                12/92  -0.25  1.00  -1.25
-CINEPLEX ODEON         3/28/91  SEIDLER AM  J LOGSDON                             12/92   0.40  0.45  -0.05
+CINEPLEX ODEON         3/28/91  SUTRO & CO  S HILL     12/91  -1.00  -1.25  0.25
-CINEPLEX ODEON         3/ 1/91  SEIDLER AM  J LOGSDON  12/91   0.05   0.16  -0.11  12/92   0.45  N/A   N/A
-CINEPLEX ODEON         2/28/91  SUTRO & CO  S HILL     12/91  -1.25  -1.00  -0.25
-CINEPLEX ODEON         2/25/91  SEIDLER AM  J LOGSDON  12/91   0.09   0.16  -0.07
 Zacks Consensus:      QTR  6/91:  0.05               ANNL:  -0.25                  ANNL:  0.13

+CINTAS CORP     1.25  4/25/91  BAIRD R W   J SCOTT     5/91   1.48   1.47   0.01   5/92   1.75   1.73   0.02
-CINTAS CORP           4/ 9/91  BARRINGTON  A PARIS JR  5/91   1.47   1.50  -0.03   5/92   1.75   1.77  -0.02
+CINTAS CORP           3/12/91  ADVEST GRO  A BEJA      5/91   1.48   1.47   0.01   5/92   1.73   1.67   0.06
+CINTAS CORP           3/ 4/91  ADVEST GRO  A BEJA                                  5/92   1.70   1.67   0.03
 Zacks Consensus:      QTR  5/91:  0.44               ANNL:   1.49                  ANNL:  1.76

-CIPRICO        -0.09  5/ 6/91  PIPER JAFF  M SABBANN   9/91  -0.10   0.05  -0.15 *
 Zacks Consensus:      QTR  6/91:  0.00               ANNL:  -0.08                  ANNL:  0.27

-CIPSCO INC      1.93  3/22/91  PRUDENTIAL  B ABRAMSON  12/91  2.10   2.15  -0.05   12/92  2.20   N/A   N/A
 Zacks Consensus:      QTR  6/91:  0.38               ANNL:   2.12                  ANNL:  2.14

+CIRCON          N/A   4/30/91  NEEDHAM &   S NAVARRO   12/91  0.40   0.35   0.05   12/92  0.60   0.55   0.05
 CIRCON                3/ 4/91  NEEDHAM &   S NAVARRO                               12/92  0.55   N/A   N/A
 Zacks Consensus:                                     ANNL:   0.40                  ANNL:  0.60

-CIRCUIT CITY ST  1.35  4/18/91  WESSELS AR  E LAURANCE  2/92   1.30   1.35  -0.05
+CIRCUIT CITY ST        4/15/91  PRUDENTIAL  B BRYANT    2/92   1.50   1.25   0.25
-CIRCUIT CITY ST        4/11/91  RAYMOND JA  H KATICA    2/92   1.40   2.15  -0.75   2/93  1.70
+CIRCUIT CITY ST        3/28/91  WHEAT FIRS  K GASSMAN   2/92   1.45   1.20   0.25
 Zacks Consensus:      QTR  5/91:  0.18               ANNL:   1.41                  ANNL:  1.73

-CIRCUS CIRCUS    3.05  4/19/91  RAYMOND JA  J UPHOFF    1/92   4.00   4.10  -0.10   1/93   4.60   N/A   N/A
 CIRCUS CIRCUS          4/11/91  SUTRO & CO  D FORST                                1/93   4.65   N/A   N/A
 CIRCUS CIRCUS          3/28/91  SEIDLER AM  J LOGSDON   1/92   3.80   N/A   N/A
 CIRCUS CIRCUS          3/11/91  SUTRO & CO  D FORST     1/92   3.90   N/A   N/A
 Zacks Consensus:      QTR  7/91:  1.10               ANNL:   3.91                  ANNL:  4.63

 CIRRUS LOGIC     1.19  4/30/91  NEEDHAM &   R RAJARATN  3/92   1.49   N/A   N/A
 CIRRUS LOGIC           3/29/91  HAMILTON I  J OBERWEIS  3/92   N/A    1.50  N/A
 Zacks Consensus:      QTR  6/91:  0.33               ANNL:   1.42                  ANNL:  1.85

+CISCO SYSTEMS    0.50  5/16/91  WESSELS AR  T ERIKSON   7/91   1.35   1.30   0.05 * 7/92   1.80   1.75   0.05
-CISCO SYSTEMS          4/30/91  NEEDHAM &   P JOHNSON                              7/92   1.88   2.16  -0.28
-CISCO SYSTEMS          4/ 1/91  NEEDHAM &   P JOHNSON   7/91   1.28   1.36  -0.08
 CISCO SYSTEMS          3/29/91  HAMILTON I  J OBERWEIS  7/91   N/A    1.15  N/A
 CISCO SYSTEMS          3/28/91  WHEAT FIRS  T CLARK     7/91   N/A    1.15  N/A     7/92  N/A    1.50  N/A
+CISCO SYSTEMS          3/ 9/91  NEEDHAM &   P JOHNSON   7/91   1.36   1.28   0.08   7/92   2.16   N/A   N/A
 Zacks Consensus:      QTR  7/91:  0.38               ANNL:   1.33                  ANNL:  1.74

 CITADEL HLDGS    7.07  3/28/91  SUTRO & CO  C CHANEY    12/91  N/A    7.75  N/A
 Zacks Consensus:      QTR  6/91:  1.40               ANNL:   6.65                  ANNL:  8.00

 CITICORP         1.53  4/30/91  INTERSTATE  J MASON                            *  12/92  1.00   N/A   N/A
 CITICORP               4/30/91  SHEARSON L  J ROSENBER                           12/92  1.55   N/A   N/A
-CITICORP               4/22/91  PRUDENTIAL  G SALEM     12/91  1.00   1.50  -0.50   12/92  2.25   N/A   N/A
-CITICORP               4/ 4/91  RAYMOND JA  F MEINKE
-CITICORP               3/11/91  SHEARSON L  J ROSENBER  12/91  1.00   1.40  -0.40
-CITICORP               3/ 8/91  DAVIDSON D  J BELLESSA  12/91  1.50   2.00  -0.50
-CITICORP               2/28/91  INTERSTATE  J MASON     12/91  0.75   1.00  -0.25
 Zacks Consensus:      QTR  6/91:  0.29               ANNL:   1.27                  ANNL:  1.91

 CITIZENS BCRP    N/A   3/28/91  WHEAT FIRS  D STUMPF                             12/92  2.40   N/A   N/A
 Zacks Consensus:      QTR  6/91:  N/A                ANNL:   2.10                  ANNL:  2.40

+CITIZENS BKNG    3.02  5/13/91  A.G. EDWAR  A POLINI    12/91  3.05   2.85   0.20 *
 CITIZENS BKNG          4/22/91  A.G. EDWAR  A POLINI                             12/92  3.10   N/A   N/A
 Zacks Consensus:      QTR  8/91:  N/A                ANNL:   2.69                  ANNL:  3.10

 CITY NATIONAL    1.35  3/28/91  SUTRO & CO  C CHANEY    12/91  N/A    1.25  N/A
 Zacks Consensus:      QTR  6/91:  0.09               ANNL:   1.12                  ANNL:  1.41

-CLAIRE'S STORES  1.01  4/25/91  RAYMOND JA  H KATICA    1/92   1.10   1.15  -0.05   1/93   1.35   1.40  -0.05
-CLAIRE'S STORES        4/11/91  RAYMOND JA  H KATICA    1/92   1.15   1.35  -0.20   1/93   1.40   N/A   N/A
 Zacks Consensus:      QTR  7/91:  0.15               ANNL:   1.28                  ANNL:  1.53

 CLARCOR INC      1.94  4/22/91  A.G. EDWAR  J COLE                              11/92  2.40   N/A   N/A
-CLARCOR INC            4/ 9/91  BARRINGTON  J O'HARE    11/91  2.10   2.30  -0.20   11/92  2.25   2.55  -0.30
 CLARCOR INC            3/ 7/91  CO FORECST  NOT IDENT   11/91  2.15   N/A   N/A     11/92  2.40   N/A   N/A
 Zacks Consensus:      QTR  5/91:  0.54               ANNL:   2.17                  ANNL:  2.37

-CLARK EQUIPMENT  2.67  4/30/91  SHEARSON L  K UBELHART  12/91  -1.40   0.25  -1.65 *
-CLARK EQUIPMENT        4/29/91  PRUDENTIAL  S COLBERT   12/91  -0.90   0.75  -1.65   12/92  2.75   3.20  -0.45
-CLARK EQUIPMENT        4/25/91  BAIRD R W   L HOLLIS    12/91  -0.60   1.35  -1.95
-CLARK EQUIPMENT        4/23/91  BARRINGTON  A PARIS JR  12/91   0.25   1.54  -1.29   12/92  2.00   N/A   N/A
-CLARK EQUIPMENT        3/22/91  PRUDENTIAL  S COLBERT   12/91   0.75   1.50  -0.75   12/92  3.20   N/A   N/A
-CLARK EQUIPMENT        3/ 4/91  SHEARSON L  K UBELHART  12/91   0.25   1.25  -1.00   12/92  2.50   N/A   N/A
-CLARK EQUIPMENT        2/28/91  BAIRD R W   L HOLLIS    12/91   1.35   3.00  -1.65
 Zacks Consensus:      QTR  6/91: -0.17               ANNL:  -0.46                  ANNL:  2.42

+CLAYTON HOMES    0.98  4/19/91  MORGAN KEE  N OVERTON   6/91   1.11   1.10   0.01
+CLAYTON HOMES          4/16/91  J.C. BRADF  J DIFFENDA  6/91   1.14   1.12   0.02   6/92   1.32   1.27   0.05
-CLAYTON HOMES          4/10/91  MORGAN KEE  N OVERTON                             6/92   1.26   1.28  -0.02
 CLAYTON HOMES          4/ 1/91  J.C. BRADF  J DIFFENDA                            6/92   1.27   N/A   N/A
-CLAYTON HOMES          3/28/91  MORGAN KEE  N OVERTON                             6/92   1.26   1.28  -0.02
+CLAYTON HOMES          3/ 1/91  EQUITABLE   A CARLISLE  6/91   1.12   1.10   0.02   6/92   1.32   1.28   0.04
 Zacks Consensus:      QTR  6/91:  0.39               ANNL:   1.12                  ANNL:  1.31

+CLEAN HARBORS    0.80  4/18/91  RAYMOND JA  J BERG      2/92   0.75   0.70   0.05   2/93   1.00   N/A   N/A
 CLEAN HARBORS          4/ 1/91  BLUNT ELLI  R EASTMAN   2/92   N/A    0.60  N/A
 Zacks Consensus:      QTR  5/91:  0.14               ANNL:   0.64                  ANNL:  0.93

 CLIFF ENGLE LTD -0.63  5/10/91  PIPER JAFF  NOT IDENT   4/91   0.78   N/A   N/A  *  4/92   0.95   N/A   N/A
 Zacks Consensus:      QTR  7/91:  N/A                ANNL:   0.78                  ANNL:  0.95

-CLIFFS DRILLING -2.19  4/30/91  HOWARD WEI  G DUTT                             *  12/92  0.55   1.69  -1.14
+CLIFFS DRILLING        3/ 1/91  MORGAN KEE  M HARRIS    12/91  0.25   0.12   0.13   12/92  0.75   N/A   N/A
+CLIFFS DRILLING        2/28/91  HOWARD WEI  G DUTT      12/91  0.50  -0.35   0.85
 Zacks Consensus:      QTR  6/91:  N/A                ANNL:   0.38                  ANNL:  0.65

-CLOROX CO        2.80  4/22/91  A.G. EDWAR  G SIGMUND                           6/92   2.85   2.90  -0.05
-CLOROX CO      1.030d  4/17/91  A.G. EDWAR  G SIGMUND   6/91   2.45   2.55  -0.10   6/92   3.00   N/A   N/A
-CLOROX CO              3/18/91  PRUDENTIAL  A SHORE     6/91   2.45   2.65  -0.20   6/92   3.10         -0.10
 Zacks Consensus:      QTR  8/91:  0.80               ANNL:   2.56                  ANNL:  2.98

 CLOTHESTIME INC  0.01  4/ 4/91  WESSELS AR  E LAURANCE                          1/93   0.10   N/A   N/A
+CLOTHESTIME INC        3/21/91  WESSELS AR  E LAURANCE  1/92   0.05  -0.25   0.30
 Zacks Consensus:      QTR  7/91:  N/A                ANNL:   0.15                  ANNL:  0.10

                                                                                                      PAGE  19
```

Reprinted with permission from Zacks Investment Research, Inc.

Stock Market Letters

By far the largest number of investment letters deal with stock market advice. They also offer the most incredible diversity of opinion and techniques. Stock letters written for followers of technical analysis are especially prevalent, and several provide detailed charts for hundreds of individual securities. One of the most popular charting services is the *Daily Graphs* series, published weekly by O'Neil & Company. O'Neil also publishes *Investor's Daily*, and smaller versions of these charts can be seen in the daily paper for those firms which are noteworthy on that particular day. Other widely followed charting services include Standard & Poor's *Trendline* series and a variety of *Chartcraft* products, from a publisher of the same name. The following discussion focuses on well-known services which take a more fundamental approach, and which provide extensive data for research purposes.

Value Line Investment Survey (Value Line, Inc.— Weekly).

If a public or college library has only one investment service, it is almost certain to be the *Value Line Investment Survey.* The late Arnold Bernhard founded the publication in the 1930s, and it has appeared in its present format since the mid-1960s. The service provides in-depth coverage of 1,700 stocks, grouped into approximately 90 industries. For sheer volume of information, few sources can compare with this extensive publication.

Value Line is issued weekly in three parts. Part I, the "Summary and Index," serves as a cumulative index to the entire set. The index leads the user to the page on which each company report appears, as well as summarizing key data for all 1,700 stocks. This section lists the Value Line ratings, recent price, EPS, dividends, and other measures for each stock. The second section of Part I consists of about 20 screening lists that rank stocks by various characteristics such as "best performers," "lowest P/E," "highest dividend yield," and "widest discount from book value."

Part II, "Selection and Opinion," is a weekly newsletter of approximately ten pages that contains articles on the economic outlook, the state of the market, current investing trends, and statistical indicators, including data on the Value Line Stock Index. Part II also offers a "stock highlight" which recommends an especially good investment buy, with an article discussing the company's virtues. A table listing all stocks which received a rating change in the previous week rounds out this section. The third part of *Value Line*, "Ratings and Reports," carries full-page coverage for every one of the 1,700 companies,

plus an industry overview for the 90 industry groups. Each company analysis is updated four times per year on a rotating schedule.

Exhibit 12-2 illustrates a typical page from the "Ratings and Reports." The box in the middle of the page marked "Business" is a succinct description of what the company does, including major brand names, subsidiaries, and, in some cases, market share. Below that is a narrative analysis of the firm's current position and outlook, explaining why the company receives the assigned ratings. Much of the remaining information consists of current and historical financial data—15 years or more of summarized balance sheet and income statement data, capitalization figures, the volume of institutional holdings of the company's stock, quarterly dividend and earnings information, and sales by line of business. Note that much of the current year's data shown in this Exhibit are estimates calculated by Value Line. The core of the *Value Line* analysis appears in the upper left corner, where each stock receives three ratings. The timeliness rating, on a scale of 1 to 5, indicates the projected price performance of the stock over the next 12 months as compared to the other 1,700 stocks. The safety rating, also on a scale of 1 to 5, measures the amount of fluctuation in the stock's price over time. The Beta Coefficient represents the price fluctuation relative to the other 1,700 stocks. Other ratings, such as "financial strength" and "growth persistence" are shown in the lower right corner. Finally, the graph at the top of the page compares the price history of the stock to its so-called "value line." The value line is a unique statistical measure which serves as a basis for predicting the future price of the stock. Because of the amount of detail contained in a *Value Line* report, the publisher sends every subscriber a 70-page booklet that explains how to interpret the reports.

Despite its complexity, *Value Line* offers the best of both types of investment newsletters. It recommends specific stocks, provides a variety of screening lists, rates each stock covered, and at the same time provides enough background data for the reader to reach an independent decision. Because reports are arranged by industry group, *Value Line* is a convenient source for industry analysis. For every grouping, the publisher also provides a single page outlook for the industry, together with composite statistics and ratios.

Data from *Value Line* can be viewed online as the *Value Line DataFile.* This service is most widely available via CompuServe. The reports can be searched by company name or ticker symbol, and can be displayed in three formats: annual data for four years, quarterly data

EXHIBIT 12-2. *Value Line Investment Survey*

SHERWIN-WILLIAMS NYSE-SHW	RECENT PRICE **36**	P/E RATIO **13.0** (Trailing: 14.3 / Median: 10.0)	RELATIVE P/E RATIO **1.02**	DIV'D YLD **2.2%**	VALUE LINE **530**

TIMELINESS	2	Above Average
(Relative Price Performance Next 12 Mos.)		
SAFETY	2	Above Average
(Scale: 1 Highest to 5 Lowest)		
BETA 1.20	(1.00 = Market)	

| High: | 3.6 | 5.0 | 5.9 | 12.5 | 15.9 | 16.2 | 23.5 | 32.3 | 38.5 | 31.6 | 35.8 | 36.4 |
| Low: | 2.5 | 2.9 | 4.0 | 4.5 | 9.1 | 11.1 | 13.9 | 21.3 | 20.1 | 24.0 | 25.0 | 30.6 |

Target Price Range 1992 | 1993 | 1994 | 1995

1992-94 PROJECTIONS

	Price	Gain	Ann'l Total Return
High	75	(+110%)	22%
Low	50	(+40%)	11%

Insider Decisions

	J	J	A	S	O	N	D	J	F
to Buy	0	0	0	0	0	0	0	0	1
Options	0	0	1	0	1	0	1	0	0
to Sell	1	0	0	0	0	0	0	0	0

Institutional Decisions

	2Q'89	3Q'89	4Q'89
to Buy	68	47	63
to Sell	58	56	42
Hld's(000)	25113	25252	26645

Percent shares traded 12.0 8.0 4.0

Options: CBOE

1974	1975	1976	1977	1978	1979	1980	1981	1982	1983	1984	1985	1986	1987	1988	1989	1990	1991	© VALUE LINE, INC.	92-94E
18.66	20.11	22.06	23.99	26.22	30.71	32.15	38.81	42.17	43.32	46.07	47.64	35.23	41.00	45.32	49.55	54.00		Sales per sh (A)	75.00
.97	.93	.70	.18	.53	.94	1.11	1.32	1.47	1.74	2.00	2.19	2.29	2.81	3.21	3.55	3.85		"Cash Flow" per sh	5.75
.57	.56	.37	d.22	.10	.37	.53	.68	.88	1.13	1.40	1.60	1.66	2.09	2.30	2.52	2.80		Earnings per sh (B)	4.50
.25	.28	.28	.21	--	.02	.15	.20	.25	.30	.38	.46	.50	.56	.64	.70	.76		Div'ds Decl'd per sh (C)■	1.10
.45	.64	.95	.67	.34	.26	.56	1.09	.70	.70	1.05	1.28	1.15	1.15	1.66	1.55	1.75		Cap'l Spending per sh	2.25
5.93	6.29	6.42	5.69	5.79	6.45	6.69	7.17	7.59	8.12	8.97	10.10	11.15	12.57	13.97	15.75	17.65		Book Value per sh	23.80
42.99	43.10	43.15	43.19	43.19	38.95	39.31	39.60	43.92	45.56	45.04	46.07	44.08	43.72	43.04	42.90	42.50		Common Shs Outst'g (D)	40.00
7.8	8.4	12.6	--	32.3	8.0	7.7	7.6	7.8	11.2	9.8	11.4	16.2	15.3	11.9	12.1	*Bold figures are*		Avg Ann'l P/E Ratio	14.0
1.09	1.12	1.61	--	4.40	1.16	1.02	.92	.86	.95	.91	.93	1.10	1.02	.98	.92	*Value Line estimates*		Relative P/E Ratio	1.15
5.6%	5.8%	5.9%	5.1%	--	.6%	3.7%	3.9%	3.7%	2.4%	2.8%	2.5%	1.9%	1.8%	2.3%	2.3%			Avg Ann'l Div'd Yield	1.7%

CAPITAL STRUCTURE as of 9/30/89
Total Debt $127.8 mill. Due in 5 Yrs $54.0 mill.
LT Debt $127.8 mill. LT Interest $12.0 mill.
Incl. $.5 mill. 6¼% sub. debs. ('95), callable 100.63, cv. into 173.91 com. shs. at $5.75.
Incl. $2.2 mill capitalized leases.
(LT interest earned: 14x) (16% of Cap'l)

Leases, Uncapitalized Annual rentals $48.4 mill.
Pension Liability None in '88 vs. None in '87

Pfd Stock None
Common Stock 43,084,448 shs. (84% of Cap'l)

	1263.7	1536.8	1851.8	1973.5	2075.2	2194.9	1552.9	1792.7	1950.5	2123.5	2300		Sales ($mill) (A)	3000
	5.6%	5.6%	5.7%	6.8%	7.1%	7.6%	10.7%	10.0%	8.8%	9.5%	9.5%		Operating Margin	10.0%
	20.0	21.7	22.4	24.2	24.9	26.3	24.6	29.0	36.9	42.0	44.0		Depreciation ($mill)	50.0
	24.9	31.4	42.9	55.4	65.0	74.6	76.4	93.8	101.1	108.9	120		Net Profit ($mill)	180
	48.6%	45.6%	43.8%	45.3%	44.0%	42.0%	45.6%	42.0%	38.0%	36.0%	35.0%		Income Tax Rate	36.0%
	2.0%	2.0%	2.3%	2.8%	3.1%	3.4%	4.9%	5.2%	5.2%	5.1%	5.2%		Net Profit Margin	6.0%
	307.4	291.6	324.9	339.6	344.2	371.6	323.2	387.0	388.1	440	480		Working Cap'l ($mill)	600
	212.9	230.1	196.2	175.3	168.9	145.4	119.7	89.2	129.6	120	110		Long-Term Debt ($mill) (A)	100
	286.9	305.0	348.8	371.0	404.1	465.4	491.6	549.7	601.3	675	750		Net Worth ($mill)	950
	6.7%	7.5%	9.6%	11.7%	12.7%	13.4%	13.5%	15.3%	14.8%	14.5%	14.5%		% Earned Total Cap'l	17.5%
	8.7%	10.3%	12.3%	14.9%	16.1%	16.0%	15.5%	17.1%	16.8%	16.5%	16.0%		% Earned Net Worth	19.0%
	6.8%	7.9%	9.5%	11.2%	11.8%	11.5%	10.9%	12.6%	12.2%	11.5%	11.5%		% Retained to Comm Eq	14.5%
	28%	28%	26%	25%	26%	28%	30%	26%	28%	27%	27%		% All Div'ds to Net Prof	24%

CURRENT POSITION ($MILL.)

	1987	1988	9/30/89
Cash Assets	208.5	154.2	168.1
Receivables	177.7	195.7	256.1
Inventory(LIFO)	281.4	323.0	309.5
Other	89.6	93.2	93.6
Current Assets	757.2	766.1	827.3
Accts Payable	145.5	153.4	163.8
Debt Due	7.2	7.4	--
Other	217.5	217.2	246.2
Current Liab.	370.2	378.0	410.0

ANNUAL RATES

of change (per sh)	Past 10 Yrs.	Past 5 Yrs.	Est'd '86-'88 to '92-'94
Sales	5.5%	-5%	11.0%
"Cash Flow"	19.5%	13.0%	13.0%
Earnings	37.5%	17.5%	14.5%
Dividends	9.0%	18.0%	11.5%
Book Value	7.5%	10.5%	11.0%

QUARTERLY SALES ($ mill.)

Cal-endar	Mar.31	Jun.30	Sep.30	Dec.31	Full Year
1986	332.2	432.0	438.2	350.5	1552.9
1987	380.5	491.5	512.3	408.4	1792.7
1988	413.4	544.5	548.0	444.6	1950.5
1989	464.8	584.0	596.0	478.7	2123.5
1990	495	640	650	515	2300

EARNINGS PER SHARE (B)

Cal-endar	Mar.31	Jun.30	Sep.30	Dec.31	Full Year
1986	.11	.58	.66	.31	1.66
1987	.17	.67	.81	.44	2.09
1988	.19	.82	.86	.43	2.30
1989	.20	.90	.96	.46	2.52
1990	.23	1.00	1.07	.50	2.80

QUARTERLY DIVIDENDS PAID (C)■

Cal-endar	Mar.31	Jun.30	Sep.30	Dec.31	Full Year
1986	.125	.125	.125	.125	.50
1987	.14	.14	.14	.14	.56
1988	.16	.16	.16	.16	.64
1989	.175	.175	.175	.175	.70
1990	.19				

BUSINESS: The Sherwin-Williams Company, world's largest producer of paints and varnishes, also makes application equipment, and chemical and automotive coatings. Has 1,865 company-operated retail paint and wallcovering stores in 48 states, and 139 automotive coatings outlets. Paint sold in company stores under *Sherwin-Williams* label. Also makes *Dutch Boy, Martin-Senour,* and *Kem-Tone* brands for sale through independent dealers. R&D, .9% of sales. '88 depr. rate: 6.1%. Est. plant age: 7 years. Insiders and employees control 17% of stock; Cooke & Bieler, 7.2%. Has 16,607 employees, 12,606 stockholders. Chmn. & C.E.O.: John G. Breen, Pres.: Thomas A. Commes. Incorp.: Ohio. Address: 101 Prospect Avenue, N.W., Cleveland, Ohio 44115. Telephone: 216-566-2000.

We look for earnings to advance about 11% this year at Sherwin-Williams. Sales, even in a soft economy—the housing sector has been weak for some time now—ought to advance by 8%–9% in 1990. The operating margin might widen a bit despite higher advertising costs this year, as the pace of raw-material price hikes has moderated in recent months. We estimate share net will reach $2.80 in 1990. Note that the company typically makes most of its money in the spring and summer months, when exterior painting can be done in much of the country. Although its price hasn't changed much in the past few months, this good-quality stock remains ranked 2, Above Average, for year-ahead relative performance.

Sherwin continually takes away market share from its competitors in a slow-growing industry. The company is able to grow faster than the average paint firm by closely attending to the needs of its customers, especially professional painting contractors. Over 70% of the sales in company-owned paint stores is wholesale business. The pros are frequently more interested in product quality than are retail do-it-yourselfers. Thus, Sherwin's position as the largest firm in the industry and a vertically integrated one at that (the company is both a manufacturer and a retailer), give it the financial muscle to constantly improve its products and its production processes to provide the best quality product at a competitive price.

The company's external trucking business may soon be sold. Sherwin purchased a less-than-truckload carrier a few years ago to improve delivery of goods to the stores. It has outside customers as well, but competition in the trucking industry makes that business little more than a breakeven proposition. The unit probably would fare better as part of a larger trucking firm; apparently there are some interested parties.

Sherwin-Williams stock offers decent 3- to 5-year appreciation potential. We project that continued market share gains combined with improvements in the production of paint will result in stock price growth in line with the market averages over the next few years.

Michael Schiffman *April 6, 1990*

(A) Fiscal year ended Aug. 31st prior to '77. Includes real estate subsidiary since 1988. (B) Fully diluted earnings. Excludes nonrecurring net gain (loss): '82, (2¢); '86, 43¢. Next earnings report due late April. (C) Next dividend meeting about April 18. Goes ex about May 21. Dividend payment dates: March 20, June 9, Sept. 8, Dec. 1. ■ Dividend reinvestment plan available. (D) In millions, adjusted for stock splits.

Company's Financial Strength	A+
Stock's Price Stability	65
Price Growth Persistence	95
Earnings Predictability	50

Factual material is obtained from sources believed to be reliable, but the publisher is not responsible for any errors or omissions contained herein.

for four quarters, or estimates and projections for the next three to five years. While the CompuServe system does not allow financial screening, Value Line produces a PC-based system which does. The product, which provides software and data on floppy diskette, is called *Value/Screen II*. Subscribers may receive updated diskettes weekly, monthly, or quarterly.

For the amount and quality of information, *Value Line* remains one of the best bargains in the advisory field. The publisher also produces several specialized newsletters, including *Options and Convertibles* and the *OTC Special Situations Service*.

Standard & Poor's Stock Reports (Standard & Poor's Corporation—Quarterly).

This series covers every company listed on the New York and American exchanges, together with over 1,600 OTC companies. Each company profile consists of a standardized, two-page report. The emphasis is on factual analysis, but investment advice appears in the "Summary" and "Current Outlook" sections. Each firm is also given an "S&P Ranking" from A+ to D (with D used to designate firms undergoing bankruptcy or reorganization). For many companies, S&P analysts also provide projections of EPS and dividend payments for the coming year-end. The *Stock Reports* summarize "Important Developments," and provide an excellent description of company activities in the "Business Summary" section. Other major features include a breakdown of sales by line of business (similar to the presentation in *Value Line*), and information on the largest institutional stockholders.

Each two-page summary provides ten years of abbreviated financial data from the income statement and balance sheet, and ten years of investment indicators such as Book Value, dividends, P/E ratio, and EPS. Standard & Poor's now calculates Beta Coefficients for nearly every company; values are based on the universe of stocks represented in the *Compustat* database. The *Stock Reports* are also a handy source of ready-reference facts about each company, such as ticker symbol, address, names of officers, transfer agent, state of incorporation, and number of shareholders. The *Stock Reports* summarize important information in an easy-to-read format, quickly telling the reader what the company does, what it is known for, its strengths and weaknesses, recent events of importance, and financial trends. For this reason, it is especially recommended to the layperson who needs a brief picture of a company's background.

Standard & Poor's Stock Reports is available in paperback and loose-leaf formats. New paperback volumes are mailed quarterly, while revised loose-leaf pages are sent weekly, on a rotating basis. In both formats,

every company report is updated quarterly, but loose-leaf subscribers receive them as soon as they are written. Every company profile includes the approximate date when the revised report will be issued. In both formats, the reports are issued in three editions, one each for NYSE, AMEX, and OTC firms. An additional service, *OTC ProFiles*, provides briefer coverage of approximately 750 smaller OTC and regional stocks of interest to investors. Standard & Poor's also sells an annual *Stock Market Encyclopedia*, which reproduces pages from the *Stock Reports*, but only for those companies in the S&P 500 Index.

Data from the *Stock Reports* can be found online through Dow Jones, CompuServe, and several other vendors as *Standard & Poor's Online*. Users can also subscribe to a service called *S&P MarketScope*, available directly through the publisher. This version includes profiles from the *Stock Reports*, general market trends, and data from other S&P publications, including the *Daily News*, *The Outlook*, and their popular *CreditWeek* service. The file is updated continuously throughout the day. S&P has also announced the imminent release of a CD-ROM version of the *Stock Reports*.

Moody's Handbook of Common Stocks (Moody's Investors Service—Quarterly).

The briefer and less expensive *Moody's Handbook* is often an acceptable alternative to the higher priced *Standard & Poor's Stock Reports*. The Moody's publication provides summary descriptions and advice for only about 900 stocks, affording single-page coverage to each firm. Despite the briefer treatment, Moody's is able to present much of the same information found in Standard & Poor's. *Moody's Handbook* provides a concise description of the firm, a rundown of recent events, a capitalization summary, a graph of price history, quarterly dividend data, and the outlook for the future. The *Handbook* also provides ready-reference information, stock price history, and abbreviated financial data, though not in the amount seen in the Standard & Poor's publication. For example, Moody's does not include summary data from the income statement or balance sheet, choosing instead to cite a few key figures and ratios. Where Standard & Poor's assigns a letter to rank each stock, Moody's uses a grading system of High, Investment, Medium, or Speculative. Moody's offers an additional rating mechanism, namely a measure of long- and short-term price growth, as compared to the NYSE index.

Although the *Handbook of Common Stock* does not cover as many companies or include as much data, it does contain additional features not found in the *Stock Reports*. Every issue contains graphs of the Dow Jones

Averages and other market indicators. Moody's also compiles investment screening lists, such as the 25 highest and lowest price performers, and stocks with the highest dividends. Several convenient reference lists are provided, including an index of companies by industry, and guides to stocks with recent quality grade changes, company name changes and mergers, and stock splits. The *Handbook* also contains an appendix called the "Condensed Statistical Tabulation," which briefly covers all NYSE firms not listed in the main section. This "Tab Section" resembles an abbreviated version of the *Standard & Poor's Stock Guide* introduced in Chapter 10. Advice and analysis from the *Handbook* are also incorporated into two electronic products introduced in Chapter 9: *Moody's Corporate Profiles* online, and *Moody's Company Data* on CD-ROM.

The Market Guide (Market Guide, Inc.—Quarterly).

This guide to approximately 800 selected OTC companies includes many firms not widely followed by Wall Street analysts. Basic guidelines for inclusion are significant average monthly trading volume; financial strength, evidenced by low debt and strong earnings; a high growth rate based on three years of sales data; or high dividend yields.

Each company is given a two-page profile. Data include a narrative description, the capital structure of the firm, officers' names, five years of quarterly earnings, five years of summary income statements, and two years of summary balance sheets. Other statistics include recent price and trading volume, basic investment ratios, per share sales and earnings data, several growth rates, and number of shares outstanding. An especially helpful feature is a listing of market makers in each stock, together with their phone numbers. The profiles are written by members of the Market Guide staff, and every report is signed by its author. Entries are arranged alphabetically by company name, with indexes by state and broad industry category. Subscribers can receive the service as a loose-leaf version with weekly mailings, or a single-volume paperbound book updated quarterly. Profiles in both formats are revised quarterly.

The electronic version, *Market Guide Database*, is available online, on magnetic tape, or on floppy diskette. It contains the same data found in the printed version, plus similar profiles for all companies on the New York and American exchanges and leading NASDAQ firms, a total of 6,600 firms. Profiles of the 800 companies in the printed edition can be found online as a separate database on the LEXIS/NEXIS system, and as part of the *Investext*

database via DIALOG and other vendors. Reports from *The Market Guide* also appear on CD-ROM through *CD/Corporate*.

The Outlook (Standard & Poor's Corporation—Weekly).

The Outlook is a more traditional weekly newsletter of 10 to 20 pages with articles and recommendations on the stock market. It has appeared since the late 1930s and boasts more than 30,000 subscribers, making it one of the oldest and best-known advisory services. In addition to a weekly article on the economic outlook, and major investment news, the bulk of the information consists of specific stock recommendations. Each issue recommends at least three stocks of exceptional value, and occasionally a list of "stocks to avoid" will also appear. A key feature of *The Outlook* is the "Master List of Recommended Issues," which presents two recommended stock portfolios of 12 stocks each. The portfolios fulfill different investment objectives—long-term capital appreciation, and long-term total return. Standard & Poor's carefully tracks all the stocks it recommends. *The Outlook* advises when to sell previously recommended stocks and regularly reviews every recommendation it makes, both in depth, and in a more frequent chart of "Advice on Previous Recommendations."

A feature introduced in early 1989 is called "STARS," the STock Appreciation Ranking System. The 800 stocks followed by *The Outlook* staff receive a STARS rating ranging from 1 to 5, with 5 being the highest recommendation. Every two weeks, *The Outlook* publishes a list of "buy" recommendations based on STARS, and once a month a corresponding "sell" list appears. A guide to all STARS ratings appears quarterly.

The Outlook also includes articles on how to invest; occasional information on bonds, mutual funds, and other securities; useful screening lists of stocks; and an annual forecast of the coming year. The service is also useful for ready-reference purposes. Specialized directories frequently appear, such as lists of companies offering dividend reinvestment plans, and periodic guides to the companies which comprise the S&P 500. Statistical summaries of the stock and bond markets appear each week, and a monthly table of S&P indexes by industry category is also published. The diversity of information is enhanced by a weekly index with quarterly cumulations. Indexing is by subject, company name, and special feature.

Industry Analysis

There are many ways to research the performance and activity of an entire industry. One method is to consult periodical indexes like *Predicasts F&S Index* or *ABI/INFORM*, which are organized by industry category. Special "review" issues of trade journals offer another convenient approach. More detailed analyses can be found in market research reports, which will be introduced in Chapter 18. Another component of industry research involves financial analysis, and the guides to industry norms and financial ratios described in Chapter 8 are especially helpful here. Finally, a broad picture of an industry should include aggregate data on production, sales, and other economic indicators. Sources for this type of research can be seen in Chapter 16.

What does this have to do with investment advice? Fundamental stock analysis deals not only with company performance, but with industry-wide developments as well. Understanding the structure of the industry, its vulnerabilities, and the activities of its key players is essential to making sound investment decisions. To one degree or another, industry surveys should include a comparison of major companies in the field. Once again there are many ways to conduct such investigations. General business magazines publish special issues which offer brief analysis for leading industries. The most popular of these is the "Annual Report on American Industry," which appears in the first January issue of *Forbes. Business Week* and other popular magazines also issue comparative overviews. Another basic method, described in Chapter 8, is to examine company rankings.

One of the best ways to evaluate companies is to utilize investment guides which take an industry approach. An invaluable source of narrative and financial information is brokerage house reports, because securities analysts at major brokerage firms are in a unique position to analyze the prospects of individual industries. *TWST* and *Investext* both carry extensive industry reports from Wall Street. Another method is to consult statistical or advisory services which are organized by industry group, which allow comparisons of competing firms, or which provide summary data for industries. Publications of this type include *Value Line, Media General*, and even *Investor's Daily*. The resources listed below offer more detailed analysis than most, and are specifically designed for industry-wide comparisons.

Standard & Poor's Industry Surveys (Standard & Poor's Corporation—Annual, with Updates).

The most encyclopedic source of narrative and financial industry analysis is published by Standard & Poor's. Its *Industry Surveys* provides concise investment profiles for a wide range of key industries, with considerable attention given to non-manufacturing activities. Fully one-half of the reports are on the retail and service trades. The 20 industry reports are divided into 5 to 10 industry subgroups and coverage is extensive, The report on Aerospace and Air Transport, for example, has sections on diversified aerospace companies, components manufacturers, builders of airframes, engine and propulsion firms, major air carriers, regional airlines, and air freight companies. The focus is on the current situation and outlook, together with summary data on the major companies within each industry. A total of 1,200 companies are compared.

For each industry group, the reports are divided into two parts: an annual "Basic Analysis," and updates called "Current Analysis." The latter are issued anywhere from one to three times per year, depending on the industry. Every Basic Analysis begins with a brief discussion of the outlook for the whole industry, followed by coverage of major segments. The Basic Analysis also provides composite industry statistics (both current and historical), financial ratios for the industry and for major companies, and brief financial data on each company. The Current Analysis consists of a four- to six-page report which brings the reader abreast of current developments in the field. The information in both sections is compiled from many sources, but the analysis is strictly the product of Standard & Poor's industry experts. S&P analysts offer their own opinions, and each report is signed by its author. The set includes a quarterly "Earnings Supplement," which summarizes the latest quarterly and annual earnings data for all 1,200 companies. Information includes total revenues, net income, return on equity, and company rankings within the industry.

Industry Surveys is published in two different formats, offering the subscriber a choice of delivery modes. The first option appears in loose-leaf form, with reports updated on a rotating basis through weekly mailings. The second format is a paperback edition received four times each year; approximately half of the reports are updated between each quarterly revision. The paperback version is less expensive than the loose-leaf service, because loose-leaf subscribers receive two added benefits: new updates are mailed as soon as they are produced; and a monthly economic newsletter called *Trends and Projections* appears as part of the service. Subscribers to the paperback edition may receive the newsletter separately for an additional charge. Otherwise the two formats are identical, including the quarterly "Earnings Supplement."

The biggest weakness of the service is that some revisions do not appear as regularly as they once did. Though most of the "Basic" reports appear annually, three or four are usually 1½ to 2 years behind. The "Current" updates are intended to appear three times per year, but less than half of them do. The others are updated only once or twice per year. Although this may seem like a minor flaw, subscribers pay a hefty price to receive current information, and a few reports are always woefully out of date. Except for this drawback, *Standard & Poor's Industry Surveys* is an excellent product. Users will find it interesting, authoritative, and convenient.

Standard & Poor's Industry Report Service (Standard & Poor's Corporation—Biweekly).

In 1990, S&P introduced the *Industry Report Service* (commonly known as *Industry Reports*). It is geared much more specifically to an investment audience. Where *Industry Surveys* offers lengthy analysis, with an emphasis on the financial characteristics of companies, this service provides much briefer reports, focusing on the investment performance of each company. In fact, *Industry Reports* summarizes data found in the *Stock Reports*, the *Industry Surveys*, and *The Outlook*. The core of the service is a collection of two-page reports on major industries, similar in format to the company profiles seen in the *Stock Reports*. As of this writing, nearly 40 industry groups are surveyed, with plans to double this number in the future. Each report provides an investment rating for the industry, a discussion of industry outlook, a brief guide to recent developments, and a table comparing the performance of leading stocks. Additional sections highlight the best and worst performing stocks, and summarize important characteristics of the industry. Every report is revised six times per year.

The service also offers a biweekly newsletter entitled "At a Glance," which quickly identifies the best and worst industry groups for investment purposes. It also rates the best and worst individual stocks by industry group, using the "STARS" system. A second supplement, "Performance and Rankings," ranks all companies in each industry according to total revenue, profit margin, P/E Ratio, and return on equity. This supplement is updated quarterly. Because only a few companies are reviewed in the *Industry Reports*, the publisher also includes a semiannual industry index to all the companies covered in the *S&P Stock Reports*, a helpful guide for those wishing to analyze additional companies in the same category. A "User's Guide" lists all the stocks which make up the S&P 500 Index, arranged by industry

group. The *Industry Reports* are not for everyone, but they offer a more action-oriented approach to investors who may find the *Industry Surveys* too general.

Moody's Industry Review (Moody's Investors Service—Biweekly).

While Moody's publishes nothing quite like S&P's *Industry Surveys* or *Industry Reports*, it does issue a different tool of value to both investors and researchers. *Moody's Industry Review* is most similar to the "Performance and Ratings" section of the *Standard & Poor's Industry Reports*, but it is actually much more detailed. First, it covers 4,000 companies in nearly 150 industry groups. And second, it compares companies according to 12 performance measures instead of 4.

Every company is ranked within its industry by five financial characteristics (revenues, net income, total assets, cash and marketable securities, and long-term debt), five ratios (profit margin, return on capital, return on assets, P/E, and dividend yield), and Moody's ratings for long-term and short-term stock performance. Every industry report also provides additional data in an unranked display, including EPS, Book Value, and 12-year stock price summaries. All reports are updated twice per year, with biweekly mailings on a rotating basis. Exhibit 12-3 shows comparative statistics for publicly traded firms in the auto industry. General Motors ranks highest for those categories dealing with sheer size—revenues, gross plant, and so on. For ratios which measure financial or stock performance, however, GM is not rated number 1. The single-page presentation allows users to make comparisons quickly and easily. Moody's varies the ratios for some industries to allow more meaningful analysis. In the case of the auto industry, plant facilities are considered more important than total assets, so a ratio for return on net plant is calculated.

Many other investment services compile company rankings by industry, or otherwise allow user's to quickly compare market performance. Among them are *Value Line*, *Media General*, and *Compact D/SEC*. However, researchers will find that *Moody's Industry Review* is among the most comprehensive and convenient sources available.

Mutual Fund Services

Next to stock services, guides to mutual funds are the most commonly published advisory letters. Standard newsletters are available in abundance, from traditional services like the *United Mutual Fund Selector* to specialized letters which recommend timing for switching from one fund to another, such as the *Mutual Fund Switch*

EXHIBIT 12-3. ***Moody's Industry Review***

MOODY'S INDUSTRY REVIEW

May 11, 1990

AUTOMOBILES & TRUCKS

COMPARATIVE STATISTICS

COMPANY	FISCAL DATE	EXCH	SYMBOL	PRICE RANGE (12 MOS.) HIGH	PRICE RANGE (12 MOS.) LOW	RECENT PRICE	EARNINGS PER SHARE LATEST 12 MOS.	EARNINGS PER SHARE 1989	EARNINGS PER SHARE 1988	EARNINGS PER SHARE 1987	IND. CASH DIV.	1989 BOOK VALUE PER SH.	1989 STKHLDRS' EQUITY ($ MILL)	1989 LONG-TERM DEBT (%)
CHRYSLER CORP.	12/31	NYS	C .	27⅛	15⅞	16⅝	0.17	...	4.66	5.90	1.200	†21.00	†7582.30	†63.61
COLLINS INDUSTRIES, INC.	10/31	ASE	GO	3⅞	3⅛	3⅝	0.34	0.33	0.18	0.17	Nil	2.45	9.34	69.51
ESI INDUSTRIES, INC.	12/31	ASE	ESI	3	1¼	1⅜	0.25	0.19	0.24	0.61	Nil	1.89	20.77	43.46
FORD MOTOR CO.	12/31	NYS	F	54⅝	41⅜	47¼	8.15	8.22	10.96	9.05	3.000	48.07	22727.80	59.84
FORD MOTOR CO. OF CANADA, LTD.	12/31	ASE	FC	170	137	149	37.87	...	32.54	14.93	11.000	†170.86	†1416.60	†2.12
GENERAL MOTORS CORP.	12/31	NYS	GM	50½	39⅜	45⅞	6.33	6.33	6.82	5.03	3.000	45.60	34982.50	0.74
HONDA MOTOR CO., LTD.	3/31	NYS	HMC	30⅜	20⅜	22⅛	1.49	...	0.75	0.45	0.159	†7.20	†6829.23	†24.38
MACK TRUCKS INC.	12/31	NAS	MACK	13⅛	5⅛	6½	d7.39	...	0.84	0.13	Nil	†17.76	†525.20	†51.70
NAVISTAR INTERNATIONAL CORP.	10/31	NYS	NAV	5⅞	3¼	4⅛	0.01	0.23	0.89	0.50	Nil	2.61	914.00	48.51
PACCAR INC.	12/31	NAS	PCAR	52½	37	44⅞	6.90	6.90	4.90	3.13	2.500	28.87	1007.31	41.07
SUBARU OF AMERICA, INC.	10/31	NAS	SBRU	8½	5	6⅝	d0.42	d0.87	d1.19	d0.62	Nil	2.63	187.58	15.72
TECH/OPS SEVCON, INC.	9/30	ASE	TOC	6⅞	6⅛	6⅝	0.77	0.68	0.50	0.27	Nil	2.76	7.10	...

† Indicates previous year's data.
Ind. cash div. excludes stk. splits & stk. divs.

FINANCIAL DATA–LATEST ANNUAL RANKINGS

REVENUES ($ MILL.)

RANK	COMPANY	'89 AMT
1	General Motors Corp.	126931.90
2	Ford Motor Co.	96145.90
3	Chrysler Corp.	†35472.70
4	Honda Motor Co., Ltd.	†26433.77
5	Ford Motor Co. Of Can	†15943.30
6	Navistar International	4241.00
7	Paccar Inc.	3564.72
8	Mack Trucks Inc.	†2188.00
9	Subaru Of America, Inc.	1728.99
10	Collins Industries, Inc.	134.48
11	ESI Industries, Inc.	113.15
12	Tech/Ops Sevcon, Inc.	14.32

NET INCOME ($ MILL.)

RANK	COMPANY	'89 AMT
1	General Motors Corp.	4224.30
2	Ford Motor Co.	3835.00
3	Chrysler Corp.	†1050.20
4	Honda Motor Co., Ltd.	†737.11
5	Ford Motor Co. Of Can	†269.80
6	Paccar Inc.	241.92
7	Navistar International	87.00
8	Mack Trucks Inc.	†24.94
9	Tech/Ops Sevcon, Inc.	1.38
10	Collins Industries, Inc.	1.14
11	ESI Industries, Inc.	0.88
12	Subaru Of America, Inc.	d42.37

OPERATING PROFIT MARGIN (%)

RANK	COMPANY	'89 AMT
1	Tech/Ops Sevcon, Inc.	13.89
2	General Motors Corp.	11.94
3	Chrysler Corp.	†11.87
4	Paccar Inc.	8.34
5	Navistar International	6.20
6	Ford Motor Co.	5.93
7	Honda Motor Co., Ltd.	†5.07
8	Collins Industries, Inc.	4.76
9	Mack Trucks Inc.	†4.62
10	ESI Industries, Inc.	4.03
11	Ford Motor Co. Of Can	†2.42
12	Subaru Of America, Inc.	d3.64

RETURN ON CAPITAL (%)

RANK	COMPANY	'89 AMT
1	Tech/Ops Sevcon, Inc.	18.61
2	Ford Motor Co. Of Can	†16.69
3	Paccar Inc.	13.87
4	General Motors Corp.	11.53
5	Honda Motor Co., Ltd.	†7.87
6	Ford Motor Co.	5.90
7	Navistar International	4.90
8	Chrysler Corp.	†4.02
9	Collins Industries, Inc.	3.72
10	ESI Industries, Inc.	2.17
11	Mack Trucks Inc.	†2.12
12	Subaru Of America, Inc.	d14.61

GROSS PLANT ($ MILL.)

RANK	COMPANY	'89 AMT
1	General Motors Corp.	63390.70
2	Ford Motor Co.	29918.40
3	Honda Motor Co., Ltd.	†12404.13
4	Chrysler Corp.	†10330.50
5	Ford Motor Co. Of Can	†2169.00
6	Navistar International	962.00
7	Mack Trucks Inc.	†518.84
8	Paccar Inc.	501.24
9	Subaru Of America, Inc.	88.71
10	Collins Industries, Inc.	27.19
11	ESI Industries, Inc.	25.11
12	Tech/Ops Sevcon, Inc.	3.14

NET PLANT ($ MILL.)

RANK	COMPANY	'89 AMT
1	General Motors Corp.	33994.50
2	Ford Motor Co.	18605.20
3	Chrysler Corp.	†6687.10
4	Honda Motor Co., Ltd.	†6561.33
5	Ford Motor Co. Of Can	†1621.90
6	Navistar International	526.00
7	Mack Trucks Inc.	†262.93
8	Paccar Inc.	260.29
9	Subaru Of America, Inc.	55.97
10	Collins Industries, Inc.	16.86
11	ESI Industries, Inc.	15.71
12	Tech/Ops Sevcon, Inc.	1.09

RETURN ON NET PLANT (%)

RANK	COMPANY	'89 AMT
1	Tech/Ops Sevcon, Inc.	126.14
2	Paccar Inc.	92.94
3	Ford Motor Co.	20.61
4	Ford Motor Co. Of Can	†16.63
5	Navistar International	16.54
6	Chrysler Corp.	†15.70
7	General Motors Corp.	12.43
8	Honda Motor Co., Ltd.	†11.23
9	Mack Trucks Inc.	†9.49
10	Collins Industries, Inc.	6.75
11	ESI Industries, Inc.	5.57
12	Subaru Of America, Inc.	d75.70

WORKING CAPITAL ($ MILL.)

RANK	COMPANY	'89 AMT
1	General Motors Corp.	20322.10
2	Chrysler Corp.	†14266.10
3	Honda Motor Co., Ltd.	†1680.23
4	Paccar Inc.	1508.39
5	Navistar International	1234.00
6	Mack Trucks Inc.	†590.44
7	Ford Motor Co. Of Can	†206.70
8	Subaru Of America, Inc.	64.14
9	ESI Industries, Inc.	12.12
10	Collins Industries, Inc.	9.46
11	Tech/Ops Sevcon, Inc.	4.73
12	Ford Motor Co.	d63273.60

PRICE-EARNINGS RATIO

RANK	COMPANY	'89 AMT
1	Chrysler Corp.	†97.79
2	Honda Motor Co., Ltd.	†14.85
3	Collins Industries, Inc.	10.66
4	Tech/Ops Sevcon, Inc.	8.60
5	General Motors Corp.	7.25
6	Paccar Inc.	6.50
7	Ford Motor Co.	5.80
8	ESI Industries, Inc.	5.75
9	Ford Motor Co. Of Can	†3.93
10	Mack Trucks Inc.	...
10	Navistar International	...
10	Subaru Of America, Inc.	...

YIELD (%)

RANK	COMPANY	'89 AMT
1	Ford Motor Co. Of Can	†7.38
2	Chrysler Corp.	†7.22
3	General Motors Corp.	6.54
4	Ford Motor Co.	6.35
5	Paccar Inc.	5.57
6	Honda Motor Co., Ltd.	†0.72
7	Collins Industries, Inc.	...
7	ESI Industries, Inc.	...
7	Mack Trucks Inc.	...
7	Navistar International	...
7	Subaru Of America, Inc.	...
7	Tech/Ops Sevcon, Inc.	...

12-MONTH PRICE SCORE

RANK	COMPANY	'89 AMT
1	Collins Industries, Inc.	107.16
2	General Motors Corp.	103.94
3	Tech/Ops Sevcon, Inc.	103.03
4	Subaru Of America, Inc.	99.81
5	Navistar International	97.71
6	Ford Motor Co.	96.90
7	Ford Motor Co. Of Can	†95.93
8	Paccar Inc.	93.88
9	Honda Motor Co., Ltd.	†85.32
10	Mack Trucks Inc.	†72.02
11	Chrysler Corp.	...
11	ESI Industries, Inc.	...

7-YEAR PRICE SCORE

RANK	COMPANY	'89 AMT
1	Ford Motor Co.	111.95
2	Honda Motor Co., Ltd.	†108.83
3	Paccar Inc.	107.88
4	Ford Motor Co. Of Can	†102.13
5	Subaru Of America, Inc.	35.96
6	Chrysler Corp.	...
6	Collins Industries, Inc.	...
6	ESI Industries, Inc.	...
6	General Motors Corp.	...
6	Mack Trucks Inc.	...
6	Navistar International	...
6	Tech/Ops Sevcon, Inc.	...

Copyright 1990 by MOODY's INVESTORS SERVICE, INC.
Publication, Editorial and Executive Offices, 99 Church Street, New York, NY 10007

Reprinted with permission from Moody's Investors Service.

Service. Investors can also track changes in a fund's portfolio using services such as the Vickers guides introduced in the previous chapter. Other formats include charting services like *Johnson Charts*, and annual summaries such as *Donoghue's Mutual Funds Almanac* or the *Guide to No-Load Funds*.

Perhaps the best-known name in the mutual fund arena is the Lipper Analytical Service, Inc., but reports from this company are made available only to the professional investment community, and are not sold to libraries or the general public. However, summary analyses from Lipper are published on a quarterly basis in *Barron's*, and in an advisory service entitled the *Standard & Poor's/Lipper Mutual Fund ProFiles*. The latter service presents summary data for approximately 800 mutual funds, in a format similar to S&P's *OTC ProFiles*. The reports include ratings and performance measures provided by Lipper.

Prices for mutual fund services range from $900 per year to as little as $15. One of the simplest ways to obtain quick advice on funds is to consult popular investment magazines which provide extensive mutual fund surveys on an annual or quarterly basis. In addition to *Barron's*, investors can turn to *Forbes, Financial World, Business Week, Money*, and even *Changing Times* for ongoing surveys. The publications listed below were chosen for the wealth of detailed information they provide.

Wiesenberger Investment Companies Service
(Wiesenberger Financial Services—Annual, with Updates).

Wiesenberger has been publishing information on mutual funds and related securities since the passage of the Investment Company Act of 1940. It differs from most services by eschewing specific investment recommendations. Instead, it provides the user with detailed background and analysis on over 2,200 investment companies, including mutual funds, money market funds, closed-end funds, fixed unit trusts, and insurance company variable annuity accounts. The first section of the annual book presents introductory articles that explain the nature of investment companies, how each type differs, and how to choose investments. It includes a glossary of investing terms and statistics on the mutual fund industry. Other sections of the book provide an excellent directory of funds with their addresses, telephone numbers, toll-free numbers (if available), and handy charts comparing the performance of individual funds grouped by investment objective.

The main feature of *Wiesenberger* is the single-page profile of each fund. The analysis includes a history of the security, its investment objectives, and the charac-

teristics of its portfolio, including its makeup by industry and the five largest holdings. *Wiesenberger* also lists ten years of financial information—total net assets, number of shareholders, Net Asset Value per share, yield, amount of dividends paid (both income and capital gains disbursements), expense ratio, and the portfolio distribution by type of investment. Another table shows how an initial investment of $10,000 would have grown over the ten-year period, assuming both reinvestment of dividends and no reinvestment. Because it covers so many securities, *Wiesenberger* provides a less-detailed profile than some of its competitors, but it remains the most diverse, comprehensive guide published today.

The publisher also issues several newsletters. The monthly *Current Dividend Record* updates data in the annual edition, but only for mutual funds and money market funds. Figures include the latest Net Asset Value and dividends, the percent yield over the past 12 months, and the percent change in NAV. The monthly *Management Results* compares investment performance by fund category, including Beta Coefficients for individual funds. A quarterly charting service for equity funds, entitled the *Wiesenberger Mutual Fund Investment Analyzer*, and a monthly letter called the *Wiesenberger Mutual Funds Investment Report*, are also available.

Mutual Fund Values (Morningstar, Inc.—Biweekly).

Morningstar is one of the most highly regarded and frequently quoted mutual fund advisory services—a remarkable feat considering that the company is less than ten years old. Its premier publication, *Mutual Fund Values*, tracks more than 1,000 mutual funds, with an emphasis on those listed through the NASDAQ system. Every two weeks, subscribers receive a numbered update containing profiles of approximately 100 funds; after ten issues, the cycle is repeated, ensuring that profiles are revised once every 20 weeks. Subscribers also receive a biweekly summary, similar to the index section of *Value Line*. This includes an alphabetical list of all funds together with their key performance measures, and a broad assortment of screening lists.

What makes the service so valuable is the high quality of the fund profiles. Morningstar maintains a large staff of investment analysts, each of whom follows a certain number of funds. Every one-page report contains a wealth of data and analysis on a single fund. Most of the information found in the *Wiesenberger* reports can be found here, plus much more. Basic data include a description of the fund's objective, recent price and dividend information, ten years of performance figures, and background on portfolio composition. An especially useful feature is a list of the largest investment holdings

for each fund. In the case of equity funds, the top 30 stocks are listed; for bond funds, the top 12 appear. Morningstar calculates a diversity of performance measures, including the Beta Coefficient for every fund. Net Asset Value and total return are charted in relation to total market performance, and to other funds in the same category. Overall ratings are assigned for risk and return. A concise narrative assessment is also provided.

Mutual Fund Values covers an extensive list of funds, updates each report frequently, offers objective recommendations together with mounds of statistical and financial measures, and tops it off with numerous screening lists by objective and performance. Without question it is the best value in mutual fund publications. For those who don't require such detailed analysis, Morningstar offers the annual *Mutual Fund Sourcebook*, which provides abbreviated profiles for all funds seen in the parent service. Included in this two-volume guide are biographical information on fund managers, a list of the top 50 securities in each portfolio, and 12 years of comparative data. Morningstar's newest publication is a monthly statistical service called the *Mutual Fund Performance Report*. It provides comparative data on 1,200 funds in tabular form. Four types of listings are given. The "General Information" tables cite summary data on every fund, in a format similar to the mutual fund section of the *Standard & Poor's Stock Guide*. An "Alphabetical Performance Summary" assigns rankings to funds based on total return over seven periods, from the previous month to the latest ten years. The final two sections consist of screening lists with funds ranked by various performance measures; the first examines all funds, the second compares them by investment objective.

A new CD-ROM product, *Morningstar Mutual Funds On Disc*, will be released in late 1991. Investors may also purchase summary Morningstar data on floppy diskette through the *Business Week Mutual Fund Scoreboard*.

Bond Advisory Services

The final category of investment advice deals with bonds and other fixed-income securities. The bond services introduced in Chapter 10 provide summary financial data, together with bond ratings. The following two sources are more advisory in nature, tracking developments in the bond market, descriptions of new bond issues, changes in bond ratings, and risk analysis of individual securities. The third major bond rater, Fitch Investors Service, Inc., does not publish an advisory service, but does produce individual reports for many

issuers who are given a new or revised rating. The company specializes in rating municipal bonds, public utilities, and banks. Fitch reports are fairly brief, and can be seen on *Investext* and LEXIS. The company also publishes a complete list of its ratings in the monthly *Fitch Rating Register*.

Moody's Bond Survey (Moody's Investors Service—Weekly).

Moody's *Bond Survey* offers news and advisory information on corporate, municipal, and foreign bonds, as well as some short-term debt securities and preferred stocks. A company or municipality is typically covered in the *Bond Survey* when it issues a new bond or when Moody's changes its rating. Each weekly issue contains an article on the general bond market, statistical tables and graphs on average bond yields and interest rates, comprehensive lists of new bond issues, shelf registrations, new Moody's ratings, and changes in existing ratings. Information is arranged by type of security.

For selected securities, Moody's provides more detailed information in a separate section. Descriptions of new issues frequently cite the details of the bond indenture, the purposes of the bond issue, a summary of the issuer's activities and finances, Moody's "Outlook and Opinion," an explanation of why a rating was changed, and the rating. Every edition of the *Bond Survey* contains a detailed table of contents and a cumulative index so users can locate articles on specific bonds. The index also provides a cumulative year-to-date list of all debt instruments which have received a new or revised rating. For these reasons, the publication serves as both a current newsletter and a ready-reference guide.

CreditWeek (Standard & Poor's Corporation—Weekly).

Standard & Poor's *CreditWeek* is similar in purpose to the Moody's publication, but generally offers more detailed information. The advisory information, which S&P terms "Credit Analyses," tends to be lengthier, for example. Special reports called "Credit Reviews" focus on a specific industry, and provide commentary, credit analyses, and comparative statistics. Standard & Poor's also includes news stories and publishes signed articles on market conditions, written by nationally known economists. On the other hand, S&P does not publish a comprehensive list of new offerings and shelf registrations, though it does provide a cumulative index to the companies and municipalities appearing in the publication. A weekly feature called the "Credit Watch" lists companies whose bond ratings have not yet been revised, but which are in danger of being downgraded. This action receives a fair amount of media attention, so Standard & Poor's promises to take prompt action in all cases. Any

bond placed on Credit Watch status will be either downgraded or "cleared" within 90 days. Approximately 50% of the bonds on Credit Watch are ultimately downgraded.

SELECTING INVESTMENT PUBLICATIONS

Selecting from the more than 1,000 investment newsletters currently published in the United States can be a difficult chore. The most obvious criterion is the kind of information needed—both the type of investment and the level of coverage. For those wishing a specific type of service, the hunting is simpler because there may be only a few publications that fit those requirements. But even seemingly specialized investment topics are covered by an assortment of newsletters.

An objective way to gather intelligence about investment newsletters is through the *Hulbert Financial Digest*, published by Mark Hulbert. It tracks the performance of about 70 different newsletters by "investing" on paper what each one recommends. The *Digest* ranks each publication according to the percentage of gains (or losses) logged by the recommended portfolios, and by the clarity of the advice. Hulbert's reports make fascinating reading, and the results are often reported in the media. An overview of approximately 100 of the best letters is called the *Hulbert Guide to Financial Newsletters*, and is released annually by Probus Publishing.

The problem with using a system like Hulbert's is that the performance of investment newsletters can be highly erratic. The best-performing letters of one year are frequently the losers of the next. An alternative to this method is to subscribe to the *Davis Digest*, a newsletter published by syndicated columnist Dick Davis. Davis examines over 300 investment advisory sources on a regular basis, and reprints portions of several publications each month, based upon what he considers the best advice being offered at the time.

Another method of evaluating newsletters is to determine whether they have large followings. Of the hundreds of services available, probably only 50 or so enjoy genuinely wide readership. Some investors purposely avoid widely disseminated advice, but a newsletter usually can't maintain long-term popularity unless it's doing something right. Unfortunately, investment letters often do not participate in circulation audits, so the exact number of subscribers may not be publicized. One way to find circulation figures is to check sources like the *Oxbridge Directory of Newsletters*.

Similarly, you may want to see which letters are owned by major public libraries, on the theory they will subscribe to the more popular services. All of the sources described in this chapter are available in many libraries. Other common library selections include the *Growth Stock Outlook*, the *United & Babson Investment Report*, *Dow Theory Forecasts*, *Market Logic*, the *Prudent Speculator*, and the *Zweig Forecast*. Several warnings are necessary, however: first, even the largest library cannot afford all the investment services it would like; second, a library's collection will reflect what is popular in that locality; and third, libraries tend to avoid newsletters that are strictly action-oriented, choosing instead to purchase broader analytical services. Another way to judge is to visit the libraries of larger brokerage firms. They too will subscribe to an assortment of financial services. Lastly, come to recognize the names of popular publishers and their newsletters by the coverage they receive in the media. Newsletters with large followings are often quoted in newspapers and magazines. Some are recognized as unique or authoritative sources of specialized information, such as William Donoghue's *Money Fund Report* or Robert Heady's *Bank Rate Monitor*. Many publishers are also authors of books which were erstwhile best-sellers, including Howard Ruff, Harry Browne, Richard Ney, Norman Fosback, and Elliot Janeway.

Newsletter publishers of every stripe advertise in financial publications like *Barron's* and *Investor's Daily*, but most solicit customers through direct-mail advertising. Once you purchase a subscription to a newsletter, the chances are good that you'll be inundated with mailings from other services, because most sell their customer lists to one another. Many publishers will send a complimentary sample copy, and others offer limited trial subscriptions. An interesting way to preview newsletters is offered by the Select Information Exchange. For a modest fee, SIE will supply you with a sample copy of 20 investment newsletters of your choice. They publish a free catalog of 350 newsletters that participate in the program.

There are several questions one should ask before selecting an advisory service. The number of years a newsletter has been published is an important consideration. Next, does the newsletter spell out its point of view or investment strategy? Does it specify the methodology used to make recommendations, or explain the reasoning behind specific advice? Similarly, does it periodically review its own recommendations, or rate its own performance? A balanced newsletter should have both "buy" and "sell" recommendations. Another criterion is whether the advice is clear and easy to understand, or vague,

confusing, and wishy-washy. Also, one should consider whether the publication follows its own advice. Is it consistent in its reasoning, or does it disregard past strategies without warning or explanation? Finally, does the newsletter concentrate on short-term gains, advising the reader to pop in and out of the market with breakneck speed? Most investors look for more stability from their advice. The price of a typical newsletter ranges from $100 to $300 per year, so "buyer beware" is a word to the wise.

FOR FURTHER READING

For specific books and articles on the topics in this chapter, the following titles are suggested. Mark Hulbert writes a regular column on investment advisory letters for *Forbes* magazine. A few of his most pertinent columns are listed below. Among the other subjects touched upon here are the value of Wall Street analysts' reports, the effect of news on the market, how bond ratings are assigned, and background information on key market barometers.

Sources of Investment Advice

Dorfman, John R. "When Wall Street Says 'Sell,' It's Usually Too Late." *The Wall Street Journal* (January 8, 1991): C–1+.

Explores the widely held belief that analysts' reports seldom recommend selling a stock, and finds it to be generally true. Because analysts must cope with potential conflict of interest when making stock recommendations, most use euphemisms for the word "sell." A study of sell signals in major analysts' reports conducted by Zacks Investment Research indicates the word is only used when a stock is in serious trouble.

Hulbert, Mark. "Hotlines Aren't So Hot." *Forbes* (October 29, 1990): 173.

Hulbert explains why telephone hotlines sponsored by newsletter publishers don't necessarily help investors. He notes that 75 of the 120 newsletters he follows now offer such phone services.

Monk, J. Thomas, Kenneth M. Landis, and Susan Monk. *The Dow Jones-Irwin Investor's Guide to Online Databases* (Homewood, IL: Irwin, 1988).

Like all works covering online databases, this one is prone to rapid obsolescence, but much is enduring. Several chapters are devoted to the standard discussions of the pros and cons

of online searching and how it works, but the real value is in the extensive profiles of producers and their databases. Two appendices compare databases and producers by topic and function. Provides an important framework for selecting the right database from among the teeming possibilities.

Thomsett, Michael C. *Investor Factline: Finding and Using the Best Investment Information* (New York: Wiley, 1989).

A very basic guide to major sources of investment information, including advisory newsletters, financial newspapers, and magazines. Also contains chapters on investment seminars, investment clubs, and financial planners.

Market Barometers

Berlin, Howard M. *The Handbook of Financial Market Indexes, Averages, and Indicators* (Homewood, IL: Dow Jones-Irwin, 1990).

Virtually all leading market barometers are described here, including standard measures of the stock market, bonds, mutual funds, commodities, and money markets. Also included are lesser-known indexes and an assortment of the more frivolous measures such as the "Misery Index," the "Big Mac Index," and various Super Bowl barometers. The introductory chapter provides a good overview of the mathematics of indexes and averages.

Hill, Joanne M., Frank J. Fabozzi, and Jonathan C. Jankus. "Stock Market Indicators." In *The Handbook of Stock Index Futures and Options*, edited by Frank J. Fabozzi and Gregory M. Kipnis. (Homewood, IL: Dow Jones-Irwin, 1989): 81–101.

Describes the purpose of stock market indicators, the difference between indexes and averages, how they are constructed, and examples of popular indicators.

Advisory Letters

Brimelow, Peter. *The Wall Street Gurus: How You Can Profit from Investment Newsletters* (New York: Minerva, 1988).

Financial reporter Brimelow investigates the world of investment newsletters, their methods, performance, and value as a source of investment advice. Contains entertaining descriptions of leading newsletters and their often eccentric publishers.

Hoffer, William. "Watcher of the Watchmen." *Nation's Business* (February 1988): 76.

Mark Hulbert's *Hulbert Financial Digest* is the *Consumer Reports* of the investment newsletter industry. Hulbert himself is frequently quoted and profiled in the popular press. This short piece briefly describes how he got started and the philosophy behind his service.

Hulbert, Mark. "Following the Value Line." *Forbes* (October 23, 1989): 398.

Hulbert examines the remarkable long-term record of *Value Line*. In a follow-up article ("Proof of Pudding," *Forbes* [December 10, 1990]), he compares the newsletter's own performance claims to the standard rating method used in the *Hulbert Digest*.

————. "How Much Is Astrology Worth?" *Forbes* (October 2, 1989): 259.

Hulbert addresses whether a newsletter's price has any relationship to its performance. He provides several examples of inexpensive letters which offer outstanding value, and vice versa. To clinch the argument, he cites *Harmonic Research*; this expensive service bases much of its advice on astrology and is one of the poorest performers tracked by Hulbert.

Kosnett, Jeff. "Investment Newsletters: Beyond the Hype." *Changing Times* (November 1990): 59–62.

About once every three years, *Changing Times* does an article which provides basic advice on selecting an investment newsletter. This installment explains do's and don'ts for prospective subscribers and describes several popular letters.

Related Topics

Bryson, Deborah H. "Mutual Funds." *RQ* 30 (Winter 1990):181–88.

A thorough survey of information sources on mutual funds. Included are books, directories, advisory services, magazines, and databases. An excellent table compares the salient features of nine leading mutual fund performance guides.

Ishmael, Cheryl. *Ratemaking: A Review of Credit Ratings with Emphasis upon New York State* (Albany, NY: New York State Senate Finance Committee, 1984).

This remarkable legislative document examines the impact of bond rating agencies and the way in which they operate.

Klein, Frederick C., and John A. Prestbo. *News and the Market* (Chicago: H. Regnery, 1974).

A fascinating study of the effect of news on financial markets, highly recommended for anyone interested in how the stock market works.

Shaw, Alan R. "Market Timing and Technical Analysis." In *Financial Analyst's Handbook*, 2nd ed., edited by Sumner N. Levine. (Homewood, IL: Dow Jones-Irwin, 1988): 312–72.

A fairly detailed introduction to technical analysis, including the basic assumptions behind this approach, the types of charts available, and key methods of analysis.

PART IV
Statistical Information

CHAPTER 13
Introduction to Statistical Reasoning

TOPICS COVERED

1. Advantages and Disadvantages of Numbers
2. Logic and Statistics
3. Statistical Abuses and Mistakes
   a. Averages
   b. Percents, Percent Change, and Ratios
   c. Index Numbers
   d. Rankings
   e. Charts and Graphs
   f. Tables
4. Evaluating Statistical Sources
5. For Further Reading

All business researchers must have a basic understanding of statistics, yet few of us are sophisticated analysts of numeric data. Like most people, we use, cite, and accept statistics in our daily lives with little judgment or forethought. Fortunately, it is not that difficult to approach statistical information in an intelligent fashion. Learning to apply common sense and a questioning attitude is a start. The basic concepts discussed in this chapter will help you to avoid common statistical mistakes, recognize possible abuses of data, understand the limitations inherent in the use of numbers, and evaluate sources of statistical information.

For the purposes of this discussion we will define a statistic as a numerical statement which summarizes a collection of measurements. The problem with using statistics comes from their ability to summarize detailed information. Whenever data are summarized, the possibility of error, misinterpretation, and outright fraudulent manipulation exists. Researchers must be wary of these possibilities when using statistical sources and look at any data with a critical eye.

ADVANTAGES AND DISADVANTAGES OF NUMBERS

When it comes to proving a point, describing something, or comparing two or more items or events, most people would say that numbers are more precise than words. Words can be symbols for both concrete objects and complex bundles of ideas. Numbers avoid much of the danger inherent in using words. In addition to being more exact and objective than words, numbers are usually more concise. A complex economic relationship can be explained far more easily with a simple graph than with a detailed discourse. Large groups of numbers can be summarized to show patterns and relationships from which conclusions may be drawn. Empirical analysis often contradicts erroneous conclusions reached on an intuitive basis. Numbers can also serve as more accurate standards of comparison than words. To say something is "five times more expensive" or "90% percent more efficient" brings added understanding to an otherwise vague comparison. The use of numbers also allows the application of mathematical techniques that can be powerful analytical tools. Statistical methods such as regression analysis can sort out multiple interdependencies among variables and measure their relative effects. Statistical methods can even be used to construct confidence intervals which measure the possibility of random error in an estimate.

Objectivity, clarity, brevity, standardization, and analytical power are all advantages to recommend the use of numbers. Unfortunately, these virtues are often taken to be unassailable, and numbers are accepted at face value. Few people would place complete trust in every number seen, but there are subtle flaws in the use of numbers that even experienced analysts can overlook. Numbers resemble words by being symbols for real world things and events. How closely a number represents the reality it is measuring is based largely upon

whether the person taking the measurement has made correct assumptions. All numbers have inherent weaknesses. Users of statistical information must be alert to potential shortcomings. The key questions are "Where do the numbers come from?" and "What assumptions were made to generate them?"

The first assumption to question involves classification. How are categories of numbers grouped together? What is included or excluded? Why is an observation placed in one category and not another? Has the scope of the classification system changed over time? The best example of this problem in the business world is the use of industry classifications. What is meant by "the communications industry," for example? Is it restricted to companies that provide telephone service and other forms of telecommunication? Should it be expanded to include manufacturers of telecommunications equipment? Does it include television and radio media? What about publishers of newspapers, books, and magazines? Can we throw in advertising agencies, consulting firms, or computer software designers? Without defining the scope of the industry, arguments can be made for making it as broad or as restrictive as desired.

One way to resolve the problem is to create an explicit and detailed classification structure. The best known of these is the Standard Industrial Classification System (SIC), introduced in Chapter 4. Even a system as rigorous as the SIC leaves many unanswered questions for compilers of statistics. Individual decisions must be made to classify each component company of an industry study. Is a firm that manufactures rubber printing rolls grouped in the "printing equipment industry" or with "rubber products not elsewhere classified?" Is it double counted in every applicable industry or assigned to one primary grouping? What about newly emerging industries for which no classification has been created, or those which are difficult to classify? In analyzing any statistical report, a researcher must consider whether an existing classification system was used, or one was made up for the study; whether individual classification decisions were made correctly; and whether the method chosen makes sense for the particular study. This task is particularly frustrating because the answer to such questions usually cannot be determined. Even the most meticulously designed studies are prone to classification errors; the problem is inherent in the use of numbers.

A related problem concerns definitions. How are the terms used in a statistical report defined? Are they defined at all? If so, do the definitions make sense for the study at hand? The more abstract the concept to be measured, the more difficult it is to define. Even ideas that seem clear at first glance may be quite complex. Accountants, for example, wrestle with the concept of asset valuation. On the surface it seems obvious how one places a dollar value on a physical asset such as a factory. But is the factory worth what it cost to build 30 years ago? Should that value be depreciated to reflect 30 years of use and deterioration? Or does the accountant value the plant at current replacement costs? Does "replacement" mean reproducing the factory brick by brick, or designing a modern factory encompassing new technology? There is probably nothing measurable which is not open to alternative definitions.

Even standard units of measurement can be subject to definition problems. The concept of a "person" seems obvious enough, yet our 1790 Census counted slaves as three-fifths of a person and Indians not at all. The story of inventorying pigs in Bulgaria, as retold by Oskar Morgenstern, illustrates that even basic concepts of time are subject to reinterpretation. An agricultural census taken on January 1, 1920 showed Bulgaria had slightly over one million pigs. Officials were delighted because the census of January 1, 1910 counted only a half million pigs. The intervening destruction of war made such doubling highly suspect. The increase actually came from a redefinition of the Bulgarian year. After World War I, Bulgaria adopted the Gregorian calendar, as most of the Western world had done long before. By this time, the difference between the two calendars amounted to 14 days. December 19 under the Julian calendar became January 1 under the new system. The change had a drastic effect on the counting of pigs because about half of the pig population was traditionally slaughtered for Christmas. Because the Bulgarians continued to celebrate Christmas according to the Julian calendar (i.e., January 6 by the new calendar), pigs were counted after the slaughter in 1910 and before the slaughter in 1920.

Changing definitions is a common problem in statistical measurement. The National Planning Association made local headlines in 1985 by saying that the population of Rochester, New York, had overtaken that of Buffalo for the first time. But this announcement was based on a change of definition. The federal government redefined the Buffalo metropolitan area as a single county, while Rochester's definition as a five-county area remained unchanged.

The anecdotes of Bulgaria and Buffalo raise an additional point about the trouble with definitions. The meaning of terms change over time, making long-term historical comparisons a tricky business. Statistics on disease are suspect for time-series analysis, for example, due to advances in medical knowledge and diagnosis.

Malaria and cholera were once loosely used terms describing a wide range of ailments. Many types of cancer were unknown 100 years ago and mental illness frequently went unreported or undiagnosed. Similarly, comparing data from one country to another is subject to the same type of problem. Deciding whether London is larger than New York City depends entirely on the definitions used for each, because the political boundaries of the two cities are not comparable.

Another unavoidable limitation when using numbers is the problem of model building. Almost every statistical picture is an incomplete representation of reality, based upon the model-builder's assumptions of the world it represents. The National Income and Product Accounts of the United States, which measures the nation's Gross National Product, is perhaps the ultimate example of the limitations of mathematical models. The GNP attempts to measure the total output of goods and services in the U.S. economy. To do so it gathers thousands of statistical series from hundreds of sources. Regardless of how intricate this model is, can it really ever approximate the complex workings of our massive economy?

Trying to estimate the behavior of real world systems mathematically is a difficult task. This is certainly true when attempting to measure abstract notions such as quality of life or job satisfaction, but it is equally so of more readily understandable concepts such as productivity, inflation, or poverty. The idea of unemployment, for example, is defined to an exacting degree by the Bureau of Labor Statistics. Among the assumptions made in measuring this concept is that individuals who have given up looking for a job for whatever reason are no longer part of the labor force. And by definition, someone who is not part of the labor force cannot be unemployed. Many critics think this is a restrictive and unwarranted assumption, but it is nevertheless a key to the construction of unemployment statistics by the government.

Assumptions are often made because they facilitate the collection of data, not because they result in more realistic models. In other cases assumptions are made because the characteristic to be measured is truly unknowable and some surrogate must be used. Measuring the cost of pollution to society at large requires many simplifying assumptions. On the other hand, complex models are not necessarily better than simple ones. Users of statistical information need to question the assumptions behind any model. Was the basic structure designed years ago without subsequent revision? Do we really understand what is being measured?

The process of data collection is also fraught with potential error. Mistakes creep into even simple tasks like counting. To complicate matters, most statistics are estimates generated from a sample survey; it is usually far too expensive or even impossible to study an entire population. The sample's fit—how closely it parallels the total universe—has an enormous effect on the accuracy of the estimate. The *Literary Digest*'s presidential poll of 1936 illustrates this point in dramatic fashion. During the presidential election between Franklin Roosevelt and Alf Landon, the *Digest* conducted a random poll of its subscribers. Realizing the subscribers might not be an accurate representation of the population, the magazine also selected random names from telephone books. The results indicated a landslide victory for Landon. When FDR won a devastating victory, the already weakened *Literary Digest* folded within the month. Analysts later concluded that because of the depression, magazine subscribers and owners of telephones were from predominantly high-income households, and more likely to vote Republican. The magazine's conscientious attempt to avoid sampling error was an abysmal failure.

The way a survey is conducted also has an effect on the outcome. How it is transacted—whether by phone, mail, or face-to-face—may result in significant differences. The way questions are worded is also extremely important. For example, in an attempt to measure the Hispanic population, the Census Bureau asked people whether they were of Spanish origin or descent. Specifically, they provided a list of Spanish-speaking countries or regions from which respondents could choose. A surprising number of non-Hispanic individuals living in the southern United States marked the box labeled "South America." The timing of a survey can also alter results due to seasonal or other cyclical variations. Seasonally mobile population groups such as students or "snowbirds" are examples of this, as were the Bulgarian pigs. In addition to problems of questionnaire design and survey methods, human (and machine) error in the collection, data entry, tabulation, and reporting of results are also worth remembering.

One last statistical pitfall is the matter of spurious accuracy. Most sensible people would look scornfully at a survey which stated the average household was comprised of 4.682973 people. Clearly, such a level of precision is both impossible to obtain and meaningless. On the other hand, few people would question a study showing 4,682,973 families below the poverty level. The order of magnitude makes the number appear more reasonable, but is it any more precise than the first figure

because the decimal place changed? In other words, can estimates based on sample surveys and complex models justify the use of such exact figures? When measurements deal in billions or trillions of units, such as the federal budget or the GNP, a small percentage of error can result in large whole number discrepancies. It's easy to fall into the trap of believing exact numbers are more authoritative than rounded figures.

LOGIC AND STATISTICS

So far the words "statistics" and "data" have been used rather loosely. For the following discussion, let's make a distinction between the two. Data are raw numbers awaiting analysis; statistics are summaries of the data, which implies conclusions have been reached. Statistics are used when arguments are being made: to prove a point, win a bet, or persuade a customer. Statistics are therefore inextricably tied to the process of logic. Whether conclusions are spelled out in a report or drawn by users for themselves, numerous logical fallacies may creep into the analysis. It is therefore worthwhile to introduce some basic examples of faulty statistical reasoning.

The nonstatistic, sometimes called the meaningless or disembodied statistic, is a precise figure used in conjunction with a vague phrase or idea, resulting in a completely meaningless statement. Commonly heard assertions such as, "Human beings only use 10% of their brains" and "75% of American workers are engaged in the information sector" are perfect examples of the nonstatistic. The advertising industry has been a long-time champion of the nonstatistic and of the dangling comparison. A dangling comparison is a statement which does not clarify the object to which the subject is being compared. To say, "Users of Fang Toothpaste have 20% fewer cavities" is a completely meaningless sentence. Twenty percent fewer than who? (or what?, or when?)

A second type of illogical statistic is the farfetched figure. This fallacy is typically based on wild guesses or ludicrous estimates. Farfetched statistics typically count something immeasurable, such as the number of cockroaches in New York City. In some instances people are unwilling to report data that would be embarrassing or self-incriminating. Figures on deviant or socially unacceptable behavior, so-called "victimless" crimes, and cases of broken rules or policies are particularly difficult to track. Examples include employee theft, abuse of sick-leave privileges, and tax evasion. Carefully designed surveys may capture data of this type to some extent, but

researchers should always be wary of the results. Another form of farfetched statistic comes from making broad generalizations not supported by the facts. A special category of the farfetched figure is the absurd projection, which assumes that a short-term trend will continue into the future. Taken to its extreme, this type of reasoning begets ridiculous results, such as predicting a child will grow to be 15 feet tall based on its current rate of growth.

A third type of faulty statistic is caused by using numbers for purposes they are not intended to address. "Good" data are frequently put to bad use because their true purpose is not understood. For instance, the most widely used measure of inflation in this country is the Consumer Price Index (CPI) compiled by the U.S. Bureau of Labor Statistics. The CPI measures the change in price of a standardized "market basket" of goods from month to month in a selected number of cities in the United States. Because numbers are available at the individual metropolitan level, many people assume the data can be used to compare the cost of living from one city to another. But the CPI measures changes over time within each place, and data on one geographic area have no bearing on any other. If the latest CPI figure was 118 for Boston and 123 for New York City, one cannot conclude that it costs more to live in New York than Boston. The correct interpretation is that since the base year, prices have increased more in New York than Boston.

Other statistical fallacies arise from oversimplification. Attributing a simple explanation to events often underestimates the complexities of the real world. The common fallacy of bifurcation—dividing the world into black and white—is an example of oversimplification. So too is the error of *post hoc ergo propter hoc*. This fallacy occurs when one assumes A causes B simply because A preceded B. Attributing false cause to an event is a common mistake because cause and effect are slippery notions. A and B may be correlated but have no causal relationship. They may be related by chance, related to a third (but undiscovered event), or there may be a dozen other valid explanations.

Numerous other errors of reasoning can creep into a statistical analysis, including begging the question, improper comparisons, and irrelevant theses. It is easy to reach the wrong conclusion based on perfectly good data. The conscientious researcher must be alert to this possibility in his or her own reasoning as well as in the conclusions of others.

STATISTICAL ABUSES AND MISTAKES

Let's turn now to the more specific question of how data are presented. This is the area where most problems occur when using statistics, but it is also the area where fallacies and mistakes are most easily recognized. While it may be virtually impossible to detect errors in reasoning or model construction, inaccuracies in format are simpler to spot.

Averages

An average implies a sense of the norm, or some "middle" value in a range of numbers. Problems arise because in ordinary usage there are many meanings to the word; and in statistical terms, many types of averages can be computed. Statisticians refer to an average as a measure of central tendency, and there are three commonly used forms. The arithmetic average, or mean, is what is typically thought of when measuring an average. The mean is calculated by adding each value in a group of numbers together and dividing the sum by the number of values in the set. A median value is obtained by arranging all the numbers in a set in ranked order, then choosing the number in the middle. In the case of a set with an even number of values, the median is calculated by adding the two middle values together and dividing by two. A mode is the value that occurs most frequently in a group of numbers. In the special case of a normal frequency distribution, the values of the mean, median, and mode are identical, but in most groups of numbers this is not the case.

Depending on the circumstances, any one of these measurements may describe a group of numbers better than the other two. The problem is that people typically choose the value which best presents their case, whether or not it is the most appropriate to use. When summarizing data with averages, it is best to present more than one value in order to portray a more descriptive picture. As an example of the statistical chicanery possible in the use of averages, take the case of a company that sells and installs garage doors. Payroll data for the firm's owner and 12 employees appear in the table below.

UP AND DOWN DOOR COMPANY

Position	Wage or Salary
Owner	$60,000
General Manager	$35,000
Office Manager	$28,000
Salesman	$26,000
Installer 1	$17,000
Installer 2	$17,000
Installer 3	$17,000
Service Rep.	$14,000
Stock Clerk 1	$14,000
Stock Clerk 2	$14,000
Secretary	$14,000
Part-time Bookkeeper	$ 5,000
Part-time Installer	$ 5,000
Total	$266,000

The mean of $20,462 is calculated by dividing 13 into $266,000. The median is the $17,000 of Installer 3 because there are exactly six values above and below this number. The mode is $14,000 because it occurs four times, more than any other amount.

Depending on the intended purpose, one of these three values will be preferable to the others, yet all are "correct." The owner's salary and the wages of the two part-time workers are very different from the other values in the group. These outlying values have a tendency to distort the mean, though perhaps not in drastic fashion. To show the effect of the outliers on the mean, consider the following options.

People Included	Mean Value
All workers & Owner	$20,462
Full-time & Owner	$23,273
Full-time, No Owner	$19,600
All workers, No Owner	$17,167

As the structure of the group changes, so does the mean income. While these fluctuations may not seem enormous, to the employee negotiating a raise or the owner defending his pay scale the difference is important.

Aside from being outlying values, strong arguments can be made to include or exclude the owner and part-timers in the calculations. What is the fairest way to calculate the average amount of pay? One suggestion is to divide the list into salaried employees and hourly wage earners. Doing this would result in a mean salary of $29,667 and a mean wage of $15,286 when ignoring the outlying figures. This calculation would be more descriptive of the situation, but a thoughtful analyst might ask further questions. How is the owner's salary determined? Is it a straight salary or does it include his profits as owner? Do the managers' salaries include bonuses?

Does the salesman earn commissions? Should fringe benefits be included in the computations? Changing definitions could affect the data quite a bit. Numerous averages can be generated, even without muddying the water with medians and modes.

The garage-door example underlines another point about statistics. In this case we can judge for ourselves what each average represents because we have the underlying data to examine for ourselves. If we had no idea what the individual amounts were, the average wouldn't tell us much no matter which method were chosen (unless we also had a measure of dispersion or "scatter"). Clearly, averages can be extremely deceptive. To use a more blatant example, the average amount given to a local charity might be $1,300. But if only three donors contributed to the fund, one could guess the individual amounts were $3,880, $15, and $5, or that each in fact gave $1,300, or any other possible combination. For very small numbers of observations, averages are not particularly useful. To accept average values without question is a foolish policy indeed.

Percents, Percent Change, and Ratios

Percents are among the most commonly used and abused statistical measures. Percents are helpful when comparing the relative size of two different numbers, or the relative size of component parts of a whole. A percent is essentially a proportion, where the denominator (or base) is the combined value, and the numerator is one of the individual values. For example, if a classroom of 31 students was composed of 18 men and 13 women, percents would be calculated in the following way:

Percentage of men = 18/31 = .58 = 58%

Percentage of women = 13/31 = .42 = 42%

The three figures on each line are equivalent because percents can be expressed as fractions, decimals, or whole numbers with percent signs.

In some cases, "per mille" (meaning "per thousand") is a more useful measure than percent because when expressed in hundredths the numbers are so small they appear similar. Birth and death statistics are commonly expressed in this fashion. The 1986 birth rate for whites in the United States was 1.45%, versus 2.12% for blacks. This means there were slightly less than 1.5 white children born for every 100 white people living. Although a comparison of the two numbers seems reasonably straightforward, if they were listed in a table filled with dozens of similar values, the difference in magnitude might become less apparent. Demographers therefore recast the figures as 21.2 and 14.5 per thousand. For similar reasons, chemists frequently express numbers in "parts per million."

Sometimes the underlying numbers from which percents are derived have no meaning in themselves. This is typically the case in survey results. If an election pollster said 510 voters prefer the incumbent, it tells the reader nothing. Only by saying 510 respondents out of a sample of 1,200 does the statement have meaning. Because percentages are usually easier to grasp than fractions, the pollster would probably not bother to say anything more than "42.5% of those polled preferred the incumbent." If one knows the total amount, the individual figures can be calculated from the percentages. Percentages are like averages; when they are presented without the underlying data from which they are computed, information is lost.

As with averages, information can be reshuffled through the use of percentages. A frequent trick is the manipulation of base numbers. One might read, for example, that one-third of all teenage girls in a small community are pregnant. What the report might fail to mention is this town is predominantly a retirement community with only three residents who are teenage girls. It is obviously misleading to draw any conclusions based on the isolated case of one teenager's behavior. In this instance, the individual numbers are more informative than a percentage.

A similar abuse is to compare two items with very different base amounts. The following case compares the sales histories of two companies in the same industry. Company A has been in business for 30 years; Company B was established three years ago.

COMPARATIVE SALES VOLUME

Year	Company A	Company B
1989	$800,000	$ 10,000
1990	$900,000	$ 30,000
1991	$980,000	$100,000

Over this period Company A increased sales by $180,000 and Company B increased sales by $90,000. One conclusion would be to say that A's increase in sales was twice that of B's, or 200% greater. Comparing absolute growth of one to another is misleading because the beginning amounts are so different. It may make more sense in this instance to compare each company to itself, by measuring the rate of change. Percent change calculations are computed by subtracting an earlier value from

a later value and dividing the result by the earlier value. Such a comparison would be obtained in our example in the following manner:

$$\text{Rate of Change A} = \frac{(\$980,000 - \$800,000)}{\$800,000}$$

$$\text{Rate of Change B} = \frac{(\$100,000 - \$10,000)}{\$10,000}$$

The calculations show that Company A had a respectable growth rate over the two-year period of 22.5%, while Company B enjoyed a spectacular increase of 900% over the same period—not unusual for a successful new company. Which comparison is better, the absolute or the relative? Both are correct, both tell us something useful, and both can be used to mislead the reader.

Honest mistakes are often made in percentage calculations. First, the numbers are not reversible; it matters which is the earlier and which is the later value, and they should not be confused. Second, a percent change cannot decrease beyond 100%. A store that advertises "150% off all merchandise" is really saying they will pay you half the original price of the item to take it off their hands. You can be sure the store has no intention of holding to such a bargain. Third, mistakes in calculating percent change can go undetected because the numbers seem believable, especially when the wrong denominator is used.

It is relatively easy to make mistakes when figuring percents or percent changes. Percents cannot be added together, for example, unless the base values are the same. In the case of Companies A and B, one cannot add their individual rates to get a total growth of 922.5%. Similarly, percentages representing parts of a whole unit cannot sum to greater than 100%. Another common oversight occurs when comparing two quantities which are not part of a whole. In any such case, the compiler has the option of determining which value will serve as the denominator and which as the numerator, as long as the fraction is correctly labeled. Either way is appropriate since the two calculations will be the reciprocal of one another. But two possible mistakes can ensue with this type of analysis. One occurs when this calculation is repeated for several values and the numerators and denominators are not chosen consistently. The second is where one loses track of what the number is supposed to represent. A common example can be found in calculating foreign exchange rates for currency. When comparing the value of U.S. dollars to British pounds, two possible numbers can be generated based on the prevailing exchange rate on any given day.

$$\frac{\text{U.S. Dollar Value}}{\text{British Pound Value}} = 1.61 \qquad \frac{\text{British Pound}}{\text{U.S. Dollar}} = .623$$

If you wish to change pounds into dollars, a bank would be willing to pay approximately .62 pounds for every 1 dollar (i.e., a dollar is worth 62% of a pound). Both exchange rates are valid, they are simply reciprocals of one another. (To demonstrate this, divide .623 into 1.00; the result equals 1.61.) On the other hand, if you want to change pounds into dollars, 1.61 is the proper conversion factor—a pound is worth $1.61 on that day. A British book priced at £30.00 should cost approximately $48.30.

When making direct comparisons of unlike numbers, as in the case above, ratios may be used as easily as percents. Just as percentages are convenient ways to express fractions, ratios can sometimes be more readily understood than percentages. In the case of our two companies, we can say that Company A's increase was two times that of Company B instead of saying Company A's growth was 200% greater. Ratios are especially helpful with percentages greater than 100%, or when a one-to-one relationship is considered the standard of comparison. Take the case of a factory which employs 320 men and 40 women in the production process. The relationship of men to women can be expressed as a percentage (11% of the production workers are women), or a ratio (there are eight times as many men as women working in production). In this case, the ratio is simply a more dramatic way of expressing an equivalent concept.

Like the case of the foreign exchange rates, it is crucial to understand which value is which in a ratio. It probably doesn't matter whether you measure the number of doctors per 1,000 members of the population, or whether you measure the number of people per doctor. What does matter is that you label the comparison properly. Your choice has significance when tracking the change in the ratio over time. Because the two values are reciprocals, graphing the ratio one way would produce an increasing line while the opposite technique will result in a decreasing line. In this manner ratios can be used to manipulate a visual image. The compiler of ratios frequently has no choice in the selection of numerators and denominators: ratios often appear as commonly accepted standard measures. In finance, for example, Price/Earnings Ratios and Earnings Per Share are conventionally defined investment comparisons.

Index Numbers

Another way in which numerical relationships can be expressed is through index numbers. An index is used to compare data over time, to measure a multifaceted concept—in which case it is called a composite index—or both. The method used to score events in Olympic competition such as diving and gymnastics is an example of a composite index. Each athlete's performance is judged by a combination of the level of difficulty and the degree of excellence; the two judgments are combined to produce a single index number. In the world of economics, composite indices are used to track the performance of complex systems. Examples of commonly seen economic indices are the Consumer Price Index, the Producer Price Index, the Index of Industrial Production, the Employment Cost Index, and the Index of Leading Economic Indicators.

Here's how an index number is constructed: assume you have a sizable garden in your back yard and you want to measure its output over the past five years. Index numbers are calculated by dividing the value for each period by that of a constant base period and multiplying the result by 100. In this instance, by defining the base period as 1985, we create the following index:

INDEX OF GARDEN OUTPUT (1985=100)

Year	Bushels	Index Number
1985	31	100.0
1986	32	103.2
1987	35	112.9
1988	32	103.2
1989	28	90.3
1990	33	106.5

Using our formula for creating an index, the base year will always be 100. The first two index numbers were calculated in the following manner:

$$1985 = (31/31) \times 100 = 100.0$$

$$1986 = (32/31) \times 100 = 103.2$$

Composite index numbers are created in the same way except each component is assigned a relative weight to designate its proportional effect on the composite, then all weighted values for each period are multiplied together before the conversion to an index is made. (This is an oversimplification; there are actually several ways a composite index can be constructed.) Why go to the trouble of making an index? One reason is to enable comparisons of concepts with many different components. A second is to show the change in an item compared to a fixed point in time. The third reason is to make changes over a long period of time more readily apparent, similar to the use of per mille instead of per cent.

If an index series is tracked for a large number of periods (e.g., several decades), the size of the most recent index numbers can become ungainly. The accepted solution is to periodically redefine the base period. But look what happens in the case of the garden example when the base year is adjusted to 1989.

INDEX OF GARDEN OUTPUT (1989=100)

Year	Bushels	Index Number
1985	31	110.7
1986	32	114.3
1987	35	125.0
1988	32	114.3
1989	28	100.0
1990	33	117.9

Obviously, index numbers can be manipulated to present a more positive picture by changing the base year. However, in most cases the base year has no particular significance; the choice is somewhat arbitrary. Common reasons for selecting a particular year are that it represents a point near the time when the data were first available, or it is a few years prior to the time the index was first constructed.

A common mistake related to index numbers occurs when computing the rate of change between periods. Calculating the percent change is not a simple matter of subtracting the two index numbers. The way an index number is constructed makes it easy to calculate the change from the base year to any other period, but calculating the change from two nonbase years is not. Using the second garden output table, the change from 1989 to 1990 appears to be a 17.9% increase if we merely subtract the numbers. If one were to use the same method to calculate this period's change based on the data in the first table, the result (106.5 - 90.3) would equal 16.2%. Logic indicates that the two rates of increase should be identical; therefore, a mistake must have been made somewhere. The explanation to the mystery lies with the percent change. If we simply subtract the two numbers, we obtain a point change rather than a percent change. Rate of change is calculated by subtracting the two values and dividing the result by the earlier value. Using the base year of 1989, when we subtract 100 from 117.9, divide the difference by 100 and then multiply by 100, the last two values in the equation cancel out. In this instance, 17.9 is the correct answer. In the case of the 1985 base year, no such magic happens. The proper calculation is:

$$[(106.5 - 90.3)/90.3] \times 100 = 17.9\%$$

The only time the percent change between two index numbers can be computed by simply subtracting the two numbers is when one of the two numbers is 100. This distinction is one of the advantages to constructing index numbers.

When reading reports which show percent changes in index numbers, the user should maintain a healthy skepticism. Percent and percent change calculations are vulnerable to convenient manipulation. Unfortunately, expressing index numbers as percents of change is usually the most understandable way of communicating the information.

Assume it is the spring of 1982 and someone asks you for a recent measurement of inflation. (This date is used because it was a time of rapidly increasing prices.) Based on the government's inflation data in Figure 13-A, you could respond that the latest CPI was 283.4. To most people, the answer would not make sense because they wouldn't understand the concepts behind the Consumer Price Index. An index figure only has meaning in relation to other numbers in the same series. You could say the cost of living had increased 183.4% since the base year of 1967, meaning that prices had almost doubled since that time. Your questioner might then ask how inflation had changed lately. You could answer that between January and February 1982, the rate of change in the CPI was .32%, or thirty-two one-hundredths of one percent.

By now your companion would probably be getting impatient. Giving it one more try, he asks what the recent annual rate of inflation has been. One answer would be to "compound," or annualize the monthly data available so far for 1982. Multiplying .0032 by 12 results in a projected annual rate for 1982 of 3.8%. This seems a little low compared to other numbers you've heard, and there is no way to guarantee the January trend will continue for the year. It turns out the most sensible and widely accepted measurement would be to calculate the percent change between the most recent month and the same month a year earlier. Doing so, you see that the annual rate of inflation during the month of February 1982 is 7.7%.

All of the numbers cited above, from 283.4 to .0032, are correct interpretations of the CPI data, and all forms can be seen reported by the news media. Using the "January-to-January" approach yields a different annual rate for each month of the year. In 1981 that rate fluctuated from a high of 11.7% to a low of 8.9%. Does this mean when someone cites a CPI figure they can choose the most suitable number for their needs? In practice, yes. A preferable alternative is to average the monthly rates of change for the year to determine a mean annual CPI. For 1981 the mean is 10.4%, which certainly seems to be a more correct summary of the year's inflation rate. Be-

FIGURE 13-A. Consumer Price Index Data, All Cities (1967=100)

Year	Data	Jan.	Feb.	March	April	May	June	July	Aug.	Sept.	Oct.	Nov.	Dec.	Annual Average
1980	Index	233.2	236.4	239.8	242.5	244.9	247.6	247.6	249.4	251.7	253.9	256.2	258.4	246.8
	%	13.9	14.2	14.7	14.7	14.4	14.3	13.2	12.8	12.7	12.6	12.6	12.4	13.5
1981	Index	260.5	263.2	265.1	266.8	269.0	271.3	274.4	276.5	279.3	279.9	280.7	281.5	272.4
	%	11.7	11.3	10.6	10.1	9.8	9.6	10.7	10.9	11.0	10.2	9.6	8.9	10.4
1982	Index	282.5	283.4											
	%	8.5	7.7											

Percent change is calculated from same month of previous year. (i.e., a twelve-month percent change)

SOURCE: U.S. BUREAU OF LABOR STATISTICS

cause the data for 1982 were not yet complete at that time, the same could not be done for the current year. However, an attempt could be made at averaging the available months to obtain a projected mean for the year. This technique would certainly yield better results in November than in February. And if this discussion hasn't been complicated enough, consider that the 1967 base year used in 1982 has since changed. The base year currently in effect for the CPI is 1983.

The previous discussion makes an important point for users of statistical information. Any of the options mentioned above can and do get cited to describe the current inflation rate. Worse, the numbers are usually given with no attempt at clarification. Newspapers frequently report the December figure (8.9% in 1981) to imply an annual average (which we have shown is actually 10.4% for 1981). This incredible smorgasbord of statistics is just one example of the manipulation possible with index numbers and percents.

Rankings

Americans love ranked lists because they like to know how things "rate." Some lists of rankings have even become part of our language, such as the "Fortune 500" industrial corporations and the "big three" auto makers. Chapter 8 offered some cautionary thoughts on the nature of ranked lists, but a few points can be added from a statistical point of view. The first question is, "By what characteristic are these items ranked, anyway?" A company's size can be evaluated by assets, net worth, sales, profits, number of employees, number of customers, or by rate of growth of any of the preceding. Where a company appears on such a list will depend on which criterion is used. Determine if the ranking characteristic makes sense. It may be appropriate to rank fast-food franchises by number of outlets, but ranking steel companies by number of factories is not.

Another consideration is from what universe the candidates are selected. If a list of companies is to be compiled, are they chosen from among all companies, or only companies which sell stock? Giant firms such as American Express and Metropolitan Life Insurance are conspicuously absent from the Fortune 500 list each year because the list only includes industrial companies. Geography can also be important. A list of the top five banks in the world will be very different from a list of the top U.S. banks. One might also ask why a particular list contains only 10 or 100 items (or 3, or 500). This is

usually due to tradition, convenience, or the symmetry of round numbers rather than any rationally chosen cut-off point.

A commonly encountered limitation of rankings can be seen in studies which assign numbers to nonnumeric attributes in a rating scale. If a market survey asked people to rate a product according to several characteristics, indicating whether each one was excellent, satisfactory, or poor, the marketer could then give each response a numeric rating. The first person's responses might have been 3-2-3, the second person's 1-2-2, etc. If this was done for several different products, composite rankings could be calculated to determine which product received the best overall rating. By placing each response on an equal-interval scale, the survey is making assumptions that may not be warranted. The real danger, however, is that subjective impressions of good-better-worse have been converted into more objective sounding numbers. Although a reader might be somewhat wary of a vague comparison showing A is "better" than B, once the comparison is quantified in some arbitrary fashion, the results seem more scientific.

To show the disparities which composite rankings can produce, let's take the specific case of the well-known *Places Rated Almanac*, a publication described in greater detail in Chapter 17. First published in 1981, this guide to "the best places to live in America" sold briskly, and was followed by several revised editions. Each revision was accompanied by considerable fanfare. Local media, chambers of commerce, and economic development agencies either lauded or deplored the results, depending upon where their city ranked on each new list. The 1985 edition, for example, ranked Pittsburgh as the top city in the United States, with other northeastern industrial cities showing in the top 25.

The study compares some 300 different metropolitan areas using approximately 50 standard measures of crime, economic conditions, weather, education, and other categories. Even a casual examination of the results raises numerous questions about the study's validity. The most striking issue involves the differences among the 1981, 1985, and 1989 rankings. Are we to believe that the quality of life in cities throughout the nation underwent such enormous shifts in this short time? Next one wonders about the variables chosen. Is the presence of a large airport a major factor in metropolitan living? Why was the availability of bowling and golf measured and not the presence of horse racing or roller skating? Only certain numbers are available for all cities, but any group of characteristics would be somewhat arbitrary by nature. Third, why were each of the categories weighted equally?

Does the presence of a symphony orchestra have as much impact on a community as the level of medical care or the cost of living? And if not, who can say what the correct weighting should be?

Places Rated points out a common weakness of composite rankings. In 1985, though Pittsburgh ranked number one, it never placed within the top three for any single category. Its high score was more the result of not receiving a terrible score for any characteristic. The design of the study created some additional biases. Because only metropolitan areas were measured, small towns and rural areas were exempt from consideration. And because most variables were more likely to be present in large cities, the list heavily favors the largest metropolitan areas. Of course the ultimate criticism is that quality of life is a subjective topic, and choosing the best place is a highly personal matter. No city is perfect, and every advantage has a corresponding disadvantage. Even given the same data, each person could no doubt create a completely different list.

Places Rated is an easy target, because it received such notoriety, and because it attempts to measure subjective issues in an objective way. Actually, the authors address many of these issues in their book. Of greater importance, the publication is far more useful for the detailed comparisons of individual communities by characteristic. Unfortunately, it is the composite rankings that attract the most attention because people prefer a simple means of making comparisons. The general conclusions to be drawn are that any ranking based on composite characteristics should be evaluated carefully, and that it is generally unwise to trust a single number. Beyond that, even the most straightforward rankings have a limited value.

Charts and Graphs

Graphic representation of data comes in many forms. Just as averages, percents, and index numbers can be altered, so too can graphs. If anything, the potential for abusive manipulation is even more severe. Graphic displays can be very useful; they help make sense of large masses of data, bring out hidden facts, and show relationships that would go unnoticed if buried in a table. They can also generate interest on the part of the reader; tabular information is frequently skipped, but graphics usually capture one's attention.

The drawback to graphic information is that minor changes in a chart's design can cause dramatic changes in its visual impact. Subtle image adjustments can create subliminal responses in the viewer. By changing scales,

altering horizontal and vertical proportions, or simply choosing another form of graph, alternative impressions can be conveyed. Like any statistical summary, the underlying numbers are usually not available to the researcher. But even where individual numbers are provided, the visual image is generally more memorable than the numbers.

The cardinal rule of graphic design is all axes should be labeled. The variables being measured, the units of measurement, and the numbering of scales are the basics of any graph. A graph without labels is not a graph. The second rule is that the independent variable is usually measured on the horizontal axis, and the dependent on the vertical. In other words, the subject of the graph is plotted vertically. The third rule of graphic presentation is that the scales should be proportional unless there is a good reason for them not to be. The scales on the x and y axes should be equally spaced and proportions should reflect real-world relationships. The most common form of graphic tomfoolery involves altering the proportions of the axes. By contracting or expanding the vertical, horizontal, or both scales, dramatic changes will result. By compressing the vertical axis, for example, a steep line can be made to appear almost flat; by expanding the vertical axis, the opposite effect can be achieved. Another popular device is to "cut" the zero line. The scale on most graphs should start at zero for both the x and y axes. By starting the vertical axis at a higher point (also called breaking the axis), the graph appears in a lower position than it would otherwise.

Be wary of the type of graph chosen to present data. Two examples of specialized graphs that can be misused are the semilogarithmic scale and the cumulative frequency ogive. The graphs most of us are familiar with utilize an arithmetic scale, meaning equal spacing between each unit of measurement. A semilogarithmic graph uses an arithmetic scale on the horizontal and a logarithmic (or ratio) scale on the vertical. It is characterized by a narrowing of distance between each unit as the scale progresses. The purpose of a semilogarithmic graph is to show rates of change, or compare values significantly different in magnitude. It may be thought of as the graphic equivalent to the percent change. Exhibit 13-1, taken from the U.S. Council of Economic Advisors' publication *Economic Indicators*, shows a typical ratio scale. The graph depicts the rate of change in the CPI by plotting the index numbers on a logarithmic scale. The same picture could be obtained by plotting the percent-change figures on an arithmetic scale. Generally, semilogarithmic graphs should not be used unless a

EXHIBIT 13-1. *Economic Indicators*—Semilog Graph

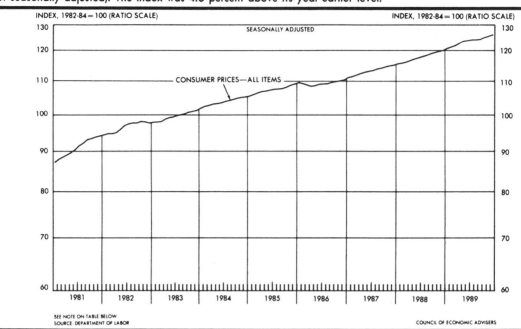

CONSUMER PRICES—ALL URBAN CONSUMERS

In December, the consumer price index for all urban consumers rose 0.4 percent, seasonally adjusted (0.2 percent not seasonally adjusted). The index was 4.6 percent above its year-earlier level.

[1982–84 = 100, except as noted; monthly data seasonally adjusted, except as noted]

Period	All items [1] Not seasonally adjusted (NSA)	All items [1] Seasonally adjusted	Food	Housing Total [1]	Shelter Total	Shelter Renters' costs (Dec. 1982=100)	Shelter Homeowners' costs (Dec. 1982=100)	Maintenance and repairs (NSA)	Fuel and other utilities	Apparel and upkeep	Transportation Total [1]	Transportation New cars	Transportation Motor fuel	Medical care	Energy [2]	All items less food, shelter, and energy
Rel. imp. [3]	100.0	....	16.2	42.3	27.8	7.9	19.7	0.2	7.6	6.4	17.2	4.3	3.1	6.0	7.3	48.7
1980	82.4	....	86.8	81.1	81.0	....	....	82.4	75.4	90.9	83.1	88.4	97.4	74.9	86.0	80.6
1981	90.9	....	93.6	90.4	90.5	....	....	90.7	86.4	95.3	93.2	93.7	108.5	82.9	97.7	88.3
1982	96.5	....	97.4	96.9	96.9	....	....	96.4	94.9	97.8	97.0	97.4	102.8	92.5	99.2	95.1
1983	99.6	....	99.4	99.5	99.1	103.0	102.5	99.9	100.2	100.2	99.3	99.9	99.4	100.6	99.9	100.0
1984	103.9	....	103.2	103.6	104.0	108.6	107.3	103.7	104.8	102.1	103.7	102.8	97.9	106.8	100.9	105.0
1985	107.6	....	105.6	107.7	109.8	115.4	113.1	106.5	106.5	105.0	106.4	106.1	98.7	113.5	101.6	109.0
1986	109.6	....	109.0	110.9	115.8	121.9	119.4	107.9	104.1	105.9	102.3	110.6	77.1	122.0	88.2	112.7
1987	113.6	....	113.5	114.2	121.3	128.1	124.8	111.8	103.0	110.6	105.4	114.0	80.2	130.1	88.6	117.0
1988	118.3	....	118.2	118.5	127.1	133.6	131.1	114.7	104.4	115.4	108.7	116.9	80.9	138.6	89.3	121.9
1989	124.0	....	125.1	123.0	132.8	138.9	137.3	118.0	107.8	118.6	114.1	119.2	88.5	149.3	94.3	127.3
1988:																
Dec	120.5	120.7	121.2	120.6	129.4	134.9	133.9	115.8	106.3	117.7	110.4	118.1	79.7	142.9	89.2	124.6
1989:																
Jan	121.1	121.4	122.1	120.9	129.7	135.2	134.2	116.1	106.9	117.7	111.2	118.9	80.5	144.0	89.9	125.4
Feb	121.6	121.9	122.6	121.3	130.3	136.4	134.7	117.1	106.7	117.5	111.9	119.3	81.8	145.2	90.4	125.8
Mar	122.3	122.5	123.6	121.7	131.1	138.2	135.1	117.1	106.9	119.1	112.6	119.7	83.6	145.9	91.4	126.3
Apr	123.1	123.3	124.2	121.8	131.2	137.3	135.6	117.3	107.4	119.4	115.0	119.8	93.0	146.6	96.1	126.6
May	123.8	124.0	125.0	122.3	131.8	137.3	136.5	117.4	107.6	120.4	116.1	119.6	96.6	147.6	97.6	127.2
June	124.1	124.2	125.3	122.6	132.3	138.1	136.9	118.3	107.1	119.1	115.9	119.3	95.4	148.7	96.6	127.4
July	124.4	124.5	125.7	123.3	133.2	140.2	137.5	118.4	107.6	118.1	115.2	118.8	93.3	149.8	95.9	127.6
Aug	124.6	124.5	125.9	123.5	133.5	139.6	138.1	118.5	107.5	116.3	114.3	118.5	89.5	150.8	94.0	127.7
Sept	125.0	124.7	126.2	123.6	133.7	138.5	138.8	118.6	107.6	118.3	113.7	118.0	87.6	152.0	93.2	128.2
Oct	125.6	125.3	126.7	124.1	134.4	139.3	139.4	118.6	107.7	119.5	114.5	118.7	88.6	153.0	93.8	128.8
Nov	125.9	125.8	127.4	124.7	135.0	140.1	140.1	119.3	108.7	119.6	114.7	119.6	86.7	154.2	93.7	129.3
Dec	126.1	126.3	128.0	125.3	135.7	141.0	140.7	119.5	109.7	118.8	114.8	120.8	85.1	155.0	93.7	129.7

[1] Includes items not shown separately.
[2] Household fuels—gas (piped), electricity, fuel oil, etc.—and motor fuel. Motor oil, coolant, etc. also included through 1982.
[3] Relative importance, December 1988.

NOTE.—Data beginning 1983 incorporate a rental equivalence measure for homeownership costs and therefore are not strictly comparable with figures for earlier periods. Data beginning 1987 and 1988 calculated on a revised basis.

Source: Department of Labor, Bureau of Labor Statistics.

Reprinted from *Economic Indicator*s, published by the U.S. Council of Economic Advisors.

percent change comparison is warranted, and the actual data should be examined to see the relationships more clearly.

An ogive, also called a frequency distribution curve, should also be used only for specific purposes. A frequency distribution is created by dividing the data under consideration into categories, then counting the number of observations which fall into each category. "Ogive" refers to the shape of the resulting graph; a frequency distribution curve generally appears as a pointed arch. A cumulative frequency distribution goes one step further, and counts all the values that are less than (or greater than) each category. The problem in graphic interpretation lies with *cumulative* frequency ogives, as the following example illustrates.

Suppose the board of directors of a local civic organization was composed of 15 members who had various years of college education. If the frequency of educational level were tabulated, the result would appear as the following two tables:

YEARS OF COLLEGE COMPLETED

FREQUENCY DISTRIBUTION		CUMULATIVE FREQUENCY DISTRIBUTION	
Years Completed	Frequency	Years Completed	Frequency
1	3	less than 2	3
2	2	less than 3	5
3	4	less than 4	9
4	5	less than 5	14
5	1	less than 6	15

Frequency distributions are typically graphed in one of the following ways: using a type of bar chart called a histogram (shown in Figure 13-B), or as an ogive, constructed by connecting the midpoints at the top of each bar. Cumulative frequency distributions are also graphed as ogives (again illustrated in Figure 13-B). Notice that the ogive appears as a steadily increasing line. By definition, it must be so. Because of their cumulative nature, "less than" ogives appear as increasing lines and "greater than" ogives are decreasing. Notice also that the cumulative frequency distribution we constructed could just as easily be recast in "greater than" form, completely changing the appearance of the ogive. By misrepresenting information in the form of a cumulative frequency ogive, the unwarranted illusion of a steadily increasing or decreasing trend can be depicted.

Numerous additional abuses can be perpetrated through the use of graphs and charts. Truncating the range of data shown can eliminate those values which contradict the impression the compiler wishes to portray. In this way, sudden upturns or downturns in a graph's direction can simply be cut off before they occur. Researchers should always question whether the range of values depicted in a chart is long enough to present a trend, and whether the beginning and end points make sense. If a graph begins with values for October instead of January, or the latest six months of available data do not appear, the possibility of manipulation should be considered. Bar charts and pictograms are also subject to alteration. For example, bar charts should always be

FIGURE 13-B. Histogram and Cumulative Frequency Ogive

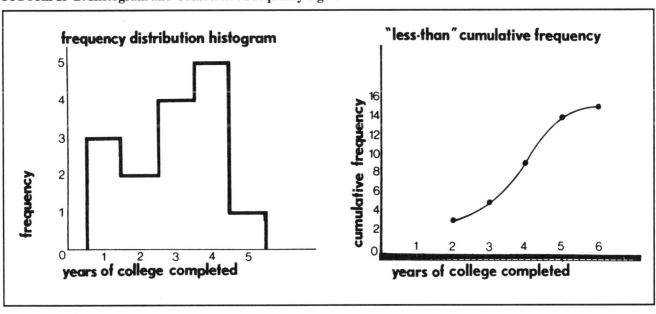

plotted so the bars have equal width, and pictograms should be proportioned as though they were three-dimensional objects.

Tables

Tabular information is less subject to blatant abuse because raw data are usually presented in addition to any summary statistics. This is not to imply that chicanery involving tables does not take place. However, the danger in using statistical tables is more likely to result from careless mistakes. Errors can certainly be made by the compiler, but mistakes made by the user are far more common. Below are guidelines for using statistical tables.

1. Read the table headings to make sure you have the correct table. Make certain the statistics are measuring what you think they are.
2. Understand the definitions and concepts used in the report.
3. Notice the unit of measurement used (dollars, tons, percents, etc.) and the order of magnitude (thousands, millions, billions). Often large numbers are abbreviated to fit in the table. Labels in the heading or boxhead will usually indicate this. For example, the number 37,904 appearing in a table which measures amounts in "millions of dollars" is reporting a figure of $37.9 billion.
4. Read any headnotes and footnotes that explain the limitations of the data, exceptions made, etc.
5. Use a straightedge to underscore the data you are reading, especially if the table is crowded or has small print.
6. Avoid giving or receiving large amounts of tabular information over the telephone. The possibility of transposing numbers or making other mistakes is too great.
7. Don't confuse subtotals or totals with individual amounts. Don't double count by adding subtotals together with individual values.
8. When percentages appear, understand the total universe (i.e., the denominator) used in calculating them.

These guidelines may seem unnecessary, but simple mistakes are the most common. The following examples, using two respected sources of economic information, illustrate how such mistakes occur.

In the first example, monthly job-absence data are reported by the Bureau of National Affairs (BNA), a commercial publisher. Figures are gathered from a quarterly survey of 1,000 employers in the United States, and the results are widely quoted in other publications. The results for all responding companies over a period of several months might look something like the fictitious numbers seen below.

Median Job Absence Rates

January	2.1
February	2.3
March	2.1
Annual Average	1.9

One might conclude the average worker is absent about two days each month. That figure seems high, so perhaps we are interpreting the information incorrectly. What if the number is approximately two days each year, but it is adjusted each month when new survey results are received? That number seems too low, so neither conclusion makes much sense. The heading of the table provides a clue to the proper interpretation of the data. "Median Rates" implies a percentage, but a percentage of what? The answer is found in the footnotes to the table, which cite the following formula used in calculating the figures:

$$\frac{\text{Work days lost in month x 100}}{\text{Average \# of workers x Work days}}$$

Thus, absenteeism is presented as a percentage of the total work days lost each month, not as a per worker measurement: in a given month, the average employer loses 1.9% of total work days to absenteeism. This is an appropriate method because the work force of most employers varies over time, as does the number of work days in a month. If the data still seem unaccountably low, that is because the survey does not count individual long-term absences beyond the first four days. There are other ways to measure absenteeism, of course, but this method is fairly standard.

The second example is taken from the annual *Survey of Buying Power Data Service*, from Bill Communications. Exhibit 13-2 depicts the Buying Power Index (BPI), a series created especially for the survey. The BPI is a composite measure of three characteristics of local areas: population, household disposable income, and retail sales. It serves as a crude measure of the percentage of the total U.S. consumer market that each geographic area represents. Without reading the explanatory preface in detail, it is unclear what exactly the BPI is. What's more, without looking at the entire table to see how the parts sum to 100%, it is unclear what each value is a percentage of, and whether the amounts appear as decimals or percentages. By examining the table in its entirety, however, we can safely assume that the .3738 BPI

EXHIBIT 13-2. ***Survey of Buying Power Data Service*—Buying Power Index**

S&MM METRO MARKET RANKING

BUYING POWER INDEX (BPI)

Area	BPI	Rank
Los Angeles - Long Beach, Cal.	3.9019	1
New York, N.Y.	3.6279	2
Chicago, Ill.	2.7058	3
Philadelphia, Pa.	2.1747	4
Washington, D.C.	1.9756	5
Boston - Lawrence - Salem - Lowell - Brockton, Mass.	1.9099	6
Detroit, Mich.	1.8451	7
Nassau - Suffolk, N.Y.	1.4180	8
Houston, Tex.	1.3299	9
Atlanta, Ga.	1.2487	10
Anaheim - Santa Ana, Cal.	1.1313	11
Minneapolis - St. Paul, Minn.	1.1151	12
Dallas, Tex.	1.0901	13
San Diego, Cal.	1.0776	14
St. Louis, Mo.	1.0363	15
Oakland, Cal.	.9928	16
Baltimore, Md.	.9923	17
San Francisco, Cal.	.9286	18
Newark, N.J.	.9224	19
Seattle, Wash.	.9033	20
Riverside - San Bernardino, Cal.	.9007	21
Phoenix, Ariz.	.8796	22
Tampa - St. Petersburg - Clearwater, Fla.	.8523	23
Pittsburgh, Pa.	.8291	24
Miami - Hialeah, Fla.	.8181	25
Cleveland, Ohio	.7683	26
San Jose, Cal.	.7518	27
Bergen - Passaic, N.J.	.7297	28
Denver, Colo.	.7206	29
Kansas City, Mo.-Kans.	.6798	30
Sacramento, Cal.	.6190	31
Fort Lauderdale - Hollywood - Pompano Beach, Fla.	.6085	32
Milwaukee, Wisc.	.5977	33
Cincinnati, Ohio	.5925	34
Hartford - New Britain - Middletown - Bristol, Conn.	.5538	35
Norfolk - Virginia Beach - Newport News, Va.	.5455	36
Columbus, Ohio	.5371	37
Fort Worth - Arlington, Tex.	.5248	38
Middlesex - Somerset - Hunterdon, N.J.	.5202	39
Indianapolis, Ind.	.5128	40
Portland, Ore.	.5123	41
Monmouth - Ocean, N.J.	.4939	42
Bridgeport - Stamford - Norwalk - Danbury, Conn.	.4938	43
New Orleans, La.	.4850	44
Charlotte - Gastonia - Rock Hill, N.C.-S.C.	.4567	45
San Antonio, Tex.	.4529	46
Orlando, Fla.	.4316	47
West Palm Beach - Boca Raton - Delray Beach, Fla.	.4259	48
Rochester, N.Y.	.4215	49
Nashville, Tenn.	.3959	50
Total Top 50	**50.4387**	
Louisville, Ky.	.3873	51
Greensboro - Winston-Salem - High Point, N.C.	.3828	52
Providence - Pawtucket - Woonsocket, R.I.	.3805	53
Oklahoma City, Okla.	.3788	54
New Haven - Waterbury - Meriden, Conn.	.3779	55
Memphis, Tenn.	.3742	56
Buffalo, N.Y.	.3739	57
Salt Lake City - Ogden, Utah	.3738	58
Dayton - Springfield, Ohio	.3728	59
Richmond - Petersburg, Va.	.3724	60
Albany - Schenectady - Troy, N.Y.	.3664	61
Jacksonville, Fla.	.3644	62
Honolulu, Haw.	.3617	63
Birmingham, Ala.	.3295	64
Austin, Tex.	.2972	65
Raleigh - Durham, N.C.	.2948	66
Worcester - Fitchburg - Leominster, Mass.	.2934	67
Oxnard - Ventura, Cal.	.2848	68
Allentown - Bethlehem, Pa.	.2822	69
Grand Rapids, Mich.	.2758	70
Las Vegas, Nev.	.2751	71
Scranton - Wilkes-Barre, Pa.	.2749	72
Omaha, Neb.	.2664	73
Tulsa, Okla.	.2653	74
Harrisburg - Lebanon - Carlisle, Pa.	.2627	75

Area	BPI	Rank
Syracuse, N.Y.	.2626	76
Toledo, Ohio	.2560	77
Springfield, Mass.	.2541	78
Akron, Ohio	.2495	79
Wilmington, Del.	.2489	80
Tucson, Ariz.	.2446	81
Knoxville, Tenn.	.2436	82
Fresno, Cal.	.2400	83
Lake County, Ill.	.2394	84
Greenville - Spartanburg, S.C.	.2319	85
Gary - Hammond, Ind.	.2302	86
New Bedford - Fall River - Attleboro, Mass.	.2147	87
Jersey City, N.J.	.2122	88
Tacoma, Wash.	.2028	89
Little Rock - North Little Rock, Ark.	.2021	90
Bakersfield, Cal.	.2020	91
Baton Rouge, La.	.1924	92
Wichita, Kans.	.1916	93
Albuquerque, N.M.	.1914	94
Youngstown - Warren, Ohio	.1875	95
Columbia, S.C.	.1812	96
Manchester - Nashua, N.H.	.1809	97
Charleston, S.C.	.1774	98
Mobile, Ala.	.1753	99
Lansing - East Lansing, Mich.	.1743	100
Total Top 100	**64.0943**	
Stockton, Cal.	.1718	101
Flint, Mich.	.1713	102
Trenton, N.J.	.1710	103
El Paso, Tex.	.1708	104
Santa Barbara - Santa Maria - Lompoc, Cal.	.1707	105
Vallejo - Fairfield - Napa, Cal.	.1694	106
Santa Rosa - Petaluma, Cal.	.1685	107
Portsmouth - Dover - Rochester, N.H.	.1684	108
Lancaster, Pa.	.1680	109
Des Moines, Iowa	.1647	110
Madison, Wisc.	.1627	111
Chattanooga, Tenn.	.1623	112
Johnson City - Kingsport - Bristol, Tenn.	.1593	113
Saginaw - Bay City - Midland, Mich.	.1592	114
York, Pa.	.1563	115
Melbourne - Titusville - Palm Bay, Fla.	.1529	116
Davenport - Rock Island - Moline, Iowa-Ill.	.1521	117
Colorado Springs, Colo.	.1520	118
Peoria, Ill.	.1483	119
Canton, Ohio	.1473	120
Beaumont - Port Arthur, Tex.	.1472	121
Aurora - Elgin, Ill.	.1463	122
Joliet, Ill.	.1453	123
Lakeland - Winter Haven, Fla.	.1451	124
Augusta, Ga.	.1445	125
Jackson, Miss.	.1440	126
Lexington-Fayette, Ky.	.1424	127
Fort Wayne, Ind.	.1423	128
Reading, Pa.	.1423	128
Atlantic City, N.J.	.1415	130
Daytona Beach, Fla.	.1408	131
Salinas - Seaside - Monterey, Cal.	.1388	132
Fort Myers - Cape Coral, Fla.	.1354	133
Spokane, Wash.	.1349	134
Pensacola, Fla.	.1316	135
Modesto, Cal.	.1290	136
Shreveport, La.	.1274	137
Corpus Christi, Tex.	.1269	138
Portland, Me.	.1254	139
Sarasota, Fla.	.1238	140
Appleton - Oshkosh - Neenah, Wisc.	.1236	141
Orange County, N.Y.	.1188	142
Rockford, Ill.	.1183	143
Ann Arbor, Mich.	.1171	144
Reno, Nev.	.1157	145
Utica - Rome, N.Y.	.1157	145
New London - Norwich, Conn.	.1152	147
Evansville, Ind.	.1142	148
Anchorage, Alas.	.1137	149
Huntington - Ashland, W.Va.-Ky.	.1124	150
Total Top 150	**71.2609**	
Macon - Warner Robins, Ga.	.1123	151
Poughkeepsie, N.Y.	.1121	152
Montgomery, Ala.	.1087	153

Area	BPI	Rank
Erie, Pa.	.1077	154
Binghamton, N.Y.	.1049	155
Santa Cruz, Cal.	.1019	156
Charleston, W.Va.	.1015	157
Lorain - Elyria, Ohio	.1015	157
Visalia - Tulare - Porterville, Cal.	.1001	159
McAllen - Edinburg - Mission, Tex.	.0999	160
Huntsville, Ala.	.0994	161
Eugene - Springfield, Ore.	.0979	162
Savannah, Ga.	.0968	163
Kalamazoo, Mich.	.0966	164
South Bend - Mishawaka, Ind.	.0963	165
Hamilton - Middletown, Ohio	.0961	166
Roanoke, Va.	.0954	167
Duluth, Minn.	.0953	168
Boulder - Longmont, Colo.	.0940	169
Fayetteville, N.C.	.0934	170
Fort Pierce, Fla.	.0921	171
Springfield, Mo.	.0906	172
Salem, Ore.	.0901	173
Lincoln, Neb.	.0885	174
Tallahassee, Fla.	.0879	175
Columbus, Ga.	.0872	176
Hickory, N.C.	.0859	177
Galveston - Texas City, Tex.	.0849	178
Lubbock, Tex.	.0841	179
Lafayette, La.	.0829	180
Bradenton, Fla.	.0823	181
Killeen - Temple, Tex.	.0823	181
Amarillo, Tex.	.0798	183
Springfield, Ill.	.0793	184
Boise, Ida.	.0792	185
Gainesville, Fla.	.0788	186
Johnstown, Pa.	.0776	187
Vancouver, Wash.	.0775	188
Brownsville - Harlingen, Tex.	.0773	189
Green Bay, Wisc.	.0770	190
Niagara Falls, N.Y.	.0767	191
Brazoria, Tex.	.0755	192
St. Cloud, Minn.	.0737	193
Asheville, N.C.	.0711	194
Biloxi - Gulfport, Miss.	.0711	194
Ocala, Fla.	.0701	196
Topeka, Kans.	.0694	197
Cedar Rapids, Iowa	.0693	198
Racine, Wisc.	.0693	198
Fort Collins - Loveland, Colo.	.0691	200
Total Top 200	**75.6533**	
Champaign - Urbana - Rantoul, Ill.	.0689	201
Beaver County, Pa.	.0682	202
Provo - Orem, Utah	.0670	203
Longview - Marshall, Tex.	.0667	204
Waco, Tex.	.0664	205
Bremerton, Wash.	.0661	206
Chico, Cal.	.0650	207
Pittsfield, Mass.	.0644	208
Yakima, Wash.	.0638	209
Houma - Thibodaux, La.	.0637	210
Naples, Fla.	.0635	211
Burlington, Vt.	.0631	212
Wheeling, W.Va.	.0625	213
Richland - Kennewick - Pasco, Wash.	.0623	214
Olympia, Wash.	.0620	215
Odessa, Tex.	.0614	216
Fort Walton Beach, Fla.	.0612	217
Lake Charles, La.	.0607	218
Fort Smith, Ark.	.0606	219
Fargo - Moorhead, N.D.-Minn.	.0597	220
Lima, Ohio	.0596	221
Benton Harbor, Mich.	.0594	222
Tyler, Tex.	.0594	222
Elkhart - Goshen, Ind.	.0592	224
Lynchburg, Va.	.0591	225
Waterloo - Cedar Falls, Iowa	.0589	226
Merced, Cal.	.0577	227
Charlottesville, Va.	.0573	228
Parkersburg - Marietta, W.Va.-Ohio	.0566	229
Janesville - Beloit, Wisc.	.0565	230
Midland, Tex.	.0563	231
Bangor, Me.	.0561	232
Muskegon, Mich.	.0559	233
Sioux Falls, S.D.	.0559	233
Battle Creek, Mich.	.0554	235
Eau Claire, Wisc.	.0545	236
Terre Haute, Ind.	.0543	237
Vineland - Millville - Bridgeton, N.J.	.0542	238

Area	BPI	Rank
Jackson, Mich.	.0540	239
Athens, Ga.	.0537	240
Kenosha, Wisc.	.0536	241
Bloomington - Normal, Ill.	.0535	242
Clarksville - Hopkinsville, Tenn.-Ky.	.0530	243
Decatur, Ill.	.0527	244
Redding, Cal.	.0527	244
Abilene, Tex.	.0515	246
Steubenville - Weirton, Ohio-W.Va.	.0511	247
Medford, Ore.	.0501	248
Anderson, S.C.	.0498	249
Wilmington, N.C.	.0495	250
Total Top 250	**78.5820**	
Jamestown - Dunkirk, N.Y.	.0493	251
Mansfield, Ohio	.0491	252
Altoona, Pa.	.0490	253
Wichita Falls, Tex.	.0489	254
Anderson, Ind.	.0488	255
Tuscaloosa, Ala.	.0488	255
Joplin, Mo.	.0483	257
Bryan - College Station, Tex.	.0477	258
Rochester, Minn.	.0477	258
Billings, Mont.	.0475	260
Panama City, Fla.	.0473	261
Dothan, Ala.	.0472	262
Florence, Ala.	.0471	263
Lafayette - West Lafayette, Ind.	.0470	264
Santa Fe, N.M.	.0464	265
Monroe, La.	.0463	266
Muncie, Ind.	.0463	266
Burlington, N.C.	.0446	268
Alexandria, La.	.0443	269
Bellingham, Wash.	.0443	269
Glens Falls, N.Y.	.0441	271
Pascagoula, Miss.	.0441	271
Sharon, Pa.	.0437	273
Albany, Ga.	.0436	274
Williamsport, Pa.	.0434	275
Hagerstown, Md.	.0433	276
Texarkana, Tex.-Ark.	.0432	277
Greeley, Colo.	.0431	278
Kokomo, Ind.	.0430	279
Sioux City, Iowa	.0430	279
Columbia, Mo.	.0427	281
Yuba City, Cal.	.0425	282
Pueblo, Colo.	.0423	283
Laredo, Tex.	.0417	284
Florence, S.C.	.0414	285
Wausau, Wisc.	.0413	286
Fayetteville - Springdale, Ark.	.0408	287
San Angelo, Tex.	.0408	287
State College, Pa.	.0408	287
Lewiston - Auburn, Me.	.0405	290
La Crosse, Wisc.	.0397	291
Jacksonville, N.C.	.0396	292
Sheboygan, Wisc.	.0395	293
Danville, Va.	.0386	294
Lawton, Okla.	.0377	295
Anniston, Ala.	.0376	296
Bloomington, Ind.	.0376	296
Las Cruces, N.M.	.0376	296
Sherman - Denison, Tex.	.0371	299
Kankakee, Ill.	.0362	300
Cumberland, Md.	.0358	301
Elmira, N.Y.	.0351	302
Owensboro, Ky.	.0347	303
Rapid City, S.D.	.0346	304
Bismarck, N.D.	.0345	305
Decatur, Ala.	.0345	305
St. Joseph, Mo.	.0338	307
Dubuque, Iowa	.0324	308
Iowa City, Iowa	.0324	308
Gadsden, Ala.	.0321	310
Jackson, Tenn.	.0319	311
Great Falls, Mont.	.0295	312
Grand Forks, N.D.	.0292	313
Victoria, Tex.	.0291	314
Pine Bluff, Ark.	.0288	315
Cheyenne, Wyo.	.0277	316
Lawrence, Kans.	.0268	317
Casper, Wyo.	.0254	318
Enid, Okla.	.0222	319
Total Above Areas	**81.3489**	
Percent of U.S.	**81.3489**	
U.S. Total	**100.0000**	

© COPYRIGHT, SALES & MARKETING MANAGEMENT MAGAZINE, 1989.
1989 SURVEY OF BUYING POWER DATA SERVICE 3-11

Reprinted with permission from *Survey of Buying Power Data Service*, copyright *Sales & Marketing Management* magazine, 1989.

for the Salt Lake City area (the 58th largest market) means .3738% of the national total, not 37.38%. Aside from its ranking on the list, what does this figure tell us? An amount of .003738 seems pretty small, so we need to question whether the number appears reasonable. One way to put the number in perspective would be to determine what the value would be if each of the 319 areas in the survey had an equal share of the market. To find out, divide 100% by 319; the result would be .3134%, so the Salt Lake City number does appear to make sense. (Actually, the last assertion is not strictly true, since the combined total of these 319 metro areas only represents 81.35% of the total U.S. market, but it does help to put the numbers in perspective.)

This table points out several statistical pitfalls. First, adding together all bold-faced numbers (subtotals for the Top 50, 100, 150, and so on) results in a sum greater than 100% because each one is a cumulative total. In other words, the top 100 includes the top 50, so double counting occurs. Second, the reader might question whether the degree of accuracy represented here is warranted to four decimal places. Clearly, however, at least three decimal places are needed to construct the ranking. Finally, given the three variables used in the calculations, the underlying assumptions of the model should be examined. As the preceding examples have shown, statistical tables may seem simple at first glance, but by making unjustified assumptions or careless errors, the user can produce gravely distorted results.

EVALUATING STATISTICAL SOURCES

Statistical information is produced by a wide range of organizations, and the same type of data is often available from several different sources, though the numbers may not be the same. In selecting and evaluating data sources, the researcher must ask many questions. Which source is most appropriate for present needs? Which has the most accurate data? How can the reliability of the numbers be determined? Some general guidelines for the evaluation of documents can be established.

The first way to judge a publication is to investigate the reputation of the organization that produced it. Does the organization possess the wherewithal to create a high quality study? Is it well known or respected for what it does? Does it have the staff and financing to conduct such a project? How long has it been doing this type of work? Does the publisher have an ax to grind on this particular topic? Assumptions of bias can be made by examining the stated purpose of the group, whether previous studies have appeared slanted, who asked for the study, and for what possible motives it was undertaken.

Other clues to the reliability of the data must be found in the report itself. Check to see if there is a long gap between the time the information was collected and published. Determine whether the figures are secondary, or obtained from primary research. If secondary data are used, are the sources identified? Are they reliable themselves? How was the research conducted? Does the publication provide explanatory material? The better the report, the more it should tell about itself, including the methodology, terminology, assumptions made, limitations, estimated sampling error, and even examples of the questionnaires used. Obviously, the more you know about these issues, the more intelligently you can judge the results. Clues to objectivity can also be found in the text of the document. Be wary of reports that use inflammatory or emotional language, or vague statements. Those which highlight some areas of the data and downplay others for no apparent reason should also be questioned. Look to see whether the conclusions are justified by the data presented in the report. Look for statistical shenanigans of the type we have discussed. The presentation of raw numbers in the report helps you reach these judgments more easily.

Another question is whether the information provided or conclusions reached are true. Decide whether the assumptions made are defensible. Then consider whether the results make sense. Do they fit what you know about the world? This can be a dangerous question because your intuitive understanding may itself be faulty, but it is a question every researcher must ask. Plausibility is a good starting point in judging information. A final test is whether the information can be confirmed by other studies, or by bits and pieces gathered from other sources. The numbers don't have to coincide, but they should be similar. These questions are also helpful in gauging a related concept known as validity. Validity is the measure of whether the study is truly doing what it set out to.

Unfortunately, it is often difficult to make such judgments in workaday situations, and data can be manipulated without the user's knowledge. An organization with preconceived beliefs can design a study so the desired results will be confirmed. Survey instruments can be reconstructed and administered again until the "right" answers appear. "Statistical leverage" can be applied by changing definitions, assumptions, or sampling techniques to suit present needs. This chapter could

not cover all the ways in which statistics can be misused, but the reader should now be sensitive to possible abuses. In this increasingly quantifiable world, hard data tend to crowd out the softer side of things. There are other ways to view the world, and words are as important as numbers. But when we do look to numbers, we should strive to use them correctly.

FOR FURTHER READING

Hundreds of textbooks on statistical methods have been published, but most are not well suited for independent study. The titles presented here are included for their readability or interest to the novice as well as for their content.

Logic and Critical Thinking

Capaldi, Nicholas. *The Art of Deception: An Introduction to Critical Thinking*. Revised ed. (Buffalo, NY: Prometheus Books, 1987).

The blurb on the title page says it all: "How to: Win an Argument, Defend a Case, Recognize a Fallacy, See Through Deception, Persuade a Skeptic, Turn Defeat into Victory."

Damer, T. Edward. *Attacking Faulty Reasoning*. 2nd ed. (Belmont, CA: Wadsworth, 1987).

A thorough catalog of the most common fallacies, arranged by type. For each error, a definition is given, followed by an example. An explanation of how to counter the faulty reasoning is then provided.

Dow, Gwyneth M. *Uncommon Common Sense: Signposts to Clear Thinking* (Melbourne, Australia: Cheshire, 1962).

A delightful work written for both student and general reader. Many of its charming examples are taken from the works of poets, essayists, and playwrights.

Engel, S. Morris. *With Good Reason: An Introduction to Informal Fallacies*. 2nd ed. (New York: St. Martins, 1982).

This work offers a concise treatment of fallacies in reasoning, with plenty of entertaining examples.

Kelly, David. *The Art of Reasoning* (New York: Norton, 1988).

A text that's readable, well organized, and broad in scope. Among the diversity of important topics are classification, definition, grammar and word meaning, diagramming arguments, fallacies, deductive and inductive reasoning, and explanation. Numerous exercises are provided, with the answers found at the back of the book.

Statistical Reasoning

Barnard, Douglas St. Paul. *It's All Done by Numbers* (New York: Hawthorn Books, 1966).

An entertaining exploration of the development and meaning of numbers, this book will appeal to readers with inquiring minds.

Campbell, Stephen K. *Flaws and Fallacies in Statistical Thinking* (Englewood Cliffs, NJ: Prentice Hall, 1974).

A well-organized and interesting guide to statistical abuse, highly recommended despite the sexist cartoons.

Morganstern, Oskar. *On the Accuracy of Economic Observations*. 2nd ed. (Princeton, NJ: Princeton University Press, 1963).

A difficult book to tackle, but it is the classic treatment of the limitations of macroeconomic statistics and worth the effort to read.

Ziesel, Hans. *Say It with Figures*. 6th ed. (New York: Harper and Row, 1985).

This classic guide for the nonstatistician goes beyond introductory concepts and examines important analytical issues.

Survey Research Methods

Alreck, Pamela L., and Robert B. Settle. *Survey Research Handbook* (Homewood, IL: Richard D. Irwin, 1985).

A step-by-step guide to designing, conducting, and analyzing surveys. Discusses why surveys are conducted, types of surveys, sampling, question composition, scaling techniques, data collection methods, statistical analysis, and report writing.

Lansing, John B. *Economic Survey Methods* (Ann Arbor, MI: University of Michigan Survey Research Center, 1971).

A classic handbook on the collection and analysis of data. This guide should be owned by anyone who conducts or uses economic surveys.

Orlich, Donald C. *Designing Sensible Surveys* (Pleasantville, NY: Redgrave Publishing, 1978).

A slim yet thorough introduction to survey methodology and questionnaire design, recommended for its nuts-and-bolts approach to the topic.

Stephen, Elizabeth Hervey, and Beth J. Soldo. "How to Judge the Quality of a Survey." *American Demographics* 12 (April 1990): 42-43.

Discusses key methodological issues, but focuses on sampling techniques. Also describes the difference between sampling error (random error) and nonrandom error (bias).

Miscellaneous Topics

Alonso, William, and Paul Starr, eds. *The Politics of Numbers* (New York: Russell Sage Foundation, 1987).
An extraordinary collection of essays commissioned for the National Committee for Research on the 1980 Census. Examines the relationship between politics and the quality of government statistics. The essays explore a diversity of statistical series besides the Census of Population, including economic indicators, voting data, education statistics, and measures of government finance. Also discussed are the ramifications of the private data industry, the role of technology, and the history of U.S. statistical policy.

Schmid, Calvin F. *Handbook of Graphic Presentation*. 2nd ed.(New York: Ronald Press, 1979).
This extensive manual should serve as a basic guide for all drafters of charts and graphs. A companion work is Schmid's *Statistical Graphics: Design Principles and Practices* (Wiley, 1981). The latter title explores the conceptual aspects of chart design in greater detail.

CHAPTER 14
The Census of Population and Housing

TOPICS COVERED

1. How Census Data Are Collected
2. Types of Data Available
3. Basic Census Concepts
   a. Census Geography
   b. Other Census Terminology
   c. 1990 Content and Program Changes
4. Decennial Census Publications
   a. 1980 Printed Reports
   b. Summary Tape File Microfiche
   c. New Products for 1990
5. Population Estimates and Projections
   a. Estimation and Projection Techniques
   b. Current Population and Housing Reports
6. Pitfalls in Using Census Information
7. Finding Census Data
   a. Census Catalogs and Subject Indexes
   b. Electronic Access to Census Data
   c. Finding Answers Quickly
8. Mastering the Census
9. For Further Reading

MAJOR SOURCES DISCUSSED

- *Characteristics of the Population:*
  Chapter A: *Number of Inhabitants*
  Chapter B: *General Population Characteristics*
  Chapter C: *General Social and Economic Characteristics*
  Chapter D: *Detailed Population Characteristics*
- *Characteristics of Housing Units:*
  Chapter A: *General Housing Characteristics*
  Chapter B: *Detailed Housing Characteristics*
- *Census Tracts*
- *Block Statistics*
- *Current Population Reports*
  Series P-26: *Local Population Estimates*
  Series P-25: *Population Estimates and Projections*
  Series P-60: *Consumer Income*
- *Current Housing Reports*
  Series H-150: *American Housing Survey*
  Series H-170: *Housing Characteristics of Selected Metropolitan Areas*

One of the most important categories of business information is statistics on people and their characteristics. The mother lode of demographic data in the United States is the decennial Census of Population and Housing. Only the federal government could attempt to collect systematic information about every man, woman, and child. The results of such an immense undertaking are necessarily complex. Census materials are widely regarded as the most difficult and frustrating of all statistical publications. It is essential, however, for researchers to have a clear understanding of what they contain and how they can be used. No other single body of data is as comprehensive as the decennial Census.

This chapter will concentrate on the concepts essential to understanding the Census: the types of data available, how they are collected, and unique Census terminology. The discussion will continue with a look at Census information products and how to use them. The chapter will summarize the array of demographic publications issued by the Bureau of the Census (hereafter referred to as the Bureau), and describe how they are organized. Included will be an introduction to intercensal reports—the monthly, annual, and irregular publications based on the Bureau's ongoing surveys, estimate programs, and projections. Common mistakes made by users of Census publications will be addressed, together with tips on locating needed information quickly.

HOW CENSUS DATA ARE COLLECTED

The fundamental purpose of the U.S. Census is stated in Article I of the Constitution: to provide an enumeration of the population for the apportionment of representation in Congress. However, from the very beginning, its value as a source of information on the condition and resources of the country was recognized. The Census has been conducted every ten years since 1790, in years ending with zero. It has grown in complexity with each succeeding decade, though its size and format have varied enormously over the years. The 1790 Census only recorded number of inhabitants, name of each head of household, number of persons in each household, sex of freeholders, and age of free white males. By 1890, the Census questionnaire grew to gargantuan proportions, overwhelming the ability of the government to collect or tally it. Since that time, the burden of questions has been reduced significantly; many have been eliminated as being nonessential, or because the data are available through other sources.

Counting every person in the country is a nearly impossible job, as the Bureau readily admits. Distrust of the government, mobility of the population, people with something to hide, and general apathy are among the obstacles to a 100% count. The best hope is to miss as few people as possible—a goal the Bureau has had 200 years of experience to achieve.

Planning for a decennial Census begins with an evaluation of the successes and failures of the previous Census. The Bureau then begins the field work necessary to improve upon past results. Concerns include how to get a better response rate, how to count individuals who are typically missed, how to reduce processing errors, how to phrase questions more clearly, and how to obtain more cooperation from local governments and the public. Accurate geographic boundaries are essential; if the underlying geography is bad, the accompanying data will be bad as well. Thousands of municipalities change their boundaries between Censuses, and the Bureau must ensure that maps used by enumerators are current and accurate. Boundaries must be clearly marked, whether they are city streets, telephone lines, or dry riverbeds. Changes are reported to the Bureau by local planning agencies throughout the nation.

The next phase is public review. The Bureau publishes issue papers outlining problems and suggestions for change. Bureau representatives then meet with other federal agencies, local planning officials, and profes-

sional statisticians to seek advice. Public hearings are held throughout the country to obtain feedback from data users of all types. Topics to consider include what questions should no longer be asked, what new questions should be added, at what geographic level should data be reported, and how much should appear in published form. Designing the questionnaire attracts the most public attention. The Bureau does not select questions for its own purposes, or because the information is useful to the business community. Questions are included because data are needed by federal, state, and local governments to establish public policies and programs. The Bureau must decide two other issues: Should a question be asked of 100% of the respondents or only a sample? And, how can the question be made comparable to data from previous Censuses, yet still reflect contemporary concerns?

A final area of preparation is publicity. The public must be informed of the importance of the Census to their communities, as well as the confidentiality of the information obtained. Data collected through the Census are used for nothing more than the compilation of statistical information. Social security numbers never appear on any Census form and individual names are stripped from each record before it is tabulated. Bureau employees face strict legal penalties for releasing personal information to anyone, including other federal agencies. An immense publicity campaign is launched to assure the public that responses will not be used for income tax, selective service, immigration, or law enforcement purposes.

Once planning is completed, the Bureau establishes nearly 500 local offices across the country, employing over 390,000 temporary workers. Commercial mailing lists are purchased for all major cities. The objective is not to specify who lives at each address, but to identify every housing unit so it won't be missed in the count. In areas outside major cities, an army of Census "listers" compile address information street by street. In both cases, lists are turned over to local post offices for verification by mail carriers, then sent to local governments to be checked against building permits, property tax payments, water bill receipts, and similar administrative records.

By Census Day (April 1st) every household in the United States receives a questionnaire in the mail. Most households (83%) receive the "short form," which asks basic questions only; the remaining 17% receive the "long form," which contains additional questions. Most respondents are directed to fill out the questionnaire and return it by mail, but those living in rural areas are instructed to keep the questionnaire until an enumerator

picks it up. Those who do not respond, and those whose answers exhibit internal discrepancies, are visited by an enumerator or contacted by phone.

Special methods are used to query unconventional housing units. Residents of group quarters such as nursing homes, army barracks, college dormitories, and ships at sea are counted separately. Two special nights are also designated when enumerators count transient and homeless individuals. This includes counts of mobile home parks, residential hotels, city missions, jails, and even park benches, doorways, and bridge underpasses where the homeless may sleep.

Data processing now begins, most of which is done at the regional and national level. Bureau staff sort and microfilm all returns, and the film is optically scanned and digitized by computer. A computer editing program checks each questionnaire for consistency, and where necessary, returns problem forms to district offices. Data are then ready for tabulation, a process which results in Summary Tape Files (STFs). These are the tapes from which the published products are produced, and as the name suggests, they contain statistical summaries only.

While this process is under way, additional steps ensure the completeness and accuracy of the data. In August, a Post-Census enumeration is conducted to estimate the undercount (and in some areas, the overcount). A random sample of 150,000 households is used to determine the characteristics of areas where significant undercount took place. A second evaluation begins in September, when the preliminary count of housing units is given to every local government for review. Governments may challenge the preliminary numbers, but they must have concrete data to support their claims. Examples might include overlooking new housing subdivisions, missing institutions like hospitals or prisons, or working with incorrect geographic boundaries. When the local review process is complete, the Bureau begins to release final population counts. By law, the president must receive apportionment data by December 31st of the Census year. The "PL 94-171" count (designated by the Public Law number which authorizes it) contains data on the number of inhabitants at the state level. The law also stipulates that individual states must receive more detailed data on population at the municipality level by the following April. The first local-level data are not officially released until a year after Census day. Preliminary (unofficial) population counts for states, metropolitan areas, and some municipalities may be announced in the press by August or September, before the local review process is completed.

TYPES OF DATA AVAILABLE

The decennial Census provides information on the number and basic characteristics of both the people and the housing stock of the United States. There are two reasons the Census is unique among statistical resources: it is the only complete survey of all people in the nation, and it is the only one which provides data at the city block level. The format varies from decade to decade, but generalizations can be made regarding the type of data researchers may find from recent Censuses.

Several rules of thumb are worth keeping in mind. First, the more detailed the information, the more likely it was asked of the 17% sample and not the full population. Second, the smaller the geographic area, the less data will be available. For example, more will be published about Florida than about Dade County, and much more will be available on Dade County than on city blocks within Miami. An important reason for this is the confidentiality doctrine—the Bureau suppresses data in cases where publication could reveal information about any individual. The threshold of confidentiality for any geographic level is five households or 15 people. If there were only three Hispanic households in a town, the number of Spanish Origin households would be suppressed in published reports. The data would be included in the counts for larger areas of geography only, such as the county and state. Another reason less is available at smaller geographic levels is because the smaller the sample size, the less valid the estimates it generates, so data at smaller levels are ruled out as inaccurate.

An understanding of the Census begins with a reasonable knowledge of the questionnaire itself. A list of the major questions asked in 1990 on the short and long forms can be seen in Figure 14-A. Questions on the number of people residing in each geographic area, the number of households and families, and general population characteristics are asked of 100% of the households. General characteristics include sex, age, race, Spanish Origin, marital status, and the familial relationships of household members to one another. Detailed questions regarding social and economic characteristics appear on the long form, and are asked of the sample population. Among the categories in this group are education (years of school completed, degrees earned, and current enrollment status), nativity (place of birth, citizenship, and year of immigration), ancestry (nationality and language spoken at home), labor force (employment status, place of work, and occupation), and income. Questions on veteran status, disabilities, travel to work, the number of

FIGURE 14-A. 1990 Census Questionnaire: Complete Count versus Sample Questions

COMPLETE COUNT ITEMS

Population
Relationship to householder
Sex
Race
Age
Marital status
Hispanic origin
Family size (D)
Household size (D)
Family type (D)
Household type (D)

Housing
Type/size of building
Number of rooms in unit
Large acreage or commercial use
Tenure (Rented or owned)
Presence of mortgage
Value of property if owned
Monthly rent if not owned
Meals included in rent
Vacancy status and reason vacant
Duration of vacancy
Persons in unit (D)
Persons per room (D)

SAMPLE ITEMS

Population
School enrollment
Educational attainment
State or country of birth
Citizenship & year immigrated
Language spoken at home
Ability to speak English
Ancestry/ethnic origin
Where resided 5 years ago
Veteran status/period served
Disability
Children ever born
Current employment status
Hours worked per week
Place of employment
Travel time to work
Means of travel to work
Persons in car pool
Year last worked
Industry/employer type
Occupation/class of worker
Self-employed
Weeks worked last year
Total income by source
Poverty status (D)
Type of group quarters (D)

Housing
Type of structure
Complete plumbing facilities
Use of property as farm
Source of water
Method of sewage disposal
Year structure built
Year householder moved into unit
Type of heat and heating fuel
Cost of utilities and fuel
Complete kitchen facilities
Number of bedrooms
Number of bathrooms
Presence of telephone
Number of cars, vans, & trucks
Amount of real property taxes
Property insurance costs
Monthly mortgage payment
Taxes/insurance in mortgage
Second mortgage payment
Condominium status
Condominium fee
Mobile home shelter costs
Total housing costs (D)

(D) indicates information not asked on form but derived from available data

children ever born to adult female respondents, and where each person lived and worked five years ago are also asked.

Housing questions follow a similar pattern. The 100% questions provide data on number of housing units, the size and type of building, whether the occupant owns or rents, and the amount of rent paid or the dollar value of the home. Data on vacant units are compiled by Census enumerators on a 100% basis. Sample questions are more numerous and include information on the source of water and of sewage disposal, whether the unit is a condominium, the year the structure was built, the year the present occupant moved in, heating facilities and fuel used, the cost of utilities, number of bedrooms, and the presence of telephone, kitchen, and plumbing facilities. The sample housing questions also ask about number of cars, trucks, and vans owned by each household.

From this reasonably small group of questions, and the ability to cross-tabulate responses, many important public policy facts can be derived. How many people live below the poverty level? How many change jobs or travel to work in car pools? How many women are heads of households with no husband present? Much of this information does not come from explicitly asked questions, but is derived from the raw data. Household and family characteristics, for example, are derived from the responses of the individuals and their relationship to the "householder." The quality of housing in a neighborhood can be derived from such factors as age of the dwellings, the absence of plumbing or heating facilities, and number of vacant and boarded-up units. Overcrowding can be determined by comparing the size of the household to the number of rooms.

Despite the acknowledged expertise of the Bureau in designing questionnaires, developing sample surveys, and conducting the Census, users must be aware of many potential errors and limitations. The most serious is the inevitable undercount, estimated in recent Censuses to be about 2% of the population. Unfortunately, most of those missed are transients, the poor, minorities, non-English speakers, or rural inhabitants. In 1990, these groups were targeted through special awareness programs and assistance centers in local communities. Another significant problem is sampling error. For detailed characteristics, estimates of the total population are generated based upon the sample data collected. Accuracy depends on how closely the composition of the sample reflects the reality of the total population.

Problems also occur during data collection and processing. Because 90% of the questionnaires are returned by mail, "fictitious answers" do happen. It is believed that deliberately false answers are few, and many can be caught in the editing process, but the possibility must be recognized by Census users. A more likely problem is that enumerators and other temporary workers will make mistakes through a lack of understanding. Training short-term employees in the complexities of the Census is a challenging task. Errors can also occur when questionnaires are being edited and coded for entry into the computer.

Problems caused by the nature of the questions asked are more difficult to identify. The way a question is phrased can cause confusion, and Census terminology can be a particular source of difficulty. For example, the Bureau considers a bedroom to be any room used for sleeping, whether it was intended for that purpose or not. Conversely, if a bedroom is being used for purposes other than sleeping, it is not counted as a bedroom. A related problem is due to the self-reporting nature of the Census. Questions on race and ethnic background are answered based on what respondents feel best describes their characteristics. A man of one-eighth Irish stock who strongly identifies with this heritage could thus call himself Irish. The ethnicity question instructs respondents to designate mixed ethnic background, but this is not an option for racial questions. Individuals of mixed race have no way to identify themselves except to write a response in the "other" box. Questions about disabilities, personal income, and valuation of property are other self-identified questions which have a tendency to be under or overstated, but the Bureau has little recourse but to take each respondent's word.

The most frequent objection to the quality of the Census is that it only appears every ten years and that by the time information is released, it is already several years old. The Bureau meets these problems in two ways: by releasing reports on a flow basis, as soon as data are available, and by providing annual and sometimes monthly estimates for basic population and housing characteristics at the national and state levels.

BASIC CENSUS CONCEPTS

It is impossible to correctly locate and interpret Census data without a grounding in basic concepts, geographic units, and definitions. Many of these are unique to the Census, and are quite bewildering when first encountered. It is difficult to grasp certain concepts in a single reading, so this discussion is designed to alert researchers to key areas of concern. Never take terminology for granted; consult Census definitions to ensure

correct understanding. Also, don't expect to master subtle distinctions instantly. Refer to user guides frequently until differences in terminology are understood.

Census Geography

Any discussion of Census concepts must begin with the geography used by the Bureau. There are three categories of Census geography: administrative, governmental, and statistical. Administrative units are used solely for purposes of collecting and tabulating the Census. The basic units used for this purpose are enumeration districts (EDs), which do not appear in any published data products. Governmental units are legal entities with politically defined boundaries. Examples are states, counties, cities, towns, and villages. In addition to the 50 states, the Bureau designates six "state equivalents." These are the District of Columbia, and U.S. foreign territories, including Puerto Rico and Guam. Although counties are the major political subdivision of most states, the Bureau has designated county-equivalents where this is not the case. In Louisiana, counties are known as parishes, and Alaska has no counties. Five states have independent cities which are autonomous from their surrounding counties, and these are also considered county equivalents. Other governmental units reported in Census publications include American Indian Reservations, Alaska Native Villages, and Congressional Districts.

Statistical units are geographical areas defined by the Bureau for statistical reporting purposes. These units include Blocks, Block Groups, Tracts, and metropolitan areas. The Bureau divides the U.S. into four regions which are further divided into two or three divisions. Beyond this, statistical units become confusing and require some explanation. Because urban growth has expanded far beyond city limits, a better measurement of urban geography is necessary. The federal government addressed this problem in 1949 by creating the standard metropolitan area, defined as a large Central City, together with its surrounding "socially and economically integrated" county or counties. Integration is determined by the commuting and trade patterns of the population. Up to and including the 1980 Census these areas were termed Standard Metropolitan Statistical Areas (SMSAs). By definition, an SMSA was built around a Central City of 50,000 or more population, but, in a few cases, cities with populations greater than 25,000 could serve as the Central City of an SMSA. In 1980 there were 323 SMSAs.

The minimum boundary of an SMSA is one county or county-equivalent; it can be comprised of more than one county, but never less than a single county, and never combined fragments of counties. SMSAs can also cross state boundaries if the area meets the definition of economic integration. Metropolitan areas such as New York City, St. Louis, and Minneapolis are examples of the many SMSAs which are made up of counties in two or more states. SMSAs are important for at least four reasons: first, many federal assistance programs are available only to metropolitan areas; second, in Census publications, more data are reported for SMSAs than for nonmetropolitan areas; third, many states and local areas also use SMSAs for planning and statistical purposes; and finally, the private sector finds the concept a convenient way to standardize urban areas.

In 1983 the criteria for metropolitan areas was redefined by the U.S. Office of Management and the Budget, but basic concepts remain the same. The term SMSA was eliminated as of June 30, 1983 and replaced with three new designations: the Metropolitan Statistical Area (MSA), the Primary Metropolitan Statistical Area (PMSA), and the Consolidated Metropolitan Statistical Area (CMSA). MSAs are roughly equivalent to most old SMSAs and they are independent of one another. MSAs with populations greater than one million are now eligible for status as a CMSA; CMSAs are then broken up into two or more PMSAs. For example, the Buffalo, New York SMSA was made up of Erie and Niagara Counties. This is equivalent to the new Buffalo CMSA, which is an amalgamation of the Buffalo PMSA (Erie County) and the Niagara Falls PMSA (Niagara County).

At first glance there may seem to be little difference between the new terminology and the old. The driving force behind the change was the fact that many communities which were metropolitan in character were ineligible for metropolitan status under the old definition because they didn't have a sufficiently large Central City. The new definition eases past restrictions, creating more MSAs. The second reason is that as areas grew in size, neighboring SMSAs were merging with one another and losing their separate identities. Under the new guidelines, merged areas can be called CMSAs, thus reflecting their unity as massive metropolitan areas; at the same time, their component PMSAs retain past identity. The various designations are confusing, but it is vitally important to remember that there is more than one definition of a metropolitan area. When a report refers to the Baltimore metro area, be sure you understand the boundaries in-

cluded. In this book, the MSA designation will be used generically for all metropolitan areas, except when 1980 publications are discussed.

Another unit of Census geography is the Census Tract, a small sub-county area with relatively homogeneous demographic, economic, and housing characteristics. Tract boundaries are determined by the Bureau in cooperation with local authorities. Each Tract contains roughly 4,000 inhabitants. Generally speaking, every county which is part of an MSA is completely divided into Tracts. Tracts do not cross MSA borders, nor do they cross county lines, but they may extend beyond other political boundaries such as towns or villages. Tracts which lie in two separate governmental units are called Split Tracts. In Census publications, data on Split Tracts are reported separately for each political unit of which they are a part.

Census Tracts are important to statistical analysis for two reasons. First, they constitute the smallest level of geography for which fairly detailed data are available. Second, their boundaries do not change from one decade to the next, making them the only level of geography comparable across Censuses. In some cases, Tracts become too large, or lose their homogeneous characteristics and must be divided into smaller Tracts. When this occurs, their boundaries remain comparable to those of past Censuses. For example, if Tract 142 of an MSA were to become too large or diverse, it would be divided into Tracts 142.01 and 142.02. These are called Divided Tracts, and should not be confused with the Split Tracts defined earlier.

In nonmetropolitan areas, Tracts are called Block Numbering Areas (BNAs), but the idea behind them is the same. In the 1980 Census, data on BNAs do not appear in most published reports or summary tapes. To counter this limitation, the Bureau allowed state and local governments to pay a fee to have their BNAs treated as Tracts. In 1980, five states contracted with the Bureau to have all nonmetropolitan areas completely tracted, as did 252 other counties in the U.S. Data on these pseudo-Tracts can thus be found in Census publications. In the 1990 Census, much more data will appear for BNAs.

The smallest area of Census geography is the Census Block. In urbanized areas it is usually a city block. In nonurbanized areas it is a unit of about 70 people and is circumscribed by natural or man-made boundaries. Census Blocks do not cross Tract or BNA boundaries. In the 1980 Census, only the urbanized portion of SMSAs are blocked, together with all incorporated places of 10,000 or more which lie outside SMSAs. As with Census Tracts, some states and local governments paid the Bu-

reau to create 100% blocking for their areas. One of the biggest changes in the 1990 Census is that the entire nation has been blocked from shore to shore. This has created more than 7.5 million Census Blocks, compared with approximately 2 million in 1980.

No sample data are published at the Block level, and complete-count data are suppressed where necessary for purposes of privacy, but the decennial Census is the only source of nonestimated demographic information at such small levels of geography. Between Blocks and Tracts is another useful level of Census geography called Block Groups. These are created by combining Blocks to form larger units. Every Tract is divided into approximately nine Block Groups, and like Tracts, some sample data are reported for these units. Data on Block Groups cannot be found in printed reports from the Bureau, but they are published in certain microfiche and electronic products.

Blocks have the additional value of being the basic unit from which larger custom-built territories can be constructed. For example, if Tracts do not provide adequate boundaries for your needs, you may contract with the Bureau to obtain data for any aggregation of Blocks you wish. While you could, of course, sum the data available from published Block reports yourself, the problems of suppressed data and no sample data would limit the usefulness of your compilation. Because many local communities have special needs for data in other configurations (police precincts, sewer districts, etc.), municipalities can contract with the Bureau to create Block aggregations to their specifications. In 1980, the venture was known as the Neighborhood Statistics Program; for 1990, it is called the User Defined Areas Program.

Aside from the basic units of Census geography, it is necessary to distinguish between several pairs of geographic terms. The first is the Census concept of "Place." This is important because Census publications provide separate tables for areas that are Places and for those which are not, and because more data are reported for Places than non-Places. To further complicate matters, there are two types of Places. An Incorporated Place is a political unit which is legally incorporated as a city, village, or similar form. In most states, with the exception of New York and Alaska, boroughs are incorporated. Towns are incorporated in all states except New York, Wisconsin, and the New England states; townships are not incorporated. A Census Designated Place (CDP) is an unincorporated area defined as a Place by the Bureau at the request of a local government. CDPs are densely settled communities with a minimum population of 1,000.

A CDP may be a township or other unincorporated political unit, or even a well defined part of a larger area. CDPs frequently have no legal status but are recognized as places by their residents. Approximately 3,400 CDPs were designated in the 1980 Census.

There are also two types of areas which are not Places: Minor Civil Divisions (MCDs), and Census County Divisions (CCDs). An MCD is an unincorporated subdivision of a county. They are usually called townships, but they are towns in the states of New York, Wisconsin, and the New England area. Six states call MCDs by unique designations such as magisterial district or supervisor's district. In contrast, Census County Divisions are created by the Bureau as county subdivisions for states where MCDs don't exist, where they are not well-known political units, or where boundaries change frequently. In the 1980 Census, 30 states have MCDs and 20 states have CCDs. As a final note in an already confusing discussion, Incorporated Places may be a legal part of the MCD which surrounds them or they may be independent of any MCD.

The preceding explanation may be unavoidably baffling to first-time Census users. Geographic concepts in the Census are complex because the Bureau is attempting to impose uniformity on an otherwise diverse system of nomenclature and legal structure across 50 states. Figure 14-B shows the hierarchy among various Census terms and may be helpful in sorting out geographical relationships. In addition, the reader may want to review this discussion by identifying examples of each term in his or her own community; bear in mind that some terms may have no relevance in your particular state.

Other Census Terminology

The Bureau is notorious for using commonly understood terms in specially defined ways. Therefore, it is vital to understand the precise meaning of any term used in the Census before interpreting data. For example, metropolitan area, urban area, and Urbanized Area are *not* synonymous terms and treating them as such will result in enormous errors. To help users avoid this trap, every published Census report has an appendix which defines important words and phrases. It is recommended that researchers consult these definitions frequently.

Certain Census relationships are particularly confusing. Figure 14-C outlines key concepts involving housing units and households; Figure 14-B clarifies geographic terminology. To show distinctions found in these and other Census concepts, a few of the more commonly misunderstood terms are described below.

Householder: Whichever person in a household chooses to fill out column 1 of the Census questionnaire. This system is used to determine the characteristics of each household, as well as the relationships among household and family members.

Group Quarters: Institutions such as hospitals, nursing homes and orphanages, and any living place occupied by ten or more unrelated individuals, including military barracks, dormitories, rooming houses, communes, and religious orders. By definition, Group Quarters are not Housing Units.

Housing Unit: A house, apartment, or rooms intended as separate living quarters and which possesses independent access from the outside or from a public area.

Occupied Housing Unit: A housing unit occupied at the time the Census is taken and which is the person's usual place of residence. If the unit is temporarily vacant due to vacation or similar reasons, it is counted as occupied. Only year-round units are counted in the occupied category, but summer homes can be counted in the vacant category.

Household: All persons living within a single housing unit. Since group quarters are not housing units by definition, individuals living in group quarters are not members of households.

Family: Two or more persons living together in a household and related by marriage, birth, or adoption. In most cases, relatives not living within the household are not defined as family members. It is also important to remember that families are defined through the relationship of household members to the householder.

Spanish Origin: Any individual born in Puerto Rico, Cuba, Mexico, or other Spanish-speaking country, of that country's descent, or self-identified as Spanish speaking or Spanish surnamed. Spanish Origin is not a racial characteristic because a Hispanic individual may be white, black, Native American, Asian, etc.

Income: Includes wages, salaries, earnings from self-employment, interest, rents, royalties, social security, public assistance, etc. Income as defined by the Bureau does not include nonmonetary payments such as food stamps and expense accounts.

FIGURE 14-B. Geographic Units in the Census

These figures illustrate the principal hierarchical or "nesting" relationships among census geographic areas. Note that the hierarchies overlap, e.g., counties are subdivided into MCD's or CCD's (part A), into urban and rural components (part C), and, inside SMSA's, also into census tracts (part B).

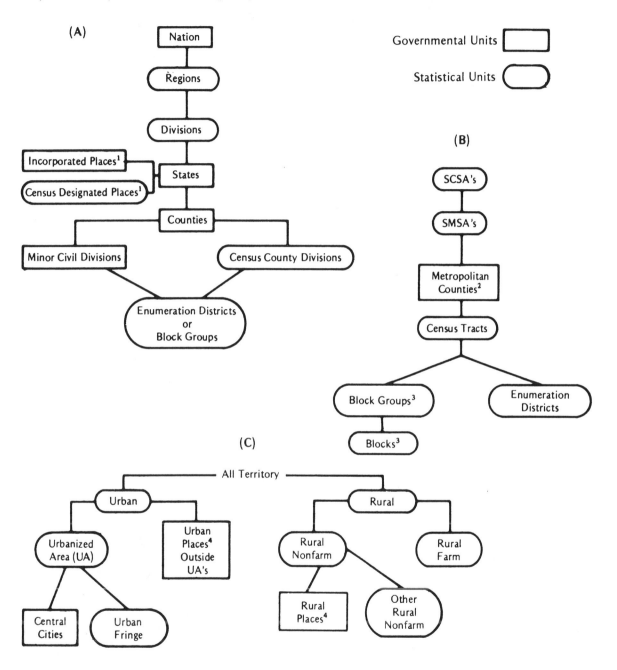

[1] Places are not shown in the county, MCD, and CCD hierarchy since places may cross the boundaries of these areas.
ED and BG summaries do, however, respect place boundaries.
[2] In New England, metropolitan towns (MCD's) and cities replace counties as the components of SMSA's.
[3] In SMSA's, blocks and block groups generally cover only the urbanized area and places of 10,000 or more.
[4] Includes both incorporated places (governmental units) and census designated places (statistical units).

Courtesy of the U.S. Bureau of the Census.

FIGURE 14-C. Important Census Relationships

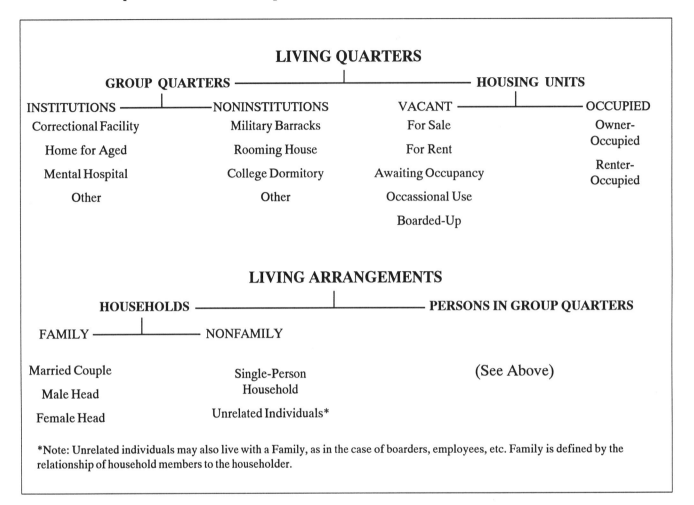

*Note: Unrelated individuals may also live with a Family, as in the case of boarders, employees, etc. Family is defined by the relationship of household members to the householder.

Central City: The largest city or cities in an SMSA, MSA, PMSA, CMSA, or Urbanized Area. Metropolitan Areas may have more than one Central City.

Metropolitan Area: An SMSA, MSA, PMSA, or CMSA.

Rural Area: Any area with fewer than 2,500 people. Rural Areas may be located within a Metropolitan Area, but they must lie outside the urbanized portion of the MSA. Remember that MSAs are made up of entire counties, and many counties contain both urban and rural portions. In contrast, an Urban Area is any area not rural.

Urbanized Area: An area of at least 50,000 people, consisting of a Central City and its contiguous closely settled surroundings (called suburbs or urban fringe). Urbanized Areas (UAs) are based strictly on the shifting patterns of population density. UAs are the most populated portion of a metro area, and typically have unusual boundaries which do not conform to other political or statistical units. Urbanized Areas should not be confused with Urban Areas.

1990 Content and Program Changes

Every decennial Census differs from those which have gone before. This discussion will examine major changes in 1990 concepts, policies, and processes. Changes in data products will be described in a later section.

All Census data flow from the questions asked on the short and long forms, so questionnaire content is the logical starting point for Census comparisons. Little is fundamentally different between the 1980 and 1990 questionnaire—few questions are new, and few existing questions have been lost. Many of the differences are changes in wording designed to reflect shifting social and economic patterns. Perhaps the most noteworthy involve

new realities in household composition, including the addition of "Unmarried Partner," stepchild, grandchild, and foster child as relationship options. The question on educational attainment formerly asked the highest grade attended; the 1990 questionnaire asks the highest grade completed and the degrees earned. A new question asks if the respondent works at home. In 1980, questions about handicapped individuals asked whether the disability presented a barrier to working or using public transportation. In 1990, the question also asks whether the disability prevents the person for caring for him- or herself in the home or in leaving the home. Several questions reflect the increasing number of elderly persons in the United States. One asks whether rents include the cost of meals; another specifies income from pension plans. New housing questions deal with solar heating, second mortgages, mobile home and condominium fees, and whether residents own their homes "free and clear."

A few questions from 1980 did not appear on the 1990 questionnaire. Only one—the question on marital history—was from the population side. The others were housing questions, including the number of stories in a dwelling and the presence of elevators and air conditioners. These were deemed expendable, so were deleted to make room for new questions. A subtler difference is the "downgrading" of certain 100% questions to the sample questionnaire. Among the subjects affected in this way are condominium status and plumbing facilities.

One of the biggest changes in 1990 was mentioned earlier—the entire nation would be completely blocked for the first time. In conjunction with this effort, the Bureau has developed the most detailed geographic database in the world. The system is called TIGER, an acronym for Topologically Integrated Geographic Encoding and Referencing System. TIGER contains machine-readable data for every map feature used in the 1990 Census, including physical features, political boundaries, and Census statistical units. The system provides latitude and longitude coordinates, feature names, place names, classification codes, zip code ranges, and, for major metropolitan areas, address ranges. Users can purchase TIGER/Line files in CD-ROM format or as magnetic tapes. By accessing TIGER data through commercially available geographic software programs, planners and researchers will be able to plot their own detailed boundary and line maps, identify specific addresses within larger units of geography, create thematic maps based on Census statistics, and superimpose their own information on Census maps. The product has fantastic possibilities for marketing, transportation planning, and many other applications.

A third change in the Census involves the User Defined Area Program (UDAP). In 1980, the Neighborhood Statistics Program was free to qualifying municipalities; in the 1990s, the Bureau will charge a fee for creating customized UDAP statistics. The UDAP program is now available to private companies, nonprofit organizations, and other nongovernment groups.

A major controversy surrounding the 1990 Census was whether the official population count would reflect actual enumerated responses, or would be adjusted to account for the estimated over- or undercount. Following the 1980 Census, the Bureau was sued by some 50 municipalities and states challenging the population figures. Because billions of dollars in federal aid are dependent on these numbers, the issue has continued to rage. With New York City leading the charge, major cities demanded that the Bureau use data from Post-Census surveys to incorporate estimates of the undercount into official population reports. The Bureau opposed this course of action, and went to court to defend its position. The commerce secretary appointed a blue-ribbon commission of professional statisticians and data users to make an independent recommendation, and the secretary's final decision was announced in July 1991: the official counts from the 1990 enumeration will not be adjusted to incorporate estimated undercount.

DECENNIAL CENSUS PUBLICATIONS

Two hundred years ago, the first decennial Census publication consisted of a single report about 50 pages in length. Published data from the 1980 Census comprise nearly 1,700 separate reports, totaling over 300,000 pages. This prodigious output represents only a small fraction of data available from the 1980 tabulation. The bulk of the information is available on microfiche and computer tape, both of which are distributed on a more limited basis. In 1990, the outpouring of data will rival that of the previous decade, with the added benefits of CD-ROM products and a greater number of geographic reports.

Decennial Census publications provide answers to the most frequently asked demographic inquiries. Formats vary from decade to decade, but their arrangement is fairly consistent. Because the printed reports from the 1990 Census will not begin to appear until late 1991, the 1980 Census will be used to explain how data are published. The 1980 products will then be compared to the announced changes for 1990. Decennial publications

follow a logical pattern, so an overview of their organization will help users become familiar with them more quickly.

Almost all Census publications appear in geographic format. Most are issued as 58 separate books: one for each state or state-equivalent, and a U.S. summary. Two report series cover population and housing data, respectively, and the third contains summary data of both types. All publications are identified by a report number, which designates the series, volume, chapter, and part. As an example, the 1980 report PC(1)-A34 represents the *Population Census* series, volume 1, chapter A, part 34 (part numbers indicate the state covered).

The full set takes several years to produce. Basic reports from the 1980 enumeration were not completed until mid-1984, and specialized reports continued to be released through 1987. The need to wait four years for detailed figures is obviously one of the most serious drawbacks of the Census. In 1990, the arrangement of reports has been modified to ensure that the most sought-after data will appear first. All major publications are scheduled for release by the end of 1993.

Each Census report has three finding aids to assist users. A Table of Contents (Exhibit 14-1) lists every table by title. A Table Finding Guide (Exhibit 14-2) relates each category of question to the level of geography sought, and a Data Index summarizes the statistics available for each geographic level. In addition, every publication includes several appendices with definitions of terms, copies of the questionnaire, and a discussion of sampling error and methodology.

A closer look at the two exhibits will provide a better understanding of the structure of the printed reports. Notice in Exhibit 14-1 that most tables are devoted to fairly narrow topics. Table 60 contains data on ancestry, Table 64 on family composition, Table 65 on mobility, and so on. This means that a researcher who needs a variety of data for a single geographic unit must consult numerous tables. The presentation is further divided into several levels of geography. Tables 61 through 65 focus on data at the state level; the sequence is then repeated for other geographic levels. For example, Table 63, "Nativity and Language," presents information on the principal language spoken at home, but only at the state level. Table 116 provides the same data for SMSAs and large cities, while Table 172 does so for counties. All state tables appear first, followed by tables for MSAs and smaller levels.

This structure is complicated by the fact that not all tables are presented for every geographic level, and by the fact that similar data can be found on several tables.

This makes the Table Finding Guide extremely important. Looking at Exhibit 14-2 under "Language spoken at home," we find Tables 63, 116, and 172 listed under state, SMSA, and county, as expected. We also find Tables 156 and 166 for smaller Places, and 192 for Indian Reservations. These tables differ from those entitled "Nativity and Language," however. Tables 156, 166, and 192 are called "Social Characteristics," and provide a greater diversity of data on a single page. Because of the different title, users trying to locate information on language for Places under 50,000 in population would find nothing explicit through the Table of Contents. Depending on geographic level, data on personal income can be found under more than 12 different table headings in Chapter C alone.

If this seems confusing, be patient; making sense of the tables should become clearer as the discussion unfolds. In the meantime, remember that reports are arranged by geographic level, but that each table deals with a specific topic. The most effective way to locate a particular type of information is usually to consult the Table Finding Guide, then the Table of Contents. The following summary of each major report will clarify how the publications are related.

1980 Printed Reports

The first series of decennial publications, the *Population Census*, is divided into two sub-series, called "volumes." Volume 1 contains several hundred reports by geographic area; volume 2 offers subject reports at the national level. The *Housing Census* follows a similar pattern. Although the numbering structure differs slightly, Volume 1 consists of detailed tables by geographic level, and most of the remaining volumes provide broader subject coverage.

The third Census series was designed for users interested in summary information, or for data reported at different levels of geography. The *Population and Housing Census* encompasses four types of report. The first is *Congressional Districts of the 98th Congress*, which provides both 100% and sample data for selected characteristics, reported by Congressional District. One report is issued for each state and for the District of Columbia. Eleven additional reports were issued for the 99th and 100th Congresses, reflecting boundary changes due to post-Census redistricting. The second title in the combined series, *Summary Characteristics for Governmental Units*, lists 80 summary characteristics from both the complete and sample counts, covering key popula-

EXHIBIT 14-1. *Census of Population*—Table of Contents

General Social and Economic Characteristics

NEBRASKA

PC80-1-C29

Contents

(Page numbers listed here omit the State prefix number which appears as part of the page number for each page. The prefix for this State is 29)

MAPS   **Page**

Standard Metropolitan Statistical Areas, Counties, and Selected Places.   9

TABLES

56. Summary of Social Characteristics: 1980   11
    The State
    Urban and Rural and Size of Place
    Inside and Outside SMSA's
    SCSA's
    SMSA's
    Urbanized Areas
    Places of 2,500 or More
    Counties

57. Summary of Economic Characteristics: 1980   14
    The State
    Urban and Rural and Size of Place
    Inside and Outside SMSA's
    SCSA's
    SMSA's
    Urbanized Areas
    Places of 2,500 or More
    Counties

58. Race by Sex: 1980   17
    The State
    Urban and Rural and Size of Place
    Inside and Outside SMSA's
    SCSA's
    SMSA's
    Urbanized Areas
    Places of 2,500 or More
    Counties

TABLES   **Page**

59. Persons by Spanish Origin, Race, and Sex: 1980 . .   24
    The State
    Urban and Rural and Size of Place
    Inside and Outside SMSA's
    SCSA's
    SMSA's
    Urbanized Areas
    Places of 2,500 or More
    Counties

60. Selected Ancestry Groups: 1980   31
    The State
    Urban and Rural and Size of Place
    Inside and Outside SMSA's
    SCSA's
    SMSA's
    Urbanized Areas
    Places of 2,500 or More
    Counties

61. Selected Social and Economic Characteristics by Race: 1980 and 1970.   37
    The State

62. General Characteristics: 1980   39
    The State
    Urban and Rural and Size of Place
    Inside and Outside SMSA's

63. Nativity and Language: 1980.   40
    The State
    Urban and Rural and Size of Place
    Inside and Outside SMSA's

64. Fertility and Family Composition: 1980   41
    The State
    Urban and Rural and Size of Place
    Inside and Outside SMSA's

65. Geographical Mobility and Commuting: 1980. . . .   42
    The State
    Urban and Rural and Size of Place
    Inside and Outside SMSA's

Reprinted from *Census of Population*, published by the U.S. Bureau of the Census.

EXHIBIT 14-2. *Census of Population*—Table Finding Guide

Table Finding Guide— Subjects by Type of Area and Table Number

The guide lists all subjects covered in the report but does not indicate all cross-classification (e.g., by sex, age, ancestry) or the historical data shown in table 61. Additional information is given in the footnotes. Table numbers identified here with boldface type (e.g., **73**) present data for racial groups and/or Spanish origin. Tables identified with an asterisked number (e.g., 56*) present data for the State by urban, rural, and rural farm residence and by inside and outside SMSA's. Data on allocation rates appear in tables C-3. For definitions of terms, see appendixes A and B.

Subject	The State		SCSA's, SMSA's, Urbanized areas, Central cities of SMSA's, Places of 50,000 or more[1]	Places[1] of—		Counties		American Indian reserva-tions[2]
	Total	Urban and rural		10,000 to 50,000	2,500 to 10,000	Total	Rural and Rural farm	
SUMMARY								
Social	56*		56	56	56	56		
Economic	57*		57	57	57	57		192
Race	**58***		**58**	**58**	**58**	**58**	**188, 190**	**193**
Spanish origin	**59***		**59**	**59**	**59**	**59**	**188, 190**	
Ancestry	60*		60	60	60	60		
GENERAL								
Age	62*, **73, 83,** 93, 99, 105	**73, 83**	115, **126, 132, 138, 144, 150**			171, **182**	**188, 190**	192
Household type and relationship .	64*, **74, 84,** 93, 99, 106	**74, 84**	117, **126, 132, 138, 144, 150**			173, **182**	**188, 190**	
Persons in households	62*, **73, 83,** 105	**73, 83**	115			171	**188, 190**	
Characteristics of persons 60 years and over								
SOCIAL								
Ancestry	105 to 114							
Nativity and place of birth	61, 65* **75,** 85, 94, 100, 107	**75, 85**	118, **127, 133, 139, 145, 151**	156, **162**	166	174, **183**		
Nativity and citizenship	63*		116			172		
Country of birth	61, 63*		116	156		172		
Year of immigration	63*		116			172		
Residence in 1975	61, 65*, **75,** 85, 94, 100, 107	**75, 85**	118, **127, 133, 139, 145, 151**	156, **162**	166, **169**	174, **183**	**188, 190**	
Language spoken at home and ability to speak English	63*		116	156	166	172		192
Family type and presence of own children	64*, **74, 84,** 94, 100, 106	**74, 84**	117, **127, 133, 139, 145, 151**	157, **162**	166	173, **182**		
Fertility	61, 64*, **74,** 84, 93, 99, 106	**74, 84**	117, **126, 132, 138, 144, 150**	157, **162**	166	173, **182**	**188, 190**	192
Marital history	64*, **74, 84,** 106	**74, 84**	117			173		
Type of group quarters								
School enrollment and type of school	61, 66*, **76,** 86, 93, 99, 108	**76, 86**	119, **126, 132, 138, 144, 150**	157, **162**	166, **169**	175, **182**		

III

Reprinted from the *Census of Population*, published by the U.S. Bureau of the Census.

tion and housing data. One report was issued for each state and state-equivalent, with data presented for political units, including Minor Civil Divisions. This is the only published report for 1980 which contains data from the 100% count for Places with fewer than 1,000 population, and sample count data on MCDs and Places smaller than 2,500. In 1990, this popular report will be replaced by two summary publications containing similar data presented in much the same format. The other combined reports cover Tract and Block data.

The most important remaining publications in all three series are described below.

Characteristics of the Population (Volume 1 of the *Population Census*).

For most researchers, this is the most frequently consulted portion of the Census. It consists of one report for every state or state-equivalent, plus a United States Summary. Every report is divided into four "chapters," each appearing as one or more separate books. Chapters A and B present data from the 100% count, Chapters C and D from the sample. The reports are lengthy and detailed, with a total of 251 tables. Lengths vary, depending on the size of the state. Information on Texas, for example, is issued as six paperback books, with a total of 4,395 pages. Descriptions of each chapter are as follows:

Chapter A: *Number of Inhabitants*
PC(1)-A-Number.

Contains three types of data only: final population counts for each state, SMSA, county, Urbanized Area, county subdivision, and Place; land area in square miles for every political unit; and corresponding population densities. Also provides outline maps for counties, county subdivisions, and urbanized areas. Especially useful to identify the component parts of SMSAs. All data are from the 100% count.

Chapter B: *General Population Characteristics*
PC(1)-B-Number.

Contains data from the 100% count on age (by individual year and by age group), sex, race, Spanish Origin, marital status, number of households, household relationship, and family type and composition. Depending on the table, as many as seven racial groups are listed. Separate tables are given for specific population groups (blacks, whites, Hispanics, and aged). Limited cross-tabulation of data is provided. Summary data are also given for individuals living in institutions and other group quarters.

Chapter C: *General Social and Economic Characteristics*
PC(1)-C-Number.

Contains sample data only, taken from the long form. Social characteristics include ancestry, place of birth, citizenship, language, fertility (children ever born), marital history, school enrollment, years of education completed, presence of disability, and veteran status. Economic data include labor force status (employed, unemployed), occupation group and type of worker, industry, travel time to work and means of transportation, income, and poverty status. Also contains more detailed data on characteristics of population in group quarters. Cross-tabulations are provided by age, race, sex, educational attainment, etc.

Chapter D: *Detailed Population Characteristics*
PC(1)-D-Number.

Contains detailed cross-tabulations for states, SMSAs with population greater than 250,000, and their Central Cities. Information is available only for large geographic areas due to the extensive detail presented. Examples include specific occupations of employed workers; and school enrollment by individual years of age, individual grades, sex, race, and type of school. Data are obtained from the long form. Because of its geographic limitations and specialized tables, this is the least-used Chapter in the set. It will not appear in the 1990 series.

Population Subject Reports (Volume 2 of the *Population Census*) PC(2)-Number.

This part of the Census provides detailed data at the national level for special topics. Each report is on a different subject, and each has a distinctive title. Examples of titles produced for the 1980 Census are *Income by Occupation, Marital Status,* and *Journey to Work.* Reports range in size up to 1,250 pages, with most in excess of 500 pages. In 1980, 13 subject reports were released. Thirty reports are planned for 1990, including detailed studies of the disabled population, the foreign born, and the aged.

The Bureau published another subject-oriented series in 1980 called *Supplementary Reports.* These are briefer pamphlets, usually under 25 pages. Instead of surveying topics at the national level, they provide comparative tables for states, metropolitan areas, counties, or other levels of geography across the country. Twenty reports were issued. Topics include summary data on American Indian Reservations and Alaska Native Villages, Congressional District profiles, and persons of Spanish Origin.

Characteristics of Housing Units (Volume 1 of the *Housing Census*).

This "volume" constitutes the most frequently cited portion of the *Housing Census,* with one report for every state or state-equivalent plus a U.S. Summary. Chapter A is based upon the 100% count, while Chapter B represents sample data.

Chapter A: *General Housing Characteristics*
HC(1)-A-Number.

Contains complete count data for housing questions asked on the short form. Data are presented in 53 tables, including the following information: total housing units; year-round units; occupied, owner-occupied, and vacant units; persons in unit, number of rooms, and persons per room; value and rent; and absence of complete

plumbing. Format parallels that of Chapter B of *Characteristics of the Population*, providing separate tables for blacks, whites, Hispanics, and the aged.

Chapter B: *Detailed Housing Characteristics* HC(1)-B-Number.

Contains sample count data on housing units collected on the long form. Coverage is extensive, with data on duration of occupancy, year structure was built, number of bedrooms, source of water, type of sewage disposal, type of heating and cooking fuel, mortgage status, and utility costs. Extensive cross-tabulation is provided.

Metropolitan Housing Characteristics (Volume 2 of the *Housing Census*) HC(2)-Number.

Corresponds to Chapter D of *Characteristics of the Population*, with detailed cross-tabulations of housing data for SMSAs and states only. A total of 375 reports were issued—one for each state and for each SMSA. Like its population counterpart, this series was infrequently used, and will not appear in 1990.

Housing Subject Reports (Volume 3 of the *Housing Census*) HC(3)-Number.

Identical in purpose to the *Population Subject Reports,* it provides detailed data on specific topics for the nation as a whole. Examples of 1980 titles are *Mobile Homes, Condominium Housing,* and *Mover Households.* Five reports were issued in 1980; ten are planned for 1990.

Additional special reports appear as volumes 4 and 5 of the *Housing Census.* Volume 4, entitled *Components of Inventory Change,* is based upon a special survey conducted by the Bureau in the fall of 1980. It provides summary data at the national level on new housing units and units removed from the housing stock. Volume 5, *Residential Finance,* is also based on a special survey .It provides national data on the mortgage status of residential housing units.

Census Tracts (Volume 2 of the *Population and Housing Census*) PHC(2)-Number.

Tract data are among the most heavily used categories of Census information. Most variables from the complete count are represented (covering both housing and population questions), as are a variety of sample variables. Data are presented at the Tract level, and for SMSAs, counties, and selected Places. Tables are arranged by subject. Population data include family and household type, nativity, school enrollment, journey to work, labor force status, income, and population below the poverty level. Among the housing variables are homeownership, value, vacancy status, contract rent, persons per room, year structure was built, and vehicles

available. One report is issued for every SMSA, plus 50 statewide reports covering those nonmetropolitan areas which contracted with the Bureau to receive Tract status. Used together with their accompanying Tract maps, these reports are simple to use, and excellent for comparing neighborhood characteristics. The Bureau also publishes a *Census Tract Street Index* for every major metropolitan area. Each index provides an alphabetic listing of street names, together with the address ranges located in each Tract.

Block Statistics (Volume 1 of the *Population and Housing Census*) PHC(1)-Number.

This is the only other standard report providing data at small levels of geography. Figures are cited for individual blocks for every area which was blocked in 1980. A limited number of characteristics is reported, all of which come from the complete count. Among them are race, Spanish Origin, number of inhabitants older than 65 and younger than 18, one-person households, owner-occupied housing units, units with more than one person per room, and units lacking complete plumbing. One report is issued for each SMSA, with additional reports for every state which contracted for additional blocked areas. Reports are available on microfiche only, but the accompanying 1980 Block maps are available on fiche or paper. Unlike Tract maps, which appear on a single sheet for every metro area, Block maps are both voluminous and cumbersome to use. For this reason, the Bureau issued a *Finder's Guide to Block Statistics Reports,* giving state-by-state listings of all counties, places, and county subdivisions which have been blocked.

Summary Tape File Microfiche

One of the best-kept secrets of the 1980 Census is the availability of extensive microfiche reports derived from the Bureau's Summary Tape Files. For most purposes, microfiche products are more detailed and more convenient to use than the printed Census reports. Tables are not organized by subject, but by geographic area. Researchers seeking a profile of a specific area will find all reported information in the same set of tables. A second benefit is increased detail; STF fiche provide more data for smaller geographic units, and population characteristics are broken down to a finer level. Many more racial groups are specified, for example, and the Hispanic population is divided into Mexican, Cuban, and other component groups. Finally, certain levels of geography can be found which are absent from the printed reports. The most notable of these are Block Groups and Block Numbering Areas.

Four microfiche products contain STF data from the 1980 Census. The two most popular are STF 1-A and STF 3-A. Both files display data in a geographic hierarchy, beginning with the state, and moving down to counties, Minor Civil Divisions, Tracts, and Block Groups. In this way, users can obtain profiles for larger units or for their component parts. STF 1-A cites 100% data and STF 3-A uses sample data. As a consequence, the sample report is lengthier; each table in 3-A consists of six pages of data, while 1-A provides two pages. STF 1-A lists 30 data categories, including age (by age group), race (for 15 racial groups), characteristics of persons under 18 years and over 65, household type, value of owner-occupied housing, and persons per room. STF 3-A lists 150 data categories from the long form. Among them are household size, group quarters population, ancestry, journey to work, educational attainment, and occupational group. A variety of basic cross-tabulations are found on 3-A, including age group by sex, family-type by presence of children, race by age, and family income by race. The other microfiche files are STF 1-C and STF 3-C. These provide remarkably detailed information at the national level, based on complete count and sample data, respectively. Exhibit 14-3, taken from the STF 3-A microfiche, shows the first page of the six-page table for the town of Amherst, New York. This presentation is well suited for geographic profiles, and the hierarchical arrangement enables quick review of neighboring areas.

The size of the complete STF fiche collection is staggering. While the complete output of printed reports from the 1980 Census approximates 300,000 pages, the output from the STF 1-A microfiche comprises 900,000 pages, and that of STF 3-A contains 2.7 million pages. Although the complete set costs several thousand dollars, users can purchase fiche for individual states, counties, or groups of counties.

New Products for 1990

The organization of major reports for 1990 will not be terribly different from their 1980 predecessors. Most differences represent improvements over the old products. The Bureau intends to release all products more quickly than in 1980, and most changes were designed with this goal in mind. In 1980, data release was hastened by the creation of *Advance Reports*, brief pamphlets containing key variables for each state. For 1990, an alternative method will be used. The Bureau will publish a new title in the *Population and Housing* series called *Summary Population and Housing Characteristics*. It will contain selected data from the 100% count, reported down to the local government level. The first is scheduled for release in late 1991, with one report for each state and one U.S. Summary report. This title will also partially replace the popular *Summary Characteristics for Governmental Units*. Because the latter publication also provided selected data from the long form, the Bureau will issue another new product called *Summary Social, Economic, and Housing Characteristics*. The second report will appear later in the production cycle. The two new products offer timely and convenient access to summary data.

Other new reports designed to speed data release are *General Population Characteristics for Metropolitan Statistical Areas* and *Social and Economic Characteristics for Metropolitan Statistical Areas*. With earlier Censuses, metropolitan areas which crossed state boundaries caused delays in the release of some state reports. This is because reports are issued on a flow basis, generally beginning with the smaller states. In the past, reports for smaller states were delayed if they contained SMSAs which crossed into larger states. The new report will provide complete count data for MSAs in their entirety, while the state reports will only cite data for the portion of the metropolitan areas within their state. Another advantage to the new titles is that they each consist of a single report, allowing quick comparisons of all MSAs. Similar reports will appear for Urbanized Areas, and for American Indian Reservations and Alaska Native Areas. The net effect is that most data will appear more quickly, but details for many of the largest MSAs will be delayed. On the other hand, MSA data will be easier to locate and compare.

Two additional changes affect the appearance of the former *Characteristics of the Population* set. The first is that Chapter A (*Number of Inhabitants*), will be moved to the combined *Population and Housing* series under a new title—*Population and Housing Unit Counts*. Once again, metro areas, Urbanized Areas, and Indian Reservations which cross state boundaries will be reported only partially in the individual state reports. The second change is the loss of Chapter D, which was dropped due to lack of use. With the exception of the change in the way cross-boundary units are reported, Chapters B and C will remain the same, but with different titles. Although changes might seem disruptive, they have been made for good cause, and experienced users should adapt to the new pattern with little difficulty.

Housing Reports will undergo changes similar to those of the Population Reports for exactly the same reasons. Chapters A and B will be much the same as in 1980, with the exception of the treatment of MSAs and

EXHIBIT 14-3. *Census of Population and Housing, Summary Tape File 3-A*

```
              CENSUS OF POPULATION AND HOUSING, 1980--SUMMARY TAPE FILE 3A
              (FOR DEFINITION OF ITEMS AND FOOTNOTES, SEE TECHNICAL DOCUMENTATION)

  SUMMARY LEVEL: 12  STATE: NEW YORK        COUNTY: ERIE           MCD/CCD: AMHERST

          PLACE:                      TRACT/BNA:        BG:    ED:

       URBAN/RURAL:      CD:   URBANIZED AREA:      WARD:      SMSA: 1280

     INDIAN RESERVATION/ANV:        INDIAN SUBRESERVATION:       SCSA:
```

1. PERSONS BY URBAN AND RURAL [50]		**14. PERSONS OF SPANISH ORIGIN BY RACE**		**19. PERSONS BY HOUSEHOLD TYPE AND RELATIONSHIP**	

TOTAL	108706
INSIDE URBANIZED AREAS	103092
RURAL	5614

2. UNWEIGHTED SAMPLE COUNT OF PERSONS	17759

3. 100-PERCENT COUNT OF PERSONS [38]	108706

4. HOUSING UNITS (INCLUDING VACANT SEASONAL AND MIGRATORY UNITS) BY URBAN AND RURAL [1,50]

TOTAL	38028
INSIDE URBANIZED AREAS	36345
RURAL	1683

5. UNWEIGHTED SAMPLE COUNT OF HOUSING UNITS (INCLUDING VACANT SEASONAL AND MIGRATORY UNITS) [1]

	6235

6. 100-PERCENT COUNT OF HOUSING UNITS (INCLUDING VACANT SEASONAL AND MIGRATORY UNITS) [1,38]

	38028

7. PERSONS IN RURAL AREAS BY FARM RESIDENCE (CURRENT FARM DEFINITION) [2]

RURAL FARM	15
NONFARM	5599

8. PERSONS IN RURAL AREAS BY FARM RESIDENCE (1970 CENSUS FARM DEFINITION) [2]

RURAL FARM	59
NONFARM	5555

9. FAMILIES	28536

10. HOUSEHOLDS [3]	37066

11. YEAR-ROUND HOUSING UNITS BY OCCUPANCY STATUS

TOTAL	38007
OCCUPIED [3]	36958
VACANT	1049

12. PERSONS BY RACE

WHITE	105022
BLACK	2704
AMERICAN INDIAN, ESKIMO AND ALEUT:	
AMERICAN INDIAN	107
ESKIMO	-
ALEUT	-
ASIAN AND PACIFIC ISLANDER: [4]	
JAPANESE	180
CHINESE	874
FILIPINO	148
KOREAN	382
ASIAN INDIAN	892
VIETNAMESE	99
HAWAIIAN	-
GUAMANIAN	-
SAMOAN	-
OTHER [47]	72
OTHER (RACE, N.E.C.): [5]	
SPANISH [6,47]	166
NOT SPANISH [47]	60

13. PERSONS BY SPANISH ORIGIN AND RACE

NOT OF SPANISH ORIGIN	107553
MEXICAN	203
PUERTO RICAN	260
CUBAN	94
OTHER SPANISH:	
WHITE, BLACK, AMERICAN INDIAN, ESKIMO, ALEUT, AND ASIAN AND PACIFIC ISLANDER [4]	539
OTHER (RACE, N.E.C.) [5]	57

14. PERSONS OF SPANISH ORIGIN BY RACE

TOTAL	1153
WHITE	971
BLACK	4
AMERICAN INDIAN, ESKIMO, ALEUT, AND ASIAN AND PACIFIC ISLANDER [4]	6
OTHER (RACE, N.E.C.) [5]	172

15. PERSONS BY SEX BY AGE

	TOTAL	FEMALE
UNDER 1 YEAR	1155	578
1 AND 2 YEARS	2211	1034
3 AND 4 YEARS	2494	1222
5 YEARS	1302	637
6 YEARS	1261	606
7 TO 9 YEARS	4328	2063
10 TO 13 YEARS	7458	3837
14 YEARS	1969	912
15 YEARS	2042	991
16 YEARS	2113	985
17 YEARS	2164	1116
18 YEARS	2512	1206
19 YEARS	2551	1172
20 YEARS	2219	1064
21 YEARS	1913	968
22 TO 24 YEARS	5265	2509
25 TO 29 YEARS	7464	3807
30 TO 34 YEARS	8553	4496
35 TO 44 YEARS	13227	6962
45 TO 54 YEARS	12944	6755
55 TO 59 YEARS	6317	3278
60 TO 61 YEARS	2186	1153
62 TO 64 YEARS	2996	1479
65 TO 74 YEARS	7062	4078
75 TO 84 YEARS	3893	2608
85 YEARS AND OVER	1107	873

16/17. PERSONS OF SPECIFIED RACES AND SPANISH ORIGIN BY SEX BY RACE AND SPANISH ORIGIN BY AGE [14]

	TOTAL	FEMALE
WHITE:		
UNDER 5 YEARS	5414	2669
5 TO 14 YEARS	15356	7616
15 TO 59 YEARS	65258	33392
60 TO 64 YEARS	5092	2588
65 YEARS AND OVER	11902	7455
BLACK:		
UNDER 5 YEARS	140	17
5 TO 14 YEARS	478	240
15 TO 59 YEARS	1956	1024
60 TO 64 YEARS	62	22
65 YEARS AND OVER	68	49
AMERICAN INDIAN, ESKIMO AND ALEUT:		
UNDER 5 YEARS	-	-
5 TO 14 YEARS	10	10
15 TO 59 YEARS	86	36
60 TO 64 YEARS	-	-
65 YEARS AND OVER	11	5
ASIAN AND PACIFIC ISLANDER: [4]		
UNDER 5 YEARS	274	132
5 TO 14 YEARS	436	167
15 TO 59 YEARS	1828	781
60 TO 64 YEARS	28	22
65 YEARS AND OVER	81	50
SPANISH ORIGIN (OF ANY RACE):		
UNDER 5 YEARS	158	81
5 TO 14 YEARS	201	119
15 TO 59 YEARS	753	381
60 TO 64 YEARS	10	4
65 YEARS AND OVER	31	31

18. HOUSEHOLDS BY PERSONS IN HOUSEHOLD [7]

1 PERSON	7348
2 PERSONS	11900
3 PERSONS	6426
4 PERSONS	6304
5 PERSONS	3203
6 OR MORE PERSONS	1885

22. MEAN NUMBER OF OWN CHILDREN BY FAMILY TYPE [10]

IN MARRIED-COUPLE FAMILY	1.0
IN FAMILY WITH MALE HOUSEHOLDER, NO WIFE PRESENT	.5
IN FAMILY WITH FEMALE HOUSEHOLDER, NO HUSBAND PRESENT	.9

19. PERSONS BY HOUSEHOLD TYPE AND RELATIONSHIP

IN FAMILY HOUSEHOLD:	
HOUSEHOLDER	28536
SPOUSE	24958
OTHER RELATIVES [8]	39645
NONRELATIVES [9]	549
IN NONFAMILY HOUSEHOLD:	
MALE HOUSEHOLDER	3084
FEMALE HOUSEHOLDER	5446
NONRELATIVES [9]	1515
IN GROUP QUARTERS:	
INMATE OF INSTITUTION	947
OTHER	4026

20PT/21PT. FAMILY HOUSEHOLDS BY PRESENCE OF OWN CHILDREN BY RACE AND SPANISH ORIGIN OF HOUSEHOLDER BY FAMILY TYPE [10,11,21]

	WITH OWN CHILDREN	WITHOUT OWN CHILDREN
TOTAL:		
MARRIED-COUPLE FAMILY	12497	12569
FAMILY WITH MALE HOUSE- HOLDER, NO WIFE PRESENT	231	514
FAMILY WITH FEMALE HOUSE- HOLDER, NO HUSBAND PRESENT	1475	1250
WHITE:		
MARRIED-COUPLE FAMILY	11729	12212
FAMILY WITH MALE HOUSE- HOLDER, NO WIFE PRESENT	202	471
FAMILY WITH FEMALE HOUSE- HOLDER, NO HUSBAND PRESENT	1344	1206
BLACK:		
MARRIED-COUPLE FAMILY	316	212
FAMILY WITH MALE HOUSE- HOLDER, NO WIFE PRESENT	23	5
FAMILY WITH FEMALE HOUSE- HOLDER, NO HUSBAND PRESENT	118	38
AMERICAN INDIAN, ESKIMO, AND ALEUT:		
MARRIED-COUPLE FAMILY	13	27
FAMILY WITH MALE HOUSE- HOLDER, NO WIFE PRESENT	-	-
FAMILY WITH FEMALE HOUSE- HOLDER, NO HUSBAND PRESENT	6	-
ASIAN AND PACIFIC ISLANDER: [4]		
MARRIED-COUPLE FAMILY	419	107
FAMILY WITH MALE HOUSE- HOLDER, NO WIFE PRESENT	6	38
FAMILY WITH FEMALE HOUSE- HOLDER, NO HUSBAND PRESENT	-	6
SPANISH ORIGIN (OF ANY RACE):		
MARRIED-COUPLE FAMILY	112	61
FAMILY WITH MALE HOUSE- HOLDER, NO WIFE PRESENT	-	6
FAMILY WITH FEMALE HOUSE- HOLDER, NO HUSBAND PRESENT	13	17

20PT/21PT. NONFAMILY HOUSEHOLDS BY RACE AND SPANISH ORIGIN OF HOUSEHOLDER [11,21]

TOTAL	8530
WHITE	8263
BLACK	117
AMERICAN INDIAN, ESKIMO, AND ALEUT	6
ASIAN AND PACIFIC ISLANDER [4]	126
SPANISH ORIGIN (OF ANY RACE)	63

23/24/25. SUBFAMILIES BY SUBFAMILY TYPE AND PRESENCE OF OWN CHILDREN [10]

MARRIED-COUPLE SUBFAMILY:	
WITH OWN CHILDREN	52
MEAN NUMBER OF OWN CHILDREN	1.6
WITHOUT OWN CHILDREN	119
FATHER-CHILD SUBFAMILY	5
MOTHER-CHILD SUBFAMILY	134
PERSONS PER SUBFAMILY	2.3

26. PERSONS 15 YEARS AND OVER BY SEX BY MARITAL STATUS

	MALE	FEMALE
SINGLE	12920	12066
NOW MARRIED, EXCEPT SEPARATED	25579	25499
SEPARATED	457	652
WIDOWED	800	5242
DIVORCED	1232	2051

```
  SUMMARY TAPE FILE 3A    ERIE, NEW YORK                              PAGE:  5205 A
```

Reprinted from *Census of Population and Housing, Summary Tape File 3-A,* published by the U.S. Bureau of the Census.

related cross-boundary areas. For both series, *Subject Reports* will appear as before, though more are planned for both. Microfiche for STF 1-A and 3-A will once again be available. *Census Tracts* and *Block Statistics* will appear virtually unchanged, but will be larger because data on BNAs will be published, and because the entire country has been blocked. Map products will also be similar, with the notable exception that Block maps will no longer be issued by the Government Printing Office. Instead, interested individuals can place special orders to the Bureau. Customized maps will be produced on demand using TIGER. However, recent public opposition has caused the Bureau to rethink its position on Block maps. A series of outline maps on CD-ROM is now planned, but as of this writing, no details are available.

The 1990 Census is the first for which sophisticated analysis can be performed without large computers. CD-ROMs will enable researchers to access greater amounts of data in greater detail, and to create customized reports and maps. The first CD-ROMs were released in the spring of 1991. The PL 94-171 files contain the preliminary data used for state redistricting, and provide complete count data to the Block level. The ten disks, arranged by groups of states, represent the most detailed data ever available to end-users at such an early date. Other CD-ROM products include extracts from the TIGER/Line files and disks for six STF files. One of the latter products contains summary data from the STF 3-B tapes, which will result in zip-code-level data being published by the Bureau for the first time. Excluding the proposed Block maps and the TIGER/Line files, approximately 53 CD-ROM disks will be available for the 1990 Census.

The Bureau originally intended to offer little programming support for its CD-ROM products. Menu-driven software would allow users to produce basic, pre-formatted reports for various geographies, but additional manipulation would require commercial software (preferably *dBase III*). A compromise was reached for the PL 94-171 disks, however. Included with every disk is the Bureau's *EXTRACT* program, which is fairly easy to use and provides extensive searching, limiting, sorting, and arithmetic capabilities. As of this writing, the Bureau has not determined whether *EXTRACT* will be available on forthcoming demographic disks.

As in previous decades, computer tape products will be released before printed reports or other media, and 100% data will appear before sample data. As of June 1991, tapes are available for the PL 94-171 redistricting data and for STF 1-A. The first printed report will be *Summary Population and Housing Characteristics* (in late 1991), followed by *Population and Housing Unit Counts*. The first sample data are due in early 1992, and by the end of the following year, all major products should be available. The Bureau will issue revised calendars of release dates as conditions change, and newly released products will be listed in the Bureau's *Monthly Product Announcements* newsletter. A better way to check on new products and anticipated release dates is to consult *CENDATA*, the Bureau's online database. More will be said about *CENDATA* later in the chapter.

POPULATION ESTIMATES AND PROJECTIONS

No population enumeration, however massive, can provide researchers with all the information they need. Many characteristics are not studied by the Bureau in sufficient detail, and others are not measured at all. Beyond that is the unavoidable problem of stale information; in a rapidly changing society, ten-year intervals are inadequate for tracking current trends or anticipating future demographic shifts. To combat these deficiencies, numerous organizations conduct sample surveys or employ other statistical techniques to arrive at population estimates and projections. Federal and state agencies, universities, nonprofit research centers, and commercial publishers are all involved in generating population estimates and projections. The Bureau itself compiles estimates at the national, state, county, and sub-county levels, and projections at the national and regional levels. Two major tasks confronting population analysts are computing estimates of current population between Census years, and creating projections of future population trends. This section will focus on the Bureau's programs and publications in this area. Chapter 17 will return to the topic of population estimates, highlighting some of the leading private sector publications available.

Estimation and Projection Techniques

The Bureau conducts a monthly Current Population Survey to estimate characteristics of the national population, but the sample is nowhere near large enough to provide usable local information. A more direct source of state and local data is an actual census conducted in a non-Census year. Several states perform their own mid-decade census programs to obtain current data. An alternative to a state-sponsored census is for a local commu-

nity to pay the Bureau to mount a "Special Census." Any municipality may contract with the Bureau to do this at any time, though the number of Special Censuses increases as the decennial data become more dated. During the mid-decade years, the Bureau may be called upon to conduct several hundred of these enumerations. The results are no longer published by the Bureau.

In cases where mid-decade censuses are unavailable, the starting point for generating local population estimates or projections must be the decennial Census itself. Its breadth of coverage, degree of specificity, and unsurpassed geographic detail make it a benchmark for any demographic analysis. Because the Census is the only complete enumeration of the U.S. population, demographers must look to less complete sources of information to shed light on current conditions. By applying mathematical models to local data, demographers can estimate what has taken place since the previous decennial Census.

A prime source of raw demographic data is the tabulation of vital events. In the strictest sense, vital statistics cover the compulsory recording of births, deaths, and fetal deaths, but the definition can be extended to include statistics on marriages, divorces, and the incidence of sickness and disease. Vital statistics provide a record of the flow of natural population changes, as opposed to the Census, which provides a static picture of the population at a moment in time. Vital statistics are extremely important to demographic analysis because they show changes in the total number of people on a continuing basis, they describe major characteristics of the people involved, and they are often available for small geographic areas. For approximately half of the incorporated Places and Minor Civil Divisions in the U.S., vital statistics are collected at the municipal level; data for the remaining areas are recorded at the county level. Local records are sent to the state bureaus of vital statistics, which then forward the tabulations to the National Center of Health Statistics. Data are reported in its *Vital Statistics of the United States*. Due to the plodding process of national reporting, data in this annual publication typically describe events from four years earlier.

A second source of demographic data comes from administrative records kept by other federal agencies. The Social Security Administration keeps statistics on Medicare recipients, for example, and the Department of Defense has data on persons serving in the armed forces. Demographic information collected by the Internal Revenue Service includes the number of income tax filers and their dependents, the place of residence for each, and income data. Information from these three agencies comprise an important source of current data for the government's population estimates. As with the Bureau's own files, administrative records are strictly confidential; only summary statistics are shared with other agencies.

A third source is data collected at the state and local level. Governments and private organizations tabulate a variety of statistics, which then can be applied to demographic analysis. The number of housing starts, registered voters, property taxpayers, and electric meters in use are all examples of this category, referred to as symptomatic data.

Many statistical techniques have been developed for estimating local population, and the Bureau utilizes several. A simple, yet effective model is called the housing unit method. Local data on building permits and demolitions are combined with estimates of vacancy rates to determine the net change in occupied housing units. The result is multiplied by average household size (from the decennial Census) to obtain a population estimate. Because the group quarters segment of the population is not included in household or housing unit data, its size must be calculated separately and added to the estimate.

A more sophisticated method is regression analysis, which generates a value for a dependent variable based upon its relationship to one or more known variables. The final equation is determined mathematically, by drawing a line which best fits a cluster of observed variables. For example, suppose the demographer decides that the most important factors affecting local population growth are the number of manufacturing plants in the area, the local birth rate, and the number of property taxpayers. By comparing annual historical data for the three independent variables with historical population figures, the computer can generate an equation which estimates the relationship between those variables and total population. All types of symptomatic data can be used as independent variables in a regression study. Examples include school enrollment, labor force, motor vehicle registrations, and building permits.

A final technique of population estimation is called the component method. Component analysis examines the additions to and subtractions from the total "inventory" of people. The two components are natural change and net migration. Natural change consists of the difference between the number of people who are born during a time period and the number who die. Because the

recording of vital statistics is compulsory, this information is readily available for counties, and in many cases for sub-county units. Net migration is the difference between the number of people moving into an area and those moving out. At the national level this means immigrants coming into the U.S. and American residents who are leaving the country. For smaller areas, net migration measures the number of people moving from one locality to another, called internal migration.

Net migration is far more difficult to measure than natural increase or decrease. Because the decennial Census asks respondents where they resided five years prior to the Census date, a picture of migration patterns can be obtained. This is combined with data from individual tax returns. The IRS provides the Bureau with computer tapes which measure "Area-to-Area Migration Flow." The tapes compare each tax filer's return from one year to the next via their social security numbers. The place of residence for both years is then scanned to determine how many individuals moved during that time, and of those, which ones migrated out of their area. The number of exemptions claimed on each return (excluding additional exemptions for blindness and age) are then totaled. In this way, a net migration rate is estimated for every area.

How does the Bureau employ these methods to create local population estimates? Actually, a combination of techniques is employed. Sub-county estimates are generated by using component analysis, with adjustments for group quarters populations. Results of any recent special or local census are incorporated into the current estimate. County estimates are generated through a different technique which utilizes the assistance of state agencies in collecting data. For each state, the Bureau works with a single designated agency—typically a state bureau of vital statistics, commerce department, or division of budget and planning—which provides county data used in the model. Population estimates are calculated using four independent methods, which are then reconciled to obtain a revised figure. The first technique is a regression model using births, deaths, school enrollments, auto registrations, and retail sales as variables. The second method is a variation of the component technique which uses both vital statistics and school enrollment. The third is called the administrative records method, which utilizes IRS and Medicare data for each county. Only 30% of the population over age 65 file income tax returns, so Medicare records are viewed as a much more comprehensive source of data on this segment of the population. The final technique is the housing unit method, which examines the number of building

permits and housing demolitions in the county, together with residential electric meter connections. Because estimates of larger areas are generally more accurate, and because the county estimates are arrived at in four different ways, sub-county population estimates are "controlled" to the county total (i.e., sub-county estimates are adjusted so they sum to the independently generated county totals).

The Bureau also uses mathematical models to create population projections. The most commonly used method is a variation of the component model. Demographers look at age cohorts—all people born in the same year—and then "age" each cohort year by year into the future. Everyone born in 1980, for example, will be 20 years old in the year 2000, assuming they live to that age. By applying age-specific mortality rates to each cohort, the number of survivors at each point in time can be projected. In a similar fashion, age-specific birth and migration rates are also applied to each cohort as it moves through its life cycle.

All of the Bureau's estimation and projection methods have limitations, both in the data used and the assumptions employed. For example, IRS data are flawed because individuals who file income tax returns may not be representative of the total population, and an individual's mailing address may not reflect his or her place of residence. And because cohort aging is so dependent upon age-specific information, projections are extremely sensitive to changing population characteristics.

Current Population and Housing Reports

The Bureau publishes a number of reports designed to provide current information between decennial Censuses. These series are called *Current Population Reports* and *Current Housing Reports*. Both appear in several parts at varying intervals. Coverage in most is limited to the national and regional level. Summary data from many of the current reports can also be found on *CENDATA*, the Bureau's online database.

Three types of *Current Population Reports* are produced. The first provides recent information on national population characteristics, and is based upon monthly, annual, or nonrecurring sample surveys. The two ongoing surveys conducted by the Bureau are the Current Population Survey (CPS) and the Survey of Income and Program Participation (SIPP). The CPS is a monthly household sample survey, and is used to collect

unemployment data for the U.S. Bureau of Labor Statistics as well as demographic data for the Bureau. A core of questions are asked every month, and a variety of special questions are asked annually, on a rotating basis. For example, the June survey contains questions on fertility and expected births, and the October survey asks about school enrollment. Detailed data from the CPS are available on computer tape dating back to 1973. The tape is especially useful for data on the states and the 44 largest MSAs. Printed reports contain much less detail, and generally provide data for the entire country or regions. SIPP, the other major survey, is collected partly on behalf of the Social Security Administration. It collects data on sources and uses of income as they relate to household characteristics, covering both money income and in-kind benefits. A major difference in survey methodology is that each participating household is interviewed approximately eight times over a two-and-a-half year period. SIPP data are also available on tape.

The second type of report calculates population estimates for the nation and for states and local areas. These reports utilize the complex estimation techniques described earlier. The third category of report produces long-term population projections for the nation, again based on statistical models.

Major titles in the *Current Housing Reports* and *Current Population Reports* series are introduced below. Each type of report is identified by a series number. Non-Census sources of population estimates and projections are described in Chapters 15 and 17.

Local Population Estimates (Current Population Reports, Series P-26) Annual or Biennial.

The Bureau's official population estimates for local areas appear in this series. The P-26 reports actually contain two types of date, covering estimates for counties and sub-county areas; the two are calculated using different techniques, as described above. County-level figures are published annually in individual reports for each state, and sub-county data are published biennially in the same fashion.

Series P-26 actually appears in four parts. *County Population Estimates* (Part A) is a single-volume pamphlet published annually. It provides data from the most recent decennial Census, plus estimates as of July 1st for the latest two years, and the percent change from the base year. Researchers should note that the data appear first in preliminary form; slightly revised figures are published in the following year's issue, as well as in other parts of the series. *Population Estimates for Metropolitan Statistical Areas* (Part B) is another single-volume pamphlet,

containing data derived from Part A. It is similar in format, but includes components of population change— births, deaths, and net migration. Part C consists of a set of 51 pamphlets and is called *Estimates of the Population of [State] Counties and Metropolitan Areas*. It contains the revised figures referred to above, but is published after considerable delay; the 1985 data appeared in 1988, for example. Each pamphlet gives detailed statistics on a single state, including annual estimates for every year since the latest decennial count, the percent change, and components of change. Finally, the fourth segment is called *Population and Per Capita Income Estimates for Counties and Incorporated Places* (Part SC). This biennial publication is issued as five volumes, arranged by Census Region. The title is misleading because it gives data for unincorporated MCDs as well as for Places. Sub-county estimates are provided for both total population and per capita personal income.

Population Estimates and Projections (Current Population Reports, Series P-25) Monthly or Irregular.

The Bureau also calculates population estimates for the U.S. and the 50 states, as well as projections for the same areas. This series reports the results of these studies, presenting the data in several types of publications. The first is a monthly release which cites the most current estimate of the U.S. population as a whole, based on the component method. A second type of publication provides estimated data on basic characteristics of national and state populations. This includes an annual report on state estimates by age, race, and sex. A third category consists of short- and long-term population projections for the nation and for states. National projections are published every five years, under the title *Projections of the Population of the United States by Age, Sex, and Race*. The projections are tabulated using the cohort component method. Because of the uncertainty regarding future fertility rates, life expectancies, and related factors, the Bureau calculates three major sets of projections based on varying assumptions. Each of the three major assumptions is further adjusted to create a series of 30 separate population projections. Results are given by sex, race, and age group, but the most detailed data are provided for the middle set of projections. Projections are calculated for each year up to 25 years in the future, then in five year increments for the next 50 to 75 years. The series also includes periodic reports on projections at the state level, nation-wide projections of households and families, and projections for the Hispanic populations. Also covered in the series are background reports which explain the methodology for estimates and projections, and which evaluate the accuracy of earlier estimates.

Population Characteristics (Current Population Reports, Series P-20) Annual or Irregular.

A series of reports on various characteristics of the national population. Reports recur with varying frequency, but most appear annually. The premier title in the series is *Household and Family Characteristics*, which is based on the Annual Demographic Survey, a supplement to the CPS conducted in March. It reports on the size and composition of households and families, with data presented for the nation and by region. Approximately eight additional annual surveys appear in this series, together with some irregular publications. Examples of other annual titles are *Marital Status and Living Arrangements, Geographic Mobility*, and *School Enrollment*. A survey of *Voting and Registration* is conducted every two years, following congressional elections.

Consumer Income (Current Population Reports, Series P-60) Annual or Irregular.

Recurring reports on personal income characteristics at the national level. The major title in this series is *Money Income of Households, Families, and Persons in the United States*. This annual survey reports on median money income and relates income to household, family, and individual characteristics. Another important annual survey is *Poverty in the United States*, which looks at the incidence of poverty and compares demographic characteristics of individuals, households, and families above and below the poverty level.

Household Economic Studies (Current Population Reports, Series P-70) Irregular.

The P-70 series consists of special onetime studies based on SIPP data. Most reports examine the relationship between household economic status and social characteristics, with an emphasis on households receiving government benefits. Examples of reports are *Who's Minding the Kids?*, which studies child care arrangements, and *What's It Worth?*, which examines the relationship between educational attainment and economic status.

Special Studies (Current Population Reports, Series P-23) Irregular.

This series covers onetime studies usually conducted under contract for another federal agency. Studies can be based on sample surveys or special analyses of the decennial Census tapes. Examples of recent titles are *Migration Between the United States and Canada, Computer Use in the United States*, and *America's Centenarians*.

American Housing Survey (Current Housing Reports, Series H-150) Biennial.

This fascinating report is based on personal interviews with household residents across the country. The survey is conducted on behalf of the U.S. Department of Housing and Urban Development (HUD), and the national sample consists of approximately 55,000 households. For many years it was known as the *Annual Housing Survey*; now it is conducted once every two years. The survey provides a detailed look at the nation's housing stock, reporting on many of the same structural and financial characteristics covered in the decennial Census. These include type of unit, tenure, property value or rent paid, fuels used, presence of air conditioning, and other familiar attributes. The report also covers demographic data such as household composition, characteristics of householders, and personal income.

What makes the survey unique, however, is that it deals with issues of neighborhood and housing quality which are not seen in other Census publications. Characteristics of neighborhood quality, as provided by survey respondents, include noise levels, commercial activities, odors or smoke, trash, vandalism, and boarded-up buildings. Measures of building quality include the condition of plumbing, electrical and heating systems, and interior floors and ceilings. The survey also asks specific questions of recent movers—why they moved, why they chose their present location, and characteristics of their previous residence. Data are presented at the national and regional levels. Separate tables provide information by race, Spanish Origin, owner- versus renter-occupied units, Central Cities versus suburbs, and metropolitan versus nonmetropolitan information. Cross-classifications are tabulated and an excellent table finding guide leads users to the appropriate data. The survey does have its limitations, however. Not only is the survey now conducted less frequently, the printed report is less detailed. In earlier years, it was published in five volumes; now it appears as a smaller, single-volume publication. Another drawback is the delay in reporting; the publication typically appears about three years after the survey is taken.

Housing Characteristics of Selected Metropolitan Areas (Current Housing Reports, Series H-170) Annual, on a rotating basis.

This series provides data similar to that in Series H-150, but for individual metropolitan areas. Unlike the national survey, it doesn't include characteristics of nonmetropolitan areas. The results are based on completely different samples than the national study. At one

time, the series studied more than 60 metropolitan areas, with each one conducted every three years. Now it covers 44 MSAs, on a four-year rotation. A separate publication is issued for each area, plus an annual summary based on the 11 MSAs studied that year. As with its national counterpart, it takes several years for the results to be published. A less noticeable change has been the reduction of the sample size for most areas. Despite its deficiencies, it is an excellent source of comparative data on American cities.

Housing Vacancies and Homeownership (*Current Housing Reports*, Series H-111) Quarterly and Annual.

This survey presents data on vacant housing units by type of unit (rental and homeowner housing). Reported characteristics include duration of vacancy, number of bedrooms, plumbing facilities, year built, and monthly rent or sales price asked. Historical tables compare vacancy rates over the past 30 years, and current rates are cited by type of unit. The report also includes a brief table comparing historical rates of homeownership, and current rates by geographic area.

PITFALLS IN USING CENSUS INFORMATION

Census publications are especially vulnerable to misinterpretation by data users. Misuse of Census data by the business world and those in public life abounds. A press release from the Bureau can be reported by the media in so many ways that the original facts become unrecognizable. Researchers can do little to counteract the inherent limitations of Census data other than to be aware of them. However, errors in using the data can be avoided by taking the time to understand important concepts, becoming familiar with the idiosyncrasies of table layout, and exercising due care.

One of the most common mistakes in quoting Census reports results from incorrectly using sample data. Only a small portion of the population receives the long-from questionnaire, but some of the most important data fields are estimates obtained from this sample. The Bureau utilizes a variable sampling method, based on the population of the area surveyed. For the 1980 Census, one in every six people received the long form in urban areas; in areas with population less than 2,500, one out of two people received it. Simplistically stated, estimates of the total population are generated by multiplying sample results by 6 in urban areas and by 2 in rural areas.

Published reports are generated from the STF computer tapes; STF 1 and 2 report data from the complete count, while STF 3 and 4 report sample data. The publications based on the sample tapes use that data to generate estimates for all numbers appearing in the report, even if 100% figures are available on another tape. For example, Chapter C of *Characteristics of the Population* (one of the sample reports) presents estimated data on total population and number of households, even though the actual counts for these characteristics appear in Chapter A and Chapter B. Because Census sampling is very precise, estimates and total counts can sometimes be equivalent, but they are frequently not. This is especially true of small levels of geography—Tracts, smaller MCDs and Places, and counties of less than 2,500 people. An additional problem is that estimates in the housing reports can differ from the estimates in the population reports measuring the same characteristic. Discrepancies are particularly vexing in the few publications, such as *Census Tracts,* which publish data from both types of STF files. This results in sample tables and complete count tables in the same book. The user can find three different numbers for the same characteristic in the same publication: a complete count figure, an estimate from a population table, and an estimate from a housing table. The solution is a cardinal rule of Census research—use only complete count publications for complete count data. The basic 100% reports for 1980 are Chapters A and B of the population series, Chapter A of the housing series, and the STF 1-A microfiche. Once again, readers are referred to Figure 14-A for a list questions in each category.

The importance of understanding Census geography and terminology has already been covered, but it is worth repeating. Mistakes are made easily if the terms and concepts are not fully understood. Because definitions and geographic boundaries change over time, it is also unwise to compare Census data from one decade to another without determining conceptual differences. The definition of "rural" has changed over the years, for example, and geographic boundaries often shift dramatically.

Many errors in using Census reports result from reading tables incorrectly. A common error is to cite what appears to be characteristics of the whole population, when the table only covers characteristics of a specific group. For example, Table 121 of *Characteristics of the Population* is titled "Occupation of Employed Persons," yet the same table is repeated five times elsewhere: Table 129 (Whites only), Table 135 (Blacks), Table 141 (American Indians), and so forth. A similar mistake comes from

using data for an MSA or Urbanized Area when data for the Central City is wanted. This can happen when the name of the city and SMSA are the same, which is often the case.

Exhibit 14-4, taken from Chapter B of *Characteristics of the Population* for Nebraska, illustrates how easy it is to make this mistake. The researcher seeking data on the city of Lincoln should be looking at the right-hand side of the table rather than the left-hand side, which contains data on the Lincoln Urbanized Area. A third source of confusion in reading tables comes from failure to note indentations in table stubs (i.e., the column of labels which describes the data found on each row of the table). When a characteristic is divided into more specific subcategories, the subdivisions are represented by indentations in the stub, but the data in the table itself are not indented. Once again, Exhibit 14-4 illustrates this problem. Notice that the number of householders is broken down by age category, but the total number of householders is also given. The distinction is represented by the format of the stub. In the case of the Lincoln Urbanized Area, the user could easily add the total value of 65,377 householders to the seven age groupings, which results in double counting.

Another common mistake related to table layout occurs when Tracts, Places, or MSAs are split by political boundaries. Depending on which table is used, the entire unit or only part of the split unit may be reported. For example, the New York City PMSA includes counties in Connecticut and New Jersey. Some tables may give figures only for the part of the PMSA which lies within New York State, others provide data for the whole PMSA, and still others subdivide the information by each of the three states. The problem will become more pronounced in the 1990 publications, because the portion of any split statistical units outside the state's boundary will not be listed in the publications for that state. Split units are frequently encountered in *Census Tracts*, where Tracts are displayed for major cities first, then for the balance of each county. Split units are always clearly labeled in Census publications, but is easy to misread the tables.

A trickier pitfall involves data carried onto another page without the user's knowledge. A good example appears in the tables for "Selected Ancestry Groups," which divide data into single ancestry and multiple ancestry. A researcher looking for the number of German-Americans might stop at the single ancestry category for "German" and fail to notice the category for "German and other group(s)" (e.g., German/Irish, German/Polish, etc.) listed on the following page. The mistakes cited above may seem foolish, yet they are made frequently by reasonably sophisticated data users. Such problems can be side-stepped by paying careful attention to the structure of the table, and the clues found in their titles, headings, stubs, and footnotes.

A more difficult problem to guard against is making unwarranted assumptions when interpreting data. The Bureau offers an example of how even they have been led astray in analyzing results. In the 1970 Census, the section on "Journey To Work" identified respondents who said they lived in San Francisco, worked in Viet Nam, and commuted by car. The confusion resulted from the wording of the questions, one of which asked, "Where did you work last week?" Recently returning war veterans answered the questions properly, but their answers produced strange results. To avoid such problems, the researcher must refer to the way questions are phrased on the Census form as well as definitions of terms.

Two final pitfalls are somewhat related: summing component parts to reach a total figure and dealing with percents. The first problem arises when individual items on a table are not parts of the same whole. An example can be seen in Exhibit 14-4. Using the data in the left-hand column, the user might attempt to add together the number of white persons, black persons, and persons of Spanish Origin to obtain the total number of people in the Lincoln Urbanized Area, as follows:

$$165,681 + 3,500 + 2,775 = 171,956$$

However, the first row in the column indicates that the actual number of persons is 173,550. First, Spanish Origin is not a racial characteristic. Hispanic people may be white, black, Asian, or any other race. Second, several racial groups are not shown on the table, including American Indians and Asians.

A final pitfall is the problem of misusing percentages and other comparative measures. Many Census tables present data in percents, so it is important to determine just what percentage is being reported. Is a table with data on women workers citing the percent of all women who are in the labor force, or the percentage of the labor force which is made up of women? Caution is particularly advised when calculating your own percentages based on values in a table. Make sure the numerator and denominator compare what you want them to. If you are measuring the percentage of housing units with complete kitchen facilities, make certain both numerator and denominator represent all housing units, and are not taken from a table which measures Occupied Housing Units only. This type of error is likely to occur when comparing data from two different tables, but it can also happen within a single table.

EXHIBIT 14-4. *Census of Population, Chapter B: General Population Characteristics*

Table 27. Household Relationship of Persons by Race and Spanish Origin for Areas and Places: 1980—Con.

[For meaning of symbols, see Introduction. For definitions of terms, see appendixes A and B]

SCSA's SMSA's Urbanized Areas Places of 50,000 or More and Central Cities of SMSA's	Lincoln, Nebr.	Omaha, Nebr.–Iowa Total	Iowa (pt.)	Nebraska (pt.)	Sioux City, Iowa–Nebr.–S. Dak. Total	Iowa (pt.)	Nebraska (pt.)	South Dakota (pt.)	Places Lincoln city	Omaha city
Total persons	173 550	512 438	62 173	450 265	96 746	84 419	10 335	1 992	171 932	314 255
In households	161 380	501 134	61 385	439 749	93 973	81 786	10 195	1 992	160 007	306 246
Householder	65 377	184 758	22 623	162 135	35 331	30 918	3 738	675	64 934	118 465
15 to 24 years	10 584	20 444	2 468	17 976	3 625	3 076	445	104	10 519	12 942
25 to 34 years	18 026	48 261	4 996	43 265	8 204	6 977	1 039	188	17 813	27 333
35 to 44 years	9 414	31 761	3 361	28 400	5 034	4 368	567	99	9 354	17 437
45 to 54 years	8 107	27 597	3 620	23 977	5 085	4 489	495	101	8 057	17 862
55 to 64 years	7 833	24 908	3 444	21 464	5 471	4 879	482	110	7 803	18 013
65 to 74 years	6 438	18 683	2 688	15 995	4 365	3 913	402	50	6 420	14 484
75 years and over	4 975	13 104	2 046	11 058	3 547	3 216	308	23	4 968	10 394
Family householder: Male	35 753	107 452	13 714	93 738	21 167	18 398	2 299	470	35 383	62 606
Female	6 413	23 348	2 954	20 394	4 213	3 740	401	72	6 392	16 378
Nonfamily householder: Male	10 051	22 783	2 187	20 596	3 672	3 179	413	80	10 019	15 973
Female	13 160	31 175	3 768	27 407	6 279	5 601	625	53	13 140	23 508
Spouse	35 735	106 998	13 605	93 393	21 178	18 452	2 271	455	35 360	62 215
Child	47 504	178 358	21 200	157 158	31 893	27 589	3 552	752	47 000	104 170
Other relatives	4 163	16 159	2 296	13 863	3 015	2 627	324	64	4 139	11 248
Nonrelatives	8 601	14 861	1 661	13 200	2 556	2 200	310	46	8 574	10 148
Inmate of institution	3 334	4 714	757	3 957	1 429	1 292	137	–	3 094	3 366
Other, in group quarters	8 836	6 590	31	6 559	1 344	1 341	3	–	8 831	4 643
Persons 75 years and over living alone	2 992	7 786	1 230	6 556	2 066	1 875	184	7	2 988	6 220
Persons per household	2.47	2.71	2.71	2.71	2.66	2.65	2.73	2.95	2.46	2.59
Persons per family	3.07	3.31	3.23	3.32	3.21	3.20	3.28	3.35	3.07	3.25
White persons	165 681	456 674	60 960	395 714	93 126	81 253	9 957	1 916	164 155	268 591
In households	154 561	446 817	60 198	386 619	90 446	78 709	9 821	1 916	153 249	261 467
Householder	63 019	167 273	22 264	145 009	34 320	30 041	3 621	658	62 590	103 740
15 to 24 years	10 086	17 900	2 427	15 473	3 480	2 948	431	101	10 022	10 870
25 to 34 years	17 151	43 255	4 897	38 358	7 915	6 734	1 000	181	16 945	23 434
35 to 44 years	9 021	28 370	3 299	25 071	4 852	4 213	544	95	8 965	14 756
45 to 54 years	7 857	24 928	3 560	21 368	4 940	4 353	488	99	7 809	15 492
55 to 64 years	7 644	23 066	3 415	19 651	5 367	4 789	469	109	7 614	16 244
65 to 74 years	6 339	17 384	2 644	14 740	4 280	3 838	392	50	6 321	13 255
75 years and over	4 921	12 370	2 022	10 348	3 486	3 166	297	23	4 914	9 689
Family householder: Male	34 671	100 098	13 527	86 571	20 686	17 994	2 234	458	34 314	56 950
Female	6 007	17 939	2 877	15 062	3 931	3 479	385	67	5 986	11 506
Nonfamily householder: Male	9 469	20 261	2 145	18 116	3 532	3 060	392	80	9 438	13 787
Female	12 872	28 975	3 715	25 260	6 171	5 508	610	53	12 852	21 497
Spouse	34 774	99 786	13 408	86 378	20 721	18 071	2 207	443	34 414	57 016
Child	44 966	154 560	20 716	133 844	30 368	26 266	3 392	710	44 490	84 441
Other relatives	3 721	12 356	2 199	10 157	2 685	2 323	302	60	3 699	7 846
Nonrelatives	8 081	12 842	1 611	11 231	2 352	2 008	299	45	8 056	8 424
Inmate of institution	2 791	4 190	733	3 457	1 395	1 262	133	–	2 581	2 969
Other, in group quarters	8 329	5 667	29	5 638	1 285	1 282	3	–	8 325	4 155
Persons 75 years and over living alone	2 959	7 383	1 217	6 166	2 036	1 851	178	7	2 955	5 831
Persons per household	2.46	2.68	2.71	2.67	2.64	2.63	2.72	2.92	2.45	2.52
Persons per family	3.06	3.27	3.22	3.28	3.19	3.18	3.26	3.32	3.05	3.18
Black persons	3 500	43 794	424	43 370	1 172	1 120	45	7	3 444	37 864
In households	2 900	42 802	402	42 400	1 123	1 071	45	...	2 868	37 286
Householder	1 145	14 330	139	14 191	386	358	26	...	1 137	12 521
15 to 24 years	234	1 975	18	1 957	52	49	3	...	233	1 649
25 to 34 years	399	3 867	18	3 849	77	70	6	...	395	3 163
35 to 44 years	178	2 782	22	2 760	55	54	1	...	176	2 301
45 to 54 years	127	2 259	23	2 236	65	63	1	...	126	2 070
55 to 64 years	112	1 610	11	1 599	51	48	3	...	112	1 570
65 to 74 years	68	1 189	29	1 160	50	45	5	...	68	1 142
75 years and over	27	648	18	630	36	29	7	...	27	626
Family householder: Male	437	5 535	62	5 473	176	169	6	...	430	4 471
Female	239	4 850	33	4 817	102	99	2	...	239	4 446
Nonfamily householder: Male	309	2 042	17	2 025	60	50	10	...	308	1 812
Female	160	1 903	27	1 876	48	40	8	...	160	1 792
Spouse	340	4 972	58	4 914	117	113	4	...	332	4 043
Child	1 058	18 982	158	18 824	469	451	13	...	1 044	16 578
Other relatives	161	3 025	33	2 992	81	81	–	...	160	2 827
Nonrelatives	196	1 493	14	1 479	70	68	2	...	195	1 317
Inmate of institution	419	452	22	430	9	9	–	...	395	362
Other, in group quarters	181	540	–	540	40	40	–	...	181	216
Persons 75 years and over living alone	17	353	11	342	18	13	5	...	17	342
Persons per household	2.58	3.01	2.87	3.01	2.99	3.06	1.85	...	2.58	2.99
Persons per family	3.40	3.63	3.62	3.63	3.57	3.57	3.25	...	3.39	3.64
Spanish origin persons[1]	2 775	11 379	1 100	10 279	1 413	1 094	294	25	2 745	7 319
In households	2 636	11 037	1 096	9 941	1 388	1 069	294	25	2 608	7 124
Householder	868	3 150	292	2 858	395	316	74	5	861	2 144
15 to 24 years	189	568	43	525	82	64	16	2	188	394
25 to 34 years	293	1 006	81	925	142	108	32	2	289	623
35 to 44 years	117	565	47	518	51	37	14	–	117	354
45 to 54 years	130	473	47	426	40	37	2	1	128	343
55 to 64 years	79	286	30	256	28	24	4	–	79	233
65 to 74 years	35	136	22	114	23	20	3	–	35	107
75 years and over	25	116	22	94	29	26	3	–	25	90
Family householder: Male	475	1 834	184	1 652	245	183	59	3	469	1 146
Female	120	514	48	466	62	55	5	2	120	402
Nonfamily householder: Male	157	494	32	462	54	47	7	–	156	363
Female	116	306	28	278	34	31	3	–	116	233
Spouse	422	1 792	184	1 608	217	158	55	4	418	1 031
Child	1 052	5 100	519	4 581	590	436	139	15	1 036	3 227
Other relatives	148	591	62	529	114	97	16	1	147	423
Nonrelatives	146	404	39	365	72	62	10	–	146	299
Inmate of institution	57	92	2	90	3	3	–	–	55	34
Other, in group quarters	82	250	2	248	22	22	–	–	82	161
Persons 75 years and over living alone	16	62	9	53	11	10	1	–	16	49
Persons per household	2.89	3.16	3.20	3.15	3.21	3.06	3.78	4.00	2.87	3.10
Persons per family	3.54	3.72	3.63	3.73	3.61	3.48	4.05	4.00	3.52	2.73

[1]Persons of Spanish origin may be of any race.

Reprinted from *Census of Population, Chapter B: General Population Characteristics*, published by the U.S. Bureau of the Census.

The best way to avoid problems in summing components parts or calculating percentages is to understand the relationships among Census terms. Two of the most commonly misinterpreted concepts involve the definitions of Households and Housing Units. Figure 14-C depicts some of the major conceptual relationships of both.

FINDING CENSUS DATA

Researchers can obtain help locating or interpreting Census data from the Bureau's Data User Services Division (DUSD), which provides answers to basic questions relating to Bureau programs, products, and services. Information officers are also employed at the Bureau's 12 Regional Offices. For users with more sophisticated questions about methodology, unpublished data, or other research concerns, the best source is often the professionals who produce the information. A phone call to the DUSD may result in a referral to another division within the Bureau, or users can contact staff members directly. The Bureau publishes an annual "Telephone Contacts" list which provides the names and numbers of professionals within the various geographic, demographic, and economic divisions. The list usually appears in one of the fall issues of *The Census and You*.

The following sections focus on alternative methods of finding Census data, including the use of published indexes and catalogs, electronic access, and developing short-cuts when using the printed reports.

Census Catalogs and Subject Indexes

Numerous directories, indexes, and other research aids have been produced to assist users in locating Census information. The titles described below constitute the most helpful publications of this type. Some are published by the Bureau and others are produced by commercial firms.

Catalog of Publications, 1790–1972 (U.S. Bureau of the Census, 1973).

This comprehensive catalog of Census publications is based on the outstanding research done by Henry J. Dubester at the Library of Congress in the 1940s. The catalog contains the full text of Dubester's original work, with updated information through 1972. It is an essential tool for anyone who uses older Census materials.

Census Catalog and Guide (U.S. Bureau of the Census, Annual).

This annual catalog contains descriptions and ordering information for current Census publications, as well as for important materials still in print from previous years. Coverage includes paper reports, microfiche, and magnetic tape files. In addition to the catalog, this guide provides a number of helpful finding tools such as agency directories. Here the user can find addresses of State Data Centers and Affiliates, Clearinghouse Agencies, Regional Offices of the Bureau, and U.S. Depository Libraries. The annual catalog is updated throughout the year by *Monthly Product Announcements*.

Subject Index to the 1980 Census of Population and Housing, by Polly-Alida Farrington (Specialized Information Products, 1985).

This detailed and well-executed publication accomplishes what the Bureau has not been able to do. It is a subject index to the tables found in every major publication of the 1980 Census. The outstanding achievement of this index is its ability to describe cross-tabulations available for each subject. The arrangement takes some getting used to, but this is a unique and worthwhile tool for all Census researchers.

Guide to 1980 Decennial Census Publications (Congressional Information Service, 1986).

The *American Statistics Index* covers the decennial Cenus with the same detail afforded to other federal statistical publications. The problem is that Census products are released over several years, so researchers would need to look through four or five annual volumes of *ASI*. To counter this drawback, the publisher issued this special guide containing all *ASI* listings for decennial publications. Like its parent, the service is divided into two parts—abstracts, and indexes by subject, title, category, and report number.

Population Information in Twentieth Century Census Volumes, 1950-1980, by Suzanne Schulze (Oryx Press, 1988).

This unique work represents a monumental research effort. The author has provided excellent descriptions of every population table from the decennial Censuses during the period covered. Users are led from a broad table-finding guide to the subject listings for every Census publication. Companion titles cover the 19th century and the period from 1900 to 1940. Together with the Bureau's *Twenty Censuses* (cited at the end of this chapter), these volumes are an indispensable tool for historical investigations.

Electronic Access to Census Data

Approximately 90% of the 1980 Census output does not appear in paper format. The 1980 Census contains more data at smaller geographic levels than ever before, and 1990 will continue with this trend. Published reports are intended to answer only the most common data needs. There are three main areas in which published reports are limited. First is the amount of detail in subject content. For example, published reports contain a great deal of data on the Hispanic community, but numbers are not broken down by components such as Cuban and Mexican. Next is the problem of geographic detail. The smaller the level of geography, the less information is published; in some cases, certain types of geography are not covered at all. For both problems, the STF fiche can help, but even these large files are not all-inclusive. The third limitation involves cross-classification of data. The Bureau cannot publish data in five-, four-, or even three-way classifications for every population and housing characteristic. Researchers expecting to find a table citing the number of black females by individual occupation and age, or similar multiple relationships, will be disappointed. Availability of STF data on computer tape, as well as various public use microdata files, can provide the Census user with a partial solution to these problems.

In addition to the CD-ROM products mentioned earlier, several other electronic resources are available. Summary Tape Files (STFs) have been mentioned in several contexts, but nothing has been said about STF data on tape. STFs are called summary files because they contain the aggregate data from which the actual publications are produced, with all confidential information suppressed. For 1990, four major files will be produced, each divided by level of geography and subjects covered. The STF number indicates the subject content of the tape and the letter-suffix designates the level of geography. STF 1 and 2 contain 100% count data on population and housing, while STF 3 and 4 contain data from the sample count. A trade-off occurs between subject detail and geographic detail. STF 1 and 3 contain broad coverage of all geographic units, while STF 2 and 4 contain detailed subject data for fewer geographic levels. A breakdown of the STF 1 tapes parallels how the others are organized. STF 1-A and B are "state-specific," providing data at the county and county subdivision level. STF 1-C is the national summary, and STF 1-D covers Congressional Districts.

The Bureau sells reels of tape for each STF on a state-by-state basis. Prices and specifications are cited in the *Census Catalog and Guide*. Tapes can be purchased together with documentation and the Bureau's own software, called CENSPAC. Users can also write their own coding to merge files or reformat tables, or use commercially produced statistical software such as the *Statistical Package for the Social Sciences*. Researchers without computer capabilities or expertise can also utilize the power of the STF tapes. One recourse is to consult the network of State Data Centers, also known as Business and Industry Data Centers. The Bureau has designated one agency in each state as a State Data Center and has provided the Centers with complete tape files for their states. The Centers (also called Lead Agencies) choose local organizations to serve as Affiliate Data Centers; the Affiliates then acquire the tapes they desire for their own purposes, though not all Affiliates have computing capabilities. Census users can contact Affiliates or Lead Agencies to purchase customized reports from the tapes. Most Lead Agencies have also created standard reports for their states, which they may sell as paper printouts, bound publications, or, in some cases, Computer Output Microfiche.

The Bureau has also established a second network called the National Clearinghouse for Census Data Service. The Clearinghouse is a registry of one or more organizations per state which can produce reports from STFs. Clearinghouse organizations differ from State Data Centers and their Affiliates because they usually provide data on more than a single state, they can frequently provide more services than the SDC network, and they are sometimes for-profit organizations. A list of local SDC Affiliates and Clearinghouse organizations can be found in the *Census Catalog and Guide*.

The availability of STF data, whether on fiche, paper, CD-ROM, or magnetic tape, can solve the problem of subject and geographic detail, but not necessarily that of cross-classification. Because STFs contain aggregated data only, they can only provide the cross-tabulations which the Bureau has performed. Tables in the printed reports and tapes typically cross-classify two (sometimes three) data items at a time, the second and third classifications usually being age and sex. Some characteristics are also classified a fourth way—by race or Spanish Origin—because separate tables repeat the same data for particular segments of the population. For 1980, two publications focused on more detailed cross-tabulations, but only for states and large SMSAs and their Central Cities. Those two—*Detailed Population Characteristics* and *Metropolitan Housing Characteristics*—will not be available for 1990.

Users in need of additional cross-classifications can contact the Bureau to produce a customized report from the confidential source tapes (an expensive recourse), or they can turn to another kind of tape file. Three *Public Use Microdata Sample* (*PUMS*) files contain samples of partial responses from individual household questionnaires, stripped of their identification to preserve confidentiality. Using *PUMS* for a given geographic area is similar to conducting a survey yourself; raw data can be retabulated in any form wanted. Many State Data Centers or Clearinghouse agencies can also create customized reports from *PUMS* on a contractual basis. The creation of these two data networks and the wide distribution of tape products has made previously inaccessible data more readily available to the general public.

What about other electronic Census media? No decennial data can be obtained from the Bureau on floppy diskette, because diskettes hold comparatively little data. However, smaller Census files, notably the *County and City Data Book* and local area population estimates, are published on diskette.

The electronic medium with which the Bureau has worked the longest is online information delivery. *CENDATA*, an online database offered through DIALOG and CompuServe, provides immediate access to news releases from the Bureau, new product announcements and ordering information, and an increasing array of Census data, primarily from the *Current Population Reports* and other ongoing surveys. A large assortment of economic and industry figures can be found here as well. No detailed data from the 1980 Census can be seen on *CENDATA*, but summary data for 1990 is already appearing. On DIALOG, the database can be searched as a menu-driven file or a command-based system; on CompuServe, it is menu-driven only. *CENDATA* is updated daily. The Bureau also sponsors its own Electronic Bulletin Board with daily updates. Like *CENDATA*, it offers news releases, product announcements, and smaller data sets. Some State Data Centers also offer Bulletin Boards with current demographic data.

Finding Answers Quickly

Sooner or later most Census users ask, "Isn't there some foolproof way to locate the proper report and table without plowing haphazardly through innumerable publications?" The honest answer is sometimes there is no simple way to instantly find needed data, but search-time can be reduced. Everything discussed so far has been introduced with this goal in mind. A clear understanding of how the Census is generated, the meanings of terms and geographical concepts, and the formats of published reports will make a systematic search strategy possible.

Researchers can turn to the subject indexes mentioned above, or to the useful summary tables in the *1980 Census Users' Guide*. However, the more you deal with the Census, the more adept you will become. Experienced users may seldom need to consult secondary finding tools to locate appropriate publications or tables. Proficient researchers develop their own shortcuts, and discover their own favorite publications. The same answer might be found in several Census reports. As an example, the 1980 population of Monroe County, New York can be found in Chapter A of New York State's *Characteristics of the Population*, the *Summary Characteristics* report for the state, the *Census Tracts* volume for Rochester, or the STF 1-A fiche for Monroe County.

A basic approach to locating Census information should follow these steps, although not always in the order listed:

1. Determine whether the information sought is available in the Census. Searching for data on religion will be fruitless because nothing about religion appears on Census questionnaires. Certain questions may be asked, but not in the detail you require. For example, information on college enrollment is available, but not by academic major. Data on persons with disabilities can be found, but not what type of disability. If you intend to use the Census on a regular basis, familiarize yourself with questionnaire content.

2. Determine whether the request pertains to a housing question or a population question. While this may seem simple, in some cases it will require a moment's thought. Information on people in group quarters is a population question, for example, as is information on household characteristics. Sometimes the distinctions between housing and population are even less obvious. Data on the number of vehicles owned by people in a household is a housing question, while data on how people travel to work is a population question.

3. Decide whether the data sought is from the complete count or the sample count. Again, Figure 14-A summarizes the questions asked on the long and short forms. Based on this information, the researcher can determine which Census reports should be consulted. To recap the contents of the major 1980 products, 100% data will be found in Chapters

A and B of *Characteristics of the Population*, Chapter A of *Characteristics of Housing Units*, and the STF 1-A and 1-C microfiche. Sample data are published in Chapters C and D of the Population Reports, Chapter B of the Housing Reports, *Metropolitan Housing Characteristics*, and STF 3-A and 3-C.

4.   Choose the level of geography needed. If information on Chicago is needed, verify that it is the Central City and not the MSA which is being investigated. This will determine what section of which table you will consult.

5.   Translate your problem into Census terminology. Data on the number of foreign-born residents is found under nativity, while information on ethnic heritage is listed under ancestry. Information on homeownership is listed under tenure. Figure 14-D is a brief guide to translating common questions into Census terminology.

6.   Use the Table Finding Guide or Data Index, in conjunction with the Table of Contents, to locate the most likely tables where data will be found.

When using printed reports, remember that table numbers remain the same from state to state. If Table 24 of *General Population Characteristics* for Texas contains "General Characteristics by Spanish Origin," so will Table 24 in the California report. This is not true of the U.S. Summary volumes, which have a numbering sequence of their own. Many other tips can be given, but only a few more will be mentioned. First, becoming familiar with the data elements of frequently repeated tables will cut down on search-time. Related tables frequently present the same data in different ways. The beginning tables in each volume are always summary tables containing general data, including percentages.

Within any Census publication, the same tables may be repeated several times for various segments of the population, and the same tables are also reproduced for different geographies. One of the more baffling aspects of geographic coverage is that data on Places are reported separately from non-Places. Because towns are not incorporated in New York State, and townships are not in Pennsylvania, they are not found in the Census tables for "Place." However, tables for Places and for MCDs are always located next to one another. If Table 32 covers age by race and sex for Places larger than 10,000 people, Table 32a will provide identical information on MCDs of the same size.

Finally, it helps to know that certain characteristics equal others by definition. Number of households is always equal to number of occupied housing units, which is equal to number of householders. Tautologies such as

this can save time when you can't seem to find figures one way but they are readily available in another form. Consider once again the numbers in Exhibit 14-4. The column of figures farthest to the left shows statistics for the Lincoln, Nebraska Urbanized Area. Although the number of households is not given, number of householders (65,377) is. This type of exercise is good for another purpose: it strengthens the user's knowledge of Census data and what they measure. By corroborating equivalent data which are presented on another table in different form, researchers can make sure they understand Census concepts. For example, by checking the number of households for the Lincoln Urbanized Area, which is listed explicitly in Table 14 of the same book, the user will see that the number does indeed equal 65,377. But remember, Census users can reach erroneous conclusions by manipulating data incorrectly.

If this sounds like too much to cope with, plenty of excellent user's guides are available to clarify terminology and concepts. Even the broadest understanding will reduce wasted time and erroneous results. Researchers who consult Census publications on a reasonably frequent basis will be pleased to discover how quickly such an understanding falls into place.

MASTERING THE CENSUS

Whether you are using population estimates, projections, or the decennial Census, and whether the data represent a sample survey or 100% count, a thorough understanding of the numbers is vital to producing quality research. Hasty assumptions can lead to disastrous results. This doesn't mean you should shrink from using Census data, only that you should have a healthy respect for their complexity. Still, Census users have an advantage over researchers who turn to alternative sources: Census publications are among the best-documented statistical reports in the world. As previously mentioned, every major publication from the Bureau includes a dictionary of the terms used. The methodology employed in every decennial enumeration, sample survey, estimate, and projection is also meticulously explained. For example, a five-volume procedural history of the 1980 Census was published in 1986/87, and a similar guide will eventually appear to document the 1990 Census. The Bureau also undertakes studies to measure undercount, sampling error, and other statistical problems encountered in previous reports. Numerous user's guides are published by the Bureau and by outside organizations. Several are mentioned at the end of this chapter.

FIGURE 14-D. Translating Demographic Questions into Census Format

Question Asked:	Census Language:
Children per household	Household relationship; Family composition
Families with children	Family type by presence of children
Female head of household	Family type; Household type
Size of household	Persons in unit
Currently divorced	Marital status
Ever divorced	Marital history
Foreign-born	Nativity
Mother tongue	Language spoken at home
Ethnic group	Ancestry
Geographic mobility	Residence in 1975
Commuting patterns	Means of transportation to work; Travel time to work
Self-employed	Class of Worker
Two-income family	Workers in family
White collar worker	Occupation
Unemployment	Labor force status
Welfare recipients	Income type
Institutional population	Group quarters type
Age of house	Year structure built
Home ownership	Tenure
Number of apartments	Units in structure
Size of building	Stories in structure
Substandard housing	Lacking complete bathroom; Boarded up; etc.

The material covered in this chapter will serve as a starting point for those approaching the Census for the first time. After that, the experience of using the Census becomes one of continuing discovery. In the process of learning, it may be comforting to remember that even people who work with the information daily are quick to point out that no one is an expert on all aspects of the Census.

FOR FURTHER READING

This reading list is intended to offer a broad sampling of basic books and articles for the beginning Census user. In addition to providing background on Census concepts, the following materials describe the 1990 Census procedures, some of the changes which have taken place over the past decade, and the major controversies associated with the decennial Census. As of this writing, few guides have appeared which describe the yet-to-be-seen 1990 Census products, so several guides to the 1980 Census are also mentioned.

Census Basics

Dailey, George, Leah Engelhardt, and James Giese, eds. "Celebrating the Bicentennial of the U.S. Census." *Social Education* 53 (November/December 1989): 413–79.
Social Education, a journal aimed at social studies teachers, has devoted an entire issue to the Census of Population. A variety of articles provide an excellent abbreviated history of the Census, discussions of applications of Census data, and suggestions for classroom exercises at all levels and covering a diversity of disciplines. An annotated bibliography of instructional materials for classroom use is also provided.

Kaplan, Charles P., and Thomas L. Van Valey. *Census '80: Continuing the Factfinder Tradition* (Washington, DC: U.S. Bureau of the Census, 1980).
This book represents the first attempt by the Bureau to write a textbook for college-level instruction. On the whole, the work is quite successful. The amount of detail provided is one of the book's best features; there is a great deal of information here which will not be found in other Census guides. Another useful feature is an extensive section of case studies which illustrate specific applications of Census data in a variety of settings.

Overbeek, Johannes. *Population: An Introduction* (New York: Harcourt, Brace, Jovanovich, 1982).

There are many textbooks on demographic methods and concepts, but this brief, easy-to-read treatment is an excellent first book on the topic. Overbeek also includes a concise, understandable chapter on basic statistical concepts.

U.S. Bureau of the Census. *Factfinder for the Nation* (Washington, DC: The Bureau, Irregular).

A series of approximately 20 pamphlets providing brief introductory information on a number of Census topics. Subjects covered in the series range from using Census records for genealogical research to understanding Census geography. Each pamphlet is revised frequently.

———. *Twenty Censuses: Population and Housing Questions, 1790–1980* (Washington, DC: U.S. Government Printing Office, 1979).

Intended as a guide for historical research, this publication reproduces the Census questionnaires from every decennial Census and their corresponding instructions to enumerators. It is quite useful for identifying the availability of historical records and for comparing data from one decade to another.

Young, Gary M. *Census ABC's: Applications in Business and Community* (Washington, DC: U.S. Bureau of the Census, 1989).

This instruction booklet for teachers introduces basic Census concepts and suggests classroom exercises designed to show students how to find, analyze, and apply Census data to business and community research.

The 1990 Census

Abramowitz, Molly. *Census '90 Basics* (Washington, DC: U.S. Bureau of the Census, 1990).

The first of many primers which will be produced to explain the 1990 Census. This booklet covers Census concepts, geography, the enumeration process, and the major products for 1990.

Exter, Thomas. "The Survey That Measures the Census." *American Demographics* 12 (November 1990): 12–14.

A concise, understandable explanation of the Bureau's post-enumeration survey, which the author likens to a biologist's capture/recapture method of tagging and counting wildlife. (A comparison not meant to be taken literally.) The post-enumeration survey is one of the most important aspects of the decennial Census, used to estimate the amount and characteristics of the Census undercount.

Haupt, Arthur. "S-Night: Counting the Homeless." *Population Today* (May 1990): 3–4.

Examines the Bureau's methods for counting the homeless in 1990, and the controversy which accompanied the effort.

Lewis, Sylvia. "Can You Trust the Census?" *Planning* (January 1991): 14–18.

Discusses how the Bureau's Local Review Program works, giving examples of several cities which challenged the Bureau's 1990 count of housing units during local review.

Marx, Robert W. "The TIGER System: Automating the Geographic Structure of the United States Census." *Government Publications Review* 13 (1986): 181–201.

An excellent overview of the TIGER mapping system, written by the chief of the Bureau's Geography Division. Includes a brief history of Census mapping, and discussions of how the file was created, how it is structured, and its strengths and weaknesses. Complex concepts are explained well, making this a good starting point for nonspecialists who want to learn about this important innovation.

"1990 Census Questionnaire." *American Demographics* 11 (April 1989): 24–31

A question-by-question explanation of the 1990 Census form, including comparisons to the 1980 questions. A prototype form is reproduced.

Selected Census Issues

Beale, Calvin. "Poughkeepsie's Complaint: Or, Defining Metropolitan Areas." *American Demographics* 6 (January 1984): 29–31+.

This provocative article describes why the changes in metropolitan definitions were made by the Office of Management and Budget and questions whether those changes have gone too far in redressing the complaints of smaller communities.

Bean, Frank D., and Rodolfo O. de la Garza. "Illegal Aliens and Census Counts." *Society* 25 (March/April 1988): 48–53.

Explores the legal and technical reasons why illegal aliens should or should not be counted in the decennial Census. (*Note*: The Bureau of the Census attempts to count all residents of the United States. The Census does not distinguish between legal and illegal residents, but asks only whether they are citizens. To the extent that undocumented residents respond to the questionnaire, they are included in the total count of our population.)

Gleick, James. "The Census: Why We Can't Count." *New York Times Magazine* (July 15, 1990): 22–26+.

A thought-provoking analysis of why a 100% enumeration may no longer be the best way to conduct the decennial Census. Although this may sound like a radical notion, many demographers endorse the idea, and the Bureau has begun exploring alternatives for 2000.

Hamilton, David P. "Census Adjustment Battle Heats Up." *Science* 248 (March 18, 1990): 807–08.

One of the most succinct and understandable explanations of the proposed methodology for statistical adjustments to the 1990 Census. Despite the political and professional controversy accompanying this issue, Hamilton points out that the Bureau has utilized minor adjustment techniques for several decades.

Paris, James A. "The Group Quarters Quandary." *American Demographics* 7 (February 1985): 34–37.

An excellent summary of the problems of interpreting group quarters data for local areas.

Estimates and Projections

Batutis, Michael J. "Estimating Population." *American Demographics* 4 (April 1982): 42–44.

This brief article outlines a handful of common population estimation techniques. The discussion of techniques used by the Bureau of the Census is presented in concise, readable style. A companion article, published in the May 1982 issue of the magazine, provides an excellent summary of the popular housing units technique.

Lee, Everett S., and Harold F. Goldsmith, eds. *Population Estimates: Methods for Small Area Analysis* (Newbury Park, CA: Sage Publications, 1982).

Based on a 1978 conference sponsored by the National Institute of Mental Health, the essays in this volume assume a familiarity with demographic methods. However, the interested reader will find the discussion of limitations in the various estimating methods to be especially enlightening.

Raymondo, James C. "How to Choose a Projection Technique." *American Demographics* 12 (February 1990): 38-39.

A quick, painless look at the four basic methods of calculating population projections.

Rives, Norfleet W., and William J. Serow. *Introduction to Applied Demography: Data Sources and Estimation Techniques* (Newbury Park, CA: Sage Publications, 1984).

A short but thorough guide covering basic demographic sources. Includes the decennial Census, the Current Population Survey, and vital statistics publications. The easy-to-read explanations of estimation techniques are especially worthwhile.

Smith, Stanley K. *Population Estimates: What Do We Really Know?* (Gainesville, FL: University of Florida Bureau of Economic and Business Research, 1984).

Contains an explanation of basic projection methods, together with the results of an empirical study which compares the accuracy of various techniques. Serious users of demographic data will be interested in the conclusions of the study, and should find it both readable and concise.

Guides to 1980 and 1990 Census Publications

American Demographics. *Researchers Guide to the 1980 Census* (Ithaca, NY: American Demographics, 1981).

This booklet is one of the best of many brief guides to the 1980 Census. Coverage includes basic topics such as how the data are compiled, who uses Census information, and the types of products available. The discussion of computer tape products and special services from the Bureau are especially good.

Manka, Paul T. "A Fiche Story." *American Demographics* 5 (May 1983): 36–41.

This article provides a detailed description of the STF data available for purchase on microfiche.

McClure, Charles R., and Peter Hernon. *Use of Census Bureau Data in GPO Depository Libraries: Future Issues and Trends* (Washington, DC: U.S. Government Printing Office, 1990).

The final report of a study conducted by private consultants under contract for the Bureau's "21st Century Decennial Census Planning Staff." The study surveyed federal depository librarians across the nation to determine their concerns regarding the ability to cope with current Census reports and with emerging information technologies. Much of the report focuses on the various formats of Census reports, including paper, microfiche, CD-ROM, online, and computer tape products, and their impact on libraries and data users. Numerous recommendations are made regarding future Census products, the structure of the Depository system, coordination with State Data Centers, and related issues of information dissemination.

Redmond, Mary. "State Data Centers: Improving Access to Census Information." *Government Information Quarterly* 3 (August 1986): 291–303.

Summarizes the development, structure, and services of the Bureau's SDC program and how it makes Census data available to the public.

Schwartz, Joe. "A Guide to the 1990 Census." *American Demographics* 12 (April 1990): 16–21.

Describes the basic content of the STF computer tapes to be issued for the 1990 Census.

U.S. Bureau of the Census. *1980 Census of Population and Housing Users' Guide* (Washington, DC: U.S. Government Printing Office, 1982).

An invaluable handbook for all researchers. Part A of the guide contains brief but clear explanations of important Census concepts, from enumeration procedures to geographic terms. This section also contains helpful descriptions of all 1980 products and a number of excellent charts and finding aids. Part B is simply the best glossary of 1980 Census terminology to be found anywhere. Part C is a guide to the Summary Tape Files and what is found on each.

————. *1990 Census of Population and Housing Tabulation and Publication Program* (Washington, DC: U.S. Government Printing Office, 1989).

To date, this is the most detailed guide to the publications and other data products planned for the 1990 Census. Covers print, microfiche, map, CD-ROM, and tape products. This booklet is most useful for its point-by-point comparisons with the 1980 data products.

————. *Product Primers* (Washington, DC: The Bureau, Irregular).

A series of pamphlets designed explicitly for classroom use. Each title provides a remarkably good introduction to a specific publication such as *Census Tracts*. In addition to describing the item in question, each *Product Primer* contains a handful of exercises which illustrate important concepts in superb fashion.

CHAPTER 15
General Economic Statistics

TOPICS COVERED

1. The Federal Statistical System
2. The Business Cycle and Economic Indicators
3. Pitfalls in Using Economic Statistics
4. Important Economic Statistics
   a. The Index of Leading Economic Indicators
   b. GNP: The National Income and Product Accounts
   c. Labor Force Data
   d. Price Levels and Inflation
   e. Other Key Indicators
5. Basic Sources of Economic Statistics
   a. General Economic Compendia
   b. Subject-Specific Data Sources
   c. Economic Forecasts
6. Locating Statistical Information
7. For Further Reading

MAJOR SOURCES DISCUSSED

- *Statistical Abstract of the United States*
- *Business Statistics*
- *The Economic Report of the President*
- *Standard & Poor's Statistical Service*
- *EconBase: Time Series and Forecasts*
- *Survey of Current Business*
- *Monthly Labor Review*
- *Employment and Earnings*
- *Federal Reserve Bulletin*
- *Budget of the United States Government*
- *National Economic Projections Series*

Few areas of business information capture the public attention the way economic statistics can. The major indicators of U.S. economic performance are widely recognized (at least in name) by the general public. When released, the latest economic measurements always become "news" of the highest order. But all this publicity does not mean the figures are understood by most people. The average American has a dim understanding of how the economy works, but even regular users of economic indicators are likely to misunderstand the meaning and purpose of these sophisticated measures.

The goal of this chapter is to shed some light on the familiar but confusing world of general economic statistics. The focus will be on measurements which track the broad performance of the economy as a whole. Statistics on specific industries and other specialized topics (including the Economic Census) will be introduced in Chapter 16. The majority of economic indicators are produced by the federal government, but some significant data are also compiled by the private sector. The focus of this chapter is on government generated economic times series. (A time series is a set of variables consistently reported over a long period of time.) Such important concepts as the structure of the federal statistical system, the nature of economic indicators, and their uses and limitations will be covered.

THE FEDERAL STATISTICAL SYSTEM

The United States collects, analyzes, and disseminates more economic data than any country on earth. Until the 1920s, however, the federal government did not regularly produce detailed measures of economic performance, and many current measures did not exist until the late 1940s. While most countries have central statistical

offices, this has never been the case in the United States. The remarkable range and extent of the government's statistical efforts grew piecemeal, according to the dictates of legislation and in response to emerging needs. Thus evolved the far-flung, highly decentralized federal statistical system. Only about a half dozen federal agencies exist solely to create statistics, but over 100 other governmental units also participate in the statistical process.

The major agencies involved in the dissemination of federal statistics are the Bureau of the Census, the Bureau of Labor Statistics, the National Center for Health Statistics, the National Center for Education Statistics, the Department of Agriculture's Statistical Reporting Service, and the Energy Information Administration. Some agencies analyze data from other sources. Examples are the Council of Economic Advisors, the Congressional Budget Office, the Bureau of Economic Analysis (part of the Department of Commerce), and the Department of Agriculture's Economic Research Service. However, most agencies produce statistics as a by-product of their administrative and regulatory duties.

Many problems are associated with such a large, diverse system. First, there is the paperwork burden imposed on citizens and businesses. Major studies have shown that the key statistical gathering agencies do keep the reporting burden to a minimum, but paperwork is a continuing political concern. A second problem is the overlapping of statistical programs among different agencies. This can occur when alternative methods are used as cross-checks to complex but important series, or when different agencies study problems from varying perspectives. Also, many programs are required by law to monitor compliance or to allocate funds according to a predetermined formula. A third problem is the frequent difficulty in determining the proper source of needed statistical information. With so many agencies involved, the appropriate one may not be obvious.

The decentralized activities of federal statistical agencies have been supervised by the U.S. Office of Management and Budget (OMB) since 1942. The Federal Reports Act requires the government to collect only the information it needs to perform its regular functions. This basic philosophy was strengthened by the Paperwork Reduction Act of 1980 and its subsequent amendments. Under these laws, OMB has the authority to approve or disapprove any statistical programs or publications agencies wish to initiate. OMB also monitors duplication and waste, evaluates effectiveness of statistical programs, and develops standards and policies agencies must follow. The designation of Metropolitan Statis-

tical Areas and the design of the Standard Industrial Classification System are examples of OMB's role in statistical affairs. The most serious limitation to OMB's statistical coordination has been the significant reduction in the staff to administer these duties. Consequently, many of the agency's planning and policy activities now receive less attention.

The integrity of U.S. statistical programs has also been endangered by drastic reductions in the number and quality of government statistical series. Program reductions stem from continuing pressure for federal budget cuts, mandated quotas for reduced reporting systems, and a political philosophy committed to reducing the government's role in the everyday lives of citizens. The deregulation movement has indirectly reduced statistical programs by eliminating regulatory requirements that were tied to many statistical series.

The specific cutbacks caused by these policies are widespread and significant to users of business information. Entire series have ceased to exist. The amount of detail in other series has diminished and the timeliness and frequency of published data has been jeopardized. The quality of statistics has been affected by reductions in sample sizes and by the delay or cancellation of needed revisions of important programs. It is unlikely that the government's role in the collection and dissemination of statistics will cease, but all business researchers should be aware of the continuing decline in many statistical programs.

The final outcome of this trend is difficult to foresee. Certain budget casualties have been reinstated by the Bush administration, though OMB still enforces the Paperwork Reduction Act assiduously. One thing is certain: the private sector is not the solution to the problem. Private organizations cannot mount the massive nationwide effort necessary to conduct a population census or compile the GNP. Even for less ambitious projects, the quality of data produced by private groups may be inferior to government statistics. The business sector cannot afford to devote the resources to design and evaluate surveys in the thorough way the government does. For example, the *ACCRA Cost of Living Index* compiled by the American Chamber of Commerce Researchers Association is not as carefully controlled as the BLS "Urban Family Budget" which it replaces. What's more, respondents may not be as willing to answer nongovernment surveys, nor are users as likely to trust them as disinterested studies. Finally, the cost of private surveys to the data user will be greater than their government-produced counterparts.

Despite these reservations, the private sector produces certain data series regularly and well. The government itself relies on the private sector for various statistical series. Many companies and nonprofit organizations have developed excellent reputations for providing specialized data for use as economic indicators. Examples are Dun & Bradstreet's data on business failures and new incorporations, R.L. Polk's figures on new car registrations, and the Conference Board's index of help wanted ads. The role of government in collecting economic statistics is indispensable, but private groups can also make worthy contributions.

THE BUSINESS CYCLE AND ECONOMIC INDICATORS

National economies exhibit long-term cyclical patterns. These fluctuations, known as the business cycle, manifest themselves as a continuous series of irregular but recurring phases, alternating from growth to contraction ("boom to bust"). Until modern times, the reasons for such fluctuations were poorly understood, and statistics for measuring the business cycle were crude or nonexistent. The unprecedented severity and length of the Great Depression spurred increased study of business cycle behavior, which identified a vast array of statistical measures, called economic indicators. These indicators have the proven ability to track and forecast the nation's economic well-being.

Much of the work on economic indicators was conducted at the National Bureau of Economic Research (NBER), a nonprofit organization that provides unbiased research on economic problems. The specific charge given to the NBER in 1937 was to determine a statistical method able to predict the end of the Depression, and in general to provide a way to consistently forecast changes in the business cycle. This research identified certain statistical series which could serve as Leading Indicators by consistently changing direction in advance of the business cycle itself.

What statistics constitute the group of Leading Indicators, and why do they have this predictive power? Most of them lead because they record economic activities which have direct consequences on future events. For example, the issuance of building permits, new business incorporations, orders by manufacturers for new equipment, and changes in inventory levels are all events which will result in future economic changes. They are preliminary activities which set economic forces in motion. Statistics which measure these events have the

proven ability to signal changes in the economy as a whole. Some are predictive because they measure expectations or intentions. For example, the Survey Research Center of the University of Michigan conducts a monthly survey of consumer expectations, upon which an important leading indicator is based.

Other Leading Indicators are less obvious because they measure more indirect relationships. The average work week of production workers is a Leading Indicator because employers tend to reduce or increase the hours of current workers before they lay them off or hire new employees. To do so is more flexible, less permanent, and an all-around simpler response to anticipated changes. Average work week thus becomes a reliable early warning system for overall changes in the labor market. Another indirect measure which serves as a Leading Indicator is the performance of the stock market. Stock prices lead the business cycle because they reflect investors' expectations of future performance.

The NBER studies also identified two other categories of indicator. Coincident Indicators are statistics which fluctuate in conjunction with the business cycle. Examples are industrial production and personal income. Coincident Indicators are used to describe the current state of the economy. Several of them together are used in the NBER's official definition of recession. The Lagging Indicator is a statistic which reaches its peak or trough after the business cycle does. Examples are the average duration of unemployment and the amount of commercial loans outstanding. Most Lagging Indicators are measures of imbalances in the economy. Because economic systems naturally move toward a state of equilibrium, such imbalances provide clues to future fluctuations. Paradoxically, Lagging Indicators can foreshadow changes in the Leading Indicators. A final category of economic indicator exhibits no consistent relationship to movements in the business cycle, though this type of statistic can be quite meaningful of itself.

PITFALLS IN USING ECONOMIC STATISTICS

Providers of economic statistics are under considerable public pressure to release figures as quickly as possible. At the same time, they must ensure that the information is accurate. Unfortunately, speed seldom goes hand-in-hand with accuracy, so statistical agencies are faced with a fundamental trade-off. Most organizations resolve this dilemma by releasing preliminary data on a timely basis, then revising the early statistics in

subsequent months. Users should be alert to the difference between preliminary and revised data, especially when doing historical research.

Aside from long-term business cycles, the national economy exhibits seasonal fluctuations which are fairly constant from one year to the next. These variations are due to recurring events such as holidays, the weather, summer vacations, and tax deadlines. To make economic data comparable from one month to the next, and to enable monthly data to be "annualized," mathematical models have been developed to smooth out such seasonal fluctuations. Statistical series which are presented in this seasonally adjusted form are also available in their unadjusted condition.

Economic indicators represent a summary measurement of complex events. Regular users of economic series should take time to learn how data are compiled. The assumptions made in building a model, the definitions which are adopted, and the methodology used all contribute to a particular view of the economy which the resulting numbers present. Because of the variety of similar statistics, there is a real danger in using data inappropriate to the researcher's true needs.

An excellent example of this difficulty can be seen in the multitude of statistics on earnings and income. The Bureau of Labor Statistics collects data on employee earnings, while agencies such as the Bureau of the Census provide information on all types of income. BLS data on hourly earnings are frequently misunderstood. The BLS conducts a national survey of employers, from which gross average hourly earnings and real earnings adjusted for inflation are obtained. How are these figures to be interpreted? They are not an average wage rate because overtime payments are included. Neither should they be construed as a wage figure for a typical family because many workers have two jobs, many families have more than one wage earner, and the survey counts part-time employees. They are not a measure of total household income because all nonwage sources are excluded. Finally, they are not the employer's average cost of labor, since payroll taxes and other employment costs are omitted. The limitations of this particular series make clear why the BLS (and other agencies) produce so many versions of statistics on wages, earnings, and income.

Other sources of personal income include interest payments, dividends, rents, pension benefits, and social welfare payments of all types. Several federal agencies compile income statistics which reflect these broader definitions. The U.S. Bureau of Economic Analysis (BEA) computes personal income as part of the National Income and Product Accounts, better known as the GNP.

The Census Bureau also collects data on personal income using the decennial Census, the Current Population Survey (CPS), the American Housing Survey, and the Survey of Income and Program Participation (SIPP). The IRS tabulates data on total gross income and adjusted gross income from individual tax returns. One of the best known of the many commercial sources of income estimates is the measure of "Effective Buying Income" computed by the Market Statistics division of Bill Communications, Inc. The data can be found in the annual *Survey of Buying Power*, described in Chapter 17.

Income data can also be reported in numerous configurations: on a per capita basis; as a mean value for persons, households, or families; as a median value; or as an income range. The diversity of possible income figures is illustrated by the following 1988 data. Per capita data come from the BEA, the Bureau of the Census, and Bill Communications. Median household income is reported by the latter two sources.

Per Capita Income		Median Household Income	
BEA	$14,116	Census	$27,225
Census	$13,123	Bill	$24,488
Bill	$12,359		

The discrepancies stem largely from the use of different definitions. The BEA examines income in the broadest possible sense, including noncash benefits such as food stamps. Both Bill and BEA are reporting "disposable income," meaning income minus deductions for income taxes and social security contributions; the Census Bureau makes no deductions of this type. All three collect their data in completely different ways and at different times of the year. The numbers change even more dramatically when different population segments are studied. According to the Bureau of the Census, the median personal income for men in 1988 was $18,908 while only $8,884 for women.

Government statistics on earnings and income can be found in a myriad of publications. BLS data are issued monthly in their journal *Employment and Earnings*. BEA figures are published in the annual *Local Area Personal Income* as well as the April issue of *Survey of Current Business*. IRS tabulations can be found in the annual *Statistics of Income* and the quarterly *SOI Bulletin*. Census data appear in the annual *Money Income of Households, Families and Persons in the U.S.* Numerous commercial publications also produce estimates of personal income. With such a diversity of sources, it is important for researchers to fully understand which one will best serve their information needs.

IMPORTANT ECONOMIC STATISTICS

Economic indicators serve as measures of the quality of life, standards of compliance for regulatory requirements, yardsticks for planning government assistance programs, and guidelines for establishing national policies. The business community relies on indicators for forecasting sales, budgeting for capital expenditures, and timing long-term expansion programs. Economic indicators present a picture of the nation's economic health and the direction toward which it is heading. The federal government has a statutory and moral commitment to maintain economic prosperity, and economic indicators are the key barometer to measure its success in meeting this goal. Whether the economy can be "fine-tuned" using monetary and fiscal policies is unclear, but officials can certainly take steps to ameliorate the length and severity of economic downturns and to prolong periods of prosperity. For these reasons, the publication of key economic indicators deserve the media attention they receive. On the other hand, a single month's figure for an individual series does not necessarily indicate a trend, and should not be viewed as a portent.

The government regularly collects and publishes data on several hundred individual indicators. Many statistical series measure the same or similar characteristics from different points of view. Depending on the user's needs at any particular time, one may be preferable to another and each presents a slightly different view of economic conditions. Economic indicators are a vast storehouse of information on economic and business activity in the United States. They are released weekly, monthly, or quarterly, depending upon their characteristics. A handful of the most important indicators are briefly introduced below.

The Index of Leading Economic Indicators

The modern economy is a complex system with numerous forces acting upon it. Each component has an effect on every other as well as on the whole. No one completely understands how our economy functions and no one can predict the full consequences of actual events. Furthermore, no single measurement conveniently describes all economic conditions. Economic analysis is difficult because even indicators which are similar to one another can move in opposite directions. To make sense of these complexities, economists have developed composite indexes which measure the behavior of a group of

statistics in a single number. The Consumer Price Index, the Employment Cost Index, and the Index of Industrial Production are examples of composite indexes. The most widely reported composite figure is probably the Index of Leading Economic Indicators, which is compiled by the U.S. Bureau of Economic Analysis.

While many time series have demonstrated leading behavior, the BEA has chosen 11 to make up its composite index. All 11 meet several useful criteria: they are published monthly, in a relatively timely manner; they exhibit strong leading characteristics; and they represent diverse segments of the economy. Each one is weighted to reflect its relative importance as a predictor, then added together to create the composite index. Despite its proven ability, the Index of Leading Indicators is not foolproof. It cannot predict the exact timing of projected upswings or downturns. Leading indicators typically signal changes several months in advance, but the Index can never identify exactly when a change will take place. To counter this problem, the Center for International Business Cycle Research (CIBCR) has recommended that the BEA publish two composite measures—a short-leading index and a long-leading index. The government has not adopted these recommendations, but CIBCR publishes its own indexes based on its assumptions. Regardless of how the Index is fine-tuned, it is only a tool and cannot explain the extent, meaning, or causes of impending change.

The Bureau of Economic Analysis also tracks two other indexes of cyclical activity: the Index of Coincident Indicators (composed of four statistical series), and the Index of Lagging Indicators (six series). The BEA indexes serve as basic measures of changing economic conditions, but their value depends upon the skill of the user. The meaning of a particular index number is always open to interpretation.

For many years the three indexes (and the individual indicators from which they are derived) were published monthly in a BEA journal entitled *Business Conditions Digest*, but this popular guide was discontinued in early 1990. Abbreviated data from *Business Conditions Digest* now appear in a supplemental section of the *Survey of Current Business*, the new official source of data on the three composite indexes. The Index of Leading Economic Indicators also receives broad media coverage in sources such as *The Wall Street Journal*.

GNP: The National Income and Product Accounts

The centerpiece of U.S. economic statistics is the Gross National Product (GNP), a quarterly measure of the total value of all goods and services produced by the national economy. It is difficult to imagine a more involved statistical chore than counting the total output of our enormous economy. Once again, the Great Depression provided the impetus and the National Bureau of Economic Research provided the solution. The NBER designed two different measures of national output. Instead of counting the actual production of individual items, two shortcuts were devised. The first was to measure broad categories of expenditures for goods and services, since the amount paid for the items equals the value of output by definition. The second method was to measure the income earned by the factors of production which generated the output. Accounting principles indicate that the sources of funds must equal their uses (i.e., total income in the system must equal total output). This equality enabled the designers of the model to measure two separate accounts which could be reconciled with one another.

Because two methods are used, the GNP accounts are more properly called the National Income and Product Accounts (NIPA). The product side is calculated by summing the expenditures of the four basic participants in the economic system: households, businesses, governments, and the foreign sector. In the language of NIPA, the four expenditure components of the GNP are personal expenditures, domestic private investment, government purchases, and net exports. On the income side of the accounts, the two basic factors of production are labor and property. The labor component consists of employee compensation and proprietors' income, while the property segment is derived from corporate profits, rental income, and net interest income.

Of course this is a very simple picture of an extremely complex model. A variety of detailed accounting devices make the model as realistic as possible. What's more, it would be truly amazing if both sides of such a complex model balanced automatically. To deal with this, a figure for "statistical discrepancy" is added to the income side of the equation to balance the accounts.

NIPA values are calculated by the U.S. Bureau of Economic Analysis; in fact, tracking GNP is the BEA's most important function. The model utilizes hundreds of statistical series gathered from many sources. Most data are collected by government agencies for other purposes; few are produced explicitly for the GNP. The government also relies on dozens of private organizations which are dependable producers of economic data. Most are trade associations, but reputable commercial firms are used as well. The BEA does not simply apply statistics to the model in a mechanical fashion. Considerable judgment and analysis is required to produce the Accounts.

The model counts only expenditures for final goods and services. For example, steel, rubber, and other products used in the production of automobiles would be double counted if the value of the component parts were added to the value of the finished product. By counting only the finished good (or final transaction), the GNP is essentially measuring only the value added by each stage of processing.

Data are calculated quarterly, but GNP is always presented as a seasonally adjusted annual amount. GNP figures are presented in two basic formats. Amounts are first presented in terms of current dollar values, called nominal GNP. The Accounts are also calculated using price levels in effect during a base year, which is presently 1982. This is called constant dollar GNP, or real GNP. Using this measure allows for comparison of national output over long periods of time regardless of inflation rates. GNP statistics are revised many times after they are first released. In the interests of expediency, a preliminary figure (called a flash report) is released within 20 days of the quarter's end. As calculations are revised, it is then adjusted to reflect incoming data two more times over the next several months. Because GNP is composed of so many figures, and because some of the data are collected only once each year, the numbers are revised a third time on an annual basis. Finally, every five years or so, historical GNP values undergo benchmark revisions to reflect refinements in the model. As revised figures become available, they are published in the BEA's monthly journal *Survey of Current Business*.

A model of such sophistication has many limitations. The most significant is that GNP misses entire categories of output in the economy. Two major overlooked transactions are those for which there are no dollar expenditures, and those which go unreported. Examples of the former are the value of a homemaker's labor, the efforts of do-it-yourselfers, food grown for family consumption, and barter. The second category of overlooked transactions covers the underground economy: cash payments not reported to the IRS, and ill-gotten gains from criminal activities. Another weakness in the Income and Product Accounts is that negative output is not subtracted from the total. Outputs such as pollution, which actually deplete the nation's total worth, should not be counted as positive values.

Labor Force Data

Labor statistics are an important component of economic analysis, but most indicators of labor force conditions are misunderstood by the public. For that reason, it is just as important to stress what each figure does *not* measure. Even more true for labor data is the warning that no single economic indicator can ever provide a full picture of current conditions and what they mean for the business cycle.

The widely publicized monthly unemployment rate is a key bellwether of economic well-being and the success of public policy measures. The government uses three major sources to generate employment and unemployment data. The first is the monthly Current Population Survey conducted for the BLS by the Bureau of the Census. The CPS is a carefully designed nationwide sample which surveys respondents' employment status, earnings, and demographic characteristics. It is the principal source for determining the unemployment rate for the United States, for the 10 most populous states, and for the New York and Los Angeles metropolitan areas. Data for the other 40 states, metropolitan areas, and cities with populations greater than 50,000 are obtained from a combination of the Current Population Survey and two additional sources. One is a monthly sample survey of U.S. employers conducted by the Bureau of Labor Statistics. This is called the Current Employment Statistics program (CES), but is usually referred to as the Establishment Survey. It covers those establishments responsible for 40% of the civilian employment in the U.S. and provides data on the number employed, the average weekly earnings, hours worked, and overtime hours. The other source is data on claims for unemployment insurance provided by local employment security offices. Taken together, the three provide a more accurate picture of the labor force than the CPS alone can give. Based on these sources, unemployment rates are calculated at the local level by regional economists of each state labor department, using BLS guidelines.

The Bureau of Labor Statistics has devised detailed definitions of employment and unemployment. People are counted as employed if they did any work for pay during the previous week. The unemployed are those individuals who did not work, but are available for work and seeking a job. All people over 16 who are not institutionalized or serving in the armed forces, and who are either employed or unemployed are by definition part of the civilian labor force. However, many people of working age are not part of the labor force. These include full-time students, homemakers who are not working, individuals who cannot work due to disabilities or family responsibilities, and those who simply are not looking for work. Since 1983, the BLS has provided separate figures for the total labor force (including the armed forces) as well as the traditional data on the civilian labor force. For either group, the unemployment rate is obtained by dividing the number of people unemployed by the number in the labor force. The labor force participation rate is calculated by dividing the number of people in the labor force by the noninstitutional population of working age.

The definitions outlined above result in a number of limitations in labor force data. The seriousness of the limitations depends on the user's intent and point of view. Some critics claim the number of unemployed is exaggerated by these definitions, while others insist the unemployed are undercounted. There is a measure of truth to both of these claims. The question to consider is what unemployment statistics are supposed to count. Is the unemployment rate an indicator of the utilization of our nation's human resources? If so, it should make distinctions between part-time and full-time work, temporary and permanent jobs, how many people are working in their chosen fields, and whether they are utilizing their marketable skills. Another point of view would be to simply count all those people who are not earning income but would like to. A narrower view would be to look at only those unemployed who have lost their jobs through no choice of their own. In reality, the unemployment rate measures none of the above, though the BLS does collect data which can shed light on such concerns.

The unemployment rate is insufficient by itself to fully describe the state of the U.S. labor market. For this reason, many additional indicators are compiled. The number of employed married men, the number of unemployed black youth, the average duration of unemployment, the number of discouraged workers, and the number of newly created jobs are some of the more frequently encountered labor statistics.

Whether the number of employed or the number of unemployed is the more important figure depends upon the user's purpose; neither presents a complete view. Employment and unemployment can both be on the rise if there are many new entrants to the labor force (i.e., the labor force participation rate increases). Similarly, the unemployment *rate* can increase when employment is increasing if the duration of unemployment is on the rise. Because the analysis can be so complex, the quality of unemployment information in the U.S. is frequently criticized, especially during times of high unemployment.

Price Levels and Inflation

Inflation has been one of the most difficult economic problems of the post-Viet Nam era. The double-digit inflation of the late 1970s and early 1980s eroded purchasing power, undermined economic stability, and frustrated corporate planning. Even when comparatively low, inflation remains a worry for economic policy makers. Consequently, economic indicators which measure price changes are an important tool of economic analysis. And though everyone understands the effect of rising prices on buying power, few grasp the concepts used to measure inflation.

Like other economic indicators, statistics which track inflation are based upon theoretical models of real world behavior. Since it would be impractical to monitor the price changes of every item sold in the U.S., simpler methods have been devised to measure inflation. Three basic series track changes in price levels over time: the Consumer Price Index, the Producer Price Index, and the Implicit Price Deflator for Personal Consumption Expenditures.

The most widely used indicator of inflation is the Consumer Price Index (CPI), formerly called the Cost of Living Index. The CPI is a composite index (like the Index of Leading Indicators), and is computed monthly by the Bureau of Labor Statistics. It is based on the prices of a fixed "market basket" of consumer goods and services representing common items purchased for everyday living. The components of the market basket are determined by an annual Consumer Expenditure Survey. Major categories include food, clothing, furniture, shelter, health care, entertainment, and transportation. A total figure called the All Items Index is calculated as well as detailed numbers for each component.

The present CPI base year is designated as 1982-1984. This means that the values for some mid-point between the two dates (usually June 1983) are set equal to 100. Since 1978, the BLS has calculated two series: the traditional one based on the buying habits of Urban Wage Earners (CPI-W); and a newer series based on the behavior of a larger group designated as All Urban Consumers (CPI-U). Data are available on an "All Cities" basis, and for individual metropolitan areas. Since 1987, local data have been reported for 29 cities—issued monthly for five cities and bimonthly for 10 others. Data for the 14 remaining CPI cities are now published semi-annually. The Bureau also gathers price data for additional cities for which no local index is published, thus enhancing the quality of the All Cities Index.

The CPI has a number of conceptual limitations. An important but subtle problem is the change in product quality over time. For example, fruit drinks are now being made with natural juices (presumably an improvement), but the size of many packaged food items has shrunk. The BLS has developed some ways of measuring the relationship between price changes and quality, but the issue is still a major weakness of the CPI. As pointed out in Chapter 13, the CPI is not intended to compare the cost of living from one city to another, even though statistics for individual areas are published. The Index is designed only to measure the change in price within each city, not the comparative cost of living between geographic areas.

One long-standing problem has been partially corrected. Prior to 1980, the Consumer Expenditure Survey was conducted infrequently. Thus the market basket used in constructing the CPI did not reflect changing tastes and buying behavior, or new products. The fact that the Survey is now being done annually means that the BLS has extensive new data which can be used to update the model. While this is an improvement, it causes problems because the CPI is intended to be comparable over long periods of time. Major changes in the design and composition of the CPI can undermine comparability. For this reason, the annual survey results are used to make minor adjustments in the market basket. The reluctance with which the BLS makes drastic changes to the CPI is a reflection on its importance as an economic indicator. The value of the Index affects literally billions of dollars in payments every year. Cost of Living Adjustment (COLA) clauses in collective bargaining agreements tie employee wage increases directly to the CPI. Residential and commercial leases, long-term contracts, and alimony and child-support payments have similar escalators based on changes in the Index. The government ties Social Security benefits and income tax policy to the CPI. These are among the reasons the Index is watched so carefully every month.

The Producer Price Index, formerly called the Wholesale Price Index, is also generated by the BLS and has been issued monthly since the turn of the century. The PPI measures the wholesale prices of goods and services purchased by the business sector. Data are available on a national basis only, but detailed figures are published for more than 3,000 commodities. Separate indexes are published for crude materials, intermediate goods, and finished products. The PPI is used for setting contract prices for commercial transactions, estimating business costs, and also as an effective predictor of consumer price changes. Because PPI data are so detailed, the series can

be used to track wholesale price changes for specific products over long periods of time. Individual indexes are calculated for items as varied as toilet bowls, high school textbooks, and ice cream.

Considered by many to be a truer indicator of inflation, yet virtually unknown by the general public, the Implicit Price Deflator (IPD) is calculated in conjunction with the National Income and Product Accounts. The Implicit Price Deflator includes a much broader range of prices than the CPI or PPI. The IPD is calculated for the entire GNP, and for its Personal Consumption Expenditures component. The latter is seen by many economists as a more realistic measure of changing consumer prices than the CPI.

As mentioned previously, current values of the GNP are also presented in constant dollars. This is done by "deflating" the individual components of the GNP using detailed CPI and PPI figures as well as price indexes developed by the Bureau of Economic Analysis. The IPD is then calculated by dividing Current Dollar GNP by Constant Dollar GNP to obtain the broader price index. Data on the various Implicit Price Deflators can be found monthly in the *Survey of Current Business*. Summary figures for the CPI and PPI are released monthly in issues of *BLS News*. Detailed data for specific commodities are published somewhat later in the monthly journals *CPI Detailed Report* and *Producer Prices and Price Indexes*. Annual averages for all CPI cities are published in the January issue of the *Detailed Report*.

Other Key Indicators

Three other economic indicators deserve special mention. The federal budget deficit, the balance of payments accounts, and the money supply all play a critical role in economic analysis and policy decisions.

The staggering size and persistent growth of the federal deficit remains the central economic issue of the 1990s. A deficit occurs when the government spends more in a fiscal year than it generates in revenues. If this situation continues each year, the size of the cumulative deficit mounts. The federal debt is the amount the U.S. Treasury must borrow in order for the government to operate. The borrowing is done through the issuance of short-term securities, such as Treasury Bills, and longer-term bonds. The biggest cause of the national debt is the federal deficit, but debt financing is utilized for other purposes. The national debt and the deficit are not equivalent values. To make an analogy, most households do not operate under a deficit—that is, under normal circum-

stances they do not spend more than they earn. Yet they do incur short- and long-term debts to finance homes, cars, and other purchases.

The key resource for analyzing the size and structure of the deficit is the Federal Budget, but two measures of the deficit can be used. One is the budget information compiled by OMB, and the other is the government accounts data used in the NIPA calculations. The two values differ due to certain assumptions built into the NIPA model.

The estimated budget for the coming year, together with actual revenues and expenditures for previous years, can be found in the annual *Budget of the United States Government*. Summary data on the deficit and national debt can be seen in sources such as the monthly *Federal Reserve Bulletin* and the more detailed *Treasury Bulletin*, which appears quarterly. NIPA values for the federal accounts can be located in the monthly *Survey of Current Business*.

The U.S. Balance of Payments is another important, but complex economic series. The balance of trade (more correctly called the balance of merchandise trade) comprises only one aspect of international payments. The merchandise trade balance is the difference between the value of goods the U.S. exports and the goods it imports. If the value of net exports is positive, the U.S. has a trade surplus; the opposite situation results in a trade deficit. However, international money transactions involve far more than the flow of tangible goods. The Current Accounts series track services, such as travel and tourism, and foreign aid to other governments. Capital Accounts include the monetary transactions of central banks (such as the Federal Reserve Board and the Bank of England), direct investment abroad (either in real estate, factories and equipment, or the purchase of foreign securities), and assets held in foreign bank accounts. Together, these current and capital accounts make up the total Balance of Payments. To understand the terminology of these accounts, it is important to see the following relationships:

Merchandise Trade + Services = Balance on Goods & Services

Goods & Services + Foreign Aid = Balance on Current Account

Current Account + Capital Account = Balance of Payments

For any of these accounts, payments received by residents of the U.S. from other nations constitute credits in the U.S. Balance of Payments. Conversely, payments made by U.S. residents to foreign nations are counted as debits. Exports are always credits and foreign aid is a debit. Balance of payments data are released on a quarterly basis in the monthly journals *Economic Indicators*

and *Survey of Current Business.* Merchandise trade data are reported monthly in the previous two journals and in the monthly *U.S. Export and Import Merchandise Trade* from the Bureau of the Census.

One other indicator which merits special attention is the Money Stock (commonly called the money supply). The Federal Reserve Board (hereafter called the Fed) began compiling this information in 1960, but definitions have since undergone major changes. The most commonly seen measure of Money Stock is what the Fed calls M-1. The original definition of M-1 was the amount of currency in circulation plus the value of all demand deposits (checking accounts). This definition made the distinction between money available for transaction purposes (i.e., as a medium of exchange), and money stored for future use in savings accounts. Fundamental changes in banking during the 1970s made the old money supply definitions inadequate, so the Fed redefined M-1 in 1980. In addition, the other measures of Money Stock were also redefined. There are presently four other indicators of the money supply which are successively broader in scope. M-1 represents currency and checkable accounts, while the others include measures of "near monies." For example, M-2 includes M-1 plus all passbook and statement savings accounts, time deposits of less than $100,000, deposits in IRAs, and other liquid accounts. Unfortunately, continuing innovations in financial markets mean that even these new definitions have serious limitations. On one hand, new types of transaction accounts may still be excluded from M-1 calculations. On the other hand, the broader definitions of the money supply include funds that are clearly not intended for transaction purposes.

Despite these limitations, many economists ardently believe that Money Stock measures are the most important type of economic indicator. The supply of money has a profound effect on interest rates, inflation, business expansion, and general economic growth.The Fed publishes money supply data weekly because of its importance as a policy measure and barometer of economic performance. Statistics are released by the Fed on Fridays and appear in *The Wall Street Journal* every Monday. Detailed figures appear in the Federal Reserve Board's weekly *Statistical Release* number H.6, entitled *Money Stock Measures and Liquid Assets.* Summary data can also be seen in the monthly publications *Economic Indicators* and the *Federal Reserve Bulletin.*

Dozens of additional series measure other important components of the U.S. economy, such as banking, housing, and retail trade. Some indicators track very specific industries which have a demonstrated effect on the economy at large. Examples include steel production, auto sales, and paper and paperboard production. As they're released, many of these statistics are published on the front page of *The Wall Street Journal.* Major indicators can also be found in weekly business sources such as *Barron's, Business Week,* and *Industry Week.* All may also be located in the official journals and news releases published by the agencies which compile the data. Several excellent guides to major economic indicators explain how various statistical series are compiled, why they are important, and in what sources the data may be found. The best of these are discussed in the "Further Reading" section of this chapter.

BASIC SOURCES OF ECONOMIC STATISTICS

Many primary and secondary sources present economic data for public use. Most are published by the government agencies or other organizations which produce the numbers. Many are specialized publications which concentrate on a narrow category of indicator, while others provide a wide array of statistical tables. Because of the abundance of resources, only a few of the best known sources will be described in detail. The documents are divided into three categories for the purpose of this discussion. The first group is comprised of encyclopedic publications which provide summary data for hundreds of indicators. The second consists of sources with narrower focus, offering detailed information on fewer series. The third deals with resources which contain short- and long-term forecasts for the economy. In all cases, the emphasis is on national conditions. Sources which compare data for states, cities, counties, or metropolitan areas are introduced in Chapter 17.

General Economic Compendia

With the huge number of statistical publications available, there is a genuine need for reference books which gather together important economic data from diverse sources. Several excellent compilations are produced on a regular basis by both the federal government and private publishers.

Statistical Abstract of the United States (U.S. Bureau of the Census—Annual).

The *Statistical Abstract* provides data on population, vital statistics, health, law enforcement, education, politics, and other areas of general interest. Although it contains much more than economic statistics, fully two-thirds of the material can be characterized as economic or industrial. Most of the information is provided by government agencies, but nongovernment sources are utilized also. Organizations as diverse as the National Hockey League and the National Council of Churches contribute material to the compendium. Each table cites the titles of the publications where the information was found, so researchers may consult the original source for greater detail. When data are obtained from unpublished sources, the name of the issuing organization is provided.

The *Statistical Abstract* is divided into numerous topical sections such as "Immigration and Naturalization," "Social Insurance and Welfare," and "Agriculture." Although most data are given at the national level only, some regional and state information can also be seen. A special feature lists state rankings for 50 different statistical measures. Most tables provide both current and historical data. The book also contains an excellent bibliography of statistical publications arranged by subject, a list of state and foreign statistical abstracts, and a fairly detailed subject index to tables in the book. It is not always the best source for general economic statistics, but with 1,600 tables it is a likely and convenient starting point.

Another useful compendium from the Bureau of the Census is *Historical Statistics of the United States: Colonial Times to 1970.* Although the *Statistical Abstract* has been published since 1878, data in each year's edition are not necessarily comparable over long periods of time. *Historical Statistics* presents information in a single publication, with footnotes to each table indicating when definitions and methodologies have changed. A narrative history of each time series explains when data were first collected and how. A subject index to the tables and an index by time period are included. A third general guide, the *County and City Data Book*, is discussed in Chapter 17.

Business Statistics (U.S. Bureau of Economic Analysis—Biennial).

This amazing collection of economic and industrial statistics covers 1,900 separate data series used by the BEA in calculating the Gross National Product. It appears every other year as a supplement to the monthly *Survey of Current Business*, though there is some lag in publishing. The edition covering data through the end of 1988 came out in early 1990.

The main section of *Business Statistics* provides monthly statistics for each time series for the previous five years, as well as annual data for the preceding 20 years. Though it is clear how most of the numbers are relevant to the GNP model, many series are quite unexpected. The publication also provides summary data for individual industries, offering information on production, inventories, imports, and exports. U.S. foreign trade data are also presented for major countries and regions of the world.

An additional section of historical data provides approximately 20 years of monthly figures for 250 of the most important series, and presents a full 30 years of monthly data for those few series compiled by the BEA itself. An extensive discussion of each statistical series outlines the definitions and methodology used. The book also contains a table of contents and subject index, though neither is terribly detailed. Given the variety and number of important economic statistics it contains, *Business Statistics* should be one of the first sources which researchers consult to obtain historical data.

The Economic Report of the President (U.S. Council of Economic Advisors—Annual).

The Economic Report of the President, released each February, is a report on the state of the economy, sent by the President and his advisors to the Congress. About two-thirds of the publication is a narrative analysis of economic issues and conditions. The discussion is readable and well-organized by topic. Individual chapters cover the major economic concerns of the moment. *The Economic Report* is definitely a partisan document, so readers should be alert to the usual political exaggeration and obfuscation. Still, the report is a useful and succinct review of economic conditions, and an outline of the President's current and future economic policies. The narrative section also contains a five-year outlook for the U.S. economy, including projections for the GNP and other key indicators.

The remainder of the publication is a collection of over 100 statistical tables which track the most important economic indicators. Each table offers monthly or quarterly data for the previous two or three years, together with 20 years or more of annual data. Like the *Statistical Abstract* and *Business Statistics*, it is a secondary source, obtaining data from other agencies. It covers fewer series than the other two sources, but the statistics are those

most frequently used. Convenient, authoritative, inexpensive, and easy to use, it is one of the few titles which should be in every business library.

More recent data can be found in the Council's monthly periodical *Economic Indicators*. The presentation parallels that of the annual report, though there are fewer tables, and some are less detailed. Monthly or quarterly figures are given for one to three years, with annual data from five to ten years. Some information is also presented in graphic form.

Standard & Poor's Statistical Service (Standard & Poor's Corporation—Monthly, with Cumulations).

Standard & Poor's Statistical Service is issued in two parts: a monthly report on *Current Statistics*, and a set of pamphlets called *Basic Statistics*, which provides historical information. Each current issue contains monthly data for the past three years, together with annual averages or totals for each of those years. The latest monthly issue supersedes the previous month's, and the historical volumes provide data beyond the latest three years. Sometimes there is a gap in coverage between the latest monthly issue and the corresponding *Basic Statistics*, so subscribers should also keep the most recent January issue of the monthly service.

The *Current Statistics* section is a thorough compendium of economic indicators, though heavily weighted toward banking and investment statistics. The publication also carries fairly detailed data on the CPI and PPI, hourly earnings by major industry groups, and production figures for most industries. The companion set of *Basic Statistics* is published in 10 parts, ranging from "Building and Building Materials" to "Agricultural Products." Data in the historical volumes are given for at least 20 years, with some time series going back to the 1920s. A third section of the publication is the annual *Security Price Index Record*, which was described in Chapter 10.

Since most Standard & Poor's data come from government sources, why pay for the more expensive commercial service instead of relying on *Business Statistics* or *The Economic Report of the President*? The most important reason is convenience; Standard & Poor's provides both current and historical statistics in one package. The publication is also extremely simple to use. Tables are well-indexed, and many are presented in simpler formats than in the official sources. The monthly issues of *Current Statistics* usually contain more timely data than the official government periodicals. The *Statistical Service* also lists more monthly data for historical series than the government sources do. The S&P service is not the ideal solution to all data needs; *Business Statistics*, for example, covers more types of data than the

S&P publication. But certain S&P series cannot be found in the BEA publication, particularly for financial information. Perhaps the biggest drawback to the *Statistical Service* is the amount of detail which is omitted. In an effort to be simple and succinct, S&P sacrifices headnotes, footnotes, and other labeling which would explain the data more completely. Still, many researchers consider it the fastest, most convenient way to locate important economic data.

EconBase: Time Series and Forecasts (The WEFA Group—Monthly).

This online database is compiled by the WEFA Group, a respected econometric forecasting firm formed in 1987 through the merger of Wharton Econometric Forecasting Associates and Chase Econometrics. Although *EconBase* covers a wide variety of economic time series, almost all historical data come from government sources. Data are not limited to broad economic indicators; many industry-specific series are also included. Among the latter are detailed price indexes from the CPI and PPI, industrial production indexes, employment by industry, and manufacturers' shipments and inventories. A limited amount of data for states, metropolitan areas, and for foreign countries can also be found. Depending on the source, series are monthly, quarterly, or annual. There are approximately 10,000 time series, and numbers may date back to 1948, including those for monthly series. Approximately 10% of the *EconBase* records include one- or two-year projections produced by WEFA's own economists. Economic forecasting is the WEFA Group's major activity, and *EconBase* is one of the few econometric files available through a popular database vendor.

EconBase is a small subset of data from the WEFA Group's larger proprietary database, which covers a much broader range of forecasts and historical data. *EconBase* is a more affordable product, accessible to a wider audience. At present, it is available exclusively on DIALOG, and is surprisingly inexpensive to search. For a few dollars, the researcher can obtain a monthly time series for a single variable dating back 20 years or more. The system was not designed for sophisticated searching, though records can be retrieved by issuing agency, unit of measurement, and SIC code. Searchers can locate specific information by combining keywords in the series title with other characteristics such as agency name or frequency of publication, but with so many similar economic measures, this is not recommended. The most effective method of searching is usually by series code, because every time series is assigned a unique identification number. To obtain code numbers, users must either

consult WEFA's *EconBase Data Directory*, or call the company's customer service hot line. For those using the database frequently, purchasing the directory is a modest and worthwhile investment. An especially useful feature of *EconBase* is the ability to limit searches to records containing forecasts. Records can also be limited to those containing only domestic data. Several standard formats are available for displaying search results.

Subject-Specific Data Sources

Numerous publications provide detailed information on a narrower range of topics. The handful of resources discussed on the following pages are among the most important and popular publications of this type.

Survey of Current Business (U.S. Bureau of Economic Analysis—Monthly).

This monthly periodical from the BEA is the primary source for information on the National Income and Product Accounts. Although the Accounts are tabulated quarterly, they are revised each month, and the revisions are presented here. The *Survey of Current Business* contains the most extensive breakdown of current NIPA values found in any ongoing publication. Each segment of the model is shown in considerable detail, because many components are themselves important economic indicators. The model is also presented from various points of view. GNP is tabulated by stage of processing, by business sector, and by type of expenditure. National Income is given by type of income as well as income source.

The *Survey of Current Business* includes several other important features. The yellow pages (or "C-pages"), contain a new section called "Business Cycle Indicators." The "C-pages" list the BEA's three composite indexes, including the Index to Leading Economic Indicators. Key data sets which make up the composite indexes are also listed, and 30 years of cyclical indicators are presented in graphic form. Information is not as detailed as that formerly found in *Business Conditions Digest*, nor is it as current, but it is sufficient for most research purposes.

The *Survey of Current Business* also serves as a wonderful compendium of general economic and industrial statistics. The blue pages (or "S-pages") contain a section called "Current Business Statistics," providing current information for every series seen in the biennial *Business Statistics*. Exhibit 15-1 illustrates the diversity of economic indicators found here. On that single page, researchers can find monthly and annual figures for

manufacturers' unfilled orders, new business incorporations, business failures, prices received by farmers for selected commodities, and the CPI.

The *Survey*'s monthly "Business Situation" offers an overview of economic conditions. The balance of each issue consists of narrative and statistical articles on special topics. Many are quite technical, explaining the methodology of NIPA revisions or similar topics, but most are understandable to the serious reader, and are quite worthwhile. Ongoing studies conducted by the BEA, such as the Plant and Equipment Expenditure Survey and a study of U.S. international trade with major countries, are summarized on a quarterly basis. Other, more detailed studies are presented annually. Examples of recurring reports are "Pollution Abatement Expenditures," "Foreign Direct Investment in the U.S.," and "U.S. Direct Investment Abroad." The most frequently cited annual article is the analysis of "State, County and Metropolitan Area Personal Income;" preliminary income data appear in the April issue, and revised tables are published in August. The back cover of every issue provides a calendar of release dates for pending BEA data. The December issue provides a subject index to the special features and narrative articles of the previous year. Users of the blue pages will also find a brief but serviceable index to the statistical series.

Monthly Labor Review (U.S. Bureau of Labor Statistics—Monthly).

The highly respected *Monthly Labor Review* is the official organ of the BLS. Each issue includes a summary of recent BLS activities, a list of major collective bargaining agreements due to expire, a discussion of new developments in labor relations, highlights of notable BLS research, book reviews, and a list of new BLS publications. Two main sections are the statistical tables and the timely articles on labor topics. Articles are generally well-written and engaging and the conclusions are frequently quoted in the national media. A variety of special articles are issued on a recurring basis. Some are annual forecasts, others serve as "year-in-review" articles. Topics covered in this fashion are prices, employment and unemployment, collective bargaining, and changes in state unemployment insurance laws. A subject index to all *MLR* articles appears in the December issue.

The statistical section presents summaries of the more detailed tables found in other BLS journals, such as *Employment and Earnings*, the *CPI Detailed Report*, and *Compensation and Working Conditions.* This section is a convenient distillation of the most useful and widely sought series. For many researchers, the 40 or so sum-

EXHIBIT 15-1. *Survey of Current Business*

Unless otherwise stated in footnotes below, data through 1988 and methodological notes are as shown in BUSINESS STATISTICS, 1961-88	Units	Annual 1988	Annual 1989	1989 May	June	July	Aug.	Sept.	Oct.	Nov.	Dec.	1990 Jan.	Feb.	Mar.	Apr.	May	June
GENERAL BUSINESS INDICATORS—Continued																	
MANUFACTURERS' SHIPMENTS, INVENTORIES, AND ORDERS—Continued																	
Unfilled orders, end of period (unadjusted), total	mil. $ ..	463,934	509,942	490,531	491,250	496,816	492,888	493,140	492,279	499,483	509,942	516,493	516,492	522,268	r523,388	522,637	
Durable goods industries, total	do	443,957	490,624	469,868	470,213	475,754	471,779	472,195	472,112	479,895	490,624	496,945	497,023	502,271	r503,170	502,782	
Nondurable goods industries with unfilled orders ‡	do	19,977	19,318	20,663	21,037	21,062	21,109	20,945	20,167	19,588	19,318	19,548	19,469	19,997	r20,218	19,855	
Unfilled orders, end of period (seasonally adjusted) total	mil. $ ..	468,860	514,499	487,913	491,834	496,359	495,002	495,794	497,866	504,750	514,499	515,367	512,654	516,426	r518,193	520,266	
By industry group:																	
Durable goods industries, total #	do	447,868	494,196	467,500	470,917	475,834	474,253	475,087	477,509	484,475	494,196	495,389	492,947	496,730	r498,308	500,471	
Primary metals	do	25,737	22,510	26,114	25,705	25,115	24,151	23,572	22,775	22,525	22,510	22,620	22,362	22,756	r23,047	23,343	
Blast furnaces, steel mills	do	10,903	8,730	10,520	10,520	10,086	9,655	9,117	8,795	8,718	8,593	8,730	8,958	8,815	8,829	9,149	
Nonferrous and other primary metals	do	12,591	11,444	13,140	13,190	13,059	12,634	12,431	11,737	11,611	11,444	11,357	11,214	11,396	r11,549	11,603	
Fabricated metal products	do	28,406	25,550	27,459	27,567	26,995	26,210	25,960	25,852	25,538	25,550	25,756	25,462	25,500	r25,533	25,192	
Machinery, except electrical	do	59,963	61,472	61,857	62,647	61,978	61,779	62,088	61,579	61,900	61,472	61,730	61,624	60,853	r60,295	60,386	
Electrical machinery	do	93,498	94,322	90,662	90,416	90,625	89,985	90,571	90,772	92,387	94,322	93,800	93,128	92,473	r92,720	92,700	
Transportation equipment	do	212,120	262,703	233,720	237,131	244,047	245,266	245,654	249,020	254,657	262,703	264,445	263,525	268,513	r269,926	272,162	
Aircraft, missiles, and parts	do	174,722	224,779	196,185	198,610	206,512	208,617	209,565	212,498	218,199	224,779	226,718	225,352	231,022	r232,037	234,228	
Nondurable goods industries with unfilled orders ‡	do	20,992	20,303	20,413	20,917	20,525	20,749	20,707	20,357	20,275	20,303	19,978	19,707	19,696	r19,885	19,795	
By market category:																	
Home goods and apparel	do	8,387	8,679	8,234	8,124	8,151	8,097	8,263	8,493	8,564	8,679	8,160	7,636	7,269	r7,320	7,191	
Consumer staples	do	836	867	921	·1,004	920	949	913	914	927	867	805	796	r727	682		
Equip. and defense prod., excl. auto	do	286,731	328,716	304,197	308,388	310,782	310,586	311,763	313,753	319,075	328,716	330,634	329,126	332,980	r332,125	332,693	
Automotive equipment	do	8,888	7,677	8,395	8,294	8,115	7,972	7,817	7,672	7,697	7,677	7,670	7,440	7,263	r7,479	7,844	
Construction materials, supplies, and intermediate products	do	15,541	13,989	14,806	14,670	14,351	13,789	13,872	13,790	13,665	13,989	14,010	13,487	13,299	r13,451	13,312	
Other materials, supplies, and intermediate products	do	148,477	154,571	151,360	151,354	154,040	153,609	153,166	153,244	154,822	154,571	154,068	154,160	154,819	r157,091	158,544	
Supplementary series:																	
Household durables	do	6,122	6,099	5,925	5,817	5,913	5,908	6,043	6,157	6,154	6,099	5,783	5,457	5,289	r5,304	5,201	
Capital goods industries	do	345,037	398,602	367,050	371,150	377,765	377,769	378,787	381,909	389,202	398,602	399,757	398,543	402,485	r403,250	404,818	
Nondefense	do	179,640	231,182	203,007	207,394	214,576	215,560	215,171	216,975	221,754	231,182	234,342	233,610	238,345	r239,622	240,348	
Defense	do	165,397	167,420	164,043	163,756	163,189	162,209	163,616	164,934	167,448	167,420	165,415	164,933	164,140	r163,628	164,470	
BUSINESS INCORPORATIONS @																	
New incorporations (50 States and Dist. Col.): Unadjusted	number	685,095	r678,421	62,242	61,041	51,373	56,755	51,014	53,175	50,214	54,017	62,189	54,150	r63,755	56,177		
Seasonally adjusted	do			57,738	57,586	54,478	56,642	54,502	53,282	55,180	57,040	59,397	56,821	r56,271	54,968		
INDUSTRIAL AND COMMERCIAL FAILURES @																	
Failures, total	number	57,099	49,719	4,406	4,180	3,679	4,231	3,676	4,226	3,989	3,684						
Commercial service	do	22,782	17,399	1,655	1,441	1,281	1,394	1,230	1,299	1,325	1,229						
Construction	do	6,828	6,829	573	586	539	628	532	607	530	498						
Manufacturing and mining	do	4,719	4,184	357	321	300	387	336	387	380	291						
Retail trade	do	11,487	10,803	948	962	820	920	832	968	832	799						
Wholesale trade	do	4,459	3,606	304	304	236	314	275	319	287	264						
Liabilities (current), total	mil. $ ..	35,908.1	35,663.6	1,873.2	2,186.0	4,073.4	2,960.0	1,751.2	2,223.9	2,000.8	5,085.4						
Commercial service	do	7,987.2	6,310.0	428.8	441.5	413.2	596.8	453.6	487.4	566.0	554.4						
Construction	do	1,878.6	2,583.1	141.1	100.9	141.9	188.9	169.7	225.7	115.0	914.2						
Manufacturing and mining	do	4,550.0	3,802.6	234.0	290.9	312.7	264.8	259.8	159.9	185.9	945.5						
Retail trade	do	3,936.4	3,203.3	139.5	259.8	235.2	1,091.6	229.9	201.1	158.7	235.5						
Wholesale trade	do	2,071.7	1,026.6	106.2	81.1	59.0	86.2	45.6	93.9	104.9	110.2						
Failure annual rate	No. per 10,000 concerns	98.0															
COMMODITY PRICES																	
PRICES RECEIVED AND PAID BY FARMERS †																	
Prices received, all farm products	1910-14 = 100	632	674	682	674	673	661	656	662	672	681	705	693	686	689	r703	693
Crops #	do	546	582	613	r595	592	554	547	552	555	551	587	577	555	566	r580	563
Commercial vegetables	do	716	775	778	r744	835	698	663	714	691	742	1,260	1,119	722	591	r620	606
Cotton	do	485	502	492	483	502	508	540	555	552	519	505	512	541	549	r552	527
Feed grains and hay	do	378	405	436	r414	398	379	378	371	373	375	379	379	387	406	r428	423
Food grains	do	378	428	441	426	421	417	416	418	411	420	414	399	392	391	r382	356
Fruit	do	683	704	751	r747	658	675	736	771	771	673	616	638	662	727	r754	718
Tobacco	do	1,295	1,400	1,395	r1,393	1,392	1,377	1,441	1,416	1,398	1,400	1,398	1,396	1,396	1,432	1,432	1,432
Livestock and products #	do	721	769	752	r755	757	773	769	778	794	817	827	814	822	818	r831	829
Dairy products	do	746	826	746	r759	771	807	856	899	948	985	960	881	838	820	r826	832
Meat animals	do	949	983	966	972	980	996	968	984	988	1,017	1,042	1,059	1,072	1,088	r1,120	1,113
Poultry and eggs	do	269	314	335	328	314	316	316	293	306	309	316	298	330	302	288	289
Prices paid: Production items	do	908	956			959			955			974			980		
All commodities and services, interest, taxes, and wage rates (parity index)	1910-14 = 100	1,165	1,220			1,227			1,224			1,246			1,259		
Parity ratio §	do	54	55	56	55	55	54	53	54	55	56	57			55		
CONSUMER PRICES *(U.S. Department of Labor Indexes)* **Not Seasonally Adjusted**																	
ALL ITEMS, WAGE EARNERS AND CLERICAL WORKERS (CPI-W)	1982-84 = 100	117.0	122.6	122.5	122.8	123.2	123.2	123.6	124.2	124.4	124.6	125.9	126.4	127.1	127.3	127.5	128.3
ALL ITEMS, ALL URBAN CONSUMERS (CPI-U)	1982-84 = 100	118.3	124.0	123.8	124.1	124.4	124.6	125.0	125.6	125.9	126.1	127.4	128.0	128.7	128.9	129.2	129.9
Special group indexes: All items less shelter	do	115.9	121.6	121.7	122.0	122.0	122.0	122.6	123.1	123.3	123.5	125.0	125.7	126.2	126.5	126.7	127.3
All items less food	do	118.3	123.7	123.5	123.9	124.2	124.3	124.8	125.4	125.6	125.8	126.7	127.3	128.1	128.4	128.7	129.4
All items less medical care	do	117.0	122.4	122.3	122.6	122.9	123.0	123.4	124.0	124.2	124.4	125.7	126.2	126.9	127.1	127.3	128.0

See footnotes at end of tables.

Reprinted from *Survey of Current Business*, published by the U.S. Bureau of Economic Analysis.

mary tables are sufficient for most information needs. Coverage includes employment and unemployment, price indexes, wages and other compensation, and labor productivity. There is no subject index to the statistical tables, but a detailed table of contents is given in every issue. Data in the *Monthly Labor Review* are cumulated in a retrospective publication called the *Handbook of Labor Statistics*. The *Handbook* appears on an irregular basis, every three to four years. The latest edition was published in 1989.

Employment and Earnings (U.S. Bureau of Labor Statistics—Monthly).

Strictly a statistical journal, *Employment and Earnings* presents employment data from the Current Population Survey, the Establishment Survey, and from the local state unemployment insurance offices. Most data are given in two separate tables, one seasonally adjusted, the other unadjusted. The level of detail seen in *Employment and Earnings* is quite extensive. For example, characteristics of the labor force (both the employed and unemployed), obtained from the Current Population Survey, are tabulated by marital status, age, race, sex, Spanish Origin, and median family income. Data are presented separately for target population groups such as women, Blacks, Viet Nam-era veterans, and youth. For unemployed persons, the duration and reason for unemployment are tallied. Persons outside the labor force are also counted, with reason for nonparticipation given.

Statistics from the Establishment Survey include nationwide hours and earnings for major industry groups, and labor productivity by industry. A third section provides composite labor force data for each state and metropolitan area. This series reports the number of people in the civilian labor force, and the number and percent who are unemployed. The inside front cover of each issue outlines special features which appear on a recurring basis. For example, annual averages for state and local unemployment data typically appear in the May issue. Finally, an appendix offers background on methodology, sampling techniques, and definitions used in compiling data.

Companion publications are also available. A convenient microfiche set called *Unemployment in States and Local Areas* presents estimates of unemployment for smaller levels of geography. In addition to states and metropolitan areas, it covers counties, cities, and even Minor Civil Divisions. It is published monthly, with an annual supplement. Monthly figures cite the total labor force, number employed, number unemployed, and the unemployment rate. Because it is more difficult to create estimates for smaller areas, preliminary numbers are

revised annually during the following year. *Employment, Hours and Earnings: States and Areas* is an annual publication in paper format. It presents data from the Establishment Survey as far back as 1939. *Employment, Hours and Earnings: United States* provides similar data by SIC groupings for the nation, with data back to 1904. The latter volume is revised periodically, but updated annually by a supplement to *Employment and Earnings*.

Federal Reserve Bulletin (U.S. Board of Governors of the Federal Reserve System—Monthly).

The *Bulletin* is the official publication of the Federal Reserve Board. It contains announcements of new regulations, a directory of the 12 Federal Reserve Banks and their branches, a list of staff members, and summaries of recent staff studies. It has readable and provocative articles, though some are quite technical. The *Bulletin* also contains over 50 pages of summary statistical tables in each issue. Tables cover the money supply, interest rates, bank conditions, the mortgage market, foreign exchange rates, U.S. government finances, and the stock market. A section of tables called "Policy Instruments" tracks monetary policy measures established directly by the Fed, such as the all-important Open Market Activities, where the Board buys and sells Treasury securities in order to adjust the money supply. The journal also publishes a list of special statistics which do not appear in every issue, together with the dates they can be found in the *Bulletin*. Finally, a calendar of release dates for important indicators is published in June and December, and a subject index to articles appears in December.

More detailed financial data can be seen in the Fed's *Statistical Release* series. These publications appear weekly, monthly, or quarterly, depending on the frequency of the data they report. Examples of titles are the weekly *Money Stock Measures and Liquid Assets* and the monthly *Industrial Production*. The weekly *Selected Interest and Exchange Rates* reports day-by-day foreign exchange rates for more than 30 currencies for the previous week. Historical data from the *Federal Reserve Bulletin* and *Statistical Releases* can be found in a monumental work entitled *Banking and Monetary Statistics, 1914-1979*. This retrospective guide is updated yearly by the Fed's *Annual Statistical Digest*.

Budget of the United States Government (U.S. Office of Management and Budget—Annual).

The federal budget, an enormous document of more than a thousand pages, generally appears in several volumes, though the format and arrangement can vary

from year to year. The narrative sections also vary in content and theme, because the report is intended as a presentation to the Congress and the American people.

Much of the information in the *Budget* is required by law, so certain generalizations can be made about the report. The main section consists of the annual budget message of the President, a message from the budget director, an overview of budget proposals, estimates of revenues for the coming year, actual data for previous years, and an analysis of the budget in terms of national goals and policies. This section also outlines the economic assumptions behind the budget estimates, including short-term forecasts of economic conditions. Finally, this section presents proposed expenditures by function and agency.

The basic information is supplemented by an Appendix, which provides an in-depth look at funding for each agency's programs, including the proposed language of appropriation bills, new programs, and objectives for each. The document also contains a section of "Special Analyses," which presents alternative views of the budget. First, it introduces a Current Services Budget, which has been mandated by law since 1974. This presents the proposed budget as though no new programs were added and none were deleted. Second, it presents the budget information appearing in the NIPA calculations, and discusses how the two series differ. Finally, it looks at the impact of the budget on the entire economy, in terms of the national debt, federal employment, aid to states and local governments, and national income tax policy.

Major changes in format and content occurred in the report for the 1991 fiscal year. A popular report entitled the *United States Budget in Brief* was discontinued, for example. The narrative portion of the main budget report no longer describes activities in a functional arrangement, but it is otherwise much improved. A section analyzing the impact of the President's proposals on the states has also been added.

Researchers can obtain background on important budget decisions from several independent sources, including various arms of Congress. The staff of the House Budget Committee issues an annual summary and analysis which is issued as a Committee Print. The Congressional Budget Office produces two important reports: the *Analysis of the President's Budgetary Proposals* examines the economic assumptions behind the budget, as well as the impact of major proposals; the *Economic and Budget Outlook* offers five-year projections for economic growth, revenues, and expenditures. Data on government finances can also be found in the *Treasury Bulletin*, a quarterly publication of the Treasury Department. This journal provides detailed information on federal revenues and expenditures, the composition and size of the national debt, government financial transactions with citizens of foreign countries, and coins and currency in circulation. Information on Treasury Department transactions is updated five times each week by the *Daily Treasury Statement*, which tabulates deposits and withdrawals in federal cash accounts and public debt transactions.

Economic Forecasts

A major concern for users of current statistics is where to obtain reliable forecasts for future economic activity. Many elaborate databases are available from respected forecasting firms. Among the best-known are DRI/McGraw-Hill (formerly Data Resources, Inc.) and the WEFA Group. Unfortunately, most services of this type charge substantial annual fees, so they are not widely accessible. Some producers of econometric databases have begun offering alternative pricing packages, including the ability to specify a small number of individual files in a subscription plan. But services remain expensive, and more affordable files such as *EconBase* are a rarity.

While most economic forecasting is based on massive econometric models, a variety of less elaborate publications provide estimates of future economic conditions. The most affordable are typically produced by the government or by nonprofit research centers. Both *The Economic Report of the President* and the *Budget of the United States Government* offer brief glimpses at official projections for a few key indicators, as do several reports from the Congressional Budget Office. Most government forecasts focus on specific areas of the economy, however. The Department of Agriculture issues separate *Situation and Outlook Reports* for more than 15 agricultural commodities, and also publishes a monthly periodical called the *Agricultural Outlook*, and an annual *Agricultural Outlook Yearbook*. Other popular government publications containing economic projections include *Employment Projections* and *Occupational Projections and Training Data*, biennial compilations from the Bureau of Labor Statistics; the *Annual Energy Outlook* from the Energy Information Administration; and the *U.S. Industrial Outlook*, from the Commerce Department. The latter publication is examined in Chapter 16.

Federal agencies also publish population projections. The Bureau of the Census's *Projections of the Population of the United States by Age, Sex, and Race*

was introduced in Chapter 14. The Social Security Administration produces long-term forecasts using methods similar to the Bureau's. These projections, revised annually, appear in a series called *Actuarial Studies*. The main title in the series is an annual report called *Social Security Area Population Projections*. It forecasts population by age group, sex, and marital status in twenty-year increments for the next century. Yearly short-term projections are given for the coming decade. Data are reported at the national level only. The Bureau of Economic Analysis produces a major series of demographic and economic projections entitled *OBERS BEA Regional Projections*. This title is described in Chapter 17.

The nonprofit Conference Board publishes forecasts in the *Economic Times*, a monthly newsletter which partially replaces its venerable *Statistical Bulletin*. The newer title contains most of the same figures which made its predecessor so popular. It compares economic projections from eight respected research organizations, including the Conference Board's own economists. Data are limited to forecasts of the GNP, the Implicit Price Deflator, and the unemployment rate. Projections are given for the coming nine quarters, and figures are revised monthly. The Conference Board also produces several annual forecasts as part of their *Research Bulletin* series. The *U.S. Economic Outlook* polls a panel of 12 prominent economists (known collectively as the "Conference Board Economic Forum") to obtain a consensus view of the economy. Two years of forecasts are given for GNP, inflation, corporate profits, unemployment, interest rates (as measured by the Prime Rate), and the federal budget deficit. Other annual reports in the series are the *U.S. Corporate Earnings Outlook* and the *Human Resource Outlook*.

Another option is to subscribe to a forecast newsletter. These publications range from broad-based analyses to more narrowly focused publications, such as the monthly *BCA Interest Rate Forecast*. Several major newsletters base their data on the assumption that combined forecasts from many people are likely to be more accurate than any single projection, a technique sometimes referred to as the Delphi Method. This method is used by *Blue Chip Economic Indicators*, a monthly service from Capitol Publications, Inc. that prints projections on approximately 15 important indicators made by 50 leading economists. Projections are given for the current year and two years in the future. The editor also computes consensus forecasts for most indicators, together with averages of the 10 highest and 10 lowest projections. Another source of composite forecasts is the National Association of Business Economists. Their quarterly *NABE Outlook* provides one- and two-year projections generated by a panel of 60 member-economists; 21 major variables are covered.

Econometric firms also publish newsletters, but these are typically offered in conjunction with other services, making them quite expensive. The *U.S. Economic Outlook*, an extensive monthly report from Laurence H. Meyer & Associates, Ltd., allows subscribers to select from a variety of additional services, including access to an online database or monthly updates to a PC-based data program. Meyer's forecasts, based on a model containing 252 major variables, are read by many leading policy-making bodies throughout the world. Meyer's firm is also one of the eight organizations polled monthly for the Conference Board survey described above.

Economic projections from all kinds of sources are reported in business periodicals and trade journals. One of the best ways to identify these is through *Predicasts Forecasts*, a quarterly index introduced in Chapter 4. It is best-known for its summaries of industry-specific projections, but extensive coverage is also given to general economic conditions. Although Predicasts no longer computes consensus forecasts, it is a simple matter for the user to generate them on his or her own.

Descriptions of other publications and databases which provide economic forecasts can be found elsewhere in the book. Those dealing with the investment outlook are described in Chapter 12. Forecasts for states and local areas are discussed in Chapter 17. Publications on marketing trends, including executives' expectations and consumer intentions, are introduced in Chapter 18. The following two publications demonstrate the diversity of published economic forecasts.

Standard & Poor's Trends and Projections (Standard & Poor's Corporation—Monthly).

This popular and affordable newsletter from Standard & Poor's is available as part of the loose-leaf version of their *Industry Surveys* or as a separate subscription. The newsletter provides a two- to four-page narrative economic outlook, plus a table of key forecasts from S&P economists. The list of variables is extensive, including GNP and its major components, various measures of personal and corporate income, the personal savings rate, the CPI, several key interest rates, the Index of Industrial Production, housing starts, auto sales, and the unemployment rate. Projections are given for the coming two years (both quarterly and annually). Actual data for the latest current year are provided for comparative purposes.

National Economic Projections Series (NPA Data Services, Inc.—Semiannual and Annual).

A leading source of economic projections for more than two decades has been the nonprofit National Planning Association. In 1987, several economists from the group formed a separate corporation called NPA Data Services, which now carries on much of the forecasting work formerly done by the Association. The major NPA publication dealing with the national economy is called the *National Economic Projections Series* (*NEPS*). A companion service, the *Regional Economic Projections Series*, will be introduced in Chapter 17. *NEPS* focuses on the long-term outlook; a diversity of annual projections are calculated for the coming 20 years. The forecasts are based on a sophisticated econometric model which studies three major forces behind economic growth: labor, capital formation, and technological innovation.

NEPS is issued as a three-volume set of data tables, with accompanying narrative. Volume 1 is a semiannual summary report, Volume 2 presents detailed tables for all variables, and Volume 3 cites selected projections broken down by 12 major sectors of the economy. The latter two reports appear annually. Among the statistics presented in Volume 2 are total population, labor force participation, federal government expenditures, the federal deficit, GNP, labor productivity, capital investment, research & development expenditures, and personal income. Thirty years of historical data are also presented. In Volume 3, the summary measures focus on output, employment, productivity, and earnings. The sectors studied are broad industry categories such as farming, mining, construction, and manufacturing. Subscribers receive a separate volume describing the methodology of the model. The complete *NEPS* database is also available online through Reuters.

LOCATING STATISTICAL INFORMATION

With statistical information, a critical concern is obtaining numbers as soon as they are released. To do this requires an awareness of the ways in which economic statistics are announced. Because of their importance to so many people, key statistical measures are first reported in press releases to the media, so one way to obtain this information as soon as it's released is to consult news wire services. A broad spectrum of online databases provides updated news stories throughout the day. Some of the major services were introduced in Chapter 5. Most are appropriate for locating recently-announced indicators, but the best resource is usually Dow Jones.

Since wire services usually provide inadequate subject indexing, it can be challenging to differentiate between the government's announcement of an indicator and news stories which mention the topic in passing. A few databases allow users to retrieve stories containing statistical tables, and the most relevant articles can be identified by searching for key words in the headlines or lead paragraphs. Unfortunately, most headlines fail to mention the name of the indicator itself. The best method of locating indicators online is to search by release date.

Another option is to use daily media sources: television and radio news, cable news networks, and newspapers. Unfortunately, the amount of detail afforded to economic stories is often minimal, and many media sources fail to supply the most important aspects of a statistical release. One of the most consistently reliable printed sources is *The Wall Street Journal*. All major indicators are covered as they are released, and the information is presented clearly. A disadvantage to the *Journal*, however, is that it is a morning paper published five days per week. Many economic statistics are typically released on Friday mornings, after the *Journal* has gone to press, so they do not appear until the following Monday's issue. An excellent guide to the economic data appearing in the paper is Michael Lehman's *Dow Jones-Irwin Guide to Using the Wall Street Journal*, which is described at the end of the chapter. A third way to obtain the information is to contact the issuing agencies themselves. Some, like the BLS, offer telephone services with tape recorded messages. Others, like the U.S. Commerce Department, maintain Electronic Bulletin Boards with current economic data.

Determining when various economic indicators are scheduled to appear is fairly simple because each agency has standard release dates. For example, the Consumer Price Index is announced by the BLS during the third week of each month, and covers prices for the previous month. Several sources provide the schedules for major series, including Lehman's guide, and some of the other titles which appear in the "Further Reading" section. Many official government journals provide calendars of release dates at least once a year, and sometimes once a month. The most closely followed indicators can be found through Dow Jones News/Retrieval; a list of major release dates is updated monthly in the *Dow Jones News* file. A short-term outlook can be found in *Investor's Daily*. Every Monday readers can find a front page column called "The Week Ahead," which includes the key indicators scheduled for release that week.

Some users of economic statistics are not so concerned with obtaining immediate information, but timeliness is still a concern. If researchers rely on the official journals of government agencies, they will be waiting a long time to receive statistical information. Because such publications usually contain narrative articles and analysis, they are not published until a month or more after current data are released. To ameliorate this problem, several agencies utilize an intermediate stage of publishing to get information to the public. Within a week or so of initial release, they publish a brief newsletter with more detailed data than a press release. The Federal Reserve Board's *Statistical Releases* series is an example. The Bureau of Labor Statistics publishes a series of newsletters under the general title *BLS News*. These provide timely access to statistics on a variety of topics. Researchers may also turn to commercial sources of statistical information. Large money center banks issue monthly Bank Letters with current economic statistics. Another option is to consult popular business magazines, such as *Business Week*, which publish weekly tables of key indicators. And for monthly updates, researchers can turn to the familiar *Standard & Poor's Statistical Service*.

With so many publications covering so many data series, it is often difficult to know how to begin a search. One suggestion is to determine which government agency or private organization is responsible for collecting the data, then consult that group's publications. Though useful, this strategy presents problems. Agencies such as the Bureau of the Census publish a large number of statistical sources. Also, it is unclear which agencies do what. The Federal Reserve Board is responsible for compiling the Index of Industrial Production, for example.

An alternative is to rely on guides to statistical sources. The handbooks listed in the bibliography to this chapter are excellent for identifying the sources of major indicators. The footnotes to the *Statistical Abstract of the United States* also provide helpful clues for tracking down detailed statistical information. The *Predicasts Basebook*, introduced in Chapter 16, can be another excellent guide to primary sources of information. Many of the indexes and finding guides discussed in Chapter 4 are also useful starting points. *Statistics Sources* and the *American Statistics Index* are particularly helpful in this regard.

A different approach is to bypass print sources entirely and use online databases. Unfortunately, many of the most popular vendors offer little in the way of statistical databases. Of the more than 350 databases on

DIALOG, only four—*EconBase, CENDATA, PTS U.S. Forecasts* and *PTS U.S. Time Series*—are exclusively devoted to economic data. In contrast, a few vendors specialize in providing statistical databases. One example is Reuters, which receives data from dozens of sources and supplies numerous databases for United States, Canadian, and foreign economic statistics. A variety of CD-ROM products containing economic time series have also made an appearance, and more will surely follow. Slater Hall Information Products (SHIP) has several economic disks on the market, including the monthly *Business Indicators*. This service provides three types of data: historical statistics (annual, quarterly, and monthly) from the National Income and Product Accounts; income and employment figures by industry at the state level; and 30 years of selected monthly data from the *Survey of Current Business*.

Whatever the need for economic statistics, products are available in print, online, and in other media. And many are quite affordable, especially those from government agencies. Researchers may not always be able to acquire the exact economic data they would like, but the diversity in price and format ensures that the most important numbers are usually within reach.

FOR FURTHER READING

Researchers who must use general economic statistics on a regular basis are encouraged to learn about the U.S. economy and how it works. Many excellent textbooks on macroeconomics provide a good grounding in basic concepts. The following list is highly selective; the books and articles emphasize the statistics themselves: their purpose, how they are compiled, and where they can be found. To place the discussion in proper perspective, information on the federal statistical system is included.

Federal Statistical Policy: Collection and Reporting

American Library Association Commission on Freedom and Equality of Access to Information. "Access to Government Information." In *Freedom and Equality of Access to Information*. (Chicago: American Library Association, 1986): 55–80.
In this thought-provoking study, a distinguished group of executives and information professionals examines the effects of present government policies on the dissemination of information in the U.S. An especially interesting segment presents an overview of recent policies toward federal statistical agencies.

Duncan, Joseph W. "Gatekeepers for Federal Statistics." *Business Economics* 25 (April 1990): 51–2.

Duncan, former chairman of the National Association of Business Economists' Statistics Committee, summarizes the results of his study on media coverage of major economic data. He queried journalists who routinely report on federal economic statistics for leading business publications about their sources of information and their reporting methods.

U.S. Commission on Federal Paperwork. *Statistics: A Report of the Federal Paperwork Commission* (Washington, DC: U.S. Government Printing Office, 1977).

Still an excellent introduction to the federal statistical system and how it works.

Wallman, Katherine K. *Losing Count: The Federal Statistical System.* Population Trends and Public Policy, no. 16. (Washington, DC: Population Reference Bureau, 1988).

Describes the federal statistical system, the role of OMB, and the effect of cuts in major government statistics programs.

Reference Guides to Economic Statistics

Fabozzi, Frank J., and Harry I. Greenfield, editors. *The Handbook of Economic and Financial Measures* (Homewood, IL: Dow Jones-Irwin, 1984).

This massive work contains in-depth articles from over 20 expert contributors on important indicators. Articles explain the economic concepts involved, the methodology of data collection, and the major sources of statistical series. The most detailed reference work of its kind.

Frumkin, Norman. *Guide to Economic Indicators.* (Armonk, NY: M.E. Sharpe, 1990).

One of the most recent entries to the handbook field is also one of the best. In addition to fairly lengthy profiles of 42 key indicators, the author provides an excellent introduction to underlying concepts. Among the basics covered in this introductory section are the construction of index numbers, the difference between annualized and annual data, current and constant dollars, seasonal adjustment, revised data, sampling methods, and evaluating government figures.

Hoel, Arline A., Kenneth W. Clarkson, and Roger L. Miller. *Economic Sourcebook of Government Statistics* (Lexington, MA: Lexington Books, 1983).

A more modest endeavor than the Fabozzi work, this guide offers brief articles (up to four pages) on nearly 50 key government series. For each indicator, the purpose of the data is discussed, as well as how they are compiled, when they are issued, and their limitations. An excellent appendix provides a lengthy list of statistical publications.

Lehman, Michael B. *The Dow Jones-Irwin Guide to Using The Wall Street Journal.* 3rd ed. (Homewood, IL: Dow Jones-Irwin, 1990).

A guide to economic statistics seen in the *Journal.* Written primarily for investors, it includes several chapters describing investment data. The information is presented in the context of the business cycle, and the interrelated nature of economic data is stressed. Numerous tables are reproduced from the newspaper, and appendices summarize the reporting schedule of key statistics. It is extremely readable, with clear explanations of complex topics.

O'Hara, Frederick M., and Robert Sicignano. *Handbook of United States Economic and Financial Indicators* (Westport, CT: Greenwood Press, 1985).

This guide is more of a dictionary and finding tool than the other handbooks on this list. It covers some 200 indicators produced by 55 organizations, both government and private. Each entry provides a brief description of the indicator, together with a list of the major publications in which the data can be seen on a regular basis.

Basic Concepts and Information Sources

Bernstein, Peter L., and Theodore H. Silbert. "Are Economic Forecasters Worth Listening To?" *Harvard Business Review* 62 (September/October 1984): 32–40.

A well-written analysis of the value of economic forecasts, based on the results of several studies. Although no forecaster is consistently accurate, economic projections can be extremely useful. Among the major conclusions are that consensus forecasts are surprisingly good, and short-term projections are easier to make than long-term.

Moore, Geoffrey H. *Business Cycles, Inflation and Forecasting.* 2nd ed. (Cambridge, MA: Ballinger, 1983).

A collection of previously published essays by the author and his colleagues at the National Bureau of Economic Research. The topics range from "What is a Recession?" to "Five Little-known Facts about Inflation." The articles are interesting and informative and make a surprisingly cohesive presentation.

———. *Leading Indicators for the 1990s* (Homewood, IL: Dow Jones-Irwin, 1990).

In 1986, the Center for International Business Cycle Research at Columbia University sponsored a project to evaluate the government's leading, lagging, and coincident economic indicators. A committee of eminent economists ultimately recommended several major changes to the U.S. Department of Commerce. Some of the recommendations were adopted in full or in part, while others were not. Moore summarizes the results of this important effort, including the argument for creating both short- and long-leading indexes. Anyone interested in understanding these key government figures will benefit from reading this brief, well-written work.

Nelson, Charles R. *The Investor's Guide to Economic Indicators* (New York: Wiley, 1987).

This primer explains why basic indicators are important to investors. The guide covers various interest rates, inflation, the money supply, the federal deficit, and a handful of other key measures, as they relate to investment performance. Though some of the analysis of current events have become outdated, most of the presentation is still relevant. The

author's easy-going style makes this a quick read for those too busy to wade through the more technical works listed in this section.

O'Leary, Mick. "Surveying the Numeric Databanks." *Database* 10 (October 1987): 65–68.

O'Leary focuses on econometric services, but surveys a number of more traditional time series databases as well.

Sommers, Albert T. *The U.S. Economy Demystified: What Major Economic Statistics Mean and Their Significance for Business.* Revised ed. (Lexington, MA: Lexington Books, 1988).

Offers a narrative approach to economic indicators and their relationship to the economy. The book covers relatively few topics, but explains each in considerable detail. The emphasis throughout is on the National Income and Product Accounts.

Woggon, Michele. "Economic Statistical Data Online: A Primer." *Database* 10 (October 1987): 70–74.

In a companion to the O'Leary article, Woggon offers a very brief introduction to online sources of economic time series. Discusses the differences between public and proprietary databases, and between basic data files and value-added services which enable the user to manipulate the numbers.

Specific Indicators and Publications

Collender, Stanley E. *Guide to the Federal Budget* (Washington, DC: Urban Institute, Annual).

This yearly guide presents both an introduction to the federal budget process, and a technical guide to the budget documents themselves. The step-by-step explanation of how the Budget is created, together with the cogent definitions of terms, are especially useful. This is a must for anyone who wants to understand the nature of the government's budget-making activities or follow shifting trends in policy.

Herman, Edward. "Reference Sources Describing and Summarizing the Federal Budget." *Reference Services Review* 18 (Spring 1990): 55–72.

An overview of the major publications which explain or analyze the complex world of federal budget data. The article is excerpted from Herman's book on the subject, to be published in 1991 by Pierian Press.

Richey, Debora. "The 'Economic Report of the President': An Analysis." *Government Publications Review* 16 (July/ August 1989): 365–75.

Discusses the history of this important document, its contents, format, and purpose. The article also touches on the role of the Council of Economic Advisors and its impact on national economic policy.

Schwenk, Frankie N. "Two Measures of Inflation: The Consumer Price Index and the Personal Consumption Expenditure Implicit Price Deflator." *Family Economics Review* (Winter 1981): 13–18.

For readers who wish a better understanding of what inflation figures mean, here is a brief, interesting summary of the CPI and the Implicit Price Deflator. Though written before major changes in the CPI were adopted, the article provides a worthwhile comparison of the two indicators.

Slater, Courtenay. "Dollars That Count." *American Demographics* 8 (January 1986): 4–7.

This short article contains a fairly detailed look at the personal income measurements used by the Bureau of Economic Analysis and the Bureau of the Census.

U.S. Bureau of Labor Statistics. *BLS Handbook of Methods.* BLS Bulletin, no. 2285. (Washington, DC: U.S. Government Printing Office, 1988).

Explains the background and methodology of all major BLS series, including the CPI, productivity measures, employment data from the Current Population Survey, and much more.

CHAPTER 16
Industry Statistics

TOPICS COVERED

1. The Economic Census
   a. Key Census Concepts
   b. Limitations of Census Data
   c. Publications of the Economic Census
   d. Changes in the 1987 Census
2. Additional Census Publications
   a. Other Quinquennial Censuses
   b. Foreign Trade Statistics
   c. Miscellaneous Census Programs
3. Other Sources of Industry Data
   a. General Statistical Compendia
   b. Specific Industry Reports
4. Industry Statistics—Where to Look?
5. For Further Reading

MAJOR SOURCES DISCUSSED

- *Census of Manufacturers*
- *Annual Survey of Manufacturers*
- *Current Industrial Reports*
- *Census of Retail Trade*
- *Report on U.S. Merchandise Trade*
- *County Business Patterns*
- *U.S. Industrial Outlook*
- *Minerals Yearbook*
- *Predicasts Basebook*
- *Dun's Census of American Business*
- *CRB Commodity Year Book*

Previous chapters discussed narrative sources of industry information, including journal articles, brokerage reports, and investment services. Despite the simplicity and usefulness of narrative profiles, researchers often find the need for raw data from which they can reach their own opinions. Publications which report statistics for specific industries are easily obtained for virtually every major type of business activity, and many minor ones as well. Information varies, but typically includes statistics on employment, dollar volume of sales, the quantity of output, and foreign trade. More specialized data can often be found, including industry costs, use of raw materials, and even the extent to which the largest firms dominate the industry. By comparing statistics found in several publications, researchers can construct a revealing picture of the industry in question.

The material in this chapter will introduce major sources of industry-wide statistics, with emphasis on publications which survey many industries in a single report. Because the U.S. Bureau of the Census plays such

an important role in the collection and dissemination of this type of data, much of the chapter will focus on Census reports and concepts. Finally, a brief discussion of how to locate the most pertinent data for an industry will be presented.

THE ECONOMIC CENSUS

The most complete statistical information on individual industries in the U.S. is compiled by the Bureau of the Census. Industrial statistics have been an integral part of the Census since 1810. Today, the Economic Census is taken every five years for years ending in 2 and 7.

Detailed statistics on business activity are vital for making economic decisions. Numbers collected by the Census provide major building blocks for determining Gross National Product, for example. Census data also have enormous value for local governments, which study economic activity for purposes of urban planning and

industrial development. Census statistics are also essential for a wide range of marketing and financial decisions, from site location to capital expenditure plans. And without the quinquennial Census, it would be virtually impossible for many trade associations and commercial publishers to create detailed industry surveys.

Unlike the Census of Population and Housing, the Economic Census makes no attempt to contact every possible respondent by questionnaire. In most cases, only the largest businesses are sent detailed forms; statistics on smaller establishments are gathered from existing administrative records—notably from the Internal Revenue Service and the Social Security Administration. Business units receiving questionnaires represent the most significant players in the economy as measured by employment, payroll, and sales volume.

The seven major components of the Economic Census are grouped according to business activity: manufacturing, retail trade, wholesale trade, service industries, mineral industries, construction, and transportation.

Key Census Concepts

An understanding of three main ideas is essential to the proper use of the Economic Census: Establishment data, classification by primary industry, and disclosure restrictions. Census figures are collected and tabulated for individual business locations. The Bureau designates these units as Establishments. If a company owns three manufacturing plants, two warehouses, nine sales outlets, and an administrative headquarters, these would be counted in the Census as 15 Establishments rather than a single company. Conversely, if two firms share the same business address, each would be counted as an Establishment. The 1987 Census collected data on approximately 12.4 million Establishments.

Establishments in the Census are categorized according to SIC number, but these classifications represent an entire industry rather than individual products. Companies associated with a particular industry can be engaged in more than one business activity; a manufacturer can produce more than one type of product, some of which may have nothing to do with the company's main industry. The Census deals with this problem by counting each Establishment only once, classifying it in the SIC code which describes its major activity. Difficulties arising from this practice are ameliorated in two ways. First, because tabulation is done at the Establishment rather than the company level, multi-product operations are encountered less often than they would be otherwise.

Second, for manufacturing, retail, and wholesale industries, some data are presented by product as well as by industry. In this way, researchers can evaluate the extent of industry diversification, and the relationship between industries and products.

As with the Census of Population, the Bureau cannot release data which could reveal information about individual respondents. Disclosure limitations are much more common in the Economic Census simply because there are fewer Establishments than people. Data are withheld not only where confidentiality could be breached through direct observation of the numbers, but also where it could be determined by subtracting values, or comparing data across several tables. Suppression of data is indicated by the symbol "d," and the numbers are tabulated at a broader level of aggregation. If there were only two Establishments with the same four-digit SIC number in one county, information for those Establishments would be suppressed. They would be counted at the two-digit SIC level for the county, and incorporated into the four-digit figures for the state.

Other information is withheld due to space limitations. To ensure that published reports are of a manageable size, the Bureau establishes guidelines to determine which geographic areas will be included. Figures for states and MSAs are always given, but statistics for Places with fewer than 2,500 inhabitants are automatically excluded. For Places with more than 2,500 people, and for counties, data at the four-digit SIC level are generally published only for localities with a minimum number of total Establishments. For example, the *Census of Retail Trade* publishes detailed data only for those counties with a total of more than 350 retail Establishments with paid employees. Similarly, the *Census of Wholesale Trade* looks for 200 Establishments before detailed data are published. For counties and Places which don't meet these requirements, separate tables report summary findings at broader geographic levels. Users should remember, however, that unpublished data are available in electronic formats, unless the information is suppressed for reasons of confidentiality.

Limitations of Census Data

There are many other limitations to Census data. Surprisingly, every type of business is not covered by the Economic Census, and entire industries are excluded. Many do not appear because information is readily available from other sources. Examples include public utilities, colleges, and banks. Some neglected industries are not adequately covered in other statistical sources;

examples are insurance companies, certain transportation industries, and many service firms. Beginning with 1987, the Bureau noticeably expanded coverage of missing industries, and intends to continue this trend in 1992. Major additions to the 1987 Census are hospitals and trucking firms.

A second problem results from the structure of the SIC system. Many problems connected with Standard Industrial Classifications have a direct bearing on the quality of Census information. Because the system is revised so infrequently, newer types of businesses have no SIC code. Although a major revision of SIC codes occurred in 1987, many smaller industries still have not received their own classification numbers. Manufacturing industries are generally well-represented in the SIC system, but coverage of service firms is particularly weak. The 4-digit level of classification is often too general, grouping somewhat unrelated businesses together or forcing many types of businesses into Not Elsewhere Classified slots. It can also be difficult to determine where an industry will be classified, and whether similar products will be classed under different code numbers. This is partly because the SIC system often categorizes manufactured goods by the material they are made from, rather than their purpose or use. This would be a minor annoyance if similar items made from different materials could be summed together to obtain a total figure. This is usually impossible because such items are grouped together with dissimilar products made from the same material. For example, shoe laces are classified in two categories: leather laces are grouped under SIC 3021 (Boot and Shoe Cut Stock) together with shoe lifts, soles, tongues, and other component leather parts; cloth laces are found under SIC 2241 (Narrow Fabrics) along with other cloth notions.

For most industries, the Bureau provides greater detail than afforded by the official four-digit SIC codes. Census publications for retail and wholesale trades, transportation, and service industries divide many of the broader SIC categories into "parts." Product-level data are also published in the Economic Census. For manufacturing and mining, this is accomplished by extending SIC codes to seven digits. For selected retail and wholesale products, the Bureau has created unique codes for merchandise and commodity lines. The *1987 Industry and Product Classification Manual* describes these breakdowns in considerable detail.

While most Census publications are designed to be comparable with one another, this is not true of data from other agencies. Payroll data from the Economic Census, for example, is not comparable with payroll data from Bureau of Labor Statistics studies. Some publications from the Bureau of the Census itself are not comparable to the Economic Census, most notably *County Business Patterns* and the *Quarterly Financial Report*. Finally, as with any type of statistic, comparing Census data from different years can be difficult because definitions, geographic boundaries, and methodology change over time.

A final drawback is the lengthy delay before Census data are published. The deadline for returning questionnaires for the 1987 Census was February 1988, and the first publications did not appear until early 1989. The earliest reports usually cover the least complex Censuses, including Construction and Transportation. Manufacturing has the most detailed set of reports, and these are among the last to appear. Reports for individual states or regions are issued before the United States summary volumes, and subject reports tend to appear last. All 1987 Census products are scheduled for publication by late 1991.

Publications of the Economic Census have their own built-in pitfalls. Perhaps the most important is that the degree of coverage varies from one industry group to another. Some Censuses report data only for Establishments with payroll, while the retail and service Censuses also cover those with no paid employees. In some industries—business consulting, personal services, and trucking, for example—self-employed businesspeople are commonplace. Although smaller Establishments account for a tiny percentage of total business activity, researchers should make sure they understand the scope of every report used. A related problem involves the interpretation of individual tables. In some cases, a table may only report a certain segment of the industry, so take time to read table headings and footnotes carefully. Never make unwarranted assumptions just because they seem reasonable; make an effort to understand Census concepts, terminology, and methods.

Publications of the Economic Census

The Economic Census is produced as seven separate titles grouped according to type of business. The pattern of publishing is fairly uniform among the seven industry clusters. Each title consists of three subseries—geographic data for each state, detailed industry data by SIC numbers, and a subject series for special topics—though for some titles the industry and subject series are combined. Many of the publications appear first as a brief preliminary report. Because 1987 data will also be published on CD-ROM, users will have access to more detailed tables than ever before. However, the printed

reports still concentrate on fairly basic data. Most quinquennial publications are updated by sample surveys done annually, quarterly, or even monthly. Results from sample surveys are much more limited and are usually available only for the nation as a whole.

The two titles used most frequently are the *Census of Manufactures* and the *Census of Retail Trade*. They are described below in reasonable detail. Because the other titles in the Economic Census are similar in format, they will be introduced in briefer fashion.

Census of Manufactures.

Census reports covering manufacturing industries are the most complex and voluminous in the Economic Census. The *Census of Manufactures* comprises over 400 4-digit SIC groups from SIC 20 through 39. Manufacturing is defined as the mechanical or chemical transformation of materials into new products. What this encompasses is not always obvious, however; as an example, newspaper, magazine, and book publishers are classified as manufacturing industries.

The *Geographic Area Series* is published in 52 reports, one for each state, the District of Columbia, and a United States summary. Data on all manufacturing activities are presented at the state level, as well as for MSAs, counties, and Places with 2,500 or more inhabitants. Data on Establishments are displayed down to 4-digit SIC categories. Exhibit 16-1 shows the standard format of information from this series, with figures on the total number of Establishments, the number of Establishments with 20 or more employees, the number of employees in the industry, the total payroll, and the value of shipments. This table also presents useful information on the operations of each industry. New Capital Expenditures indicates the total amount spent during the Census year on new plant and equipment, while the cost of materials shows how much was spent on raw materials and parts used in manufacturing. Value Added is considered to be the best measurement of each industry's relative economic importance, and reflects the value of the processing done at that Establishment. Value Added is not equivalent to the difference between the value of shipments and the cost of materials because at the end of the year some material will still be in process, and some finished goods will be stored as inventory. Finally, because data on production workers are reported separately, labor productivity can be measured, and comparisons can be made to total employment and payroll.

The *Industry Series* provides similar statistics for the entire country, broken down to the 7-digit SIC level. This series also presents data not found in the geographic series. The value of inventories is given, as are listings of

Establishments by employment-size groupings. Supplemental data are published based on sample surveys, including energy use by manufacturers, services purchased, value of fixed assets, rental payments, and other industry-wide financial data. Another type of information in the *Industry Series* is financial and operating data in ratio form. Ratios include value added per production worker and payroll per employee. These ratios offer a convenient way of comparing inter-industry performance.

A unique table appearing in the *Industry Series*, called "Materials Consumed by Kind," offers a remarkable look at the types of raw materials used by each industry. Data include the dollar value of materials consumed, and, for some industries, the quantity consumed also. The table which describes the types of materials used by the upholstered furniture industry, for example, lists the amounts of wood, fabric, padding, springs, varnishes and other materials in significant detail. Careful reading of these tables can be invaluable for market research purposes. A manufacturer of cotton battings, for example, could scan this table for every industry covered to obtain an idea of which businesses used that product and to what extent.

Another set of unique tables shows the relationship between products and industries, some of which can be seen in Exhibit 16-2. Table 5a compares the major products manufactured within each industry and the Establishments which manufacture them. For example, the majority of cottonseed oil mills don't produce oil; 29 out of 52 produce cottonseed cake, meal, and other by-products. Table 5b examines several aspects of industry structure, including specialization and coverage ratios. Specialization measures the extent to which the industry focuses on its primary product, while coverage measures the degree to which the industry accounts for the total output for their primary product. According to the second table in Exhibit 16-2, 97% of the output of cottonseed mills are cottonseed products (a 97% specialization ratio). Conversely, cottonseed mills account for 93% of all cottonseed products, while miscellaneous industries account for the remaining 7%. Notice too, that for these industries, both ratios have increased over the past 10 years. Table 6a (not shown) takes another approach, examining products regardless of the industry which manufactured them. These tables are displayed down to the 7-digit SIC level.

The third section in the *Census of Manufactures* is the *Subject Series*, which provides detailed reports on specialized topics of interest. For 1987, seven separate reports will cover such subjects as water use by manufacturers, distribution channels utilized, and legal form of

EXHIBIT 16-1. *Census of Manufactures: Geographic Series*

Table 4. Statistics for the State, Metropolitan Statistical Areas, Counties, and Selected Places: 1987—Con.

[Includes operating manufacturing establishments and auxiliaries. Includes places with 450 manufacturing employees or more. For definitions of CMSA's, MSA's, and PMSA's, information on geographic areas followed by ▲, and explanation of terms, see appendixes. For meaning of abbreviations and symbols, see introductory text]

Geographic area	E[1]	All establishments[2] Total (no.)	With 20 employees or more (no.)	All employees Number (1,000)	Payroll (million dollars)	Production workers Number (1,000)	Hours (millions)	Wages (million dollars)	Value added by manufacture (million dollars)	Cost of materials[3] (million dollars)	Value of shipments[3] (million dollars)	New capital expenditures (million dollars)
COUNTIES—Con.												
Bureau County	–	49	22	2.9	60.7	2.0	3.6	38.9	148.7	150.9	302.8	(D)
Calhoun County	–	7	1	(D)	(D)	(D)	(D)	(D)	(D)	(D)	(D)	(D)
Carroll County	–	26	8	1.2	23.3	.9	1.6	14.0	61.2	46.8	113.4	(D)
Cass County	–	16	7	1.0	21.1	.7	1.2	15.2	36.4	93.0	126.4	.8
Champaign County	–	141	58	9.4	189.7	6.4	12.1	117.5	676.5	976.0	1 685.7	34.7
Christian County	–	26	12	1.2	24.0	.9	1.9	14.5	69.6	211.4	278.6	(D)
Clark County	E2	22	8	.8	13.2	.6	1.1	8.4	30.3	23.1	54.3	(D)
Clay County	–	27	12	1.3	23.1	.9	1.9	17.1	70.2	80.0	151.0	(D)
Clinton County	E1	40	13	(D)	(D)	(D)	(D)	(D)	(D)	(D)	(D)	(D)
Coles County	–	60	27	5.8	126.6	4.8	9.3	97.6	481.6	413.8	893.7	32.6
Cook County	E1	9 450	3 842	491.6	13 180.7	290.3	589.3	6 315.2	31 463.1	29 121.6	60 440.1	1 478.6
Crawford County	–	24	10	(D)	(D)	(D)	(D)	(D)	(D)	(D)	(D)	(D)
Cumberland County	E1	10	2	.1	1.6	.1	.2	1.0	3.0	2.4	5.3	.1
De Kalb County	–	120	55	7.0	174.2	4.4	8.6	89.9	323.8	342.6	669.4	19.1
De Witt County	E2	15	10	1.5	32.2	1.1	2.2	20.3	103.7	68.3	174.3	10.1
Douglas County	E1	35	11	1.6	39.0	1.1	2.2	23.8	69.6	150.6	224.8	5.6
Du Page County	E1	1 857	655	67.5	1 820.8	38.1	76.3	770.1	3 628.3	2 628.0	6 252.4	230.9
Edgar County	E1	24	13	1.4	27.7	1.1	2.3	18.0	78.3	73.2	149.4	(D)
Edwards County	–	14	5	(D)	(D)	(D)	(D)	(D)	(D)	(D)	(D)	(D)
Effingham County	–	48	19	3.8	99.2	2.9	5.8	63.9	220.5	248.4	461.6	14.4
Fayette County	–	19	5	1.0	16.4	.8	1.4	11.9	39.0	36.5	75.1	6.5
Ford County	E1	23	9	.8	15.0	.6	1.2	10.2	46.5	115.6	161.5	(D)
Franklin County	E2	38	6	.7	13.7	.6	1.1	9.6	43.3	26.6	67.0	(D)
Fulton County	E4	26	6	(D)	(D)	(D)	(D)	(D)	(D)	(D)	(D)	(D)
Gallatin County	E1	5	2	.1	1.9	.1	.1	.9	2.6	4.8	9.5	.1
Greene County	E1	14	5	.4	6.6	.3	.6	4.7	12.2	13.5	25.6	(D)
Grundy County	–	44	23	2.9	86.7	2.0	4.3	52.6	298.8	506.0	791.0	(D)
Hamilton County	–	7	–	.1	.8	(Z)	.1	.6	5.2	4.5	8.9	(Z)
Hancock County	E3	23	6	1.0	17.0	.7	1.2	9.3	37.5	66.0	101.9	(D)
Hardin County	E1	4	1	(D)	(D)	(D)	(D)	(D)	(D)	(D)	(D)	(D)
Henderson County	E9	2	–	(D)	(D)	(D)	(D)	(D)	(D)	(D)	(D)	(D)
Henry County	–	59	25	4.3	76.0	3.2	6.5	51.8	125.3	1 054.5	1 189.0	(D)
Iroquois County	E1	44	18	1.9	31.7	1.5	3.2	23.3	86.5	112.4	199.1	(D)
Jackson County	E1	34	11	1.4	23.6	1.1	2.0	16.2	51.1	82.8	133.6	3.7
Jasper County	E5	14	4	.6	7.3	.5	1.1	5.9	23.5	16.6	39.2	.4
Jefferson County	–	41	15	2.9	74.5	2.2	3.7	52.5	225.5	190.0	403.1	(D)
Jersey County	E7	12	2	.2	2.1	.1	.2	1.4	4.9	7.4	12.3	(D)
Jo Daviess County	–	22	11	1.3	24.0	1.1	2.1	19.1	109.4	119.5	226.5	4.4
Johnson County	E9	7	–	(Z)	.4	(Z)	.1	.3	1.4	1.8	3.2	.1
Kane County	E1	749	316	37.4	954.7	24.8	50.2	542.9	2 643.6	2 375.1	5 019.7	(D)
Kankakee County	–	111	45	7.0	170.7	4.7	9.1	108.0	606.5	671.9	1 301.6	32.0
Kendall County	E2	51	15	1.4	23.1	1.1	2.1	14.3	79.5	49.8	128.0	(D)
Knox County	–	55	23	4.6	107.7	3.6	6.7	78.9	290.9	347.4	639.3	8.2
Lake County	–	760	289	50.9	1 476.1	22.1	44.2	450.4	2 920.7	1 935.3	4 816.3	255.4
La Salle County	–	153	67	8.1	204.1	5.9	12.1	139.2	626.9	701.7	1 325.9	39.6
Lawrence County	E2	24	4	.5	7.4	.4	.6	4.0	23.2	10.3	33.2	(D)
Lee County	–	51	26	3.6	72.7	2.5	5.0	46.7	214.3	217.1	427.0	15.6
Livingston County	–	56	27	4.2	105.6	3.3	6.4	76.6	273.7	309.5	575.2	23.3
Logan County	–	21	11	1.9	44.5	1.5	2.6	33.7	242.4	126.3	373.3	10.3
McDonough County	E1	30	16	1.9	38.6	1.6	3.0	28.0	92.2	72.0	164.4	(D)
McHenry County	E1	435	161	20.8	457.2	15.4	31.9	284.4	1 127.6	1 123.5	2 243.0	71.0
McLean County	–	99	34	6.4	132.9	3.5	6.9	74.3	323.1	464.2	786.3	(D)
Macon County	–	129	47	13.1	428.2	8.2	16.7	254.7	1 281.8	2 061.9	3 345.0	135.6
Macoupin County	–	35	13	1.0	21.6	.6	1.3	10.5	36.8	79.1	115.7	3.0
Madison County	–	217	71	19.5	596.3	13.9	28.9	384.5	1 308.5	4 153.8	5 455.5	(D)
Marion County	–	68	25	4.7	107.1	3.7	7.1	75.1	298.2	174.3	469.2	17.4
Marshall County	–	16	7	.7	20.0	.5	1.0	13.0	68.9	94.2	162.4	(D)
Mason County	E2	20	4	.2	4.2	.1	.3	2.3	17.1	8.9	25.5	.3
Massac County	–	12	4	(D)	(D)	(D)	(D)	(D)	(D)	(D)	(D)	(D)
Menard County	E1	7	1	.1	1.4	.1	.1	1.1	6.2	5.5	12.6	.1
Mercer County	E3	16	3	.2	4.0	.2	.4	2.7	10.8	23.4	33.6	.6
Monroe County	E2	19	4	.2	4.5	.1	.2	2.1	9.8	6.5	16.3	(D)
Montgomery County	–	43	15	1.6	35.4	1.2	2.5	23.1	95.5	96.4	194.2	9.0
Morgan County	–	38	12	3.5	74.4	2.6	5.4	50.3	286.2	462.6	740.8	42.3
Moultrie County	–	19	4	1.0	19.5	.8	1.7	14.4	44.8	42.0	85.5	(D)
Ogle County	–	66	32	5.7	117.9	4.2	8.2	77.1	293.7	546.5	833.2	33.9
Peoria County	–	185	83	20.4	672.1	9.2	18.5	264.4	1 204.2	1 385.8	2 588.7	(D)
Perry County	–	29	7	1.5	26.4	1.1	2.3	18.4	52.9	127.6	178.6	(D)
Piatt County	–	16	5	.5	11.4	.4	.8	8.4	31.0	37.4	69.8	(D)
Pike County	E8	19	4	.3	4.8	.2	.4	3.4	13.5	72.6	85.9	.3
Pope County	–	2	–	(D)	(D)	(D)	(D)	(D)	(D)	(D)	(D)	(D)
Pulaski County	E1	3	2	(D)	(D)	(D)	(D)	(D)	(D)	(D)	(D)	(D)
Putnam County	–	10	4	(D)	(D)	(D)	(D)	(D)	(D)	(D)	(D)	(D)
Randolph County	–	30	14	3.6	85.9	2.7	5.8	59.8	202.2	311.5	516.0	21.6
Richland County	–	23	5	1.0	15.1	.8	1.3	8.5	35.4	96.3	131.7	(D)
Rock Island County	–	200	72	14.9	481.3	8.5	15.8	227.9	1 069.7	820.2	1 915.5	(D)
St. Clair County	–	194	61	7.7	188.9	5.4	10.4	120.2	557.3	817.8	1 376.4	(D)
Saline County	E2	17	8	.4	4.6	.3	.6	3.4	8.3	8.6	17.1	(D)
Sangamon County	E1	126	38	4.3	91.2	2.7	5.2	47.9	197.5	288.5	483.8	(D)
Schuyler County	E1	10	2	.1	2.1	.1	.2	1.2	1.9	13.5	15.9	(D)
Scott County	E4	8	3	.1	1.2	.1	.1	.7	3.5	2.0	5.4	(D)
Shelby County	–	16	4	(D)	(D)	(D)	(D)	(D)	(D)	(D)	(D)	(D)
Stark County	–	6	2	.2	4.0	.2	.4	3.1	15.2	10.3	24.3	.1
Stephenson County	–	63	25	7.9	195.8	5.6	11.1	122.8	488.0	398.6	899.8	(D)
Tazewell County	–	97	35	8.3	264.5	5.9	12.1	192.4	593.9	774.8	1 378.0	(D)

See footnotes at end of table.

MANUFACTURES—GEOGRAPHIC AREA SERIES

ILLINOIS IL-9

Reprinted from the *Census of Manufactures: Geographic Series*, published by the U.S. Bureau of the Census.

EXHIBIT 16-2. *Census of Manufactures*—**Product Tables**

Table 5a. **Industry Statistics by Industry and Primary Product Class Specialization: 1987**

[Table presents selected statistics for establishments according to their degree of specialization in products primary to their industry. Measures of plant specialization shown are (1) industry specialization: ratio of primary product shipments to total product shipments (primary plus secondary, excluding miscellaneous receipts) for the establishment; and (2) product class specialization: ratio of largest primary product class shipments to total product shipments (primary plus secondary, excluding miscellaneous receipts) for the establishment. See appendix for method of computing ratios. For meaning of abbreviations and symbols, see introductory text. For explanation of terms, see appendixes]

Indus-try or prod-uct class code	Industry or primary product class	All estab-lish-ments (number)	All employees Number (1,000)	All employees Payroll (million dollars)	Production workers Number (1,000)	Production workers Hours (millions)	Production workers Wages (million dollars)	Value added by manufac-ture (million dollars)	Cost of materials (million dollars)	Value of shipments (million dollars)	New capital expend-itures (million dollars)
2074	**Cottonseed oil mills:**										
	All establishments in industry	52	2.6	44.8	2.0	4.5	29.8	106.9	378.8	470.7	12.2
	Establishments with this product class primary:										
20741	Cottonseed oil, crude	10	(D)	(D)	(D)	(D)	(D)	(D)	(D)	(D)	(D)
20742	Cottonseed oil, once-refined	4	(D)	(D)	(D)	(D)	(D)	(D)	(D)	(D)	(D)
20744	Cottonseed cake and meal and other byproducts	29	1.8	30.5	1.5	3.4	21.3	82.5	240.2	308.4	9.8
2075	**Soybean oil mills:**										
	All establishments in industry	106	7.0	172.5	4.8	10.1	112.2	1 011.5	8 103.3	9 074.1	90.7
	Establishments with this product class primary:										
20751	Soybean oil	2	(D)	(D)	(D)	(D)	(D)	(D)	(D)	(D)	(D)
20752	Soybean cake, meal, and other byproducts	77	(D)	(D)	(D)	(D)	(D)	(D)	(D)	(D)	(D)
2076	**Vegetable oil mills, n.e.c.:**										
	All establishments in industry	23	.9	19.9	.5	1.1	11.4	82.7	353.3	431.5	4.9
	Establishments with this product class primary:										
20761	Linseed oil	4	.2	4.1	.1	.2	2.7	14.2	119.6	145.5	2.2
20762	Vegetable oils, n.e.c.	8	.4	10.2	.3	.6	5.5	51.0	165.3	207.0	2.1
20763	Other vegetable oil mill products, n.e.c.	4	.1	3.9	.1	.2	2.1	12.6	61.2	66.6	.5
2077	**Animal and marine fats and oils:**										
	All establishments in industry	305	10.3	215.7	6.2	12.8	111.5	752.9	1 022.9	1 763.4	60.4
	Establishments with this product class primary:										
20771	Grease and inedible tallow	92	4.2	101.1	2.2	4.8	47.0	365.2	387.3	745.5	26.4
20772	Feed and fertilizer byproducts	85	3.6	65.7	2.5	5.0	37.8	253.5	454.4	703.0	26.1
20773	Animal and marine oil products	21	1.4	28.2	1.0	1.9	18.4	84.6	85.6	169.1	5.5
2079	**Edible fats and oils, n.e.c.:**										
	All establishments in industry	100	9.3	253.3	6.6	13.7	167.4	1 260.1	2 886.3	4 151.1	86.2
	Establishments with this product class primary:										
20791	Shortening and cooking oils	56	6.8	193.8	4.7	9.9	123.9	777.5	2 336.6	3 118.7	66.5
20792	Margarine	21	2.2	54.1	1.7	3.5	40.1	452.1	479.8	931.8	18.4

Note: For qualifications of data, see footnotes on table 1a.

Table 5b. **Industry-Product Analysis—Value of Shipments and Primary Product Shipments and Specialization and Coverage Ratios for the Industry: 1987 and Earlier Census Years**

[An establishment is assigned to an industry based on shipment values of products representing largest amount considered primary to an industry. Frequently, establishment shipments comprise mixtures of products assigned to an industry (primary), those considered primary to other industries (secondary), and receipts for activities such as merchandising or contract work. Columns A-D show this product pattern for an industry, and column E shows primary product specialization ratio. The extent to which an industry's primary products are shipped by establishments classified in and out of an industry is shown in columns F-H and coverage ratio is shown in column I. For meaning of abbreviations and symbols, see introductory text. For explanation of terms, see appendixes]

Industry and product group code	Industry and census year	Value of shipments Total (million dollars) A	Value of shipments Primary products (million dollars) B	Value of shipments Secondary products (million dollars) C	Value of shipments Miscel-laneous receipts (million dollars) D	Primary product special-ization ratio col. B÷ col. B+C (percent) E	Value of primary product shipments Total made in all indus-tries (million dollars) F	Value of primary product shipments Made in this industry (million dollars) G	Value of primary product shipments Made in other indus-tries (million dollars) H	Coverage ratio col. B÷ col. F (percent) I
2074	Cottonseed oil mills									
	1987	470.7	402.6	12.2	55.9	97	434.6	402.6	32.0	93
	1982	933.3	785.6	46.9	100.9	94	812.2	785.6	26.6	97
	1977	859.2	679.7	88.9	90.5	88	763.1	679.7	83.4	89
2075	Soybean oil mills									
	1987	9 074.1	7 554.1	836.8	683.3	90	7 728.9	7 554.1	174.8	98
	1982	8 603.6	6 900.0	964.0	739.5	88	7 257.4	6 900.0	357.3	95
	1977	7 580.0	5 973.3	867.9	738.8	87	6 116.5	5 973.3	143.2	98
2076	Vegetable oil mills, n.e.c.									
	1987	431.5	351.6	50.1	29.8	88	490.0	351.6	138.4	72
	1982	556.9	426.0	32.5	98.5	93	544.3	426.0	118.3	78
	1977	360.8	231.6	37.8	91.4	86	401.0	231.6	169.4	58
2077	Animal and marine fats and oils									
	1987	1 763.4	1 535.0	60.3	168.2	96	2 148.2	1 535.0	613.2	71
	1982	1 752.5	1 593.7	48.9	109.8	97	2 337.1	1 593.7	743.4	68
	1977	1 655.0	1 440.8	91.2	123.0	94	2 102.2	1 440.8	661.4	68
2079	Edible fats and oils, n.e.c.									
	1987	4 151.1	3 618.6	404.5	128.0	90	4 694.1	3 618.6	1 075.5	77
	1982	4 905.6	4 092.0	705.3	108.3	85	5 340.5	4 092.0	1 248.5	77
	1977	4 025.0	3 290.9	423.8	310.3	89	4 272.2	3 290.9	981.3	77

Reprinted from the *Census of Manufactures*, published by the U.S. Bureau of the Census.

organization. The subject report entitled *Concentration Ratios in Manufacturing* measures the degree to which each industry is dominated by its largest firms. A fourth series, *Analytical Reports,* is new to the 1987 Census. Three publications are planned, covering exports by industry, the characteristics of exporting Establishments, and inflation-adjusted indexes which measure changes in production from 1982 to 1987.

Information from the *Census of Manufactures* is updated through ongoing sample surveys and published in the *Annual Survey of Manufacturers* (*ASM*) and *Current Industrial Reports* (*CIR*). The *ASM* is based on a survey of 55,000 manufacturing Establishments and has been conducted since 1949. Data found here are similar to the basic statistics in the *Census of Manufactures,* with less geographic detail. On the other hand, certain questions are asked of the sample Establishments which are not asked of the general manufacturing population. For example, respondents are requested to break down expenditures for new equipment by type. The *ASM* is not published for Census years, but the Establishments in the sample receive their annual questionnaire along with the quinquennial forms. In this way, information from the *ASM* is consistent from year to year, and some of the more important tables are reproduced in the *Census of Manufactures* itself.

Current Industrial Reports is a series of approximately 100 annual, quarterly, or monthly reports on specific industries. Data are limited, and cover only half the industries tabulated in the *Census of Manufactures.* For each product, *Current Industrial Reports* typically cite the value and quantity of shipments, together with imports and exports for the product. Depending on the industry, additional data may be found. The series is designed to provide rapid updating of the Census, and to compare domestic output to product imports. Several general reports are also produced in the *CIR* series, including *Plant Capacity* and *Manufacturers' Shipments, Inventories and Orders.* Both monitor key economic indicators of manufacturing activity.

Census of Retail Trade.

Retail businesses sell merchandise to the general public for personal or household use. In the SIC system they comprise classes 52 through 59. The publishing scheme for the *Census of Retail Trade* is similar to that outlined for manufacturing. The *Geographic Area Series* provides detailed data for states, MSAs, counties, and Places with 2,500 inhabitants or more. Data in the series include number of Establishments, total dollar volume of sales, payroll size, and number of paid employees. A separate column in each table outlines the number of

Establishments which are proprietorships, and the number of partnerships. Most figures are given at three- and four-digit SIC levels, but some industries are further divided for greater specificity. For example, SIC 5812 ("Eating Places") is divided into the following 6 "parts": restaurants, cafeterias, fast food operations (which the Bureau actually places in a more general category designated "refreshment places"), ice cream stands, social caterers, and contract feeding establishments (i.e., contracted services in a hospital, school, or other institution). These breakdowns are typically seen at the state and metropolitan level; they are too specific for smaller geographic areas. Definitions for "parts" are given at the back of every report.

Another useful feature in the geographic series is a set of state tables ranking counties and Places by total sales volume. The "United States Summary" volume contains these rankings for the 250 leading counties, cities, and MSAs in the nation. Operating ratios in the *Geographic Area Series* cite per capita sales, "per Establishment sales," payroll per employee, and employees per Establishment.

The *Census of Retail Trade* also has a *Subject Series* that is really a combination of industry and subject data. Three titles in the series present exceptionally useful information. *Establishment and Firm Size* provides retail data at the national level for both Establishments and companies. Within each industry group, the number of Establishments and firms is given by size category. The data answer questions such as "How many car dealerships have 100 or more employees?" and "How many grocery stores have sales greater than $5 million?" This report also analyzes concentration ratios for retail businesses by sales and payroll size.

Another report in the *Subject Series* is called *Merchandise Line Sales.* The information in this publication is analogous to the product-industry relationships given in the *Census of Manufactures*—it presents an alternative to data tabulated by primary SIC codes alone. Retail stores usually sell more than one type of merchandise, and it is helpful to know which stores sell what kinds of products. In Exhibits 16-3 and 16-4, *Merchandise Line Sales* does precisely that. The first of these exhibits shows types of retail stores and the various merchandise sold by each. Notice, for example, that furniture stores (SIC 5712) sell significant amounts of major appliances, TV and audio equipment, floor coverings, and even women's clothing in addition to furniture and household items. As to be expected, the vast majority of sales (83%) involve furniture. Exhibit 16-4 illustrates the reverse situation, outlining individual products and the types of

EXHIBIT 16-3. *Census of Retail Trade*: *Merchandise Line Sales*, **Table 1**

Table 1. **Merchandise Lines by Kind of Business: 1987**—Con.

[Includes only establishments with payroll. For meaning of abbreviations and symbols, see introductory text. For explanation of terms and comparability of 1982 and 1987 censuses, including revised methodology for presenting establishment counts, see appendix A]

ML code	Kind of business and merchandise line	Establish-ments (number)	Sales of specified merchandise line			ML code	Kind of business and merchandise line	Establish-ments (number)	Sales of specified merchandise line		
			Amount ($1,000)	As percent of total sales of—					Amount ($1,000)	As percent of total sales of—	
				Estab-lish-ments handling line	All estab-lish-ments					Estab-lish-ments handling line	All estab-lish-ments
	Family shoe stores (SIC 566 pt.)	**25 082**	**9 744 854**	**(X)**	**100.0**		**Miscellaneous apparel and accessory stores (SIC 569)** ∗	**9 057**	**2 361 696**	**(X)**	**100.0**
200	Men's and boys' wear, except footwear	2 961	200 834	11.7	2.1		**Furniture and homefurnishings stores (SIC 57)**	**109 653**	**74 782 502**	**(X)**	**100.0**
220	Women's and girls' wear, except footwear	3 756	126 360	7.1	1.3	100	Groceries and other foods	1 498	45 925	4.7	.1
260	Footwear, except infants' and toddlers'	25 082	9 354 384	96.0	96.0	220	Women's and girls' wear, except footwear	1 598	89 687	6.2	.1
261	Men's and boys' footwear	22 715	1 975 055	23.7	20.3	270	Sewing, knitting, and needlework goods	1 610	67 455	10.0	.1
262	Women's and girls' footwear	22 692	3 406 030	40.8	35.0	280	Curtains, draperies, and dry goods	17 146	2 960 006	24.6	4.0
263	Children's footwear	20 307	874 001	11.7	9.0	300	Major household appliances	22 803	8 298 246	37.3	11.1
264	Athletic footwear	19 870	2 677 298	34.1	27.5	310	Small electric appliances	12 248	922 336	10.5	1.2
265	Footwear accessories	21 352	422 000	4.9	4.3	320	TV's and video recorders and tapes	31 280	7 410 539	26.8	9.9
500	Sporting goods	254	17 753	13.8	.2	330	Audio equipment, musical instruments, and supplies	34 250	11 415 668	41.1	15.3
890	Unclassified merchandise	2 862	33 626	3.3	.3	340	Furniture and sleep equipment	38 717	22 265 348	69.7	29.8
–	Miscellaneous merchandise	(X)	11 897	(X)	.1	360	Floor coverings	27 107	8 943 528	40.5	12.0
						370	Computer hardware and software, and calculating equipment and supplies	13 550	3 448 651	37.6	4.6
	Other apparel and accessory stores (SIC 564, 9)	**15 203**	**4 463 167**	**(X)**	**100.0**	380	Kitchenware and homefurnishings	30 203	4 526 065	20.3	6.1
160	Drugs, health aids, and beauty aids	111	4 182	7.9	.1	400	Jewelry	2 659	97 279	4.7	.1
200	Men's and boys' wear, except footwear	10 128	1 329 410	42.0	29.8	440	Photographic equipment and supplies	350	81 862	6.3	.1
220	Women's and girls' wear, except footwear	14 391	2 823 178	67.2	63.3	600	Hardware, tools, and plumbing and electrical supplies	2 226	190 370	8.5	.3
260	Footwear, except infants' and toddlers'	2 561	127 390	14.7	2.9	620	Lawn and garden equipment and supplies	2 654	112 811	3.5	.2
280	Curtains, draperies, and dry goods	98	2 343	5.8	.1	640	Lumber and building materials	5 789	298 526	7.3	.4
340	Furniture and sleep equipment	308	27 761	20.6	.6	670	Paint and related preservatives and supplies	2 092	69 410	4.5	.1
400	Jewelry	852	11 155	4.2	.2	850	All other merchandise	3 689	260 378	8.0	.3
460	Toys, hobby goods, and games	221	6 868	7.7	.2	890	Unclassified merchandise	15 988	276 474	2.9	.4
500	Sporting goods	796	57 192	16.2	1.3	900	Nonmerchandise receipts	39 416	2 853 932	8.5	3.8
850	All other merchandise	334	15 489	9.7	.3	–	Miscellaneous merchandise	(X)	148 006	(X)	.2
890	Unclassified merchandise	2 097	26 016	10.6	.6						
900	Nonmerchandise receipts	784	23 555	9.1	.5		**Furniture stores (SIC 5712)**	**32 763**	**25 996 804**	**(X)**	**100.0**
–	Miscellaneous merchandise	(X)	8 628	(X)	.2	220	Women's and girls' wear, except footwear	225	16 357	9.6	.1
						280	Curtains, draperies, and dry goods	4 958	246 547	4.8	.9
	Children's and infants' wear stores (SIC 564)	**6 146**	**2 101 471**	**(X)**	**100.0**	300	Major household appliances	7 813	1 011 639	16.4	3.9
200	Men's and boys' wear, except footwear	4 377	601 976	36.3	28.6	301	Kitchen appliances	7 370	602 398	10.1	2.3
201	Boys' and young men's wear and accessories	4 351	588 646	35.7	28.0	302	Laundry appliances	6 252	303 189	6.3	1.2
202	Men's overcoats, topcoats, raincoats, and outer jackets	93	1 521	5.8	.1	303	Other major household appliances	4 512	106 052	3.1	.4
206	Men's casual slacks, jeans, and shorts	125	1 977	6.4	.1	310	Small electric appliances	1 095	24 113	2.6	.1
209	Men's sport shirts	148	2 323	5.2	.1	320	TV's and video recorders and tapes	6 256	586 476	10.8	2.3
212	Men's hosiery, pajamas, and underwear	269	4 165	4.4	.2	321	Televisions	6 132	465 309	8.7	1.8
–	Miscellaneous merchandise	(X)	3 344	(X)	.2	324	Video recorders, cameras, and tapes	3 536	121 167	3.7	.5
220	Women's and girls' wear, except footwear	6 019	1 438 880	69.6	68.5	330	Audio equipment, musical instruments, and supplies	2 797	97 352	3.6	.4
221	Infants', toddlers', girls', and subteen clothing and accessories	5 995	1 360 235	66.1	64.7	340	Furniture and sleep equipment	32 763	21 578 954	83.0	83.0
222	Furs and fur garments	40	1 086	13.4	.1	341	Upholstered furniture	24 322	7 205 689	33.4	27.7
223	Dresses	436	11 752	8.8	.6	342	Other living room, dining room, and bedroom furniture	26 781	8 155 246	36.3	31.4
224	Dress coats, jackets, and rainwear	209	3 185	4.2	.2	343	Sleep furniture and equipment	25 750	4 183 217	19.0	16.1
225	Suits, sport jackets, and blazers	164	2 117	3.3	.1	345	Office furniture	6 539	672 383	12.0	2.6
226	Slacks, jeans, shorts, and skirts	308	6 743	5.8	.3	346	Other furniture	12 093	1 362 419	12.5	5.2
227	Tops (shirts, blouses, and sweaters)	377	7 796	7.2	.4	360	Floor coverings	10 184	786 369	7.7	3.0
228	Women's active sportswear	219	4 982	9.4	.2	361	Soft-surface floor coverings	9 857	692 509	7.0	2.7
229	Hosiery, socks, and tights	343	3 556	3.9	.2	362	Hard-surface floor coverings	4 068	93 860	3.1	.4
232	Lingerie, sleepwear, and loungewear	400	5 387	3.8	.3	380	Kitchenware and homefurnishings	16 640	932 789	6.0	3.6
234	Women's accessories	1 093	24 851	6.7	1.2	383	Decorative accessories	16 522	867 560	5.6	3.3
236	Other women's wear items	242	5 187	9.4	.2	385	Other kitchenware and homefurnishings	1 614	65 229	4.0	.3
–	Miscellaneous merchandise	(X)	2 003	(X)	.1	400	Jewelry	714	19 259	3.3	.1
260	Footwear, except infants' and toddlers'	519	12 452	7.5	.6	600	Hardware, tools, and plumbing and electrical supplies	492	18 130	5.5	.1
261	Men's and boys' footwear	151	2 013	3.5	.1	620	Lawn and garden equipment and supplies	752	13 622	2.2	.1
262	Women's and girls' footwear	134	2 283	4.6	.1	640	Lumber and building materials	476	27 480	7.7	.1
263	Children's footwear	427	7 633	5.7	.4	850	All other merchandise	1 509	86 332	6.4	.3
–	Miscellaneous merchandise	(X)	523	(X)	(V)	857	Antiques	412	19 693	6.5	.1
280	Curtains, draperies, and dry goods	62	1 498	4.9	.1	858	Collectibles	298	13 793	6.3	.1
340	Furniture and sleep equipment	298	27 524	21.0	1.3	859	Art goods	981	26 200	3.0	.1
400	Jewelry	321	2 043	3.0	.1	879	All other merchandise	269	26 646	9.1	.1
460	Toys, hobby goods, and games	141	5 108	8.3	.1	890	Unclassified merchandise	2 869	99 087	3.9	.4
850	All other merchandise	93	3 879	13.4	.2						
890	Unclassified merchandise	234	3 672	5.0	.2						
900	Nonmerchandise receipts	122	2 136	3.9	.1						
–	Miscellaneous merchandise	(X)	2 303	(X)	.1						

See footnotes at end of table.

Reprinted from the *Census of Retail Trade*, published by the U.S. Bureau of the Census.

EXHIBIT 16-4. *Census of Retail Trade*: *Merchandise Line Sales*, **Table 2**

Table 2. Kinds of Business by Broad Merchandise Line: 1987—Con.

[Includes only establishments with payroll. For meaning of abbreviations and symbols, see introductory text. For explanation of terms and comparability of 1982 and 1987 censuses, including revised methodology for presenting establishment counts, see appendix A]

1987 SIC code	Merchandise line and kind of business	Establishments (number)	Sales ($1,000)	Percent of sales accounted for by specified kind of business
	Curtains, draperies, and dry goods (ML 280)	**67 605**	**13 036 768**	**100.0**
52	Building materials and garden supplies stores	5 824	189 386	1.5
521, 3	Building materials and supply stores	4 950	174 254	1.3
521	Lumber and other building materials dealers	687	29 164	.2
523	Paint, glass, and wallpaper stores	4 263	145 090	1.1
525	Hardware stores	857	14 964	.1
53	General merchandise stores	28 350	8 351 737	64.1
531	Department stores	9 788	7 169 774	55.0
531 pt.	Conventional	2 369	2 519 954	19.3
531 pt.	Discount or mass merchandising	5 614	2 921 001	22.4
531 pt.	National chain	1 805	1 728 819	13.3
533	Variety stores	9 420	357 474	2.7
539	Miscellaneous general merchandise stores	9 142	824 489	6.3
54	Food stores	917	28 918	.2
541	Grocery stores	858	28 302	.2
56	Apparel and accessory stores	6 008	495 913	3.8
562, 3	Women's clothing and specialty stores	487	24 195	.2
562	Women's clothing stores	445	22 629	.2
565	Family clothing stores	5 376	468 607	3.6
57	Furniture and homefurnishings stores	17 146	2 960 006	22.7
5712	Furniture stores	4 958	246 547	1.9
5713, 4, 9	Homefurnishings stores	11 994	2 705 752	20.8
5713	Floor covering stores	2 691	140 987	1.1
5714	Drapery and upholstery stores	3 856	896 439	6.9
5719	Miscellaneous homefurnishings stores	5 447	1 668 326	12.8
572	Household appliance stores	183	7 499	.1
591	Drug and proprietary stores	1 129	24 217	.2
591 pt.	Drug stores	1 086	23 587	.2
59 ex. 591	Miscellaneous retail stores	8 161	982 937	7.5
594	Miscellaneous shopping goods stores	1 879	83 600	.6
5947	Gift, novelty, and souvenir shops	1 146	21 424	.2
5949	Sewing, needlework, and piece goods stores	598	58 515	.4
596	Nonstore retailers	3 697	851 393	6.5
5961	Catalog and mail-order houses	2 854	572 673	4.4
5963	Direct selling establishments	843	278 720	2.1
–	All other retailers	70	3 654	(V)
	Major household appliances (ML 300)	**65 537**	**17 570 604**	**100.0**
52	Building materials and garden supplies stores	9 154	614 152	3.5
521, 3	Building materials and supply stores	3 392	372 514	2.1
521	Lumber and other building materials dealers	3 359	372 046	2.1
525	Hardware stores	5 418	233 805	1.3
53	General merchandise stores	10 788	6 450 711	36.7
531	Department stores	5 806	5 308 806	30.2
531 pt.	Conventional	1 161	330 143	1.9
531 pt.	Discount or mass merchandising	2 963	957 536	5.4
531 pt.	National chain	1 682	4 021 127	22.9
533	Variety stores	550	17 037	.1
539	Miscellaneous general merchandise stores	4 432	1 124 868	6.4
55 ex. 554	Automotive dealers	5 130	311 597	1.8
553	Auto and home supply stores	5 061	302 364	1.7
553 pt.	Tire, battery, and accessory dealers	1 951	73 711	.4
57	Furniture and homefurnishings stores	22 803	8 298 246	47.2
5712	Furniture stores	7 813	1 011 639	5.8
5713, 4, 9	Homefurnishings stores	203	16 582	.1
5713	Floor covering stores	111	13 397	.1
572	Household appliance stores	10 921	5 558 939	31.6
573	Radio, television, computer, and music stores	3 866	1 711 086	9.7
5731	Radio, television, and electronics stores	3 807	1 708 452	9.7
	Major household appliances (ML 300)—Con.			
591	Drug and proprietary stores	2 999	35 676	.2
591 pt.	Drug stores	2 879	34 380	.2
59 ex. 591	Miscellaneous retail stores	14 404	1 854 120	10.6
594	Miscellaneous shopping goods stores	2 973	119 708	.7
5949	Sewing, needlework, and piece goods stores	2 843	113 888	.6
596	Nonstore retailers	4 182	1 472 349	8.4
5961	Catalog and mail-order houses	2 435	629 025	3.6
5963	Direct selling establishments	1 738	842 866	4.8
598	Fuel dealers	3 571	141 673	.8
5983	Fuel oil dealers	193	16 164	.1
5984	Liquefied petroleum gas (bottled gas) dealers	3 306	125 289	.7
–	All other retailers	259	6 102	(V)
	Small electric appliances (ML 310)	**79 831**	**6 245 498**	**100.0**
52	Building materials and garden supplies stores	11 238	336 135	5.4
521, 3	Building materials and supply stores	2 432	175 271	2.8
521	Lumber and other building materials dealers	2 131	161 820	2.6
523	Paint, glass, and wallpaper stores	301	13 451	.2
525	Hardware stores	8 401	154 949	2.5
526	Retail nurseries, lawn and garden supply stores	402	5 873	.1
53	General merchandise stores	25 269	3 910 341	62.6
531	Department stores	8 991	2 477 636	39.7
531 pt.	Conventional	1 752	526 951	8.4
531 pt.	Discount or mass merchandising	5 550	1 662 459	26.6
531 pt.	National chain	1 689	288 226	4.6
533	Variety stores	6 528	108 314	1.7
539	Miscellaneous general merchandise stores	9 750	1 324 391	21.2
54	Food stores	3 767	186 159	3.0
541	Grocery stores	3 243	176 901	2.8
543, 4, 5, 9	Other food stores	511	9 193	.1
549	Miscellaneous food stores	506	9 152	.1
55 ex. 554	Automotive dealers	1 953	46 591	.7
553	Auto and home supply stores	1 952	46 569	.7
56	Apparel and accessory stores	471	5 815	.1
565	Family clothing stores	388	4 345	.1
57	Furniture and homefurnishings stores	12 248	922 336	14.8
5712	Furniture stores	1 095	24 113	.4
5713, 4, 9	Homefurnishings stores	1 307	70 462	1.1
5719	Miscellaneous homefurnishings stores	1 219	69 351	1.1
572	Household appliance stores	1 589	121 261	1.9
573	Radio, television, computer, and music stores	8 257	706 500	11.3
5731	Radio, television, and electronics stores	8 214	705 505	11.3
591	Drug and proprietary stores	17 199	473 341	7.6
591 pt.	Drug stores	16 783	453 861	7.3
591 pt.	Proprietary stores	416	19 480	.3
59 ex. 591	Miscellaneous retail stores	7 660	364 262	5.8
594	Miscellaneous shopping goods stores	691	20 082	.3
5944	Jewelry stores	215	11 008	.2
5947	Gift, novelty, and souvenir shops	239	5 174	.1
596	Nonstore retailers	2 726	298 535	4.8
5961	Catalog and mail-order houses	2 430	260 473	4.2
5963	Direct selling establishments	291	38 040	.6
598	Fuel dealers	90	6 093	.1
5984	Liquefied petroleum gas (bottled gas) dealers	70	5 252	.1
–	All other retailers	26	518	(V)

See footnotes at end of table.

Reprinted from the *Census of Retail Trade*, published by the U.S. Bureau of the Census.

stores in which they are sold. Merchandise Line 280 (Curtains, Draperies, and Dry Goods) lists products sold not only in department stores, home furnishing stores, and similar retail locations, but also in clothing stores, hardware stores, and a host of other outlets. To show the relationship between the two tables, compare the sales volume of draperies in furniture stores. The value ($246,547,000) is shown on both exhibits. Note that the amount sold in these stores is small, regardless of the point of view: only 1.9% of all drapery sales take place in furniture stores, and only 4.8% of furniture store revenues result from drapery sales. Still, this information might provide sales managers with an unforeseen new market, as well as portraying a more complete picture of both industries. The usefulness of this report is limited, however, because not all retail industries are analyzed by merchandise line. The coverage for 1987 has been expanded, but there are still only 41 Merchandise Lines presented.

The third major report in the *Subject Series* covers a range of topics under the title *Miscellaneous Subjects*. This report analyzes some of the more important and ubiquitous retail businesses in detail, including restaurants, gasoline service stations, and drug stores. Data for each industry vary considerably, depending on the characteristics of the business. Information on eating places, for example, covers the average cost per meal, the number of franchise holders, seating capacity, and the number of Establishments without waiter or waitress service. The variety of information found in these tables illustrates an important point about the Economic Census: different industries receive different questionnaires, and hundreds are used to compile the reports.

Another table appearing in *Miscellaneous Subjects* gives the total square footage and "selling footage" for department stores, grocery stores, and other major retail groups, together with the average dollar volume of sales per square foot. A table called "Class of Customer" provides breakdowns on the percentage of sales for broad retail groups to the following customer categories: the general public; builders and contractors; and wholesalers, institutions, and governments. A third table cites data on leased departments within main stores. These are independent businesses which lease space in supermarkets, department stores, and other retail facilities. The number of stores which allow leased departments, and the number of leased departments by type of store are given.

A new feature for 1987 is a separate *Nonemployer Statistics Series* that covers "mom and pop" stores operated by their owners without paid employees. The series is issued in four regional volumes, and provides limited information on nonemployer operations. The data cite number of Establishments and value of sales for states, MSAs, counties, and larger Places, but only for 10 industry groups. The tables in the *Geographic Area Series* exclude these operations, tabulating data for Establishments with payroll only.

The *Census of Retail Trade* can be used to identify the characteristics of stores, their locations, and the products they sell. The quinquennial Census is updated by a monthly and annual survey, but information from these studies is quite general. The basic update is called *Monthly Retail Trade: Sales and Inventories*, and is published as part of the Bureau's *Current Business Reports* series. Broad data are presented for the United States, the nine Census regions, and for the largest states, MSAs, and cities only. The Bureau also releases a preliminary report called *Advance Monthly Retail Sales*. The information is eventually cumulated in a summary report entitled *Annual Retail Trade*.

Census of Wholesale Trade.

This Census covers SIC categories 50 and 51, representing businesses which sell merchandise primarily to retail stores, institutions, farms, and to other wholesalers. The *Geographic Area Series* once again presents data for states, MSAs, counties, and larger Places. Basic information includes the number of Establishments, sales volume, payroll, number of employees, year-end inventories, and total operating expenses. Data are also broken down by type of wholesaler: merchants, manufacturer's sales outlets, or agents and brokers. The *Subject Series* is comparable to the reports found in the retail Census, including *Establishment and Firm Size* and *Miscellaneous Subjects*. The wholesale Census also reports on *Commodity Line Sales*, which is similar to the retail data found in *Merchandise Line Sales*. Quinquennial reports are updated by sample surveys and published in the *Current Business Reports* series as *Monthly Wholesale Trade: Sales and Inventory* and *Annual Wholesale Trade*.

Census of Service Industries.

This Census concerns businesses which provide services to individuals or other businesses. SIC codes 70 through 89, including lodging, repair, amusement, health care, and professional services, are covered here. Unlike other Census programs, many industries within the designated SIC groupings are not enumerated at all. Nothing is reported for real estate firms, banks, or finance companies. The *Geographic Area Series* covers states, MSAs, counties, and larger Places. Basic data include the number of Establishments, dollar value of receipts, payroll,

and number of employees. The 1987 *Census of Service Industries* offers more detailed industry breakdowns than afforded by 4-digit SIC codes. SIC 7011 (Hotels and Motels) is subdivided into four "parts," for example: hotels with 25 guest rooms or more, smaller hotels, motels and tourist courts, and motor hotels.

Because many services are provided by nonprofit organizations, separate tables present data for tax-exempt Establishments, including sales by revenue source, such as admissions, membership dues, concession sales, and government assistance. The *Subject Series* gives in-depth coverage to hotels and motels; advertising agencies; accounting, consulting, and public relations firms; photography businesses; and computer services. Like the retail series, the *Census of Service Industries* includes a separate report on *Nonemployer Statistics*, which presents limited information on Establishments with no paid employees. The quinquennial Census is updated by a brief *Service Annual Survey Report* only; no monthly surveys are taken.

Census of Mineral Industries.

The Establishments covered in this Census are engaged in the extraction of naturally occurring substances such as salt, sand, iron ore, oil, and natural gas. The presentation of data is similar to the *Census of Manufactures*, but because the scope of mining activities in the United States is less extensive, the result is a much smaller set of reports. The *Geographic Area Series* consists of nine reports, one for each region of the country. Data are presented by state and county only, and include the same type of information seen in the manufacturing Census. Industry data appear at the two, three, and four-digit SIC levels, but specific product information is listed under each primary industry. An *Industry Series* and *Subject Series* are also published. The Bureau of the Census does not undertake any sample surveys between quinquennial Censuses for mineral industries. The U.S. Bureau of Mines publishes a large amount of annual and monthly information, but it is not comparable to Census figures.

Census of Construction Industries.

This Census counts Establishments which operate as general contractors, builders, special contractors (plumbers, electricians, etc.), and real estate subdividers and developers. The *Geographic Area Series* appears in nine regional volumes and covers states and MSAs only. The *Industry Series* reports number of Establishments, employment hours, payroll, and dollar value of work completed. This series also offers more financial information than most Censuses. Data on the cost of materials, payments to subcontractors, and other operating ex-

penses can be found here as can information on capital expenditures by construction Establishments and the gross value of their fixed assets. Tables also indicate whether projects were public or private, whether they involved new construction or renovation of existing structures, and whether the work was done in the contractor's home state.

There is no real update to the quinquennial construction Census, but the Bureau publishes numerous titles in its *Current Construction Reports* series. These monthly, quarterly, and annual publications provide data on a wide range of construction activities, but are not comparable to information in the *Census of Construction Industries*. While the quinquennial Census reports on the operations of construction Establishments, the various *Current Construction Reports* examine the results of construction activities. In other words, they provide current information on new housing stock and the total value of completed construction projects. Thus they offer a wealth of vital information on the state of the economy. Examples of titles in the series are *New One-Family Houses Sold and for Sale, Housing Authorized by Building Permit, Price Index of New One-Family Houses Sold*, and the *Value of New Construction Put in Place*.

Census of Transportation.

Unlike the other parts of the Economic Census, only a portion of this series focuses on the Establishments which comprise the industry. Prior to 1987, the *Census of Transportation* emphasized broader transportation issues, including surveys of American travel habits, studies of how manufacturers transported their goods, and a Census of commercial trucks owned by all industries. The 1987 Census focuses more on the transportation industry itself.

Still, this Census covers only a segment of the industry, notably trucking (including the transport of hazardous materials), water-borne transportation, public warehousing, and transportation-related services such as travel agencies and tour operators. Excluded are railroads, air transportation, buses, and local public transit. Because this Census only covers Establishments with payroll, many independent truckers are also excluded. The single-volume *Geographic Area Series* provides data on number of Establishments, payroll, employment, and revenues for the nation and for states and MSAs. The *Subject Series*, also issued as a single volume, provides additional information on concentration ratios, Establishments by revenue size and employment size, and source of revenue. Data in this volume are reported primarily at the national level.

The second component of the 1987 transportation Census is the *Truck Inventory and Use Survey*. Not an "Establishment-based" survey, it covers all categories of truck owners, not just those in the trucking industry. In short, it is an inventory of the nation's "truck population." Data are based on a sample of all registered private and commercial trucks in the country, excluding those in government service. The report is published in 52 volumes, one for each state, the District of Columbia, and a U.S. summary. The publications describe the characteristics and use of trucks in each area, with data reported at the state level. Information includes truck size, miles traveled, hazardous material transported, and range of operation. Major use is also tallied, whether for personal travel, agriculture, construction, rental, or manufacturing.

The *Census of Transportation* is updated in part by the annual *Motor Freight Transportation and Warehousing Survey*, which is part of the *Current Business Reports* series. It covers the trucking industry and public warehousing operations only. For warehouses, the report covers total revenues, and operating expenses by major category. For trucking, it presents similar information to the quinquennial reports, plus revenues by type of commodity, which is not covered in the Census itself. All data are given at the national level.

Changes in the 1987 Census

Most of the differences between the 1982 and 1987 Censuses are minor, so users familiar with the earlier publications will have no trouble switching to the 1987 reports. One of the least visible, but most significant changes was the adoption of the revised SIC codes for 1987. The areas most affected by the SIC changes were computer-related industries, including manufacturing, retail, and service operations. Another major revision occurred in the business services area, especially for consulting services. Finally, in cases where manufacturing and mining activities are no longer as prominent as they once were, some industries have been combined into broader classifications. Researchers can turn to the "bridge tables" in the 1987 *Standard Industrial Classification Manual* to identify the industry codes which have changed. The 1987 Census reports also have bridge tables comparing data from 1982 and 1987. For retailing, wholesale trade, and service industries, these are found in the *Geographic Area Series*, with reporting at the state level. For manufacturing and mineral industries, the bridge tables are in the *Industry Series*, with data at the national

level. The 1987 Census was the first to employ the new definitions of metropolitan areas, a change to be aware of when comparing information from earlier publications.

A third noteworthy difference is expanded coverage of previously omitted industries. The most sweeping expansion took place in the transportation Census, but the *Census of Service Industries* was also broadened. Expansion will continue in 1992, when all remaining uncovered activities will be added to the Census, including finance, real estate, communications, and public utilities.

Another change corrected a large-scale error in the 1982 Census. The U.S. Internal Revenue Service, which provides the Bureau with most of the data from administrative records, made numerous mistakes in 1982 when coding information from retail and service Establishments. Detailed SIC numbers were assigned to each Establishment by IRS personnel, and many were given "Not Elsewhere Classified" numbers instead of more descriptive classifications. As a result, the Bureau decided that data on Establishments with no payroll could not be used. Because of the IRS error in 1982, information for individual industries was published only for Establishments with paid employees. For 1987, the IRS revised its forms, so nonemployers now assign their own SIC codes. Because self-employed businesspeople play a smaller role in certain industries than others, only three Censuses provide data for nonemployers—retail, service, and construction. For the first two, data appear in separate reports entitled *Nonemployer Statistics Series*. For the *Census of Construction Industries*, nonemployer data appear in the *Geographic Area Series*, but only at the state level.

The other significant change for 1987 is the introduction of CD-ROM products. Virtually all data from the printed reports can now be searched via personal computer, and some data are available only on CD-ROM. Among the unique features are zip code level reporting, smaller geographic breakdowns for Merchandise Line Sales, and greater detail for minority- and women-owned businesses. The disks will be published as two CD "volumes": Volume 1 contains every table found in the seven Economic Censuses; Volume 2 provides data by zip code, but only for retail, service, and manufacturing industries. Because the Economic Census is produced on a flow basis, CDs are being published with partial data, and early disks will be superseded by later editions until all industries are included. The Bureau plans to issue five editions of Volume 1 and two editions of Volume 2. (As of this writing, editions 1-C and 2-A have been released.

The final, cumulative editions of both volumes are scheduled for release in late 1991.)The disks also contain comparable historical data for many series.

The disks allow users to print a standard table of basic data for any state or county, but this extremely limited feature will satisfy few research needs. To create customized tables or otherwise manipulate data requires a bit of effort. The Economic Census is designed to work with *dBase III*, but disks also come with the Bureau's own *EXTRACT* program. *EXTRACT* prompts the user through each step: choosing a file, selecting data items and records, designing text labels and display formats, indexing records, and extracting data to a separate file. Users select from menus of data variables, industry codes, geographic levels, and areas of the country. A detailed definition of any data item can be called up with a simple command. Because the files are so large, certain operations can be slow, but the program is surprisingly versatile and fairly simple to learn.

Two printed series were canceled in 1987: *Major Retail Centers* and the *Commodity Transportation Survey*. Both were victims of reduced Census budgets. Other changes for 1987 are fairly minor. Several new printed reports will be issued, including a separate report on geographic rankings for retail sales. Other changes involve increased coverage. The number of Merchandise Lines for retailing was increased from 34 to 41, for example, and the service industry series now reports on ten broad business categories instead of five. In both Censuses, greater detail is reported below the four-digit SIC level. More information on imports and exports appears in the manufacturing Census, and more data on exports can be found in the service Census.

ADDITIONAL CENSUS PUBLICATIONS

The Bureau conducts a number of other economic programs in addition to the seven major Censuses. A few are also undertaken every five years, while others are done more frequently.

Other Quinquennial Censuses

Five additional Census programs are conducted every five years for years ending in 2 and 7. The *Economic Census of Outlying Areas* presents similar information to that found in the sources introduced above, but for Puerto Rico, the U.S. Virgin Islands, Guam, and the Northern Marianas. The most detailed information is

provided for Puerto Rico. Each geographic area is presented in a separate volume covering all seven industry groups for that location.

The next quinquennial report presents an alternative view of U.S. industries. With few exceptions, most data from the Economic Census are tallied by Establishment. To place this information in a more traditional perspective, the Bureau recasts Establishment data by company in a series called *Enterprise Statistics*. Companies are classified according to a variation of the SIC system called the Enterprise Standard Industrial Classification. It consists of the the the first two digits of the SIC number and a single letter—34A, for example. The main publication in this series has been split into two parts for 1987. The first, entitled *Company Summary*, contains data on the number of companies in each industry, their legal form of organization, number of firms by employee-size category, and industry sales volume. It also shows the relationship between number of Establishments in each primary industry and number of companies. Separate tabulations are given for companies with a single location (i.e., one Establishment) and multi-Establishment firms; the latter are further divided by those in a single industry and those engaged in multiple business activities. Data are reported at the national and state levels. The second report in the Enterprise series, called *Large Companies*, covers firms with more than 500 employees. It provides similar data to that of the main report, plus additional financial characteristics. The third report is *Auxiliary Establishments*, which tallies the number of Establishments existing solely to provide support services to the company of which they are a part. Examples are company-owned warehouses, sales offices, and research facilities. The volumes of *Enterprise Statistics* are among the last reports to appear after the Economic Census is conducted.

The third survey related to the Economic Census tabulates information on minority-owned and women-owned businesses, and the titles in this series also present data for companies rather than Establishments. The *Survey of Minority-Owned Businesses* for 1987 will be issued in five volumes: a general summary, plus volumes for businesses owned by blacks, Hispanics, Asian-Americans, and Native Americans and other minorities. Data are given for the nation, states, and for MSAs, counties, and Places with more than 100 minority firms. Tabulations are for 2- and 3-digit SIC codes for all types of industries. Information given includes number of companies, legal form of organization, number of employees,

payroll, and gross receipts. The other segment of this series, *Women-Owned Businesses*, is similar in format and content to the minority business volumes.

The two remaining quinquennial Censuses are not thought of as part of the Economic Census. The *Census of Agriculture* provides a detailed look at farms and farming in the United States. Since 1982, it has appeared in the same years as the Economic Census. Data from the *Census of Agriculture* are available at the national, state, and county levels. A report is issued for each state, plus a U.S. summary volume. The *Census of Agriculture* can also be received as a set of floppy diskettes or on a single CD-ROM. An enormous amount of information is collected on the number, characteristics, and output of American farms. Statistics range from total acreage in use, to financial characteristics of farms, to crop production, including grain, fruit, nut, vegetable, poultry, livestock, and dairy output. The Bureau also produces an annual survey on farm inhabitants called *Farm Population of the U.S.* (as part of the *Current Population Reports* series), but the majority of agriculture statistics are produced by various agencies within the U.S. Department of Agriculture.

The final quinquennial Census is the *Census of Governments*, a wide-ranging and voluminous enumeration of government finances and activities in the United States. The Bureau collects data on over 80,000 governmental units, including states, counties, cities and other Places, Minor Civil Divisions, and school districts. Among the statistics which can be found are total assessed valuation of real property, government revenues, expenditures, debt, number of public employees, and forms of government. The Bureau also publishes an extensive collection of annual and quarterly reports on government.

The Economic Census doesn't measure all economic activity in the nation. The 1987 program measured industries which accounted for only about 65% of the country's Gross National Product. After adding the Censuses of agriculture and government, the coverage rises to 75%. After the omitted industries are brought into the program in 1992, however, that percentage should approach 100%.

Foreign Trade Statistics

The Bureau of the Census is the principal agency which tabulates and publishes data on imports and exports in the United States. Probably no category of Census statistics is more misunderstood or more susceptible to misinterpretation than data on foreign trade.

Confusion comes from the definition of the term itself. Foreign trade does not imply a change of ownership, but rather the physical movement of merchandise across U.S. borders. The statistics in question deal with *merchandise* foreign trade—tangible goods only.

The agency which monitors the flow of goods across our borders is the U.S. Customs Service. Customs employees literally inspect every shipment of goods for import or export, and they require shippers to submit detailed documentation as well. The Customs Service has been performing this task (and collecting the accompanying statistics) since 1790. For imports, the government imposes taxes (called tariffs) on most product categories. Tariff guidelines are set at the international level by a treaty known as the General Agreement on Trade and Tariffs (GATT), but Congress imposes additional duties on certain goods to protect American manufacturers. The complete rate structure is published by the U.S. International Trade Commission in a document called the *Harmonized Tariff Schedule of the United States*. The Customs Service administers the tariff system for all imported goods arriving at U.S. ports. Products are classified according to the Harmonized Schedule, and shipping documents are submitted to Customs; copies are then passed on to the Bureau of the Census for tabulation. A similar process takes place for exported goods, even though no tariff duties are assessed.

Three key concepts are critical to the understanding of U.S. foreign trade data: valuation methods, types of imports and exports, and classification schemes. The dollar value of goods in foreign trade is established in various ways. Exports are always valued Free Along Side (F.A.S.), which includes the cost of the commodity together with all costs incurred in getting it to the point of U.S. departure (except taxes). Imports, however, can be valued in one of two ways. The first is according to "Cost, insurance, freight" (C.i.f.), which includes the cost of the item as well as the cost of insuring it and shipping it to the point of entry in the U.S. (excluding U.S. import duties). The other is termed Customs Valuation, and includes only the cost of the commodity itself. Depending on the data user's needs, one or the other method may be more appropriate. An important point when making historical comparisons is that methods used for valuation have changed several times over the past 20 years.

The second concept involves the stages of processing in the import and export cycles. There are two ways in which imported products are defined. General Imports include all arrivals at U.S. ports, including those items which are stored in a bonded warehouse at the point of entry. Imports for Consumption include only those im-

ported items which are immediately shipped to another destination, plus previously imported merchandise which is withdrawn from the warehouse. The difference is essentially a matter of timing, but depending on the statistical table used, either definition may be employed. Exports also have two important stages. Domestic Merchandise has been produced or processed in the United States for export abroad. Foreign Merchandise is imported material being re-exported without undergoing any processing in this country.

Enormous confusion arises from the fact that more than one classification system is employed to report foreign trade data in the United States. For many years, six different classification systems were used. Separate numbering was used for imports and exports, for comparing U.S. data with other countries, and for comparing U.S. foreign trade with domestic output. To make matters worse, other nations had their own unique classification structures. For purposes of international comparisons, the United Nations created the Standard International Trade Classification (SITC) in 1950. All member nations are required to submit their own foreign trade statistics to the U.N. based on this system, which uses five-digit codes grouped into 10 major categories. Unfortunately, the SITC system is not sufficiently detailed for most industrial nations, which is one reason why such a proliferation of numbering schemes arose in the U.S. After many years of attempting to create an acceptable uniform system, most countries adopted the Harmonized Commodity Description and Coding System (HS) in 1985. The United States finally did so in January 1989.

The HS classification consists of approximately 5,000 six-digit numbers, arranged in 96 categories (or "chapters"). Unlike the SIC system, it is completely product-based, organized in most cases by the type of materials from which the items are made. Despite adoption of the Harmonized System by this country, its structure is deemed too general for most purposes. As a result, the United States has extended the basic HS numbers, in some cases up to the 10-digit level. In fact, two separate classification structures are used for imports and exports. This is because the nature of products leaving the country can be quite different than those entering, and because the import classification must also serve as a detailed tariff schedule. However, both classifications are identical up to the first six digits, and are usually similar thereafter.

The code numbers for imported products appear in the *Harmonized Tariff Schedule of the United States: Annotated for Statistical Reporting Purposes*. It is revised annually, with loose-leaf updates as required. The classification system for export data is called Schedule B, and its structure is enumerated in *Schedule B: Statistical Classification of Domestic and Foreign Commodities Exported from the United States*. It is reissued on an irregular basis, but loose-leaf updates are again supplied as needed. The latest complete revision appeared in 1990. In addition to detailed definitions of each classification number, both works provide alphabetical indexes to product names.

As of this writing, the Bureau's foreign trade publications are in a state of transition. Almost all printed statistical reports (called FTs) have ceased publication, and the remaining few have been revamped. The primary means of dissemination is now by CD-ROM. Selected statistics can also be found online through *CENDATA* or through the Department of Commerce Electronic Bulletin Board.

The Bureau has moved away from a paper-based reporting system because it was so cumbersome and complex. In contrast, the CD-ROM products offer significant advantages. First, large amounts of data can appear on a single disk. Second, customized reports can be created. Third, the disks include a complete alphabetical index to the classification systems, plus a concordance linking SIC codes to the HS structure. Fourth, and most important, data are released on a more timely basis, many months before the old printed reports typically appeared. In fact, the CD-ROMs are used to supply the most current statistics to key government officials such as the United States Trade Representative. Three CD products are described below. For those interested in receiving printed reports, the major paper publication in the FT series is also introduced.

Foreign Trade Data (Monthly).

Foreign trade data from the federal government are officially released on two monthly disks: *U.S. Exports of Merchandise* and *U.S. Imports of Merchandise*. The two databases are structured the same and are searched in identical fashion. Both utilize the Harmonized System, though the export file actually uses the new HS-based Schedule B. Both files work with the Bureau's *EXTRACT* software or with *dBase III*. Unlike the Economic Census disks, *Foreign Trade Data* also provides a fairly detailed menu-driven search system. Disks are distributed to Depository Libraries and can also be purchased on a subscription basis from the Bureau of the Census. Customers who don't need or can't afford monthly updates can receive the annual summary disks at an extremely reasonable price.

In the menu search mode, the user is prompted with a series of windows which lead to different levels of data. The opening screen presents a list of two-digit commodity codes; from there the user is led to four-digit subdivisions, and finally, to the specific six-digit tables. Every commodity report consists of two basic tables: the first presents data for the latest month and the second repeats the same variables for the year-to-date. Export tables cite the quantity and value of shipments for both domestic and foreign exports, then subdivide the totals by two modes of transport—sea and air. Import figures cover both general imports and imports for consumption, citing unit quantity, customs value, and import charges. Once again, data are subdivided by mode of transport. After viewing the two basic tables, country-specific data can be selected. Here the choice is to view country totals for the commodity, or to select figures for specific U.S. Customs Districts. This means tables can be displayed which show the value of toys exported from Buffalo to Canada or the value of orange juice concentrate imported from Brazil to Miami. A significant amount of information is not retrievable through the menus, including data for many countries. To utilize the disks fully, *EXTRACT* must be used.

The third foreign trade file from the government is the remarkable *National Trade Data Bank* (*NTDB*), a monthly disk produced by the Commerce Department's Office of Business Analysis. It contains an incredible array of economic and industrial data of interest to foreign traders. Numbers are provided by approximately 20 organizations, including the Federal Reserve Board, the Department of Agriculture, and the Office of the U.S. Trade Representative. The database is too extensive to describe in detail here, but a few remarks will illustrate its diversity. Among the subfiles are country profiles from the CIA and a current directory of foreign companies seeking to purchase American products and services. (The latter comes from the Commerce Department's Trade Opportunities Program.) One of the most important files is compiled by the nonprofit Massachusetts Institute for Social and Economic Research (MISER). MISER estimates the value of U.S. exports produced by each of the 50 states, displayed by 2-digit SIC and country of destination. *NTDB* utilizes its own unique search software, which has undergone considerable improvement since its first release.

U.S. Export and Import Merchandise Trade (Monthly).

This print publication, more commonly referred to as "FT 900," is intended as a monthly summary of the detailed data available from the Bureau. The main tables show total imports, exports, and the merchandise trade

balance by month for the current year and the preceding two years. A second set of tables gives current import, export, and balance of trade information for 25 selected countries, plus regions of the world. A third set tabulates imports and exports for broad commodity groupings, based on the SITC system. (Revision 3 of the SITC is also based on the Harmonized System. The five-digit codes are used to compare U.S. data to that published by foreign countries.) Three time-periods are reported: the current month, the same month a year ago, and the year-to-date cumulation. A final section reports statistics on imports and exports of petroleum products. The publication is typically released a little less than two months after the end of the reporting period. Subscribers also receive a monthly supplement which is mailed at a later date. The supplement provides commodity breakdowns by SIC code, exports by state of origin, and more complete coverage of foreign countries.

The other general-interest printed report is FT 925, *U.S. Merchandise Trade: Exports, General Imports, and Imports for Consumption*. It provides more detailed country/commodity figures, similar to those seen in the CD-ROM files, except that the broader 5-digit SITC codes are employed. This report is also published monthly, but is typically released five months after the period covered.

Miscellaneous Census Programs

The Bureau also publishes several other prominent sources of industry statistics. Neither of the two series introduced below provide data that are comparable to the Economic Census. However, each gives useful information on industrial activity and conditions in the United States.

County Business Patterns (Annual).

An excellent source of detailed industry data at the local level is *County Business Patterns*. *County Business Patterns* is not based on a sample survey, but generated from a complete count of business Establishments taken every March. Data are obtained primarily from administrative records. The results are invaluable not only because they provide annual SIC breakdowns at the county level, but because they cover many more industries than the quinquennial Census itself. On the other hand, government and nonprofit organizations are excluded, as are businesses with no paid employees. Self-employed professionals are not covered unless they have a payroll.

Data in *County Business Patterns* are tabulated at the two-, three-, and four-digit SIC levels; information is suppressed where confidentiality is an issue. Statistics

are recorded according to the Establishment's primary industry. The series is published as 52 reports, with one for each state, the District of Columbia, and a U.S. summary. Information is limited to the following data elements, all reported by industry: the total number of Establishments, the number of Establishments by employment size category, the number of employees, and the total industry payroll. A major weakness is the lengthy delay in releasing reports; it generally takes two years from the survey date until all 52 titles are issued. Several other limitations should also be pointed out. Establishments which are administrative headquarters or auxiliary units are not counted in their primary industry, but are grouped together in a single category at the end of each broad industry division (e.g., manufacturing, construction, etc.) Next, data are not reported for SIC groupings with fewer than 50 employees in the county or state, but are aggregated at a broader level. For this reason, the sum of individual Establishments may be less than the county total. Also, new Establishments which have not yet been classified according to the SIC system are listed at the end of each table under an Unclassified heading.

The CD-ROM version offers a menu search system which prompts users to select a year, state, county, and industry. Only one table can be viewed at a time, in the same format seen in the print edition. To create customized tables or compare data, *EXTRACT* must be used. *County Business Patterns* is also available from the Bureau as a set of floppy diskettes, though data are only reported at the two-digit SIC level.

Quarterly Financial Report for Manufacturing, Mining and Trade Corporations (Quarterly).

Essentially a guide to industry-wide financial data, the *Quarterly Financial Report* (*QFR*) is based on an ongoing survey of 13,500 corporations in manufacturing, mining, retail trade, and wholesaling. The *QFR* covers corporations only, and not other forms of business. Corporations with assets less than $250,000 are excluded. Because the study deals with financial characteristics, activity is reported at the company level, not by Establishment. Responses are classified according to the SIC code representing each firm's largest single activity. This is important because unlike the Establishment tabulations used in other Bureau publications, multi-industry companies present a more serious barrier to interpreting data in a meaningful way.

The *QFR* contains composite balance sheets and income statements for each industry, plus a small number of industry ratios. Balance sheet data include broad categories of current and fixed assets, liabilities, and equity. Data from the income statements cover total sales, net income, taxes paid, dividends paid, and retained earnings. Dollar totals for each industry are presented as well as percentages displayed in traditional common-size fashion. Data in every financial statement are given for the total industry, then broken down by size of company. Current Assets/Current Liability, Equity/Debt, Profit/Equity, and Profit/Total Assets are among the few ratios calculated. Summary tables give rates of change in sales and profits, and profit per dollar sales for each industry. The *QFR* has been published regularly since 1947, though prior to 1983 it was compiled by the U.S. Federal Trade Commission.

OTHER SOURCES OF INDUSTRY DATA

The Bureau of the Census is the most prolific producer of industry statistics in the United States, but other government agencies, trade associations, trade journals, and commercial publishers are also excellent sources of additional information. Examples of each will be introduced below.

General Statistical Compendia

Few publishers outside the Bureau of the Census compile guides which cover a broad range of industries. The *Standard & Poor's Statistical Service* and a few other publications introduced in Chapter 15 report on a variety of industries, but the amount of information is limited. The following titles represent additional sources with wide industry coverage.

U.S. Industrial Outlook (U.S. Dept. of Commerce—Annual).

This narrative and statistical guide to 350 industries is published by the government each January. Although coverage represents all major business activities, some 80% of the text deals with manufacturing and mining industries. The reports are written by industry specialists at the Commerce Department and all articles are signed by their authors. Discussion of each industry is brief, but includes a description of the current situation, outlook for the coming year, and long-term prospects for the next five years. The narratives are especially helpful because they provide a quick overview of the industry. For manufacturing industries, most articles describe the nature of the products, how they are used, and who the principal users are. Statistical information, based on Census data, reflects historical figures, current estimates,

and short-term projections. Another useful feature is the list of sources for further research included in every article.

Figures for each SIC grouping include the total output of that industry, regardless of whether Establishments in that industry manufacture other products. Unlike many government reports, however, the *U.S. Industrial Outlook* shows data for both the total industry and the product itself. Just as the industry data count output regardless of the product made, product data show output regardless of which industry produced the item. Basic information displayed in the statistical tables include the dollar value of shipments or revenues, employment, annual growth, foreign trade data, and capital expenditures.

Predicasts Basebook (Predicasts—Annual).

The *Basebook* is one of the most extensive compendia of industry statistics compiled by a commercial publisher. It makes no effort to provide current monthly or quarterly figures, but focuses on annual historical data from a diversity of organizations. Much of the information comes from the U.S. government, but a great deal is generated by trade associations, commercial firms, and other private sources. The *Basebook* summarizes statistics from trade journals, government periodicals, annual statistical reports, and other publications. To appear in the *Basebook*, the data must have been produced by the issuing organization for at least 10 years. Approximately 27,000 data series are covered in each annual issue.

A major advantage is the length of time for which statistics are presented. Each volume covers 14 years of annual figures, but the series has been published for many years, and the earliest data go back to 1958. Thus it is one of the most convenient sources for compiling lengthy time series. Many variables in the *Basebook* are general economic indicators, but the majority are industry-specific figures. Some of the frequently encountered characteristics for individual industries and products include production or shipments; consumption or sales; exports and imports; employment, payroll, and hours worked; raw materials consumed; expenditures for new plant and equipment, research, or materials; and wholesale prices. Depending on the source, data may be presented in dollar amounts, unit quantities, or as index numbers.

The *Basebook* format resembles that of *Predicasts Forecasts*, introduced in Chapter 4. Arrangement is by the publisher's seven-digit product codes, which are based on the SIC system. For general economic measures (including demographic and labor force data), variables are assigned coined numbers beginning with

the letter E. The first column describes the variable (e.g., "Cottonseed Oil Mills—Expenditures for Electric Power"), followed by 14 columns for the yearly figures. The next two columns indicate the units of measurement and the source of the data. The final column provides an average annualized growth rate. A footnote in this column indicates the time period for which the growth rate was calculated. Unlike *Predicasts Forecasts*, the *Basebook* is not truly an index to the sources it covers. Because so many years of data are given, the source column does not specify publication dates or pages.

The *Basebook* is also produced as an online database called *PTS U.S. Time Series*. Aside from the additional search capabilities which an online system provides, the *PTS* service differs from its printed equivalent in several ways. The most noticeable is quarterly updating, which means researchers can locate current annual figures sooner. The other differences involve the fact that data series undergo changes over long periods of time. Both versions present numbers as far back as 1958, but the online edition does so in a single file, which has several implications. First, Predicasts product codes have changed over the years, so users of the printed version may run into dead ends when transitions occur. In the online version, all retrospective data are automatically indexed to the latest code number. Second, the online version cites the dates and pages of the publications where each number was found, including changes in titles. Third, the online system includes defunct series, which do not show up in the latest printed editions. While the variables in the *Basebook* are well-established time series, even the most venerable economic and industrial measures can die. The online version is approximately twice the size of the current printed edition. This means that the publisher has witnessed the demise of nearly as many time series in 30 years as it presently tracks. *PTS U.S. Time Series* can be found on DIALOG and Data-Star, and the file can be searched by series title, product code, event code, unit of measure, year, or name of source.

Dun's Census of American Business (Dun's Marketing Services—Annual).

Dun & Bradstreet is one of the few organizations with a database large enough to rival the Bureau of the Census. Its *Dun's Census of American Business* tabulates information from D&B's file of company records to create industry profiles at the national and state levels, with summary information for individual counties. A major difference between this report and statistics produced by the government is that both primary and secondary SIC categories are counted. In other words, if an

Establishment is engaged primarily in one activity, but is involved to a lesser degree in three other activities, D&B will count it under each of the four SIC categories. This gives marketers a more complete picture of the number of participants in each industry. At the national level, tables cite the data both ways for comparative purposes.

Dun's Census of American Business is divided into several sections. National data appear in two sets of tables, both presented for two- and four-digit SIC groupings. The first shows number of Establishments by employee size, the second by sales category. In both cases, seven size ranges are given. Because some records in the D&B database have no employee-size data, the tables also include a column for Establishments where the data are not reported. Exhibit 16-5 shows a page from the national sales volume tables. For SIC 3716, note that 214 Establishments manufacture motor homes in the United States, but according to the last column, 31 of these do so as a secondary activity. Also note that while most of them have sales greater than $500,000, 19 Establishments did not report sales figures. The second set of tables provides similar data at the state level, but for the nine SIC divisions only. In these tables, only primary Establish-

ments are shown. A third state table gives total number of Establishments at the four-digit SIC level, with no size breakdowns.

The next set of tables presents summary information for counties. In this case, Establishments are listed by employee and sales ranges, but no SIC breakdowns are given. Users can determine that Lincoln County, Oklahoma has eight Establishments with 100 or more employees, but can find no data on the types of industries in Lincoln. The final set of tables is a statistical summary of the companies which comprise the *Million Dollar Directory*. Eight tables show data at the national and state levels, by employee size and sales range. Breakdowns are given for all 160,000 companies in the directory, and for the top 50,000 firms. In this way, users can compare the characteristics of the entire industry to the largest companies in each.

Users of *Dun's Census of American Business* should remember that Dun & Bradstreet does not collect sales data on branch locations, which means that single-Establishment companies will be counted in the sales-range categories, as will headquarters of parents and subsidiaries, but divisions, branch offices, and plant locations will

EXHIBIT 16-5. *Dun's Census of American Business*

4 SIC	DESCRIPTION	$1- 49K	$50K- 99K	$100K- 249K	$250K- 499K	$500K- 999K	$1.0M- 4.9M	$5.0M+OVER	NOT SHOWN	TOTAL	SEC SIC
3652	PRERECORDED RECORDS	98	175	404	175	115	157	84	149	1,357	174
3661	TEL, TELEGRAPH EQP	12	90	70	108	122	319	358	255	1,334	323
3663	RADIO & TV COMM EQP	56	107	367	208	215	539	444	200	2,136	473
3669	COMM EQP NEC	21	78	246	118	127	256	203	138	1,187	230
3671	MFG ELECTRON TUBES	2	4	44	15	11	26	25	16	143	21
3672	PRINTED CIRCUIT BDS	32	89	231	242	256	665	395	156	2,066	340
3674	SEMICONDTS, REL DV	34	60	155	195	185	445	433	345	1,852	321
3675	ELCR CAPACITORS	3	1	12	13	9	44	53	39	174	33
3676	ELECTRONIC RESISTOR	2	4	8	8	6	28	35	13	104	34
3677	ELCR COIL, TRANSFMR	9	21	62	56	71	183	119	47	568	129
3678	ELCR CONNECTORS	4	7	21	23	16	75	93	22	261	65
3679	ELCR COMPONENTS NEC	104	193	505	465	512	1,107	775	532	4,193	939
3691	STORAGE BATTERIES	6	11	43	44	35	44	64	18	265	35
3692	DRY, WET PRIM BATTS	2	9	36	22	15	17	16	21	138	28
3694	ENGINE ELC EQP	52	43	130	104	90	155	135	113	822	223
3695	MAG, OPT RECORDING	14	13	50	75	51	83	59	36	381	86
3699	ELC EQP & SUPS NEC	56	153	322	309	307	593	370	820	2,930	517
36	ELECTRICAL EQUIPMENT	861	1,677	4,262	3,569	3,601	7,685	6,182	4,402	32,239	7,060
37	TRANSPORTATION EQPT										
3711	MOTOR VH,CAR BODIES	30	111	373	186	112	199	192	124	1,327	273
3713	TRUCK & BUS BODIES	20	52	171	133	154	366	200	77	1,173	283
3714	MOTOR VH PARTS, ACC	88	276	688	556	554	977	925	1,715	5,779	953
3715	MFG TRUCK TRAILERS	32	63	223	115	121	211	147	73	985	250
3716	MFG MOTOR HOMES	1	4	17	13	27	63	70	19	214	31
3721	MFG AIRCRAFT	11	36	55	47	40	57	66	106	418	52
3724	AIRCRAFT ENG, PARTS	6	26	66	52	49	129	185	73	586	131
3728	AIRCRAFT PARTS, EQP	39	91	236	226	246	477	396	185	1,896	377
3731	SHIP BLD, REPAIRING	11	48	115	103	84	181	209	155	906	172
3732	BOAT BLD, REPAIRING	289	488	1,061	481	353	475	243	304	3,694	589
3743	RAILROAD EQUIPMENT	2	8	17	17	27	73	105	45	294	74
3751	MOTORCYCLES,BCY,PRT	31	95	196	90	57	92	53	49	663	128
3761	GUIDED MIS,SPACE VH	2		8	9	2	6	25	9	61	17
3764	SPACE PROPULSION UN			5	7	4	9	25	4	54	23
3769	SPACE VEHICLE EQP	1	3	6	3	6	20	43	8	90	47
3792	TVL TRAILERS,CAMPER	63	85	189	116	96	117	92	45	803	152
3795	TANKS & COMPONENTS		1	1	2	4	9	11	9	37	13
3799	TRANSPORTATION EQP	38	92	208	147	128	154	64	334	1,165	173
37	TRANSPORTATION EQPT	664	1,479	3,635	2,303	2,064	3,615	3,051	3,334	20,145	3,738
38	INSTRUMENTS RLTD PDTS										
3812	SEARCH, NAVIGN EQP	29	44	119	119	82	201	281	89	964	268
3821	LAB APPARATUS & FRN	25	53	92	56	68	157	120	86	657	153
3822	ENVIRONMENTAL CTRL	15	42	103	128	88	189	148	63	776	159
3823	INDUS CONTROL INSTR	43	98	237	248	303	710	456	304	2,399	539
3824	FLUID METERS & DVS	14	23	53	69	38	92	83	35	407	106
3825	ELCT MEASURE INSTRS	53	85	231	213	220	451	412	222	1,887	447
3826	ANALYTICAL INSTR	16	35	59	67	65	169	143	51	605	114
3827	OPTICAL INSTRS	21	65	206	107	115	218	130	66	928	169
3829	MEASUR, CTRL DV NEC	66	111	307	219	265	523	334	249	2,074	456

COUNT BY PRIMARY AND SECONDARY   RANGE BY SALES IN THOUSANDS   PAGE   13

Excerpted from *Dun's® Census Book of American Business*™. © 1991 by Dun's Marketing Services, Inc. Reprinted with permission.

not. This publication presents an alternative to government reports. Because D&B includes Establishments with no employees, and because secondary SIC activities are counted, the totals will generally be quite a bit higher than those seen in *County Business Patterns*. Even those inclined to distrust the data will find it valuable for comparing economic activity from one year to the next, whether for entire industries or geographic locations.

CRB Commodity Year Book (Commodity Research Bureau—Annual, with Updates).

The Commodity Research Bureau, a private organization owned by Knight-Ridder, has been producing this invaluable resource for over 50 years. It offers summary data and brief narrative information on some 100 different commodities from arsenic to zinc, giving an overview of the industry and worldwide statistics and charts. The majority of products are agricultural or mineral commodities, but it also covers steel, lumber, electric power, paper, plastics, foreign currencies, and world interest rates. Although many commodities have options or futures contracts listed on major exchanges, others do not.

The short narrative section of each commodity report summarizes the previous year's activities, and frequently explains how the product is used. Statistical tables generally offer production data by country, average U.S. cash prices, and where applicable, prices on major futures exchanges. Depending on the commodity, a diversity of additional information can be given, including foreign trade data, consumption, inventories, and utilization of quantities sold (i.e., how much of the product is purchased for various manufacturing purposes). Tables frequently give monthly or annual figures for as many as 15 years. The *CRB Year Book* is a wonderfully concise guide for historical analysis, worldwide comparisons, or quick industry profiles. Several updating services are also available.

Specific Industry Reports

Federal agencies of all types collect and publish data on a wide range of industries. The Department of Agriculture alone churns out an incredible number of statistical reports on farm output, prices, consumption, and the outlook for agricultural commodities. These reports cover statistics on virtually every imaginable product which can be grown or raised. Data from dozens of the Department's publications are summarized yearly in a handbook called *Agricultural Statistics*. Likewise, the U.S. National Marine Fisheries Service collects data on commodities gathered from the sea. When seeking statistics from the federal government, it is not necessarily obvious which agency collects data for particular industries. Sometimes this is due to an overlap of jurisdictions. For example, the Federal Reserve Board publishes some data on member banks, but most detailed statistics on the banking industry are generated by the Federal Deposit Insurance Corporation. Other times, identifying the appropriate agency can result in a complete surprise. One of the best sources of statistics on synthetic organic chemicals, for example, is the U.S. International Trade Commission, which is charged with monitoring the impact of imports on key domestic industries.

Trade associations, another major source of industry statistics, exist for just about every possible type of business activity and many produce detailed statistical compilations. Examples include the International Tin Council's *Tin Statistics*, the Cigar Association of America's *Statistical Record Bulletin*, and the American Meat Institute's *Meatfacts*. Data from trade associations are often the most authoritative sources available. A publication from the National Association of Realtors called *Home Sales* is essentially the only publication which reports on the sale of existing homes (as opposed to newly constructed houses). Data from many associations are utilized by the government in compiling the Gross National Product, particularly for industries not covered by the Census. For example, although the U.S. Energy Information Administration tabulates a great deal of data on public utilities and other energy-related industries, the government also relies on reports from the Edison Electric Institute, the American Gas Association, and the American Petroleum Institute. Association data can also be inexpensive to obtain or even free. For example, the American Council of Life Insurance publishes the *Life Insurance Fact Book*, sent annually at no charge to interested parties. Although not all association publications are inexpensive, and many are distributed to members only, the importance of statistical publications from trade associations should not be underestimated.

Many commercial publishing companies also specialize in a narrow industry and produce a variety of statistical and narrative guides. Examples include Fairchild Publications, which produces data on the textile, apparel, and retail industries, and the Jobson Publishing Corporation, which tracks the liquor industry. These and other firms have developed reputations for providing comprehensive and reliable information.

Trade journals regularly provide detailed data on the industries they cover, and they are abundant and easily obtainable. Some journals are well-known for the statistical tables which appear in every issue. Others compile special statistical issues on an annual basis. Special issues of trade journals are usually inexpensive and often can be purchased without a subscription to the magazine.

A special category of trade journal is devoted to reporting current prices for commodities within an industry. Although general newspapers like the *Journal of Commerce* and *The Wall Street Journal* give brief coverage to commodity cash prices, numerous specialized periodicals offer detailed listings. They may be well-known newspapers such as the *Chemical Marketing Reporter*, or more obscure newsletters such as *Rough Lengths* (lumber). Two excellent guides to the contents of these unusual publications are the *Commodities Price Locator*, by Karen J. Chapman (Oryx Press, 1989) and *Commodity Prices* by Catherine Friedman (Gale Research, 1990). Both contain detailed subject indexes to price data on commodities ranging from buttermilk to methanol.

To illustrate the diversity of quality publications with industry-specific data, the following publications are offered as examples. The first is a government document, the second a trade association report, and the third a commercial publication.

Minerals Yearbook (U.S. Bureau of Mines—Annual).

The Bureau of Mines conducts a statistical survey which in many ways is more comprehensive and detailed than the Census itself. A battery of questionnaires is sent to every relevant, identifiable Establishment, though not everyone responds. The resulting *Minerals Yearbook* offers an unparalleled look at all metals and nonfuel minerals of importance to the United States economy. More than 70 product categories are examined. Some are fairly broad, such as abrasives or gem stones, but most cover an individual mineral. The massive *Yearbook* is issued in three volumes: the first is arranged alphabetically by commodity, the second offers state profiles for the United States, and the third summarizes the mineral industries of 150 foreign countries.

The *Minerals Yearbook* is much more than a dry statistical compilation; like the *U.S. Industrial Outlook*, it offers informative articles describing the characteristics of each industry and product, and every article is signed by the author. These profiles discuss the uses of each commodity, consumption patterns, and worldwide production capacity. Outside forces which have an effect on the industry are examined, including environmental concerns, legislative initiatives, government programs, new technology, and transportation issues. Company information is also provided, including lists of the top 10 producers of each commodity, and in some cases, news of important mergers. Statistical tables are quite detailed, covering quantity and value of production, foreign trade, employment, and number of Establishments. Output is typically broken down by state of origin and by grade or type of product. Many articles even provide statistics by usage. For example, data on sand and gravel production are divided into construction and industrial applications; both are further divided into specific uses such as highway construction. Every article indicates the survey response rate and the resulting industry coverage. Volume 1 also contains an annual overview of mining and quarrying trends.

The state profiles cite the major metals and minerals, together with the quantity and value of output for every state. Maps identify locations of major producing regions by commodity. The leading companies in each state are listed, with information on the their products, headquarters address, county of operation, and type of activity (e.g., mine, pit, quarry, manufacturing plant, etc.). Like the articles in Volume 1, state profiles discuss legislative issues and other environmental factors specific to the state.

One drawback to the *Yearbook* is the publication lag; the full hardbound set may not appear until two years after questionnaire responses are received. To offset this delay, every chapter is released first as a separate paperback report called a Preprint. The Bureau of Mines also compiles more current information in its *Mineral Industry Surveys*, which appear annually, monthly, or quarterly, depending on the commodity. Researchers should view all of these publications as a complement to the *Census of Mineral Industries*; statistics from the two agencies are not comparable.

Electronic Market Data Book (Electronic Industries Association—Annual).

This outstanding publication combines narrative articles and statistical tables to present a wide-ranging look at the electronics industry. Among the fields covered are consumer electronics, communications equip-

ment, computers, and defense electronics. New technological developments are discussed at length, and important trends such as robotics and fiber optics are described. The articles are written for a lay audience, offering a wonderful introduction to readers unfamiliar with the subject. Among the statistics found are the value of factory shipments and imports by product category, employment (including number of scientists employed), and research expenditures. International comparisons are also given, including balance of trade for electronics products by country.

Ward's Automotive Yearbook (Ward's Communications, Inc.—Annual).

Many fine statistical compilations are published on the auto industry, but *Ward's* is widely recognized as the best in its field. Like many commercially produced yearbooks, it provides both narrative and statistical information. Every aspect of the U.S. and Canadian auto industries is covered. Tables provide data on production, retail sales, and auto registrations by manufacturer, size, and model of car, for both domestic and foreign cars. Market share data are also given down to the brand level. In all, more than 100 detailed tables can be found. Narrative information is also wide-ranging, from new product information to major industry events. Brief profiles of all major auto makers are included. In addition to automobiles, *Ward's* provides sections on light trucks, recreational vehicles, medium and heavy trucks, and farm and construction vehicles. The yearbook offers more than statistical and narrative information; coverage is rounded out with a buyers' guide to automotive equipment suppliers, and descriptions and specifications for all new cars introduced that model year.

INDUSTRY STATISTICS—WHERE TO LOOK?

The sheer abundance of industrial information can make locating specific data a troublesome chore. A logical first step is to read a narrative profile of the industry, particularly if one knows little about it. By setting the stage in this fashion, the researcher is better able to place subsequent facts in perspective, and obtain clues for likely avenues of investigation. Narrative reports also offer general background on an industry and what makes it unique—its structure, problems, and current situation. Even if in-depth profiles cannot be found, basic overviews can help. Two sensible starting points are *Standard & Poor's Industry Surveys*, introduced in Chapter 12, and the *U.S. Industrial Outlook*. Industry

studies from Wall Street analysts, also described in Chapter 12, offer another approach. Even general encyclopedias such as *World Book* can be helpful to those completely unfamiliar with an industry.

From there, the researcher can move to more specialized technical encyclopedias. A diversity of these exist in various fields of chemical technology and manufacturing; many are produced by trade journal publishers. An excellent example is McGraw-Hill's annual *Modern Plastics Encyclopedia*. Because it provides suppliers' addresses and technical specifications of products, the *Encyclopedia* is used primarily as a buyer's guide. However, it also contains extensive background data, including detailed descriptions of major materials, equipment, and processes employed by the industry. For each type of plastic, product applications are discussed, together with a brief summary of industry structure. Although such publications are not available for all industries, they are quite common. If these options fail, journal and newspaper articles may provide brief background information. For example, the business section of the Sunday *New York Times* profiles a different industry every week.

Once the researcher is ready to consult statistical publications, the principal question is, "Of all the possible sources, which is the most useful?" To cite a specific case, the individual who seeks economic data on the coal industry has numerous choices. Should the *Census of Mineral Industries* be consulted? What about the *Minerals Yearbook*? Or the U.S. Energy Information Administration's *Coal Production*? Nongovernment information is also available in the *CRB Commodity Year Book* and the National Coal Association's annual *Coal Data*. Beyond looking to the publication closest at hand, the best source depends upon the nature of the information being sought: recency, detail, form of geography, and similar considerations.

Publications from the Economic Census are often a wise starting point for many reasons. As a rule, they generally offer more complete coverage of an industry than other sources. The amount of detail, both by SIC breakdowns and by small geographic areas, is another important advantage. Finally, a great deal of information in the Economic Census cannot be found in other sources. When turning to the Economic Census, the researcher can take several simple steps to help locate data more quickly. Before consulting the Census, ask whether the industry under consideration is covered, and if so, in which report. Now consider whether data are needed at the national level or some smaller level of geography. Some published reports do not provide data at the county

level, for example. Finally, become familiar with the basic information categories which can be found in the Economic Census. There is no point in looking for data on industry profitability in the quinquennial publications, but it can be found easily in the *Quarterly Financial Report*.

The overwhelming drawback to the Economic Census is its lack of timeliness. The enumerations are conducted every five years, but the resulting data may not be published for several years after the Census is taken. Users can attempt to construct current estimates using quinquennial data as a benchmark, together with more current sources such as annual Census surveys or *County Business Patterns*, but this is a tricky business. Data such as concentration ratios, sales per employee, and other analytical figures can help researchers in making their own estimates, but it is recommended that you immerse yourself in the industry before making hasty assumptions. This means following news about leading companies in the field, reading trade journals, and otherwise keeping abreast of recent news. Econometric research firms such as DRI/McGraw-Hill employ sophisticated mathematical models to generate estimates in non-Census years, and sell data to users who need more current information. However, no matter how reputable the organization, such figures are estimates only. Data of this type should be viewed with a questioning attitude, particularly for local areas.

Aside from the Census, how does one locate statistics from other organizations? When general information is sought, a broad economic compendium, such as those introduced in the previous chapter, may be perfectly adequate for research needs. Publications like *Business Statistics* and the *Standard & Poor's Statistical Service* are easy to use and widely available. The *Predicasts Basebook* is especially useful for identifying additional sources of data. A compendium with a narrower focus, such as *Agricultural Statistics* or the *CRB Commodity Year Book* may be equally appropriate. When general sources fail, the next step is to identify more specific publications. A convenient way to do this is through the finding guides introduced in Chapter 4. The *Statistical Reference Index* and the *American Statistics Index* are among the best to consult, but remember, no guide covers everything. Researchers should utilize all the finding tools possible when pursuing elusive data, because each has unique information to impart. Even general guides such as the *Encyclopedia of Business Information Sources* can help in a statistical search. For an overview of leading industry yearbooks, one of the best guides is *Business Information Sources* by Lorna Daniells; the chapter on

industry statistics does an admirable job describing dozens of the most important and useful publications for a variety of major industries. Finally, a great deal depends on the researcher's familiarity with pertinent publications. Too many are produced to enable first-hand experience of every one, but users should have a working knowledge of basic sources in their fields of interest. The key to using sources well is knowing how they differ and what each has to contribute.

Once a publication has been found which provides the required information, researchers must still question the value of the data. Again, users of statistical information must understand the nature of the information in order to properly evaluate it. This is essential for determining whether the publication really answers the question being posed. In other words, where do the numbers come from, and what do they purport to do? To use the example of *Home Sales*, data are obtained from the records of local Boards of Realtors in communities throughout the country. While on the surface this may seem like a reasonably comprehensive source of information, it excludes "for sale by owner" transactions and sales by real estate brokers who are not Realtors.

And of course the researcher must assess the accuracy and reliability of individual publications. As with all statistics, it is wise to question the objectivity of the organization doing the study, as well as the methodology used. If the researcher makes no other critical analysis of secondary data, one final question should always be asked: "Do the numbers make sense?"

FOR FURTHER READING

Several of the sources listed at the end of Chapter 15 provide useful information on industry statistics. The following publications are more specific, describing basic guides to industry data available from the Bureau of the Census and other sources. Also listed are background readings which describe industry structure and methods of industry analysis.

Industry Structure and Analysis

Adams, Walter. *The Structure of American Industry*. 8th ed. (New York: Macmillan, 1990).
   This classic work, first published in 1950, discusses the structure, conduct, and performance of representative industries in the United States. Eleven broad industry types are profiled and a twelfth chapter discusses the behavior of

conglomerates. The format varies for each chapter, but descriptions may include industry concentration, barriers to entry, factors affecting supply and demand, the impact of government regulation and policies, and much more. Anyone conducting industry research will find this a wonderful model for analysis.

Clarke, Richard N. "SICs as Delineators of Economic Markets." *Journal of Business* 62 (January 1989): 17-31.

Results of a study designed to test whether SICs describe distinctive, homogeneous markets. Based on the assumption that companies in the same industry display similar rates of change in sales, profits, or stock prices, the author analyzes data from 985 companies in 126 industries. The conclusion: except at the two-digit level, firms grouped within a single SIC category demonstrate weak market similarities. Its methodology can be questioned, but the study raises an interesting and important question for serious users of SIC-based company data.

Losman, Donald L., and Shu-Jan Liang. *The Promise of American Industry: An Alternate Assessment of Problems and Prospects* (Westport, CT: Quorum, 1990).

From the title, readers might assume this is another prescription for improved U.S. competitiveness. Instead, it is a concise and astute description of the current state of our industrial economy (both good and bad). Much of the book is devoted to explaining important economic and management concepts—types of markets, sources of capital, legal forms of business, vertical integration, and the relative importance of different industries. Anyone wishing to research or analyze a particular industry would do well to understand these key ideas.

Mattera, Philip. *Inside U.S. Business: A Concise Encyclopedia of Leading Industries*, 2nd ed. (Homewood, IL: Dow Jones-Irwin, 1990).

Describes 25 major American industry groups. For each industry, the book provides a brief, well-written discussion of its history, current trends, labor conditions, and leading companies. Where the Adams book provides more sophisticated analysis, Mattera's work is intended for a popular audience and much of the information is synthesized from stories in the popular press. A guide to major trade journals, books, directories, and data sources follows every industry summary.

Porter, Michael E. "How to Conduct an Industry Analysis." In *Financial Analyst's Handbook*, 2nd ed., by Sumner N. Levine. (Homewood, IL: Dow Jones-Irwin, 1988): 375-88.

Covers basic sources of industry information, as well as the process of industry research. One cogent observation is particularly worth quoting: "Experience shows that the morale of researchers...often goes through a U-shaped cycle as the study proceeds. An initial period of euphoria gives way to confusion and even panic as the complexity of the industry becomes apparent and mounds of information accumulate." (Reprinted from the author's *Competitive Strategy*, Free Press, 1980.)

The Economic Census

Hernon, Peter. "Symposium on the Economic Censuses, United States Bureau of the Census." *Government Information Quarterly* 4 (November 1987): 213-340.

A collection of articles on the 1987 Economic Census, contributed especially for this special issue. Among the topics covered are a brief history of the Economic Census, its uses, planning and conducting the Census, making the data available to the public, and a comparison of economic censuses conducted by other nations. All contributors are current or former employees of the Bureau.

U.S. Bureau of the Census. *Business Data Finder* (Washington, DC: U.S. Government Printing Office, 1984).

This slim booklet provides a basic description of the Census data available for retail, wholesale, and service industries. The summary charts are especially useful for ready-reference purposes. The Bureau also publishes other booklets in this series, including the *Industrial Statistics Data Finder*.

Zeisset, Paul T. *Guide to the 1987 Economic Censuses and Related Statistics* (Washington, DC: U.S. Bureau of the Census, 1990).

The Bureau's basic guidebook to the 1987 Census publications offers brief but helpful information on the format, content, and methodology of the Economic Census. Sample tables are provided, as are helpful charts for comparing the features of the various reports. Also included are short discussions of related publications such as *County Business Patterns*. This is recommended to all users of industry data.

Foreign Trade Data

Bailey, Victor B. and Sara R. Bowden. *Understanding Foreign Trade Data* (Washington, DC: U. S. International Trade Administration, 1985).

An excellent introduction to foreign trade data, though it was written prior to the adoption of the Harmonized system. This outstanding manual explains the older classification systems and other fundamental concepts in a clear and detailed manner. Most readers will find certain sections more technical than they need, but this is unquestionably the source which beginners to the FT data should consult first. An excellent feature of the book is a thorough discussion of the limitations of FT statistics.

Chadwick, Terry Brainerd. "Trade Data: Not What It's Cracked Up to Be." *Proceedings of the Tenth National Online Meeting, 1989* (Medford, NJ: Learned Information, 1989): 83-93.

The author points out the surprising paucity of detailed data on worldwide trade, but goes on to point out that new databases are emerging at a brisk pace. Descriptions of major databases are provided, including several specialized, lesser-known products. Especially noteworthy are the author's comments on foreign trade statistics.

Finegan, Jay. "Garbage In, Gospel Out." *Inc.* (April 1988): 51-52.

An articulate and probing critique of the accuracy of U.S. foreign trade statistics. Some of the potential errors in collecting merchandise trade data are given. Also discussed are the fundamental problems of capturing information on trade in services.

Gelinne, Michael S. "A Selected Guide to Foreign Trade Statistical Sources." *Journal of Business & Financial Librarianship* 1 (No. 1, 1990): 33-44.

Describes the Harmonized Classification System, together with basic government and nongovernment sources of import/export statistics. The article was written before the Bureau of the Census made major changes to its array of foreign trade publications, but the article remains a useful introduction to this complex area of business research.

Torrence, Dale O. "New Tariff Code Streamlines Global Trading System." *Business America* (November 23, 1987): 2-5.

A quick explanation of the Harmonized System, written by an official with the U.S. Customs Service.

PART V
Special Topics

CHAPTER 17
Information on States and Local Areas

TOPICS COVERED

1. Analyzing Geographic Markets
2. General Market Comparisons
   a. State Economic Conditions
   b. Local Area Profiles
3. Market Estimates and Projections
   a. Estimates of Population and Buying Power
   b. Long-Term Forecasts
4. Special Topics
   a. Industrial Development
   b. Real Estate and Construction
   c. Cost of Living Comparisons
   d. Wage and Salary Surveys
5. Judging the Quality of Local Data
6. For Further Reading

MAJOR SOURCES DISCUSSED

- *Almanac of the 50 States*
- *Rand McNally Commercial Atlas and Marketing Guide*
- *Metro Insights*
- *Editor and Publisher Market Guide*
- *County and City Data Book*
- *Survey of Buying Power Data Service*
- *MEI Marketing Economics Guide*
- *Sourcebook of Zip Code Demographics*
- *Donnelley Demographics*
- *Market Profile Analysis*
- *Regional Economic Projection Series*
- *ACCRA Cost of Living Index*
- *Area Wage Surveys*

When seeking information on local business and economic conditions, the natural inclination is to consult organizations in the locality itself. After all, who knows a community better than the people who live and work there? Published and unpublished local information is frequently abundant, though scattered across government and nongovernment sources alike. Chapter 1 suggested a number of local information sources. But what about researchers who need to investigate many geographic locations, perhaps even in different states? Or those trying to identify municipalities with similar characteristics? Happily, a surprising amount of comparative information on local areas can be found in national publications.

Users have a wide assortment of resources to choose from, but this chapter will concentrate on publications which compare economic, demographic, or market conditions. Because these three categories are interrelated, many publications and databases combine aspects of each in their analysis. Typical subjects include popula-tion estimates, household characteristics, retail sales and buying power, market forecasts, labor force statistics, housing conditions, construction activity, and industrial structure. But most sources which compare geographic areas either provide individual profiles of many communities, or compare specific features in tabular form, often providing ranked lists of geographic areas.

ANALYZING GEOGRAPHIC MARKETS

Almost any type of business publication can be used to research local economic conditions. Many of the sources introduced throughout this book are well suited to this type of analysis. Among the best are periodical indexes which focus on local newspaper and magazine stories; services such as *NewsBank* and *Business Dateline* are outstanding resources for investigating current local conditions and events. Business directories of all

kinds provide access to companies by geographic area. Even telephone books and city directories can offer clues about the economic structure and vitality of individual areas. Many statistical publications containing local area information have already been covered, including the decennial Census, which offers unparalleled detail on demographic characteristics. General economic conditions can be found in sources as diverse as *Unemployment in States and Local Areas* and the *American Housing Survey*. Local industrial data are published in such basic statistical compilations as the Economic Census, *County Business Patterns*, and *Dun's Census of American Business*.

The incredible diversity of sources on local business information reflects the wide range of individuals who need data of this type—marketers, regional planners, economists, real estate developers, government officials, and job hunters, to name a few. The uses to which local data can be applied are also varied. Marketing professionals alone use local information to select sites for service outlets, plan distribution networks, identify promising new markets, define sales territories, establish goals and quotas, and forecast product demand. Though certain types of data are important to all local research projects, the information needs of users can differ greatly. A manufacturer in search of new factory locations wants to know about electric utility rates, transportation infrastructure, corporate income taxes, government assistance programs, state and local regulations, and labor force characteristics. A retailer moving into a new area wants to know about existing competition, population growth, household characteristics, disposable income, and consumer spending. Most families and individuals seeking to relocate want to research comparative costs of living, but beyond this their concerns quickly diverge. Some are interested in recreational and cultural attractions, others in the quality of school systems. Some worry about pollution, some about crime, others about climate.

Seldom will a single source answer all questions about a locality. Few resources provide a broad range of information in a single publication, and few materials offer lengthy analyses of geographic areas. In fact, most compendia of local area information are statistical, requiring researchers to synthesize data from a variety of sources and draw their own conclusions.

GENERAL MARKET COMPARISONS

Researching local communities should begin with a summary of basic information. Brief overviews of geographic areas appear in many general reference tools. Even travel guides from organizations like Fodor's, Mobil, and the AAA can be used for this purpose. Another important source for preliminary research is a good atlas; maps portray useful information in a way which narrative reports and statistical tables frequently cannot. The following publications represent common sources of local information, including encyclopedias with brief narrative articles, ready-reference fact books, and statistical yearbooks. Publications comparing state information will be introduced, along with those covering smaller geographic levels.

State Economic Conditions

Research on a single community should often begin with a survey of state conditions. The best source of information on state economic conditions is usually the state government itself. State departments of commerce, taxation, budget, and other agencies all produce statistical publications and economic reports. For example, every state has a labor department which collects data on employment, unemployment, and characteristics of the labor force. All produce monthly, quarterly, and annual statistical guides describing current labor conditions, recent trends, and future needs. Data range from industry-specific employment figures and wage rates to information on supply and demand for individual occupations. A good way to approach the large body of information from state agencies is to obtain the statistical abstracts for individual states. Every state produces at least one abstract, and some have several. Most are compiled by state governments, though some are published by state universities or other nonprofit organizations. Almost all state statistical abstracts are updated annually. A complete list of titles, together with ordering information, can be found in each year's *Statistical Abstract of the United States*. More specialized resources from state governments can be located by using the guides to state agencies described in Chapter 2, or the *Statistical Reference Index*, introduced in Chapter 4.

Of course other organizations besides state agencies compile state data. The federal government publishes comparative state data in many of its major compendia, with titles as varied as the *Sourcebook of Crimi-*

nal Justice and the *Digest of Education Statistics.* Many nonprofit groups study economic and political concerns at the state and regional levels. The Council of State Governments' biennial *Book of the States* focuses on political and governmental issues. This indispensable guide is a gold mine of information on the functioning of all branches of state governments. In addition to convenient comparative charts, it provides authoritative review articles on political trends and numerous statistical tables. Data include government revenues, expenditures by service category, public employment, and salaries of key officials.

The problem with the sources mentioned above is that the information is too fragmented—either the researcher must examine separate books for each state, or the publication covers a fairly narrow topic. Broad comparisons of all 50 states are scarce. Traditional sources such as standard encyclopedias and almanacs present background information for all states, but coverage tends to be fairly limited. However, a few specialized reference tools focus on general profiles. The *Worldmark Encyclopedia of the States* summarizes political, economic, geographic, and demographic characteristics in fairly lengthy articles. It is published by Worldmark Press, Ltd., and is updated approximately every five years. The briefer *Facts about the States*, published by the H.W. Wilson Company, provides standardized 10-page synopses for every state in a single volume. The breadth of facts is extensive, including state holidays, minimum ages for various activities, locations of military installations, population characteristics, data on government finance, and transportation facts. An appendix provides approximately 20 statistical tables comparing attributes ranging from crime rates to average teachers' salaries. The first edition appeared in 1989, and it will be updated on an irregular basis.

Worldmark and *Facts about the States* cite a diversity of statistical measures, but this is not their main purpose. Several publications offer a broader range of data for all states. The *Statistical Abstract* is primarily a guide to national economic and social conditions, but it includes a fair amount of data for individual states. A particularly useful feature is a section which tabulates state rankings for approximately 60 key demographic, economic, and social variables. A more detailed publication from the Bureau of the Census is the *State and Metropolitan Area Data Book.* It provides state comparisons for approximately 1,600 variables, but is only published once every four to five years. The 4th edition appeared in 1991. Three additional guides to conveniently arranged state data are described below.

Almanac of the 50 States (Information Publications—Annual).

Since its debut in 1985, this annual compendium has become one of the most popular guides to general statistical information. For each state, the District of Columbia, and the United States, a variety of data is presented in a standard eight-page format. Statistics are gathered from the federal and state governments, trade and professional associations, private research centers, and even commercial data companies. Nongovernment sources include the American Hospital Association, the National Committee for Adoption, and the Joint Center for Political Studies. Topics from crime to education are covered, but most data focus on economic and political issues. More than 450 variables are reported for each state, including such infrequently encountered measures as the number of elected officials who are black or female. Only statistics that can convey meaningful information about state conditions are included. A second section of the *Almanac* provides state rankings for approximately 50 of the most important indicators. The *Almanac* is enhanced by a bibliography listing more detailed publications on each topic.

States in Profile (Brizius & Foster Public Affairs—Annual, with Mid-year Update).

States in Profile is designed specifically for government policy-makers. This compendium of comparative statistics was originally compiled in cooperation with State Policy Research, Inc. (as a supplement to their *State Policy Reports* newsletter), but is also available from Brizius & Foster as a separate subscription. Almost all data come from the federal government; most can be found in basic statistical publications such as the *Statistical Abstract* and *Bureau of Labor Statistics Bulletins*, though a few unpublished figures are used. In many cases, raw numbers are recast as percentages, ratios, percent changes, or per capita figures.

No state summaries are found in *States in Profile.* Instead, it presents approximately 500 comparative tables, most of which rank states by specific characteristics. The publication is arranged in more than 15 topical sections, covering standard subjects like demographics and health care, but also exploring unexpected topics such as technology, natural resources, and government administration. Among the more unusual tables are spending by foreign visitors, the number of millionaires, the percentage of households without telephones, and the number of residents who own stock. Examples of government figures recast in another form include business failures per million residents, service employment as a percent of total civilian employment, and labor force participation

reported as the difference between male and female rates. Each section also presents at least one thematic map summarizing key relationships. For its choice of variables and its interesting manner of presenting them, *States in Profile* is recommended as an alternative to more traditional statistical sources. The publication is also available on floppy diskette as *States in Profile: The State Policy Data Diskette.*

State Rankings: A Statistical View of the 50 States
(Morgan Quitno Corporation—Annual).

State Rankings takes a more conventional approach to comparative state data, ranking the states according to major political and economic attributes. Each table presents comparisons for a single characteristic, with approximately 275 tables in all. Most numbers are presented in both their original form, and as percentages of the national total. Variables include population characteristics, vital statistics, number of reported AIDS cases, social welfare payments by type of program, school enrollment, grants to state and local governments, and motor vehicle deaths.

State Rankings relies on a limited number of sources. All data are taken from two Bureau of the Census publications: the *Statistical Abstract of the United States* and *Federal Expenditures by State*, with most figures coming from the first title. Each table derived from the *Statistical Abstract* refers to the table number in the government's compendium, plus the original source of the data. So why not go straight to the *Statistical Abstract*? Many researchers and librarians will do just that, but *State Rankings* is still popular because of the convenience it offers. For example, the *Statistical Abstract* only ranks one-fifth of the variables seen in the Quitno publication, and the government tables present the rankings in alphabetical order.

Local Area Profiles

State comparisons are useful for various types of economic analysis, but marketers and business researchers generally prefer to examine smaller levels of geography. A later section of this chapter will introduce specialized guides to local market data, but there is more to evaluating local communities than examining consumer buying potential. Researchers should investigate broader economic trends, such as components of the labor force, major industries, and government finance. Noneconomic factors also play a role in business decisions, ranging from the strength of political leadership to the severity of the climate. Whatever the research question, a good starting point is to obtain a general overview of the area.

In any given year, several new reference books may appear which compare cities or metropolitan areas. Most of these are one-time efforts and others are infrequently updated. The following publications represent some of the better guides to ongoing information. All are of interest for their summary descriptions of numerous places. Some offer brief narrative profiles, some are strictly numerical, and others combine both approaches. The first publications in this section are general encyclopedias, covering a range of economic and noneconomic concerns, from history to recreational facilities. The remaining sources focus more directly on business and economic concerns. Formats include an atlas, an analytical report, a ready-reference guide, and a statistical compendium.

Flying the Colors Series (Clements Research, Inc.—Irregular).

This ambitious encyclopedic series of local area profiles is extremely useful for beginning research. As of this writing, separate volumes are available for 20 states, with each giving some 400 pages of county profiles. The publisher plans to cover the remainder of the nation within the next few years, though less populous states will be combined in regional volumes. Individual books in the series are entitled "State Fact Books"—*New York Facts, Connecticut Facts/Rhode Island Facts*, and so on. Most states will be updated every three or four years. The format of each title is the same: more than 50 pages are devoted to the economic conditions and government structure of the state, followed by five-page profiles of every county. Coverage is rounded out by brief narrative reports on every MSA, several comparative statistical tables, and an extensive chronology of state history. County economic data range from descriptions of the transportation system to analyses of industry structure. Noneconomic information covers schools, libraries, health care, and recreational facilities. Although the profiles are presented in narrative form, much of the presentation is in statistics-packed sentences which are difficult to read. The ease of use would improve greatly by moving most of the data to tables, and reserving the narrative portion for summary information.

A more recent encyclopedia is a four-volume set from Gale Research called *Cities of the United States.* The set is arranged by geographic region, with each title describing 25-30 of the largest cities. Volumes are released individually as they are completed. The first edition of the set was published in 1988/89; a revised edition is scheduled to appear beginning in 1992. Although profiles are briefer, the Gale publication covers many of the same topics as its competitor, including

government, education, health care, and recreation. Clements covers every county within the state, while Gale only examines major cities. However, the Gale profiles are more readable, and easier on the eye.

Places Rated Almanac, Richard Boyer and David Savageau (Prentice Hall, Inc.—Irregular).

Some of the negative aspects of the *Places Rated Almanac* were introduced in Chapter 13, but the work offers sufficient advantages to recommend its use. The study is geared toward a popular audience—specifically those considering relocating to another city—but the information is useful to business researchers as well. The first two editions were published by Rand McNally, and the third (1989) by Prentice Hall. It is updated approximately every four years.

When the *Places Rated Almanac* debuted in 1981, it received phenomenal attention from local newspapers and community leaders. Subsequent editions have continued to capture the public's interest, and their appearance is announced at press conferences with great fanfare. The reason for this is that the authors devised a system which assigns a composite ranking to every metropolitan area in the country. The variables used in determining the metropolitan rankings and the weights assigned to each variable can be questioned, but the usefulness of this unique publication should not be doubted. A great deal of information is given on each locality. And even if the reader chooses to ignore the composite rankings, the raw data are extremely helpful for comparative purposes. The authors gather information on important community characteristics from a variety of government and nongovernment sources, and present them in an extremely understandable fashion.

Nine chapters present comparisons by broad topic, then assign combined rankings for that topic. The methodology employed for ranking each characteristic is fully explained. Most categories are not economic at all, but examine different aspects of the quality of community life. Noneconomic topics are climate, health & environment, crime, education, the arts, recreation, and transportation. The two chapters explicitly devoted to economic conditions cover general living costs, housing, taxes, and employment opportunities. The diversity of information is fascinating, from air quality and pollen counts to capital punishment and handgun laws. Special lists highlight the best and worst locations in each category (e.g., states with the worst traffic laws, cities with no public transportation systems, etc.). Another useful feature is that concepts are carefully explained; not only are terms defined, but their relationship to living conditions are examined. *Places Rated* also offers suggestions on how to evaluate communities intelligently, including tips on rating school systems, coping with life in a boom town, and creating personalized metropolitan rankings. Despite the weaknesses inherent in any composite rankings method, *Places Rated* presents an entertaining look at metropolitan living conditions, with plenty of information for the serious researcher. And though the book is revised infrequently, it refers to the sources of more current data. Perhaps the book's greatest contribution is that it will suggest ways of studying a community that the researcher might not otherwise consider.

Rand McNally Commercial Atlas and Marketing Guide (Rand McNally and Company—Annual).

An authoritative atlas is indispensable to the proper understanding of information on geographic markets. The *Rand McNally Commercial Atlas*, first published in 1876, is the finest atlas of the United States. It presents the most detailed, accurate, and up-to-date geographic information possible. This comprehensive sourcebook is revised annually to reflect changes in place names and political boundaries, and to present the most current economic data. Each state map is large, clear and enormously detailed, showing both political and physical features. Map indexes list thousands of place names, including unpopulated places. For each place, the index indicates the county in which it is located, together with pertinent characteristics such as the presence of banks, hospitals, prisons, and railroad terminals. For most populated places, a measure of population is also given. Data from the latest decennial Census are used, together with current estimates from other sources. For cities with a population greater than 25,000, Rand McNally uses data from Market Statistics, a highly respected producer of local estimates. For smaller communities, estimates come from local government officials.

The *Commercial Atlas* also offers a wealth of useful marketing data. It is chock-full of unexpected information, including directories of colleges, military installations, railroads, and major corporations by city. One of the more useful directories is a guide to cities with airports, together with a list of airlines servicing that city. For many of these lists, a thematic map is also provided. Other maps include guides to zip code and telephone area code boundaries, time and mileage maps showing driving and railroad distances between major cities, and a guide to international time zones. Demographic and economic data are also depicted in map form. Among the more interesting are maps of manufacturing activity, population change, and college enrollment.

The *Commercial Atlas* contains extensive marketing information. Rand McNally obtains estimates of local demographic characteristics and economic conditions from Market Statistics, a division of Bill Communications, Inc. Market Statistics produces the famous *Survey of Buying Power*, which is introduced later in this chapter. Selected data from the *Survey* are reproduced in the *Commercial Atlas*, and include the number of households, per capita income, median household income, car registrations, and total retail sales by type of store. Figures are given for counties and MSAs. The *Commercial Atlas* offers ranked lists of these characteristics for various levels of geography, as well as rankings of the fastest growing areas. Market Statistics also compiles certain figures expressly for Rand McNally.

Information is tabulated for 500 so-called Basic Trading Areas, which reflect retail trade patterns in metropolitan areas. These are then grouped into 50 Major Trading Areas. Another useful feature is the inclusion of basic data by three-digit zip code, an extremely popular breakdown for marketing purposes. Finally, Rand McNally assigns every city an alphanumeric rating which measures the locality's contribution to the national economy as a "Business Center." For the recency and quality of geographic information, as well as for the variety of marketing data provided, nothing comes close to the *Rand McNally Commercial Atlas*.

Metro Insights (DRI/McGraw-Hill—Annual).

One of the few published resources which combines data on metropolitan areas with a narrative analysis of market conditions is *Metro Insights*. This annual review is published by DRI/McGraw-Hill, one of the nation's premier econometric forecasting firms. Utilizing information from DRI's extensive economic database, the company creates estimates and forecasts for key indicators of the local economies, then compares these measures to national and regional averages. DRI analysts summarize the results in a standardized, 10-page report. *Metro Insights* covers the 100 largest MSAs in the United States. It is published in four regional volumes, which can be purchased separately or as a set. The publisher also issues the numeric data as a floppy diskette called *Metro Insights City Analyzer*. With it, researchers can identify cities exhibiting similar characteristics, rank cities by key attributes, and perform economic screening. DRI has also announced plans for a new product, tentatively called *Metro Insights II*, which will provide summary reports on smaller MSAs.

For each metropolitan area covered, *Metro Insights* describes population, income, retail sales, employment trends, economic growth, cost of living, indus-

trial operating costs, major employers, and key industries. Data are gathered from a variety of government and private sources. For most variables, DRI computes a current year estimate. One-year forecasts are also calculated for several key variables, including population, retail sales, personal income, and growth by industry sector. Reports highlight the strengths and weaknesses of each MSA, summarize the geographic location and economic infrastructure, and present "Business Report Cards" which compare local economic performance to regional and national averages. The standard format is convenient for making city-to-city comparisons, and is easy to use. Data sources are usually not identified in the reports and some tables are not labeled clearly, but a separate "User's Guide" provides adequate definitions of terms and explanations of concepts and methodology.

Researchers will undoubtedly encounter mistakes in some of the reports, and those familiar with specific markets may take exception to certain conclusions drawn by DRI analysts. But on the whole, *Metro Insights* provides reliable information and its conclusions are generally quite accurate. DRI/McGraw-Hill has an outstanding reputation for economic analysis and forecasting. For researchers who need a concise overview of local economies, who require comparative information, or who are seeking reputable forecasts, *Metro Insights* is one of the best possible resources.

Editor & Publisher Market Guide (Editor and Publisher Co.—Annual).

This annual guide from the company which issues *Editor & Publisher* magazine offers profiles of every city in the United States and Canada which has a daily newspaper. The "Survey of Cities" section gives a few short paragraphs of basic data for each location, but the amount of information packed into this brief treatment is admirable. The enormous range of topics includes climate, water quality, and geographic location; total population and number of households; average weekly wages by industry; total value of bank deposits; number of registered automobiles, electric and gas meters, and banks; principal industries and transportation facilities; names of major shopping centers and chain store outlets; principal shopping days; and names of daily newspapers and their circulations.

The *Editor & Publisher Market Guide* also contains two extensive sections of comparative statistics for states, MSAs, counties, and major cities. Data are gathered from the decennial Census, the *Census of Retail Trade*, and the *Census of Agriculture*, but current estimates are calculated by Editor & Publisher's own market research staff. The first section of statistics provides

rankings for MSAs, cities, and counties in each of the following areas: population, total disposable income, income per household, total retail sales, and sales by type of store. The second section offers state-by-state comparisons of all MSAs, counties, and major cities. These tables cite current population estimates, the change in population since the previous decennial Census, population in five age groups, the number of households, several measures of personal income, retail sales for nine categories of stores, the number of farms, and the total value of crops and livestock.

County and City Data Book (U.S. Bureau of the Census—Quinquennial).

The *County and City Data Book*, published every five years, offers statistics for all states and counties in the United States, and for cities with populations greater than 25,000. Beginning with the 1988 edition, brief data are also given for Minor Civil Divisions with populations greater than 2,500. Much of the information is obtained from the decennial and quinquennial Censuses, but other sources are also used. The *Data Book* covers population, vital statistics, health, employment, income, social welfare, housing, crime, education, government finance, and business establishments. To compare the quality of life from one community to another, the book offers information on climate, cost of electricity, poverty status, and number of physicians. Separate tables provide rankings by various characteristics. The top 25 counties are listed in each of 80 categories, while the top 75 cities are ranked in 30 categories. Rankings include the worst and smallest as well as the best and biggest. For example, counties with the fewest people per square mile are listed, as are counties with the largest decline in manufacturing employment. County outline maps are also provided for each state.

The *County and City Data Book* is quite detailed, but limited by the infrequency of publication. Also, the staggered schedule of major Censuses makes it impossible to coordinate this publication with the release of both the Economic and the Population Censuses. For example, the 1983 edition included 1980 population data soon after they became available, but figures from the 1982 Economic Census didn't appear until the 1988 issue of the *Data Book*. To counter this problem, the Bureau also publishes the *State and Metropolitan Area Data Book* approximately every four years. This volume presents similar information at the MSA level.

Statistics from the *County and City Data Book* are also available from the government in three electronic formats: magnetic tape, floppy diskette, and CD-ROM. Diskettes can be purchased in one of six file sets. Five of

the sets represent different levels of geography (counties, cities, small places, states, or census regions). The sixth set is divided by type of information, with a subset for demographic data only and another for economic data. The size of each file varies; the 1988 county file is issued as 18 diskettes, for example, while the state file is complete in a single diskette. The entire contents of the 1988 book can also be found on a single CD-ROM disk. Simple menu choices on the CD will retrieve a selection of standard tables identical to those in the printed book, but the Bureau's *EXTRACT* software allows more sophisticated searching. The disk is also compatible with *d-Base III*.

MARKET ESTIMATES AND PROJECTIONS

Demographic data for use in marketing are abundantly available in the Census publications outlined in Chapter 14, but marketers usually require more current information. The sources that appear below not only serve the need for updated consumer demographics, but are presented in formats specifically designed for market research. Used together with the more detailed Census materials, they can be powerful marketing tools, limited only by the researcher's diligence and imagination.

How do commercial services differ from traditional Census products? A major difference is in the type of data presented. First, the basic unit of measurement is typically the household, because many purchasing decisions are made at the household level. Second, most marketers focus on a narrow group of characteristics rather than examining a diversity of economic and social attributes. Among the most notable are age distribution, income levels, educational attainment, and race. Furthermore, many commercial products summarize data in broad groupings—those with college education versus those without; households above and below certain income levels, families with or without children. Commercial publishers usually combine demographic and economic information in their profiles, including information on retail sales, labor force characteristics, or other market measures. Beyond this, many commercial products calculate unique indexes or ratios for identifying and ranking markets. Typical composite indexes combine the total number of households, some measure of personal income for the area, and total retail sales.

Nongovernment data sources frequently examine specialized geographic areas. Political boundaries are not particularly meaningful for market analysis. Of greater relevance are geographic levels which reflect consumer

behavior: How far do people travel to go shopping? How much territory does a particular advertising medium cover? The concept of metropolitan areas is frequently useful for this type of analysis, and many commercial services utilize the government's definitions of MSAs. Unique geographic constructs are also devised, as with Rand McNally's Major Trading Areas. The impact of broadcast media has spawned new levels of marketing geography. The A.C. Nielsen Company and Arbitron, Inc. have each created their own geographic boundaries to measure television viewership patterns. These areas are constructed by grouping together the counties (and in some cases, portions of counties) which receive the broadcast signals of a dominant metropolitan area. Arbitron's groupings are called Areas of Dominant Influence (ADIs), while Nielsen's are Designated Market Areas (DMAs). The two are constructed differently, but are quite similar in most respects. Both are broader in scope than the government's definitions of metro areas. For example, the Buffalo, New York CMSA area consists of two counties, while the ADI for Buffalo is comprised of ten counties, including two in Pennsylvania. ADIs are utilized by marketers more frequently than DMAs, but both appear in a variety of commercial data products. Several of the sources described in this chapter (and in Chapter 18) present data by ADI and/or DMA, including the *Survey of Buying Power, Donnelley Demographics*, the *Sourcebook of County Demographics*, and the *MEI Marketing Economic Guide*. Tabulations by zip code are especially important for direct mail companies and telemarketers. Unfortunately, standard Census products did not provide zip code data prior to 1990. In fact, the absence of zip code information spurred the growth of many private data companies during the past two decades.

Most leading data firms can also provide demographic information in customized reports based on the geographic requirements of the client. One of the most frequently requested constructs for marketing analysis is a circular area surrounding some central point. Marketers specify the size of the area they are interested in, and data companies estimate the characteristics of the population within that radius. How can they provide data for areas which don't match any standard geographic, political, or statistical boundaries? A common technique is called the centroid method. Research firms begin with a small unit of geography for which data are available, such as Blocks, Block Groups, or Census Tracts. Next they plot the geographic center of each of these units, and superimpose the specified circle over this map. If the centroid for an individual unit falls within the circle, that unit is included in the analysis; centroids outside are excluded. Data for the individual units are then totaled to obtain a profile of the specified area. The resulting area is not actually a circle, merely the approximation of one. Clearly, the smaller the units upon which this analysis is based, the more meaningful the resulting estimate.

Estimates of Population and Buying Power

Firms offering population estimates and projections were virtually nonexistent in 1970, but are now a thriving segment of the information industry. These companies provide an alternative to the estimates and projections available from the government. Most combine traditional demographic data with other market information, giving researchers a more complete picture of local conditions. In addition to the companies described below, well-known names in this field include the Claritas Corporation, the National Planning Data Corporation, Urban Decision Systems, and Equifax Marketing Decision Systems (formerly National Decision Systems). The *Best 100 Sources for Marketing Information*, a brief annual directory from the publishers of *American Demographics* magazine, describes the research capabilities, services, and information products of the leading demographic data suppliers in the United States.

How do private companies compute estimates and projections for local areas? Individual techniques vary, but the decennial Census serves as the benchmark upon which estimates all are constructed. Chapter 14 discussed some of the methods used by the Bureau of the Census, and many of these are utilized by private publishers to some degree. Some data providers rely strictly on arithmetic techniques, such as extrapolation and ratios. Others utilize econometric models, such as regression analysis. Arithmetic methods are based more heavily on historical population figures, while econometric models incorporate current symptomatic data. The companies creating market estimates usually do not collect local symptomatic data themselves, but purchase data sets from other organizations. For example, R.L. Polk sells a database with statistics on motor vehicle registrations by county and the U.S. Postal Service sells data on the number of delivery addresses by zip code. Many demographic firms also purchase data summaries compiled by commercial mailing list companies.

Producers of market estimates mainly provide clients with custom-designed reports, but many publish standardized products as well. Researchers can subscribe

to online databases, or they can acquire computer tapes outright. Subsets of larger files are available on diskettes or CD-ROM. These services offer the client enormous flexibility, including the opportunity to examine data for alternative geographic boundaries.

Survey of Buying Power Data Service (Bill Communications, Inc.—Annual).

The *Survey of Buying Power* is the most famous and widely used source of consumer market data in the U.S. It is also the oldest service of its type, appearing annually since 1929. Bill Communications offers the results in two publications: a detailed report called the *Survey of Buying Power Data Service*, and an abbreviated version released as two special issues of *Sales & Marketing Management* magazine. Both versions offer data on population, income, and retail sales for states, MSAs, counties, major cities, and ADIs.

For each geographic area, the following statistics are given: the total population; the number of households; the median age of the population; the percentage of population by sex and age group; the distribution of households by income category and by age of householder; a measure of disposable personal income which the publisher calls Effective Buying Income (EBI); total retail sales; and sales by type of store. The data are generated by a division of Bill Communications known as Market Statistics. The *Survey* also ranks every metropolitan area in the nation by more than 25 different characteristics, ranging from the number of single-person households to retail sales per household. A unique and popular feature is the calculation of a Buying Power Index (BPI) for every geographic area. The BPI is a weighted index combining local population, EBI, and retail sales data into a composite measure expressed as a percentage of the national total. It compares the potential consumer buying power of a particular area to other areas, or to the nation as a whole. (An example of BPI rankings for the nation can be seen in Chapter 13, Exhibit 13-2.) The *Data Service* also calculates a "graduated BPI," listing separate indexes for three income levels—economy, moderate, and premium households.

The *Data Service* offers a set of county outline maps for each of the 50 states, and an analysis of merchandise sales by type of store. The latter figures are similar to those found in the *Merchandise Line Sales* report from the *Census of Retail Trade*, but at a broader level of aggregation. The final feature is a set of five-year projections for MSAs, ADIs, and counties. Forecasted characteristics include total population, number of households, average household EBI, and total retail sales.

Much of the information contained in the *Data Service* can also be seen in *Sales & Marketing Management* magazine. Part I, appearing in a July or August issue, cites population, income, and retail sales figures for most levels of geography covered in the *Data Service*. Part II, published in October or November, provides figures on merchandise line sales, television market estimates, and five-year projections. The differences between the two formats involve the amount of detail: retail sales are given for only six store types rather than ten, age breakdowns are less detailed, population figures are not given by sex, and some household characteristics are omitted. The Buying Power Index is also less specific; a single BPI is given for each area, rather than the graduated indexes by income level. A variety of specialized tables are also lacking in the magazine version, including local area data expressed as a percentage of the national total, and merchandise line sales by metropolitan area. The absence of certain amenities, such as the county outline maps, also limit the magazine version. On the other hand, the magazine contains a few features which the *Data Service* lacks, such as a series of articles which identify emerging economic trends and a section on newspaper market profiles. Whether the researcher turns to the *Survey of Buying Power* in the issues of *Sales & Marketing Management*, or to the separate *Data Service*, the same consistently reliable market estimates will be found.

Information from the *Survey of Buying Power* can also be purchased on floppy diskette or CD-ROM. In both versions, the product is called *YMC—Your Marketing Consultant: Advanced Consumer. YMC* provides the same type of data for the same levels of geography seen in the *Data Service*. Customers can also contract with the publisher to obtain special reports by zip code, purchased in units of 50 zip codes each.

MEI Marketing Economics Guide (Marketing Economics Institute, Ltd.—Annual).

Though not as well known as the *Survey of Buying Power*, the *Marketing Economics Guide* is similar in most respects. Produced by a private data company called the Marketing Economics Institute, it provides estimates of population, income, and retail sales for all states, MSAs, and counties in the United States, and for 1,500 major cities. Data can be accessed by geographic location, or through ranked lists by type of characteristic. MEI lists most demographic characteristics only as a percentage of total population, or as a ratio of two characteristics. For example, the user can find the percentage of the black population within each place, the percent living in group quarters, the percent living in

urban areas, and the percent of households in several income categories. The other demographic variables are population density, per capita disposable income, and income per household. Retail sales for each area include the local percentage of total U.S. sales, sales per household, and dollar volume of sales in each of nine categories. Finally, MEI constructs an index measuring the relationship of retail sales to disposable income for every locality. This source also provides county outline maps and suggestions for applying the data to specific marketing problems.

Sourcebook of Zip Code Demographics (CACI Marketing Systems—Annual).

CACI (pronounced "khaki") is one of the leading providers of demographic data in the United States. The company offers a diversity of information products and services, including customized reports, online databases, and microcomputer systems. It provides demographic estimates by five-digit zip code, and is the only major company to publish this data in book form for the entire nation. For every zip code area, tables provide current-year estimates for total population, population growth, number of households, age distribution by 13 groupings, median age, population by race (black and white), and several measures of personal income (including income distribution in seven categories). For many variables, comparative data from the latest decennial Census are given. In some cases, CACI does not offer current estimates, but provides summary figures from the Census. These latter variables deal with education, labor force, and housing characteristics. CACI also computes a five-year forecast at the zip code level for total population, number of households, median age, and median household income.

Another section of the tables presents various indexes of "Market Potential" for every zip code. These measure an individual locality's potential for retail sales compared to a national average. CACI creates the indexes in conjunction with Mediamark Research, Inc., a leading producer of data on consumer buying behavior. The indexes are given for 14 product or service categories, ranging from footwear to video rentals. A number greater than 100 indicates a zip code where the product group is likely to sell better than average; a lower number suggests a less lucrative market. Exhibit 17-1 illustrates this analysis for various zip codes in Kentucky, many of which represent rural areas with high poverty rates. As expected, the market potentials for savings and investments for most localities falls far below the national average. But consider zip code 41394 (Wolverine).

Three areas reflect market potentials significantly above the norm: loans, sporting goods, and pet ownership. Notice how these results differ from most other zip codes in the area, and show how the CACI *Sourcebook* can target pockets of sales potential within a broader geographic area. More will be said about this technique in Chapter 18.

The *Sourcebook* also includes summary tables for national and state demographic estimates, and an appendix which lists the top ranked industry in every zip code by employment size. CACI's *Sourcebook of County Demographics* presents the same information by county, MSA, ADI, and DMA breakdowns. Data from both publications can be purchased on diskette or magnetic tape. Diskettes are divided into approximately 30 standardized files by type of characteristic. Users must specify not only the file category, but the geographic area and level of reporting. For example, a single disk might contain current estimates of household income distribution for the Dallas MSA, broken down by either zip code or Census Tract.

Annual information is also available through CACI's online databases, such as *SUPERSITE*, offered through CompuServe and several corporate-oriented database vendors. In addition to the variables found in the *Sourcebooks*, *SUPERSITE* identifies characteristics of the Hispanic population, income by age breakdown, age by sex, percent of the population below the poverty level, and greater detail on employment and educational attainment. Data on market potential are also more detailed, with each product category further divided into specific types of products. These reports indicate both the Market Potential Index and estimated expenditures on each product per person and per household. Reports are available by state, MSA, ADI, county, Minor Civil Division, Census Tract, or zip code group. Users can choose from any one of 35 report formats, containing either historical data, current estimates, or forecasts. On CompuServe, *SUPERSITE* is divided into two subfiles for demographic and market potential information. A third subfile on *SUPERSITE*, *ACORN Target Marketing*, is described in Chapter 18. Finally, CACI produces customized reports which provide data for geographic areas within a specified radius of a targeted site.

Donnelley Demographics (Donnelley Marketing Information Services—Annual).

The first company to offer direct electronic access to customized demographic data on local markets was Donnelley Marketing. Their population estimates are

EXHIBIT 17-1. ***Sourcebook of Zip Code Demographics***

DEMOGRAPHIC AND BUYING POWER PROFILE — KENTUCKY

41363-41529 B

ZIP CODE		NUMBER OF HOUSEHOLDS				RACE (%)				1990 MARKET POTENTIAL INDEX													
#	POST OFFICE NAME	1980	1990	1995	% ANNUAL GROWTH RATE 80-90	WHITE 1980	WHITE 1990	BLACK 1980	BLACK 1990	INVEST-MENTS	SAVINGS	LOANS	APPAREL	FOOT-WEAR	SPORTS GOODS	GROCERY	DRUG STORES	DINING OUT	PET OWNER-SHIP	VIDEO RENTALS	AUTO AFTER-MARKET	FURNI-TURE	HOME IMPROVE-MENT
41363	QUICKSAND	258	410	544	4.7	99.2	99.2	0.5	0.4	99	95	119	91	85	110	93	102	92	121	104	104	101	91
41364	RICETOWN	255	249	268	-0.2	99.6	99.6	0.4	0.4	37	45	60	81	77	68	65	100	33	109	71	88	81	48
41365	ROGERS	155	184	204	1.7	99.8	100.0	0.0	0.0	37	44	60	81	77	68	66	100	33	109	71	88	81	48
41366	ROUSSEAU	47	34	29	-3.2	99.4	100.0	0.0	0.0	37	44	60	82	77	68	66	100	33	109	71	88	81	48
41367	ROWDY	43	52	58	1.9	100.0	100.0	0.0	0.0	37	44	60	81	77	68	66	100	33	109	71	88	81	48
41368	SAINT HELENS	11	12	12	0.9	100.0	100.0	0.0	0.0	38	46	62	84	79	70	66	103	34	109	71	88	81	48
41369	SALDEE	60	57	55	-0.5	100.0	100.0	0.0	0.0	38	47	59	83	82	69	67	98	43	106	71	88	82	48
41370	SEBASTIANS BRANCH	169	139	126	-1.9	99.8	99.8	0.2	0.2	39	50	57	83	85	69	69	96	51	103	70	88	82	49
41377	TALBERT	100	82	74	-2.0	99.7	100.0	0.3	0.0	40	50	58	84	86	69	69	97	51	103	70	88	82	49
41378	TALLEGA	9	10	10	1.1	100.0	100.0	0.0	0.0	38	45	61	83	78	69	66	101	33	109	71	88	81	48
41383	VADA	5	5	5	0.0	100.0	100.0	0.0	0.0	38	45	60	82	78	69	66	101	33	109	71	88	81	48
41385	VANCLEVE	428	367	337	-1.5	99.1	98.8	0.1	0.2	37	44	60	81	77	68	66	100	33	109	71	88	81	48
41386	VINCENT	302	332	378	1.0	99.9	99.9	0.0	0.0	37	44	60	81	77	68	66	100	33	109	71	88	81	48
41390	WHICK	154	146	142	-0.5	100.0	100.0	0.0	0.0	38	47	58	82	81	69	67	98	43	106	71	88	82	48
41391	WIDECREEK	3	2	2	0.0	0.0	0.0	0.0	0.0	0	0	0	0	0	0	0	0	0	0	0	0	0	0
41393	WOLF COAL	60	57	55	-0.5	100.0	100.0	0.0	0.0	38	47	58	82	81	69	67	98	42	106	71	88	82	48
41394	WOLVERINE	242	385	511	4.8	99.2	99.2	0.4	0.4	99	95	119	91	85	110	93	102	92	121	104	104	101	91
41396	ZACHARIAH	330	354	381	0.7	99.3	99.3	0.6	0.6	44	54	64	82	75	69	60	101	47	109	70	93	77	57
41397	ZOE	128	137	147	0.7	99.2	99.2	0.5	0.5	43	53	64	82	75	69	60	101	47	109	70	93	77	56
41401	BETHANNA	86	91	97	0.6	100.0	100.0	0.0	0.0	37	44	60	82	77	68	66	100	33	109	71	88	81	48
41403	BLAZE	33	34	35	0.3	100.0	100.0	0.0	0.0	38	45	60	82	78	69	66	101	33	109	71	88	81	48
41405	BURNING FORK	9	10	12	1.1	100.0	100.0	0.0	0.0	49	54	69	87	84	76	71	105	46	109	78	90	84	57
41406	BUSKIRK	113	123	132	0.9	99.1	99.1	0.6	0.6	37	44	60	81	77	68	66	100	33	109	71	88	81	48
41407	CANEY	538	576	609	0.7	99.9	99.9	0.0	0.0	52	59	73	84	77	75	67	100	54	111	76	96	81	65
41408	CANNEL CITY	24	24	25	0.0	98.5	100.0	0.0	0.0	62	69	82	86	78	81	68	102	67	112	79	100	81	76
41409	CARVER	134	158	178	1.7	99.8	99.8	0.0	0.0	47	52	66	83	80	73	70	100	44	109	76	90	84	55
41410	CISCO	8	9	10	1.2	100.0	100.0	0.0	0.0	50	55	69	87	83	76	69	104	47	109	75	89	83	53
41411	CONLEY	82	97	109	1.7	100.0	99.6	0.0	0.0	47	52	66	84	80	73	70	100	44	109	76	90	84	54
41412	COTTLE	55	57	59	0.4	100.0	100.0	0.0	0.0	59	67	79	86	78	79	67	101	65	111	78	98	81	72
41413	CROCKETT	171	183	193	0.7	99.6	99.5	0.0	0.0	39	48	58	82	82	69	68	98	44	105	70	88	81	48
41414	CUTUNO	33	35	37	0.6	99.1	100.0	0.0	0.0	38	45	60	83	78	69	66	101	33	109	71	88	81	48
41417	DINGUS	100	106	112	0.6	99.4	99.7	0.0	0.0	40	48	58	82	82	69	68	98	44	105	70	88	81	48
41419	EDNA	34	36	38	0.6	99.1	100.0	0.0	0.0	38	45	60	82	77	69	66	101	33	109	71	88	81	48
41421	ELKFORK	155	166	175	0.7	99.6	99.6	0.0	0.0	39	48	58	82	82	69	68	98	44	105	70	88	81	48
41422	ELSIE	18	19	20	0.5	100.0	100.0	0.0	0.0	38	45	60	82	77	68	66	100	33	109	71	88	81	48
41425	EZEL	477	506	533	0.6	98.7	98.6	0.8	0.9	39	46	61	82	77	69	66	100	35	109	71	89	81	50
41426	FALCON	7	9	10	2.5	100.0	100.0	0.0	0.0	49	54	69	88	85	77	69	106	46	109	75	89	83	53
41427	FLAT FORK	7	8	9	1.3	100.0	100.0	0.0	0.0	50	55	70	88	85	77	69	106	47	109	75	90	83	53
41429	FORAKER	308	363	408	1.7	99.9	99.8	0.0	0.0	47	52	66	83	80	73	70	100	44	109	76	90	83	54
41430	FREDVILLE	172	180	191	0.5	99.8	99.6	0.0	0.0	38	46	59	82	80	68	67	99	39	107	71	88	81	48
41431	FRITZ	2	2	2	0.0	0.0	0.0	0.0	0.0	0	0	0	0	0	0	0	0	0	0	0	0	0	0
41433	GAPVILLE	42	44	47	0.5	100.0	99.3	0.0	0.0	39	47	59	82	80	69	67	99	39	107	71	88	81	48
41434	GIFFORD	75	88	99	1.6	99.6	100.0	0.0	0.0	46	51	65	83	80	73	70	100	44	109	76	90	83	54
41435	GRASSY CREEK	28	28	30	0.0	100.0	100.0	0.0	0.0	62	69	82	86	78	81	68	102	68	112	79	100	82	76
41438	GYPSY	3	3	3	0.0	0.0	0.0	0.0	0.0	0	0	0	0	0	0	0	0	0	0	0	0	0	0
41439	HAGER	39	42	44	0.7	100.0	100.0	0.0	0.0	38	45	60	82	78	69	66	101	33	109	71	88	81	48
41440	HARPER	67	74	80	1.0	100.0	99.5	0.0	0.0	41	47	62	83	78	70	67	100	37	109	73	89	82	50
41441	HENDRICKS	111	131	147	1.7	100.0	100.0	0.0	0.0	47	52	66	84	80	73	70	100	44	109	76	90	84	54
41443	INSKO	136	156	171	1.4	100.0	100.0	0.0	0.0	37	44	60	81	77	68	66	100	33	109	71	88	81	48
41444	IVYTON	6	8	8	2.9	100.0	100.0	0.0	0.0	48	53	67	85	81	74	69	101	45	109	75	90	83	53
41447	LENOX	130	138	145	0.6	99.5	99.5	0.0	0.0	42	50	61	83	81	70	68	98	47	106	71	90	81	51
41451	MALONE	448	494	530	1.0	100.0	99.9	0.0	0.0	46	53	67	83	77	72	66	100	45	110	74	93	81	58
41452	MARSHALLVILLE	2	3	3	0.0	0.0	0.0	0.0	0.0	0	0	0	0	0	0	0	0	0	0	0	0	0	0
41453	MASHFORK	161	190	214	1.7	99.8	99.8	0.0	0.0	47	52	66	84	80	73	70	100	44	109	76	90	84	55
41456	MIMA	23	25	26	0.8	100.0	100.0	0.0	0.0	40	48	58	83	82	69	68	98	44	105	70	88	81	48
41457	MOON	148	159	168	0.7	99.6	99.6	0.0	0.0	40	48	58	82	82	69	68	98	44	105	70	88	81	48
41459	OPHIR	54	58	61	0.7	99.4	99.4	0.0	0.0	40	48	58	83	83	69	68	98	45	105	70	88	81	48
41464	ROYALTON	388	416	448	0.7	99.8	99.7	0.0	0.0	40	47	60	82	80	69	67	99	40	107	72	88	82	49
41465	SALYERSVILLE	1866	2205	2484	1.7	99.8	99.8	0.0	0.0	47	52	66	83	80	73	70	100	44	109	76	90	84	55
41466	SEITZ	142	150	160	0.5	100.0	100.0	0.0	0.0	37	44	60	82	77	68	66	100	33	109	71	88	81	48
41467	SILVERHILL	45	48	51	0.6	100.0	99.3	0.0	0.0	40	48	58	83	82	69	68	98	44	105	70	88	81	48
41469	STELLA	100	105	112	0.5	99.7	100.0	0.0	0.0	37	44	60	82	77	68	66	100	33	109	71	88	81	48
41472	WEST LIBERTY	467	482	500	0.3	99.8	99.8	0.0	0.0	59	66	78	85	77	79	67	101	63	111	78	98	81	72
41473	WHEELERSBURG	47	56	63	1.8	100.0	100.0	0.0	0.0	47	52	66	84	80	73	70	100	44	109	76	90	84	55
41474	WHITE OAK	95	98	102	0.3	100.0	100.0	0.0	0.0	61	68	80	85	78	80	67	101	66	111	78	99	81	74
41475	WONNIE	9	10	12	1.1	100.0	100.0	0.0	0.0	49	54	69	87	84	76	71	105	46	109	78	90	84	57
41477	WRIGLEY	488	500	518	0.2	99.9	99.9	0.1	0.1	39	46	61	82	77	69	66	100	35	109	71	89	81	49
41501	PIKEVILLE	6091	6465	6903	0.6	98.7	98.6	1.0	1.0	81	82	100	94	88	97	88	100	83	113	97	102	93	84
41503	PIKEVILLE	50	51	54	0.2	97.9	97.8	1.4	1.5	76	77	98	89	83	97	78	102	66	115	92	97	89	79
41510	AFLEX	37	39	41	0.5	97.2	98.0	1.8	1.0	77	78	99	89	83	97	78	102	67	115	91	97	89	78
41511	ARGO	15	17	19	1.3	100.0	100.0	0.0	0.0	48	69	82	90	94	85	74	97	85	111	87	96	88	78
41512	ASHCAMP	702	857	982	2.0	99.9	99.8	0.0	0.0	51	74	92	92	94	90	75	99	91	117	95	100	90	90
41513	BELCHER	237	251	268	0.6	99.6	99.6	0.0	0.0	61	79	100	93	92	97	72	100	85	117	97	100	86	96
41514	BELFRY	315	326	343	0.3	98.1	97.9	1.4	1.4	76	77	98	89	83	96	78	101	66	115	92	97	89	79
41517	BURDINE	20	20	20	0.0	96.6	98.1	3.4	1.9	61	66	84	88	82	87	68	100	51	110	84	94	80	73
41518	BURNWELL	41	43	45	0.5	98.3	98.2	1.7	1.8	76	77	98	89	83	97	78	101	67	115	92	98	89	79
41519	CANADA	170	195	216	1.4	100.0	100.0	0.0	0.0	51	76	95	92	94	92	75	99	92	118	96	101	90	93
41520	DORTON	458	525	581	1.4	99.9	99.9	0.0	0.0	46	65	68	88	97	78	74	93	84	102	79	92	86	65
41521	DRAFFIN	33	33	35	0.0	99.0	100.0	0.0	0.0	64	81	102	94	92	99	71	102	84	116	97	100	84	97
41522	ELKHORN CITY	576	595	628	0.3	99.7	99.6	0.0	0.0	62	80	101	93	92	98	72	101	84	117	97	100	85	97
41523	ETTY	194	213	231	0.9	99.8	99.7	0.0	0.0	43	59	54	86	99	71	73	90	79	94	70	87	85	50
41524	FEDSCREEK	152	156	164	0.3	99.8	99.8	0.0	0.0	83	90	117	97	87	106	84	100	87	121	104	106	92	100
41525	FISHTRAP	22	23	24	0.4	100.0	100.0	0.0	0.0	64	82	103	95	93	100	71	102	84	117	98	100	85	98
41526	KEWANEE	207	248	282	1.8	100.0	100.0	0.0	0.0	77	87	114	96	89	103	86	100	90	122	104	106	94	98
41527	FOREST HILLS	258	269	284	0.4	98.3	98.0	1.3	1.3	74	77	98	89	83	96	77	101	68	115	92	98	89	80
41528	FREEBURN	225	258	286	1.4	99.9	100.0	0.0	0.0	49	69	82	90	94	85	74	97	84	111	88	96	88	79
41529	GOODY	24	25	26	0.4	98.6	98.5	1.4	1.5	77	78	99	90	84	98	77	103	67	115	91	97	88	79
	KENTUCKY				1.2	92.3	92.4	7.1	6.9	83	85	93	94	93	95	88	100	86	107	94	99	94	88
	UNITED STATES				1.6	83.1	82.0	11.7	11.1	100	100	100	100	100	100	100	100	100	100	100	100	100	100

135-B

The *Sourcebook of Zip Code Demographics*, copyright 1990 by CACI Marketing Systems, (800) 292-CACI. Reprinted with permission.

based upon the company's enormous file of consumer mailing lists. With names and addresses for some 78 million occupied housing units in the United States, Donnelley boasts specific information on 90% of the country's households. The firm is now a subsidiary of Dun & Bradstreet, which means it can also draw on D&B's enormous data resources when constructing local market profiles.

Their best-known product is an online database called *Donnelley Demographics*, available exclusively through DIALOG. Like CACI, Donnelley provides summary data from the most recent decennial Census, current-year estimates, and selected five-year projections. Estimates and projections are given for total population, number of households, mean and median household income, average household size, median age, age distribution by five-year groupings (for the total population and by sex), race, Spanish Origin, and household income distribution (for the total population and by age of householder). Decennial data are also cited for all of the preceding variables, plus marital status; household composition; employment status by industry and occupation; transportation to work; and cross tabulations by age, race, and sex. Each report is seven pages, though users can request segments of any report or create customized tables of their own. Reports are available for every state, MSA, ADI, DMA, county, Place, and zip code, and for most Minor Civil Divisions. Absent from the database is the Census Tract, though Donnelley does present Tract-level data in its other demographic products. Another weakness is the lack of information on retail sales or buying power, but again this can be found in other Donnelley products. Despite these omissions, *Donnelley Demographics* presents more detailed demographic estimates and projections than most other services.

Donnelley Demographics offers powerful search capabilities through DIALOG. Nearly 200 variables can be searched numerically; the user can either specify a range of values or use numeric operators such as "greater than" or "less than." Approximately 85 sortable variables enable the searcher to rank results in descending or ascending order. The flexibility offered by such a powerful system is remarkable. As an example, the user can quickly identify all counties with a population between 100,000 and one million, a median household income greater than $29,000, and a change in population greater than 30%. The results can then be ranked by median income within each state, and displayed as comparative tables. Searching the database is straightforward, with the exception of one idiosyncrasy. Every geographic entity is indexed to the larger units of which it is a part.

Therefore, the user must specify both the place name (or code) and the level of geography. For example, a search for the city of Miami, Florida, will retrieve numerous records because it will include the individual reports for every zip code within the city, as well as the city itself. To limit the results to the single report for Miami, the searcher must specify "Level = City."

Two other Donnelley databases are accessible through the Control Data Corporation. *American Profile* provides information similar to that seen in *Donnelley Demographics*, together with summary statistics on business characteristics provided by Dun & Bradstreet. *ClusterPLUS*, discussed briefly in Chapter 18, combines demographic data with information on consumer buying behavior. Both *American Profiles* and *ClusterPLUS* are also available on CD-ROM as part of Donnelley's *Conquest* system. Statistics from all three databases are available in a variety of customized printed reports. For any report, the customer can specify the unit of geography, from Census Tracts to concentric circles.

Market Profile Analysis (Donnelley Marketing Information Services—Annual).

Donnelley Marketing also offers a set of standardized reports collectively known as the *Market Profile Analysis (MPA)* series. A separate report is produced for every MSA in the country, each issued as an 8$1/2$" by 17" spiral-bound book. The books combine data from Donnelley Marketing and Dun & Bradstreet with several other sources. Depending on the type of statistic, information is presented by Census Tract, zip code, or Minor Civil Division, and for the MSA and its component counties. Four types of data can be found in *MPA*: characteristics of households, statistics on business establishments, summary information on new construction activity, and detailed listings of bank deposits by branch. Household data come from Donnelley itself, and business statistics are compiled from *Dun's Market Identifiers*. Construction information is provided by the Bureau of the Census, which collects its data from local governments. Financial deposits are obtained from the same federal regulatory agencies utilized by the *Branch Directory and Summary of Deposits* described in Chapter 8.

MPA is divided into six sections. The first is a table of summary data arranged by place name and zip code. Variables found here are current estimates of total population, number of households, number of business establishments, total employment size, number of branches of financial institutions by type, and ratios of people to branches. "Retail Market Factors I" is arranged by Tract within place and zip code. For both the most recent decennial Census year and the current year's estimate, it

reports total population, households, and median household income. From the decennial Census it also cites median age and median home value of owner-occupied housing units. Household mobility, derived from Donnelley's mailing list information, reports the percentage of households new to the area, the percentage which have left, and the turnover ratio. Every Tract is also ranked within the MSA on each of the reported variables. "Retail Market Factors II" also lists data by Tract. Current-year estimates are given for income distribution (in five size categories), the length of residence in four categories, and the percentages of single-family and multiple-family dwellings. Decennial Census data include age distribution in five categories, the percentage of college graduates, and selected labor force characteristics.

The fourth section consists of business statistics broken down by ten broad SIC groupings for each zip code area. The variables are total number of employees, number of establishments by employee size, total sales volume, and number of establishments by sales volume range. "New Construction Information" is one of the most useful portions of the report. For each Minor Civil Division, it cites data on residential and nonresidential construction by type of dwelling. The four residential categories are grouped by size of dwelling, from single-family to multiple-family with five or more units. Non-residential data are divided into industrial, office, retail, institutional, and other. This section also reports data on building additions, alterations, and conversions. For every category, three figures are given: the number of structures, the number of units, and the dollar value of the construction. All of the information in this section is provided as a measure of economic strength, but can also be used to calculate changes in housing stock since the previous Census. It is one of the few sources to report both number of buildings and number of units.

The final section of *MPA* contains profiles of branch bank operations. Data are given for commercial banks, thrifts, and credit unions. The parent institution, branch name, address, date opened, and dollar value of deposits by type are given for each branch. Information is arranged by zip code. Access to the information in *MPA* is enhanced by several geographic indexes. An "Index of Place Names" relates smaller communities to the Minor Civil Division of which they are a part. An "Index of Zip Codes" links zip codes to the MCDs where they are found. An "Index of Census Tracts by Zip Code" shows the relationship between zips and Tracts. A final index matches Tracts with the MCDs where they are located.

Individual reports in the *Market Profile Analysis* series are expensive, with prices based on the size of the MSA. For this reason, and because many counties in the United States lie outside metropolitan areas, Donnelley produces a companion series called the *Community Profile Analysis* (*CPA*). An individual *CPA* publication is available on demand for every county in the United States.

Given their expense, what do the *Market Profile Analysis* and the *Community Profile Analysis* offer that's different from other Donnelley or D&B products? Although they provide nowhere near the demographic detail seen in *Donnelley Demographics*, *MPA* and *CPA* present information at the Tract level, which the online service does not. The statistics on business establishments in both are more detailed than the data seen in *Dun's Census of American Business*, plus they are presented at the zip code level. By presenting both demographic and economic data at such small geographic levels, *MPA* and *CPA* offer a closer look at local communities than many other data products. Finally, the two services contain a greater diversity of market information than almost any other printed guide to local areas, including several unique measures. The *Market Profile Analysis* is one of the most convenient sources of local market data available.

Long-Term Forecasts

Many guides to local area market conditions contain demographic and economic projections, but they usually focus on the short term—one to five years. The farther one peers into the future, the more difficult it becomes to make meaningful or accurate forecasts, an axiom especially true for smaller levels of geography. Nevertheless, several organizations are well-known for long-term projections depicting local economic conditions 20 to 50 years in the future. For population projections, an excellent source is state government. Almost every state produces official projections at the state and county levels. The issuing agency varies, but is typically the State Data Center, the Commerce Department, or Planning Department. In some states, projections are generated by a research center affiliated with the State University. All three of the sources described below utilize a step-down approach to arrive at figures for smaller areas. This means that projections are calculated first at the the national level; state projections are derived from the national figures, and local data from the state projections.

Regional Economic Projection Series (NPA Data Services, Inc.—Annual).

A frequently cited source of long-term projections is NPA Data Services, a spinoff of the nonprofitNational Planning Association. Their major guide to local area forecasts, the *Regional Economic Projection Series* (*REPS*), is also known by several other names, including *Regional Economic Growth in the United States*. The report provides 30-year projections for key economic variables, in some cases down to the county level. Population projections are generated using the cohort component method, while economic forecasts are based on a regression model. The key engines of economic growth are examined in the model, including the size of the labor force, labor productivity, capital investment, technological advances, and government expenditures.

REPS is issued annually in three volumes. The first provides summary data for the United States, Census regions, states, MSAs, and counties. For each area, four variables are reported—total population, employment, the total value of personal income, and per capita income. Figures are given for the previous two decennial Census years, together with a current-year estimate and 30 years of projections, reported in five-year intervals. Income figures are reported in constant dollars. This volume also provides a brief narrative summary of trends and projections, and lists of the leading metropolitan areas ranked by long-term projected growth. Volume 2 provides more detailed employment and income information down to the MSA level, and for the same reporting years. Employment data are broken down by industry sector (including government employment), while income is projected by source of funds. This volume also reports the projected value of employee earnings by industry sector. The third volume provides detailed population information, with data reported again for the nation, regions, states, and MSAs. Figures are given for age groups, which are further broken down by race and sex. The number of households, persons per household, and income per household are also given. Projections are reported in ten-year intervals for three decades.

Summary data from *REPS* are also published in a biennial service called *Key Indicators of Economic Growth*. For each state and county, it reports ten variables, including total population, number of households, per capita income, income per household, and employment. Census benchmarks are cited, together with two years of current estimates, 20-year projections, and three measures of population growth.

A companion set of forecasts, the *National Economic Projection Series* (*NEPS*), was introduced in Chapter 15. Information from *REPS* and *NEPS* is also available online, and can be searched via Reuters. Data are presented in two files, *NPA/Economic* and *NPA/ Demographic*. The content of the databases resembles the printed products, though more years of annual figures are presented online. Data are also available on computer tape and diskette.

MSA Profile: Metropolitan Area Forecasts (Woods & Poole Economics, Inc.—Annual).

The highly respected firm of Woods & Poole is the major competitor to NPA Data Services. The company publishes several printed reports, but the most popular is the single-volume *MSA Profile*. It covers every CMSA, PMSA, and MSA in the nation, together with data for states and regions. Each area is profiled in a single table covering population, employment, earnings, income, and retail sales. Historical data from the previous two decennial Censuses are given, along with two years of current estimates and 20 years of forecasts reported in five-year intervals. Among the 80 variables reported are total population, number of households, persons per household, age distribution in five-year groupings, median age, race, Spanish Origin, employment and earnings by industry category, total personal income, income per capita, mean household income, income by source, and retail sales in ten categories. Several characteristics are also reported as percentages, growth rates, or national rankings. Additional features include a narrative summary of national economic and demographic trends, and a complete list of MSAs and their component counties.

Although the tables in the *MSA Profile* look similar to those in *REPS*, the two publications use different econometric models. The Woods & Poole model uses employment forecasts to derive the measures of population, earnings, income, and retail sales. The methodology is explained in fair detail in the published report. Also, certain data elements found in the *MSA Profile* are absent from the NPA product, notably the estimates and projections of local retail sales. On the other hand, *REPS* cross-tabulates age groups by both sex and race, which Woods & Poole does not.

Another Woods & Poole series, *State Profiles*, is published in 50 separate volumes. Each volume provides a narrative overview of the state economy, together with tables similar to those in *MSA Profiles*. Data are presented for the entire state, for MSAs (including those crossing state boundaries), and for every county in the state. National data are also cited for comparative purposes. The *Complete Economic and Demographic Source*

is a three-volume report that includes all the data found in the other two publications, plus a series of rankings for MSAs and other areas. Researchers can also obtain data on magnetic tape or floppy diskette.

OBERS BEA Regional Projections (U.S. Bureau of Economic Analysis—Quinquennial).

Every five years the U.S. Bureau of Economic Analysis issues its *OBERS BEA Regional Projections*. "OBERS" is an acronym based on the names of the two agencies which formerly produced the report—the Commerce Department's Office of Business Economics (now called the BEA) and the Agriculture Department's Economic Research Service. *OBERS* employs a complex regression model, making it an important alternate source of population projections. It presents forecasts up to 50 years in the future for the United States, individual states, and every MSA in the nation. The variables covered are similar to those in *REPS*, but are less detailed. At the state and national level, projections are given for total population, population for three age groups, per capita income, employment by industry, sources of income, and earnings by place of work. For metropolitan areas, similar, but less detailed projections are made. Employment and earnings data by place of work are not broken down as finely, for example, and population by age group is not given. Historical estimates are reported in five-year intervals for the previous four periods, and projections are given for 5, 10, 15, 20, 30, and 50 years hence. Though only published every five years (in years ending in five and zero), *OBERS* is the only report from the federal government which provides long-term forecasts for local areas.

SPECIAL TOPICS

The publications and databases described so far have concentrated on broad economic, demographic, and social conditions for states and local areas. An incredible diversity of additional publications can be used to compare more specialized characteristics of local markets. For example, such publications as *Facts & Figures on Government Finance* (the Tax Foundation), *Moody's Municipal & Government Manual*, and the *Municipal Yearbook* (the International City Management Association) analyze the financial health and structure of state and local governments. The following section will briefly mention a variety of sources covering industrial development, real estate and construction, prevailing wage and salary rates, and comparative cost of living.

Industrial Development

Published sources on industrial development compare such factors as general business climate, economic growth, and the cost of doing business. Companies seeking to relocate, expand facilities, or build new plants need an enormous amount of information. Categories include the availability of financial assistance and incentives, the condition of transportation systems, labor productivity, and wage rates. Much of this information is only published at the state level, but some comparative sources cover larger metropolitan areas. For example, Dun & Bradstreet compiles the number of new business incorporations for every state, but reports monthly and annual business failures for the largest metropolitan areas.

Several high-quality reports compare business conditions for each state, combining insightful narrative with meaningful economic indicators. For over 10 years, the national accounting firm Grant Thornton has issued the annual *Grant Thornton Manufacturing Climate Study*. It ranks regions and states according to the economic climate for manufacturing firms. Factors measured include state policies on unemployment insurance and workers' compensation, energy costs, the percentage of unionized workers, and the effect of work stoppages (strikes, lockouts, etc.) on productivity. Since 1987, the nonprofit Corporation for Enterprise Development has issued the annual *Making the Grade: Development Report Card for the States*. This study looks beyond manufacturing concerns when evaluating business climate, but is otherwise similar in its approach. Characteristics studied include employment growth, the percentage of employees covered by health insurance, new company formation, educational expenditures, the number of working scientists, government expenditures for research and development, and the miles of deficient highways and bridges. In addition to ranking the states on various measures, it assigns "report card grades" in economic performance, business vitality, growth capacity, and government support. Both publications are popular for the same reason as the *Places Rated Almanac*—they assign composite scores based on numerous variables. All of the caveats pertaining to *Places Rated* are relevant here.

Though less prevalent, comparative studies of metropolitan areas are also published. "Metro Hot Spots" has appeared in the March issue of *Inc.* magazine since 1987. The research is conducted by the consulting firm Cognetics, Inc., and the survey focuses on the climate for small business growth. It examines approximately 190

metropolitan areas, ranking such characteristics as new business start-ups and the number of young companies with high employment growth. *Fortune* magazine publishes an annual "Best Cities for Business" in an October issue. It compares about 40 metro areas, and focuses on labor force issues. Among the factors examined are population growth, salaries, high school SAT scores, unemployment, and chief executives' opinions of worker quality.

Many printed guides and databases are designed specifically to assist corporate planners make site selection decisions. One of the oldest producers of publications and databases in this field is Conway Data, Inc., whose *Site Selection and Economic Development* has appeared under various titles since 1956. *Site Selection* is a bimonthly magazine which combines articles on trends and techniques in industrial development with economic profiles of states and counties throughout the nation. Each of the year's six issues focuses on one aspect of local development, combining directory information with statistics on local markets. For example, issue number 1 always contains Conway's "Geo-Corporate Directory," which lists the facilities directors (i.e., real estate managers) of major corporations across the country, together with news of major plant expansion projects arranged geographically. The other five issues present local area surveys of government agencies and officials specializing in economic development; major research facilities; statistics on the economy and quality of life; tax incentives, loans, and other inducements available to relocating companies; and office and industrial parks.

Despite its popularity, *Site Selection* is cumbersome to use. *Plant Locations*, a semiannual booklet from Simmons-Boardman Publishing, is simpler and more concise. This service gives summary data on transportation facilities, tax rates, electric utility rates, and other information of interest to companies wishing to open a facility in the state. It also gives population, employment, and wage rate data for major cities, and addresses of state and local development agencies.

Real Estate and Construction

Comparative information for real estate and construction markets is essential for builders, investors, real estate brokers, property managers, and companies and individuals making relocation decisions. Real estate and construction statistics are also strong indicators of general economic health. A breathtaking array of published products covers such topics as average home prices, office vacancy rates, construction costs, and new building projects. Producers of information include the Bureau of the Census, national real estate franchises, relocation consultants, and investment companies. Trade associations are an especially fruitful source of local market information. Important annual association publications include the *Guide to Industrial and Office Real Estate Markets* from the Society of Industrial and Office Realtors, and the *Income/Expense Analysis* series from the Institute of Real Estate Management. Nonprofit research organizations also study national and local real estate conditions. One of the oldest is the Urban Land Institute (ULI), whose mission is to conduct research on urban land use and development. ULI issues special studies and recurring reports on a variety of topics, and produces an annual guide to local real estate conditions called *ULI Market Profiles*. It provides narrative and statistical summaries for more than 25 major metropolitan areas, with brief updates on smaller markets. Profiles are written by leading real estate consultants familiar with the city they analyze. Authors follow a standard format which includes the general climate for economic development, followed by the real estate activities and trends in the residential, retail, hotel, and industrial markets. Numerous statistical tables make it simple to compare localities.

Numerous commercial publishers provide local real estate information, and many compile extremely detailed data. The F.W. Dodge Group, a syndicated intelligence firm owned by McGraw-Hill, maintains local offices throughout the country where staff members compile progress reports on every major construction project planned or under way in the community. Collected data include project cost, structural type, square footage, and the names of project owners, builders, architects, and engineers. The information is available as individual *Dodge Reports* or via the company's online service, *Dodge Dataline*. Dodge also produces statistical reports in print and online, and economic forecasts compiled in conjunction with DRI/McGraw-Hill.

The Westgate Publishing Company produces a monthly newsletter called the *Sales Prospector*. Issued in 15 regional editions, it lists proposed construction projects in the private and public sector, arranged by state and city. Announcements indicate the nature of the construction, the companies involved, a contact person, address and phone number, and cost information when available. The newsletters are intended to provide sales leads for companies seeking new customers. The information is also useful for job hunting, competitive intelligence, and market research. The *Sales Prospector* can also be

searched online in full text through the *PTS Newsletter Database* on DIALOG and Data-Star, and directly through NewsNet.

A final category of real estate information is cost comparison guides, of which there are many types. A basic service, *Home Sales*, was mentioned in Chapter 16. This monthly report from the National Association of Realtors compares the number of home sales and the average price of a home in states and metropolitan areas. A second type of cost guide compares the cost of new construction, either on a total project basis, or by listing the costs of labor and materials by type. Leading producers of this type of data are the R.S. Means Company, Inc. and the E.H. Boeckh Company, which both issue numerous comparative cost guides. A third type of cost service examines the cost of renting office or commercial space in major cities. One of the best-known publications of this kind is the *BOMA Experience Exchange*, an annual guide from the Building Owners and Managers Association International.

Cost of Living Comparisons

Cost of living is a fundamental issue confronted by anyone contemplating a move to another city. Such information is also important to employers, site-selection managers, marketers, and economic analysts. Unfortunately, finding information at the local level can be enormously difficult. One method is to obtain copies of a daily newspaper from the city in question and compare prices as shown in advertisements. Publications which afford a more systematic approach are few, and most focus on a single aspect of living expenses. For example, gasoline prices in major cities can be found in monthly issues of the *Oil and Gas Journal*. The federal government reports scant information on local prices, and most of it is narrow in focus. As an example, the U.S. Energy Information Administration publishes an annual report called *Typical Electric Bills*, which summarizes average electric utility costs for 6,000 communities. The Bureau of Labor Statistics's *CPI Detailed Report* has a small section of retail price information in the back of each issue. Four tables list average prices for utilities, gasoline, and selected food items by region and major city.

A bimonthly newsletter from Cost Comparison Counselors, Inc. called the *Cost of Living News* reprints cost-of-living surveys from government agencies, research centers, real estate firms, moving companies, and other private sources. Many of the surveys examine costs

at the national or state levels, but inter-city comparisons are reprinted also. Topics range from the cost of auto insurance to home prices.

ACCRA Cost of Living Index (American Chamber of Commerce Researchers Association—Quarterly).

The most extensive on-going survey of its kind is this quarterly study of over 250 urban areas. Researchers from local chambers of commerce conduct the survey during a three-day period each quarter, based on ACCRA's specifications. Participation is voluntary, so the number of cities varies from one quarter to the next. Also, some major cities do not participate at all. However, ACCRA indicates a typical report covers between 70-80% of the urban U.S. population. The *ACCRA Cost of Living Index* measures inter-city differences in the cost of maintaining a middle management standard of living. Data are based on average prices of approximately 60 representative goods and services, ranging from a pound of hamburger to a city bus fare. One section of the quarterly publication lists the actual retail prices of these 60 items for every reporting city. The main portion of the report, however, consists of the ACCRA indexes shown in Exhibit 17-2. For each of the six component categories, weighted averages are used to compare local prices to their corresponding national averages. Weights are based on typical consumption patterns of managerial and professional households, and are shown in the column headings. The composite column in Exhibit 17-2 indicates the all-items index for Manchester, New Hampshire is 22.3% higher than the national average, while the index for Hobbs, New Mexico falls 5% below the average.

Wage and Salary Surveys

Knowledge of prevailing wage or salary rates is vital to job seekers and employers alike, but information sources are scarce indeed. Numerous guides to nationwide earnings are published, but data seldom appear in sufficient detail. Chapter 15 introduced several publications from the U.S. Bureau of Labor Statistics which provide earnings information, but they are inappropriate for evaluating prevailing wage rates for two reasons. Most reports cite figures which include overtime pay and part-time work. Also, the data found in publications such as *Employment and Earnings* are reported by industry rather than specific occupation. The BLS series *Industry Wage Surveys* reports occupational wages within a single industry, but only 10 studies of this type are issued each year. Likewise, most nongovernment sources lack the level of detail researchers seek. For example, several

EXHIBIT 17-2. *ACCRA Cost of Living Index*

ACCRA COST OF LIVING INDEX   FOURTH QUARTER 1989   PAGE 1.6

COMPONENT INDEX WEIGHTS MSA/PMSA URBAN AREA AND STATE	100% COMPOSITE INDEX	17% GROCERY ITEMS	22% HOUSING	11% UTILITIES	13% TRANS- PORTATION	7% HEALTH CARE	30% MISC. GOODS AND SERVICES
Nonmetropolitan Areas							
Clinton MO	90.9	90.3	84.6	112.5	83.6	78.9	93.8
Jefferson City MO	91.2	92.8	88.2	86.7	102.4	90.7	89.4
Kennett MO	86.6	99.4	81.4	65.2	82.4	71.3	96.5
Kirksville MO	89.3	95.9	87.6	99.5	87.6	81.1	85.6
Nevada MO	89.5	98.9	69.2	98.2	80.5	81.9	101.5
Poplar Bluff MO	86.2	103.2	75.7	68.6	89.3	78.9	91.2
Lincoln NE MSA							
Lincoln NE	93.2	92.2	88.7	97.9	98.6	84.7	95.1
Omaha NE-IA MSA							
Omaha NE	91.7	92.4	86.2	89.9	107.3	84.3	90.8
Nonmetropolitan Areas							
Grand Island NE	91.1	95.3	77.5	98.7	100.1	84.1	93.6
Hastings NE	88.1	98.1	76.2	84.6	90.9	84.8	91.9
Scottsbluff NE	88.8	100.5	71.0	88.7	94.9	82.6	94.0
Las Vegas NV MSA							
Las Vegas NV	104.4	94.5	123.0	85.9	105.3	116.7	99.9
Reno NV MSA							
Reno-Sparks NV	102.9	95.8	113.3	93.4	99.3	110.7	102.6
Nonmetropolitan Areas							
Carson City NV	103.7	96.7	113.0	91.5	104.5	125.4	99.9
Manchester NH MSA							
Manchester NH	122.3	102.5	161.4	129.3	113.8	115.5	107.4
Middlesex-Somerset-Hunterdon NJ PMSA							
Warren NJ	138.8	118.1	211.2	113.2	109.3	121.9	123.5
Albuquerque NM MSA							
Albuquerque NM	100.9	97.6	106.8	100.4	100.6	103.8	98.1
Las Cruces NM MSA							
Las Cruces NM MSA	100.8	104.6	97.0	91.2	106.9	105.4	101.3
Santa Fe NM MSA							
Los Alamos NM	116.4	110.6	150.8	85.0	108.6	122.5	107.9
Santa Fe NM	112.9	108.8	137.7	87.6	115.2	111.8	105.6
Nonmetropolitan Areas							
Alamogordo NM	101.6	108.7	90.9	117.5	100.0	107.1	98.9
Carlsbad NM	95.1	110.4	80.1	79.4	105.7	109.3	95.3
Espanola NM	104.6	111.3	112.7	95.8	105.9	102.7	98.0
Farmington NM	98.2	102.3	98.1	97.1	105.9	95.0	93.8
Hobbs NM	95.0	105.8	82.2	91.1	101.6	97.9	96.3
Portales NM	95.7	108.7	86.0	85.7	92.5	92.2	101.4
Roswell NM	96.2	106.4	90.8	90.5	97.5	90.8	97.2
Ruidoso NM	104.5	117.0	91.1	108.3	106.5	117.9	101.8
Albany-Schenectady-Troy NY MSA							
Albany NY MSA	105.3	107.9	107.9	123.9	90.3	106.6	101.2
Binghamton NY MSA							
Binghamton/Broome County NY	103.7	99.8	106.3	109.4	103.3	98.3	103.5

organizations publish starting salaries for college graduates, including the College Placement Council, Northwestern University, Michigan State University, and the consulting firm Abbott, Langer and Associates. These studies generally report data for broad degree categories, industry groupings, and geographic regions.

Why is such fundamental and seemingly simple information so difficult to locate? Because there are too many types of work to survey. Moreover, every type of work has different job grades, reflecting varying levels of skill, responsibility, and experience. Wages paid for the same tasks may also differ greatly across different industries. Varying salaries from region to region and even city to city make the dimensions of the problem even more apparent.

Ultimately, what is needed is an annual survey covering hundreds of occupations and reflecting disparities in job grade, industry, and geographic area. Unfortunately, nothing so detailed is available in a single source. Instead, hundreds of specialized surveys cover narrow fields. Many are conducted by trade associations or management consultants. The cost and number of these surveys make it unlikely that most will be found in public and academic libraries. An alternative to detailed studies is the summary data found in trade and professional journals. Many periodicals conduct salary surveys as annual features; others do so on an irregular basis. The most helpful studies provide data for various job grades as well as for different types of businesses. Unfortunately, most findings are reported at the national level, or at best, for large regions.

One of the few sources of local, multi-job salary information is *Inter-City Wage and Salary Differentials*, based on a survey conducted by Abbott, Langer and Associates. This report reviews salaries for 90 occupations in nearly 200 U.S. cities. The range of job titles includes positions in clerical, technical, maintenance, and materials handling areas. Another annual study is conducted by the Administrative Management Society, a national association of personnel officers. Called the *AMS Office, Professional, and Data Processing Salaries Report*, it draws on figures submitted by members in approximately 100 local chapters of the Society. It provides salary data for 60 job titles, including middle management positions, clerical occupations, and such data processing jobs as computer operators, data entry clerks, programmers, and database managers. The salary figures are reported as mean and median values, plus upper and lower quartiles. Data are presented by region

and type of firm, with summary information for individual cities. In all cases, salaries are reported as annual amounts.

Area Wage Surveys (U.S. Bureau of Labor Statistics— Annual and Biennial).

Although limited in the range of occupations studied, *Annual Wage Surveys* is a readily available source of inter-city comparisons. It consists of approximately 90 reports on individual metropolitan areas, with data on representative jobs common to all industries. The same 50 occupations are studied in every area of the country. Uniform job descriptions and survey methods provide a standard of comparison found in few other studies. Since 1988, only the 32 largest areas are surveyed every year; the rest are done biennially, with each half of the remainder done in alternate years.

The basic job families covered are clerical, professional, technical, custodial, materials movement, and maintenance. Although the number of positions is limited, the diversity of those chosen is impressive, including switchboard operator, warehouse worker, and computer systems analyst. Tables in each volume list weekly and hourly straight-time earnings for every position. The BLS computes mean and median values, a "middle range" representing the two central quartiles, and a frequency distribution by salary range. Separate tables show the earnings relationships of similar jobs. For example, a chart comparing clerical jobs in a given metropolitan area might show that a Typist I earns 88% of a Word Processor's salary. *Area Wage Surveys* also present tables showing fringe benefits by occupation. Benefits include overtime wage rates, health insurance and retirement programs, and the number of paid vacation days and holidays. The benefits survey is conducted for each MSA on a rotating basis, every third or fourth year.

The BLS also conducts less detailed surveys for selected additional cities on an intermittent basis. Results are issued as brief *Area Wage Survey Summaries*. Finally, summary results for all MSAs are compared in *Occupational Earnings in Selected Areas*.

A government document with the uninspired title of *General Wage Determinations Issued under the Davis-Bacon and Related Acts* is a loose-leaf publication of the U.S. Employment Standards Administration. While it has a limited purpose, the amount of detail found here is absolutely unequaled. The Davis-Bacon Act mandates that contractors and subcontractors working on projects which receive federal funding must pay workers the prevailing wage rates in that area. To facilitate compli-

ance with this law, *General Wage Determinations* lists prevailing union scales for the building trades by county or county grouping. The information is remarkably specific, covering dozens of occupations including skilled trades such as Bricklayer, Cable Splicer, and Tile Finisher, as well as various categories of unskilled laborer. Data for each position include the basic hourly rate and the hourly dollar equivalent of paid benefits. For each geographic area, a list of paid holidays negotiated for the building trades is also given.

American Salaries and Wages Survey, *Arsen J. Darnay* (Gale Research, Inc.—Irregular).

A new product from Gale Research provides an ingenious solution to many of the difficulties inherent in published salary surveys. Using abbreviated comparative tables, the *American Salaries and Wages Survey* (*ASWS*) provides both occupational and geographic details for 4,500 job classifications. Data are gathered from 300 sources falling into four categories: *Area Wage Surveys* from the BLS, published and unpublished data from state employment agencies, articles from leading trade journals, and published reports from trade associations. Occupations are arranged by job title, then broken down by industry, job setting, and geographic area. Depending on the occupation, figures are cited for the U.S., for states, and/or metropolitan areas. In most cases, low, middle, and high salaries are reported. Because wage and salary data are published in numerous ways, the *ASWS* utilizes a battery of standard abbreviations to designate the time periods, reporting methods, and units of measurement found in each report. Although somewhat annoying, this technique is definitely necessary; even with abbreviations and codes, the resulting book is over 900 pages. Confusion is minimized by repeating definitions for all abbreviations at the bottom of every two-page spread.

The *ASWS* is the first publication to summarize salary data from such a diversity of sources. It is also the first to present such an eclectic array in a standard format. A great deal of thought went into this publication, and editor Arsen Darnay clearly understands his topic. An excellent preface explains many of the idiosyncrasies of the sources used, including the distinction between state governments' employer surveys and their corresponding job bank data. Complete bibliographic listings are also provided, so researchers can obtain the original publications. The first edition of this remarkable guide appeared in 1991, and researchers can hope it will continue to be published on a regular basis.

JUDGING THE QUALITY OF LOCAL DATA

Researchers must consider which of the many available sources of local data provide the most reliable information. Some publications are intended to provide a general introduction to a given locality, while others are designed to impart more in-depth, sophisticated analyses. Regardless of the source, an obvious question is: "How familiar can a national research firm be with market conditions throughout the country?" State and local sources will certainly provide more detailed data than a nationwide compendium, and local analysts will know their own markets better than economists at national firms. Information from a county planning agency, a local university research center, or even a state agency may reflect a greater depth of understanding than *Metro Insights* or *Cities of the United States*. On the other hand, data in some national publications are contributed directly by local sources according to a prescribed format. Examples include ULI's *Market Profiles*, the *ACCRA Cost of Living Index, Home Sales*, and the *BOMA Experience Exchange Report*. Estimates, projections, and commentary made from afar are not necessarily inferior to local observations because local analysts are frequently biased in one way or another. Furthermore, local data providers may not have the skills or resources to conduct sophisticated analyses. Serious investigators are advised to examine both local and national information sources.

How different can the information from various data providers really be? Two analysts can arrive at conclusions that are miles apart. Differences may be due to the level of care taken in the analysis, the recency of the raw data used, or other matters of quality control, but more often the discrepancies can be attributed to methodology. This can be illustrated with small area population estimates. The demographic firms described in this chapter are all respected organizations with good track records, but each utilizes different techniques. For example, CACI adjusts the population estimates created by the Bureau of the Census. To create those adjustments, they utilize a combination of four statistical techniques—two based on extrapolation, two using ratio analysis—then average the results. In contrast, the model used in the *Survey of Buying Power* incorporates symptomatic data, and *Donnelley Demographics* builds upon the company's extensive consumer mailing lists to create its estimates.

Estimates for a single location from three data companies can yield three widely different figures. The question of which is correct is difficult to answer. Esti-

mates from the Bureau of the Census itself are subject to error, and the only way to tell is after the fact—by comparing 1980 or 1990 estimates to the results of the decennial Census itself. Every good data company will do that, but even the best will have an error rate somewhere between 10 and 20%. The Bureau's own error rate for sub-county population estimates in 1980 averaged around 11%.

Certain problems are common to all methodologies: the smaller the geographic area, the less accurate the estimate; and the farther from a Census year, the less accurate. Beyond these general considerations, there is little the researcher can do to determine which source has the best data for a given locality. Even though an overall error rate may be known, there is no way to determine how those errors are distributed. Any company's specific errors will vary from place to place. Estimates for one area will be very accurate, while high or low for others. Unfortunately, one can never be sure which is which.

If no single source is head-and-shoulders above the rest, how can the user be assured of the overall accuracy of any guide to local markets? Start with the methodology employed. Some publishers include fairly detailed explanations in the data products—CACI and Woods & Poole are good examples. For others, the researcher should always ask for a summary of the methods used. Reputable firms will provide this on request, though some details may be proprietary. Why is methodology so important? Some techniques may be well suited to certain types of geographic areas and not at all suited to others. Extrapolation is especially weak for areas experiencing abrupt economic changes, for example.

Every researcher should compare the results of several studies whenever possible. For estimates which seem unusually high or low, call the producer and ask why. Sometimes it is the fault of the methodology; other discrepancies may be the result of procedural glitches which were subsequently corrected. When estimates for a particular location seem suspect, customers should determine if revisions or corrections were issued. To evaluate market firms that have been in business for over a decade, ask for comparisons to decennial Census data.

Find out if information is primary or secondary. Most publications which offer summary comparisons are secondary by nature. In some cases, standard reference publishers employ their own market analysts and demographers to generate current estimates, but many rely on outside sources. For many years, both Rand McNally and Standard Rate & Data Service had their own marketing divisions, but now they rely on others. Even sophisticated marketing guides may purchase some of their

numbers from other producers—data from Woods & Poole has been used in sources as varied as *Places Rated Almanac* and the *Editor & Publisher Market Guide.* Users should pay careful attention to where numbers come from. Does the publisher utilize certain information because it is readily available, or because it is a reputable product? Estimates from the Market Statistics division of Bill Communications are widely quoted in many sources because Bill's *Survey of Buying Power* is highly regarded by marketing professionals.

Commercial estimates may themselves be based on other estimates. CACI, for example, builds its population projections based on the official county projections made by each state government. There is nothing necessarily wrong with this, but users should consider whether the errors of one data producer are being perpetuated by another.

Beyond accuracy, researchers should consider price, format, and convenience. Price should never be the overriding decision rule, but it can't be ignored. Certain sources of market estimates are affordable to even the smallest company or library. Examples include *Local Population Estimates* from the Bureau of the Census, the *Editor & Publisher Market Guide,* and the *MEI Marketing Economics Guide.* Other sources are affordable because they appear as part of a publication with more general applications, such as the *Rand McNally Commercial Atlas,* the special issues of *Sales & Marketing Management,* and many of the media guides introduced in Chapter 18. For years, researchers really had few options when choosing data sources, but today the field is wide open.

Format and type of data are also important considerations. Given the common features of many of the sources described in this chapter, is there really much difference between any two? Most contain the same types of basic information, cover the same levels of geography, and include a variety of ranked lists. Almost all are produced by well-known, respected research organizations. Despite these similarities, almost every source has unique features to recommend it. Donnelley's *Market Profile Analysis* combines demographic data with information on business establishments, new construction, and bank deposits. CACI's *Sourcebook of Zip Code Demographics* includes its "Market Potential Index," and the *Survey of Buying Power* computes its famous "Buying Power Index." A few publications are extremely similar to one another—the *Survey of Buying Power* and the *MEI Marketing Economics Guide,* for example, or the publications of Woods & Poole and NPA Data Services. Even these present differences when examined

carefully. Therefore, researchers should make their own judgments based on individual needs. Required data will vary from one situation to another, and a single source will rarely answer all information needs. More often, researchers will need several publications or databases to retrieve market information.

Which brings us back to a point made earlier—it is generally unwise to rely on market estimates from a single source. It is also unwise to look at data for a single year, rather than comparing the trend over a longer time period. Finally, it makes sense to combine a variety of approaches and examine more than a few factors. Population characteristics may be just as important as buying power, and the strength of the real estate market may tell as much about an area as employment growth. Whatever the need, the products in this chapter can offer enormous assistance. But remember to resist the seeming certainty of the information presented; there is no substitute for healthy skepticism, careful reasoning, and patient analysis.

FOR FURTHER READING

A surge in research and discussion on the rating of community quality is due in large part to the phenomenal popularity of the *Places Rated Almanac* and the sustained debate it inspired. At the same time, social scientists have shown a renewed interest in the measurement of quality of life. Information on both topics is included in the list.

Measuring Local Markets

Papke, Gary, and Cheryl Inghram. "Detecting the Flaws in Market Analysis." *Planning* (June 1990): 18–22.
Tips on evaluating local area research reports. Common shortcomings include conflicts of interest, lack of familiarity with local conditions, and a tendency toward standardized "cook book analysis." Readers are advised to recognize the leaps from fact to judgment which all report writers make.
Paris, James A. "How to Read a Demographic Report." *American Demographics* 8 (April 1986): 22+.
Explains typical products and services available from data companies, together with a brief guide to interpreting demographic information.
Waldrop, Judith. "How Good Are the Numbers You're Buying?" *American Demographics* 12 (July 1990): 20–21.
A few brief, but important guidelines for anyone intending to purchase or use demographic estimates from commercial sources.

Wickham, Penelope, ed. *Insider's Guide to Demographic Know-How.* 2nd ed. (Ithaca, NY: American Demographics Press, 1990).
A wide-ranging collection of articles reprinted from *American Demographics* magazine. Most focus on sources of local area demographic and marketing data.

Quality of Life and Community Ratings

Landis, John D., and David S. Sawicki. "A Planner's Guide to the 'Places Rated Almanac'." *American Planning Association Journal* 54 (Summer 1988): 336–46.
This critique of the 1985 edition of *Places Rated* suggests that several of the key indicators don't measure what they are intended to, and that many variables are biased in favor of large metropolitan areas. The authors then report the results of a survey of local planning officials that found *Places Rated* was quite well-known among planners, but had no impact on local planning policies.
Myers, Dowell. "Building Knowledge about Quality of Life for Urban Planners." *American Planning Association Journal* 54 (Summer 1988): 347–58.
Myers discusses ways in which local planners can assess quality of life within their own communities. A five-stage method is recommended, including interviews with community leaders to determine factors important to the community; attempts to collect data which measure those factors; and surveys of citizens to learn their perceptions. The article then examines different approaches to quality-of-life studies.
Sawicki, David S. "Places Rated Almanac [Book Review]." *American Planning Association Journal* 56 (Summer 1990): 396–97.
This follow-up review of *Places Rated* covers the 1990 edition. Several key measures were changed due to earlier criticism. Some of the changes represent improvements, but others do the opposite. The reviewer demonstrates that many changes in a metro area's ranking from one edition to the next are actually attributable to the change in methodology. For example, Los Angeles is ranked #1 in "health care and environment" because air pollution was dropped as a variable.

Specific Information Sources

Crispell, Diane. "The World of Demographic Data." *Database* 10 (April 1987): 36–43.
This introduction to demographic databases covers popular files offered through major online vendors and the proprietary databases available directly from private data companies.

Harris, Laura A. *The Real Estate Industry: An Information Sourcebook* (Phoenix, AZ: Oryx Press, 1987).

An annotated bibliography covering most aspects of the real estate industry. The "Core Library Collection" includes descriptions of publications containing local market comparisons.

Robinson, Mark, and Jill Holden. "Donnelley Demographics and CENDATA: A Demographic Duo." *Database* 12 (December 1989): 13–27.

Detailed descriptions of two leading online databases, including sample searches and search results.

U.S. Bureau of the Census. *State and Local Agencies Preparing Population and Housing Estimates.* Current Population Reports, Series P-25, no. 1063. (Washington, DC: U.S. Government Printing Office, 1990).

A directory of nearly 300 state and local organizations which make population and/or housing unit estimates. Entries list geographic areas covered, levels of geography, demographic characteristics measured, and methodology employed.

CHAPTER 18
Marketing Information

TOPICS COVERED

1. Advertising and Media Sources
   a. Advertising Expenditures
   b. Comparing Advertising Costs
   c. Audience Measurement and Media Guides
2. Consumer Behavior and Attitudes
   a. Consumer Expenditure Surveys
   b. Public Opinion and Consumer Attitudes
   c. Consumer Confidence and Buying Plans
3. Market Segments
   a. Segmentation Techniques
   b. Lifestyle Analysis
4. Estimating Market Share
   a. Company Comparisons
   b. Brand Comparisons
5. Shopping for Market Research
6. For Further Reading

MAJOR SOURCES DISCUSSED

- *LNA/Arbitron Multi-Media Service*
- *Adweek Client/Brand Directory*
- *Standard Rate & Data Service Directories*
- *Television & Cable Factbook*
- *American Radio*
- *Broadcasting Yearbook*
- *Consumer Expenditure Survey*
- *Gallup Poll Monthly*
- *American Public Opinion Index*
- *Surveys of Consumers*
- *Lifestyle Market Analyst*
- *Market Share Reporter*
- *Simmons Study of Media and Markets*

Marketing requires an enormous amount of up-to-date information for planning and decision-making purposes. Every business researcher will find that marketing information comprises an important part of search activities. One reason for this is that marketing is all-encompassing, dealing with much more than just advertising and merchandising. In its broadest sense, the topic covers every function connected with bringing a product or service to the customer, from setting prices to determining channels of distribution. The need for current, accurate information appears at every stage of the marketing process. Nearly all publications mentioned in this book have relevance to marketing in some fashion. Sales representatives use business directories to determine potential customers and to research a company before paying a sales call. The strategic planning staff uses news articles and financial publications to keep abreast of the competition. And statistical sources are crucial to a wide range of marketing decisions.

Some of the most common forms of marketing publications were introduced in Chapter 1, including off-the-shelf research reports based upon one-time studies. An excellent source of research reports is the *Market Analysis and Information Database* (*M.A.I.D.*), from M.A.I.D. Systems Ltd. This full-text online system contains approximately 40,000 one-time and recurring reports from more than 20 leading U.S. and European research firms, including Frost & Sullivan and Packaged Facts. *M.A.I.D.*'s annual subscription fee is quite expensive, but heavy users of market reports will find this a useful alternative to purchasing print publications.

The most interesting, diverse, and important market research reports are ongoing studies known as syndicated intelligence services. These reports are the result of

extensive, standardized surveys sold on a subscription basis. Some research organizations specialize in narrow fields, while others are broad-based in their pursuits. For example, J.D. Power & Associates is the leading provider of data on new car buyers, while the Simmons Market Research Bureau tracks several hundred categories of products and services. Regardless of their subject focus, most research firms concentrate on a particular type of survey technique.

The complete results of syndicated studies rarely appear in published reference books or serials; instead the producers maintain large databases from which customized reports can be supplied. In some cases, information may be accessible online through the research firm itself, or subscribers may receive summary data on diskette or CD-ROM. More often, clients obtain printouts designed to address their particular marketing needs. Because of the cost of such services, and their customized nature, products of this type are seldom seen in public or academic libraries. In many instances, syndicated services are controlled publications unavailable to the general public. But readers should not assume that specialized market information falls outside the province of business libraries. On the contrary, an amazing wealth of survey-based information is found in reference publications. With the possible exception of investment data, marketing information constitutes the largest body of published business information.

A vast fund of intelligence is available through syndicated market reports, whether published or not. Virtually any information imaginable is likely to be found in some form or another. For these reasons, this chapter will discuss both published and unpublished resources. The material presented here is uniquely geared toward solving particular marketing problems. The topics covered focus on some of the most common information needs: making advertising and media decisions, understanding and anticipating consumer behavior, and determining market share of products or services.

ADVERTISING AND MEDIA SOURCES

The advertising industry is highly visible, and the activities of leading ad agencies capture a great deal of attention in published sources. One of the most popular directories in business libraries is the *Standard Directory of Advertising Agencies*, which describes ad agencies across the country and ranks the largest firms by gross billings. Annual rankings of leading agencies can also be found in special issues of *Advertising Age* and the regional editions of *Adweek*. Another way to survey the industry is through publications that highlight award-winning advertising, public relations, and design campaigns. A good example is the *Art Directors Annual*, produced by ADC Publications. This handsomely designed pictorial guide presents winning works judged at New York's "The One Show," a competition sponsored by the Art Directors Club, Inc. and the Copy Club of New York.

The following discussion will focus on three frequently encountered topics in advertising research: advertising expenditures by individual companies, the cost of placing an ad, and measuring media penetration.

Advertising Expenditures

Company-specific data on the amount of money spent on advertising by major companies can be found in the *Standard Directory of Advertisers*, introduced in Chapter 6. Publicly-traded firms do not divulge total advertising expenses in their annual Income Statements, but such data can sometimes be found in the Management Discussion or financial footnotes portions of the Annual Report. *Advertising Ratios & Budgets* from Schoenfeld & Associates, Inc., tracks advertising expenditures for nearly 6,000 publicly traded companies. This annual study also reports current and historical ad budgets, the ratio of ad spending to net sales, the ratio of spending to gross margin, and the annual average compound growth in ad spending for each company. Information is arranged by SIC category, so researchers can compare company performance to industry norms. Company data within industry are reported in ranked order as well as alphabetically. The publication also ranks the top 1,000 public firms by total ad spending and spending growth.

A diversity of market research firms track advertising expenditures for specific types of media. Among the many firms which track magazine advertising are Burrelle's Advertising Analysis Service, the Publishers Information Bureau, and Bacon's PR and Media Information Service. Most data of this type are sold on a contract basis as syndicated intelligence services, but the publications of two companies which report summary data in book form are described below.

LNA/Arbitron Multi-Media Service (Leading National Advertisers, Inc.—Quarterly).

This unique service, commonly referred to as *LNA*, consists of three different titles, each appearing quarterly. The set reports corporate advertising expenditures

for each of the following media: daily newspapers and Sunday supplements; major consumer magazines; network, syndicated, and cable television; spot television (local TV); network radio; and outdoor advertising (billboards). Broadcast data are gathered by the Arbitron Company; information on other media is collected by LNA and its subsidiaries. The data-gathering methods vary, depending on the type of media. Television and radio expenditures are obtained by monitoring broadcasts and applying the known ad rates for each. Data on magazine advertising are collected by the Publishers Information Bureau (PIB), which receives reports from some 160 contributing magazines. PIB magazines tend to be the more popular, high-circulation publications. Data on billboard advertising come from the Institute for Outdoor Advertising and the Outdoor Advertising Association of America.

With few exceptions, the figures in *LNA* represent a sampling of media firms, and are not the total expenditures of each advertiser. Despite this limitation, *LNA* is the most comprehensive, authoritative survey of multimedia expenditures; its data are used by financial, economic, and market analysts, and are widely quoted in numerous publications. Many trade journals rely heavily on LNA data for special reports on advertising trends within their respective industries. It is an important source of comparative data, whether the researcher is examining individual companies or entire industries.

The three LNA titles present similar information in slightly different formats. *Company/Brand $* lists advertising expenditures by company name, then by brand within each company, for firms with total ad spending of $25,000 or more. *Class/Brand YTD $* cites expenditures by industry grouping, followed by company name, then brand within company. The classification system is divided into seven broad industries, each of which is subdivided into major classes and sub-classes. *Ad $ Summary* presents information alphabetically by brand name, with no company or industry groupings. The quarterly issues of these three titles tabulate data as year-to-date figures, so that the fourth quarter publication carries total expenditures for the year. Only *Class/Brand $* lists both quarter-by-quarter and year-to-date statistics.

Exhibit 18-1 is a typical page from *Ad $ Summary*. For every brand name listed, total advertising outlays are given, as well as codes for the media categories used. Note that the company name is listed below the brand, and the industry code number is cited in the second column. Brand-level data are very specific. Motion pic-

ture advertising, for example, is listed by the name of the movie, and special ad campaigns such as coupon promotions can be found as separate listings.

The *LNA/Arbitron Multi-Media Service* is a controlled publication available primarily to ad agencies, media companies, and advertisers. Researchers outside these areas may subscribe to the *Ad $ Summary* portion of the service, however. Unfortunately, this is the most limited title in the set, with no analysis by company or industry. It is also the only title which presents only the media totals, omitting expenditures by individual media category. To offset these weaknesses, LNA does include some summary information on companies and brands in the year-end issue of *Ad $ Summary*. For every major class, aggregate expenditures are cited by industry, with classes appearing in ranked order. A second section ranks the top 1,000 advertising companies, together with expenditure breakdowns by type of media. A third section ranks the top 100 companies in each of the ten media categories. The top 10 brands in every industry sub-class are also given. The *LNA/Arbitron Multi-Media Service* is also available online through *M.A.I.D.*.

Trade journals also provide summary information on leading advertisers. A special issue of *Advertising Age*, appearing in September, lists the 100 largest spenders by total expenditures and media category, together with the top 25 firms within each medium. *Advertising Age* rankings differ from LNA's because the journal supplements LNA data with other sources. Based on contacts with the advertisers themselves, government filings for publicly traded companies, and other sources, *Advertising Age* estimates spending on direct mail campaigns, special promotions, and other categories omitted by LNA. Figures are broken down into LNA-reported data and the magazine's own "unmeasured estimates."

Of the many other periodicals which rely on LNA data, one other is worth mentioning for its unique approach. The *Public Relations Journal* analyzes LNA reports to create its "Annual Review of Corporate Advertising Expenditures." This interesting study reports company expenditures on campaigns designed to promote the image of the entire firm, rather than specific products, services, or brands.

Adweek Client/Brand Directory (A/S/M Communications, Inc—Annual).

An alternative to LNA data comes from the publishers of the *Adweek* trade journals, though the results are far less extensive. Brand-level figures are reported for 6,000 brands with at least $250,000 in annual expenditures. Information is provided by the advertisers them-

EXHIBIT 18-1. *LNA/Arbitron Multi-Media Service*

LNA/ARBITRON MULTI-MEDIA SERVICE
January - December 1990

AD $ SUMMARY
BRAND INDEX

BRAND/PARENT COMPANY	CLASS CODE	10-MEDIA YTD $ (000)	MEDIA USED	BRAND/PARENT COMPANY	CLASS CODE	10-MEDIA YTD $ (000)	MEDIA USED
MAXWELL HOUSE CULTURAL EVENTS	F171-8	42.0	M	MAYBELLINE MASCARA	D112	8,744.6	MNSYC
PHILIP MORRIS COMPANIES INC				MAYBELLINE			
MAXWELL HOUSE DECAF INSTANT COFFEE	F171	504.0	NSC	MAYBELLINE MOISTURE WHIP LIPSTICK	D112	2,690.1	MNSYC
PHILIP MORRIS COMPANIES INC				MAYBELLINE			
MAXWELL HOUSE DECAF REG & INSTANT COFFEE	F171	39.6	SC	MAYBELLINE NAIL COLOR	D115	2,476.3	MSC
PHILIP MORRIS COMPANIES INC				MAYBELLINE			
MAXWELL HOUSE DECAF REGULAR COFFEE	F171	8,494.6	NSYC	MAYBELLINE PERF 10 NAIL SYS & NAIL COLOR	D115	72.6	M
PHILIP MORRIS COMPANIES INC				MAYBELLINE			
MAXWELL HOUSE FILTER PACK COFFEE	F171	11,238.3	PNSYC	MAYBELLINE SHINE FREE EYE MAKE-UP	D112	234.3	M
PHILIP MORRIS COMPANIES INC				MAYBELLINE			
MAXWELL HOUSE INSTANT COFFEE	F171	15,668.6	NSYC	MAYBELLINE SHINE FREE LIPSTICK & NAIL PO	D112	234.3	M
PHILIP MORRIS COMPANIES INC				MAYBELLINE			
MAXWELL HOUSE REG & DECAF INSTANT COFFEE	F171	112.9	M	MAYBELLINE SHINE FREE MAKE-UP	D114	595.1	M
PHILIP MORRIS COMPANIES INC				MAYBELLINE			
MAXWELL HOUSE REGULAR & INSTANT COFFEE	F171	151.4	SR	MAYBELLINE SHINE FREE MASCARA	D112	325.2	M
PHILIP MORRIS COMPANIES INC				MAYBELLINE			
MAXWELL HOUSE REGULAR COFFEE	F171	10,126.1	MWNSYCR	MAYER & MEYER ASSOC INC	B152	27.1	W
PHILIP MORRIS COMPANIES INC				COMPANY UNKNOWN			
MAXWELL HOUSE RICH FRENCH ROAST COFFEE	F171	11,588.5	NSYC	MAYFAIR HOUSE HOTEL MIAMI	T431	190.4	MW
PHILIP MORRIS COMPANIES INC				HUSA INTERNATIONAL HOTELS			
MAXWELL HOUSE RICH FRENCH ROAST REG & DC	F171	37.1	W	MAYFAIR SHOPS (MISC)	G729	8.8	M
PHILIP MORRIS COMPANIES INC				MAYFAIR SHOPS IN THE GROVE			
MAXWELL HOUSE WHOLE BEAN	F171	555.2	S	MAYFAIR SHOPS APPAREL FAMILY	G721-3	17.5	M
PHILIP MORRIS COMPANIES INC				MAYFAIR SHOPS IN THE GROVE			
MAY CO (HH)	G724	13,445.7	PWSD	MAYFAIR SUITES SAINT LOUIS	T431	41.6	PW
MAY DEPARTMENT STORES CO				MAYFAIR SUITES			
MAY CO (MISC)	G729	4,301.8	PWOSD	MAYFAIR THEATRE	G321	91.1	W
MAY DEPARTMENT STORES CO				COMPANY UNKNOWN			
MAY CO APPAREL CHILDREN	G721-4	840.8	PWS	MAYFIELD DAIRY FRZN YOGURT	F133	57.9	S
MAY DEPARTMENT STORES CO				DEAN FOODS CO			
MAY CO APPAREL MEN	G721-1	5,042.4	MPWS	MAYFIELD DAIRY ICE CREAM	F133	7.6	S
MAY DEPARTMENT STORES CO				DEAN FOODS CO			
MAY CO APPAREL MEN & WOMEN	G721-3	67.6	PS	MAYFIELD DAIRY PRODUCTS	F139	46.0	OS
MAY DEPARTMENT STORES CO				DEAN FOODS CO			
MAY CO APPAREL WOMEN	G721-2	12,031.3	PWS	MAYFIELD MILK	F131	55.5	S
MAY DEPARTMENT STORES CO				DEAN FOODS CO			
MAY CO AUTOMOTIVE	G723	31.1	W	MAYFLOWER HOTEL NEW YORK	T431	168.4	MW
MAY DEPARTMENT STORES CO				MAYFLOWER HOTEL			
MAY CO DRUGS & TOILETRIES	G728	2,744.5	PWS	MAYFLOWER HOTEL WASHINGTON DC	T431	99.6	W
MAY DEPARTMENT STORES CO				MAYFLOWER HOTEL			
MAY CO FOOD	G726	34.2	WS	MAYFLOWER MOVING SERVICE	B613	27.1	S
MAY DEPARTMENT STORES CO				MAYFLOWER GROUP INC			
MAY CO INSTITUTIONAL	G729-8	10,418.9	PWS	MAYNARD ELECTRONICS INC TAPE BACKUP SYS	B311	15.9	M
MAY DEPARTMENT STORES CO				ARCHIVE CORPORATION			
MAY CO JEWELRY	G722	2,063.1	PWS	MAYORS JEWELRY	G712	576.8	MSD
MAY DEPARTMENT STORES CO				MAYORS JEWELERS			
MAY CO SHOPPING CENTERS	G719	18.3	O	MAYORS WATCHES	G712	8.1	M
MAY DEPARTMENT STORES CO				MAYORS JEWELERS			
MAY CO SPORT TOY HOBBY	G727	242.1	W	MAYPO OATMEAL	F122	134.5	S
MAY DEPARTMENT STORES CO				AMERICAN HOME PRODUCTS CORP			
MAY CO WORLD TRAVEL BUREAU	G729	4,575.9	W	MAYS DRUG STORE	G718	63.4	OS
MAY DEPARTMENT STORES CO				MAYS DRUG STORE INC			
MAY D&F (HH)	G724	2,505.8	WS	MAYTAG APPLIANCES LOCAL DEALERS	H219	1,188.1	WOS
MAY DEPARTMENT STORES CO				MAYTAG CO LOCAL DEALERS			
MAY D&F (MISC)	G729	1,438.7	PWS	MAYTAG DISHWASHER	H215	3,766.8	NSYC
MAY DEPARTMENT STORES CO				MAYTAG CO			
MAY D&F APPAREL CHILDREN	G721-4	207.8	W	MAYTAG MAJOR APPLIANCES	H219	8,484.6	MPWNSYC
MAY DEPARTMENT STORES CO				MAYTAG CO			
MAY D&F APPAREL MEN	G721-1	1,030.4	MW	MAYTAG MAJOR APPLIANCES TV PROGRAM	H219-8	52.7	M
MAY DEPARTMENT STORES CO				MAYTAG CO			
MAY D&F APPAREL WOMEN	G721-2	2,906.4	PWS	MAYTAG REFRIGERATOR-FREEZER	H211	7,823.3	NSYC
MAY DEPARTMENT STORES CO				MAYTAG CO			
MAY D&F DEPT INSTITUTIONAL	G729-8	1,578.6	PWS	MAYTAG WASHER	H214	13.4	SC
MAY DEPARTMENT STORES CO				MAYTAG CO			
MAY D&F DRUGS & TOILETRIES	G728	437.7	PWS	MAYTAG WASHER & DISHWASHER	H214	16.4	SC
MAY DEPARTMENT STORES CO				MAYTAG CO			
MAY D&F JEWELRY	G722	561.5	PW	MAYTAG WASHER & DRYER	H214	3,538.6	MWNSYC
MAY DEPARTMENT STORES CO				MAYTAG CO			
MAY D&F SPORT TOY HOBBY	G727	77.4	W	MAYWOOD PARK	G329	34.0	W
MAY DEPARTMENT STORES CO				COMPANY UNKNOWN			
MAY D&F WORLD TRAVEL BUREAU	G729	551.5	PW	MAZATLAN MEXICO RESORT PROMOTION	T432	1,079.5	WOS
MAY DEPARTMENT STORES CO				MEXICO REPUBLIC OF			
MAY FOOLS MOVIE	G310	125.1	W	MAZDA 323	T112	13,588.6	MNSYC
COMPANY UNKNOWN				MAZDA MOTOR CORP			
MAYBELLINE CO GEN PROMO	D119-8	72.5	S	MAZDA 323 & 626	T112	967.1	S
MAYBELLINE				MAZDA MOTOR CORP			
MAYBELLINE COSMETICS	D119	413.4	MS	MAZDA 626	T112	22,541.7	MWONSYC
MAYBELLINE				MAZDA MOTOR CORP			
MAYBELLINE EYE MAKE-UP	D112	7,885.2	MNSYC	MAZDA 626 & PROTEGE	T112	59.4	S
MAYBELLINE				MAZDA MOTOR CORP			
MAYBELLINE LIP MAKEUP	D112	35.7	SC	MAZDA 929	T112	7,883.6	MONSC
MAYBELLINE				MAZDA MOTOR CORP			
MAYBELLINE LIPSTICK	D112	1,745.4	M	MAZDA 929 & RX-7	T112	374.8	SC
MAYBELLINE				MAZDA MOTOR CORP			
MAYBELLINE MAKE-UP	D114	4,404.0	MNS	MAZDA B2200	T117	23.4	S
MAYBELLINE				MAZDA MOTOR CORP			

339

M = MAGAZINES	O = OUTDOOR	C = CABLE TV NETWORKS	
P = SUNDAY MAGAZINES	N = NETWORK TV	R = NETWORK RADIO	
W = NEWSPAPERS	S = SPOT TV	D = NATL SPOT RADIO	
A = ALL	Y = SYNDICATED TV		

Source: *LNA/ARBITRON Multi-Media Service*, as compiled and published by Leading National Advertisers. Reprinted with permission.

selves, based on an exclusive *Adweek* survey of companies with large advertising budgets. The directory is available in six regional editions as well as a single nationwide compilation. Within each geographic region, entries are arranged alphabetically by brand. The name and address of the company is then given, together with the total media expenditures for the brand, the key marketing executives, the lead advertising agency, and, where relevant, the ultimate parent company. An alphabetical index to brand names is provided. The national edition provides a separate listing of the 200 largest multi-brand companies ranked by ad expenditures. A/S/M also publishes an annual guide to "Superbrands," which appears as a September supplement to *Adweek's Marketing Week*. It provides expenditures data on the top 2,000 U.S. brands, grouped by 20 industry categories.

Comparing Advertising Costs

Potential advertisers need to know how much it costs to place an ad in a specific medium. In addition to allocating advertising budgets, such information can also be used to design the most cost-effective campaign, and to evaluate a completed campaign. For example, marketing managers can determine the "cost per exposure" by comparing advertising costs with the number of people reached by the ad. Many media directories, from the *Gale Directory of Publications* to the *Television & Cable Factbook*, list general advertising rates for individual publications or broadcasting stations. However, only one series provides detailed and current information on the cost of placing an ad for the full spectrum of advertising media.

Standard Rate & Data Service Directories (Standard Rate & Data Service—Frequency Varies).

For years, the Standard Rate & Data Service has provided the advertising industry with authoritative information on rates for thousands of newspapers, magazines, television stations, and other media. Major titles in the series include:

- *Newspaper Rates and Data*
- *Community Publication Rates and Data*
- *Business Publications Rates & Data*
- *Consumer Magazine and Agri-Media Rates and Data*
- *Spot Radio Rates and Data*
- *Spot Radio Small Markets*
- *Spot Television Rates and Data*
- *Network Television and Radio Rates and Data*

All publications are issued monthly, with the exception of *Spot Radio Small Markets* and *Community Publications*, which cover media in smaller communities and are published semiannually.

Each title gives a succinct description of individual publications or broadcast stations, detailed ad rates, and brief production specifications. The descriptions for print publications include the frequency of the publication, editorial policy, circulation figures, and deadlines for submission of ads. Rate information covers the price schedule for both black and white and color ads, the number of times the ad is run, and the position it appears in the publication. For television and radio stations, SRDS describes broadcast formats and rate structure, listed according to the number of times the ad is aired and the time of day. SRDS guides to printed media are fairly simple to use, but those for broadcast media are more complex. While general information on rates is given for comparative purposes, the user will almost always need to contact individual stations for more specific data.

The SRDS guides serve as excellent directories of newspapers, magazines, and broadcast stations. Since most editions are revised monthly, directory information reflects recent address and personnel changes. Several SRDS titles also contain helpful market data similar to the *Survey of Buying Power* and other statistical publications introduced in Chapter 17. Data are compiled by National Decision Systems, Inc., a well-known provider of demographic estimates. Information includes estimates of total population, number of households, aggregate household income, income per household, income distribution, total household expenditures, and expenditures in seven retail categories. These data elements are given for the United States, and for Census regions, states, counties, and cities. Additional demographic breakdowns are given for MSAs, ADIs, and DMIs. Special tables provide rankings by population, households, income, and expenditures for a variety of geographic levels. This market analysis can be found in the following SRDS titles: *Spot Television, Spot Radio, Newspapers*, and a special service called *Circulation [Year]*. Estimates are revised annually, but can be found in every issue of these publications.

Newer SRDS publications cover rates for alternative media. The semiannual *Card Deck Rates and Data* tracks rates for direct mail card packs, newspaper inserts, and other cooperative ad techniques. The annual *Advertising Options Plus* covers "out of home" media, such as billboards, in-store advertising, and posters in malls and airports, and on taxis and bus shelters. It also follows miscellaneous media such as college newspapers, airline magazines, and videotext systems.

Standard Rate & Data Service also publishes *Direct Mail List Rates & Data*, which describes the availability and cost of several thousand mailing lists of individuals or companies. Each entry indicates the source of the mailing list, the characteristics of the names, the geographic areas covered, and the cost per thousand names. This monthly directory is divided into two sections: a consumer directory which describes mailing lists of households available by characteristic, and a business directory which describes lists of companies by type of firm.

Audience Measurement and Media Guides

Marketing managers must consider the potential effectiveness of their ad campaigns. This can be done after the fact by surveying consumers to see if they remember a particular ad. Research firms such as Television Storyboard and Starch/INRA/Hooper do so on a syndicated basis. Another method is simply to estimate the number and characteristics of the viewers an ad could reach. Most media organizations conduct their own research and are happy to share it with potential advertisers, but many independent research firms provide unbiased information on audience characteristics.

Print media readership figures can be obtained from audit bureaus that monitor both the number of subscribers and the newsstand sales of newspapers, magazines, and other periodicals. Leading names in this field are the Audit Bureau of Circulation and Business Publications Audit of Circulation. Data from these organizations are reported in many directories, from Standard Rate & Data Service publications to the *Standard Periodical Directory*. For circulation data on daily newspapers and newspaper supplements, several specialized guides are available. One of the best is SRDS's *Circulation [Year]. American Newspaper Markets' Circulation*, published by American Newspaper Markets, Inc., is similar. Both compare circulation in a variety of ways. For every newspaper, readership is broken down by counties reached. Conversely, for every county, the circulation for all papers in the area is reported. Similar comparisons are given by MSA and ADI. Both publications include rankings of papers and markets, and both are issued annually.

Print publications are also read by individuals who don't purchase them; magazines are often read by more than one person in a household or organization, and are frequently passed on to friends, relatives, or coworkers. People read magazines in barber shops, doctors' offices, and on airplanes. In addition to total readership, market-

ers need to know how much of a publication is read, how long readers spend with it, and the demographic characteristics of the readers. This information can only come from survey data, and many research firms conduct ongoing studies of this type. The two most popular surveys of reader behavior for magazines are conducted by the Simmons Market Research Bureau and Mediamark Research, Inc. Major publications from these companies are described later in the chapter, though most of their information is disseminated through syndicated intelligence services and customized reports.

The best-known sources of audience measurement data are in the broadcasting field. Most people are familiar with the television ratings reported by the A.C. Nielsen Company, but other firms provide similar information for various media. Nielsen and the Arbitron Ratings Company are the powerhouse sources for data on television viewing patterns. The results of their surveys have enormous impact on what is seen on local and network television. Arbitron and Birch/Scarborough Research are the prime sources of information on local radio listenership. Nielsen, Arbitron, and Birch use different methods to conduct their surveys, including electronic monitoring, household diaries, and telephone interviews. Each method depends upon a random sample of cooperating households.

Information from audience surveys can tell the client not only which stations and programs are popular, but also the characteristics of the audience. Unfortunately, detailed data on how many and what types of people watch or listen to specific programs at the local level are only available to broadcast stations and advertising agencies. However, summary results are reprinted in numerous publications. A.C. Nielsen issues an inexpensive annual guide called the *Nielsen Report on Television*. It describes national viewing habits, including hours of TV usage by household type, most popular viewing times, audience composition by type of program, cable viewership, and use of VCRs. It also reports the top network and syndicated programs by audience type. Program ratings for network television at the national level can also be found weekly in *Broadcasting* magazine and *Variety*. Ratings and market data for television and radio are also reported less frequently by such trade journals as *Television/Radio Age* and *Radio & Records*.

Although local area ratings for television and radio are generally restricted to syndicated information services, local newspapers and business magazines frequently report summary data. Similarly, audience participation at the station level is reproduced in several

national publications which are readily available to outside subscribers. The following titles comprise the best-known sources of this nature.

Television & Cable Factbook (Warren Publishing, Inc.—Annual).

This two-volume guide to the television industry covers an enormous range of topics. The profiles of local television stations and cable systems in the United States are arranged by state and city in both volumes. TV stations are afforded single-page coverage which includes a map depicting the broadcast range, technical information on the station's broadcast frequency and power, station owner, founding date, network affiliation, news services, and key personnel. Summary figures on station viewership are provided by Arbitron, and population estimates for each ADI and county come from Market Statistics. Market data for stations are presented in three groups: counties where 50% or more of the households receive the station, counties where 25%-49% receive it, and those where 5%-24% of the homes are reached. For each county, an estimate of the number of households is given, together with the number which own televisions. The average daily circulation (i.e., households watching that station) is also cited. The same county breakdowns can be found for "Super Stations" which broadcast nationwide. Separate sections provide briefer coverage of public and educational stations, low-power stations, and Canadian stations. Again all three sections are arranged geographically.

Descriptions of cable systems are also fairly detailed. For each system, the *Factbook* identifies areas served; number of subscribers by level of service; fees charged; names of the local stations, satellite stations, and cable networks carried; local advertising information; and technical specifications. Cable listings identify the operating company and key executives, and indicate parent companies and degree of ownership.

The *Television & Cable Factbook* also contains numerous business directories, including listings of producers, networks, satellite earth stations, equipment manufacturers, companies which own more than one station, and firms which provide special services to the industry, such as attorneys and consultants. A buyer's guide offers classified listings by product or service. Special sections list new stations applying for FCC licenses and summarize station sales and mergers. The *Factbook* includes a complete list of stations by call letter, and a list of station allocations (indicating which stations in the United States can be found on channel 7, for example). Statistical tables summarize industry-wide data, such as aggregate station revenues and expenses for the nation and major ADIs, the number of TV sets sold each year, the number of video cassette recorders in use, and ADIs ranked by size. An international section offers background on the broadcasting industry in foreign countries. Country profiles cite the number of sets in use and descriptions of broadcast networks, including whether they are government-owned and the number of programs they carry. Complete subject and company name indexes are provided. The publisher is also known for its journals and newsletters on the broadcasting industry, including *Television Digest*.

American Radio (Duncan's American Radio, Inc.–Quarterly).

The main section of this guide to local radio stations consists of listenership data arranged by geographic market. Both Arbitron and Birch ratings are cited for each station, with Arbitron data reported for the most recent four quarters and Birch data given for the latest quarter only. In both cases, ratings are presented in percentages by share of the total audience. Individual station descriptions are brief, containing information on network affiliation, station owner and manager, spot advertising rates, broadcast power, height above the average terrain for broadcast signals, and station format. For every ADI, Duncan also ranks stations by listenership in six age groups, ten categories by sex and age, and five categories for time of day. A statistical breakdown of the number of stations and total listeners is also given by format for both AM and FM stations. In this way researchers can quickly determine how many country & western stations broadcast in that market, how many people listen to country music, and what percentage of the market they represent. Additional data for each geographic market include median household income, retail sales, population per station, and total revenues for all stations. Information comes from Market Statistics, Arbitron, and Duncan's own surveys.

Within every market profile, *American Radio* lists additional reference information on station purchases, format changes, and call letter changes. The Spring and Fall issues also contain a second section of statistics on broadcasting trends, as well as ranked lists of stations and markets. Examples of the more useful rankings are the top 50 stations in the country by local market share, leading stations by format, the leaders in each metro area, and the best markets for each format. The strength of this interesting tool is not simply the amount of detail it provides, but the analysis of the data by the publisher.

Broadcasting Yearbook (Broadcasting Publications, Inc. —Annual).

The *Broadcasting Yearbook*, from the publishers of *Broadcasting* magazine, provides less detail than the two sources listed above, but is convenient for its combined coverage of television and radio. The *Broadcasting Yearbook* does not give audience data for individual stations. The main section consists of brief descriptions of television and radio stations and cable services, each listed by state and city. An index to call letters for TV and radio stations is also given. Special tables list group owners of stations and cross owners—companies which own both broadcast and print media. Another section reproduces maps and demographic data for individual ADIs. For each county in the marketing area, the number of TV households is cited. Ranked lists compare ADIs by size within each region. The *Broadcasting Yearbook* contains numerous other directories of organizations such as TV film producers and distributors, television manufacturers, trade associations, ad agencies, market research firms, and even colleges which offer degrees in broadcasting. It also provides a summary of major FCC regulations affecting the broadcast industry.

CONSUMER BEHAVIOR AND ATTITUDES

A key objective of marketing research is to assess the potential market for a given product or service. A market is a group of people with the ability and desire to purchase that product or service. Each company is competing for its market with other firms selling similar or substitute goods and services. Researching the competition involves a supply-oriented perspective; researchers need to identify the leading companies in their geographic and product markets, monitor their activities, and keep abreast of trends in the industry. Sources and techniques for tackling this component of market analysis have been introduced in previous chapters. Researchers also need to compare the percentage of the market each company controls, a topic discussed in a later section. Demand-oriented market research examines the characteristics of potential or actual buyers.

There are two types of basic markets: industrial and consumer. Industrial markets concern businesses which sell their goods or services to other companies. Data on industrial market potential at the national, regional, or local level can be found in a variety of sources, from the *Annual Survey of Manufactures* to *Trinet U.S. Businesses*. The focus of this section will be on consumer markets, meaning the characteristics and behavior of individuals and households.

The most obvious way to investigate consumer behavior is to conduct surveys of people's attitudes, beliefs, buying habits, and media preferences. Indeed, consumer surveys are linked so frequently with the idea of market research that the public often perceives the two activities as identical. This is a fertile area for secondary information sources and the diversity of syndicated intelligence services and off-the-shelf market studies is amazing. For decades, marketers have dreamed of instantaneous access to detailed information on buyer behavior. New technologies, including interactive cable television, smart credit cards, product bar-coding, and the ability to match data from unrelated mailing lists or databases, have brought the dream close to reality.

Despite these breakthroughs, most data on consumer behavior are still gathered through more traditional survey methods. Market research firms employ a battery of specialized techniques—focus interviews, consumer panels, and the like—to create detailed reports. A consumer study could be designed and carried out for just about any subject a client could imagine. Many studies are custom designed for individual clients and become proprietary information. Others are published on a syndicated basis, but are sold to a limited audience of marketing professionals. A small number of services are disseminated on a wider basis, but even summary publications can be expensive.

An abundance of popular periodicals report on general consumer trends. Several glossy magazines are devoted to the topic, including the well-known *American Demographics* and the newer *Marketing Insights*. Many specialized newsletters gather information from all manner of sources and report brief accounts of shifts in consumer tastes and interests, including *The Public Pulse* (the Roper Organization, monthly), *Research Alert* (Alert Publications, Inc., biweekly), and the *American Marketplace* (Business Publishers, Inc., monthly). Such newsletters identify emerging trends before they become widely recognized. The *Future Survey*, introduced in Chapter 5, is an excellent index to articles on consumer trends.

The next sections will examine three broad categories of consumer study: general trends in household expenditures or consumption patterns; opinion polls which measure consumer attitudes and beliefs; and surveys of buying intentions.

Consumer Expenditure Surveys

One approach to the study of consumer expenditures is to examine total sales by product or industry. The *Census of Retail Trade* offers an all-encompassing look at retail sales data, but more specialized surveys are conducted by trade associations and commercial publishers. The drawback to studies of this type is lack of detail; most cite data for broad product categories only, and few examine sales at the brand level.

Another way to study buying patterns is to actually track individual products as they are sold, a process made easier by the widespread use of the Universal Product Codes on consumer packaging. At the retail level this technique is called a store audit, in which a market research firm collects data from a sampling of cooperating retailers across the country. Audits and Surveys, Inc., NPD Research, Inc., and A.C. Nielsen are well known for this type of research, and all offer customized product reports with data broken down by product category, brand name, and geographic area. Manufacturers can also use such reports for a variety of other purposes, including evaluating their distribution channels. Market reports generated through this method can compare sales by type and size of store, by type of location (suburban versus downtown, shopping mall versus business district), and by geographic region. A related methodology is to study sales at the wholesale level by tracking warehouse withdrawals. One of the leading firms conducting research of this nature is SAMI/Burke.

Whether collected at the retail, wholesale, or manufacturing level, sales data can provide valuable information on consumer trends, but cannot answer all marketing questions. Aggregate trade statistics, store audits, and warehouse withdrawal surveys can't explain who purchases particular products and services. Determining the characteristics of customers, and how they make purchasing decisions, is vital to market research. The best way to gather data on consumer behavior is through direct surveys of consumers. Commonly seen survey techniques include diaries kept by the consumers themselves, personal and telephone interviews, and questionnaires inserted in manufacturers' products. Grocery stores are now offering shoppers bar-coded discount cards, from which data can be tabulated at the point of purchase. The advantages of gathering information directly from consumers are many. This approach enables researchers to create demographic profiles of consumers, study behavior as it relates to different brands or grades of the same product, and study the complete buying patterns of household units, including amounts spent on different categories.

These surveys are regularly conducted for food products, health and beauty aids, and other common household merchandise, as well as consumer services such as banking and travel. Studies are also frequently done on "big ticket" items such as major appliances and consumer electronics. Several national research firms conduct extensive, ongoing surveys of 20,000 or more households, including Mediamark Research, the Simmons Market Research Bureau, and NFO Research. One-time studies are also likely to be conducted on just about any product or service. Examples of sophisticated publications which combine the results of expenditure surveys with other types of market research are introduced in later sections of this chapter. Among them are the *Lifestyle Market Analyst* and *Simmons Study of Media and Markets*.

While syndicated intelligence services and off-the-shelf market reports are quite expensive, many reliable studies can be found in periodicals and other readily accessible sources. Trade associations can be an affordable source of consumer expenditure surveys. Among the organizations noted for their detailed studies are the National Sporting Goods Association, the Food Marketing Institute, and the Photomarketing Association International. Another important source of data on expenditure patterns is the trade journal. In some cases trade journals summarize conclusions found in more extensive studies, in others they commission surveys of their own. Leading journals with recurring consumer surveys are *Discount Store News*, *Apparel Merchandising*, *Automotive News*, and *Lawn & Garden Marketing*.

The caliber of consumer data available in trade publications can be seen in two reports on the grocery industry. *Supermarket Business* has conducted an extensive "Annual Consumer Expenditure Study" for many years. The September issue reports statistics on total food expenditures, retail sales by product, and sales data for each state. Of particular interest to marketers is information on where consumers buy their food (whether in supermarkets, convenience stores, restaurants, etc.) and the estimates of average household expenditure by product category. A more detailed study of food expenditure patterns is *Progressive Grocer*'s "Guide to Product Usage," which usually appears in an August or September issue. It utilizes data from both SAMI/Burke and Simmons Market Research to provide total consumption information and characteristics of consumers. The analysis of each product includes the percentage of consumers who

are exclusive one-brand users, the percent who use the product daily, and a comparison of heavy usage for each product to the norm of heavy usage of all products. Demographic characteristics for product users include income, age group, employment status, household size, education, and region of the country. Similar analysis for consumers of health products and general merchandise can also be seen.

Although federal agencies don't focus on buying behavior by brand, the Department of Agriculture, the Bureau of the Census, and the Bureau of Labor Statistics study broad areas of consumer spending. In particular, they survey the percentage of household income spent on different categories of products and services, differences in spending patterns by type of household, and the types of stores in which certain products are purchased. While some of these topics might seem beyond the legitimate interest of the government, two public policy concerns dictate the type of data collected. One is the administration of social service programs such as food stamps, and the other is the design of the model for the Consumer Price Index. The following publications report the results of the government's major expenditure surveys.

Consumer Expenditure Survey (U.S. Bureau of Labor Statistics—Annual).

The Bureau of Labor Statistics has collected expenditure data since 1888 in order to design an effective measure of consumer price changes. The *Consumer Expenditure Survey* (CES) remains the basis for the market basket of goods that determines the Consumer Price Index. Previously, the CES was conducted approximately every 10 years, but in 1979 the BLS announced its intention to do the study annually. The CES is actually two surveys utilizing different methodologies. The Diary Survey is based on a sample of 5,000 households asked to keep a detailed record of their purchases for two consecutive weeks. The Interview Panel Survey is generated from a separate sample of 5,000 households interviewed every three months for five quarters. Slightly more than 100 metropolitan areas are included. The survey measures household spending patterns for food and beverages consumed at home, food away from home, tobacco, apparel, household supplies, personal products, housing, utilities, household furnishings, transportation, health care, insurance, education, and entertainment.

At first, the results of the two annual surveys were published on an irregular basis. The 1980/81 study was released in two parts, in September 1983 and April 1985. The two segments of the 1982/83 survey were published simultaneously in May 1986. The next detailed study covered 1984 through 1986 and was issued in August 1989. Now the report is published according to its long-promised annual schedule, appearing approximately three years after the end of the survey period. Although the reports were formerly issued in two parts to reflect the dual methodology, results are now integrated into a single report. The publication is issued as part of the *BLS Bulletins* series, though summary results can be seen in a press release from the BLS and in *Monthly Labor Review* articles.

Data are presented as average annual expenditures for each category and are tabulated by household characteristics. These include the age of the householder, race, household size, family composition, number of earners, income levels, home-owning status, occupational group, and region of the country. The survey also reports total household income by source, income taxes paid, and income after taxes. Detailed expenditure categories range from postage and stationery to floor coverings. Summary results are also given for 26 metropolitan areas.

Food Consumption, Prices and Expenditures (U.S. Department of Agriculture Economic Research Service—Annual).

The government's second major survey of consumer expenditures focuses on food products. The majority of this annual study deals with consumption rather than expenditures, estimating per capita consumption (in pounds) for major food categories. The total stock of food at the beginning of the year is compared to what is available at year end, an extremely complex task. The Department of Agriculture begins by examining supply at the processing level—grain mills, canneries, slaughterhouses, etc., then adds this beginning inventory to the amount produced that year and the amount imported from abroad. From this total they subtract the amounts used for nonfood purposes, including industrial uses, farm inputs (seed and feed), and exports. The year-end inventory is also subtracted, and the remaining amount is assumed to be food consumed in the United States. The methodology incorporates commodity-specific formulas to adjust for spoilage, processing waste, and related concerns. Raw data are obtained from the Agriculture Department's own surveys, from the Bureau of the Census, and from trade associations. This "residual approach" is crude but effective. The resulting estimates are not necessarily intended to measure the actual amounts consumed, but are extremely useful for comparing relative consumption of different commodities and for tracking changes over time. The survey has been conducted since the 1940s and each annual report cites 20 years of data.

Several other topics are examined in the study. Data from the Consumer Expenditure Survey are analyzed to show average percentage of household income spent on food items. Analysis of Census figures compares sales of food for home consumption to meals and snacks away from home. Unpublished data from the Consumer Price Index is used to present average retail prices of various foods from year to year. This report presents a detailed time series for studying long-term changes in dollar prices, not price indexes. It also measures aggregate retail sales of food items by commodity. The study documents changing patterns in consumption and expenditures, and uses alternatives to traditional consumer surveys to do so. Marketers can employ *Food Consumption, Prices and Expenditures* to track important changes over time—the dramatic switch from whole milk to low fat milk, for example. Researchers can also utilize price data to analyze the impact of changing prices on consumption.

A related Department of Agriculture publication, the annual *Food Cost Review*, provides detailed analysis of changes in food prices and the effect on expenditures. Its unique tables calculate the "farm value" of food, meaning the prices received by farmers. A "farm-to-retail price spread" shows the percentage of the final price accounted for by processing, packaging, advertising, distribution, and other nonfood costs.

Public Opinion and Consumer Attitudes

An alternative method of researching consumer markets is to study people's attitudes and beliefs. Opinion polling is an accepted part of modern life, and survey results are widely reported in the media. Most major news organizations sponsor national opinion surveys in conjunction with the leading polling companies. Business publications which cosponsor major surveys include *The Wall Street Journal*, *Business Week*, and *Fortune*. Most people associate polls with political opinion, but opinion surveys also cover social issues of vital interest to marketers because they gauge both what is popular and what is acceptable to the American public. Surveys are also conducted to measure consumer issues, including specific studies of products, packaging, and customer service.

Consumer attitudes differ from actual consumer behavior. For example, people may express considerable concern for environmental protection, but do little as consumers to reduce the levels of solid waste or air pollution. Still, opinion polls are an important way to monitor market trends, identify emerging opportunities, anticipate changing tastes, and modify existing products

and services before their popularity wanes. Sometimes it is difficult to draw clear distinctions between surveys of beliefs and behaviors because some studies track both. Combined polls are known as surveys of Activities, Interests, and Opinions, or AIO Surveys.

Several AIOs are produced especially for marketers, and are made available as online databases, syndicated reports, or both. These ongoing polls generally cover a large sampling of households on a monthly or quarterly basis. They are sometimes referred to as "omnibus surveys" because they ask a diversity of questions and may be sponsored by several clients. The following organizations are the better-known producers of sophisticated (and expensive) syndicated surveys. Yankelovich Clancy Shulman conducts the annual *Monitor* survey, which tracks more than 50 social and economic trends and their effect on consumer behavior. The venerable Roper Organization makes its *Roper Report* available online and updates it 10 times per year. Cambridge Reports, Inc. conducts quarterly and annual omnibus surveys which are made available as reports or online databases.

An alternative source of AIO surveys is the nonprofit sector. Approximately 30 state governments sponsor ongoing polls for their areas, and dozens of university research centers conduct opinion polls of all types. Several academic institutions are particularly well known for their nationwide omnibus studies. Perhaps the most distinguished is NORC: A Social Science Research Center (formerly the National Opinion Research Center), at the University of Chicago. NORC has conducted its "General Social Survey" annually since 1972. Approximately 1,500 respondents are surveyed each year through lengthy personal interviews. Core questions are asked every year, but each survey also contains a different module of special questions which focus on a particular topic being studied that year. In any given year, the survey reports more than 1,000 variables, from detailed demographic characteristics to social attitudes and behavior. The results are available primarily in machine-readable form, but summary data can be found in the annual *General Social Surveys Cumulative Codebook*. A guide to using the data tapes, the *Codebook* also compares the results of the current survey with those of previous years. Another summary of this important survey is *An American Profile: Opinions and Behavior*, from Gale Research. It reports yearly results from 1972 to 1989 for 300 key questions, with breakdowns by 18 demographic characteristics. The first volume appeared in 1990 and future editions are planned.

Another prominent academic pollster is the Survey Research Center (SRC), part of the Institute for Social Research at the University of Michigan. Its series of marketing studies, "Surveys of Consumer Attitudes and Behavior," has been conducted since the late 1940s. Most SRC studies combine opinion questions with those on consumer, social, or political behavior. A prime example is an annual project called "Monitoring the Future: A Continuing Study of the Lifestyles and Values of Youth." This ambitious poll surveys approximately 16,000 students at 130 high schools across the continental United States. It asks dozens of questions about academic performance, college and career plans, absenteeism, health, drug use, church attendance, employment, income, and use of leisure time. The survey also investigates attitudinal areas—personal preferences, levels of satisfaction, and values—regarding family relationships, political and social concerns, and quality of life. Detailed results are reported annually in *Monitoring the Future: Questionnaire Responses from the Nation's High School Seniors*.

Whatever the source, survey data can be delivered in various ways. Clients can subscribe directly with the polling agency to obtain summary results through syndicated services, online databases, or special reports. Computerized data tapes containing the individual responses to national surveys are also available. Machine-readable files are useful not only because they afford greater detail than summary reports and services, but because the user can perform additional analysis of the data. For example, responses to several questions can be cross-tabulated to examine relationships between different beliefs and attitudes. Likewise, the user can cross-tabulate demographic characteristics of the respondents to compare the beliefs and opinion of different segments of the population.

Many polling organizations can provide users with tapes directly, but several national archives collect tapes from producers. A major source of machine-readable data sets is the Inter-university Consortium for Political and Social Research (ICPSR). Their catalog of products and *ICPSR Variables*, their online database, were introduced in Chapters 1 and 3. A more specialized provider of data tapes for opinion surveys is the Roper Center for Public Opinion Research, a nonprofit organization located at the University of Connecticut. Though founded by Elmo Roper and still connected with the Roper Organization, it is an independent research center which collects survey results from dozens of companies and institutions around the world. They receive hundreds of tapes each year, from the three leading polling firms (Roper, Harris, and Gallup), all major media-sponsored

surveys, specialized polling firms such as Yankelovich Clancy Shulman, market research companies such as Leo Shapiro & Associates, and nonprofit organizations such as NORC. This archive constitutes the largest collection of public opinion tapes in the United States. Users can acquire the actual tapes and code books, or contract with the Center to obtain customized printouts and summaries. The Center also produces a wonderful online service called *POLL*, described below.

How else can researchers obtain results of opinion polls and consumer surveys? Summary results from hundreds of surveys can be found each year in newspapers, business magazines, and trade journals, and these articles are amply covered by periodical indexes and full-text databases. For those willing to spend more for printed information, several specialized periodicals are available. Louis Harris & Associates and the Gallup Organization each produce weekly press releases of their recent surveys, known respectively as the *Harris Poll* and the *Gallup Poll. Cambridge Reports Trends and Forecasts*, a monthly newsletter containing summary information from the omnibus and special surveys conducted by Cambridge Reports, is also available as a full-text database on the NewsNet system.

The publications and databases described below are among the resources most likely to be found in public and academic libraries. They include periodicals and newsletters which summarize major survey results, as well as specialized indexing and abstracting services. Each serves as a convenient guide for monitoring public opinion and consumer intentions.

Public Opinion Online (POLL) (Roper Center for Public Opinion Research—Monthly).

The Roper Center maintains the nation's largest collection of opinion polls in machine-readable format. In addition, the Center's staff compiles a database called *POLL*, which contains summary data from hundreds of surveys in the Roper archive. For many years, information from this important resource was not widely disseminated. The Roper Center provided direct online access to those who paid an annual fee, but few organizations subscribed to the service. However, since late 1990 the database has also been available on DIALOG. The major difference between the DIALOG file and Roper's own version is timeliness: on DIALOG the information is updated monthly; through Roper the updates are daily.

Each record in the database represents an individual question asked in a particular survey, together with a breakdown of responses to the question. The responses are generally shown as percentages. Also

given are the name of the organization conducting the survey, the sponsor (if any), and the title of the publication or data file where complete results can be found. Dates given include the beginning and ending dates of the survey and the date results were released. Characteristics of the poll include the population sampled, number of respondents, and interview method. Subject descriptors are assigned from a list of 105 general terms. Users can search by virtually any field in the record, including descriptor, polling organization, or dates. One of the most powerful features is the capability to search on key words or phrases in the poll questions and/or responses. Another useful access point is survey population and subgroup, which enables users to compare the responses of a particular group to different polls. Researchers wishing to compare different survey characteristics can search by respondent size or polling method. Although records summarize the responses to a single question, searchers can easily retrieve information on all the questions asked in a particular poll. (Average survey size is about 15 questions.) The file contains 140,000 records, with approximately 12,000 new records added per year. Comprehensive coverage begins in 1960, with partial holdings going back to 1940.

Gallup Poll Monthly (The Gallup Poll—Monthly).

Only results from polls conducted by Gallup appear in this affordable guide to current public opinion. The magazine has been published for many years under a variety of titles, including the *Gallup Report*. In any given year Gallup conducts over 100 major surveys on topics as diverse as the closeness of family relationships and general satisfaction with the quality of life. Recurring Gallup polls cover religion in America (annual), confidence in major institutions (annual), alcohol consumption (annual), the President's performance (bimonthly), and the most admired men and women in America (annual). Several in-depth Gallup surveys are not summarized in the monthly journal, but must be purchased separately. Among them are an annual survey of American's book-buying and reading habits, and an annual study of teenagers' beliefs, habits, and consumption patterns.

Gallup's monthly magazine presents summary results only. Each issue contains four to five articles of three to four pages in length. Each article provides a narrative summary, a demographic and geographic profile of the respondents, the wording of each question asked, and the frequency distribution of responses. In most cases, results are cross-tabulated by several demographic characteristics, and for recurring polls, a historical trend is given. The dates of the survey, sponsor (if

any), sample size, and polling method are cited. Most Gallup surveys draw on samples of 1,000 to 1,500 people. The monthly publication lacks a subject index, though the articles are indexed selectively in *PAIS* and *PTS PROMT*.

Gallup results are also summarized in an annual compilation from Scholarly Resources Inc. entitled *Gallup Poll: Public Opinion* (not to be confused with Gallup's own weekly and monthly publications). The annual compilation contains a fairly detailed subject index and summaries of survey results. The format is similar to that of the monthly journal, though the results are more abbreviated. Information is arranged chronologically by the date of the survey. Each abstract cites the questions asked, tabular results, and a brief narrative overview. Responses are summarized according to age, sex, income, region of the country, and where appropriate, political affiliation. A fairly lengthy preface describes Gallup's survey methods and sampling techniques, and a chronology of key economic and political events which might have influenced responses.

Public Opinion (American Enterprise Institute— Bimonthly).

Several periodicals combine the results of polls conducted by a variety of organizations with thoughtful commentary and analysis of their meaning. *Public Opinion*, a respected journal of this type, is produced by the nonprofit American Enterprise Institute for Public Policy Research. Its editorial board includes some of the most prominent names in American conservatism, but the journal is basically nonpartisan and frequently presents a diversity of perspectives. A mix of articles can be found in every issue, from explanations of how well-known surveys are conducted to what trends in public opinion mean for society. Several articles report the results of recent surveys. An important feature in every issue is the "Opinion Roundup," which compares survey results from different polls on the same topic. For example, a recent overview of opinion on income taxes included questions asked by Yankelovich, Harris, Gallup, Roper, NBC News/Wall Street Journal, ABC News/Washington Post, NORC, and several other polls. This feature is compiled jointly with the Roper Center.

A similar, though more scholarly journal, is published by the American Association for Public Opinion Research. Called the *Public Opinion Quarterly*, it offers articles on polling methodology and the impact of public

opinion, as well as summary results of recent opinion studies. It too contains a regular feature comparing the results of similar surveys, called in this case, "The Polls: A Report."

The Roper Center itself has begun publishing a bimonthly newsletter called *Public Perspective*. It contains signed articles from many contributors. Almost all articles summarize results from recent polls on topics of public interest. The articles (and the data contained therein) are brief, but *Public Perspective* reports on a wide array of topics, with more than a dozen surveys abstracted in each issue. A feature called the "American Enterprise Public Opinion and Demographic Report" is similar to the "Opinion Roundup" section of *Public Opinion*.

American Public Opinion Index (Opinion Research Service—Annual).

This well-designed publication is an index to thousands of public opinion surveys conducted by some 40 research firms in the United States. Pollsters include prominent market research firms, trade associations, universities, and media companies. The index is arranged by broad topic, followed by references to individual questions from surveys taken during that year. The index section cites the actual question, together with a code indicating the source and date of the survey. A second section is a guide to the survey sources, indicating the polling organization, the date it was taken, the size of the sample, and whether it was conducted by phone or in person. The annual index does not provide actual survey results, but pollster addresses are given for further information. The index is intended as a guide to a corresponding microfiche collection published by the Opinion Research Service. The collection is called *American Public Opinion Data*, and it provides summary results for the questions described in the annual index.

A second index to opinion polls is published by Greenwood Press and is called the *Index to International Public Opinion*. Compiled by Survey Research Consultants International, this annual guide covers surveys from 125 different countries. The compilers draw upon the work of nearly 100 research firms from around the world, utilizing only those pollsters with a reputation for technical competence. An impressive variety of subjects is dealt with, from religious and moral beliefs to consumer product surveys. Unlike the *American Public Opinion Index*, brief results of each poll are reported in the index itself, with answers tabulated by the demographic characteristics of the respondents. Results are grouped in broad categories, but detailed subject and geographic indexes are provided. Because it contains such broad-based representation from other countries, the *Index to International Public Opinion* serves as an excellent source for cross-cultural comparisons. The complete contents are also indexed in *DataMap*, an annual statistical service described in Chapter 4.

Opinions [Year] (Gale Research, Inc.—Quarterly).

Most of the guides mentioned above suffer from a lack of timeliness. For current subject access to recent opinion surveys, the best source is the Roper Center's *POLL* database, which has no printed equivalent. Periodical indexes are another option, because poll results are widely reported in popular newspapers and magazines. The *Business Periodicals Index*, *PAIS*, and the *Business Index* all provide standard subdivisions for articles which summarize public opinion surveys. For example, the user can look under a topic such as "Savings and Loan Associations—Public Opinion." The drawback is that articles on public opinion can be lost among the other subject headings, even with standard subdivisions. And of course, the user must still retrieve the original article to obtain survey results.

Many of the problems mentioned above are addressed by a new reference service debuting in 1990 under the title *Opinions '90*. Its editors systematically scour 1,700 newspapers and magazines for articles on public opinion. In every quarterly issue, the results of 150 polls of general or topical interest are summarized in single-page abstracts. The fourth issue cumulates the abstracts from the preceding year as well as reporting on 150 new surveys. The title is somewhat misleading because surveys of consumer behavior are also included. Topics in the premiere issue ranged from the use of condoms by teenagers to the amount of time (per trip) spent in shopping malls. Arrangement is by broad topic, with a detailed keyword index to subjects, titles, and organizations. Every abstract highlights the major questions and responses in tabular or graphic form, together with a narrative summary of additional results. Poll descriptions include the survey organization, sponsor, date, and sample size. The publication in which the story appeared is cited. An appendix lists addresses and phone numbers for survey compilers and the publications in which the articles appeared.

Consumer Confidence and Buying Plans

A related area of consumer polling is the ongoing survey of consumer buying plans and their expectations about the economy. Chapter 15 introduced publications which summarized economic forecasts made by economists and industry experts. In contrast, these studies ask

average consumers what they believe the future holds, and how they plan to react to these expectations. A variety of organizations conduct research of this nature because consumer intentions can be an excellent indicator of future economic activity. If people are worried about the state of the economy or their personal financial security, they tend to spend less. This type of data is useful not only as an indicator of economic conditions, but as a key variable in forecasting consumer demand.

One prominent source of consumer outlook is the Gallup organization. Two to three times per year, Gallup conducts a survey of "Financial Optimism." This poll asks the degree to which respondents worry about their personal finances, whether they had insufficient funds to buy food, clothing, or medical care during the past year; whether they feel better off financially now than a year ago; and if they believe their financial situation will be better a year hence. An interesting feature tabulates data for "Super Optimists"—those who feel they are better off now and will be still better in the future. Summary results can be seen in the *Gallup Poll Monthly*.

For industrial marketers, similar surveys are conducted to measure attitudes and perceptions of business executives. Several popular magazines sponsor ongoing surveys of this type, from *Business Week* to *Fortune*. A November issue of *Industry Week* asks 400 CEOs their expectations for sales and capital expenditures in their industry. Nonprofit organizations and trade associations also conduct surveys of executives' expectations. Two of the most prominent are reported in the Conference Board's quarterly *Business Executives' Expectations* and the National Association of Purchasing Management's monthly *Report on Business*.

Consumer Confidence Survey (The Conference Board—Monthly).

One of the best-known surveys of consumer intentions and expectations is conducted by NFO Research, Inc. on behalf of the Conference Board. The results are published in this two-page monthly newsletter. The survey sheds light on both consumer views toward general economic conditions and on short-term buying plans. Consumers' beliefs regarding the current business and employment situation are measured, together with their expectations for six months hence. Respondents are also asked if they think their personal income will increase, decrease, or remain unchanged in the coming months. The second part of the survey explores purchasing plans in the coming six months. Respondents are asked if they plan to purchase a new or existing home, a new or used auto, or a major appliance. For appliances, the responses

are broken down for seven specific types, from vacuum cleaners to air conditioners. This section also asks whether respondents plan to take a vacation soon, whether the destination is in the United States or abroad, and the means of transportation. Based on the survey, the Conference Board constructs a Consumer Confidence Index and a Buying Plan Index which can be used as basic economic barometers. These indexes are presented in graphic form in another Conference Board publication, the monthly *Economic Times*. Summary figures are also published monthly in the government's *Survey of Current Business* and in *The Wall Street Journal*.

Surveys of Consumers (University of Michigan Survey Research Center—Monthly).

A second major survey of general consumer confidence comes from the University of Michigan's Survey Research Center. Detailed information from the monthly study of confidence and expectations can be found in a 60-page newsletter. It measures consumer attitudes toward employment and general financial conditions, together with plans for purchasing a home, vehicle, or other durable goods. An Index of Consumer Sentiment and an Index of Consumer Expectations are then constructed and charted over time. Among the opinions solicited are respondents' assessments of the current economic situation compared to a year ago and their outlook for the coming year. Specific factors include expectations for family income, unemployment, price levels, and interest rates. Consumers are also asked whether they have heard favorable or unfavorable news reports which have influenced their expectations. The second component of this survey deals with the outlook for buying automobiles, homes, and large household goods. Unlike the Conference Board study, the Michigan interview merely asks if the respondent feels now is a good time to buy the items, not whether they actually plan to do so. Since early 1989, the Center's Index of Consumer Expectations has been a component of the government's Index of Leading Economic Indicators, so summary figures can also be found in the monthly *Survey of Current Business*.

MARKET SEGMENTS

Making sense of the torrent of information on consumer behavior and attitudes is no simple task. Knowing who buys a product or service doesn't necessarily suggest ways of identifying others with similar characteristics, or of focusing marketing efforts. Without target marketing, companies would waste a large portion of their advertising and promotion budgets on an audience

with no interest in their products or services. Marketing managers categorize the total market into identifiable segments and design a program to reach the most important groups. Companies tailor their marketing efforts to capture the attention of specific groups within the population—families with young children, senior citizens, unmarried urban professionals. The ability to target specific segments has become a fundamental part of the marketing process. Analyzing the characteristics and buying habits of particular segments helps companies create new products and services, design effective advertising and promotional campaigns, and utilize the most appropriate distribution channels. This type of analysis has progressed well beyond the study of basic demographic characteristics such as age, race, and sex. Marketers now focus on consumer behavior according to social, economic, and even psychological attributes.

Segmentation Techniques

The simplest approach to market segmentation is to conduct demographic research that focuses on the social and economic characteristics of the population—income, occupational type, educational attainment, household composition, etc. If the primary users of a product are affluent teenagers, then the marketer can study the growth of this segment of the population and identify local areas with the highest concentration of teenagers in affluent households. Among the resources for accomplishing this task are the decennial Census of Population, *Current Population Reports*, and many of the commercial products introduced in Chapter 17.

Few people would question the logic or usefulness of demographic analysis for marketing purposes, but in recent years many marketers have begun to view it as too simplistic. Alternative techniques have arisen to bring greater sophistication to market segmentation. One variation is to classify market segments by psychographic characteristics. Psychographics defines the characteristics of standard personality types by combining demographic analysis with psychological factors such as people's beliefs, attitudes, needs, and aversion to risk. In the strictest application of this technique, consumers are asked how they see themselves—the needs and values which motivate them most strongly. Based on these perceptions, researchers identify common patterns in consumer and social behavior, and create segments based on these categories. The first syndicated intelligence service to employ psychographic research was the VALS

Program. VALS stands for Values and Lifestyles, and was developed in the late 1970s at the nonprofit Stanford Research Institute (now called SRI International).

A variety of other segmentation typologies can be employed by market researchers. In recent years, marketers have found that the ways people spend their time can be an even more powerful predictor of consumer behavior than demographic or psychographic characteristics. This method allows marketers to relate consumers' activities and interests with actual buying behavior. Among the factors examined in "lifestyle" classifications are people's hobbies; their specific reading, listening, and viewing preferences; how they spend their leisure time; and the groups they belong to. Data are combined with demographic characteristics to construct profiles of differing ways of life.

Lifestyle Analysis

"Lifestyles" was one of the more irritating and overused buzzwords of the 1980s, but for marketers the notion has important applications. The ability to link different lifestyles with specific consumer behaviors was a tremendous breakthrough in market research. The term lifestyle analysis is now used to describe any segmentation technique that relates consumer behavior to personal characteristics. A variety of methodologies exist to categorize lifestyles, identify the households in each category, and study their buying habits. At the heart of each is the ability to pigeonhole consumers into one of several standard categories, then predict their market behavior based on the profile of that category.

Lifestyle analysis combines the efforts and expertise of demographic data companies with those of large market research firms. Companies which analyze decennial Census data and create population and housing estimates join forces with companies which conduct surveys of consumer behavior in order to build lifestyle profiles. Two especially interesting techniques for comparing local area lifestyle trends across the country are the analysis of manufacturers' warranty cards and a form of geodemographic analysis known as cluster analysis. Both methods will be described briefly in this section, together with major publications and databases which utilize them.

Manufacturers of consumer goods often include a brief questionnaire on the registration card the purchaser must file in order to be covered under the manufacturer's warranty program. The leading collector of data from warranty cards in the United States is a subsidiary of the R.L. Polk Company known as National Demographics

and Lifestyles (NDL). The company works with major manufacturers to design and collect response cards for a broad spectrum of consumer goods, from appliances to sporting goods. From 30 million completed forms received each year, NDL has built an enormous consumer database. In addition to supplying clients with information about their customers, NDL uses the database to compile consumer mailing lists by category, and to tabulate statistics on consumer behavior. After applying statistical sampling methods, the company cross-tabulates demographic characteristics with consumer behavior and preferences for the nation and for local areas. Profiles of households with particular lifestyles are thus constructed.

A second method of lifestyle segmentation is geodemographic cluster analysis. This system is grounded on the theory that the majority of people living in a small geographic area (a Block Group, Census Tract, or even a zip code territory) will exhibit similar consumer behaviors because most of us prefer to live in neighborhoods with people like ourselves. Neighborhoods made up of similar households are called lifestyle clusters. How are they identified? A sampling of households across the country is surveyed to gather information about people's beliefs, attitudes, buying habits, and leisure activities. At the same time, the surveys collect data on the social, economic, and housing characteristics of the respondents. Next, the results are analyzed to determine whether a strong correlation exists between certain demographic characteristics and consumer behaviors. College-educated white-collar professionals living in affluent suburbs tend to be heavy book buyers, for example. Combining all of the highly correlated responses of this population group results in a profile of that group's lifestyle. Finally, data from the latest decennial Census are used to locate geographic areas which contain a large percentage of households with those socioeconomic and housing characteristics.

The model for geographic clustering was devised by researcher and computer scientist Jonathan Robbin in the early 1970s. Robbin, founder of the Claritas Corporation, created a system he called PRIZM—the Potential Rating Index for Zip Markets. Using extensive surveys of consumer behavior and expenditure patterns, he divided households into 40 lifestyle clusters with such catchy names as "Furs & Station Wagons," "Blue Blood Estates," and "Shotguns & Pickups." The profiles of each cluster provide insights into the characteristics of each market segment. People in the cluster labeled "Bohemian Mix," for example, tend to read magazines like *Atlantic Monthly*, belong to environmentalist groups, eat whole

wheat bread, ski, and drive Saabs. While some of these profiles might seem obvious (or even stereotypical), they are widely used by major corporations across the country. Geographic clustering is probably the most popular form of market segmentation in the U.S. By associating every zip code in the United States with a single lifestyle cluster, systems like PRIZM help users target their marketing efforts to specific localities.

Several other demographic data firms have created clustering systems of their own. The major competitors are Donnelley Demographics (*ClusterPLUS*), CACI (*ACORN*), and National Decision Systems (*VISION*). One of the most common uses of all four systems is the analysis of a client's own customer base. Geodemographic databases can be compared against the zip codes in a company's customer mailing list to determine the predominant lifestyle clusters in their present market.

A certain faddishness is associated with geodemographic clustering, psychographics, and other lifestyle segmentation techniques. The proprietary systems created by major market research firms are named with distinctive acronyms and utilize flashy terminology. Some researchers are deeply suspicious of the gimmicky nature of lifestyle analysis. A reasonable person might conclude that this approach is too crude to yield accurate results—after all, people are individuals, and Americans tend to resist stereotyping. Even small neighborhoods exhibit great diversity. Yet independent studies have shown that various models do work, and that homogeneous groups can be identified. Most people living in a particular neighborhood or enjoying a specific style of living do exhibit similar consumer behaviors. These theories aren't suggesting that all people with a particular lifestyle are identical, but that individuals within one cluster are more likely to behave in certain ways than people in other segments. Marketers can therefore target their advertising, promotion, and distribution efforts to reach those areas with the highest concentration of potential customers. Lifestyle analysis is not a panacea, but combined with other research methods, it can be a powerful marketing tool.

Lifestyle analysis offers the ability to identify characteristics of target markets. Do certain households watch television more than others? What type of people are active in their community's affairs? Do they shop through mail-order services more than retail stores? Are they more likely to read *Architectural Digest* or the *National Enquirer*? Matching demographic characteristics to consumer surveys can provide the answers to questions such as these. Lifestyle profiles are useful in other ways. If people who enjoy gourmet food also tend to hold season

tickets to the philharmonic, then a specialty food shop can reach new customers by advertising in the orchestra's program, or renting its membership list.

Another advantage is the ability to pinpoint geographic locations nationwide, identifying large concentrations of households with the lifestyles marketers are most interested in. Other techniques are appropriate for local studies, from store audits to household interviews, but few methods allow the user to compare local markets across the country in a systematic way. Just as large research firms design sample surveys to track nationwide behavior patterns, local marketing companies can do the same for their own metropolitan areas. But locally generated surveys cannot be compared with the results from other communities. Conversely, most national surveys utilize samples too small to provide valid data at the local level. Geodemographic clustering offers an ingenious solution to these problems; relating the results of national consumer surveys to local demographic estimates conveniently sidesteps the limitations of a small sample.

The remainder of this section is devoted to descriptions of two specific research products which utilize lifestyle analysis. *ACORN* relies on geodemographic clustering, while the *Lifestyle Market Analyst* uses data from warranty cards.

Lifestyle Market Analyst (Standard Rate & Data Service—Annual).

This unusual marketing guide combines data on demographic characteristics with information on consumer behavior patterns. Although published by Standard Rate & Data Service, most of the information comes from the warranty-response database compiled by National Demographics and Lifestyles (NDL).

Lifestyle Market Analyst is divided into three sections. The first is arranged geographically, with two-page profiles of every ADI in the country. Data on two of the demographic variables—Race/Spanish Origin and Educational Attainment—are obtained from the decennial Census, but all other information comes from the NDL database. Among the characteristics reported are sex, marital status, age groups, household composition, occupational group, household income, and credit card usage. In addition to the raw numbers, data are presented as percentages of the total, and as an index comparing local conditions to the nationwide breakdowns. The user can thus determine that 10.6% of the labor force in a specific ADI are blue-collar workers, a higher percentage than in most geographic areas. The second page reports consumer behavior by 57 lifestyle activities. Lifestyles are grouped into five categories, from "high-tech" to "outdoor." Activities include Bible/devotional

reading, working on automobiles, attending cultural events, and foreign travel. Again data are presented as percentages, comparative index figures, and raw numbers. For every ADI, the top 10 lifestyles are ranked, and the average number of interests per respondent are cited.

The second section analyzes data for each of the 57 lifestyle interests. The researcher can use these profiles to determine the demographic characteristics of coin and stamp collectors, gourmet cooks, or fishing enthusiasts, for example. Each activity is also cross-tabulated with all other interests, and again the top 10 lifestyles are ranked. This type of analysis is wonderful for countering preconceived notions about one's market. For example, the profile of people who enter sweepstakes shows that they like to explore money making opportunities, shop by catalog, do crossword puzzles, read science fiction, and wear fashionable clothing. While the first three characteristics might seem predictable, the latter two are much less so. The final component of this section ranks every ADI according to that lifestyle interest.

The third section, called "Consumer Segment Profiles," presents a similar analysis by household characteristics. More than 40 segments are described and each is based on a combination of age, income, marital status, and family composition. As an example, one segment analyzes the characteristics of dual-income households with children under 13 years of age. Data are given by demographic characteristics and lifestyle activities, with the top 10 interests ranked for each segment. All ADIs are also ranked by segment. Subscribers to the basic report can also request customized analyses from the publisher at a reduced rate. These special reports are available by zip code, zip code groups, MSAs, or states.

Information in the *Lifestyle Market Analyst* is easy to use and well presented. Arrangement in three segments makes the publication useful for a variety of marketing situations. It is also one of the few marketing services of this type available to a wide audience, being neither a controlled publication nor prohibitively expensive.

ACORN (CACI Marketing Systems—Annual).

CACI is a well-known supplier of population estimates, projections, and marketing data for local areas, and a leading source of lifestyle profiles for geographic clusters. The clustering system devised by CACI is called *ACORN*, "A Classification of Residential Neighborhoods." The company has categorized every Census Block Group or Enumeration District into one of 44 predetermined market segments, based on homogeneous demographic, social, economic, and housing characteristics. While PRIZM utilizes flashy names for its clusters,

CACI's terminology is more straightforward. The classification is organized into 13 broad categories, which are then subdivided into the more specific clusters. For example, "Upper-Middle Income, High Value Suburbs" are subdivided into five clusters—newer suburbs, postwar suburbs, highly mobile young families, families with older children, and middle-income, blue collar households.

CACI creates lifestyle profiles for each cluster through a cooperative venture with well-known consumer research firm Mediamark Research, Inc. Mediamark conducts a semiannual survey of consumer buying habits and media behavior based on interviews and questionnaires with 40,000 households. Every respondent is matched to a particular *ACORN* cluster based on his/her address, and the buying behavior of that cluster is then analyzed. Information derived from the *ACORN* system is available in a variety of formats, but CACI provides most services on a customized basis. Summary *ACORN* data are available in standardized reports for individual units of geography. These summary reports can be obtained as printed reports and floppy diskettes, or can be retrieved online as a subset of CACI's *SUPERSITE* database, partially described in Chapter 17.

SUPERSITE focuses on consumer characteristics for virtually all levels of geography, from state to Census Tract. *ACORN* data are available for each of these units, but the most commonly requested reports are by zip code. For any geographic area, *SUPERSITE* can indicate the distribution of *ACORN* clusters. But the basic unit of *ACORN* analysis is the Block Group, so even a zip code may be comprised of several different clusters of Block Groups. A given zip code may be made up of 42.6% "Upper-middle income, high value suburbs," 46.9% "Wealthy areas," and smaller percentages of two other lifestyle clusters.

On the CompuServe system, the *ACORN* subfile of *SUPERSITE* provides limited information. For any specified geographic area, it lists the distribution of *ACORN* clusters as described above. Several standard formats are available; current estimates of cluster distribution can be retrieved by number of people or number of households, and five-year projections are also available. Subscribers can then turn to the printed *ACORN Users Guide* or the abbreviated version online to examine the consumer characteristics of each lifestyle cluster. Unfortunately, the *ACORN* subfile on CompuServe does not allow the searcher to create a list of zip codes with the highest percentage of a given cluster, nor does it offer detailed profiles of each market segment. Still, it is one of the only widely published sources of geodemographic clusters.

ESTIMATING MARKET SHARE

For librarians and researchers, the most frequently encountered marketing questions involve market share: What share of the market is held by company X? What are the best-selling brands of product Y? Who are the leading companies in industry Z? The answers to such questions can be difficult to find. And once data are found, researchers must seriously question their meaning. A significant problem is determining what is being measured, or what should be measured. First comes the issue of defining the market. For example, a small printing firm may be selling within a single metropolitan area. To obtain share data, the owner could compare his sales figures to data from the Bureau of the Census on total industry revenues for the MSA. He might discover that he commands 20% of the market, which is impressive considering there are 165 printing Establishments in the area. For the owner of a corner convenience store, this method is inappropriate; her market might be a 20-block neighborhood. These examples may seem fairly obvious, but others are less so.

Next, the market needs to be defined as to the scope of the industry under consideration. Competition can come from firms outside the industry. The convenience store is also competing with local drug stores, supermarkets, newsstands, and other retail outlets. Third, the product or service being measured must be defined. For the print shop, the owner's total market share will differ from his share of business in specific areas—wedding invitations, letterhead, business forms.

Defining the market should never be taken for granted, even where it might appear obvious. For large companies, the geographic market is usually considered to be nationwide, but it could be regional, or even international. Product markets are especially fragmented for consumer goods. It doesn't mean much to compare market share for athletic footwear, because there are many market segments, including high-tech shoes for professional athletes, high-priced designer products, and inexpensive knock-around shoes. Even a seemingly homogeneous product like deodorant has segments—men versus women, roll-on versus spray. And many products have substitute goods which might command an important share of the total market. For example, the market for soft drinks may not be a simple matter of colas versus non-colas. Carbonated beverages may receive stiff competition from noncarbonated soft drinks, fruit juices, or even from bottled water. Before any market share data are used, the researcher should ask, "What market is being measured?"

The methodology used in gathering data is also important. All of the many ways to arrive at a figure for market share involve estimates. Depending on the market definition and the estimation methods used, three different sources are likely to yield wildly different results. And the issue is not only how well a particular method is executed, but whether it is a reasonable approach.

A company may be able to estimate its own market share by comparing internal sales data to industry totals reported by the Economic Census, trade associations, or other reliable sources. But how can the firm obtain the same information on its competitors? Similarly, how can an outside researcher find this type of information? Broadly speaking, there are two approaches to measuring market share; one is to compare data at the company level, the other is to examine sales by individual brand. Both will be discussed in turn.

Company Comparisons

One of the simplest and most frequently used ways to estimate share data is to compare sales for leading companies with total industry sales. Unfortunately, it is also one of the least accurate techniques. The two main deficiencies of this method are related to one another. First, industry sales in most cases cannot be equated with product sales. And second, most companies are engaged in more than one industry—they make more than one type of product, or provide more than one type of service. It would be incorrect to say that Quaker Oats sells more cold cereal than Kellogg simply because Quaker is a bigger company. Quaker Oats manufactures a diverse line of food products, including frozen pizza, pancake mixes and syrup, canned beans, prepared foods, beverages, and, of course, oats and oatmeal. Quaker is also a leading producer of pet foods, and until recently, owned many nonfood subsidiaries, from toy companies to clothing stores.

The degree of industry concentration plays an important role in market share. In some industries, relatively few companies dominate the entire market, and smaller firms compete for very small portions of the remaining pie. A surprising number of U.S. industries are highly concentrated, with markets controlled by a handful of companies. In some cases, this concentration may be hidden by a proliferation of brand names owned by a small number of firms. The more concentrated the industry, the easier it will be to find share data. A related point is that some products are so specialized there may be very few competitors. For example, dozens of firms may produce telecommunications systems, but only a few will make a specific type of equipment.

When seeking data on market share, it helps to understand the characteristics of the industry. Is it highly concentrated? Are firms in the industry highly diversified (that is, do they make or do lots of other things)? How specialized is the industry—do lots of other industries engage in this activity as a secondary venture, or is most of the output accounted for by the primary industry alone? Knowing the basic structure of the industry will enable you to select the most appropriate source of market share information, interpret data much more accurately, and evaluate its reliability with greater confidence. The best place to find background on industry composition is the Economic Census and other sources covered in Chapter 16.

The only way to use company sales to accurately determine market share is to obtain breakdowns of each firm's revenues by type of product. Unfortunately, such information is rarely reported by the companies themselves. For large, publicly held corporations, the researcher might locate sales data by business segment (also called line of business), but segment data are rarely comparable—segments are loosely defined by each company and are purposely designed to be as broad as possible. Quaker, for instance, includes cold cereal in a broad "food products" segment. Trinet, Inc. has attempted to side-step this problem by using Establishment-level sales data to estimate both industry and company sales. The *Trinet U.S. Businesses* database, introduced in Chapter 6, offers standardized reports which calculate industry market share by company. This analysis is based on the premise that an individual plant location will usually restrict its activities to a single product category. If ten Establishments within a company are engaged in the same activity, then the sum of their revenues should equal the firm's total sales for that product. But sales data at the Establishment level are equally difficult to come by, so Trinet must rely on its own estimates in most cases.

Wall Street analysts' reports, discussed in Chapter 12, can offer a more reliable source of company comparisons. Investment analysts frequently have access to data on company sales by product type. And because every analyst specializes in a particular industry, they can obtain comparable figures for most, if not all leading companies in the industry. This gives them a unique vantage point from which to estimate market share. And though brokerage reports focus on publicly traded companies, analysts usually include information on major

privately held competitors. Trade associations may also be able to collect and compile market share data for specific industries because they promise their members complete confidentiality. Editors of trade journals and newsletters may also obtain detailed company sales data. In fact, some newsletters focus almost entirely on market issues; an excellent example is *Beer Marketer's Insights*, a biweekly publication by a firm of the same name.

Trade journals and newsletters can also be a valuable source of secondary information. They may summarize the results of more extensive (and costly) market research reports which may be otherwise unavailable. General periodical indexes, from *Predicasts F&S Index* to *ABI/INFORM*, can provide access to articles which mention market share. Online and CD-ROM versions are especially helpful because the searcher can look for any occurrence of the phrase "market share" (or similar phrases), regardless of whether the indexer assigned that subject heading. Other useful finding tools include the *Statistical Reference Index, Industry Data Sources*, and the *Business Rankings Annual*.

Market Share Reporter, Arsen J. Darnay   (Gale Research, Inc.—Irregular).

The only reference tool devoted exclusively to market share data is the *Market Share Reporter*, which covers 2,000 product and service categories in all industries. Most of the data are obtained from several hundred trade journals, newsletters, business magazines, and newspapers, but approximately one-fourth of the listings are based on analysts' reports, as published in the *Investext* database. Arrangement is by two-digit SIC grouping, with indexes by subject, company, geographic area, and information source.

Market share is loosely defined here, and researchers may be slightly confused or disappointed by the hodge-podge of information. Market information includes more than company-specific comparisons; among the other categories are product types, usage, production capacity, distribution outlets, organization types, and places. Users can find such diverse percentages as newspaper circulation by type of paper, steel production by country, greeting card sales by type of store, number of pancake restaurants by region, and lawn mower sales by price range. Still, numerous listings focus on more traditional market share concerns. Most of these compare data by company, but some brand-level analysis is given.

Each listing cites the companies, brands, products, or other topics being compared, together with market data reported as percentages. Brief notes explain what is being measured and cite data sources (including both the publication where the numbers were found and the original data supplier). While casual users will be content to use the summary data listed in the *Market Share Reporter*, serious researchers will want to consult the primary sources for further information. The principal value of this unique publication is convenience. It covers a remarkable range of topics gathered from a diversity of sources, summarizes data in easily scanned lists (often accompanied by bar or pie charts), and offers extensive, detailed indexing. The first edition of *Market Share Reporter* was published in 1991.

Brand Comparisons

For most consumer products and services, market share is more meaningful when reported at the brand level, or at least by groups of brands. Obtaining information for brand analysis can be surprisingly easy. This is because brand-level information can be gathered at the point of purchase or from the actual consumers. Once again, all techniques employed for this analysis involve sample surveys of some type.

As mentioned earlier, a common method of gathering market data by brand name is to enlist the aid of cooperating retailers or wholesalers, and to tabulate product movement at selected stores or warehouses. Audits and Surveys, Inc., A.C. Nielsen, SAMI/Burke, and other companies use this approach to provide market share reports. Typical data available for each brand include number of units sold, dollar volume of sales, average price, percentage of stores stocking that brand, average number of brands per store, and percentage of the total market.

An alternative approach is to survey consumers directly. Surveys may involve mailed questionnaires, personal interviews, asking families to keep detailed diaries of household purchases, or a combination of methods. Obtaining brand data directly from consumers allows other information to be collected at the same time. Commonly studied attributes and behaviors include socioeconomic characteristics, information on lifestyles and personalities, and exposure to different advertising media. Marketers can cross-tabulate data to create profiles of frequent buyers, at both the product and brand level. Companies providing this type of report are the Market Research Corporation of America and NFO Research, Inc.

Results from market surveys are usually available as customized reports, but may also appear as standardized summary publications, or as online databases. They can usually be characterized as syndicated intelligence services rather than one-time market studies. Unfortunately, these reports are often either controlled publications or extremely expensive. Thus, they are seldom found in academic or public libraries, though they may be common in specialized corporate libraries. The one product available from a leading market research firm introduced below was chosen because it is probably the most detailed, versatile, and powerful resource of its type.

Simmons Study of Media and Markets (Simmons Market Research, Inc.—Annual).

This remarkable publication is based on an extensive annual survey of 19,000 households in the United States. Data are gathered through a combination of personal interviews, telephone surveys, self-administered questionnaires, and consumer diaries. The surveys measure usage of products and services by brand name, characteristics of the respondents, and their exposure to different media. Simmons then cross-tabulates results to report information on the demographic and psychographic characteristics of individuals who use each product, and their media behavior. The annual publication is enormous, appearing as 43 separate reports, plus one volume of technical documentation. The set is divided into two types of reports: 13 volumes focusing on media behavior, and 30 examining product or service usage.

The Media Reports cover newspapers, magazines, television and radio, billboards and more. Data are given not only for categories of programs or publications, but for specific periodicals or shows. Television coverage includes weekly series, movies, and special programming. The various reports measure demographic characteristics of readers, listeners, and viewers, as well as exposure patterns. Reports on magazine readership, for example, indicate whether the publication was read in the home, in someone else's home, at work, or at a barber shop/beauty parlor. For TV viewership, the level of attentiveness is reported, indicating whether each member of the household was present in the room, and, if so, whether they were paying full or partial attention to the program. Another report, entitled "Media Imperatives," measures the type of media that respondents follow most heavily, then compares specific publications or programs to other media. The user can thus determine that readers of a certain magazine are not heavy readers in general, but that they watch lots of television.

The Product Reports cover the gamut of household items, from cold remedies to packaged Mexican foods. Services are also tracked, including insurance, banking, and auto repair. In fact, the full spectrum of consumer activity is measured—pay television subscriptions, credit card use, where and when grocery shopping is done, chronic medical problems, book club membership, charitable donations, and much more. Each product analysis begins with a single page summary of the market. For example, the report on packaged rice first asks whether the product is used, and if so, which kinds (white, brown, long grain, or flavored varieties). Brand data are then presented, showing the percentage of households which use each brand. Finally, the summary page asks how many times the product category was used during a specified period.

The remainder of the product analysis consists of detailed user characteristics, both demographic and media-related. By correlating characteristics of the respondent with product usage, companies can learn a great deal about their market. For example, marketers can determine that heavy users of fabric softeners tend to be married women, but that there is no strong relationship between usage and the presence of children in the home. Like all studies of this type, some results are fairly predictable, while others are not. This type of analysis can be used to compare differences between heavy and light users, differences among users of different brands, and even differences by type of use (e.g., whether fabric softener is used in the wash cycle, rinse cycle, or in the dryer). Simmons not only reports the percentage of respondents using each brand, but also whether it is the only brand used, and if not, whether it is a primary or secondary product in the household. For most products, the list of brand names is fairly comprehensive.

At first glance, the format of *Simmons Study of Media and Markets* is confusing because of the enormous amount of information presented and the variety of cross classifications. The publisher must condense a great deal of data on a single page and has adopted several conventions for doing so that require getting used to. Column B always presents data elements as a percentage of the column total, or as a percentage of that section of the column; in other words, percentages are read down the page. Column C always casts information as a percentage of the total in that row, so percentages are read across the page. Column D, the most complex of the three, creates index numbers which compare the percentage in column C to the percentage of the total population, with 100 representing complete correspondence. Exhibit 18-2 shows a table which reports on the age characteris-

EXHIBIT 18-2. *Simmons Study of Media and Markets*

PORK & BEANS OR BAKED BEANS (IN JARS OR CANS): USAGE IN LAST 30 DAYS (FEMALE HOMEMAKERS)

	TOTAL U.S. '000	ALL USERS A '000	B % DOWN	C % ACROSS	D INDX	HEAVY USERS THREE OR MORE A '000	B % DOWN	C % ACROSS	D INDX	MEDIUM USERS TWO A '000	B % DOWN	C % ACROSS	D INDX	LIGHT USERS ONE OR LESS A '000	B % DOWN	C % ACROSS	D INDX
TOTAL FEMALE HOMEMAKERS	85281	49979	100.0	58.6	100	17975	100.0	21.1	100	13749	100.0	16.1	100	18255	100.0	21.4	100
18 - 24	8692	4661	9.3	53.6	92	1789	10.0	20.6	98	1478	10.7	17.0	105	1394	7.6	16.0	75
25 - 34	20269	11640	23.3	57.4	98	4425	24.6	21.8	104	2713	19.7	13.4	83	4501	24.7	22.2	104
35 - 44	16808	9996	20.0	59.5	101	3831	21.3	22.8	108	2633	19.2	15.7	97	3532	19.3	21.0	98
45 - 54	12038	7361	14.7	61.1	104	2872	16.0	23.9	113	1970	14.3	16.4	102	2519	13.8	20.9	98
55 - 64	11596	7076	14.2	61.0	104	2379	13.2	20.5	97	2210	16.1	19.1	118	2487	13.6	21.4	100
65 OR OLDER	15879	9245	18.5	58.2	99	2679	14.9	16.9	80	2745	20.0	17.3	107	3821	20.9	24.1	112
18 - 34	28961	16301	32.6	56.3	96	6214	34.6	21.5	102	4191	30.5	14.5	90	5895	32.3	20.4	95
18 - 49	52046	30228	60.5	58.1	99	11669	64.9	22.4	106	7804	56.8	15.0	93	10755	58.9	20.7	97
25 - 54	49115	28997	58.0	59.0	101	11128	61.9	22.7	107	7317	53.2	14.9	92	10552	57.8	21.5	100
35 - 49	23085	13927	27.9	60.3	103	5454	30.3	23.6	112	3613	26.3	15.7	97	4860	26.6	21.1	98
50 OR OLDER	33235	19752	39.5	59.4	101	6307	35.1	19.0	90	5946	43.2	17.9	111	7500	41.1	22.6	105
GRADUATED COLLEGE	13522	7675	15.4	56.8	97	2425	13.5	17.9	85	1879	13.7	13.9	86	3372	18.5	24.9	116
ATTENDED COLLEGE	15391	8872	17.8	57.6	98	2847	15.8	18.5	88	2321	16.9	15.1	94	3705	20.3	24.1	112
GRADUATED HIGH SCHOOL	35720	21667	43.4	60.7	104	7805	43.4	21.9	104	6336	46.1	17.7	110	7526	41.2	21.1	98
DID NOT GRADUATE HIGH SCHOOL	20648	11765	23.5	57.0	97	4899	27.3	23.7	113	3214	23.4	15.6	97	3651	20.0	17.7	83
EMPLOYED	47042	27500	55.0	58.5	100	9965	55.4	21.2	101	7258	52.8	15.4	96	10278	56.3	21.8	102
EMPLOYED FULL-TIME	38298	21943	43.9	57.3	98	8060	44.8	21.0	100	5720	41.6	14.9	93	8163	44.7	21.3	100
EMPLOYED PART-TIME	8745	5557	11.1	63.5	108	1905	10.6	21.8	103	1538	11.2	17.6	109	2114	11.6	24.2	113
NOT EMPLOYED	38239	22479	45.0	58.8	100	8010	44.6	20.9	99	6492	47.2	17.0	105	7977	43.7	20.9	97
PROFESSIONAL/MANAGER	12060	7272	14.6	60.3	103	2483	13.8	20.6	98	1821	13.2	15.1	94	2967	16.3	24.6	115
TECH/CLERICAL/SALES	20779	11896	23.8	57.3	98	4060	22.6	19.5	93	3112	22.6	15.0	93	4724	25.9	22.7	106
PRECISION/CRAFT	1122	*740	1.5	66.0	113	**245	1.4	21.8	104	**215	1.6	19.2	119	**280	1.5	25.0	117
OTHER EMPLOYED	13081	7593	15.2	58.0	99	3177	17.7	24.3	115	2110	15.3	16.1	100	2306	12.6	17.6	82
SINGLE	11092	5610	11.2	50.6	86	2016	11.2	18.2	86	1677	12.2	15.1	94	1918	10.5	17.3	81
MARRIED	53215	33132	66.3	62.3	106	12006	66.8	22.6	107	9174	66.7	17.2	107	11952	65.5	22.5	105
DIVORCED/SEPARATED/WIDOWED	20973	11238	22.5	53.6	91	3954	22.0	18.9	89	2899	21.1	13.8	86	4385	24.0	20.9	98
PARENTS	33799	20212	40.4	59.8	102	8405	46.8	24.9	118	5011	36.4	14.8	92	6796	37.2	20.1	94
WHITE	73654	43488	87.0	59.0	101	14773	82.2	20.1	95	12145	88.3	16.5	102	16571	90.8	22.5	105
BLACK	9568	5350	10.7	55.9	95	2649	14.7	27.7	131	1354	9.8	14.2	88	1347	7.4	14.1	66
OTHER	2059	1142	2.3	55.5	95	*554	3.1	26.9	128	**251	1.8	12.2	76	**337	1.8	16.4	76
NORTHEAST-CENSUS	18475	9913	19.8	53.7	92	3795	21.1	20.5	97	2534	18.4	13.7	85	3584	19.6	19.4	91
MIDWEST	21369	13544	27.1	63.4	108	4313	24.0	20.2	96	3746	27.2	17.5	109	5484	30.0	25.7	120
SOUTH	28918	17878	35.8	61.8	105	7791	43.3	26.9	128	4830	35.1	16.7	104	5257	28.8	18.2	85
WEST	16519	8644	17.3	52.3	89	2076	11.5	12.6	60	2640	19.2	16.0	99	3929	21.5	23.8	111
NORTHEAST-MKTG.	19219	10274	20.6	53.5	91	4259	23.7	22.2	105	2584	18.8	13.4	83	3431	18.8	17.9	83
EAST CENTRAL	12301	7732	15.5	62.9	107	2697	15.0	21.9	104	2093	15.2	17.0	106	2943	16.1	23.9	112
WEST CENTRAL	14286	8980	18.0	62.9	107	2703	15.0	18.9	90	2561	18.6	17.9	111	3716	20.4	26.0	122
SOUTH	24891	15398	30.8	61.9	106	6554	36.5	26.3	125	4161	30.3	16.7	104	4683	25.7	18.8	88
PACIFIC	14583	7595	15.2	52.1	89	1763	9.8	12.1	57	2350	17.1	16.1	100	3482	19.1	23.9	112
COUNTY SIZE A	34940	18997	38.0	54.4	93	6428	35.8	18.4	87	5317	38.7	15.2	94	7252	39.7	20.8	97
COUNTY SIZE B	26036	15550	31.1	59.7	102	5585	31.1	21.5	102	4153	30.2	16.0	99	5813	31.8	22.3	104
COUNTY SIZE C	12853	7909	15.8	61.5	105	3078	17.1	23.9	114	2176	15.8	16.9	105	2656	14.5	20.7	97
COUNTY SIZE D	11451	7524	15.1	65.7	112	2885	16.1	25.2	120	2104	15.3	18.4	114	2534	13.9	22.1	103
METRO CENTRAL CITY	26124	14046	28.1	53.8	92	5272	29.3	20.2	96	3877	28.2	14.8	92	4898	26.8	18.7	88
METRO SUBURBAN	38980	22898	45.8	58.7	100	7794	43.4	20.0	95	6134	45.0	15.7	98	8920	48.9	22.9	107
NON METRO	20177	13035	26.1	64.6	110	4909	27.3	24.3	115	3689	26.8	18.3	113	4437	24.3	22.0	103
TOP 5 ADI'S	19126	9902	19.8	51.8	88	3303	18.4	17.3	82	2630	19.1	13.8	85	3969	21.7	20.8	97
TOP 10 ADI'S	26945	13908	27.8	51.6	88	5002	27.8	18.6	88	3730	27.1	13.8	86	5176	28.4	19.2	90
TOP 20 ADI'S	38767	21189	42.4	54.7	93	7373	41.0	19.0	90	5724	41.6	14.8	92	8092	44.3	20.9	98
HSHLD INC. $60,000 OR MORE	7959	4620	9.2	58.0	99	1561	8.7	19.6	93	1029	7.5	12.9	80	2030	11.1	25.5	119
$50,000 OR MORE	12735	7408	14.8	58.2	99	2309	12.8	18.1	86	1891	13.8	14.8	92	3207	17.6	25.2	118
$40,000 OR MORE	22430	13138	26.3	58.6	100	4216	23.5	18.8	89	3557	25.9	15.9	98	5366	29.4	23.9	112
$30,000 OR MORE	35197	20800	41.6	59.1	101	6907	38.4	19.6	93	5771	42.0	16.4	102	8122	44.5	23.1	108
$30,000 - $39,999	12768	7662	15.3	60.0	102	2692	15.0	21.1	100	2215	16.1	17.3	108	2756	15.1	21.6	101
$20,000 - $29,999	17025	10234	20.5	60.1	103	3555	19.8	20.9	99	2760	20.1	16.2	101	3920	21.5	23.0	108
$10,000 - $19,999	19772	11246	22.5	56.9	97	4447	24.7	22.5	107	3063	22.3	15.5	96	3736	20.5	18.9	88
UNDER $10,000	13286	7699	15.4	57.9	99	3466	17.1	23.1	109	2156	15.7	16.2	101	2477	13.6	18.6	87
HOUSEHOLD OF 1 PERSON	12976	6543	13.1	50.4	86	1690	9.4	13.0	62	1843	13.4	14.2	88	3010	16.5	23.2	108
2 PEOPLE	28489	17202	34.4	60.4	103	5197	28.9	18.2	87	5209	37.9	18.3	113	6796	37.2	23.9	111
3 OR 4 PEOPLE	32778	19365	38.7	59.1	101	7626	42.4	23.3	110	5132	37.3	15.7	97	6608	36.2	20.2	94
5 OR MORE PEOPLE	11038	6870	13.7	62.2	106	3463	19.3	31.4	149	1566	11.4	14.2	88	1841	10.1	16.7	78
NO CHILD IN HSHLD	50278	29116	58.3	57.9	99	9251	51.5	18.4	87	8586	62.4	17.1	106	11279	61.8	22.4	105
CHILD(REN) UNDER 2 YRS	7441	4404	8.8	59.2	101	1788	9.9	24.0	114	1160	8.4	15.6	97	1456	8.0	19.6	91
2 - 5 YEARS	13029	7867	15.7	60.4	103	3221	17.9	24.7	117	1941	14.1	14.9	92	2705	14.8	20.8	97
6 - 11 YEARS	16386	9785	19.6	59.7	102	4423	24.6	27.0	128	2332	17.0	14.2	88	3031	16.6	18.5	86
12 - 17 YEARS	15168	9135	18.3	60.2	103	4113	22.9	27.1	129	2198	16.0	14.5	90	2823	15.5	18.6	87
RESIDENCE OWNED	59052	36183	72.4	61.3	105	12809	71.3	21.7	103	9850	71.6	16.7	103	13524	74.1	22.9	107
VALUE: $60,000 OR MORE	32773	19533	39.1	59.6	102	6384	35.5	19.5	92	5201	37.8	15.9	98	7948	43.5	24.3	113
VALUE: UNDER $60,000	26279	16650	33.3	63.4	108	6425	35.7	24.4	116	4649	33.8	17.7	110	5576	30.5	21.2	99

SIMMONS MARKET RESEARCH BUREAU, INC. 1988

*PROJECTION RELATIVELY UNSTABLE BECAUSE OF SAMPLE BASE-USE WITH CAUTION
**NUMBER OF CASES TOO SMALL FOR RELIABILITY-SHOWN FOR CONSISTENCY ONLY

Reprinted with permission from Simmons Market Research Bureau, Inc.

tics of female users of canned pork and beans. In the 25-34 age group, the value in column B for "All Users" is 23.3, which means that 23.3% of all women who use this product are in that age group. Column C reports a value of 57.4, indicating that 57.4% of women in that age bracket use the product. The value in Column D is 98, meaning women in this age range are 2% less likely to use canned beans than all other female users. This presentation is further complicated by the fact that different characteristics may be measured in each report, so it is difficult to make generalizations about the tables. Researchers should always be careful to interpret the meaning of percentages in *Simmons* correctly. Because the actual numbers are given in column A and in the first row, individuals can verify their understanding by computing sample percentages for themselves.

Simmons Study of Media and Markets is one of the few syndicated marketing services found in selected academic libraries. The publisher sells a limited number of superseded sets to university libraries as part of a special instructional program. Though superseded copies contain older information, the program allows students and researchers an opportunity to see how such surveys are conducted and reported. The program is not available to public libraries.

Data from the Simmons surveys can also be received in customized reports, on floppy diskette, or as an extensive CD-ROM system called *Choices*. The CD-ROM includes psychographic data from VALS, and geodemographic estimates from *PRIZM*. Because Simmons questionnaires are coded to correspond to the typologies utilized by the latter two products, users can cross-tabulate buying habits with demographic, psychographic, and lifestyle characteristics. Summary data from the surveys can be retrieved online through the *M.A.I.D.* system.

A direct competitor to *Simmons Study of Media and Markets* is the *National Media and Marketing Study*, produced by Mediamark Research, Inc. The service is similar in most important respects, including format, type of products covered, and media measured. Sampling techniques and survey methods vary slightly, but the basic methodologies are similar. The most noteworthy difference involves the way the two firms study magazine readership. Mediamark asks respondents to sort through a deck of cards with journal logos to pick out titles they have read. Simmons shows respondents "stripped" issues containing selected articles from each magazine, minus the advertising content. The distinction is quite important to the advertising and magazine indus-

tries. Mediamark typically reports higher readerships, but Simmons estimates are probably more accurate. The Mediamark study is also available as an online database known alternately as *MRI* and the *Mediamark Research Data Base*. Like Simmons, Mediamark cooperates with other data companies to provide detailed demographic and lifestyle profiles of consumers. Both the CACI *Sourcebook* and the *ACORN* database utilize Mediamark estimates, and the *MRI* service likewise contains data from CACI, as well as from National Decision Systems and several other data providers.

SHOPPING FOR MARKET RESEARCH

The tools covered in this chapter reinforce two noteworthy points about business research in general. First, published sources of business information can be utilized to address an infinite variety of very specific requests. Though many tools are quite narrow in focus, when the need arises, a publication such as *LNA* or the *Art Directors' Annual* can be indispensable. Second, if there is a recognized need for a category of business information, sooner or later someone will find a way to collect and disseminate it.

The greatest strength of published market research can also be its greatest weakness. Because market research publications frequently provide users with exactly the type of data they seek, it is easy to overlook where the numbers come from. The types of sources discussed in this chapter represent secondary information, which has its limitations. Because secondary information is gathered for general purposes, it may not strictly match the user's needs, even though it may give that impression. Readers must further remember that most market research figures are mere estimates, based on the assumptions of a particular data-gathering model.

Despite the specialized nature of these products, seldom is one market study unique, and users can generally choose from several competitors. Researchers need to select their tools carefully. In some cases, several companies are known for using similar methods to provide the same types of information. In these instances, the user can contact the companies for point-by-point comparisons. More often, however, data companies arrive at their results in completely different ways. Two measures of market share for a particular product may give widely different results depending on the definition of the market. Similarly, lifestyle profiles for a geographic market can paint completely different pictures of the area, based

on the questions asked of the inhabitants. The mode of data collection also plays a major part in the outcome—a consumer survey may yield very different results from a store audit, for example. It is worth the trouble to investigate the methodology used to arrive at the published numbers, and to assess whether that technique seems appropriate for your purposes.

By failing to look at the methodology of a study, users frequently misunderstand the results and may apply conclusions to situations they weren't intended to address. A good example involves the frequently encountered assertion that Americans enjoy less leisure time than their parents. Numerous studies have appeared to support this statement, but most are based on opinion surveys. In other words, such reports indicate that people believe they have less free time. In fact, time-use studies, which track how people actually spend their days, show that leisure time has steadily increased in recent decades. Both types of study are valid, and both provide important market insights. But depending on whether the user is interested in people's perceptions or in how they actually use their time, one is preferable to the other.

Another way of evaluating a market study is to examine whether the conclusions conform to what is already known. This can be done by comparing the results to those of similar studies. A simpler approach is to ask whether the results make sense in light of your own experience and understanding. The danger in the latter technique is that some of the best market studies uncover previously undiscovered trends, or reach conclusions which seem counter-intuitive. One of the great virtues of market research is its ability to dispel "Aunt Janeisms"—commonly-held beliefs which are simply not true.

A third evaluation method is to judge the reputation of the information producer. All of the firms introduced in this chapter are respected sources of market data. The results of many market research studies are incorporated into other respected reports. Data from such companies as Leading National Advertisers, Nielsen, Simmons, and Claritas are frequently encountered in other publications. Major information providers even contract with these organizations to conduct original research on their behalf. For example, Gallup conducts an annual *Air Travel Survey* for the Air Transport Association of America, an ongoing study of book buying behavior for Bowker's *Publishers Weekly*, and monthly surveys of religious issues for the Princeton Religion Research Center. A related phenomenon is the large number of joint ventures among market research providers. The *LNA/Arbitron Multi-Media Service* is an excellent example. Examples of the partnership between consumer behavior studies and demographic estimates are the joint ventures of Simmons/Claritas and Mediamark/CACI.

This chapter has introduced representative examples of sources which address common marketing concerns. Additional categories that could have been discussed include specialized guides for sales force management, publicity, direct mail marketing, product promotion, and advertising law. There are many more publications of all types, and prices range from very affordable to prohibitively expensive. Most tools introduced in this chapter are relatively affordable, though few can be considered cheap. Except for the syndicated services, most can be found in larger academic and public libraries. But syndicated publications can be a vital part of a corporate library's collection, and all librarians and researchers need to be aware of their existence. Information on specific studies of this type can be located in directories such as *FINDEX* and *Industry Data Sources*, introduced in Chapters 3 and 4, respectively.

Researchers shouldn't feel constrained by the high cost and limited distribution of certain marketing information sources. The specialized tools described here are not the only resources for marketers, nor are the best data necessarily found in controlled publications. Alternative sources are special issues of business magazines and trade journals, and association publications. How can the researcher locate such materials? *Industry Data Sources* is excellent for locating inexpensive guides to audience measurement, consumer expenditures, public opinion, and related topics. Another outstanding finding tool is the *Statistical Reference Index*, described in Chapter 4. *SRI* serves as a guide to an assortment of popular consumer studies in journals, special reports, and annual surveys. The *Business Rankings Annual* is also useful for company comparisons and market share by brand name. A newsletter published by the Special Libraries Association, *What's New in Advertising and Marketing*, is published 10 times per year and contains ordering information for dozens of market studies, reference books, and other publications pertinent to marketing. Many of these are brief reports which are available free from their compilers. Finally, don't underestimate the power of periodical indexes and full-text databases to provide access to marketing data. Virtually every topic discussed in this chapter can be researched in periodical sources, from market share to advertising expenditures. Syndicated intelligence services and off-the-shelf market reports may be better known in the corridors of corporate America, but a surprising amount of quality marketing information can be found in basic business tools.

FOR FURTHER READING

Studying the characteristics of markets is one of the most fascinating areas of business research. To illustrate the richness of this field, and to provide the reader with more information on the diverse topics mentioned in the chapter, the following materials are recommended.

Market Research Basics

Aaker, David A., and George S. Day. *Marketing Research.* 4th ed. (New York: Wiley, 1990).

Market researchers devote most of their attention to collecting and analyzing primary data, but virtually every leading textbook includes a brief introduction to secondary research methods and information sources. One of the better treatments can be found in this popular text. Chapter 4 discusses the strengths and weaknesses of secondary information, together with short descriptions of selected statistical publications. Chapter 5 presents profiles of representative syndicated intelligence services. Another popular textbook with a good chapter on secondary sources is *Marketing Research: Measurement and Method*, 4th ed., by Donald S. Tull and Del I. Hawkins (Macmillan, 1987).

Cravens, David W. "Defining and Analyzing Markets." In his *Strategic Marketing*, 2nd ed. (Homewood, IL: Irwin, 1987): 157-94.

A key to researching market share is a proper understanding of the appropriate product-market. Craven offers a particularly good discussion of how to define the scope of the market and analyze its characteristics.

Franchese, Peter, and Rebecca Piirto. *Capturing Customers: How to Target the Hottest Markets of the '90s* (Ithaca, NY: American Demographics Press, 1990).

An outstanding guide to secondary information for market research. Topics include data sources on consumer expenditures, media preference, psychographics, market trends, and much more. In addition to describing major suppliers of market information and their data products, this unique guide explains how to incorporate secondary information in the research process.

Lazer, William. *Handbook of Demographics for Marketing and Advertising: Sources and Trends on the U.S. Consumer* (Lexington, MA: Lexington, 1987).

Explains basic demographic concepts and trends important to market research. Among the topics introduced are population growth, life expectancy, age distribution, occupational mobility, the aging labor force, shifting geographic patterns, living arrangements, and household size. One interesting chapter describes the difference between personal income and wealth, and why this distinction is important to marketers. Also covered are trends and issues related to specific market segments, including blacks, Hispanics, working women, and "mature consumers."

Market Segments

Lee, Paula Munier. "The Micro-Marketing Revolution." *Small Business Reports* 15 (February 1990): 71-82.

A primer on geodemographic market segmentation, its uses, and the major data companies which provide market profiles by zip code.

Piirto, Rebecca. "Measuring Minds in the 1990s." *American Demographics* 12 (December 1990): 31-35.

Explores the latest trends in syndicated services which track psychographic market segments, including SRI's revised VALS 2 program.

Rice, Berkeley. "The Selling of Life-Styles." *Psychology Today* (March 1988): 45-50.

An introduction to psychographic segmentation techniques. The bulk of the article describes the popular VALS Program and how it is used by marketers.

Settle, Robert B., and Pamela L. Alreck. *Why They Buy: American Consumers Inside and Out* (New York: Wiley, 1986).

Explores ways to segment markets, and gives examples of each approach. Included are demographics, life stages, personality, family type, social affiliations, and many more. The book is especially useful for the explanations of such subtly different consumer characteristics as beliefs and attitudes.

Swenson, Chester A. *Selling to a Segmented Market: A Lifestyle Approach* (New York: Quorum, 1990).

An introduction to lifestyle market segmentation, with separate chapters on the consumer behavior of various groups, including college students, sports fans, Hispanics, and women.

Weiss, Michael J. *The Clustering of America* (New York: Harper and Row, 1988).

Free-lance writer Weiss investigates the validity of geodemographic clustering as portrayed in the PRIZM model. Selecting a random sample of zip codes in each of the PRIZM clusters, the author criss-crosses the country to interview cluster residents. He finds clustering to be surprisingly effective, and in the process offers an entertaining profile of American market segments. For those curious about geodemographic marketing techniques, this is a fast-paced introduction.

Public Opinion Polls

Barry, John M. "The Roper Center: The World's Largest Archive of Survey Data." *Reference Services Review* 16, No. 1/2 (1988): 41-50.

A wonderful tour of the resources and services of the Roper Center, including an introduction to the *POLL* database.

Bradburn, Norman M., and Seymour Sudman. *Polls & Surveys: Understanding What They Tell Us* (San Francisco: Jossey-Bass, 1988).

An excellent introduction to polls and opinion surveys aimed at the nonspecialist. Included are discussions of the history of polls; their growing importance in modern society; how they can be used and misused; their effect on politics, business, and the media; and profiles of major polling organizations. Five chapters explain basic concepts in polling methodology, written for users of opinion surveys rather than would-be poll-takers.

Walden, Graham R. "Public Opinion Polls: A Guide to Accessing the Literature." *Reference Services Review* 16, No. 4 (1988): 65-74.

A wide-ranging review of significant published sources of public opinion data and the organizations which produce them. Covers periodicals, indexes, yearbooks, and intelligence services.

Special Topics

Celente, Gerald. *Trend Tracking: The System to Profit from Today's Trends* (New York: Wiley, 1990).

Once you move beyond the hype, this is a fascinating and useful guide to the world of trend spotting. Consultant Celente describes his multidisciplinary "Globalnomic" tracking system and demonstrates how anyone can implement it to identify and profit from emerging trends. Although professional trend watchers develop complex monitoring systems, Celente asserts that most important clues can be found in the daily newspapers. The middle portion of the book is devoted to a summary of trends the author sees in many fields.

Frichtl, Paul. "Ad Tracking Services Add Competitive Edge." *Folio* (September 1987): 121-31.

An introduction to the various types of ad-tracking services which monitor advertising in magazines, by periodical title and/or advertiser. A directory of major tracking services is included.

Gieseman, Raymond. "The Consumer Expenditure Survey: Quality Control by Comparative Analysis." *Monthly Labor Review* (March 1987): 8-14.

An introduction to the government's Consumer Expenditure Survey and the methods used to evaluate the results after each survey is taken. Includes brief descriptions of nongovernment surveys to which the CES is compared.

Robinson, John P. "Time's Up." *American Demographics* 11 (July 1989): 32-35.

Describes the work of the University of Maryland's "Americans' Use of Time Project," in which a large national sample of Americans are asked to keep a detailed diary of daily time usage. Robinson, the project director, is a frequent contributor to *American Demographics*, where he reports on a variety of Project findings.

CHAPTER 19
Business Law Sources

TOPICS COVERED

1. The Structure of American Legal Institutions
2. Basic Legal Publications
    a. General Finding Aids
    b. Statutes and Codes
    c. Legislative History
    d. Court Reports, Digests, and Annotations
    e. Regulations and Administrative Decisions
    f. Law Citators
3. Beyond the Basics
    a. Loose-Leaf Services
    b. Online Databases
4. Labor Law in the United States
    a. Major Provisions of Labor Relations Law
    b. Collective Bargaining and Arbitration
    c. Labor Statutes, Regulations, and Case Law
    d. Loose-Leaf Services for Labor Law
    e. Miscellaneous Labor Publications
5. Legal Research for the Nonlawyer
6. For Further Reading

MAJOR SOURCES DISCUSSED

- *Current Law Index*
- *United States Code*
- *Congressional Index*
- *CIS Index*
- *United States Code Congressional and Administrative News*
- *United States Reports*
- *Code of Federal Regulations*
- *Decisions and Orders of the NLRB*
- *Labor Relations Reference Manual*
- *Labor Arbitration Reports: Dispute Settlements*
- *Labor Relations Reporter*
- *Employment Coordinator*
- *Collective Bargaining Negotiations and Contracts*
- *Current Wage Developments*

The system of published law in the United States is vast and enormously complex. While this publication system is well-organized, with many excellent finding tools, it can be cumbersome and frustrating to deal with. The precise language of the law, with all its carefully developed concepts and principles, also presents a major barrier to the nonlawyer who must confront these publications. Thus, sophisticated legal research is best left to experts. It is beyond the scope of this book to provide a detailed introduction to legal research; many specialized textbooks accomplish that task quite well. Instead, this chapter will outline the framework of the American legal system in cursory fashion, follow with a brief introduction to the basic categories of legal publications, and close with a look at a specific area of business law, namely labor relations.

THE STRUCTURE OF AMERICAN LEGAL INSTITUTIONS

The foundation of law in this country (and in others which adhere to the British system of common law) is the doctrine of *stare decisis*. This principle holds that court rulings should be based on legal precedent. To achieve fair treatment for all people, current rulings must take past decisions into effect. *Stare decisis* ensures that the law is constantly evolving to reflect changes in society. Prior rulings are modified or overturned; existing laws are reinterpreted, struck down, amended or repealed; and regulations are rewritten to reflect current statutes and administrative policies. In legal research, the past can

never be ignored. Several million published statutes, regulations, and judicial decisions exist and thousands more are issued each year, creating a vast archive of jurisprudence which the researcher must confront.

All branches of government—legislative, judicial, and executive—have important responsibilities in the legal system. The legislative branch enacts the law, the judiciary interprets the law, and the executive branch enforces it. Of the three tasks, the legislative function is perhaps the easiest to understand. A legislature introduces bills, which if passed by both houses and signed by the executive, become statutes. The legislative process occurs at all levels of government: federal, state, and local. The resulting laws have effect only on the jurisdictions over which the legislature has authority. Another type of statute, called a uniform law, has wide applicability to the business world. To achieve consistency in certain state laws throughout the country, over 100 uniform laws have been passed. The National Commission on Uniform State Laws proposes and drafts such laws, which can then be adopted as statutes by individual state legislatures. The Uniform Commercial Code, for example, has been passed by all 50 states; the Model Business Corporations Act is currently in force in fewer states.

It is impossible to foresee all the specific situations to which new laws will apply. The judiciary interprets statutes when two contesting parties disagree on their meaning. Court rulings are recorded on a case-by-case basis and become as much a part of the law as the statutes themselves. Judicial decisions may strike down an existing law as unconstitutional, or interpret the language of the statute in an unforeseen way; they may also affirm or reverse the prior ruling of a lower court. There is a hierarchy of courts at each level of government. At the bottom of the pyramid is a series of trial courts, followed by one or more intermediate appellate courts, and finally, a court of last resort. There may also be special purpose courts such as Family Court or Probate Court.

The executive branch participates in the legal system primarily through the activities of administrative agencies. Because these agencies exhibit characteristics of all three branches of government, they are often said to constitute the fourth branch of government. Administrative agencies create regulations, a quasi-legislative function. Regulations are guidelines promulgated to administer specific statutes enacted by the legislature. The enormous impact of the Food and Drug Administration, the Environmental Protection Agency, the Occupational Safety and Health Administration, and other regulatory agencies is frequently bemoaned by the business com-

munity. Before establishing a new regulation, agencies must follow a series of steps to ensure due process under the law. The text of the proposed regulation must be published for public comment. In some cases, hearings are convened to solicit public opinion; in others, responses come by letter. For every proposed rule, the agency must establish a Docket Number, under which all ensuing testimony, correspondence, and internal communications are filed. The contents of the Docket are not published, but they are available for public inspection.

Administrative agencies also serve a quasi-judicial function. When the effect of regulation or other administrative action is contested, the case may be adjudicated by one or more Administrative Law Judges (ALJs), or by an administrative board with special powers. Dozens of agencies hand down decisions that are published in much the same way as decisions of a court.

The activities of a single branch in this trilateral system cannot be viewed in isolation. Statutory, judicial, and administrative law are each part of an interlocking network. Court decisions can affect statutes and prior rulings and may also affect regulations and administrative decisions. To counteract the adverse effects of judicial decisions, statutes and regulations can be amended. The ever-changing mosaic which results makes "finding the law" a challenging assignment.

BASIC LEGAL PUBLICATIONS

The major drawback to most government publications on law is that current statutes, decisions, and regulations are printed in chronological order as they are issued. Most research problems require a subject approach, however, so there is an ongoing need for tools which can lead the user to the appropriate body of law on a given issue. Happily, a sophisticated and all-embracing system of annotated codes, court digests, citators, and other guides are published for every category of the law. The serious researcher must ultimately consult the official source to which any finding guide leads. And while commercial publications offer helpful editorial commentary, the researcher should never rely entirely on someone else's legal analysis.

The most obvious characteristic of legal publications is their continual need for updating. They typically appear as loose-leaf services, newsletters, or books which are revised by supplements or pocket parts. A second characteristic is that commercially produced publications are usually better organized, more timely, and

easier to use than their government counterparts. More surprisingly, some types of legal information have no official publications. The decisions of many courts and regulatory agencies appear in commercial publications only.

The three leading publishers of legal guides in the United States are West Publishing Company, Lawyers Co-operative Publishing Company, and Shepard's/McGraw-Hill, Inc. Each of the three is noted for a particular type of law service; without them, modern legal research could not take place.

General Finding Aids

When beginning any legal investigation, it is sensible to look for an overview of the topic in secondary sources. One method is to find treatises devoted to a specific subject. These may be scholarly treatments or basic handbooks. Several publishers produce extensive series of introductory legal guides. West Publishing's "Nutshell Series" offers dozens of current titles in virtually every area of the law. The Practicing Law Institute's "Course Handbook Series" provides especially strong coverage of business topics, from structuring a merger to handling employment problems. Several publishers focus on narrower aspects of business law. The Bureau of National Affairs, for example, issues introductory guides to labor law, covering current topics such as drugs in the workplace, childcare benefits, and pre-employment screening.

The *Index to Legal Books* is a six-volume looseleaf service from R.R. Bowker which debuted in 1990. The set provides detailed subject indexing to the contents of approximately 1,000 legal treatises and manuals, selected by an editorial panel for their authoritative treatment. The index is divided into more than 50 chapters, each one covering a broad area such as accounting, securities law, environmental concerns, or corporate law. Approximately 20 books are indexed in every section, with page references to the pertinent sections of each book. The *Index to Legal Books* is more than a merger of individual "back-of-the-book" indexes, however; standard subject headings provide uniformity throughout.

An alternative approach to beginning a research project is to determine how the structure of government relates to the question at hand. Many of the government directories introduced in Chapter 2 are well-suited to this task, including the *U.S. Government Manual*, the *Federal Regulatory Directory*, and the *State Legislative*

Sourcebook. A related guide, the *Book of the States*, was described in Chapter 17. It offers a broad look at the organization, powers, and constitutional limitations of individual state governments.

A third way to begin investigating a question of law is to consult a legal encyclopedia. The *American Jurisprudence Second*, from Lawyers Co-operative Publishing, consists of 82 volumes and 6 index volumes. *Corpus Juris Secundum*, from West Publishing, has 101 volumes with 5 index volumes. Both works cover broad topics in an alphabetical subject arrangement. Each article presents a general introduction to the topic, a detailed scholarly analysis of all aspects of the issue, and references to authoritative cases. The individual volumes in both services are updated by pocket supplements and are completely revised when necessary. Although the subject indexes are quite detailed, neither encyclopedia provides a table of case names. Another drawback is lack of recency; despite the annual updates, many years can elapse before an individual volume is completely rewritten. Although intended for lawyers, the general researcher may find these resources useful for ideas on how to proceed with a search. Some encyclopedias cover state laws in the same in-depth manner. For the layperson, West publishes a 12-volume *Guide to American Law*, which provides a basic introduction to major legal concepts and issues.

A final technique to gain an overview of a legal issue is to look for survey articles in legal periodicals. Law reviews, especially those published by prestigious universities, have an important impact on the American judicial process. The articles are written by scholars, judges, and practicing lawyers and provide detailed analyses of narrow topics. The legal detail in law reviews can be difficult for the layperson to grasp, but many articles present understandable, timely overviews of specific topics. Of greater importance, they often deal with issues not readily found in other sources. For these reasons, law reviews should not be overlooked by the researcher. The two leading indexes to the journal literature in law, covering both law reviews and other types of journals, are described below.

Current Law Index (Information Access Company—Monthly, with Cumulations).

This outstanding service is sponsored by the American Association of Law Libraries and released in four different formats. In book form, it is entitled the *Current Law Index*, and appears monthly, with quarterly and annual cumulations. It is also available as a cumulative reel of microfilm, with each monthly update superseding

the previous reel. Its arrangement is similar to the microfilm version of IAC's *Business Index*, introduced in Chapter 5. The microfilm console covers several years of articles, while a companion set of archival microfiche provides access to older stories. The third format is an online database available through DIALOG, BRS, LEXIS, and WESTLAW. Both the microfilm edition and the online database are known as the *Legal Resources Index*. The final format is a monthly CD-ROM product known as *LegalTrac*. All four versions index approximately 700 legal periodicals, but the electronic and microfilm editions cover an additional seven legal newspapers not found in the printed index, plus legal articles found in popular journals and newspapers. Access is by subject and author, with additional indexing by case name and statute.

Index to Legal Periodicals (H.W. Wilson Company—Monthly, with Cumulations).

This classic guide is one of Wilson's oldest periodical indexes, dating back to 1908. Approximately 500 periodicals are represented, and law reviews are covered especially well. Its frequency and format are similar to other standard Wilson indexes, with monthly, quarterly, and annual cumulations. Like the *Current Law Index*, the bulk of each issue is a combined subject/author index, with separate indexes to case names and statutes. A guide to standard subject headings appears at the front of every bound volume. The index is also available in online format through WILSONLINE, LEXIS, and WESTLAW, and as a WILSONDISC CD-ROM.

Statutes and Codes

The publishing system for statutes in the United States is fairly consistent, with the states following the pattern set by the federal government. In general, statutes are published as they are enacted, in the form of individual slip laws. These are then collected and reprinted in bound volumes called session laws. Session laws are then reorganized according to subject matter to create a code of statutes. Federal session laws are published chronologically in a bound set entitled *United States Statutes at Large*, which contains an annual volume for each session of Congress. The codified laws of the federal government can be found in the *United States Code*, which is described below. Many state governments publish session laws only, and commercial publishers assume the task of compiling a code service for the state.

United States Code (U.S. House of Representatives, Judiciary Committee—Irregular, with Annual Supplements).

The House Judiciary Committee is charged with codifying all U.S. laws currently in force and of general public interest. A complete revision is issued every six years, with annual updates between revisions. The 50 Titles in the *U.S. Code* each represent a specific subject area. For example, Title 17 contains all the laws relating to copyrights, while Title 31 deals with money and finance. Each part of the Code includes the original laws as revised by subsequent amendments. Furthermore, the Code is often rewritten so that the codified language is clearer, though these changes are always minor. To locate the exact text of the law as originally enacted, the *Statutes at Large* must be consulted. For this reason, the *U.S. Code* sections always cite the volume and page in the *Statutes at Large* where the law was first published.

The *U.S. Code* enables users to locate statutes on a given subject. The publication contains a number of finding aids, including a seven-volume subject index and a table which links references in the *Statutes at Large* to their appropriate Code sections. Another helpful aid is the index to laws by their short titles or popular names. Although a number of commercial publications provide this type of information, including the well-known *Shepard's Acts and Cases by Popular Name*, the name index to the *U.S. Code* is usually just as effective for tracking down a specific law.

A number of problems are associated with using the *U.S. Code*. The biggest drawback is the lack of timeliness in its release. Although annual supplements are compiled, there is considerable delay before each year's issue appears. The other weakness is that the official edition of the Code does not provide the researcher with information on how the courts have construed the various laws. To address these shortcomings, commercial publishers have created annotated code services that contain the same wording and numbering system used in the *U.S. Code*, but also include digests of important court cases, as well as references to articles in law reviews and other sources which analyze the Code. The major services of this type are the *United States Code Annotated* from West Publishing and the *United States Code Service* from Lawyers Co-op.

Legislative History

Besides locating the text of a statute or code, other typical legal research questions include determining the current status of a bill before Congress, finding the text

of a hearing held on a particular bill, following the congressional debate and the roll call vote, and tracking down amendments to existing laws. Many of these issues surface when investigating a statute's legislative history. Judging the intent of Congress when enacting a law, or interpreting ambiguous language in a statute may require tracing the law's development as it passed through the legislative process. The published information generated by the U.S. House and Senate is voluminous, as is the output of commercial publishers which summarize or index congressional activities. Whether documents are published by the government or private firms, many contain much of the same information. In spite of similarities, each one offers unique features, which may recommend it for certain research situations. A full chapter could be devoted to the topic of conducting legislative research; however, space permits only the following brief sketch of major publications.

Every bill is printed in slip form when introduced in Congress. These bills are published on microfiche by the Government Printing Office, as well as by commercial firms such as the Congressional Information Service, Inc. Summary language from every bill and resolution of general public interest can be found in a publication of the Library of Congress called the *Digest of Public General Bills and Resolutions*, which is issued in several parts during each session of Congress. Transcripts of hearings sponsored by congressional committees may or may not be published; those which are can be ordered on an individual basis from the Government Printing Office.

The most important document for determining legislative intent is the *Committee Report*. Every bill introduced in the House or Senate must be reported out of committee before it can be voted upon. *House Reports* and *Senate Reports* are series which contain the full text of *Committee Reports* in chronological order. These reports are also republished, together with other congressional documents, in a bound collection called the *Serial Set*.

The official source of information on House and Senate debate is the daily *Congressional Record*. However, this famous transcript does not necessarily provide a verbatim report of what was said on the floors of Congress; legislators are allowed to edit and embellish their remarks for publication. They may also insert additional information into the record, including editorials from local newspapers and testimonials to leading constituents. Another government document useful for legislative history is the *Weekly Compilation of Presidential Documents*. This publication includes Presidential statements made upon signing a bill into law, veto messages, and Executive Orders and Proclamations.

Most of the above-mentioned documents contain indexes and finding tables to assist in their use. Following the text of each law, the *U.S. Statutes at Large* provides a list of pertinent *Committee Report* numbers and references to debate in the *Congressional Record*. The *Digest of Public General Bills* contains a chronological list of the actions taken on every bill, together with indexes by subject, short title, and sponsor/cosponsor. The *Congressional Record* offers a biweekly index of subjects, titles of bills, and cosponsors' names, together with a tabular "History of Bills and Resolutions." Each of these is cumulated annually. Published hearings and *Committee Reports* can be located by subject, title, and committee name in the *Monthly Catalog of U.S. Government Publications*, described in Chapter 4.

Tracing important legislative developments can be a rigorous chore despite the finding aids within the documents themselves. To meet the need for improved accessibility, many commercial publishers have created outstanding services which index and/or summarize congressional activities. Three leading publications, each taking a different approach, are described below.

Congressional Index (Commerce Clearing House—Weekly, with Cumulations).

While this popular loose-leaf service from CCH does not provide the text of bills or public laws, its convenience as a finding tool cannot be matched. The strength of the publication is its ability to identify the status of a current bill by title, bill number, subject matter, or name of sponsor. Every two years, when a new Congress is convened, subscribers receive a revised set of binders. In this way, a historical record of congressional activity can be maintained.

For the current Congress, the service is organized in three sections. The first covers the activities of the Senate, while the second covers the House. The third section describes enacted statutes, treaties, nominations, and vetoed legislation, and provides combined indexes to the set. The "Enactments" section lists public laws by P.L. number together with their original bill numbers and the date each law was passed. The arrangement of the House and Senate sections parallel one another. Each begins with directory information, listing state delegations, committee assignments, and biographical information. A calendar of congressional hearings and a list of *Committee Reports* are also included. The next sections provide brief digests of bills and resolutions, together with their sponsors, arranged by bill number. The "Status of Bills" tables are also organized by bill number and list the actions taken on each piece of legislation. The final

section in each part of the *Congressional Index* summarizes the voting record for every bill, with the names of members of Congress who voted for it.

CIS Index (Congressional Information Service—Monthly, with Quarterly and Annual Cumulations).

The best detailed summary of the contents of legislative publications is the *CIS Index*. Similar in format to the *American Statistics Index*, introduced in Chapter 4, the *CIS Index* offers subject access to congressional documents of all types, including bills, public laws, hearings, and *Committee Reports*. In addition to fairly specific subject indexing, documents can be located by titles, geographic areas affected or discussed; authors, sponsors or cosponsors of publications or bills; names of witnesses appearing before congressional hearings, together with their affiliations; names of executive agencies affected by the action; official titles and popular names of bills and laws; and document number (including bill, report, and hearing numbers).

The *CIS Index* also creates an abstract of every document. Abstracts of hearings, for example, provide a list of witnesses and a summary of their testimony. Abstracts for public laws contain a brief legislative history, but a separate volume, *CIS Annual Legislative Histories*, offers more detailed background information. As each law is enacted, the staff at CIS compiles an expert documentary history of the hearings, reports, and debates associated with the law, from both the current year and previous sessions of Congress. The publisher also compiles a companion microfiche collection called the *CIS Legislative History Service*. All documents are reproduced in their entirety, including every version of the bill itself from the time it was introduced until its passage. The combined index and microfiche collection represent a one-stop approach to researching legislative intent and meaning.

The *CIS Index* is also available online exclusively through DIALOG and via a CD-ROM version called *Congressional Masterfile 2*. In both formats, searchers can retrieve information by keyword or through CIS subject terms. Full Boolean searching is supported, and entries include both the standard abstracts and the legislative histories. The online file is updated monthly. The disk version is updated quarterly, with a current disk covering 1990 to the present and a retrospective disk for 1970 through 1989.

United States Code Congressional and Administrative News (West Publishing Company—Monthly, with Annual Cumulations).

This monthly paperback series is both popular and relatively inexpensive. Known alternately as *U.S. Cong. News* or *USCCAN*, it reprints the full text of enacted laws and their *Committee Reports*, as well as Executive Orders of the President, and significant regulations from the *Federal Register*. *USCCAN* is not the best source for tracing legislative history, but the text of *Committee Reports* and congressional debates make it a useful source for many purposes. Laws are indexed according to their classification within the *U.S. Code*, so *USCCAN* serves as an update to West's own *United States Code Annotated*.

Laws are listed numerically and alphabetically by title, as are the original bills. The index of popular names is especially helpful. An excellent classification table links bill numbers to the section of the *U.S. Code* in which they will appear, and a list of amendments and repeals is also organized by Code section. Like CCH's *Congressional Index*, *USCCAN* also includes a convenient table summarizing the actions taken on each law prior to its passage.

Several other popular commercial publications should be thought of as current awareness services rather than as finding tools. *United States Law Week*, by the Bureau of National Affairs, reproduces the text of public laws. Actually, a very small section of this service deals with laws; the bulk of the coverage is on actions of the Supreme Court, digests of administrative agency rulings, and the decisions of other courts. *U.S. Law Week* only contains the text of those laws deemed by BNA to have widespread interest, but the service's broad popularity ensures its availability in numerous local libraries and law firms. Many popular periodicals and news services provide summary information on current political and legislative events. Among the most useful are the *CQ Weekly Report*, by Congressional Quarterly, Inc. and the *National Journal*, a weekly magazine from the Center for Political Research.

Court Reports, Digests, and Annotations

Case law is only one aspect of the legal system, but it is an essential one. Judicial decisions (mostly at the appellate level and higher) are published in court reports, sometimes known as law reports. They may be official publications of the federal or state governments, or they may be produced by commercial firms. With thousands of appeals being heard each year, only those dealing with

significant issues of law are published. The information contained in court reports is limited; exhibits, testimony, and attorneys' briefs are usually not seen. Court reports typically include the names of the plaintiff and defendant, the name of the court and the docket number, the names of the judge (or judges) and the attorneys involved, and the text of the judicial opinion. Another important part of the published decision is the headnotes. Every court opinion is based on one or more rules of law called holdings. The holdings are summarized by headnotes appearing before the text of the opinion. Headnotes identify the important legal issues of each case.

Publication of important federal decisions is fairly comprehensive. However, not even the U.S. Supreme Court publishes all its decisions. The official source of information on the decisions of the U.S. Supreme Court is called *United States Reports*. Cases are reported in chronological order, with five bound volumes for each year's term of court. Before cases appear in the *United States Reports*, they are issued in pamphlet form as "slip decisions." After this, they are republished as "Preliminary Prints," paperback advance reports issued every two to three months. This is necessary because the final bound volumes are not published for several years after the decisions are handed down. For every case reported, the information includes a case syllabus, which summarizes the facts of the case and the Court's holdings. In addition, the full text of the Court's majority opinion can be found, together with any dissenting opinions. Exhibit 19-1 shows the opening page of a typical case in *U.S. Reports*. This case, identified hereafter as Reis, will be mentioned again later in the chapter in conjunction with other Exhibits. As can be seen from the syllabus, the case deals with a trucking firm which sued its employees for engaging in an illegal (wildcat) strike. The docket number for Reis is No. 79-1777, but the official citation for the decision is 451 US 401. This indicates that the opinion of the Court can be found in volume 451 of *U.S. Reports*, beginning on page 401. Following the syllabus is the complete text of the Supreme Court decision (not shown in Exhibit 19-1).

Decisions of the Supreme Court can also be found in commercial services called the *Supreme Court Reporter* (West Publishing) and *U.S. Supreme Court Reports, Lawyers Edition* (Lawyers Co-op). There are several advantages to using commercial report services: they appear much sooner than the official government reports; the headnotes are written by the publishers' own editorial staffs, which gives the researcher alternatives to the official summary; and they contain added features not

seen in *U.S. Reports*. For example, the *Supreme Court Reporter* provides tables of the statutes construed by the Court and the *Lawyers Edition* contains summaries of the briefs presented by the opposing lawyers. Another category of information on Supreme Court decisions is the loose-leaf service which covers the activities of the Court. Two examples of this type of publication are the *United States Law Week* from the Bureau of National Affairs, and the *U.S. Supreme Court Bulletin* from Commerce Clearing House.

The government does not publish official reports for decisions of the U.S. Court of Appeals or the U.S. District Courts. Significant decisions from these bodies can be found in the *Federal Reporter 2d* and the *Federal Supplement*, both from West Publishing. However, the government does publish official reports for specialized courts such as the Court of International Trade and the U.S. Court of Claims. The publication of state appellate court opinions is sporadic. Official reports are available in less than half the states; for those states where government reports are not compiled, the researcher must turn to commercial publications. West has resolved the problem of uneven coverage by creating a nationwide report structure consisting of seven regional publications covering every state in the country. Known collectively as the *National Reporter System*, this remarkable series offers the researcher uniform treatment of significant legal decisions from one state to another. West also publishes individual reports for many states, including New York and California. Figure 19-A summarizes the major reporting services which are available for the various federal and state courts.

Because judicial decisions are published chronologically, the researcher once again needs subject access. One way to locate important decisions by title is to consult legal encyclopedias or journal articles, both of which cite authoritative cases. A more thorough approach is to utilize index-digests, which group related cases together by the rules of law concerned and present brief summaries of the decisions. West's *American Digest System* is an impressive series of publications that provides subject access to the entire body of case law in the United States. Volumes are issued monthly in paperback form and cumulated into bound volumes. West also publishes separate digests for individual state and federal courts.

At the heart of the *American Digest System* is West's unique Key Numbering System, a remarkable classification scheme covering the entire universe of legal issues. The Key Numbering System divides the law into seven broad categories, which are then subdivided

EXHIBIT 19-1. *United States Reports*

COMPLETE AUTO TRANSIT, INC. *v.* REIS   **401**

Syllabus

COMPLETE AUTO TRANSIT, INC., ET AL. *v.* REIS ET AL.

CERTIORARI TO THE UNITED STATES COURT OF APPEALS FOR THE
SIXTH CIRCUIT

No. 79-1777.   Argued February 24, 1981—Decided May 4, 1981

Petitioner trucking companies are parties to a collective-bargaining agreement with the Teamsters Union that contains a no-strike clause. Respondent employees of petitioners commenced a wildcat strike because they believed the union was not properly representing them in negotiations to amend the collective-bargaining agreement. Thereafter, petitioners brought an action against respondents in Federal District Court under § 301 (a) of the Labor Management Relations Act, which confers jurisdiction on federal district courts to decide suits alleging violations of collective-bargaining agreements. Petitioners sought, *inter alia*, damages against respondents in their individual capacities for all losses arising out of the wildcat strike. The District Court dismissed the damages claim, and the Court of Appeals affirmed, holding that Congress had not intended through § 301 to create a cause of action for damages against individual union members for breach of a no-strike agreement.

Held: Section 301 (a) does not sanction damages actions by employers against individual employees for violating the no-strike provision of a collective-bargaining agreement, whether or not the union participated in or authorized the strike. The legislative history of § 301 clearly reveals Congress' intent to shield individual employees from liability for such damages, even though this results in leaving the employer unable to recover for his losses. While § 301 (b), which provides that any money judgment against a union for violation of a collective-bargaining agreement shall be enforceable only against the union and not against any individual member, explicitly addresses only union-authorized violations, the "penumbra" of § 301 (b), as informed by its legislative history, establishes that Congress meant to exclude individual strikers from damages liability, whether or not they were authorized by their union to strike. The history demonstrates that Congress deliberately chose to allow a damages remedy for breach of a no-strike provision only against *unions*, not *individuals*, and, as to unions, only when they participated in or authorized the illegal strike. Pp. 405–417.

614 F. 2d 1110, affirmed.

FIGURE 19-A. Sources of Federal Judicial Decisions

Court	Official Reporter	Unofficial Reporter
Supreme Court	United States Reports	Supreme Court Reporter (West) U.S. Supreme Court Reports Lawyers' Edition (Lawyers Co-operative)
Court of Claims	U.S. Court of Claims Reports	Federal Reporter (West)
Court of Appeals	slip decisions	Federal Reporter (West)
District Courts	slip decisions	Federal Supplement (West)

into hundreds of narrower topics. This classification technique links the *American Digest System* and the *National Reporter System*. The headnotes for every case in West's court reports list the Key Numbers for the rules of law involved. The researcher can then turn to the *American Digest System* to find a comprehensive list of other cases dealing with the same issues. Under each classification number, the cases are arranged by court, with the various federal courts appearing first and followed alphabetically by each state court system. For every case, a brief abstract of the decision is provided. The *American Digest System* also contains a descriptive keyword index and alphabetical case-name tables. The *American Digest System* is first and foremost a lawyer's tool, and the researcher must look at dozens, perhaps hundreds of cases to identify the appropriate ones. However, no discussion of legal sources can ignore this monumental research guide.

An alternative to the digest approach is to consult an annotated case service. Annotated law reports, like legal encyclopedias, approach the law by the issues involved, rather than on a case-by-case basis. The most complete annotated service in the U.S. is *American Law Reports Annotated* (*A.L.R.*) from Lawyers Co-op. This series is not intended to offer a comprehensive listing of cases on all subjects. Instead, *A.L.R.* examines a limited number of critical issues and traces the development of those issues in every legal jurisdiction. For each topic, it provides the text of all pertinent cases covering that point of law. Unlike most reporting systems, *A.L.R.* includes a summary of facts in each case and the arguments of opposing counsel. The resulting coverage of each subject is detailed and exhaustive, often filling several hundred pages of narrative. *A.L.R.* focuses on narrow topics not likely to be handled by legal encyclopedias or textbooks. Issues covered in the past are updated on a continual basis and a detailed indexing system is provided.

Regulations and Administrative Decisions

Perhaps the most pervasive aspect of law in the United States is generated by administrative agencies of the federal government. Although federal agencies usually promulgate regulations, they also issue quasi-judicial rulings on cases arising from enforcement of the regulations. These administrative decisions are reported in much the same way as decisions of the court system; they can be found in official reports as well as commercial sources. Examples of annual law reports published by the agencies themselves are *Federal Trade Commission Decisions* and *Interstate Commerce Commission Reports*. A variety of weekly and daily news services also report decisions of administrative agencies. However, a surprising number of administrative agencies do not publish their rulings. For example, private publishers issue loose-leaf services covering the Equal Employment Opportunity Commission and the Consumer Product Safety Commission. Another concern involves researching state administrative rulings. The researcher interested in comparing similar rulings from several states would have a difficult time doing so through primary documents. Once again, commercial publica-

tions address the problem. A leading example of such a service is *Public Utilities Reports*, from a firm of the same name.

Regulations of federal agencies are widely published in a number of formats. In some cases they are issued in codified form as loose-leaf services from the agencies themselves. Examples of this type of service are the *Customs Regulations of the United States* issued by the U.S. Customs Service and the *Federal Acquisition Regulations*, published jointly by the General Services Administration and the Department of Defense. Many agencies issue weekly or daily news services which combine the opinions of Administrative Law Judges or Commissioners with the text of new and proposed regulations, public notices, and news. Examples include the *Internal Revenue Bulletin*, the *Customs Bulletin*, the *SEC Docket*, the *FCC Record*, and the *ICC Register*.

Administrative agencies also respond to petitions from individuals, companies, and other groups. Under the law, organizations as diverse as stock exchanges, television stations, and interstate motor carriers must obtain permission or seek waivers from their regulatory bodies before engaging in certain activities. In many cases, these rulings are not published, but a few agencies do list such actions in their news services. Among them are the above-mentioned periodicals from the SEC, the ICC, and the FCC. In many cases, regulated companies or individuals can circumvent unpleasant legal disputes with the government by requesting an opinion before engaging in a planned activity. A good example of the specific nature of such requests involves import duties. Importers who are concerned about the classification code the government will assign to products they wish to bring into the country can petition the Commercial Rulings Division of the U.S. Customs Service for an advance ruling. They submit samples of the product, together with supporting arguments for the classification code they desire. The resulting decisions are reported by the government in *Commodity Classification Under the Harmonized System: The Harmonized System Rulings Packet*. Why is this important public information? In this instance, because different codes will result in higher or lower tariff rates. But in general, the published responses of regulatory agencies can give other companies clues about the agencies' future behavior.

Specialized publications such as these do not constitute the most widely used source of government announcements. That honor goes to the daily *Federal Register*, which by law must publish all United States regulations when they are first issued or amended. All proposed regulations must also appear to allow public

comment. The *Federal Register* is cumulated annually by the *Code of Federal Regulations* (*CFR*). Both of these important documents are described below, together with related finding tools designed by commercial publishers.

Code of Federal Regulations (Office of the Federal Register—Annual).

The *CFR*, as updated by the *Federal Register*, is the official source of all general federal regulations currently in force. Like the *United States Code*, it is organized by subject, though the *CFR* takes up approximately three times the shelf space of the *U.S. Code*. This fact alone indicates the relative output of regulations compared to statutes in the United States.

The *CFR*'s 50 Titles roughly parallel the organizational structure of the *U.S. Code*. While most Titles are the same in both publications, the correspondence is not always complete. For example, federal securities laws can be found as part of Title 15 of the *U.S. Code* ("Commerce and Trade"), but regulations based on these laws are assigned a Title of their own in the *CFR* (Title 17, "Commodity and Securities Exchanges"). Given the specific responsibilities of most administrative agencies, a close relationship usually exists between the topics covered in each Title of the *CFR* and the individual agencies. As examples, Title 21 contains the regulations issued by the Food and Drug Administration and Title 39 covers the Postal Service.

The Titles in the *CFR* are divided into chapters, parts, and sections. A single Title may be published in several large volumes. They are revised on a rotating basis, but each one is completely updated every year. Each Title provides a detailed table of contents and a historical list of changes made to *CFR* sections. A master index to the set provides access by subject and agency. The annual index also contains finding lists which link *United States Code* and *Statutes at Large* citations to the appropriate *CFR* sections.

More current information is published five days per week in the *Federal Register*. New regulations and changes to existing ones are listed numerically according to their Titles in the Code. A table of contents lists each day's changes by agency name. At the back of every issue is a numerical list of all changes issued in the calendar month to date. At the end of the month, a separate *List of CFR Parts Affected* is published; this is a cumulative record of all changes which have occurred since the last revision of the *CFR*. Using the latest daily list of changes in conjunction with the most current cumulative monthly list will identify all changes made since the latest edition

of the *CFR*. The *Federal Register* also publishes a monthly index to regulations and notices by agency name, which covers the current year to date.

The *CFR* and the *Federal Register* contain useful finding tools, but the enormous output of regulatory agencies makes these documents difficult to use. One way to locate specific information within these massive publications is to search their electronic equivalents. The complete text of the *CFR* can be searched in its entirety or by specific Title on LEXIS and WESTLAW. The complete text of the *Federal Register* is also available online through the above two services and via DIALOG. Several commercial publishers also produce current, detailed indexing to the two works. One of the best is compiled by the Congressional Information Service in its weekly *CIS Federal Register Index*. It is extremely current and uses many of the same indexing features seen in other CIS publications. Access is by subject, geographic area, industry, company name, and product, as well as by agency name and *CFR* section affected. A separate numeric index lists Docket Numbers, together with specially numbered regulations such as OMB Circulars and Treasury Decisions. A weekly calendar gives deadline dates for comments on proposals and effective dates of new regulations. An electronic version of the index is available on both DIALOG and BRS. The CIS index is invaluable because the *Federal Register* provides no subject indexing of its own. Another resource of interest is intended more as a current awareness service than as a finding tool. Each monthly issue of the *U.S. Code Congressional and Administrative News* includes textual information on major regulations from the *Federal Register*, but it is not as helpful for locating specific regulations as the CIS publication.

Although the government produces a subject index to the *Code of Federal Regulations*, commercial publications offer greater detail. CIS publishes an annual *Index to the Code of Federal Regulations* in four volumes. It provides subject access down to the individual paragraph level, plus geographic and proper name indexes. Because the *CFR* is issued sequentially over the year, the CIS index doesn't appear until the complete annual set is released. A similar service is the *Code of Federal Regulations Index* from R.R. Bowker. This version's quarterly supplements make it a more timely resource.

Law Citators

It is not enough to find applicable statutes, regulations, or court rulings; legal researchers must also verify that what is found constitutes the current authority on the issue. Has the statute or case been affected in some way by subsequent rulings? Such verification is done with a citator, which provides comprehensive lists of every court decision mentioning an existing statute, regulation, or previous court case. The premier publisher of legal citation services is Shepard's Citations, a subsidiary of McGraw-Hill. In fact, verifying the authority of a law or ruling is known as "Shepardizing."

Shepard's publishes citators for various types of law and for various jurisdictions. For example, individual publications are available which cover the U.S. Supreme Court, other federal courts, state court decisions published in West's *National Reporter System*, federal administrative agency rulings, and other types of case law. Shepard's also produces citation services for laws and regulations. They trace subsequent court rulings according to provisions of the *U.S. Code*, *U.S. Statutes at Large*, and the *Code of Federal Regulations*. Most volumes are updated monthly, with frequent cumulations.

To use Shepard's citators, the researcher begins with a reference to the case in question, called the cited case. By looking in all issues of *Shepard's* since the cited case occurred, the researcher can find listings of subsequent court decisions which mention the cited case. These later cases are called the citing cases. The citator gives two essential types of information. First, "history citations" show subsequent developments of the same case as it moved through the appeals process. This section indicates whether the case in question is still a good authority. Abbreviations included by the Shepard's editors show whether the original decision was affirmed, modified, or reversed by a higher court. The second type of information traces decisions of subsequent, related cases which mention the cited case. The Shepard's editors frequently use letters and numbers attached to each citing case to indicate what issue of law was involved and the nature of the court's decision. Shepard's publications usually provide separate tables for both the official case reporting service and the most popular commercial reporters. Researchers can thus utilize the citators regardless of which case reporting service is readily available.

Exhibit 19-2 is taken from *Shepard's Federal Labor Law Citations*, which covers labor cases tried in all federal courts and administrative tribunals. If recent citations to the Reis case were being sought, the researcher would begin by turning to the section which covers *U.S. Reports*. Under the official designation of the case (volume 451, page 401), a list of citing cases can be seen. On the sixth line down, for example, is a citation to a subsequent Supreme Court decision which cited Reis, designated as 457 US 768. The letter j indicates that the citation appeared in a dissenting opinion.

EXHIBIT 19-2. *Shepard's Federal Labor Law Citations*

Vol. 451   UNITED STATES SUPREME COURT REPORTS (Labor Cases)

543FS853	f603FS¹873	95LC¶34296	j52USLW	569FS1330	38EPD	s103LRM	f104LC
568FS¹14	h622FS¹1149	97LC¶10175	[4778	597FS¹655	[¶35609	[2722	[¶11819·
582FS¹630	643FS¹536	97LC¶34363	53USLW	628FS¹313	40EPD	i258Bd1080	109LRM2355
f592FS¹592	d109FRD¹539	112LRM2608	[4951	639FS¹658	[¶36308	No 141	109LRM3197
f594FS¹474	Cir. 10	113LRM2771	j53USLW	Cir. 6	27FEP1049	263Bd1308	110LRM2673
f599FS¹919	e749F2d¹1454	113LRM2772	[4957	690F2d¹105	27FEP1059	No 188	110LRM2908
602FS¹500	751F2d317	f115LRM3400	54USLW	d697F2d¹721	29FEP499	j263Bd1314	110LRM2912
611FS¹1223	798F2d¹1323	j115LRM5124	[4620	715F2d1041	31FEP1336	No 188	f110LRM3042
12BRW272	567FS463	25WHC1115	j54USLW	755F2d1230	32FEP1649	457US¹723	e112LRM
63BRW¹603	e580FS¹20	139Il₳291	[4634	j785F2d1371	32FEP1662	j457US768	[2057
Cir. 3	f603FS¹873	383Mas609	j54USLW	538FS1117	33FEP834	460US703	112LRM2721
f654F2d¹944	608FS¹1486	132McA255	[4637	43BRW720	d34FEP1708	Cir. 1	112LRM3269
717F2d781	19BRW¹638	88NYAᴾ65	Cir. D.C.	Cir. 7	d34FEP1713	708F2d¹8	113LRM2454
543FS1378	Cir. 11	169WV708	f734F2d¹1578	689F2d729	j34FEP1720	e528FS862	113LRM2622
d604FS¹875	j734F2d574	Ill	d735F2d	729F2d¹1139	36FEP994	536FS1211	113LRM2824
d613FS¹1154	796F2d¹399	486N₤1381	[¹1461	741F2d¹990	36FEP1038	e536FS¹1212	114LRM2787
642FS¹1262	18MJ731	Mass	749F2d56	742F2d¹320	38FEP740	Cir. 2	115LRM2474
648FS¹952	5EBC1091	421N₤71	522FS32	753F2d¹1404	39FEP1268	663F2d396	d115LRM
102FRD¹885	5EBC1359	Mich	636FS¹822	794F2d¹269	41FEP409	581FS¹240	[2487
Cir. 4	e5EBC1447	347NW214	Cir. 1	808F2d¹1278	d96LC¶13934	597FS283	117LRM2502
664F2d1212	5EBC2614	NY	703F2d¹643	548FS¹582	d101LC	Cir. 3	117LRM2682
731F2d215	5EBC2620	452NYS2d89	715F2d9	565FS382	[¶11066	658F2d¹165	118LRM2809
799F2d940	6EBC1739	ND	733F2d¹173	622FS¹441	d112LRM	522FS108	118LRM3067
554FS¹951	f26EPD	315NW288	522FS¹208	Cir. 8	[2459	647FS240	120LRM2282
Cir. 5	[¶31395	W Va	535FS¹584	673F2d973	113LRM3340	Cir. 4	120LRM2529
750F2d1323	j27EPD	289S₤685	f599FS741	771F2d¹413	116LRM2552	e683F2d¹829	120LRM2534
756F2d¹1122	[¶32289	35LLJ617	Cir. 2	774F2d¹254	d116LRM	547FS675	e121LRM
515FS735	j28EPD	34NYCn265	q687F2d¹653	f774F2d¹307	[2592	Cir. 6	[2159
619FS¹833	[¶32496	74CaL327	f718F2d¹27	j799F2d1231	e119LRM	674F2d¹564	f121LRM2578
628FS¹220	f28EPD	52ChL30	719F2d¹46	591FS1470	[2557	697F2d733	122LRM3245
Cir. 6	[¶32667	67Cor570	732F2d¹1101	e15BRW882	122LRM3276	718F2d823	123LRM3086
686F2d¹429	30EPD	70Cor406	761F2d101	Cir. 9	189Ct27	f564FS¹1174	36LLJ908
707F2d¹916	[¶33010	71Cor98	801F2d629	743F2d1369	189Ct547	567FS¹584	34NYCn195
738F2d¹725	31EPD	82CR295	518FS¹1174	753F2d728	68N₳402	598FS¹220	36NYCn
790F2d¹546	[¶33377	84CR1502	554FS¹765	784F2d¹1017	16OA3d228	Cir. 7	[§5.07
556FS¹35	31EPD	71Geo1315	578FS¹440	528FS480	Colo	755F2d1290	36NYCn
592FS¹99	[¶33545	95HLR1223	595FS¹1131	639FS¹558	690P2d240	e779F2d¹1278	[§6.02
604FS719	32EPD	99HLR890	110FRD¹36	Cir. 10	Conn	f601FS¹1064	
24BRW¹838	[¶33684	99HLR1168	57BRW¹628	658F2d1377	453A2d771	Cir. 8	**– 679 –**
26BRW781	34EPD	81IlLR318	Cir. 3	678F2d¹850	456A2d1203	804F2d¹461	(68L₤538)
65BRW¹334	[¶34298	1985IlLR598	d659F2d¹313	710F2d¹1465	DC	641FS806	(101SC2088)
Cir. 7	35EPD	66MnL1004	665F2d449	739F2d¹1479	434A2d1381	Cir. 9	(91LC
d670F2d¹731	[¶34723	67MnL885	677F2d319	808F2d753	Fla	664F2d1369	¶12741)
695F2d¹1089	e35EPD	58NYL18	688F2d¹210	Cir. 11	423So2d929	f680F2d¹624	(107LRM
709F2d¹1135	[¶34848	59TxL851	747F2d¹155	695F2d539	423So2d931	743F2d¹708	2385)
f732F2d¹1336	f35EPD	60TxL740	795F2d¹297	707F2d1185	449So2d838	771F2d¹1257	s623F2d563
737F2d643	[¶34878	92YLJ1148	540FS924	716F2d¹1579	478So2d459	771F2d¹1264	s104LRM
752F2d¹1178	f37EPD	AgD§18.27	567FS¹968	720F2d1520	478So2d1201	f777F2d¹1400	[2118
752F2d¹1183	[¶35252	DEEC§2.21	596FS¹1015	734F2d¹782	487So2d376	567FS¹458	i269Bd939
789F2d¹548	f37EPD	TT§10.12	Cir. 4	791F2d¹1459	Mont	Cir. 10	No 161
e803F2d¹288	[¶35311		526FS989	639FS¹658	630P2d229	725F2d1263	272Bd901
f531FS356	h38EPD	**– 390 –**	553FS¹327	27EPD	Ohio	Cir. 11	No 138
d618FS¹1065	[¶35508	(68L₤175)	572FS¹173	[¶32337	475N₤191	793F2d¹1207	f452US912
f622FS¹1495	40EPD	(101SC1830)	Cir. 5	29EPD	Tex	92LC¶13181	f452US934
e624FS¹1004	[¶36089	(25EPD	650F2d¹767	[¶32697	669SW402	94LC¶13582	e459US¹226
628FS¹220	j27FEP899	[¶31725)	651F2d345	j29EPD	29CLA15	f94LC¶13703	j459US232
30BRW¹168	f27FEP1419	s453US921	651F2d¹346	[¶32697	69Cor414	96LC¶13982	460US708
Cir. 8	j28FEP212	s69L₤1003	662F2d302	30EPD	73Geo1055	96LC¶14130	462US¹163
j664F2d683	28FEP1490	s101SC3156	662F2d314	[¶33067	45LCP(3)38	96LC¶14142	Cir. D.C.
700F2d1200	d30FEP1035	s616F2d127	694F2d80	31EPD	81McL1439	97LC¶10155	721F2d¹824
d775F2d¹971	30FEP1383	s16EPD¶8336	d695F2d¹955	[¶33365	59TxL1060	98LC¶10405	603FS80
535FS821	31FEP1548	s24EPD	703F2d¹831	32EPD	RPHP§1.06	99LC¶10500	Cir. 1
546FS86	32FEP1787	[¶31228	704F2d1407	[¶33624	RPHP§3.22	100LC	626FS¹302
604FS¹847	33FEP1414	452US¹716	725F2d262	32EPD		[¶10756	Cir. 2
616FS¹31	33FEP1735	j457US667	532FS¹470	[¶33857	**– 401 –**	f100LC	785F2d¹33
619FS¹224	34FEP519	463US¹1333	544FS¹1014	33EPD	(68L₤248)	[¶10871	f795F2d¹1133
65BRW¹495	34FEP858	d467US572	553FS788	[¶33973	(101SC1836)	101LC	547FS¹711
Cir. 9	f35FEP439	d467US¹585	554FS104	d34EPD	(91LC	[¶11193	563FS¹1337
660F2d743	36FEP102	j467US601		[¶34415	¶12708)	102LC	594FS¹1168
e660F2d747	36FEP902	f471US¹149		j34EPD	(107LRM	[¶11385	646FS¹1464
j663F2d870	f36FEP1251	j471US150		[¶34415	2145)	103LC	Cir. 3
677F2d697	f37FEP419	d52USLW		36EPD	s571F2d580	[¶11677	d669F2d131
f696F2d¹705	40FEP779	[4770		[¶35032	s614F2d1110	103LC	670F2d¹402
528FS482	f40FEP958	d52USLW		37EPD	s88LC¶11847	[¶11677	d716F2d¹185
	e40FEP1177	[4773		[¶35246		e104LC	
	j92LC¶34106					[¶11771	*Continued*

BEYOND THE BASICS

Most of the publications and finding guides covered so far deal with the law as issued by a single type of institution. However, given the interlocking relationship of the three branches of government, there is a genuine need for research tools which examine all aspects of a legal question, or allow the researcher to locate a diversity of materials simultaneously. The other problem with basic sources is the sheer volume of published information. Even with the extensive array of indexes, digests, and citators, finding the law for a specific situation can be a major undertaking. Two specialized categories of research tools are custom-designed to address these concerns—loose-leaf services and online databases.

Loose-Leaf Services

The loose-leaf format is especially suited to legal research. Because they focus on specific topics, loose-leaf services can bring together all pertinent statutes, court decisions, and other legal matters related to the subject under investigation. A particular strength of the loose-leaf service is its expert coverage of regulations and administrative rulings. The resulting unified system of information represents a powerful tool for business and legal research.

Loose-leaf services are so termed because they are issued as loose pages in ring-binders; when information needs to be updated, the affected pages are replaced by revised material. Most legal loose-leafs are updated weekly, though some are revised monthly, biweekly, or even daily. Because superseded information is discarded, there is often no way to retain retrospective pages for historical research. But historical developments are important in legal research, so loose-leaf publishers have found several ways to deal with this problem. One is to remove older information from the ring-binders and reprint it in permanent bound volumes; this method is most commonly used for preserving older court decisions. A similar technique is to remove portions of the older loose-leaf material to a so-called "transfer binder." A third method is to issue a completely new set of binders every year, preserving the previous binders as a retrospective record. The *Congressional Index, U.S. Law Week,* and some income tax services do this. Still, many loose-leafs are current awareness tools, with no provisions for saving obsolete information.

Almost all legal loose-leaf services provide the full text of statutes and regulations, together with either the full text or digests of important judicial and administrative rulings. They also provide editorial commentary and explanatory text, which makes them more useful to the nonlawyer. Some services also contain information not readily found in other sources. This is especially important for areas of law where the government does not publish cases or administrative rulings. For example, *Trade Regulation Reports,* published by Commerce Clearing House, contains consent decrees issued by the Antitrust Division of the Department of Justice.

Loose-leaf publications also offer excellent systems of finding guides. Most publications contain a detailed master index to the set, which provides subject and name access to the material being sought. Because updating this master index is an enormous task, most publishers include separate, less-detailed indexes to the most current information in the publication. For example, a "Recent Additions" index will cover the previous week's listings. Each month, this index is folded into a "Current Matters" index, which in turn is cumulated into the "Basic" index at the end of the year. The user must consult three different indexes to locate all pertinent material, but this is an effective way to keep track of recent information. Loose-leaf services present a total information package for the topic at hand, but like other legal finding tools, they should not be considered substitutes for the official documents containing cases, statutes, or regulations.

The 1990 edition of *Legal Looseleafs in Print* (described in Chapter 3) lists 3,700 titles from 320 different publishers. Approximately two dozen loose-leaf publishers regularly produce major services in business law. The largest loose-leaf firms produce scores of publications for every type of law imaginable. For any subject category, several publishers usually offer similar services. Despite extensive competition, most firms have established enduring reputations for specific types of publications. The following list briefly describes the leading publishers in the field.

> *Commerce Clearing House, Inc.*—The oldest and largest loose-leaf publisher, with over 150 different titles available in virtually every area of the law. Examples of publications: *Consumer Product Safety Guide, Federal Banking Law Reporter, Common Market Reporter,* and *Government Contracts Reports.*

Prentice Hall Information Services—The major competitor to CCH with 75 loose-leaf publications. Noted for tax services and guides to business practice. Owned briefly by Maxwell Macmillan, PHIS is now a division of Thomson International. Examples of titles: *Charitable Giving and Solicitation; Corporate Acquisitions, Mergers and Divestitures*; and *Divorce Taxation.*

Bureau of National Affairs—The third firm of the "Big Three" in loose-leaf publishing, with approximately 70 major titles. Most noted for its coverage of labor law, but also active in international trade law, environment, and safety. The weekly *Environment Reporter*, a massive 29-volume set, is the definitive guide to environmental law. A BNA subsidiary, Tax Management, Inc., is a leading producer of loose-leaf tax services and newsletters. Other services: *Export Shipping Manual, Pension Reporter*, and *Media Law Reporter.*

Matthew Bender & Co., Inc.—Another broad-based loose-leaf supplier. Noted for publishing in fields of accounting, securities law, taxation, and legal practice. Some publications are classic works, like *Nimmer on Copyright* and the *Collier Bankruptcy Manual.* Other representative titles: *Accounting Systems for Law Offices* and *Cable Television Law.*

Research Institute of America, Inc.—Now a subsidiary of the Lawyers Co-operative Publishing Company. Publisher of several extensive sets in the areas of taxation, labor law, and personnel practices. Publications noted for their ease of use and readability.

Other publishers of loose-leaf services in business law are Warren, Gorham & Lamont, Inc., Clark Boardman Company, Ltd., and Panel Publishers, Inc.

Online Databases

Computer databases can relieve much of the tedium of locating relevant cases, tracing subsequent citations, and bringing together related aspects of a complex legal issue. Because of the huge number of publications and the enormous amount of detail they contain, legal research is ideally suited for full-text retrieval capabilities.

The two major legal database systems in the United States are LEXIS, from Mead Data Central, and WESTLAW, from West Publishing. The two services are generally similar in coverage and methodology, but each continues to offer refinements. Both are enormous

full-text services, offering the complete spectrum of primary legal documents and secondary finding tools. They provide the text of current federal and state court decisions, including some not available in print form. Federal statutes are available through the online *U.S. Code* as well as commercial Code services, and many state laws can also be found. Regulatory information is abundant, including electronic versions of the *CFR* and the *Federal Register.* LEXIS and WESTLAW also provide online versions of *Shepard's Citations.* Retrospective coverage varies for each area, but both publishers continue to add older materials to their files. The availability of these automated systems has revolutionized legal research. Searchers can now combine terms to narrow their investigations, limit searches to specific jurisdictions or types of documents, and retrieve documents containing specified words or phrases as they appear anywhere in the text. LEXIS and WESTLAW have become common fixtures in law libraries and legal firms throughout the world.

The structure of the LEXIS service will illustrate how far-flung, yet flexible these major systems can be. LEXIS databases are grouped together in electronic "Libraries." For example, the *LA WREV* Library contains the text of some 60 major law reviews. Some Libraries cover broad areas such as court decisions, while others deal with fairly narrow publications or topics. Individual Libraries are available for each of the 50 states. The coverage in State Libraries varies; they may contain court reporters, codified statutes, administrative decisions from state agencies, and/or the state constitution. Topical Libraries cover such fields as banking, securities, labor, and taxation. Separate Libraries contain the text of CCH and BNA loose-leaf services. Finally, an assortment of foreign and international Libraries are offered, including databases from the European Economic Community. Users can select individual Libraries, groups of Libraries, or all files simultaneously, or they can limit searches to a specific document.

Many other publications mentioned in this chapter are available online from various vendors. The Bureau of National Affairs offers information from many of its loose-leaf services, newsletters, and case reporters online via several vendors, including LEXIS, WESTLAW, and HRIN. On the DIALOG system, BNA has grouped seven of its case reporters together in a database called *LABORLAW.* A newer file on DIALOG is *BNA Daily News*, the electronic equivalent of 15 of BNA's newsletters, updated daily. LEXIS and WESTLAW also offer these files, plus selected loose-leafs and additional case reporters. A number of standard government documents

can be searched electronically through traditional online vendors. The complete text of the *Congressional Record* can be found on LEXIS and WESTLAW, among others. Abstracts of the *Congressional Record* can be seen on DIALOG and BRS. DIALOG also provides access to important legal and government finding tools, including the *CIS Index*, the *Monthly Catalog*, and the *GPO Publications Reference File*. The potential for improved searching which these sources provide is virtually unlimited.

The preceding discussion of legal institutions and publications, while necessarily brief, has tried to impart a general understanding of the basic structure of the law and the categories of research tools available. Even if such specialized resources as the *American Digest System* or *Shepard's Citations* are never consulted, it is important for business researchers to have a sense of where different types of information can be found.

At this point, the discussion can be tied together by looking at a specific area of business law in greater detail. Labor law was singled out for several reasons. First, labor publications exhibit some unique characteristics. Second, labor law is enormously complex and presents an excellent opportunity to build on the concepts already introduced. Third, it is a frequent topic of research requests. And finally, it is a subject that can be easily identified with and one which is inherently interesting.

LABOR LAW IN THE UNITED STATES

The body of law affecting the workplace is diverse, covering such wide-ranging topics as trade unions and collective bargaining, employment discrimination, minimum wages, maximum work hours, safety on the job, and occupational illness. Each of these subjects is complex and is governed by its own set of laws, regulations, and court decisions. The immediate impact of this legal structure upon our everyday lives is perhaps more noticeable than any other area of the law.

Labor law has several distinct characteristics. For one thing, there is considerable overlapping between state and federal laws. The statutes governing a single state may be far more stringent than the national legislation, or vice versa. What's more, it is often unclear which jurisdiction prevails in a given situation. A second distinction is that federal regulatory bodies such as OSHA, the NLRB, and the EEOC often have significant and far-reaching powers granted by Congress. In many cases, statutes intentionally limit the role of the courts in adjudicating labor issues, instead granting such powers to administrative agencies. Third, American work rules are

established not only by public law, but by labor contracts between unions and managements. The provisions of U.S. collective bargaining agreements are extremely detailed, covering all manner of work situations. The parties to a contract must be conscious of the terms of the agreement under which they live. This aspect of labor relations is commonly called shop law. Finally, many labor disputes are settled outside the judicial and regulatory structure, through mediation and binding arbitration. Published decisions of labor arbitrators can serve as legal precedent just as judicial decisions do.

Labor law provides an excellent example of the uses and interrelationships of legal publications. All of the categories of resources introduced earlier in the chapter have applications to labor law. Many of the following publications are specialized sources unique to this topic, but they serve to demonstrate in greater detail the basics of the legal research process. Before exploring some of the leading labor law resources, a few important concepts will be discussed.

Major Provisions of Labor Relations Law

Federal laws protecting the rights of workers to organize and bargain collectively are a fairly recent phenomenon in the United States. The Norris-LaGuardia Act, the landmark legislation limiting the government's ability to interfere with striking workers, was passed in 1932. Since that time, a series of laws established the basic structure of labor relations in this country. The first systematic look at labor-management issues was undertaken by the National Labor Relations Act of 1935, better known as the Wagner Act. This law was completely revised in 1947 as the Labor Management Relations Act, popularly designated the Taft-Hartley Law. Other important labor laws cover employees in special areas such as hospitals, railroads, airlines, and the public sector. But Taft-Hartley remains the principal federal legislation dealing with union-management issues for most American workers.

The Wagner Act created the National Labor Relations Board, the primary regulatory body governing union-management relations. The Board consists of five members appointed by the President and confirmed by the Senate. The NLRB is also composed of a vast administrative system, including an Office of the General Counsel, and a network of Administrative Law Judges. To avoid confusion in the remainder of this discussion, the term Board will refer to the five members appointed by the President and the name NLRB will designate the agency in its entirety.

The jurisdiction of the NLRB is narrowly defined. The agency can intervene in two types of situations: a petition for representation under Section 9 of the Taft-Hartley Law, and a charge of unfair labor practices under Section 8 of the same Law. These two areas constitute the most frequent sources of conflict between unions and management, or between two unions.

Representation petitions involve employees' rights to select a union. When a nonunion shop wants to become unionized, or unionized workers wish to change the union which represents them, an election must take place. The election process is complicated and is overseen at every step by the NLRB. Unfair labor practices may be committed by a union or by management, and either side may file a charge against the other. Charges are filed at the local level, where they are investigated by a Regional Office of the NLRB. Facts are gathered and affidavits taken from the parties involved. If the Regional Director determines the case has merit (and falls within the jurisdiction of the NLRB), a hearing takes place before an Administrative Law Judge. The ALJ then makes a written report to the Board, stating the Judge's finding of facts and conclusions of law, together with a recommended order stating the actions, if any, which must be taken to rectify the situation. In typical cases, three members of the Board then review the recommendation, although in complex cases the full Board may be involved. The Board either accepts the recommendations of the ALJ in full, or makes modifications to the findings. The resulting decision and order of the Board is binding on the parties. The decision may be appealed to the U.S. Court of Appeals, but the Court has limited powers to vacate or modify Board actions because Congress intended the NLRB to serve as the principal adjudicating body in labor disputes.

Collective Bargaining and Arbitration

The power to negotiate a successful labor contract is every union's ultimate reason for existing. When an existing collective bargaining agreement is due to expire, the parties must notify an independent government agency known as the Federal Mediation and Conciliation Service (FMCS). By law, both parties are bound to bargain in good faith. Federal laws strictly define what constitutes good faith bargaining, but both sides have complete freedom in choosing the makeup of their negotiating teams. If an impasse is reached, the parties may call in a representative of the FMCS to help reach a compromise. If the impasse cannot be resolved, a work stoppage may occur, initiated either by the union (a strike or slowdown)

or the employer (a lockout). A testament to the workability of the U.S. labor relations system is the relatively small number of major work stoppages which take place in any year.

After a contract is ratified, labor and management must live under its terms for the life of the new agreement, usually one, two, or three years. A fairly universal feature of labor contracts is the provision of detailed procedures for filing and resolving a grievance. The grievance must cite the specific provision of the contract under which the aggrieved party seeks redress. As a consequence, contracts are lengthy documents defining seniority rights, work rules, employee discipline procedures, and other day-to-day practices. Most collective bargaining agreements provide for binding arbitration as the final step in the grievance process. If a dispute reaches this stage, a trained labor arbitrator is brought in to decide the issue. Labor contracts outline the steps which must be taken to obtain an arbitrator. A common method is to ask the FMCS or the American Arbitration Association to supply a list of qualified consultants with demonstrated expertise in labor practice. (Many arbitrators are not full-time practitioners; typically they are lawyers, academics, or retired labor professionals.) From this list, both sides reject unsuitable choices until a mutually agreeable arbitrator is designated.

Once an arbitrator is chosen, both sides of the dispute are presented in an informal hearing. The arbitrator takes into account the laws pertaining to the issue at hand, the language of the collective bargaining agreement, the decisions of other arbitrators in similar situations, and the history of past practices in the workplace. The arbitrator's decision (called an award) is final and binding. When appropriate, the award includes an order for remedial action. Awards involving unique, important, or complex issues are printed by commercial publishers in the same way as court decisions. These published decisions can serve as useful precedents for future labor disputes.

Labor Statutes, Regulations, and Case Law

Most statutes relating to the workplace can be found in Title 29 of the *U.S. Code* ("Labor"), but labor laws can be found in other Titles as well. The researcher who seeks information on amendments to the Equal Employment Opportunity Act of 1972, for example, needs to consult the Popular Name Index to the *U.S. Code*, since the EEOA is found in Title 42 with civil rights legislation. The Index also lists the Public Law

number for the Act (P.L. 92-261) and where the text of the original law can be found in the *U.S. Statutes at Large* (86 Stat 103). Labor regulations are printed in the annual *Code of Federal Regulations*, again in Title 29. There is not always complete correspondence between the *CFR* and the *U.S. Code*; for example, the regulations of the Equal Employment Opportunity Commission are found in Title 29, Chapter 14, rather than in Title 42.

Court decisions involving labor law appear in a variety of general case reporters, but more specialized services are available from the Bureau of National Affairs and Commerce Clearing House. Cases heard before the National Labor Relations Board are also published in book form, by both the government and commercial firms. An excellent guide to the diverse publications of labor case law is *Shepard's Federal Labor Law Citations*. Like other Shepard's publications, it traces the current authority of judicial decisions, including rulings of the NLRB, the U.S. Supreme Court, and lower federal courts.

The following publications constitute the most widely used labor case reporters from the Government Printing Office and private publishers.

Decisions and Orders of the NLRB (The National Labor Relations Board—Irregular).

These massive volumes constitute the official reports of cases decided by the Board, printed in chronological order. The reports contain the full text of the Board's decisions, but the bulk of the information is actually the recommendation of the original Administrative Law Judge who heard the case. The table of case names is a "forward and backward" index, providing access by the names of both parties in the dispute. Cross-references from varying forms of company names are also included. The bound volumes are published four to six times per year, but the time lag in coverage is approximately two years. More recent information can be found in the *Weekly Summary of NLRB Cases*, though it contains abbreviated reports only.

Another NLRB publication, *Court Decisions Relating to the National Labor Relations Act*, doesn't cover decisions of the Board, but rather decisions of the Supreme Court and U.S. Court of Appeals which construe sections of the Taft-Hartley Law. A small number of significant state court rulings can also be found. It appears annually, but once again has a two-year lag in coverage. The decisions are printed in chronological order, with an alphabetical index to case names, and an index by court. Since this publication is not the official reporter for the various courts in question, a conversion table is presented which lists the location of each case in the appropriate official court report. The Government Printing Office once published several law reports of this type, but the labor relations title is one of the few remaining government documents which covers the decisions of more than a single court. An extremely useful resource for labor law research, it offers an inexpensive alternative to the commercial publications introduced later in this chapter.

Subject access to the above publications is offered in a companion series from the NLRB called the *Classified Index of NLRB and Related Court Decisions*. This quarterly guide is an index-digest system to the law reports, with cases grouped together according to the NLRB's own classification system. Each case is given a brief abstract and a reference to its location in the bound reports. The quarterly indexes are cumulated every three years and the NLRB publishes a separate outline of its classification numbers to assist users.

Labor Relations Reference Manual (Bureau of National Affairs, Inc.—Three Times per Year).

Much of the information from the three NLRB publications just introduced can be found in a popular series from BNA referred to as the *LRRM*. It provides digests of the NLRB decisions, together with the full text of significant court decisions, each in roughly chronological order. The *LRRM* includes a detailed index to case names similar to that found in the NLRB publications. A parallel table of case locations in official law reports is also given. Exhibit 19-3 shows the *LRRM* presentation of the Reis case which was seen earlier in the chapter. The correct citation for this report is 107 LRRM 2145, indicating the volume and page of the publication. Note that the case digest is different from the syllabus found in *U.S. Reports*.

Subject access to the *LRRM* is published annually in a companion paperback volume entitled the *Labor Relations Cumulative Digest and Index*. This service is cumulated quinquennially. Like the NLRB's *Classified Index*, the information from BNA is arranged according to a classification system by topic. The numbering is different from the government's, but serves the same function. For example, cases involving union representation elections are grouped under Class 62 in the BNA numbering system, and Class 370 in the NLRB system. Information in the BNA cumulative digest consists of the headnotes to each case. The researcher must then consult the *LRRM* or other reporting service to obtain the text of the decision. An added feature of the *Labor Relations Cumulative Digest and Index* is a guide to union names by their popular designations. Exhibit 19-4 illustrates the

EXHIBIT 19-3. *Labor Relations Reference Manual*

COMPLETE AUTO TRANSIT v. REIS   107 LRRM 2145

COMPLETE AUTO TRANSIT v. REIS

Supreme Court of the United States

COMPLETE AUTO TRANSIT, INC., et al. v. REIS, et al., No. 79–1777, May 4, 1981

LABOR MANAGEMENT RELATIONS ACT

Section 301 action — Wildcat strike — Breach of contract — Damages against individual employees ▶ 80.554 ▶ 80.8430

Section 301 of LMRA does not sanction damages against individual employees for violating no-strike provision of collective bargaining contract, whether or not their union participated in or authorized strike. Legislative history of Section 301 clearly reveals Congress' intent to shield individual employees from liability for damages arising from their breach of no-strike clause, even though this results in leaving employer unable to recover for his losses; legislative debates and process of legislative amendment demonstrate that, after balancing competing advantages and disadvantages inherent in possible remedies to combat wildcat strikes, Congress deliberately chose to allow damages remedy for breach of no-strike provision of contract only against "unions", not "individuals", and, as to unions, only when they participated in or authorized strike.

On writ of certiorari to the U.S. Court of Appeals for the Sixth Circuit (103 LRRM 2722, 614 F.2d 1110). Affirmed.

R. Ian Hunter (C. John Holmquist, Jr., and Matheson, Bieneman, Parr, Schuler & Ewald, with him on brief), Bloomfield Hills, Mich., for petitioners.

Hiram S. Grossman (Draper, Daniel, Ruhala & Seymour, P.C., with him on brief), Flint, Mich., for respondents.

J. Albert Woll, Washington, D.C., Laurence Gold, Washington, D.C., and George Kaufmann, Washington, D.C., filed brief for AFL-CIO, as amicus curiae, seeking affirmance.

Before BURGER, Chief Justice, and BRENNAN, STEWART, WHITE, MARSHALL, BLACKMUN, POWELL, REHNQUIST, and STEVENS, Justices.

Full Text of Opinion

JUSTICE BRENNAN delivered the opinion of the Court.

In Atkinson v. Sinclair Refining Co., 370 U.S. 238, 50 LRRM 2433 (1962), the Court held that §301(a) of the Labor Management Relations Act of 1947, 29 U.S.C. §185, does not authorize a damages action against individual union officers and members when their union is liable for violating a no-strike clause in a collective-bargaining agreement. We expressly reserved the question whether an employer might maintain a suit for damages against "individual defendants acting not in behalf of the union but in their personal and nonunion capacity" where their "unauthorized, individual action" violated the no-strike provision of the collective-bargaining agreement. Id., at 249, n.7. We granted certiorari to decide this important question of federal labor law. —— U.S. —— (1980).

I

Petitioners are three companies engaged in the transportation by truck of motor vehicles. All three are parties to a collective-bargaining agreement with the Teamsters Union that covers operations at their respective facilities in Flint, Mich. Respondents are employees of petitioners and members of Teamsters Local Union No. 332. The collective-bargaining agreement contains a no-strike clause[1] and subjects all disputes to a binding grievance and arbitration procedure.

On June 8, 1976, respondents commenced a wildcat strike, because they believed that "the union was not properly representing them in . . . negotiations for amendments to the collective bargaining agreement." Complete Auto Transit, Inc. v. Reis, 614 F.2d 1110, 1111, 103 LRRM 2722 (CA6 1980). Soon thereafter, petitioners brought this §301(a) action in the United States District Court for the Eastern District of Michigan, seeking injunctive relief and "damages against the [employees], in their individual capacity, for all losses arising out of the unlawful work stoppage and for attorneys fees." Joint App. 21. Petitioners alleged that the strike was neither authorized nor approved by the union and, therefore, sought no damages from the union. See 614 F.2d, at 1115; Joint App. 18, 20–21. After a hearing, the District Court found that "the issue which had caused the work stoppage was not arbitrable" because it was "an internal dispute between factions in the Local," App. to Pet. for

---

[1] The no-strike clause provides that "[t]he Unions and the Employers agree that there shall be no strike, tie-up of equipment, slowdowns or walkouts on the part of the employees, nor shall the Employer use any method of lockout or legal proceeding without first using all possible means of a settlement, as provided for in this Agreement, of any controversy which might arise." See Exhibit A to Complaint of Complete Auto Transit, Inc., at 24–25.

Reprinted with permission from *Labor Relations Reference Manual,* Vol. 107, p. 2145. Copyright 1981 by The Bureau of National Affairs, Inc. (800-372-1033).

EXHIBIT 19-4. *Labor Relations Cumulative Digest and Index*

callback work —Elevator Mfrs. Assn. of New York, Inc. v. Elevator Constructors, Local 1 [CA 2 (1982)] 111 LRRM 2631

Contract's prohibition against work stoppage does not invalidate right to conduct work stoppage to protest matters which cannot be resolved under contractual grievance procedure; work stoppage precipitated by nonarbitrable dispute does not come within purview of contract —Ryder Truck Lines, Inc. v. Teamsters, Local 480 [CA 6 (1983)] 113 LRRM 2193

▶80.553 —Conditional no-strike agreements
[For obligation to exhaust grievance and arbitration remedies, see ▶80.555.]

U.S. District Courts

Unions are liable for damages caused by sympathy strikes by employees, where unions aided strike in violation of contracts' no-strike provisions, despite claim that collateral oral agreement existed permitting observance of members of sanctioned picket lines —Owens-Illinois, Inc. v. Glass Bottle Blowers, Local 29 [DC Calif (1983)] 114 LRRM 3454

▶80.554 —Union and union officers' responsibility; unauthorized strikes
[For union responsibility for picketing, see ▶81.04. For union unfair practices, see ▶57.932 and 58.1603.]

U.S. Supreme Court

LMRA Sec. 301 does not sanction damages against individual employees for violating no-strike provision of contract —Complete Auto Transit, Inc. v. Reis [US SupCt (1981) aff 103:2722] 107 LRRM 2145

Union may waive statutory protection afforded union officials against imposition of more severe sanctions for participating in unlawful work stoppage —Metropolitan Edison Co. [US SupCt (1983), sub nom Metropolitan Edison Co. v. NLRB, aff 108:3020] 112 LRRM 3265

Union did not waive statutory protection afforded union officials against imposition of more severe sanctions for participating in unlawful work stoppage, despite claim that union's failure to change general no-strike clause in face of two prior arbitration awards constitutes implicit contractual waiver —Ibid.

U.S. Courts of Appeals

Local union president who allegedly tortiously induced union to violate contract with publisher by participating in establishment and operation of strike newspaper while engaged in contract negotiations is not individually liable in damages —Wilkes-Barre Publishing Co. v. Newspaper Guild, Local 120 (Wilkes-Barre) [CA 3 (1981)] 107 LRRM 2312

LMRA precludes newspaper publisher from maintaining damage action under either federal common labor law or Pa. law against officers of unions that allegedly tortiously induced labor

organization to breach its contract with publisher —Ibid.

Norris-LaGuardia Act does not bar grant of injunctive relief against local union president and officers of other labor organization in newspaper publisher's action alleging that president, officers, and other unions tortiously induced local union to breach contract by publishing strike newspaper during negotiations —Ibid.

Norris-LaGuardia Act precludes grant of injunctive relief against local unions in newspaper publisher's action alleging that unions tortiously induced another local union to breach contract —Ibid.

LMRA does not deprive federal district court of jurisdiction over claim that council, which is composed of several unions, tortiously induced one of unions to breach its contract with newspaper publisher —Ibid.

Court has jurisdiction over newspaper publisher's claim that international union, local unions, and officers tortiously induced another local union to breach contract by operating strike newspaper while negotiating —Ibid.

Court's decision that Sec. 301 does not permit damage award against local union officials for violation of no-strike provision of contract is not authority for proposition that lower court lacks jurisdiction to fine union officers in civil contempt proceedings arising from their violation of temporary injunction against strike —Consolidation Coal Co. v. Mine Workers (UMW) Local 1702 [CA 4 (1982)] 110 LRRM 2911

Civil contempt conviction of union and officers for violation of court's temporary injunction against strike is appealable —Ibid.

Court properly found union and its officials in civil contempt of temporary injunction against wildcat strike —Ibid.

Absent specific contractual obligations to contrary, union officers may not be disparately disciplined for mere participation in or failure to take affirmative steps to end illegal work stoppage —South Central Bell Telephone Co. [CA 5 (1982), sub nom NLRB v. South Central Bell Telephone Co., enf 106:1164] 111 LRRM 2609

Arbitrator's decision upholding union president's discharge that relied heavily on official's failure to exert his influence to end illegal strike was based on erroneous premise of law that official had affirmative duty to end illegal strike —Babcock & Wilcox Co. [CA 6 (1983), sub nom NLRB v. Babcock & Wilcox Co., enf 104:1199] 112 LRRM 2713

Collateral estoppel bars portion of employer's action against union alleging that union violated contract by failing to make every effort to persuade wildcat strikers to return to work, where, in prior action by employer, lower court found that union took all available steps to abide by court's temporary restraining order —Anchor Motor Freight, Inc. v. Teamsters, Local 377 [CA 6 (1983)] 112 LRRM 2928

Lower court erred in entering summary judgment in employer's damage action against union for its alleged failure to immediately make every effort to persuade wildcat strikers to return

For Guidance See Introduction

coverage of the Reis case in the *Cumulative Digest and Index*. Under BNA's Class 80, which deals with strikes and slowdowns, the user will find subdivision 80.554, covering union responsibility in a wildcat strike. Note that this classification number can also be seen in the headnotes shown in Exhibit 19-3. The *LRRM* is updated weekly by a loose-leaf called *Labor Relations Reporter*, which includes subject indexes and case tables.

The Commerce Clearing House equivalent to the *Labor Relations Reference Manual* appears as two separate publications: *Labor Cases* provides the full text of court cases dealing with labor relations and wage-hour issues; *NLRB Decisions* prints CCH digests of NLRB decisions and orders.

BNA and CCH also produce court reports for other areas of labor law. The reporters from BNA follow the *LRRM* format, but with varying frequencies: the texts of cases appear chronologically in bound volumes issued one to three times per year. A separate classified index-digest accompanies each bound reporter, and these are cumulated annually and quinquennially. BNA's *Fair Employment Practices Cases* provides information on discrimination decisions from the Equal Employment Opportunity Commission. This is a significant publication because the EEOC does not produce an official reporter of its own. Other labor law reports from BNA include *Wage and Hour Cases, Individual Employment Rights Cases, Employee Benefit Cases*, and *Occupational Safety and Health Cases*. Except for the latter two titles, which have their own corresponding loose-leaf services, all are updated weekly by the *Labor Relations Reporter*. The case reporters from Commerce Clearing House are similar in most respects to those from BNA.

Labor Arbitration Reports: Dispute Settlements (Bureau of National Affairs—Semiannual).

The most frequently cited guide to noteworthy arbitration decisions is BNA's *Labor Arbitration Reports (LAR)*. This hardcover series reprints the full text of decisions from labor arbitrators and government-appointed fact-finding boards. The vast majority of cases involve privately appointed arbitrators dealing with labor disputes in both the private and public sectors. *LAR* also includes court cases ruling on arbitration awards. BNA obtains most of its cases from professional arbitration societies such as the American Arbitration Association, or from the arbitrators themselves. Not all submissions are accepted for publication. The case must deal with a significant issue of interest to the general public. Unique situations with no outside applicability, or cases

hinging on the believability of the testimony rather than legal issues, will not be included in *Labor Arbitration Reports*. Routine cases contributing nothing to the body of labor law are also rejected. Finally, the award itself must be well written, so outside parties can readily understand the facts and issues.

BNA reproduces the complete text of each arbitration award verbatim. The format of the reports can differ, depending on the writing style of the arbitrator. However, standard segments of a report include introductory information (identifying the parties involved, the date and place of the hearing, the witnesses who testified, and the arbitrator's name), a statement of the issues, the sections of the contract in dispute, the facts of the case, the key positions of both parties, the arbitrator's discussion or analysis, and the award itself. BNA also adds editorial information of its own. The key issues of law in each case are outlined in numbered headnotes, utilizing the same classification system seen in *LRRM*. A cumulative index-digest system is published annually and quinquennially. A name index to parties in the disputes is included in the main case volumes, and cumulated in the index-digest volumes. The bound volumes of *Labor Arbitration Reports* are updated weekly as part of the *Labor Relations Reporter* loose-leaf set, including current indexes by topic and case name.

An index by arbitrators' names appears in the case volumes, with cumulations in the index-digest. This feature is important when both parties in a dispute must agree on an arbitrator, to be selected from an approved list. *Labor Arbitration Reports* allows the parties to review each candidate's notable awards from the past. BNA also produces a biographical directory of the arbitrators whose awards are published in *LAR*. The biographies, which are found in the hardcover index-digest volumes, cite each individual's address, occupation, birth date, professional affiliations, experience, areas of specialization, publications, and a cumulative list of cases found in *LAR*. The text of the cases, together with the biographical data on the arbitrators, can also be searched online through LEXIS.

Commerce Clearing House publishes a competing semiannual service called *Labor Arbitration Awards*. The CCH and BNA titles are not necessarily similar in content; each publisher covers many cases the other does not. The minimal overlap is because the reports are submitted to the publishers by the arbitrators themselves, and because the selection process is somewhat subjective. Otherwise, the format of the CCH service is similar.

The complete text of each award is reproduced, together with standard introductory matter and CCH headnotes. A minor difference is CCH's indication of how the arbitrator for the case was chosen. Another difference is the absence of a companion index-digest. Instead, CCH provides a topical index in every volume, with a single-sentence annotation rather than a lengthier digest. Like BNA, this is presented in a classified arrangement, though CCH of course utilizes its own numbering system. For retrospective research, 10-year cumulations are published for the topical and case name indexes.

Several other major guides to dispute resolution are published. For example, the American Arbitration Association publishes three major reporters: *Summaries of Labor Arbitration Awards*, *Labor Arbitration in Government*, and *Arbitration in the Schools*.

Labor Arbitration Information System (LRP Publications—Monthly, with Annual Cumulations).

Rather than consulting the same topic in numerous sources, researchers can turn to the *Labor Arbitration Information System*, a collective index to several major arbitration series. This helpful guide provides summaries of all the cases reported in seven major services, plus a small number unique to LRP. Included are the major publications from BNA, CCH, and the AAA. Approximately 2,500 cases are summarized per year.

The digests are arranged using a key classification system unique to the publisher, with a master subject index. Additional indexes are provided for the parties in the dispute; unlike some services, which afford access only by the official case name, the *Labor Arbitration Information System* compiles separate indexes to employer and union names. Every monthly issue appears in two parts: one contains the summary decisions and indexes; the other contains the full text of decisions published exclusively by LRP. Twenty new cases are reported each month; twelve from the private sector and eight from the public sector. The monthly issues are superseded by a year-end hardcover edition, also issued in two parts.

Loose-Leaf Services for Labor Law

Because of the extensive body of laws affecting labor situations, this subject area is ideally suited for coverage by loose-leaf services. Loose-leaf labor services bring together state and federal law in one series, providing up-to-date coverage of statutes, regulations, and case law in a unified system. There are two types of loose-leaf publications for labor topics: those which emphasize the legal framework of labor relations, and those which focus on practical advice for the nonlawyer. Between the two extremes are hybrid services which combine aspects of both.

The array of products designed expressly for the personnel manager has mushroomed in recent years because of the increased importance of legal concerns in the day-to-day operations of the firm. In the past, labor law was governed by a principle known as "employment at will." It stated that, barring specific covenants of collective bargaining agreements, companies could fire employees whenever they wanted, with little or no cause. This is an oversimplification, of course, but recent legislation and judicial rulings have greatly limited the employer's freedom to terminate workers, and lawsuits for wrongful discharge are now commonplace. To protect against such suits, employers need to document their work rules and policies thoroughly, and to communicate these rules to their labor force. And while many excellent publications explain how to design a personnel handbook, the current environment demands a more sophisticated approach to the subject, combining practical "how-to" advice with specific legal information.

The diversity of loose-leaf products created for labor relations and human resource management is mind-boggling. Some are quite broad in their coverage, others focus on narrower topics. Numerous publishers compete for this lucrative market, and a single publisher may offer a variety of similar titles for every need, ranging from multi-volume legal sets to abbreviated services of various sizes. Unlike most areas of loose-leaf publishing, competing labor law services are not easily compared.

Labor Relations Reporter (Bureau of National Affairs, Inc.—Weekly).

BNA launched the first comprehensive labor law service, the *Labor Relations Reporter*, in 1937. Today the company is recognized as the leading producer of labor relations resources. The *LRR* is an 18-volume set covering all aspects of employment law and serving as a weekly updating service to many of BNA's bound case reports. In addition to providing the text of current judicial decisions, arbitration awards, and digests of NLRB decisions, the *LRR* contains the full text of federal statutes, Executive Orders, and regulations. These various types of law are grouped together in a topical arrangement. BNA also offers editorial commentary and examples to help the reader interpret the enormous amount of legal information. A sense of the publication's scope can be gathered from the following list of titles available in the set.

Labor Relations Expediter (2 vols.) The first volume of the *Expediter* provides the full text of major federal laws for quick reference. Relevant portions of the laws are also interspersed throughout the remainder of the set on a subject basis. The second volume of the *Expediter* is an alphabetical summary of basic topics in labor relations, intended to lead users to the more detailed information found in the remaining volumes. Many subscribers find it invaluable as a stand-alone desk top reference manual. This volume includes numerous dictionaries of common labor terms and directories of labor organizations and agencies. The *Expediter* may also be purchased independently.

State Laws (2 vols.) Significant portions of state labor laws are reproduced verbatim, along with brief editorial comments. The material is organized by state and by broad topic within each state. State laws on job discrimination appear in the *Fair Employment Practices* volumes described below.

Analysis/News and Background Information (1 vol.) This title contains two weekly newsletters: one provides a summary of recent events, the other analyzes important trends and issues.

Labor-Management Relations (2 vols.) Current laws and decisions on unfair labor practices, union recognition, labor disputes, and related issues can be found here. Cases printed here are reissued in bound form as the *Labor Relations Reference Manual.*

Labor Arbitration and Dispute Settlements (1 vol.) This title publishes the full text of current labor arbitration awards dealing with union-management disputes. The cases are later reprinted in the bound volumes of *Labor Arbitration Reports.* Subscribers may also purchase this volume separately.

Wages and Hours (3 vols.) Here are found state and federal laws, regulations, and decisions on matters of fair labor standards. Topics include minimum wage, overtime and holiday pay, employees working at home, and child labor. Judicial decisions later appear in the bound volumes of *Wage and Hour Cases.*

Individual Employment Rights (2 vols.) The newest addition to the service is this title covering issues related to employee rights outside the collective bargaining arena. Among the topics covered are employee privacy; drug, alcohol, and polygraph testing; and employment at will. These concerns are among the most hotly contested issues in the workplace and comprise a complex and rapidly changing body of law. This service may also be purchased separately.

Fair Employment Practices Manual (4 vols.) This title is similar in format to *Wages and Hours.* Subjects covered include all areas of state and federal employment discrimination laws. Older cases are reprinted in the bound volumes of *Fair Employment Practices Cases* can also be purchased separately.

Master Index (1 vol.) This is the current and retrospective index to the entire set, including the bound law reports. A "Topic Finder" provides subject access to the set, while a cumulative classified index lists cases according to the classification system used in the annual index-digest volumes. An alphabetical table of cases leads the user to named cases within the set as well as providing parallel references to their location in official court reports.

The massive loose-leaf set, together with the corresponding bound volumes of law reports, constitute a stand-alone resource for most labor law topics. The three-way approach to indexing is especially helpful. Given the name of a relevant case, the section of related laws, regulations, and cases can be found easily in the loose-leaf set. The numbered headnotes to each case provide the classification numbers under which all related cases may be found. The "Topical Index" constitutes the third segment of the finding system, leading the researcher directly to the pertinent section of the loose-leaf service, or to the appropriate classification numbers for bound court decisions.

Commerce Clearing House provides a similar 16-volume loose-leaf called *Labor Law Reporter.* Subject coverage is the same as in the BNA set, but the arrangement differs. The following titles are found in the CCH service: *Labor Relations* (5 volumes), *Employment Practices* (4 vols.), *Wages/Hours* (2 vols.), *State Laws* (3 vols), a master index (1 vol.), and a *Quick Finder* volume, which is similar in purpose to BNA's *Expediter* volumes, but arranged topically. The *Labor Law Reporter* is also integrated with a series of bound case reporters, including arbitration awards.

Employment Coordinator (Research Institute of America—Weekly).

A clear alternative to the BNA and CCH services is this 17-volume set from RIA. It provides less emphasis on the text of the law, choosing instead to provide extensive narrative coverage of labor law matters. These well-written discussions are understandable to the researcher uncomfortable with the language of laws and judicial decisions. The RIA service does not provide case reporters in either loose-leaf or bound formats. Researchers who need to read the text of a court decision must refer to other publications. For this reason, RIA provides parallel case tables, citing both official publications and commercial services, including BNA, CCH, and West. References to cases and statutes appear as footnotes to each page, so the narrative flow is not interrupted. The service is updated weekly and covers job discrimination, wages and hours, compensation and benefits, occupational safety and health, unfair labor practices, labor disputes, and personnel policies.

Each volume is devoted to a particular topic, with narrative reports summarizing the basics of the law. Discussions begin with an overview of the topic, followed by narrative summaries of the statutes, regulations, and notable cases. Detailed contents guides in every volume and numerous cross-references throughout the text make the service extremely easy to use. Instead of placing the latest developments in a separate binder, RIA places them at the back of each subject volume, with finding tables linking the new matter to the old. In addition to the finding guides in the individual subject volumes, users can turn to separate master indexes, with one volume by topics and another by case names, statutes, and regulations.

The *Employment Coordinator* also offers suggestions for implementing the law, from sample forms to suggested language for personnel handbooks. Despite the practical touches, the RIA service is first and foremost a law service, and should be viewed as a competitor to BNA's *Labor Relations Reporter*.

For a less detailed look at labor law, Prentice Hall has recently created an abbreviated service which follows the RIA approach. The two-volume set is called the *Guide to Employment Law and Regulation*. The first volume presents a topical arrangement of laws, regulations, and cases dealing with fair employment, wages and hours, equal pay, labor relations, and other subjects. The volume concludes with brief summaries of state laws. References to cases and statutes appear as footnotes to the narrative. The standardized format for each topic describes who is covered under the law, forbidden prac-

tices, do's and don'ts, administration, procedures, and enforcement. The second volume reproduces the text of major federal laws.

BNA Policy and Practice Series (Bureau of National Affairs—Biweekly).

BNA's *Policy and Practice Series* is clearly intended for the nonlawyer, but BNA finds it difficult to abandon the legal approach it has perfected. This 10-volume set covers much the same subject matter as the *Labor Relations Reporter*, but with an emphasis on specific applications. It discusses both the legal guidelines for labor issues and common practices utilized in the business world. Under each topic are found the text of labor laws, summary "Ground Rules" for common situations, an "Application of Policy" section with real-world examples, and sample employment forms. An excellent bibliography concludes every topic. Several binders also contain relevant labor statistics on areas such as employee turnover and absenteeism.

The first three titles in the set are quite similar to their counterparts in the *Labor Relations Reporter*, though the information is less detailed. These are *Fair Employment Practices* (3 vols.), *Wages and Hours* (2 vols.), and *Labor Relations* (2 vols.). The remaining titles are unique to the *Policy and Practice Series*, and emphasize recommended labor practices. *Compensation* (2 vols.) offers background information on establishing a wage administration program, conducting job evaluations, planning executive compensation packages, and creating an employee profit-sharing plan. *Personnel* (2 vols.), covers such common situations as hiring, promotion, discipline, training, working conditions, morale, and termination. Titles may be purchased separately, or as a complete set. Subscribers to any of the items in the *Policy and Practice Series* receive a biweekly newsletter entitled *Bulletin to Management*.

BNA also publishes the three-volume *Payroll Administration Guide*, which covers such practical aspects of payroll management as withholding taxes, workers' compensation, and unemployment insurance. The single-volume *Job Safety and Health* covers law and practice relating to occupational safety. Neither of the latter titles are part of the *Policy and Practice Series* but both follow a similar format.

Personnel Management (Prentice Hall Information Services—Biweekly).

Both Prentice Hall and CCH offer competing services to BNA's *Policy and Practice Series*. The P-H version, *Personnel Management*, consists of *Policies and Practices* (2 vols.) and *Communications* (1 vol.). The first covers a broad range of practical topics, includ-

ing hiring, training, promotion, working hours, morale, benefits, employee problems (substance abuse, AIDS, etc.), absenteeism, discipline, and termination. *Communications* deals with preparing personnel handbooks and communicating work policies to the staff. This volume takes a topical approach to written policies and stresses both what to say and how to say it. *Personnel Management* combines the latest legal information with clear suggestions on putting the law into practice, including model forms. In many respects the Prentice Hall series is easier to use than the BNA service. The writing is generally clearer, with lots of user-friendly section headings and sidebars. Standard features include new ideas, pointers, and guides to finding additional information on the topic. A recent reorganization discontinued several volumes and moved their contents to other loose-leaf products. For example, much of the former *Industrial Relations* title has been shifted to a newer series called the *Guide to Employment Law and Regulation*.

The CCH version of the standard policy-oriented loose-leaf is *Human Resources Management*. This five-volume monthly service covers much the same territory as BNA and P-H. The main volume, *Personnel Practices/Communications*, is like an abbreviated version of its Prentice Hall counterpart, though case law is emphasized more.

Personnel Management Guide (Prentice Hall Information Services—Quarterly).

Several firms have created handy single-volume products aimed at the owner of the small business. While most small companies may not have a separate personnel department, they can't afford to ignore issues of employment law. To meet their needs, Prentice Hall has devised a single-volume resource called the *Personnel Management Guide*. The work is especially well-written and understandable, being designed for a popular audience. Section headings have such catchy titles as "Paying competitive wages without going broke," and "Hiring the best and the brightest." The chapters focus on issues of interest to the small employer, including wages, benefits, training, and improving productivity.

BNA's newer *Employment Guide* is also geared toward the small employer. It too provides basic facts in short, readable chapters. Each topic includes a brief overview, a discussion of policy considerations, and a sample policy statement. Much of the information is presented in tables and checklists. Among the broad subjects are recruitment, promotion, discipline procedures, and dealing with a union. A diversity of specific topics are explored, including keeping personnel files and records, mandatory benefits under the law, establishing a safety program, sexual harassment, employee theft, and workplace smoking.

Collective Bargaining Negotiations and Contracts (Bureau of National Affairs—Biweekly).

A perfect example of the situation-oriented labor service is *Collective Bargaining Negotiations and Contracts* from BNA. This unique two-volume loose-leaf is an outstanding manual of practical information on contract negotiation. By monitoring bargaining activity in several thousand organizations, BNA is able to provide the latest information on practices and methods in contract situations. Volume 1, *Techniques and Trends*, offers specific pointers on bargaining strategy. BNA's concise guidelines on preparing for negotiations, making demands, and dealing with counter-proposals have become classics of the literature. Similar guidelines on "Administering the Contract" provide an excellent explanation of the arbitration process and how to use it. Another valuable section contains summaries of the latest trends in bargaining issues, including job security, wage concessions, and other topics in the news. BNA also adds extensive statistical information in Volume 1. A section labeled "Background for Bargaining" gives data on the Consumer Price Index, employment costs, absenteeism, and similar labor statistics. "Industry Wage Patterns" provides current wage information for major industry groupings. Data are gathered from government publications, trade journals and other news sources, and from BNA's own surveys. "Current Contract Settlements" prints news of recently negotiated settlements involving most unionized employees in the U.S. The final segment of Volume 1 reproduces the full text of 10 or more representative labor contracts from different industries. The editorial staff at BNA has chosen well-constructed contracts to serve as models for other bargaining groups in the country.

Volume 2, the *Clause Finder*, offers hundreds of narrow clauses from actual labor contracts in a topical arrangement. Over a dozen subject areas are covered, including employee discipline, union security, grievance procedures, seniority, working conditions, and fringe benefits. The clauses represent a diversity of settlements culled from some 3,000 labor contracts. They serve as a fertile source for bargaining ideas and model contract language, as well as a survey of trends in contract settlement. This remarkable publication is intended as a manual for both union and management negotiators. Subscribers also receive a biweekly newsletter entitled *What's New in Collective Bargaining*.

Miscellaneous Labor Publications

The Bureau of National Affairs publishes a variety of additional resources for labor researchers. The annual *Directory of U.S. Labor Organizations* is an outstanding guide to approximately 300 major unions in the United States. BNA also publishes an excellent (though expensive) newsletter called the *Daily Labor Report*. This service provides information found in BNA's various loose-leaf publications, but on a more timely basis. Coverage includes the status of bills before Congress, recent court rulings, major bargaining settlements, the latest statistical data, and general news items relating to labor. The size of each issue ranges from four pages to more than 50. Summary information from the daily service is available in the more affordable *Labor Relations Week*. Two other BNA newsletters related to labor relations and personnel management are *Benefits Today* and the *Employment and Training Reporter*. The first reports the latest news relating to employee benefits, including alternative health insurance, childcare, and employee stock ownership plans. The service also contains interviews with prominent experts, summaries of research findings, and analysis of legislative and economic issues. The second title covers a broader range of topics, but focuses on fair employment issues, training policies, and government-sponsored employment programs. The first is issued biweekly, the second weekly. Both are filed in loose-leaf binders with cumulating indexes.

Electronic databases can also be an important source of current information on labor trends. An online vendor that focuses almost exclusively on employment topics is Executive Telecom Systems, Inc. Their system, the Human Resources Information Network (HRIN), carries a diversity of useful databases, including research reports from the Conference Board, directories of consultants and labor unions, and an extensive collection of newsletters and loose-leaf services from BNA, including *Collective Bargaining Negotiations and Contracts*.

As with any subject, one of the best approaches to current information is through periodical articles. In addition to general business magazines, academic journals, and trade publications aimed at labor practitioners, a useful source of labor news is the union newspaper or magazine. Most national trade unions produce publications which offer information not found in more traditional sources. A periodical index which covers all these formats, including union publications, is *Work Related Abstracts*, described in Chapter 5.

Another source of current labor information is the federal government. For example, the results of union representation elections are reported in a monthly publication from the National Labor Relations Board called the *NLRB Election Report*. Much of the government's information on trends and statistics is compiled and reported by the Bureau of Labor Statistics, which publishes the indispensable *BLS Bulletins* series. Titles in this series include the *Area Wage Surveys* (Chapter 17) and the *Consumer Expenditure Survey* (Chapter 18), as well as a surprising variety of other recurring reports and one-time research studies. Annual reports in the series include *Employee Benefits in Medium and Large Firms*, the *Geographic Profile of Employment and Unemployment*, *Occupational Injuries and Illnesses in the United States*, and *Productivity Measures for Selected Industries*.

For those who can't afford such commercial services as the *Daily Labor Report*, the BLS produces an extremely useful monthly report called *Compensation and Working Conditions* (formerly *Current Wage Developments*). It contains little narrative information, but is jam-packed with statistics on collective bargaining activity. The focus is on recent contract settlements, with tables summarizing the wage and benefits packages negotiated by specific unions. Data on individual contracts are grouped together by industry, but only those settlements involving 1,000 workers or more are covered. Other tables cite summary statistics on the average percentage of wage increases negotiated by unions in the United States and the number of work stoppages in effect during the month. Another section lists major union contracts due to expire. The government also publishes an annual *Bargaining Calendar* which appears within the *BLS Bulletins* series. Most of the information from *Compensation and Working Conditions* can also be found in *Collective Bargaining Negotiations and Contracts*; in fact, the BNA service reports on more settlements than the government publication. However, for those without access to the loose-leaf service, the BLS periodical is an inexpensive way to monitor recent bargaining trends.

LEGAL RESEARCH FOR THE NONLAWYER

The strategic impact of changing laws and regulations on the business community can be staggering. All firms must monitor such changes and analyze their potential effects, either as threats or opportunities. The

law also has a direct influence on the daily operations of the firm, making a fundamental knowledge of legal issues essential. Nor is it enough to conduct business in a lawful manner. In our increasingly litigious society, managers must be sensitive to the day-to-day procedures and record-keeping requirements which must be followed to provide a defense in case of legal suits. For these reasons, all business researchers should have a basic understanding of how the law works and a familiarity with major information sources.

For the nonspecialist, legal research can be both confusing and perilous. Simply knowing where to begin becomes an obstacle. Determining the questions to ask, the resources to consult, or even whether the issue is a legitimate concern of the law may not be obvious. Even verifying the proper jurisdiction for a legal problem is no simple task. On the other hand, researchers can lull themselves into a false security, assuming that they really know how to "find the law." If legal research is usually best left to experts, the question is, "Just how far should I go in conducting legal research for myself or someone else?" As the chestnut goes, "He who would serve as his own lawyer has a fool for a client." Yet businesspeople cannot afford to overlook important areas of the law; at the very least, they should be monitoring the environment for legal changes which could affect their business. To ignore this is to invite disaster. Likewise, librarians and researchers should be familiar with the structure of legal publishing. Whether monitoring current events for an employer or locating facts for a library patron or client, researchers must become comfortable with important publications.

The discussion of legal sources in this chapter was intentionally brief. Many are designed for attorneys or experienced paralegals. But as we have seen, numerous publications address the needs of the nonspecialist. When dealing with a specific branch of the law, selecting the proper tool is not always obvious. Even a seemingly basic task like locating a statute can be fraught with twists. The labyrinth of administrative law is far worse, and keeping up with the deluge of changes is daunting. Many businesspeople scan the *Federal Register* every day. Others turn to specialized notification services like the *FCC Record* or the *SEC Docket*. Despite the availability of commercial tools like the *CIS Federal Register Index*, online databases are among the most efficient methods of locating a specific regulation. Modern legal research would be difficult without the powerful capabilities of WESTLAW and LEXIS.

Another tack is to utilize sources which relate statutes, regulations, and case law. For current awareness, publications like *U.S. Law Week* and *USCCAN* are notable for their coverage of many aspects of the law. When beginning a research project, consulting a "nutshell" or law review can be a good way to obtain a broad overview. From there, a loose-leaf service frequently offers the best approach for the nonspecialist. Their topical arrangement is ideal for following current developments in a narrow, but complex area. Unfortunately, their very specificity presents a problem; published looseleafs number in the hundreds, and identifying and locating the best one can be a challenge in itself. Also, many are designed for attorneys, despite their inviting titles. So what does all this mean? With so many specialized tools at their disposal, researchers shouldn't be intimidated by legal questions. At the same time, neither should they become overconfident; knowing your limitations is an important virtue. Researchers should understand the nature of any information product before using it. Finally, readers should remember that legal research is a process. Few questions of law involve a quick solution. Instead, the researcher must be prepared to consult a variety of sources and to follow leads to their logical conclusions. More than any other topic in this book, legal research requires careful planning and diligent execution.

FOR FURTHER READING

The reader interested in learning more about legal resources has a large number of textbooks to choose from, most of them written for students in law school. Another helpful source is promotional material from major legal publishers. Firms such as West and Shepard's have created booklets explaining how to use their products. The following titles represent a small sampling of resources which should be especially helpful to the nonlawyer. A few handbooks on labor relations law are also listed.

General Research Texts

Cohen, Morris L., and Robert C. Berring. *Finding the Law*, 9th ed. (St. Paul, MN: West Publishing, 1989).
This abridged version of a popular law school text offers a well-organized introduction to legal research methods and sources. The clear prose and numerous sample pages make this an excellent first choice for the beginning researcher.

Corbin, John. *Find the Law in the Library: A Guide to Legal Research* (Chicago: American Library Association, 1989). This guide offers a nontraditional approach to legal research. The first section presents an overview of the American legal system, basic legal publications, and a detailed flow chart describing a nine-step research process. The remainder of the book is divided into 20 case studies, each covering a specific legal problem. These topics represent common research situations, ranging from divorce law to labor relations.

Jacobstein, J. Myron, and Roy M. Mersky. *Fundamentals of Legal Research.* 5th ed. (Westbury, NY: Foundation Press, 1990). One of the best textbooks on legal research, noteworthy for its simple, step-by-step approach. The introduction to the legal research process is especially good, as is the chapter on loose-leaf services. A discussion of computer-assisted research services is also provided.

Special Topics

Bluh, Pamela. "Legal Looseleafs: No Grounds for Intimidation!" *Serials Review* 15 (Fall 1989): 63-66. Excellent review of the characteristics of legal loose-leafs and the problems in maintaining a loose-leaf collection.

Carrick, Kathleen M. *LEXIS: A Legal Research Manual* (Dayton, OH: Mead Data Central, 1989). This outstanding work, commissioned by the publisher of the LEXIS database system, was written by a university law librarian. It describes the resources available through LEXIS, provides step-by-step instructions for searching, and places electronic research methods within the broader picture of legal publishing. Brief discussions of basic concepts in legal research make an excellent introduction for the nonspecialist.

Maclay, Veronica. "Selected Sources of United States Agency Decisions." *Government Publications Review* 16 (May/June 1989): 271-301. This superb annotated bibliography of the published sources of federal administrative decisions profiles over 30 agencies. For each one, the following resources are listed: official reporters (if any), commercial reporters and loose-leafs, and full-text databases. This monumental effort brings together heretofore scattered information on an important area of legal research.

Thomas, Terry, and Marlene G. Weinstein. *Computer-Assisted Legal and Tax Research: A Professional's Guide to Lexis, Westlaw, and PHINet* (Paramus, NJ: Prentice Hall Information Services, 1986). A primer on computer databases for legal research. Part I covers hardware and software basics, together with introductory chapters on WESTLAW, LEXIS, PHINet, and DIALOG. Part II offers instruction on search techniques and strategies, with lots of examples. One of the best chapters explains how to translate legal issues into search queries. The third part describes the pricing policies of major vendors and briefly discusses how to choose the right system.

U.S. Office of the Federal Register. *The "Federal Register": What It Is and How to Use It* (Washington, DC: The Office, 1985). Describes the purpose and content of the *Federal Register* and how it relates to the *CFR*. Generous use of sample pages clarifies how to use the *Register*. Additional chapters explain the federal rulemaking process and summarize the Freedom of Information Act.

Labor Law Sources

Feldacker, Bruce. *Labor Guide to Labor Law.* 3rd ed. (Englewood Cliffs, NJ: Prentice Hall, 1990). Intended for union representatives taking labor courses, this exceptionally readable textbook is recommended as an introduction to the topic.

Kenny, John J., and Linda G. Kahn. *Primer of Labor Relations.* 24th ed. (Washington, DC: Bureau of National Affairs, 1989). Each chapter in this helpful guide is devoted to a broad topic, which is further broken down into capsule discussions of major issues. The authors are senior labor editors with BNA.

CHAPTER 20
Taxation and Accounting

TOPICS COVERED

1. The Legal Structure of Federal Taxation
2. Primary Sources for Tax Research
   a. Statutes, Regulations, and Administrative Rulings
   b. Judicial Decisions
3. Loose-Leaf Services and Tax Citators
   a. Code-Based Loose-Leaf Services
   b. Topical Loose-Leaf Services
   c. Tax Citators
4. Miscellaneous Tax Publications
   a. Journals and Newsletters
   b. Periodical Indexes
   c. IRS Publications
   d. Tax Preparation Guides
5. Basic Accounting Information
   a. Accounting Standards
   b. Guides to Accounting Practices
6. What Researchers Should Know
7. For Further Reading

MAJOR SOURCES DISCUSSED

- *Internal Revenue Bulletin*
- *United States Tax Court Reports*
- *Tax Court Memorandum Decisions*
- *U.S. Tax Cases*
- *Standard Federal Tax Reports*
- *Federal Taxes 2nd*
- *Federal Tax Coordinator 2d*
- *Tax Notes*
- *Index to Federal Tax Articles*
- *Tax Information Publications*
- *FASB Accounting Standards: Original Pronouncements*
- *FASB Accounting Standards: Current Text*
- *Accounting Trends and Techniques*

This final chapter deals with two highly technical topics—tax research and accounting information. Because both areas are dependent on legal concepts, the discussion builds upon ideas introduced in the previous chapter. All taxation information flows from the tax laws passed by Congress, which are then cumulated in the Internal Revenue Code. For this reason, tax research is more legal than financial. Although accounting is not based on actual laws, accounting principles are presented in a body of published rules which work in similar fashion. This chapter will sketch the broad structure of both topics, together with some of the most important information tools.

THE LEGAL STRUCTURE OF FEDERAL TAXATION

The modern federal income tax was enacted in 1913, with major revisions of the law occurring in 1939, 1954, and 1986. Each of these revisions resulted in a completely new tax code. Specific sections of the existing Code are revised continuously. Changes may occur as a result of "technical amendments" to earlier legislation or through the passage of new statutes. In any given year, an average of ten major laws have significant impact on the Internal Revenue Code. Some are written specifically as tax laws, and are typically called "revenue acts" or "tax reform acts." Others are introduced as part

of broader legislation, often dealing with areas such as the federal budget or specific entitlement programs such as Social Security.

The Internal Revenue Code of 1986, as amended, is the starting point for all current tax research. All rulings of the IRS and all court decisions on tax issues are grounded in specific sections of the Code. The overriding importance of the statutes themselves makes the investigation of legislative intent an essential part of tax research. *Committee Reports* from the House and Senate are invaluable for understanding the meaning of specific Code sections.

The second area of tax law is the regulatory system based on the Code. Tax regulations are formulated by the Internal Revenue Service, and approved by the Secretary of the Treasury. Called Treasury Decisions, they are numbered sequentially and are so designated in the literature (e.g., T.D. 8306, T.D. 8307, etc.).

Other types of administrative law have less force than Treasury Decisions. A taxpayer or tax consultant may query the IRS regarding the likely tax outcome of a proposed course of action. The IRS answers such queries with official written responses called Private Letter Rulings. These are not published by the IRS, but are available for examination at the IRS Reading Room in Washington and are also reprinted by several commercial publishers. Private Letter Rulings may not be used or cited as legal precedent, but are useful for determining the government's position on a specific tax matter. If an inquiry is deemed to have broad public interest, the IRS responds with a Revenue Ruling, which *is* published by the government and is valid as legal precedent. Confidential information, including the inquirer's identity, is not divulged in either the published Revenue Rulings or the publicly disclosed Letter Rulings. Both types of rulings include the following information: the legal issue involved, the facts of the case, a statement of the prevailing law, an analysis of the situation, and the IRS ruling or "holding." Revenue Rulings are important in tax research, but constitute a slippery area of law for two major reasons. First, existing Revenue Rulings are constantly revoked or amended by the IRS because of changes in IRS policies, adverse court decisions, or revisions of the Code. Second, they are written in response to a specific set of facts; in order to apply a ruling to a different situation, the facts must be substantially the same.

The third element in the legal structure of the tax system is the judiciary. The courts typically become involved when a taxpayer disputes the results of a tax audit. When the IRS determines that back taxes are owed, the audited individual may attempt to resolve the dispute through a hearing before the Internal Revenue Service Appeals Office. If the taxpayer loses, he or she must first pay the deficiency (and the interest charges) before redress may be sought through the judicial system. Cases involving federal income tax may be introduced in the U.S. District Courts or the U.S. Court of Claims, but the court created specifically to deal with tax matters is the U.S. Tax Court (formerly the U.S. Board of Tax Appeals). Individual cases are heard by a single judge, who renders a written opinion to the Chief Judge. The Chief Judge decides whether the case should be reviewed by the entire court; if not, the original judge's opinion, called a Memorandum Decision, stands as written. If the case is presented to the full court, a majority opinion is reached, which is called a Regular Decision.

The IRS may or may not agree with the decision of the Tax Court. This has no bearing on the outcome of the case, but it is important for future occurrences. If the IRS announces "acquiescence" to the decision, the government will abide by the Court's decision in future, similar cases. If the IRS announces "nonacquiescence," it means the government will continue to contest this type of situation, forcing other individuals to also seek a court decision. Obviously, a decision to which the IRS has acquiesced serves as a much stronger legal precedent.

PRIMARY SOURCES FOR TAX RESEARCH

The complexity and importance of tax law necessitates a wide assortment of published documents and finding tools. Many of the general law sources introduced in Chapter 19 are appropriate for tax research. For example, the *U.S. Code*, the *Code of Federal Regulations*, and West's *National Reporter System* are all relevant to tax work. However, publications and databases which specialize in taxation are more convenient and simpler to use. The two leading online legal services provide extensive electronic libraries with the complete text of primary documents dating back to 1954. On LEXIS, the service is found in the *FEDTAX* library; on WESTLAW the service is called *TAXATION*. Both supply the complete text of most documents, including court rulings and IRS pronouncements. A huge assortment of specialized print publications are also available. The resources covered below include government and com-

mercial publications focusing on primary information: the statutes, regulations, administrative rulings, and court decisions upon which tax law is built.

Statutes, Regulations, and Administrative Rulings

The text of the Internal Revenue Code appears in Title 26 of the *United States Code*, but more current information can be found in commercial publications. The general Code services produced by West Publishing and Lawyers Co-op are the most timely, but researchers typically consult specialized publications which are devoted exclusively to the Internal Revenue Code. Several commercial publishers issue annual paperback editions of the Code, including Prentice Hall and the Research Institute of America, Inc. (RIA). West publishes a similar single-volume annual guide as a supplement to their *U.S. Code Congressional and Administrative News* service. An even better option is to subscribe to a loose-leaf service which updates the Code throughout the year as new legislation is passed; these will be described later in the chapter.

All Treasury Decisions currently in force are cumulated annually in Title 26 of the *Code of Federal Regulations*, one of the largest components of the *CFR*. Commercial publishers reproduce Treasury Decisions in annual guides, such as the four-volume *Federal Income Tax Regulations* from RIA. However, the most frequently used primary sources for retrieving the text of regulations and rulings come from the IRS itself.

Internal Revenue Bulletin (U.S. Internal Revenue Service—Weekly, with Semiannual Cumulations).

Current announcements from the IRS are issued in the weekly *Internal Revenue Bulletin*. Treasury Decisions can appear up to a month earlier in the daily issues of the *Federal Register*, but most tax practitioners prefer the IRS's own periodical. It is more convenient to use, and contains more information. In addition to Treasury Decisions and proposed regulations, the *Internal Revenue Bulletin* prints the complete text of Revenue Rulings, and of administrative releases such as Revenue Procedures and Notices. Private Letter Rulings are not covered by the *Internal Revenue Bulletin*.

Most information in the *Internal Revenue Bulletin* is reprinted twice per year in a hardbound set called the *Cumulative Bulletin*. Each semiannual issue is arranged in three parts. The first covers all Revenue Rulings and Treasury Decisions issued during that period, arranged

according to the pertinent section of the Internal Revenue Code. The second part reproduces the text of tax treaties, statutes, and their corresponding congressional *Committee Reports*. When legislation is extensive, this part may appear as a separate volume. The third section deals with administrative releases and administrative announcements, including Revenue Procedures. Every issue of the *Cumulative Bulletin* includes a Finding List which cites the regulations and rulings by number. A separate list serves as a guide to "Current Action on Previously Published Rulings," citing the earlier ruling and the subsequent action which changed it during that period.

Although the indexes in the *Cumulative Bulletin* are helpful, each issue only covers a six-month period. Fortunately, the IRS produces retrospective indexes to the weekly and semiannual *Bulletins*. They appear as four separate guides by type of tax: income, estate and gift, employment, and excise. The set, called the the *Bulletin Index-Digest System*, provides brief abstracts to all Revenue Rulings and Revenue Procedures, grouped according to subject. Excluded from the "Digest" portion are Public Laws, Treasury Decisions, and international Tax Conventions (i.e., treatises). However, a separate table lists all Laws and Treasury Decisions according to their related Internal Revenue Code sections. Similar tables cite Revenue Rulings and Procedures by relevant Code section. A numeric list of all Revenue Rulings issued since 1935 and currently in force is provided. Another list cites all Rulings which were subsequently superseded, revoked, modified, or otherwise amended, together with the number of the amending Ruling. Finally, an alphabetical index to Tax Court and Supreme Court decisions by case name is provided.

The *Bulletin Index-Digest System* is published every two years, but its research power is enhanced by retrospective coverage; each biennial issue includes digests of all Revenue Rulings from 1953 to the present. The biennial digests are updated by supplements issued between editions. The supplement to income tax rulings is published four times per year; the supplements for gift and estate, employment, and excise taxes are published twice per year. Every new issue of these supplements supersedes the preceding ones. This means the researcher needs to consult only the basic volume going back to 1953, and the most recent supplement. The bound issues of the *Cumulative Bulletin* or the weekly updates can then be used to find the complete text of the pertinent rulings. For the most current information, the tables of contents of all weekly *Bulletins* issued since the latest index must be scanned.

IRS Letter Rulings (Commerce Clearing House—Weekly).

CCH prints Private Letter Rulings verbatim in the weekly *IRS Letter Rulings*. Subscribers may choose to bind the weekly reports, or opt to purchase the retrospective collection on microfiche. A cumulative loose-leaf index provides access by subject and by relevant Code section. CCH also reproduces IRS Technical Memoranda, which are similar to Letter Rulings, in a service called *IRS Positions*.

Private Letter Rulings, a competing publication from Prentice Hall, resembles the CCH service in most respects, except that the weekly reports are cumulated in annual bound volumes. Another source of Letter Rulings is the *Tax Notes Microfiche Data Base*, described later in the chapter. Private Letter Rulings are also available on LEXIS and WESTLAW. Each of the preceding services reproduces Rulings in their entirety, but digests can also be found in several publications. Among the best are the *Daily Tax Report* from BNA and the weekly *Tax Notes* from Tax Analysts.

Judicial Decisions

The text of judicial opinions issued in federal tax cases can be found in the official and unofficial case reporters introduced in the previous chapter. Because of the importance of the U.S. Tax Court in these matters, publications which cover its decisions will be discussed below. Specialized services covering tax cases tried outside the Tax Court will also be introduced.

United States Tax Court Reports (U.S. Tax Court—Monthly, with Semiannual Cumulations).

The official source of decisions from the Tax Court is *U.S. Tax Court Reports*. Similar in form and content to other official case reporters, it provides the following information on every case: a statement of the Court's "finding of fact," the text of the Court's opinion, and any dissenting opinions. Both the monthly issues and the semiannual bound volumes contain alphabetical lists of cases by name of petitioner and an index-digest which provides brief abstracts of the cases by broad topic.

This series covers only the Regular Decisions of the Tax Court; Memorandum Decisions are printed in mimeograph form for limited distribution. However, every volume of *U.S. Tax Court Reports* contains a list of recently issued Memorandum Decisions by name. The complete text of all Memorandum Decisions are available from CCH and Prentice Hall.

Court Reports from Commercial Publishers

Most tax researchers prefer to consult specialized tax publications from Commerce Clearing House and Prentice Hall because both have created unified reporting systems which are integrated with their other tax services to form complete research systems. These reporters can be confusing because separate publications are issued for each of three different types of court decisions, and because every title has a current loose-leaf component and a retrospective component.

CCH reporters are issued as four separate titles. The first title is a weekly loose-leaf service covering the current year's Regular and Memorandum Decisions of the Tax Court. Unlike most commercial case reporters, the *Tax Court Reporter* does not reprint the Regular Decisions in permanent bound form; instead, the decisions from earlier years can be preserved in "transfer binders." Because Memorandum Decisions of the Tax Court are not published by the Government Printing Office, this portion of the *Tax Court Reporter* is preserved in more permanent form. The semiannual bound volumes are called *Tax Court Memorandum Decisions*. The third part of the CCH reporting service brings together important cases heard in other federal courts (and some from state courts). Again, the most current cases appear in weekly loose-leaf volumes. In this instance, they are found as part of CCH's *Standard Federal Tax Reports*, a service described later in the chapter. The cases are reprinted in bound form in a semiannual series entitled *U.S. Tax Cases*. All four publications offer alphabetical tables of case names, a parallel case table which serves as a cross-reference from West Publishing's case numbers to CCH's numbers, and a detailed subject index. The text of the decisions is identical to that seen in the official reporters, but the headnotes are written by the CCH editorial staff.

Prentice Hall offers an equivalent set, virtually identical to the CCH service in format and content. All current decisions of the Tax Court are published by P-H in a loose-leaf service called *Tax Court Reported Decisions*. As with CCH, Prentice Hall does not republish the Regular Decisions in permanent hardcover volumes, but previous years are retained in transfer binders. Memorandum Decisions are reissued in a bound set called *T.C. Memorandum Decisions*. The rulings of other federal courts are found in Prentice Hall's *American Federal Tax Reports 2d*, first in loose-leaf, then in bound volumes.

FIGURE 20-A. Sources of Federal Tax Decisions

SOURCES OF FEDERAL TAX DECISIONS

Category	Official Reporter	CCH	Prentice-Hall	Other
U.S. Tax Court (Regular Decisions)	U.S. Tax Court Reports	Tax Court Reporter (loose-leaf)	Tax Court Reported Decisions (loose-leaf)	Federal Reporter (West Publishing)
U.S. Tax Court (Memorandum Decisions)	Slip Decisions	Tax Court Memorandum Decisions	T.C. Memorandum Decisions	None
Other Federal Courts	See Figure 19-A	U.S. Tax Cases	American Federal Tax Reports 2d	See Figure 19-A
Case Citators	None	Standard Federal Tax Reports	Federal Taxes 2nd: Citator	Shepard's Federal Tax Citations

To summarize the availability of judicial decisions from the various publishers, Figure 20-A compares the titles from the Government Printing Office, CCH, Prentice Hall, and West Publishing by the topics covered. Since the popular CCH and Prentice Hall reporters are nearly identical, the choice of one set over the other might seem of little significance. However, because each set is an integral part of its publisher's complete tax research package, the choice is largely determined by which total system is used. There are notable differences between the packages offered by Prentice Hall and CCH and these will be discussed in the following section.

LOOSE-LEAF SERVICES AND TAX CITATORS

The biggest advantage to loose-leaf publications for legal research is their ability to bring together all areas of law according to subject. Nowhere is this assistance more welcome than in tax research. Loose-leaf tax guides organize the constant flow of statutes, Treasury Decisions, court cases, and administrative rulings in a coherent, timely system. Furthermore, they are compiled and edited by staffs of tax experts who include commentary and interpretation throughout. Because of the sheer mass of tax information, these publications are enormous— usually 15 volumes or more—and relatively expensive.

But most services are completely revised on an annual basis. Purchasers receive weekly updates throughout the year, but, unlike most loose-leaf publications, subscribers also receive a complete replacement set (including binders) every December. This enables major research libraries to build a retrospective collection, a feat not possible with most loose-leaf publications. Users can consult obsolete editions to conduct historical research or determine a point of law as it existed at an earlier date.

Three types of loose-leaf services are published for tax research. The first is organized according to the provisions of the Internal Revenue Code. For each section of the Code, the full text of the law is given, followed by all the regulations, rulings, and court decisions based on that Code section. The two major publications with this type of arrangement are produced by Commerce Clearing House and Prentice Hall. An alternative to the Code-based service is a topical reporting system, intended for people unfamiliar with tax research. The leading publisher of topically arranged tax services is the Research Institute of America (RIA). Scholarly services, somewhat analogous to the legal encyclopedias introduced in the previous chapter, also take a topical approach. Scholarly tax guides provide in-depth, narrative treatises on a range of individual tax subjects. References to the appropriate laws, regulations, and court decisions appear as footnotes to the main text.

Tax lawyers and accountants generally use Code-based services to conduct exhaustive tax research. This is because the IRS and the courts refer to the Code when making a ruling. A topical service may be simpler to use and easier to read, but it may not result in a thorough search. Users who find the Code-based approach confusing may want to begin a search using the RIA service, but will need to follow up by consulting CCH or Prentice Hall. On the other hand, the clear prose of the RIA service may provide a fuller understanding of a complex issue; what eludes the reader in one publication may become apparent in another. Lawyers may likewise find the scholarly approach more comfortable because of its narrative form, but these publications are not as current as the Code-based services. In any event, haphazard tax research is to be avoided at all costs. Thorough investigation of a tax issue is time-consuming and requires a knowledge of tax laws and familiarity with the publications used.

Code-Based Loose-Leaf Services

The two tax guides organized according to the provisions of the Internal Revenue Code are *Standard Federal Tax Reports* by Commerce Clearing House and *Federal Taxes 2nd* by Prentice Hall.

Standard Federal Tax Reports (Commerce Clearing House—Weekly).

Of the two services, *Standard Federal Tax Reports* is the more widely used for two reasons: it was the first loose-leaf tax guide ever produced, making its debut in 1913 with the passage of the first income tax law; and it was the first service to organize its contents by Code section, beginning in 1954. Because of these innovations, *Standard Federal Tax Reports* is entrenched in law offices, libraries, and accounting firms throughout the country.

The CCH service is a massive set which grows larger with each passing year. The 1991 edition appears in 18 volumes, with additional volumes available on federal excise, gift, and estate taxes. The first 12 volumes are known as the compilation section, because they combine the basic information on the Code, the regulations, the judicial decisions, and the CCH explanations, all organized by Code section. Volume 12 ends with a reference section of IRS procedures, Tax Court procedures, a list of current IRS forms, a directory of key IRS personnel, and other miscellaneous information. Volume 13 contains the latest updated information ("New Matters"), the text of current-year IRS rulings, proposed regulations, digests of recent Tax Court decisions, new

legislation, and a topical index to current developments. A separate, unnumbered volume contains the cumulative subject index to the set, current rate tables (including income tax rates, withholding tables, and Applicable Federal Rates), a tax calendar, tax planning tips, and checklists for tax practitioners. Five additional unnumbered volumes round out the set. Two of these contain the full text of the Internal Revenue Code; this is intended for quick reference, since sections of the Code are also interspersed throughout the compilation volumes. Another unnumbered volume provides Advance Sheets of federal court cases; these are ultimately reprinted in the semiannual bound volumes entitled *U.S. Tax Cases*. The remaining two volumes consist of CCH's tax case citator. Because of the importance of citators in tax research, these volumes will be discussed in detail later in this chapter.

Information in the compilation volumes is displayed in a standard format. For each Code section, the full text of that portion of the Code is reprinted, followed by the text of congressional *Committee Reports* pertaining to that section. Next can be found all appropriate regulations for that section, any proposed regulations, CCH's editorial explanation of the information, and digests of relevant Revenue Rulings and court decisions. The editorial staff of Commerce Clearing House provides helpful tips throughout the publication. For example, the text of the Code includes cross-references to related Code sections and comments from CCH called "cautionary notes." The text of regulatory materials also contains cautionary notes, together with historical comments explaining when major rules went into effect. Editorial explanations also discuss specific tax situations and how they are treated under the law. While information on court cases appears only in digest form in *Standard Federal Tax Reports*, users can turn to the full text of judicial decisions found in CCH's own bound reporters, or the law reports from West Publishing or the Government Printing Office. Information from the loose-leaf set can also be found online as part of the *CCH Tax Day* database. It is available through LEXIS and WESTLAW, updated daily on both.

Federal Taxes 2nd (Prentice Hall Information Services—Weekly).

Prentice Hall's *Federal Taxes 2nd*, formerly *Federal Taxes*, is similar in most respects to the CCH service. The 1991 edition is issued in 16 volumes, but the structure is virtually identical to the competing service. The size difference is because Prentice Hall's *Citator* appears separately in bound volumes. The first 11 volumes of the loose-leaf set constitute the compilation volumes—the

fundamental information and explanation arranged by Code section. Volume 12 contains the most recent updates, labeled "Recent Developments," in much the same way as CCH's Volume 13. As with CCH, a separate, unnumbered volume contains the subject index to the set. The index to the Prentice Hall set also provides a comprehensive case-name table for court decisions, a numerical index to IRS rulings, and a cross-reference guide to changes in rulings. Some of the items seen in CCH's index volume can be found in Prentice Hall's "Recent Developments" volume. For example, the tax rate tables and tax calendar are found there. *Federal Taxes* has three additional unnumbered volumes: one contains Advance Sheets for the bound set of *American Federal Tax Reports 2d,* and two reprint the text of the Internal Revenue Code. Prentice Hall's case citator will be discussed later. The arrangement of the compilation volumes is similar to CCH. Within each Code section, the full text of the Code's provisions, the congressional *Committee Reports,* and the regulations are printed. A minor difference is that P-H's editorial explanation appears at the beginning of each section and is sometimes less detailed than the editorial matter in *Standard Federal Tax Reports.* On the other hand, Prentice Hall includes a "Pilot Chart" at the beginning of each section which summarizes the information in clear, readable fashion.

Given the basic similarities between the two publications, choosing one over the other can be a difficult purchasing decision. If the bound court reports from CCH or P-H are already near at hand, the decision is already made; users of the loose-leaf service must turn to the publisher's own case reporting system. Another criterion for deciding is based on who will use the publication; if the users are already familiar with a particular service, they will tend to use the set they are comfortable with. If neither situation applies, the choice can be a toss-up. Both are updated weekly and both contain much the same information. They are widely regarded as comprehensive, authoritative sources, with excellent editorial explanations. The commentary in CCH tends to be lengthier, but Prentice Hall provides numerous small touches to make the researcher's job simpler. For example, the print is larger, the typeface is crisper, section headings are bolder, and pages are laid out better, all of which make the P-H service easier on the eye. Prentice Hall also utilizes a better internal numbering system, making it simpler to differentiate among the various parts of each Code section. Subscribers to the loose-leaf service also receive a password to PHINet, Prentice Hall's menu-driven online tax information service.

Prentice Hall's user-friendly approach can be seen by comparing the subject indexing in the two publications. Prentice Hall's index tends to be much more specific, particularly where actual tax situations are concerned. The CCH index focuses more on broad tax issues rather than individual situations. Prentice Hall's index also offers more access points to a particular topic.

Despite the added Prentice Hall features, the differences mentioned above are minor; they probably won't sway the prospective purchaser's decision one way or the other. A more significant difference is the superiority of the Prentice Hall case citator. On the other hand, the editorial content of the CCH service tends to be greater, and the set is both better known and more widely available than *Federal Taxes.* Long-time users could cite many other attractive features for either one; both services have attributes to recommend them and the selector must weigh these advantages in light of his or her situation.

Both sets provide a powerful tool for investigating tax questions, with access by case name, Code section, or subject. Searching in either service requires a two-step process: once the relevant discussion is found in the basic volumes, the researcher must turn to the updating volume to find more recent information. Many law libraries, law practices, and accounting firms subscribe to both publications. This sizable investment makes sense because serious researchers find it helpful to consult both services; what is overlooked in one can be found in the other, guaranteeing more thorough results.

Topical Loose-Leaf Services

Many tax research tools are arranged by subject rather than by Internal Revenue Code sections, but only the *Federal Tax Coordinator 2d* by the Research Institute of America is viewed as a competitor to CCH and Prentice Hall. The other categories of topical publications are scholarly reports and tax planning services. Examples of these will also be given.

Federal Tax Coordinator 2d (Research Institute of America, Inc.—Weekly).

RIA's marketing strategy is to concentrate on the research needs of the nonlawyer and the *Federal Tax Coordinator* is a perfect example of this approach. It has become quite popular because it is simple to use and easy to understand. Like the publications from CCH and Prentice Hall, it provides verbatim text of the Internal Revenue Code and IRS regulations, but here the similarity ends. The set is organized into approximately 30 loose-leaf volumes, with information arranged by sub-

ject, regardless of how many sections of the Code touch on the topic. Emphasis is on specific tax situations. For example, Volume 15 contains RIA's discussion of personal deductions, including medical expenses. Here the user can find sections on who may deduct expenses, what is deductible, and when to deduct.

Each subject volume is divided into three parts. The main part is the analysis by subject. Topics are presented in a logical progression, with clearly written summaries of the applicable law. Unlike CCH and P-H, the discussion is not divided by type of law. Explanations of the governing statutes, regulations, rulings, and judicial decisions are interspersed as appropriate. In fact, it is not clear from the narrative itself what aspect of the law is being discussed. All references are cited in footnotes at the bottom of each page. This makes the service much easier to read, yet still provides the user with the necessary legal citations. RIA highlights its analysis with boxed summaries of practical information using the following notations: "Observations," which clarify questionable areas of the law; "Illustrations," which provide examples of actual tax situations; "Cautions," which warn of possible tax pitfalls; and "Recommendations," which suggest appropriate courses of action.

The second part of each subject volume contains the full wording of relevant Internal Revenue Code sections and Treasury Decisions. The third part contains the most recent developments for that volume. A finding table lists all paragraphs in the main analysis which are affected by later rulings. As with CCH and P-H, this means users must look in two places to ensure seeing the latest information. However, the method of updating is simpler to follow in the RIA service. The final three volumes in the set are not subject-oriented; they contain the text of proposed regulations, major revenue rulings, and revenue procedures. Transfer binders can be used to retain the text of older rulings.

Access to the set is obtained in one of three ways. The first is to go to the volume which covers the broad topic under investigation; the user then consults a detailed table of contents within the volume to locate the topic being sought. A second method is to check the subject index to the set, which is published as a separate, unnumbered volume. A third way is to use the finding table of Code provisions in Volume 1. Because RIA does not publish the full text of judicial decisions, the user must turn to other publishers for case law. For this reason, Volume 1 contains parallel case tables indicating where the decisions can be found in CCH, P-H, West's *National Reporter System*, and the government's own law reports.

A second RIA service called the *Tax Action Coordinator* is a ten-volume guide to specific tax transactions. It illustrates the tax consequences of various actions, provides a variety of tax planning tables, sample letters to use in correspondence with the IRS, and numerous filled-in tax forms. Throughout the subject volumes of the *Federal Tax Coordinator*, users will find references to the *Tax Action Coordinator*, indicating which forms or agreements to use.

The *Federal Tax Coordinator* is not recommended as a sole source for in-depth tax research, despite the publisher's claims to the contrary. This is not to imply that RIA is sloppy or incomplete in its coverage; in fact, it is quite thorough. However, the structure of tax law makes a Code-based service the preferred choice for legal research. On the other hand, for the professional tax preparer who needs current, authoritative analysis presented in a clear manner, RIA's *Tax Coordinator* is highly recommended. The nonspecialist looking for a detailed discussion of a specific tax topic will also find the RIA service a better choice than its competitors. Even the experienced tax lawyer can turn to it with confidence for an understandable introduction to an unfamiliar topic or as a starting point to more detailed research. Used in conjunction with the Prentice Hall or CCH services, the *Tax Coordinator 2d* is a powerful tool. Next to the CCH *Standard Federal Tax Reports*, it is the best-selling multi-volume tax service in the United States.

Mertens Law of Federal Income Taxation (Callaghan & Company—Monthly and Quarterly).

This massive set is the preeminent source of scholarly information on federal taxes. It is published in more than 50 loose-leaf and bound volumes and is arranged in five parts. The first three parts are uncomplicated; they consist of the full text of the Internal Revenue Code, the income tax regulations, and, most importantly, the full text of all Revenue Rulings issued since 1954. These volumes are updated monthly and offer cross-references to the other volumes in the set. The fourth part is a multi-volume "Code Commentary," which provides a concise narrative analysis of Code provisions and their meaning. The fifth part is the heart of the *Mertens* service and is updated quarterly. It contains scholarly treatises on all aspects of tax law, with references to important judicial decisions. The treatises are written by the most respected tax lawyers in the country and *Mertens* is commonly cited in legal briefs. The IRS itself recommends the use of *Mertens* to its own staff. It provides the most thorough, insightful analyses of tax issues to be found in a single set.

Mertens is not designed to supplant the Code-oriented services; Callaghan & Company suggests the publication as a complement to the CCH or P-H guides. The major limitations to *Mertens* are its less frequent updates, its lack of a companion case reporter, and its failure to bring all relevant information together by Code section. However, *Mertens* is still the finest tool of its kind.

A more modest example of the scholarly loose-leaf service is the 17 volume *Federal Income, Estate, and Gift Taxation* published by Matthew Bender & Company. Commonly known as "Rabkin & Johnson," after editors Jacob Rabkin and Mark H. Johnson, this set offers treatises by topic as well as the full text of the tax code and regulations. A feature not found in *Mertens* is the complete text of congressional *Committee Reports*, which can be found together with the Code. This service is updated monthly.

Tax Management Portfolios (Tax Management, Inc.—Irregular).

Two other major publications utilize the treatise approach, but these focus on various aspects of tax planning and the tax consequences of specific transactions. A series of publications by Tax Management, Inc., a subsidiary of the Bureau of National Affairs, consists of some 300 different monographs, called *Portfolios*. Each slim volume covers a specific aspect of tax law, providing narrative analysis, a discussion of planning opportunities and pitfalls to avoid, authoritative references to case law, checklists, sample forms, and a bibliography for additional reading. Every treatise is written by an acknowledged tax expert. Volumes are issued in spiral binders so updated pages can be inserted. A master index to the set is issued in loose-leaf form. The *Portfolios* are also available online through LEXIS and WESTLAW.

A newer service from Commerce Clearing House is the *CCH Tax Transactions Library*. Again, each volume covers a specific topic, ranging from failing businesses to reporting passive losses. The series also covers tax aspects of specific industries, including coal, health care, and motion pictures. As with BNA's *Portfolio* series, each treatise is written by experts. Narratives provide an overview of the topic, a discussion of critical tax issues, and transactional analysis. Every volume includes planning aids, forms, a case finding table, and a topical index. As of this writing, about 25 volumes have been issued. Aside from the smaller size of the set, a second difference between the two services is orientation. The *Portfolio* series is written primarily for attorneys, with a strong emphasis on case law. The CCH series also covers cases and IRS rulings, but can be read easily by the nonspecialist.

Both services include examples of worked-through transactions, but the CCH series tends to include more of these.

Tax Citators

An essential part of tax research is the verification of the latest authority on an issue of law. Has the tax code been interpreted by the courts in an adverse manner? Has an important judicial decision been questioned or overturned by a higher court? The way to conduct this type of research is through a citation service. Citators can identify two important pieces of information: whether the case in question was appealed (and the result of the appeal), and what subsequent cases have mentioned the cited case as a precedent. The premier publisher of case histories is Shepard's Citations. For tax specialists, the firm compiles *Shepard's Federal Tax Citations*, which covers decisions of the U.S. Tax Court, the Supreme Court, and lower federal courts. It also provides citations to Treasury Decisions, Revenue Rulings, and the Internal Revenue Code. In these instances, it shows both cases which mention the laws or rulings, plus subsequent regulations and laws which amend the original. The full set appears in 10 bound volumes which are completely revised every few years. Between revisions, the service is updated through monthly paperback issues, which are cumulated quarterly. This Shepard's publication is designed for use with all major case reporting services. Separate volumes are issued for official publications of the government, for West's law reports, and for the court reports of Commerce Clearing House and Prentice Hall. In addition to government and commercial case reporters and primary documents from Congress and the IRS, Shepard's cites references in authoritative legal periodicals and leading law textbooks.

Since Shepard's publications are primarily designed for lawyers, many tax accountants rely on the more familiar case citators published by CCH and Prentice Hall. One of the most significant differences between *Standard Federal Tax Reports* and *Federal Taxes 2nd* is the quality of their citators, so a comparison of the two is worth making. The most striking difference is size: CCH issues its citator in two loose-leaf volumes, while the Prentice Hall citator now appears as a cumulative monthly paperback volume with hardcover historical volumes. Because of space limitations, CCH must continually review the contents of its citator and eliminate older, less important cases. Prentice Hall, on the other hand, cumulates older cases in the bound volumes. For *Federal Taxes 2nd*, two bound volumes are issued. The first

covers citations to decisions issued between 1954 and 1977. The second begins with 1978 and covers through the latest complete calendar year. The monthly paperbacks update the second bound volume, which itself is reprinted annually. For older cases, the user must consult three volumes to trace the history of the decision, but using the Prentice Hall service can result in many more citations.

Another drawback to the CCH citator is that it simply lists the cases which cite the original decision; no indication is given regarding the nature of the citation. Prentice Hall improves upon this in two ways. First, the nature of all subsequent citations is indicated by the use of symbols. Thus the user can determine whether the later cases affirmed the original decision, explained it at greater length, modified it in some way, or reversed it. Both CCH and P-H do this for appeals of the case itself, but only Prentice Hall provides the additional information for other, related cases. Second, Prentice Hall indicates what point of law was involved in the later citations. A tax case may involve several legal issues; subsequent cases which cite a previous decision may refer only to one of those issues. By indicating the issues involved in the later cases, the Prentice Hall citator saves the effort of tracking down irrelevant information.

A sample page from the Prentice Hall citator is illustrated in Exhibit 20-1. All cases are identified by name, then by the publications where the court decision can be located. References to both the official law reporter (e.g., 797 F2d 920) and the Prentice Hall reporter (e.g., 58 AFTR 2d 86-5548) are provided. Using the example of Beech Aircraft, two listings are found: the original case, tried in the U.S. District Court for Kansas in 1984 (the second entry); and its subsequent appeal in the U.S. Court of Appeals in 1986. In this way the researcher can trace the history of the case itself as well as the other cases which later cited it. Notice that the Court of Appeals decision for Beech cited the original District Court decision, as one might expect; the sa notation indicates the original decision was affirmed (upheld) on appeal.

The remaining listings under both cases refer to the other decisions which have cited Beech. Because the two cases are entered separately, the researcher can easily tell which one is being cited. The letter codes show the nature of the citing decision. The letter e in the Gulf Oil listing indicates the 1986 Beech decision was cited favorably by the court in this ruling. The g designation in the Malone and Hyde case means it differed from Beech on some

matter of fact or law. Prentice Hall is able to distinguish which points of law are involved in the citing cases by the simple technique of numbering each headnote in the cited case. Assume that the Beech appeal centered on two legal issues. When the researcher consults the text of the decision in Prentice Hall's *American Federal Tax Reports 2d*, those issues will be summarized in the headnotes by numbers 1 and 2. If the researcher was tracing subsequent opinion on issue 2, none of the cited cases would be appropriate since they all revolve around issue 1 (as in the "e-1" designation for the Gulf Oil case). These features result in enormous time-savings for researchers using the *Federal Taxes 2nd* citator.

MISCELLANEOUS TAX PUBLICATIONS

An amazing array of other tax guides is available for all kinds of users with all manner of information needs. The following section will introduce a variety of publications, from research tools like periodical indexes, to tax preparation aids such as instruction manuals and forms books.

Journals and Newsletters

Journal literature is one of the most useful sources of detailed information on tax law. Many respected journals provide current, detailed articles on complex tax issues. Some are more scholarly in their approach, such as law reviews and academic journals. Others are written for practitioners. Two better known periodicals are the American Institute of Certified Public Accountants' *Tax Adviser* and the American Bar Association's *Tax Lawyer*. Warren, Gorham & Lamont produces several fine journals, including the *Journal of Taxation, Taxation for Accountants*, and *Taxation for Lawyers*. For those who need to keep abreast of the latest tax developments, newsletters are an ideal resource. Many loose-leaf publishers produce weekly tax newsletters; most, like Commerce Clearing House's *Taxes on Parade* and RIA's *Weekly Tax Alert*, come automatically with a subscription to the loose-leaf. Others, like Matthew Bender's *U.S. Tax Week*, are purchased separately. One of the best known newsletters is the brief, but popular *Kiplinger Tax Letter*, a biweekly service from the publishers of *Changing Times*. In addition to specialized newsletters, many general business magazines and newspapers report on

EXHIBIT 20-1. *Federal Taxes 2nd Citator, 2nd Series*

| BEDELL—BEER | 215 |

BEDELL—contd.
e—Hatchett, Richard J., Est. of, 1989 PH TC Memo 89-3234
BEDELL v COMM., 30 F2d 622, 7 AFTR 8469 (USCA 2)
n—Hirst, Edna Bennett v Comm., 41 AFTR2d 78-562, 572 F2d 439 (USCA 4) [See 30 F2d 624, 7 AFTR 8471]
e—McShain, John & Mary, 71 TC 1010, 71 PH TC 564 [See 30 F2d 625, 7 AFTR 8472]
f—Steffens, Fred W. & Margaret T., 1981 PH TC Memo 81-2485 [See 30 F2d 625, 7 AFTR 8472]
f-2—Hatchett, Richard J., Est. of, 1989 PH TC Memo 89-3234
BEDELL, HARRY M., JR., 86 TC 1207, ¶ 86.70 PH TC (A) 1987-1 CB 1
e—Allen, Robert L., Est. of, 1989 PH TC Memo 89-544 [See 86 TC 1221]
BEDELL, HARRY M., JR., TRUSTEE, 86 TC 1207, ¶ 86.70 PH TC (A) 1987-1 CB 1 (See Bedell, Harry M., Jr.)
BEDELL, HARRY M., SR., EST. OF, TRUST, 86 TC 1207, ¶ 86.70 PH TC (A) 1987-1 CB 1 (See Bedell, Harry M., Jr.)
● BEDFORD, EST. OF; COMM. v, 325 US 283, 33 AFTR 832
q—Shimberg, Mandell, Jr. v U.S., 42 AFTR2d 78-5581, 577 F2d 290 (USCA 5)
l-4—Clark, Donald E.; Comm. v, 63 AFTR2d 89-862 (US) 109 S Ct 1457
q-4—Johnson, James Hervey, 78 TC 575, 78 PH TC 303
l-6—Clark, Donald E. v Comm., 60 AFTR2d 87-5593, 828 F2d 223 (USCA 4)
q-7—Sellers, William D., Jr. v U.S., 42 AFTR2d 78-6197 (DC Ala)
f-7—Rose, Stanley B. v U.S., 43 AFTR2d 79-455 (DC Wash)
c-7—Clark, Donald E. & Peggy S., 86 TC 143, 86 PH TC 71
BEDFORD, MAURICE F. v U.S., 39 AFTR2d 77-1246, (DC Wis)
e-1—Bradford, Virgil, In re, 52 AFTR2d 83-6246 (Bkt Ct Va)
BEDOTTO, REMO v COMM., 54 AFTR2d 84-5305, 734 F2d 1377 (USCA 9) (See Strimling, Murton D. v Comm)
BEDOTTO, REMO & ESTHER Z., 1983 PH TC Memo ¶ 83,281 (See Strimling, Murton D. & Brenda)
BEDSON, JAMES E., 1981 PH TC Memo ¶ 81,064
a—Court Order, 4-1-85 (USCA 11)
e-1—Epstein, Michael, 1989 PH TC Memo 89-2515
BEEBE, RICHARD L; U.S. v, 61 AFTR2d 88-349, 835 F2d 670 (USCA 6, 12-22-87), reh den, 2-18-88
BEECH AIRCRAFT CORP. v U.S., 58 AFTR2d 86-5548, 797 F2d 920 (USCA 10, 8-6-86)
sa—Beech Aircraft Corp. v U.S., 54 AFTR2d 84-6173 (DC Kan)
g-1—Humana Inc. v Comm., 64 AFTR2d 89-5145, 89-5148, 881 F2d 251, 254
e-1—Clougherty Packing Co. v Comm., 59 AFTR2d 87-668, 87-670, 87-672, 811 F2d 1298, 1300, 1303 (USCA 9)
f-1—Humana Inc. & Subsidiaries, 88 TC 207, 88 PH TC 107
n-1—Humana Inc. & Subsidiaries, 88 TC 223, 88 PH TC 115
e-1—Gulf Oil Corp., 89 TC 1023, 1025, 1039, 89 PH TC 525, 526, 534
g-1—Malone & Hyde, Inc. & Subs., 1989 PH TC Memo 89-3053
e-1—Letter Ruling 8837057, 1988 PH 196,366
e-1—Rev Rul 88-72, 1988-2 CB 31
BEECH AIRCRAFT CORP. v U.S., 54 AFTR2d 84-6173 (DC Kan, 7-3-84)
a—Beech Aircraft Corp. v U.S., 58 AFTR2d 86-5548, 797 F2d 920 (USCA 10)
e-1—Clougherty Packing Co. v Comm., 59 AFTR2d 87-668, 87-670, 87-672, 811 F2d 1298, 1300, 1303 (USCA 9)
g-1—Crawford Fitting Co. v U.S., 55 AFTR2d 85-1977, 606 F Supp 144 (DC Ohio)
f-1—Mobil Oil Corp. v U.S., 56 AFTR2d 85-5643, 85-5644, 85-5646, 8 Cl Ct 563, 565, 568
f-1—Clougherty Packing Co., 84 TC 955, 84 PH TC 500
e-1—Anesthesia Service Medical Group, Inc., Employee Protective Tr., 85 TC 1041, 85 PH TC 580

BEECH—contd.
e-1—Gulf Oil Corp., 89 TC 1025, 1035, 1039, 89 PH TC 526, 532, 534
e-1—Pariseau, Raymond C. & Carol, 1985 PH TC Memo 85-551, 85-552
e-1—Humana Inc. & Subsidiaries, 1985 PH TC Memo 85-1897
BEECHAM, INC. v U.S., 32 AFTR2d 73-5916 (DC Tenn)
g-1—Fieland, Louis C. & Ruth F., 73 TC 755, 73 PH TC 418 [See 32 AFTR2d 73-5918]
BEECHER, EXEC. v U.S., 6 AFTR2d 6113, 280 F2d 202 (USCA 3)
g-1—Luce, Dorell C. v U.S., 41 AFTR2d 78-1497, 78-1498, 444 F Supp 351, 352 (DC Mo)
l—Quinn, Jess H., Est. of, 1982 PH TC Memo 82-109
BEEGHLY FUND; COMM. v, 10 AFTR2d 6090, 310 F2d 756 (USCA 6)
l—Hartwick College v U.S., 55 AFTR2d 85-822, 588 F Supp 931 (DC NY)
BEEGHLY, L. A. & MABEL L., 36 TC 154, ¶ 36.14 PH TC 1961
l—Letter Ruling 8237004, 1982 PH 55,433
BEEGHLY, LEON A., FUND, THE, 35 TC 490, ¶ 35.56 PH TC 1961
e—Orange Cty. Agricultural Society, inc., 1988 PH TC Memo 88-1879 [See 35 TC 513]
g-1—Sound Health Assn., 71 TC 186, 71 PH TC 105 [See 35 TC 518]
BEEGHLY v WILSON, 152 F Supp 726, 51 AFTR 992 (DC Iowa)
e-3—Drexler, William E., Sr.; U.S. v, 60 AFTR2d 87-5100 (DC Okla)
f-7—Westinghouse Credit Corp. v B. F. Leasing, Inc., 42 AFTR2d 78-5245 (DC Wis)
BEEK, BARTON v COMM., 55 AFTR2d 85-1004, 754 F2d 1442 (USCA 9, 3-4-85)
sa—Beek, Barton & Dorothy M., 80 TC 1024, ¶ 80.53 PH TC
e—Norgaard, Preben & Sandra C., 1989 PH TC Memo 89-1890
e-1—Fox, Frederick M. & Michele B., 1989 PH TC Memo 89-1093
2—Wetterholm, Dennis H. & Geraldine A., 1986 PH TC Memo 86-799
2—Sels, Della Walker van Loben, Est. of, 1986 PH TC Memo 86-2268
BEEK, BARTON & DOROTHY M., 80 TC 1024, ¶ 80.53 PH TC
a—Beek, Barton v Comm., 55 AFTR2d 85-1004, 754 F2d 1442 (USCA 9)
e—Sels, Della Walker van Loben, Est. of, 1986 PH TC Memo 86-2268 [See 80 TC 1033]
e—Norgaard, Preben & Sandra C., 1989 PH TC Memo 89-1890 [See 80 TC 1034]
e-1—Cameron, Thomas W. & Ingrid L., 81 TC 258, 81 PH TC 135
l—Webber, Douglas G. & Betty J., 1983 PH TC Memo 83-2582
e-1—Wetterholm, Dennis H. & Geraldine A., 1986 PH TC Memo 86-799
e-1—Fox, Frederick M. & Michele B., 1989 PH TC Memo 89-1093
BEEKER, JAMES O. v U.S., 54 AFTR2d 84-5602, 582 F Supp 1132 (DC Ariz) (See Aune, George v U.S.)
BEEKMAN, CHARLES K., 17 BTA 643
e—Carroll, Leroy & Juanita B., 1981 PH TC Memo 81-1233 [See 17 BTA 648]
BEER v U.S., 132 F Supp 282, 47 AFTR 1678 (DC Ala)
f-4—Walsh, Richard F., Exec. v U.S., 42 AFTR2d 78-5770 (DC Tex)
BEER, WILLIAM J., 1982 PH TC Memo ¶ 82,735
a—Beer, William J. v Comm., 53 AFTR2d 84-1464, 733 F2d 435 (USCA 6)
d—1983 PH 61,000 (USCA 1)
rc—Beer, William J. & Dora, 64 TC 879, ¶ 64.83 PH TC
e-1—Stefan, George N., 1984 PH TC Memo 84-2204
e-1—Anderson, David R., 1985 PH TC Memo 85-734
e-1—Holtsinger, Inc., 1986 PH TC Memo 86-1217
e-1—Short, Jack M., 1988 PH TC Memo 88-248
BEER, WILLIAM J. v COMM., Court Order, 11-22-76 (USCA 6)
x—Beer, William J. v Comm., 431 US 938, 97 S Ct 2650, 53 LEd2d 255, 5-31-77 (T); reh den, 434 US 1052, 98

current tax developments. The best example is the "Tax Report" column found on the front page of *The Wall Street Journal* every Wednesday.

Two newsletters are worth special notice for the detail and diversity of their coverage.

Tax Notes (Tax Analysts—Weekly).

Each weekly issue of *Tax Notes* provides over 100 pages of commentary, news, and digests of primary documents. Summary information is extracted from the *Congressional Record*, the *Internal Revenue Bulletin*, congressional hearings, tax journals, and many other sources. Digests of judicial decisions, Revenue Rulings, and Private Letter Rulings are included. Both state and federal tax developments are followed. A detailed index appears monthly, with quarterly, semiannual, and annual cumulations.

Subscribers can also purchase a comprehensive microfiche collection which reprints the full text of most primary documents and journal articles cited in the newsletter. In this way, subscribers can not only keep abreast of current developments, but develop a comprehensive tax library. Also on the fiche are hard-to-find documents such as IRS Private Letter Rulings. The text service is called the *Tax Notes Microfiche Data Base* and is published weekly. *Tax Notes Today*, the online version, is updated daily, and contains the news stories, commentaries, and digests seen in the printed newsletter. It too provides full-text access to selected primary documents and journal articles. *Tax Notes Today* is available through DIALOG, LEXIS/NEXIS, NewsNet, and PHINet.

Daily Tax Report (Bureau of National Affairs—Five Times per Week).

BNA's *Daily Tax Report* also covers the full spectrum of tax news and digests of official releases, conveniently arranged by type of document. The highlights of each day's issue are reported on the front page, followed by a detailed table of contents and index to case names. The service is enhanced through biweekly and bimonthly topical indexes. A daily legislative calendar indicates activities of the previous day, meetings scheduled, and bills and resolutions introduced. Digests of tax decisions and rulings are also reported daily, arranged by Code section. For the most important judicial decisions and Revenue Rulings, the complete text is reproduced. Digests of IRS Private Letter Rulings are listed by Code section. A separate index to these rulings appears monthly, with bimonthly cumulations. The *Daily Tax Report* is also accessible online, through BNA itself, and via LEXIS and WESTLAW.

Periodical Indexes

Subject access to the periodical literature can be gained through a number of indexes. General publications and databases such as *Business Periodicals Index*, *ABI/INFORM* and *PAIS* include tax subjects in their coverage. Because tax information services are often arranged by Internal Revenue Code sections, several periodical indexes offer the same type of access. This enables researchers to locate independent commentary on changes in the law, recent court decisions, and specific Revenue Rulings. An excellent example is the AICPA's quarterly *Accountants' Index*. This service, described in Chapter 5, groups articles on federal income tax together under the broad heading "Taxation, United States." The broader term is then subdivided in four ways: by topic

(e.g., "stock transfers"), by the name of a tax law (e.g., "Revenue Act of 1987"), by Code section (e.g., "Section 401"), or by IRS Ruling (e.g., "Revenue Ruling 88-32"). All four types of subheadings are interfiled in a single alphabet. A typical annual edition of the index contains nearly 300 pages of citations to federal tax articles.

Another excellent publication is the *Current Law Index* from the Information Access Company. This index, together with its electronic counterparts, was introduced in Chapter 19. Like the *Accountants' Index*, the IAC index lists tax articles by section of the Internal Revenue Code or statute name, in this case in a separate section called "Table of Statutes." Court decisions are also indexed in a separate section by case name.

Aside from these sources, there are two indexing services devoted exclusively to tax matters.

Index to Federal Tax Articles (Warren, Gorham & Lamont—Quarterly).

This in-depth guide to tax literature was first published in 1975 as a three-volume, retrospective set covering articles from 1913 to 1974. The service is now updated quarterly, with irregular cumulations. Bound volumes have been published covering 1973 to 1981, 1982 to 1983, and 1984 to 1987. Each quarterly issue is also cumulative, dating back to the most recent hardcover volume. The service indexes over 300 different journals, plus published proceedings of annual tax symposia. The emphasis is on law journals, but selected accounting and economic periodicals are covered. Indexing is by subject and author's name. Although no access is provided by Code section, the subject headings are quite detailed, and general headings are subdivided. For example, the section on "Capital Gains and Losses" is further divided into "Capital Loss Carryforward," "Definition of Capital Assets," "Imputed Interest," and other subtopics. A complete list of headings and cross-references is printed in the front of every issue. However, the index is best used by those familiar with tax terminology. A small percentage of listings include lengthy abstracts of the articles.

Federal Tax Articles (Commerce Clearing House—Monthly).

This loose-leaf index covers some 400 periodicals of all types, plus tax symposia. Brief abstracts are given for every article. Besides the abstracts, the advantage to this service is the broader journal coverage, including general financial periodicals and pertinent trade journals. The principal drawback is its confusing arrangement, which is virtually identical to CCH's *Accounting Articles* (described in Chapter 5). Listings are published in a single loose-leaf binder, with older articles reprinted in

bound cumulations approximately every five years. The loose-leaf volume is best used as a current awareness service. The latest monthly updates are easy to use, with sections labeled by Code section. The abstract for an individual article is duplicated in every section of the Code to which it relates. However, the monthly reports are cumulated every six months, and the entries in the cumulations are renumbered in consecutive order, so the Code-specific numbering is lost. To conduct retrospective research, the user must consult the latest months, plus all semiannual cumulations over several years until the five-year volume is issued. In the loose-leaf volume, both subject and author indexing is provided, but both are divided into current and cumulative indexes. *Federal Tax Articles* does offer an alternative to traditional subject access, and those who use it frequently will adapt to the cumbersome arrangement.

IRS Publications

The Internal Revenue Service produces an extensive series of *Taxpayer Information Publications*. These range from single-page instruction sheets to extensive books with detailed information. Their purpose is to assist taxpayers and tax preparers in the income tax process. Most publications in the series deal with a specific topic, such as nontaxable income (Publication 525) or deductions for investors (Publication 550). The guides are free and most are revised annually. IRS Publications are not always as lucid as they could be, but they can provide valuable assistance with complex topics. Since the early 1980s, the IRS has collected its most popular pamphlets in an annual set called *Tax Information Publications*, which itself is identified as Publication 1194. This invaluable resource saves taxpayers the frustration of ordering needed pamphlets individually. Publication 1194 is distributed to libraries and tax preparers free on request.

IRS Publication 1132, *Reproducible Tax Forms for Use in Libraries*, is an annual loose-leaf set providing durable copies of the most commonly used federal income tax forms and instructions. The forms are designed to be photocopied, filled out, and submitted to the IRS. Publication 1132 is distributed to libraries at no charge. A similar IRS publication, the strangely titled *Package X: Informational Copies of Federal Tax Forms*, contains nearly all the forms found in Publication 1132, but it is intended for professional tax preparers rather than libraries. Both publications contain a full set of tax rate tables in addition to forms and instructions. For tax preparers who need large quantities of an individual form, there is Publication 1045, *Information and Order Blanks for Preparers of Federal Tax Returns*.

Publication 17, *Your Federal Income Tax*, is an excellent manual on how to prepare personal income tax returns. It contains nearly 200 pages of detailed information on declaring income, establishing gains and losses, calculating adjustments to income, and determining itemized deductions. Examples of specific tax situations are given throughout, together with the official IRS position on each. A companion to *Your Federal Income Tax* is Publication 334, *Tax Guide for Small Business*. Both sources are updated annually. For a complete catalog of additional IRS publications, the researcher can turn to Publication 1200, the *Reference Listing of Federal Tax Forms and Publications*, which contains both alphabetical and numerical listings.

Tax Preparation Guides

For the user who doesn't need a full-service loose-leaf set, any number of alternative tax guides are available. BNA's Tax Management subsidiary publishes an excellent "expediter" service for practitioners called the *Tax Practice Series*. This 12-volume loose-leaf is similar in approach to RIA's *Federal Tax Coordinator*, but emphasizes tax preparation. The explanations and examples are brief and clear, with footnotes citing the tax authority, and references to a more complete discussion in the *Portfolio* series. For ready reference purposes, several loose-leaf publishers produce scaled-down versions of their flagship publications. The two best known are Prentice Hall's *Federal Tax Guide* and RIA's *Tax Guide: Federal Taxes*. The Prentice Hall service is updated weekly, while the RIA publication is revised monthly; both are issued in two volumes. Commerce Clearing House publishes a brief, annual paperback summary to its voluminous tax service, called the *U.S. Master Tax Guide*.

A number of publishers also produce annual handbooks for the part-time tax preparer and the sophisticated taxpayer. Examples of this type of publication are *Bender's Tax Return Manual*, J.K. Lasser's *Your Income Tax: Professional Edition*, and the *Prentice Hall 1040 Handbook*. Dozens of publishers issue inexpensive guides for the do-it-yourselfer, and during tax season, such manuals dominate the display areas of local bookstores. The grandfather of the "how-to" tax guides is the familiar yellow-and-red *Your Income Tax* from J.K. Lasser. Other popular titles are Ernst & Young's *Arthur Young Tax Guide*, the *H&R Block Income Tax Guide*, and the *Guide*

to Income Tax Preparation, by the editors of Consumer Report Books. The format, content, and readability of these guides vary tremendously. Most are arranged in a topical fashion, usually following the steps on the tax form itself. Others are alphabetical guides to tax deductions; examples are the *Complete Book of Tax Deductions* by Robert S. Holzman, and *Bender's Dictionary of 1040 Deductions*. Many guides contain filled-in tax forms; others usually provide worked-through examples or step-by-step instructions. Almost all commercial publications include a section on recent changes in the tax laws, and all leading titles are updated annually. The unadorned IRS Publication 17 offers more than adequate guidance for free. However, there is simply no best choice; each person must select the book which suits his or her needs. Indeed, users may find a combination of publications offers the best approach.

The IRS publication *Reproducible Tax Forms for Use in Libraries* fills the need for blank copies of the most commonly used tax forms. Several commercial publishers issue more comprehensive sets of federal tax forms, with as many as 2,000 reproducible documents. They are published in loose-leaf binders and updated as new and revised forms appear. Among the most extensive collections are *Federal Tax and Related Forms* (Tax Form Library), *Federal Tax Forms* (Commerce Clearing House), and *IRS Forms* (Tax Management, Inc.). Several publishers also produce collections of filled-in tax forms which illustrate how to complete major forms. One of the best examples is the previously mentioned *Tax Action Coordinator* set from RIA, which also provides an extensive library of reproducible forms and instructions.

Many publishers issue loose-leaf or paperback guides for an individual state, or for groups of states, but only a few cover all 50. Both CCH and P-H produce a series of loose-leaf guides to state income taxes, with one or more volumes for each state. The CCH series is entitled *State Tax Reports* and the Prentice Hall service is called *State and Local Taxes*. Both publishers also sell intermediates guides that are less detailed than the full loose-leaf service. These series appear as paperback handbooks for each state. For comparable tax information on all states, RIA publishes the *State Tax Action Coordinator*, a fairly detailed guide issued in six regional loose-leaf volumes. Briefer information on state taxes is available from Commerce Clearing House and Prentice Hall. CCH has an excellent two-volume summary set called the *State Tax Guide* and Prentice Hall publishes a single-volume *All States Tax Guide*. Both services provide basic information on all types of taxes on a state-by-state basis, including income taxes, franchise taxes, sales taxes, and other excise taxes.

Locating specific state tax forms can be difficult, especially for out-of-state filers. Numerous commercial firms offer assistance. Among the most extensive guides to popular forms from all 50 states are *State Tax Forms: Individual* (Tax Form Library), *State Personal Income Tax Forms* (CCH), and *Allstate Personal Income Tax Forms* (National Tax Training School). Taken together, the various services of the major tax publishers constitute an enormous range of resources for every imaginable research and tax preparation need.

BASIC ACCOUNTING INFORMATION

Accountants are concerned with more than taxation. When most people think of accounting, they mean financial accounting, which involves reporting an organization's financial activities to those outside the organization. Another branch of the discipline, management accounting, creates reports for use by the company itself, to assist management in making decisions, establishing budgets, and controlling financial operations. A subset of this field is cost accounting, which identifies costs by type—labor, materials, and overhead—and allocates them by departments, functions, products, or other units within the organization. Auditing is the systematic investigation of an organization's activities and accounting records to determine whether they conform to prescribed criteria. Internal auditors are employees of the organization who investigate whether internal controls are functioning properly. An external audit is performed by a public accountant (i.e., a CPA), who then issues a formal opinion that the organization's financial statements meet generally accepted accounting principles. All of these accounting activities are relevant to every type of economic organization, including nonprofit corporations, government entities, and public and private companies. The remainder of this chapter will focus on financial accounting in general, and the sources of information for identifying standard accounting principles and practices in particular.

Accounting Standards

As defined in Chapter 8, generally accepted accounting principles (or GAAP, for short) represent the body of concepts, rules, and procedures followed by the accounting profession. GAAP ensures uniformity in

financial reporting, so that statements from one organization can be compared to those from all others. Generally accepted accounting principles are not static; they evolve over time to reflect changes in financial and economic conditions. Today, the authority for establishing GAAP is the Financial Accounting Standards Board (FASB), a nonprofit body created by various accounting organizations. FASB (pronounced FAS-bee) is not a government agency; accounting is a self-regulated profession.

Prior to the creation of FASB in 1973, other organizations were charged with promulgating accounting standards. These earlier rule-making bodies are important because many of their pronouncements remain part of GAAP. In 1930, the American Institute of Accountants (predecessor of the American Institute of Certified Public Accountants) established the Committee on Accounting Procedure (CAP). The Committee was charged with publishing a set of uniform accounting principles, the first of which appeared in 1938. During its tenure, CAP issued 51 separate standards in the form of *Accounting Research Bulletins*. In 1953, Bulletin 43 codified all previously issued bulletins into a single statement of principles, and much of its contents remain in force today. In 1959, the AICPA replaced CAP with the Accounting Principles Board (APB), which continued to issue standards under the title *APB Opinions*. Thirty-one Opinions were issued prior to the APB's demise in 1973. The APB also issued numerous *Accounting Interpretations*, which clarified specific points in the *Opinions*. The group was dissolved because of the widespread belief that GAAP should not be determined by the AICPA alone; after all, public accountants are not the only members of the profession, and users of financial data also have a stake in accounting standards.

The composition of FASB reflects the interests of the entire accounting profession. Actually, FASB is an affiliate of the Financial Accounting Foundation, which was also created in 1973. The 13 members of the Foundation's Board of Trustees are selected by eight sponsoring organizations, representing various branches of the financial and accounting communities. Among the sponsoring groups are the AICPA, the National Association of Accountants (management accountants), the American Accounting Association (primarily academic accountants), the Securities Industry Association, and the Financial Analysts Federation. Other members represent the banking industry, corporate financial executives, and accountants working for government agencies. The Trustees appoint seven individuals from outside their group to serve on the Board of FASB. FASB is the "action arm" of the Foundation, charged with the cre-

ation of new accounting standards and the modification of existing rules. To ensure its independence, all Board members must resign from previous employment and work full-time for FASB.

Noticeably absent from the membership of both FASB and the parent Foundation is any official from the U.S. Securities and Exchange Commission. This is in keeping with FASB's mission as a self-regulating body. On the other hand, FASB has a close working relationship with the SEC. The government may suggest issues for FASB to investigate, and FASB typically seeks input from the SEC when determining standards, but such cooperation is strictly voluntary. What makes FASB pronouncements binding is their acceptance by both the accounting profession and the government. Though the SEC occasionally issues accounting rules of its own, it has traditionally left this responsibility to FASB and its predecessors. Similarly, the AICPA recognizes FASB as the source of generally accepted accounting principles. Rule 203 of the AICPA's Code of Professional Ethics states that an auditor cannot express the opinion that a particular financial report conforms to GAAP if it departs in any way from authoritative FASB pronouncements.

The most important rules promulgated by FASB appear as a *Statement of Financial Accounting Standards*, also referred to as a FASB Statement, FAS, or SFAS. As of this writing, slightly more than 100 *Statements* have been issued. Each one deals with a major area of financial reporting, such as accounting for changing prices, pension funds, research and development expenses, and so on. Many FASB *Statements* are issued to modify or revoke older pronouncements.

Because FASB *Statements* have such a far-reaching impact on the financial community, and because many pronouncements are controversial, FASB has established a formal system to ensure due process. This means that careful consideration is given to the opinions of all interested parties before a rule is issued. The process begins with the identification of an accounting problem. Since 1984, FASB has designated an Emerging Issues Task Force to examine current topics in light of existing standards. If the Task Force feels that generally accepted accounting principles do not address the topic clearly, the Board may choose to take further action. The next step is a description of the issues involved, and an outline of alternative positions which FASB could take. This information is published in a *Discussion Memorandum* written by the FASB staff. Based on responses received from the public, the Board begins deliberations and issues a *Proposed Statement*, generally referred to as an *Exposure Draft*. A deadline date is set for receiving

written comments on the draft, after which changes may be incorporated into a revised statement. The Board then approves the amended version by a majority vote, and a final *Statement* is released. The entire procedure may take many months, especially for controversial issues.

FASB issues other publications with varying degrees of authority. FASB *Interpretations* clarify, explain, or elaborate upon previously issued FASB *Statements*, as well as those APB *Opinions* and CAP *Research Bulletins* still in force. FASB *Technical Bulletins* present rules on issues of less significance. They tend to be narrowly focused, dealing with situations of interest to specific industries or less common activities. they are seldom controversial, and do not represent a major change in accounting principles. Another FASB pronouncement is called a *Statement of Financial Concepts*, or SFAC, and is not considered an official part of GAAP. Each SFAC presents an overview of broad concepts in financial accounting and is intended to establish a conceptual framework for the profession. For example, SFAC 2, entitled *Qualitative Characteristics of Accounting Information*, outlines the desired qualities of a financial report. As of this writing, six *Statements of Financial Concepts* have been issued. All publications of FASB are available through one of several blanket subscription plans.

Additional rule-making bodies issue pronouncements on topics outside the purview of FASB. One of the most important is the AICPA's Auditing Standards Board, which issues *Statements on Auditing Standards*. Rule 202 of the AICPA Code of Professional Ethics states that members must conform to these standards when conducting an audit. Others include the Governmental Accounting Standards Board and the Cost Accounting Standards Board. The latter was created by Congress to establish specific accounting rules for federal contractors.

Because generally accepted accounting principles change over time, and because portions of the standards from FASB's predecessors remain in force, accountants need a comprehensive guide to current GAAP. FASB has codified all accounting standards by topic, incorporating changes made to the original pronouncements, just as the *Code of Federal Regulations* organizes current government regulations.

Accounting students, faculty members, and even practicing accountants may also need to trace the development of a particular concept or standard. Code services provide a "legislative history" for standards currently in force. Researchers can then read amended pronounce-

ments as they were first issued. Most accounting libraries maintain a set of original pronouncements in addition to the latest codification. Supporting documents, such as *Discussion Memoranda* and *Exposure Drafts*, are also available. A second way to locate the text of the original publications is through a subset of the *NAARS* database on the LEXIS/NEXIS system. The "Literature" file contains the complete text of all AICPA and FASB pronouncements and is updated weekly. Another important source is periodical literature. Newsletters from major accounting firms, leading accounting magazines, and trade journals in the affected industries will contain commentaries written during the drafting process as well as analysis of the rule's impact after it's promulgation. An excellent way to identify articles and letters of this type is to consult *Accountants' Index* under the pronouncement number. Another useful source is *ABI/INFORM*, though it covers only the most prominent accounting journals.

A diversity of official and unofficial resources covers accounting standards of one type or another. The following titles represent some of the most popular.

FASB Accounting Standards: Original Pronouncements (Financial Accounting Standards Board—Quarterly).

Official pronouncements from FASB are published in separate booklets which are released as the new standards are approved. For accountants and researchers without access to a full set of the original publications, a loose-leaf service reproduces all relevant documents in their entirety, including those issued by FASB's predecessors. The complete text of all AICPA *Accounting Research Bulletins*, *APB Opinions*, and *Accounting Interpretations* are found here, together with all FASB *Standards*, *Technical Bulletins*, *Interpretations*, and *Concepts*. As an alternative, an annual paperback edition is issued in two volumes. Volume 1 deals with FASB *Statements* from June 1973 to the present; Volume 2 covers pre-FASB standards. The paperback set is published on behalf of FASB by Business One Irwin.

In both versions, *Original Pronouncements* offers an important benefit. Any sections of the original documents which have been amended or rescinded are designated through shaded text. In this way, the standards are continuously updated, but at the same time the user can see the changes which have taken place over time. A summary page for every pronouncement indicates the earlier standards that it revises as well as the later standards which affect it. Both versions of *Original Pronouncements* also provide a topical index, a list of pronouncement dates, and several other appendices.

FASB Accounting Standards: Current Text (Financial Accounting Standards Board—Quarterly).

As a companion to the *Original Pronouncements*, FASB produces an official codification of GAAP in this loose-leaf service. It provides an integrated, topical presentation of currently effective standards, including the AICPA's *Accounting Research Bulletins, APB Opinions,* and FASB *Statements, Interpretations,* and *Technical Bulletins. Statements of Financial Accounting Concepts* are omitted because they are not considered part of GAAP. The service is divided into two volumes. The first covers broad accounting principles arranged by topic. The second lists standards which apply to specific industries. In both, the topics are arranged alphabetically, and given an alphanumeric code. For example, the section on Intangible Assets is designated I60, while the section on Interim Financial Reporting is coded I73. A detailed topical index in Volume 2 not only leads the user to the pertinent section of the *Current Text*, but to the original pronouncement and the report of the Emerging Issues Task Force as well. Rounding out the service are several useful finding tools: a list which links original pronouncements to the sections of *Current Text* in which they are discussed, a list of all paragraphs which have been amended or superseded, a chronology of pronouncements by publication number, and a calendar of major topics considered by the Emerging Issues Task Force.

Under each code section, *Current Text* cites a list of source documents, an excellent summary of the accounting principle, its applicability and scope, and the specific issues it covers. Illustrations and exhibits show how the principle is applied. Subscribers can opt to receive the service in loose-leaf form, or as a two-volume annual paperback, published by Business One Irwin. Since *Current Text* presents FASB-written abridgments of the complete rules, it is not considered an authoritative source. The underlying authority is the latest version of the full pronouncements.

A final publication from FASB is called *EITF Abstracts*. It contains summary descriptions of every topic considered by the Emerging Issues Task Force since its inception in 1984, including issues for which no subsequent action was taken. This is not an essential publication, but it is important for researchers tracing the development of accounting principles.

GAAP: Interpretation and Application of Generally Accepted Accounting Principles, *Patrick R. Delaney, et al.* (John Wiley & Sons—Annual).

FASB's *Current Text* is the best way to determine the latest GAAP, but readers may find certain principles difficult to understand. This is certainly true for account-

ing students and nonaccountants, but may also be the case for experienced practitioners. For this reason, several unofficial guides to GAAP are available, most of which are updated on an annual basis. These publications explain accounting principles in basic language, comment on their importance, development, and applicability, and provide computational examples. They may be compiled by accounting professors, prominent practitioners, or a combination of both.

One of the best introductory guides is *GAAP: Interpretation & Application,* by Patrick R. Delaney and others. It covers only the most widely applicable principles, but the explanations are detailed and lucid. Unlike the *Current Text*, topics are not arranged alphabetically, but presented in the order they would appear on financial statements. Each section provides an overview of the principle, a list of the ruling pronouncements, an explanation of the issues, a discussion of the reporting requirements, and extensive examples. An excellent introductory chapter offers suggestions on accounting research methods. The book also provides a detailed subject index, a list of authoritative pronouncements by number, and a simplified disclosure checklist, arranged by items on the financial statements.

Commerce Clearing House's *Financial Accounting Standards: Explanation and Analysis,* by Bill D. Jarnigan, is also arranged to follow the major items on the financial statements. Like the Wiley publication, it offers a general discussion of the GAAP provisions, together with worked-through examples. A unique feature is a flow chart presented for every topic, illustrating the decision process in applying the principles under discussion.

Perhaps the most popular unofficial handbook is the *Miller Comprehensive GAAP Guide,* written by Martin A. Miller and published by Harcourt, Brace, Javonovich. It covers all current standards, restating the original text in more basic terms. It differs from the first two publications by presenting the topics in alphabetical order, much like FASB's *Current Text*. The arrangement differs slightly from the FASB publication, however. It presents general background, explanation, and detailed illustrations, as well as a topical index, a disclosure checklist, and a finding table of original pronouncements. Miller also compiles a *Comprehensive GAAS Guide,* covering the AICPA's auditing standards. All four unofficial publications are updated annually.

Codification of Statements on Auditing Standards (Commerce Clearing House—Annual).

Just as the Financial Accounting Standards Board codifies its existing standards, so does the AICPA's

Auditing Standards Board. *Statements on Auditing Standards*, originally issued as individual booklets, are updated and brought together as the *Codification of Statements*. General standards are presented first, followed by standards of field work, standards of reporting, and special topics. The *Codification* is published on behalf of the AICPA by Commerce Clearing House. Subscribers may receive it as an annual paperback book, or as part of a CCH loose-leaf service called *AICPA Professional Standards*. The latter edition also reproduces the AICPA's Code of Professional Ethics, Rules of Conduct, Bylaws, and related standards.

SEC Accounting Rules (Commerce Clearing House—Monthly).

The principles of accounting for publicly traded corporations should be comparable to those for privately held firms. In some cases, however, FASB has remained silent regarding certain issues specific to public companies, and in a few others, the SEC has taken exception with FASB pronouncements. To deal with these situations, the government has issued accounting rules of its own. These appear as regulations (notably Regulations S-X and S-K) or as less formal published rules. The latter have been brought together as the *Codification of Financial Reporting Policies*, and are updated through *Financial Reporting Releases*. The releases are also published in the government's *SEC Docket*.

A two-volume loose-leaf service from Commerce Clearing House brings together all SEC accounting regulations and policies in a single publication. Volume 1 presents information in a topical arrangement and provides digests of all relevant case law, including Commission rulings and major court decisions. Volume 2 reproduces original pronouncements of the policies and regulations, plus correspondence between accounting firms and the SEC on the subject of auditors' independence. To avoid conflicts of interest, auditors cannot have any ties to the companies they audit, including business, family, investment, or legal relationships. When such conflicts are not clear-cut, accountants describe the situation in detail, and request an opinion from the SEC. Because this correspondence is public record, CCH reprints the most noteworthy exchanges of letters. *SEC Accounting Rules* contains a topical index, an index to case names, and a section of proposed regulations. An alternative to printed sources is the *NAARS* Literature file, which contains the full text of all SEC accounting regulations and policy statements.

Guides to Accounting Practices

Accountants need an enormous amount of specific information in order to prepare financial statements, ranging from industry-wide financial ratios to handbooks of basic accounting formulas. Three areas deserving special mention are the legal aspects of accounting, current trends in accounting practice, and directories of auditors and their clients.

A variety of loose-leaf services examine the legal concerns of the accounting profession, such as the auditor's liability in cases where he or she failed to detect serious financial problems due to management incompetence or criminal activity. More traditional services help users navigate the complex laws of new securities registration, insider trading, and related topics. One of the most comprehensive is the seven-volume *Federal Securities Law Reporter* from Commerce Clearing House. An excellent guide to securities law at the state level is *Blue Sky Law Reports*, another service from CCH. This four-volume set covers both the Uniform Securities Act adopted by most states and state-by-state regulations.

Loose-leaf services of the types described above are written primarily for attorneys rather than accountants, and are difficult for the layperson to decipher. A different category of loose-leaf focuses on the disclosure requirements of publicly traded companies. These publications cover the types of reports which must be filed and the mandatory contents of each report. *SEC Financial Reporting*, by Robert K. Hardman and others, is published by Matthew Bender and covers the requirements for submitting Form 10-K Reports, Annual Reports to Shareholders, and quarterly income reports. Separate sections cover the special reporting requirements of banks and insurance companies.

Accountants can take several approaches to determine how other firms have handled situations similar to ones they are facing. One method is to use electronic databases to identify publicly traded companies which have experienced a particular set of circumstances. *Compact D/SEC* is helpful for this type of research, but a better resource is the *NAARS* Annual Reports file. Both databases are described in detail in Chapter 9. A second approach is to consult manuals which recommend the best way to deal with each situation. The Practitioner Publishing Company specializes in authoritative publications of this type, including their annual *Guide to Preparing Financial Statements*. A third approach is to consult annual guides which highlight the best annual reports of the previous year.

Accounting Trends and Techniques (American Institute of Certified Public Accountants—Annual).

For many years the AICPA has culled the Annual Reports to Shareholders of 600 publicly traded companies to detect changing patterns in financial accounting practice. *Accounting Trends and Techniques* summarizes the results of this analysis and describes noteworthy trends in financial reporting. All audited sections of the report are scrutinized. Corporate treasurers and comptrollers consider it an honor to have their reports highlighted in this fashion. The publication is divided into three sections. The first examines the accounting treatment of general topics, such as business segment reporting, related-party transactions, corporate reorganizations, financial contingencies, and inflation reporting. The second and third sections cover major items from the Balance Sheet and Income Statement. In all three sections, excerpts from actual reports illustrate notable reporting techniques. Depending on the topic, illustrations may show the portions of the financial tables, auditors report, or management discussion, but most focus on the footnotes to the statements. For each topic, trends are shown by the use of statistical tables which compare the number of companies using a particular reporting method or experiencing a specific event. The publication also includes indexes by topic and by company name.

Who Audits America (Data Financial Press—Semiannual).

One method of determining who audits a particular company is to consult basic business directories such as the *Standard & Poor's Register*. For publicly traded companies, researchers can turn to the Annual Report to Shareholders, or to summary services such as *Moody's Manuals*. Electronic databases like *Compact D/SEC* can generate lists of clients by accounting firm, or rank major clients by size. The problem with services based on Annual Reports is that a surprising number of companies switch auditors every year. A semiannual directory called *Who Audits America* indicates the current auditor, the former auditor (where relevant), and basic directory information for all companies which file a 10-K Report. Companies which are no longer public continue to appear in the directory for several editions. The second major section of *Who Audits America* is arranged by auditor, with listings of their major clients. This section is arranged in two parts, one for "Big Eight" firms, the other for smaller auditors. In both parts, clients are ranked by sales volume. A third section provides geographic access to auditors by city, again in two parts. For national firms, a list of local offices is presented; smaller firms are listed geographically in the second part. Nu-

merous special features add to the versatility of this unique publication. A guide to companies which have switched auditors lists changes both by the old firm and the new. A ranked comparison of all auditing firms covered in the book lists the total number of public clients, and the number of clients by size category.

WHAT RESEARCHERS SHOULD KNOW

Taxation and accounting present many problems for researchers. The language of the tax law tends to be long, densely worded, and complicated. The body of regulations and court decisions which affect the statutes is voluminous and rapidly changing. And despite the myriad of specific tax situations covered in various publications, all eventualities simply cannot be dealt with in explicit fashion. For these reasons, finding and understanding the law for a given tax question can be exceedingly difficult. Most of the sources introduced in this chapter are sophisticated tools designed for experienced tax practitioners. Even accountants and lawyers who don't specialize in taxation will find them challenging to use. Some detailed publications are intended for the nonspecialist, but these simpler tools are not definitive sources for exhaustive research. Similarly, original accounting pronouncements are written for professional accountants, and even explanatory guides assume a basic knowledge of accounting concepts.

Is there any point in knowing about such specialized materials if one does not intend to concentrate on tax or accounting work? Both fields exert a pervasive influence on business activities, so librarians and researchers should have more than a nodding acquaintance with these important topics. There are a number of broad categories where tax research comes into play: applying the law to an individual circumstance, evaluating the tax result of a proposed decision, planning to minimize the total tax burden of a firm or individual, following the twists and turns of legislative debates, and investigating public policy issues. Likewise, fundamental accounting rules play a role in many situations: understanding the meaning behind the numbers seen in an annual report, comparing the performance of different companies, or studying the impact of accounting changes on a sector of the economy. Significant changes in accounting principles are frequently important enough to become major news stories in the business press.

For the expert and novice alike, a basic understanding of these reference publications is essential. But what constitutes "basic?" In the field of taxation, researchers

should know the difference between Treasury Decisions and Revenue Rulings. They should know that the *Federal Register* publishes tax regulations quickly, but that the *Internal Revenue Bulletin* publishes many additional tax announcements and rulings. Familiarity with the *Cumulative Bulletin* and the *Index-Digest System* is important. And finally, an understanding of the difference between Code-based and topical loose-leafs is fundamental. In the field of accounting, researchers should remember that accounting principles change over time, but that many older pronouncements remain in force substantially unchanged. They should also be comfortable with finding the original text of a pronouncement, the text as currently amended, and the codified arrangement of the text.

Whether conducting preliminary research, answering a ready-reference question, or guiding a nonspecialist to the appropriate source, sooner or later the need for familiarity with key resources will surface. However, as with most areas of the law, in-depth research is best left to the experts.

FOR FURTHER READING

Numerous textbooks, handbooks, and nutshells are published on tax law and tax accounting. Some are updated annually, others less frequently. Rather than describe leading works on tax practice, this list focuses on fundamental concepts related to the income tax and tax policy, plus guides to research techniques. Similarly, the accounting materials emphasize the conceptual framework of this discipline, including major issues facing the profession.

Tax Concepts and Policies

Conlan, Timothy J., Margaret T. Wrightson, and David R. Beam. *Taxing Choices: The Politics of Tax Reform* (Washington, DC: CQ Press, 1990).

Several excellent books chronicle the events leading up to the monumental Tax Reform Act of 1986, but this book is notable for its thorough and engrossing treatment. The emphasis is on the political process of tax reform and the negotiations which took place during each step of the journey. The chapter on the historical development of the income tax is also worth reading.

Pechman, Joseph A. *Federal Tax Policy.* 5th ed. (Washington, DC: Brookings Institution, 1987).

Pechman was an outspoken and well-known proponent of tax reform. This classic text describes the workings of the federal tax system, including the impact of the political

system and the relationship between taxation and economic policy. A brief historical overview of the federal income tax is also provided.

Witte, John F. *The Politics and Development of the Federal Income Tax* (Madison, WI: University of Wisconsin Press, 1985).

Here is an exceptionally lucid and well-researched account of the development of the income tax, from the Civil War through the first term of the Reagan presidency. The role of the political system in the tax-making process is emphasized. Witte also includes excellent background material on theories of taxation and the problems of creating a just system of taxes.

Tax Publications and Research Methods

Hedberg, Augustin. "Your Guide to the 1989 Tax Guides." *Money* (January 1989): 101-05.

A variety of popular magazines offer periodic comparisons of the best-known tax preparation guides. Some (*Consumer Reports* and *U.S. News & World Report*) actually rate the publications, while others (*Business Week* and *Money*) merely describe some of the leading contenders. The *Money* article is published annually in a January or February issue.

Research in Federal Taxation. 17th ed. (Paramus, NJ: Prentice Hall Information Services, 1988).

Prentice Hall designed this convenient booklet to assist customers in using its "Complete Federal Tax Library." Researchers will find this an excellent guide to understanding how the various types of publications are used in concert. The booklet is revised approximately every three years.

Richmond, Gail Levin. *Federal Tax Research: Guide to Materials and Techniques.* 4th ed. (Westbury, NY: Foundation Press, 1990).

This important research guide is geared toward attorneys, focusing on the institutional framework of the law and the primary and secondary publications where legal information can be found. Specific titles are described, including the major citators, loose-leaf services, newsletters, computerized databases, and commercial reproductions of primary documents. Brief explanations are given on tracing legislative history and tracking pending legislation.

Scanlan, Jean M. "Comparison Shopping of Tax Research Databases." *Database* 13 (February 1990): 13-17.

A brief guide to major databases and online systems covering tax information, written by the director of Price Waterhouse's Information Center. It compares the two specialized sources of tax information (PHINet and CCH ACCESS) to the broader legal services of LEXIS and WESTLAW. Several databases on DIALOG and ORBIT are also discussed.

Sommerfeld, Ray M., et al. *Tax Research Techniques*. 3rd ed. (New York: American Institute of Certified Public Accountants, 1989).

Sommerfeld is an eminent author in the field of taxation. Although intended for accountants, the book is clearly aimed at the novice tax practitioner. It discusses the difficulties of conducting tax research, the steps in the process, and the resources used. Interesting examples are used to clarify the points being made.

Accounting Principles

Belkaoui, Ahmed. *Public Policy and the Practice and Problems of Accounting* (Westport, CT: Quorum, 1985).

Belkaoui is one of the accounting profession's most articulate voices, and here he summarizes some of the central public policy issues related to accounting standards and practices. Among the problems he tackles are whether there should be more than one set of GAAP, the roles of the FASB and the SEC, competition and conflict of interest in large CPA firms, and the changing nature of the AICPA.

Flegm, Eugene H. *Accounting: How to Meet the Challenges of Relevance and Regulation* (New York: Wiley, 1984).

Another thoughtful exploration of the current challenges facing the profession. The author presents a fairly detailed history of accounting standards, misconceptions surrounding GAAP, and FASB's attempts to define a conceptual framework for accounting. An eminently readable discussion, with numerous case studies.

Miller, Paul B., and Rodney J. Redding. *The FASB: The People, the Process, and the Politics*. 2nd ed. (Homewood, IL: Irwin, 1988).

An interesting and well-rounded description of FASB—its history, purpose, organization, and decision-making mechanisms. Especially useful is the chapter describing FASB's due process procedures. The work of FASB is brought to life through a discussion of several accounting controversies and how they were handled by FASB.

APPENDIX
Keeping Up to Date

Business research and publishing change so rapidly that keeping current can be a full-time job. Every professional researcher must make an effort to keep abreast of new information products, publishing trends, technological advances, and research methods. A host of current awareness techniques can be employed. Maintaining regular contact with your colleagues in other institutions is an important resource, especially if you are self-employed or work in a one-person library or research department. To this end, researchers are encouraged to belong to the professional associations best suited to their needs and temperaments. Attending conferences and workshops can be one of the most intensive methods of keeping current and building a network of contacts. Some of the newsletters listed below offer clues about appropriate associations to consider; many others are also worth investigating. Aside from national and regional associations, you may be able to tap into informal collegial networks in your city. Similarly, electronic bulletin boards and E-mail lists can be worth joining.

An often overlooked resource is the publisher's representative. Some are less than competent, and others can be too aggressive or annoying, but a good sales rep is a treasure. The best ones realize the importance of developing a strong relationship with their customers; they are knowledgeable about their products and those of their competitors, and they generally pick up a great deal of useful intelligence in their travels. Remember, however, that information is a two-way street, and that a sales rep's job is to sell products. Don't abuse your publisher contacts: share what you know, be frank, and don't make false promises of potential purchases.

For systematic and continuous monitoring of your environment, the best resource is trade and professional periodicals. Innumerable journals, newspapers, and newsletters are of interest to business researchers and librarians. It is also vital for business researchers and librarians to be aware of general business and economic news. The best way to become "business literate" is to follow the news regularly. At the very least, skim one daily newspaper and one news magazine. If you follow one or two industries as part of your research activities, read a few of the leading trade journals. Cover-to-cover reading isn't necessary—look at headlines and lead paragraphs of important stories, and give fuller attention only to stories which interest you. The pages of *The Wall Street Journal*, *Business Week*, *Fortune*, and others can become your best instructors. A regular reading program will make an invaluable contribution to your fund of knowledge and your awareness of what's going on. As a result, you will not only become more comfortable with information requests, you'll actually find the answers to a variety of queries lurking in the back of your mind.

FOR FURTHER READING

The following list is highly selective (and somewhat idiosyncratic). The focus is on the most significant topics covered in this book. One of the largest problems of keeping up to date is remaining aware of new information products and changes in existing products. For this reason, the emphasis is on publications which contain reliable product reviews, or at the least, new product announcements. Other titles are listed because they report the latest developments related to underlying concepts discussed in the book. These selections highlight publications which are understandable and even enjoyable.

Without doubt some of your favorite titles will not appear on this list; many more could have been included. But you may discover new and valuable current awareness publications. One bit of advice is not to overindulge; the more titles you add to your personal library or in-house routing list, the fewer you are likely to read. Stick with the ones which yield the best results over the long

haul. For less important topics, consider searching periodical indexes and databases when the need arises, or develop an SDI profile with your favorite online vendor.

General Business Research

Business Information Alert. (Chicago: Alert Publications—10 times/year).
Aimed at business librarians and researchers, this well-written newsletter covers all aspects of business information, from obtaining SEC filings to finding market share data online. Each issue contains a lead article, news, and book reviews.
Information Advisor. (Rochester, NY: The Winters Group—Monthly).
This brief newsletter focuses on how to evaluate business information, with an emphasis on economic, financial, and marketing data. With lots of comparative reviews and how-to articles, it is an eminently practical resource.
The Information Report. (Washington, DC: Washington Researchers—Monthly).
Contains brief announcements on reference books, newsletters, pamphlets, and seminars of interest to business researchers. Emphasis is on government information, market reports, and company intelligence.

Business Librarianship

Topics relating to business research can be found in a wide array of professional journals, including such standards as *RQ, Reference Services Review, College & Research Libraries,* and *Library Journal.* Articles can be few and far-between in any general title. The following periodicals are aimed predominantly at business librarians.
Business and Finance Division Bulletin. (Washington, DC: Special Libraries Association—Quarterly).
The official newsletter of SLA's Business and Finance Division contains news of the Division's activities, and frequently offers reference bibliographies and brief guides to resources.
Journal of Business & Finance Librarianship. (Binghamton, NY: Haworth Press—Quarterly).
A balanced mix of theoretical and practical articles on business librarianship in all settings. Coverage includes library management, reference techniques, collection development, and information products.

Online Databases and CD-ROMs

One of the most prolific areas of journal publishing for the information specialist is in electronic databases. Titles range from the theoretical (*Journal of the American Society for Information Science* and *Online Review*) to trade journals aimed at database producers and corporate end-users (*CD-ROM Review* and *CD-ROM End-User*). Most online vendors also provide newsletters or magazines to their customers. Two of the most informative are *Chronolog* (DIALOG Information Service—Monthly) and *Dowline* (Dow Jones News Retrieval—Quarterly). The most appropriate journals for business researchers tend to be those with hands-on searching advice and lengthy product reviews.
CD-ROM Librarian. (Westport, CT: Meckler Corporation—Monthly).
A glossy magazine with new product announcements, product reviews, and a few feature articles. Each issue also provides updated listings to Meckler's annual *CD-ROMs in Print.*
CD-ROM Professional. (Weston, CT: Pemberton Press—Bimonthly).
The leading journal for users of CD-ROM products offers extensive reviews of new CD-ROM databases, product evaluations for hardware, and articles on trends in the industry. Formerly called *Laserdisk Professional.*
Database. (Weston, CT: Online, Inc.—Bimonthly).
Examines all aspects of electronic information delivery, with strong coverage of business databases. Detailed product reviews and creative searching tips are the hallmark of this excellent tool. A must-read for all online searchers.
Information Today. (Medford, NJ: Learned Information—Monthly).
Probably the best source for keeping up with the rapid changes in online and CD-ROM technologies. Reliable and timely reporting on new products, corporate changes, and industry trends.
Inside Business. (Palo Alto, CA: DIALOG Information Systems—Quarterly).
A glossy magazine aimed at DIALOG business searchers. Each issue focuses on a theme such as competitive intelligence or strategic planning, and offers tips on using DIALOG databases to conduct research in that area. Also contains interviews with DIALOG's searchers in business and industry.
Online. (Weston, CT: Online, Inc.—Bimonthly).
Similar in every respect to its companion journal (*Database*), with strong coverage of business databases and trends in electronic information.

Government Publications

Government Information Quarterly. (Greenwich, CT: JAI Press—Quarterly).
Explores all aspects of government publications and documents librarianship. Special issues, called "symposia," are frequently devoted to a single topic such as the Economic Census or the federal information system.
Government Publications Review. (Elmsford, NY: Pergamon Press—Bimonthly).
Similar in many ways to the above-mentioned publication, but with a stronger emphasis on reviews of specific publications. Also tends to discuss international documents more frequently.

Investments

Among the many excellent investment periodicals mentioned in the preceding chapters, *Barron's* and *Investor's Daily* are especially notable. Additional publications abound, geared to satisfy every taste and interest. General guides to personal finance, such as *Money* and *Changing Times*, are extremely popular. Innumerable magazines are written for small investors. *Better Investing*, *Fact*, and *Stock Market Magazine* are good examples. Researchers specializing in investment research will gain much from such professional journals as *Securities Week, Institutional Investor,* and *Investment Dealers' Digest*. Other journals focus on specific topics, including *Pensions and Investment Age* and *Futures*. For high quality coverage of a diversity of topics, the following are recommended:

Financial World. (New York: Financial World—Biweekly).
This sophisticated and widely read magazine covers corporate financial news and all categories of investment information. Articles and regular columns are well written, and aimed at both financial professionals and individual investors.
Forbes. (New York: Forbes, Inc.—Biweekly).
Forbes is one of the premiere business journals in the United States, ranking with *Business Week* and *Fortune* as an indispensable information source for business leaders. In addition to colorful, often irreverent coverage of general business news, corporate events, and biographical profiles, *Forbes* focuses strongly upon investing. Trends in corporate financing are followed very well, including innovative investment strategies and new types of securities. Mark Hulbert's column on investment newsletters is recommended. *Forbes* is also one of the few general magazines with insightful reporting on accounting trends which affect investment information.

Statistics and Data Use

APDU Newsletter. (Princeton, NJ: Association of Public Data Users—10 times/year).
The APDU was founded to encourage the availability and use of government statistics. Members include economists and other data users in government, industry, and academia, as well as commercial data producers and consultants. The newsletter reports developments in government statistical programs, upcoming conferences, and major new publications and computer products.
Chance: New Directions for Statistics and Computing. (New York: Springer-Verlag—Quarterly).
A lively new magazine which focuses on the analysis of statistical data. Articles cover statistical methods, new software packages, graphic presentation of data, the misuse of data, and statistical trends in the social sciences, sciences, medicine, and business. For example, a recent issue contained articles on the probability of human risk from electric/magnetic fields, and sports fans' perceptions of "shooting streaks" in basketball.
IASSIST Quarterly. (Princeton, NJ: International Association for Social Science Information Service and Technology—Quarterly).
For those interested in machine-readable data files, this newsletter keeps readers abreast of collections, trends, and techniques. Brief articles also provide tips for data archive managers. Another useful newsletter is the *ICPSR Bulletin,* a quarterly publication of the Inter-university Consortium for Political and Social Research in Ann Arbor, Michigan. An extensive portion of the newsletter lists new computer tapes acquired by the Center, but every issue also contains a feature article and brief news items.
News From COPAFS. (Alexandria, VA: Council of Professional Associations on Federal Statistics—Approximately 6 times/year).
COPAFS is the major lobbying organization for users of federal statistics. The newsletter alerts readers to changes in government statistical policies, including pending legislation and administrative actions. It also effectively encourages readers to respond to proposed curtailments in federal statistical programs. In addition, the newsletter describes new data products and services from government agencies.

Demographics and Marketing

Several worthwhile marketing titles were suggested in Chapter 18, but the following publications are especially recommended for business researchers.

American Demographics. (Ithaca, NY: Dow Jones—Monthly). A wonderful guide to marketing trends and sources of marketing/demographic data. Articles present summary statistics on the demographics of market segments as well as tips on how to conduct research. Provides excellent coverage of government information sources, including the Bureau of the Census. The publisher also issues a monthly newsletter called the *Numbers News*.

Census and You (Washington, DC: U.S. Bureau of the Census— Monthly). The official newsletter of the Bureau, with informative articles on new programs and products, as well as background on the operations of the Bureau. A companion publication, *Monthly Product Announcements*, provides a comprehensive list of newly issued publications and data files.

Marketing News. (Chicago: American Marketing Association—Biweekly). Many outstanding journals cover developments in marketing and advertising, but for the widest window on current happenings, this tabloid-sized periodical is recommended. In addition to reporting industry news, brief articles explore the latest market research techniques, new sources of marketing data, software for market analysis, and legal and policy issues affecting marketing managers.

Population Today. (Washington, DC: Population Reference Bureau—Monthly). Offers short news articles and opinion pieces on all aspects of population studies and follows the progress of controversial issues related to the decennial Census. Also provides a fascinating look at census-taking programs in other countries.

Title Index

A NOTE ON FILING CONVENTIONS: All acronyms and initialisms are filed as words, whether or not they are pronounced as words. All titles beginning with "U.S." are filed as though written "United States." Because business publications frequently have variant titles, numerous cross-references have been provided.

ABI/INFORM, 13-14, 18, 19, 54, 84, 87-89, 95, 102, 264, 418, 463, 467
ABI/INFORM Ondisc, 87-89
ABPR. See *American Book Publishing Record*
ABS. See *Information Bank Abstracts*
Academic Index, 19
Accountants, 95
Accountants' Index, 95, 463, 467
Accounting Articles, 95, 463
Accounting Interpretations (APB), 466, 467
Accounting Principles Board Opinions. See *APB Opinions*.
Accounting Research Bulletins, 466, 467, 468
Accounting Review, 94
Accounting Systems for Law Offices, 438
Accounting Trends and Techniques, 470
ACCRA Cost of Living Index, 327, 391, 392, 394
ACORN, 384, 414, 415-16, 421
ACORN Target Marketing. See *ACORN*
ACORN Users Guide, 416
Acquisitions/Divestitures Weekly Report, 241
Across the Board, 10
Actuarial Studies, 342
Ad Change, 120
Ad $ Summary. See *LNA/Arbitron Multi-Media Service—Ad $ Summary*
Advance Monthly Retail Sales. See *Current Business Reports—Advance Monthly Retail Sales*
Advertiser Red Book. See *Standard Directory of Advertisers*
Advertising Age, 10, 399, 400
Advertising and Marketing Intelligence Abstracts, 97
Advertising Options Plus. See *Standard Rate & Data Service—Advertising Options Plus*
Advertising Ratios & Budgets, 399
Adweek, 399, 400, 402
Adweek Client/Brand Directory, 400, 402
Adweek's Marketing Week, 402
Aerospace/Defense Markets and Technology, 92, 101

Aerospace Facts and Figures, 174
AFTR 2d. See *American Federal Tax Reports 2d*
Agency Red Book. See *Standard Directory of Advertising Agencies*
Agribusiness USA, 101
Agricultural Outlook, 341
Agricultural Outlook Yearbook, 341
Agricultural Situation and Outlook Reports, 341
Agricultural Statistics, 73, 75, 366, 369
AICPA Accounting Research Bulletins. See *Accounting Research Bulletins*
AICPA Professional Standards, 469
AICPA Statements on Auditing Standards. See *Statements on Auditing Standards*
Air Travel Survey, 422
All States Tax Guide, 465
Allstate Personal Income Tax Forms, 465
Almanac of American Politics, 29
Almanac of Business and Industrial Financial Ratios, 174, 176
Almanac of the 50 States, 377
A.L.R. See *American Law Reports Annotated*
Alternative Press Index, 94
American Banker, 96, 177
American Bankers Association Banking Literature Index, 96
American Banker's Top Numbers. See *Top Numbers* (American Banker)
American Book Publishing Record, 66, 67
American Book Trade Directory, 142
American Business Disk, 124
American Demographics, 382, 405, 476
American Digest System, 431, 433, 439
American Federal Tax Reports 2d, 455, 456, 458,
American Funeral Director, 10
American Heritage Dictionary, 149
American Housing Survey. See *Current Housing Reports—American Housing Survey*
American Institute of Real Estate Appraisers' Directory of Members, 142
American Jurisprudence Second, 427

American Law Reports Annotated, 433
American Library Directory, 33
American Marketplace, 405
American Metal Market, 10
American Newspaper Markets' Circulation, 403
American Profile, 386
American Profile: Opinion and Behavior, 408
American Public Opinion Data, 411
American Public Opinion Index, 411
American Radio, 404
American Salaries and Wages Survey, 394
American Statistics Index, 70, 75-76, 94, 319, 344, 369
American Universities and Colleges, 36
America's Centenarians, 315
America's Corporate Families: The Billion Dollar Directory, 146, 148
Ameritech Industrial Yellow Pages, 139
AMI. See *Advertising and Marketing Intelligence Abstracts*
AMS Office, Professional and Data Processing Salaries Report, 393
Analysis of Investor-Owned Electric and Gas Utilities. See *P.U.R. Analysis of Investor-Owned Electric and Gas Utilities*
Analysis of the President's Budgetary Proposals, 341
Annual Consumer Expenditure Study. See *Supermarket Business Annual Consumer Expenditure Study*
Annual Energy Outlook, 341
Annual Housing Survey. See *Current Housing Reports—American Housing Survey*
Annual Report on American Industry. See *Forbes Annual Report on American Industry*
Annual Reports Abstracts. See *PTS Annual Reports Abstracts*
Annual Retail Trade, 356
Annual Statement Studies. See *RMA Annual Statement Studies*
Annual Statistical Digest (Federal Reserve Board), 340
Annual Survey of Manufacturers, 353, 405
Annual Wholesale Trade, 356

APB Accounting Interpretations. See
    Accounting Interpretations (APB)
APB Opinions, 466, 467, 468
APDU Newsletter, 475
Apparel Merchandising, 406
Applied Science and Technology Index,
    100
Arbitration in the Schools, 445
Architectural Digest, 414
Area Wage Survey Summaries, 393
Area Wage Surveys, 393, 394, 449
Art Directors Annual, 399, 421
Arthur D. Little/Online, 50
Arthur Young Tax Guide, 464
Artificial Intelligence Abstracts, 100
ASI. See *American Statistics Index*
Asia-Pacific Database, 100
ASM. See *Annual Survey of*
    Manufacturers
Association of Public Data Users
    Newsletter. See *APDU Newsletter*
Association Periodicals, 48
ASWS. See *American Salaries and Wages*
    Survey
Atlanta Constitution, 101, 104
Atlantic Monthly, 414
Automotive News, 10, 406
Auxiliary Establishments. See *Enterprise*
    Statistics—Auxiliary Establishments
Ayer Directory of Publications. See *Gale*
    Directory of Publications and
    Broadcast Media

Babson Staff Letter. See *United & Babson*
    Investment Report
Bank Quarterly Ratings and Analysis. See
    Sheshunoff Bank Quarterly Ratings
    and Analysis
Bank Rate Monitor, 216, 269
Bankcard Monitor, 216
Bankers Blue Book. See *Thomson Bank*
    Directory
Banking and Monetary Statistics, 1914-
    1979, 340
Banking Literature Index. See *American*
    Bankers Association Banking
    Literature Index
BAR/LNA Multi-Media Service. See
    LNA/Arbitron Multi-Media Service
Bargaining Calendar, 449
Barron's Guide to Graduate Business
    Schools, 36
Barron's Index. See *Wall Street Journal*
    Index
Barron's National Business and Financial
    Weekly, 103, 209, 215-16, 220, 224,
    232, 243, 252, 254, 267, 269, 335,
    475
Basebook. See *Predicasts Basebook*
BCA Interest Rate Forecast, 342
Beer Marketers' Insights, 418
Bell & Howell Phonefiche. See
    Phonefiche
Bender's Dictionary of 1040 Deductions,
    465
Bender's Tax Return Manual, 464
Benefits Today, 449
Best 100 Sources for Marketing
    Information, 382
BestLink, 168
Best's Advance Company Reports, 168

Best's Insurance Management Reports,
    168
Best's Insurance Reports, 168
Best's Rating Monitor, 168
Best's Review, 168
Better Investing, 475
Bibliographic Guide to Business and
    Economics, 67, 68
Bibliographic Guide to Government
    Publications, 67, 70
Bibliographic Guide to Law, 67
Bibliographic Index, 68
Billboard, 10
Billion Dollar Directory. See *America's*
    Corporate Families: The Billion
    Dollar Directory
Biobusiness, 101
BioCommerce Abstracts and Directory,
    101
Biography and Genealogy Master Index,
    36, 145
Biography Index, 15
BioScan, 144
BIP. See *Books in Print*
BIR. See *Dun & Bradstreet Business*
    Information Reports
Block Statistics. See *Census of Population*
    and Housing—Block Statistics
BLS Bulletins, 377, 391, 393, 407, 449
BLS News, 334, 344
Blue Chip Economic Indicators, 342
Blue List of Current Municipal and
    Corporate Offerings, 232
Blue Sky Law Reports, 469
BNA Daily Labor Report. See *Daily*
    Labor Report
BNA Daily News, 438
BNA Daily Tax Report. See *Daily Tax*
    Report
BNA Policy and Practice Series, 447
BNA Tax Management Portfolios. See
    Tax Management Portfolios
BOMA Experience Exchange Report, 391,
    394
Bond Buyer. See *Daily Bond Buyer*
Bond Guide. See *Standard & Poor's*
    Bond Guide
Book of the States, 377, 427
Book Publishers Directory. See
    Publishers Directory
Book Review Digest, 68
Book Review Index, 68
Book World. See *Washington Post Book*
    World
Booklist, 68
Books and Periodicals Online: A Guide to
    Publication Contents of Business
    and Legal Databases, 54, 56, 108
Books in Print, 42, 43, 50, 66-67, 68
Books in Print Plus, 67
Boston Globe, 14, 101, 102, 104
BPI. See *Business Periodicals Index*
BPO. See *Books and Periodicals Online*
Bradford's Directory of Marketing
    Research Agencies, 38
Branch Directory and Summary of
    Deposits, 165, 386
Brands and Their Companies, 150-51
Broadcasting, 403, 405
Broadcasting/Cable Yearbook. See
    Broadcasting Yearbook

Broadcasting Yearbook, 405
Budget of the United States Government,
    334, 340-41
Bulletin Index-Digest System (IRS), 454,
    471
Bulletin to Management, 447
Bureau of Labor Statistics Bulletins. See
    BLS Bulletins
Bureau of Labor Statistics News. See
    BLS News
Burwell Directory of Information Brokers,
    37, 84
Business & Economics: An Abstract
    Newsletter, 73
Business and Finance Division Bulletin
    (SLA), 474
The Business Collection, 87
Business Conditions Digest, 330, 338
Business Dateline, 17, 54, 105, 375
Business Dateline Ondisc, 105
Business Executives' Expectations, 412
Business Horizons, 10
Business Identification Service. See
    Dun's Business Identification Service
Business Index, 85-87, 101, 104, 108-09,
    411, 428
Business Indicators, 344
Business Information Alert, 474
Business Information Reports. See *Dun &*
    Bradstreet Business Information
    Reports
Business Information Sources, vii, 43, 68,
    369
Business International Publications Index,
    67, 95
Business Library Review, 68
Business Lists-On-Disc, 124
Business Marketing, 10
Business Month, 10, 54
Business NewsBank, 105
Business NewsBank Index, 105
Business One Irwin Investor's Handbook,
    223, 253
Business Organizations, Agencies, and
    Publications Directory, 26
Business Periodicals Index, 15, 17, 19, 68,
    84, 85, 86, 95, 108-09, 411, 463
Business Periodicals Ondisc, 18, 89, 105
Business Profiles. See *TRW Business*
    Profiles
Business Publication Rates and Data. See
    Standard Rate & Data Service—
    Business Publication Rates and Data
Business Rankings Annual, 50, 418, 422
Business Statistics, 336, 337, 338
Business Week, 10, 50, 103, 177, 215, 220,
    251, 264, 267, 335, 344, 408, 412,
    473, 475
Business Week Mutual Fund Scoreboard,
    268
Business Wire, 107

Cable Television Law, 438
CACI Sourcebook of County
    Demographics. See *Sourcebook of*
    County Demographics
CACI Sourcebook of Zip Code
    Demographics. See *Sourcebook of*
    Zip Code Demographics
CAD/CAM Abstracts, 100

Cambridge Reports Trends and Forecasts, 409

Canadian Business Index, 100

Candy Industry Buying Guide, 142

CAP Research Bulletins. See *Accounting Research Bulletins*

Capital Adjustments, 242, 243, 245

Capital Changes Reports, 241-42, 243, 245

Card Deck Rates and Data. See *Standard Rate & Data Service—Card Deck Rates and Data*

Catalog of Data Files on Floppy Diskette. See *NTIS Listing of Data Files on Floppy Diskette*

Catalog of Publications, 1790-1972 (Bureau of the Census) , 319

CBI. See *Cumulative Book Index*

CCH Tax Day, 457

CCH Tax Transactions Library, 460

CD/Banking, 166

CD/Corporate, 18, 84, 89, 92, 145, 188, 222, 257, 263

CD/Corporate: SEC Filings, 195

CD/M&A, 239

CD/Newsline, 18

CD-ROM End-User, 474

CD-ROM Librarian, 56, 474

CD-ROM Professional, 474

CD-ROM Review, 474

CD-ROMs in Print: An International Guide, 56

CDMARC Subjects, 65

CENDATA, 311, 313, 321, 344, 361

The Census and You, 319, 476

Census Catalog and Guide, 319, 320

Census of Agriculture, 360, 380

Census of Construction Industries, 357
  Geographic Area Series, 357, 358
  Industry Series, 357

Census of Governments, 360

Census of Housing, 304, 307, 308. See also *Current Housing Reports*
  Characteristics of Housing Units, 307, 308
  Characteristics of Housing Units, Chapter A, 307-08, 322
  Characteristics of Housing Units, Chapter B, 308, 322
  Components of Inventory Change, 308
  Housing Subject Reports, 308, 311
  Metropolitan Housing Characteristics, 308, 320, 322
  Residential Finance, 308

Census of Manufactures, 350-53, 357
  Analytical Reports, 353
  Concentration Ratios in Manufacturing, 353
  Geographic Area Series, 350, 351
  Industry Series, 350, 352, 358
  Subject Series, 350, 353

Census of Mineral Industries, 357, 367, 368
  Geographic Area Series, 357
  Industry Series, 357, 358
  Subject Series, 357

Census of Outlying Areas. See *Economic Census of Outlying Areas*

Census of Population, 304, 305-06. See also *Current Population Reports*
  Advance Reports, 309
  Characteristics of the Population, 73, 307, 308, 309
  Characteristics of the Population, Chapter A, 307, 309, 316, 321, 322
  Characteristics of the Population, Chapter B, 307, 308, 309, 316, 317-18, 322,
  Characteristics of the Population, Chapter C, 307, 309, 316, 322
  Characteristics of the Population, Chapter D, 307, 309, 320, 322
  General Population Characteristics for Metropolitan Statistical Areas (1990), 309
  Population Subject Reports, 307, 308, 311
  Social and Economic Characteristics for Metropolitan Statistical Areas (1990), 309
  Supplementary Reports, 307

Census of Population and Housing, 304, 309
  Block Statistics, 308, 311
  Census Tracts, 308, 311, 316, 317, 321
  Congressional Districts of the 98th Congress, 304
  Population and Housing Unit Counts (1990), 309, 311
  Public Use Microdata Sample, 321
  Summary Characteristics for Governmental Units, 304, 321
  Summary Population and Housing Characteristics (1990), 309, 311
  Summary Social, Economic, and Housing Characteristics (1990), 309
  Summary Tape Files, 311, 316, 320
  Summary Tape Files Microfiche, 308-9, 310, 311, 316, 321, 322

Census of Population and Housing Users' Guide. See *1980 Census of Population and Housing Users' Guide*

Census of Retail Trade, 348, 350, 353-356, 380, 406
  Establishment and Firm Size, 353
  Geographic Area Series, 353, 356, 358
  Major Retail Centers, 359
  Merchandise Line Sales, 353-56, 383
  Miscellaneous Subjects, 356
  Nonemployer Statistics Series, 356, 358
  Subject Series, 353, 356

Census of Service Industries, 356-57, 358
  Geographic Area Series, 356-57, 358
  Nonemployer Statistics Series, 357, 358
  Subject Series, 357

Census of Transportation, 357-58
  Commodity Transportation Survey, 359
  Geographic Area Series, 357
  Subject Series, 357
  Truck Inventory and Use Survey, 358

Census of Wholesale Trade, 348, 356
  Commodity Line Sales, 356
  Establishment and Firm Size, 356
  Geographic Area Series, 356, 358
  Miscellaneous Subjects, 356
  Subject Series, 356

Census Tract Street Index, 308

Census Tracts. See *Census of Population and Housing—Census Tracts*

Census Users' Guide. See *1980 Census of Population and Housing Users' Guide*

Center for Research in Securities Prices Master File. See *CRSP Common Stock Master File*

Center Line (NTIS), 57

CES. See *Consumer Expenditure Survey*

CFR. See *Code of Federal Regulations*

Chain Store Guides, 142-143

Chance: New Directions for Statistics and Computing, 475

Changing Times, 267, 461, 475

Characteristics of Housing Units. See *Census of Housing—Characteristics of Housing Units*

Characteristics of the Population. See *Census of Population— Characteristics of the Population*

Characteristics of the Population Below the Poverty Level. See *Poverty in America*

Charitable Giving and Solicitation, 438

Chartcraft, 260

Chemical Business Newsbase, 101

Chemical Industry Notes, 101

Chemical Marketing Reporter, 10, 78, 368

Chemical Week, 78

Chicago Tribune, 101, 102

Chilton's Jewelers' Circular/Keystone, 76

Choice: Books for College Libraries, 68

Choices, 421

Christian Science Monitor, 99, 101, 102, 105

Chronolog, 474

CIA World Data Bank, 18

Cigar Association of America Statistical Record Bulletin. See *Statistical Record Bulletin*

CIR. See *Current Industrial Reports*

Circulation: Annual Circulation and Penetration Analysis of Print Media. See *American Newspaper Markets' Circulation*

Circulation [Year]. See *Standard Rate & Data Service—Circulation [Year]*

CIS Annual Legislative Histories, 430

CIS Federal Register Index, 435, 450

CIS Index, 430, 439

CIS Legislative History Service, 430

Cities of the United States, 378-79, 394

City & State Directories in Print, 45, 138

Class/Brand YTD $. See *LNA/Arbitron Multi-Media Service—Class/Brand YTD $*

Classified Index of NLRB and Related Court Decisions , 441

Clause Finder. See *Collective Bargaining Negotiations and Contracts—Clause Finder*

ClusterPLUS, 386, 414

Coal Data, 368

Coal Production, 368

Code of Federal Regulations, 27, 28, 434-35, 438, 441, 453, 454, 467

Code of Federal Regulations Index
(Bowker), 435
*Codification of Financial Reporting
Policies,* 469
*Codification of Statements on Auditing
Standards,* 468-69
Coffeeline, 99
*Collective Bargaining Negotiations and
Contracts,* 448, 449
Clause Finder, 448
Techniques and Trends, 448
College & Research Libraries, 474
College Blue Book, 36
Collier Bankruptcy Manual, 438
*Colt Microfiche Library of State
Directories,* 138
COMLINE, 92
Commerce Business Daily, 16
*Commerce Register Directory of (State)
Manufacturers,* 137
Commercial and Financial Chronicle,
212, 232
Commercial Atlas and Marketing Guide.
See *Rand McNally Commercial
Atlas and Marketing Guide*
*Committee Reports (U.S. House and
Senate),* 429, 430, 453, 454, 457,
458, 460
Commodities Price Locator, 367
*Commodity Classification Under the
Harmonized System: The Harmonized
System Rulings Packet,* 434
Commodity Line Sales. See *Census of
Wholesale Trade—Commodity Line
Sales*
Commodity Prices, 367
Commodity Transportation Survey. See
*Census of Transportation—
Commodity Transportation Survey*
Commodity Year Book. See *CRB
Commodity Year Book*
Common Market Reporter, 437
*Common Stock Newspaper Abbreviations
and Trading Symbols,* 208
Communication Abstracts, 98
Community Cross-Reference Guide, 140
Community Profile Analysis, 387
Community Publication Rates and Data.
See *Standard Rate & Data Service—
Community Publication Rates and
Data*
Compact D/Canada, 189
Compact D/SEC, 18, 188-89, 194, 195,
196, 197, 230, 235, 236, 241, 246,
258, 265, 469, 470
Compact D/'33, 189, 232
Compact D/Worldscope, 189, 196
Compact Disclosure. See *Compact D/SEC*
Companies and Their Brands, 151
Company/Brand $. See *LNA/Arbitron
Multi-Media Service—Company/
Brand $*
Company Intelligence, 14-15, 84, 122
Company ProFile, 85, 107, 122
Company Summary (Enterprise Statistics).
See *Enterprise Statistics—Company
Summary*
Compensation and Working Conditions,
338, 449
Complete Book of Tax Deductions, 465

*The Complete Economic and
Demographic Source,* 388-89
Components of Inventory Change. See
*Census of Housing—Components of
Inventory Change*
Comprehensive GAAP Guide. See *Miller
Comprehensive GAAP Guide*
*Compu-Mark Directory of U.S.
Trademarks,* 153-54
Compu-Mark U.S. On-Line, 154
Compustat, 117, 193, 197, 262
Compustat Corporate Text, 195, 246
Compustat PC Plus, 196-97, 220, 246, 258
Computer and Control Abstracts, 99
Computer Database, 86, 100
Computer Literature Index, 100
*Computer Readable Databases: A
Directory and Data Sourcebook,* 52-
53, 56, 57
Computer Select, 18, 100
Computer Use in the United States, 315
Computing Reviews, 100
Concentration Ratios in Manufacturing.
See *Census of Manufactures—
Concentration Ratios in
Manufacturing*
*Condominium Housing (Housing Subject
Report),* 308
Conference Board Chart Collection, 116
*Conference Board Consumer Confidence
Survey.* See *Consumer Confidence
Survey*
Conference Board Cumulative Index, 67
Conference Board Research Bulletin, 342
Conference Board Statistical Bulletin. See
Statistical Bulletin (Conference
Board)
Congressional Committee Reports. See
*Committee Reports (U.S. House and
Senate)*
Congressional Directory, 29
*Congressional Districts of the 98th
Congress.* See *Census of Population
and Housing—Congressional
Districts of the 98th Congress*
Congressional Index, 429-30, 437
Congressional Information Service Index.
See *CIS Index*
Congressional Masterfile 2, 430
*Congressional Quarterly Service: CQ
Weekly Report.* See *CQ Weekly
Report*
Congressional Record, 429, 439, 462
Congressional Staff Directory, 27, 29
Congressional Yellow Book, 30
Connecticut Facts/Rhode Island Facts,
378
Conquest, 386
Construction Reports. See *Current
Construction Reports*
*Consultants and Consulting Organizations
Directory,* 38
Consultants News, 38
Consumer Attitudes and Buying Plans.
See *Consumer Confidence Survey*
Consumer Confidence Survey, 412
Consumer Expenditure Survey, 19, 407,
449
Consumer Income. See *Current
Population Reports—Consumer
Income*

*Consumer Magazine and Agri-Media
Rates and Data.* See *Standard Rate &
Data Service—Consumer Magazine
and Agri-Media Rates and Data*
Consumer Price Index Detailed Report.
See *CPI Detailed Report*
Consumer Product Safety Guide, 437
*Consumer Reports Guide to Income Tax
Preparation.* See *Guide to Income
Tax Preparation*
Contacts Influential, 142
Contemporary Authors, 36
*Core Collection (Harvard Business
School).* See *Harvard Business
School Core Collection: An Author,
Title, and Subject Guide*
*Corporate Acquisitions, Mergers and
Divestitures,* 438
Corporate Action, 146, 241
Corporate Affiliations, 146
*Corporate Directory of U.S. Public
Companies,* 196
Corporate Earnings Estimator. See *Zacks
Earnings Forecaster*
Corporate Finance Blue Book, 144
Corporate Growth Report, 241
Corporate 1000 Yellow Book, 196
Corporate Ownership Watch, 237
Corporate Technology Directory, 144, 156
CorpTech. See *Corporate Technology
Directory*
Corpus Juris Secundum, 427
Cost of Living Index. See *ACCRA Cost of
Living Index*
Cost of Living News, 391
County and City Data Book, 73, 321, 336,
381
County Business Patterns, 19, 349, 362-
63, 366, 369, 376
County Population Estimates. See
*Current Population Reports—Local
Population Estimates*
*Court Decisions Related to the National
Labor Relations Act,* 441
CPA. See *Community Profile Analysis*
CPI Detailed Report, 334, 338, 391
CQ Weekly Report, 430
Crain's Chicago Business, 85, 104
CRB Commodity Year Book, 73, 366, 369
Credit Advisory. See *Dun & Bradstreet
Credit Advisory*
CreditWeek, 232, 262, 268-69
Criminal Justice Sourcebook. See
Sourcebook of Criminal Justice
Criss+Cross Directories. See *Haines
Criss+Cross Directories*
CRSP Common Stock Master File, 219
Cumulative Book Index, 66, 67, 68
Cumulative Bulletin (IRS), 454, 471
Cumulative Bulletin Index-Digest System.
See *Bulletin Index-Digest System*
Cumulative List of Organizations (IRS),
132
Current Biography Yearbook, 36
Current Business Reports, 356, 358
Advance Monthly Retail Sales, 356
*Monthly Retail Trade: Sales and
Inventories,* 356
*Monthly Wholesale Trade: Sales and
Inventories,* 356

Motor Freight Transportation and Warehousing Survey , 358
Current Construction Reports, 357
   Housing Authorized by Building Permit, 357
   New One-Family Houses Sold and for Sale, 357
   Price Index of New One-Family Houses Sold, 357
   Value of New Construction Put in Place, 357
Current Contents: Social and Behavioral Sciences, 100
Current Dividend Record. See *Wiesenberger Current Dividend Record*
Current Economic Indicators, 10
Current Housing Reports, 313, 314, 315-16
   American Housing Survey, 315, 376
   Housing Characteristics of Selected Metropolitan Areas, 315-16
   Housing Vacancies and Homeownership, 316
Current Index to Statistics: Applications, Methods, and Theory, 100
Current Industrial Reports, 353
   Manufacturers' Shipments, Inventories, and Orders, 353
   Plant Capacity, 353
Current Law Index, 94, 427-28, 463
Current Population Reports, 313-15, 321, 413
   Consumer Income, 315
   Farm Population of the United States, 360
   Household Economic Studies, 315
   Local Population Estimates, 314, 395
   Population Characteristics, 315
   Population Estimates and Projections, 314, 341
   Special Censuses, 312
   Special Studies, 315
Current Population Surveys (data files), 19
Current Statistics. See *Standard & Poor's Statistical Service*
Current Text (FASB). See *FASB Accounting Standards: Current Text*
Current Wage Developments. See *Compensation and Working Conditions*
Customs Bulletin, 434
Customs Regulations of the United States, 434

D & B Report. See *Dun & Bradstreet Business Information Reports*
Daily Bond Buyer, 6, 232
Daily Graphs, 260
Daily Labor Report, 449
Daily Quotation Service. See *National Daily Quotation Service*
Daily Stock Price Record, 217, 218, 224, 253
Daily Tax Report, 455, 463
Daily Treasury Statement, 341
Daily Variety, 10
Data Book: Operating Banks and Branches, 165
Data User News. See *Census and You*
Database, 474

DataBase Directory Service, 53
DataMap: Index of Published Tables of Statistical Data, 73, 75, 411
Datapro Directory of On-Line Services, 53
Davis Digest, 269
DCA. See *Directory of Corporate Affiliations*
Dealerscope Merchandising, 10
Decennial Digest. See *American Digest System*
Decisions and Orders of the NLRB, 441
Defense Markets and Technology. See *Aerospace/Defense Markets and Technology*
Denver Post, 104
Detailed Housing Characteristics. See *Census of Housing—Characteristics of Housing Units, Chapter B*
Detailed Population Characteristics. See *Census of Population Characteristics of the Population, Chapter D*
Development Report Card for the States. See *Making the Grade: Development Report Card for the States*
DFR. See *Duns Financial Records Plus*
DIALOG Quotes and Trading, 219
Dickman Criss-Cross Directories, 141
Dictionary of Occupational Titles, 19
Digest of Education Statistics, 377
Digest of Public General Bills and Resolutions, 429
Direct Mail List Rates and Data. See *Standard Rate & Data Service— Direct Mail List Rates and Data*
Direct Marketing Market Place, 144
Directories in Print, 26, 45, 57, 138, 143
Directory of American Book Publishing. See *Literary Market Place*
Directory of American Firms Operating in Foreign Countries, 146
Directory of American Research and Technology, 144, 155
Directory of Blue Chip Companies, 122, 132
Directory of Central Atlantic States Manufacturers, 138
Directory of Companies Required to File Annual Reports with the Securities and Exchange Commission, 197
Directory of Computer Software, 57
Directory of Computerized Data Files: A Guide to U.S. Government Information in Machine-Readable Format, 57-58
Directory of Corporate Affiliations, 146-47, 155, 197, 241
Directory of Corporate Financing, 233
Directory of Directories. See *Directories in Print*
Directory of Directors in the City of New York and Tri-State Area, 145
Directory of Fee-Based Information Services in Libraries. See *FISCAL Directory of Fee-Based Information Services in Libraries*
Directory of Foreign Manufacturers in the United States, 146
Directory of Government Document Collections and Librarians, 33

Directory of Information Brokers. See *Burwell Directory of Information Brokers*
Directory of Investment Research, 255
Directory of Japanese Affiliates and Offices Operating in the U.S. and Canada, 146
Directory of Library & Information Professionals, 33
Directory of Management Consultants, 38
Directory of Market Research Reports, Studies and Surveys. See *Findex*
Directory of New England Manufacturers, 138
Directory of Obsolete Securities, 242
Directory of Online and Portable Databases, 53, 56
Directory of Online Databases, 53, 54, 56, 108
Directory of Periodicals Online; Indexed, Abstracted, and Full-Text: News, Law & Business, 54-55, 56, 108
Directory of Portable Databases, 56, 57
Directory of Publicly Traded Bonds, 216
Directory of Publicly Traded Stocks, 216
Directory of Research Services Provided by Members of the Marketing Research Association, 38
Directory of Special Libraries and Information Centers, 33
Directory of the Pickle Industry, 142
Directory of United States Exporters, 144, 156
Directory of United States Importers, 144
Directory of United States Labor Organizations, 449
Directory of U.S. Trademarks. See *Compu-Mark Directory of U.S. Trademarks*
Directory of Wall Street Research. See *Directory of Investment Research*
Disclosure Online, 122, 179, 189, 192, 195
Disclosure/Spectrum Ownership, 188, 235-36
Disclosure/Worldscope. See *Compact D/ Worldscope*
Discount Store News, 406
Divorce Taxation, 438
DJNEWS. See *Dow Jones News*
DMI. See *Dun's Market Identifiers*
DMMP. See *Direct Marketing Market Place*
Dodge Dataline, 390
Dodge Reports, 390
Domestic Public New Issues Database, 233
Donnelley Demographics, 382, 384, 386, 387, 394
Donnelley Market Profile Analysis. See *Market Profile Analysis*
Donoghue's Money Fund Report, 269
Donoghue's Mutual Funds Almanac, 267
D.O.T. See *Dictionary of Occupational Titles*
Dow Jones Averages, 1885-1990, 253
Dow Jones Enhanced Current Quotes, 219
Dow Jones Historical Quotes, 219, 224
Dow Jones Investor's Handbook. See *Business One Irwin Investor's Handbook*

Dow Jones-Irwin Guide to Using the Wall Street Journal, 343
Dow Jones News, 103-04, 106, 343
Dow Jones News Service, 106-07
Dow Jones Text-Search Services, 103, 104, 107, 245
Dow Theory Forecasts, 269
Dowline, 474
DPO. See Directory of Periodicals Online
Drug & Cosmetics Industry, 78
DSPR. See Daily Stock Price Record
Dun & Bradstreet Business Information Reports, 161-62, 163, 164
Dun & Bradstreet Credit Advisory, 162
Dun & Bradstreet Key Business Ratios. See Industry Norms and Key Business Ratios
Dun & Bradstreet Payment Analysis Report, 162
Dun & Bradstreet Reference Book of American Business , 126, 162-63
Dun & Bradstreet Reference Book of Corporate Managements. See Reference Book of Corporate Managements
Dun & Bradstreet Reference Book of Manufacturers. See Reference Book of Manufacturers
Duncan's American Radio. See American Radio
Dun's Business Identification Service, 126, 132, 155, 163
Dun's Business Month. See Business Month
Dun's Business Rankings, 177-78
Dun's Census of American Business, 364-366, 376, 387
Dun's Consultants Directory, 38
Dun's Electronic Business Directory, 124-25, 155
Dun's Electronic Yellow Pages. See Dun's Electronic Business Directory
Duns Financial Records Plus, 163-64, 174
Dun's Market Identifiers, 125-26, 138, 145, 155, 163, 386
Dun's Microcosm. See Microcosm
Dun's Million Dollar Disc. See Million Dollar Disc
Dun's Reference Plus, 18, 163
Dun's Regional Business Directories, 139-140, 142
DunsPrint, 162, 163

Earnings Forecaster. See Zacks Earnings Forecaster
Earthquake Database, 18
EBSCO Index and Abstract Directory. See Index and Abstract Directory
EBSCO Librarians' Handbook. See Librarians' Handbook
EBSCONET, 47
EconBase Data Directory, 338
EconBase: Time Series and Forecasts, 337-38, 341, 344
Economic and Budget Outlook, 341
Economic Census of Outlying Areas, 359
Economic Indicators, 285-86, 334, 335, 337
Economic Report of the President, 336-37, 341
Economic Times, 342, 412

Economist, 99
Edison Electric Institute Statistical Yearbook, 165
Editor & Publisher, 380
Editor & Publisher International Year Book, 49, 84
Editor & Publisher Market Guide, 380-81, 395
Editor & Publisher Syndicate Directory, 49
EITF Abstracts, 468
Electronic Market Data Book, 367-68
Electronic News Financial Fact Book and Directory, 196
Electronic Washington Post. See Washington Post
Electronic Yellow Pages. See Dun's Electronic Business Directory
Emerging and Special Situations. See Standard & Poor's Emerging and Special Situations
Emerging Issues Task Force Abstracts. See EITF Abstracts
Emerson's Directory of Leading U.S. Accounting Firms, 38
Employee Benefit Cases, 444
Employee Benefits in Medium and Large Firms, 449
Employment and Earnings, 10, 329, 338, 340, 391
Employment and Earnings Supplement, 340
Employment and Training Reporter, 449
Employment and Unemployment in States and Local Areas. See Unemployment in States and Local Areas
Employment Coordinator, 447
Employment Guide (BNA), 448
Employment, Hours and Earnings: States and Areas, 340
Employment, Hours and Earnings: United States, 340
Employment Projections, 341
Encyclopedia of Associations, 33-35, 48, 132, 141
Encyclopedia of Business Information Sources, 43-44, 47, 82, 108, 369
Encyclopedia of Geographic Information Sources, 43
Encyclopedia of Health Information Sources, 43
Encyclopedia of Information Systems and Services. See Information Industry Directory
Encyclopedia of Legal Information Sources, 43
Encyclopedia of Public Affairs Information Sources, 43
Energy Information Abstracts, 100
Engineering Index, 100
Enterprise Statistics, 359
   Auxiliary Establishments, 359
   Company Summary, 359
   Large Companies, 359
Environment Abstracts, 100
Environment Reporter, 438
Ergonomics Abstracts, 100
Establishment and Firm Size. See Census of Retail Trade—Establishment and Firm Size

Estimates of the Population of [State] Counties and Metropolitan Areas. See Current Population Reports— Local Population Estimates
European Index of Management Periodicals. See SCIMP: European Index of Management Periodicals
Existing Home Sales. See Home Sales
Export Shipping Manual, 438
Exposure Drafts (FASB). See FASB Proposed Statements of Financial Accounting Standards

F & S Index of Corporate Change. See Predicasts F&S Index of Corporate Change
F & S Index Plus Text, 90, 92
F & S Index United States. See Predicasts F&S Index United States
Fact: The Money Management Magazine, 475
Facts about the States, 377
Facts & Figures on Government Finance, 389
Fair Employment Practice Cases, 444, 446
Fair Employment Practices Manual, 446
Fairchild's Financial Manual of Retail Stores, 196
Fairchild's Textile & Apparel Financial Directory, 196
Far Eastern Economic Review, 99, 101
Farm Population of the United States. See Current Population Reports—Farm Population of the United States
FASB Accounting Standards: Current Text, 468
FASB Accounting Standards: Original Pronouncements, 467, 468
FASB Discussion Memorandum, 466-67
FASB Exposure Drafts. See FASB Proposed Statements of Financial Accounting Standards
FASB Interpretations, 467, 468
FASB Proposed Statements of Financial Accounting Standards, 466, 467
FASB Statements of Financial Accounting Concepts. See Statements of Financial Accounting Concepts
FASB Statements of Financial Accounting Standards. See FASB Statements of Financial Accounting Standards
FASB Technical Bulletins, 467, 468
Fastock II, 219
FCC Record, 434, 450
FDIC Data Book. See Data Book: Operating Banks and Branches
FDIC Statistics on Banking. See Statistics on Banking
Fed in Print, 96, 108
Federal Acquisitions Regulations, 434
Federal Banking Law Reporter, 437
Federal Data Base Finder, 52, 57
Federal Executive Directory, 28, 29, 30
Federal Expenditures by State, 378
Federal Filings, 230-31, 232, 241, 246
Federal Income, Estate, and Gift Taxation, 460
Federal Income Tax Regulations, 454
Federal Regional Executive Directory, 28

Federal Register, 430, 434-35, 438, 450, 454,471
Federal Regulatory Directory, 27-28, 427
Federal Reporter 2d, 431, 433, 456
Federal Reserve Annual Statistical Digest. See *Annual Statistical Digest* (Federal Reserve Board)
Federal Reserve Bulletin, 334, 335, 340
Federal Reserve Statistical Releases, 335, 340, 344
  Industrial Production, 340
  Money Stock Measures and Liquid Assets, 335, 340
  Selected Interest and Exchange Rates, 340
Federal Securities Law Reporter, 230, 469
Federal Staff Directory, 27
Federal Statistical Data Bases: A Comprehensive Catalog of Current Machine-Readable and Online Files, 57-58
Federal Statistical Directory, 28-29
Federal Supplement, 431, 433
Federal Tax and Related Forms, 465
Federal Tax Articles, 463-64
Federal Tax Coordinator 2d, 458-59, 464
Federal Tax Forms, 465
Federal Tax Guide, 464
Federal Taxes Citator. See *Federal Taxes 2nd—Citator*
Federal Taxes 2nd, 457-58, 460
  Citator, 456, 457, 460-61, 462
Federal Trade Commission Decisions, 433
Federal Yellow Book, 28
FEDFILES. See *Federal Filings*
FEDTAX, 453
Financial Accounting Standards: Explanation and Analysis, 468
Financial Accounting Standards Board: Current Text. See *FASB Accounting Standards: Current Text*
Financial Industry Information Service. See *FINIS*
Financial Reporting Releases (SEC), 469
Financial Statistics of Selected Electric Utilities, 165
Financial Studies of the Small Business, 176
Financial Times, 99, 102
Financial Times Company Abstracts, 102
Financial World, 177, 220, 267, 475
Finders Guide to Block Statistics Reports, 308
Findex: The Directory of Market Research Reports, Studies and Surveys, 51, 78, 422
FINIS: Financial Industry Information Service, 95-96, 104, 108
FirstSearch Catalog, 66
FISCAL Directory of Fee-Based Information Services in Libraries, 37
Fisher Manual of Valuable and Worthless Securities. See *Robert D. Fisher Manual of Valuable and Worthless Securities*
Fitch Rating Register, 268
Five Percent Ownership. See *Spectrum Ownership Profiles—Spectrum 5: Five Percent Ownership*
Flying the Colors Series, 378

FMI Monthly Index Service. See *Reference Point: Food Industry Abstracts*
Food Consumption, Prices and Expenditures, 407-08
Food Cost Review, 408
Food Industry Abstracts. See *Reference Point: Food Industry Abstracts*
Forbes, 10, 50, 99, 177, 215, 264, 267, 270, 475
Forbes Annual Report on American Industry, 264
Foreign Trade Data, 361-62
Forthcoming Books, 67
Fortune, 10, 103, 177, 215, 390, 408, 412, 475
Fortune Directory, 177
FT 900. See *U.S. Export and Import Merchandise Trade*
FT 925. See *U.S. Merchandise Trade: Exports, General Imports, and Imports for Consumption*
FTC Decisions. See *Federal Trade Commission Decisions*
Fulltext Sources Online, 54, 56
Funk & Scott Index of Corporations and Industries. See *Predicasts F&S Index United States*
Future Survey, 94, 104, 405
Futures: The Magazine of Commodities and Options, 475

GAAP: Interpretation & Application of Generally Accepted Accounting Principles, 468
Gale Directory of Publications and Broadcast Media, 49, 402
Gale GlobalAccess: Associations, 34
Gale International Directory of Publications, 49
Gallup Poll, 409
Gallup Poll Monthly, 410, 412
Gallup Poll: Public Opinion, 410
Gallup Report. See *Gallup Poll Monthly*
General Business File, 85
General Digest. See *American Digest System*
General Housing Characteristics. See *Census of Housing—Characteristics of Housing Units, Chapter A*
General Periodicals Index, 86, 87, 104
General Population Characteristics. See *Census of Population— Characteristics of the Population, Chapter B*
General Population Characteristics for Metropolitan Statistical Areas. See *Census of Population—General Population Characteristics for Metropolitan Statistical Areas*
General Social and Economic Characteristics of the Population. See *Census of Population— Characteristics of the Population, Chapter C*
General Social Surveys Cumulative Codebook, 408
General Wage Determinations Issued under the Davis-Bacon and Related Acts, 393-94

Genetic Technology Sourcebook, 45
GeoBase, 99
Geographic Mobility (Population Characteristics), 315
Geographic Profile of Employment and Unemployment, 449
Geographical Abstracts: Human Geography, 98-99
Globe and Mail, 54
Going Public: The IPO Reporter, 232
Government Contract Reports, 437
Government Documents Catalog Service, 71
Government Information Quarterly, 475
Government Manual. See *U.S. Government Manual*
Government Periodicals and Subscription Services, 72
Government Publications Index, 71
Government Publications Review, 475
Government Reports: Announcements & Index, 72, 80
Government Research Centers Directory, 36
GPO Monthly Catalog (database), 66
GPO on SilverPlatter, 71
GPO Sales Publications Reference File, 72, 439
GPO Subject Bibliographies. See *Subject Bibliographies*
GRA&I. See *Government Reports: Announcements & Index*
Grant Thornton Manufacturing Climate Study, 389
Granville Market Letter, 250
The GreenBook. See *International Directory of Marketing Research Houses and Services*
Growth Stock Outlook, 269
Guide to American Directories, 45
Guide to American Law, 427
Guide to Employment Law and Regulation, 447, 448
Guide to Income Tax Preparation, 464-65
Guide to Industrial and Office Real Estate Markets, 390
Guide to Microforms in Print, 51
Guide to 1980 Decennial Census Publications, 319
Guide to No-Load Funds, 267
Guide to Preparing Financial Statements, 469
Guide to Special Issues and Indexes of Periodicals, 49-50
Guide to U.S. Government Directories, 70
Guide to U.S. Government Publications, 70
Guide to Using the Wall Street Journal. See *Dow Jones-Irwin Guide to Using the Wall Street Journal*

H & R Block Income Tax Guide, 464
Haines Criss+Cross Directories, 141
Handbook of Common Stocks. See *Moody's Handbook of Common Stocks*
Handbook of Labor Statistics, 340
Hardware Age Who Makes It Buyer's Guide, 142
Harfax Industry Data Sources. See *Industry Data Sources*

Harmonized System Rulings Packet. See
    *Commodity Classification Under the
    Harmonized System: Harmonized
    System Rulings Packet*
*Harmonized Tariff Schedule of the United
    States: Annotated for Statistical
    Reporting Purposes,* 360-61
Harris Poll, 409
Harris (State) Industrial Directories, 137,
    138
Harvard Business Review, 10, 97
Harvard Business Review Online, 54
*Harvard Business School Core Collection:
    An Author, Title, and Subject Guide,*
    67
Health Index, 86
Health Planning and Administration, 100
HEP: Higher Education Directory, 36
Higher Education Directory. See *HEP:
    Higher Education Directory*
*Historical Statistics of the United States:
    Colonial Times to 1970,* 336
Home Sales, 366, 369, 391, 394
Hospital Literature Index, 100
House Reports, 429. See also *Committee
    Reports (U.S. House and Senate)*
Household and Family Characteristics,
    315
Household Economic Studies. See *Current
    Population Reports—Household
    Economic Studies*
Housing Authorized by Building Permit.
    See *Current Construction Reports—
    Housing Authorized by Building
    Permit*
Housing Census. See *Census of Housing*
*Housing Characteristics of Selected
    Metropolitan Areas.* See *Current
    Housing Reports—Housing
    Characteristics of Selected
    Metropolitan Areas*
Housing Subject Reports. See *Census of
    Housing—Housing Subject Reports*
Housing Vacancies and Homeownership.
    See *Current Housing Reports—
    Housing Vacancies and
    Homeownership*
*How to Find Business Intelligence in
    Washington,* 28
*How to Find Company Intelligence in
    State Documents,* 32
*How to Find Information about
    Companies,* 28
Hulbert Financial Digest, 269
Hulbert Guide to Financial Newsletters,
    269
Human Resource Outlook, 342
Human Resources Abstracts, 98
Human Resources Management, 448

IASSIST Quarterly, 57, 475
IBC/Donoghue's Mutual Funds Almanac.
    See *Donoghue's Mutual Funds
    Almanac*
I/B/E/S. See *Institutional Broker's
    Estimate System*
ICC Register, 434
ICC Reports. See *Interstate Commerce
    Commission Reports*
ICPSR Bulletin, 58, 475

ICPSR Guide to Resources and Services,
    58
ICPSR Variables, 19, 409
*IDD Domestic and International New
    Issues,* 233
IDD M&A Transactions, 239, 246
IHS Vendor Catalog Service. See *Vendor
    Catalog Service*
IMPACT. See *Government Documents
    Catalog Service*
Impact of Travel on State Economies, 76
Inc. Magazine, 177, 389-90
*Income by Occupation (Population Subject
    Report),* 307
Income/Expense Analysis (Institute of Real
    Estate Management), 390
INCORP, 170
Index and Abstract Directory, 108
Index of Corporate Change. See
    *Predicasts F&S Index of Corporate
    Change*
Index of Economic Articles, 100
Index to Current Urban Documents, 12
Index to Federal Tax Articles, 463
Index to International Public Opinion, 73,
    411
Index to International Statistics, 76
Index to Legal Books, 427
Index to Legal Periodicals, 94, 428
Index to 1980 Census Publications. See
    *Subject Index to the 1980 Census of
    Population and Housing*
*Index to Periodical Articles Related to
    Law,* 94
Index to the Code of Federal Regulations
    (CIS), 435
Index to Trademark and Service Classes,
    150
*Index to Trademarks Registered in the
    United States Patent and Trademark
    Office,* 153
Index to U.S. Government Periodicals, 94
Index to Who's Who Books, 145
Individual Employment Rights, 446
Individual Employment Rights Cases, 444
Individual Investor, 217
Industrial Equipment News, 130
Industrial Production. See *Federal
    Reserve Statistical Releases—
    Industrial Production*
Industrial Relations (Prentice Hall), 448
*Industrial Research Laboratories in the
    U.S..* See *Directory of American
    Research and Technology*
*Industry and Product Classification
    Manual.* See*1987 Industry and
    Product Classification Manual*
Industry Data Sources, 49, 50, 78,
    418, 422
Industry Norms and Key Business Ratios,
    174, 176
Industry Wage Surveys, 391
Industry Week, 335, 412
INFOBANK. See *Information Bank
    Abstracts*
Infomat International Business, 100
Information Advisor, 474
Information America, 170
*Information and Order Blanks for
    Preparers of Federal Tax Returns.*
    See *Taxpayer Information
    Publications—Publication 1045*

Information Bank Abstracts, 99, 101, 102,
    104
Information Broker, 37
Information Industry Directory, 36, 51-52,
    56, 57
Information Report (Washington
    Researchers), 474
Information Today, 56, 474
*Informational Copies of Federal Tax
    Forms.* See *Package X*
INFOSERV, 46
Initial Public Offerings Annual, 233
Inside Business, 474
Insider Ownership. See *Spectrum
    Ownership Profiles—Spectrum 6:
    Insider Ownership*
Insider Trading Monitor, 236-37, 246
Insiders' Chronicle, 237, 246
INSPEC, 99
Instant Yellow Page Service. See *Online
    Information Network*
Institutional Broker's Estimate System, 16,
    197, 258
Institutional Investor, 475
Institutional Portfolios. See *Spectrum
    Ownership Profiles—Spectrum 4:
    Institutional Portfolios*
Institutional Stock Holdings Survey. See
    *Spectrum Ownership Profiles—
    Spectrum 3: Institutional Stock
    Holdings Survey*
Insurance Periodicals Index, 95, 101
Inter-City Cost of Living Index. See
    ACCRA Cost of Living Index
Inter-City Wage and Salary Differentials,
    392
Internal Revenue Bulletin, 434, 454, 460,
    471
*Internal Revenue Service Cumulative
    Bulletin.* See *Cumulative Bulletin*
*International Abstracts in Operations
    Research,* 100
*International Association for Social
    Science Information Service and
    Technology Quarterly.* See *IASSIST
    Quarterly*
International Bankers Directory. See
    Thomson Bank Directory
International Bibliography of Economics,
    100
*International Brands and Their
    Companies,* 151
*International Companies and Their
    Brands,* 151
International Development Abstracts, 100
*International Directory of Corporate
    Affiliations,* 146
*International Directory of Marketing
    Research Houses and Services: The
    GreenBook,* 37-38
*International Directory of Nuclear
    Utilities,* 165
International Executive, 84, 100
*International Financial Statistics
    Yearbook,* 73
International Literary Market Place, 69
International Monetary Statistics (data
    file), 19
International Organizations, 34
International Periodicals Directory. See
    *Ulrich's International Periodicals
    Directory*

International Research Centers Directory, 36

Interstate Commerce Commission Register. See *ICC Register*

Interstate Commerce Commission Reports, 433

Investext, 6, 85, 92, 179, 256-57, 263, 264, 268, 418

Investment Company Portfolios. See *Spectrum Ownership Profiles— Spectrum 2: Investment Company Portfolios*

Investment Company Stock Holdings. See *Spectrum Ownership Profiles— Spectrum 1: Investment Company Stock Holdings*

Investment Dealers' Digest, 232, 233, 246, 475

Investment Statistics Locator, 224

Investor's Daily, 15, 102, 209, 214-15, 220, 232, 243, 252, 260, 264, 269, 343, 475

Investor's Daily Database, 102, 215

Investor's Guide to Stock Quotations and Other Financial Listings, 208, 212

IPO Reporter. See *Going Public: The IPO Reporter*

IRS Corporate Financial Ratios, 174, 176

IRS Cumulative Bulletin. See *Cumulative Bulletin* (IRS)

IRS Cumulative List of Organizations. See *Cumulative List of Organizations* (IRS)

IRS Forms, 465

IRS Letter Rulings, 455

IRS Positions, 455

IRS Taxpayer Information Publications. See *Taxpayer Information Publications*

J. K. Lasser's Your Income Tax. See *Your Income Tax*

Jewelers' Circular/Keystone. See *Chilton's Jewelers' Circular/ Keystone*

Job Safety and Health, 447

Johnson's Charts, 267

Johnson's World Wide Chamber of Commerce Directory. See *World Chamber of Commerce Directory*

Journal of Applied Psychology, 97

Journal of Business and Finance Librarianship, 474

Journal of Commerce and Commercial, 102, 367

Journal of Economic Literature, 100

Journal of Taxation, 461

Journal of the American Society for Information Science, 474

Journey to Work (Population Subject Report), 307

Judicial Staff Directory, 27

Keep Watching, 11

Key Business Ratios. See *Industry Norms and Key Business Ratios*

Key Indicators of Economic Growth, 388

Key Ratio Survey of the Folding Carton and Rigid Box Industry, 176

Keystone Coal Industry Manual, 142

Kiplinger Tax Letter, 461

Kirkus Reviews, 68

Knight-Ridder Financial News, 107

Knowledge Industry Publications Database, 53

Labor Arbitration and Dispute Settlements, 446

Labor Arbitration Awards, 444-45

Labor Arbitration in Government, 445

Labor Arbitration Index. See *Labor Arbitration Information System*

Labor Arbitration Information System, 445

Labor Arbitration Reports: Dispute Settlements, 444, 446

Labor Cases, 444

Labor Law Reports, 446

Labor-Management Relations, 446

Labor Relations Cumulative Digest and Index, 441, 443, 444

Labor Relations Expediter, 446

Labor Relations Reference Manual, 441- 42, 444, 446

Labor Relations Reporter, 444, 445-46, 447

Labor Relations Week, 449

LABORLAW, 438

LACE Financial Rating Service. See *Quarterly Bank and Savings & Loan Rating Service*

LAIS. See *Labor Arbitration Information System*

LAR. See *Labor Arbitration Reports*

Large Companies (Enterprise Statistics). See *Enterprise Statistics—Large Companies*

Laser D/Banking, 165, 194

Laser D/International, 194

Laser D/SEC, 194, 195, 246

Laser Focus World, 92

LaserDisclosure. See *Laser D/SEC*

Laserdisk Professional. See *CD-ROM Professional*

Lasser's Your Income Tax. See *Your Income Tax*

Law & Business Directory of Corporate Counsel, 144

Lawn & Garden Marketing, 406

LAWREV, 438

LC MARC-Books, 66

Leading National Advertisers Multi-Media Service. See *LNA/Arbitron Multi- Media Service*

Left Index, 94

Legal Looseleafs in Print, 51, 437

Legal Newletters in Print, 48

Legal Resource Index, 428

LegalTrac, 428

Librarians' Handbook, 46

Library Journal, 68, 80, 474

Library of Congress Subject Headings, 65

Life Insurance Fact Book, 366

Lifestyle Market Analyst, 406, 415

Lipper Mutual Fund ProFiles. See *Standard & Poor's/Lipper Mutual Fund ProFiles*

List of CFR Parts Affected, 434

Listing of Data Files Available on Floppy Diskette. See *NTIS Listing of Data Files Available on Floppy Diskette*

Literary Digest, 277

Literary Market Place: The Directory of American Book Publishing, 69, 84

Little (Arthur D.)/Online. See *Arthur D. Little/Online*

LMP. See *Literary Market Place*

LNA/Arbitron Multi-Media Service, 399- 400, 401, 421, 422
  Ad $ Summary, 400, 401
  Class/Brand YTD $, 400
  Company/Brand $, 400

Local Area Personal Income, 329

Local Population Estimates. See *Current Population Reports—Local Population Estimates*

Los Angeles Times, 99, 101, 102

Lotus One Source: CD/Corporate. See *CD/Corporate*

LRR. See *Labor Relations Reporter*

LRRM. See *Labor Relations Reference Manual*

M & A Data Base, 239

M & A Filings, 240, 246

M & A Transactions. See *IDD M&A Transactions*

Machine-Readable Data Files (RLIN), 57, 58

Macmillan Directory of Leading Private Companies, 122-23, 145, 155, 179

MacRae's Blue Book, 130, 148, 155

MacRae's (State) Industrial Directories, 137, 138

Magazine ASAP, 54

Magazine Collection, 87

Magazine Index, 85, 108

M.A.I.D.. See *Market Analysis and Information Database*

Major Retail Centers. See *Census of Retail Trade—Major Retail Centers*

Making the Grade: Development Report Card for the States, 389

Management Accounting, 10

Management Contents, 54

Management Results. See *Wiesenberger Management Results*

Manual of Extinct or Obsolete Securities. See *Marvyn Scudder Manual of Extinct or Obsolete Securities*

Manual of Valuable and Worthless Securities. See *Robert D. Fisher Manual of Valuable and Worthless Securities*

Manufacturers' News (State) Manufacturer Registers, 137, 138

Manufacturers' Shipments, Inventories and Orders. See *Current Industrial Reports—Manufacturers' Shipments, Inventories and Orders*

Manufacturing Climate Study. See *Grant Thornton Manufacturing Climate Study*

MARCIVE GPO CAT/PAC, 71

Marital Status (Population Subject Report), 307

Marital Status and Living Arrangements (Current Population Reports), 315

Market Analysis and Information Database (M.A.I.D.), 398, 399, 421

Market Guide, 256, 263

Market Guide Database, 263

Market Logic, 269
Market Profile Analysis, 386-87, 395
Market Research Abstracts, 97
Market Share Reporter, 50, 418
Marketing and Advertising Reference Service. See *PTS Marketing and Advertising Reference Service (MARS)*
Marketing Economics Guide. See *MEI Marketing Economics Guide*
Marketing Economics Key Plants: Guide to Industrial Purchasing Power, 128
Marketing Insights, 405
Marketing News, 476
Marketing Research Association Directory of Research Services. See *Directory of Research Services Produced by the Members of the Marketing Research Association*
MarketScope, 262
MARS. See *PTS Marketing and Advertising Reference Service (MARS)*
Martindale-Hubbell Law Directory, 38
Marvyn Scudder Manual of Extinct or Obsolete Securities, 242
Materials Business File, 99
MDF. See *Machine-Readable Data Files (RLIN)*
Meatfacts, 366
Media General Financial Services Database, 196, 219, 220, 222, 224, 235, 246, 253, 254, 264, 265
Media General Financial Weekly, 212
Media General Plus, 222
Media Law Reporter, 438
Mediamark Research Database, 421
MEI Marketing Economics Guide, 382, 383-84, 395
MEI Marketing Economics Key Plants. See *Marketing Economics Key Plants: Guide to Industrial Purchasing Power*
Merchandise Line Sales. See *Census of Retail Trade—Merchandise Line Sales*
Merchandising Magazine. See *Dealerscope Merchandising*
Merger & Acquisition Sourcebook, 241
Merger and Corporate Transactions Database, 239-40, 241
Merger Management Report, 241
Merger Yearbook, 6, 241
Mergers & Acquisitions Report, 239
Mergers & Acquisitions: The Journal of Corporate Venture, 238-39, 240
Mergers and Corporate Policy, 241
Mergerstat Review, 240, 241
Mertens Law of Federal Income Taxation, 459-60
Metro Insights, 380, 394
Metro Insights City Analyzer, 19, 380
Metropolitan Area Forecasts. See *MSA Profile: Metropolitan Area Forecasts*
Metropolitan Housing Characteristics. See *Census of Housing—Metropolitan Housing Characteristics*
Microcomputer Index, 100

Microcosm, 139, 141-42
Microform Market Place: An International Directory of Micropublishing, 51
Micropublishers' Trade List Annual, 51
Migration Between the United States and Canada, 315
Miller Comprehensive GAAP Guide, 468
Miller Comprehensive GAAS Guide, 468
Million Dollar Directory, 119-20, 125, 132, 138, 146, 155, 156, 365
Million Dollar Directory Top 50,000 Companies, 119
Million Dollar Disc, 17, 120, 145
Mineral Industry Surveys, 367
Minerals Yearbook, 367, 368
MLR. See *Monthly Labor Review*
Mobile Homes (Housing Subject Report), 308
MoCat. See *Monthly Catalog of U.S. Government Publications*
Modern Plastics Encyclopedia, 368
Money, 267, 475
Money Fund Report. See *Donoghue's Money Fund Report*
Money Income of Households, Families and Persons in the United States, 315, 329
Money Magazine. See *Money*
Money Stock Measures and Liquid Assets. See *Federal Reserve Statistical Releases—Money Stock Measures and Liquid Assets*
Monitor, 408
Monitoring the Future: Questionnaire Response from the Nation's High School Seniors, 409
Monthly Catalog of U.S. Government Publications, 70-71, 72, 75, 429, 439
Monthly Labor Review, 338, 340, 407
Monthly Product Announcements, 311, 319, 476
Monthly Retail Trade: Sales and Inventories. See *Current Business Reports—Monthly Retail Trade: Sales and Inventory*
Monthly Wholesale Trade: Sales and Inventories. See *Current Business Reports—Monthly Wholesale Trade: Sales and Inventories*
Moody's Bond Record, 222
Moody's Bond Survey, 232, 268
Moody's Company Data, 192, 263
Moody's Corporate News: International, 190, 192
Moody's Corporate News: U.S., 190, 192
Moody's Corporate Profiles, 190, 192, 263
Moody's Dividend Record, 243-45
Moody's Handbook of Common Stocks, 192, 262-63
Moody's Industry Review, 253, 265, 266
Moody's International Plus, 192
Moody's Manuals, 189-92, 193, 232, 241, 246, 470
  Moody's Bank & Finance Manual, 165, 189, 205
  Moody's Complete Corporate Index, 189, 197
  Moody's Industrial Manual, 189
  Moody's International Manual, 189, 192

Moody's Municipal & Government Manual, 189, 389
Moody's News Reports, 189, 190, 192
Moody's OTC Industrial Manual, 189
Moody's OTC Unlisted Manual, 189
Moody's Public Utility Manual, 165, 189, 190, 193
Moody's Transportation Manual, 189, 190, 193
Morningstar Mutual Funds On Disc, 268
Motor Freight Transportation and Warehousing Survey. See *Current Business Reports—Motor Freight Transportation and Warehousing Survey*
Mover Households (Housing Subject Report), 308
MPA. See *Market Profile Analysis*
MRA Blue Book. See *Directory of Research Services Provided by the Members of the Marketing Research Association*
MRI Data Base. See *Mediamark Research Data Base*
MRI National Media and Marketing Study. See *National Media and Marketing Study*
MSA Profile: Metropolitan Area Forecasts, 388
Municipal/County Executive Directory, 32
Municipal Yearbook, 389
Mutual Fund Performance Report, 268
Mutual Fund Sourcebook, 268
Mutual Fund Switch Service, 265, 267
Mutual Fund Values, 267-68
Mutual Funds Almanac. See *Donoghue's Mutual Funds Almanac*

NAARS, 195-96, 246, 467, 469
NABE Outlook, 342
NAPM Report on Business. See *Report on Business*
National Association of Business Economists Outlook. See *NABE Outlook*
National Automated Accounting Research System. See *NAARS*
National Business and Financial Weekly. See *Barron's National Business and Financial Weekly*
National Business Telephone Directory, 126
National Daily Quotation Service, 216
National Directory of Corporate Public Affairs, 144
National Economic Projections Series, 343, 388
National Enquirer, 414
National Faculty Directory, 34
National Five-Digit ZIP Code and Post Office Directory, 126
National Journal, 29, 430
National Media and Marketing Study, 421
National Monthly Bond Summary, 216
National Monthly Stock Summary, 198, 216, 224, 241
National Newspaper Index, 101, 104, 107
National OTC Stock Journal, 216-17, 224, 232
National Reporter System, 431, 433, 435, 453, 459

National Stock Summary. See *National Monthly Stock Summary*

National Trade & Professional Associations of the United States. See *NTPA: National Trade & Professional Associations of the United States*

National Trade Data Bank, 362

National Union Catalog: Books, 66, 67

Nation's Business, 10

Nelson Directory of Investment Research. See *Directory of Investment Research*

NEPS. See *National Economic Projections Series*

Network Television and Radio Rates and Data. See *Standard Rate & Data Service—Network Television and Radio Rates and Data*

New England Business, 54, 56, 104

New Issues Investor. See *Standard & Poor's Emerging and Special Situations*

New One-Family Houses Sold and for Sale. See *Current Construction Reports—New One-Family Houses Sold and for Sale*

New Research Reports, 257

New York Facts, 378

New York Stock Exchange Fact Book, 177, 223

New York Stock Exchange Weekly Bulletin. See *NYSE Weekly Bulletin*

New York Times, 15, 85, 99, 101, 102, 206, 214, 224, 368

New York Times Index, 99

News From COPAFS, 475

NewsBank, 375

NewsBank CD News, 102

NewsBank Electronic Index, 105

NewsBank Index, 105

Newsearch, 54, 86, 101

Newsletters in Print, 48

NewsNet, 15, 106, 391

Newspaper Abstracts, 101, 102, 103

Newspaper Abstracts Ondisc, 101, 104

Newspaper and Periodical Abstracts, 101, 104

Newspaper Circulation Analysis. See *Standard Rate & Data Service—Circulation [Year]*

Newspaper Rates and Data. See *Standard Rate & Data Service—Newspaper Rates and Data*

Newswire ASAP, 106, 107

Nielsen Report on Television, 403

Nimmer on Copyright, 438

1980 Census of Population. See *Census of Population*

1980 Census of Population and Housing Users' Guide, 321

1987 Industry and Product Classification Manual, 349

NLRB Decisions, 444

NLRB Election Report, 449

NNI. See *National Newspaper Index*

NORC General Social Surveys. See *General Social Surveys Cumulative Codebook*

NPA/Demographic, 388

NPA/Economic, 388

NQB Monthly Price Report, 216

NTDB. See *National Trade Data Bank*

NTIS Abstract Newsletters, 72-73

NTIS Bibliographic Data-Base, 72

NTIS Listing of Data Files on Floppy Diskette, 57

NTPA: National Trade & Professional Associations in the United States, 34

NUC. See *National Union Catalog: Books*

NUEXCO International Directory. See *International Directory of Nuclear Utilities*

Number of Inhabitants. See *Census of Population—Characteristics of the Population, Chapter A*

Numbers News, 476

NYSE Fact Book. See *New York Stock Exchange Fact Book*

NYSE Weekly Bulletin, 232

OBERS BEA Regional Projections, 342, 389

Occupational Earnings in Selected Areas, 393

Occupational Injuries and Illnesses in the United States, 449

Occupational Projections and Training Data, 341

Occupational Safety and Health Cases, 444

OCLC EASI Reference, 66

OCLC Online Union Catalog, 65-66, 68

O'Dwyer's Directory of Public Relations Firms, 38

Office, Professional, and Data Processing Salaries Report. See *AMS Office, Professional, and Data Processing Salaries Report*

Official Congressional Directory. See *Congressional Directory*

Official Directory of the American Institute of Architects. See *Pro File: The Official Directory of the American Institute of Architects*

Official Gazette of the Patent and Trademark Office: Trademarks, 149, 150, 151-53, 154, 155

Official Summary of Securities Transactions and Holdings, 237, 246

Oil and Gas Journal, 10, 391

Online, 474

Online Database Search Services Directory, 37

Online Information Network, 122, 123-24, 128, 132, 138, 155

Online Review, 474

Operating Banks and Branches. See *Data Book: Operating Banks and Branches*

Operating Ratios for the Typographic Industry, 174

Operating Results of Mass Retail Stores, 176

Operations Research, 47

Operations Research/Management Science: International Literature Digest, 83, 100

Opinions [Year], 411

Optical Publishing Directory, 56

Options and Convertibles. See *Value Line Options and Convertibles*

Original Pronouncements (FASB). See *FASB Accounting Standards: Original Pronouncements*

OR/MS: International Literature Digest. See *Operations Research/Management Science: International Literature Digest*

OTC ProFiles. See *Standard & Poor's OTC ProFiles*

OTC Special Situations. See *Value Line OTC Special Situations*

The Outlook (S&P), 262, 263, 265

Oxbridge Directory of Newsletters, 48, 269

Oxford English Dictionary, 17

Package X: Informational Copies of Federal Tax Forms, 464

PAIS Bulletin. See *PAIS International in Print*

PAIS Foreign Language Index. See *PAIS International in Print*

PAIS International in Print, 49, 54, 84, 94, 104, 410, 411, 463

PAIS International on SilverPlatter, 94

PAIS International Online, 94

PAIS on CD-ROM, 94

Papers, 104

Payment Analysis Report. See *Dun & Bradstreet Payment Analysis Report*

Payroll Administration Guide, 447

Pension Reporter, 438

Pensions and Investment Age, 475

Penthouse, 94

Periodical Abstracts Ondisc, 85

Personnel Journal, 10

Personnel Literature, 98

Personnel Literature Index, 98, 104

Personnel Management Abstracts, 97-98

Personnel Management: Communications, 447-48

Personnel Management Guide, 448

Personnel Management: Policies and Practices, 447-48

Peterson's Graduate Programs, 36

Pharmaceutical News Index, 101

Phonefiche, 140

The Pink Sheets. See *National Daily Quotation Service*

Places Rated Almanac 284-85, 379, 389, 395, 396

Plant Capacity. See *Current Industrial Reports—Plant Capacity*

Plant Locations, 390

Platt's Oilgram News, 11

Playboy, 94

PNI. See *Pharmaceutical News Index*

Policy and Practice Series. See *BNA Policy and Practice Series*

Polk City Directories, 140-41

Polk's World Bank Directory, 143, 165

POLL. See *Public Opinion Online (POLL)*

Pollution Abstracts, 100

Poor's Register. See *Standard & Poor's Register of Corporations, Directors, and Executives*

Population and Housing Census. See *Census of Population and Housing*

Population and Housing Unit Counts. See *Census of Population and Housing— Population and Housing Unit Counts*

Population and Per Capita Income Estimates for Counties and Incorporated Places. See *Current Population Reports—Local Population Estimates*

Population Census. See *Census of Population*

Population Characteristics. See *Current Population Reports—Population Characteristics*

Population Estimates and Projections. See *Current Population Reports— Population Estimates and Projections*

Population Estimates for Metropolitan Statistical Areas. See *Current Population Reports—Local Population Estimates*

Population Index, 57, 100

Population Information in Twentieth Century Census Volumes, 319

Population Statistics, 17

Population Subject Reports. See *Census of Population—Population Subject Reports*

Population Today, 476

Poverty in the United States, 315

PR Newswire, 85, 86, 107, 179

Predicasts Basebook, 78, 344, 364, 369

Predicasts F&S Index Europe, 90

Predicasts F&S Index International, 90

Predicasts F&S Index of Corporate Change, 242

Predicasts F&S Index United States, 89-91, 92, 97, 104, 264, 418

Predicasts Forecasts, 62, 78-79, 342, 364

Predicasts Overview of Markets and Technology. See *PROMT: Predicasts Overview of Markets and Technology*

Predicasts Source Directory. See *Source Directory of Predicasts*

Predicasts Worldcasts. See *Worldcasts*

Prentice Hall Federal Taxes 2nd. See *Federal Taxes 2nd*

Prentice Hall OnLine, 170

Prentice Hall Tax Citator. See *Federal Taxes 2nd—Citator*

Prentice Hall 1040 Handbook, 464

PRF. See *GPO Publications Reference File*

Price Index of New One-Family Houses Sold. See *Current Construction Reports—Price Index of New One-Family Houses Sold*

Price List 36. See *Government Periodicals and Subscription Services*

Private Letter Rulings, 455

Private Placement Letter, 232

PRIZM, 414, 415, 421

Pro File: The Official Directory of the American Institute of Architects, 38

Probe Directory of Foreign Direct Investment in the United States, 146

Producer Prices and Price Indexes, 334

Productivity Measures for Selected Industries, 449

Professional Carwashing, 10

Progressive Grocer, 10

Progressive Grocer Guide to Product Usage, 406-07

Progressive Grocer's Marketing Guidebook, 142, 179

Projections of the Population of the United States by Age, Sex, and Race. See *Current Population Reports— Population Estimates and Projections*

PROMT: Predicasts Overview of Markets and Technology, 83, 90, 92. See also *PTS PROMT*

ProQuest Newspapers Ondisc, 102, 103, 104

Prudent Speculator, 269

Psychological Abstracts, 98

PTS Annual Reports Abstracts, 179, 193-94, 246

PTS F&S Index, 90

PTS Marketing and Advertising Reference Service (MARS), 92, 96-97

PTS New Product Announcements, 107

PTS Newsletter Database, 106, 391

PTS PROMT, 54, 90, 92-93, 97, 99, 102, 104, 107, 194, 232, 256, 410. See also *PROMT: Predicasts Overview of Markets and Technology*

PTS U.S. Forecasts, 78, 344

PTS U.S. Time Series, 344, 364

Public Affairs Information Service Bulletin. See *PAIS International in Print*

Public Opinion, 410, 411

Public Opinion Online (POLL), 409-10, 411

Public Opinion Quarterly, 410-11

Public Perspective, 411

Public Pulse, 405

Public Relations Journal, 400

Public Use Microdata Sample. See *Census of Population and Housing—Public Use Microdata Sample*

Public Utilities Reports, 434

Publications Reference File. See *GPO Sales Publications Reference File*

Publishers Directory, 69

Publishers, Distributors & Wholesalers of the United States, 68

Publishers' International ISBN Directory, 68

Publishers' Trade List Annual, 68

Publishers Weekly, 68, 80, 422

PUMS. See *Census of Population and Housing—Public Use Microdata Sample*

P.U.R. Analysis of Investor-Owned Electric and Gas Utilities, 165

QFR. See *Quarterly Financial Report for Mining, Manufacturing and Trade Corporations*

Qualitative Characteristics of Accounting Information, 467

Quarterly Bank and Savings & Loan Service, 165-67

Quarterly Financial Report for Mining, Manufacturing and Trade Corporations, 176, 349, 363, 369

Quotdial, 219

Radio & Records, 403

RAND Abstracts. See *Selected RAND Abstracts*

Rand McNally Commercial Atlas and Marketing Guide, 379-80, 395

Rand McNally International Bankers Directory. See *Thomson Bank Directory*

Random House Dictionary of the English Language, 149

Rate%Gram, 216

Readers' Guide Abstracts, 85

Readers' Guide to Periodical Literature, 83, 108

Recent Additions to Baker Library, 67

Recent Releases from the Federal Computer Products Center, 57

Reference Book of American Business. See *Dun & Bradstreet Reference Book of American Business*

Reference Book of Corporate Managements, 120, 145

Reference Book of Manufacturers, 128-29, 163

Reference Listing of Federal Tax Forms and Publications. See *Taxpayer Information Publications— Publication 1200*

Reference Point: Food Industry Abstracts, 101

Reference Services Review, 474

Regional Economic Growth in the United States. See *Regional Economic Projections Series*

Regional Economic Projections Series, 343, 388, 389

Regional Industrial Buying Guides. See *Thomas Regional Industrial Buying Guides*

Regional, State, and Local Organizations, 34

Report on Business, 412

Reproducible Tax Forms for Use in Libraries. See *Taxpayer Information Publications—Publication 1132*

REPS. See *Regional Economic Projections Series*

Research Alert, 405

Research Centers and Services Directory, 36

Research Centers Directory, 36, 57, 132

Research Service Directory (MRA). See *Directory of Research Services Provided by Members of the Marketing Research Association*

Research Services Directory (Gale), 36

Residential Finance. See *Census of Housing—Residential Finance*

Restaurant and Institutions, 76

Restaurant Industry Operations Report, 176

Reuters Financial Report, 101

RIA Weekly Tax Alert. See *Weekly Tax Alert*

RLIN Machine-Readable Data Files. See *Machine-Readable Data Files*

RMA Annual Statement Studies, 172-74, 176

Robert D. Fisher Manual of Valuable and Worthless Securities, 242

Robert Morris Associates Annual Statement Studies. See *RMA Annual Statement Studies*

Robotics Abstracts, 101

Roper Report, 408

Rough Lengths, 367

RQ, 474

RSR. See *Reference Services Review*

Rural Development Abstracts, 100

S & P Register. See *Standard & Poor's Register of Corporations, Directors, and Executives*

Sage Human Resources Abstracts. See *Human Resources Abstracts*

Sage Public Administration Abstracts, 100

Sage Urban Studies Abstracts, 100

Sales & Marketing Management, 383, 395

Sales Prospector, 390-91

Sandblasting Companies Directory, 45

Savings and Loans Quarterly Ratings and Analysis. See *Sheshunoff Savings and Loans Quarterly Ratings and Analysis*

SBBI/PC, 223

SBBI Yearbook. See *Stocks, Bonds, Bills, and Inflation Yearbook*

SCAD Bulletin, 100

Schedule B: Statistical Classification of Domestic Commodities Exported from the United States, 361

School Enrollment (Population Characteristics), 315

SCIMP: European Index of Management Periodicals, 100

Scrip World Pharmaceutical News, 11

Scudder Manual of Extinct or Obsolete Securities. See *Marvyn Scudder Manual of Extinct or Obsolete Securities*

SDA. See *Standard Directory of Advertisers*

SDC Domestic Public New Issues Database. See *Domestic Public New Issues Database*

SDC Merger and Corporate Transactions Database. See *Merger and Corporate Transactions Database*

SEC Abstracted Filings. See *SEC Abstracts*

SEC Abstracts, 230-31, 232, 240, 246

SEC Accounting Rules, 469

SEC Docket, 434, 450, 469

SEC Filing Companies, 197

SEC Financial Reporting, 469

SEC Financial Reporting Releases. See *Financial Reporting Releases*

SEC News Digest, 229, 230, 232, 246

SEC No-Action Letters Index and Summaries, 230

SEC Online, 194-95, 230, 246

SEC Online on SilverPlatter, 195

SEC Today, 229-30, 232, 246

Securities and Exchange Commission News Digest. See *SEC News Digest*

Securities Industry Yearbook, 179

Securities Week, 230, 475

Security Owner's Stock Guide. See *Standard & Poor's Security Owner's Stock Guide*

Security Price Index Record, 223, 337

Selected Interest and Exchange Rates. See *Federal Reserve Statistical Releases—Selected Interest and Exchange Rates*

Selected RAND Abstracts, 67

Selected Research in Microfiche (SRIM), 70

Selective Cooperative Index of Management Periodicals. See *SCIMP: European Index of Management Periodicals*

Senate Reports, 429. See also *Committee Reports (U.S. House and Senate)*

Serial Set, 429

Serials Directory: An International Reference Book, 46-47, 54, 108

Serials Directory/EBSCO CD-ROM, 47

Service Annual Survey Report, 357

Shepard's Acts and Cases by Popular Name, 428

Shepard's Citations, 435, 438, 439

Shepard's Federal Labor Law Citations, 435-37, 441

Shepard's Federal Tax Citations, 456, 460

Sheshunoff Bank Quarterly Ratings and Analysis, 6, 166

Sheshunoff Savings and Loans Quarterly Ratings and Analysis, 166

SIC Manual. See *Standard Industrial Classification Manual*

Simmons Study of Media and Markets, 406, 419-21

Site Selection and Economic Development, 390

Situation and Outlook Reports. See *Agricultural Situation and Outlook Reports*

SLA Business and Finance Division Bulletin. See *Business and Finance Division Bulletin (SLA)*

Sludge, 11

Small Business Advisory Reports, 162

Soap/Cosmetics/Chemical Specialties, 78

Social and Economic Characteristics for Metropolitan Statistical Areas. See *Census of Population—Social and Economic Characteristics for Metropolitan Statistical Areas*

Social Science Computer Review, 57

Social Sciences Citation Index, 84

Social Sciences Index, 100

Social Security Area Population Projections, 342

Socioeconomic Characteristics of Medical Practice, 76

Sociological Abstracts, 98, 100

SOI Bulletin, 176, 329

Source Book of Franchise Opportunities, 169

Source Directory of Predicasts, 47

Sourcebook of County Demographics, 382, 384

Sourcebook of Criminal Justice, 376-77

Sourcebook of Zip Code Demographics, 384, 385, 395, 421

SPD. See *Standard Periodical Directory*

Special Censuses. See *Current Population Reports—Special Censuses*

Special Libraries Association. Business and Finance Division Bulletin. See *Business and Finance Division Bulletin (SLA)*

Special Studies (Series P-23). See *Current Population Reports—Special Studies*

Spectrum Ownership Profiles, 6, 188, 235-36, 246

Spectrum 1: Investment Company Stock Holdings, 235, 236

Spectrum 2: Investment Company Portfolios, 235, 236

Spectrum 3: Institutional Stock Holdings Survey, 235, 236

Spectrum 4: Institutional Portfolios, 235, 236

Spectrum 5: Five Percent Ownership, 235

Spectrum 6: Insider Ownership, 235

Spot Radio Rates and Data. See *Standard Rate & Data Service—Spot Radio Rates and Data*

Spot Radio Small Markets. See *Standard Rate & Data Service—Spot Radio Small Markets*

Spot Television Rates and Data. See *Standard Rate & Data Service—Spot Television Rates and Data*

SRDS. See *Standard Rate & Data Service*

SRI. See *Statistical Reference Index*

SRIM. See *Selected Research in Microfiche (SRIM)*

Standard & Poor's Bond Guide, 222

Standard & Poor's Corporate Descriptions, 193

Standard & Poor's Corporation Records, 117, 192-93, 197, 241

Standard & Poor's Corporations, 117, 193, 197, 246

Standard & Poor's CreditWeek. See *CreditWeek*

Standard & Poor's Daily News, 192-93, 197, 232, 262

Standard & Poor's Dividend Record, 243, 245

Standard & Poor's Earnings Guide, 258

Standard & Poor's Emerging and Special Situations, 232

Standard & Poor's Industry Report Service, 265

Standard & Poor's Industry Reports. See *Standard & Poor's Industry Report Service*

Standard & Poor's Industry Surveys, 253, 264-65, 342, 368

Standard & Poor's Insurance Rating Service, 168

Standard & Poor's/Lipper Mutual Fund ProFiles, 267

Standard & Poor's MarketScope. See *MarketScope*

Standard & Poor's News, 179, 193

Standard & Poor's Online, 262

Standard & Poor's OTC ProFiles, 262, 267

Standard & Poor's Outlook. See *The Outlook*

Standard & Poor's Register of Corporations, Directors and Executives, 117-19, 120, 132, 145, 193, 197, 470

Standard & Poor's Security Owner's Stock Guide, 208, 220-21, 222, 224, 235, 258, 263, 268

Standard & Poor's Security Price Index Record. See *Security Price Index Record*

Standard & Poor's Statistical Service, 253, 337, 344, 363, 369

Standard & Poor's Stock Guide. See *Standard & Poor's Security Owner's Stock Guide*

Standard & Poor's Stock Market Encyclopedia. See *Stock Market Encyclopedia*

Standard & Poor's Stock Reports, 232, 254, 262, 265

Standard & Poor's Trendline. See *Trendline*

Standard & Poor's Trends and Projections, 264, 342-43

Standard & Poor's Weekly Dividend Record. See *Standard & Poor's Dividend Record*

Standard Directory of Advertisers, 120-21, 132, 148, 156, 399

Standard Directory of Advertising Agencies, 38, 399

Standard Federal Tax Reports, 455, 456, 457, 458, 459, 460

Standard Industrial Classification Manual, 62-64, 124, 128, 358

Standard Periodical Directory, 47, 48, 403

Standard Rate & Data Service, 402-03
  Advertising Options Plus, 402
  Business Publication Rates and Data, 47, 82, 402
  Card Deck Rates and Data, 402
  Circulation [Year], 402, 403
  Community Publication Rates and Data, 402
  Consumer Magazine and Agri-Media Rates and Data, 402
  Direct Mail List Rates and Data, 403
  Network Television Rates and Data, 402
  Newspaper Rates and Data, 48, 402
  Spot Radio Rates and Data, 402
  Spot Radio Small Markets, 402
  Spot Television Rates and Data, 402

State Administrative Officials Classified by Function, 30-31

State and Local Taxes, 465

State and Metropolitan Area Data Book, 377, 381

State and Regional Associations, 34

State Business Directory Series, 139

State Data and Database Finder, 32, 52

State Elective Officials and Legislatures, 30

State Executive Directory, 30

State Legislative Leadership, Committess, & Staff, 30

State Legislative Sourcebook, 32, 427

State Personal Income Tax Forms, 465

State Policy Reports, 377

State Profiles, 388

State Rankings: A Statistical View of the 50 States, 378

State Tax Action Coordinator, 465

State Tax Forms: Individual, 465

State Tax Guide, 465

State Tax Reports, 465

State Yellow Book, 30

Statements of Financial Accounting Concepts, 467, 468

Statements of Financial Accounting Standards, 466, 467, 468

Statements on Auditing Standards, 467, 469

States in Profile, 377-78

States in Profile: The State Policy Data Diskette, 378

Statistical Abstract of the United States, 73, 336, 344, 376, 377, 378

Statistical Bulletin (Conference Board), 342

Statistical Classification of Domestic and Foreign Commodities Exported from the United States. See *Schedule B: Statistical Classification of Domestic and Foreign Commodities Exported from the United States.*

Statistical Masterfile, 76

Statistical Record Bulletin (Cigar Association of America), 366

Statistical Reference Index, 49, 76-78, 176, 369, 376, 418, 422

Statistical Releases (Federal Reserve Board). See *Federal Reserve Statistical Releases*

Statistical Services Directory, 73

Statistical Theory and Methods Abstracts, 100

Statistical Yearbook of the Edison Electric Institute. See *Edison Electric Institute Statistical Yearbook*

Statistics of Income Bulletin. See *SOI Bulletin*

Statistics of Income: Corporation Income Tax Returns, 174-75

Statistics of Income: Individual Income Tax Returns, 329

Statistics of Income Source Book, 176

Statistics on Banking, 176

Statistics Sources, 29, 52, 73-74, 344

Statutes at Large. See *U.S. Statutes at Large*

STFs. See *Census of Population and Housing—Summary Tape Files*

Stock Guide. See *Standard & Poor's Security Owner's Stock Guide*

Stock Market Encyclopedia, 262

Stock Market Magazine, 475

Stock Reports. See *Standard & Poor's Stock Reports*

Stocks, Bonds, Bills, and Inflation: Historical Returns, 223

Stocks, Bonds, Bills, and Inflation Yearbook, 222-23

Subject Bibliographies (GPO), 72

Subject Directory of Special Libraries and Information Centers, 33

Subject Index to the 1980 Census of Population and Housing, 319

Summaries of Labor Arbitration Awards, 445

Summary Characteristics for Governmental Units. See *Census of Population and Housing—Summary Characteristics for Governmental Units*

Summary of U.S. Export and Import Merchandise Trade. See *U.S. Export and Import Merchandise Trade*

Summary Population and Housing Characteristics. See *Census of Population and Housing—Summary Population and Housing Characteristics*

Summary Social, Economic, and Housing Characteristics. See *Census of Population and Housing—Summary Social, Economic, and Housing Characteristics*

Summary Tape Files. See *Census of Population and Housing—Summary Tape Files*

Summary Tape Files Microfiche. See *Census of Population and Housing— Summary Tape Files Microfiche*

Supermap, 17

Supermarket Business Annual Consumer Expenditure Study, 406

SUPERSITE, 16, 384, 416

Supreme Court Bulletin. See *U.S. Supreme Court Bulletin*

Supreme Court Reporter, 431, 433

Survey Methodology Information System, 19

Survey of Buying Power, 329, 380, 382, 383, 394, 395, 402

Survey of Buying Power Data Service, 288-90, 383

Survey of Consumer Attitudes and Behavior, 19

Survey of Consumers, 412

Survey of Current Business, 329, 330, 331, 334, 335, 336, 338, 339, 344, 412

Survey of Minority-Owned Businesses, 359-60

Sweet's Catalog File, 130

SweetSearch, 130

Taft Corporate Giving Directory, 144

Tariff Schedule of the United States Annotated. See *Harmonized Tariff Schedule of the United States: Annotated for Statistical Reporting Purposes*

Tax Action Coordinator, 459, 465

Tax Adviser, 461

Tax Court Memorandum Decisions, 455, 456

Tax Court Reported Decisions, 455, 456

Tax Court Reporter (CCH), 455, 456

Tax Guide: Federal Taxes, 464

Tax Guide for Small Business. See *Taxpayer Information Publications— Publication 334*

Tax Information Publications. See *Taxpayer Information Publications— Publication 1194*

Tax Lawyer, 461
Tax Management Portfolios, 460, 464
Tax Notes, 455, 462-63
Tax Notes Microfiche Data Base, 455, 463
Tax Notes Today, 463
Tax Practice Series, 464
Tax Transactions Library. See *CCH Tax Transactions Library*
TAXATION, 453
Taxation for Accountants, 461
Taxation for Lawyers, 461
Taxes on Parade, 461
Taxpayer Information Publications, 464
   Publication 17: Your Federal Income Tax, 464, 465
   Publication 334: Tax Guide for Small Business, 464
   Publication 1045: Information and Order Blanks for Preparers of Federal Tax Returns, 464
   Publication 1132: Reproducible Tax Forms for Use in Libraries, 464, 465
   Publication 1194: Tax Information Publications, 464
   Publication 1200: Reference Listing of Federal Tax Forms and Publications, 464
T.C. Memorandum Decisions, 455, 456
Technology Forecasts, 78
Television & Cable Factbook, 402, 404
Television Digest, 404
Television/Radio Age, 403
Tent Rental Directory, 45
TEXT. See *Dow Jones Text-Search Services*
Textile and Apparel Financial Directory. See *Fairchild's Textile and Apparel Financial Directory*
Thesaurus of Financial Marketing Terms, 96
Thomas Food Industry Register, 129
Thomas Grocery Register. See *Thomas Food Industry Register*
Thomas New Industrial Products, 130
Thomas Regional Industrial Buying Guides, 139
Thomas Register of American Manufacturers, 129- 30, 132, 133, 138, 139, 148, 155
Thomson Bank Directory, 143, 165, 177
Thomson Credit Union Directory, 143
Thomson Savings Directory, 143
Times Literary Supplement, 68
Tin Statistics, 366
Today's Investor, 217
Top 50,000 Companies. See *Million Dollar Directory Top 50,000 Companies*
Top Numbers (American Banker), 177
Toronto Globe and Mail. See *Globe and Mail*
Trade & Industry ASAP, 54, 86
Trade & Industry Index, 54, 68, 86, 99, 102, 104, 107,
Trade Directories of the World, 45
Trade Names Database, 151
Trade Names Dictionary. See *Brands and Their Companies*
Trade Names Directory Series, 151

Trade Regulation Reports, 437
Tradeline, 219
Trademark Design Register, 153
Trademark Owners Register, 153
Trademark Register, 150, 153, 154
Trademarks/CD-ROM, 154-55
Trademarkscan—Federal, 6, 150, 154, 155, 156
Trademarkscan—State, 154
Transdex Index, 12
Treasury Bulletin, 334, 341
Trendline, 260
Trends and Projections (S&P). See *Standard & Poor's Trends and Projections*
Trinet Company Database, 127
Trinet U.S. Businesses, 126-27, 133, 155, 162, 178, 405, 417
Truck Inventory and Use Survey. See *Census of Transportation—Truck Inventory and Use Survey*
TRW Business Profiles, 162
Twenty Censuses—Population and Housing Questions, 1790-1980, 319
TWST. See *The Wall Street Transcript*
Typical Electric Bills, 391

ULI Market Profiles, 390, 394
Ulrich's Annual and Irregular Serials. See *Ulrich's International Periodicals Directory*
Ulrich's International Periodicals Directory, 46, 47, 50, 54, 56, 108
Ulrich's Plus, 46
Unemployment in States and Local Areas, 340, 376
United & Babson Investment Report, 269
United Business Service. See *United & Babson Investment Report*
United Mutual Fund Selector, 265
U.S. and Canadian Business in South Africa, 144
U.S. Budget in Brief, 341
U.S. Code, 428, 430, 434, 435, 438, 440, 441, 453, 454
U.S. Code Annotated, 428, 430
U.S. Code Congressional and Administrative News, 430, 435, 450, 454
U.S. Code Service, 428
U.S. Congressional Committee Reports. See *Committee Reports (U.S. House and Senate)*
U.S. Congressional News. See *U.S. Code Congressional and Administrative News*
U.S. Corporate Earnings Outlook, 342
U.S. Court of Claims Reports, 433
U.S. Economic Outlook: A Monthly Forecast Update (Meyer & Associates), 342
U.S. Economic Outlook [Year] (Conference Board), 342
U.S. Export and Import Merchandise Trade, 335, 362
U.S. Exports of Merchandise. See *Foreign Trade Data*
U.S. Federal Trademarks Official Gazette, 153
U.S. Government Manual, 27, 28, 427

U.S. House of Representatives Reports. See *House Reports*
U.S. Imports of Merchandise. See *Foreign Trade Data*
U.S. Industrial Directory, 130
U.S. Industrial Outlook, 78, 341, 363-64, 367, 68
U.S. Law Week, 430, 431, 437, 450
U.S. Manufacturers Directory, 128, 132, 138, 155
U.S. Master Tax Guide, 464
U.S. Merchandise Trade: Exports, General Imports, and Imports for Consumption, 362
U.S. Regional Projections: Population, Employment and Income. See *Regional Economic Projections Series*
U.S. Reports (Supreme Court), 431, 432, 435, 441
U.S. Senate Reports. See *Senate Reports*
U.S. Serial Set. See *Serial Set*
U.S. Statutes at Large, 428, 429, 434, 435, 441
U.S. Supreme Court Bulletin, 431
U.S. Supreme Court Reports, Lawyers Edition, 431, 433
U.S. Tax Cases, 455, 456, 457
U.S. Tax Court Reports, 455, 456
U.S. Tax Week, 461
U.S. Time Series. See *PTS U.S. Time Series*
University Research in Business and Economics, 67
Unlisted Market Guide. See *Market Guide*
Urban Affairs Abstracts, 100
Urban Documents Microfice Collection, 12
Urban Transportation Abstracts, 95, 100
USA Today, 101
USCCAN. See *U.S. Code Congressional and Administrative News*

Value Line DataFile, 16, 260
Value Line Investment Survey, 196, 220, 254, 260-262, 264, 265, 267
Value Line Options and Convertibles, 262
Value Line OTC Special Situations, 262
Value of New Construction Put in Place. See *Current Construction Reports— Value of New Construction Put in Place*
Value/Screen II, 19, 262
Variety. See *Daily Variety*
Vendor Catalog Service, 131
Vickers Institutional Holdings, 236
Vickers Portfolio Guide, 236, 246
Vickers Securities Report, 236
Vickers Stock Traders Guide, 236, 246
Virginia Business Directory, 139
VISION, 414
Vital Statistics of the United States, 312
Voting and Registration (Population Characteristics), 315

Wage and Hour Cases, 444, 446
Wages and Hours, 446
Walker's Manual of Western Corporations and Securities, 196

Wall Street Journal, 10-11, 15, 85, 89, 92, 99, 101, 102, 103-04, 106, 162, 206-14, 215, 220, 232, 233, 245, 251, 252, 253, 254, 330, 335, 343, 367, 408, 412, 462, 473

Wall Street Journal Index, 102-3, 104, 197, 243, 253

The Wall Street Transcript, 256, 257, 264

Wall Street Week with Louis Rukeyser, 250

Ward's Automotive Yearbook, 368

Ward's Business Directory: Ranked by Sales within 4-Digit SIC, 178

Ward's Business Directory of U.S. Private and Public Companies, 85, 122, 124, 132, 133, 155, 178

Warndex, 256

Washington Information Directory, 26-27

Washington Post, 54, 99, 101, 102, 103, 105

Washington Post Book World, 68

Washington [Year]: A Comprehensive Directory of Key Institutions and Leaders of the National Capital Area, 27

Webster's New Collegiate Dictionary, 149

Weekly Compilation of Presidential Documents, 429

Weekly Summary of NLRB Cases, 441

Weekly Tax Alert, 461

What's It Worth? (Household Economic Studies), 315

What's New in Advertising and Marketing, 422

What's New in Collective Bargaining, 448

Who Audits America, 144, 470

Who Knows: A Guide to Government Experts, 28

Who Owns Whom, 148

Who Owns Whom Red Book. See *Directory of Corporate Affiliations*

Who's Minding the Kids (Household Economic Studies), 315

Who's Who in America, 36, 144

Who's Who in Economics, 36

Who's Who in Finance and Industry, 145

Who's Who in Special Libraries, 33

Who's Who in the East, 145

Wiesenberger Current Dividend Record, 267

Wiesenberger Investment Companies Service, 6, 267

Wiesenberger Management Results, 267

Wiesenberger Mutual Fund Investment Analyzer, 267

Wiesenberger Mutual Funds Investment Report, 267

Wilson Business Abstracts, 85

Wires, 231, 245

Women-Owned Businesses, 360

Women Studies Abstracts, 98

Women's Wear Daily, 10

Woods & Poole MSA Profile. See *MSA Profile: Metropolitan Area Forecasts*

Work Related Abstracts, 84, 98, 108, 449

Working Press of the Nation, 49

World Almanac and Book of Facts, 73, 75

World Book Encyclopedia, 368

World Chamber of Commerce Directory, 32, 141

World Military and Social Expenditures, 76

Worldcasts, 78

Worldmark Encyclopedia of the States, 377

Worldscope Company Profiles, 196, 220

WWD. See *Women's Wear Daily*

Yearbook on Corporate Mergers, Leveraged Buyouts, Joint Ventures and Corporate Policy. See *Merger Yearbook*

YMC-Your Marketing Consultant: Advanced Consumer, 383

Your Federal Income Tax. See *Taxpayer Information Publications— Publication 17*

Your Income Tax (Lasser), 464

Your Income Tax: Professional Edition, 464

Your Marketing Consultant: Advanced Consumer. See *YMC-Your Marketing Consultant: Advanced Consumer*

Zacks Earnings Estimates, 188, 258

Zacks Earnings Forecaster 188, 257-58, 259

Zweig Forecast, 269

Subject Index

by Joan K. Griffitts

Please note: All federal agencies are listed under U.S.

ABD (American Business Directories, Inc.), 122
Abott, Langer and Associates, 393
Abstracts, 83
Academic libraries, 8–9
Accounting
  financial ratios, 171–76
  financial statements, 158–61
  indexes, 95
  practice, 469–70
  standards, 465–69
ACCRA (American Chamber of Commerce Researchers), 391
Activities, Interest and Opinions (AIO) surveys, 408
ADIs (Areas of Dominant Influence), 382
Administrative Management Society, 393
ADP (Automatic Data Processing, Inc.), 217
Advertising
  audience measurement, 403–05
  costs, comparing, 402–03
  expenditures, 399–400
  indexes, 96–97
  media sources, 399–405
Advertising agencies directory, 120–21
Agency bonds, 205
Agriculture, 360
Almanacs, 174
American Bankers Association, 96
American Bar Association, 461
American Business Directories, (ABD) Inc., 122
American Business Information, Inc., 123, 128
American Chamber of Commerce Researchers Association (ACCRA), 391
American Directory Publishing Co., 139
American Enterprise Institute, 410
American Institute of Certified Public Accountants (AICPA), 95, 195, 461, 463, 470
American Institute of Real Estate Appraisers, 142
American Stock Exchange (AMEX), 202, **203, 214**
AMEX (American Stock Exchange), 202, 203, 214
Andriot, John, 70

Annual Report to Stockholders (ARS), 184–86
  financial information in, 185
  microforms, 185–86
Arbitron, Inc., 382, 403
Areas of Dominant Influence (ADI)s, 382
ARS (Annual Report to Stockholders), 184–86
Arthur D. Little, Inc., 9, 50
Association for University Business and Economic Research, 67
Associations, directories, 33–34
Auditors, 470
Audits & Surveys, Inc., 406
Auto–Graphics, Inc., 71
Automatic Data Processing, Inc. (ADP), 217
Automobiles, 368

Balance of payments accounts, 334
Balance sheet, 159
Bank Marketing Association, 95–96
Banking. See also U.S. Federal Reserve Board
  directories, 143, 165–68
  indexes, 95–96
BEA. See U.S. Bureau of Economic Analysis
Bernhard, Arnold, 260
A.M. Best Co., 168
Beta Coefficient, 254
Bibliographic databases, 14
Bibliographic resources, 64–65
Bibliographic utilities, 65
Bill Communications, Inc., 383
Biographical directories, 144–45
Birch/Scarborough, 403
BLS. See U.S. Bureau of Labor Statistics
Blue books, 30
Blue List Publishing, 232
Blue Sky Laws, 169, 183
BNA. See Bureau of National Affairs
Board of directors, 233
Bonds. See also Securities; Stocks
  advisory services, 268–69
  coupon rate, 204
  current yield, 204
  government-issued, 205
  interest rates, 204
  price, 204
  primary vs. secondary markets, 204

quotations, 212
ratings, 254–55
types, 205
Books
  finding, 61–81
  reviews, 68
Boolean operators, 13–14
R.R. Bowker, 33, 66, 68, 69
Brands. See also Trademarks
  advertising directory, 400–01
  comparisons, 418–21
  name use, 419–21
  names, 150–51
Bresser Company, 141
Broadcast media directory, 49, 405
Broadtape, 106–07
Brokerage reports, 255–58
BRS Search Service, 15, 16
Buckmaster Publishing, 169
Bunker Ramo Corporation, 219
Burwell, Helen, 37
Business cycle, 328
Business indexes, general, 85–94
Business information
  CD-ROMs, ix, 17–18
  characteristics, 5–7
  computer disks and tapes, 18–19
  computer use, 7
  controlled publications, 5–6
  cost, 3–4
  current awareness service, 84
  external, 4–5
  forms of, 3–22
  government agencies, 7–8
  guides, 43–44
  internal, 4
  libraries, 8–9
  locating, 7–9
  microforms, 12
  nonprofit organizations, 9
  online databases, 12–17
  periodical sources, 10–11
  primary sources, 4–5
  private companies, 9
  proprietary sources, 5
  publications, 11–12
  secondary sources, 4–5
  services, 11–12
  trade associations, 9
  trade journals, 10
  value, vii, 3–4

Business law. *See* Labor law; Legal information; Taxes
Business One Irwin, 169, 223
Buying power, 382–87

CACI Marketing Systems, 384, 414
Cahners Publishing, 130
Call Reports, 164–65
Callaghan and Company, 459
CAMEL, 166
Carroll Publishing Co., 28, 30
Catalog directories, 129–31
Catalogs of current publishing, 66
CDA Investment Technologies, 235
CD-ROMs
    banking information, 166
    business information, change in, ix
    company directories, 117, 119–20, 122
    directories, 56–58
    financial information, 163, 189, 192–94
    national directories, 123–25
    source of business information, 17–18
    trademarks, 154–55
Census. *See also* Economic Census; Population statistics; Statistics
    administrative units, 298
    Block Groups, 298
    Block Numbering Areas (BNAs), 299
    Block statistics, 308
    Blocks, 298
    catalogs, 319
    Census Tract, 299
    classification by primary industry, 348
    County Divisions, 300
    data collection, 294–95
    data, types available, 295–97
    disclosure restrictions, 348
    electronic access, 320–21
    establishment data, 348
    finding answers quickly, 321–22
    geographical units, 297–301
    governmental units, 298
    indexes, 319
    information, pitfalls in using, 316–19
    limitations of data, 348–49
    mastering, 322–23
    1980 printed reports, 304
    1990 content and program changes, 302–03
    population estimates and projections, 311–16
    products for 1990, 309–11
    questionnaires, 295–97
    relationships, 302
    Summary Tape Files (STF)s, 295, 320
    statistical units, 298–301
    terminology, 300
Census Bureau Data User Services Division (DUSD), 319–22
Chamber of commerce directories, 32, 141
Chapman, Karen, 224
Charts and graphs, 285–88
Citation indexes, 83–84
Cities
    directories, 140–41
    guides, 380–81
    statistics, 381
Classification systems
    legal, 431, 433

Library of Congress, 65
Standard Industrial Classification, 62–64
    structure in statistics, 276
Closed–end funds, 205
CMSA (Consolidated Metropolitan Statistical Area), 298
Coincident Indicators, 328
COLA (Cost of Living Adjustment), 333
College and university directories, 36
Colt Microfiche Corporation, 138
Columbia Books, Inc., 27
Commerce Clearing House, Inc, 95, 444, 455, 460, 463
Commerce Register, Inc., 137
Commercial advisory sources, 258–63
Commodities, 366
Commodity Research Bureau, 366
Common–size analysis, 171
Common stock, 202
    handbooks, 262–63
Communication indexes, 98
Companies. *See also* Industries; Industry statistics
    affiliated firms, 115–16, 145–48
    annual reports, 184–86
    board of directors, 233
    catalog directories, 129–30
    city directories, 140–41
    companies versus corporations, 114–15
    corporate changes, 241–42
    defined, 114–15
    detailed company research, 133
    directories, 113–44
    financial statements, 158–61
    international, 197
    national directories, 123–27
    leading firms, 116–23
    local directories, 141–42
    management, 116
    manufacturing firms, 127–31
    marketing information, 120–21
    mergers and acquisitions, 237–41
    organizational charts, 116
    ownership, 233–37
    private, 122–23, 158–81
    profiles, other sources, 196–97
    proxy statements, 187
    public, 182–99
    rankings, 176–79
    ready-reference searches, 132–33
    regulated, 164–68
    sales comparisons, 417–18
    service directories, 138–40
    state industrial directories, 137–38
    subsidiaries, 115
    telephone book directories, 140
    10–K reports, 186–87
    trade directories, 142–43
    women–owned, 360
Composite index, 330
Composite trading, 206
CompuServe, 16
Computer science indexes, 99
Computer software directories, 57–58
Computer tapes, 18–19
    as source of business information, 18–19
    from government, 71
Computerized information sources, guides, 51–58

Conference Board, 116, 341
Congressional directories, 29–30
Congressional Information Service, Inc., 75, 76, 430
Congressional Quarterly, Inc., 26, 27
Consolidated Metropolitan Statistical Area (CMSA), 298
Consolidated statements, 184
Construction, 357, 387
Consultants, 38
Consumer behavior
    attitudes, 408–11
    confidence and buying plans, 411–12
    expenditure surveys, 333, 406–08
    public opinion, 408–11
    trends, 94, 406–08
Consumer Price Index (CPI), 333
Contacts Influential Marketing Information Services, 142
Contract negotiation, 448
Conway Data, Inc., 390
Corporate affiliations, 145–48
Corporation, defined, 114–15
Cost of Living Adjustment (COLA), 333
Cost of living comparisons, 391
Council of Planning Librarians, 67
Council of State Governments, 30
Counties
    business patterns, 362–63
    statistics, 381
CPI (Consumer Price Index), 333
Credit reports, 161–64
Credit unions, 143
Croner Publications, 45
Cross–reference directories, 141
Cuadra Associates, 53
Cuadra/Gale, 56
Current awareness services, 84
CUSIP numbers, 188

Daniells, Lorna, 43
Darnay, Arsen J., 394, 418
Data, 278
Data Courier, Inc., 87
Data–Star, 15
DataTimes, 15
Davis, Dick, 269
Dealers' Digest, Inc., 232–33
Decennial census publications, 303–11
Decision Research Sciences, Inc., 165
Delaney, Patrick R., 468
Demographic data, 384–87
Designated Market Areas (DMAs), 382
DIALOG, 15, 16, 101–02
Dickman Criss–Cross Directories, Inc., 141
Digests, 83
Directories
    associations, 33–34
    banking, 143
    biographical information, 144–45
    companies, 113–35
    corporate affiliations, 145–48
    fee-based research services, 36–38
    franchises, 169
    government agencies, 26–32
    guides to, 45
    imports and exports, 360–62
    libraries and librarians, 33
    local business information, 141–42

manufacturers, 127–31
nonprofit research organizations, 34–36
online databases, 52–56
periodicals, 82
problems using, 131–32
state business information, 137–40
trade directories, 45, 143–44
trade names, 150–51
universities, 34–36
Directory of Directors Co., Inc., 145
Disclosure data
  Annual Report to Stockholders (ARS), 184–86
  Form 10-K reports, 186–87
  forms and reports, 228
  full-text systems, 194–96
  proxy statements, 187
  secondary sources, 188–97
  statements, 184–87
Disclosure, Inc., 187, 188–89
Dividend announcements, 242–45
DJIA (Dow Jones Industrial Average), 252
F.W. Dodge Group, 390
Donnelly Demographics, 384–86, 414
Dow Jones & Company, Inc., 212, 215
Dow Jones Industrial Average (DJIA), 252
Dow Jones News/Retrieval, 15, 16, 103–04, 106, 219
DRI/McGraw-Hill, 341
Dun & Bradstreet Corporation
  company directories, 119–20
  comprehensive national directories, 123–26
  consultants directory, 38
  corporate affiliations, 145–48
  credit services, 144, 161–64
  executive information, 145
  industry profiles, 364–66
  local business directories, 141–42
  manufacturing firm directories, 128–29
  state and local filings, 170

Earnings Per Share (EPS), 253
EBSCO, 46–47
Economic Census. *See also* Census
  CD-ROM products, 358–59
  changes in 1987, 358–59
  construction industries, 357
  key concepts, 348
  manufacturers, 350–53
  mineral industries, 357
  publications, 349–58
  retail trade, 353–56
  revised SIC codes, 58
  service industries, 356–57
  transportation, 357–58
  wholesale trade, 356
Economic statistics
  balance of payments accounts, 334
  business cycle and, 328
  coincident indicators, 328
  compendia, general, 335–38
  federal deficit, 334
  forecasts, 341–43
  general, 326–46
  Gross National Product, 331
  Index of Leading Economic Indicators, 330
  indicators, 328
  inflation, 333–34

labor force data, 332
Leading Indicators, 328
money supply, 334
National Income and Product Accounts (NIPA), 331
pitfalls in using, 328–29
price levels, 333–34
sources, 335–43
subject-specific data sources, 338–41
EDGAR (Electronic Data Gathering, Analysis and Retrieval), 187
Editor & Publisher Co., Inc., 49
Electonic bulletin boards, 16
Electronic clipping services, 84, 104–05
Electronic Data Gathering, Analysis and Retrieval (EDGAR), 187
Electronic quote systems, 217–19
Electronic sources, guides, 51–58
Employment, 448
End-user systems, online databases, 16
Engineering indexes, 99
EPS (Earnings Per Share), 253
Equity and debt financing, 201–02
Ernst & Young, 464
Evinger, William R., 28, 57
Executive Sciences Institute, 83
Executive Telecom Systems, Inc., 449
Executives, 145, 255
Experts, sources of
  associations, 33–34
  experts, 25–41
  fee-based research services, 36–38
  government agencies, 26–32
  how and when to ask for help, 38–40
  libraries and librarians, 33
  nonprofit research organizations, 34–36
  universities, 34–36

Faculty directories, 34
Fairchild Publications, 196
Farm populations, 360
FASB (Financial Accounting Standards Board), 159, 466–69
FDIC (Federal Deposit Insurance Corporation), 164, 176
Federal Computer Products Center, 57
Federal Deposit Insurance Corporation (FDIC), 164, 176
Federal government. *See also* names of Federal agencies beginning with U.S.
  agencies, resident experts, 8
  budget, 340–41
  budget deficit, 334
  computer products, 18
  data products, 52
  directories, 26–27
  legislative history, 428–30
  population statistics, 294–322
  regulatory agencies, 27–28
  as source of company financial information, 168–70
  statistical programs, 28
  statistical system, 326–28
  telephone listings, 28
Federal Home Loan Bank Board (FHLBB), 165
Federal Information Center (FIC), 27
Federal Mediation and Conciliation Service (FMCS), 440
Fee-based research services, 36–38

FHLBB (Federal Home Loan Bank Board), 165
FIC (Federal Information Center), 27
Financial Accounting Standards Board (FASB), 159, 466–69
Financial comparisons, 170–79
  rankings, 176–79
  ratios, 171–76
Financial information
  comparisons, 170–79
  credit reports, 161–64
  franchises, 169
  from government records, 168–70
  private companies, 158–81
  public companies, 182–99
  regulated companies, 164–68
Financial quotations
  electronic sources, 217–19
  guides, 208
  how to read, 206–12
  sources of, 212–20
  telephone inquiry services, 219
Financial ratios, 171–76
Financial Research Associates, 176
Financial statements, 158–61
  balance sheet, 159
  income statement, 159–60
  Statement of Cash Flows, 161
  Statement of Stockholders' Equity, 160
FIND/SVP Information Clearinghouse, 50
Fitch Investors Service, Inc., 254, 268
Fixed income securities, 268–69
Fixed-unit investment trusts, 205
FMCS (Federal Mediation and Conciliation Service), 440
Food product surveys, 407
Foreign trade statistics, 360–62
Form 8-K, 229
Form 10-K reports, 186–87
Format-specific finding guides, 50–51
Franchises, 169
Frequency distribution curve, 287
Frost & Sullivan, Inc., 50

GAAP (Generally Accepted Accounting Procedures), 158–59, 468
Gale Research, Inc., 26, 33, 45, 68, 69, 73, 122, 126
Gallop Organization, 409, 410
Gates, Jean Key, 58
Generally Accepted Accounting Principles (GAAP), 158–59, 468
Geodemographic cluster analysis, 414
Geographic directories, 137–42
Geographic markets, 375–76
Glanville Publications, 94
GNP (Gross National Product), 331
Gordon and Breach Publishers, 68
Government. *See also* Federal government; Local government; State government; and names of Federal agencies beginning with U.S.
  business information available, 7–8
  CD-ROMs, 71
  directories, 26–32
  documents, 61–81
  as source of experts, 26, 28
  tape files, 57–58
Government Documents Catalog Service, 71

GPO. *See* U.S. Government Printing Office
Granville, Joseph, 250
Grocery stores, 406
Gross National Product (GNP), 331
Guides to literature
    business literature, 43–44
    computerized information sources, 51–58
    directories, 45–49
    government publications, 69–73
    periodicals and serials, 45–50
    specialized business publications, 50–51

Haines and Company, 141
George D. Hall Company, 137
G.K. Hall, 67
Harmonie Park Press, 98
Harmonized Commodity Description and Coding System, 361
Louis Harris & Associates, 409
Harris Publishing Company, 137
Harvard Graduate School of Business Administration Baker library collection list, 67
Heady, Robert, 269
Hellebust, Lynn, 32
High-technology companies, 144
Holman, Richard A., 256
Housing, 307–08, 314–16
Hulbert, Mark, 269
Human geography indexes, 98–99
Human resources, 97–98

Ibbotson Associates, Inc., 222
ICPSR (Inter-university Consortium for Political and Social Research), 58, 409
IDD Information Services, 219, 239
Implicit Price Deflator (IPD), 334
Imports and exports, 144, 360–62
Income statement, 159–60
Income statistics, 174
Income tax reporting services, 11
Index numbers, 282–84
Index of Coincident Indicators, 330
Index of Lagging Indicators, 330
Index of Leading Economic Indicators, 330
Indexes
    according to type of research, 108
    accounting and finance, 95–96
    characteristics, 64–65
    general business, 85–94
    marketing and advertising, 96–97
    microforms, 12
    to news sources, 99–107
    periodical literature, 83–99
    personnel and labor relations, 97–98
    quality of, 107–09
    types, 83–84
Industrial development, 389–90
Industries. *See also* Companies
    analysis, 264–65
    state directories, 137–38
Industry newspapers
    source of business information, 10
Industry statistics, 347–71
    agriculture, 366, 399
    automobiles, 368

construction industries, 357
electronics, 367–68
enterprise statistics, 359
foreign trade, 360–62
governments, 360
manufacturers, 350–53
mineral industries, 357, 367
minority-owned businesses, 359–60
outlying areas, 359
retail trade, 353–56
service industries, 356–57
trade associations, 366
transportation, 357–58
where to look, 368–69
wholesale trade, 356
women-owned businesses, 360
Inflation, 333–34
Information Access Company, 71, 78, 85–87, 101, 122, 463
Information America, 170
Information brokers, 37
Information Handling Services, 131
InfoTrac system, 86
Initial Public Offerings (IPO), 231–32
Insider trading, 234, 236–37
Instinet System, 203
Institute for Scientific Information, 84
Insurance industry, 168
Intelligence gathering, 4
Intermarket Trading System (ITS), 203
Inter-university Consortium for Political and Social Research (ICPSR), 58, 409
Internal Revenue Code of 1986, 453
International Access Co., 106
International Thomson Organization, Ltd., 6
Interviewing techniques for researchers, 38–39
Investment information
    advisory services, 249–51
    basic, 200–26
    bonds, 212, 268–69
    brokerage reports, 255–58
    charting services, 260
    choosing right source, 223–24, 245
    commercial advisory sources, 258–69
    data summary, 220–23
    equity and debt financing, 201–202
    financial intermediation, 210
    financial quotations, 206–19
    industry analysis, 264–65
    investment companies, 205
    market indicators, 252–55
    money market, 206
    mutual funds, 209–12, 265–68
    news, 227–31
    performance predictions, 251–52
    process, 200–02
    publications, 269–70
    securities, 202–06
    special situations, 227–48
    stock indexes, 252–53
    stock quotations, 206–09
    stocks, 202–04
    telephone inquiry, 219
Invest/Net Group, Inc., 236
Investor Responsibility Research Center, 144
IPD (Implicit Price Deflator), 334

IPO (Initial Public Offerings), 231–32
IRS. *See* U.S. Internal Revenue Service

Jarnigan, Bill D., 468
Jarrell, Howard R., 208
Journal of Commerce, Inc., 144
Journals. *See* Periodicals

Key Numbering System, 431
B. Klein Publications, 45
Knight-Ridder Financial News, 107
Knowledge Industry Publications, 53

Labor force data, 332
Labor law
    arbitration, 440, 444
    case reporters, 441–45
    characteristics, 439
    collective bargaining, 440
    indexes, 97–98
    loose-leaf services, 445–48
    newsletters, 449
    online databases, 449
    provisions of labor relations law, 439–40
    publications, 449
    statutes and regulations, 440–45
Labor unions, 449
LACE Financial Corporation., 165–68
Lagging Indicators, 328
Lasser, J.K., 464
Lawyers Co-operative Publishing, 427, 431
Leading Indicators, 328
Leading National Advertisers, Inc., 399–400
Lebhar-Friedman, Inc., 142
Legal information
    administrative decisions, 433–35
    citators, 435–37
    court decisions, 430–33
    indexes, 427–28
    legislative history, 428–30
    loose-leaf services, 51
    newsletters, 48
    online databases, 438
    regulations, 433–35
    research for nonlawyer, 449–50
    statutes and codes, 428
Lesko, Matthew, 52
Letter rulings, 453
LEXIS/NEXIS, 15, 438, 453
Libraries and librarians
    acquisitions lists, 67
    catalogs, 17, 65–66
    directories, 33
    research guides, 58
    as source of business information, 8–9
    source of experts, 26
Library cataloging records database, 57
Library of Congress, 66
Library of Congress Subject Headings (LCSH), 65
    for periodicals, 84
Licensing agreements, 148
Lifestyle analysis, 413–16
Lipper Analytical Service, Inc., 267
Listing Application, 231
Local areas
    almanacs, 379
    analyzing geographic markets, 375–76
    atlases, 379–80

business directories, 141–42
  data quality, 394–96
  encyclopedias, 378
  marketing information, 380
  profiles, 378–81
Local filings, 170
Local government agencies, 8
  as source of company financial
    information, 168–69
Logic and statistics, 278
Logical operators, 13–14
Long-term forecasts, 387–89
Loose-leaf services, 11
  business law, 437
  directories, 51
  labor law, 445–48
  labor relations, 445–46
Lotus Development Corporation, 18
Lynch, Jones & Ryan, 258

MacLean Hunter Media, Inc., 142
MacRae's Blue Book, Inc., 130, 137
Magnetic tape file directories, 57–58
Mail order companies, 144
Management consultants, 38
Management literature, 87–89, 98
Mann, Thomas, 58
Manufacturers, 350–53, 363
  directories, 127–31
Manufacturers News, Inc., 137
Market Research Society, 97
Marketing
  advertising and media sources, 399–
    405
  analysis of geographic markets, 375–76
  consumer behavior, 405–12
  directories, 37–38, 51
  estimates and projections, 381–89
  indexes, 96–97
  intelligence reports, 11–12
  lifestyle analysis, 413–16
  local area profiles, 378–81
  market comparisons, 376–81
  market research, 421–22
  market segments, 412–16
  market share, 416–21
  state economic conditions, 376–78
Marketing Research Association, Inc., 38
Marquis Who's Who, 145
Matthew Bender & Company, 460
Maxwell Macmillan, 438
Mead Data Central, Inc., 15
Meckler Corp., 51, 56
Media General Financial Services, 220–
  21, 254
Media guides, 403–05
Mediamark Research, 406
Median value, 279
Merchandise licensing, 148
Merchandise statistics, 353–56
Mergers and acquistions (M&A), 237–41
  major filings, 238
Metropolitan Statistical Area (MSA), 298
Laurence H. Meyer & Associates, Ltd, 342
Microcomputer software guides, 57
Microforms, 12
  company directories, 126–27
  directories, 51
  indexes, 12
  state industrial directories, 138

Miller, Martin A., 468
Mineral industries, 357
Minor Civil Divisions (MCDs), 300
Mode, 279
Model building, 277
Money market, 206
Money Stock, 335
Money supply, 334
Monitor Publishing Co., 28, 30, 196
Moody's Investors Service, 189–90, 222,
  254
Morningstar, Inc., 267–68
Robert Morris Assoicates (RMA), 172
MSA (Metropolitan Statistical Area), 298
Multidisiplinary indexes, 98–101
Municipal and county directories, 32
Municipal bonds, 205
Mutual funds, 205
  listings, 209–12
  services, 265–68

NASD (National Association of Stock
  Dealers), 203, 223
NASDAQ Automated Quotation
  (NASDAQ), 203, 209
  quotes, 214
NASDAQ National Market System
  (NMS), 209
National Association of Stock Dealers
  (NASD), 203, 223
National Bureau of Economic Research
  (NBER), 328
National Decision Systems, 414
National Demographics and Lifestyles
  (NDL), 413–14, 415
National Income and Product Accounts
  (NIPA), 331
National Labor Relations Board (NLRB),
  439–41
National Quotation Bureau, 216, 219
National Register Publishing Co., 120, 122
National Technical Information Service
  (NTIS), 57–58, 69
NBER (National Bureau of Economic
  Research), 328
NDL (National Demographics and
  Lifestyles), 413–14, 415
Nelson Publications, 255
Net Asset Value (NAV), 205, 209
New York Society of Securities Analysts
  (NYSSA), 255
New York Stock Exchange (NYSE), 202,
  203
  quotes, 214
The New York Times Company, 97, 99
News services
  searching, 82–110
NewsBank, Inc., 101–02
Newsletters, 11. *See also* Newspapers;
    Periodicals
  databases, 105–06
  directories, 48
  investment advisory services, 258–69
NewsNet, 15, 106
Newspaper reporters, 26
Newspapers. *See also* Newsletters;
    Periodicals
  directories, 48–49
  indexes, 99–105
  searching, 82–110

NEXIS, 104
  wire services, 106
A.C. Nielsen Company, 12, 382, 403
NIPA (National Income and Product
    Accounts), 331
NLRB (National Labor Relations Board),
  439–41
Non-NASDAQ stock quotations, 216–17
Nonprofit organizations, 9, 16–17, 34–36
Nonstatistics, 278
NORC, 408
North American Securities
    Administrator's Association, 183
NPA Data Services, Inc., 388
NTIS (National Technical Information
    Service), 57–58, 69
NUEXCO, 165
John Nuveen Co., 205

Obsolete securities, 242
OCLC, 65–66
Office of the Federal Register, 434–35
Off-the-shelf Publications, Inc., 50
OMB. *See* U.S. Office of Management
    and Budget
O'Neil & Company, 260
O'Neil, William J., 214–15
Online databases, 12–17
  accounting, 467
  benefits, 13–14
  bibliographic, 14
  books, 54
  company directories, 117–20, 122,
    146–48
  directories, 52–56
  factual, 14
  filings, 170
  financial services, 189, 192–94, 215
  full-text, 14
  insider trading, 236–37
  insurance directories, 168
  investment data, 220, 222
  manufacturing directories, 128
  menu-driven systems, 15–16
  multifile searching, 108
  national directories, 123–27
  nonprofit databases, 16–17
  ownership, 235–36
  securities, 232, 245
  for stock quotes, 219
  subscription services, 15
  taxation, 453, 455, 458, 460, 463
  trademarks, 154
  types of databases, 14–15
Online library networks, 65–66
Opinion Research Service, 411
Oryx Press, 70, 73
Over-the-Counter (OTC) market, 202–04
  stock quotes, 209

Partnerships, 114, 183
Penny stocks, 203–204
Percent changes, 280–81
Percents, 280
Pergamon Financial Data Services, 15
Periodicals. *See also* Newsletters;
    Newspapers
  current awareness services, 84
  directories, 82

(Periodicals *continued*)
full-text databases, 54, 56
indexes, 83–99
online directory, 54
as source of business information, 10–11
sources, 10–11
types of indexes, 83–84
Personnel indexes, 97–98
PMSA (Primary Metropolitan Statistical Area), 298
R.L. Polk Co., 140–41, 143
Population statistics. *See also* Census; Statistics
data collection, 294–95
estimates and projections, 311–16, 382–87
housing unit method, 302
monthly surveys, 311
pitfalls in using, 316–19
publishied Census reports, 313–19
regression analysis, 312
reports, 313–15
sources of, 319–22
vital statistics, 312
PR Newswire Association, 107
Predicasts, Inc., 47, 78, 89–93, 96, 106, 107
industry statistics, 364
product codes based on SIC codes, 64
Preferred stock, 202
Prentice Hall, 170, 455, 460, 461
Price/Earnings Ratio, 253
Price levels and inflation, 333–34
Price volatility, 254
Primary Metropolitan Statistical Area (PMSA), 298
Principal trademarks, 149
Privacy and public disclosure, 182–84
Private companies. *See also* Companies; Public companies
business information available, 9
research strategies, 179–80
Private letter rulings, 453, 455
Problem solving in information, 4
Producer Price Index, 333
Product directories, 129–31
Proprietary information, 5
Prospectus, 231
Proxy statements, 187
Psychology indexes, 98
PTO. *See* U.S. Patent and Trademark Office
Public Affairs Information Service (PAIS), 94
Public companies. *See also* Companies; Private companies
corporate finances, 182–99
and private companies, 182–84
problems with, 197–98
research strategies, 197–98
Public information, 5
Public libraries, 8–9
Public opinion and consumer attitudes, 408–11
Public utilities, 165, 190
Public Utilities Reports, Inc., 165
Publicity services, 107
Publishers, 6, 68–69
Putnam, Barron, 166

Q-Data Corporation, 187
Quotron Systems, Inc., 217, 219

Radio, 404–05
Ratio analysis, 171
Ready-reference searches, 132–33
Real estate
and construction, 390–91
cost comparison guides, 391
REDI Real Estate Information Service, 6–7
Reference materials
computerized information sources, 51–58
directories, 45
guides to literature, 43–44
periodicals and serials, 45–50
specialized business publications, 50–51
Regional Bell Operating Companies (RBOCs), 140
Registered versus unregisterd trademarks, 148–49
Registration Statements, 231
Regression analysis, 312
Regulated companies, researching, 164–68
Regulatory agencies, 27–28
Research Institute of America, Inc., 456, 458
Research Libraries of the New York Public Library, 67
Research organizations, nonprofit, 36
Retail directories, 142
Retail trade, 353–56
Reuters Ltd., 15, 219
Rights, 243
RLIN (Research Libraries Information Network), 57
Robbin, Jonathan, 414
Roper Center for Public Opionion Research, 408, 409
Rukeyser, Louis, 250

Sage Publications, 98
SAMI/Burke, 406
K.G. Saur (publisher), 68
Savings and loans, 165–68
directories, 143
Schonfeld & Associates, Inc., 174
SEC. *See* U.S. Securities and Exchange Commission
Secondary markets, 202
Securities. *See also* Investment information; Stocks
bonds, 204–05
investment companies, 205
money market, 206
new offerings, 231–33
primary markets, 202
secondary markets, 202
stocks, 202–04
types, 202–06
Securities Data Company, 241
Selected Research in Microfiche (SRIM), 70
Selective Dissemination of Information (SDI), 84
Serials. *See* Periodicals
Service directories, 143
Service industries, 356–57

Shell corporations, 238
Shepard's Citations, 435, 460
Sheshunoff Information Services, Inc., 166
SIC (Standard Industrial Classification), 62–64, 348–49
Simmons Market Research Bureau, 406, 419
Charles E. Simon & Company, 240
SITC (Standard International Trade Classification), 361
Small businesses, 176
SMSA (Standard Metropolitan Statistical Area), 298
Sociology indexes, 98
Special issues of periodicals, 49–50
Special libraries, 33
Special purpose directories, 144
Staff Directories, Ltd., 27, 29
Standard & Poor's Corporation
company directory, 117–19
financial quotations, 217
Standard & Poor's 500, 252
stock guide, 222
Standard Industrial Classification (SIC), 62–64, 348–49
Standard International Trade Classification (SITC), 361
Standard Metropolitan Statistical Area (SMSA), 298
Standard Rate & Data Service (SRDS), 47, 48, 402–03
Stare decisis, 425
State government
administrative officials, 30
almanacs, 377
data and databases, 32
directories, 30–32
economic conditions, 376–78
filings, 170
legislative processes, 32
nonmanufacturing directories, 138–40
personnel, 30–32
rankings, 378
service directories, 138–40
as source of company financial information, 168–70
Statement of Financial Position, 159
Statistics. *See also* Census; Economic statistics; Industry statistics; Population statistics
abuse and mistakes, 279–90
advantages and disadvantages of numbers, 275–78
averages, 279–80
charts and graphs, 285–88
classification, 276
compendia, general, 363–66
data, 278
definition, 275
faulty, 278
index numbers, 282–84
indexes, 75–80
information, 73–79, 343–44
and logic, 278
percentages, 280
rankings, 284–85
ratios, 281
reasoning, 275–92
reports, finding, 61–81
sources evaluating, 290–91

tables, 288–90
tracking inflation, 333
Statutes and codes, 428
Stock market
historical information, 222–23
letters, 260–63
Stock split, 242
Stocks. *See also* Investment information;
Securities
computer trading networks, 203
dividends, 242
exchanges, 202–03
indexes, 252–53
price per share, 03
quotations, 206–09
Store audits, 406
Subject bibliographies, 67–68
Subject-oriented indexes, 94–99
Subscription agents, 46–47
Subsidiary companies, 115
Summary Tape Files (STF)s, 308–09
Supplemental trademarks, 149
Sweet's Group, 130
Syndicated intelligence services, 11–12,
398–99

Tax Analysts, 462
Tax Management, Inc., 460
Taxes
citators, 460–61
IRS publications, 465
journals and newsletters, 461–63
judicial decisions, 455–56
legal structure, 452–53
loose-leaf services, 456–60
periodical indexes, 463–64
preparation guides, 464–65
research primary sources, 453–56
statutes, regulations, and administrative
rulings, 454–55
Technical information
indexes, 99
reports, 70
Telephone directories, 140
Telerate, Inc., 219
Television industry, 404–05
Thesaurus, 84
Thomas Publishing Co., 129, 139
Thomson Financial Networks, 256
Thomson International, 438
Ticker services, 217–19
TIGER (Topologically Integrated
Geographic Encoding and
Referencing System) database, 303
Time series, 326
Topologically Integrated Geographic
Encoding and Referencing System
(TIGER) database, 303
Tracts, 298
Trade associations, 9
directories, 34
source of experts, 26
Trade directories, 45
Trade journals
business information available, 10
directories, 47
Trademarks, 148–55
classification system, 149–50
Patent Depository Libraries (PDLs),
150

publications, 150–55
registered vs. unregistered, 148–49
searching, 155–56
Transportation, 190, 357–58
Treasury Bonds, 205
Treasury Decisions, 453–54
Treasury Notes, 205
Trinet America, Inc., 126
Troy, Leo, 174
TRW Business Credit, 162

Uhlan, Miriam, 49
UMI/Data Courier, 101, 105
Unemployment rate, 332
Uniform Commercial Code, 170
Uniform Securities Act, 183
Universities, 34–36
University Microfilms International, 17–
18, 102, 104, 140
University of Chicago Center for
Reasearch in Security Prices (CRSP),
219
University of Michigan Survey Research
Center, 409, 412
Urban Land Institute (ULI), 390
U.S. Bureau of Economic Analysis, 329,
330, 331, 336, 338, 389
U.S. Bureau of Labor Statistics, 329, 332,
333, 338, 407
U.S. Bureau of National Affairs, 441, 463,
464
U.S. Bureau of the Census, 57, 329, 336
U.S. Congress, 29–30
U.S. Congressional Budget Office, 341
U.S. Council of Economic Advisors, 285–
86
U.S. Customs Service, 360
U.S. Department of Agriculture, 403
U.S. Energy Information Administration,
165
U.S. Federal Reserve Board, 164, 340
U.S. Government Printing Office (GPO),
8, 69, 70, 72
U.S. Internal Revenue Service (IRS), 174,
454–55, 464, 465
U.S. Joint Committee on Printing, 29
U.S. Office of Management and Budget
(OMB), 62, 327
U.S. Office of Personnel Management, 98
U.S. Office of the Federal Register, 27
U.S. Patent and Trademark Office (PTO),
148, 150–55
U.S. Securities and Exchange Commission
(SEC), 164, 229
accounting rules, 469
documents, 188
EDGAR, 187
filings, 227
U.S. Supreme Court, 431
U.S. Treasury bills (T-bills), 206

Value Line, Inc., 219, 260–62
Vendor Catalog Service, 131
Vickers Stock Research Corporation, 236
Videotext systems, 16
Vital statistics, 312
VU/TEXT, 15, 104

Wage and salary surveys, 391–94
Walker's Western Research, 196

Warfield, Gerald, 208
Warren, Gorham & Lamont, 461, 463
Washington Researchers Publishing, 28,
32
Washington Service Bureau, 229–30
The WEFA Group, Inc., 341
West Publishing, 427, 430, 431
WESTLAW, 438, 453
Wiesenberger Financial Services, 267
Wholesale Price Index, 267
Wholesale trade, 356
Williams, Martha E., 52
Williams Act filings, 238, 240
H.W. Wilson Company., 66, 85
WILSONLINE, 15
Wire services, 106–07
Women-owned businesses, 360
Women studies indexes, 98
Woods & Poole Economics, Inc., 388
World Future Society, 94
Wright Investor's Service, 196

Yankelovich Clancy Shulman, 408

Zacks Investment Research, 257–58